BIBLIOTHECA EPHEMERIDUM THEOLOGICARUM LOVANIENSIUM

CXVI

THE SIGNS SOURCE
IN THE FOURTH GOSPEL

HISTORICAL SURVEY AND CRITICAL EVALUATION
OF THE SEMEIA HYPOTHESIS

BY

GILBERT VAN BELLE

1425

LEUVEN
UNIVERSITY PRESS

UITGEVERIJ PEETERS
LEUVEN

1994

CIP KONINKLIJKE BIBLIOTHEEK ALBERT I, BRUSSEL

ISBN 90 6186 624 3 (Leuven University Press)
D/1994/1869/43
ISBN 90 6831 649 4 (Uitgeverij Peeters)
D/1994/0602/111

Leuven University Press / Presses Universitaires de Louvain
Universitaire Pers Leuven
Krakenstraat 3, B-3000 Leuven-Louvain (Belgium)

© Uitgeverij Peeters, Bondgenotenlaan 153, B-3000 Leuven (Belgium)

THE SIGNS SOURCE IN THE FOURTH GOSPEL

PREFACE

The starting point of the present study was a survey on *De Semeia-bron in het vierde evangelie* I published on the occasion of the Collo-quium Biblicum Lovaniense on the Gospel of John in August 1975. Since R. Bultmann's commentary on John, the semeia or signs source hypothesis is without doubt the most important literary theory in Johannine studies. "The broad agreement with Bultmann's hypothesis is striking. The list of authors who concur is impressive by its length and the number of well-known names. The spread of the hypothesis is like the description of a triumphal procession. The consensus is interconfes-sional as well as international" (H.-P. Heekerens). Since 1975, more than before, critical voices have been raised against the assumed self-evidence of the signs source. Even R.T. Fortna, who continues to defend a pre-Johannine signs gospel, now concedes that "despite wide accep-tance, the hypothesis has never been universally accepted". In view of this situation, Professor Frans Neirynck suggested that I supplement and translate my earlier study. Chapters I-IV of *De Semeia-bron* have been revised and expanded, Chapter V (The Semeia Hypothesis Criticized in Recent Research) and Chapter VI (Evaluation of the Semeia Hypothe-sis), as well as a Bibliography of pertinent literature, have been added. Two Appendices are included: a presentation of the Johannine notion of σημεῖα and an updated catalogue of Johannine style characteristics.

A very special word of thanks goes to Peter J. Judge for translating my text into English. From his own interest in the topic, he was able to offer valuable suggestions for this new edition.

My special gratitude is due to my mentor Professor F. Neirynck. I appreciate his encouragement and the time he has devoted to the present work.

G. Van Belle

TABLE OF CONTENTS

CHAPTER V

THE SEMEIA HYPOTHESIS CRITICIZED
IN RECENT RESEARCH

G.M. Burge (330-331). – M. Hengel (331-332). – J. Engelbrecht (332-333). – W.J. Bittner (333-334). – A. Marchadour
(334-335). – U. Schnelle (335-341). – G.S. Sloyan (342). –
J.R. Michaels (342-343). – K. Grayston (343-344). – D. Marguerat (344-346). – R. Kühschelm (346-347). – T.M. Dowell
(347-348). – J.W Pryor (348-349). – K.-M. Bull (349-350). –
F. Vouga (351). – A.T. Hanson (351). – M. Davies (351). –
J.A. Trumbower (351). – J. Konings (351-352). – T.L. Brodie
(352). – I. Dunderberg (352).
Negative Reactions to R.T. Fortna's "The Fourth Gospel and
Its Predecessor": J. Painter (352-354). – C. Niemand (354-
355). – F.F. Segovia (355-356). – M. FitzPatrick (356). – R.
Kysar (356). – K. Matsunaga (356-357).

CHAPTER VI
EVALUATION OF THE SEMEIA HYPOTHESIS

INDEXES

CHAPTER I

THE ORIGIN OF THE SEMEIA HYPOTHESIS

The first suggestion of a signs source in the Fourth Gospel is usually attributed to A. Faure (1922)[1]. But as early as 1923 H. Windisch compared the opinion of Faure with that of J.M. Thompson[2], and further antecedents of the semeia hypothesis can be found already in the nineteenth century.

I. ANTECEDENTS OF THE THEORY

The first author who deserves mention is Alexander SCHWEIZER (1841)[3]. From C.H. Weisse, originator of the Johannine "Partition Theory", he adopted the idea that two authors can be distinguished in the Gospel of John, though not in the sense that one is responsible for the discourses and the other for the narrative material. In his opinion the coherent composition of the evangelist was interrupted by interpola-

---

1. "This source was first detected by Alexander Faure" (J.M. ROBINSON, *Kerygma*, 1965, p. 136; = 1971, pp. 51-52; GT: 1965, p. 321). Cf. BECKER, *Wunder*, 1970, p. 131 (= 1980, p. 437): "Bultmann (hat) eine These von Alexander Faure aufgegriffen". For Bultmann's reference to Faure, see below, p. 25 n. 141.

2. WINDISCH, *Erzählungsstil*, 1923, p. 210 n. 2 (ET: 1993, p. 61 n. 1): "Vgl. hierzu jetzt die Hypothese von Faure... Ähnlich vor ihm schon Thompson im Expositor Jan. 1916". In *Johannes und die Synoptiker*, 1926, p. 55 n. 1, he refers also to Soltau and Meyer. See below, pp. 15-16 n. 92. – TEEPLE, *Methodology*, 1962, p. 281, thinks that the signs source was first described by A.T. OLMSTEAD, but this is perhaps based on an error (cf. KONINGS, *Joh. verhaal*, I, 1969, p. 107 n. 2); in Teeple's *Origin* (1974) Olmstead is not even mentioned. I could find only two articles and one book on the Gospels by Olmstead: *ATR* 24 (1942) 1-26; *JNES* 1 (1942) 41-75; *Jesus in the Light of History*, New York, 1942. The author defends the position that the discourses are a later interpolation into an older historical framework; cf. BULTMANN, *Johannes. Ergänzungsheft*, [2]1957, p. 20 (p. 78 n. 4) (ET: 1971, p. 113 n. 2); GRANT, *The Gospels*, 1957, p. 159.

3. A. SCHWEIZER, *Das Evangelium Johannes nach seinem innern Werthe und seiner Bedeutung für das Leben Jesu kritisch untersucht*, Leipzig, 1841. – Cf. JACQUIER, *Histoire*, IV, [3]1908, pp. 37-38; BOUSSET, *Evangelium*, 1909, pp. 1-4; CLEMEN, *Entstehung*, 1912, p. 10; LOISY, *Quatrième évangile*, [2]1921, p. 22; GOGUEL, *Introduction*, II, 1923, pp. 26, 57; BROMBOSZCZ, *Einheit*, 1927, p. 11; HOWARD, *Fourth Gospel*, [4]1955, p. 95; MERLIER, *Question*, 1961, p. 68 nn. 5-6; KONINGS, *Joh. verhaal*, I, 1969, pp. 29-30; III, 1972, pp. 52-54 (Jn 6,1-16); TEEPLE, *Origin*, 1974, pp. 32-33; VAN BELLE, *Parenthèses*, 1985, pp. 156-157; KUHN, *Christologie*, 1988, p. 11 (Jn 1,35-51); ASHTON, *Understanding*, 1991, p. 28; SCHMITHALS, *Johannesevangelium*, 1992, pp. 47, 89, 118, 127. On Schweizer, cf. FLÜCKIGER, in LEIMGRUBER – SCHOCH (eds.), *Gegen die Gottesvergessenheit*, 1990, pp. 68-85.

tions[4]. Schweizer begins his investigation with ch. 21, whose secondary character is obvious[5]. Then, within the body of the gospel, he points to similar but smaller additions attributable to the same hand (19,35-37; 18,9; 16,30; 2,21-22)[6]. He also suspects that 20,19-29 was inserted later[7].

Similarly, Schweizer admits some larger interpolations, the Galilean sections 2,1-12; 4,44-54; and 6,1-26[8]. He offers various criteria, which later defenders of the signs source will also employ[9].

1. The *aporias*: The Galilean pericopes can easily be detached from the context, where they interrupt the continuous chronology of the original gospel. With reference to 2,1-11 Schweizer gives six arguments. First, after 1,50, where Nathanael was promised greater *acta Christi*, a more exalted glory than is visible in the miracles, one expects no further sign. Second, faith originates on the basis of a sign (2,11) although in 1,50 Jesus criticized such faith. Third, the disciples believe in Jesus already in ch. 1; why mention it again in 2,11? Fourth, the sympathy of the relatives for Jesus does not fit with their rather hostile and mocking attitude in 7,3-10; cf. Mk 3,21. Fifth, it is historically impossible that Jesus is recognized as the master of his disciples already at Cana (2,2), since he had just gathered disciples when he decided to travel to Galilee. Sixth, "on the third day" makes no sense, for the third day has already been mentioned in 1,43. With the interpolation of 2,1-11 the author changed ἐξῆλθεν to κατέβη in 2,12 and added καὶ ἡ μήτηρ καὶ οἱ ἀδελφοὶ αὐτοῦ (cf. 2,1)[10].

---

4. *Johannes*, pp. 8-23, esp. 12. For C.H. Weisse, see below, p. 12 n. 61.

5. *Ibid.*, pp. 55-60, 117-125. Schweizer refers to the following *aporias*: 21,25 is pleonastic after 20,30 (pp. 57, 119); and how could the evangelist write about his own death (p. 57)? In 21,1, μετὰ ταῦτα is rather vague and joins ch. 21 only externally with the gospel: nowhere is there mention of a journey by the disciples from Jerusalem (ch. 20) to Galilee (ch. 21). In John's use μετὰ ταῦτα means more precisely "after these events" (pp. 117-118, 120-121). Further, ch. 21 does not correspond with John's style of presentation: (1) the stories of ch. 21 are too legendary and not graphic enough (pp. 120, 123); (2) John gives more prominence to Andrew, Philip and Thomas than to Peter; he never mentions the sons of Zebedee (21,2) (p. 120); (3) the numbering in 21,14 does not designate the appearance (after ch. 20 it would rather be the fourth), but the miracle; such an emphasis is strange in John (p. 118). Finally, ἐφανέρωσεν ἑαυτόν (21,1), ἐφανέρωσεν δὲ οὕτως (21,1), παιδία in place of τεκνία (21,5), and ἐγερθείς (21,14) are non-Johannine (p. 120).

6. *Ibid.*, pp. 60-65. Perhaps also 6,64.71; 12,6 have been interpolated (p. 65); cf. VAN BELLE, *Parenthèses*, 1985, pp. 156-157.

7. *Johannes*, pp. 95-96, 216-219.

8. *Ibid.*, pp. 65-96, 105-117.

9. "Auffallend ist es nun, dass ... einige Erzählungen ganz lose und abgerissen dastehen, in keine Reden verflochten, ja ohne irgend ein bedeutendes Wort Jesu, und von einer wesentlich andern Werthschätzung und Idee des Wunders getragen, endlich sogar stylistisch abweichend sind; so dass das Evangelium durch die Ausscheidung dieser Abschnitte nur gewinnt und seine klare Einheit des Planes wie des Charakters wieder erhält" (p. 66).

10. For Jn 2,1-12: (1-2), cf. p. 68; (3-5), p. 69; (6), pp. 100, 108-109. See also pp. 106-107. – That 4,44-54 is an addition is indicated among other things by the contra-

2. The Galilean stories display a different narrative technique, lacking characteristic elements of Johannine narration such as vivid presentation, a higher conception of faith, dialogue that leads into discourse, a significant saying of Jesus[11]. These stories have more in common with ch. 21 than with the rest of the gospel[12].

3. The Galilean interpolations carry a differing conception of σημεῖον and attach a special importance to the (magic) miracle; in the Judean narratives, faith which arises from seeing a sign is only preliminary. John prefers the testimony of the Father and the ἔργα τοῦ πατρός[13].

4. There are also some stylistic criteria: in 2,1-11, ἡ ὥρα μου (in place of ὁ καιρός μου) is a non-Johannine element; elsewhere John uses ἡ ὥρα only for the death of Jesus (7,30; 12,27; 13,1)[14]. In 4,48 σημεῖα καὶ τέρατα is a Synoptic expression: John indeed uses σημεῖα but never τέρατα; the pleonasm τοῦτο πάλιν δεύτερον κτλ. (4,54) recalls Mt 26,42 and Jn 21,16[15]. Also ὀψία ἐγένετο (6,16), σκοτία ἤδη ἐγεγόνει (6,17) and the Semitic paratactic καί (6,17.18.19.21) are non-Johannine[16].

diction between 4,43 and 4,44: why does Jesus still go to Galilee if he knows that a prophet is not honored in his own country (pp. 74-75)? Contrary to John's custom, there is a reference to the wine miracle (4,46.54), which has nothing to do with the healing story; where John makes such a reference (11,2; 12,1; 18,14) it is always to something that has a function within the narrative (p. 78). The emphasis on miracle faith in 4,53-54 is strange in the Gospel of John (p. 79). – Jn 6,1-26 also interrupts the composition of the evangelist: in 5,47 Jesus is in Jerusalem and in 6,1 he goes to the opposite side of the sea, without mention of his journey to Galilee (pp. 81-82, 87-88); the reference to the approaching Passover (6,4) is improbable after the Passover or Pentecost of 5,1 (pp. 82, 116); nor does 6,1-26 correspond with the theme of the following discourse (p. 85); finally, at 7,1 Jesus is suddenly back in Jerusalem (p. 88). One can best suppose that 6,1-26 was inserted into the discourse of 5,1-47; 6,27-58.60-71; and, together with that interpolation, 6,59 was added (pp. 86, 100).

11. *Ibid.*, pp. 66, 68, 78-79, 80, 81-82, 90.

12. "Diese Erzählungen verrathen ihre Fremdartigkeit überdies durch gänzlichen Mangel an Reden, Gesprächen oder irgend einem bedeutenden Worte Jesu; durch schlechte Übereinstimmung mit dem, was ihnen vorhergeht und nachfolgt, und durch Auffallendes im Styl, in all diesen Hinsichten weit mehr dem Anhangscapitel verwandt als dem Evangelium selbst" (pp. 67-68).

13. "Vorzüglich unterscheidet sich der *Wunderbegriff*. Johannes legt zwar auch Werth auf σημεῖα aber durchweg nur einen sekundären Werth, so dass von ihnen aus auf die 'grössern Werke' hingewiesen wird, welche Christus im Seelenleben verrichte. ... Noch lieber beruft er sich aber auf das Zeugniss des Vaters überhaupt, auf die ἔργα τοῦ πατρός, die er verrichte. ... Mitten in diese durchgängig festgehaltene Idee und Schätzung des Wunders treten nun einige wenige Erzählungen, welche die σημεῖα als das Höchste schätzen, beim Glauben, welcher durch σημεῖα geweckt ist, als bei einem befriedigenden stehen bleiben, das Wunder selbst als magisches geben" (pp. 66-67). Cf. pp. 68, 80, 81, 96, 99.

14. *Ibid.*, pp. 73-74.

15. *Ibid.*, p. 79.

16. *Ibid.*, p. 94. Note in 6,18: τέ in place of καί.

5. The numbering of the signs in 2,11 and 4,54[17]: In 2,11 the narrator characterizes the story as the beginning of the signs; this does not fit after 1,48, where the miraculous knowledge of Jesus has been mentioned. Similarly, in 4,54 the healing is counted as the second sign, even though signs are already mentioned in 2,23; 3,2 and assumed in 4,48. In both these cases the signs could be numbered because the other miracles were not narrated in detail, but in 6,1-26[18] it was not possible to continue the count because of the preceding healing narrative from the original gospel in 5,1-9. The *Überarbeiter* numbered the Galilean miracle stories to underscore their importance: "Cana in Galilee has the honor of seeing the first manifestation of Jesus' δόξα; Cana has the honor as well with the second miracle"[19]. It is evident already from 21,14 that the interpolator himself readily numbered the signs[20].

According to Schweizer, the author of the Fourth Gospel is not John the son of Zebedee, but the μαθητής who appears in the gospel as the Beloved Disciple (21,24); he originates from Judea and is possibly of prominent rank[21]. After the death of the "other disciple", and before the Judean *Grundschrift* was published, a Pseudo-Johannine redactor added the Galilean narratives[22]. The tradition he used was perhaps the same as that behind the Synoptics; it is uncertain whether he knew the Synoptic Gospels themselves[23].

Schweizer's theory found few followers[24], and he himself retracted his composition theory in 1864[25]. His chief critics were A. Schwegler

17. *Ibid.*, pp. 100-105.

18. The numbering here would have been: τοῦτο ἤδη τρίτον σημεῖον ἐποίησεν ὁ Ἰησοῦς ἐλθὼν ἐκ τῆς Ἰουδαίας εἰς τὴν Γαλιλαίαν (p. 104).

19. *Ibid.*, p. 102.

20. *Ibid.*, p. 104. See above, p. 2 n. 5. The narrator added τῆς Γαλιλαίας to Κανά in 2,11 (cp. 4,46) (p. 102).

21. *Ibid.*, pp. 235-239. Cf. NEIRYNCK, in *ETL* 51 (1975), p. 122 n. 44 (= 1982, p. 344 n. 44).

22. *Ibid.*, pp. 80, 85, 98, 118.

23. *Ibid.*, pp. 276-277.

24. According to HOLTZMANN, *Einleitung*, ³1892, p. 435, Schweizer's hypothesis was adopted by KRÜGER-VELTHUSEN in *Das Leben Jesu*, 1872; cf. CLEMEN, *Entstehung*, 1912, p. 10; LOISY, *Quatrième évangile*, ²1921, p. 22; MERLIER, *Question*, 1961, p. 68. I was not able to consult the work of Krüger-Velthusen; regarding it, cf. SCHWEITZER, *Von Reimarus zu Wrede*, 1906, p. 215 n. 1 (ET: 1936, p. 217); = *Geschichte*, I, 1913, p. 215 n. 1.

25. Holtzmann, Clemen, Loisy and Merlier (see above, n. 24; cp. more recently TEEPLE, *Origin*, 1974, p. 34; KUHN, in *TTZ* 95, 1987, p. 155) refer for this to A. SCHWEIZER, *Das Johannesevangelium. Eine Erwiederung*, in *PKZ* (1864), no. 17 (Sonnabend, 23. April), 362-363. Schweizer notes there, with reference to Strauss's critique in *Das Leben Jesu für das deutsche Volk bearbeitet* (1864): "Die frühere Kritik, welche mittelst Hypothesen einzelne neutestamentliche Bücher zu verstehen suchte und blos die übrigen neutestamentlichen Schriften zur Vergleichung herbeizog, ist offenbar veraltet; so namentlich die von *Weisse*, *Schenkel* und *mir* seiner Zeit angestellten Versuche das

(1842), W.M.L. de Wette (1848), C.E. Luthardt (1852), D.F. Strauss (1864), and J.H. Scholten (1864)[26]. Schwegler argues with the starting point. If chapter 21 was added by a later hand, this does not necessarily lead to the conclusion that the same hand made other additions within the gospel. The latter are *Einschaltungen*; chapter 21 is an *Anhang*. If both were from the same redactor, chapter 21 would have been inserted like the other so-called additions. As this did not occur, Schweizer's hypothesis should be expanded to several stages of redaction[27]. As for the smaller interpolations, the authors are divided: for Schwegler[28] and

Johannesevangelium, dessen unbedingte Bevorzugung durch Schleiermacher, Lücke, u.A. nicht mehr haltbar erschien, das vielmehr wie ein Räthsel vorlag, durch Ausscheidung älterer [sic] und jüngeren Bestandtheilen zu begreifen" (c. 362); cp. c. 363: "Wäre meine Schrift jetzt erschienen, so würde sie unstreitig die derbste Abfertigung verdienen". He refers also to his *Glaubenslehre*, I, 1863, p. 164, where he expressly recognizes "Baurs Kritik als eine Epochmachende", and particularly describes the Gospel of John as a book in which "die historische Auffassung einer eigenthümlichen Gnosis oder Mystik assimilirt werde".

26. A. SCHWEGLER, *Die neueste Johanneïsche Literatur*, in *TJb(T)* 1 (1842) 140-170, 288-309, pp. 154-170; W.M.L. DE WETTE, *Lehrbuch der historisch-kritischen Einleitung in die kanonischen Bücher des Neuen Testaments*, Berlin, [5]1848, pp. 216-218 (§ 110*f*); [6]1860, pp. 235-237 (§ 110*f*); C.E. LUTHARDT, *Das johanneische Evangelium nach seiner Eigenthümlichkeit geschildert und erklärt*, I, Nürnberg, 1852, pp. 6-13; D.F. STRAUSS, *Das Leben Jesu für das deutsche Volk bearbeitet*, Leipzig, 1864, pp. 103-106 (FT: I, s.d., pp. 131-135); J.H. SCHOLTEN, *Het evangelie naar Johannes. Kritisch historisch onderzoek*, Leiden, 1864, pp. 30-31, 64-71 (GT: 1867, pp. 29, 61-67). – In addition, see the rejection by GUERIKE, *Einleitung*, 1843, p. 314: "eine Sisyphusarbeit, worin der Verfasser eben so unglücklich, als kühn, durch das ganze Evangelium hindurch ein Aechtes und Unächtes, und damit zwei Verfasser, Johannes selbst und einen armseligen Ueberarbeiter, der etwa den verachteten Synoptikern gleichstehe, scheidet"; LÜCKE, *Johannes*, II, [3]1843, pp. 830-832; MAIER, *Johannes*, I, 1843, pp. 70-71, who notes with reference to Weisse and Schweizer, among others: "Alle diese Kritiker stehen auf einem Standpunkte, bei welchem mehr oder weniger die Unmöglichkeit vorwaltet, zu einem wahren Resultate zu kommen; die Negation geht der Untersuchung voraus"; SCHWEITZER, *Von Reimarus zu Wrede*, 1906, pp. 126-127 (ET: 1936, pp. 127-128); = *Geschichte*, I, 1913, pp. 131-132.

27. Thus, for example, ch. 21 could have been introduced between 20,29 and 20,30. Schwegler continues: "Da diess nicht geschieht, so sind wir berechtigt anzunehmen, der Verf. des Anhangs-Capitels habe das übrige Evangelium als ein fertiges Ganzes schon vorgefunden, sei also verschieden von dem Dritten, von dem die übrigen Einschaltungen, wenn deren vorhanden wären, herrühren müssten. Die Schweizer'sche Hypothese muss sich also dahin erweitern, den Johanneïschen Grundstock zwei Epochen, zwei Redaktionen durchlaufen zu lassen, wovon die eine die galiläischen Erzählungen eingewoben, die andere das Schluss-Capitel hinzugefügt habe" (*Literatur*, pp. 155-156). This, however, is impossible: "Wie aber beides möglich gewesen sei bei dem anerkannten Werke eines Apostels oder apostolischen Augenzeugen, bei einem Werk, das in der kleinasiatischen Kirche verbreitet und um seines pneumatischen Charakters willen hochgehalten sein musste, das überlässt der Urheber jener Hypothese unserer eigenen Phantasie" (p. 156).

28. Schwegler discusses only 19,35-37 (pp. 166-168) and concludes: "Man wird dann aufhören, Sätze wie IX,7 für Glosseme, Typen, wie XIX,36 für Einschiebsel, und Teleologieen, wie XVIII,9 für Anzeichen einer spätern Hand zu erklären, und jede dieser Ausmerzungen mit der Bemerkung zu motivieren, von solcher Liebhaberei zeige *sonst* der Evangelist keine Spur" (p. 168). On Schwegler, cf. VAN BELLE, *Parenthèses*, 1985, pp. 187-188.

Luthardt[29] they should be attributed to the evangelist; Scholten agrees with Schweizer that they were added later[30].

There is disagreement with Schweizer above all with regard to the interpolation of the Galilean stories. Schwegler remarks that Schweizer's hypothesis makes the "Judean Gospel of John" even less reconcilable with the Synoptic Gospels[31], and Luthardt does not see why the original author would not have employed any Galilean passages since Galilean sections remain even in Schweizer's reconstruction[32]. If it was the interpolator's intention to bring the *Grundschrift* more into agreement with the Synoptic Gospels, then Luthardt wonders why he did not employ more Synoptic material and why he did not bring it more into agreement than he did[33].

Particularly called into question were the criteria Schweizer gives for the secondary character of the Galilean pericopes[34].

29. LUTHARDT, *Das johanneische Evangelium*, I, pp. 7-8 (he discusses 19,35-37; 18,9; 16,30 and 2,21-22); see especially pp. 43-44 on the "Zwischensätze" as characteristic of the Gospel of John; cf. VAN BELLE, *Parenthèses*, 1985, pp. 25-26.

30. SCHOLTEN, *Johannes*, p. 67: "Moeten wij aan *Schweizer*, wat de hoofdzaken betreft, onzen bijval weigeren, zoo blijft de verdienste zijner kritiek bestaan in de aanwijzing, dat, wanneer de latere oorsprong van Hdst. XXI wordt toegestemd, de mogelijkheid van latere interpolatie ook elders in dit evangelie niet kan geloochend worden, en dat dus voor den criticus het regt en de verplichting bestaan, hiernaar opzettelik onderzoek te doen" (GT: p. 64). For more detail about the smaller interpolations which Scholten accepts with Schweizer, cf. VAN BELLE, *Parenthèses*, 1985, pp. 157-158. See also the reaction to Scholten by HILGENFELD, in ZWT 11 (1868) 434-455; cf. VAN BELLE, *op. cit.*, p. 188.

31. "Durch diese Annahme entsteht jedoch eine ungleich grössere Schwierigkeit, als diejenige ist, der sie abhelfen will. Hat man nämlich bisher darüber geklagt, dass das Johanneïsche Evangelium die galiläische Tradition hinter die judäische ungebührlich zurückstelle, und hat man hierin ein Zeichen grösserer Zeitferne finden wollen, insofern die erstere weit leichter von der letztern verschlungen, als neben ihr habe fingirt werden können, so würde diese Incongruenz der synoptischen und Johanneïschen Darstellung noch viel unversöhnlicher werden durch eine Hypothese, welche ihnen ihre wenigen bisherigen Berührungspunkte entzieht" (*Literatur*, pp. 158-159).

32. Cf. 1,43; 4,43; 6,27-71; 7,1-9 (LUTHARDT, *Das johanneische Evangelium*, pp. 8-9). Moreover it seems that Galilean passages should follow 1,43 and 4,43.

33. LUTHARDT, *op. cit.*, pp. 8-9, with reference to BAUR, *Kritische Untersuchungen*, 1847, p. 122.

34. Cf. the summary of criticism by DE WETTE, *Einleitung*, [5]1848, p. 217 (= [6]1860, p. 236): "Aber theils sind von diesen besondern örtlichen Beweisgründen manche unrichtig oder doch nicht ganz überzeugend, theils ist der wiederhergestellte ursprüngliche Zusammenhang des Stückes VI,27ff. unbefriedigend, theils ist der Hauptgrund, dass diese galiläischen Wunder durch ihre magische Beschaffenheit sich von den übrigen des Evangeliums unterscheiden, und dass auf sie ein grösserer Werth gelegt sein soll, als sonst im Evang. auf die Wunder gelegt werde, unhaltbar. Endlich möchte die Rettung des Uebrigen von allen Angriffen schwerlich durchweg gelungen, mithin diese Hypothese für Viele unbefriedigend sein". – I limit my discussion here to the critique of Schweizer's analysis of the wine miracle. SCHWEGLER, *Literatur*, pp. 164-166, also discusses 4,44-45; LÜCKE, *Johannes*, II, [3]1843, pp. 830-832: 19,35-37; 20,19-29; LUTHARDT, *Das johanneische Evangelium*, pp. 6-13: 19,35-37; 18,9; 16,30; 6,1-15.16-26; DE WETTE, *Einleitung*, [6]1860, pp. 236-237: 6,1-26; SCHOLTEN, *Johannes*, pp. 65-67 (GT: pp. 62-64): 4,48; 6,1-16; 6,41.52; 20,19-29.

1. The *aporias* he perceives can be explained within the present form of the gospel. (a) Schwegler notes that the wine miracle, as a revelation of Jesus' glory, does not contradict the greater works promised in 1,50[35]. (b) Nor, according to Schwegler, is the declaration that the disciples believe superfluous after 1,41.45.50. If such an "aporia" were so striking, it would have struck the interpolator. Rather, the evangelist has indicated different stages in the development of the disciples' faith[36]. (c) The demeanor of Jesus' relatives (2,11-12) actually contrasts with Synoptic tradition, with which the interpolator is supposed to have been familiar. Schweizer accepts 2,12 as essentially authentic, because the trip to Galilee has already been announced in 1,43; he attributes only the words καὶ ἡ μήτηρ καὶ οἱ ἀδελφοὶ αὐτοῦ to the interpolator. But why this small addition? It has not the least reference to the Synoptic tradition. According to Schwegler, Schweizer would have been more consistent if he had ascribed 1,43a with all of 2,12 to the interpolator. If only the Cana story were interpolated we would have the following itinerary: Jesus desires to go to Galilee (1,43), he meets Philip and Nathanael (1,43-51), goes with the disciples to Capernaum where he stays only a few days (2,12) and then returns to Jerusalem (2,13). All this amounts to nothing. Why does the evangelist prepare a journey to Galilee if he says nothing about it[37]? (d) Schwegler and Scholten both reject Schweizer's opinion that the third day in 2,1 does not connect with the enumeration

35. Schwegler explains the connection between 1,50 and 2,11 as follows: "Der Gegensatz, der in den Worten: μείζω τούτων ὄψῃ aufgestellt wird, ist nicht derjenige des physikalischen und geistigen, sondern allerdings derjenige des kleinern und grössern Naturwunders. Diess zeigen schon die erläuternden Worte: ἀμὴν ἀμὴν – ἀπ' ἄρτι ὄψεσθε τὸν οὐρανὸν κτλ. 1,52; denn statt von 'der *religiösen Kraft*' zu sprechen, 'die von *Christus* auf *die Gläubigen* übergeht', ist hier, viel allgemeiner, von der schöpferischen *Allmacht* die Rede, die vom *Vater* auf den *Sohn* überströmt. Jenes ἰδεῖν ὑποκάτω τῆς συκῆς will eigentlich der Evangelist als gar keine specifische That Christi betrachtet wissen. Einer höheren Erkenntnis, wenn auch nur auf einzelne Momente, erfreute sich auch der Täufer, aber eine That göttlicher Allmacht hat er nicht verrichtet (x,41), eine solche ist vielmehr das ausschliessliche Vorrecht, das specifische Kriterium des Gottessohns. Mit einem Wort, die Anknüpfung des Hochzeitwunders passt nicht nur in den Zusammenhang, sondern sie wird von ihm sogar gefordert" (*Literatur*, pp. 161-162).

36. The belief of the disciples is mentioned once again in 11,15; 14,29; cp. 13,19. These passages would also have to be inauthentic if the disciples already believe fully at the Jordan. But the evangelist also uses the verb πιστεύω for a weak and superficial faith, as is apparent at 2,23-25, among other places (*Literatur*, p. 162).

37. Schwegler concludes: "Die Klage des Kritikers: 'dass das ganze Hochzeitwunder weder ein Gespräch, noch eine Rede Christi über irgend einen Punkt des Heils enthalte', muss, und zwar durch seine Schuld, zu der noch grösseren fortgehen, dass das Reise-tagebuch des Evangelisten nicht nur kein Gespräch, sondern nicht einmal eine bemerkenswerthe Thatsache enthalte" (*Literatur*, p. 163). Cp. DE WETTE, *Einleitung*, ⁵1848, p. 218 n. *b* (= ⁶1860, p. 237 n. *b*): "Durch Ausscheidung von II,1-11. scheint doch eine fühlbare Lücke zu entstehen, und II,12. wenn auch von Zusätzen gereinigt will sich nicht gut an I,52. anschliessen".

of days in chapter 1[38]. They take up the explanation of F.C. Baur[39]: as proof of the divine mission of Jesus, the evangelist first mentions three testimonies delivered on three successive days by the Baptist (1,19-28.29-34.35-39), and then he enumerates three demonstrations, which likewise take place on three successive days (1,40-42.43-51; 2,1-12)[40].

2. With regard to the narrative technique, Luthardt remarks that no dialogue follows the raising of Lazarus either. Moreover, the wine miracle itself is a σημεῖον that contains its own proclamation[41].

3. Schweizer's critics especially reject the third criterion. For Luthardt, a miracle always surpasses the senses, and one cannot make a distinction between a greater and a lesser miracle, whether Jesus cures a sick person, raises the dead, changes water into wine, or gives sight to one born blind. Jesus reveals his glory no less at Cana than at the grave of Lazarus[42]. For Schwegler, moreover, it is unthinkable in itself that the miracles of the Fourth Gospel would have had only a subordinate significance: they, like the discourses, express a unity between the Father and

---

38. SCHWEGLER, *Literatur*, pp. 160-161 (to which DE WETTE, *Einleitung*, [5]1848, p. 218 n. c [= [6]1860, p. 237 n. c], reacts); SCHOLTEN, *Johannes*, p. 65 (GT: p. 61).

39. BAUR, *Kritische Untersuchungen*, 1847, p. 110.

40. Scholten still weighs the possibility of reckoning the third day from 1,43 (*Johannes*, p. 65; GT: p. 61).

41. "Derselbe Cirkel ist in dem andren Argument, welches *Schweizer* gegen das Hochzeit-Wunder geltend macht, dass nämlich keine Rede sich anschliesse; denn dasselbe ist bei 4,47ff. 6,1-15 u. 16-21 der Fall; aber auch bei der Auferweckung des Lazarus. Und welcher innere Grund wäre auch vorhanden, der eine sich anschliessende Rede mit Nothwendigkeit erforderte, wenn das Wunder als ein σημεῖον, welches etwas anzeigt, selber eine Verkündigung ist?" (*Das johanneische Evangelium*, p. 9).

42. *Ibid.*, p. 9. Cp. SCHWEGLER, *Literatur*, p. 158: "'Jedenfalls aber verrathen die in Rede stehenden Erzählungen ihre Fremdartigkeit durch ihre magische Wundertheorie'. Auf den ersten Anblick kann man über diese Behauptung nicht genug staunen. Wie? die Weinverwandlung sollte magisch sein und die Heilung des Blindgeborenen nicht, die Speisung magisch, und die Auferweckung eines Gestorbenen nicht? Das Staunen mindert sich, wenn man im Verlaufe erfährt, dass der Verf. sich der ächt-Johanneïschen Wunder durch eine mehr als kühne Exegese zu entledigen weiss; aber der unbefangene Beobachter dieses Verfahrens wird sagen müssen, dass dieselben Schultern, welche die Naturalisierung einer Todtenerweckung zu tragen im Stande waren, wohl auch die Naturalisirung einer Weinverwandlung über sich zu nehmen vermocht hätten"; see also DE WETTE, *Einleitung*, [5]1848, p. 218 n. c (= [6]1860, p. 237, n. c): "Magisch ist gerade die Heilung des Blindgebornen (vgl. Vs. 6. mit Marc. VIII,23.), und den Wunderglauben im höchsten Grade in Anspruch nehmend Cap. IX. Auf den Wunderbeweis wird IX,16.31ff. XI,15.41f. ein hoher Wert gelegt, und das in Anspruch genommene καὶ ἐπίστευσαν κτλ. II,11. rechtfertigt sich durch XI,15. XIV,29. vollkommen"; STRAUSS, *Das Leben Jesu*, 1864, pp. 105-106 (FT: I, pp. 134-135); SCHOLTEN, *Johannes*, p. 66: "Eindelijk baat de weglating dier stukken niet, om de erkenning der authentie gemakkelijker te maken, daar, na het wegvallen dier feiten, nog even groote wonderen, zoo als V:1 verv., IX:1 verv., XI:1 verv., voor rekening van de schrijver blijven" (GT: p. 62); see also SCHWEITZER (see above, p. 5 n. 26).

the Son (cf. 10,37-38; 5,31.32.36)[43]. The conclusion of the wine miracle, ἐφανέρωσεν τὴν δόξαν αὐτοῦ (2,11), which Schweizer attributes to the "Falsarius", corresponds to ἵνα φανερωθῇ τὰ ἔργα τοῦ θεοῦ (9,3) in the healing of the blind man and to 11,41-42 in the pericope of Lazarus' raising, which are both genuinely Johannine. In the latter texts, the σημεῖα are in no way "indicated as the smaller, less significant kind, besides which the effects on the life of the soul would be incomparably greater and more manifest"[44]. More particularly, the wine miracle has no independent significance, but serves as external confirmation of an already existing conviction and is very closely connected with chapter 1[45].

4. The stylistic evidence which Schweizer manipulates in order to attribute the Galilean pericopes to the interpolator is also refuted. Thus Schwegler notes that the evangelist correctly uses ἡ ὥρα μου (in place of ὁ καιρός μου) at 2,4; in fact, contrary to what Schweizer thinks, the hour refers to Jesus' death[46].

43. "An und für sich schon ist es undenkbar, dass das vierte Evangelium den Wundern Christi nur eine untergeordnete Bedeutung beilege. Denn wie die Einheit des Sohns mit dem Vater, welche die Grundanschauung des Evangeliums bildet, als Einheit des Wissens sich offenbart in der Lehre, so offenbart sie sich als Einheit des Willens im Wunder. Beide Seiten, die theoretische und praktische, Lehre und Wunder, sind nur die correlaten Manifestationen einer und derselben Offenbarungsthatsache. Es hängt folgerichtig damit zusammen, wenn diese Bedeutung des Wunders, ein Zeugniss des Vaters von seiner Einheit mit dem Sohne zu sein, im Johanneïschen Evangelium selbst ausdrücklich und sehr bestimmt ausgesprochen wird" (*Literatur*, p. 156).
44. Cited by Schwegler, from A. SCHWEIZER, *Johannes*, p. 67: "Unter diese ἔργα gehören die σημεῖα zwar auch, aber nur als die kleinere, minder bedeutende Art, neben welcher die Wirkungen auf das Seelenleben unvergleichlich grösser und beweisender seien".
45. SCHWEGLER, *Literatur*, p. 157. For the significance of the sign in 2,1-11 according to Schwegler, see above, p. 7 n. 35. With reference to 4,46-54 and 6,1-15, he notes: "bei der Heilung nach Kapernaum könnte jene beschränktere Anschauung, die Schweizer den spätern Einschaltungen zuschreibt, nicht bestimmter abgewiesen werden, als mit den Worten Christi: ἐὰν μὴ σημεῖα καὶ τέρατα ἴδητε, οὐ μὴ πιστεύσητε (ιν,48); das Speisungswunder endlich hätte bei jener Voraussetzung nicht ungeschickter eingeflochten werden können, als in der Nähe der Abendmahls-Reden, an eine Stelle, wo der Gegensatz des Lebensbrodes und des gemeinen Brodes, des leiblichen und geistigen Speisungswunders unmittelbar sich aufdrängt" (pp. 157-158).
46. *Ibid.*, pp. 163-164; LUTHARDT, *Das johanneische Evangelium*, pp. 9-10, notes: "Aber es soll 2,4 ἡ ὥρα μου in einer dem johanneischen Sprachgebrauch zuwiderlaufenden Bedeutung gebraucht sein; denn hier stehe es für ὁ καιρός μου, während der Evangelist jenes Wort ausserdem immer von Jesu Todesstunde brauchte... Beides aber ist ein Irrthum. Denn fürs erste steht ἡ ὥρα μου in keinem andern Sinn, als in welchem es der Evangelist immer gebraucht; und zum andern bezeichnet es nicht geradezu Jesu Todesstunde"; see also DE WETTE, *Einleitung*, [6]1860, p. 236 n. *a*; SCHOLTEN, *Johannes*, p. 65; cp. p. 66: "Tegen het gevoelen, dat deze stukken oorspronkelijk niet zouden behoord hebben tot het evangelie pleit voorts: 1° de gelijkheid van stijl met de andere

5. With reference to 2,11 and 4,54, Luthardt[47] remarks that if these two statements are non-Johannine, then 7,21.23; 10,32.40 would have to be as well, and that does not appear to be the case. De Wette notes that 4,54 conflicts not only with 2,23 and 3,2 but with 4,48 itself, making it an unsteady argument for interpolation of the story[48].

Schweizer's opinion about the Judean author of the original gospel was further developed by Hugo DELFF (1883)[49]. Later additions are: 1,1-5.9-18; **2,1-11**.17.21-22; **4,44.46-54**; 5,19-29; **6,1-29**.37-40.44.54.59; 7,39; (7,53-8,11); 12,16.25-30.33.38-41; 13,20; 18,19 (?); 19,20.35-37; 20,9-10.11-18; **21**[50]. They would have been borrowed from some apocryphal gospel[51], the gospel book of a popular Galilean tradition[52].

deelen" (GT: p. 61; cp. p. 62). – LUTHARDT, *Das johanneische Evangelium*, pp. 20-69, who himself devoted much attention to the language of the evangelist, objects to the way in which Schweizer manipulates the criterion of style characteristics: "Nach diesem wollen nun auch die sprachlichen Ausstellungen wenig sagen". He points to the following inconsequences in Schweizer's thinking (pp. 12-13): (1) The use of ὡς δὲ ὀψία ἐγένετο (6,16) and σκοτία ἤδη ἐγεγόνει (6,17), in place of the genitive absolute οὔσης οὖν ὀψίας (20,19) and σκοτίας ἔτι οὔσης (20,1), does not necessarily indicate an interpolator, for, on the one hand, the latter uses a genitive absolute in 2,3; 4,51; 6,18; 21,4 and, on the other hand, John himself avoids this construction where he could easily have used it (5,1; 7,2; vgl. 7,14.45; 11,41; 13,31; 19,23.31.42). Moreover, Luthardt rejects the idea that we should expect an author too consistently use the same construction. (2) The frequent use of καί does not necessarily point to an interpolator. Apart from the fact that John writes in a Hebraizing style, Luthardt refers to the absence of periods and to short sentences (cf. 1,10; 2,12-16). (3) With reference to the "non-Johannine" σημεῖα καὶ τέρατα in 4,48, Luthardt remarks that Schweizer fails to notice that τέρας appears only once also in Mt and Mk, and there likewise in connection with σημεῖα (Mt 24,24; Mk 13,22) (p. 10).

47. LUTHARDT, *Das johanneische Evangelium*, p. 10.

48. DE WETTE, *Einleitung*, ⁶1860, p. 236, n. *a*.

49. H. DELFF, *Grundzüge der Entwicklungsgeschichte der Religion dargestellt*, Leipzig, 1883, pp. 264-272, 284-290, 329-343; *Geschichte des Rabbi Jesus von Nazareth. Kritisch begründet, dargestellt und erklärt*, Leipzig, 1889. For other studies by Delff, see *Bibliography*. – Cf. A. MEYER, *Behandlung*, 1889, pp. 259-261; BOUSSET, *Evangelium*, 1909, pp. 5-6; HOLTZMANN, in *ZWT* 26 (1893) 503-507; SANDAY, *Criticism*, 1905, pp. 17-20, 99-108; JACQUIER, *Histoire*, IV, ³1908, pp. 37-38; CLEMEN, *Entstehung*, 1912, p. 11; MOFFATT, *Introduction*, ²1912 (³1918), p. 559; GOGUEL, *Introduction*, II, 1923, pp. 45, 57-58; LOISY, *Quatrième évangile*, ²1927, pp. 28-29; HOWARD, *Fourth Gospel*, ⁴1955, pp. 297-298; MERLIER, *Question*, 1961, pp. 63-64; TEEPLE, *Origin*, 1974, pp. 35-36; NEIRYNCK, in *ETL* 51 (1975), p. 122 (= 1982, p. 344); TEMPLE, *Core*, 1975, pp. 24, 34; KUHN, *Christologie*, 1988, p. 23 (Jn 1,35-51); SCHMITHALS, *Johannesevangelium*, 1992, p. 89. Delff's hypothesis has been taken up by A. Mayer in 1988 (see below, pp. 268-269).

50. References in bold correspond to Schweizer's Galilean pericopes.

51. *Geschichte*, p. 106.

52. *Ibid.*, p. 109. With these additions the later author wanted to harmonize the Judean gospel with the Galilean tradition and adapt it to Alexandrian philosophy and chiliasm; cf. A. MEYER, *Behandlung*, 1889, pp. 260-261; CLEMEN, *Entstehung*, 1912, p. 11.

Hans Heinrich WENDT, in a number of publications (1886, 1900, 1911), took up Weisse's distinction between narrative and discourse material[53]. For the special Johannine material the evangelist used an expanded written source of mostly dialogues and discourses, set in the life of Jesus with only a brief narrative framework[54]. This is of the same nature as the collection of Matthean *logia* that was used by the First and Third Evangelists[55]. Perhaps the Johannine *Redequelle* was written by the Beloved Disciple[56]. In order to work this tradition into the present gospel form, the evangelist added narrative material[57]. J. Becker, W. Nicol and G. Richter count Wendt among the forerunners of the semeia hypothesis[58], perhaps on account of the criteria he used to distinguish narrative from discourse material. In fact, however, he posited no narrative source for the Johannine Gospel and thus, in the strict sense, cannot count as a precursor of the semeia hypothesis. Wendt was particularly struck by the distinction between σημεῖα and ἔργα

---

53. H.H. WENDT, *Die Lehre Jesu*. I. *Die evangelischen Quellenberichte über die Lehre Jesu*, Göttingen, 1885, pp. 215-343; ²1901, pp. 33-44 (ET: 1893, pp. 22-28; cf. p. 25: "a valuable older source"; see pp. 8-12: "Translator's Preface", esp. 9: "Wendt's original hypothesis of a 'third main source' underlying the Gospel of John ... shows that the last word has not been said on that important department of New Testament Criticism"); *Das Johannesevangelium. Eine Untersuchung seiner Entstehung und seines geschichtlichen Wertes*, Göttingen, 1900 (ET: 1902); *Die Schichten im vierten Evangelium*, Göttingen, 1911. In the main, the presentations of *Johannesevangelium* and *Schichten* are similar; in the latter work, however, some narrative portions are added to the source as necessary context for the sayings of Jesus (cf. KONINGS, *Joh. verhaal*, I, 1969, p. 48). – Cf. A. MEYER, *Literatur*, 1902, pp. 497-501; 1912, pp. 292-293; JACQUIER, *Histoire*, IV, ³1908, p. 42; BOUSSET, *Evangelium*, 1909, pp. 6-10; CLEMEN, *Entstehung*, 1912, p. 11; GOGUEL, *Introduction*, II, 1923, p. 56; LOISY, *Quatrième évangile*, ²1921, p. 28; BROMBOSZCZ, *Einheit*, 1927, pp. 11-12; HOWARD, *Fourth Gospel*, ⁴1955, pp. 95-97; KONINGS, *Joh. verhaal*, I, 1969, pp. 46-48; NICOL, *Sēmeia*, 1972, p. 9; TEEPLE, *Origin*, 1974, pp. 34-35; TEMPLE, *Core*, 1975, pp. 34, 39; HEEKERENS, *Zeichen-Quelle*, 1984, p. 11; VAN BELLE, *Parenthèses*, 1985, p. 158; SCHNELLE, *Christologie*, 1987, p. 105[-106] n. 105 (ET: 1992, p. 91[-92] n. 105); KUHN, *Christologie*, 1988, pp. 25-26 (Jn 1,35-51); WAGNER, *Auferstehung*, 1988, pp. 51-52 (Jn 11,1–12,19); ASHTON, *Understanding*, 1991, p. 28; SCHMITHALS, *Johannesevangelium*, 1992, pp. 90-91. On Wendt as precursor of the semeia hypothesis, see below, p. 15 n. 92.

54. *Johannesevangelium*, pp. 154-157; *Schichten*, pp. 3-4, 88-106. Before *Die Lehre Jesu* (I, 1885), Wendt had already defended this hypothesis in various lectures beginning in 1879 (cf. *Schichten*, p. 3).

55. *Johannesevangelium*, p. 154; *Schichten*, p. 91.

56. *Johannesevangelium*, pp. 190-215; *Schichten*, pp. 103-106.

57. He can rightly call his gospel εὐαγγέλιον κατὰ Ἰωάννην because he took up and commented upon the old tradition of the apostle. In the same way, the First Evangelist characterized his gospel as κατὰ Μαθθαῖον, because he took up the Matthean *logia* (*Johannesevangelium*, p. 196; *Schichten*, p. 106).

58. BECKER, *Wunder*, 1970, p. 131 n. 3; = 1980, p. 437 n. 8 (see below, p. 15 n. 92); NICOL, *Sēmeia*, 1972, p. 9; RICHTER, *Semeia-Quelle*, 1974, p. 64 n. 3 (= 1977, p. 281 n. 2).

respectively in the narratives and the discourses[59]. In the narratives a special emphasis has been laid on Jesus' miraculous works and knowledge, and in the closing verses (20,30-31) the evangelist states his intention: he wants to assemble the most significant σημεῖα in order to demonstrate Jesus' Messiahship and divinity so that all might believe. This interest in the miraculous is foreign to the *Redequelle*, which speaks about ἔργα, not σημεῖα. Jesus accomplishes the works the Father commissioned (5,36): his prophetic preaching activity (4,34; 17,4), in which he communicates ἀλήθεια (8,46). The ἔργα will be equated with the λόγοι (8,28; 14,10-11; 15,22.23). Wendt's other arguments are the erroneous interpretation of certain words of Jesus[60] and the disturbance of the original order[61]. Besides the *Redequelle*, the evangelist knew and used the Synoptic Gospels[62]. In the narrative material, for the most part, it is probable that the evangelist simply rendered the historical interpretation of the discourses that already existed in his community[63].

59. *Johannesevangelium*, pp. 54-61; cf. *Schichten*, pp. 35-42, esp. 36: "Die ursprünglichen Schlussworte des Evangeliums 20,30f. bestätigen ausdrücklich, dass dies, was sich uns als tatsächliche Hauptgedanke des Geschichtsberichtes darstellt, für den Verfasser der bewusst leitende Gesichtspunkt bei seiner Auswahl des Stoffes war. Er wollte die wichtigsten 'Zeichen' Jesu zusammenstellen, aus denen man den Glauben an seine Messianität gewinnen kann. Viele einzelne Erzählungszüge, die geflissentlich immer wieder hervorgehoben werden, sind offenbar bedingt durch die Absicht, den Einwänden zu begegnen, denen ein auf die Wunder Jesu gestellter Beweis für seine Messianität und Göttlichkeit ausgesetzt war"; and pp. 37-38: "Für den *ganzen* geschichtlichen Erzählungsbericht des vierten Evangeliums ist dieses Interesse für die mirakulöse Art des Wirkens und Wissens Jesu charakteristisch. Zwischen den Ergänzungsstücken, die zu der synoptischen Überlieferung in Beziehung stehen, und den anderen, welche zur Sonderüberlieferung des vierten Evangeliums gehören, besteht hinsichtlich dieses charakteristischen Interesses kein Unterschied. Dagegen ist dieses Interesse den Redenstücken des Evangeliums ganz fremd. Sie sind beherrscht von einer eigentümlichen anderen Anschauungsweise".

60. *Johannesevangelium*, pp. 62-27; *Schichten*, pp. 28-30, 43-49. Cf. VAN BELLE, *Parenthèses*, 1985, p. 158.

61. *Johannesevangelium*, pp. 67-101; *Schichten*, pp. 57-87. The insight that the evangelist used a discourse source was not new; Wendt himself (*Johannesevangelium*, p. 49; *Schichten*, p. 3 n. 1) refers to WEISSE, *Die evangelische Geschichte*, 1838; *Die Evangelienfrage*, 1856. Weisse was followed by, among others, SCHENKEL, in *TSK* 13 (1840) 736-808. Before Weisse, a similar hypothesis was defended by ECKERMANN (1796), and AMMON (1811). – Regarding the "Redequelle" before Wendt, cf. A. SCHWEIZER, *Johannes*, 1841, pp. 8-23; JACQUIER, *Histoire*, IV, ³1908, p. 25; CLEMEN, *Entstehung*, 1912, p. 9; GOGUEL, *Introduction*, II, 1923, pp. 19, 26, 57; BROMBOSZCZ, *Einheit*, 1927, p. 11; ASHTON, *Understanding*, 1991, p. 28 n. 58; SCHMITHALS, *Johannesevangelium*, 1992, pp. 51, 54, 55, 88.

62. *Johannesevangelium*, pp. 29-44; *Schichten*, pp. 107-108.

63. Wendt refers to 2,22.23-25; 4,44-45; 6,64b.70-71; 7,30-32.44-52; 8,20b; 10,19-21.39; 12,36b-43; 13,11; and 4,16-18.26-30.39-42; 5,8-16; 9,6-38; 11,4-6.11-15.28-34.36-57 (*Schichten*, pp. 106-107). Jn 1,43-51; 2,1-11; 18,1-9.12-13.19-24; 19,31-37.39; 20,11-18.24-29 probably were not created by the evangelist, but taken over from one or another tradition (p. 110).

Contrary to Wendt, Wilhelm SOLTAU (1916)[64] considered the discourses secondary[65]. At the origin of the Gospel of John lay seven legends which stem from the oral preaching of the evangelist: 2,1-11; 3,1-12; 4,1-9.16-30.39-43; 5,1-8; 13,3-20; 18,25 and 19,25-33; 20,11-18[66]. Windisch compared Soltau's collection of Johannine legends with the source identified by Thompson, Meyer, and Faure[67].

More important for the semeia hypothesis is the work of Friedrich SPITTA (1910)[68]. He studied the Gospel of John as "a source for the history of Jesus". In contrast to Wendt, he seeks the historical kernel not only in the discourses but also in the narratives. Like Schweizer, he begins his study with ch. 21, and, for several reasons, considers it an addition to the gospel by a redactor[69]. The gospel plainly ends with

64. W. SOLTAU, Das vierte Evangelium in seiner Entstehungsgeschichte dargelegt (SHAW.PH, 7/6), Heidelberg, 1916. This synthetic article was preceded by a number of other studies (see Bibliography). – Cf. A. MEYER, Literatur, 1902, p. 501; 1910, p. 72; SANDAY, Criticism, 1905, p. 21; MOFFATT, Introduction, [2]1911, p. 560; [3]1918, p. 560; CLEMEN, Entstehung, 1912, pp. 12-13; LOISY, Quatrième évangile, [2]1921, p. 28; GOGUEL, Introduction, II, 1923, pp. 68-69; LAGRANGE, Dissection littéraire, 1924; BROMBOSZCZ, Einheit, 1927, pp. 13-14; HOWARD, Fourth Gospel, [4]1955, pp. 65, 299-300; MERLIER, Question, 1961, pp. 70-71; KONINGS, Joh. verhaal, I, 1969, pp. 48-50; SELONG, Cleansing, I, 1971, pp. 23-24; TEEPLE, Origin, 1974, p. 37; TEMPLE, Core, 1975, p. 34; KUHN, Christologie, 1988, pp. 30-31 (Jn 1,35-51); ASHTON, Understanding, 1991, p. 33; SCHMITHALS, Johannesevangelium, 1992, pp. 124, 135.

65. For the recapitulation of his literary theory, see especially Das vierte Evangelium, p. 38.

66. Ibid., p. 23.

67. See above, p. 1 n. 2. Soltau sketches the further progress of the Gospel of John as follows: after A.D. 80, these legends (L) were completed with Synoptic pericopes (S) and so originated a Grundschrift, which was not so much a life of Jesus, but a devotional collection of σημεῖα καὶ τέρατα without chronological connections. Around A.D. 130, the evangelist added anti-Synoptic material, and also some passages from the Redestücke (R). Ten years later R was completely taken up into the gospel. After A.D. 150, a Continuator (C) added ch. 21 to the gospel, and 13,23; 20,2-3 and perhaps ch. 11 were interpolated as well (p. 38).

68. F. SPITTA, Das Johannes-Evangelium als Quelle der Geschichte Jesu, Göttingen, 1910. – Cf. A. MEYER, Literatur, 1912, pp. 286-292; WENDT, Schichten, 1911, pp. 13-15; CLEMEN, Entstehung, 1912, p. 15; LOISY, Quatrième évangile, [2]1921, p. 32; GOGUEL, Introduction, II, 1923, pp. 56, 69-71; LAGRANGE, Dissection littéraire, 1924, pp. 327-329; HOWARD, Fourth Gospel, [4]1955, pp. 62, 96, 298; MERLIER, Question, 1961, p. 71; BOISMARD, Saint Luc, 1962, p. 204 (see below, p. 56 n. 89); KONINGS, Joh. verhaal, I, 1969, pp. 53-55 (cp. p. 108, see below, pp. 15-16 n. 92); SELONG, Cleansing, I, 1971, p. 27; TEEPLE, Origin, 1974, pp. 89-90; NEIRYNCK, Jean et les Synoptiques, 1979, pp. 121 n. 212, 154 n. 322, 160 n. 341, 169 n. 375; Semeia-bron, 1983, p. 9 (ET: 1991, p. 657); VAN BELLE, Parenthèses, 1985, pp. 165-166; SCHNELLE, Christologie, 1987, p. 105[-106] n. 105 (ET: 1992, p. 91[-92] n. 105); KUHN, Christologie, 1988, pp. 29-30 (Jn 1,35-51); MARCHADOUR, Lazare, 1988, pp. 40-42 (Jn 11); WAGNER, Auferstehung, 1988, pp. 48-51 (Jn 11,1–12,19); ASHTON, Understanding, 1991, p. 33; SCHMITHALS, Johannesevangelium, 1992, p. 91.

69. Johannes-Evangelium, pp. 1-20.

20,30-31[70], and ch. 21 is only apparently linked by μετὰ ταῦτα (21,1) without mention of a journey of the disciples to Galilee[71]. The appearance of Jesus at the Sea of Gennesaret is called "the third" in 21,14, although three appearances have already been mentioned: one to Mary Magdalene (who also belongs with the disciples) and two to the eleven disciples[72]. The redactor joined this chapter to the *Grundschrift*[73] in order to supplement the appearances of the Lord with Galilean narratives and to give an important testimony about the author of the *Grundschrift* as well[74]. This addition stems, for the most part, from an older document containing Galilean narratives, wherein the miraculous catch of fish together with the call of Peter, as in Lk 5,1-11, took place in the beginning of Jesus' public life in Galilee[75]. The saying about the Beloved Disciple also originated from this document[76]. In this literary-critical view it is clear that the activity of the redactor did not remain restricted to the addition of this chapter: he expanded the *Grundschrift* (= A) with doublets of A, with Synoptic material and other traditions (= B), and with his own reflections (= C)[77]. Among the other traditions, Spitta counted the Galilean gospel document, in which the miraculous catch of fish (21,1-14) was narrated as the third example of Jesus' revelation following the wine miracle and the healing of the royal official's son (21,14; cf. 2,11; 4,54)[78]. The redactor's insertion of the wine miracle (2,1-11) disturbs the original context of the *Grundschrift*: the time indication τῇ ἡμέρᾳ τῇ τρίτῃ is not understandable after ch. 1[79]; after 1,11 (εἰς τὰ ἴδια ἦλθεν, καὶ οἱ ἴδιοι αὐτὸν οὐ παρέλαβον) it is surprising that Jesus is accompanied in 2,1-11 by his mother and brothers[80]; the disciples' belief (2,11) is a repetition of ch. 1 where their belief is already specifically expressed[81]; the performance of a miracle is strange immediately after Jesus' promise to Nathanael (1,51)[82]. In the Galilean source, 4,46-54 followed upon 2,12a[83]. As in the Synoptics, Mt 8,5-13 and Lk 7,1-10, the miracle took place in Capernaum and the redactor is responsible for all the additions with regard to the change of

70. *Ibid.*, p. 1.
71. *Ibid.*, pp. 2-3.
72. *Ibid.*, p. 2.
73. *Ibid.*, p. 16.
74. *Ibid.*, p. 2.
75. *Ibid.*, p. 3.
76. *Ibid.*, p. 10.
77. *Ibid.*, p. 17. For the presentation of the literary layers see Spitta's translation: text (A), footnotes (B), and italics (C) (pp. IX-XLVII).
78. *Ibid.*, pp. 16-17. On pp. 63-70 Spitta gives literary analyses of 2,1-11 and 4,45-46.
79. *Ibid.*, pp. 64-65.
80. *Ibid.*, p. 65.
81. *Ibid.*, p. 65.
82. *Ibid.*, p. 65.
83. *Ibid.*, pp. 65-66.

venue[84]. Thus, with J. Wellhausen, Spitta thinks that both pericopes, 2,1-11 and 4,46-54, belong together[85], but, in contrast to Wellhausen, he attributes the numbering of the signs to the Galilean source[86] and not to the redactor[87]. How could, after 2,23; 3,2 and 4,45, the redactor have been so inconsequent that he himself added verse 4,54[88]? Neither pericope was in the *Grundschrift*, as J. Wellhausen and E. Schwartz thought; both were introduced by the redactor[89]. According to Spitta, the numbering of the signs, above all, indicates that the three Galilean pericopes belong together[90]. Finally, it must be noted that Spitta is inclined to expand the source. He suspects that it contained an account of the call of the disciples, parallel with 1,45-51; from that narrative the redactor would have derived 1,48.49.50[91].

In *The Expositor* of 1915 James Matthew THOMPSON studied the authenticity of ch. 21[92]. Non-Johannine language and style are no criteria

84. *Ibid.*, pp. 66-67.
85. *Ibid.*, p. 66. Spitta cites WELLHAUSEN, *Das Evangelium Johannis*, 1908, p. 23: "Da diese Erzählung [4,46-54] in Galiläa spielt, so mag sie der Grundschrift entstammen. Dann muss sie dicht hinter 2,1-12 gestanden haben und Jesus muss in Kapernaum (nicht in Kana) gedacht werden, so dass die Angabe von seiner Übersiedelung dahin 2,12 nun Sinn und Inhalt gewinnt".
86. *Johannes-Evangelium*, pp. 68-69.
87. Concerning the numbering, Wellhausen notes (p. 24): "Auf ihn [Bearbeiter] geht ferner die Zählung der galiläischen Wunder in 4,54 und 2,11 zurück. Denn sie hat in der Grundschrift, wo die beiden Wunder dicht auf einander folgen, keine Stelle; sie hat nur Sinn, wenn die grosse Einschaltung 2,13–4,45, dazwischen liegt. Übrigens genügt ἐλϑὼν ἐκ τῆς Ἰουδαίας εἰς τὴν Γαλιλαίαν, um die Herkunft von 4,54 zu erkennen".
88. Spitta refers to SCHWARTZ, *Aporien*, 1908, p. 510: "Wenn es also im vierten Evangelium (4,54) als das zweite bezeichnet wird, so ist die Zählung nicht müssige Spielerei, sondern ausdrückliche Polemik gegen Lucas oder die Vorlage des Matthaeus und Lucas: die Zählung ist ausserdem alt, da sie die erste Reise nach Jerusalem ignoriert (cf. 2,23; 3,2; 4,45) und die Geschichte nahe an die der Hochzeit von Kana heranrückt".
89. *Johannes-Evangelium*, p. 68.
90. "Dass die drei galiläischen Perikopen unmittelbar neben einander gestanden haben, beweist die Zählung der drei Wunderthaten" (p. 70). Cf. pp. 66-67. For the reconstruction of the original text, cf. pp. XI-XII; additions of the Redactor are: 2,4-5.12c; 4,46a.48-49.52-53; 21,13. – Spitta's hypothesis was rejected by B. WEISS, *Das Johannesevangelium als einheitliches Werk*, 1912, p. 355; JUNCKER, *Zur neuesten Johanneskritik*, 1912, p. 27, and STRACHAN, in *Exp*, 8th ser., 4 (1912) 363-369, 554-561, p. 368: the τρίτον (Spitta's main argument) applies to the appearances to the disciples (not to Mary Magdalene); cf. NEIRYNCK, *Semeia-bron*, 1983, p. 9 n. 18 (ET: 1991, p. 657 n. 18). See also the reaction of STANGE, *Die Eigenart*, 1915, p. 15, who considers "Numerierungen von Handlungen" (2,11; 4,54; 21,14) as a characteristic of the evangelist; cf. VAN BELLE, *Parenthèses*, 1985, pp. 27-29, esp. 28.
91. *Johannes-Evangelium*, pp. 59, 70.
92. J.M. THOMPSON, *Is John XXI an Appendix?*, in *Exp*, 8th ser., 10 (1915) 139-147. – Thompson is mentioned as precursor of the semeia hypothesis (cp. above, p. 1 n. 2) by RUCKSTUHL, *Einheit*, 1951 ([2]1987), p. 107 n. 3 (cp. p. 9); BECKER, *Wunder*, 1970, p. 131 n. 3 (= 1980, p. 437 n. 8: "Vor Faure haben schon H.H. Wendt ... und J.H. [sic] Thompson... von einer Semeiaquelle gesprochen"); KONINGS, *Joh. verhaal*, I, 1969, pp. 107-109

for considering ch. 21 an addition: non-Johannine words occur in the body of the gospel as well, and one must take account of John's varying style[93]. The Galilean setting of ch. 21 and the precedence of the Beloved Disciple likewise correspond with Johannine presentation[94]. Moreover, the three-fold question of Jesus to Peter in 21,15.16.17 is analogous to Peter's denial, and ἀκολούθει in 21,19 (cf. v. 22) recalls ἀκολουθήσεις δὲ ὕστερον in 13,36[95]. The numbering in 21,14 is construed in the same way as 2,11 and 4,54. Reference to a third appearance in 21,14 is no problem for Thompson: either the evangelist did not include the appearance to Mary Magdalene or 20,24-29 was introduced later as a doublet of 20,19-23[96]. Nor is the inconsistency between 20,30-31 and ch. 21 troublesome, since 20,30-31 (with the concepts σημεῖα, χριστός, and ζωή) did not originally close the entire gospel but only the first part, where it followed 12,36-43, with which it formed a unit of 728 letters, precisely the length of the units of the accidental dislocations[97].

In another contribution the same year, Thompson mentioned a narrative source or narrative gospel as the foundation of Jn 1–12[98]. His point of departure was that there are doctrinal differences between the prologue (1,1-18) and the closing (12,36-43): a (higher) logos doctrine on the one hand, and a (lower) view of Jesus' Messiahship based on signs on the other. One has the impression that the prologue introduces the discourses and the closing concludes the narratives[99]. Thompson then studies the concept σημεῖον in the Synoptic Gospels and Acts, Paul, and John; he concludes that in Jn 1–12, with the exception of 2,18; 6,30; (10,41), σημεῖον is used with a special meaning, which is thematized in 20,30-31: the miracle is a proof for Jesus' divine mission and basis for faith in him. This, for Thompson, indicates the presence of an older literary layer in the Gospel of John[100].

(refers also to Spitta and Goguel); FORTNA, *Gospel of Signs*, 1970, pp. 22-23; NICOL, *Sēmeia*, 1972, p. 9; RICHTER, *Semeia-Quelle*, 1974, p. 64 n. 3 (= 1977, p. 281 n. 2); KYSAR, *Fourth Evangelist*, 1975, p. 14 n. 8; TEMPLE, *Core*, 1975, p. 39 (cp. p. 34); HEEKERENS, *Zeichen-Quelle*, 1984, p. 11; SCHNELLE, *Christologie*, 1987, p. 105[-106] n. 105 (ET: 1992, p. 91[-92] n. 105); ASHTON, *Understanding*, 1991, p. 33 n. 78; SCHMITHALS, *Johannesevangelium*, 1992, p. 124. On Thompson, see also HOWARD, *Fourth Gospel*, [4]1955, pp. 71-72; TEEPLE, *Origin*, 1974, pp. 36-37; VAN BELLE, *Parenthèses*, 1985, p. 29.

93. *John XXI*, pp. 139-141.
94. *Ibid.*, pp. 141-143.
95. *Ibid.*, p. 143.
96. *Ibid.*, p. 144.
97. *Ibid.*, pp. 145-146. Cf. *Accidental Disarrangements in the Fourth Gospel*, in *Exp*, 8th ser., 9 (1915) 421-437, pp. 424, 433.
98. *The Structure of the Fourth Gospel*, in *Exp*, 8th ser., 10 (1915) 512-526, pp. 523, 526.
99. *Ibid.*, pp. 512-516.
100. *Ibid.*, pp. 525-526.

A further article (1916) clarified his hypothesis by an analysis of the main ideas in 20,30-31[101]. Thompson summarizes as follows: "It therefore appears that all three heads of the Conclusion (xx.30-31), σημεῖα, χριστός, and ζωή, are appropriate summaries of a point of view which characterises an earlier narrative gospel underlying John i.–xii., but which does not characterise the overlying portions of these chapters, or any part of John xiii.–xxi. We may therefore suggest (1) that xx.30-31 ought to stand at the end of xii.: (2) that the main 'fault' in the structure of the gospel lies between xii. and xiii., the ministry-narrative and the passion-narrative: and (3) that i.–xii. consists of an earlier source or narrative-gospel, whose point of view was, roughly speaking, Synoptic, edited from a later point of view, which is specifically Johannine"[102].

According to Eduard MEYER (1921) John used not only the Synoptic Gospels (above all Luke) and oral tradition but also a written source or *Sonderquelle*[103]. Meyer enumerates the following items from the source[104]: 1. the indication of place in the healings of the paralytic and the man born blind[105]; 2. certain facts in the passion narrative (the addition of the wife, or mother, of Clopas in 19,25, the supersession of the high priest Caiaphas by his father-in-law Annas in 18,13 and the dating of the crucifixion on the day before Passover); 3. Nicodemus (ch. 3; 7,50; 19,39); 4. 12,20-21, which perhaps was continued in 12,28ff.; 5. 2,1-11; 4,45-54 and the raising of Lazarus; 6. perhaps the conversation with the Samaritan woman; 7. Nathanael (1,45-51; cf. 21,2); 8. the story of doubting Thomas (20,24-29; cf. 11,16; 14,15; 21,2); 9. some geographical indications: Cana (2,1; 4,46), Sichar (4,5), Bethany (11,8), Ephraim (11,54), the pools in Jerusalem (5,2; 9,7), the portico of Solomon (10,23), Gabbatha (19,13), and the precise description of the location of the grave (19,41).

Meyer attributed both Cana stories to the source because of the numbering of the signs in 2,11 and 4,54, and supposes that the source

101. *The Composition of the Fourth Gospel*, in *Exp*, 8th ser., 11 (1916) 34-46.
102. *Ibid.*, p. 46.
103. E. MEYER, *Ursprung und Anfänge des Christentums*. I. *Die Evangelien*, Stuttgart - Berlin, 1921, pp. 332-340: "Die Sonderquelle des Johannesevangeliums", esp. 340. – Cf. GOGUEL, *Introduction*, II, 1923, p. 71; BULTMANN, *Johannes*, 1941, p. 78 n. 4 (ET: 1971, p. 113 n. 4); MERLIER, *Question*, 1961, pp. 76-77; TEEPLE, *Origin*, 1974, pp. 37-38; KYSAR, *Fourth Evangelist*, 1975, p. 15 n. 2; SCHNELLE, *Christologie*, 1987, p. 105[-106] n. 105 (ET: 1992, p. 91[-92] n. 105); KUHN, *Christologie*, 1988, p. 33 (Jn 1,35-51); SCHMITHALS, *Johannesevangelium*, 1992, pp. 120, 122.
104. *Ursprung*, I, pp. 334-339.
105. The healing of the paralytic and the man born blind are parallel with the Synoptic Gospels (Mk 2,1-12; 8,22-26), where they actually take place in Capernaum and Bethsaida; the evangelist placed them at Jerusalem and thereby used the place-indications from the source (p. 334).

enumerated even more miracles[106]. He called the wine miracle a "crude miracle story" and the Lazarus story a "blatant intensification" of the Synoptic accounts of raising the dead[107]. Indeed, John employed these miracle stories literally, but interpreted them symbolically by adding (among others) 2,4 and 11,4[108]. The source may not have reported the entry into Jerusalem and it probably had Jesus staying in Jerusalem's environs a half-year before the passion[109]. This *Sonderquelle* was a complete gospel. Perhaps it was of the same nature as the sources to which Luke refers in his prologue (1,1-4). The source can be compared with the apocryphal gospels, according to Meyer, but in contrast to them it contained more valuable data, such as the dating of Jesus' death on the day before Passover[110].

II. A. FAURE'S THEORY: A BOOK OF MIRACLES

Alexander FAURE (1922) was the first to speak of a *Wunderbuch* as the basis for the narrative portions of the Fourth Gospel[111]. He thought that Johannine literary criticism lacked a firm starting point and sought to find it in the formulas introducing quotations from the Old Testament. He distinguishes between reminiscence quotations (1,23; 2,17; 6,31.45; 7,38.42; 10,34; 12,14.16; as well as 8,17) and fulfillment quotations

---

106. "Dieser Quelle wird auch die Zählung der Wunder (σημεῖα) angehören... In dieser werden vermutlich noch weitere Wunder gezählt worden sein, die der Verfasser nicht aufgenommen hat; vielmehr hat er durch Einschiebung des Aufenthalts in Jerusalem und Samaria den Zusammenhang zerstört" (p. 337).

107. *Ibid.*, pp. 336, 337.

108. *Ibid.*, p. 337.

109. *Ibid.*, p. 334.

110. *Ibid.*, p. 340.

111. A. FAURE, *Die alttestamentlichen Zitate im 4. Evangelium und die Quellenscheidungshypothese*, in *ZNW* 21 (1922) 99-121. – Cf. LAGRANGE, *Dissection littéraire*, 1924, pp. 339-341; MENOUD, *L'évangile de Jean*, ²1947, p. 18 n. 4; RUCKSTUHL, *Einheit*, 1951 (²1987), p. 107; NOACK, *Tradition*, 1954, p. 71; SMITH, *Composition*, 1965, p. 66, 111 n. 183; FORTNA, *Gospel of Signs*, 1970, pp. 23-25; *Predecessor*, 1988, p. 5 n. 12; KONINGS, *Joh. verhaal*, I, 1969, pp. 109-110; BECKER, *Wunder*, 1970, p. 131 n. 3 (= 1980, p. 437 n. 8); NICOL, *Sēmeia*, 1972, p. 10; TEEPLE, *Origin*, 1974, pp. 38-40; REIM, *Hintergrund*, 1974, pp. 1, 206; RICHTER, *Semeia-Quelle*, 1974, p. 64 n. 3 (= 1977, p. 281 n. 2); KYSAR, *Fourth Evangelist*, 1975, p. 15 n. 12; *ANRW* II, 25/3, 1985, p. 2399 n. 38; TEMPLE, *Core*, 1975, p. 39; CORSANI, *I miracoli*, 1983, p. 15; HEEKERENS, *Zeichen-Quelle*, 1984, p. 11; NEIRYNCK, *Semeiabron*, 1983, p. 4 (ET: 1991, p. 652); SCHNELLE, *Christologie*, 1987, p. 105[-106] n. 105 (ET: 1992, p. 91[-92] n. 105); ASHTON, *Understanding*, 1991, pp. 33-35, 88, 163; SCHMITHALS, *Johannesevangelium*, 1992, pp. 116, 124, 168; see also CARSON, in *FS B. Lindars*, 1988, p. 245. See esp. the reaction of SMEND, in *ZNW* 24 (1925) 147-150, who rejects the separation of a source from Johannine redaction on the basis of the biblical citation formulas.

(12,38; 13,18; 15,25; 19,24.36.28; and 17,12)[112]. On the basis of the different formulas, Faure identifies two authors, each responsible for one half of the Fourth Gospel: 1,1–12,37 and 12,38–20,31[113]. He also discerns a distinctive use of language in each part, the unity of Johannine style notwithstanding. Characteristic for the first part are ὄχλος (ὄχλοι), λέγω (εἶπον) with πρός and the accusative, Μωϋσῆς and σφραγίζω[114]. References to the "Beloved Disciple" and the "other disciple" are specific to the second part[115]. It is very significant that a vocabulary similar to that of chapters 1–12 appears in the close of the gospel: χριστός and σημεῖον[116]. Jn 20,30-31 is inappropriate in its present context, not only because there are resurrection narratives still to follow in chapter 21 but also because the appearances in chapter 20 can hardly be called "signs that Jesus did". Therefore, Faure supposes that 20,30-31 was originally joined to 12,37, where it formed the conclusion of a *Quellenschrift*, a book in which the miracles of Jesus were recorded (ἐν τῷ βιβλίῳ τούτῳ). It was an apologetic tract with a missionary interest, intended to stimulate faith in Jesus as the Christ[117]. The Gospel of John still shows traces of such a miracle book. It contained two Galilean miracle stories (2,1-11; 4,46-54), two healings in Jerusalem (the paralytic and the man born blind) and the raising of Lazarus. Jn 7,21-24 is a continuation of the sabbath healing in chapter 5[118]. On the other hand, the miracle narratives in chapter 6 are borrowed from the Synoptic Gospels, where they also appear together in one block. Faure also refers to the close connection between the two Galilean miracle stories, apparent from the numbering of the signs (2,11 and 4,54) and

112. *Zitate*, pp. 99-100. The reminiscence quotations in 12,39 and 19,37 were added to the fulfillment quotations 12,38 and 19,36; this is apparent not only from the introduction formulas but from the quotations themselves: in 12,38 and 19,36 the Septuagint has been used, but a different text was the basis of 12,39 and 19,37 (pp. 103-105).

113. *Ibid.*, p. 105. In the Gospel of John the words of Jesus have the same authority as the prophecies of the Old Testament (2,22) and are introduced in the same way in both halves of the gospel: as a reminiscence in 2,22 and as a fulfillment in 18,9.32 (pp. 101-102).

114. ὄχλος (ὄχλοι): 5,13; 6,2.5.22.24; 7,12.20.31.32.40.43.49; 11,42; 12,9.12. 17.18.29.34; λέγειν (εἰπεῖν) with πρός and the accusative: 3,3.4; 4,15.33.48.49; 6,5.28.34; 7,3.33.50; 8,31.57; 10,35; 11,21; 12,19; exceptions are: 16,17; 19,24; Μωϋσῆς: 1,17.45; 3,14; 5,45.46; 6,32; 7,19.22.22.23; [8,5]; 9,28.29; σφραγίζω: 3,33; 6,27 (pp. 105-106).

115. ὁ μαθητὴς ὃν ἠγάπα ὁ Ἰησοῦς (13,23; 19,26; 20,2; 21,7.20) or ἐφίλει (20,2) ὁ Ἰησοῦς (p. 106).

116. ὁ χριστός: 1,20.25; 3,28; 4,29; 7,26.27.31.41.42; 10,24; 11,27; 12,34; χριστός: 1,41; 4,25; 9,22; Ἰησοῦς Χριστός: 1,17; 17,3; σημεῖον: 2,11.18.23; 3,2; 4,48.54; 6,2.14.26.30; 7,31; 9,16; 10,41; 11,47; 12,18.37; 20,30. See also ὁ ἅγιος τοῦ θεοῦ (6,69); ὁ σωτὴρ τοῦ κόσμου (4,42). In the second part, Jesus' miracles are referred to as ἔργα (pp. 107-108).

117. This miracle book was perhaps meant to be a reply to the objections of the Jews and the disciples of John the Baptist against the Messiahship of Jesus (pp. 108-109, 111).

118. *Ibid.*, p. 109 n. 1.

their similar location[119]. He considers the existence of the *Wunderquelle* confirmed by the presence of differing theologies of the signs: in the miracle book, faith in Jesus as the Messiah is based on signs, whereas the evangelist rejects this "miracle faith" as imperfect[120].

In 1929, W. Bauer wrote that there were many enthusiasts for the semeia hypothesis at that time[121], but prior to Bultmann's commentary we hear only a few voices that corroborate such a statement.

One year after Faure's article, Hans WINDISCH, referring to the numbering of the two Cana miracles, held open the possibility that John used a collection of Galilean miracle stories[122]. Unlike Faure, Windisch

119. *Ibid.*, p. 110. According to Faure, the author of the source made a selection from a larger number of miracles: "Vielleicht hat aber auch der Verfasser unter den vorliegenden Berichten die für seine Zwecke geeignetsten ausgewählt: das Wunderbare erscheint ja bei fast allen besonders gesteigert" (p. 110 n. 4).

120. *Ibid.*, pp. 110-112. Faure thinks it possible that John used the Synoptics and other sources. He likewise proposes later redactions: a rereading by the evangelist and a redaction by a "more consciously dogmatic" editor; this explains the relative unity of the Gospel of John (p. 120). He identifies the following traces of the evangelist's redaction: καὶ οὐκ ... ὕδωρ in 2,9; cf. εἰδέναι and οὐκ εἰδέναι πόθεν ἐστίν in 7,27-28; 8,14; 9,29-30; 19,1. The Jerusalem miracles in particular have been redacted (p. 110 n. 2). The time indication καὶ τῇ ἡμέρᾳ τῇ τρίτῃ (2,1) was not in the source. Faure remarks that from the closing verses of the source (20,30-31) we can be inclined to conclude that the miracle book was a letter. – Faure mentions the *Wunderquelle* again in *Das 4. Evangelium im Muratorischen Fragment. (Ein nicht genug beachteter Bericht über die Entstehung des Johannesevangeliums)*, in *ZSysT* 19 (1942) 143-149, pp. 147-148. He distinguishes two distinct lines of development in regard to the origin of Jesus: the common tradition (that Jesus came from Galilee) and a special tradition related to that behind Lk 1–2 according to which Jesus originated from Judea and began his ministry there. Both traditions found their way into the Fourth Gospel via non-harmonized *Quellenschriften*, in precisely the same way as the Galilean miracles of the signs source (4,33ff. [sic]) were disregarded in ch. 7: there Jesus speaks only about the healing of the paralytic, as if no miracles had yet taken place in Galilee (p. 148). Cf. MENOUD, *L'évangile de Jean*, ²1947, p. 18 n. 4.

121. BAUER, in *TR* 1 (1929), p. 140: "für die sich manche in der Gegenwart erwärmen".

122. H. WINDISCH, *Der johanneische Erzählungsstil*, in *FS H. Gunkel*, II, 1923, pp. 174-213, esp. 209-210 (ET: 1993, pp. 25-64, esp. 60-61): "Warum der Evangelist diese Geschichte und auch noch in dieser Form in sein Evangelium aufgenommen hat, ist schwer zu sagen. Dass zwischen Kap. 4 und 5 eine galiläische Szene erwünscht war, dass, wie V. 54 hervorgehoben wird, noch ein zweites galiläischen Zeichen geboten werden sollte, erklärt noch nicht alles. Vielleicht hat der Evangelist eine Sammlung von galiläischen Zeichen vor sich, die er noch einmal verwerten wollte; vielleicht wollte er die galiläischen Zeichen auf drei bringen (das dritte das Brotwunder). Oder sollte die Perikope erst später eingesetzt sein?" (with reference to Faure and Thompson; see above, p. 1 n. 2). – On Windisch, cf. HOWARD, *Fourth Gospel*, ⁴1955, pp. 71-74, 135-136; NOACK, *Tradition*, 1954, pp. 116-119; KONINGS, *Joh. verhaal*, I, 1969, pp. 69-71; NICOL, *Sēmeia*, 1972, p. 10; TEEPLE, *Origin*, 1974, pp. 23, 60, 63, 95; TEMPLE, *Core*, 1975, pp. 50, 302 n. 5; SCHNELLE, *Christologie*, 1987, p. 105[-106] n. 105 (ET: 1992, p. 91[-92] n. 105); KUHN, *Christologie*, 1988, pp. 32-33 (Jn 1,35-51); SCHMITHALS, *Johannesevangelium*, 1992, p. 124; SMITH, *John among the Gospels*, 1992, pp. 19-31 (pp. 31-37: "Reaction to Windisch").

places the count in 2,11 and 4,54 at the level of Johannine redaction. True, John took the narrative of 2,1-11 from the tradition, but he arranged it chronologically in his composition by connecting it with the preceding in 2,1 and by adding the numbering in 2,11. John thus placed the first link of a chain that runs through the whole gospel[123]. In 1926, in presenting his Replacement Theory, Windisch's opinion about the signs source is a great deal more positive. A non-Synoptic tradition or a written source must have had greater influence on the Gospel of John than did the Synoptic Gospels. This source or tradition was a collection of signs (2,11; 4,54; 7,31; 9,31-32; 12,37; 20,30). The evangelist attached much importance to adapting it; the Synoptic tradition was only auxiliary[124]. A year later, Windisch refers again to his 1923 article, in which he considered the author of the discourses responsible for the dramatic design of the narratives. He now concedes that his thesis is not as sure as he had thought at that time and admits that in all probability John used a collection of signs, or at any rate a non-Synoptic *Vorlage*; the interruptions and additions in many narratives are an indication of redactional adaptation[125].

Maurice GOGUEL (1923) thought that the Gospel of John was partly composed from sources and redactions that are independent of the Synoptics[126]. He rejects the *Grundschrifthypothese* of Spitta and Wellhausen[127], but, with Spitta, accepts a separate source for 2,1-11; 4,46-54; and, with great probability, 21,1-14[128]. Indeed, the first two narratives are closely bound to one another by the localization in Cana (in the second story, Capernaum is of lesser importance) and the numbering of the signs. The author who numbered the signs had no knowledge of σημεῖα that took place in Jerusalem (4,45)[129]. On the basis of the

---

123. *Erzählungsstil*, p. 208 (ET: 1993, p. 59).

124. *Johannes und die Synoptiker. Wollte der vierte Evangelist die älteren Evangelien ergänzen oder ersetzen?* (UNT, 12), Leipzig, 1926, pp. 54-55.

125. *Die Absolutheit des Johannesevangeliums*, in *ZSysT* 5 (1927) 3-54, p. 12. He refers (p. 12 n. 3) to BAUER, *Johannesevangelium*, ²1925 and FAURE, *Zitate*, 1922.

126. M. GOGUEL, *Introduction au Nouveau Testament. II. Le quatrième évangile*, Paris, 1923, p. 470. For other studies by Goguel about source criticism, see *Bibliography*. – Cf. LOISY, *Quatrième évangile*, ²1921, p. 32; HOWARD, *Fourth Gospel*, ⁴1955, pp. 81, 88, 131, 133-134, 157; MERLIER, *Question*, 1961, pp. 82-83, 98-99; KONINGS, *Joh. verhaal*, I, 1969, pp. 86-89; SELONG, *Cleansing*, I, 1971, p. 28; NICOL, *Sēmeia*, 1972, p. 12 n. 3; TEEPLE, *Origin*, 1975, pp. 40, 63, 74, 95, 99; NEIRYNCK, *Semeia-bron*, 1983, p. 9 n. 18 (ET: 1991, p. 657 n. 18); KUHN, *Christologie*, 1988, pp. 39-40 (Jn 1,35-51); SCHMITHALS, *Johannesevangelium*, 1992, p. 121; SMITH, *John among the Gospels*, 1992, p. 117 n. 15.

127. *Quatrième évangile*, pp. 355-382, 383-470, esp. 470.

128. *Ibid.*, pp. 269-279, 389-390, 396-398. Jn 2,4 (an interruption in the story) and 4,43-45.48 (borrowed from an older tradition parallel with Mk 6,1-6; Mt 13,53-58 and Lk 4,16-30) are attributed to the evangelist (p. 390 n. 1, 395-396. 270); 2,12 can be from either the evangelist or the source (p. 390); see also *ZNW* 12 (1911) 321-324, pp. 321-322.

129. *Ibid.*, pp. 269-270.

numbering in 21,14, which is inconsistent with chapter 20 but follows well after 2,11 and 4,54, one may also assign 21,1-14 to the source[130].

Walter BAUER, in the first edition of his commentary (1912), held that John was dependent on the Synoptics[131]. In the second edition (1925), he accepted that the evangelist had obtained gospel material, already fixed literarily, from non-Synoptic traditions or *Vorlagen* as well. This is apparent, first, from the great freedom with which John employed the Synoptics and, second, from the passages that are missing in the other gospels. Lk 1,1, the oldest apocryphal gospels, and the gospel quotations in Ignatius and 2 Clement confirm the existence of a non-Synoptic tradition around 100[132]. Bauer remains skeptical about the semeia hypothesis because one can hardly reconstruct a *Grundschrift* or source from these *Vorlagen*; the evangelist employed these with the greatest freedom and borrowed only what was useful for him[133]. Bauer ascribes the following passages to written non-Synoptic tradition: the conversation with the Samaritan woman (chapter 4); the healing of the paralytic (chapter 5); Jesus at the Sea of Tiberias (chapter 6); Jesus and the brothers (chapter 7); the healing of the man born blind (chapter 9); the raising of Lazarus (chapter 11); the footwashing and the prediction of the betrayal (chapter 13); Peter and Mary at the tomb (chapter 20); and two stories which lay at the basis of 21,1-14[134].

130. *Ibid.*, p. 299. The evangelist likewise knew and used the Synoptic Gospels, especially Luke, and added some passages himself. Because he used the Synoptics, we cannot date the evangelist's redaction before 90 (p. 531). Goguel noted the following additions by the evangelist: 1,1-18; 2,23-25; 3,1-21; 4,4-42; 5,9b-16.34-35.37-38.41-44; 7,10.11-13.16-18; 10,25-35; 11,57; 12,34-50; 13,1-17; ch. 14–17; 18,13b-14 (pp. 383-470). Later, the evangelist revised his gospel and perhaps added 11,1-45.54 (pp. 430-431). An editor is responsible for the final redaction; he added ch. 21 and 19,35 (pp. 359-365).

131. W. BAUER, *Das Johannesevangelium erklärt* (HNT, 2), Tübingen, 1912, pp. III, 51 (4,46-54), 63 (6,1-13), 137 (12,3). – Cf. HOWARD, *Fourth Gospel*, [4]1955, pp. 78-82, 109, 171-172; RUCKSTUHL, *Einheit*, 1951 ([2]1987), pp. 10-11, 30; HAENCHEN, *Literatur*, 1955, pp. 304-305; KONINGS, *Joh. verhaal*, I, 1969, p. 66; SELONG, *Cleansing*, I, 1971, pp. 14-15; KUHN, *Christologie*, 1988, pp. 36-37 (Jn 1,35-51); SCHMITHALS, *Johannesevangelium*, 1992, p. 121; SMITH, *John among the Gospels*, 1992, p. 34.

132. *Johannesevangelium*, [2]1925, esp. pp. 238-239; the third edition remained essentially unchanged (1933, pp. 246-247).

133. *Johannesevangelium*, [2]1925, p. 241 ([3]1933, pp. 249-250): "Ein Vergleich mit den Synoptikern zeigt deutlich, dass Jo schriftliche Vorlagen bearbeitet hat. Man kann daraus aber auch lernen, wie er dabei verfahren ist. Er schaltet willkürlich mit dem überlieferten Stoff, entnimmt, was ihm brauchbar erscheint, und gibt ihm die ihm gutdünkende Form. Steht er aber seinem Gewährsmännern derartig frei gegenüber, dann ist von vornherein wenig glaubhaft, dass er sich auf weite Strecken hin der Führung einer 'Grundschrift' sollte anvertraut haben. Jedenfalls würden uns die sicheren Massstäbe fehlen, die uns gestatteten, eine solche Grundschrift von dem Erzeugnis letzter Hand abzulösen. Wir kommen schwerlich weiter als dahin, festzustellen, wo im Einzelfall nicht-synoptischen Vorlagen bearbeitet zu sein scheinen, und müssen mannhaft den Wunsch unterdrücken, aus den auf diesem Weg gewonnenen Materialien 'Quellen' oder eine 'Grundschrift' zusammenzustellen".

134. For this summary, cf. p. 241 ([3]1933, p. 250). Bauer points to the following traces of redaction upon older material: (1) the priority given to the Jews (4,22b): according to

In a review of Johannine studies (1929), Bauer defended the same opinion: we can hardly say that John was dependent on the Synoptics in the same way that Matthew and Luke were dependent on Mark; John made a free choice of Synoptic material. His presentation of the self-revealing Jesus is also entirely different from the teaching Jesus of the Synoptics. With regard to the miracle stories, one could think that John was more dependent on the Synoptic material, but he also omits a great deal (e.g., the exorcisms) and he introduces new stories which he can hardly have borrowed from one and the same σημεῖα source. Perhaps the evangelist used older, non-Synoptic material that was already composed in written form[135].

John salvation comes from the heavenly σωτὴρ τοῦ κόσμου (4,42) (²1925, p. 67); the disciples' marvelling at Jesus talking with a woman (4,27) (p. 68); the narrative detail that the woman left her water jar at the well (4,28) (p. 69); the emphasis on Jesus' omniscience in 4,29 in place of his testimony about himself (4,25.26) (p. 69); the conclusion (4,35-38) is difficult to understand in the present context, and θερίζω, θερισμός, σπείρω, κόπος, and κοπιάω are not Johannine words (pp. 69-70). (2) In 5,1-18 there is no mention that the healed man joins Jesus (pp. 79-80). (3) The descent of the disciples (6,16) does not fit after 6,15, but does indeed after 6,3 (p. 89). (4) The unclear references to Jesus' brothers in 7,3.4.5 (pp. 103-104). (5) The story of the man born blind perhaps originally dealt with someone who became blind (pp. 128-129); the healed man's confession that Jesus is a prophet goes back to a *Vorlage* which treated of ideas about believers and sinners in regard to Jesus (cf. Sir 15,7.12; 27,30) (p. 131). (6) With reference to 11,1-45 Bauer notes: "Hat Jo jene Geschichten durch eine sie weit übertreffende ersetzt, so hat er die ihm nötigen Elemente doch der älteren Tradition entnommen" (p. 150), and after a comparison with Lk 10,38-42 and 16,19-31 he concludes: "Wird doch hier besonders deutlich, dass Jo vorliegenden Erzählungsstoff, der nicht den Synoptikern entnommen ist, benützt hat (s. 2f.16.20.22.24.28.32.34.35.39 verglichen mit 44). Er hat in einer seiner Quellen von der Erweckung eines Gestorbenen durch Jesus gelesen und diesen Bericht, die Einzelheiten, so gut es ging, verwertend, ausgestaltet zu dem göttlichen Allmachtswunder, durch das Jesus erneut seine Herrlichkeit offenbart" (p. 150). In vv. 1-2 not only the names of the two sisters but also the reference to the anointing story and the following reference to Lazarus (v. 2) point to redaction (p. 143); the saying of Thomas in v. 16 takes up v. 15 and connects well with v. 8, but takes no account of Jesus' calming explanation in vv. 9.10 (p. 145); after v. 17 the reader no longer expects v. 20 (p. 146); that Jesus' deeds are the result of his prayer (v. 22) does not fit well with the Johannine presentation (p. 146; cp. p. 149); Martha's expectation that Lazarus will rise in the resurrection on the last day does not accord with Jesus' declaration in v. 23 (p. 146); Martha's communication to Mary (v. 28) does not correspond to an instruction of Jesus (p. 147); the saying of Mary in v. 32 is a repetition of Martha's in v. 21 (p. 147); Jesus' question in v. 34 points likewise to older material (p. 148); τεταρταῖος (v. 39) is non-Johannine (p. 148). (7) In 13,1-20 verses 6-11 appear to have been added (p. 166). (8) What some thought in 13,29 is incomprehensible after 13,23-26 (p. 170). (9) Jn 20,2-10 seems to have been inserted (p. 223). (10) In 21,1-14 perhaps two stories, with differing points, have been worked together (vv. 1-8.9-14): the Beloved Disciple (v. 7) is not mentioned in v. 2; the result of Peter's sudden action is not described; in vv. 5.10 Jesus requests something to eat, but in v. 9 there are already fish at hand (p. 231).

135. *Johannesevangelium und Johannesbriefe*, in *TR* NF 1 (1929) 135-160, p. 140.

Perhaps we should also mention here the less known Edward Selwyn
HOERNLE (1931)[136]. According to him, the Gospel of John, originating at
Ephesus, is a compilation of two sources: "R" or the witness of the
Beloved Disciple, and "P" or the Gospel of Philip. "P" appears to deserve
some place in our discussion of the signs source hypothesis because it
contained a series of miracle stories which portray Jesus' divinity.

III. R. BULTMANN'S SEMEIA HYPOTHESIS

Rudolf BULTMANN, who had declared himself in favor of the signs
source as early as 1931[137], made the first attempt to circumscribe it by
content and form in his important commentary (1941). Portions of that
work that are significant for the semeia hypothesis had already appeared
in 1937[138]. Bultmann never provided a systematic exposition, however:
references to the σημεῖα-*Quelle* are scattered throughout the commentary. On the basis of disparate notations, mostly in footnotes, we will
attempt to give a description of his theory[139].

136. E.S. HOERNLE, *The Record of the Loved Disciple together with the Gospel of
St. Philip: Being a Reconstruction of the Sources of the Fourth Gospel*, London, 1931. –
R = *Record of the Loved Disciple*; P = *Gospel of Philip*. R was meant to describe Jesus'
personality and itself consisted of two parts: RD (= *Discourses in R*), a collection of
sayings on the doctrine of the relationship of the Father to the Son, and RN (= *Narratives
in R*), the account of the Beloved Disciple. RN was composed perhaps of "poetical stan-
zas" and likewise contained two parts, of which the first reported Jesus' public ministry
and the second the passion narrative. The compilation of the gospel progressed in two
phases. First, all Jesus' works from P were illustrated with logia from RD. Second, P was
reedited and amplified by the incorporation of all of RD, parts of the first half of RN, and
the entire second half, except for a few narratives (e.g., the institution of the Eucharist). –
I borrowed my information on Hoernle from HOWARD, *Fourth Gospel*, [4]1955, pp. 49-50;
KONINGS, *Joh. verhaal*, I, 1969, p. 101 n. 6; TEEPLE, *Origin*, 1974, pp. 40-41. Reviews:
cf. MALATESTA, no. 675.
137. R. BULTMANN, *Die Geschichte der synoptischen Tradition* (FRLANT, 29), Göttingen, [2]1931, p. 347 n. 2 (ET: 1963, p. 321 n. 2; FT: 1973, p. [391-]392 n. 2): "Jedenfalls hat Joh. eine σημεῖα-Quelle benutzt" (note added to [1]1921, p. 194).
138. *Das Evangelium des Johannes* (KEK, 2), Göttingen, 1941 (= 10th edition of the
Meyer commentary). – Bultmann's commentary was a long time in being completed (cf.
EASTON, in *ATR* 22, 1940, 223-224, p. 223). More information has recently been provided
by EVANG, *Rudolf Bultmann*, 1988, pp. 72-73; cp. SCHMITHALS, *Johannesevangelium*,
1992, p. 164). The first five fascicles (up to 12,19; pp. 1-320) appeared in 1937. The commentary ([10]1941) remained unchanged in the later editions ([21]1986). According to
Schmithals (*op. cit.*, p. 164) the "Gesamtauflage" amounts to 40,000 copies. In *Das Evangelium des Johannes. Ergänzungsheft*, Göttingen, 1950; [2]1957 (= 1966, 1969, 1979),
Bultmann made some changes and additions. In 1971, the commentary was translated from
the 1964 printing (with the supplement of 1966) by G.R. BEASLEY-MURRAY (see, however,
below, p. 41 n. 1); cf. EISENBEIS, *A Translation*, 1982. – Reviews: cf. MALATESTA, nos.
960 (the first five fascicles, 1937), 974 (the complete commentary [10]1941), 994 ([11]1950),
1039 ([17]1962; VAN BELLE, no. 1923 (English translation). See also below, pp. 41-45.
139. For the lack of a systematic introduction to the Gospel of John, see Bultmann's
motivation in his "Nachwort" (Marburg, July 1951), reproduced by SCHMITHALS, *Johan-*

The semeia hypothesis must be situated within the whole of Bultmann's literary theory, which is a combination of theories on sources, redaction, and text displacements. According to Bultmann, canonical John is the reworking of an original gospel by an "ecclesiastical redactor", who is responsible for some interpolations, the addition of chapter 21, and the present order of pericopes[140]. The original gospel itself was composed from three sources: the σημεῖα-*Quelle* for the narrative portions of Jn 1–12[141]; the *Offenbarungsreden*, a pre-Christian gnostic source, for the Johannine discourses; and the Passion source. Besides these sources the evangelist used other traditions[142]. Bultmann doubts

---

nesevangelium, 1992, p. 166. Schmithals wrote the *Introduction* to the English translation (1971, pp. 3-12) and Thyen added a *Postscript* (pp. 741-744). For Bultmann's theory, see esp. SMITH, *Composition*, 1965 (see below, p. 53 n. 69). A few quotations demonstrate the importance of Bultmann's commentary: KÄSEMANN, in *VF* (1942-1946, ed. 1947), p. 182: "Es gibt keine bessere Einführung in den gegenwärtigen Stand der joh. Frage, ihre Motive und Problemverschiebungen; kein Werk, das in gleich meisterhafter Prägnanz den Ertrag eines ebenso langwährenden wie verschlungenen exegetischen Ringens zusammenfasst"; JEREMIAS, *Literarkritik*, 1941, p. 39: "Ohne alle Frage ist R. Bultmanns Kommentar zum JohEv eine der wichtigsten Erscheinungen auf dem gesamten Gebiet der theologischen Literatur der letzten Zeit". Thirty years after its publication the opinion of exegetes appears not to have changed: "So bleibt – bei aller im einzelnen zu übenden Kritik – Bultmanns Kommentar nach wie vor der beste Weg zur Interpretation des vierten Evangeliums" (BECKER, *Wunder*, 1970, p. 148; = 1980, p. 461). See also below, pp. 44-45 n. 20. Yet J. LEVIE could remark in *NRT* 73 (1951), p. 876: "Il faut bien avouer que ce commentaire est resté un premier jet, une première mise en œuvre du riche fichier réuni par l'auteur; l'ouvrage de 1941 n'était pas 'fait', mais seulement 'préparé' pour la rédaction".

140. *Johannes*, p. 4 n. 2 (ET: p. 17 n. 2).

141. "Für den Nachweis der σημεῖα-Quelle s. A. Faure" (p. 78 n. 4; ET: p. 113 n. 2). See above, p. 1 n. 1.

142. For references, see the key words in the index (pp. 557-563; ET: pp. 733-740): *Literarkritik, Quellen: Offenbarungsreden, σημεῖα-Quelle, andere Quellen, Redaktion des Evangelisten* and *kirchliche Redaktion*). See also Bultmann's article *Johannesevangelium*, in *RGG*³ 3 (1959) 840-450, and *Theologie des Neuen Testaments*, Tübingen, 1948-1953; ²1954; ³1958; ⁴1959; I cite the 5th edition, 1965, which is practically unchanged (ET: 2 vols., 1952, 1955). – For Bultmann's literary theory see, among others: JEREMIAS, *Literarkritik*, 1941, cc. 39-43; MICHAELIS, *Einleitung*, 1946, pp. 106-111, esp. 108-109; MENOUD, *L'évangile de Jean*, ²1947, pp. 17-21; RUCKSTUHL, *Einheit*, 1951 (²1987), pp. 14-17, 20-179; NOACK, *Tradition*, 1954, pp. 9-42; HOWARD, *Fourth Gospel*, ⁴1955, pp. 166-167, 171-172, 250-258; HAENCHEN, *Literatur*, 1955, pp. 305, 310; MENOUD, *Les études johanniques*, 1958, p. 14; BRAUN, *Jean le théologien*, I, 1959, p. 10; SMITH, *Sources*, 1964 (= 1985, pp. 39-61); *Composition*, 1965, *passim*; BLANK, *Krisis*, 1964, pp. 15-16; BECKER, *Wunder*, 1970, pp. 131-135 (= 1980, pp. 437-443); KONINGS, *Joh. verhaal*, I, 1969, pp. 111-113; FORTNA, *Gospel of Signs*, 1970, pp. 1 n. 1, 24; SELONG, *Cleansing*, I, 1971, pp. 163-164; NICOL, *Sēmeia*, 1972, pp. 10-11; REIM, *Hintergrund*, 1974, pp. 233-236, 269-282; TEEPLE, *Origin*, 1974, pp. 41-43; KYSAR, *Fourth Evangelist*, 1975, pp. 14-16; TEMPLE, *Core*, 1975, pp. 4-5, 26, 31, 35, 39, 51; COTHENET, *Le quatrième évangile*, 1977, pp. 103-107; *L'évangile selon saint Jean*, 1984, pp. 46-47; CARSON, *Current Source Criticism*, 1978, pp. 414-420; HOEFERKAMP, *Relationship*, 1978, pp. 29-33; LEIDIG, *Jesu Gespräch*, 1979, pp. 2-3 (Jn 4,1-42); SMALLEY, *John*, 1978, pp. 51-56, 103-113; HAENCHEN, *Johannesevangelium*, 1980, pp. 37-41 (ET: I, 1984, pp. 34-37); NEIRYNCK, *Semeia-bron*, 1983, pp. 3-8 (ET: 1991, pp. 651-656); CORSANI, *I*

that John knew the Synoptics; if he had, he surely has not used them as a source in the way Matthew and Luke have used Mark[143]. Contrary to the defenders of a *Grundevangelium*, Bultmann thinks that the unity of the gospel is obtained at the end of the evolution and not at the beginning. Although he was convinced that one can hardly distill the sources from the present gospel, he nonetheless defined them rather precisely[144].

To determine the signs source, Bultmann makes use of four criteria[145].

1. His first criterion is undoubtedly that of style. In 1927 he wrote that the collection of style characteristics is the only way to a more objective source criticism[146]. He develops this in his commen-

---

miracoli, 1983, pp. 13-22; HEEKERENS, *Zeichen-Quelle*, 1984, pp. 11-16, 17-43; J.A.T. ROBINSON, *Priority*, 1985, p. 15; VAN BELLE, *Parenthèses*, 1985, pp. 35-42; BITTNER, *Jesu Zeichen*, 1987, pp. 2-3; KUHN, *Christologie*, 1988, p. 39 (Jn 1,35-51); MARCHADOUR, *Lazare*, 1988, pp. 44-46 (Jn 11); WAGNER, *Auferstehung*, 1988, pp. 54-57 (Jn 11,1–12,19); ASHTON, *Understanding*, 1991, pp. 44-66, 161; BOTHA, *Jesus and the Samaritan Woman*, 1991, pp. 14-16; RUCKSTUHL – DSCHULNIGG, *Stilkritik*, 1991, pp. 10-11; SLOYAN, *What Are They Saying about John?*, 1991, pp. 8-11; KOSKENNIEMI, *Apollonios von Tyana*, 1992, pp. 115-118; SCHMITHALS, *Johannesevangelium*, 1992, pp. 164-174; SMITH, *John among the Gospels*, 1992, pp. 48, 65-66. See also the *Introduction* by SCHMITHALS in the English translation of Bultmann's Commentary (pp. 3-12, esp. 6-7). – For the reconstruction of the different literary layers, see esp. SMITH, *Composition*, 1965, pp. 23-34: *Offenbarungsreden* (cp. EASTON, in *JBL* 65, 1946, 143-156); pp. 38-44: semeia source; pp. 48-51: passion source; pp. 54-56: other sources and traditions; pp. 179-212: the original order of the gospel.

143. *Johannesevangelium*, c. 841.

144. *Ibid.*, c. 842.

145. Cf. RUCKSTUHL, *Einheit*, 1951 (²1987), pp. 98-99; SMITH, *Composition*, 1965, pp. 35-38; KONINGS, *Joh. verhaal*, I, 1969, pp. 111-113; BECKER, *Wunder*, 1970, pp. 133-134 (= 1980, pp. 439-441). – Bultmann abandons Faure's argument based on the introductory formulas for Old Testament quotations: "Dass die Einführungsformeln der Zitate verschieden sind, wird freilich nicht als Kriterium der Quellenscheidung gelten können", at least with reference to 12,38.40: ἵνα πληρωθῇ (v. 38) was also written by the evangelist (13,18; 15,25; 17,12). Otherwise, he distinguishes between the source (v. 38) and the evangelist (v. 40) because the Septuagint has been used in the first quotation and not in the second (*Johannes*, p. 346 n. 4; ET: p. 452 n. 2).

146. *Das Johannesevangelium in der neuesten Forschung*, in *CW* 41 (1927) 502-511. At that time, Bultmann judged that a *Quellenanalyse* is indispensable, and that the basic fault of the older literary criticism lay in the fact that it almost never paid attention to criteria of style. According to Bultmann, one should "in sorgfältiger Arbeit" collect "stilistische Merkmale", in which "die Kriterien für die Unterscheidung von Tradition und Redaktion, von Quellen und Verfasser geliefert werden" (p. 503). See also RUCKSTUHL, *Einheit*, 1951 (²1987), p. 39; NICOL, *Sēmeia*, 1972, p. 10; HEEKERENS, *Zeichen-Quelle*, 1984, p. 27; SCHNELLE, *Christologie*, 1987, p. 173 (ET: 1992, p. 156). In his analysis of 1 John (1927), Bultmann carefully studied the style of the author (and of the *Vorlage*): *Analyse des ersten Johannesbriefes*, in *FS A. Jülicher*, 1927, pp. 138-158, esp. 141-143 (= 1967, pp. 105-123, esp. 108-109). For the importance of style criticism, see also his *Hirsch's Auslegung des Johannesevangeliums*, in *EvT* 4 (1937) 115-142, p. 121: "Die Analyse kann sich nur an der Hand der *Stilkritik* vollziehen. H[irsch] macht zwar gelegentlich, wenn es sich um die Ausscheidung eines 'redaktionellen' Zusatzes handelt,

tary[147]. Whenever he considers a certain pericope for the signs source he enumerates the style characteristics. This is obvious in his commentary on the wine miracle, the starting point of his hypothesis: the style of the semeia source is clearly distinguishable from the language of the evangelist or of the *Redenquelle*, which is at the basis of the Prologue and the discourses; it is equally clearly distinguishable from the miracle stories of the Synoptic tradition[148]. The language of the source is especially characterized by Semitisms, but Bultmann rejects the opinion that the source was originally drafted in Aramaic and later translated into Greek. If that were the case, we should encounter more Greek sentence connections on one hand, and translation errors on the other. Rather, the signs source was written in Greek by a Greek-speaking Semite[149]. Bultmann notes the following characteristics[150]: (a) the place of the verb, usually at the beginning of the sentence; (b) short sentences without connection (asyndeton) or joined only with the conjunctions καί, οὖν, and δέ (not μέν); (c) redundant αὐτοῦ and ἡμεῖς; (d) the use of ποιέω; (e) the

---

gute stilkritischen Bemerkungen; er hat aber die Aufgabe einer durchgehenden stilkritischen Analyse des Evangeliums nicht ergriffen. Eine solche würde zeigen, dass viele Stücke, die H[irsch] dem Redaktor zuschreibt, dem Evangelisten selbst angehören, und dass der Text, den H[irsch] für den ursprünglichen hält, in Wahrheit der Text der vom Evangelisten benutzten Quelle ist".

147. Nevertheless he remarks: "Die Frage nach den Quellen ist deshalb so schwer zu beantworten, weil die Sprache des J.s eine so einheitliche zu sein scheint, dass zu kritischen Scheidungen kein Anlass geboten ist. Indessen kann die Einheit der Sprache darauf beruhen, dass der Evangelist seine Quellen in durchgreifender Weise redigiert hat, und eine genauere Beobachtung zeigt auch erhebliche Unterschiede der Sprache in einzelnen Partien, vor allem zwischen den erzählenden Berichten und den Reden und Diskussionen" (*Johannesevangelium*, c. 842). – When NOACK, *Tradition*, 1954, pp. 21-22, remarks that Bultmann attributes the substantive ἐκεῖνος, a clear trait of the evangelist, to the source, and thus carries style criticism to inconsequence, Bultmann replies that his use of style criticism as subordinate to the total literary criticism is completely justified; cf. *Zur johanneischen Tradition*, in *TLZ* 80 (1955) 521-526. For him the arguments from style criticism must always converge with the other arguments: it is possible that the evangelist regularly inserted ἐκεῖνος into a source text, while elsewhere it can be an indication for assigning a passage to the evangelist (esp. cc. 522-523).

148. *Johannes*, p. 78. Cp. pp. 68 n. 7, 131 n. 5, 155 n. 5, 177 n. 4, 250 n. 1, 301 n. 2, 541 n. 2 (ET: p. 113. Cp. pp. 89 n. 6, 180 n. 2, 211 n. 1, 238 n. 1, 329 n. 2, 395 n. 2, 698 n. 2).

149. "Aber Übersetzung aus einem aram. Original liegt offenbar nicht vor; denn ein griech. Übersetzer hätte wohl gerade die Satzverbindungen hergestellt; auch fehlen Übersetzungsfehler. Also ist die Quelle wohl von einem griech. redenden Semiten griech. verfasst" (with reference to 1,35-49; p. 68 n. 7; ET: p. 98 n. 7). Cp. pp. 131 n. 5, 155 n. 5, 177 n. 4, 250 n. 1, 301 n. 2 (ET: pp. 180 n. 2, 211 n. 1, 238 n. 1, 329 n. 2, 395 n. 2).

150. References: (a) pp. 68 n. 7, 131 n. 5, 155 n. 5, 177 n. 4, 250 n. 1, 301 n. 2; (b) pp. 68 n. 7, 131 n. 5, 155 n. 5, 177 n. 4, 250 n. 1, 301 n. 2; (c) pp. 155 n. 5, 250 n. 1; (d) pp. 155 n. 5, 301 n. 2; (e) pp. 177 n. 4, 180 n. 6, 253 n. 8, 301 n. 2; (f) p. 541 n. 2 (ET: [a] pp. 98 n. 6, 180 n. 2, 211 n. 1, 238 n. 1, 329 n. 2, 395 n. 2; [b] pp. 98 n. 6, 180 n. 2, 211 n. 1, 238 n. 1, 329 n. 2, 395 n. 2; [c] pp. 211 n. 5, 329 n. 2; [d] pp. 211 n. 1, 395 n. 2; [e] pp. 238 n. 1, 241 n. 6, 334 n. 1, 395 n. 2; [f] p. 698 n. 2).

non-Greek Semitic phrases ἐν τῇ ἀσθενείᾳ αὐτοῦ (5,5) and ἦν δὲ σάββατον ἐν ἐκείνῃ τῇ ἡμέρᾳ (5,9), ἴδε (11,3.36) and ἔρχου καὶ ἴδε (11,34), prolepsis of the object by αὐτόν (9,13), absolute ἀποστέλλω (11,3), the time indications in 11,7 and φωνῇ μεγάλῃ (11,43); (f) ἐνώπιον τῶν μαθητῶν (20,31).

2. The second criterion is the numbering of the signs. Like Wellhausen, Schwartz, Spitta and Meyer[151], Bultmann accepts the original connection of 2,1-12 and 4,46-54 because of the numbering of the signs in 2,11 and 4,54[152]. He ascribes the numbering to the source because 4,54 contradicts 2,23 and 4,45. The source is a collection of signs with 20,30-31 as its conclusion[153]. Contrary to Spitta and Goguel, he does not assign 21,1-14 to the signs source, because 21,14 does not refer to a third "sign" but to an appearance of the Risen Lord[154]. He wonders, as well, whether miracles were not enumerated and counted already in Judaism[155].

3. Bultmann likewise employs a content criterion, ascribing to the signs source pericopes with a specific θεῖος ἀνήρ christology. Jesus is primarily pictured as a miracle worker who behaves according to his own laws. He therefore shuns premature requests, even from his relatives (2,3-4)[156]; the presence of this motif indicates that the *Traditionsstück* behind 7,1-13 and the raising of Lazarus should be derived from the signs source[157]. In line with this theme, Jesus always takes the initiative, so much so that belief in the miracle worker by the sick person is no longer mentioned. The initiative of Jesus is obvious in 6,5, but also in 5,6 and 9,6, indicating that the narratives of the paralytic and the man born blind belong to the signs source along with the multiplication of the loaves[158].

---

151. See above, pp. 15 nn. 85-88 (Wellhausen and Schwartz), 15 nn. 89-90 (Spitta), 18 n. 106 (Meyer).

152. *Ibid.*, pp. 78, 83, 151 (ET: pp. 113, 118, 205).

153. *Ibid.*, pp. 78 (esp. n. 4), 346, 541 (ET: pp. 113 [esp. n. 2], 452, 698).

154. If 21,1-14 comes from the source, the redactor would have added not only ἐγερθεὶς ἐκ νεκρῶν (21,14) but also ἐφανερώθη ... τοῖς μαθηταῖς; the miracle would be characterized expressly as a σημεῖον (cf. 2,11; 4,54), and something like ἐφανέρωσεν τὴν δόξαν αὐτοῦ would be expected (p. 546 n. 1; ET: p. 705 n. 2).

155. He cites *Joma* 29a: "R. Asi (c. 300) said: Esther is the last of all the (OT) miracles" (p. 78 n. 4; ET: p. 113 n. 2).

156. *Ibid.*, p. 81 n. 3 (ET: p. 116 n. 5).

157. "Die Gleichheit des Motives dürfte dafür sprechen, dass alle diese Geschichten aus der σημεῖα-Quelle stammen" (p. 217 n. 1; ET: p. 289 n. 1). Cf. p. 85 n. 4 (ET: p. 121 n. 4): "Deutlich ist die Parallelität von 2,1-11 mit 7,1-10: beiderwärts die Aufforderung an Jesus, seine Macht zu erweisen, in Kap. 2 von Seiten der Mutter, in Kap. 7 von Seiten der Brüder; beiderwärts die Abweisung mit dem Hinweis auf die ὥρα (2,4) bzw. den καιρός (7,6); und beiderwärts unmotiviert nachher die Erfüllung der Aufforderung. Da 7,1-10 viel stärker die Arbeit des Evglisten zeigt, ist es möglich, dass er diese Parallelität geschaffen hat. Aber es ist wahrscheinlicher, dass in 7,1-10 ein Traditionsstück benutzt ist, das ursprünglich die Einleitung zu einer Wundergeschichte war" (i.e., 5,1-18).

158. *Ibid.*, pp. 155 (6,5), 181 (5,6), 250 (9,6) (ET: pp. 210, 242, 329).

In 1,35-51 supernatural knowledge appears as a characteristic of the miracle worker, and the same motif is present in 4,5-42. Bultmann, therefore, attributes the traditional material behind both the conversation with the Samaritan woman and the call of the first disciples to the signs source[159].

4. Naturally the literary aporias and inconsistencies in the gospel text play an important role, too. In this regard, Bultmann counts additions which interpret the text wrongly or differently, points in the narrative which are broken or altered, lack of clarity in construction, and lack of inner coherence[160]. We give illustrations with the delimitation of the source.

The following verses, indicated by pericope, are ascribed to the signs source by Bultmann:

1,35 (without τῇ ἐπαύριον πάλιν). 36-37. 38 (without ὅ λέγεται μεθερμηνευόμενον διδάσκαλε). 39 (perhaps without ὥρα ἦν ὡς δεκάτη). 40. 41 (without ὅ ἐστιν μεθερμηνευόμενον χριστός). 42 (without ὅ ἑρμηνεύεται Πέτρος). 43 (perhaps without τῇ ἐπαύριον and ἠθέλησεν ἐξελθεῖν εἰς τὴν Γαλιλαίαν; the original subject of εὑρίσκει is one of the disciples mentioned before). 44-48. 49 (perhaps without σὺ εἶ ὁ υἱὸς τοῦ θεοῦ)[161].

---

159. *Ibid.*, pp. 71, 73, 75, and esp. 131 (ET: pp. 101-102, 104, 106, and esp. 180): "Dann wäre das zugrundeliegende Traditionsstück dem in 1,35-51 verwendeten Quellenstück verwandt in dem sich Jesus auch durch seine übernatürliche Kenntnis der ihm begegnenden Menschen als θεῖος ἄνθρωπος und dadurch als Messias erweist. Stammt 1,35-51 aus der σημεῖα-Quelle, so könnte das auch für die Grundlage von 4,5-42 vermutet werden".

160. Cf. RUCKSTUHL, *Einheit*, 1951 (²1987), pp. 98-99.

161. In 1,35-51 (pp. 68-76; ET: pp. 97-108) there are only minor additions by the evangelist. In v. 35 he links the account with the preceding section by adding τῇ ἐπαύριον πάλιν (p. 68; ET: p. 97). The translation of the Aramaic words in vv. 38.41.42 comes from either the evangelist or the redactor (p. 68 n. 6; ET: p. 98 n. 5). The indication of the hour, ὥρα ἦν ὡς δεκάτη (v. 39), has perhaps been inserted by the evangelist (p. 70; ET: p. 100). V. 43 creates more difficulties. Why is Jesus expressly named at the end of the verse, although he was the subject of the preceding sentence (43a)? Jesus himself finds Philip, in contrast to an evidently deliberate pattern otherwise, that one disciple brings another to Jesus. This makes the plural εὑρήκαμεν (v. 45) unfitting as spoken by Philip, and there is no reason for πρῶτον in v. 41 because there is no logical follow-up. And finally, if Jesus meets Philip on the way to Galilee (εὑρίσκει), how would Philip be able to find Nathanael and bring him back to Jesus (vv. 45-46) (p. 68; ET: p. 98)? Thus, v. 43 has been altered by the evangelist. All difficulties are removed, according to Bultmann, if the subject of εὑρίσκει (v. 43) was originally one of the previously mentioned disciples, either Andrew or the disciple who was called with him. The evangelist wanted simply to prepare for the following section by inserting ἠθέλησεν ἐξελθεῖν εἰς τὴν Γαλιλαίαν and by suppressing the name of the original subject of εὑρίσκει, who was perhaps Andrew's companion (pp. 68 n. 5, 69 n. 1, 70 n. 8, 72 n. 4; ET: pp. 98 n. 4, 99 n. 1, 101 n. 3). Whether τῇ ἐπαύριον (v. 43) was already in the source or was introduced by the evangelist in the interest of his enumeration of days (cp. 2,1) is difficult to say (p. 68 n. 5; ET: p. 98 n. 4). In his commentary, Bultmann assigns v. 51 (cp. 5,20) to the

2,1-2 (perhaps οἱ ἀδελφοί in place of οἱ μαθηταὶ αὐτοῦ, and perhaps without τῇ ἡμέρᾳ τῇ τρίτῃ). 3-8. 9 (without καὶ οὐκ ᾔδει ... τὸ ὕδωρ). 10. 11 (either καὶ ἐφανέρωσεν κτλ. has been added or οἱ μαθηταὶ αὐτοῦ alone). 12 (perhaps without μετὰ τοῦτο, καὶ οἱ μαθηταὶ αὐτοῦ and οὐ πολλὰς ἡμέρας)[162].

4,(4). 5-7. 9. 16-19. (25-26). 28-30. (40)   (in the source the text of this verse was ἐξῆλθον ἐκ τῆς πόλεως καὶ ἠρώτων κτλ.)[163].

evangelist (pp. 68 n. 6, 74 n. 3), but in his *Ergänzungsheft*, [2]1957 pp. 18 (68), 19 (74 n. 2) (ET: pp. 98 n. 5, 105 n. 1) he also considers 1,50 an addition, because it limits the importance of the miracle that has just been related. For v. 49, he leaves open the possibility that σὺ εἶ ὁ υἱὸς τοῦ θεοῦ was already in the source; there, this title had the same significance as "King of Israel" and "Messiah" (pp. 74 n. 1, 75; ET: pp. 104 n. 7, 107).

162. In the wine miracle (pp. 78-85; ET: pp. 113-121) τῇ ἡμέρᾳ τῇ τρίτῃ (v. 1) is perhaps from the evangelist (p. 79; ET: p. 114). The disciples were likely not mentioned in v. 2 (cf. Wellhausen), but the correction of the original ἀδελφοί by μαθηταί might well have occurred already in the redaction of the signs source (p. 79 nn. 5-6; ET: p. 114 nn. 5-6). The interrupted sentence construction in v. 9 indicates that καὶ οὐκ ᾔδει ... ὕδωρ has been added, for it is not possible to take ὡς (δὲ ἐγεύσατο) as temporal in relation to ἐγεύσατο and as causal in relation to οὐκ ᾔδει (pp. 79, 82 n. 9; ET: pp. 114-115, 118 n. 5). In v. 11 the evangelist added καὶ ἐφανέρωσεν κτλ., or perhaps only οἱ μαθηταὶ αὐτοῦ (cf. p. 79; *Ergänzungsheft*, [2]1957, p. 20 [79 n. 7]; ET: p. 115, esp. n. 5). If the former was already in the source, then δόξα meant the power of the miracle worker and πιστεύω had the primitive meaning of belief on the basis of an external miracle, which does not fit with the evangelist's view (cp. 6,26) (p. 83 n. 7; ET: p. 119 n. 5). Verse 12 was already in the source as the transition to 4,45-54 (pp. 79 n. 4, 85, 151; ET: pp. 114 n. 4, 121, 206), but the evangelist has perhaps added οὐ πολλὰς ἡμέρας in order to prepare for the temple cleansing (cf. Wellhausen) (p. 85 n. 5; ET: p. 121 n. 5). Μετὰ τοῦτο is a Johannine transitional formula (p. 85 n. 6; ET: p. 121 n. 6) and καὶ οἱ μαθηταὶ αὐτοῦ is text-critically secondary (p. 79; ET: p. 114).

163. With Wendt, Schwartz, Wellhausen, and Spitta (p. 127 n. 7; ET: p. 175 n. 2) Bultmann thinks that the evangelist thoroughly reworked the account of Jesus' meeting with the Samaritan woman (pp. 127-149; ET: pp. 175-202). The evangelist introduces the geographical setting from the *Grundlage* with 4,1-3(4) (p. 127; ET: p. 175). V. 4 belongs to the introduction written by the evangelist, but he may have used a sentence from the source (p. 128 n. 4; ET: p. 176 n. 2). The point of vv. 5-9 is to describe Jesus' attitude toward the Samaritan woman; but another idea (the living water) appears in vv. 10-15. These verses are apparently the evangelist's own composition because of the Johannine devices of double-meaning and misunderstanding of Jesus' words (p. 128; ET: p. 175). It is difficult to reconstruct the remainder of the original story; there was no need to mention that Jesus received a drink, but the account must have included Jesus' reply to the woman, which has dropped because of the addition of vv. 10-15 (p. 131; ET: p. 179). Vv. 4-9 were continued in vv. 16-19 (p. 128; ET: p. 175). This was the second part of the conversation, in which Jesus reveals himself to be a prophet, and this was followed by a final exchange which the evangelist replaced by vv. 20-26 (p. 131; ET: p. 179). It is likely that vv. 25-26 are based on traditional material; these verses treat of Jesus' messiahship, as does the original conclusion vv. 28-30.40 (pp. 131, 139 n. 1; ET: pp. 179-180, 189 n. 1). In the source v. 40 ran: ἐξῆλθον ἐκ τῆς πόλεως καὶ ἠρώτων αὐτὸν μεῖναι παρ' αὐτοῖς κτλ. (pp. 128 esp. n. 1, 131, 142, 148; ET: pp. 175 esp. n. 3, 180, 192-193, 200). The evangelist uses this conclusion to work out two further ideas about the mission: vv. 31-38 (Jesus and the disciples or first- and second-hand faith) and vv. 39.41-42 (Jesus and the Samaritans or the task of mission) (p. 128; ET: p. 175). The first implies that the evangelist likewise added v. 8 and 27 (pp. 128, 130, 142; ET: pp. 175, 178, 193).

4,46 (without ἦλθεν οὖν ... οἶνον). 47 (without ἐκ τῆς ... Γαλιλαίαν and καταβῇ καί, which perhaps replaced the original ἐλθών). 50-51. 52 (without ἐχθές). 53. 54 (without ἐλθὼν ... Γαλιλαίαν)[164].

5,2-3 (through ξηρῶν). 5-10. 11 (without ἐκεῖνος). 12-15, followed by: καὶ διὰ τοῦτο ἐζήτουν οἱ Ἰουδαῖοι ἀποκτεῖναι τὸν Ἰησοῦν, ὅτι ταῦτα ἐποίει ἐν σαββάτῳ in place of vv. 16-18[165].

6,1 (perhaps without τῆς Τιβεριάδος). 2 (without ὅτι ἐθεώρουν κτλ.). 3. 5. 7-13. 16-17. 19-22. 25[166].

164. In 4,46-54 (pp. 151-154; ET: pp. 204-209) the redaction of the evangelist is not always clearly distinguishable. In the source the story takes place at Capernaum (2,12) (pp. 79 n. 4, 85, 151; ET: pp. 114 n. 4, 121, 206). The additions in vv. 46.47.52.54 are from the evangelist (pp. 151-152; ET: p. 206). The redactional character of ἦλθον ... οἶνον (v. 46) demonstrates the evangelist's habit of referring to earlier passages (cf. 1,30; 6,65; 13,33; 15,20; 16,15; 18,9) (p. 151 n. 11; ET: p. 206 n. 4). In v. 47, καταβῇ καί may have replaced an original ἐλθών (cp. Mt 8,7; Lk 7,3) (pp. 151-152; ET: p. 206). In contrast to Spitta, who regarded vv. 52-53 as entirely redactional because they presuppose the distance between Cana and Capernaum, Bultmann thinks it sufficient to assign only ἐχθές to the evangelist (p. 152 n. 1; ET: p. 206 n. 5). V. 48, which plays no further role in the story, and v. 49 also are from the evangelist; these verses have perhaps suppressed an original dialogue, which must have corresponded with Mt 8,7-10 (pp. 152-153; ET: pp. 206-207). Contrary to SMITH, *Composition*, 1965, p. 39, I think that Bultmann also assigns ἐλθὼν κτλ. (4,54) to the evangelist (p. 154; ET: p. 209); cf. KONINGS, *Joh. verhaal*, II, 1972, p. 215; NEIRYNCK, *Jean et les Synoptiques*, 1979, p. 169 n. 376; *Semeiabron*, 1983, p. 14 n. 38 (ET: 1991, p. 662 n. 38).

165. In the healing of the lame man (5,1-18) (pp. 177-179, 179-185; ET: pp. 237-239, 240-247) v. 1 is an editorial addition by the evangelist, for the feast plays no role in what follows (p. 179 n. 2; ET: p. 240 n. 2). V. 3b is a Western reading (p. 180 n. 2; ET: p. 241 n. 2), and v. 4 is a gloss clarifying v. 7 (p. 180 n. 4; ET: p. 241 n. 4). In v. 11, ἐκεῖνος, typical of the evangelist, has been inserted (pp. 181 n. 7, 53 n. 5; ET: pp. 243 n. 2, 79 n. 3). Vv. 16-18 are a reworking of the original text of the source: the evangelist made one sentence into two and inserted v. 17 so that now the decision to kill Jesus rests on his claim to be the Revealer, and in this way he leads into the discourse (pp. 177, 182; ET: pp. 238, 243-244).

166. In the account of the feeding of the multitude and the walking on the sea (6,1-26) (pp. 155-161; ET: pp. 210-218) the evangelist or editor has added τῆς Τιβεριάδος to v. 1 (p. 156 n. 2; ET: p. 211 n. 3) and ὅτι ἑώρων κτλ. to v. 2 (p. 93 n. 3, 156 n. 3; ET: p. 103 n. 3, 211 n. 4). With v. 4 he prepared the way for the feast in 5,1 (pp. 155, 156; ET: pp. 210, 211). Bultmann places ch. 5 in the original gospel between chs. 6 and 7 (pp. 177, 154-156; ET: pp. 237, 209-210). V. 6 is a note added by the evangelist which shows his own typical style; its purpose is to make clear the παράδοξον of the miracle (pp. 155, 157 n. 1; ET: pp. 210, 212 n. 4). Vv. 14-15 are likewise from the evangelist: (a) in contrast to the early tradition, which is interested only in the effect of the miracle on the witnesses, the further consequences are reported here; (b) the typical interest of the evangelist appears in these verses: the stance for or against the Revealer with reference to the σημεῖα (cf. 6,26); (c) vv. 14-15 have no consequences for Jesus' meeting with the people on the following day (vv. 25ff) (pp. 155, 157 n. 8; ET: pp. 210, 213 n. 5). Contrary to SMITH, *Composition*, 1965, p. 41, I would not assign v. 18 to the signs source; Bultmann indeed notes: "Heitmüller will mit Recht V. 18 als Glosse streichen; die Stillung des Sturmes wird ja nachher nicht erzählt, und stilistisch fällt V. 18 mit dem Gen. absol. aus dem Rahmen" (p. 159 n. 1; ET: p. 215 n. 4); cf. KONINGS, *Joh. verhaal*, II, 1972, p. 409 n. 1; III, 1972, p. 115. The evangelist wrongly understands εἶδον (6,22), and

7,(2). 3 (without οἱ μαθηταί σου). 4 (without εἰ ταῦτα ποιεῖς κτλ.). 6 (without ὁ καιρὸς κτλ.). 8 (without ὅτι ὁ ἐμὸς καιρὸς οὔπω πεπλήρωται). 9. 10 (without τότε καὶ αὐτὸς ἀνέβη κτλ.)[167]. **7**,19 (without οὐ Μωϋσῆς ... νόμον). 21 (without ἀπεκρίθη ... αὐτοῖς). 22 (without οὐχ ... πατέρων). 23[168]. **9**,1-3 (without ἀλλ᾽ ἵνα κτλ.). 6. 7 (without ὃ ἑρμηνεύεται ἀπεσταλμένος). 8-15. 16 (without ἄλλοι δὲ ... ἐν αὐτοῖς; perhaps without οὐκ ἔστιν ... παρὰ θεοῦ ὁ ἄνθρωπος). 17 (without ὁ δὲ εἶπεν ὅτι προφήτης ἐστίν). 18 (without οὖν οἱ Ἰουδαῖοι). 19-21. 24-28. 34 (without ἀπεκρίθησαν ... διδάσκεις ἡμᾶς;). (35-38)[169].

---

interprets πέραν as the eastern shore of the lake. Thus he has to bring the ὄχλος over to the western shore and therefore adds vv. 23-24: like a *deus ex machina*, the ships come from Tiberias to near the place where the feeding occurred and carry the crowd over to Capernaum (pp. 155, 160-161; ET: pp. 210, 216).

167. Bultmann agrees with Wellhausen and Goguel that the evangelist used an earlier tradition in 7,1-13 (p. 216-222; ET: pp. 288-295). V. 1 is a redactional link between ch. 5 and ch. 7 (p. 217 n. 2; ET: p. 289 n. 2). It is possible that μετάβηθι (v. 3) means a "change of abode" rather than a "journey to the feast". If so, then the dating of the narrative (v. 2) is the evangelist's redaction (so Wellhausen) (p. 218 n. 5; ET: p. 290 n. 5). The source made no mention of disciples in v. 3: why should only disciples and not everyone see the miracles? Thus, the evangelist inserted οἱ μαθηταί (p. 218 n. 9; ET: p. 290 n. 9). The idea of revelation to the κόσμος (v. 4b) is from the evangelist (pp. 217 n. 2, 219 n. 2; ET: pp. 289 n. 2, 291 n. 2) and v. 5 is one of his typical motivations (cp. 5,22; 8,42; 20,9) (pp. 217 n. 2, 218 n. 6; ET: pp. 289 n. 2, 290 n. 6). V. 7 is from the *Offenbarungsreden* and v. 6b and 8b are from the evangelist (cf. v. 4b) (pp. 217 n. 2, 220 nn. 1, 2, 5; ET: pp. 289 n. 2, 292 nn. 2, 3, 293 n. 1). The evangelist tries to relieve the contradiction between v. 8 and v. 10 by adding οὐ φανερῶς ἀλλὰ ὡς ἐν κρυπτῷ. The source itself must have related a journey by Jesus to Jerusalem (pp. 216-217, 221 n. 8; ET: pp. 288-289, 294 n. 4). Finally, Bultmann assigns vv. 11-13 to the evangelist (cp. 7,43; 7,31; 10,19-21) (p. 221 n. 8; ET: p. 294 n. 4). Observe, however, that Bultmann notes (p. 217 n. 2; ET: p. 289 n. 2) that "vv. 10b.13 probably come from the evangelist".

168. The original conclusion of the healing narrative in 5,1-18 is to be found in 7,19-24 (pp. 208-209; ET: pp. 276-277). Originally following ἐζήτουν ... ἀποκτεῖναι (5,18) was Jesus' answer: τί με ζητεῖτε ἀποκτεῖναι (7,19) and then ἓν ἔργον ἐποίησα καὶ πάντες θαυμάζετε (7,21) and 7,22-23 which have been reworked by the evangelist (pp. 178, 208; ET: pp. 238, 276). This clear line of thought has been disturbed by the evangelist, because he wanted to portray the Jews as transgressors of the Mosaic law (5,45-47). For that reason the evangelist added οὐ Μωϋσῆς ... ποιεῖ τὸν νόμον to 7,19. He underlines the enormity of the decision to kill Jesus with v. 20, which has no importance for the argument. Jesus' reply (v. 21) ignores this and takes up the thread of the argument as it comes from the source (pp. 208-209; ET: pp. 276-278). Bultmann remarks that we could ascribe 7,20-21a to the redactor, who put the story in its present position (in the original gospel 7,15-24 followed the discourse in ch. 5) (pp. 177-178, 209 n. 2; ET: pp. 237-239, 278 n. 1). In v. 22, οὐχ ὅτι ... πατέρων is one of the evangelist's typical parenthetical expressions (p. 209 n. 3; cp. p. 173 n. 1; ET: p. 278 n. 2; cp. p. 232 n. 3).

169. The story about the healing of the man born blind (pp. 249-260; ET: pp. 329-342) has been more extensively reworked than the similar miracle story in ch. 5 (p. 250; ET: p. 329). In 9,3b we find an elliptic clause (ἀλλ᾽ ἵνα ... ἐν αὐτῷ) characteristic of the evangelist. The original continuation of Jesus' reply has been suppressed by the evangelist's addition of vv. 4-5, for which he used the *Offenbarungsreden* (pp. 251 n. 4, 250, 252

(**10**,40-42)[170].

11,1. 3. 5 (perhaps without τὴν Μάρθαν ... αὐτῆς καί). 6. ἔπειτα (from v. 7). 11 (without ταῦτα εἶπεν, καί). 12. 14. 15 (perhaps without ἵνα πιστεύσητε). 17-19. 33-34. 38 (without πάλιν ἐμβριμώμενος ἐν ἑαυτῷ). 39. 41 (only ἦραν οὖν τὸν λίθον). 43 (perhaps Ἰησοῦς [οὖν] in place of [καὶ] ταῦτα εἰπών). 44 (perhaps without ὁ Ἰησοῦς)[171].

n. 1; ET: pp. 331 n. 4, 329, 332 n. 1). The interpretation of Σιλωάμ, by the evangelist or the redactor, raises the symbolism of the story to the level of allegory (p. 253; ET: p. 333). Vv. 16-17 have been worked over by the evangelist (p. 250; ET: p. 329). One might wonder whether the evangelist has replaced another formulation from the source with οὐκ ἔστιν οὗτος παρὰ θεοῦ ὁ ἄνθρωπος (p. 254 n. 1; ET: p. 334 n. 3). He added the motif of dissension (v. 16b), as well as the conclusion of v. 17 (pp. 254 n. 4, 255 n. 3; ET: pp. 334 n. 6, 336 n. 2). In the source, therefore, v. 17 followed upon v. 16a, and was not a question but a shout of horror. In v. 18, the evangelist also inserted οὖν οἱ Ἰουδαῖοι (p. 254 n. 4; ET: p. 334 n. 6). The change from Pharisees to Jews indicates the evangelist's addition of vv. 22-23; thus, Bultmann rejects the view of Wellhausen and Spitta that the whole of vv. 17-23 (or 18-23 respectively) is an addition by the evangelist (pp. 250 n. 2, 254 n. 6; ET: pp. 329 n. 3, 335 n. 1). The evangelist has created vv. 22-23 in order to explain that the parents' caution is a result of their fear of being cast out of the synagogue. The evangelist's style is also apparent here (p. 254 n. 10; ET: p. 335 n. 5). V. 29 certainly comes from the evangelist, with its characteristic τοῦτον δὲ οὐκ οἴδαμεν πόθεν ἐστίν (cp. 8,14; 7,27-28; 2,9; 3,8; 19,9) (p. 255 n. 5, 82 n. 9; ET: pp. 336 n. 4, 118 n. 5). If that is so, then Bultmann also ascribes v. 30 to the evangelist; Spitta is probably correct in suggesting that v. 28 was followed immediately by καὶ ἐξέβαλον αὐτὸν ἔξω from v. 34, for the intervening verses until that point certainly sound Johannine (pp. 250, 254 n. 1, 255 n. 5; ET: pp. 329, 334 n. 3, 336 n. 4). In the source, ἐκβάλλω had the same sense as in Mk 1,43, but for the evangelist it means "exclusion from the congregation of the synagogue" (p. 255 n. 5; ET: p. 336 n. 4). Vv. 35-38 are partly attributable to the evangelist, whose style is evident (pp. 250, 256; ET: pp. 329, 338 n. 1). The basic portion is, nevertheless, from the source: as in 5,1-16(18), the meeting between Jesus and the healed man in ch. 9 must have been related there. However, the original text of the source is difficult to reconstruct (p. 256 n. 7; ET: p. 338 n. 1). Finally, vv. 39-41, as an introduction to the following discourse on the Light (cp. 5,16-18), stem from the evangelist (pp. 250, 258; ET: pp. 329, 339).

170. About these verses, Bultmann is rather reserved: "Man kann fragen, ob in diesem redakt. Stück des Evglisten die σημεῖα-Quelle benutzt ist, in der eine Aussage wie 10,41 gestanden haben könnte" (p. 299 n. 2; ET: p. 393 n. 2).

171. The literary-critical analyses of Wendt, Wellhausen, Schwartz, and Spitta offer no satisfying elucidation of ch. 11 (pp. 300-313; ET: pp. 394-409), and it is questionable whether one can be reached: "Die sprachliche Untersuchung liefert nicht hinreichende, wenngleich bestätigende Kriterien. ... Der Stil des Evglisten aber hebt sich nicht durchweg scharf von dem der σημεῖα-Quelle ab" (p. 301 n. 4; ET: p. 395 n. 4). We might perceive the text of the source in vv. 1.3.5-6.11-12.14-15.17-19.33-39.43-44. Yet, many obscurities show that these verses are not an original report; presumably an old narrative had already been edited when it was taken up into the σημεῖα source, and the evangelist further reworked it (p. 301 n. 4; ET: p. 395 n. 4). The κύριος title betrays v. 2 as a gloss by the "ecclesiastical redactor"; its purpose is to identify Mary with the woman in Mk 14,3-9; Lk 7,37-38 (p. 301 n. 4, 302 n. 1, 128 n. 4; ET: pp. 395 n. 4, 396 n. 1, 176 n. 2). It is probable that the sisters (αἱ ἀδελφαὶ αὐτοῦ in v. 3), if they were mentioned at all, were anonymous, and their identification with Martha and Mary is secondary; or did the original text simply run: ἀπέστειλαν οὖν πρὸς αὐτὸν λέγοντες ("man schickte zu

12,37-38[172].

20,30-31 (perhaps without καὶ ἵνα πιστεύοντες κτλ.)[173].

With the analysis of the content, Bultmann also gives some indications about the order. The first sign in the source was the wine miracle,

ihm")? (pp. 301 n. 4, 302 n. 4; ET: pp. 395 n. 4, 397 n. 1). V. 4 is from the evangelist (cf. 9,3-5); he anticipates the ὡς οὖν ἤκουσεν of the source (v. 6) with ἀκούσας δέ in order to connect to the ἀσθενεῖ of v. 3 his explanation of the meaning of the sickness. The verse shows his characteristic style (pp. 301 n. 4, 302 n. 7; ET: pp. 395 n. 4, 397 n. 4). After v. 3, one would expect in v. 5 that Lazarus would be the only, or at least the first, object of Jesus' love; this suggests that mention of the sisters is secondary (pp. 301 n. 4, 306 n. 6; ET: pp. 395 n. 4, 397 n. 3). In the source, v. 11 followed immediately upon v. 6 (ἔπειτα from v. 7 and then μετὰ τοῦτο κτλ.) (p. 303 n. 6; ET: p. 398 n. 3). Vv. 7-10 were added by the evangelist (p. 301 n. 4; ET: p. 395 n. 4). In v. 7, he anticipates the ἄγωμεν of the source (v. 15) (p. 305 n. 3; ET: p. 400 n. 5). In vv. 9-10, he used the discourse on Light from the *Offenbarungsreden* (pp. 301 n. 4, 304 n. 1; ET: pp. 395 n. 4, 399 n. 1). He also added v. 13 to explain the misunderstanding of the disciples (cp. 2,21; 7,39; 12,16.33) (pp. 304 n. 7, 301 n. 4; ET: pp. 400 n. 1, 395 n. 4; SMITH, *Composition*, 1965, p. 44, wrongly ascribes this verse to the signs source). V. 15 has been expanded by the evangelist with ἵνα πιστεύσητε (p. 305 n. 1; ET: p. 400 n. 3). In the source, v. 17 immediately followed v. 15, as αὐτόν shows, and has no relation with v. 16, which is therefore from the evangelist (pp. 301 n. 4, 305 n.4; ET: pp. 395 n. 4, 400 n. 6). Wellhausen gives several indications for including v. 17 in the signs source. In v. 17, Jesus goes immediately to the grave; this is inconsistent with 11,34.38. Vv. 18-19 are secondary. The original story thus related that when Jesus came to the grave he met the mourners who had just buried Lazarus. Consequently, τέσσαρας ἤδη ἡμέρας ἔχοντα (v. 17) and v. 39 are likewise secondary additions. This reconstruction by Wellhausen might be right; rather, this *Urform* would hardly have come from the evangelist, as Wellhausen thought, but would already have been edited in the signs source. The enhancement of the greatness of the miracle, by the statement that Lazarus was already dead for three days, corresponds to the tendency of the source, and not to that of the evangelist, who regarded the miracle as a symbol. By mentioning Martha and Mary, the source offered the evangelist the opportunity for composing vv. 20-32 (pp. 305 n. 9, 311 n. 3, 309 nn. 2, 5; ET: pp. 401 n. 3, 407 n. 6, 405 nn. 1, 4). At v. 33 the evangelist resumes the source he had left at v. 20. In this already edited source, v. 33 followed upon v. 19, and began with Ἰησοῦς οὖν ὡς εἶδεν αὐτὰς κλαίουσας κτλ. How far the evangelist has edited vv. 33-40 cannot be established with certainty. Vv. 33-34 come completely from the signs source. Vv. 35-37 are from the evangelist; v. 34 is taken up again in v. 38 with πάλιν ἐμβριμώμενος ἐν ἑαυτῷ. V. 40 is also from the evangelist (pp. 310 nn. 3, 4, 301 n. 4; ET: pp. 406 nn. 3, 4, 395 n. 4); v. 39, on the other hand, is from the source (pp. 311 n. 4, 305 n. 9; ET: pp. 407 n. 7, 401 n. 7). Like v. 40, vv. 41-42 are also from the evangelist, clearly because of their theology and terminology. Only ἦραν οὖν τὸν λίθον in v. 41 is from the source; v. 43 was joined to that, but perhaps Ἰησοῦς (οὖν) stood in place of (καὶ) ταῦτα εἰπών (pp. 311 n. 6, 312 n. 6; ET: pp. 407 n. 9, 409 n. 4). The effect of the miracle and the influence upon the sisters, from the signs source, are dropped in the evangelist's redaction. Something may remain in v. 45 (p. 313, but see n. 2; ET: p. 409, but see n. 8).

172. *Ibid.*, pp. 78 n. 4, 346 n. 4, 541 n. 2 (ET: pp. 113 n. 2, 452 n. 2, 698 n. 2).

173. 12,37-38 and 20,30-31 together conclude the source; perhaps the evangelist added καὶ ἵνα πιστεύοντες κτλ. (20,31) (pp. 541-542, 346 n. 4, 78; ET: pp. 698-699, 452 n. 4, 113).

an epiphany miracle correctly mentioned as the first (2,11)[174]. In 2,12 the second sign is introduced, the healing of the son of the βασιλικός (4,46-54)[175]. There is no order indicated in the commentary for the other miracle stories. Bultmann certainly regarded 7,1-13 as a piece of traditional material which served as the introduction to the healing of the paralytic (ch. 5) and 7,19-24 as its original conclusion[176]. Because of the similarity of style between 1,35-49 and 2,1-12 he concluded that 1,35-49 was perhaps the introduction to the signs source: its content and conclusion certainly go well with the source[177]. Finally, Bultmann accepted with Faure that the source was concluded by 12,37-38 and 20,30-31[178].

According to Bultmann, then, the signs source was a collection of miracle stories[179], a written source[180], which he compared with the pre-Markan collections[181]. The "redaction" of the source consisted in collecting the miracle stories, numbering the signs, adding framing verses and interpretations, and providing the conclusion[182]. Sometimes more important changes are made, as noted in the raising of Lazarus. Compare also the possible correction of ἀδελφοί to μαθηταί in 2,2[183].

In the theology of the signs source, Jesus is a θεῖος ἀνήρ with supernatural knowledge and omniscience (1,40-42.47-48; 4,17-19; 5,6)[184].

174. *Ibid.*, pp. 78, 83 (ET: pp. 113, 118).
175. *Ibid.*, pp. 79 n. 4, 85, 151 (ET: pp. 114 n. 4, 121, 206).
176. *Ibid.*, pp. 85 n. 4, 177-178, 217, 208 (ET: pp. 121 n. 4, 238, 289, 276).
177. *Ibid.*, p. 78 (ET: p. 113).
178. See nn. 172-173 above.
179. *Johannes*, p. 78 (ET: p. 113). Cp. *Johannesevangelium*, c. 842: "eine *Sammlung von Wundergeschichten*, deren Stil mit dem der synoptischen verwandt, jedoch weiterentwickelt ist".
180. *Johannes*, p. 68 (ET: p. 97) (with reference to 1,35-49); *Theologie*, p. 355 (ET: II, p. 3).
181. *Geschichte*, ²1931, p. 347 n. 2 (ET: p. 321 n. 2; FT: p. 391 n. 2 [on p. 392]).
182. *Johannes*, p. 78 (ET: p. 113).
183. With reference to 2,2: "Natürlich könnte die Korrektur der 'Brüder' in die 'Jünger' schon in der σημεῖα-Quelle erfolgt gewesen sein, wenn in dieser die einzelnen σημεῖα zu einem fortlaufenden Zshg verbunden waren" (p. 79 n. 6; ET: p. 114 n. 6; see above, p. 30 n. 162). Referring to ch. 11: "Vermutlich war eine alte Erzählung schon bei der Aufnahme in die σημεῖα-Quelle redigiert worden, und der Evglist hat sie weiter bearbeitet" (p. 301 n. 4; cp. 305 n. 9; ET: p. 395 n. 4; cp. 401 n. 4; see above, p. 33 n. 171). – Bultmann thinks that the wine miracle has been taken from a pagan legend (p. 83; ET: pp. 118-119; cf. *Geschichte*, 1921, pp. 145-146; ²1931, p. 253; ET: p. 238; FT: p. 292; see below, p. 38 n. 198) and that the walking on the sea is related after the feeding miracle because both stories were already joined to one another early in the tradition (*Johannes*, p. 158; ET: p. 214; *Theologie*, p. 397; ET: II, pp. 44-45).
184. *Johannes*, pp. 71, 73, 75, 131, 138 (ET: pp. 102, 104, 106, 180, 187). – Bultmann uses the term θεῖος ἄνθρωπος on pp. 71, 75, 81 n. 3, 131, 138, 223 n. 2, 225 n. 7, 306, 310 n. 4, 512 n. 1 (ET: pp. 102, 106, 116 n. 5, 180, 188, 296 n. 4, 299 n. 5, 402, 406 n. 4, 661 n. 4); θεῖος ἀνήρ on pp. 202, 206 n. 1, 561 (ET: pp. 269, 273 n. 5, 737); both terms appear on pp. 223 n. 1, 225 n. 7 (ET: pp. 296 n. 4, 299 n. 5). In *Theologie* he uses only θεῖος ἀνήρ (pp. 132-133, 394-396, xiv; ET: I, p. 130; II, pp. 42-43).

This is a Hellenistic notion. Ancient Israel also knew such a concept, yet it was superseded by prophecy. Therefore it was missing later in Judaism, although this motif sporadically appears[185]. As θεῖος ἀνήρ, Jesus also performs miracles. Miracles, supernatural knowledge, and omniscience are proofs of Jesus' Messiahship; the messianic prophecies and expectations have been fulfilled in him[186]. In this line, various titles for Jesus appear: Rabbi, Messiah, Lamb of God, King of Israel, Prophet, and Son of God[187]. The source presents encounters with the miracle worker very pregnantly and creates a mysterious impression: as soon as Jesus appears in everyday life there are higher powers at work[188].

As for form, the miracle stories of the signs source exhibit a more developed stage than those of the Synoptic Gospels[189]. Bultmann never says explicitly that the further evolution is the result of the redaction of the signs source, but his formulation is sufficiently vague to leave the possibility open. He calls the wine miracle a typical *Wundergeschichte* and indicates the following division[190]: 1. exposition (vv. 1-2); 2. preparation (vv. 3-5): the tension has been built up in order to describe the παράδοξον of the miracle, and Jesus takes the initiative by refusing the early request for a miracle[191]; 3. the miracle proper (vv. 6-8): it is only indirectly described, the divine behavior of the miracle worker remaining concealed; 4. closing (vv. 9-10) with the demonstration and the astonishment of those present. A similar structure appears more or less in the other miracle stories. Form-critically speaking the miracle stories in chapters 5 and 9 are secondary compositions. In contrast to Synoptic apophthegms which have a brief healing story as the starting point of a

185. For example in 1 Sam 9,19-20 (*Johannes*, p. 71 n. 4; ET: p. 102 n. 1). Occasionally, it is said of a rabbi that he knows someone he meets without ever having seen him. Nevertheless, this portrayal differs from the Hellenistic: for the rabbi, this ability is attributed to the Holy Spirit; in Hellenism, to the divine quality of the miracle worker himself. The gift of the prophet is something different.

186. *Ibid.*, p. 76 (ET: p. 107).

187. *Ibid.*, pp. 75-76 (ET: p. 107). Rabbi (1,38.49; 6,25; 9,2), Messiah (1,41; 4,25.30), Lamb of God (1,36), King of Israel (1,49), Prophet (4,19), and Son of God (1,49). It is not sure whether this last title was found in the source.

188. *Ibid.*, p. 75 (ET: p. 107) (referring to 1,35-51).

189. *Ibid.*, p. 78 (ET: p. 113); *Theologie*, p. 355 (ET: II, p. 3). Cp. *Johannesevangelium*, c. 842 (see above, p. 35 n. 179).

190. *Johannes*, pp. 79-82, esp. 79 (ET: pp. 115-118, esp. 115).

191. Bultmann thinks this characteristic reveals the secondary character of the miracle story: "Es ist ein Zeichen sekundärer Bildung, wenn Jesus selbst die Initiative ergreift. ... Der sekundäre Stil zeigt sich deutlich bei Joh, wo Jesu Handeln ganz der eigenen Initiative entspringt (5,6; 9,6) und voreilige Bitte abgewiesen wird (2,3f.; 7,3ff.; 11,3f.)" (*Geschichte*, 1921, p. 36; ²1931, p. 70; ET: p. 66; FT: p. 90). Cp. *Johannes*, p. 250 (ET: p. 330) (with reference to 9,1-7): "Ein Zeichen fortgeschrittenen Stadiums ist es, dass Jesus selbst die Initiative zum Wunder ergreift, sodass das Wunder zur Demonstration wird, was durch die dem Evangelisten zugehörigen Verse 4f. noch besonders betont wird. Demgemäss fehlt wie 5,6ff. die Erwähnung der πίστις des Kranken".

controversy, here "a controversy has been attached later to a detailed miracle story". The appended reference to the sabbath (5,9b and 9,14) and the obscurity of the situation (5,15ff.) are characteristic of this development[192].

On one rare occasion, in connection with the narrative of the call of the disciples, Bultmann gives some precise indications about the Sitz-im-Leben of the source, although it remains unclear whether "the source which he [the evangelist] takes over here" refers to the whole signs source or to the account of chapter 1. This source would have originated as a propaganda document in the circle of John the Baptist's disciples who had embraced faith in Jesus[193].

The marks of a separate Sitz-im-Leben for the individual miracle stories of the signs source are rather meager. The story of the epiphany at Cana belongs in a community where Mary, the mother of Jesus, was especially held in regard[194]. The discussions and the interrogations of the healed men in chapters 5 and 9 reflect the relation of the first Christians to a hostile, Jewish environment; they demonstrate the adversaries' method of interrogating people who came into contact with the first Christians in order to gather information for an indictment against the Christian community[195].

In his commentary, Bultmann explains the customs and concepts that appear in the signs source, chiefly against a Jewish background[196]. But he explains the typical uniqueness of the miracle from the perspective of Hellenism. So, for example, it is striking that he completely rejects the symbolism of wine as it might be seen from Old Testament texts; he does not accept that the wine would be a symbol of the eschatological end time[197]. He explains the wine miracle against a Hellenistic back-

---

192. *Ibid.*, pp. 178 n. 4, 249 (ET: pp. 239 n. 2, 329); *Geschichte*, 1921, p. 139; ²1931, p. 242 (ET: p. 227; FT: p. 280).

193. *Johannes*, p. 76, esp. n. 6 (ET: p. 108, esp. n. 6). Cp. SMITH, *Composition*, 1965, pp. 37-38.

194. *Johannes*, p. 80 n. 7 (ET: p. 116 n. 2).

195. *Ibid.*, p. 178 (ET: p. 239).

196. 2,6 (p. 82; ET: p. 117); 2,10 (p. 82 n. 8; ET: p. 118 n. 4); 6,11 (p. 157 n. 5; ET: p. 213 n. 2); 6,12 (p. 157 n. 6; ET: p. 213 n. 3); 5,10 (p. 181 n. 6; ET: p. 243 n. 1); 5,14 (p. 182; ET: p. 243); 9,2 (p. 251; ET: p. 330); 9,31 (p. 256 n. 2; ET: p. 337 n. 2); 11,17 (p. 305 n. 6; ET: p. 400 n. 8); 11,31 (p. 309 n. 6; ET: p. 405 n. 5); 11,41 (p. 311 n. 7; ET: p. 407 n. 10); 11,44 (p. 312 n. 7; ET: p. 409 n. 5). – According to Bultmann τί ἐμοὶ καὶ σοί (2,4) and γύναι are best understood in terms of Jewish and Rabbinic literature (p. 81 nn. 2, 3; ET: p. 116 nn. 4, 5). We can grasp the significance of οὔπω ἥκει ἡ ὥρα μου (2,4) from other texts about miracle workers, where it is likewise reported that the time must be suitable for the performance of miracles (p. 81 n. 4; ET: p. 117 n. 1). The ἄρτους κριθίνους (6,9) does not necessarily have to be a reminiscence of 2 Kgs 4,42 (p. 157 n. 3; ET: p. 212 n. 6). Bultmann does accept the analogy of sending the blind man to the pool (9,7) with sending Naaman to the Jordan (2 Kgs 5,10) (p. 252 n. 4; ET: p. 333 n. 1).

197. *Ibid.*, p. 84 n. 1 (ET: p. 120 n. 1).

ground; the changing of the water into wine is a typical motif that we find frequently in the Dionysus legends[198]. He thus neglects Jewish and Old Testament motifs which could be taken into consideration in the miracle stories of the signs source.

In fact, for Bultmann, source criticism serves only as a background for his theological conclusions: the Fourth Evangelist is the example of the Christian preacher and exegete. He received traditional material which he interpreted existentially in order to proclaim Jesus Christ as the Word that comes to humankind (1 Jn 4,2: ἐν σαρκὶ ἐληλυθότα) and calls persons to faithful obedience. Therefore, what is important in Bultmann's literary theory is not to reconstruct the source but to trace and understand the reaction of the evangelist in his redaction.

The evangelist used the miracle narratives from the signs source in a two-fold way: as the beginning of a section[199], or as the introduction to a discourse[200]. As in the signs source, Jesus is presented by the evange-

198. Each year at the Dionysus feast the temple springs of Andros and Teos were said to have poured out wine instead of water. In Elis on the eve of the feast three empty jars were set up in the temple, and were then found full of wine on the next morning. Bultmann thinks that this Hellenistic interpretation of the wine miracle is confirmed by the concurrence of the Feast of Epiphany and the Dionysus feast on January 6th (p. 83, esp. n. 3; ET: p. 119, esp. n. 1; *Geschichte*, 1921, pp. 145-146; ²1931, p. 253; ET: p. 238; FT: p. 292).

199. Together with the temple cleansing, the epiphany at Cana forms a diptych that introduces the first part of the gospel, the revelation of Jesus' δόξα to the world, chs. 1–12. The evangelist has reported this miracle as the first because it was also the first miracle story in the signs source; this is a very appropriate place for an epiphany miracle (*Johannes*, pp. 77-78; ET: pp. 111-112). By the evangelist's arrangement and in analogy with the wine miracle, the raising of Lazarus has also received the character of an epiphany miracle. It belongs to the fourth section of the first part ("The Revealer's Secret Victory over the World": 10,40–12,33; 8,30-40; 6,60-71). This section is at the same time the transition to the second part ("The Revelation of the δόξα before the Community", ch. 13–20). Seen in this way, the raising of Lazarus, together with the entrance into Jerusalem, forms an overture as well as a diptych that, by way of *inclusio* with the first diptych, treats of the same theme: Jesus as the giver of life (pp. 77-78, 298-299; ET: pp. 111-112, 392-393). The healing miracle in 4,46-54 should also be mentioned. Bultmann rejects the interpretation that this pericope introduces the discourse in ch. 5; rather, he places it as the introduction and prelude to the second section: "The Revelation as Crisis" (4,43–6,59; 7,15-24; 8,13-20) (pp. 77-78, 151-152; ET: pp. 111-112, 204-206).

200. Three (four) miracle stories have been used by the evangelist as introductions to discourses: the feeding miracle (with the walking upon the sea), the paralytic, and the man born blind. In the latter two stories we find a remarkable parallel structure (pp. 178, 249; ET: pp. 239, 329). Each case has to do with a Sabbath healing, indicated by the appended note (5,9b; 9,14); already in the signs source both stories reported a controversy after the healing. The attack is directed first toward the healed person. The difference between chs. 5 and 9 is that the controversy in ch. 9 is much more detailed, and the Jews do not plot against Jesus' life but expel the healed man. The evangelist has expanded the source with the conversation between Jesus and the healed man in 9,35-38, followed by a short exchange of words which, as in ch. 5, leads into a discourse of Jesus. The feeding miracle (and the walking on the sea) introduces the Bread of Life discourse; the healing of the paralytic, a discourse about Jesus' power to judge; and the healing of the blind man, the discourse on Light (for the structure, cf. esp. pp. 5*-8*; ET: pp. VII-XII).

list as a miracle worker and as all-knowing; his divinity is also illustrated in his mysterious elusion of harm or arrest until his hour has come[201]. The σημεῖα reveal Jesus' δόξα (2,11; cf. 9,3; 11,4), and non-belief in the signs is censured (12,37). This θεῖος ἀνήρ theology, nevertheless, is not taken over without critique; repeatedly in the Gospel, we encounter reactions to faith based on miracles (4,48; 20,29; 6,26.30; 2,18)[202]. For the evangelist, in contrast to the signs source, the miracles are not proofs but σημεῖα, i.e., symbols which, as *verba visibilia*, are subject to the same misunderstanding as the words of the Johannine Jesus[203]. According to John, Jesus in his pure humanness paradoxically lays claim to the status of Revealer who brings χάρις and ἀλήθεια. The miracle stories serve this christology. They are no longer legitimations of faith, and are tolerated only to arouse "a first shock" (*Anstoss*). As concessions to human weakness they are merely of preliminary importance and, for believers, superfluous[204].

201. Jesus sees through the people he meets (1,42.47-48; 2,24-25; 5,42; 6,61-62; 16,19), he knows the Samaritan woman's past (4,17-18), he is all-knowing (16,30), he has supernatural knowledge at his disposal (2,19-21; 11,4.11-14; 6,64.70; 13,18; 15,18–16,4a; 16,32; 13,1; 18,4; 19,28), he is elusive (7,30.44; 8,20.59; 10,39), he is a miracle worker (besides the miracle stories, 2,23; 3,2; 4,45; 7,3.31; 10,41; 11,47; 12,37; 20,30) (*Theologie*, pp. 394-396; ET: II, pp. 42-44).

202. *Ibid.*, p. 396 (ET: II, p. 44).

203. The wine miracle symbolizes what occurs in Jesus' entire life: the revelation of his δόξα, not so much as a miracle worker but as the revealer of truth. The stories of the official's son and the paralytic are σημεῖα in the general sense that they point to the Revealer's life-giving work. The feeding miracle, the healing of the blind man, and the raising of Lazarus represent the revelation symbolically as food, light, and life. And perhaps the walking on the sea was meant as an illustration of the Revealer's power over the laws of nature (*Theologie*, p. 397; ET: II, pp. 44-45).

204. Bultmann found the key to this existential interpretation in 1,14a: καὶ ὁ λόγος σάρξ ἐγένετο. This means that Jesus was "nothing but a man" (*Johannes*, p. 40; ET: p. 62) and that his δόξα was completely concealed in his σάρξ; the divinity of the Revealer is "completely lacking in visibility" (*Theologie*, p. 394; ET: II, p. 42), and the revelation occurs openly but not in "demonstrative obtrusiveness" (p. 398; ET: p. 45). Nevertheless, John proclaims that this mere human being is God's revelation and this is a total paradox, an "offense" (*Johannes*, p. 40: "Ärgernis"; ET: p. 62). To accept this message, one must abandon "his claim to self-glorification"; this frees him from the world and brings him to himself and to God (p. 41; ET: p. 64). – It is clear that in such a christology there is no place for miracles. Bultmann emphasizes that "die σημεῖα als wunderbare Vorgänge kein Ausweis, keine Legitimation Jesu sind" (*Theologie*, p. 397; ET: II, p. 45). Therefore, as actual occurrences, the miracles are "im Grunde entbehrlich" (p. 409; ET: p. 56). The meaning of the signs does not lie in the miraculous occurrence (p. 396; ET: p. 44); they are pictures, symbols (p. 397; ET: p. 44) of what Jesus means for believers (see above, n. 203). Note here that Bultmann doubts whether John saw a historical occurrence in the Cana miracle: "Die Frage, ob der Evglist das Wunder für ein wirkliches historisches Ereignis gehalten habe, scheint mir nicht so selbstverständlich bejaht werden zu dürfen, wie gewöhnlich geschieht; doch mag sie dahingestellt bleiben" (*Johannes*, p. 83 n. 4; ET: p. 119 n. 2). – NICOL, *Sēmeia*, 1972, p. 97, remarks that "the miracles were one of the most difficult obstacles Bultmann had to overcome in his existential interpretation of John. An exegete such as Bultmann could not deny that John

[n. 204 contd]

sometimes emphasizes the miracles. He breaks his interpretative principle of 'nichts als ein Mensch' and admits this: 'so wird doch der menschlichen Schwäche unter Umständen das σημεῖον konzediert' (*Jh.*, 173 [ET: p. 233]). The miracles can give 'den ersten Anstoss zur Aufmerksamkeit auf Jesus, zum Anfang des Glaubens' (*Theol.*, 397 [ET: p. 45]) although a faith based on miracles is 'kein wirklicher Glaube' (*Jh.*, p. 83, 7 [ET: p. 119 n. 5])".

CHAPTER II

CRITICAL REACTIONS TO R. BULTMANN'S COMMENTARY

We will review first the immediate reactions to Bultmann's commentary[1], then studies of Johannine style criticism, and finally variations on the semeia hypothesis.

I. REVIEWS OF BULTMANN'S COMMENTARY

In his review of the commentary, Martin DIBELIUS[2] (1942) was not convinced that all the narratives Bultmann attributes to the signs source must stem from the same source[3]. He observes that stylistic similarities can best be explained by literary form. Further, he does not believe that the text of the source can be precisely reconstructed, verse-by-verse, as Bultmann thinks. Dibelius would rather postulate a non-Synoptic tradition as *Grundlage* for some of these stories[4].

1. According to SMITH, *Composition*, 1965, p. 85 n. 105, the Second World War made Bultmann's commentary, like many German books, difficult to obtain and so it waited a long time for thorough critique. Nevertheless, Bultmann's literary theory was already widely known. I note here but two important authors who acquainted the English-speaking world with the commentary even before its complete publication: K. GROBEL, in *JBL* 59 (1940) 434-436; B.S. EASTON, in *ATR* 22 (1940) 223-224; cp. also *JBL* 65 (1946) 73-81, 143-156 (see below, pp. 42-43). – Easton observed in 1946 that Bultmann's commentary was not easy to obtain: "very few complete copies appear to be available in English-speaking countries; although publication in fascicles began before the war, it was less than half complete in September of 1939 and only unusual good fortune enabled subscribers to obtain the remaining portions. Moreover the reported destruction of the book stocks in Leipsic [sic] and elsewhere leaves the future possibility of procuring additional copies in some doubt, even after commercial relations with Germany are reestablished" (*JBL* 65, p. 73). Cp. B. LINDARS, in *Theology* 75 (1972) 149-150, p. 149: "Because of war conditions, Bultmann's commentary did not become generally accessible in this country until its second printing in 1950". – Already in 1940, Grobel mentioned a translation: "Before the war began, a translation of this commentary into English was already under way in Scotland. It is to be hoped that the war not prevent its ultimate completion" (p. 436). An English translation appeared in 1971 (see above, p. 24 n. 138, and below, pp. 44-45).

2. M. DIBELIUS, *Ein neuer Kommentar zum Johannes-Evangelium*, in *TLZ* 67 (1942) 257-264, cc. 258-259. – Cf. SMITH, *Composition*, 1965, pp. XI n. 2, 58; FORTNA, *Gospel of Signs*, 1970, p. 1 n. 1; CORSANI, *I miracoli*, 1983, p. 20; VAN BELLE, *Parenthèses*, 1985, pp. 191-192.

3. Dibelius enumerates the following pericopes: the wine miracle, perhaps the *Grundlage* of the conversation with the Samaritan woman, the healing of the royal official's son, the paralytic, the feeding miracle and the walking on the sea, the blind man, and the raising of Lazarus (cc. 258-259).

4. Dibelius was also skeptical about the *Offenbarungsreden*, but thought the use of a passion source more probable: "Weit sicherer als diese Hypothese der Offenbarungs-

A year later, Joachim JEREMIAS[5] reacted in a similar way. Not every exegete would defend the hypothesis that John used written sources, though the signs source, as postulated by Faure on the basis of 20,30-31, still has the best chance. Moreover, not everyone who admits the use of sources would distill the source word-for-word from the Gospel of John as optimistically as Bultmann[6]. Nonetheless, Jeremias thinks that Bultmann's commentary is important for Johannine research, above all because ample attention has been paid to style characteristics[7].

In 1946, Burton Scott EASTON presented a "somewhat extended analysis" of Bultmann's commentary[8]. He gives attention mostly to the *Offenbarungsreden* (RQ), and, in a subsequent article, presents a reconstruction of it in English[9], wondering whether the bulk of "RQ" may not be the evangelist's own composition, in which he used portions from one or several gnostic works[10]. Easton especially criticizes "Dr. Bultmann's drastic rearrangement of the text"[11], but describes Bultmann's semeia source without criticism: "The evidence for the existence of SQ is found usually in a lack of smoothness in the narrative, especially where the interruptions show characteristic conceptions of the evangelist; anyone interested enough to mark in a text of the gospel the SQ passages listed above will usually see with little difficulty the course of Dr. Bultmann's reasoning. In addition, however, Dr. Bultmann detects a peculiar Greek style in SQ; chiefly placing the verb before the subject,

---

reden scheint mir die Annahme, dass der johanneischen Passion eine vorjohanneische Leidensgeschichte zugrunde liegt. Denn hier bietet das wesentliche Argument die Beobachtung, dass die johanneische Leidensgeschichte gewisse Elemente enthält, die vom Evangelisten gar nicht ausgewertet, sondern einfach weitergegeben werden (Verleugnung, Verlosung des Mantels, Begräbnis)" (c. 260).

5. J. JEREMIAS, in *DLZ* 64 (1943) 414-420, cc. 416-417.

6. For Jeremias, the existence of the *Offenbarungsreden* is also impossible to prove (cc. 418, 419). By reconstructing the original gospel with the aid of numerous rearrangements of the text, we arrive in fact at a gospel "κατὰ Bultmann" (c. 417).

7. "Das Wesentliche sind nicht die Einzelheiten der literarkritischen Ergebnisse und Operationen B.s., sondern die Energie, mit der das literarkritische Problem von ihm aufgegriffen ist, und die bewundernswerte stilkritische Einzelarbeit, mit der B. seine Quellenscheidung unterbaut. ... Hier der künftigen johanneischen Forschung grundlegend wichtiges Material geliefert zu haben, ist ein bleibendes Verdienst des B.schen Werkes" (c. 418). In *Ein bisher unbekanntes Evangelienfragment. Einblicke in die Arbeitsweise eines alten Evangelisten*, in *TBl* 15 (1936) 38-45, c. 44, Jeremias was more reserved with regard to separating sources: one should "mit der Annahme der Benutzung schriftlicher Quellen bei der Abfassung der Evangelien noch erheblich zurückhaltender sein, als üblich. Wir müssen radikal brechen mit der Vorstellung, als ob die Evangelisten wie ein moderner Gelehrter gearbeitet hätten, der verschiedenen Quellen am Schreibtisch neben sich liegen hat und in einander arbeitet". In a 1941 article, however, Jeremias accepted a written narrative source (see below, pp. 47-48).

8. B.S. EASTON, in *JBL* 65 (1946) 73-81.

9. *Bultmann's RQ Source*, in *JBL* 65 (1946) 143-156.

10. *Ibid.*, p. 156.

11. *JBL* 65, p. 79.

the absence or scanty use of connecting particles, and other 'Semitizing' characteristics. Incidentally, in the Lazarus story Dr. Bultmann detects behind SQ's version a still earlier form, in which the raising took place *before* burial, much as in Luke 7,11-17"[12].

Another reaction came from Wilhelm MICHAELIS (1946)[13], who devotes several pages of his *Einleitung* to Bultmann's literary theory. The enumeration of the signs, "a hinge of the entire Semeia-Quelle hypothesis", cannot prove the existence of the source. If a continuous count appeared in the source, why has the evangelist taken it over only in 2,11 and in 4,54 (where, moreover, it contradicts 2,23 and 4,45 according to Bultmann)? Rather, the numbering originated with the redaction: the evangelist chose seven signs and by numbering the first two wished to alert the reader to the importance of the seven[14]. For the evangelist the miracles are actually signs, referring to "a higher reality". Michaelis observes that the count does not contradict the signs in 2,23 and 4,45 because these are only summarily mentioned and not really described[15]. He further wonders how to explain the evangelist's combination of narratives from the signs source with discourses in chapters 5 and 6 only. This difficulty disappears if the evangelist is accorded freedom as a literary composer. Lastly, Michaelis refers to E. Schweizer's examination of style, which pointed out the difficulty of distinguishing sources within the gospel. Only the discourses exhibit a certain independence, but that is to be understood from their specific content and form[16].

Among the reviews of the first edition of Bultmann's commentary we should also mention Ethelbert STAUFFER, who, referring to Jeremias,

---

12. *Ibid.*, pp. 80-81. See also p. 77 for a reconstruction of the σημεῖα-*Quelle* by verse numbers.

13. W. MICHAELIS, *Einleitung in das Neue Testament. Die Entstehung, Sammlung und Überlieferung des Neuen Testaments*, Bern, 1946, esp. pp. 106-110. – Cf. SMITH, *Composition*, 1965, p. 118 n. 12; FORTNA, *Gospel of Signs*, 1970, p. 9 n. 2; HEEKERENS, *Zeichen-Quelle*, 1984, p. 24 n. 26.

14. "Das Ergebnis ist, dass die Existenz einer Semeia-Quelle sich nicht beweisen lässt, dass die Annahme der Benutzung einer Semeia-Quelle nur neue Schwierigkeiten schafft, die sich nicht gleichzeitig behebt, dass aber alle Schwierigkeiten schwinden, sobald mit der Möglichkeit gerechnet wird, dass der Evangelist selbst diese Auswahl von 7 Semeia getroffen hat und durch die Zählung der beiden ersten den Leser auf die besondere Bedeutung aller 7 Semeia hat aufmerksam machen wollen" (pp. 108-109).

15. "Diese dem Joh-Ev eigentümliche Auffassung der Wunder bringt der Evangelist durch die fast überall mit den Semeia verbundenen Reden in wohlüberlegter Steigerung zum Ausdruck. An den nur summarisch erwähnten Semeia kann der Evangelist das nicht dartun, sie bleiben für den Leser daher blosses äusseres Geschehen; dass der Leser aber nicht auf die summarisch erwähnten, sondern auf die wirklich erzählten und gedeuteten Semeia achten soll, das macht der Evangelist ihm dadurch klar, dass er die ersten beiden Semeia dieser Art zählt und das zweite über 2,23; 4,45 hinweg als zweites Semeion bezeichnet" (p. 108).

16. *Ibid.*, p. 109.

denigratingly reviewed Bultmann's literary theory: "one must wonder at the boldness with which he enters anew into source-critical work and further advances a completely new source hypothesis, invents completely new authors, and untertakes completely new divisions and rearrangements. The result is a Fifth Gospel, built from Johannine material – the Gospel 'kata Bultmann', as Joachim Jeremias (in DLZ) has named it"[17].

Jean LEVIE reacted similarly in his review of the second edition (1951): "Despite the respect one spontaneously feels for the critical ingenuity of the author and the wealth of his information, one remains astonished at the self-assurance with which he pretends to recover the original order of the Johannine chapters and the sources used by the final redactor"[18].

The English translation by George R. BEASLEY-MURRAY appeared in 1971. Reaction by English-speaking commentators was enthusiastic[19]: Charles Kingsley BARRETT, Raymond E. BROWN, and Barnabas LINDARS all agree that Bultmann's commentary has lasting value[20]. In these and

---

17. E. STAUFFER, in *ZKG* 62 (1943, ed. 1947) 347-352, p. 348 (for the reference to Jeremias, see above, p. 42 n. 6). With Dibelius and P. Althaus (*Deutsches Pfarrerblatt*, January, 1943), he rejects Bultmann's rearrangement of the gospel.

18. J. LEVIE, in *NRT* 53 (1951) 876 (see also above, p. 25 n. 139).

19. See above, p. 24 n. 138.

20. C.K. BARRETT noted in the first edition of his commentary (*John*, 1955, p. VII): "Dr. Rudolf Bultmann's commentary is beyond question one of the greatest achievements of biblical scholarship"; cp. ²1978, p. VII, and the preface of the German translation (1990, p. 9). D.M. MACKINNON ("who revived the publisher's enthusiasm for the project when translation difficulties seemed insuperable"; see "Publisher's Note", in BULTMANN, *John*, 1971, p. XIV) referred to Barrett's comment on the dust jacket of the English translation: "The last thirty years have seen a number of major works on the Fourth Gospel. But it was not for nothing that the author of another massive commentary on this Gospel, Professor C. Kingsley Barrett, referred to Bultmann's commentary in the German *Meyer-Kommentar* as one of the greatest on any book of the Bible to be written in this century". In his review of the ET, Barrett added: "After nearly twenty years I am still of the same opinion; and if I were ever driven from my study as a refugee and allowed to take only half a dozen books with me, two at least would not take a moment to choose – Barth's *Romans* (the big one), and Bultmann's *John*" (*ExpT* 83, 1971-72, 185; also quoted by B.M. NEWMAN, Jr., in *BTrans* 24, 1973, 336-337, p. 336). Even for the second edition of Barrett's commentary Bultmann remains an important guide: "This does not mean that I have ceased to be grateful to earlier guides, of whom now none survives: Hoskyns, and his editor – to me, much more than editor – Noel Davey; C.H. Dodd; and Rudolf Bultmann, who died about a week after the manuscript of the new edition left my hands" (*John*, ²1978, p. VII). – R.E. BROWN, in *TTod* 28 (1971-72) 517-519, p. 519: "But these minor failings are swept away by overall admiration for the consistency of Bultmann's thought, for his ability to detect the important ideas in the text, and for his compactness of expression. Despite all that has appeared since, this is a great and lasting commentary". – B. LINDARS, in *Theology* 75 (1972) 149-150, p. 149: "The year 1971 will be remembered for a number of notable events. Amongst them should be counted the appearance of the long-awaited English translation of Bultmann's celebrated commentary, thirty years after the original publica-

other reviews little criticism is given or nothing is said about the signs source. Yet, Lindars and, among others, John ASHTON, Edward MALATESTA, and Barclay M. NEWMAN, especially question Bultmann's literary criticism[21]. C.K. Barrett has strikingly described the influence of Bultmann's commentary: "There is hardly any aspect of Johannine study which has not in the last thirty years borne the marks of Dr. Bultmann's work. His view of the sources used by the evangelist, his theory of a process of ecclesiastical redaction that brought the gospel into line with contemporary orthodoxy, his understanding of John's complex relation to primitive gnosticism – these especially have provoked sometimes agreement, sometimes dissent, but always lively argument. Many valuable things have been said by many people in the course of the debate, but no single contribution has yet eclipsed this one"[22].

II. STYLE CRITICISM: THE UNITY OF THE GOSPEL OF JOHN

Together with the appearance of Bultmann's commentary we observe the definite beginning of style-critical research[23]. To be men-

tion". – Compare, e.g., also J.C. KIRBY, in *StudRel/SciRel* 1 (1971) 140: "It would be superfluous to write a review of this book which first appeared some thirty years ago and has only now been translated into English. It has been referred to by so many New Testament scholars and has influenced so much theological writing, both positively and negatively, that there must be few readers of theological books who have not heard of its basic ideas"; J. ASHTON, in *HeythJ* 13 (1972) 196-197, p. 196: "the most remarkable commentary ever to have been written on a single New Testament author".

21. LINDARS, in *Theology* 75, p. 150 (with reference to the prologue and the *Offenbarungsreden*): "We may complain that Bultmann has erected a false antithesis, and that he has done it by splitting into source and reworking by the Evangelist what is really a seamless robe"; ASHTON, in *HeythJ* 13, p. 197: "He built grand and imposing edifices upon a tenuous and insubstantial theory of Gnostic influences; his drastic reshuffling of the text of the Gospel is influenced by theological presuppositions, among them an arbitrary assignment of any hints of sacramentalism or futuristic eschatology to the 'ecclesiastical redactor'"; E. MALATESTA, in *BTB* 2 (1972) 93-94, p. 94: "His options especially regarding the order of the text, the stages of its composition, and its sources have been seriously challenged and often shown to be wrong. His most basic theological presuppositions and many of his conclusions have been rejected by competent scholars"; NEWMAN, in *BTrans* 24, p. 337: "Dr. Bultmann's source analysis and reconstruction of the 'original' order of the text is often highly subjective and unnecessary".

22. C.K. BARRETT, in *ExpT* 83 (1971-72) 185.

23. Style criticism was practiced before Schweizer by CREDNER, *Einleitung*, 1836; ABBOTT, *Johannine Vocabulary*, 1905; *Johannine Grammar*, 1906; BROOKE, *Johannine Epistles*, 1912; CHARLES, *Revelation*, 1928; BROMBOSZCZ, *Einheit*, 1927; BERNARD, *John*, 1928. – CREDNER, *op. cit.*, pp. 225-235 ("§ 96. Sprache und Aechtheit"), esp. 223-229, gave a list of Johannine style characteristics numbered 1 to 78. He himself refers to such predecessors as SCHULZE (1803; [2]1811), WEGSCHEIDER (1806), and WEBER (1823). Credner's list was reproduced completely by DAVIDSON, *Introduction*, II, 1849, pp. 341-346, and in short form by GUERIKE, *Einleitung*, 1843, p. 310 n. 3, and DE WETTE, *Einleitung*, [5]1848; [6]1860, p. 213.

tioned first is Bultmann's student, Eduard SCHWEIZER[24], with his dissertation *Ego Eimi* (1939). Without rejecting source theories a priori, he points out the homogeneous character of the Gospel of John. He compiles a list thirty-three style characteristics[25], which he finds scattered almost evenly among all the components of the respective source theories of Spitta, Wendt and Hirsch[26]. Schweizer thinks that the Gospel of John is not a completely free literary creation; it was composed on the basis of a (presumably written) tradition, which, nonetheless, is difficult to ferret out because of the uniform style of the evangelist. He considers it possible that John used a special source for the narrative portions[27]. In several passages the presence of source material can be established because Johannine style characteristics are missing: in 2,1-10 and in the short pericopes 2,13-19; 4,46-53; 12,1-8.12-15[28].

24. E. SCHWEIZER, *Ego Eimi. Die religionsgeschichtliche Herkunft und theologische Bedeutung der johanneischen Bildreden, zugleich ein Beitrag zur Quellenfrage des vierten Evangeliums* (FRLANT, NF 38), Göttingen, 1939; ²1965. – Reviews: cf. MALATESTA, no. 2290. Cf. MENOUD, *L'évangile de Jean*, ²1947, pp. 14-16; JEREMIAS, *Literarkritik*, 1939, c. 35; RUCKSTUHL, *Einheit*, 1951 (²1987), pp. 16, 180-219; NOACK, *Tradition*, 1954, pp. 7, 20-21; HOWARD, *Fourth Gospel*, ⁴1955, pp. 167, 173; HAENCHEN, *Literatur*, 1955, pp. 307-309; MENOUD, *Les études johanniques*, 1958, pp. 14-16; BLANK, *Krisis*, 1964, pp. 17-18; BRAUN, *Jean le théologien*, I, 1959, p. 11; SMITH, *Composition*, 1965, pp. 57, 66-71; BECKER, *Wunder*, 1970, p. 132 n. 1 (= 1980, p. 437 n. 9); KONINGS, *Joh. verhaal*, I, 1969, pp. 114-117, 140-141; FORTNA, *Gospel of Signs*, 1970, pp. 13-14, 17-19, 23, 24 n. 2, 203-214; WEAD, *Literary Devices*, 1970, p. 9; NICOL, *Sēmeia*, 1972, pp. 10-11; TEEPLE, *Origin*, 1974, pp. 19-22; KYSAR, *Fourth Evangelist*, 1975, p. 16; *ANRW* II, 25/3, 1985, p. 2398; TEMPLE, *Core*, 1975, pp. 34, 119; COTHENET, *Le quatrième évangile*, 1977, pp. 106, 123-125; *L'évangile selon saint Jean*, 1984, p. 31; CARSON, *Current Source Criticism*, 1978, p. 414; SMALLEY, *John*, 1978, pp. 97, 101, 107, 109; HAENCHEN, *Johannesevangelium*, 1980, pp. 65-66, 66-74 (ET: I, 1984, pp. 60, 61-66); CORSANI, *I miracoli*, 1983, pp. 20, 21-22, 29, 31, 32, 52-53; HEEKERENS, *Zeichen-Quelle*, 1984, pp. 27-32; BEUTLER, *ANRW* II, 25/3, 1985, pp. 2518-2519, 2523; ROBINSON, *Priority*, 1985, p. 18; VAN BELLE, *Parenthèses*, 1985, p. 194; SEGALLA, *Panorama*, 1986, p. 206; BITTNER, *Jesu Zeichen*, 1987, p. 7; HENGEL, *Interpretation*, 1987, p. 92 n. 31; SCHNELLE, *Christologie*, 1987, p. 172 (ET: 1992, pp. 154-155); KUHN, *Christologie*, 1988, p. 45 (Jn 1,35-51); WAGNER, *Auferstehung*, 1988, p. 21 (Jn 11,1–12,19); BOTHA, *Jesus and the Samaritan Woman*, 1991, p. 22; RUCKSTUHL – DSCHULNIGG, *Stilkritik*, 1991, pp. 10, 11, 23-24, 27; SCHMITHALS, *Johannesevangelium*, 1992, p. 128. – Schweizer began his study of the Johannine parable-discourses in a seminar with Bultmann; in 1939 he defended *Ego Eimi* as a dissertation at Basel under the direction of K.L. Schmidt (see the foreword of the 1st and 2nd editions, pp. IV-V). Schweizer made use of a few notes from the manuscript of Bultmann's commentary (ἐγώ εἰμι, ἄρτος and ποιμήν and 1,1–2,4); later, he could consult the commentary itself for 2,5–8,44 (p. IV).

25. *Ego Eimi*, pp. 87-99: positive characteristics (87-89), negative characteristics (97-98), less characteristic traits (98-99).

26. *Ibid.*, pp. 103-105. Cp. p. 108: "Der Stil ist im wesentlichen durchgängig einheitlich. Es kann also die Einheit nicht in einer 'Grundschrift' gesucht werden, sondern nur in einer Zusammenfassung am Ende des Entwicklungsprozesses bzw. in einer einheitlichen Abfassung". Cp. Bultmann himself (see above, p. 27 n. 147).

27. *Ibid.*, p. 108.

28. *Ibid.*, p. 100. – Schweizer thus reacted to Thompson: "Deutlich wird zweitens auch, dass Kap. 12 nicht, wie Thompson meint, eine Grenze bildet; in 13,1ff. fehlt von

In a later article, Schweizer would defend the connection of the two Cana stories[29].

In 1941, even before Bultmann's commentary appeared in complete form, Joachim JEREMIAS[30] had examined his literary theory from the style-critical point of view[31]. He comes to almost the same result as Schweizer[32]. From the presence of Johannine style characteristics in the entire gospel it appears that the evangelist homogeneously reworked his sources or traditions. The gospel was written by the author of 1 John[33]. The linguistic and stylistic differences between the discourses and a portion of the narratives – especially 2,1-11 and the short "Synoptic" pericopes – allow for the possibility that the evangelist drew his narrative material mostly from the tradition. Jn 20,30-31 leads us to suppose that he used a written source[34]. It is also probable that he used a source for the Prologue[35]. In a few pericopes, the gospel was reworked anew by

unseren Eigentümlichkeiten nur Nr. 8, die viermal vorkommt und in den betr. Kapiteln noch drei sehr nahe Analogien hat, und 24, die im ganzen achtmal (wovon drei wohl sekundär wiederholt) sich findet" (p. 100).

29. See below, pp. 54-55.

30. J. JEREMIAS, *Johanneische Literarkritik*, in *TBl* 20 (1941) 33-46. At that time six fascicles of Bultmann's commentary had already appeared: 1,1–14,21; 15,1–17,26 (c. 39 n. 22). – Cf. COPPENS, in *ETL* 18 (1941) 180-182; MENOUD, *L'évangile de Jean*, ²1947, pp. 7 n. 3, 16 n. 1; RUCKSTUHL, *Einheit*, 1951 (²1987), pp. 16, 181; HAENCHEN, *Literatur*, 1955, p. 307; BRAUN, *Jean le théologien*, I, 1959, p. 11; SMITH, *Composition*, 1965, pp. XI n. 2, 57-58, 59, 66; KONINGS, *Joh. verhaal*, I, 1969, pp. 113-114, 141; FORTNA, *Gospel of Signs*, 1970, pp. 1 n. 1, 4 n. 1, 11 n. 2, 13, 22 n. 3, 23 n. 2, 24 n. 2, 49 n. 2, 204; NICOL, *Sēmeia*, 1972, p. 11; TEEPLE, *Origin*, 1974, pp. 21, 74, 94-95, 131; TEMPLE, *Core*, 1975, p. 35; COTHENET, *Le quatrième évangile*, 1977, p. 124; HAENCHEN, *Johannesevangelium*, 1980, p. 66 (ET: I, 1984, pp. 60-61); CORSANI, *I miracoli*, 1983, p. 21; HEEKERENS, *Zeichen-Quelle*, 1984, p. 31; VAN BELLE, *Parenthèses*, 1985, pp. 170-171; RUCKSTUHL – DSCHULNIGG, *Stilkritik*, 1991, p. 23; SCHMITHALS, *Johannesevangelium*, 1992, pp. 124, 137. – In his later review, Jeremias seems to give the signs source more credence, even though he was still rather reserved (see above, p. 42).

31. See esp. cc. 39-43 (Bultmann's commentary), 45-46 ("Ergebnisse").

32. Cp. KONINGS, *Joh. verhaal*, I, 1969, p. 113 n. 4: "In feite neemt hij de opinie van E. Schweizer, *Ego Eimi* over, behalve voor 20,30 e.v.".

33. Jeremias refers to three characteristics of Johannine style that were not noticed by Schweizer: γύναι "als völlig singuläre Anrede der Mutter Jesu", πιστεύειν εἴς τινα and ὥρα with personal pronoun (cc. 35, 40-41). Further, he examines the presence of seven style characteristics in Bultmann's various sources: personal pronoun after substantive with repetition of the article, ἀφ᾽ ἑαυτοῦ (ἀπ᾽ ἐμαυτοῦ), ὑπάγω used metaphorically, οὐκ ... οὐδείς, (ἐ)άν (μή) τις, οὐ δύναται ... ἐὰν μή, πιστεύειν εἴς τινα. He concludes: "Keine der genannten Stileigentümlichkeiten beschränkt sich also auf *eine* Quelle" (cc. 40-41, esp. 41).

34. "Der Abschluss 20,30f. ... lässt vermuten, dass u.a. eine schriftliche Quelle benutzt ist" (c. 46).

35. *Ibid.*, c. 46. In *Der Prolog des Johannesevangeliums (Johannes 1,1-18)* (CwH, 88), Stuttgart, 1967, Jeremias reconstructs an *Urprolog* consisting of vv. 1-5.9-12b. 14.16.18.

an editor, perhaps the writer of 2 and 3 John: 21,24 and presumably 4,2.37-38.44; 6,51c-58; 7,22.39b; 12,16; 19,35[36].

In the same year, Philippe-H. MENOUD[37] carried the style-critical research of Schweizer and Jeremias further and added a few style characteristics to Schweizer's list[38]. He examines Bultmann's source criticism (with special attention to the *Offenbarungsreden*)[39] and concludes that Johannine style characteristics are not absent in any literary layer and that no characteristic is unique to any one of the sources[40]. His evaluation of Bultmann's work is therefore rather reserved[41].

In turn, Eugen RUCKSTUHL (1951)[42] defended the literary unity of the Gospel of John in a larger work that successively studies Bultmann's

36. *Literarkritik*, cc. 43, 46. On 6,51c-58, see below, p. 48 n. 43. He also supposes two instances where pages have been confused: 7,15-24 originally followed 5,47, and 10,19-29 came before 10,1. Jn 7,53–8,11 and 5,4 were added later (cc. 41-42, 46).

37. P.-H. MENOUD, *Le problème johannique*, in *RTP* 29 (1941) 236-256; 30 (1942) 155-175; 31 (1943) 80-101; see esp. pp. 29, 247-252 (for the discussion of Bultmann's commentary). These articles were bound in one volume in *L'évangile de Jean d'après les recherches récentes* (CTAP, 3), Neuchâtel - Paris, 1943; I cite the second edition (1947), which was thoroughly reworked but remained unchanged in regard to Bultmann. See also *Les études johanniques de Bultmann à Barrett*, in BRAUN (ed.), *L'évangile de Jean*, 1958, pp. 11-40. – Reviews: cf. MALATESTA, nos. 39, 45. Cf. RUCKSTUHL, *Einheit*, 1951 (²1987), pp. 16, 181; HAENCHEN, *Literatur*, 1955, p. 307; BRAUN, *Jean le théologien*, I, 1959, p. 11; SMITH, *Composition*, 1965, pp. XI n. 2, 59, 66; KONINGS, *Joh. verhaal*, I, 1969, p. 142; FORTNA, *Gospel of Signs*, 1970, pp. 1 n. 1, 9 n. 2, 13 n. 1; COTHENET, *Le quatrième évangile*, 1977, p. 124; HAENCHEN, *Johannesevangelium*, 1980, p. 66 (ET: I, 1984, pp. 60-61); CORSANI, *I miracoli*, 1983, pp. 20, 21; HEEKERENS, *Zeichen-Quelle*, 1984, p. 31; J.A.T. ROBINSON, *Priority*, 1985, 18 n. 62; SEGALLA, *Panorama*, 1986, p. 206; SCHNELLE, *Christologie*, 1987, p. 172 n. 446 (ET: 1992, p. 155 n. 446); WAGNER, *Auferstehung*, 1988, p. 22 (Jn 11,1–12,19); RUCKSTUHL – DSCHULNIGG, *Stilkritik*, 1991, p. 23; SMITH, *John among the Gospels*, 1992, pp. 49-50.

38. For the discussion of Schweizer's style criticism, cf. *L'évangile de Jean*, ²1947, pp. 14-16. The following characteristics have been added: πιστεύειν εἴς τινα (Jeremias, see above, p. 47 n. 33), ἀπεκρίθη καὶ εἶπεν (λέγει), ἀμὴν ἀμήν, εἰς τὸν αἰῶνα, μαρτυρία (p. 16).

39. For his description of Bultmann's literary theory, cf. pp. 17-21.

40. Jeremias performs this test on the basis of seven characteristics (see above, p. 47 n. 33), Menoud on the basis of forty; but the latter gives the results from only eight characteristics: ἐμός, (ἐ)ὰν (μή) τις, οὐκ ... οὐδείς, ὑπάγειν, ἀφ᾽ ἑαυτοῦ, πιστεύειν εἴς τινα, ἀπεκρίθη καὶ εἶπεν (p. 19 n. 2). Only one trait, λαμβάνω τινα (with the accusative of person and with a theological meaning) appears exclusively in the *Offenbarungsreden* (1,12; 5,43.43; 13,20.20) (pp. 19-20, esp. 19 n. 3).

41. "C'est donc avec réserve que nous accueillons les idées neuves présentées par le professeur Bultmann" (p. 211).

42. E. RUCKSTUHL, *Die literarische Einheit des Johannesevangeliums. Der gegenwärtige Stand der einschlägigen Forschungen* (SF, NF 3), Freiburg/Schw., 1951 (dir. F.-M. Braun); reprinted with the same pagination in *NTOA* 5, Freiburg/Schw. - Göttingen, 1987. Ruckstuhl received the preparatory research work for *Ego Eimi* from Schweizer (*Einheit*, p. VII; = ²1987, p. XV). – Reviews: cf. MALATESTA, no. 552. Cf. NOACK, *Tradi-*

source theory, the style criticism of Schweizer, and Jeremias's opinion on 6,51c-58[43]. Ruckstuhl thinks that Bultmann erred methodologically by attributing all (in his opinion) characteristic sentences to the evangelist and by parcelling out the neutral, colorless remainder to the sources[44]. Bultmann did not succeed in indicating the distinctive style characteristics of the differing sources, even though this is indispensable for source criticism[45]. Wherever features that are typical of the evangelist appear in source material, Bultmann attributes them to the redaction of the evangelist. In Ruckstuhl's opinion, such a procedure is arbitrary[46].

With reference to the signs source he observes that Bultmann has also failed to distinguish its style characteristics from those of the other narrative sources[47]. The distinction between the miracle stories and the

---

tion, 1954, pp. 7, 11 n. 7; HAENCHEN, *Literatur*, 1955, pp. 307-309; MENOUD, *Les études johanniques*, 1958, p. 15; BLANK, *Krisis*, 1964, pp. 17-18; BRAUN, *Jean le théologien*, I, 1959, p. 11; SMITH, *Composition*, 1965, pp. 66-72; BECKER, *Wunder*, 1970, pp. 132-133 (= 1980, pp. 438-439); KONINGS, *Joh. verhaal*, I, 1969, pp. 142-144; FORTNA, *Gospel of Signs*, 1970, pp. 13-14, 17-19, 21, 204-214; WEAD, *Literary Devices*, 1970, p. 9; NICOL, *Sēmeia*, 1972, p. 11; TEEPLE, *Origin*, 1974, pp. 20-22; KYSAR, *Fourth Evangelist*, 1975, p. 16; *ANRW* II, 25/3, 1985, p. 2398; TEMPLE, *Core*, 1975, p. 34; COTHENET, *Le quatrième évangile*, 1977, pp. 106, 123-125; *L'évangile selon saint Jean*, 1984, p. 31; CARSON, *Current Source Criticism*, 1978, p. 414; SMALLEY, *John*, 1978, pp. 97, 101, 107; HAENCHEN, *Johannesevangelium*, 1980, pp. 66-74 (ET: I, 1984, pp. 61-66); CORSANI, *I miracoli*, 1983, pp. 21-22, 26-27, 31-33; HEEKERENS, *Zeichen-Quelle*, 1984, pp. 27-32; BEUTLER, *ANRW* II, 25/3, 1985, pp. 2518-2519, 2423; J.A.T. ROBINSON, *Priority*, 1985, p. 18; VAN BELLE, *Parenthèses*, 1985, p. 195; SEGALLA, *Panorama*, 1986, p. 206; BITTNER, *Jesu Zeichen*, 1987, p. 7; HENGEL, *Interpretation*, 1987, p. 92 n. 31; SCHNELLE, *Christologie*, 1987, p. 172 (ET: 1992, pp. 154-155); KUHN, *Christologie*, 1988, pp. 40-41 (Jn 1,35-51); WAGNER, *Auferstehung*, 1988, pp. 22-23 (Jn 11,1–12,19); NEIRYNCK, in *ETL* 65 (1989) 170-171 (review of the second edition); RUCKSTUHL – DSCHULNIGG, *Stilkritik*, 1991, pp. 10, 12, 23-24, 27; BOTHA, *Jesus and the Samaritan Woman*, 1991, pp. 22-23; SCHMITHALS, *Johannesevangelium*, 1992, pp. 137-138. On Ruckstuhl, see also below, pp. 302-312.

43. *Ibid*, resp. pp. 20-179, 180-219, 220-271. In the first part, after describing Bultmann's literary theory (pp. 20-37), Ruckstuhl gives a detailed discussion of the discourses (pp. 38-97), the narratives (pp. 98-134), and the work of the ecclesiastical redactor (pp. 134-179); pp. 107-111 are especially important for the semeia hypothesis. – The second part, devoted to Jeremias's theory concerning the secondary character of 6,51c-58, is a reprint of Ruckstuhl's article in *DivThom* 23 (1945) 153-190, 301-333. Under Ruckstuhl's influence, Jeremias accepted the original character of 6,51c-58; cf. *ZNW* 44 (1952-53) 256-257. See now also SCHWEIZER, in *ZNW* 82 (1991) 274. Jn 6,56 means: "Whoever eats my flesh and drinks my blood, in him I abide and he in me". From this unusual sequence (cf. 14,20; 15,4.5.7), Schweizer concludes: "Joh 6,51c-58 (ist) eher vom Evangelisten aus der Abendmahltradition aufgenommen als von einem Redaktor zugefügt".

44. *Einheit*, p. 105.

45. Ruckstuhl refers to the articles by Bultmann noted above (see above pp. 26-27 n. 146).

46. *Ibid*., p. 206.

47. *Ibid*., pp. 98-100.

Synoptics is also not relevant, for *all* Johannine narratives differ from the Synoptic stories[48]. Besides the stylistic aspect, Ruckstuhl treats the other arguments of Faure and Bultmann[49]. First, 20,30-31 could have been written by the evangelist as the original ending of the gospel before the addition of chapter 21. The reference to σημεῖα is not unintelligible: the appearances are revelations of the resurrection miracle and the evangelist could also have conceived of the preaching of Jesus as σημεῖα. It is incorrect to conclude that 20,30-31 refers back to 12,37. Next, the numbering of the signs (2,11; 4,54) is not a convincing argument: in 4,54 "the second miracle in Cana" is intended. If 4,54 belongs to the source, how could the evangelist not have noticed the contradiction with 4,45 (and 2,23)? And if more miracles were numbered, why has the evangelist omitted the numbering? Jn 4,54 and 2,11 are rather the closing verses of narratives which are characteristic for the evangelist. Finally, how can one place 1,35-51 and 4,1-42 in a "miracle book"? Ruckstuhl also notes the difference of opinion between Faure and Bultmann with reference to the "Synoptic" account in 6,1-26[50].

Ruckstuhl arrives at a list of 50 style characteristics, wherein those of Schweizer, Jeremias, and Menoud are accepted, corrected, and supplemented[51]. Following Menoud, he distributes the characteristics over passages from the evangelist and the various sources. His conclusion is quite firm: the stylistic unity of the gospel precludes the existence of written sources[52]. For parallels with the Synoptic Gospels he does not reject reminiscences of Synoptic pericopes, but dependence on oral *Urkatechese* appears more likely to him[53].

---

48. *Ibid.*, pp. 100-101.

49. *Ibid.*, pp. 107-111.

50. In order to disprove Bultmann's source analysis, Ruckstuhl studies 1,35-51; 4,1-42; 6,1-26; 13,1-20; 13,21-30; 18,1-11; 20,1-18 (pp. 111-134).

51. *Ibid.*, pp. 190-205. BRAUN, *Jean le théologien*, I, 1959, pp. 401-403, prints Ruckstuhl's list ("Appendice I: Les caractéristiques johanniques"), and adds one number more, with reference to HOWARD, *Fourth Gospel*, ⁴1955, pp. 278-280: "51. Alternance de deux synonymes (αἰτέω-ἐρωτάω, λέγω-λαλέω, ἀγαπάω-φιλέω, ποιέω-πράσσω, βόσκω-ποιμαίνω, ἀποστέλλω-πέμπω, γινώσκω-οἶδα, ἀρνία-προβάτια, dans la même sentence, le même contexte immédiat, ou un texte parallèle (Howard): 18+1(1)".
– In the *Anhang* to the second edition of *Einheit*, pp. 291-303, Ruckstuhl now gives the "Liste der johanneischen Stilmerkmale mit allen Belegstellen aus dem johanneischen Schrifttum".

52. "An *schriftlichen Quellen* wird man angesichts der stilistischen Einheit des Ev und der Widerlegung aller bisherigen Aufteilungen *kaum* mehr denken. Unzweifelhaft ist die Annahme *stilkritisch nicht erweisbar*, vornehmlich auch deswegen, weil die joh Eigentümlichkeiten einigermassen vollständig gesammelt sein dürften" (p. 219).

53. *Ibid.*, p. 219.

Heinz BLAUERT (1953)[54] treats the Johannine motif of time[55] in dialogue with the literary theory of Bultmann and the style-critical method of Schweizer and Ruckstuhl. He admits the possibility of literary-critical separation between tradition and redaction[56], but remarks that the wine miracle, because of its special character, cannot accurately serve as an argument for the semeia hypothesis[57]. Also, in his examination of 11,1-44 he finds no indications of a larger source[58].

Bent NOACK (1954) comes independently to the same conclusion as Schweizer and Ruckstuhl[59]. In the foreword to his monograph, he notes that he had just learned of Schweizer's work after he had already critically examined Bultmann's commentary, and only after his manuscript was ready had he become acquainted with the work of Ruckstuhl[60]. Noack would claim that the Gospel of John originated directly out of oral tradition without the use of sources[61]. His critique of Bultmann strongly resembles the reaction of Ruckstuhl. Literary analysis itself is

54. H. BLAUERT, *Die Bedeutung der Zeit in der johanneischen Theologie. Eine Untersuchung an Hand von Joh 1–17 unter besonderer Berücksichtigung des literarkritischen Problems*, diss. Tübingen, 1953. I base these remarks on Blauert's summary in *TLZ* 78 (1953) 689-690; see also KONINGS, *Joh. verhaal*, I, 1969, pp. 114-146; SCHMITHALS, *Johannesevangelium*, 1992, p. 123.

55. Blauert studies: 2,13-22; 3,31-36; 5,19-30; 6,27-59; 7,1-9; 11,1-44; 12,20-36a; 13,31-32; 14,1-9.15-26; 16,16-24.

56. "Sie [the literary-critical analyses] zeigen, dass unter Beachtung der joh. Stilcharakteristika eine Scheidung von Tradition und Interpretation im Joh.ev. durchaus möglich ist (anders Schweizer und Ruckstuhl)" (*TLZ* 78, c. 689).

57. "Gegen die σημεῖα-Quelle spricht u.a. der verschiedentlich beobachtete Sondercharakter ihres angeblich ersten Wunders, nämlich der Perikope vom Weinwunder" (*Bedeutung*, p. 118 n. 35).

58. *Ibid.*, p. 118.

59. B. NOACK, *Zur johanneischen Tradition. Beiträge zur Kritik an der literarkritischen Analyse des vierten Evangeliums* (LSSK.T, 3), Copenhagen, 1954. He successively discusses the analysis of the gospel (pp. 7-42), the Johannine logia, the Old Testament quotations, the Synoptic logia, the narrative material (pp. 43-125), and the tradition of the material (pp. 126-142). On pp. 11-17, he gives a brief description of Bultmann's literary theory, followed by a critique of it on pp. 18-42, and discusses the semeia hypothesis more particularly on pp. 112-114. – Cf. MENOUD, *Les études johanniques*, 1958, p. 15; BLANK, *Krisis*, 1964, pp. 18-21; BRAUN, *Jean le théologien*, I, 1959, p. 12; SMITH, *Composition*, 1965, pp. 72-77; BECKER, *Wunder*, 1970, p. 134 n. 4 (= 1980, p. 441 n. 21); KONINGS, *Joh. verhaal*, I, 1969, pp. 203-206; FORTNA, *Gospel of Signs*, 1970, pp. 1 n. 1, 3 n. 5, 9 n. 2, 12, 14 n. 3; WEAD, *Literary Devices*, 1970, p. 9; SELONG, *Cleansing*, I, 1971, pp. 164-165; NICOL, *Sēmeia*, 1972, p. 4 n. 1; TEEPLE, *Origin*, 1974, pp. 70-71; KYSAR, *Fourth Evangelist*, 1975, pp. 11 n. 4, 55, 58; TEMPLE, *Core*, 1975, p. 10; SMALLEY, *John*, 1978, p. 97 n. 55; BEUTLER, *ANRW* II, 25/3, 1985, pp. 2523-2524; J.A.T. ROBINSON, *Priority*, 1985, p. 11 n. 27; VAN BELLE, *Parenthèses*, 1985, p. 36 n. 221; KUHN, *Christologie*, 1988, p. 41 (Jn 1,35-51); RUCKSTUHL – DSCHULNIGG, *Stilkritik*, 1991, p. 12; SMITH, *John among the Gospels*, 1992, pp. 48-49.

60. *Tradition*, p. 7.

61. *Ibid.*, pp. 157-162, esp. 157.

not called into question, but the self-assuredness with which the literary units are ascribed to the reconstructed sources. Bultmann regards grammatical and stylistic characteristics as the exclusive attributes of a specific literary layer. Moreover these characteristics are absolutized as if they had a constant meaning, not determined by the context[62]. Most of the evangelist's style characteristics also appear in the source material. Bultmann sometimes attributes them to the redactional intervention of the evangelist and sometimes not[63]; occasionally he appeals to the explanation that the evangelist has been influenced by the style and content of the source[64].

In the narratives, Noack distinguishes between Synoptic[65] and non-Synoptic material[66], and declares that Bultmann escapes the difficulty that arises from this distinction by acceptance of a signs source[67]. According to the semeia hypothesis the evangelist has employed almost the entire signs source. He even used its conclusion, which stresses the importance of the signs (20,30-31), as the conclusion of his gospel, which sets special value upon words of revelation. Noack does not understand why the evangelist would conclude his work with a remark that accords neither with his intention nor with the content of the gospel. One can only conclude, therefore, that emphasis on the "signs" is not foreign to the evangelist but was "his own interest". Nothing pleads against this interpretation once the artificial distinction between Jesus as a miracle worker and Jesus as a revealer is abandoned. It is also difficult to accept that the evangelist used a written source in which the signs were numbered and that he adopted the numbering only with the first two. One can easily explain the numbering on the level of the evangelist's redaction: he wanted to call attention to the first sign, which expresses the entire activity of Jesus (as miracle worker and revealer!) in one event. Thereby he pointed to Jesus' glorification (2,11) and the provisional character of the revelation (2,4: οὔπω ἥκει ἡ ὥρα μου). In 4,54 the evangelist indicated that the healing miracle occurred in the same place. After he had called his readers' attention to the significance of the signs by the numbering in 2,11 and 4,54, the evangelist had no more interest in further counting[68].

62. *Ibid.*, p. 20.
63. Thus, for example, ἐκεῖνος (used independently) appears in the signs source (5,11) and in the *Offenbarungsreden* (8,42.44). – For Bultmann's reaction, see above, p. 27 n. 147.
64. *Ibid.*, p. 31.
65. 2,14-16; 4,46-53; 6,1-13.16-21; 12,1-8.12-16; 13,21-30.36-38; 18,1.3-11.12-27; 18,28–19,15; 19,16-30.38-42; 21,13 (pp. 109-110). In a few cases it can be doubted whether or not a narrative is Synoptic: 1,19-34.35-51; 5,6-9; 6,66-70 (pp. 110-111).
66. Jn 2,1-11; 4,4-42; 7,1-10; 11,1-44; 11,45-53; 12,20-22; 13,4-11; chs. 18–19 (*passim*); chs. 20–21 (the resurrection narratives) (p. 111).
67. *Ibid.*, pp. 112-113.
68. *Ibid.*, pp. 113-114. From these observations Noack concludes: "Wir bezweifeln daher die Existenz einer Semeia-Quelle als einer schriftlichen Sammlung von Wun-

With reference to style criticism as a curb to arbitrary reconstruction of sources and redactions, one can also mention Dwight Moody SMITH. In 1965 he presented Bultmann's literary theory by a thorough analysis and presentation of the different literary layers in the Gospel of John, and then discussed the influence of, and the reaction to, Bultmann's literary criticism[69]. Preceding this work, in 1964, was an article that presented the "status quaestionis" of Johannine literary criticism[70]. According to Smith, Schweizer and Ruckstuhl correctly pointed out that the entire Gospel of John is dominated by a single style. This does not entirely mean that there were no sources (contra Ruckstuhl), but that the evangelist has reworked his sources. Thus style criticism must make the exegete critical of "source distillation"[71]. From this viewpoint, with Käsemann and others, Smith rejects the *Offenbarungsreden*[72]. There is more to be said, however, for a *semeia* source[73]: the miracle stories have retained their unique character and the order of the source has been preserved[74].

Nevertheless, Bultmann's signs hypothesis exhibits some rather weak points. First, he has abandoned the main argument of Faure (the differing introductory formulas for quotations from the Old Testament); Bultmann assigns these quotations to the evangelist, to the ecclesiastical redactor, or to other sources or traditions. Second, with reference to the

---

dergeschichten und müssen einen anderen Weg zum Verständnis des Erzählungsstoffes suchen" (p. 114).

69. D.M. SMITH, *The Composition and Order of the Fourth Gospel: Bultmann's Literary Theory* (YPR, 10), New Haven, CT - London, 1965. – Cf. BECKER, *Wunder*, 1970, p. 132 n. 1 (= 1980, p. 457 n. 9); KONINGS, *Joh. verhaal*, I, 1969, pp. 123-124; FORTNA, *Gospel of Signs*, 1970, pp. 1 n. 1, 9 n. 2, 15 n. 4, 18 n. 1, 24 n. 2; NICOL, *Sēmeia*, 1972, p. 12 n. 3; TEEPLE, *Origin*, 1974, p. 43; THYEN, *Literatur*, 1974, pp. 289-291; KYSAR, *Fourth Evangelist*, 1975, p. 15 n. 10; CARSON, *Current Source Criticism*, 1978, p. 414; SMALLEY, *John*, 1978, pp. 103 n. 76, 104 n. 79; HEEKERENS, *Zeichen-Quelle*, 1984, p. 31 n. 66; BEUTLER, *ANRW* II, 25/3, 1985, p. 2531; SCHMITHALS, *Johannesevangelium*, 1992, p. 127.

70. *The Sources of the Gospel of John: An Assessment of the Present State of the Problem*, in *NTS* 21 (1963-64) 336-351 (= 1984, pp. 39-61).

71. "If Bultmann goes further than the evidence warrants in defining extensive sources down to the most minute detail, Ruckstuhl goes too far in concluding from a demonstrable stylistic unity of the Gospel that such sources not only cannot be proved, but, in fact, never existed at all" (*Sources*, p. 341; = 1984, p. 46). Cp. *Composition*, p. 108.

72. *Sources*, pp. 343-345 (= 1984, pp. 48-51); *Composition*, pp. 108-110.

73. "Certainly something positive may be said for the semeia-source" (*Composition*, p. 110). Cp. *Sources*, p. 245 (= 1984, p. 52): "While there may be alternative explanations of the narrative material in John, the semeia-source proposal is surely not implausible".

74. "In the semeia-source we have miracle stories which have been commented upon and altered by the evangelist but without any of the stories having lost their essential character or individuality. Neither has the source lost its essential order" (*Composition*, p. 111).

content, Smith gives a few critical remarks. On the basis of the word σημεῖον, only the two Cana narratives can be assigned to the signs source. Jn 12,37 and 20,30-31 give no further clarification about the content of the source (if they were derived from it); these verses are perhaps from the evangelist. It is thus difficult to assign 1,35-51; 4,1-42; 5,1-18; 6,1-26; 7,1-13; chs. 9 and 11 to the source because there is no mention of signs in these passages (except in 6,2.14.26; 9,16, but these are redactional verses of the evangelist; in 7,3 "works" are mentioned). Third, the stylistic data provide little help in determining the source, because they are not decisive and cannot be determined with certainty. On the other hand, it is not true that, because signs are not mentioned in 12,37–20,29, no material from the signs source can appear in these chapters[75]. Thus, Smith finds it difficult to imagine a primitive Christian document without an account of the passion and resurrection. He is not opposed to a signs source, but subjects Bultmann's elaboration to critical question, and in the end is content to allow a choice for the pre-Johannine narrative tradition between a source with a passion-resurrection report (an *Urevangelium* rather than a semeia source; cf. Wellhausen, Wilkens, and Haenchen) and a loose collection of individual traditions[76]. We note, finally, that Smith makes a positive judgement about the existence of a signs source in his later articles[77].

III. THE TWO CANA MIRACLES: A SHORT SIGNS SOURCE

In an article about the second Cana miracle, Jn 4,46-54, Eduard SCHWEIZER (1951) gives several indications for the presence of a source: v. 48 demonstrates a viewpoint different from the context; the numbering of signs; and the absence of Johannine style characteristics[78]. As in 1939, he defends the presence of sources in the Fourth Gospel, but limits the signs source to the two Cana stories. Many exegetes would follow him in this. In the foreword to the second edition of *Ego Eimi* (1965) he refers to Ruckstuhl: "What I held in general, has indeed come to light: the unity of style is of the kind that the separation of sources on the basis of these characteristics appears impossible. Only the prologue and the miracle stories are an exception; in all probability one can point to a source in the first two miracle stories. In any case – and here I am more

---

75. *Ibid.*, p. 111 n. 183.
76. *Ibid.*, pp. 112-113; *Sources*, pp. 348-349 (= 1984, pp. 54-55).
77. See below, pp. 165-166, 194-197, 241-242.
78. E. SCHWEIZER, *Die Heilung des Königlichen: Joh. 4,46-54*, in *EvT* 11 (1951-52) 64-71 (= 1963, pp. 407-415); ET (summarized in part): *Orthodox Proclamation: The Reinterpretation of the Gospel by the Fourth Evangelist*, in *Interpr* 8 (1954) 387-409. – Cf. KONINGS, *Joh. verhaal*, I, 1969, pp. 114-116.

cautious than E. Ruckstuhl – the conclusion that the sources are difficult to demonstrate linguistically does not imply that they do not exist. Outside the prologue and the miracle stories, the existence of written sources remains for me very improbable"[79]. Schweizer also amends the theological argument for the semeia hypothesis by stressing a possible continuity between sign and faith[80].

In 1958, Otto MICHEL published a brief but noteworthy article on the wine miracle, wherein he accepts Spitta's Galilean source[81]. It is striking that Cana, absent from the Synoptics, appears in three stories in John (2,1.11; 4,46; 21,2). This may indicate a separate tradition[82]. From the numbering of the signs, inconsistent with 2,23 and 4,45, Michel thinks it probable that 2,1-11 and 4,46-54 originally followed one another[83]. Edward F. SIEGMAN[84] follows the opinion of Schweizer, for the most part (in an article on 4,46-54 written about 1958-1959 and published posthumously in 1968): he rejects Bultmann's source theory, but accepts a source for 4,46-54[85]. In 1961, Octave

79. SCHWEIZER, *Ego Eimi*, ²1965, p. VI.

80. *Heilung*, pp. 68-71 (= 1963, pp. 411-414). Note that Schweizer, in his *Theologische Einleitung in das Neue Testament* (Grundrisse zum Neuen Testament. NTD Ergänzungsreihe, 2), Göttingen, 1989, p. 141, again defends the signs source on the basis of the absence of Johannine characteristics in the two Cana miracles and the numbering in 2,11; 4,54 (ctr. 2,23; 3,2): "Dass eine 'Zeichenquelle' vorlag, ist höchstwahrscheinlich". But he no longer limits the source to the two Cana miracles: "Wahrscheinlich gehörte auch die Speisung der Fünftausend mit dem anschliessenden Seewandel Jesu und der Zeichenforderung (6,1-31) dazu, die in Einzelheiten anders erzählt werden als in den übrigen Evangelien, aber in gleicher Reihenfolge. Auch der Grundstock anderer Wundererzählungen mag auf diese Quelle zurückgehen, so dass 20,30-31 vielleicht deren Schluss bildete. Der Satz, dass diese Zeichen hier niedergeschrieben seien, damit die Leser zum Glauben kämen, könnte also stärker der Überzeugung des Verfassers dieser Quelle entsprechen als der des Evangelisten".

81. O. MICHEL, *Der Anfang der Zeichen Jesu (Joh 2,11)*, in *FS A. Köberle*, 1958, pp. 15-22 (= 1986, pp. 148-153). – Cf. FORTNA, *Gospel of Signs*, 1970, pp. 25, 98; NICOL, *Sēmeia*, 1972, p. 12 n. 1; TEMPLE, *Core*, 1975, p. 35; HEEKERENS, *Zeichen-Quelle*, 1984, p. 24 n. 26.

82. *Anfang*, pp. 15-17 (= 1986, pp. 148-149).

83. "Man könnte vermuten, dass beide Anekdoten ursprünglich dicht nebeneinander standen, ja dass vielleicht der zeitliche Hinweis: 'Als Jesus aus Judäa nach Galiläa kam' auf beide Anekdoten gemeinsam zutrifft" (p. 17; = 1986, p. 150). – In contrast to W. Bauer and Bultmann, who explained the wine miracle against the background of the Dionysus cult, Michel thinks that the Old Testament stories of Moses and Elijah are the first *religionsgeschichtliche* parallels to be considered (p. 17; = 1986, p. 151).

84. E.F. SIEGMAN, *St John's Use of the Synoptic Material*, in *CBQ* (1968) 182-198. See the editor's note for the dating of the article, p. 182 n. *. – Cf. KYSAR, *Fourth Evangelist*, 1975, p. 64; TEMPLE, *Core*, 1975, p. 119.

85. "From what we have already said, it is clear that we are impressed with the opinion that the author of the IV Gospel found 4,46-53 in a pre-existing source which probably included also 2,1-11. This does not mean that we accept Bultmann's postulate of a special *Semeia-Quelle*, which included these and the other miracles described in Jn. E. Schweizer showed by a careful analysis of the literary characteristics of Jn that Bult-

MERLIER[86] published his 1945 doctoral dissertation. He views the gospel as a composite work[87] and gives attention to the first two miracle stories: he thinks that they were joined in the first redaction of the gospel[88].

A year later (1962), Marie-Émile BOISMARD accepted the original sequence of 2,1-11 and 4,46-54[89]. Also in 1962, Sydney

mann's dissection of Jn into the *Semeia-Quelle* and the *Offenbarungsreden* is unwarranted. Nevertheless, Schweizer defends the distinctive character of 2,1-11 and 4,46-53" (pp. 194-195).

86. O. MERLIER, *Le quatrième évangile. La question johannique*, Athens, 1961. This dissertation was defended at the Sorbonne in 1945. Merlier refers frequently to two works (on language and vocabulary) which he wrote before the Second World War and intended to publish soon afterward (cf. p. 6: "Avertissement"). To my knowledge, these have never appeared. See by the same author: *Itinéraires*, 1961. – Cf. SMITH, *Composition*, 1965, p. 243 n. 89; BECKER, *Wunder*, 1970, p. 132 n. 1 (= 1980, p. 437 n. 9); FORTNA, *Gospel of Signs*, 1970, p. 3 n. 8; SELONG, *Cleansing*, I, 1971, p. 30; KONINGS, *Joh. verhaal*, III, 1972, p. 133; NICOL, *Sēmeia*, 1972, p. 12 n. 1; TEEPLE, *Origin*, 1974, pp. 98-99; KYSAR, *Fourth Evangelist*, 1975, p. 15 n. 11; TEMPLE, *Core*, 1975, p. 35; COTHENET, *Le quatrième évangile*, 1977, p. 112; BEUTLER, *ANRW* II, 25/3, 1985, p. 2528.

87. In the first place there was an anonymous collection of logia and narratives, like those attested in the Unkown Gospel. An author (A) composed a life of Jesus, which differed from the Synoptic Gospels, and later expanded it with logia. A first redactor (R1) tried to harmonize this composition with the Synoptics. Then a second redactor (R2) added chs. 14–17. A third redactor (R3) reordered the gospel, introduced it with the prologue, and perhaps also added 7,53–8,11. A group of believers (Merlier labels them R4) was responsible for ch. 21; their intention was to present the book of R3 as a gospel by the Beloved Disciple (cf. spec. *Question*, pp. 429-432).

88. "Il est probable que le verset 2,11 était suivi de 4,46 et suiv." (p. 407). Cp. p. 409: "Il nous paraît que 46b faisait suite, dans la première rédaction, à 2,12)".

89. M.-É. BOISMARD, *Saint Luc et la rédaction du quatrième évangile (Jn. IV,46-54)*, in *RB* 69 (1962) 185-211, p. 204: "Sans en donner preuves ici, je dirai simplement que les conclusions de mes analyses rejoignent celles de Fr. Spitta, R. Bultmann, E. Schweizer, W. Wilkens: primitivement, le récit de la guérison du fils du fonctionnaire royal de Capharnaüm suivait immédiatement le récit des noces de Cana (II,1-11), le v. II,12 faisant le lien entre les deux épisodes: 'Après cela, il descendit à Capharnaüm, avec sa mère et ses frères'. Ce verset n'a plus aucune signification dans l'évangile actuel; primitivement, il introduisait le deuxième miracle galiléen". – Cf. SMITH, *Composition*, 1965, pp. [242-]243 n. 85; KONINGS, *Joh. verhaal*, I, 1969, p. 201; FORTNA, *Gospel of Signs*, 1970, pp. [9-]10 n. 2; TEEPLE, *Origin*, 1974, pp. 99-100; KYSAR, *Fourth Evangelist*, 1975, pp. 13 n. 3, 39 n. 1; TEMPLE, *Core*, 1975, p. 11; COTHENET, *Le quatrième évangile*, 1977, pp. 181-182, esp. 181 n. 12; NEIRYNCK, *John and the Synoptics*, 1977, pp. 82-93, esp. [82-]83 n. 37 (= 1982, pp. 374-385, esp. [374-]375 n. 37); SMALLEY, *John*, 1978, p. 115 n. 116; HEEKERENS, *Zeichen-Quelle*, 1984, pp. 53-54. See also RUCKSTUHL, *Einheit*, 1951 ([2]1987), p. 146 n. 1 (pp. 146-149).

Boismard's view on the literary origin of Jn 4,46-54 has changed many times. Besides his articles in *AssSeign* 17 (1962) 29-44; 75 (1965) 26-37, see esp. *Synopse des quatre évangiles en français*. II. *Commentaire*, Paris, 1972, where he writes that the original story of 4,46-54 (without vv. 48-49.51-54) comes from "un recueil de miracles" (p. 160b: § 84, IV,1; but on p. 161b: § 84,V, he notes: "ce récit pourrait provenir, soit d'un recueil de miracles, soit du Document C"); the stories of the paralytic and the man born blind in chs. 5 and 9 would also originate from a primitive collection of miracles (p. 160b: § 84, IV,1; cp. p. 107b: § 40, I,2*b*, where he supposes that the healing of the

TEMPLE[90] studied the Cana narratives in a thorough fashion. He draws attention to the numbering and remarks that, in itself, it is already an indication of the distinct literary character of these two accounts[91]. In contrast to the other Johannine miracles, they are not followed by an explanatory discussion. They have a length similar to 7,53–8,11 (11 and 9 verses respectively) and are similar in type to the pericopes in the Synoptic Gospels[92]. For Temple, this is an indication of a tradition that differs from the rest of the Fourth Gospel (*Core*)[93]. The

paralytic belonged with the exorcism and the raising of Jairus' daughter in Mk 5; see also p. 109b: § 40, IV,1; p. 321b: § 268, I,5*b*). Later, in his commentary on John (1987), Boismard further works out and corrects this view (see below, pp. 271-276). Recently, he has replied to Neirynck's *Jean et les Synoptiques* (1979) in *Jean 4,46-54 et les parallèles synoptiques*, in DENAUX (ed.), *John and the Synoptics*, 1992, pp. 239-259. For his presentation in 1962, 1965, 1972 and 1977, see NEIRYNCK, *Jean et les Synoptiques*, 1979, pp. 93-120, esp. 94 n. 143 (= *ETL* 53, 1977, 451-478, esp. p. 452 n. 143), and for his 1992 presentation, cf. P.J. JUDGE, *A Note on Jn 20,29*, in *FS F. Neirynck*, III, 1992, pp. 2183-2192, esp. 2183 n. 3: "Now he has reverted to his earlier opinion".

90. S. TEMPLE, *The Two Signs in the Fourth Gospel*, in *JBL* 81 (1962) 169-174. – Cf. KONINGS, *Joh. verhaal*, I, 1969, pp. 194-196; FORTNA, *Gospel of Signs*, 1970, pp. 9 n. 1, 10 n. 3, 25, 98; NICOL, *Sēmeia*, 1972, p. 12 n. 3; TEEPLE, *Origin*, 1972, pp. 47-49; KYSAR, *ANRW* II, 25/3, pp. 2396, 2397, 2402; TEMPLE, *Core*, 1975, p. 35; CARSON, *Current Source Criticism*, 1978, pp. 415, 416-420; SMALLEY, *John*, 1978, p. 114 n. 113; HEEKERENS, *Zeichen-Quelle*, 1984, pp. 13, 15, 39, 132; SMITH, *John among the Gospels*, 1992, p. 75 n. 110. – Fortna compares Temple's article with that of Michel (see above, p. 85): "Two recent studies (those of Michel and Temple) stop with the first two signs in looking for a source – and it is true that the formula found in 2,11 and 4,54 does not appear again (except in a different form in 21,14) and that the structural relation of these two stories to their contexts is unique" (*Gospel of Signs*, 1970, p. 25).

91. *Two Signs*, p. 169: "The particular numbering of the two signs and no more would suggest that the author was drawing attention to the fact that there was something different about the two episodes so numbered". He notes the numbering in 21,14 (pp. 169-170), but omits consideration of the "third" appearance story (cp. FORTNA, *Gospel of Signs*, 1970, p. 98, n. 3).

92. Jn 7,53–8,11 is also not connected with a discourse, but, for text-critical reasons, this pericope did not belong to the original gospel (p. 170).

93. Based on a study of 6,24-71, Temple enunciated his literary theory in *A Key to the Composition of the Fourth Gospel*, in *JBL* 80 (1961) 220-232 (cf. KONINGS, *Joh. verhaal*, I, 1969, p. 195). The *Core* is an early independent tradition which may be based on an eyewitness account. It is characterized by Aramaisms and direct discourse between Jesus and the people, or the disciples, which is simple and terse. In the second stage, the evangelist used the *Core* to write a theological treatise to convince his readers that Jesus is the Jewish Messiah (20,31). He stresses *works* in place of *signs*, calls Jesus the Son of God, and especially emphasizes the last day. The gospel is written in a smooth Greek. Finally, 6,48-59, intended as a homiletic interpretation of the Eucharist, is introduced in a third stage at the same time as the addition of ch. 21 (p. 232). – Temple treats his theory more comprehensively in his study *The Core of the Fourth Gospel*, London - Oxford, 1975 (reviews: cf. VAN BELLE, no. 1736). In section 9, "The Search for a Sign Source in the Fourth Gospel" (pp. 39-50, esp. 41-43), he repeats the arguments for a "two-sign-source" (or "Cana-sign-source") from his 1962 article. For the "Original Text of the Core" in English, see pp. 255-282.

absence of the formula ἀπεκρίθη καὶ εἶπεν[94] and the presence of the expressions σημεῖα καὶ τέρατα[95] and ἐφανέρωσεν τὴν δόξαν αὐτοῦ[96] also point to the unique character of the two Cana narratives. Independent of the *Core* material, they are closely bound with one another. Jn 4,46 and 54 refer expressly to the first sign; this is an indication that the two stories were inserted into the Fourth Gospel at the same moment. In contrast to Q (Mt 8,5-13; Lk 7,1-10), Jn 4,46-54 takes place in Cana, nevertheless the βασιλικός comes from Capernaum[97]. The formula μετὰ τοῦτο/ταῦτα in 2,12 and 5,1 is striking. According to Temple, it re-introduces the *Core* material each time after the insertion of the Cana tradition. In the original order of events Jn 2,12-13 followed the call of the disciples, and the dialogue with the Samaritan woman was followed by Jn 4,43; 5,1. The *Core* material was limited to the events and discourses which took place in Judea, with two exceptions: the Samaritan journey and the one Passover that Jesus spent in Galilee. In two places a journey to Galilee is mentioned, but without any account of what happened. At these places the evangelist has inserted the Cana narratives[98].

In his Introduction to the New Testament (1963)[99] Werner Georg KÜMMEL is rather opposed to Bultmann's semeia hypothesis[100]. Like the style critics, he deems the search for coherent sources extremely problematic. Nevertheless, characteristics of Johannine style are missing in 2,1-10.13-19; 4,46-53; 12,1-8.12-15 (cp. Schweizer) and therefore he thinks that older traditions lay at the origin of these passages[101]. Only in

94. We meet its variations 33 times in John, while ἀπεκρίθη alone occurs 43 times (*Two Signs*, p. 171 n. 9).

95. *Ibid.*, p. 171.

96. *Ibid.*, p. 171.

97. *Ibid.*, p. 172.

98. "Now the evangelist also had at hand reports of the events which took place in Galilee (perhaps from a tradition preserved in Cana)" (p. 173). Cp. p. 174: "It appears, therefore, that these sections come from a different tradition to that which provided the main source for the Gospel and that in writing the gospel the evangelist inserted the two at appropriate places in his main source, the Core".

99. W.G. KÜMMEL, *Einleitung in das Neue Testament*, Heidelberg, [12]1963, pp. 146-147; [17]1973 ([21]1984), pp. 179-180 (ET: [[14]1965] by A.J. MATTILL, JR., 1966, p. 152; [[17]1973] by H.C. KEE, 1975; 5th printing, 1984, pp. 213-214). On Kümmel, see, e.g., SCHMITHALS, *Johannesevangelium*, 1992, p. 192.

100. He observes in *Das Neue Testament im 20. Jahrhundert. Ein Forschungsbericht* (SBS, 50), Stuttgart, 1970, p. 47: "Aber während die Annahme einer Abhängigkeit des Johannes von einer Wunderquelle und einer Leidensgeschichte weite Zustimmung fand, ist die Hypothese einer, womöglich vorchristlichen, Offenbarungsquelle mit Recht auf starken Widerstand gestossen".

101. He strongly notes however: "Aber auf eine dem Evangelisten vorliegende schriftliche 'Zeichenquelle' führt das keineswegs. Und auch für die Leidensgeschichte reichen die Hinweise auf eine Sonderüberlieferung schwerlich aus, um eine zusammenhängende schriftliche Vorlage neben der Kenntnis des Mk. und Lk. zu erweisen" (*Einleitung*, [12]1963, p. 147; ET: 1966, p. 152).

this sense should one count Kümmel among the defenders of the "short" signs source[102]. His view remains unchanged in the new editions of his Introduction[103].

In the first volume of his commentary, Raymond E. BROWN (1966)[104] presents a literary theory which can be seen as an attempt to combine the tradition hypothesis of P. Gardner-Smith and C.H. Dodd with the multiple-redaction theory of P. Parker and W. Wilkens[105]. Brown dismisses Bultmann's semeia hypothesis: he considers it improbable that the miracle stories and the discourses are attributable to separate sources[106]. For the Cana narratives, however, he makes an exception. The two pericopes are indeed the strongest argument for the signs

---

102. Cf. J.M. ROBINSON, *Kerygma*, 1965, p. 136 (= 1971, p. 53; GT: 1965, p. 322); NICOL, *Sēmeia*, 1972, p. 12 n. 1; VAN BELLE, *Parenthèses*, 1985, p. 220, n. 753.

103. KÜMMEL, *Einleitung*, [17]1973, pp. 178-180. He pays extensive attention to Fortna's *Gospel of Signs*. But his opinion about the signs source remains unchanged: "die Bearbeitung einer 'Zeichenquelle' oder eines 'Zeichenevangeliums' durch den Evangelisten (ist) keineswegs wahrscheinlich gemacht" (p. 180; ET: pp. 213-214).

104. R.E. BROWN, *The Gospel according to John: Introduction, Translation, and Notes* (AB, 29-29A), 2 vols., Garden City, NY, 1966, 1972. – Reviews: cf. VAN BELLE, no. 1921. See also KONINGS, *Joh. verhaal*, I, 1969, 235-237; SELONG, *Cleansing*, I, 1971, pp. 157-158; TEEPLE, *Origin*, 1974, pp. 71-72, 103-104; REIM, *Hintergrund*, 1974, p. 235 n. 10; THYEN, *Literatur*, 1974, pp. 316-317; KYSAR, *Fourth Evangelist*, 1975, pp. 39-42; *ANRW* II, 25/3, pp. 2392, 2403-2404; TEMPLE, *Core*, 1975, p. 35; COTHENET, *Le quatrième évangile*, 1977, pp. 112, 190-191; *L'évangile selon saint Jean*, 1984, p. 50; NEIRYNCK, *John and the Synoptics*, 1977, p. 76 n. 13 (= 1982, p. 368 n. 13); SMALLEY, *John*, 1978, p. 116; HAENCHEN, *Johannesevangelium*, 1980, pp. 41-42 (ET: I, 1980, p. 37); BEUTLER, *ANRW* II, 25/3, 1985, pp. 2531-2532; VAN BELLE, *Parenthèses*, 1985, pp. 50-51; KUHN, *Christologie*, 1988, pp. 60-61 (Jn 1,35-51); MARCHADOUR, *Lazare*, 1988, pp. 55-56 (Jn 11); MORGEN, *L'exégèse johannique*, 1989, pp. 247-250; LÉON-DUFOUR, *Où en est la recherche johannique?*, 1990, pp. 22-23; LINDARS, *Trends*, 1990, p. 333; ASHTON, *Understanding*, 1991, pp. 82-83, 161-162; SLOYAN, *What Are They Saying about John?*, 1991, pp. 19-24; SCHMITHALS, *Johannesevangelium*, 1992, pp. 192-193; SMITH, *John among the Gospels*, 1992, p. 64.

105. He explains the origin of the Fourth Gospel in five stages: (1) There first arose a body of traditional material (perhaps by John the Apostle) pertaining to the words and deeds of Jesus; this tradition, although independent of the Synoptics, shows similarities to them. (2) This traditional material was developed, under influence of preaching and teaching, into patterns typical of Johannine form and style. (3) The same "master preacher and theologian" responsible for the developments at stage 2 organized this material into a consecutive Gospel, written in Greek. Brown refers to him as the "evangelist". (4) This same evangelist re-edited his gospel after 80 A.D., when a complete break with Judaism occurred. (5) A "redactor", other than the evangelist, produced a final edition. He was most likely a close friend or disciple of the evangelist. To this redactor Brown attributes the insertions or duplications (like 6,51-58 next to 6,35-50; or 16,4-33, a variant duplicate of ch. 14); the placement of the discourses at 3,31-36 and 12,44-50; the addition of chapters 11 and 12; the placement of 2,13-22 and 6,51-58; and the addition of ch. 21. The redactor could have known the Synoptic Gospels, but Brown does not stress this since, in his opinion, "close parallels can also be explained in terms of dependence on similar early traditons" (I, pp. XXXIV-XXXIX).

106. *Ibid*, p. XXXI; cp. p. XXIX.

hypothesis[107]. The similarity of the two stories (they are not followed by a discourse and display the same structure) has been emphasized by the evangelist himself in the two-fold reminiscence of the wine miracle in 4,46.54. They could originate from the same tradition; 4,54 ("the second sign") also points in this direction. Originally, perhaps, the two miracles belonged together and, at a certain phase of the composition, they were disengaged in order to form the beginning and the end of a section: from Cana to Cana. Brown mentions the hypothesis of Faure and Bultmann in the second volume of his commentary (1970), but explains 20,30-31 simply as the conclusion of the evangelist. It appears from the context that he is speaking about the signs done before the disciples: the appearances of the Risen One[108]. In 1971 Brown also reacted against G.W. Buchanan's reconstruction of a signs source with fourteen signs[109].

IV. THE MIRACLE STORIES IN A PRIMITIVE GOSPEL

Although the semeia hypothesis knew a wide circulation[110], many exegetes rejected Bultmann's literary theory, chiefly on the basis of style criticism[111]. The existence of the *Offenbarungsreden*, above all, was called into question[112].

107. "However, it is reasonable to suppose that there were collections of miracles in the corpus of Johannine material that was edited to give us the Gospel. In one of the stages of editing two closely related miracles may have been split up to form the beginning and the end of Part Two of the Book of Signs, 'From Cana to Cana', in the Gospel" (p. 195).

108. *John*, II, pp. 1058-1059.

109. BROWN, *Jesus and Elisha*, in *Perspective* 12 (1971) 85-104, p. 94: "Finally, to emphasize the conjectural character of Buchanan's reconstruction of a pre-Johannine source containing fourteen signs or miracles, I would note that R. Fortna's recent and painstaking attempt to reconstruct the narrative source underlying the Fourth Gospel admits the indeterminability of the exact content of that source and yet suggests that John has reproduced the entire structural framework of the source which consisted of only seven signs!". For Buchanan, see below, p. 91. – See now also Brown's reaction against the reconstruction of a pre-Johannine Gospel in *The Death of the Messiah: From Gethsemane to the Grave. A Commentary on the Passion Narratives in the Four Gospels* (The Anchor Bible Reference Library), New York, 1994, p. 84: "Most who attempted this do so by stripping of from the present Gospel what is distinctively Johannine by way of wording, style, and theology and emerge with a source much closer to the Synoptic Gospels"; cp. p. 85: "There is no convincing reason to posit an alien source that the evangelist spent his time correcting".

110. See below, pp. 71-72.

111. See above, pp. 45-54.

112. Among exegetes who accept the semeia hypothesis but expressly reject the *Offenbarungsreden* are Haenchen, Käsemann, Marxsen, Schnackenburg, Schulz.

In 1956, at the conclusion of the Leuven Biblical Colloquium, F.-M. Braun declared: "On vient de le dire, malgré sa prodigieuse érudition et ses vues pénétrantes, R. Bultmann paraît aujourd'hui dépassé. Ceci vise tout d'abord sa critique littéraire du quatrième évangile"; cf. *L'évangile de Jean*, 1958, p. 250 (and p. 251: "L'unité de l'évangile johannique n'est plus guère contestable"). P.-H. MENOUD, in his lecture at the Colloquium, *Les études johanniques de Bultmann à Barrett*, pointed out that the literary theories of Bultmann were still being keenly discussed (p. 14). Most exegetes, according to Menoud, refuse to accept sources and text displacements, even though they have attended to the unevennesses and incomplete character of the gospel no less than the *Literarkritiker*. They reason as follows: the Gospel of John has a long history behind it; without doubt it was preached beforehand, and perhaps written down in various phases; the author probably died before his work was complete and a disciple published it (p. 16). Menoud, in n. 4, refers to the commentaries of STRATHMANN, *Johannes*, [6]1951, p. 6; LIGHTFOOT, *St. John's Gospel*, 1956, pp. 4-5; MOLLAT, *L'évangile selon saint Jean*, 1953, pp. 61-62 ([2]1960, pp. 61-62; [3]1973, p. 66); MICHAELIS, *Einleitung*, 1946, pp. 117-118 (see above, p. 43); BOISMARD, *Du Baptême à Cana*, 1956, pp. 8-9.

It is striking that the three great British commentators on John, HOSKYNS, *The Fourth Gospel*, 1940; [2]1947, pp. 4-5; BARRETT, *John*, 1955, pp. 16-17 (Barrett's view remains unchanged in the second edition of 1978; see below, pp. 166-167); and DODD, *Interpretation*, 1953 (FT: 1975); *Tradition*, 1963, eschew any source criticism. We read in Dodd's *Interpretation*: "Bultmann's massive commentary on the Fourth Gospel did not come to my hand as a whole until this book was complete" (p. 121 n. 2; FT: p. 162 n. 24). He does cite some other articles by Bultmann (see esp. pp. 121 n. 2, 151, 171, 172 n. 2, 174, 184; FT: pp. 161 n. 23, 198, 223, 225 n. 4, 227, 241), but he does not go into the latter's literary criticism. In *Tradition*, he refers to Bultmann's commentary several times (pp. 60 n. 2, 179 n. 1, 211 n. 4, 241 n. 1, 381 n. 3, 386 n. 1, 389 n. 1) and mentions the semeia hypothesis (see esp. p. 211, on 6,1-21; cp. pp. 179, n. 1, on 5,1-9; 241 n. 1, on 7,1-2), but does not discuss it. Cp. the commentary of MORRIS, *John*, 1971, p. 58: "If John did take sources he has so re-worked them and made them his own that in the judgment of many competent scholars it is now impossible to discern which were sources and which was John's own material. ... It seems much safer to take the Gospel as it stands and assume it comes from the Evangelist. There is no need to deny that he made use of sources. He may have done this. But he has so thoroughly made them his own that they cannot now be recovered. Any criticism of this Gospel which rests on the detection of sources must be regarded as suspect".

In his programmatic paper *The New Look on the Fourth Gospel*, presented at the Oxford Conference on the Four Gospels (1957) and published in *StEv*, I, 1959, pp. 338-350 (= 1962, pp. 94-106), J.A.T. ROBINSON notes with regard to John's "non-Gospel sources", i.e., Bultmann's *Offenbarungsreden* and σημεῖα-*Quelle*, that there is "an increasing reluctance to admit the evidence for such sources" (p. 341; = 1962, p. 96). Robinson quotes Parker (*JBL* 75, 1956, p. 304): "It looks as though, if the author of the Fourth Gospel used documentary sources, he wrote them all himself". (On this quotation, Robinson notes in *Priority*, 1987, p. 19: "He [Parker] tells me, thanks to my quotation of it, this is the remark for which he is now famous!") From the detailed examination of the Johannine characteristics undertaken by Schweizer, Menoud, and Ruckstuhl, and the study of Noack we may conclude that "Bultmann's 'source criticism' ... cannot stand. In John we are dealing with a man who is not piecing together written sources but placing his stamp upon an oral tradition with a sovereign freedom. As Menoud puts it, it is as if he is saying to us from beginning to end: *'La tradition, c'est moi!'*" (p. 341; see also pp. 349-350; = 1962, pp. 97-98, 105-160; cf. MENOUD, *L'évangile de Jean*, ²1947, p. 77). Note that for Robinson, the dependence of John on the Synoptics is also a presupposition "into which the acids of criticism have themselves eaten most deeply", but P. Gardner-Smith and others have proven it "as quite unproven" (*StEv*, I, 1959, p. 340; = 1962, p. 96). On Robinson, see also below, pp. 327-328.

Bultmann's distillation of sources is similarly rejected by COLWELL – TITUS, *The Gospel of the Spirit*, 1952, p. 32; VAN DEN BUSSCHE, *Het vierde evangelie*, I, 1959, p. 63 (FT: 1967, p. 51); KLIJN, *Inleiding*, 1961, p. 54; *De wordings-geschiedenis*, 1965, p. 64 (ET: 1980, p. 51): "The trouble with accepting two sources is that this gospel has a uniform style which gives no indication of any use of sources. The 'discourse source' theory, therefore, has found very little favour. This uniformity of style is, of course, equally an obstacle to the theory of a 'signs source'. If he used such a source at all, the author must have thoroughly rewritten the material he derived from it" (with references in n. 1 to Ruckstuhl, Noack and Smith).

In addition, the opinion developed that the miracle stories were not derived from a separate source but were part of a primitive gospel: the work of the evangelist himself (Wilkens) or the gospel of the Johannine community (Haenchen).

According to Wilhelm WILKENS (1958)[113] the Gospel of John is the work of one author, accomplished in three phases. The evangelist wrote

---

113. W. WILKENS, *Die Entstehungsgeschichte des vierten Evangeliums*, Zollikon, 1958 (diss. Basel, 1957; dir. O. Cullmann). – Of the many reviews (cf. MALATESTA, no. 690) I refer to J.M. ROBINSON, in *JBL* 78 (1959) 242-246; C.K. BARRETT, in *TLZ* 84 (1959) 828-829; E. KÄSEMANN, in *VF* (1960-1962) 90-91. See also BLANK, *Krisis*, 1964, pp. 21-22; SMITH, *Composition*, 1965, pp. 96-99; KONINGS, *Joh. verhaal*, I, 1969, pp. 118-119, 221-223; FORTNA, *Gospel of Signs*, 1970, pp. 1 n. 1, 9 n. 2, 20, 24 n. 2; NICOL, *Sēmeia*, 1972, pp. 11-12; REIM, *Hintergrund*, 1974, pp. 206-207, 234-235, 237; TEEPLE, *Origin*, 1972, pp. 96-98; THYEN, *Literatur*, 1974, pp. 308-314; KYSAR, *Fourth Evangelist*, 1975, pp. 42-46; *ANRW* II, 25/3, pp. 2397-2398, 2904-2905; TEMPLE, *Core*, 1975, p. 34; COTHENET, *Le quatrième évangile*, 1977, pp. 112, 188-189; HOEFERKAMP, *Relationship*, 1978, pp. 35-37; SMALLEY, *John*, 1978, pp. 114-115; HEEKERENS, *Zeichen-Quelle*, 1984, p. 22; BEUTLER, *ANRW* II, 25/3, 1985, pp. 2526-2527; J.A.T. ROBINSON, *Priority*, 1975, p. 15 n. 44; VAN BELLE, *Parenthèses*, 1985, pp. 172-174; KUHN, *Christologie*, 1988, pp. 41-42 (Jn 1,35-51); MARCHADOUR, *Lazare*, 1988, pp. 44-46 (Jn 11); WAGNER, *Auferstehung*, 1988, pp. 57-62 (Jn 11,1–12,19); WÖLLNER, *Zeichenglaube*, 1988, p. 8; ASHTON, *Understanding*, 1991, pp. 82-83, 85, 89; SCHMITHALS, *Johannes-evangelium*, 1992, pp. 189-190; SMITH, *John among the Gospels*, 1992, p. 73. – For other studies by Wilkens, see *Bibliography*. Note esp. *Zeichen und Werke. Ein Beitrag zur Theologie des 4. Evangeliums in Erzählungs- und Redestoff* (ATANT, 55), Zürich, 1969; reviews: cf. VAN BELLE, no. 5707; see esp. the review article by R.T. FORTNA, in *JBL* 89 (1970) 457-462.

a simple *Grundschrift*, which, on the basis of its conclusion (20,30-31), can be characterized as a "signs gospel" (*Zeichenevangelium*). Later, he expanded this with discourses and, finally, refashioned it once again into a "passion gospel"[114]. As a critique of Bultmann[115], Wilkens attempts to combine Wellhausen's hypothesis of a *Grundevangelium* with the recognition of the gospel's stylistic unity. In the "signs gospel", just as in the Synoptics, the Galilean activity of Jesus was followed by a single journey to Jerusalem which resulted in the passion-resurrection narrative[116]. The structure expressed the following idea: we can understand the signs of Jesus (A) in light of the sign of his death (B), whereby Jesus reveals

---

114. For the reconstruction of the *Zeichenevangelium*, see *Entstehungsgeschichte*, pp. 32-93 ("Das johanneische Grundevangelium"), esp. 92-93 ("Übersicht über den zum Grundevangelium gehörenden Stoff"). Wilkens is not sure whether the *ur*gospel was ever published (p. 94). – In the first revision, in addition to the Prologue (1,1-5.9-14.16-18), the evangelist has added the following discourses, each joined closely to a narrative from the Signs Gospel (cf. pp. 94-122: "Der Ausbau des Grundevangeliums durch Redepartien"): the Bread of Life discourse (6,28-35.37-40.47-51b.41-46.59), the discourse on Judgment (7,21-24; 5,19-29.30-47; 7,15-18; 8,13-20), on the Light (8,12; 12,44-50; [7,33-36; 8,21-26a.26b-27]; 8,28-29; 12,34-36; 10,19-21), the conversation on the resurrection of the dead (11,5-6.18-31.38a.39-40), the address to the Greeks (12,20-24.27-32), the Farewell Discourse (ch. 14). Wilkens does not consider it his task to investigate whether the evangelist used a special source for these discourses; it is clear for him, however, that they were not composed for the first time *ad hoc* (p. 122). In the second revision, the evangelist composed a passion gospel from the expanded *Zeichenevangelium* (cf. pp. 123-170: "Die Umgestaltung zum Passionsevangelium") by anticipating three passages from the passion week of the *Grundschrift* (2,13-22; 6,51c-58; 12,1-11) and distributing the great discourses.

115. Wilkens formulates two objections against Bultmann's literary theory: (1) because of the stylistic unity of the Fourth Gospel it can hardly be accepted that the evangelist used sources; (2) the numerous displacements are very improbable (pp. 6-7). The unevennesses can be better explained by recognizing that the evangelist has expanded his own work. According to Wilkens (p. 7 n. 25), this was defended by A. BECKER, in *TSK* 62 (1889) 117-140; FAURE, *Zitate*, 1922, pp. 117-118 (see above, pp. 18-20); and STRATHMANN, *Geist und Gestalt*, 1946. – With Wellhausen, Wilkens accepts the existence of a *Grundevangelium*, but in contrast to Wellhausen he attributes its expansion to the same author (pp. XI, 7, 91). Wilkens was also influenced by the "sacramentalism" of his director, O. Cullmann, inasmuch as it corresponds with the view of his father, Joh. Wilkens, who saw the entire Gospel of John ordered around the passion narrative as a Passion Gospel. Wilkens (pp. 8 n. 27, 177, 61 n. 228) cites an unpublished dissertation by his father (1926) as well as Jn 2,1-11 (1951); see *Bibliography*. According to Wilkens himself (*Zeichen*, p. 9 n. 1), Brown has presented a variant of his theory: he accepts a two-fold edition of the gospel by the same evangelist and a final redaction by a collaborator or disciple of the evangelist. THYEN, in *TR* 39 (1974), pp. 317-318, rejects this analogy and notes that Wilkens would better have referred to J.A.T. Robinson, who likewise takes account of two editions of the gospel by the same author; cf. *NTS* 9 (1962-63) 120-129 (= 1984, pp. 65-76). – Wilkens's "Signs Gospel" can be compared to a certain extent with Fortna's *Gospel of Signs* which, however, is treated as a source used by the evangelist; cf. THYEN, in *TR* 39 (1974), p. 309.

116. *Entstehungsgeschichte*, p. 91. Wilkens rejects the *Benutzungshypothese*: "Vielmehr ist das 4. Evangelium ein Evangelium sui generis, das unabhängig neben den Synoptikern steht und von ursprünglicher Kraft ist" (p. 170). Cp. p. 174.

himself as the King of Israel (C)[117]. Jesus' declaration τετέλεσται (19,30) is the high point: like the exclamation of John the Baptist (1,36) and the dating of Jesus' death on 14 Nisan, it signals a Paschal Lamb christology that was developed further with the second redaction. By its sacramental composition the first part is already oriented toward the death of the Lord[118]. Thus, the first miracle story, in which his δόξα was revealed, makes reference already in 2,4 to the hour of Jesus' passion when his δόξα will be revealed completely. The purpose of the *Zeichen-evangelium* is described in the confession of Thomas (20,28): Jesus' ministry and life is a royal activity, Jesus the crucified is the Messiah (20,31)[119].

Wilkens's "signs gospel" must be understood within his redactional theory: this *Grundschrift* should in no way be identified with a signs source like Bultmann's[120]. Indeed, he rejects most of the arguments for the semeia hypothesis. First, there is no tension between the evangelist's concept of signs and that of a source: the demonstrative character of the signs and emphasis on the miraculous are attributable to the evangelist himself. This does not mean, however, that for him the miracles are merely proofs; they can indeed be wrongly interpreted[121]. Second, the

117. *Entstehungsgeschichte*, p. 91.

118. Wilkens very clearly indicates the kerygmatic structure of the miracle stories, four in Galilee and three in Jerusalem (pp. 60-62). As in the Synoptics, healing stories (which take place in Jerusalem, however) follow after the bread miracle and the walking on the sea. The walking on the sea is the center: it presents Jesus as the Crucified and Risen Lord. The bread miracle is the counterpart of the wine miracle; between these two stories, in 4,46-54, the notion is conveyed that the wine and the bread which Jesus gives in the eucharist provide true life to those who believe. The three signs in Jerusalem illustrate Jesus' power over the darkness of this world and result in the plot to kill Jesus. At the same time, there are thematic connections with baptism (5,1-9a; 9,1-7): just as the eucharist gives life, so does baptism. The narrative of the raising of Lazarus is again an illustration of Jesus' life-giving power. As the last and greatest miracle, it is at the same time an introduction to the passion story. In 10,40-42 and 11,54, which frame the death plot (11,47-53), Jesus' solitude is described: resurrection to life occurs in the solitude of the cross.

119. *Ibid.*, p. 92.

120. "Dem 4. Evangelium liegt also wohl keine *vorjohanneische* Zeichenquelle (Faure – Bultmann) zugrunde, sondern ein johanneisches Zeichenevangelium" (p. 31 n. 107). Cp. *TZ* 16 (1960), pp. 89-90; *Zeichen*, pp. 28, 29, 30, 41, 44, 60, 80, 82 n. 6, 83 n. 1. Wilkens does not want to engage in source criticism: "Wir sehen es als unsere Aufgabe an, diese entstehungsgeschichtlichen Voraussetzungen zu klären und betreiben daher in dieser Arbeit nicht Literarkritik im Sinne von Quellenkritik, sondern im Sinne der Entstehungsgeschichte des Evangeliums" (*Entstehungsgeschichte*, p. XI). In *TZ* 15 (1959) 22-39, Wilkens reconstructs the traditional narrative in ch. 11 before its use in the *Zeichenevangelium*: 11,1a.3.17.33a.c.34.38 (without πάλιν ἐμβριμώμενος ἐν ἑαυτῷ). 39a.41a.43 (without ταῦτα εἰπών).44 (cp. *Zeichen*, p. 43).

121. Jn 6,15.25; 12,12-19; 11,45-54 (*Entstehungsgeschichte*, pp. 63-64). Wilkens gives an analysis of σημεῖον and explicitly stresses: "*Der demonstrative Charakter der Zeichen Jesu ist mithin keineswegs Indiz einer vom Evangelisten verarbeiteten Semeia-Quelle, die am naiven Wunderglauben im Unterschied zum Glauben auf das Wort Jesu orientiert ist. Es ist der Evangelist, der an der Demonstration interessiert ist. Das gilt auch*

conclusion (20,30-31)[122] and the numbering of the signs[123] do not originate from a source but from the evangelist. Third, the arrangement of the signs in pairs is a strong argument against the semeia hypothesis[124].

In *Johanneische Probleme* (1959)[125], Ernst HAENCHEN rejected Wilkens's description of the origin of John's Gospel: the σημεῖα

da, wo er sich in weitgehendem Masse an eine überlieferte Wundererzählung anschliesst" (*Zeichen*, p. 30; cp. p. 44). In his analysis of 6,1-15 he refutes Haenchen's opinion: the "heightened" formulation of the bread miracle is not a further development of the tradition, but the "most uniquely original" and theologically consequent work of the evangelist (cf. *TZ* 16, 1960, pp. 89-90, cp. *Zeichen*, pp. 35-36; cp. p. 34 n. 24, concerning 4,46-54). In fact, Wilkens's interpretation agrees in part with that of Käsemann: the evangelist accepts the miraculous because the miracles manifest the Lordship of Jesus. Wilkens regrets that Käsemann does not see the consequences of his judgment (p. 44); such an opinion practically precludes the semeia hypothesis: "Denn theologisch lebt ja diese Hypothese gerade von dem, was wir als dem Evangelisten eigentümlich herausgestellt haben, nämlich dem demonstrativen Charakter der Semeia und dem damit gekoppelten 'naiven' Wunderglauben. Damit wird nicht bestritten, dass der 4. Evangelist auf Quellenmaterial zurückgreift. Diese Quellen dürften freilich vom Evangelisten in erheblich stärkerem Masse überarbeitet und geprägt sein als z.B. E. Haenchen meint" (p. 45). That the evangelist represents a naive docetism (as Käsemann suggests) is incorrect (p. 49). Against Bultmann, Wilkens objects that the σημεῖα do not simply symbolize Jesus' ἐγώ εἰμι but that Jesus actually reveals himself in the signs (p. 49).

122. Cf. esp. *Zeichen*, p. 60 n. 4: "Dass der Evangelist den Abschlusssatz seiner Quelle, der ursprünglich auf die Semeia folgte, dort weggebrochen und zum Abschlusssatz *seines* Evangeliums unter Einschluss von Passions- und Ostergeschichte gemacht haben soll, ist eine zu kühne Konstruktion".

123. In the *Zeichenevangelium*, 4,46b-54 immediately followed 2,12a: "Wenn der Evangelist das Zeichen 4,46-54 numerisch als zweites zählt, so wohl nicht in der Absicht, die Zeichen Jesu vom ersten bis zum siebenten zu numerieren. Tatsächlich hat er ja das nicht getan. Vielmehr dürfte in dieser Zählung die Intention zum Ausdruck gelangen, das zweite Zeichen sachlich eng mit dem ersten zusammenzuschliessen. Auch die folgenden Zeichen ordnen sich ... zwanglos zu Paaren"; cf. *Zeichen*, p. 35, with reference in n. 26 to RISSI, *Die Hochzeit*, 1967, p. 84: the evangelist wishes to stress that the second sign also took place in Cana; cp. Ruckstuhl and Noack. Cf. *Zeichen*, pp. 40-41 (see below, n. 124); cp. *Entstehungsgeschichte*, pp. 40-41.

124. "Die paarweise Zuordnung der Semeia ist ein starkes Argument gegen die Semeia-Quellen-Hypothese und für die von uns vertretene Hypothese eines johanneischen Semeia-Evangeliums" (*Zeichen*, p. 41). – The two Cana stories, joined closely by the numbering, have the theme of faith. The bread miracle and the walking on the sea express the unbelief of the disciples and the crisis of faith coupled with it. The sabbath conflicts in the healings of the paralytic and the blind man illustrate the negative working of the σημεῖα; the confession of the blind man stands over against the failing of the paralytic. The seventh sign is the climax of the signs composition, which results in the death plot, on the one hand, and the belief of many, on the other (p. 78).

125. E. HAENCHEN, *Johanneische Probleme*, in *ZTK* 56 (1959) 19-54 (= 1965, pp. 78-113). In the following notes, I refer also to the pages in Haenchen's commentary (*Joh.*, 1980; ET: 2 vols., 1984), where the same (or comparable) text is reproduced (on Haenchen's commentary, cf. below, pp. 277-281). – Cf. SMITH, *Composition*, 1965, pp. XI n. 2, 78 n. 79, 86, 88; FORTNA, *Gospel of Signs*, 1970, pp. 1 n. 1, 9 n. 2, 24 n. 2; KONINGS, *Joh. verhaal*, I, 1969, pp. 116-120; SELONG, *Cleansing*, I, 1971, pp. 150-151; NICOL, *Sēmeia*, 1972, pp. 12 n. 1, 140; TEEPLE, *Origin*, 1974, p. 78; KYSAR, *Fourth Evan-*

theology of the narrative material and the evangelist's concept of signs point in different directions; moreover, the central theme of the Gospel lies not in Jesus' death but in his glorification, which is, of course, connected with his death[126]. Haenchen studies the relationship of the Fourth Gospel and the Synoptics in four narrative pericopes[127] and draws several conclusions which he extends to all the narratives[128]. He agrees with P. Gardner-Smith (and others) that the contacts with the Synoptic Gospels are very slight and concern only certain accounts and motifs. A few brief phrases are shared with the Synoptics, but this does not indicate use of the Synoptic Gospels. Haenchen prefers, instead, a *Vorlage* or tradition, in a "later, often already obviously 'hackneyed' form", which had coincidental contact with them[129]. The *Benutzungs-*

gelist, 1975, p. 64; TEMPLE, *Core*, 1975, p. 10; HOEFERKAMP, *Relationship*, 1978, pp. 41-44; SMALLEY, *John*, 1978, p. 15 n. 25; HEEKERENS, *Zeichen-Quelle*, 1984, p. 12 n. 9; SCHNELLE, *Christologie*, 1987, p. 105[-106] n. 105 (ET: 1992, p. 91[-92] n. 105); SMITH, *John among the Gospels*, 1992, pp. 50-52. – NEIRYNCK, *John and the Synoptics*, 1992, p. 8, calls Haenchen "the propagator of Gardner-Smith in Germany (1955, 1959)". For Haenchen's references to Gardner-Smith (and Noack), see, e.g., *TR* 23 (1955), p. 303; *Probleme*, pp. 20-22, esp. 51 (= 1965, pp. 79-81, 110); *Joh.*, pp. 80, 263, 416 (ET: I, pp. 75, 238; II, p. 69).

126. *Probleme*, p. 21 n. 1 (= 1965, p. 80 n. 1). Cp. *Joh.* (see below pp. 279-280 nn. 163-164).

127. The healing of the royal official's son, the feeding miracle and the walking on the water, the cleansing of the temple, and the healing of the paralytic. He chose these because it was especially in narrative material that earlier critics saw dependence by the Fourth Evangelist upon the Synoptics (p. 22; = 1965, p. 81). – For his analysis of the healing of the official's son, see also *Faith and Miracle*, in *StEv*, 1959, pp. 495-498, esp. 497-498.

128. *Probleme*, pp. 50-54 (= 1965, pp. 109-113). Cp. pp. 51-53 (= 1965, pp. 110-112) with *Joh.*, p. 263 (ET: I, p. 238).

129. *Probleme*, pp. 51, 52 (= 1965, pp. 110, 111): resp. "die spätere, oft schon deut-lich 'zersagte' Gestalt" and "eine bereits festgewordene, ja schon 'zersagte' Überliefe-rung"); cp. *Joh.*, p. 263 (ET: I, p. 238). See also *Probleme*, p. 53 (= 1965, p. 112): "Das vierte Evangelium ist wohl ein reifes Werk, aber kein frühzeitig gereifte Treibhausfrucht" (= *Joh.*, p. 263; ET: I, p. 238). – (a) The encounter with the royal official does not take place in Capernaum but in Cana; only the sick son of the βασιλικός is in Capernaum. Nothing indicates that the man is a Gentile, and consequently there is no expression of his unworthiness. In place of the emphasis on human faith, the miraculous deed of the Lord is spotlighted. The miracle is explicitly presented as a healing at a distance, and only when the father learns about the healing of his son does he believe completely (*Probleme*, pp. 23-31, esp. 28-29; = 1965, pp. 82-90, esp. 87-88; cp. *Joh.*, pp. 83-84, 260-263; ET: I, pp. 78, 236-238). (b) The feeding miracle has details in common with the Synoptics: five loaves (6,9), 5000 men (6,10), and 12 baskets (6,13). But there are also differences that point to a later, more developed tradition: 200 denarii worth of bread would not suf-fice (6,7); after the miracle, it is not until evening that Jesus flees from the people who want to make him king (6,15-16); the mention of barley loaves (6,9; cf. 2 Kgs 4,42-44). There are also more fundamental differences: in 6,5-6 Jesus takes the initiative in order to test the disciples (*Probleme*, pp. 31-34, esp. 32-33; = 1965, pp. 90-93, esp. 91-92; cp. *Joh.*, pp. 304-309; ET: I, pp. 273-277). (c) In the walking upon the sea, which was already joined to the bread miracle in the *Vorlage*, the miraculous landing has been added (*Probleme*, p. 33; = 1965, p. 92; cp. *Joh.*, pp. 313-316; ET: I, pp. 281-282). (d) The

hypothese is thus at an end[130]; with it collapses the notion that John was a creative "poet" who borrowed appropriate motifs from the Synoptic Gospels and freely reworked them. The Fourth Gospel is not a stylistic unity. Contrary to Noack and Gardner-Smith, Haenchen emphasizes that John had an already fixed tradition before him: he is not a primary evangelist who can be dated as early as Mark; nor does his gospel have any great historical value. Likewise, as it displays its own theological message, his tradition exhibits clear traces of progressive development. The Johannine (non-Synoptic) tradition and the whole Gospel probably originated on the frontier between Syria and Palestine in a small community subsisting outside the main stream of development. Perhaps John knew a non-Synoptic type of gospel from the liturgy of his community[131].

Many elements in the article indicate that Haenchen follows the semeia hypothesis to a certain degree. Already in his survey of Johannine studies of 1955 he thought that the gospel of the Johannine

evangelist found the temple-cleansing in his *Vorlage* already at the beginning of Jesus' public ministry. The narrative especially differs from the Synoptics in its concrete description in 2,12-16. This, once again, points to a later tradition (*Probleme*, pp. 34-46, esp. 42-46; = 1965, pp. 93-105, esp. 101-103; cp. *Joh.*, pp. 204-210; ET: I, pp. 186-190). (e) The healing of the paralytic especially demonstrates a treatment of the tradition similar to that in the Synoptic-like pericopes. The story has in fact no parallel. Jn 5,5 was written by a copyist to explain v. 7. In v. 6 Jesus takes the initiative. Upon the sick man's reply follows Jesus' command, which is carried out by the sick man and by which the sabbath is broken. With the mention of the sabbath (v. 9c) a new element is introduced into the story, which was probably elaborated by the evangelist himself and by which he was able to insert Jesus' discourse (vv. 17.19-46). The original conclusion of the Jewish-Christian story may perhaps have been v. 14. For the evangelist the healing story itself is not important, he uses it only to introduce the sabbath controversy, which in its own turn is an introduction to the discourse. The controversy is parallel with the Synoptic controversies. But there are differences: in John it is Jesus' command, which takes no account of the sabbath, that instigates the controversy; in the Synoptics it is the healing itself. This narrative (5,1-3.5-9b.14) probably stems from a different tradition than 4,46-54 (*Probleme*, pp. 46-50; = 1965, pp. 105-109; cp. *Joh.*, pp. 282-291, esp. 285; ET: I, pp. 254-260, esp. 256).

130. John certainly did not know the Synoptics, and therefore he could not have written to supplement, improve, or replace them: "Damit wird der früher als selbstverständlich geltenden Annahme der Boden entzogen, Johannes habe die Synoptiker oder doch einige von ihnen 'benutzt'. Bei dieser beliebten Vermutung scheint die Vorstellung eines Schriftstellers mitgespielt zu haben, der die Werke seiner Vorgänger mindestens im Kopf, vielleicht aber sogar auf seinem Schreibtisch hat. Ausserdem setzt jene Hypothese ohne Grund voraus, dass die Evangelien des Markus, Matthäus und Lukas in jeder grösseren Gemeinde vorhanden waren. Man wird erwägen müssen, ob nicht die bescheidenere Vorstellung mehr Wahrscheinlichkeit besitzt, dass der Besitz und gottesdienstliche Gebrauch mehrerer Evangelien in ein und derselben Gemeinde während des 1. Jahrhunderts nicht zu erwarten ist. Johannes dürfte die Synoptiker gar nicht gekannt haben. Er wollte sie darum weder ergänzen noch verbessern noch verdrängen" (*Probleme*, pp. 51-52; = 1965, pp. 110-111; cp. *Joh.*, p. 263; ET: I, p. 238). See also *Joh.*, pp. 78-80, esp. 80 (ET: I, pp. 74-76, esp. 76), 305 (ET: p. 274, on 6,1-15), 315 (ET: I, pp. 282-283, on 6,16-25). See also below, p. 279 n. 167.

131. *Probleme*, pp. 52-54 (= 1965, pp. 111-113).

community was something like Bultmann's signs source; such a gospel existed already in written form, but the evangelist probably knew it only orally[132]. Like the defenders of the semeia hypothesis, Haenchen attributes differing interpretations of the miracles to the *Vorlage* and to the evangelist[133]. In the *Vorlage* the miracles are demonstrations of Jesus' power and proofs for belief (2,11; 3,2; 4,53; 6,14; 7,31; 11,45.47-48; 12,37; 20,30-31). The evangelist adopted these miracles; he did not doubt them, but for him faith based on a miracle does not suffice. He interpreted them not as proofs but as signs of the unique event of salvation[134]: hearing and believing in the Word of God that came into our world, clear and unadulterated, in Jesus Christ[135]. Next, Haenchen

132. HAENCHEN, *Aus der Literatur zum Johannesevangelium*, in *TR* 23 (1955) 295-335, pp. 303-304: "Vielleicht hat der 4. Evangelist wirklich keine schriftlichen Quellen benutzt. Aber das besagt ja nicht, dass es zu seiner Zeit noch keine solchen gab. Er kann die evangelische Überlieferung, die er benützt, im Gottesdienst seiner eigenen Heimatgemeinde gehört haben! Dass diese ein geschriebenes Evangelium besass, dürfen wir ruhig annehmen. Das, was Bultmann die 'Semeia-Quelle' nennt, kann gut das Evangelium dieser Gemeinde gewesen sein: einer Art vergröberten Markusevangeliums, ein Evangelium, das Jesu Herrlichkeit nicht mehr in geheimen Epiphanien zeigte, sondern möglichst sichtbar und greifbar. Auch die 'synoptischen' Stücke im 4. Ev. könnten jenem Evangelium entstammen. Wir dürften es freilich kaum in einer Grossstadtgemeinde suchen (Antiochia, Ephesus), sondern in irgendeiner bescheidenen syrischen Gemeinde. Hätte Johannes sein Evangelium unter Benutzung und (dogmatischer) Korrektur einer solchen ihm mündlich überlieferten schriftlichen Tradition verfasst, dann wäre freilich nicht ausgeschlossen, dass es später in einer solchen grossen Stadt veröffentlicht wurde". For Haenchen's view on the written character of the evangelist's *Vorlage* in *Joh.*, see below, p. 280 n. 172.

133. Haenchen returns to this theme on numerous occasions; see, e.g., *Probleme*, pp. 29, 34, 54 (= 1965, pp. 88, 93, 113); *StEv*, 1959, pp. 497-498; *NTS* 9 (1962-63), pp. 208-209 (= 1965, pp. 68-70); *ZTK* 60 (1963), pp. 310-311 (= 1965, pp. 119-120); *TLZ* 89 (1964), cc. 888-889 (= 1968, pp. 219-222); *Gott und Mensch*, 1965, pp. 13-15. Cp., e.g., *Joh.*, pp. 106-107 (ET: p. 95). On the different interpretation of miracles as starting-point for Johannine source criticism in his commentary, see below, pp. 278-279 nn. 163-164.

134. *Probleme*, p. 54 (= 1965, p. 113; cp. his commentary (see below, p. 281 nn. 177-178). See also the review of Bultmann's commentary ([17]1963), in *TLZ* 89 (1964) 881-898, cc. 888-889 (= 1968, pp. 206-234, esp. 219-221). In contrast to Bultmann, and in agreement with Käsemann, Haenchen thought that John was convinced of the historicity of the miracles even though he interpreted them symbolically (cp., e.g., *Gott und Mensch*, 1965, p. 14; *Joh.*, pp. 106, 335; ET: I, pp. 95, 302).

135. Cf. esp. *Probleme*, p. 54 (= 1965, p. 113). The evangelist criticizes the miracle faith of the *Vorlage* in 4,48; because of this abrupt insertion it becomes necessary for him to repeat the nobleman's question. With this redactional intervention the evangelist raises the story to a higher level: by observing the miracle we should come to see the Father in Jesus (14,9) and thus to enter into communion with Jesus and the Father (14,23) (p. 29; = 1965, p. 88). – The bread miracle signifies that Jesus is the Living Bread: 6,35.51 (p. 34; = 1965, p. 93). – In the pre-Johannine tradition 2,12-22 had to do with an actual temple-cleansing, in which Jesus proves his authority in a mysterious reference to the resurrection. With the addition of 2,17 and τῇ γραφῇ καί (2,22) it appears the evangelist sees much more in the story: Jesus does not cleanse an institution, but has actually abolished the whole Jewish cult. Through this action he realizes what is described in 4,21 as

ascribes to the *Vorlage* all the characteristics which pertain to the signs source: the numbering of the signs[136], the accent on the miraculous[137], and emphasis on the initiative of Jesus[138]. Finally, he characterizes the *Vorlage* like the signs source: it relates miracles of Jesus which reveal and prove that he is the Son of God[139].

Critics disagree on whether Haenchen subscribes to the semeia hypothesis or not. According to D.M. Smith (1965), "Although Haenchen rejects Bultmann's semeia-source hypothesis, his own understanding of the way in which the evangelist employs narrative material is, after all, not so different from Bultmann's"[140]. Contrariwise for J.M. Robinson (1965), "It gives something of a wrong impression of Haenchen's assessment of Bultmann's analysis to refer to this as a 'rejection'"[141]. In several contributions in the course of 1968-1970, Robinson argued, on the basis of the typescript of Haenchen's then unpublished commentary, that "though diverging in method and results, they [i.e., R.T. Fortna and Haenchen] confirm the existence of a written miracles source used by John"[142]. It appears, however, from letters to Robinson during the same years that Haenchen distanced himself more

---

true worship: in Jesus and his word, God is present for all time (p. 46; = 1965, p. 105). – The healing of the paralytic on the sabbath is, for the evangelist, only a typical example of the statement "God is working still" (5,17): this is evident in the imperfect ἐδίωκον and ἐποίει. The deeper significance of ἔγειρε is explained in ἐγείρειν and ζφοποιεῖν (5,21) (pp. 49-50; = 1965, pp. 108-109). Cp., e.g., *Joh.*, esp. pp. 106-107 (ET: I, p. 95).

136. *Probleme*, pp. 28, 29 (= 1965, pp. 87, 88).

137. *Ibid.*, pp. 28, 33, 34 (= 1965, pp. 87, 92, 93). Cp., e.g., *Joh.*, p. 384 (ET: II, p. 42; see below, p. 280 n. 170).

138. *Probleme*, pp. 33, 48 (= 1965, pp. 92, 107).

139. "Dass der Wundertäter Jesus hier im Mittelpunkt der Handlung steht, verbindet diese Erzählung mit der von der Hochzeit in Kana, die in 2,11 'Beginn der Zeichen' genannt war. Wahrscheinlich zeigt sich damit das Wesen der von Johannes benutzten 'Vorlage': Sie berichtete Wundertaten, die ihn als Gottessohn offenbaren und erweisen" (p. 29; = 1965, p. 88; *Joh.*, p. 260; ET: I, p. 236).

140. SMITH, *Composition*, 1965, p. 110 n. 181. – KONINGS, *Joh. verhaal*, I, 1969, pp. 116-120; BECKER, *Wunder*, 1970, p. 131 n. 1 (= 1980, p. 437 n. 9); NICOL, *Sēmeia*, 1972, p. 12 n. 1 (with the specification: "an 'Urevangelium' with the miracles as core") and SCHNELLE, *Christologie*, 1987, p. 105[-106] n. 105 (ET: 1992, p. 91[-92] n. 105) (with the specification: "vgl. aber jetzt ders., Joh, 101"; see below, p. 70 n. 144) cite Haenchen in their lists of defenders. Cp. CONZELMANN (see below, p. 75 n. 22).

141. J.M. ROBINSON, *Kerygma*, 1965, p. 136 n. 36 (= 1971, p. 52 n. 53). Not in GT: *ZNW* 62 (1965), p. 321 n. 51.

142. *On the Gattung of Mark (and John)*, 1970, p. 127 n. 10, where he refers to his paper *The Johannine Trajectory* (see below, pp. 172-174) given at the organizational meeting of the Gospel Seminar of SBL in Berkeley, December 19, 1968. Moreover, Robinson asked Haenchen "to make available the typescript of relevant sections" of his commentary. Thus, Haenchen's position was discussed at the first session of the "Gospels Seminar" at the SBL Meeting in New York, December 16, 1969, and the most important portions with reference to the miracle stories were at the disposal of several exegetes. See J.M. ROBINSON, *Vorwort*, in HAENCHEN, *Johannes*, 1980, pp. V-IX, esp. IX (ET: I, 1984, pp. IX-XIII, esp. XIII).

and more from the semeia hypothesis[143]. One can now read in his commentary: "It is inordinately risky to posit a semeia source" ("Die Annahme einer Semeia-Quelle ist ausserordentlich gewagt")[144].

143. See Robinson's Foreword to the Commentary (1980): "Haenchen, ..., like Bultmann, did initially assume the existence of a collection of miracle stories, the Semeia Source. In 1966 he said in a letter to me: 'The so-called 'Miracle Source' in the sense of 'sign' is in kind a sort of enlarged Mark; it seeks, by narrating miracles that are enlarged over against Mark, to demonstrate the divine sonship of Jesus walking on earth'. But already in a letter of 1968 the designation of the source was put in question: 'Semeia Source is an unfortunate name, since only the miracle at Cana and the healing of the son of the *Basilikos* are counted as *semeia*; 6:26 is something quite different'. Indeed he came to question the unity of the Semeia Source, as reflected in a letter of 1969: 'To be sure this does not mean that the Evangelist only had access to a single source. Probably the understanding of the *semeia* as convincing miracles was really the usual thing at that time. Hence it is very questionable to me whether one can, à la Bultmann, reconstruct the texts behind the narrative material (which is all that is now being discussed), the 'source' down to the half-verses. Hence I often have to write 'tradition' without being able to express myself more precisely as to the exact delimitation and origin of this 'tradition'" (*Vorwort*, pp. VII-VII; ET: I, p. XII). In the German text: "ging – wie auch der Bultmann-Schule – von der Semeia-Quelle ... aus"; "ihrer Art nach eine Art von gesteigertem Mk". Also BUSSE, *Ernst Haenchen*, 1981, pp. 139-140 (ET: II, pp. 250-251) refers to the evolution of Haenchen's thought.

144. *Joh.*, p. 101 (ET: I, p. 89). See also below, pp. 278 n. 162, 279-280 nn. 168-169.

THE SPREAD OF R. BULTMANN'S HYPOTHESIS

The positive reactions to Bultmann's semēia hypothesis are described in chapter III of my historical survey, *De semeia-bron*, 1975. Lists of the defenders of the hypothesis were also given by KONINGS, *Joh. verhaal*, I, 1969, pp. 107-135; BECKER, *Wunder*, 1970, p. 131 n. 2 (= 1980, p. 437 n. 9); NICOL, *Sēmeia*, 1972, pp. 9-14; MERKEL, *Urmarkus*, 1974, p. 140 n. 71[1]. In recent literature, most authors refer now to my 1975 survey. See, e.g., DE JONGE, *Signs and Works*, 1975, p. 107 n. 1 (= 1977, p. 136 n. 1); MARTYN, *History and Theology*, [2]1979, p. 168; NEIRYNCK, *Jean et les Synoptiques*, 1979, pp. 121 n. 212, 166, 171; *Semeia-bron*, 1983, p. 4 n. 2 (ET: 1991, p. 652 n. 2); WENGST, *Bedrängte Gemeinde*, 1981, p. 102 n. 326 ([2]1990, p. 190 n. 23); HEEKERENS, *Zeichen-Quelle*, 1984, p. 11 n. 5; BEUTLER, *ANRW* II, 25/3, 1985, pp. 2545 n. 263, 2546 nn. 268 and 270; KYSAR, *ibid.*, p. 2402 n. 51; WITKAMP, in *JNTS* 25 (1985) 19-47, p. 37 n. 5; *Jezus van Nazareth*, 1986, p. 5; BITTNER, *Jesu Zeichen*, 1987, pp. 3 n. 5, 7 n. 13; HENGEL, *Interpretation*, 1987, p. 92 n. 30; SCHNELLE, *Christologie*, 1987, p. 105[-106] n. 105 (ET: 1992, p. 91[-92] n. 105); WAGNER, *Auferstehung*, 1988, p. 348 n. 23; THYEN, in *TRE* 17 (1988), p. 207: "Über die Forschungsgeschichte der Hypothese einer 'Semeia-Quelle' hat Van Belle in seltener Vollständigkeit berichtet"; MUÑOZ LEÓN, *Panorama*, 1990, p. 20; SCHMITHALS, *Johannesevangelium*, 1992, p. 124: "Faures Vorschlag wurde schon bald aufgegriffen ... und ist ferner hin sehr fruchtbar gewesen, so dass *Van Belle* (1975) bereits eine Geschichte der Semeia-Quelle schreiben konnte"; FORTNA, in *ABD*, VI, 1992, p. 20 (with reference to the present "revision" of *De semeia-bron*, 1975). To my list of proponents of the

---

1. On the spread of the hypothesis, see J.M. ROBINSON, *Kerygma*, 1965, p. 136 (= 1971, pp. 51-52; GT: 1965, p. 321): "This [miracles] source was first detected by Alexander Faure, was accepted by Bultmann, and has become the one of his sources for John that has withstood best the recent trend toward discounting Johannine sources in the light of the pervasive unity of style in the Gospel of John". Cp. BECKER, *Wunder*, 1970, pp. 131-132 (= 1980, p. 437): "Diese literarkritische These hat eine erstaunlich breite internationale Zustimmung erfahren, gerade auch dort, wo man Bultmanns sonstigen tiefgreifenden literarkritischen Operationen am Johannesevangelium zu Recht mit reservierter Skepsis gegenübersteht"; *Johannes*, I, 1979, p. 113: "Keine der literarischen Grundfragen des Joh ist in jüngster Zeit so häufig bearbeitet worden wie die Analyse der joh Wundererzählungen (grundlegend sind: Bultmann, Haenchen, Fortna, Nicol). Ausserdem hat keine der literarischen Hypothesen so breite Zustimmung erfahren wie die, dass die Wundererzählungen einer gemeinsamen Quelle entstammen" (in [3]1991, p. 135, Becker adds Appold and Wöllner). See, e.g., also KOESTER, *One Jesus*, 1968, p. 231 (= 1971, p. 187); KÜMMEL, *Das Neue Testament in 20. Jahrhundert*, 1970, p. 47 (see above p. 58 n. 100); TIEDE, *The Charismatic Figure*, 1972, pp. 269, 275. – SMITH thought differently in *Sources*, 1964, p. 349 (= 1984, p. 58): "Although many would accept Bultmann's proposed passion source, or something like it, his *semeia*-source (accounting for most of the narrative material in chaps. i–xii) has not been accorded wide acceptance".

semeia source, DE JONGE, in *NTT* 30 (1976) 225-226, p. 226, added Lohse;
NEIRYNCK, *Semeia-bron*, 1983, p. 4 n. 5 (ET: 1991, p. 652 n. 5), mentioned
Perrin, Vielhauer, Conzelmann – Lindemann, Koester, Schenke – Fischer. See
also the enumeration by SCHNELLE, *Christologie*, 1987, p. 105[-106] n. 105 (ET:
1992, p. 91[-92] n. 105), who added Gnilka, Hoeferkamp, Lona, Corsani, Kysar,
Weder; FORTNA, in *ABD*, VI, 1992, pp. 19b-20b, mentioned also Attridge,
Heekerens, and Cope.

I. THE REACTION OF BULTMANN'S STUDENTS

Not surprisingly, Bultmann's students accepted the existence of the
signs source[2]. In 1947, Ernst KÄSEMANN declared his agreement with the
semeia hypothesis in a review of Bultmann's commentary[3]. He remarks,
however, that the evangelist, though he regards the miracles as symbols,
did not doubt their historicity[4]. Nor did the source's depiction of the

2. The three most prominent are Käsemann, Conzelmann, and Bornkamm. The spread
of the hypothesis can be seen in *RGG*[3] (1957-1962; *Registerband*: 1965), in which
Bultmann's article *Johannesevangelium* (1959; see above, p. 25 n. 142) appeared along
with contributions by Bornkamm (1958), Koester (1959), and Käsemann (1962), all of
whom championed the semeia hypothesis (see below, pp. 76 n. 25, 80 n. 40, 73 n. 6).
Also for Heinz BECKER, *Die Reden des Johannesevangeliums und der Stil der gnostischen
Offenbarungsrede* (FRLANT, 68; NF 50), Göttingen, 1956, p. 13 n. 2, Faure and Bultmann had demonstrated the existence of a signs source. On H. Becker, see, e.g., RUCK-
STUHL – DSCHULNIGG, *Stilkritik*, 1991, p. 14; BOTHA, *Jesus and the Samaritan Woman*,
1991, pp. 20-22. The posthumous publication of his 1941 dissertation was undertaken by
Becker's director, Bultmann (cf. *Die Reden*, p. 3).
   3. E. KÄSEMANN, review of BULTMANN, *Johannes*, in *VF* 1942-46 (ed. 1947) 182-
201, p. 186: "Zweifellos richtig ist, dass vom Ev. eine Sammlung von Wundergeschichten verwertet wurde, deren Beginn vielleicht 1,35ff., deren Schluss wohl
20,30f. gebildet hat". He doubts the existence of the *Offenbarungsreden* (p. 188);
cp. *ZTK* 54 (1957) 1-21, p. 16 (= 1964, pp. 11-31, esp. 25; ET: 1969, pp. 1-22, esp. 16).
In his review of works by HOWARD, BARRETT, and DODD, in *GGA* 211 (1957) 145-160,
p. 156 (= 1964, pp. 131-155, esp. 143) he remarks that Barrett questions a narrative
source as well as a discourse source; from Käsemann's reaction it appears that he rejects
the discourse source and tacitly accepts a narrative source: "Obgleich ich mich dem
letzten anschliessen möchte, bezweifle ich die Kraft des Argumentes, es gäbe dafür
keine Parallelen, da die Logienquelle der Synoptiker, wenn sie überhaupt existiert hätte,
doch auch Erzählungsgut enthalten habe". – Käsemann describes the pre-johannine tradition as "eine verwilderte synoptische Tradition" (*VF* 1947-48 [ed. 1950] 195-223,
p. 222). Cf. *Jesus letzter Wille* (see below, p. 73 n. 7), p. 68: "Ein Evangelist, der die
irdische Geschichte Jesu erzählen will, kann natürlich nicht auf Traditionen verzichten.
Überraschender ist schon, dass Johannes am Ende des 1. Jahrhunderts und, wie es
scheint, nicht allzu weit von Palästina entfernt, vielleicht am ehesten doch in Syrien
beheimatet, schwerlich die Synoptiker kennt, wohl aber eine verwilderte Überlieferung,
wie sie ursprünglicher sich in den Synoptikern erhalten hat" (ET: p. 36). Cf. SMITH,
Composition, 1965, pp. 59-63; KONINGS, *Joh. verhaal*, I, 1969, p. 114; NICOL, *Sēmeia*,
1972, pp. 76-77.
   4. "Hinzu kommt, dass die These vom geläuterten Offenbarungsbegriff vom Ev. selber her auf erheblichste Schwierigkeiten stösst. Man wird in diesem Zusammenhang

ϑεῖος ἀνήρ disturb him; it has been poorly disguised[5]. In 1962, Käsemann reaffirmed that John used a source of miracle stories: "John selectively used a source (20,30f) which revealed Jesus' glory stirringly and vividly by means of especially great demonstrations of power. For him 'signs' are symbols, i.e., earthly shadows of the gift of eternal life vouchsafed by the revealer, in which the miracle itself is in no way spiritualized, but even strongly heightened"[6].

Especially in his study of chapter 17 (1966) Käsemann describes the Johannine redaction of the signs source[7]. Against Bultmann, he revives the liberal characterization[8] of the Johannine Christ as "God going about

daran erinnern müssen, dass die im 4. Ev. erzählten Wundergeschichten an Massivität diejenigen der Synoptiker weit in den Schatten stellen und zweifellos der gleichen späten Gemeindeüberlieferung entstammen wie die Abendmahlsterminologie von 6,51ff. Der Evangelist hat in ihnen Symbole gesehen. Das dürfte jedoch nicht ausschliessen, dass er von ihrer Historizität überzeugt war" (review of BULTMANN, *Johannes*, in *VF* 1942-46 [ed. 1947] 182-201, pp. 198-199).

5. "Hinzu kommt, dass die Grundanschauung der Zeichenquelle von Christus als dem 'ϑεῖος ἄνϑρωπος' dem Evangelisten jedenfalls nicht untragbar erschien und nur dürftig umgebogen wurde" (p. 200).

6. *Wunder. IV. Im N.T.*, in *RGG*³ 6 (1962) 1835-1837, c. 1836: "Er [John] benutzt in Auswahl (20,30f) eine Quelle, die sehr bewegt und anschaulich Jesu Herrlichkeit an bes. grossen Machterweisen dartat. Für ihn sind 'Zeichen' Symbole, nämlich irdische Abschattungen der vom Offenbarer gewährten Gabe himmlischen Lebens, wobei das W. selbst keineswegs spiritualisiert, sondern sogar kräftig gesteigert wird".

7. *Jesu letzter Wille nach Johannes 17*, Tübingen, 1966 (²1967), p. 69: "Er [John] hat sehr wahrscheinlich die Erzählungen einer Quelle von Wundergeschichten zum mindesten teilweise und ohne tiefe Eingriffe übernommen, und dasselbe gilt für seine Passions- und Ostergeschichte in ihrem Kern" (ET: 1968, p. 37). In this work Käsemann published his lectures given as the Shaffer Lectures at the Yale Divinity School on April 26-28, 1966; it corresponds closely with his inaugural lecture at the University of Göttingen on May 30, 1951, published in *ZTK* 48 (1951) 292-311 (= 1960, pp. 168-214). Cf. *Jesu letzter Wille*, p. 5 (ET: p. vii); cp. NICOL, *Sēmeia*, 1972, p. 97 n. 1. – For his description of the Johannine redaction of the signs source, cf. esp. *Jesu letzter Wille*, pp. 43-48 (ET: pp. 21-22). See also *Aufbau und Anliegen des johanneischen Prologs*, in *FS F. Delekat*, 1957, pp. 75-99, esp. 95-96 (= 1964, pp. 155-180, esp. 175-177; ET: 1969, pp. 138-167, esp. 161-162). – Reviews of *Jesu letzter Wille*: cf. VAN BELLE, no. 3961. On Käsemann, see, e.g., SMITH, *Composition*, 1965, pp. 59-64; NICOL, *Sēmeia*, 1972, pp. 2-3, 12 n. 1, 49 n. 1, 76-77, 97-99, 134-139; TEEPLE, *Origin*, 1974, pp. 25, 43, 104, 129; KYSAR, *Fourth Evangelist*, 1975, pp. 186-192, 194-195; ANRW II, 25/3, 1985, p. 2445; TEMPLE, *Core*, 1975, pp. 39, 314 n. 5; COTHENET, *Le quatrième évangile*, 1977, pp. 113, 171, 199, 233, 271; *L'évangile selon saint Jean*, 1984, p. 88; GIBLET, *Développements*, 1977 (²1987), pp. 62-66; SMALLEY, *John*, 1978, pp. 55-56; HOEFERKAMP, *Relationship*, 1978, pp. 33-35; HEEKERENS, *Zeichen-Quelle*, 1984, p. 28 n. 45; BEUTLER, ANRW II, 25/3, 1985, p. 2546; J.A.T. ROBINSON, *Priority*, 1985, pp. 114 n. 340, 329 n. 99, 345 n. 4; 366 n. 64; WITKAMP, *Jezus van Nazareth*, 1986, pp. 13-16; SCHNELLE, *Christologie*, 1987, p. 105[-106] n. 105 (ET: 1992, p. 91[-92] n. 105). See also the reaction to Käsemann and Bultmann by J. Becker (see below, pp. 116-132); ASHTON, *Understanding*, 1991, pp. 71-74, 92-93; SMITH, *John among the Gospels*, 1992, p. 76.

8. See, e.g., his references to F.C. Baur, G.P. Wetter, E. Hirsch (*Jesu letzter Wille*, p. 22 n. 6; ET: p. 9 n. 6), J. Grill, W. Heitmüller (p. 54, n. 1; ET: p. 27, n. 1), and W. Bousset (p. 118 n. 14; ET: p. 66 n. 14).

on the earth"[9]. Depicting such a Jesus, the evangelist falls into a naive, unreflective form of docetism[10], so that the gospel's acceptance into the Church's canon took place "through man's error and God's providence" (*errore hominum et providentia Dei*)[11]. According to Käsemann, we must not overemphasize the σάρξ in Jn 1,14, as Bultmann does. The words to be accented are "we beheld his glory"[12], for the evangelist does not explicitly portray Jesus as a human being[13], but as a divine epiphany[14]. Jn 1,14a signifies only that God came to earth: "He does not really change himself, but only his place"[15]. The human features of the Johannine Jesus are not signs of his humility, but only "the absolute minimum of the costume designed for the one who dwelt for a little while among men, appearing to be one of them, yet without himself being subjected to earthly conditions"[16].

The miracle stories serve this naive docetic christology[17]: "For John, too, miracles are indispensable. They are not merely concessions to human weakness [ctr. Bultmann[18]]. If that were the case, it would have been unnecessary to heighten them to the very extreme. Nor would Jesus' passion, with deliberate intention and contrary to all traditions, have been triggered off by the miracle of the raising of Lazarus. It would also ignore the fact that the Johannine miracles in general are clearly and emphatically described in terms of demonstrations of the glory of Jesus. Human need is, to be sure, the occasion for the miracle, but the meeting of human needs is at most a subsidiary aim. God does not manifest

---

9. *Jesu letzter Wille*, p. 22 (ET: p. 9); cp. pp. 53-54 (ET: p. 27).

10. *Ibid.*, pp. 51-52 (ET: p. 26); cp. p. 118 (ET: p. 66).

11. *Ibid.*, p. 132 (ET: p. 75).

12. *Ibid.*, pp. 22-23 (ET: pp. 9-10).

13. *Ibid.*, p. 27 (ET: p. 12).

14. "Inkarnation ist für Johannes wirklich Epiphanie" (with reference to LOISY, *Le quatrième évangile*, 1903, p. 186). Cf. *Aufbau und Anliegen*, p. 95 (= 1964, pp. 175-176; ET: pp. 161-162).

15. *Jesu letzter Wille*, p. 28 (ET: p. 12).

16. *Ibid.*, p. 24 (ET: p. 10). In this view, the passion became "problematical" for the evangelist: "Fast möchte man sagen, sie klappe nach, weil Johannes sie unmöglich übergehen, die überlieferte Gestalt jedoch auch nicht organisch seinem Werk einfügen konnte". For John, the solution was to press the features of Christ's victory upon the passion story (p. 19; ET: p. 7). The death of Jesus is given with the characteristic description of "exaltation and glorification" in the verb ὑπάγω ("to go away"): "Es schliesst Erhöhung und Verherrlichung in sich, sofern es die Trennung von der Welt und die Rückkehr zum Vater meint, die als solche zugleich die Rückkehr in die Herrlichkeit des präexistenten Logos ist. Der Aspekt des Gehorsams wird dabei nicht eliminiert. ... Gehorsam ist hier die Manifestation göttlicher Herrschaft und Herrlichkeit am gottentfremdeten Ort, christologisch also Bekundung der Einheit mit dem Vater. Eben deshalb muss Jesu Passion in unserm Evangelium statt als Schmach als Siegesweg geschildert werden" (pp. 37-38; ET: p. 18).

17. *Ibid.*, pp. 43-45 (ET: pp. 21-22). Cf. *Aufbau und Anliegen*, pp. 95-96 (= 1964, pp. 175-177; ET: pp. 161-162).

18. See above, pp. 39-40 nn. 203-204.

himself on earth without the splendour of the miracles which character-ize him as the Creator"[19]. Thus, the miraculous itself is not questioned, but its incorrect interpretation: "It is indeed correct to point out that John attacks a craving for miracles. This is not done, however, on the basis of miracles in general, but in the interest of his one and only theme, namely, his christology. His dominant interest which is every-where apparent is that Christ himself may not be overshadowed by any-thing, not even by his gifts, miracles and works. Jesus alone is the true divine gift to which all other gifts can and should only point"[20]. For Käsemann, the presence of the miracles in John cannot be explained by the evangelist's faithfulness to the tradition. Indeed, "John took up that tradition freely. It was not accidental that he omitted demon exorcisms as not being illustrative enough of Jesus' glory and that he selected the most miraculous stories of the New Testament. He would hardly have done so had he wanted to use them as mere illustrations to the speeches of Jesus and thus been disinterested in the miracle itself"[21].

Hans CONZELMANN (1967)[22] also accepts that John used a written source which accented the miraculous[23]. Nonetheless, he attributes the notion of σημεῖον, the numbering of the signs and 20,30-31 (the conclu-sion of Bultmann's σημεῖα-Quelle) to the redaction of the evangelist[24].

19. *Jesu letzter Wille*, pp. 43-44 (ET: p. 21).
20. *Ibid.*, p. 44 (ET: pp. 21-22); cp. p. 45 (ET: p. 22): "Die johanneische Wun-derkritik beginnt und endet dort, wo Jesus selber um seiner Gaben willen gesucht oder vergessen wird. Umgekehrt gibt es seine Herrlichkeit nicht ohne seine Wunder, und je grösser und demonstrativer sie sind, um so besser. Denn seine Gemeinde bekennt von ihm: 'Aus seiner Fülle haben wir genommen Gnade um Gnade'".
21. *Ibid.*, p. 44 (ET: p. 22).
22. H. CONZELMANN, *Grundriss der Theologie des Neuen Testaments* (EET, 2), München, 1967; ²1968, p. 354 (ET: 1969, p. 324): "Entsprechendes [cf. the Passion] gilt auch von den gemeinsamen Wundergeschichten. Johannes verwendet eine schriftliche Quelle, die sich von der synoptischen Fassung unterscheidet". On p. 354 n. 7 (ET: p. 324 n. 1): "Bultmann: σημεῖα-Quelle", with reference to HAENCHEN, *Johanneische Pro-bleme*, 1959. See also p. 355 (ET: p. 325): "Für die *Wunder*geschichten benutzt Johannes eine Quelle, in der das mirakelhafte Element drastisch gesteigert ist (Auferweckung des Lazarus!)"; pp. 376-378, esp. 376 (ET: pp. 345-347, esp. 345): "Die Wundergeschichten des Johannesevangelium sind massiver als die der Synoptiker. Das ist sicher durch seine Quelle mit bedingt". – On Conzelmann, see, e.g., KYSAR, *Fourth Evangelist*, 1975, p. 16 n. 13; GIBLET, *Développements*, 1977 (²1987), pp. 60-61; CORSANI, *I miracoli*, 1983, p. 59; SCHNELLE, *Christologie*, 1987, p. 105[-106] n. 105 (ET: 1992, p. 91[-92] n. 105).
23. According to BECKER, *Wunder*, 1970, p. 132 n. 1 (= 1980, p. 437 n. 9), Conzel-mann also accepted the signs source in *Jesus Christus*, in *RGG*³ 3 (1959) 619-653, c. 625. But Conzelmann only puts the question of a possible source that presents Jesus' activity in the course of one year, as the Synoptics do; he says nothing specifically about a signs source: "Man kann sich fragen, ob nicht auch im JohEv noch eine Quelle durchschim-mert, welche mit *ein*jährigem Ablauf rechnete".
24. *Grundriss*, p. 377 (ET: p. 345): "Der literarkritische Befund: *Bultmann* dürfte mit seiner Annahme recht behalten, dass der Evangelist eine Quelle mit Wunderberichten

Günther Bornkamm likewise reacted positively (1958, 1968, 1971)[25]. Because the miraculous element is greatly enhanced in John's miracle stories (in comparison with the Synoptics), Bornkamm believes that the signs source used by the evangelist recalls the Hellenistic stories about the θεῖοι ἄνδρες[26]. In contrast to Käsemann, Bornkamm thinks it is the

benützt, in der das Mirakelhafte stärker ausgearbeitet war als in der synoptischen Tradition. Es ist möglich, dass sich das Stichwort σημεῖον bereits in dieser Quelle fand; sicher ist es nicht. Die Analyse macht vielmehr (gegen *Bultmann*) wahrscheinlich, dass es überall redaktionell vom Evangelisten eingefügt ist. *Bultmann* argumentiert, die Zeichen seien in der Quelle gezählt worden (2,11; 4,54), diese Zählung passe aber nicht zum jetzigen Bericht, da Johannes inzwischen weitere Wunder erwähne. Sie müsse also von ihm vorgefunden sein. Dagegen ist festzustellen, dass zwischen 2,11 und 4,46 immerhin keine weiteren Wunder erzählt werden und dass die Zählung nicht fortgesetzt wird. Sie ist deshalb als redaktionell anzusehen. Das gilt vollends vom Schluss des Buches (20,30f.). Auch die übrigen σημεῖον-Stellen stammen eindeutig vom Evangelisten. 4,48: 'Wenn ihr nicht Zeichen und Wunder seht, dann glaubt ihr nicht' ist eine gewaltsame, den Zusammenhang sprengende redaktionelle Einfügung in die Quelle''. For Becker's reaction, see below, p. 127 n. 313. – Conzelmann (with Andreas Lindemann) has not changed his stand vis-à-vis Bultmann in regard to the σημεῖα-*Quelle* in *Arbeitsbuch zum Neuen Testament* (UTB, 52), Tübingen, 1975 (= [4]1979), pp. 282-283; [5]1980 (= [8]1985), pp. 291-292; [9]1988, pp. 309-310 (ET: 1988). He does admit that John used such a source, but he continues to object against Bultmann that neither the numbering nor the concept σημεῖον nor the conclusion (20,30-31) come from the source: they are to be assigned to the evangelist. That John probably used a source, however, is apparent from the presence of "a considerable heightening of the miraculous" in comparison with the Synoptics. In addition, Johannine style characteristics do not appear in 2,1-11; 4,46-52 (except v. 48); 5,1-9a.12-15, and they are easily recognizable in 6,1-26; 9,1.41; 11,1-44. Cf. [9]1988, p. 309. Previously, Conzelmann simply noted: "In den Abschnitten 2,1-11; 4,46-52 (ausgenommen V. 48); 12,1-8; 12,12-15 fehlen joh Stilmerkmale" (1975, p. 283; [4]1979, p. 283). – Cf. Neirynck, *Semeia-bron*, 1983, p. 4 n. 5 (ET: 1991, p. 652 n. 5).
    25. G. Bornkamm, *Formen und Gattungen*. II. *Im N.T.*, in *RGG*[3] 2 (1958) 999-1005, pp. 1001-1002: "Aller Wahrscheinlichkeit nach hat Johannes eine eigene Sammlung von Wundergeschichten verarbeitet (von Bultmann als 'σημεῖα-Quelle' bezeichnet), die in ihrer novellistisch breit ausgemalten Wunderhaftigkeit die synoptische Tradition zT noch beträchtlich überbietet". – In *Zur Interpretation des Johannesevangeliums. Eine Auseinandersetzung mit Ernst Käsemanns Schrift 'Jesu letzter Wille nach Johannes 17'*, in *EvT* 28 (1968) 8-25, pp. 19-22 (= 1968, pp. 104-121, esp. 115-117; = 1985, pp. 118-135, esp. 129-131; ET: 1986, pp. 79-98, esp. 89-91), Bornkamm stresses, without explicitly speaking about the signs source however, that a pre-Johannine tradition, which differs from that of the Synoptics, is certainly to be recognized in the miracle stories. Bornkamm again speaks of the signs source in *Bibel. Das Neue Testament. Eine Einführung in seine Schriften im Rahmen der Geschichte des Urchristentums* (TdT, 9), Stuttgart - Berlin, 1971, pp. 153-155 (= 1980, pp. 323-326; ET: 1973, pp. 134-136). Also in *Die Heilung des Blindgeborenen. Johannes 9*, in *Geschichte und Glaube*, II, 1971, pp. 65-72, esp. 66, Bornkamm defends the semeia source: "in der von Johannes aller Wahrscheinlichkeit nach aus seiner Semeiaquelle übernommenen und vom Evangelisten ausgedeuteten Erzählung von der Heilung des Blindgeborenen...". This article is a reworked edition of Bornkamm's contribution in *GPM*, VI/3, 1952. – On Bornkamm, see, e.g., Corsani, *I miracoli*, 1983, p. 62; Schmithals, *Johannesevangelium*, 1992, pp. 178, 207.
    26. *Das Neue Testament*, p. 153 (= 1980, p. 323; ET: p. 135): "Alle diese [Wundergeschichten] sind gegenüber den synoptischen Wundern noch ungleich mehr ins

source, not the evangelist, which presents Jesus as "God striding over the earth". The evangelist accepted this tradition as his own but critiqued it, controverting its crude miracle faith. For him, the true significance of Jesus' deeds is brought out only in the discourses, and particularly in the ἐγώ εἰμι sayings (6,35; 8,12; 9,5; 10,11; 11,25; 14,6; 15,1)[27].

NOTE on Edwin C. BROOME, Jr., *The Sources of the Fourth Gospel*, in *JBL* 63 (1944) 107-121. Broome stands somewhat apart, defending a miracles source in his own fashion. Without any argumentation, he distinguishes seven sources lying behind the Fourth Gospel (pp. 108-109). Source 1 (S1) is a collection of independent sayings of Jesus, each beginning with the reduplicated formula ἀμὴν ἀμήν, probably written in Aramaic (pp. 109-112); S2, a collection of "Greek Logia" without the double ἀμήν formula (pp. 112-114); S3, another Aramaic collection (cf. 8,56a and possibly 5,34), the extent of which is difficult to determine (pp. 114-115); S4, a collection of eight Aramaic "I am" passages (pp. 115-116); S5, a signs source (pp. 117-118); S6, a group of possibly independent anecdotes about Jesus (pp. 118-119); and S7, the "Beloved Disciple" source, describing the fateful last days of Jesus at Jerusalem (pp. 119-120).

Broome's presentation of S5 and S6 is unclear; he identifies both with Bultmann's *Offenbarungsquelle* but must undoubtedly mean the σημεῖα-Quelle, to which the content of Broome's two sources would correspond: the seven miracle stories (S5) and the Samaritan woman story (S6). That S5 contained more miracle stories seems probable from the artificiality of the number seven and the fact that some are actually numbered (2,11; 4,54). There is a growing supernatural character in these miracles from first (water changed into wine) to last (the raising of Lazarus). As for this source's relationship to the Synoptics, Broome is not completely clear: on p. 109 he says four of the miracles appear in the Synoptics, on p. 117, five. In any case he attributes the healings of the royal official's son, the paralytic, and the man born blind to a tradition that is not dependent on the Synoptics but springs from a common origin. Jn 6,5-14 is probably from the Synoptics (p. 118). Further, he notes: "It appears that S5 represents several separate sources, possibly individual anecdotes, and not a ready-made 'collection'" (p. 118). The evangelist does not quote his sources at length, but a verse here and there, which accounts for the numerous aporias, for instance, in ch. 11 (pp. 117-118). He is interested more in the purpose of the story than in the story itself.

On Broome, cf. RUCKSTUHL, *Einheit*, 1951 (²1987), pp. 17-19; KONINGS, *Joh. verhaal*, I, 1969, p. 117; SELONG, *Cleansing*, I, 1971, p. 47; TEEPLE, *Origin*, 1974, p. 51; KYSAR, *Fourth Evangelist*, 1975, pp. 14 n. 5, 15 n. 11; TEMPLE, *Core*, 1975, pp. 35, 312 n. 30; BEUTLER, *ANRW* II, 25/3, 1985, p. 2521; SCHMITHALS, *Johannesevangelium*, 1992, p. 139.

---

mirakelhafte gesteigert. Diese stark hervortretende Tendenz verbindet die johanneische 'Zeichenquelle' mit den hellenistischen Erzählungen von göttlichen Wundermännern".

27. *Zur Interpretation*, pp. 19-22 (= 1968, pp. 115-117; 1985, pp. 129-131; ET: pp. 89-91); *Das Neue Testament*, pp. 154-155 (= 1980, pp. 324-325; ET: pp. 135-136).

II. The Signs Source as Aretalogy

The dissertation by Bornkamm's student Dieter GEORGI on the opponents of Paul in 2 Corinthians 2,14–7,4 and 10–13 (1958)[28] has influenced
consideration of the signs source, as well as the supposed pre-Markan collection of miracle stories, as an aretalogy in which Jesus is depicted as
θεῖος ἀνήρ. This was not new in the history of the semeia hypothesis.
Bultmann had already attributed a θεῖος ἀνήρ presentation to the signs
source, and had raised the question concerning Mark's use of a collection
of miracle stories[29]. In Markan exegesis, J. Weiss was one of the first to
suggest that the four miracles in Mk 4,35–5,43 constitute a small pre-
Markan collection[30]. M. Dibelius also thought it possible that the cycle of
miracle stories in Mk 4,35–5,43 had already existed before Mark[31].

According to Georgi, Paul's opponents in 2 Cor 2,14–7,4 and 10–13
were wandering Jewish-Christian missionaries who had adopted the
pattern of Hellenized Jewish propaganda[32]. By their skilled speech,
miracles, and spiritual qualities they demonstrate how *Christus praesens*
transcends the limitations of human life[33]. The letters of recommendation (2 Cor 3,1) by which they legitimized their activity were of special
importance[34]. They were written documents in which the powerful
works of the deity and the missionaries were listed and ratified by the
religious community (cf. 2 Cor 11,12). These "apostles" tried to obtain
similar documents from the Corinthians. Georgi has also pointed out that

28. This dissertation, directed by Bornkamm, was published six years later as "Neu-
fassung": D. GEORGI, *Die Gegner des Paulus im 2. Korintherbrief. Studien zur religiösen
Propaganda in der Spätantike* (WMANT, 11), Neukirchen-Vluyn, 1964 (ET: 1986). For
other studies by Georgi, see *Bibliography*. On Georgi, see, e.g., KOSKENNIEMI, *Apollonios
von Tyana*, 1992, pp. 78-80, 128.
    29. See above, p. 35 n. 181.
    30. *Das älteste Evangelium*, 1903, p. 180: "als feste Gruppe aus der Überlieferung
übernommen".
    31. *Die Formgeschichte* (1919), [2]1933, p. 220 (= [3]1959, p. 220; ET: 1935, p. 219).
For a more complete survey on the hypothesis of a pre-Markan collection in Mk
4,35–5,43, see FITZPATRICK, *The Structure of St. Mark's Gospel*, I, 1975, pp. 249-259. He
distinguishes four forms of the hypothesis: (1) a collection of four miracles, as suggested
by J. Weiss (1903), E. Wendling (1908), M. Dibelius (1919, [2]1933), K.L. Schmidt (1919),
R. Bultmann (1921), has become "a common opinion" (see the others mentioned by
FitzPatrick on p. 251 n. 22); (2) a larger collection of sea stories, as proposed by B.H.
Branscomb (1937), H. Hegermann (1960), L.E. Keck (1965), and T.A. Burkill (1968);
cp. R. Pesch (1976, see below, p. 85 n. 63); (3) the collection proposed by H.W. Kuhn
(1971); see below, pp. 84-85; (4) the double miracle-cycle of P.J. Achtemeier (1970,
1972). See also VAN OYEN, *De summaria in Marcus*, 1987, pp. 181-196: "Een voormarciaanse verzameling in Mc 4–6?"; *De studie van de Marcusredactie*, 1993, pp. 260-267:
"Voormarciaanse wonderverzameling en θεῖος ἀνήρ-christologie".
    32. *Gegner*, pp. 31-82 (ET: pp. 27-60: "The Missionary Role of the Opponents").
    33. *Ibid.*, pp. 219-300 (ET: pp. 229-313: "The Self-Understanding of the Oppo-
nents").
    34. *Ibid.*, pp. 241-246 (ET: pp. 242-246).

the θεῖος ἀνήρ presentation appeared with the "pseudo-apostles" of 2 Corinthians who had penetrated the Pauline community during his absence[35].

Nowhere in his published dissertation does Georgi expressly compare the θεῖος ἀνήρ christology of Paul's opponents with that of the signs source[36]. J.M. Robinson attributes this comparison to Koester: "Helmut Koester, 'Häretiker im Urchristentum', in RGG, 3rd ed., vol. 3 (1959), p. 19, has already associated the heresy opposed in 2 Cor. with the miracles source, as well as with Mark and parts of Acts"[37]. But Koester, who knew Georgi's dissertation from the beginning[38], attributed it to Georgi: "I am somewhat embarrassed to be credited with having discovered the connection between the sources of Mark and John and the opponents of 2 Corinthians, in my article 'Häretiker im Urchristentum' ... It was, as a matter of fact, Dieter Georgi who first suggested this relationship in his 1958 Heidelberg dissertation, which was published six years later"[39].

35. *Ibid.*, pp. 282-292 (ET: pp. 271-277: "Jesus as θεῖος ἀνήρ"); on the θεῖος ἀνήρ, see also pp. 145-167, 192-200 (ET: pp. 155-160, 220-234). Cp. the *Epilogue*, in the ET, esp. pp. 390-422: "Social Aspects of the Phenomenon of the Divine Man". – There is an array of literature on aretalogy and the portrayal of the θεῖος ἀνήρ. See, e.g., M. SMITH, in *JBL* 90 (1971) 174-199; KEE, in *JBL* 92 (1973) 403-422; GUNDRY and LANE, in LONGENECKER – TENNEY (eds.), *New Dimensions*, 1974, resp. pp. 97-114 and 144-161; HOLLADAY, *Theios anèr*, 1977; TIEDE (see below, pp. 85-86); BERGER, *ANRW* II, 25/2, 1984, pp. 1031-1432, 1831-1835, esp. 1218-1231 ("Aretalogie"). (On Berger, see KOSKENNIEMI, *Apollonios von Tyana*, 1992, pp. 61-62, 110-112, 159-160.) Note especially the critical reactions by Kee, Gundry and Berger. For a recent criticism of the θεῖος ἀνήρ concept, see esp. BLACKBURN, *Theios Anèr and the Markan Miracle Traditions*, 1991, esp. pp. 262-266: "Chapter Six: Conclusion"; cp. *"Miracle Working ΘΕΙΟΙ ΑΝΔΡΕΣ"*, in WENHAM – BLOMBERG (eds.), *The Miracles of Jesus*, 1986, pp. 185-218. See also KOSKENNIEMI, *Apollonios von Tyana*, 1992, esp. pp. 64-163 ("Die Diskussion über das Gottmenschentum"); PADILLA, *Los milagros de la "Vida de Apolonio de Tiana"*, 1991; VAN OYEN, *De studie van de Marcusredactie*, 1993, pp. 260-267.

36. However, in the *Epilogue* of the ET (pp. 333-450, esp. 445-446), Georgi notes: "The importance of the θεῖος ἀνήρ concept for the christology of the early church is now almost taken for granted. Its impact on the formation of the Jesus tradition is being thoroughly studied, including tendencies, differentiations, and influences which occurred in the development of the various genres summarily and somewhat incorrectly classified under the term 'gospel'", with n. 212 (p. 449): "Various articles by H. Koester redirect our understanding of gospel tradition and gospel formation. Gospel scholarship must follow this lead. It must break down further the artificial walls around the four canonical Gospels and see even more their variety and their correspondence with character and tradition of apocryphal and Gnostic gospels and with Hellenistic phenomena, pagan as well as Jewish".

37. J.M. ROBINSON, *Kerygma*, 1965, p. 321 n. 47 (ET: 1965, p. 136 n. 32; = *Trajectories*, 1971, p. 51 n. 50). On this article, see below, p. 83 n. 51. Note that the German edition adds to the text cited above: "Die Verbindung zur Zeichen-Quelle hat Georgi freilich ausser acht gelassen".

38. GEORGI, *Gegner*, p. 6.

39. KOESTER, *One Jesus*, 1968, p. 233 n. 106 (= 1971, p. 189 n. 106; see below, p. 80 n. 42). Cp. *HTR* 58 (1965), p. 310 n. 94 (= 1971, p. 149 n. 94): "For the following

Helmut KOESTER (1959)[40] notes in his *RGG* article that the tendency toward "heightening the historical appearance of Jesus into that of a divine miracle-man (θεῖος ἀνήρ)", as is done by the opponents of Paul in 2 Cor, appears not only in the apocryphal Gospels and Acts but also in the traditions of the Gospel of Mark, the signs source of John, and many portions of the Acts of the Apostles[41]. In *One Jesus and Four Primitive Gospels* (1968)[42], Koester describes his view on the signs source more completely. According to him, "the existence of earlier written documents as an intermediate stage between free transmission and written Gospels is beyond doubt; we can still detect, e.g., a collection of parables used in Mk. 4, a document containing miracle stories called the Johannine 'sèmeia source' (but also related to the source of large parts of Mk.), and – above all – the Synoptic source of sayings, common to Mt. and Lk."[43]. John and Mark, the oldest gospels, consist principally of a Passion story and a source of miracle narratives[44]. The use of the signs source in John is quite obvious, but there can be no doubt that Mark also employed a (different) collection of miracle stories[45]. These primitive gospel sources represent Jesus as a "man endowed with divine power who performs miracles to prove his divine quality and character"[46]. They are aretalogies and their intention is clearly expressed in a typical concluding formula (cp. Jn 20,30-31 with Sir 43,27; 1 Macc 9,22; and others). Their function is to promote a particular religion[47]. In the signs

description I am indebted to D. Georgi and to his excellent study Die Gegner..." (GT: 1968, p. 195 n. 96).

40. H. KOESTER, *Häretiker im Urchristentum*, in *RGG*[3] 3 (1959) 17-21, cc. 18-19.

41. *Ibid.*, c. 19.

42. *One Jesus and Four Primitive Gospels*, in *HTR* 61 (1968) 203-247, pp. 230-236: "Jesus as the Divine Man (Aretalogies)" (rewritten: 1971, pp. 158-204, esp. 187-193). – On Koester, see TIEDE, *The Charismatic Figure*, 1972, pp. 287-292; SCHENKE, *Wundererzählungen*, 1974, pp. 384-385; KYSAR, *Fourth Evangelist*, 1975, pp. 31 n. 41, 34 n. 49; *ANRW* II, 25/3, 1985, p. 2400 n. 42; HEEKERENS, *Zeichen-Quelle*, 1984, pp. 20, 43, 108.

43. *One Jesus*, pp. 208-209 (= 1971, p. 164).

44. *Ibid.*, pp. 230-231 (= 1971, p. 187).

45. *Ibid.*, p. 231 (1971, p. 187): "Mark's and John's sources, even though closely related to each other, certainly were not identical". For the relation between Mark's and John's source, see above, p. 80 n. 43.

46. *Ibid.*, p. 231 (= 1971, p. 187).

47. *Ibid.*, p. 231 (= 1971, p. 188). Koester rejects the term apologetic for the Sitz-im-Leben (contra Robinson, see below, p. 83 n. 53): "I would rather not use the term *apologetic* here, since the primary element is certainly that of religious propaganda" (p. 232 n. 101; = 1971, p. 188 n. 101). He limits the Sitz-im-Leben for aretalogies as follows: "Aretalogies were normally written for purposes of religious propaganda. The religious convictions which incline to the use of this literary genre for propaganda purposes are very much the same everywhere in the Hellenistic world, whether they be Jewish, pagan, or Christian. Aretalogies are not used only to defend certain religious tenets; they are not simply apologetic. Rather, these stories of extraordinary events and performances represent in themselves the essential creed and belief of a religious movement" (pp. 231-232; = 1971, p. 188).

source and the pre-Markan collection of miracles, Jesus is portrayed as θεῖος ἀνήρ. According to Koester, the meaning of the title is explained in Acts 2,22: "Men of Israel, hear these words: Jesus of Nazareth, a man attested to you by God with mighty works and wonders and signs which God did through him in your midst, as you yourselves know..."[48]. John has employed this notion from his source not uncritically; for him Jesus' revelation is in his glorification on the cross. A similar critique appears in the Gospel of Mark as well: the true "mystery of the Messiah" is visible not in his miracles but in his Passion[49]. Koester takes up the hypothesis of Georgi on the opponents of Paul in 2 Cor and proposes that the letters of recommendation (2 Cor 3,1) with which these opponents underscored their authority were none other than aretalogies. Once the collections of Jesus' miracles had been incorporated into the Gospels of Mark and John they ceased to exist as separate entities, but continued to exercise a great influence in the later literature of primitive Christianity[50].

Koester repeatedly compares the presentation of Jesus in the signs source with the christology of Paul's opponents: *ΓΝΩΜΑΙ ΔΙΑΦΟΡΟΙ. The Origin and Nature of Diversification in the History of Early Christianity*, in *HTR* 58 (1965) 279-318, p. 313 (= 1971, pp. 114-157, esp. 151; GT: 1968, pp. 205-231, esp. 197-198): "The 'Gospel' which corresponds to such a Christology must have been very similar to the narrative sources and traditions which have been used by our oldest written gospels: the Gospel of Mark and the Gospel of John"; *The Structure of Criteria of Early Christian Beliefs*, in *Trajectories*, 1971, pp. 205-231, esp. 216-219: "Jesus as the Divine Man"; cf. p. 218: "Mark and John used collections of Jesus' miracle stories, which were obviously produced in order to enhance the belief in Jesus' possession of divine power"; see also *Conclusion: The Intention and Scope of Trajectories*, in *op. cit.*, pp. 269-279, esp. 270-271, on the "divine man literature, the aretalogy genre".

Also in *Einführung in das Neue Testament im Rahmen der Religionsgeschichte und Kulturgeschichte der hellenistischen und römischen Zeit*, Berlin - New York, 1980, pp. 622-263 (ET: II, 1982, p. 184), Koester compares the signs source with Mark's tradition of miracle stories (cp. pp. 604-605; ET: II, pp. 168-169). He describes the source as "eine Sammlung von Stücken 'hellenistischer' Propaganda, die Jesus als 'göttlichen Menschen' verkündigen". It contains 2,1-11; 4,43–5,9; 6,1-21, 9,1-7; 11,1-44, and perhaps 20,30-31 as conclusion; also the older form of 4,4ff., where Jesus appears as a prophet who possesses supernatural knowledge (vv. 16-19), could have been part of this tradition, even in an earlier stage. According to Koester, the language of these traditions points to an Aramaic milieu: "Sie stammen also aus der Mission unter aramäisch sprechenden Juden und Heiden und wurden in einer Gemeinde gesammelt, die zweisprachig war". He accepts that the wine miracle at Cana derived its main features from the cult of Dionysus ("kennzeichnend für den

48. *Ibid.*, p. 232 n. 103 (= 1971, p. 188 n. 103).
49. *Ibid.*, pp. 232-233 (= 1971, p. 189).
50. *Ibid.*, pp. 233-234 (= 1971, pp. 189-190). Especially in the Gospel of Luke, in Acts, and the apocryphal Acts of the Apostles (pp. 233-236; = 1971, pp. 190-193).

Synkretismus auch gerade des nicht griechisch sprechenden syrisch-palästini-schen Raumes"). More than in the Markan parallels, the signs source empha-sized the miraculous power of Jesus. The source cannot be called "Johannine", because the author of the Fourth Gospel strongly criticizes the miracles. Koester even presumes that Mark's and John's miracle sources were different versions of the same literary collection: "Inhalt und Abfolge einer Reihe von Wunderge-schichten Jesu bei Markus und Johannes entsprechen sich so weitgehend, dass man auf die Benutzung gemeinsamen Quellenmaterials schliessen muss" (p. 481; ET: II, p. 47). In *Überlieferung und Geschichte der frühchristlichen Evangelienliteratur*, in *ANRW* II, 25/2, 1982, pp. 1463-1542, esp. 1509-1512: "Das Evangelium als Aretalogie" (on the signs source, see pp. 1509-1510), Koester remarks on the language of the source: "In der vom Johannes benutzten Form war die Semeia-Quelle griechisch verfasst. Es ist aber möglich, dass ihr ein aramäisches Original zugrunde liegt" (p. 1510). There is no literary depen-dence between the signs of John and the miracles of Mark: "Eine oder mehrere der von Markus benutzten Aretalogien sind mit der johanneischen Semeia-Quelle verwandt; denn mehrere Wundergeschichten finden sich sowohl bei Markus als auch bei Johannes, ohne dass eine literarische Abhängigkeit besteht" (p. 1510; cp. p. 1477). On Koester's *Einleitung*, see NEIRYNCK's reviews in *ETL* 57 (1981) 357-358; 59 (1983) 364-365; cp. *Semeia-bron*, 1983, p. 4 n. 5 (ET: 1991, p. 652 n. 5).

Koester further mentions the signs source in *Johannesevangelium*, in *EKL* 2 (1989) 840-843, c. 840: "Die im ersten Abschnitt [2,1-11,54] verwendete *Semeia-Quelle* ist mit den Quellen der synopt. Wunder verwandt... In der Semeia-Quelle erscheinen die wunderhaften Züge überhoht, aber Joh warnt vor blossem Wunderglauben (2,23f; 4,49 u.ö)"; cp. c. 842. See also his *Ancient Christian Gospels: Their History and Development*, London - Philadelphia, PA, 1990, pp. 201-205: "Miracle Catenae"; 251-253: "The Semeia Source". From the numbering in 2,11 and 4,54 and the gospel's closing formula (20,30-31), Koester once again concludes that it is beyond doubt that the miracle stories in 2,1-11; 4,46-54; 5,2-9; 6,5-14; 6,16-25; 9,1-7; 11,1-45 "derived from a written source" (p. 251; see also pp. 203-204). The semeia source (or source of signs) drew these stories "from the same source which provided the materials for the miracle catenae of the Gospel of Mark" (p. 204; cp. pp. 296-287). Jesus, how-ever, is not presented as a "magician" (so the pre-Markan tradition) but as a god, and his miracles are to be characterized as "epiphanies" (p. 205): "Jesus is the divine man who strides upon the face of the earth displaying supernatural power" (p. 251). The source is composed in Greek but "it is not impossible that it was originally written in Aramaic". It originated "most likely" in Syria/Pales-tine and was written "for the Hellenistic-syncretistic milieu which determined the forms of Christian propaganda in this eastern region of the Roman empire" (p. 205). According to Koester, the author of the gospel has adopted this source as the basis of Jn 2–12 (p. 251), but "on the one hand, nothing is taken away from the powerful effect of the miracles. On the other hand, it is repeatedly explained that belief in miracles is not only insufficient; it falsifies what true belief in Jesus ought to be" (see the evangelist's comments in 2,11; 2,23-24; 4,48; 6,14-15; 9,35-38) (pp. 251-252). Moreover, for the author of the gospel, the miracles become the cause of Jesus' condemnation (11,45-50) and provide "the topics for the discourses and dialogues" (pp. 252-253). Regarding the story of raising the young man in the Secret Gospel of Mark (cp. Jn 11) (pp. 293-303), Koester maintains that it "represents a stage of development of the story that corresponds to the source used by John" (p. 296).

On Koester, see also ASHTON, *Understanding*, 1991, p. 275 n. 70; KOSKENNIEMI, *Apollonios von Tyana*, 1992, pp. 61, 108-110, 125-126, 132-134, 150-153; SCHMITHALS, *Johannesevangelium*, 1992, p. 175; SMITH, *John among the Gospels*, 1992, pp. 82-83. SCHNELLE, *Perspektiven*, 1990, p. 59, remarks on Koester's 1989 *EKL*-article: "H. Köster lehnt sich in einem jüngst erschienenen Lexikonartikel so stark an die Position Bultmanns an, als hätte es seit 1941 keine weiterführende Johannesforschung gegeben").

In the same way, James M. ROBINSON (1965)[51] situated the signs source in the historical context of the early church. He refers to the original sequence of the two Cana stories[52] and notes that the numbering accords well with apologetic emphasis on the quantity of miracles (7,31; 11,47; 12,37; 20,30-31). Jn 20,30-31 is a good illustration of the *Sitz im Leben* of the source: missionary activity and apologetics[53]. In the source, "there is a direct, unambiguous, non-paradoxical, causal relation between the miracles that demonstrate Jesus to be a divine man, and the resultant faith (or credulity) in him as just such a miracle worker" (cp. 3,2; Acts 2,22). But for the evangelist "the true form of faith is faith in Jesus' word" (5,24)[54]. Using 4,46-54, Robinson elucidates the character of the source and the redactional activity of the evangelist[55]. The Q source offers a similar account, but its narrative frame was limited to a minimum. There the point consists in the belief of the centurion, whom the Lord praises (Mt 8,8 par.). In the signs source, the story has been expanded through a full description of the confirmation of the miracle,

---

51. J.M. ROBINSON, *Kerygma and History in the New Testament*, in HYATT (ed.), *The Bible*, 1965, pp. 114-150, esp. 131-146 (on the semeia source: pp. 135-146); GT: in *ZTK* 62 (1965) 294-337 (this text is expanded in the footnotes), esp. 316-333 (pp. 321-333); republication of the English text in *Trajectories*, 1971, pp. 20-70 (the most complete version), esp. 46-66: "History as the Transmission of Traditions in the New Testament" (pp. 51-66). – Robinson defends the semeia hypothesis in other articles as well: *On the Gattung of Mark (and John)*, in *Jesus and Man's Hope*, I, Pittsburgh, 1970, pp. 99-129, esp. 103-105; *The Johannine Trajectory*, in *Trajectories*, pp. 232-268 (see below, pp. 172-174); *The Literary Composition of Mark*, in SABBE (ed.), *L'évangile selon Marc*, 1974 (²1988), pp. 11-19, esp. 12, 16; see also his review of Fortna's *The Gospel of Signs*, in *JAAR* 39 (1971) 339-348: *The Miracle Source of John* (see below, pp. 172-174). – Cf. KONINGS, *Joh. verhaal*, I, 1969, pp. 124-125; TIEDE, *The Charismatic Figure*, 1972, pp. 187- 192; KYSAR, *Fourth Evangelist*, 1975, p. 34 n. 49; CORSANI, *I miracoli*, 1983, p. 82; SCHNELLE, *Christologie*, 1987, p. 105[-106] n. 105 (ET: 1992, p. 91[-92] n. 105); KOSKENNIEMI, *Apollonios von Tyana*, 1992, p. 127; SMITH, *John among the Gospels*, 1992, p. 78.

52. *Kerygma*, pp. 137 (= 1971, pp. 53-54; GT: pp. 323-324).

53. We read in 20,31, according to Robinson, "the apologetic, missionary scope or *Sitz im Leben* of the miracle source... It is the very quantity of such miracle stories that produces faith, and the narrator has assured the reader he could continue indefinitely recounting such miracle stories of Jesus" (*Kerygma*, p. 138; = 1971, pp. 55; GT: p. 323). For Koester's reaction, see above, p. 80 n. 47.

54. *Ibid.*, pp. 138-139 (= 1971, p. 55; GT: p. 324).

55. *Ibid.*, pp. 139-140 (= 1971, pp. 56-58; GT: pp. 324-327).

whereby faith in Jesus on the basis of the miracle is emphasized. The evangelist took the account from the source but criticized the miracle-faith by inserting 4,48. The same critique of the θεῖος ἀνήρ interpretation of Jesus' divine origin is present in the Temptation pericope of Q[56]. According to Robinson, the attitude of the evangelist agrees with Paul's criticism of the preaching of a "different Jesus", the θεῖος ἀνήρ predication of his opponents, which likewise appeared in the signs source and the pre-Markan miracle collection[57].

In response to Robinson's 1965 paper, Floyd V. FILSON, on the one hand, rejects Robinson's interpretation of Johannine miracles criticism: "It does not seem that the writer of the Fourth Gospel was sharply critical and negative towards the miracles or 'signs' of Jesus; otherwise it is hard to see how he could have made such a favorable reference to these signs in the climactic statement of his purpose which he presents in his gospel conclusion (John 20:30-31)"[58]. On the other hand, David M. STANLEY does not agree with Robinson's description of the nature of the signs source: "If this [signs source] hypothesis be accepted – and Robinson has provided us with a reasonable basis for accepting it – then the question must be raised concerning the theological reasons for the author's consistent and almost exclusive use of the term *sèmeion* to designate the miracles attributed to Jesus. The Synoptic tradition employed the word relatively rarely in this sense... But the tradition recorded by the author of the Fourth Gospel insisted upon the symbolic or pedagogical meaning of Jesus' miracles. The important thing for Christian faith is the seeing of the 'sign' in the bread (John 6:26). The encounter between Nicodemus and Jesus shows that the purpose of such 'signs' is not merely the construction of a scholastic apologetic (John 3:2). It is rather to enable the Christian to see the Lord's Anointed and the Son of God in Jesus (John 20:31). Accordingly, I find it difficult to accept the view that 'it is the very quantity of such miracle stories that produces faith' as the real opinion of the author of the 'Signs Source'. His insight and religious spirit is too sophisticated, theologically speaking. Whatever one may think of the 'wooden redactional style' of the writer who employed such a source to compose the Fourth Gospel, he too is no theological *ingénue* but one of the great religious thinkers of the apostolic age"[59].

According to Heinz-Wolfgang KUHN (1971)[60] it remains probable that we can recognize for Mk 4,35–5,43; 6,32-51 a pre-Markan collection of

---

56. *Ibid.*, p. 140 (= 1971, p. 58; GT: p. 326).
57. *Ibid.*, pp. 140-146 (= 1971, pp. 58-66; GT: pp. 326-333).
58. F.V. FILSON, in HYATT (ed.), *The Bible*, 1965, pp. 160-165, esp. 163.
59. D.M. STANLEY, *ibid.*, pp. 151-159, esp. 158-159.
60. H.-W. KUHN, *Ältere Sammlungen im Markusevangelium* (SUNT, 8), Göttingen, 1971 (diss. Heidelberg, 1969; dir. K.G. Kuhn), pp. 191-213: "IV. Das Problem einer

six miracle stories. These stories must be characterized as "Novellen" or "Epiphaniegeschichten", which all betray a θεῖος ἀνήρ christology[61]. The Sitz-im-Leben of these miracle stories and such a collection is to be found in the mission, and more precisely, as Georgi, Koester, and Robinson have indicated, in the circle of itinerant missionaries[62]. According to Kuhn, we know that such collections existed, for we find another σημεῖα source in the Fourth Gospel[63].

In his dissertation under Koester at Harvard University, *The Charismatic Figure as Miracle Worker* (1972), David Lenz TIEDE[64] also accepted the semeia hypothesis and compared the signs source with the pre-Markan miracle collection. In his chapter three, on Jesus as the θεῖος ἀνήρ[65], he remarks: "Redaction studies of the *Gospel of John*

vormarkinischen Sammlung in Mk 4,35–6,52". – Cf. CORSANI, *I miracoli*, 1983, p. 29; SCHNELLE, *Christologie*, 1987, p. 105[-106] n. 105 (ET: 1992, p. 91[-92] n. 105).

61. *Ältere Sammlungen*, p. 192. In characterizing the miracle stories, Kuhn depends strongly on DIBELIUS, *Die Formgeschichte*, ²1933 (³1959), pp. 91, 149.

62. *Ibid.*, pp. 211-213: "§ 19. Die Träger der Einzeltraditionen und der angenommenen Sammlung" (see esp. p. 211 n. 5).

63. *Ibid.*, p. 210: "Dass es Sammlungen von Wundergeschichten im Urchristentum gab, beweist die Semeia-Quelle im JohEv, deren Existenz erwiesen sein dürfte, nicht zuletzt auch aufgrund der theologischen Spannung zwischen Quelle und Evangelium (allerdings scheint hier mehr als eine blosse Sammlung vorzuliegen, weil doch wohl eine Redaktion zu erkennen ist)" (cp. pp. 212, 232). The same argument (cp. Bultmann; see above, p. 24 n. 137) has been used by Koch and Pesch. Cf. KOCH, *Die Bedeutung der Wundererzählungen*, 1975, pp. 30-31: "Die Annahme von Wundersammlungen im Markusevangelium gewinnt dadurch an Wahrscheinlichkeit, dass es innerhalb des Neuen Testaments ein gesichertes Beispiel für eine Sammlung von Wundererzählungen gibt: die sog. Semeiaquelle des Johannesevangeliums"; cp. p. 32); PESCH, *Das Markusevangelium*, I, 1976 (³1980: ⁴1985), pp. 277-278: "Dass es Sammlungen von Wundergeschichten in der evangeliaren Tradition des Urchristentums gegeben hat, beweist die Parallele der Sämeia-Quelle des Joh-Ev". – This argument has been criticized by Schenke, FitzPatrick (ctr. Kuhn) and Neirynck (ctr. Pesch). Cf. SCHENKE, *Die Wundererzählungen*, 1974, pp. 373-389, esp. 386: "Der Hinweis auf die vorjohanneische 'Zeichenquelle' erbringt hier gerade nichts, weil wir dort literarkritische Kriterien antreffen, die eine vorjohanneische Quelle wahrscheinlich machen (vgl. Joh 2,11f; 4,46.54; 20,30f). Solche Kriterien fehlen dagegen im Markusevangelium" (on Schenke, see also below, pp. 281-283); FITZPATRICK, *The Structure of St. Mark's Gospel*, I, 1975, p. 258: "An appeal to the existence of a σημεῖα source for the Fourth Gospel does not really add support here, since studies on this source seem frequently to appeal to a pre-Markan collection for support"; NEIRYNCK, in *ETL* 53 (1977), pp. 166-167 (= 1982, pp. 504-505): "Dans l'hypothèse de la dépendance johannique (et il me semble que des raisons sérieuses plaident dans ce sens), il devient difficile de démontrer l'existence d'une source spéciale pour les récits de miracles. D'ailleurs, et c'est également l'avis de Pesch, l'existence d'une source johannique ne dispenserait pas de fonder la *Sammlung* prémarcienne sur des indications dans le texte de Marc lui-même" (cf. PESCH, *op. cit.*, p. 278 n. 1).

64. D.L. TIEDE, *The Charismatic Figure as Miracle Worker* (SBL DS, 1), Missoula, MT, 1972. – Cf. BITTNER, *Jesu Zeichen*, 1987, p. 11 n. 23; SCHNELLE, *Christologie*, 1987, p. 105[-106] n. 105 (ET: 1992, p. 91[-92] n. 105); KOSKENNIEMI, *Apollonios von Tyana*, 1992, pp. 83-85, 108, 112, 136-137.

65. *Charismatic Figure*, pp. 241-292.

have attained a broader level of consensus, at least with respect to the existence of a pre-gospel cycle of miracles, than is true for *Mark*"[66]. He provides a brief review of the history of the semeia hypothesis after Bultmann[67]. In contrast to Bultmann's "signs source" he chooses the term "miracle source" because that term "corresponds to the under-standing of such acts that the source itself appears to imply, while the performances appear to have been re-interpreted by the evangelist as 'signs'"[68]. According to Tiede, the numbering of the miracles appears to be "the strongest evidence for such a source", and 20,30-31 is generally seen as the source's "climax and conclusion" in which "attention is focused on the miracles and an enumeration is implied"[69]. Further on, Tiede observes that "most, if not all, of these miracle accounts can be classified form-critically as 'tales' or 'novelistic miracle stories' accord-ing to Dibelius' description of that form"[70]. Twelve years later, Tiede again defended the semeia hypothesis, although with some reservation: "To be sure, miracle stories may be used in a variety of propagandistic responses to the prevailing culture. They may only be signs of the apoc-alyptic rending of the world that is just beginning. But if the author of Mark did have access to a collection of miracles and the author of John used a 'signs source', the best available parallels would suggest that these collections would have had great propaganda value for promoting the hero of the Christian tradition as equal or superior to the divinely empowered prophets and heroes and divine men of Judaism and the Greco-Roman world. At least such 'aretalogical' traditions would have been very useful to a mode of Christian religious propaganda that sought to come to terms with the prevailing religious cultures by representing its Jesus as surpassing the holy men of other traditions. Jesus is not sim-ply another charismatic figure, he is 'the very Son of God walking the earth'"[71].

---

66. *Ibid.*, p. 269.
67. *Ibid.*, pp. 269-279.
68. *Ibid.*, p. 275 n. 88.
69. *Ibid.*, pp. 279-280.
70. Tiede refers (p. 281 n. 106) to a study by a graduate student, James BRASHLER, *A Form-Critical Analysis of the Miracle Stories in Fortna's Reconstructed "Gospel of Signs"*, Course paper, Claremont Graduate School and University Center, 1969. Brashler "has attempted to show that all of the miracle stories that Fortna has included in his source still show enough traits of this form [tale or novelistic miracle story] to suggest that 'the miracle source was a collection of Novelistic Miracle Stories designed to con-vince those who read or heard them that Jesus was a θεῖος ἀνήρ in whom one should believe'" (p. 281). On pp. 287-292, Tiede describes the views of Koester and Robinson.
71. *Religious Propaganda and the Literature of the Early Christian Mission*, in *ANRW* II, 25/2, 1984, pp. 1705-1729, esp. 1715-1721: "The Tales of the Mighty Men", esp. 1720-1721. See now also his article *Aretalogy*, in *ABD*, I, 1992, pp. 372-373, esp. 373a: "John probably used a Signs Source, and Mark may have drawn upon a cycle of miracle stories but subsumed them in a cross-resurrection narrative structure".

III. THE SIGNS SOURCE AND THE OLD TESTAMENT

A few exegetes have described the signs source on the basis of the Old Testament[72]. According to Georg ZIENER (1957, 1958)[73], the Wisdom of Solomon is of special importance for understanding the Fourth Gospel and the miracle stories in particular[74]. Comparing with the Synoptic Gospels, one observes not only that John chose different miracle stories but also that he gave them a different character[75]. The evangelist reproduces the intention of the miracle stories in the conclusion: he wants to awaken faith in Jesus as the Son of God and Messiah[76]. The

72. We have noted above (p. 55 n. 83) that Michel, in contrast to Bultmann, defended the position that the Cana story should be compared first to the Old Testament tradition: Moses and Elijah do indeed stand at the origin of the Israelite miracle tradition.

73. G. ZIENER, *Weisheitsbuch und Johannesevangelium*, in *Bib* 38 (1957) 396-418, pp. 399-418; 39 (1958) 37-60; *Johannesevangelium und urchristliche Passafeier*, in *BZ* 2 (1958) 263-274. – Cf. KONINGS, *Joh. verhaal*, I, 1969, pp. 212-213; REIM, *Hintergrund*, 1974, pp. 194-204. For Reim's and J. Becker's reaction to Ziener, see below, pp. 93 n. 98, 129-130 nn. 321-322.

74. After a short survey of research (*Weisheitsbuch*, pp. 396-398), Ziener notes that there is some parallel between John and Wisdom: "Trotz seines Ursprungs im Bereich des hellenistischen Judentums reichen die Wurzeln des Weisheitsbuches in den jüdisch-palästinensischen Raum. Damit wird das Weisheitsbuch ähnlich wie die Qumran-Texte zu einem wichtigen Zeugen für jüdisches theologisches Denken unmittelbar am Eingang des neutestamentlichen Zeitalters. Wenn deshalb zwischen Johannesevangelium und Sektenschriften Beziehungen bestehen, so spricht das noch nicht gegen eine mögliche Verwandtschaft zwischen Weisheitsbuch und viertem Evangelium. Eher ist bei den inhaltlichen und terminologischen Übereinstimmungen zwischen Weisheitsbuch und Sektenschriften damit zu rechnen, dass von *beiden* Seiten Parallelen zum Johannesevangelium angeführt werden können" (p. 398). Many, however, argue against the parallel between John and Wisdom: (1) Wisdom would have arisen in Hellenistic Judaism, while John would be a Palestinian Jewish writing; (2) Wisdom, in contrast to John, contains many more philosophical terms; (3) apologetic and wisdom sayings, abundant in Wisdom, are absent in John (p. 397).

75. *Ibid.*, pp. 399-400. In the Synoptics the miracles are witnesses to God's mercy (Mt 14,14; 15,32; 20,34; Lk 7,13), they are signs of an announcement (Mt 12,28): the coming of the Kingdom of God (Mt 11,5). In John, on the other hand, the miracles have a deeper theological significance: Jesus reveals himself in his miracles as Food (ch. 6), Light (ch. 9), and Life (ch. 5 and 11).

76. *Ibid.*, p. 401. On p. 401 n. 2, Ziener refers to SAHLIN, *Zur Typologie*, 1950, who advocates a very thorough-going parallelism between the Gospel of John and the Exodus story. Sahlin's thesis stresses that "das vierte Evangelium als ganzes die Heilstat Jesu Christi als ein Gegenstück zu dem Auszug Israels aus Ägypten und seinem Einzug in das gelobte Land darstellt – ein Gegenstück also zu der heiligen Geschichte, die sich von der Gottesoffenbarung, die Mose im brennenden Dornbusch empfing, bis zur Einweihung des salomonischen Tempels erstreckt" (p. 5). But the parallels that Sahlin brings forward are not convincing. Ziener differs from Sahlin in two points: (1) John's Gospel does not parallel the Exodus story from the Pentateuch, but a late Jewish presentation of the Exodus events, which also served as *Vorlage* for the author of Wisdom; (2) Ziener does not compare the entire Gospel of John with the Exodus, but only the miracle stories. – For the Exodus typology in John (cp. Boismard, see below, pp. 275-276), see also ENZ, in *JBL* 76 (1957) 208-215, and R.H. SMITH, in *JBL* 81 (1962) 329-342. In reaction to Smith,

Johannine miracle stories are indeed signs of messianic expectation, which are prefigured in Israel's rescue from Egypt; Jesus as the Messiah performs miracles from the time of the Exodus which are recorded in Wisdom 11,2–19,22 alongside the seven plagues. Ziener gives the following miracles as parallel in Wisdom and John[77]:

	Wisdom	John
Quenching thirst	11,4-14	2,1-12
	16,2	—
Healing the sick	16,5-13	4,46-54
	—	5,1-9a
Satisfying hunger	16,20-26	6,1-13
Deliverance from darkness	18,1.3	9,1-41
Deliverance from death	18,22	11,1-44

The agreement in order further confirms that John has been influenced by the miracle cycle of Wisdom[78]. The counting of signs (2,11; 4,54; in contrast to 2,23; 3,2; 4,45) can be understood as a systematic enumeration which refers to the miracles in Wisdom[79]. The similarities between the two collections become even more obvious when one compares the structure of the stories[80].

M. KILEY, *The Exegesis of God: Jesus' Signs in John 1–11*, in *SBL 1988 Seminar Papers*, 1988, pp. 555-569, suggests that the signs of John can be explained from Ps 23 and 27 (see pp. 556-560: "Psalmic 'backbone' in John"). Cf. esp. p. 562: "The evidence suggests then that John alone in the canon intends all of Jesus' related miracles to be seen as signs of the activity of the Lord of Psalms 23/27". Kiley has been involved with this thesis since the mid-1970's. He presented it to the Upper Seminar in the Study of Religion at Harvard University in September 1980 and gave it in schematic form to the Catholic Biblical Association Conference in San Francisco. Cf. *CBQ* 47 (1985), p. 684.

77. *Weisheitsbuch*, pp. 403-405. From this comparison it appears that John lacks the first feeding miracle in Wis 16,2, but, by contrast, gives two healing miracles (pp. 403-406). Cp. *Passafeier*, p. 268.

78. With reference to the order of chapters 5 and 6 Ziener remarks: "In diesem Schema ist vielleicht die sonst schwer verständliche Stellung des sechsten Kapitels (Brotvermehrung) im Johannesevangelium *hinter* dem fünften (Krankenheilung am Teich des Bethesda) begründet" (*Weisheitsbuch*, p. 405 n. 2).

79. *Ibid.*, pp. 405-406; *Passafeier*, p. 272.

80. First, the miraculous help to the person in need is described. Second, the reader makes the transition from the level of the natural world to the spiritual level: what God (Jesus) does for the worldly, he does always for the spiritual. Finally, these good deeds are attributed in the Book of Wisdom to Wisdom (10,25–11,1) or to the Word of God (16,12.26; 18,22), and in John to Christ, the Word (λόγος) who is Bread and who satisfies hunger and quenches thirst, who is the Light, the Life, and the Resurrection (*Weisheitsbuch*, pp. 406-407). Ziener explores this structure for each miracle story (pp. 407-415). For example, in the bread miracle we observe: (1) the miracle (Wis 16,20; Jn 6,1-13); (2) the transition from the natural to the spiritual level (Wis 16,26; Jn 6,27); (3) the theological interpretation (Wis 16,26; Jn 6,35; cp. 6,48.51).

In his article *Johannesevangelium und urchristliche Passafeier* (1958)[81], Ziener combined this Old Testament interpretation of the Johannine miracle stories with the semeia hypothesis. Since the agreement between John and Wisdom is not so great, the exegete cannot posit a direct dependence of John upon Wisdom[82]. Ziener thinks that the relationship is best explained by a common *Vorlage*, namely, a Passover Haggada in which the Exodus miracles have been joined with Jewish speculations on the Word and Wisdom. The author of the Fourth Gospel was not directly in contact with the Jewish Passover Haggada used in Wisdom, but indirectly via a Christian Haggada, which was used in the Easter ceremonies of the Quartodecimans[83]. The signs source was presumably a Christian Passover Haggada that John employed for the redaction of his miracle stories[84]. In view of Schweizer's and Ruckstuhl's studies on Johannine style, one can hardly reconstruct the source because the evangelist thoroughly reworked it, but that does not mean that it did not exist[85]. According to Ziener, two considerations prove the existence of the miracle source. First, the "many formal agreements" between the wine miracle and the first Markan bread miracle indicate that miracle stories in the form of the wine miracle existed before John[86]. A second indication is the systematic numbering of the signs[87]. Ziener also proposes that the Logos hymn functioned as the introduction and a key to

81. See above, p. 87 n. 73. Ziener describes the celebration of the Passover feast in primitive Christianity (pp. 263-266), the relation between Wisdom and John (pp. 266-270), and the relation between John and the primitive Christian Passover, which is important for the history of the semeia hypothesis (pp. 270-274).

82. *Ibid.*, pp. 270-271.

83. "Es ist denkbar, dass christliche Gemeinden für ihre Passafeier nach dem Vorbild der jüdischen Passa-Haggada eine christliche Haggada schufen, in welcher den Exoduswundern die Wunder Jesu als Entsprechung und Erfüllung gegenübergestellt wurden. Von dieser christlichen Passa-Haggada ausgehend und in ihrem Geiste hätte der Evangelist sein Evangelium verfasst" (p. 271). In so doing, the evangelist had the same intention as the early Christian Passover Haggada: in connection with Ex 12, he wanted to present Jesus' saving activity as the completion and fulfillment of the delivery from Egypt. In the Passion narrative he makes it clear that Jesus is the Passover lamb, and in the miracle stories he portrays Jesus' activity in parallel with the rescue from slavery in Egypt (p. 270).

84. *Ibid.*, pp. 271-274. The Christian Passover Haggada contained the Logos hymn from the Prologue, some miracle stories (e.g., 2,1-11; 4,43-54; 5,1-9a; 6,1-13; 9,1-5), which, as in Wisdom (e.g., 16,12-13.26), were provided with a short interpretation, and perhaps also a Passion narrative in which Jesus is presented as the Passover lamb (p. 273).

85. *Ibid.*, pp. 271-272, esp. 271 n. 26, 272 n. 27.

86. "Bei einem Vergleich zwischen dem Bericht über das Weinwunder in Joh 2 und der Darstellung des 1. Brotwunders bei Mk zeigen sich so viele formale Entsprechungen zwischen beiden Berichten, dass man von einem 'joh'-Stil innerhalb des Markusevangeliums sprechen kann" (p. 272; with reference to LOHMEYER, *Das Evangelium nach Markus*, 1937, p. 129).

87. *Ibid.*, p. 272.

interpretation: the Word that performed the Exodus miracles has become flesh in Jesus; Jesus' miracles are clearly signs of his Messiahship: he is the Son of God, the Word[88].

We may note here that Douglas K. CLARK, *Signs and Wisdom in John*, in *CBQ* 45 (1983) 201-209, without reference to Ziener, has also defended the literary relationship between Wisdom and the Fourth Gospel. He proposes that "the Gospel according to John is laid out according to the same basic pattern as the *relecture* of Exodus ... in Wisdom 11–19, viz., seven (six-plus-one) *sèmeia*, with the seventh sign both fulfilling and surpassing the first six which point to it" (p. 205). Furthermore, "the contents of many, if not all, of the signs in John correspond in a surprising way to the contents of their exact equivalents in Wisdom. Signs 1, 4, 5, and, of course, 7 show strong correspondence. Sign 3 shows some verbal connection, while sign 2 is more remotely connected to its counterpart in Wisdom" (pp. 205-208, esp. 206): (1) Wis 11,5-14 (undrinkable water from Nile; drinkable water in desert), cp. Jn 2,1-11; (2) Wis 11,15 + 16,1-4 (animals sent as a plague: unappetizing frogs; animals sent as a blessing: delicious quails), cp. Jn 4,46-54; (3) Wis 16,5-14 (animals that kill: locusts and flies; animals that save: bronze serpent), cp. Jn 5,1-17; (4) Wis 16,15-29 (destructive creation: fire burns food; salvific creation: manna resists fire), cp. Jn 6,1-66; (5) Wis 17,1–18,4 (captivity in darkness; pillar of light in darkness), cp. Jn 9,1-41; (6) Wis 18,5-25 (death of first-born; Aaron stops destroyer), cp. Jn 11,1-44; (7) Wis 19,1-9 (drowning in the sea; passing through sea), cp. Jn 18–20.

For Clark, Wisdom may possibly be considered one of the principal sources (pp. 201-202, 208). He notes also that the Prologue is to be compared with Wisdom: "John's portrayal of Jesus in these *sèmeia* consistently attributes to him what Wisdom attributes to God's *logos*. Seen in this light, the *logos*-christology of John's prologue appears more congruent with the rest of the Fourth Gospel than might otherwise be the case" (p. 209). Unlike G. Ziener, however, he does not attach his source to the semeia hypothesis. On Clark, see SLOYAN, *What Are They Saying about John?*, 1991, pp. 83-84.

On Clark's description of the relationship between Wisdom and the Fourth Gospel, Martin SCOTT, *Sophia and the Johannine Jesus* (JSNT SS, 71), Sheffield, 1992 (diss. Durham, 1990; dir. J.D.G. Dunn), pp. 166-168, esp. 168, remarks: "some of the comparisons he makes are rather strained, especially 'signs' two and three, suggesting that in his enthusiasm to make the point he has stretched the evidence further than it is possible to go with any security". Discussing the number of signs (pp. 165-166, esp. 166), Scott compares Clark's counting of the seven signs, the seventh being the greatest σημεῖον of all, i.e., the hour of Jesus' glorification, his death and resurrection, with Fortna's reconstruction of the Gospel of Signs, where the "resurrection of Jesus was seen as the 'last and greatest of his christological deeds'" (FORTNA, *Predecessor*, 1988, p. 208). Regarding the origin of the Fourth Gospel, Scott presupposes (p. 35) that "the present form of the Gospel is the result of a process of redaction, which may be possible to point to at specific places in the Gospel, but which is now generally impossible to reconstruct fully", and, not without hesitation, he

88. For the parallels with Wisdom in the Prologue, see p. 271 n. 24.

accepts the signs source for 2,1-11: "The text itself seems to be based on a traditional miracle story, possibly from a 'signs source', which has been the object of redactional activity". His aim, however, is not "to discuss the merits or demerits of such a theory, but it may provide an important insight into the way in which the final compiler of the Gospel understood both the miracle itself and the role of Jesus' mother in it" (p. 176).

Heinz NOETZEL, in a posthumously published study (1960)[89], assigned Jn 2,1-11 to the signs source, without going into further detail[90]. He rejected interpretations based on the Dionysus cult (J. Grill, R. Bultmann) and referred to the Jewish symbolism of wine as the messianic gift and to the christological and eschatological contrast between old and new[91].

In the opinion of George W. BUCHANAN (1968)[92] John used a document containing fourteen miracles of Jesus, but employed only seven signs[93]. In this source John the Baptist is presented as Elijah, who accomplished seven miracles, and Jesus as Elisha, who received twice as many spiritual gifts as Elijah and performed fourteen miracles[94].

89. H. NOETZEL, *Christus und Dionysos. Bemerkungen zum religionsgeschichtlichen Hintergrund von Johannes 2,1-11* (AzT, 1), Stuttgart, 1960. K. von Rabenau edited the study of Noetzel, who died on April 11, 1959 (see p. 5: *Zum Geleit*). – Cf. SMITMANS, *Das Weinwunder von Kana*, 1966, esp. pp. 33-34, 44-45; HEEKERENS, *Zeichen-Quelle*, 1984, pp. 97, 98. For a critique of Noetzel's hypothesis, see LINNEMANN, in *NTS* 20 (1973-74) 408-418. Against Noetzel, Linnemann (esp. p. 418) argues that the similarities between Jn 2,1-11 and the Dionysus legend do not have to be explained by the categories of borrowing and identification. Rather, they should be seen as part of a dialogue between the Christian community and the devotees of Dionysus. While both Jesus and Dionysus provide wine, only with the crucified one is there fullness of life. – I can note here that Peter STUHLMACHER, in a review of Noetzel's book, accepts the semeia hypothesis; cf. *VF* 1960-62 (ed. 1965) 242-243, esp. p. 243.

90. "In welchem Sinne nun aber der Evangelist dieses Stück aus der Zeichen-Quelle ... umgestaltet bzw. erweitert hat, ..." (p. 7). Cp. pp. 22, 23, 26, 39, 43. Noetzel does not discuss the semeia hypothesis itself: "Es soll hier nicht in diese Debatte eingegriffen werden, sondern nur gefragt werden, wie das Quellenstück beschaffen sein müsste, wenn der Dionysoskult hierhinter stünde" (p. 22).

91. According to GRILL, *Untersuchungen*, II, 1923, pp. 134-138, Jesus would also have been portrayed as Dionysus in the second Cana miracle. BULTMANN, *Johannes*, 1941, p. 151 n. 6 (ET: 1971, p. 205 n. 5) rejects this: "*Grills* Vermutung is überscharfsinnig". For the Old Testament background of the wine miracle according to Noetzel, see pp. 39-56. Bultmann's dating, 5-6 January, which he employs as the decisive argument, is uncertain and hardly relevant, because the miracle story has been secondarily connected with the Dionysus feast on the basis of local customs in Egypt which were taken up by the primitive church (pp. 29-38).

92. G.W. BUCHANAN, *The Samaritan Origin of the Gospel of John*, in NEUSNER (ed.), *Religions in Antiquity*, 1968, pp. 149-175. – Cf. BROWN, *Jesus and Elisha*, 1971, pp. 93-94 (see above, p. 60 n. 109); KYSAR, *Fourth Evangelist*, 1975, pp. 160-163; HEEKERENS, *Zeichen-Quelle*, 1984, p. 105.

93. *Samaritan Origin*, pp. 166-173, esp. 172.

94. "The obvious question at this point is: if Jesus was interpreted as the new Elisha in the Gospel of John, why did he not perform fourteen miracles as Elisha had done. The answer is that originally the 'signs' section in the Gospel of John probably existed in a

We can also mention the study of Günter REIM (1974)[95] on the Old
Testament background in the Gospel of John. In his view, John made
use of a signs source as well as a "Fourth Synoptic Gospel"[96]. To the
signs source belonged: 1,19-51; 2,1-11; 4,46-54; 6,1-21; 9,1-41; 11,1-
44; 12,37-41; 20,30-31; and the travel notices in chapters 2, 4, 7 and
10[97]. Beginning with John the Baptist, the source intended to demonstrate, with the help of the miracles, that Jesus was the Messiah, the

separate document which included fourteen stories attributed to Jesus. This then was later
abridged; the number of miracles reduced in half, the prologue, the passion narrative, and
the synoptic pericope (John: 7,53–8,11) added to make a Gospel out of a document
patterned originally after I and II Kings, or at least the section of those books containing
the Elijah-Elisha narratives" (pp. 171-172). On pp. 167-168 the author gives a table of
similarities between John and the Elijah-Elisha cycle, on pp. 168-170 he compares Jn 2,1-
11 with 1 Kgs 17,1-6 and 2 Kgs 4,1-7; Jn 4,46-54 with 2 Kgs 5,1-14; Jn 6,4-14 with 2
Kgs 4,42-44; and Jn 11,1-44 with 1 Kgs 17,17-24; 2 Kgs 4,18-37. He also refers to the
similarity of the miracle stories of chapters 5 and 9 with 2 Kgs 5. The walking upon the
sea may recall 2 Kgs 2,8.14. – A similar comparison was drawn for the Markan
tradition by HARTMANN, *Der Aufbau des Markusevangeliums*, 1936, and applied to John
by HEISING, in *ZKT* 86 (1964) 80-96; *Die Botschaft der Brotvermehrung*, Stuttgart, 1966
(DT: 1968); see KONINGS, *Joh. verhaal*, II, 1969, pp. 364, 392; III, 1972, pp. 176-178.
    95. G. REIM, *Studien zum alttestamentlichen Hintergrund des Johannesevangeliums*
(SNTS MS, 22), Cambridge, 1974 (diss. Oxford, 1967; dir. G.D. Kilpatrick). On the signs
source ("Semeiaquelle", "Wunderbüchlein", or "Semeiabüchlein"), see also pp. 217-220
("Untersuchungen zur Sprache der Semeiaquelle"), 233-241 (on Bultmann, Schnackenburg, Wilkens, and Fortna), 245-246, 270, 272. – Reviews: cf. VAN BELLE, no. 1397. See
also SCHNACKENBURG, *Forschung*, 1974, pp. 276-277; *Entwicklung*, 1977, p. 25 (= 1984,
p. 15); KYSAR, *Fourth Evangelist*, 1975, pp. 59-61, 105-107; SMALLEY, *John*, 1978, p. 64
n. 120; HEEKERENS, *Zeichen-Quelle*, 1984, pp. 97, 99; SMITH, *John among the Gospels*,
1992, pp. 73-74.
    96. *Hintergrund*, pp. 206-216: the signs source (pp. 207-209), the Synoptic-like mate-
rial in John, "the Fourth Synoptic Gospel" (pp. 209-216). – To this Fourth Synoptic
Gospel, which the evangelist already possessed in written form (p. 210), belonged, among
other things, the entry into Jerusalem, the cleansing of the temple and the question about
Jesus' authority, the anointing at Bethany, the passion and resurrection narratives
(p. 211). Moreover, it contained material that is lacking in Mark: the footwashing, the
piercing with a lance, the appearance to Mary Magdalene, to the disciples and Thomas,
and material from chapter 21 (p. 212). Also contained were 1,23; 3,22ff.; 4,1-42; 5,1-16;
6,69 (p. 213). According to Reim, this Fourth Synoptic Gospel is older than Mark
(p. 215). John's Gospel existed originally as an "erweitertes Wunderbüchlein" (p. 241)
and was later transformed into its present form with the help of the Fourth Synoptic
Gospel (pp. 233-246, esp. 245-246). – For other studies by Reim, see *Bibliography*. Note
esp. his reconstruction of the "Semeiaquelle" for Jn 9 in *BZ* 22 (1978) 245-253, pp. 249-
250: vv. 1-2 (without αὐτοῦ λέγοντες). 3 (without ἀλλ᾽ ἵνα ... ἐν αὐτῷ). 4 (τοῦ θεοῦ
instead of τοῦ πέμψαντός με; without ἕως ... ἐργάζεσθαι). 6. 7 (without ὃ ἑρμηνεύεται ἀπεσταλμένος). 8. 10 (without οὖν). 11 (without ὁ ἄνθρωπος ὁ λεγόμενος). 13-
15. 18-21. 24. 31 (preceded by ἀπεκρίθη οὖν ἐκεῖνος of v. 25). 34. 35 (without σὺ
πιστεύεις ... τοῦ ἀνθρώπου;). 39 (without καὶ εἶπεν ὁ Ἰησοῦς). For Reim's hypothesis, see also his most recent article in *BZ* 36 (1992) 235-240, p. 240 n. 31.
    97. *Hintergrund*, pp. 208-209. The evangelist made a free choice from the signs
source (cf. p. 239).

Prophet, and especially the Son of God[98]. Reim himself marked the difference between his semeia hypothesis and that of Bultmann: the source does not begin with 1,35 but with 1,19; the account of the Samaritan woman and the healing of the paralytic do not come from the signs source but from a Fourth Synoptic Gospel; nor did 7,19-24 belong to the signs source[99]. All the miracle stories from the source have references to four stories of the Elijah-Elisha cycle, namely, the visit of Elijah to the widow of Zarephath (1 Kgs 17,8-24), the divine ordeal on Mount Carmel (1 Kgs 18,20-46), the multiplication of the loaves (2 Kgs 4,42-44) and the healing of Naaman (2 Kgs 5,1-26)[100]. Such references are missing in two miracle stories: the healing of the paralytic and the walking on the sea. The first does not belong to the signs source; the second does: it was already connected with the bread-miracle early in the Christian tradition[101].

IV. DISCUSSION ON THE CONTENT OF THE SIGNS SOURCE

Bultmann's semeia hypothesis was accepted but limited to miracles by Willi MARXSEN (1963)[102] and Reginald H. FULLER (1965)[103], who do

98. *Ibid.*, pp. 207-208. In reaction to Ziener (see above, pp. 87-90), Reim notes that only the following passages are "wirkliche Entsprechungen zum Weisheitsbuch": 3,14-15; 6,27; 7,37-38 (cf., respectively, Wis 16,5-7; 16,26; 11,4-7) (p. 196).

99. *Ibid.*, p. 209.

100. Reim (pp. 156-158) indicates the following parallels: 2,4 (1 Kgs 17,18); 2,5 (1 Kgs 17,15); 4,50 (1 Kgs 17,23); 6,9.11.13 (2 Kgs 4,42-44); 9,7 (2 Kgs 5,10.14); 11,41-42 (1 Kgs 18,37).

101. *Ibid.*, p. 158 (see esp. n. 89). Perhaps Luke, whose miracle stories may demonstrate a good number of parallels with the Elijah-Elisha cycle, used a similar collection of miracles (pp. 158-159 n. 90).

102. W. MARXSEN, *Einleitung in das Neue Testament. Eine Einführung in ihre Probleme*, Gütersloh, 1963, pp. 212-213 (ET: 1968). – Marxsen accepts the existence of the signs source without criticism. He points to the following characteristics and arguments: the numbering, the conclusion of the gospel (20,30-31; preceded in the source by 12,37), the heightening of the miraculous and the emphasis on the materiality of the miracles. Nothing indicates that Marxsen assigns other narrative material to the miracle book besides the miracle stories. In the signs source, the miracles are intended to arouse faith (2,11; 4,53; 6,14; 7,31; 11,45.47b-48; 12,37-38; 20,31). In the redactional commentaries (see, e.g., 2,23-25; 4,48) and especially in the conversation with Nicodemus, the evangelist corrects this traditional view of miracles (e.g., 3,2) by reference to being born from above (3,3) and the Spirit (3,5ff.). For the evangelist, the miracles are not so much legitimations of faith in Jesus, as signs of his person, and faith originates upon the basis of the word and preaching of Jesus. Marxsen doubts the existence of the *Offenbarungsreden* (p. 213). – Cf. KYSAR, *Fourth Evangelist*, 1975, p. 16 n. 13; SCHNELLE, *Christologie*, 1987, p. 105[-106] n. 105 (ET: 1992, p. 91[-92] n. 105).

103. R.H. FULLER, *Interpreting the Miracles*, London, 1963; ⁴1968, pp. 88-96 (GT: 1967; DT: 1971, pp. 86-93). – Fuller gives the numbering and the conclusion

not include the other narrative material that Bultmann had ascribed to the signs source (e.g., the call of the disciples and the encounter with the Samaritan woman). In the fourth, fully revised edition of his *Einleitung* (1978), Marxsen further confined the certain content of the source to the two Cana miracles and the conclusion (12,37; 20,30)[104].

The influential Catholic Johannine scholar Rudolf SCHNACKENBURG also restricted the signs source to the miracles. In the article *Johannes-evangelium* (1960)[105], where he remarked that style criticism should

(12,37-38; 20,30-31) as arguments. He does not know whether the evangelist employed all the stories from the *Book of Signs*, but in any case the seven miracle stories come from it (2,1-11; 4,46-54; 5,1-9; 6,1-13; 6,16-21; 9,1-34; 11,1-44). We can probably assign the following verses to the evangelist: 2,6 (with allusion to the Jewish rites of purification); 4,46 (cross-reference to Cana); 4,48; 5,17.18b.19-47; 6,4 (the allusion to "feast of the Jews"); 6,14 (qualification of the prophet as one who would come into the world); 6,26-65; 9,3b-5.16b.22-23.29-34 (without καὶ ἐξέβαλον αὐτὸν ἔξω).35-37; 11,4.7-10.16.20-27.40.41b-42 (p. 89; DT: 1971, p. 87). Fuller also notes the emphasis upon the miraculous (2,6; 4,46; 5,5; 6,7; 9,1; 11,39), and thinks that "the Book of Signs seems to have been compiled at a later stage of development" (p. 90; DT: p. 88); dependence upon Mark is rejected (p. 91 n. 2; DT: 1971, p. 89 n. 2; with reference to Gardner-Smith, 1938). Further, the miracle stories from the source are full of features which are common in pagan wonder stories, but in the signs source they are real signs of a Christian message: "They show Jesus' Messianic power which was still being manifest in the continuing life of the Christian Church" (pp. 92-96, esp. 96; DT: 1971, pp. 90-93, esp. 93). – The evangelist reacts against faith based on miracles (4,48; 2,23-25; 20,29). This miracle faith is not necessarily bad, for it can lead to real faith (Nicodemus, the official, Thomas; cf. 14,11), and it is in any case better than total unbelief. But it is only a second possibility, "a second best" (pp. 96-109, esp. 99; DT: 1971, pp. 93-104, esp. 95-96). – In *The Foundations of New Testament Christology* (Lutterworth Library), London, 1965 (= 1972), p. 228, as well as in *A Critical Introduction to the New Testament* (Studies in Theology, 55), London, 1966, p. 170, Fuller refers to his analysis of the book of signs in *Interpreting*. – On Fuller, see KYSAR, *Fourth Evangelist*, 1975, p. 16 n. 13; *ANRW* II, 25/3, 1985, p. 2400 n. 42; SCHNELLE, *Christologie*, 1987, p. 105[-106] n. 105 (ET: 1992, p. 91[-92] n. 105).

104. *Einleitung*, ⁴1978, p. 251: "Welche von den nachfolgenden Wundergeschichten der Zeichenquelle entnommen sind und welche Johannes aus anderen Traditionen kannte, lässt sich nicht sicher sagen".

105. R. SCHNACKENBURG, *Johannesevangelium*, in *LTK*² 5 (1960) 1101-1105, c. 1103. – In *Das erste Wunder Jesu (Joh 2,1-11)*, Freiburg, 1950, p. 5, referring to the counting of signs in 2,11 and 4,54, he speaks vaguely of a special tradition: "Der Evangelist scheint bei den Kana-Erzählungen einen besonderen Überlieferungsstrom zu folgen". – On Schnackenburg, see KONINGS, *Joh. verhaal*, I, 1969, pp. 120-122; SELONG, *Cleansing*, I, 1971, pp. 155-157, 171-172; TEEPLE, *Origin*, 1974, p. 49; KYSAR, *Fourth Evangelist*, 1975, pp. 17-37; *ANRW* II, 25/3, 1985, pp. 2397, 2399, 2400, 2453; COTHENET, *Le qua-trième évangile*, 1977, pp. 112, 132, 189-190; *L'évangile selon saint Jean*, 1984, p. 50; SMALLEY, *John*, 1978, p. 115; HOEFERKAMP, *Relationship*, 1978, p. 37-41; CORSANI, *I miracoli*, 1983, p. 22, and *passim*; HEEKERENS, *Zeichen-Quelle*, 1984, pp. 12, 14, 15, 18, 20, 25, and *passim*; J.A.T. ROBINSON, *Priority*, 1985, p. 21 n. 75, and *passim*; BEUTLER, *ANRW* II, 25/3, 1985, pp. 2527-2528; VAN BELLE, *Parenthèses*, 1985, pp. 47-50; BITTNER, *Jesu Zeichen*, 1987, pp. 3 n. 6 (on p. 4), 6 n. 9, 9-11; SCHNELLE, *Christologie*, 1987, p. 105[-106] n. 105 (ET: 1992, p. 91[-92] n. 105); KUHN, *Christologie*, 1988,

make the exegete critical of source theories, he did not take a position on the semeia hypothesis. In 1964, however, in a thorough study of 4,46-54, he admitted a signs source[106]. The two Cana miracles, which are numbered, contain few Johannine style characteristics and perhaps followed one another in the source with 2,12 as a transitional verse[107]. Because the evangelist separated these two accounts, he had to make some changes[108]. Schnackenburg demonstrates the Johannine character of 4,48-49 and rejects the position of Boismard who attributed these verses, together with 4,51-53, to Luke[109]. John's account reports the same event as Mt 8,5-13 par. Lk 7,1-10; the differences originate from the tradition-variant in the signs source, not from John[110]. The special relation between John and Luke is to be located at the level of sources[111]. In fact, Schnackenburg considered the two Cana narratives to be the starting point of the semeia hypothesis[112]. John did not employ all the narratives from the source. This explains why the numbering was not continued; he repeatedly mentions "many signs", so that the reader may assume that he has employed only a few significant examples[113]. Contrary to Faure and Bultmann, Schnackenburg regarded only 20,30 as the conclusion of the signs source[114]; the evangelist is responsible for

pp. 46-47 (Jn 1,35-51); MARCHADOUR, *Lazare*, 1988, pp. 48-50 (Jn 11); WAGNER, *Aufer-stehung*, 1988, pp. 69-71 (Jn 11,1–12,19); WÖLLNER, *Zeichenglaube*, 1988, pp. 8-9; NEIRYNCK, *John 21*, 1990, pp. 322 n. 6, 323 n. 12, 329 n. 31, 333-334 n. 49 (= 1991, pp. 602 n. 5, 603 n. 12, 608 n. 31, 613 n. 49); SLOYAN, *What Are They Saying about John?*, 1991, pp. 24-27; SCHMITHALS, *Johannesevangelium*, 1992, pp. 185-186; SMITH, *John among the Gospels*, 1992, pp. 66-67.

106. *Zur Traditionsgeschichte von Joh 4,46-54*, in *BZ* 8 (1964) 58-88, pp. 62-67, 76-82 (on the signs source).

107. *Ibid.*, pp. 63-64.

108. In 4,46-54, Schnackenburg attributes to the evangelist (besides vv. 48-49): vv. 46a-47a (from ἀκούσας to Γαλιλαίαν), in v. 47b καταβῇ καί, in v. 51a ἤδη δὲ αὐτοῦ καταβαίνοντος, in v. 52 ἐχθές, in v. 54 the last words after ὁ Ἰησοῦς (p. 64).

109. *Ibid.*, pp. 67-70. For the view of Boismard, see *RB* 54 (1947) 473-501, p. 500; 69 (1962) 185-211, pp. 194-200; 70 (1963) 5-42, p. 5. On Boismard, see also above, pp. 56[-57] n. 89 and below, pp. 271-276.

110. The *Vorlage* of John did not contain the word on faith, which is essential in Q. Other less important differences are: (1) βασιλικός in place of ἑκατόνταρχος; (2) a Jew in place of a Gentile; (3) the encounter in Cana instead of in Capernaum; (4) υἱός (cp. 4,51: παῖς) in place of παῖς (Mt) or δοῦλος (Lk); (5) the sickness is a fever, while in Matthew it is paralysis; (6) only in John is it announced to the father while he is returning that the son has been healed (*Traditionsgeschichte*, pp. 72-76). There are also a good number of similarities: (1) the sick person stays in Capernaum; (2) the man who seeks the healing is in the service of King Herod Antipas, as a centurion or as a court official; (3) he is a relative of the sick person; (4) ἐρωτάω in both Lk 7,3 and Jn 4,47; (5) faith is emphasized in all three stories; (6) in Lk 7,2 and Jn 4,47 the sick person is at the point of death; (7) in Mt 8,13 and Jn 4,52-53a the hour of the healing is established (pp. 71-72).

111. *Ibid.*, pp. 83-88.

112. *Ibid.*, p. 77.

113. *Ibid.*, p. 77. Cf. Jn 2,23; 3,3; 6,2.14; 7,31; 9,16: 10,41; 11,47.

114. *Ibid.*, pp. 78-79. Schnackenburg leaves the possibility open that the μαθηταί

12,37[115]. Also 5,1-9a; 9,1-3.6-7 and the *Vorlage* of chapter 11 are from the source. In the source, the healings of the paralytic and the blind man followed immediately upon one another and the raising of Lazarus was the climax of the three signs in Jerusalem[116]. Perhaps the multiplication of the loaves and the walking on the sea also belonged to the signs source[117]. The source could even have had two miraculous draughts of fish: one at the beginning of Jesus' ministry and one among the resurrection appearances[118]. On the basis of 6,2 one could also conclude that the source contained more healings in Galilee[119]. The miracles had no deep symbolic or christological meaning in the source. The evangelist took up the σημεῖα but gave them a deeper content; he critically opposed faith based on miracles. This is especially obvious in 6,26 where Jesus reproaches the people for not having seen the signs. In the view of the evangelist, the sign has an eminent christological significance: the believer experiences the glory of the Son of God who has become man (1,14; 2,11; 11,4.40). When the sign is not grasped in this way, the evangelist calls it into question (e.g., 2,23; 4,45.48)[120].

In his commentary as well (1965, 1972, 1975, 1984)[121], Schnackenburg defends the semeia theory as he described it in his 1964 article,

---

were already mentioned in the source expressly as witnesses (p. 79). See, however, below, p. 98 n. 125.

115. He advances the following reasons: (1) The entire passage 12,37-43 is a reflection by the evangelist on the unbelief of the Jews at the conclusion of Jesus' public ministry. (2) Jn 12,37 is closely connected with the quotation from Isaiah in 12,38 and can hardly have existed independently. (3) According to 20,30, the source appears not to have considered unbelief, but had an interest only in the positive significance of the miracles. (4) The immediate connection of 12,37 and 20,30 is improbable: in 12,37 τοσαῦτα σημεῖα suffice to portray unbelief as incomprehensible; thereafter, a reference to "many other signs ... which are not recorded in this book" would only be disturbing. (5) As for stylistic considerations, ἐνώπιον appears only in 20,30, while elsewhere the gospel has ἔμπροσθεν (1,15.30; 3,28; 10,4; 12,37). To be sure, ἐνώπιον is used in 1 Jn 3,22; 3 Jn 6, so this is not a clear stylistic criterion. (6) Decisive, however, is an internal theological argument: for John, the σημεῖα belong to the time of Jesus' public ministry; after ch. 12 nothing more is said of them. The signs are an expression of revelatory activity by the incarnate Son of God; for that reason they are to be experienced externally, should be performed in public, and are undeniable (ch. 9 and 11), even though their unique meaning is accessible only for those who believe. It should be obvious, then, that the evangelist, by composing 12,37, wants to express his own understanding of σημεῖα: the significance of "signs" in the activity of the earthly Jesus and for the "world" (*Traditionsgeschichte*, p. 78).

116. *Ibid.*, pp. 79-80.

117. *Ibid.*, pp. 80-82.

118. *Ibid.*, p. 87. The numbering in 21,14 should not be connected with 2,11 and 4,54 but with 20,19-23 and 26-29; it comes from the redactor (cf. Bultmann).

119. *Ibid.*, pp. 64-65.

120. *Ibid.*, pp. 65-66.

121. *Das Johannesevangelium* (HTKNT, 4/1-4), 4 vols., Freiburg - Basel - Wien, 1965, 1971, 1975, 1984 (ET: vols. I-III, 1968, 1979, 1982). For the semeia hypothesis, see esp. I, pp. 51-54 (ET: pp. 64-67) and the references given in note 124 on p. 98. See

without neglecting to refer to its hypothetical character. The hypothesis appears to be the best way to explain the origin of the Johannine narratives[122]. Once again he begins with the two Cana stories[123], and from

also I, pp. 8, 17, 19, 38-39, 59, 345 (ET: pp. 19, 28, 50-51, 72, 515); II, pp. 303, 456, 466 (ET: pp. 239, 363, 371); III, pp. 234, 357 (ET: pp. 205, 304). – Reviews: cf. VAN BELLE, no. 1999.

122. *Johannesevangelium*, I, p. 51 (ET: p. 64): "Am besten begründet ist die Annahme einer Quelle für die *Wunderberichte*. Auch wenn Bultmanns Quellenscheidungshypothese im ganzen nicht überzeugen kann, bleiben seine verstreuten Beobachtungen zugunsten einer 'σημεῖα-Quelle' beachtlich". Cp. p. 53 (ET: p. 66): "So lässt sich, freilich nur hypothetisch, für die joh. Erzählungen eine Quelle eruieren, die einfache Wunderberichte ohne Anspruch auf eine tiefere theologische Deutung geboten hätte, sicher erheblich mehr als die sieben im Joh-Ev erzählten"; p. 54 (ET: p. 67): "Wenn die σημεῖα-Quelle einige Wahrscheinlichkeit besitzt, so ist eine *Logien- oder Redenquelle* abzulehnen"; p. 59 (ET: p. 72): "Mit einiger Wahrscheinlichkeit darf man die Verwendung einer schriftlichen 'σημεῖα-Quelle' behaupten"; III, p. 464 (ET: p. 388): "Die Annahme einer Semeia-Quelle, für die ich mich schon im I. Band entschieden hatte, wurde zu stärkerer Gewissheit, auch durch neue, in der Zwischenzeit erschienene Untersuchungen. Allerdings ist über ihren Umfang noch keine Übereinstimmung erzielt". – In his *Entwicklung und Stand der johanneischen Forschung seit 1935*, in DE JONGE (ed.), *L'évangile de Jean*, 1977 (²1987), pp. 19-44, esp. 25 (= 1984, pp. 9-32, esp. 15) Schnakkenburg reacted against Fortna's rearrangements and the acceptance of the passion narrative, resurrection stories and other narrative material into his Gospel of Signs. – According to Schnackenburg, the evangelist used a good deal of traditional material. It is difficult to prove that he knew the Synoptics in written form; he perhaps knew a Synoptic tradition that was only orally handed on, and had some *traditionsgeschichtlich* relation with the Lukan traditions. In addition to the (written) signs source, the evangelist would also have employed the following traditions: independent traditional narratives, logia, and liturgical or kerygmatic traditions (e.g., the Prologue; 6,31-50.51-58). All these traditions would, for the most part, have been oral. The evangelist gave them form and structure in the Fourth Gospel; he is responsible for the typical Johannine theology. Various individual traditions, which originate with the evangelist (3,31-36.13-21; ch. 15–17), were inserted by a redactor. The redactor is likewise responsible for ch. 21 (in which he probably used the signs source for the miraculous draught of fish) and the present order of the chapters; originally, ch. 5 followed ch. 6 and 7,15-24 followed 5,47. He further added a few small glosses to the gospel: 4,2 or 4,1-2; 4,44; 6,22-23; 7,39b; 11,2 and perhaps 12,6 (*Johannesevangelium*, I, pp. 59-60; ET: pp. 72-74).

123. In the Introduction to vol. I (p. 52; ET: p. 64), Schnackenburg notes that the numbering in 2,11 and 4,54 may certainly be attributed to the evangelist (cf. HEEKERENS, *Zeichen-Quelle*, 1984, p. 25: "R. Schnackenburg [hält] die Zählung in Joh 2,11 und 4,54 *nicht* für ursprünglich"; cp. p. 24 n. 26). He refers to Michaelis's explanation that the numbering is not continued because the evangelist relied on his reader "to go on counting himself after 2:11 and 4:54 till he reached the number seven, and then recognize that the significance of the *semeia* included their being seven" (cf. MICHAELIS, *Einleitung*, 1946, p. 111; see above, p. 43). Schnackenburg replies to Michaelis that it is not easy to understand why the evangelist, who "is quite ready to indicate numbers", did not suggest this symbolism more strongly and he proposes a readier explanation: the evangelist found the first two miracles already joined (cf. 2,12, as transition) and wished to emphasize them as the "beginning" of the revelation of Jesus's glory by his miracles (I, p. 52; ET: p. 65). However, in his commentary on 2,11 and 4,54, he also considers the possibility of attributing the numbering of signs to the source. On 2,11: "Die Schlussbemerkung, die wenigstens mit der zweiten und dritten Aussage die Hand des Evangelisten verrät" (I, p. 338; ET: p. 334). On 4,54: "Die Abschlussbemerkung des Evangelisten"

them extends the source to the multiplication of loaves, the walking upon the sea, the healings of the paralytic and the man born blind, the raising of Lazarus and the story of the catch of fish[124]. He thinks it possible that it was more extensive, as would appear from (1) the summaries, where more signs, which the evangelist claims to know, are mentioned (2,23; 3,2; 6,2.26; 7,31; 11,47; 12,37; 20,30); (2) the important role allotted to the miracles in the discussions with the Jews (7,31; 9,16.30-33; 10,41; 11,47); and (3) the final remark (20,30), which mentions "signs" more with reference to the entire gospel, and especially chapters 1–12, than to the resurrection appearances[125]. Here, too, Schnackenburg ascribes no other narrative material to the signs source (ctr. Bultmann). In his literary analysis of the miracle stories he gives attention to the agreements and differences with the Synoptics[126],

(I, p. 500; ET: p. 469); but on p. 501 (ET: p. 470) he attributes only the words after ὁ Ἰησοῦς to the evangelist. Against Fortna, Schnackenburg maintains that 21,14 is "entirely editorial" (III, p. 412; ET: p. 346). See now also *Die Person Jesu Christi im Spiegel der vier Evangelien* (HTKNT Supplementband, 4), Freiburg - Basel - Wien, 1993, p. 268: "Ob den 'Zeichen' eine σημεῖα-Quelle zugrundeliegt, ist umstritten. Manches spricht dafür, wie die Zählung der ersten beiden 'Zeichen' und der Rückblick in 12,37f und 20,30f. Aber die Zählung der 'Zeichen' und der Umfang sind nicht klar (wie steht es mit dem Seewandel?). Vielmehr muss man mit der Aufnahme und Verarbeitung von bestimmten 'Zeichen'-Erzählungen durch den Evangelisten bzw. die Schlussredaktion rechnen. Tradition und Redaktion, geschichtliche Wirklichkeit und symbolische Deutung lassen sich nicht klar voneinander trennen".

124. For the analysis of tradition and redaction in the miracle stories, see vol. I, for 2,1-11, pp. 328-344, esp. 329-330 (ET: pp. 323-340, esp. 323-324); for 2,12, p. 358 (ET: pp. 342-343); for 4,46-54, pp. 496-508, esp. 500-502 (ET: pp. 464-477, esp. 469-471); II, for 6,1-15, pp. 15-33, esp. 28-33 (ET: pp. 12-24, esp. 20-24); for 6,16-21, pp. 33-40, esp. 37-38 (ET: pp. 24-30, esp. 28); for 5,1-9b, pp. 118-122, esp. 121-122 (ET: pp. 93-97, esp. 96-97); for 9,1-7, pp. 304-311, esp. 309-311 (ET: pp. 240-245, esp. 243-245); for 11,1-45, pp. 396-433, esp. 398-402, 428-433 (ET: pp. 316-346, esp. 317-321, 340-346); III, for 20,30, pp. 400-405 (ET: pp. 335-340); for 21,1-14, pp. 410-413, 417-429 (ET: pp. 345-347, 351-360). – In the source 9,1-7 was the next sign after 5,1-9a (II, p. 117; ET: p. 92).

125. Cf. I, pp. 53-54 (ET: pp. 66-67). After the literary analysis of 4,46-54 he asks again: "Es wäre zu fragen, ob jene σημεῖα-Quelle nicht noch weitere Wunder enthielt, aus denen der Evangelist noch das eine oder andere ausgewählt hätte" (I, p. 501; ET: p. 470). Cp. I, p. 53 (ET: p. 66); see above, p. 97 n. 122. Note that Schnackenburg in III, pp. 403-405 (ET: pp. 337-340), also considers 20,31 (without καὶ ἵνα κτλ.) a part of the source's conclusion. Regarding the words ἐνώπιον τῶν μαθητῶν αὐτοῦ in v. 30 he hesitates. In *BZ* 8 (1964), p. 79, he noted: "Die μαθηταί werden als Zeugen ausdrücklich erwähnt, ob schon von der Quelle oder erst vom Evangelisten, mag offenbleiben". In III, p. 405 (ET: p. 340), however, he notes: "Auf ihn selbst [the evangelist] geht vielleicht die Bemerkung 'vor den Jüngern' ... zurück"; cp. p. 403 (ET: p. 336): "[man] muss (trotz ἐνώπιον) mit der Möglichkeit rechnen, dass erst der Evangelist die Wendung 'vor den Jüngern' hinzugefügt hat"; on ἐνώπιον, see above, p. 96 n. 115.

126. He remarks that the Cana story resembles the brevity of the Synoptic miracle stories (I, pp. 51, 329; ET: pp. 64, 324). Further, he compares 4,46-54 very closely with the Synoptic tradition (I, pp. 502-506; ET: pp. 471-475), as he does with 6,1-15.16-21 (II, pp. 28-30, 37-38; ET: pp. 21-22, 28). The healing of the paralytic is also compared

Johannine style characteristics[127], and, of course, the aporias[128]. The evangelist perhaps borrowed the σημεῖα idea from the signs source[129], which called Jesus' miracles σημεῖα instead of (Synoptic) δυνά-μεις[130]. The miracle stories, which accented the miraculous[131], had no deep theological meaning in the source[132]. John used them, and for him too the signs have "a solidly 'material' aspect"[133], but underneath is hidden a deeper spiritual significance, especially obvious in the feeding miracle, the healing of the blind man, and the raising of Lazarus[134].

For Siegfried SCHULZ (1972)[135] also, the source is not as extensive as for Bultmann. Beside 12,37-38 and 20,30-31 as the closing, the signs

with the Synoptics (II, pp. 121-122; ET: pp. 96-97), as are the healing of the blind man (II, p. 309; ET: p. 244), the raising of Lazarus (II, pp. 428-431; ET: pp. 341-343), and the catch of fish (III, pp. 410-413; ET: pp. 345-347). – With reference to the feeding miracle, he describes the relationship with the Synoptics very precisely: the pre-Johannine story comes from a tradition (likely the signs source) which combined Synoptic and non-Synoptic features. As a whole it is indeed independent of the Synoptics, but has perhaps been influenced by them during the process of oral transmission (II, p. 31; ET: p. 23).

127. See esp. I, pp. 50, 51, 329, 501 (the Cana stories); II, p. 30 (6,1-15) (ET: I, pp. 62, 64, 324, 470; II, p. 22).

128. See the literary analysis, especially of ch. 11 (see above, p. 98 n. 124).

129. See I, pp. 344-356, esp. 346 ("Exkurs 4: Die johanneischen Zeichen") (ET: pp. 515-528, esp. 517). See also *Joh 12,39-41. Zur christologischen Schriftauslegung des vierten Evangelisten*, in *FS O. Cullmann II*, 1972, pp. 167-177, esp. 167 n. 1 (= 1984, pp. 143-152, esp. 143 n. 1): "Die Spannung im σημεῖον-Begriff wird sich dadurch erklären, dass der Evangelist eine σημεῖα-Quelle mit massiv-dinglichen Wundern vorfand und sie neu interpretierte".

130. *Johannesevangelium*, I, p. 355 (ET: p. 526).

131. *Ibid.*, II, p. 31 (ET: p. 23).

132. *Ibid.*, I, pp. 53, 346, 355 (ET: pp. 66, 517, 526).

133. *Ibid.*, I, p. 354 (ET: p. 525).

134. *Ibid.*, I, p. 350 (ET: p. 521).

135. S. SCHULZ, *Das Evangelium nach Johannes übersetzt und erklärt* (NTD, 4), Göttingen, 1972 (12th ed. in the series); ³1978, pp. 7-8. – Reviews: cf. VAN BELLE, no. 2001. Cf. KYSAR, *Fourth Evangelist*, 1975, p. 17 n. 18; *ANRW* II, 25/3, 1985, p. 2399; TEMPLE, *Core*, 1975, p. 35; CORSANI, *I miracoli*, 1983, p. 22, and *passim*; HEE-KERENS, *Zeichen-Quelle*, 1984, pp. 12, 34; KUHN, *Christologie*, 1988, pp. 59-60 (Jn 1,35-51); WÖLLNER, *Zeichenglaube*, 1988, p. 9; SMITH, *John among the Gospels*, 1992, p. 68. – Here Schulz gives the same description and argumentation for the semeia hypothesis as in *Die Stunde der Botschaft. Einführung in die Theologie der vier Evangelisten*, Hamburg - Zürich, 1967; ²1970, pp. 312-314. That John used a collection of miracle stories (cf. Bultmann) seems to be indicated from the numbering of the signs, the discord between a positive and negative attitude toward miracles, and the conclusion of the gospel. The *Zeichenquelle* was surely not yet a literary unity, but was already a written source with a peculiar Semitizing language. It presented Jesus as θεῖος ἀνήρ, which would indicate that the source originated among Hellenistic Jewish Christians. Schulz likewise refers to the miraculous character of the miracle stories, which are intended to arouse faith in Jesus. Schulz accepts Bultmann's *Offenbarungsreden*; cf. KONINGS, *Joh. verhaal*, I, 1969, pp. 239-240. For other studies by Schulz, see *Bibliography*.

source contained primarily miracle stories[136]. Like Bultmann, he attributes the traditional layer of 1,35-51 to the source as its introduction, on the basis of Semitizing style[137]; the other narrative material, however, did not belong to the signs source[138].

V. FURTHER ACCEPTANCE OF THE THEORY

In 1961, Wilhelm HARTKE[139] presented the semeia hypothesis in his own way; his work seems isolated from other exegetical literature[140]. According to him, John Mark, at Jerusalem in 43-44, wrote down the *Zeichenevangelium* (= Z), dictated by John the son of Zebedee shortly before his martyrdom[141]. This gospel of signs was introduced by the appearance of the Baptist and the call of the disciples (1,6.19ff.) and contained "twelve signs of Jesus the Messiah": (1) the wine miracle, (2) the cleansing of the temple, (3) the confession of Nicodemus, (4) the witness of the Baptist, (5) the confession of faith by the Samaritan woman, (6) the second sign at Cana, (7) the healing of the paralytic, (8) the multiplication of the loaves, (9) the walking on the sea, (10) the healing of the man born blind, (11) the raising of Lazarus, and (12) the messianic entry into Jerusalem. The source closed with 20,30-31[142].

136. 2,1-12 (*Johannes*, pp. 44-47); 4,46-54 (pp. 79-81); 5,1-9a (pp. 81-84); 6,1-21 (pp. 97-100); 9,1-7 (pp. 140-143); 11,1-44 (pp. 156-161); 12,37-38 (p. 169); 20,30-31 (pp. 247-248).

137. *Ibid.*, pp. 40-44, esp. 40.

138. Thus it is striking that Schulz discovers traditional material in the dialogue with the Samaritan woman, but does not assign it to the signs source as he does 1,35-51. Jn 4,5-7.9 is a brief, traditional Jesus story ("eine kleine Jesusgeschichte, eine alte judenchristliche Jakobsbrunnenerzählung"), and 4,16-19 is traditional as well. Whether they were originally connected is no longer to be determined (p. 73).

139. W. HARTKE, *Vier urchristliche Parteien und ihre Vereinigung zur apostolischen Kirche* (SSA, 24), 2 vols., Berlin, 1961, esp. I, pp. 3-145. The first volume treats the Gospel of John, its sources, and its relationship to the Synoptics. – Cf. SMITH, *Composition*, 1965, pp. 106-107; KONINGS, *Joh. verhaal*, III, 1972, pp. 120-121; TEEPLE, *Origin*, 1974, p. 44; THYEN, *Literatur*, 1974, pp. 320-322; KYSAR, *Fourth Evangelist*, 1975, p. 16 n. 13; TEMPLE, *Core*, 1975, pp. 35, 41; BEUTLER, *ANRW* II, 25/3, 1985, p. 2527.

140. On p. 3, Hartke does, however, refer to Faure: "Für diese Grundschrift sind mir im 1922 die Augen geöffnet worden durch einen Aufsatz von A. Faure".

141. *Ibid.*, pp. 129-143: "Die Grundschrift Z und ihr Verfasser". SMITH, *Composition*, 1965, p. 106, and THYEN, *Literatur*, 1974, p. 320, rightly remark that Hartke's Grundschrift Z is a variant of Bultmann's signs source.

142. *Vier urchristliche Parteien*, p. 142. On pp. 3-128 Hartke gives his literary analysis. John Mark expanded Z to an *Ur-Johannes-Evangelium* by adding the prologue and the passion narrative (= V). (According to Hartke, John Mark was the Elder of Ephesus, "the disciple whom Jesus loved", and his mother was Mary Magdalene.) Judas Barsabbas, who also published the letters of John and the book of Revelation, saw to the final redaction; he added the literary strand H, with eschatological material and a doctrine of predestination, to the existing gospel (p. 3). Hartke provides the Greek text with his analysis: Z is in bold print, V in italics, and H in normal print.

Z thus contained no exorcisms, and no passion or resurrection narratives[143]. The picture of Jesus in Z is very simple but stirring: everything he does radiates his glory. Z testifies to the deepest belief in Jesus: he is the Messiah[144]. In Hartke's view, Z was written in Koine Greek with Semitic traits[145]. Sometimes humor appears in it. Z contains forceful controversies, is clearly written, and is precise in indications of place and time. The author limits himself in his information. Although he himself has undergone higher spiritual experiences, he cannot describe them. The discourses are missing and Jesus speaks only in short sayings (e.g., 2,19; 6,36; 10,25)[146].

143. *Ibid.*, p. 141.
144. *Ibid.*, p. 132. Z presents Jesus first as the son of Joseph (1,45); he remains in the company of the Baptist, wins his disciples there, is himself a baptizer (1,35-45; 2,11; 3,22), and has much success (10,40-42). The Baptist typifies him as the Lamb of God (1,29). Z frequently characterizes Jesus as an extraordinary teacher (3,2; 7,14-16.46). He is likewise fundamentally free (e.g., 2,4; 7,8) because he comes from God (9,33; cf. 3,2). Moreover, Jesus has what people are seeking (1,41-51). He also shows a partiality toward certain persons (11,5.38). But he is no ordinary person: he possesses a supernatural knowledge (1,42; 4,17), knows events that occur at a distance (4,50; 11,11), and performs miracles. To defend the poor he opposes the greed of the Pharisees (e.g., the temple cleansing; 7,49). For Nicodemus, Jesus has come from God (3,2), for the man born blind, he is a prophet (9,17), and for the crowds, "the true prophet" (6,14; 7,40). The disciples regard Jesus as the one about whom Moses and the prophets wrote (1,45), Messiah and King of Israel (1,49; 11,27; 12,13). Jesus is indifferent and reserved about these testimonies (1,49; 11,27); he never says that he is the Messiah, even when people demand that he do so (6,30; 10,24). Nor does he do anything himself to encourage the triumphal entry into Jerusalem. Because of this attitude, many of his disciples leave him (6,66) (pp. 129-132).
145. *Ibid.*, p. 132. The following words and phrases are unique to Z (p. 190): ἀδελφοί, ἁμαρτάνειν, ἁμαρτωλός, ἀμνός, ἀναβαίνειν εἰς Ἱεροσόλυμα (τὴν ἑορτήν, τὸ ἱερόν), ἀναβλέπειν, ἀντλεῖν, οἱ ἀρχιερεῖς καὶ οἱ Φαρισαῖοι, ἀρχιτρίκλινος, ἄρχων τῶν Ἰουδαίων, βασιλεὺς τοῦ Ἰσραήλ, Βηθανία, βουλεύεσθαι, Γαλιλαία, γάμος, ἐγένετο (at the beginning of a sentence), ἐμβλέπειν, ἑορτή or τὸ πάσχα τῶν Ἰουδαίων, ἐπαίρειν τοὺς ὀφθαλμούς, with θεᾶσθαι, ἐπιχρίειν, ἑρμηνεύειν, μεθερμηνεύειν, ἔρχεσθε καὶ ἴδετε (δεῦτε ἴδετε), ζητεῖν (ἐζήτουν καὶ ἔλεγον), θερισμός, ἦν δέ τις, ἦν δὲ ἐγγὺς τὸ πάσχα (καὶ ἐγγὺς ἦν), ἰᾶσθαι, ἱερεῖς καὶ λευίται, Ἱεροσόλυμα, Ἰουδαία, καθαρισμός, καθῆσθαι, καὶ εὐθέως ἐγένετο, καλεῖν, Καφαρναούμ, κολυμβήθρα, κράβαττος, Μεσσίας, νυμφίος, ὄχλος, ὄψις, παραμυθεῖσθαι, πέραν τοῦ Ἰορδάνου, with ὅπου ἦν Ἰωάννης βαπτίζων, πέραν τῆς θαλάσσης, περιτομή, περιτέμνειν, πηλός, πιστεύειν, πλανᾶν, ὁ προφήτης, ῥαββί, Σαμάρεια, Σαμαρῖτις, στάδιοι, σημεῖα ποιεῖν (and such expressions with Jesus as the subject), σημεῖα καὶ τέρατα, Σιλωάμ, στοά, σχίσμα, ταχύ, ταχέως, τις with following substantive, ὑγιής, ὑδρία, ὑπαντᾶν, ὁ χριστός, χώρα, καί with a verb in the Semitic manner, the place of the antecedent in a relative clause, translation from Greek, οὗτος separated from the noun.
146. *Ibid.*, pp. 132-133. The author of Z is a man of action, not of letters. He is Jewish and writes with an eye to the events in Jerusalem before 70. There are various indications that he wrote for Greeks. He describes Jewish practices (2,6; 4,9) and explains them (2,5); he speaks 70 times of "the Jews", translates Semitic words, uses the Greek form for the name Jerusalem, and gives the disciples with Greek names (Andrew and Philip) an important role to play (p. 133). Hartke thinks that the christology of Z was

Z is a *Missionsschrift* which was written for the Hellenists[147]. It is a very old, independent source for our knowledge of the historical Jesus and early Christianity. From numerous miracles, Z chose twelve representative signs, with the Entry as the climax, to convince readers that Jesus is the Messiah; in 2,23; 3,2 the author of Z himself refers to this choice[148].

Referring to Faure, Bultmann and Hartke, Ernst BAMMEL (1965, 1972)[149] also accepts the semeia hypothesis. He compares Z (= *Zeichenquelle*) or the σημεῖα source with the Q source: "both sources see the ministry of Jesus from one angle and it is likely that the σημεῖα source (= Z) existed without a developed passion and resurrection story in the same way as Q almost certainly did"[150]. Bammel does not think, as Faure and Bultmann did, that 12,37 and 20,30 "were originally consecutive" and "form the end of Z"[151]. These passages, together with other miracle summaries, "reflect an interest in a miraculous view of the ministry of Jesus which is as different from the theological direction of Z as it is from the sophisticating tendency of the soliloquies"[152]. Among the σημεῖα passages Bammel distinguishes two categories. On the one hand, not all the σημεῖα passages are closely connected with a miracle (2,18; 7,31; 6,30[?]). But at least one of them (7,31) is part of a controversy with the Pharisees (cp. ch. 9). According to Bammel, "the Pharisees-passages reflect controversies between the christian community and shades of opinion within the Jewish world. They represent old valuable tradition"[153]. Also the sign request (2,18) may have arisen in such a discussion. Bammel presumes that these Pharisees-passages (he thinks especially of 7,10.22-32.40-52; 8,12-20; 9,1-3.[3b altered?].6-17.24-34.39-41) "were combined with Z at a very early stage"[154]. On the other hand, "the summaries in the true sense of the word: 2,23; 3,2; 6,2.14(?); 12,37-38; 20,30 seem to belong to the latest, the redactional

---

actually obsolete when Z was written; at that time Paul appeared in Ephesus and laid emphasis particularly on Jesus' death (1 Cor 1,22). Shortly before the redaction of Z there also appeared another writing about Jesus' signs, the *Ur-Markus-Evangelium* which, in contrast to Z, reported Jesus' death and resurrection and was directed toward the Hellenists (in Caesarea and Antioch) as well (pp. 142-143).

147. *Ibid.*, pp. 137, 141 n. 1.

148. *Ibid.*, pp. 141, 142.

149. E. BAMMEL, *John Did No Miracle*, in MOULE (ed.), *Miracles*, 1965, pp. 179-202, esp. 193-202 (for the references to the authors mentioned see p. 195 n. 2). See also *The Baptist in Early Christian Tradition*, in *NTS* 18 (1971-72) 95-128, pp. 122-126. – On Bammel, see ASHTON, *Understanding*, 1991, pp. 175, 202 n. 9, 284.

150. *John Did No Miracle*, p. 195.

151. *Ibid.*, p. 196.

152. *Ibid.*, p. 196.

153. *Ibid.*, p. 197.

154. *Ibid.*, p. 197.

level"[155]. Contrary to Bultmann, Bammel does not consider 1,35-49 the beginning of the source[156], nor 12,37-38 and 20,30-31 the conclusion. Rather, in Z, Jn 10,40-42 was "the climax and summary of the report on the ministry of Jesus"[157].

The semeia hypothesis is also accepted by the authors listed in nn. 159-168 below[158].

155. *Ibid.*, pp. 197-198.

156. In reaction to Bultmann, Bammel notes: "this theory, attractive as it seems, is unlikely to be correct. We have to be content with stating that the source may have included some of the material of chapter 1" (pp. 198-199). See above, pp. 29[-30] n. 161.

157. *Ibid.*, p. 201. Cp. *Baptist*, pp. 109-110: "In fact, this passage is the very end of one of the sources of the gospel. This source (Z) included a number of passages dealing with the Baptist and his circle. None of these reports was left without revisionary touches". Thus, ch. 11 did not belong to Z. Cp. BAMMEL, *Die Tempelreinigung bei den Synoptikern und im Johannesevangelium*, in DENAUX (ed.), *John and the Synoptics*, 1992, pp. 507-513, esp. 510: "Sie [die Lazarusgeschichte] hebt sich in ihrer komplizierten Darbietung wie dem ganzen Stil nach von der Erzählungen der Zeichenquelle (Z) ab". In this article, Bammel argues that the cleansing of the temple was placed originally between Jn 11,7 and 11,16.

158. According to BECKER, *Wunder*, 1970, p. 132 n. 1 (= 1980, p. 437 n. 9), and NICOL, *Sēmeia*, 1972, p. 12 n. 1, the signs source was also defended by GRUNDMANN, *Zeugnis und Gestalt*, 1960 (= 1961), pp. 14-15. However, Grundmann speaks rather vaguely about traditions: "Die Überlieferungen, über die der Evangelist verfügt, sind doppelter Art, Überlieferungen von Zeichen und Überlieferungen von Sprüchen, Reden und Gesprächen Jesu; ihre Mitte erhalten diese Überlieferungen in den Ich-bin-Worte" (pp. 14-15); on p. 14 n. 15 he refers to Bultmann: "Diese Schau entspricht dem Ergebnis Bultmanns über die Traditionen des Evangelisten, wobei die Frage des Umfanges der schriftlichen Quellen offenbleiben muss; Bultmann underscheidet zwischen einer Zeichenquelle und einer Redequelle" (pp. 14-15). – KAMPHAUS, *Von der Exegese zur Predigt*, 1968; ²1968, p. 145 (DT: 1971), in his analysis of the bread miracle, refers to a unique Johannine *Vorlage* and *Quelle*, but it is not clear whether he means the signs source. See also SCHLIER, *Johannes 6*, 1967, p. 75 (= 1971, p. 107).

159. Anton VÖGTLE, *Wunder im N.T.*, in *LTK²* 10 (1965) 1255-1261, c. 1259: "zumal das Jo-Ev. seine W[under] mit einiger Wahrscheinlichkeit einer gegenüber der Synopse selbständigen σημεῖα-Quelle entnahm".

160. Gerhard SASS, *Die Auferweckung des Lazarus. Eine Auslegung von Johannes 11* (BSt, 51), Neukirchen-Vluyn, 1966, p. 64 (DT: 1969, p. 72). John interprets the story in a symbolic sense so that no one should understand it as a purely historical report (pp. 24-25, 56, 64; DT: 1969, pp. 32-33, 62, 72). With the help of a traditional story, he proclaims the message that Jesus is the Lord who conquers death (pp. 68-69; DT: 1969, pp. 77-78). To the source belong: vv. 1. 3 (without αἱ ἀδελφαί). 6. 7 (without ἄγωμεν εἰς τὴν Ἰουδαίαν πάλιν). 11 (without ταῦτα εἶπεν, ... λέγει αὐτοῖς). 12. 14-15. 17. 33 (without καὶ τοὺς ... κλαίοντας). 34. 38. 39 (without λέγει αὐτῷ ... γάρ ἐστιν). 41 (without ἦραν οὖν τὸν λίθον). 43-44. 45 (without οἱ ἐλθόντες πρὸς τὴν Μαριὰμ καί). 46 (pp. 28-30; DT: 1969, pp. 30-31). Cf. MICHIELS, in *Collationes* 5 (1975) 433-447; WAGNER, *Auferstehung*, 1988, pp. 62-64 (Jn 11,1–12,19).

161. Rudolf RENNER, *Die Wunder Jesu in Theologie und Unterricht*, Lahr-Schwarzwald, 1966, pp. 188-189 (for the wine miracle), 204-205 (for the paralytic), and 218-219 (for the man born blind).

162. Franz MUSSNER, *Die Wunder Jesu. Eine Hinführung* (SK, 10), München, 1967, p. 56 n. 18, with reference to Schnackenburg.

163. Günter HAUFE, *Vom Werden und Verstehen des Neuen Testaments. Eine Einführung*, Gütersloh, 1968, p. 72. Cp. *Einführung in das Johannes-Evangelium*, in ZdZ 24 (1970) 265-271, pp. 266-267. According to Haufe it is not so certain that the numbering of the signs comes from the source. The existence of the signs source cannot be doubted because there is a thoroughgoing tension in the gospel between the tendency of the miracle stories and the leading ideas of the evangelist. In the source, as in the pre-Markan miracle stories, Jesus is portrayed as a θεῖος ἀνήρ, but more strongly: the exorcisms, which are not very representative of this image, have been omitted, the healing stories are more miraculous, and two very miraculous works (the wine miracle and the raising of Lazarus) have been added. This portrayal by the signs source demonstrates all the traits of a secondary, more evolved tradition against which the evangelist reacted. For him the miracles are not proofs for faith, but are indeed signs of Jesus as the revealer in whom God's saving activity is made present.

164. Haikki RÄISÄNEN, *Die Mutter Jesu im Neuen Testament* (AASF, B/247), Helsinki, 1969; [2]1989, p. 156, notes on the first Cana miracle: "Die Erzählung muss aus älterer Überlieferung stammen. In ihr fehlen manche für die Schreibweise des Johannes charakteristische Kleinigkeiten. In ihrer jetzigen Form bleibt die Geschichte merkwürdig unvollständig. Das Wunder selbst wird nicht geschildert, auch nicht seine Wirkung auf die Gäste. Johannes hat offenbar die zu seinen eigenen Zwecken passenden Teile ausgewählt und dadurch die Erzählung beträchtlich verkürzt". He does not clearly identify this tradition with the signs source, although he speaks of the "Quelle" (see p. 157 n. 2: "Trotzdem verhindert nichts die Annahme, dass auch die Quelle von einer 'Stunde' gesprochen hat"; cp. p. 163 n. 1).

165. Gerhard DAUTZENBERG, *Die Geschichte Jesu im Johannesevangelium*, in SCHREINER – DAUTZENBERG (eds.), *Gestalt und Anspruch*, 1969, pp. 229-248, esp. 233-234.

166. Luise SCHOTTROFF, *Der Glaubende und die feindliche Welt. Beobachtungen zum gnostischen Dualismus und seiner Bedeutung für Paulus und das Johannesevangelium* (WMANT, 37), Neukirchen-Vluyn, 1970. See pp. 228-296 (for Johannine gnosis), and esp. 245-269 ("Die Bedeutung der innerweltlichen Sichtbarkeit der σημεῖα"). According to Schottroff, the semeia hypothesis is the best explanation for the contradiction between 4,54 and 2,23 and for the sudden transition from 2,12 to 2,13 (pp. 245-246; see her reaction to Conzelmann on p. 246 n. 1). The evangelist has taken the concept of σημεῖον from the signs source (2,11; 4,54) (p. 246). Heightening of the miraculous is peculiar to the source. In it, the miracles are regarded as demonstrations of Jesus' Messiahship and are intended to arouse faith. A σημεῖον is therefore a legitimation. For Schottroff, the source must be situated within apologetic (pp. 246, 247). John employs this apologetic θεῖος ἀνήρ christology from the source but gives it a gnostic, dualistic interpretation (6,2.14; 9,16; 11,47; 12,18): Jesus' signs are indeed visible in the world, just as his "fleshly" existence is; but correct "seeing", and not simply (physical) seeing, is the ground of faith (p. 250). In contrast to Bultmann, Schottroff ascribes 12,37 and 20,30-31 to the evangelist (p. 251; cf. the redactional verse 3,2; see Conzelmann and Bammel). According to John's dualistic interpretation of the miracles two attitudes with respect to miracle are possible: the false view regards Jesus as an inner-worldly bringer of salvation (θεῖος ἀνήρ, eschatological prophet, or Messiah); the correct view regards Jesus as Revealer (pp. 251-253). Schottroff illustrates the viewpoint of the source and the evangelist's redaction upon it using 4,46-54 as an example (pp. 253-267).

On Schottroff, see NICOL, *Sēmeia*, 1972, pp. 49-50, 101, 104, 139; THYEN, *Literatur*, 1974, pp. 233-239; KYSAR, *Fourth Evangelist*, 1975, pp. 31 n. 41, 70-72, 74, 78-79; *ANRW* II, 25/3, 1985, pp. 2400 n. 42, 2441-2442, 2445; COTHENET, *Le quatrième évangile*, 1977, pp. 111, 138, 140-141, 199; GIBLET, *Développements*, 1977 ([2]1987), pp. 66-69; SCHNACKENBURG, *Entwicklung*, 1977 ([2]1987), p. 33 (= 1984, p. 22); SMALLEY, *John*, 1978, p. 135; WITKAMP, *Jezus van Nazareth*, 1986, pp. 16-18; SCHNELLE, *Christologie*, 1987, p. 105[-106] n. 105 (ET: 1992, p. 91[-92] n. 105); KOSKENNIEMI, *Apollonios von Tyana*, 1992, p. 142; SMITH, *John among the Gospels*, 1992, p. 136 n. 72.

Referring to Schottroff, Gerd PETZKE, *Die historische Frage nach den Wundertaten Jesu. Dargestellt am Beispiel des Exorzismus Mark. ix. 14-29 par.*, in *NTS* 22 (1975-76) 180-204, p. 200, notes: "Die vormarkinische und vorjohanneische Wundertradition ist nur in dem kritischen Rahmen der Evangelisten erhalten worden. Die Kritik des Johannes an der Semeia-Quelle wird z.B. in der Erzählung iv.46ff. deutlich: der Wunderglaube der Tradition wird kritisiert und ein 'Glauben im Vollsinne' wird eingetragen". Petzke, the author of *Die Traditionen über Apollonius von Tyana und das Neue Testament* (SCHNT, 2), Leiden, 1970 (diss. Mainz, 1968), clearly accepts that the pre-Markan tradition and the signs source represented a θεῖος ἀνήρ christology: "Das Jesusbild dieser Texte [the pre-Markan tradition] wird man am besten als das eines θεῖος ἀνήρ bezeichnen: Jesus is der epiphane Gottesmann, der durch seine Kraft die Kranken heilt. Dies gilt auch für die Heilungen und Naturwunder der vorjohanneischen Semeia-Quelle" (*art. cit.*, p. 199). On Petzke's article, cf. SUHL, *Einleitung*, in ID., *Der Wunderbegriff*, 1980, pp. 15-17.

167. Hartwig THYEN, *Studien zur Sündenvergebung im Neuen Testament und seinen alttestamentlichen und jüdischen Voraussetzungen* (FRLANT, 96), Göttingen, 1970, p. 250 n. 1 (only with reference to 5,14 and 9,2ff.). Thyen has expressed skepticism in later years about source hypotheses; see below, pp. 252-254, 262-266.

168. Nikolaus WALTER, *Die Auslegung überlieferter Wundererzählungen im Johannes-Evangelium*, in *TVers* 2 (1970) 93-107, pp. 93-94. From the fact that "die Wunderhaftigkeit gegenüber den synoptischen Parallelen in manchen Einzelzügen noch gesteigert ist" Walter concludes: "der Evangelist habe diese Erzählungen aus einer besonderen Quelle entnommen, die eben jene Tendenz hatte, das Wunderhafte an den Taten Jesu zu verstärken, die also – formgeschichtlich gesprochen – die überlieferten Jesus-Novellen den dieser Gattung innewohnenden Gesetzen entsprechend weiterbildete" (p. 94). He refers to Bultmann (pp. 94-95), and to Käsemann, Haenchen, Marxsen and Schnackenburg (p. 94 n. 5; cf. p. 103 n. 5).

Even after the publication of Fortna's *The Gospel of Signs* (1970)[169], Bultmann's hypothesis of a signs source that principally contained miracle stories continued to thrive. Eduard LOHSE (1972, 1975) is rather reserved. He notes, with reference to the numbering of the signs, that the postulation of a signs source is quite possible, but remains hypothetical[170]. In his *Introduction*, Norman PERRIN (1974) is convinced that

169. On Fortna and those who adopt his "Gospel of Signs" hypothesis, see Chapter IV (pp. 141-250).

170. E. LOHSE, *Die Entstehung des Neuen Testaments* (TW, 4), Stuttgart, 1972, p. 108 (= ³1979, p. 108): "Die Annahme einer Semeia-Quelle ist daher durchaus möglich, bleibt jedoch hypothetisch (Schnackenburg)". See also *Miracles in the Fourth Gospel*, in *FS C. Evans*, 1975, pp. 64-75, esp. [73-]74 n. 4 (= 1982, pp. 45-56, esp. [54-]55, n. 4): "The hypothesis that such a source [signs source] existed remains uncertain, though it has again been vigorously put forward by J. Becker. ... It is in any case obvious that the miracle stories are distinct from the Johannine discourses both stylistically and in terms of content. It must at least be allowed for that the evangelist has made use of, and joined together, different traditions or groups of traditions". Thus, Lohse notes on 4,46-54: "It is more likely that a narrative passed on in oral tradition has been recorded both in Q and in the fourth gospel, in each case provided with particular interest" (p. 65; = 1982, p. 46); on 6,1-21: "In ch. 6 the evangelist again takes up an inherited tradition, in which the miraculous feeding and Jesus' walking on the water were already joined. But the Synoptic and Johannine versions of the tradition have been formed independently, so that it is impossible to assume any literary relationship. In both cases it is more likely that an oral tradition about Jesus, handed on in a fixed form, has been worked over" (p. 66; = 1982, p. 67). On the miracles in chs. 2, 5, 9 and 11, see pp. 68-72 (= 1982, 49-53). – Cf. M. DE JONGE, in *NTT* 30 (1976), p. 226.

John knew Mark and perhaps Luke[171]. He begins the discussion on John's sources rather emphatically with the statement: "there is one source whose use must be recognized: a signs source"[172]. He acknowledges Fortna's "strong and careful" argumentation, but limits his own discussion to miracle stories[173]. Perrin refers to three arguments which "make it very probable that the author of the Gospel of John is using as a source and reinterpreting a book of signs that represents Jesus as a Hellenistic 'divine man' whose miracles induce faith"[174]. These are: (1) the numbering (2,11; 4,54) and the "summaries" (12,37; 20,30-31); (2) "the possibility that in his narrative up to 12,37 the evangelist has used a source other than the Synoptic Gospels or the tradition represented by those gospels is strengthened since all the other miracles in John that are not paralleled in the Synoptic Gospels occur before 12,37" (5,1-9; 9,1-12; 11,1-44); (3) the notion of faith differs not only from the Synoptic Gospels but also from the rest of the Gospel of John itself: "Whereas in the Synoptic Gospels the emphasis is on faith as the prerequisite for miracles (e.g., Mark 6,5-6), here in the gospel of John miracles induce faith. These references not only contrast with the Synoptic Gospels, they also contrast with the remainder of the gospel itself". In the second edition, posthumously edited by Dennis C. Duling (1982), the statement that a signs source "must be recognized" has been dropped, although the probability that the evangelist used a book of signs is maintained. Fortna's proposal of a "signs gospel" (signs source and passion narrative) is discussed, but the acceptance of an independent (from the Synoptics) passion source for John, whether connected to the signs or not, "can be accepted only with caution"[175]. Also for Philipp VIELHAUER (1975), "the existence of *a collection of miracle stories* is not to be doubted"[176]. The extent of it, however, is less easy to establish. Based on 2,11; 4,54;

---

171. N. PERRIN, *The New Testament: An Introduction. Proclamation and Parenesis, Myth and History*, New York, 1974, p. 229; ²1982 (rev. ed. by Dennis C. DULING), p. 335. – Cf. NEIRYNCK, *Semeia-bron*, 1983, p. 4 n. 5 (ET: 1991, p. 652 n. 5).

172. *The New Testament*, 1974, p. 225.

173. *Ibid.*, p. 225; the reference to Fortna is in n. 10. This has been replaced in the second edition by a reference to Kysar's review of several hypotheses (cf. KYSAR, *Fourth Evangelist*, 1976).

174. *Ibid.*, p. 225; ²1982, p. 336.

175. *Ibid.*, ²1982, pp. 336-337.

176. P. VIELHAUER, *Geschichte der urchristlichen Literatur. Einleitung in das Neue Testament, die Apokryphen und die Apostolischen Väter*, Berlin - New York, 1975, pp. 424-425, esp. 424. He gives the following arguments: (1) the numbering; (2) "die auf Jesu Wirken rückblickende Bemerkung 12,37..., die wie ein Zitat wirkt, denn der Evangelist selbst ordnet die Zeichen dem Wort Jesu unter"; (3) the conclusion of the gospel in 20,30; (4) the absence of Johannine style characteristics. That we have to do with a "Quellenschrift" is apparent from the numbering of the signs and the manner in which the evangelist inserts his own additions (cf. 4,48 and the literary seams in vv. 47b and 49a). – Cf. NEIRYNCK, *Semeia-bron*, 1983, p. 4 n. 5 (ET: 1991, p. 652 n. 5); KOSKEN-NIEMI, *Apollonios von Tyana*, 1992, pp. 108, 144-145.

12,37f.; and 20,30f. it can be said with some certainty, in agreement with Bultmann, that we are dealing with a "collection of miracle stories, whose style is related to the Synoptics, but is further developed"[177]. On the other hand, Vielhauer finds it "fraglich" to characterize the source as a gospel à la Haenchen[178], since it contained no passion and resurrection stories[179]. With reference to Bultmann, Gudrun MUHLACK (1979) ascribes the two Cana miracles to the σημεῖα-Quelle[180]. According to Otto KNOCH (1980), the evangelist borrowed the seven miracle stories from the σημεῖα-Quelle[181]. For the evangelist they are σημεῖα by which Jesus reveals his significance for salvation (the light, the life, the bread of life).

In his article on Jn 7,1-36, Harold W. ATTRIDGE (1980) concludes that Bultmann's delineation of the underlying source in Jn 7,1-36 "remains the most plausible"[182]. The source was not limited, however, to Jn 5,1-16; 7,19.21-23 (so Bultmann[183]), but may have been continued with Jn 7,32.43-46 (the plot against Jesus)[184]. Further, Attridge considers the possibility that in Jn 9–10 "there lies a source with a structure similar to that behind chaps. 5–7"[185]. He also thinks that "the elaboration of this

177. See BULTMANN, in *RGG*³ 3 (1959), c. 842 (see above, p. 35 n. 179).
178. See HAENCHEN, in *TR* 23 (1955), p. 303 (see above, p. 68 n. 132).
179. Vielhauer does agree with Haenchen, however, that the source "Jesu Herrlichkeit nicht mehr in geheimen Epiphanien zeigte, sondern möglichst sichtbar und greifbar" (p. 425).
180. G. MUHLACK, *Die Parallelen von Lukas-Evangelium und Apostelgeschichte* (Theologie und Wirklichkeit, 8), Frankfurt/M, 1979, p. 46: "Dem engen Verhältnis des ἑκατόνταρχος, von dem Matthäus und Lukas berichten, zu einem seiner Diener entspricht das des johanneischen βασιλικός zu seinem Sohn. Ferner liegt dieser zwar in Kapernaum (Joh 4,46), doch das Gespräch seines Vaters mit Jesus findet in Kana statt, wo sich schon das erste σημεῖον Jesu, die Verwandlung von Wasser zu Wein, vollzog (Joh 2,1-11). Das lässt auf die Folge beider Wunder in der σημεῖα-Quelle schliessen [with reference to Bultmann]. Neben den genannten Unterschieden spricht vor allem die Verarbeitung der σημεῖα-Quelle gegen die Existenz einer Johannes und den Synoptikern gemeinsamen Vorlage".
181. O. KNOCH, *Begegnung wird Zeugnis. Werden und Wesen des Neuen Testaments* (Biblische Basis Bücher, 6), Kevelaer - Stuttgart, 1980, pp. 85-86, esp. 85: "Daher ist die Annahme berechtigt, dass der Verfasser hier aus einer eigenen literarischen Quelle geschöpft hat, die er dann theologisch bearbeitete. Näherhin handelt es sich um ... 7 *Wunderberichte*, die Johannes aus der sogenannten Zeichen- oder Sēméia-Quelle entnahm" (p. 85). They are: 2,1-11 (numbering in 2,11); 4,46-54 (numbering in 4,54); 6,1-15 ("zwar mit Mk verwandt, doch eigenständig nach Stoff und Darbietung"); 6,16-21 ("hier fehlt der Hinweis auf den 'Zeichencharakter'"); 5,2-9 ("mit Mk 2,1-12 ... verwandt, doch ebenfalls eigenständig"); c. 9 ("Zeichencharakter deutlich herausgearbeitet"); c. 11 ("theologische Bearbeitung besonders deutlich").
182. H.W. ATTRIDGE, *Thematic Development and Source Elaboration in John 7:1-36*, in *CBQ* 42 (1980) 160-170, p. 170. For Fortna's reaction, see below, pp. 215-216 n. 380.
183. See above, pp. 32 n. 168, 35 n. 176.
184. *Ibid.*, p. 166.
185. *Ibid.*, p. 166 n. 12: (a) healing (5,1-16; cp. 9,1-7); (b) reaction (7,19-23.31-32.43-46; cp. 9,16; 10,19-20).

source took several steps"[186]. With reference to Faure and Bultmann, Craig A. EVANS (1982) attributes all quotation formulas to the evangelist, with the possible exception of Jn 12,38, which probably belongs to the *semeia* source[187].

According to Bruno CORSANI (1983)[188], the source contains three healing miracles (4,46-54; 5,1-18; 9,1-41), one resurrection story (11,1-44), and three epiphany stories (2,1-11; 6,1-15; 6,16-21)[189]. He rejects Fortna's proposal to extend the signs source with the passion narrative[190]. All miracles, though different in form, have the same apologetic scope: as is clearly expressed in the source's conclusion (20,30-31), they proclaim Jesus as the Messiah[191]. From the use of σημεῖον (cp. esp. Jn 20,30-31 with Deut 34,10-12; cf. Nicol), the source can be defined as a missionary book for first-century Jews[192]. John made use of his source in a critical way[193]. First, he takes up the source's own word σημεῖον to criticize its apologetic explanation; for the evangelist, Jesus is the sign of God's salvific will. Second, he questions the messianic significance of the signs in several redactional remarks (2,4.24-25; 4,50). Third, he explains the deeper meaning of the signs in the discourses (chs. 5, 6 and 9).

186. These steps (pp. 168-170) are: (1) separation of the healing (5,1-16) and the defense (7,19-23) by the insertion of 5,17-47; by developing the material in 7,1-18, the evangelist composed a new setting for the continuation of his source; (2) insertion of Jn 6 "at some point in the development of the material"; (3) "into the final section of his source, the evangelist has woven his discourse material" (7,24.25-30.33-42.47-52). – Recently, Herold WEISS, *The Sabbath in the Fourth Gospel*, in *JBL* 110 (1992) 311-321, departing from Attridge's suggestion that "John 7:18-23 was connected with 5:1-16 and included the sabbath motif already in John's source" (pp. 312-313; cp. p. 311), suggests that "5:1-47 represents a second elaboration of the story" (p. 314). He tries to demonstrate that this addition "reveals that the Johannine community eventually reinterpreted the notion of sabbath by untying it from its weekly moorings and using it as a description of the eschatological present in which the works of God need to be done, while it is day" (p. 313).

187. C.A. EVANS, *On the Quotation Formulas in the Fourth Gospel*, in *BZ* 26 (1982) 79-83, p. 79; cp. also pp. 80, 81. On 12,40, see *To See and not Perceive: Isaiah 6.9-10 in Early Jewish and Christian Interpretation* (JSOT SS, 64), Sheffield, 1989, pp. 129-135 ("Chapter 10: Isaiah 6.9-10 in John"), 214-216 (notes). – Cf. VAN BELLE, *Parenthèses*, 1985, p. 187.

188. B. CORSANI, *I miracoli di Gesù nel quarto vangelo. L'ipotesi della fonte dei segni* (Studi biblici, 65), Brescia, 1983. This booklet contains the author's lectures given in Madrid at invitation of the Evangelical Theological Faculty (p. 9). In the first three chapters, Corsani deals with Bultmann's semeia hypothesis (pp. 13-22), gives a survey of some recent proponents of the theory (Schnackenburg, Fortna, Teeple, Nicol, and Becker), summarizes some critical reactions (Barrett and Lindars) (pp. 23-39), and analyzes the miracle stories (pp. 41-80). In the fourth chapter, he proposes his own approach to the "fonte dei segni" (pp. 81-97, esp. 88-94). – Reviews: P.J. CAHILL, in *CBQ* 47 (1985) 727; M. DE BURGOS, in *Communio* (Spain) 18 (1985) 289-290. Cf. SCHNELLE, *Christologie*, 1987, p. 105[-106] n. 105 (ET: 1992, p. 91[-92] n. 105).

189. *I miracoli*, pp. 88-89.

190. *Ibid.*, p. 97.

191. *Ibid.*, pp. 89-91.

192. *Ibid.*, pp. 91-92.

193. *Ibid.*, pp. 92-94.

Fourth, he does not connect the δόξα primarily with the signs, but with the hour of Jesus' death, i.e., the moment of Jesus' ὑπάγειν (3,14). Fifth, the central point of the evangelist's message is to be seen in the cross (3,14; 12,31-32) and not in the miracles.

For Horacio E. LONA (1984)[194] the "Semeia-Quelle" contained seven signs and had a "catechetical" purpose (cf. 20,30-31). The author of the source, viz. the collector ("Sammler") of the miracle stories, presents Jesus as a worker of miracles in his own power, and saw no problem in the direct connection between the miracles and the faith they evoked (cf. 2,11; 4,53; 6,14; 9,38; 11,27.45). The evangelist adopts the miracles from his source, but gives them and the source's word σημεῖον a deeper meaning[195]. This change in point of view, however, does not mean that the evangelist contradicts his source[196].

In his study on John and Luke, Anton DAUER (1984)[197] believes that Jn 4,46b-54a originated from a signs source[198], where it followed 2,1-11.12 and preceded 6,1ff.[199]. In Dauer's opinion, however, the

194. H.E. LONA, *Glaube und Sprache des Glaubens im Johannesevangelium*, in *BZ* 28 (1984) 168-184, pp. 176-179: "III. Glaube und Interpretation (Die 'Semeia'-Quelle)".

195. *Ibid.*, pp. 176-177. The evangelist gives the miracles a new meaning, "entweder durch redaktionelle Eingriffe in die Erzählung selbst oder durch eine sich an die Erzählung anschliessende Szene". So, he stresses the unity of Jesus with the Father in their common works (5,19) and, under his hand, the miracles become "die Grundlage für eine geschlossene christologische Darstellung, in der Jesus als Verkörperlichung der durch die Zeichen sichtbar gewordenen Gaben erscheint. Er schenkt Brot, Licht, Leben. Er selber identifiziert sich mit diesen Gaben, die wiederum als Zeichen des Gottesheiles zu verstehen sind" (p. 178). In the Gospel, the miracle stories are to be seen as "eine Semantik für die Interpretation dieser Erzählungen... Sie wollen das Sprach- und Bedeutungssystem einer Gruppe bestätigen. Sie können missionarisch wirken, insofern sie diese eigenartige Semantik des wahren Glaubens bekannt machen, aber sie sind ursprünglich nicht 'nach aussen' ausgerichtet" (p. 179).

196. See Lona's reaction to Becker and Richter, p. 177 n. 19: "Stünde die Christologie der Quelle in einem so deutlichen Gegensatz zur Christologie des Evangelisten, hätte er die Quelle nicht übernommen".

197. A. DAUER, *Johannes und Lukas. Untersuchungen zu den johanneisch-lukanischen Parallelperikopen Joh 4,46-54/Lk 7,1-10 – Joh 12,1-8/Lk 7,36-50; 10,38-42 – Joh 20,19-29/Lk 24,36-49* (FzB, 50), Würzburg, 1984. – Reviews: cf. VAN BELLE, no. 1887. See esp. F. NEIRYNCK, *John 4,46-54 Signs Source and/or Synoptic Gospels*, in *ETL* 60 (1984) 367-375 (= 1991, pp. 678-687, 687-688: Additional Note); P. JUDGE, *Luke 7,1-10: Sources and Redaction*, in NEIRYNCK (ed.), *L'évangile de Luc*, ²1989, pp. 472-490, esp. 474-475, 486-488. – For Dauer's earlier study (*Die Passionsgeschichte*, 1972; reviews: cf. VAN BELLE, no. 4033), see esp. SABBE, in DE JONGE (ed.), *L'évangile de Jean*, 1977 (²1987), pp. 203-234 (= 1991, pp. 354-386, 387-388: Additional Note"): on Jn 18,1-11; NEIRYNCK, in *op. cit.*, pp. 73-106, esp. 93-95 "2. Dauer's Study on the Passion Narrative" (= 1982, pp. 365-400, esp. 385-387); VAN BELLE, *Parenthèses*, 1985, pp. 176-177.

198. *Johannes und Lukas*, p. 357 n. 433, refers to Bultmann, Schnackenburg, Schulz, Becker, Haenchen ("Wunderevangelium"), Muhlack, and especially Fortna.

199. See his reconstruction of the pre-Johannine story on p. 72. On the signs source, see also pp. 52-53 (description of the aporias in 4,46-54), and pp. 54 (on 4,46b; cp. 5,5; 11,1), 55 (on 4,47), 60, 71 (on the numbering of signs in 2,11; 4,54; ctr. 2,23; 3,2; 4,45, with on p. 335 n. 221, references to Bultmann, Fortna, Teeple, Lindars, and Schottroff),

pre-Johannine story was "a free rendering of Mt 8,5-13 making use of narrative elements from Lk 7,1-10"[200]. This means that the date of the signs must be later than the final redaction of the Synoptic Gospels[201]. Dauer has thus significantly revised his earlier hypothesis of an independent Johannine tradition that was later influenced by the Synoptics[202]. With reference to Fortna, Dauer remains open to the possibility of a continuous source with signs, passion and resurrection narratives[203]. Uwe WEGNER (1985)[204] simply considers the "Vorlage" of Jn 4,46-54[205] as a "Traditionsvariante" of the Q-parallel[206]; this "Vorlage" belongs to the "Semeia-Quelle", where it followed 2,1-11.12[207].

Petr POKORNÝ (1985)[208] thinks it possible that Mark and the *Zeichen-quelle* depend upon common material, given that some miracle stories

298. But on p. 358 n. 435, he notes: "Im übrigen ist die Herleitung von Joh 4,46-54 (und 2,1-12) aus der Semeia-Quelle gar nicht so unumstritten".

200. *Ibid.*, p. 121; cp. p. 297 (see his diagrams on pp. 122, 124).

201. Dauer perceived the difficulty of this late date, but answers: "Aber was wissen wir schon über die Herkunft dieser Quelle und das darin verwendete Traditionsmaterial?" (p. 109); on p. 359 n. 435, he refers to NICOL, *Sēmeia*, 1972, pp. 68-77, esp. 78, who also "an eine relativ späte Abfassung der Semeia-Quelle denkt ... (etwa zur Zeit der Abfassung der Apg geschrieben)". See below, p. 158 n. 77.

202. *Johannes und Lukas*, p. 124. In *Die Passionsgeschichte* (diss. 1969, ed. 1972), Dauer defended the Dahl-Borgen hypothesis. On the significance of Dauer's "new" hypothesis, see NEIRYNCK, in *ETL* 60, p. 368: "Dauer's own thesis of indirect dependence looks like a variation of the same basic hypothesis. It is now quite clear that the so-called Borgen-Dauer position has been split up in two different directions. For Borgen 'John is based essentially on an independent tradition, even though it had been influenced by the synoptic accounts'. In Dauer's view the pre-Johannine 'tradition' in Jn 4,46-54 is strictly post-synoptic"; on "The Borgen-Dauer Thesis", see also ID., *John and the Synoptics: A Response to P. Borgen*, in DUNGAN (ed.), *The Interrelations of the Gospels*, 1990, pp. 438-450 (= 1992, pp. 699-711).

203. *Johannes und Lukas*, pp. 298-299, esp. 299: "Diese Ergebnisse Fortnas zu verifizieren oder zu falsifizieren, würde aber die Aufgabenstellung meiner Untersuchung überschreiten und muss hier unterbleiben. Doch die Möglichkeit einer solchen durchlaufenden Quelle, in die auch meine Ergebnisse sich einfügen liessen, dürfte Fortna mit Recht deutlich gemacht haben".

204. U. WEGNER, *Der Hauptmann von Kafarnaum (Mt 7,28a; 8,5-10.13 par Lk 7,1-10). Ein Beitrag zur Q-Forschung* (WUNT, 2/14), Tübingen, 1985 (diss. Tübingen, 1982-83; dir. M. Hengel). See esp. pp. 18-57 ("Mt 8,5-10.13/Lk 7,1-10 im Vergleich mit Joh 4,46-54"), 57-74 ("Exkurs: βασιλικός und ἑκαντοντάρχης"). Cf. NEIRYNCK, *Evangelica II*, 1991, pp. 687-688; JUDGE, *art. cit.* (n. 545), pp. 480, 487, 499, 489.

205. *Der Hauptmann*, pp. 18-32; cp. p. 430. See his reconstruction on p. 32.

206. *Ibid.*, pp. 18-32; cp. p. 430.

207. *Ibid.*, p. 30: "Ohne detaillierter auf den Problemkomplex der Quellen im JohEv eingehen zu können, scheint uns die Annahme, Joh verarbeitete in 4,46-54 und in den weiteren Wundergeschichten seines Ev ein von der Tradition ihm bereits schriftlich (oder mündlich) vorgegebenes Material, gut begründet zu sein". Note, however, that Wegner's director, M. Hengel, criticized the signs-source hypothesis in 1987 and 1989 (cp. 1993) (see below, pp. 331-332).

208. P. POKORNÝ, *Die Entstehung der Christologie. Voraussetzungen einer Theologie des Neuen Testaments*, Stuttgart, 1985, p. 125 (with reference to Koester).

are common to the Synoptic Gospels and John, partly even in the same order. Moreover, he thinks that it was a literarily fixed collection[209]. For Jn 6,5-59 (cp. Mk 6,30-7,37 par.; Mk 8,1-26), however, Pokorný remarks against Achtemeier[210] that John can only be dependent on Mk and not on his *Vorlage*. Finally, he stresses that John interpreted the miracles differently than Mark[211].

In his short commentary, Felix PORSCH (1988)[212] believes that the argument for the literary unity of the Gospel of John from its so-called *Einheitssprache* is not as convincing as it appears. First, there is not the unique language of a single author only, but also that of a group living in the same cultural milieu, the so-called "sociolect". Second, the Johannine language, upon closer examination, is not so "einheitlich". More precise examination of vocabulary and style, along with consideration of peculiarities in content, reveals that the Gospel of John must have undergone a long process of development and that it therefore cannot have been written, in its present form, by a single author. Porsch thinks that an older, shorter version of the passion story underlay the present form, and that the evangelist used a "Sammlung von Wundergeschichten", commonly called the "Zeichenquelle" because of the Johannine designation of miracles as σημεῖα[213].

In his study on the significance of the Mosaic law, Markku KOTILA (1988)[214] claims, against U. Schnelle[215], that "die SQ-*hypothese* immer

209. *Ibid.*, p. 125; cp. p. 127: "Als eine schriftliche Quelle (Zeichenquelle) treten die Wundererzählungen im Johannesevangelium deutlich hervor (vgl. Joh 2,11; 4,54; 6,14; 20,30)".

210. *Ibid.*, p. 125 n. 6. Cf. ACHTEMEIER, in *JBL* 89 (1970) 265-291.

211. *Die Entstehung*, p. 127: "Der Evangelist verschmilzt jedoch bewusst die Ebene der vorletzten Hilfe mit dem Eschaton des Heils und unterstreicht ständig, dass die Wunder Jesu auf das himmlische Heil hinweisen. Er akzentuiert seine Auseinandersetzung mit der Wundertradition anders als Markus. Zum Beispiel schon in 4,49 spitzt er die Geschichte durch eine redaktionelle Notiz über den Tod zu, in 11,17-27 deutet er die Auferweckung des Lazarus bereits direkt als Zeichen der Auferstehung zum neuen Leben, und die theologische Redaktion gipfelt in 20,29... Selbst die mächtigen Taten Jesu, zu denen der Evangelist auch die Erscheinungen nach der Auferstehung rechnet, sind Gegenstand der Verkündigung, nicht der Beweis des Glaubens im äusseren Sinne. So deutet Johannes das Anliegen der Zeichenquelle, das im nächsten Vers durchschimmert (20,30). Das Entscheidende ist der Glaube, der als die bewusste Aufnahme der Taufe charakterisiert wird, als die Geburt aus dem Geist: Joh 3,1-15" (p. 127).

212. F. PORSCH, *Johannes-Evangelium* (SKK NT, 4), Stuttgart, 1988, pp. 18-19, esp. 18.

213. *Ibid.*, p. 18 (with reference to the numbering in 2,11 and 4,54). For an analysis of the notion σημεῖον, cf. pp. 52-54.

214. M. KOTILA, *Umstrittener Zeuge. Studien zur Stellung des Gesetzes in der johanneischen Theologiegeschichte* (AASF DHL, 48), Helsinki, 1988 (dir. H. Räisänen). The author studies the significance of the Mosaic law in the different layers of Johannine literature: the "Semeia-Quelle" (= SQ), the evangelist (= E), the secondary redaction(s) (= R^1 and R^2), and the Johannine Letters (see esp. pp. 201-214; cp. pp. 235-236). On 5,1-16, see pp. 11-33, esp. 14, 18 (cp. p. 201); on 7,19-24, see pp. 47-50, esp. 51; on 9,1-10,21, see pp. 61-83, esp. 67-68, 82 (cp. pp. 201-202). – On Kotila, see KOSKENNIEMI, *Apollonios von Tyana*, 1992, p. 159.

215. See below, pp. 335-341.

noch eine fruchtbare *Arbeitshypothese* darstellt"[216]. By transforming two traditional miracle stories (5,2-3b.5-9c.14-15; 9,1-3.6-8) into two discussions on the Sabbath question (5,9d-13.16; 7,19-24; 9,1-17), the author of SQ made an apology for the way of life in his community[217]. According to Kotila, 5,1-16 in SQ was not only followed by 7,19-24 (cp. Bultmann[218]) but also by 7,31-32 and 45-52, and probably in this order: 5,2-16; 7,31-32.19-24.45-52[219]. Regarding the pre-Johannine passion story, he thinks that it possibly stems from the same hand as the signs source or at least from the same community[220].

Hans-Jürgen KUHN (1988)[221] bases his literary analysis of Jn 1,35-51 on Bultmann's semeia hypothesis[222]. In contrast to Bultmann[223], however, only vv. 43 and 51 are from the author (or authors) who edited the present Gospel[224]. The source's story is not dependent upon the Synoptics[225]. It contains three episodes: a "Präsentationslegende" (1,35-39) and two christological "Erweislegenden" (1,40-42.44-50)[226]. After examination of the religion-historical background of the source's story[227], he concludes that the source was not only influenced by the Old

---

216. *Umstrittener Zeuge*, p. 204 n. 5.

217. *Ibid.*, p. 45: "Der Verf., dessen Gemeinde wegen ihrer Sabbatpraxis verfolgt wurde, will in 5,2-16; 7,19-24 beweisen, dass auch eine liberalere Sabbatpraxis theologisch legitimierbar ist"; see also p. 82 (on ch. 9): "Ebenso wie in 5,2-16; 7,19-24 verteidigt der Verf. der SQ auch hier eine liberale Sabbatpraxis, die deutlich mit der Lebensweise seiner jüdischen Umwelt in einem gespannten Verhältnis steht. Die Fragestellung ist, wie auch schon in SQ, innerjüdisch" (on the "innerjüdische Streit um die Orthodoxie" of SQ, see esp. pp. 202-203).

218. See above, pp. 32 n. 168, 35 n. 176.

219. *Ibid.*, p. 51; see also p. 203 n. 1.

220. *Ibid.*, p. 203: "Vorläufig ist als einfachste Exegese anzunehmen, dass die vorevangelische Passionsgeschichte, wenn nicht aus der gleichen Hand, so doch wenigstens aus den gleichen Gemeinde wie die SQ stammt".

221. H.-J. KUHN, *Christologie und Wunder. Untersuchungen zu Joh 1,35-51* (BibUnt, 18), Regensburg, 1988 (diss. Trier, 1985; dir. J. Eckert), pp. 69-161. See also his lecture "im Rahmen der Promotionsfeier am 30. November 1985": *Joh 1,35-51 – Literatur und Form*, in *TTZ* 95 (1987) 149-155. – Reviews: J. BECKER, in *TLZ* 114 (1989) 434; X. LÉON-DUFOUR, in *RSR* 77 (1989) 275-276; D.E. AUNE, in *JBL* 109 (1990) 145-146.

222. *Christologie*, pp. 160-161: "Die herausgearbeitete Kleine Einheit gehört als einleitendes Stück zu der von Rudolf Bultmann ermittelten Semeia-Quelle (SQ), deren Existenz in der Forschung weithin angenommen wird" (p. 161; cp. p. 552); see also *TTZ* 95, p. 152. For Jn 1,35-42.44-50 as introduction of SQ, see esp. *Christologie*, pp. 233, 234; cp. *TTZ* 95, p. 154.

223. See above, pp. 29-30 n. 161.

224. *Christologie*, p. 552. See his analysis on pp. 121-130 (1,43), 153-159 (1,51), 197-201 ("Die sprachliche Gestalt von 1,43 und 1,51"); cp. *TTZ* 95, pp. 150-152.

225. *Christologie*, pp. 201-206, esp. 206: "Eine unmittelbare literarische Beziehung ist zwischen den Berichten nicht anzunehmen, wohl aber sind traditionsgeschichtliche Zusammenhänge offensichtlich".

226. *Christologie*, pp. 207-234, 552; cp. *TTZ* 95, pp. 153-154.

227. *Christologie*, pp. 294-352: "5. Zur Prophetchristologie in Joh 1,35-42.44-50"; pp. 352-551: "6. Zur θεῖος ἀνῆρ-Christologie in Joh 1,35-42.44-50" (cp. pp. 553-555).

Testament and the Jewish tradition, but also by the Hellenistic θεῖος ἀνήρ typology[228]. Kuhn also considers the possibility that SQ was extended to a *Grundschrift* by inclusion of the passion story, but he makes no decision[229].

Burton L. MACK (1988)[230] presents a Johannine signs source which, like the two miracle chains in Mk[231], consisted of five stories (4,46-54; 5,1-9; 6,1-14; 6,16-21; 9,1-34)[232]. Two stories, 2,1-11 and 11,1-44, "differing from the others", do not belong to the source[233]. Mack's hypothesis can be compared with John D. CROSSAN's more recent suggestion (1991) of an early miracles collection embedded in Mark and John, with a fivefold sequence: Jn 5,1-18; 6,1-15.16-21; 9,1-7; 11,1-57; cf. Mk 2,1-12; 6,33-44.45-52; 8,22-26; Secret Mark[234].

In the *ABD* (1992) several authors accept the signs source[235] but limit its content to the miracles. First, we mention Dieter-Alex KOCH's article

228. *Ibid.*, p. 556: "Für Joh 1,35-42.44-50 rechnet die vorliegende Arbeit mit unbestreitbaren Merkmalen der alttestamentlich-jüdischen Tradition, glaubt aber auch, eindeutig hellenistische Vorstellungen am Werk zu sehen, ohne freilich das Ineinander beider Komponenten abschliessend geklärt zu haben. Wohl aber leistet die Beschäftigung mit dem Fragenbereich Christologie und Wunder an Hand von Joh 1,35-51 dazu einen Beitrag".

229. *Ibid.*, p. 161: "Es bleibt somit offen, ob die sogenannte Semeia-Quelle in eine Grundschrift des vierten Evangeliums eingearbeitet wurde, aus der erst in einem weiteren Schritt Joh selbst geformt wurde. Es mag Anzeichen dafür geben, da 1,43 und 1,51 allem Anschein nach nicht auf denselben Verfasser zurückgehen. Dieser Fragenkomplex bleibt unberücksichtigt. Vielmehr geht die weitere Arbeit von der Existenz einer Wunderquelle aus, ohne deren Umfang im einzelnen festzulegen".

230. B.L. MACK, *A Myth of Innocence: Mark and Christian Origins*, Philadelphia, PA, 1988, pp. 216-219, 220-222. – Reviews: A.Y. COLLINS, in *JBL* 108 (1989) 726-729; W.H. KELBER, in *CBQ* 52 (1990) 161-163; J.A. OVERMAN, in *Interpr* 44 (1990) 193-195; V.K. ROBBINS, in *RelStR* 17 (1991) 15-22. See also NEIRYNCK, *John and the Synoptics*, 1992, pp. 50-51 n. 228 (he calls Mack's presentation, "a rather curious sequel to Achtemeier's theory"). On Achtemeier, see above, p. 78 n. 31.

231. *A Myth of Innocence*, pp. 216-219: "The Miracle Chains in Mark".

232. *Ibid.*, pp. 220-222

233. *Ibid.*, p. 221. According to Neirynck (p. 50), "a theory of a signs source without including 2,1-11 is self-destructive".

234. J.D. CROSSAN, *The Historical Jesus: The Life of a Mediterranean Jewish Peasant*, San Francisco, CA, 1991, pp. 310-313, 429. Regarding Jn 6,1-15.16-21 (Mk 6,33-44.45-52), cf. p. 407: "the order of meal and sea in the *Miracles Source* used by Mark and John may have been reversed...". On the signs source, see also p. 429. On the Secret Gospel of Mark, see also CROSSAN's *Four Other Gospels: Shadows on the Contours of Canon*, Minneapolis, MN, 1985, pp. 91-121, esp. 104-106. – Cf. NEIRYNCK, *John and the Synoptics*, 1992, pp. 50-51 n. 228; ID., in *ETL* 70 (1994) 231-234, esp. p. 225 (see below, p. 321 n. 419).

235. D.N. FREEDMAN (ed.), *The Anchor Bible Dictionary* [= *ABD*], 6 vols., New York - London, 1992. Besides articles mentioned here, see also, of course, the article *Signs/ Semeia Source*, written by FORTNA (VI, pp. 18-22; see below, pp. 239-241). We must also refer to the articles *John, The Gospel of* (III, pp. 912-931), written by KYSAR (who, as in his earlier studies, is rather critical concerning Johannine source criticism; see below, pp. 189-193, 356), and *Aretalogy* (I, pp. 372-273), written by TIEDE (see above, p. 86 n. 71). On the *ABD*, see the review by NEIRYNCK, in *ETL* 68 (1992) 428-432, p. 430.

on "source criticism"[236]. As in his 1975 monograph, he doubts the existence of pre-Markan collections of miracles[237], but for the Gospel of John he seems to accept a signs source[238] which "consisted exclusively of the seven miracle stories and a limited editorial framework (John 2:11-12a; 4:54; 12:37-38; 20:30-31a)"[239]. Each of the miracles represents a different type of miracle, and Koch considers this "an argument in favor of the assumption that the source has been incorporated *completely* into the gospel of John"[240]. Moreover, "the sequence [of the miracles] appears to be the result of a conscious

236. D.-A. KOCH, *Source Criticism, New Testament*, in *ABD*, VI, 1992, pp. 165-171, esp. 169a-169b: "The Signs Source".

237. See p. 167b: "the arrangement of the traditional material in Mark 2–8 and 11+12 can be understood without the assumption of written sources". See above, p. 85 n. 63

238. The five arguments he enumerates in favor of the source are well-known: (1) "The numbering of the two miracles in John 2:11 and 4:54" (ctr. 2,23); (2) "The editorial transitional phrase in 2:12a, which is without function in its present context and obviously was intended originally to connect the first two miracle stories (2:1-11 and 4:46-54)"; (3) "Insertions by the evangelist in the miracle stories which lead to the assumption of a written *Vorlage*" (cf. 4,48; see also 6,4.6); (4) "The conclusion of the gospel of John in 20:30-31a, which cannot be understood as a summary of the whole ministry of Jesus by the evangelist, because the speeches and Passion of Jesus are nowhere else called *sēmeia*. Here the author of the speeches has made use of the conclusion of a source consisting of *sēmeia* (= signs), i.e., of miracle stories"; (5) "The critical attitude of the evangelist towards the view that faith is based on miracles (4:48; 6:26-35), which is incompatible with the view put forward in the single traditions (4:53) and in editorial remarks not deriving from the evangelist (2:11; 20:31a)" (p. 169a).

239. With regard to the extent of the signs source, Koch distinguishes three solutions. (1) He calls the one he himself seems to accept "the minimal solution" (given above). (2) The second is "a midway position, according to which the source contained additionally some further materials like the traditional layer of John 1:35-51 and 4:1-42". Koch accepts that there is indeed "a close relationship between these materials and the miracle stories", but for him that "does not prove that these materials are derived from the same source". Moreover, "the additional argument that the mentioning of the disciples in 2:1 presupposes a story that tells how they became Jesus' followers is not compelling". In *Der Täufer als Zeuge des Offenbarers. Das Täuferbild von Joh 1,19-34 auf dem Hintergrund von Mk 1,2-11*, in *FS F. Neirynck*, III, 1992, pp. 1963-1984, Koch rejects Becker's inclusion of 1,19-35 in the signs source. He explains the passage "mit einem wesentlich einfacheren diachronen Modell: als literarisch homogene Komposition durch den Evangelisten, der die synoptische Täuferüberlieferung von Mk 1,2-11 voraussetzt, diese selektiv aufnimmt und die aufgenommenen Bestandteile als disjecta membra in seine eigene darstellerische und inhaltliche Konzeption einschmilzt" (pp. 1966-1967; cp. p. 1982). (3) According to a "maximal solution", "the source additionally contained a Passion narrative so that it was a gospel resembling the Synoptics". But he also rejects this solution for two reasons. First, "in this case, however, John 20:30-31a cannot be claimed as the end of the source, and the source itself cannot be labeled 'Signs Source' any longer". Second, "as far as theology of the source is concerned, it is difficult to see how this alleged source solved the tension between the miracles which have become much more marvelous (cf. John 11) on the one hand and Jesus' suffering and death on the other hand" (p. 169b).

240. *Ibid.*, p. 169b.

composition"[241]. In the source's conclusion (20,30-31a) its intention is clearly expressed: "The collection of miracles is intended to cause faith in Jesus as the Son of God because of his mighty deeds (2:11), but the source is aware of the fact that miracles may be rejected (12:37-38)"[242]. Koch thinks that both the selection of seven different types of miracle stories and the fact that the miracles have become more marvelous in comparison with the Synoptics "point to a later date"[243]. On the source's provenance, he can only say that it is possible that the names of places in 1,28; 10,40 (Peraea) or in 4,1 (Samaria) may provide some evidence[244]. Like Koch, Dieter LÜHRMANN rejected in 1987 the pre-Markan miracle collection(s) but accepted a signs source for Jn[245]. In his *ABD* article on "faith", he again upholds the hypothesis that "John probably took [the] miracle stories out of a 'gospel of signs', of which indeed the first half of the original end of the gospel ... is to be explained as a summary. This source recounted miracles of Jesus (partially parallel to the Synoptic miracle stories) with the purpose of awakening faith in Jesus"[246]. Harold E. REMUS notes in his article on "miracles" that "the use of the distinctive term *semeion/-a* for miracle in the Fourth Gospel as well as certain clues in the narrative point to the evangelist's use of traditions, or even a collection ('signs source') containing accounts of *semeia*"[247].

---

241. It starts with 2,1-11, which reveals "Jesus' power over inanimate nature" and "leads to the disciples' faith"; it ends with "a (massively enhanced) resurrection story (chap. 11)" (p. 169b).

242. *Ibid*, p. 169b.

243. *Ibid*, p. 169b.

244. But, as he says, that "depends on the question as to whether or not these remarks can be assigned to the source" (p. 169b).

245. D. LÜHRMANN, *Das Markusevangelium* (HNT, 3), Tübingen, 1987, p. 15: "Versuche, als Vorlage des Mk eine oder zwei parallele Sammlungen von Wundergeschichten zu rekonstruieren, haben daher manches für sich, nicht zuletzt das analoge Phänomen einer Semeia-Quelle im Johannesevangelium (vgl. P. Achtemeier, Origin). Es ergibt sich aber doch keine in sich geschlossene 'Quelle' mit eigener, von der des Mk abzuhebender Intention". Cp. pp. 94-95, 118.

246. *Faith, New Testament*, in *ABD*, II, 1992, pp. 749-758, esp. 755a.

247. H.E. REMUS, *Miracles, New Testament*, in *ABD*, IV, 1992, pp. 856-869, esp. 865a. He mentions the following arguments: (1) the numbering of signs (2,11; 4,54; ctr. 2,23; 3,2); (2) the reference to the first miracle in 4,46b and the similarity of both the geographical location and the pattern of the two Cana accounts "suggest that the healing account followed the account of the wine miracle directly in a source employed by the evangelist"; (3) the conclusion (20,30) "is inappropriate insofar as much material intervenes between this passage and the last of the signs in chap. 11; such a conclusion would be appropriate to a collection of signs, however" (p. 866a).

VI. J. Becker's Christology of the "Semeiaquelle"

Of greater importance for the history of the semeia hypothesis is Jürgen Becker's article, *Wunder und Christologie* (1970)[248], in which he attempts to give a systematic presentation of the christology of the signs source and the redaction of the evangelist[249]. He compares Bultmann's existential interpretation with the more liberal approach of Käsemann[250], and attempts to decide which offers the best exegesis of the Gospel of John by examining a crucial problem in Johannine theology: the relationship between miracle and christology. Despite the nuance Becker brings to Bultmann's theory, he maintains that Bultmann's commentary is still the best exposition of the Fourth Gospel[251]. Also, in his *ÖTK* commentary (1979, 1981)[252], Becker situates himself in the line of Bult-

---

248. J. Becker, *Wunder und Christologie. Zum literarkritischen und christologischen Problem der Wunder im Johannesevangelium*, in *NTS* 16 (1969-70) 130-148 (= 1980, pp. 435-461, 461-463: *Nachtrag [1979]*). This article is an expansion of a lecture given on the occasion of the author's *Habilitation* in 1968 (cf. p. 130 n. 1; = 1980, p. 435 n. 1). – Cf. Konings, *Joh. verhaal*, III, 1972, pp. 123-126; Nicol, *Sēmeia*, 1972, pp. 12, 139; Teeple, *Origin*, 1974, p. 50; Kysar, *Fourth Evangelist*, 1975, pp. 17-37; *ANRW* II, 25/3, 1985, pp. 2397, 2400, 2411, 2451-2452; Temple, *Core*, 1975, p. 39; Cothenet, *Le quatrième évangile*, 1977, pp. 111, 125, 192, 199; Giblet, *Développements*, 1977 (²1987), p. 49; Smalley, *John*, 1978, pp. 106-107; Corsani, *I miracoli*, 1983, p. 22, and *passim*; Heekerens, *Zeichen-Quelle*, 1984, pp. 12, 18 nn. 5 and 12, 20 n. 15, 23, 24, 31, and *passim*; J.A.T. Robinson, *Priority*, 1985, p. 21 n. 75; Schnelle, *Christologie*, 1987, p. 105 [-106] n. 105 (ET: 1992, p. 91[-92] n. 105); Wöllner, *Zeichenglaube*, 1988, pp. 9-11.

249. Cf. Richter, *Der Vater*, 1973, p. 97 (= 1977, p. 267): "J. Becker, der – wohl als erster – versucht hat die Christologie der vom Evangelisten als Vorlage verwendeten Grundschrift zusammenhängend darzustellen"; Konings, *Joh. verhaal*, III, 1972, p. 124, also refers to the importance of this article because of its attention to the *redaction* of the signs source: the source is not identical with the tradition, but has been redacted by an author. See also Kuhn, *Christologie*, 1988, pp. 286-292, 289-290 (with reference to Becker's commentary): "Aus den vorhergehenden Ausführungen ergibt sich bereits, dass Becker in der SQ nicht ein Zufallsprodukt erblickt, sondern einen planmässig arbeitenden Verfasser am Werk sieht, der vorhandenen Stoff redaktionell bearbeitet". See below, p. 121 n. 277.

250. *Wunder*, pp. 130-131 (= 1980, pp. 436-437).

251. *Ibid.*, p. 148 (= 1980, p. 461): "So bleibt – bei aller im einzelnen zu übenden Kritik – Bultmanns Kommentar nach wie vor der beste Weg zur Interpretation des vierten Evangeliums".

252. J. Becker, *Das Evangelium nach Johannes. I. Kapitel 1–10. II. Kapitel 11–21* (ÖTKNT, 4/1-2), Gütersloh - Würzburg, I, 1979, pp. 1-340 (²1985; ³1991, pp. 1-397); II, 1981, pp. 341-663 (²1984; ³1991, pp. 401-776). In the second edition of the commentary, only some misprints were corrected. The third edition has been enlarged: "Dritte, überarbeitete Auflage". In the following notes, I refer to the pages of the first edition and give within brackets the pages of the third. For additions to the first edition, see below, esp. nn. 254, 259, 265, 273, 280, 282, 284-286, 297-298, 303-304, 307-309, on pp. 117-126. See also Becker's *Forschungsberichte* in *TR* 47 (1982) 279-301, 305-347; 51 (1986) 1-78 (see below, p. 132 n. 334, 133 n. 340). – Reviews: cf. Van Belle, no. 1912; see below. Neirynck, in *ETL* 58 (1982) 397-399; 61 (1985) 403. Cf. Corsani, *I miracoli*, 1983, pp. 34-36; Van Belle, *Parenthèses*, 1985, pp. 185-187; Kuhn, *Christologie*, 1988, pp. 61-62 (Jn 1,35-51), 286-292 ("Die θεῖος-ἀνήρ-Christologie nach Jürgen Becker");

mann, and distinguishes three levels in the development of the Gospel of John[253]: (1) the level of sources: *Semeiaquelle* (= SQ)[254], *Passionsbericht* (= PB)[255], and other small literary units (e.g., the hymn in 1,1-18); (2) the work of the evangelist (= E); and (3) a *Kirchliche Redaktion* (= KR)[256]. We shall present Becker's signs source hypothesis, by examining the three questions with which he structures his article[257]: (1) From where has John drawn the material for his miracle stories? (2) What was the theology of this material? (3) How has the evangelist theologically reworked the material?

1. For the answer to the first question[258] Becker accepts the semeia hypothesis[259], for which the argumentation has been worked out by Bult-

WAGNER, *Auferstehung*, 1988, pp. 82-85 (Jn 11,1–12,19); WÖLLNER, *Zeichenglaube*, 1988, pp. 17-19; BEUTLER, *Méthodes et problèmes*, 1990, p. 22; LÉON-DUFOUR, *Où en est la recherche johannique?*, 1990, p. 25; ASHTON, *Understanding*, 1991, p. 161; BOTHA, *Jesus and the Samaritan Woman*, 1991, p. 20; RUCKSTUHL – DSCHULNIGG, *Stilkritik*, 1991, pp. 213-214, 248-249; KOSKENNIEMI, *Apollonios von Tyana*, 1992, pp. 127, 158-159; SCHMITHALS, *Johannesevangelium*, 1992, pp. 126, 184; SMITH, *John among the Gospels*, 1992, pp. 68-69.

253. *Johannes*, I, pp. 32-36 [36-41]: "Die Frage nach Quellen", esp. 35 [39]: "Diese Position versteht sich als Variante zur Mehrquellentheorie von Bultmann, der mit drei Quellen (SQ, Redenquelle, PB) und einer nachevangelistischen kirchlichen Redaktion rechnet". In *TR* 47, pp. 295-296, Becker distinguished "zwei Grundmodelle" in literary criticism: (1) on the one hand, the "Grundevangeliumshypothese" (cf. Wellhausen, Schwartz), in which it is held that the different literary layers are due to the same author (Boismard, Brown) or a Johannine school (Richter, Haenchen, Thyen); (2) the "Mehrquellentheorie" of Bultmann (cp. J. Becker, Koester, Marxsen, Schenke, Schnackenburg). Later, in *TR* 51, pp. 31-37, Becker expanded this simplified schema to six models and reckoned his own literary criticism within the last: "Das sechste Modell übernimmt aus Bultmanns Gesamtthese die vor dem Evangelisten liegenden Stücke wie die Semeiaquelle und den Passionsbericht..., sowie Einzeltraditionen (z.B. Logoshymnus), lässt aber nach dem Evangelisten das Evangelium einer umfangreicheren Redaktion unterworfen sein. Diese Phasen der Entstehung des jetzigen Gesamttextes sowie die Beachtung auch der joh Briefe erlauben es, umrisshaft eine Geschichte des joh Gemeindesverbandes zu zeichnen... Die primären Vertreter dieser Ansicht sind Schnackenburg ... und Becker" (pp. 35-36).

254. In *Exkurs 1* (*Johannes*, I, pp. 112-120 [134-142]) Becker gives a precise description of "Die Semeiaquelle" with reference to (1) argumentation, (2) content and literary form, (3) the Sitz-im-Leben, (4) christology, and (5) the redactional reworking of the SQ by the evangelist. Like most authors, Becker does not accept a *Redenquelle*: "Vermieden wird damit die Annahme einer Redenquelle, die in der Forschung mit Recht kaum Anklang fand (vgl. jedoch H. Becker; Vielhauer, Geschichte)" (I, p. 35 [39, referring also to H.-M. Schenke and Koester]).

255. Cf. *Johannes*, II, pp. 531-539 [634-643]: "Exkurs 13: Der joh Passionsbericht". See below, pp. 124-125 nn. 297-301.

256. He assigns not only ch. 21 to the Ecclesiastical Redactor, but also the *Nachträge* in 3,31-36; 10,1-18; 12,44-50; chs. 15–17; and other smaller additions like 1,29b; 5,28-29; 6,51c-59; etc. (*Johannes*, I, p. 35 [40]).

257. *Wunder*, p. 131 (= 1980, p. 437).

258. *Ibid.*, pp. 131-135 (= 1980, pp. 437-443).

259. With reference to Faure and Bultmann (p. 131; = 1980, p. 437). On p. 132 n. 1 (= 1980, p. 437 n. 9) he provides a list of defenders of the semeia hypothesis (see above,

mann in short, scattered notations; since then, no further arguments have been adduced[260]. The hypothesis has been hard-pressed by the style criticism of Schweizer and Ruckstuhl, who maintain that the Fourth Gospel is a "seamless robe" out of which the different literary layers can hardly be separated[261]. But Bultmann also gave arguments from content[262]: (1) The conclusion of the gospel (20,30-31) is the conclusion of the miracle book, since the contents of the gospel can hardly be brought under the concept of "signs"[263]. (2) The extremely heightened miracles do not harmonize with sayings that definitely relativize the miracles. Such contradiction could not be the work of the same author; there must have been a source that was reworked[264]. (3) The two Cana miracles are numbered (2,11; 4,54), but this count contradicts 2,23 and 4,45. Therefore, the consecutive numbering of the two miracles must have been

p. 71 n. 1). In his commentary (*Johannes*, I, p. 113 [135]), Becker refers for the analysis of the Johannine miracle stories especially ("grundlegend") to Bultmann, Haenchen, Fortna and Nicol; in ³1991 Appold and Wöllner are added.

260. *Wunder*, p. 132 (= 1980, p. 438). See, however, below, p. 119 n. 265.

261. The image "seamless robe" comes from STRAUSS, *Vorrede zu den Gesprächen von Ulrich von Hutten*, in *Gesammelte Schriften*, VII, ³1890, p. 556 (original edition, 1860, p. XLIV), cited by HOWARD, *Fourth Gospel*, ⁴1955, p. 297; see also HENGEL, *The Johannine Question*, 1989, p. 1; cf. p. 136 n. 1; GT: 1993, p. 9; cf. p. 9 n. 1). – KÄSEMANN, in *VF* (1951-52), p. 206, cited by Becker (p. 132; = 1980, pp. 438-439) remarks, in fact, that not even Ruckstuhl explains any of the aporias in a conclusive way: "Keine einzige der zahllosen Aporien, die zur Quellenkritik getrieben haben, hat (bei Ruckstuhl) eine Lösung gefunden. Man steht erneut am Ausgangspunkt und hat im Grunde ... nichts dazugelernt ... Das Rätsel der Historie lastet weiter auf allen Fragenden". For Becker, the style-critical method itself is not free from criticism. With reference to HIRSCH, *Stilkritik*, 1950-51, and HAENCHEN, *Literatur*, 1955, pp. 307-308, he remarks: "Einmal kann diese statistische Erhebung dem Einfluss des Stils einer Schrift auf ihre Bearbeiter nicht gerecht werden. Vor allem ist aber die Erhebung der stilistischen Eigentümlichkeiten des Johannesevangeliums aufgrund eines Vergleichs nur mit den übrigen Schriften des Neuen Testaments (so Ruckstuhl) höchst fragwürdig. Zeigt sich doch, dass der johanneische Stil zwar relative Selbständigkeit innerhalb des uns erhaltenen neutestamentlichen Schrifttums besitzt, jedoch häufig die literarische Sprache der Koine verwendet. Diese Beobachtung verbietet den Rückschluss auf nur einen Verfasser, dessen individuelle Sprache durch die Statistik erhoben werden soll, und fordert zwingend, den johanneischen Stil nicht individuell, sondern soziologisch zu deuten. Die johanneische Sprache hat ihre Prägung primär durch eine Gemeindetradition erhalten, nicht durch einen einzelnen 'Schriftsteller'" (p. 133; = 1980, p. 439). On the use of style criticism, see also *Johannes*, I, p. 34 [38]. – Note, however, that Becker, in the passages he ascribes to the source, uses the absence of Johannine style characteristics as an argument in his commentary, although he says nothing about it in his *Exkurs 1* on the *Semeiaquelle*. Cf. *Johannes*, I, p. 106 [127] (on 2,1-12): "Dass E die Wundergeschichte vorgefunden hat, ist sicher: 2,1-12 gehört zu den Stücken des Joh, die kaum joh Spracheigentümlichkeiten enthalten (Schweizer)"; p. 230 [276] (on 5,9b-16): "die Sprache gehäuft unjohanneisch".

262. *Wunder*, pp. 133-134 (= 1980, pp. 439-441).

263. *Wunder*, pp. 133-134 (= 1980, p. 439-440); cp. *Johannes*, I, p. 113 [135] (argument a, with reference to Bultmann); II, pp. 632-633 [753-757] (see below, pp. 123 n. 295, 127 n. 313). See my reaction on pp. 402-403.

264. *Wunder*, p. 134 (= 1980, p. 440); cp. *Johannes*, I, pp. 113-114 [135] (argument b, with reference to Bultmann). See also below, p. 127 n. 314.

from a source. Becker contends, however, that Bultmann's postulation that the source would have had a continuous count beyond the first two is an "unproven assertion"[265].

For Becker, reconstruction of SQ in detail, as with the Q source, is frequently hypothetical[266]; yet the extent of the source can be ascertained more precisely than Bultmann has done[267]. Thus, in his commentary, he indicates the essential contours and details of the source which are certainly recognizable[268]: (1) 1,19ff. is the beginning and 20,30-31 is clearly the conclusion of the source. (2) The number of the miracles (seven) is an indication of completeness. (3) The source contained an entire itinerary[269]. (4) The parts of SQ are often concentrated around confessions and acclamations; these serve to structure entire sections[270]. (5) The relation of miracle worker, miracle, and faith has been thematized[271]. (6) The relation with the competing Baptist com-

---

265. *Wunder*, p. 134 (= 1980, pp. 440-441); cp. *Johannes*, I, p. 114 [135-136] (argument d, with reference to Bultmann). Against Bultmann, he remarks that any reader can count to seven. Even in Ex 4 (cf. 4,8-9) only the first signs are numbered and thus are placed in relation to the certainly-not-accidental number of plagues in Ex 7–14. In ³1991 [136] Becker adds: "Auch sonst zeigt SQ ein auffälliges Interesse an Zahlen (vgl. nur 1,37.39f.; 2,6; 4,6.52f.; 5,5; 6,7.9f.13.19; 11,6.17)". Cp. *Johannes*, I, pp. 106 [127: in an addition, he rejects that the numbering in 2,11 and 4,54 refers only to the miracles in *Cana*], 186 [224]. See also his reaction to Conzelmann (see below, p. 127 n. 313). In his commentary (I, pp. 113-114 [135-136]), however, he gives three further arguments for the existence of the SQ, which he identifies there as a literary source (cf. 20,30-31) (the arguments c, e, and f [in ³1991: c, f, and g]): (4) The distinction between tradition and redaction that can be made in the pericopes which probably belong to the *Semeiaquelle* (with reference to Bultmann and Haenchen). (5) The clearly identifiable structure and theological conception of the source (with reference to J. Becker, Fortna, and Nicol). (6) The lack of Johannine dualism, of the style of the *Offenbarungsreden*, of the eschatological expressions, and especially of the Johannine christology of "sending" in the *Quellenstücken*. For this last argument, he refers to his own negative description of the source in *Wunder*, p. 136 (= 1980, p. 443); see below, p. 126 n. 311. In ³1991 [136] he adds a seventh argument (= e): the miracles were already linked together by transitional verses (e.g., 2,12) and topographical indications before the redaction of E.

266. Cf. *Wunder*, p. 135 n. 1 (= 1980, p. 441 n. 23); cp. *Johannes*, I, p. 114 [136]. See also the *Nachtrag [1979]*, p. 462: "Schwierig is allerdings die Umfangsbestimmung. Sie wird naturgemäss wie bei der Logienquelle im Detail nur umrissweise rekonstruierbar sein (mit W. Nicol ...; anders R.T. Fortna ...)"; cp. *TR* 47, p. 295. – Note that Becker (*Johannes*, I, p. 13 [13]) expressly calls his literary criticism a working hypothesis: "Das Modell hat dienende Funktion und gehört zu den widerlegbaren Wahrheiten, so sicher sein Autor überzeugt ist, dieses hypothetische Modell komme der Wirklichkeit recht nahe"; cp. *TR* 47, p. 295: "Sicherlich bleiben das gewonnene Gesamtbild und seine Einzelheiten im letzten Sinne hypothetisch. Literarkritische Theorien sind Hilfsmodelle für den Zugang zum Text, als 'widerlegbare Wahrheiten'". For Schnelle's reaction, see below, p. 336 n. 516.

267. *Wunder*, p. 135 n. 1 (= 1980, p. 441 n. 23)

268. *Johannes*, I, p. 114 [136].

269. See below, pp. 120 n. 273, 121 n. 279.

270. Cf. 1,19ff.; 4,1ff.; 9,1ff.

271. See below, p. 127 n. 313.

munity is established[272]. (7) Special local traditions belong, as a rule, to this source[273].

Because the evangelist employed both the beginning and the end of the source, Becker thinks that the evangelist has probably retained the entire source[274]. He does not pursue the question of whether more material from the source is recognizable in the Gospel than he includes in his reconstruction; more could perhaps be assigned to it[275]. Form-critically, SQ consists mainly of novelistically expanded miracle stories, which have been placed together in the "Rahmengattung einer Wunderanthologie". This miracle collection is related to others in early Christianity, all of which have a missionary purpose, i.e., to draw attention to Jesus' peculiarity through his miracles[276].

272. *Johannes*, I, p. 114 [136]; cp. p. 91 [110] (1,19ff.): "Dann betrieb schon die SQ Polemik gegen den Täufer. Die SQ bekämpft diese Konkurrenz mit der Aberkennung von Würdeprädikaten für Johannes"; cp. p. 93 [112]; p. 100 [120] (1,35ff.): "So spricht der Verfasser der SQ der Johannesgemeinde ihre Existenzberichtigung ab"; p. 153 [181] (3,22-30): "Dass der Täufer in Samaria wirkte, ist eine ähnlich singuläre Angabe wie die Tauftätigkeit Jesu. Sie setzt zumindest voraus, dass der SQ noch Täufergemeinden in dieser Gegend bekannt waren (Kundsin) und dass die christliche Mission in Samaria (4,39-42) auf die Konkurrenz der Täufergemeinde stiess"; p. 340 [396] (10,40-42). See also Becker's description of the Sitz-im-Leben of the source (see below, pp. 125-126).

273. Becker frequently stresses this in his commentary. Cf. *Johannes*, I, p. 90 [109] (1,28): "Endlich zeichnet sich die SQ durch besondere Ortstraditionen aus"; cp. p. 92 [111]: "Diese Ortsangabe gehört zur Sonderüberlieferung der SQ"; p. 110 [131] (2,12): "Dass die Familie Jesu sich in Kapernaum [aufhielt oder hier sogar] ansiedelte, ist abermals eine Sonderüberlieferung der SQ"; p. 152 [180] (3,23): "Sie [SQ] enthielt nicht nur das Täuferthema, sondern zu ihr passen besonders gut die Ortsangaben"; cp. p. 153 [181]: "Besser passen die Angaben zum geographisch konkret gemeinten Itinerar der SQ"; pp. 165-166 [cp. 197] (4,5-6): "Auch das Interesse am Lokalkolorit (4,5f.) deutet in dieselbe Richtung: Die Vorlage in Joh 4 wird zur SQ gehören"; cp. p. 168 [200]: "Sie [die Erzählung] hat – für die SQ typisch – starkes Interesse an Lokaltraditionen"; p. 185 [222] (4,46a): "V. 46a dürfte [sachlich] das Itinerar der SQ sein (vgl. 2,1.11)"; p. 190 [228] (6,1): "Die Situation eingangs beginnt mit dem Itinerar, das E (vgl. 4,43.47.54) und die SQ (vgl. 4,46) für sich reklamieren können"; p. 230 [227] (7,1ff.): "Das Itinerar der SQ, das den Übergang zwischen 6,1-25(G) und Joh abgab, findet sich in 7,1ff. (G) als Torso wieder"; p. 231 [not noted in ³1991] (5,2-3): "Dass die SQ den ungewöhnlichen Bau korrekt beschreibt, zeigt, dass sie wie so oft gute Lokalkenntnisse besass, die man E selbst nich zutrauen kann"; p. 340 [396] (10,40-42): "Dabei bedient er sich offenbar eines Stückes aus der SQ... Auf sie weist die ungewöhnliche Ortsangabe"; II, p. 366 [430] (11,54): "Sie [die Ortsangabe] passt ausgezeichnet in das Bild der SQ, die singuläre Ortsangaben bei relativ guter geographischer Kenntnis enthält". See also *Nachtrag [1979]*, p. 463: "M.E. wäre es ergänzend möglich, das gesamte Milieu der SQ noch besser in den Blick zu bekommen, wenn z.B. das Itinerar und die Ortsnamen der SQ für den Standort des Verfassers und für das Milieu der Gemeinden ausgewertet werden". Cp. Gnilka's stress on the itinerary of the source (see below, p. 135 n. 354).

274. *Wunder*, p. 135 (= 1980, p. 443).

275. *Ibid.*, p. 135 n. 8 (= 1980, p. 443 n. 30): "Im jedem Fall könnte sie [this question] nur Beantwortung finden mit Hilfe des Analogieschlusses von den der Semeiaquelle relativ sicher zuzuweisenden oben genannten Stücken".

276. *Johannes*, I, p. 115 [137]. Other miracle collections are found in the Old Testament (Moses, Elijah), in the Synoptic tradition, and in the apocryphal gospels.

In both article and commentary, Becker highlights the redaction of the source[277]. According to him, the author of SQ gave the traditional material a distinct structure by "Kommentierung" and "Rahmung"[278]. There are five parts: parts 1-3 take place in Galilee, part 4 in Judea, and part 5 is the conclusion[279]. He includes in the *Semeiaquelle* the "Grundstock" of the following pericopes:

1. Jesus as the Son of God proclaimed by the Baptist:
   (a) 1,19-34[280];
   (b) 1,35-51[281];

---

277. See above, p. 116 n. 249. Against Bultmann, Becker notes (*Wunder*, p. 134; = 1980, p. 441): "Er versäumt es jedoch, Aufbau und Theologie der Quelle in Erwägung zu ziehen. Diese Konsequenz ist die Schattenseite seines Zieles, die ihm allein bedeutsame Theologie des Evangelisten zu erheben. Aber weder ist dieser damit gedient, hintergrundlos erörtert zu werden, noch kann die Semeiaquelle aus ihrem schemenhaften Dasein ohne Bemühung um ihr Profil befreit werden".

278. *Johannes*, I, p. 115 [137].

279. *Ibid.* Cp. *Wunder*, pp. 134-135 (= 1980, pp. 441-443), where Becker stresses that the twofold structure of the source (Jesus' activity in Galilee and in Judea respectively) is the same as that in the Gospel of Mark, and is clearly demarcated at 7,1-13 (see also below, p. 123 n. 289). The three Passovers on which Jesus goes to Jerusalem, however, are to be ascribed to the evangelist's composition; cf. CONZELMANN, in *RGG*³ 3, 1959, c. 625 (*Wunder*, p. 135 n. 6; = 1980, p. 442 n. 28). For the description of the five parts, cf. *Johannes*, I, pp. 115-116 [137-138]. In his article (*Wunder*, p. 134; = 1980, p. 441) Becker refers for a detailed analysis to Bultmann's commentary and to Haenchen's article, *Johanneische Probleme*.

280. Thus, Becker's reconstruction begins with 1,19: "Die Jüngerberufung in 1,35ff., die auch nach Bultmann der Semeiaquelle zuzurechnen ist, setzt eingangs ein Täuferzeugnis voraus". Jn 10,41-42, indicating the theological relevance of the Baptist's witness, strengthens this hypothesis. His entire testimony is concentrated on the anticlimax ("I am not the Christ, I am not Elijah, I am not the prophet"), and expressed in the confirmation: Jesus is the Son of God. This last title in particular, as well as an indication for christological titles in general, fits the signs source exceptionally well (*Wunder*, p. 135 n. 2; = 1980, p. 442 n. 24). – See also *Johannes*, I, pp. 89-98 [107-117], esp. 90-92 [109-111], where Becker assigns to SQ the "Grundbestand" of vv. 19-28 (p. 90 [109]) and some elements of vv. 32.34 (p. 91 [111: vv. 32f.34]). In vv. 19-28, Becker recognizes some typical redactional features of E: "So ist das Zeugnisablegen des Täufers (1,6-8.15) für ihn charakteristisch (1,19a.32a.34). Er arbeitet die Überlegenheit Jesu über den Täufer durch dessen Präexistenz heraus (V 15 und V 30). Zu ihm passt, dass Jesus nur an dem göttlichen Zeichen (V 32f.) erkannt wird, und der Täufer nur dazu da ist, den auch ihm wie allen anderen in seiner Würde vorher Unbekannten aufgrund des göttlichen Zeichens zu bezeugen (1,26c.31.33a; vgl. 5,31ff.). E und nicht die SQ spricht von 'den Juden' (V 19) durchweg so pauschal. Da erst durch ihre Einführung die Spannung zu V 24 entsteht, fällt es um so leichter, hier E am Werk zu sehen" (p. 90 [109-110]). Further, Becker thinks that SQ used two "Einzelüberlieferungen" in vv. 19-28 (p. 90-91 [not noted in ³1991, but see pp. 108-109]: (a) "ein gerahmtes Wort in V 22-24 ... mit Resten aus V 19"; (b) vv. 26-27 (and v. 20) (p. 90). On 1, 28, see above, p. 120 n. 273.

281. See *Johannes*, I, pp. 99-105 [119-125], esp. 99-101 [119-121]. From SQ are: 1,37-42.44-50. The evangelist added vv. 35-36.43.51 and "die für griechische Leser bestimmten Erklärungen in V 38.41.42" (p. 101 [121]).

(c) 2,1-11[282];
(d) 2,12[283].

2. The Baptist decreases and Jesus' activity increases:
(a) 3,22-30[284];
(b) 4,1-42[285];
(c) 4,43-54[286].

3. The prophet Jesus has no significance in his own country Galilee:
(a) 6,1-15[287];

282. In contrast to Bultmann, Becker ascribes all of 2,11 to the source: the relation "Jesus - sign - disciples" is precisely the same as in 20,30-31; cf. *Wunder*, p. 135 n. 3 (= 1980, p. 442 n. 25); *Johannes*, I³, p. 128 (not noted in the first ed.). See also *Johannes*, I, pp. 106-112 [126-133], esp. 106-107 [127-128]; cp. p. 90 [109]. – From E (I, pp. 106-107 [127-128]): the mention of the third day in v. 1 (cf. 1,29.35.43); the explanation κατὰ τὸν καθαρισμὸν τῶν Ἰουδαίων in v. 6 ("E pflegt solche Erklärungen zu geben, manchmal – wie hier – ohne grosses Geschick"; p. 107 [128]), and the parenthesis καὶ οὐκ ᾔδει πόθεν ἐστίν, οἱ δὲ διάκονοι ᾔδεισαν οἱ ἠντληκότες τὸ ὕδωρ in v. 9 ("vgl. 6,6; 12,16; 20,9 als formale und 3,8; 4,11; 7,27f. usw. als sprachliche Parallelen"; p. 107 [128]). On the absence of Johannine style characteristics in this pericope and on v. 11, see above, pp. 118 n. 261, 119 n. 265.

283. *Johannes*, I, p. 110 [131]: "V. 12 leitete schon in der SQ zur nächsten Erzählung über". Against Wellhausen and Fortna, Becker (p. 108 [128]) argues that SQ mentions Jesus' disciples already in v. 12 (cf. 1,50). For the brothers of Jesus in SQ, see also 7,3.5.10. On 2,12, see also above, p. 120 n. 273.

284. This section is not mentioned as part of SQ in *Wunder*, but, see *Johannes*, I, pp. 152-155 [180-184], esp. 153-154 [181-183]. From SQ are vv. 23. 24 ("Zwischenbemerkung der SQ"; p. 153 [182]). 25 (with Loisy and Bauer, Becker accepts the conjecture μετὰ Ἰησοῦ instead of μετὰ Ἰουδαίου; in ³1991 he adds Bentley). 26 (without ᾧ σὺ μεμαρτύρηκας = E; cf. 1,19-34). 28. 30. E added also v. 22 ("Überleitung von E") and v. 27 (cp. 6, 65; 19,11); v. 29 comes from KR (p. 155 [183]). On 3,23, see also above, p. 120 n. 273.

285. *Johannes*, I, pp. 165-184 [194-216], esp. 165-167 [194-199]. SQ contained vv. 5-7a. 7b-9b. 16-19. 27-29. 30 and fragments of vv. 40-42 ("Und viele ... glaubten (ihm) und ... sprachen...: Wir wissen, dieser ist wahrhaftig der Retter der Welt"; p. 167). In ³1991, he considers VV. 40.39.42b the end of SQ's story (cp. Fortna): "... und sie sprachen ...: Wir wissen, dieser ist wahrhaftig der Retter der Welt" [199]). Becker assigns to E (p. 168 [199]): vv. 1-4 ("im wesentlichen Itinerar von E"; p. 166 [197]). 10-15. 20-26. 31-38; to KR (p. 166 [197]: vv. 2.4 and further: ὡς οὖν ἔγνω ὁ κύριος (v. 1) (p. 166, not mentioned in ³1991 [197]); οὐ γὰρ συγχρῶνται Ἰουδαῖοι Σαμαρίταις (v. 9). On 4,5-6, see also above, p. 120 n. 273.

286. 4,48-49 is from the evangelist (cf. Haenchen); the rest can be assigned to the signs source (*Wunder*, p. 135 n. 4; = 1980, p. 442 n. 25). Cp. *Johannes*, I, pp. 185-188 [222-226], esp. 186 [223]: "Sein [E's] Kommentar ist vielmehr sehr [relativ] sparsam". Besides vv. 48-49 (in ³1991 [223], he mentions, with Dauer and Wegner, also v. 50b), E added to SQ: ἐκ τῆς Ἰουδαίας εἰς τὴν Γαλιλαίαν in v. 47; ἐλθὼν ἐκ τῆς Ἰουδαίας εἰς τὴν Γαλιλαίαν in v. 54. Also vv. 43.45 are from E ("Mit V 43.45 setzt eingangs E sein Itinerar fort"; p. 185 [222]); V. 44 is "eine Randnotiz ..., die ein Leser aus der joh Gemeinde frühzeitig an den Textbestand schrieb, und die bei der Vervielfältigung des Joh dann in den Text eingebaut wurde"; p. 185 [223]). On 4,46a.54, see above, pp. 119 n. 265, 120 n. 273.

287. Becker thinks that ch. 6 preceded ch. 5 in SQ and also in E (*Wunder*, p. 135 n. 5; = 1980, p. 442 n. 27; cp. *Johannes*, I, p. 162 [191]). In *Johannes*, I, pp. 189-194 [228-232], Becker assigns to SQ: vv. 1 (without τῆς Τιβεριάδος = KR; cf. 21,1 and also

(b) 6,16-21[288];
(c) 7,1-13[289].

4. Rejection in Jerusalem and belief among the disciples:
   (a) 5,1-18[290];
   (b) 9,1-34[291];
   (c) 10,40-42[292];
   (d) 11,1-44.54[293].

5. Conclusion of SQ:
   (a) 12,37-43[294];
   (b) 20,30-31[295].

6,23). 3. 5. 7. 8-9. 10-13 and for vv. 14-15 in SQ he gives the following reconstruction: "Als die Menschen das Zeichen sahen, das er getan hatte, sagten sie: 'Wahrhaftig, das ist der Prophet...' (Und) ... Jesus ... zog sich wieder auf den Berg zurück, er allein"; he assigns to E ("E hat das Wunder selbst – wie oft – ohne grossen Kommentar übernommen"; p. 193 [231]): vv. 2. 6 (p. 191 [230]: "eine unterbrechende Lesehilfe"; cp. 11,11-15; see also 2,21; 9,22-23); to KR: v. 4. On 6,1, see above, p. 120 n. 273.

288. *Johannes*, I, p. 195 [234]: "E hat 6,16ff. aus Treue zur SQ berichtet. Auf sie geht wohl der ganze Text zurück"; cp. p. 189 [228].

289. *Wunder*, p. 135 n. 6 (= 1980, p. 442 n. 28): "Der hier gegebene Aufriss folgt also Bultmanns Vermutung..., in 7,1-13 liege ein stark überarbeitetes Quellenstück, der Semeiaquelle zugehörig, zugrunde, das ehedem in der Semeiaquelle die Einleitung zu Joh. 5,1ff. abgab". Cp. *Johannes*, I, p. 262 [313]: "(man) wird die Hypothese wagen dürfen, dass etwa in 7,3a.4a.6.9 eine fragmentarische Einleitung der SQ zu Joh 5,1ff. vorliegt"; cp. p. 230 [277]. See also above, p. 120 n. 273.

290. In *Johannes*, I, pp. 229-233 [276-281], esp. 229-230 [276-277], Becker assigns 5,2-9b and also (ctr. Haenchen and Fortna) 9c-16 (without the mention of the Jews in vv. 10.15.16 = E) to SQ; E added vv. 1. 17-18. SQ used a traditional miracle story: "Dann hat wohl der Verfasser der SQ eine ursprüngliche ihm vorliegende vom Sabbatkonflikt freie Wundererzählung durch V 9c-16 erweitert" (p. 230 [277]). On 5,2-3, see also above, p. 120 n. 273.

291. Becker (*Johannes*, I, pp. 315-323 [370-378], esp. 315-316 [370-371]) assigns to the oldest tradition of chapter 9: vv. 1. 6-7; to SQ vv. 1. 2. 3a. 6. 7a and the "Grundstock" of vv. 8-12. 13-17. 18-23. 24-34; to E vv. 3b-5. 7b ("die Parenthese"). 9. 16b. 18a. 22-23. 27b-30. 35-41.

292. *Johannes*, I, p. 340 [396]: "Um so genauer weiss E zu erzählen, wohin Jesus entweicht (V 40-42). Dabei bedient er sich offenbar eines Stückes aus der SQ"; cp. p. 90 [109]. See also above, p. 120 n. 273.

293. Becker (*Johannes*, II, pp. 344-364 [404-426], esp. 344-350 [404-411]) presumes that SQ used a "Basistext", which contained vv. 1. 3. 17. 38b (ἦν δὲ σπήλαιον καὶ λίθος ἐπέκειτο ἐπ' αὐτῷ). 39a (λέγει ὁ Ἰησοῦς· ἄρατε τὸν λίθον). 41a (ἦραν οὖν τὸν λίθον). 43 (without ταῦτα εἰπών). 44. In SQ the following verses were added: 5. 6. 7a (ἔπειτα λέγει τοῖς μαθηταῖς·, without μετὰ τοῦτο). 11b (Λάζαρος ὁ φίλος ἡμῶν κεκοίμηται· ἀλλὰ πορεύομαι ἵνα ἐξυπνίσω αὐτόν). 12. 14. 15. 18. 19 (without ἐκ τῶν Ἰουδαίων). 20. 21 (without οὖν). 28. 29. 30. 32. 33a (Ἰησοῦς οὖν ὡς εἶδεν αὐτὴν κλαίουσαν). 33c (ἐνεβριμήσατο τῷ πνεύματι). 34. 38a (Ἰησοῦς ἔρχεται εἰς τὸ μνημεῖον·, without οὖν πάλιν ἐμβριμώμενος). 39b.c. For Becker, 11,54 is "der szenische Abschluss zu 11,1ff. (G) aus der SQ" (II, p. 365 [428]).

294. From SQ are vv. 37-38; cf. *Wunder*, p. 135 (= 1980, p. 442); *Johannes*, II, pp. 408-409 [475-476].

295. In v. 31 E added καὶ ἵνα πιστεύοντες ζωὴν ἔχητε ἐν τῷ ὀνόματι αὐτοῦ; cf. *Wunder*, p. 135 (= 1980, p. 442). Cp. *Johannes*, II, pp. 632-633 [753-757]. For Becker's reaction to Bittner and Schnelle, see below, pp. 401 n. 109, 402 n. 120.

In contrast to Bultmann's reconstruction, Becker adds the "Grundstock" of 1,19-34 and 3,22-30, but he omits 7,19-23[296]. In the *Anhang* to the reprint of his article (1980) and in his commentary, Becker notes that SQ is clearly to be distinguished from PB and related *Einzeltraditionen*. Thus, it is immediately clear for him that the E(vangelist) did not have a *Grundevangelium* at his disposal. Becker notes the following differences between SQ and PB[297]: (a) SQ has no special relationship with the Lukan tradition, as PB does, but only with the Markan tradition[298]. (b) SQ makes no reference to the PB, and on the other hand PB never speaks of the miracles[299]. (c) The title "Son of God", typical for SQ, is

296. See above, pp. 29-34.
297. *Johannes*, I, p. 114 [136-137]. Cp. *Nachtrag [1979]*, p. 462: "Doch ist es von wesentlicher Bedeutung für die Theologie der Quelle wie der des Evangelisten, welche Grundstruktur sie besitzt. Hier besteht neuerdings wieder die Tendenz, die alte Hypothese eines Grundevangeliums in Anlehnung an J. Wellhausen zu vertreten und demzufolge (nahezu) alles erzählende Material aus dem Johannesevangelium einschliesslich des Passionsberichtes (PB) der SQ, oder nun sinnvoller: dem Grundevangelium, zuzuweisen (vgl. etwa: R.T. Fortna, G. Richter, H. Thyen, W. Langbrandtner). Dieser Tendenz vermag ich mich nicht einzuschliessen, sondern sehe in R. Bultmanns Trennung von SQ und PB den besseren Weg. Eine Bestätigung gewinnt diese Ansicht bei A. Dauer ..., und bei R. Schnackenburg ... M.E. fällt schon auf den ersten Blick auf, dass der Schlüsselbegriff Semeion aus der SQ in PB ganz fehlt und auch die Titulatur Sohn Gottes nur in der SQ, nicht im PB begegnet. Dieser bezieht sich nirgends auf jesuanische Wundertradition (18,10ff.) und orientiert sich christologisch am 'König der Juden', Joh. 20f. dann am Titel Kyrios. Beide Bezeichnungen Jesu fehlen in der SQ. Auch gibt es keinen sicheren Hinweis, dass Stücke aus der SQ den PB vorbereiten sollen. Die SQ war also kein Evangelium im gattungsgeschichtlichen Sinn, sondern ein literarischer Zyklus von Wundererzählungen, der wie ein Werbeplakat Mission für Jesus betreiben wollte". See also *TR* 47 (1982), p. 297: "Die Differenzen zwischen den Wundergeschichten im Joh einerseits und dem Redenstoff sowie der Passionserzählung andererseits sind recht gross; und es will nicht gelingen, eine vor dem Evangelisten liegende Verbindung zwischen diesen drei Bereichen zu bestimmen. Macht Haenchen darum den Verzicht auf eine genaue Rekonstruktion zur Tugend solider Enthaltsamkeit, weil er diese Nagelprobe scheut?". Cp. above, p. 117 n. 255. See also his reaction to Wagner in ³1991 (II, p. 429).
298. *Johannes*, I, p. 114 [136]; cp. pp. 36-37 [43-44]: "Fragt man zunächst nach dem Verhältnis der SQ zu den Synoptikern, so ergibt sich, dass die Themenfolge eingangs der Quelle, die Akoluthie der Stoffe in Joh 6 und die Abfolge einer galiläischen und judäischen Periode des Lebens Jesu Verwandtschaft mit Mk zeigen. Diese Verwandtschaft ist offenbar traditionsgeschichtlicher Art. Die SQ zeigt nirgends ein direktes literarisches Abhängigkeitsverhältnis zu einem der Synoptiker (Haenchen). Dies gilt auch dort, wo relativ enge einzelne Formulierungen an Mk erinnern (vgl. Joh 5,8 mit Mk 2,11; Joh 6,7 mit Mk 6,37; Joh 6,20 mit Mk 6,50)" (in ³1991 [44] he adds: "Diese geringen engen Einzelbeziehungen können angesichts des gesamten Stoffes der SQ keine Basis für ein Urteil abgeben, die Wunderquelle benutzte z.B. Mk direkt"). Cp. p. 38 [45]: "So ergibt sich als Gesamtthese: Der joh Gemeindeverband kennt auf keiner theologiegeschichtlichen Stufe auch nur eines der synoptischen Evangelien. Das vierte Evangelium auf allen Ebenen ist nicht geschaffen, die Synoptiker zu ergänzen oder zu verdrängen. Seine Quellen und es selbst samt seiner Redaktion sind unabhängig von den ersten drei Evangelien konzipiert. Dabei zeigen jedoch die beiden Quellen traditionsgeschichtlich besondere Affinität, sei es zu Mk (so die SQ), sei es zu Lk (so der PB)". Cp. above, p. 121 n. 279.
299. *Ibid.*, p. 114 [136].

lacking in PB; on the other hand, SQ lacks the typical titles "King of the Jews" and "Kyrios"[300]. (d) PB does not portray the death and resurrection of Jesus as σημεῖα and is thus at some variance with 20,30-31 and SQ as a whole[301]. (e) SQ and PB each have an independent thematic, which is especially expressed in their respective christologies. (f) Both are completely different as *Gattungen*.

In his commentary, Becker gives a precise description of the Sitz-im-Leben of the source. It is clear for him that the community in which the SQ originated lived in "Konkurrenzverhältnisse"[302]. That the Baptist is not a miracle worker serves as an objection against the claims he makes (10,41). The "heightened" miracles also point in general to the field of competition with different and similar missionary activities besides the Christian community[303]. SQ accordingly belongs in the *religionsgeschichtliche* context of a certain kind of missionary activity, which at that time was widespread[304].

This milieu can be more precisely described when the Johannine miracles are compared with the Synoptic miracle stories and those of Acts. There Jesus and the apostles are persons through whom God works miracles[305]; in SQ, on the contrary, Jesus is portrayed as the miracle worker who performs miracles in his own right for self-revelation and radiation of his glory[306]. The miracle is an epiphany of the divine power of the

300. *Ibid.*, p. 114 [136]. See also below, p. 126.

301. *Ibid.*, p. 114 [136].

302. *Ibid.*, p. 116 [138]. Cp. *TR* 42, p. 341. See also above, p. 120 n. 272.

303. "Wer so mit Freude und Mässivität Wunder als Anlass, Jesus zu glauben, darstellt, will andere, die von ihren Meistern ähnliches berichten, verdrängen. Besonders gut passt solche durch das Wunder sich legitimierende Missionstätigkeit u.a. nach Samaria und Syrien (vgl. Apg 8,4-25)" (*Johannes*, I, p. 116 [138]). See also the new Excursus (8a) in ³1991: "Der Missionsgedanke im Joh" [pp. 216-221, esp. 217-218]: "Sie [SQ] versteht sich als eine Schrift, die im Eingehen auf das hellenistische Weltverstehen und Empfinden von religiösen Phänomenen Jesus Christus so zeichnet, dass die Leser solcher Herkunft zum Glauben kommen können. Natürlich ist für sie Jesus 'der König Israels' (Joh 1,49). Aber er is auch 'Retter der Welt' (4,42). Darum ist etwa die Samaritanermission (Joh 4 G) Thema der SQ, ja sind die Wunder überhaupt in missionarischer Konkurrensituation als missionarische Plakate gezeichnet". That signs and wonders served as missionary legitimation (in competition with other missionaries) is apparent from Acts 13,6-12; 14,3-4.8-13; 15,12; 16,14-20; 19,8-40; cp. Paul in Rom 15,18; 2 Cor 15,18. Such legitimation almost always meets with rejection (Acts 14,2.4; 16,19ff.; 19,9). SQ reflects this circumstance with the Isaian "hardening" motif (Jn 12,38-40; cf. Is 6,9), which was used elsewhere in the Christian tradition for such experiences (cp. Acts 19,9) and is especially encountered in the hardening of Pharoah in Ex 6–12.

304. *Johannes*, I, p. 116 [139] (with reference to Georgi, Haufe, Petzke, and Theissen; in ³1991 he adds Corrington).

305. *Ibid.*, p. 116 [139]. Cp. the Old Testament presentation of Moses in Ex 3–14.

306. *Ibid.*, p. 117 [139]. That is why the miracles are so marvelous; they are not performed out of compassion or to alleviate a need. Moreover, the description of Jesus' relationship with God is consciously relegated to the background.

miracle worker[307]. For Becker it is clear that SQ stood closer to Judaism than E did[308]; but the "Verfärbung" of this Jewish-Christian tradition by the Hellenistic portrayal of the miracle worker as a θεῖος ἀνήρ should not be lost[309].

2. What kind of christology did the source contain[310]? Becker first gives a number of negative considerations. In contrast to the other material of the Fourth Gospel, the signs source exhibits no dualism, no eschatology, no interest in describing the "coming" and "going" of the Lord (as, for instance, in 16,28), no reflection on Jesus' origin. It portrays Jesus as an earthly miracle worker; Son of Man-, κύριος-, and πατήρ-sayings are completely missing. Nowhere does Jesus speak in the style of the *Offenbarungsreden*. There is no development of the concept of church, and sacraments are not mentioned[311]. These arguments "e silentio" indicate that the source arose in a milieu different from, for exam-

---

307. Jesus is not presented as an elect of God through whom God works, but as θεῖος ἀνήρ, who makes his divine glory apparent in the miracles. In place of a manifestation of God through the miracle worker is the manifestation of the miracle worker himself. Thus the Jesus of SQ compares more to Simon Magus of Acts 8,9f. and to the typical Hellenistic miracle workers than to the Old Testament miracle workers and the Synoptic Jesus (p. 117 [139]). In [3]1991, p. 139, Becker adds: "Dazu passt die Beobachtung, dass im Unterschied zu den Synoptikern (Mk 6,7-13 parr.), zur Apg und Paulus das Joh nirgends von Wundern der Jünger bzw. Apostel erzählt. Die Fähigkeit zum Wunder ist exklusiv Jesus zugeordnet".

308. The christology (titles and expectations of salvation) betrays a Jewish-Christian background (see esp. 1,35ff.), a few miracle stories are derived from the Synoptic tradition (4,43ff.; 6,1-21), and the general Jewish milieu stands outside any discussion. SQ does not explain Jewish names and customs (these comments are from E), and it is primarily E who speaks of "the Jews" (p. 117; the last observation is omited in the [3]1991, p. 139). Cp. *Wunder*, p. 142 n. 1 (= 1980, p. 453 n. 53), where Becker also notes that the source can hardly be dated on the basis of ἐστίν in 5,2. With Bultmann, he thinks that the source was written in a Semitizing Greek. The author of the source used the Septuagint as his text for the Old Testament (12,38 = Is 53,1 LXX; and 2,5 is best explained as a free quotation of Gen 41,55 LXX). It can be doubted that the precise topographical knowledge in Jn 5 indicates that the author of the source was a Palestinian, for this data springs from his tradition and not from his own redaction. That Jesus finds no following among the Pharisees (5,9; 12,37), but does in Samaria (4,40-42), seems a sure indication for a non-Palestinian origin of the source. The source was probably the gospel in use in the Johannine community; cf. HAENCHEN, in *TR* 23 (1955), p. 303 (see above, p. 68 n. 132).

309. Becker remarks that the discussion is still in full swing (cf. Georgi, Habicht, Haufe, Kee, Mack, von Martitz, Petzke, Schüssler-Fiorenza, Tiede, and Corrington). Against O. Betz he notes: "Mögen dadurch auch die alten Arbeiten (Bieler, Wetter) überholt sein, die pauschale Leugnung des Phänomens in seiner Relevanz für die SQ ... hilft nicht weiter, vielmehr gilt es zu erkennen, dass die SQ hier nicht allein steht, sondern auch z.B. die mk Wundertradition in begrenztem Umfang ähnlich hellenisiert wurde (Luz)" (*Johannes*, I, p. 117 [139-140]). In [3]1991, p. 140, Becker adds: "Vor allem aber ist die deutliche Nähe der SQ zum Leben des Apollonios bei Philostratos unübersehbar (Kuhn)".

310. *Wunder*, pp. 136-143 (= 1980, pp. 443-454).

311. See also above, p. 119 n. 265 (argument 6).

ple, the discourses in John[312]. Positive description of the theology of the signs source can begin with an analysis of the notion σημεῖον. The passages where the idea is positively employed originate from the source (2,11; 4,54; 6,2.14; 10,41; 12,37; 20,30-31); where the sign is esteemed negatively, the evangelist is speaking (2,18.23; 3,2; 4,48; 6,26.30; 7,31; 9,16; 11,47; 12,18). Becker analyzes three aspects of the concept σημεῖον successively: the miracle itself, the person of the miracle worker, and the witness of the miracle[313]:

(a) Heightening of the miraculous and an epiphanic character are constitutive of the signs[314]. Compassion, forgiveness of sins, and exorcisms are absent.

(b) The miracle worker is central; the other persons are mere figures, and the settings are only props. He is himself a human being like

312. *Ibid.*, p. 136 (= 1980, p. 444).

313. "Semeion ist das Wort, indem sich das beschriebene Verhältnis der drei Grössen [Wundertäter, Wunder und Zeugen] zueinander verdichtet" (*Wunder*, p. 139; = 1980, p. 448; cp. *Johannes*, I, pp. 117-119 [140-141], esp. 119 [141]). Cp. *TR* 47, p. 341: "Dabei ist der Begriff Semeion vom Verfasser der Quelle redaktionell bewusst in diesem Zusammenhang eingesetzt: Er hat drei Konstituentia, die massive Steigerung des Wunders für die Transparenz der Herrlichkeit Jesu, die Qualifikation Jesu in seiner epiphanen Macht, und die glaubende Annahme des Wundertäters durch die Zeugen des Wunders". – Against Conzelmann (*Grundriss*, 1967, p. 377; see above, pp. 75-76 n. 24), who does not attribute the notion σημεῖον to the source, Becker remarks that the numbering of the signs, nevertheless, contradicts 2,23 and 4,45 even though these verses speak of miracles only summarily. There is no doubt that 4,48 is from the evangelist, but that does not imply that all other occurrences of σημεῖον should be attributed to him. The word σημεῖον in 20,30-31 is precisely the impetus for separating sources (*Wunder*, p. 136 n. 4; = 1980, p. 444 n. 34). – Regarding σημεῖον, Becker remarks in his commentary (*Johannes*, I, pp. 117-118 [140]) that the author of SQ has recast the Jewish-Christian usage in his own way and therefore avoids the otherwise customary Hellenistic understanding of miracle. The Old Testament understanding of σημεῖον is functional in a double manner. It occurs in SQ only in the redactional portions (2,11; 4,54; 6,2.14; 10,41; 12,37; 20,30-31) and thus expresses the theological function which the author ascribes to the miracles. Moreover, the concept from the tradition is a functional concept which expresses the referential character of a miraculous event. In early Christianity, a christological use of the concept akin to that of SQ appears only in Acts 2,22. Its use otherwise for apostolic works (Acts 4,30; 5,12; 6,8.13; 14,3; 15,12; Rom 15,19; 2 Cor 12,12; Heb 2,4) demonstrates, nevertheless, that SQ stands within early Christian tradition. In any case, all the aforementioned passages differ from SQ in that it is always God who performs the miracle in them. This goes as well for the use of the LXX (see esp. Ex 3–12). Josephus also knows the miracle as a sign in the functional, legitimizing sense (*Antiquities* 2,280.283f.; 9,23; 10,28).

314. The quantity of wine (2,6); the *Steigerung* of the healing at a distance (4,46-54); the insufficiency of 200 denarii to feed the crowd (6,7); the fact that the people eat their fill (6,11) and there are still twelve baskets left over (6,12; cp. Mk 8,8); the walking upon the sea with the sudden and safe arrival at the shore; the paralytic has been sick 38 years (5,5); the man is blind from birth (9,1); and Lazarus is already dead four days (11,17.39). Besides the epiphany of the wine miracle and the walking on the sea, the other miracle stories are written in the style of an epiphany (*Wunder*, pp. 137-138, esp. 137 n. 4; = 1980, pp. 445-446, esp. 446 n. 38; *Johannes*, I, p. 118 [140]).

others[315], not characterized by an extraordinary origin. Yet, Jesus is an exceptional person: he addresses his mother with the γύναι unfamiliar (2,4); his relatives may not give him orders (7,6). His exceptional character is especially apparent in his supernatural knowledge (1,47ff.; 4,16-19), which is only a means to discover something greater in his person, that is, the miracles that are promised by Jesus to Nathanael (1,50). Jn 9,33 speaks for all the miracles: "Never since the beginning of the world has it been heard that any one opened the eyes of a man born blind". Jesus is thus described as the greatest miracle worker: he accomplishes the most impossible things; he performs such a great number of miracles that one cannot describe them all (20,30); he himself takes the initiative[316]. Since prayer before the miracle and the mention of the Spirit are missing, Jesus seems very independent of God, his relation to whom is only incidentally described (e.g., 9,31). Never absent in the source, however, is a reference to his humanity.

(c) It is expected from the witnesses of the miracle that they draw conclusions about the nature of the miracle worker through the transparent character of the miracles; revelation in words is mentioned only accidentally in 4,42. There is no presupposition of faith, and the miracles have no double meaning. After the miracle, a conversion can take place among the spectators: "seeing" leads to an acclamation of the miracle worker, and the source calls this approval "faith" (2,11; 4,54; 10,42; 11,27; 12,37; 20,31). The whole signs source is a christological book of miracles, intended to incite faith (20,30-31)[317].

---

315. "The man called Jesus" (9,11); "Jesus of Nazareth, the son of Joseph" (1,45); Jesus' brothers are known (2,12; 7,25), as are his parents (1,45; 2,1) (*Wunder*, p. 138; = 1980, p. 446; *Johannes*, I, p. 118 [140]).

316. Jesus declines his mother's request and fixes the hour for the miracle himself (2,4); he addresses the paralytic (5,6); he foresees the bread miracle: the people must first follow him up the mountain and he shows unexpectedly how he procures food; the walking upon the sea also originates with the initiative of Jesus; he heals the blind man completely unsolicited; he himself sets the time for the raising of Lazarus (11,6-7.11bff.) (*Wunder*, p. 138 n. 1; = 1980, p. 447 n. 39; *Johannes*, I, p. 118 [140-141]).

317. *Wunder*, p. 139 (= 1980, p. 448): "Die Semeiaquelle ist ein christologisches Buch der Wunder, das um Glauben an diesen Wundertäter wirbt, wie ausdrücklich am Ende des Werkes in 20,30f. formuliert ist". The positive aim of the presentation in each of the parts is belief in Jesus the miracle worker (*Johannes*, I, p. 116 [138]). But discipleship in this sense undergoes threats and hostilities, which are always mentioned along with the theme of belief (p. 116 [138]): (1) The danger of a misunderstood Baptist obviously threatens the Christian community, which arose out of the Baptist group (1,19ff.; 3,22ff.; 10,40f.). (2) The distance in Galilee (6,1ff.) and especially the hostility in Jerusalem is clearly recognizable. One gets the impression that Jesus gains disciples only from the Baptist's circle (1,35ff.), in Samaria (4,1ff.), and among the Gentiles (4,43ff.). Few others are added to these (e.g., 11,1ff.). Moreover, it is striking that the places where, according to the source, something positive has happened are, in contradiction to the Synoptics, Samaria (3,23; 4,1ff.; 11,54) and the Jordan valley beyond Perea (1,28; 10,40; 11,6). It is in this, according to Becker, that a reflection can be seen of the *Gemeinde-*

Besides the notion σημεῖον, the christological titles also are constitutive of the theology of the signs source. They appear especially in the acclamations and the confessions of faith. This christological interest is present not only in 20,30-31 (Christ, Son of God), but in the whole source[318]. Above all, the titles Son of God and the Prophet are of essential importance for the source[319]. According to Becker, the interpreter must take into account that use of these titles points to a later Christian document. Most titles are only formally used. The study of G.P. Wetter[320] has more or less established that the title "Son of God" was connected with the θεῖος ἀνήρ conception; the same goes for "the Prophet"[321]. All theological characteristics of the miracles from

---

situation of SQ: "Sie setzt sich im geographischen und theologischen Sinn aus 'Randsiedlern' des Judentums zusammen" (p. 116 [138]). In ³1991, p. 138, Becker adds: "Doch sieht es so aus, als gehörte man noch zur Synagoge: Abständige Aussagen wie bei E fehlen ganz... Die SQ scheint demnach einen Geist zu atmen, der den Gemeinden der Hellenisten analog ist: Bei noch synagogaler Eingebundenheit verwischt man die Grenzen, die das offizielle Judentum zieht (typisch für die Hellenisten: Apg 8)".

318. *Wunder*, pp. 139-140 (= 1980, pp. 448-449); *Johannes*, I, pp. 118-119 [141]. John the Baptist confesses that he is not the Christ, Elijah, or the prophet (1,20-21); his task is to testify that Jesus is the Son of God (1,34). The call of the disciples begins with the Baptist's witness that Jesus is the Lamb of God (1,36), and Andrew brings Peter to Jesus with the confession: "We have found the Messiah" (1,41). Nathanael hears from Philip: "We have found him of whom Moses in the law and also the prophets wrote" (1,45); after meeting Jesus Nathanael confesses: "Rabbi, you are the Son of God! You are the King of Israel!" (1,49). In Samaria, Jesus is recognized as prophet, Messiah, and Savior of the world (4,19.30.42). The bread miracle ends with the proclamation: "This is indeed the prophet who is to come into the world!" (6,14), and the man born blind first says to the Pharisees: "He is a prophet" (9,17), but after a second encounter with Jesus he believes in the Son of Man (9,35-38). In ch. 11 Martha says: "Yes, Lord; I believe that you are the Christ, the Son of God, he who is coming into the world" (11,27). Becker mentions that according to K.G. Kuhn an intentional *Steigerung* of christological titles may be present in the signs source; however, that is improbable (*Wunder*, p. 139 n. 2; = 1980, p. 449 n. 41).

319. Prophet: 1,21.25; 4,19; 6,14; 9,17; Son of God: 1,34.49 (and King of Israel); 11,4.27 (and Christ); 20,31 (and Christ) (*Wunder*, p. 140 nn. 3-5; = 1980, pp. 449 n. 44, 450 nn. 45-46).

320. WETTER, *"Der Sohn Gottes"*, 1916.

321. Becker (*Johannes*, I, pp. 118-119 [141]) illustrates with "the Prophet" and "Son of God" SQ's formal use of the christological titles, though most are of Jewish origin and have a specific content. (1) It is not correct to see in the title "Prophet" (1,21.25; 6,14; cp. 1,45) SQ's picture of Jesus as the eschatological Prophet-like-Moses (thus Nicol; Fortna is more reserved here) or even to construe a special influence from Samaritan theology (the Moses figure). For Becker, Jesus is not described as a prophet who outdoes the miracles of Moses or Elijah or Elisha (cf. Reim, R.H. Smith, Ziener, Clark). Rather, the intention of the source must be explained in another way: "Dabei hat insbesondere neben dem oben beschriebenen Verhältnis Wundertäter – Wunder – Glaubende die Deutung der Bekenntnisse und Akklamationen insgesamt als Ausdruck der Qualifikation des Wundertäters, nicht der eine oder andere Titel allein als grundlegend zu dienen" (p. 119 [141]). (2) This goes as well for the title "Son of God" which is used most frequently in SQ and about which there has been long-running discussion in the context of the

the signs source can indeed be explained out of this Hellenistic notion[322].

3. How has the evangelist theologically reworked this source[323]? Becker replies first that the evangelist is not against miracles as such[324], but criticizes the christology of the signs source. In his view, Jesus is not an ideal man, a θεῖος ἀνήρ, but the incarnate λόγος who, against the background of a dualistic world, encounters humanity dwelling in darkness[325]. John also corrects the source by employing the early Christian proclamation of Jesus' death and resurrection: the cross as Jesus' glori-

Hellenistic θεῖος ἀνήρ portrayal (p. 119 [141-142]). In any case, the title is not original and is only accidental in the context of the charismatic and thaumaturgic θεῖος ἀνήρ (Wülfing von Martitz). Typical for SQ is the connection with the royal acclamation (1,49; 20,30-31). This tradition appears in the ancient royal cult (Egyptian origin: Wülfing von Martitz) and has also found some place in the Old Testament (Ps 2). Thus, it also came into early Christianity (Rom 1,3b-4). In this general framework, its use by SQ can be more precisely determined. The connection of royal acclamation and sonship of God with epiphanic elements occurs with the figure of Joseph in the Jewish-Christian writing *Joseph and Aseneth* (4,7; 5,5; 6,2-8; 8,2; 13,13-14; 19,11; 21,4). Moreover, the title Son of God is found in the Hellenized Markan miracle tradition as a derivation from Jewish-Christian messianic preaching (Mk 5,7). There lie the real roots for SQ's use of the title.

322. "Mit dem θεῖος ἀνήρ ist zugleich das Stichwort gefallen, das die religions-geschichtliche Voraussetzung der Semeiaquelle einzig und allein zutreffend erklären kann. Alle theologischen Wesenszüge der Wundergeschichten in der Quelle gehören in diese θεῖος-ἀνήρ-Vorstellung des Hellenismus. Vor allem das als Epiphanie geschilderte, absichtsvoll gesteigerte Wunder mit der abschliessenden stilgerechten Akklamation hat in diesem Bereich seine besten Parallelen. Es ist in der Tat nicht mehr viel, was den Jesus der Semeiaquelle von diesen Wundermännern der Antike trennt: Sein Name Jesus, seine jüdische Herkunft, seine Ankündigung durch die Propheten des Alten Testaments und dass er als Christus Sohn Gottes ist, wären zu nennen. Das ist wenig genug!" (*Wunder*, p. 141; = 1980, pp. 450-451). – On p. 141 n. 5 (= 1980, p. 451 n. 52), Becker rejects Ziener's interpretation of the signs source as a Passover Haggada (see above, pp. 87-90): the parallels with Wisdom are very hypothetical, and the Prologue certainly does not belong to the signs source.

323. *Ibid.*, pp. 143-148 (= 1980, pp. 454-461). Cp. *Johannes*, I, pp. 119-120 [142].

324. The evangelist does indeed use the miracles as the basis for the first part of his gospel. The first public activity of Jesus is the wine miracle, and there is no discourse (like that attached to the miracle in ch. 5). This miracle is an epiphany of the Lord's coming into the world. The Lazarus story also has an important place in his composition: contrary to tradition it is the introduction to the passion narrative. Moreover, the evange-list enlarged the number of miracles in the summaries (2,23; 4,45.48; 6,26; 11,47). The conclusion of the source confirms that Jesus did many more miracles; the evangelist did not censor this in using the source. In contrast to Bultmann, Becker affirms that the mir-acles were more than symbols: they constitute part of the revelation of the Johannine Christ. If the evangelist did not want to stress the miracles, he would have ignored the source or reduced it. On the contrary, he employed the miracle stories as he received them: neither the miracle itself nor its extravagantly miraculous character hindered him (*Wunder*, pp. 143-144; = 1980, pp. 454-455; see also *Johannes*, I, p. 119 [142]).

325. Based on an Old Testament quotation (12,37-38), the source declares that the miracles can also arouse disbelief. For the evangelist, Revealer and World are enemies from the beginning, and the origin of this enmity is the predestining plan of God. For that reason the evangelist adds 12,39-40 to 12,37-38 (*Wunder*, p. 144; = 1980, pp. 455-456).

fication is now the epiphany and κρίσις upon the world (12,31). Further, the miracle stories are only narrative introductions to discourses (particularly in chapters 5 and 6), wherein the One Sent from God testifies to himself that, as κρίσις upon the world, he censures a naive epiphany. For the evangelist, the miracle is a sign that, like Jesus' words, leads to κρίσις (7,31-32; 9,16.19; 11,45-46; 12,9-11.18-19). The ambivalent sign is rejected as a legitimation (4,48; cp. 2,18.23; 3,2; 6,26.30; 7,31; 9,16; 11,47; 12,38)[326]. In contrast to the independence of the miracle worker in the source, the evangelist focuses on the unity of the Father and the Son, whose obedience seeks only the glory of the Father. The Father allows the Son to perform greater works than the healing of a paralytic: giving life to the dead and judging (5,21-22); indeed, in Jesus, the eschatological judgment of mankind is achieved (5,24). As long as anyone persists in faith based on the signs he has not yet understood the revelation in Jesus. Release from darkness and death exists not in faith based on a miracle, but in a new birth (3,3.5); this release, which a person does not arrange for himself, is given to him in the word of Jesus (3,6-8). In the sequence of the wine miracle and the cleansing of the temple the same idea is expressed as in 3,1-13: the epiphany only has sense and meaning when interpreted as judgment[327]. Becker thinks that his analysis of the christology is further corroborated in chapter 6: in the gift, one must discover the giver himself[328]. The miracle in itself is, properly speaking, superfluous. In Becker's view, the evangelist polemicizes against the christology and the accompanying concept of revelation in the signs source[329]. This polemic goes so far that the evangelist even calls the meaning of the miracle into question. Becker distances himself from Bultmann's notion of symbol because it does not express the intention of the miracles sufficiently. In chapter 11, after the revelatory word of Jesus in 11,25-26, the miracle is no longer a symbol but a meaningless event. The miracle has less significance than in Bultmann's idea of symbol. On the other hand, for the evangelist, the miracle is also an actual event, and this again questions Bultmann's interpretation[330]. At the same time, however, Becker especially rejects Käsemann's interpretation[331]. The evangelist did not allow a naive-

---

326. *Ibid.*, pp. 144-145 (= 1980, pp. 455-456).
327. *Ibid.*, pp. 145-146 (= 1980, pp. 456-458).
328. *Ibid.*, p. 146 (= 1980, p. 458).
329. *Ibid.*, pp. 146-147 (= 1980, pp. 458-459).
330. *Ibid.*, p. 147 (= 1980, p. 459).
331. In Becker's opinion, Käsemann's understanding of the miracles as pointing to the Creator who reveals his glory is un-Johannine. Such an interpretation brings the purpose of creation into play, which is foreign to the Johannine miracle stories. Moreover, Jesus' glory is revealed on the cross, not in his miracles (p. 147 n. 1; = 1980, p. 459 n. 62). – Bornkamm, who simply pushes back to source what Käsemann attributes to the evangelist, is also incorrect: in Becker's opinion neither the source nor the evangelist conceived of Jesus as "ein über die Erde schreitender Gott" (p. 148 n. 2; = 1980, p. 461 n. 65). See above, pp. 76-77.

docetic miracle collection to serve as the scene for the sojourn of the Word of God among men. Rather, the miraculous knowledge and deeds are not those of a god but of a human being with divine powers. The evangelist has transformed the epiphany christology of the source to a christology by which the Son reveals himself in spoken word (i.e., in existential appeal), calls to judgment, and makes miracles superfluous[332]. In spite of his christological disagreement, the evangelist employed the source because miracles were part of the Jesus tradition[333].

J. Becker again discussed the semeia hypothesis in his surveys of Johannine scholarship. In the 1978-1980 *Forschungsbericht*, he criticizes Heekerens and Leidig[334]. Three objections are raised against H.-P. Heekerens's short signs source. First, connected as it is in its present context with verse 21,1, Jn 21,14a cannot be used to join the "Grundstock" of 21,1ff., as the third sign, to the two other Galilean miracles (2,1ff. and 4,46ff.)[335]. Second, Heekerens eliminates all "additions"

---

332. *Ibid.*, pp. 147-148 (= 1980, pp. 459-461).

333. In *Johannes*, I, pp. 119-120 [141-142], Becker gives a similar description of the redactional reworking of SQ by the evangelist. E made this source his own, but not without critique. He did not in any case champion its theology. Even for E Jesus is a miracle worker, and so he has not withdrawn the solid miraculous character from the miracles. But in each case E has contradicted SQ's endeavor to portray Jesus without presenting his teaching, i.e., as if he could be grasped only from his miracles. In other words, E has not only placed the words of Jesus in the foreground, but also made the claim of Jesus in the discourses into a real scandal for the hearer; Jesus' legitimation and the acceptance of his word go together for E. The miracle belongs to Jesus' earthly manner of appearance, but it has double meaning. One can take offence (11,45-53) in the miracle as in the earthly origin of Jesus (6,42), or one can misunderstand it in an earthly way (6,15,26). Faith that sees the question of Jesus' legitimacy solved in the miracle is decidedly rejected (3,1-8). The one, who has recognized Jesus' word as the word of divine life, which is foreign to human persons, has really recognized Jesus' sending and with it salvation for himself (6,60-71). In this sense then, the miracle effects a confession of faith (2,11; 11,1ff.). But a preliminary and fundamental function of legitimation is denied to the miracle in every case. And faith in itself does not need the miracle (14,5-9), because the word of Jesus creates faith and life (3,1-21; 5,24; 6,63.68; etc.). For Becker, this shows, again, that E proceeds with presuppositions different from the theology of SQ. He is determined not by openness for the divine epiphany miracle, but by the dualistic, and therefore negative, characterization of human persons, who live in godless darkness and are confronted by Jesus with a God who is strange to them (1,18; 5,37; 6,46). This implies that E, in distinction from SQ, energetically brings the unity of God and his Son into play. Different from SQ, likewise, the christology of sending unfolds: Jesus, as the one who has come from the Father, returns to him by way of the cross. His coming is an eschatological judgment.

334. J. BECKER, *Aus der Literatur zum Johannesevangelium (1978-1980)*, in *TR* 47 (1982) 279-301, 305-347, pp. 297-298 (cf. NEIRYNCK, *Semeia-bron*, 1983, p. 28 n. 115; ET: 1991, p. 677 n. 115). On the signs source, see also BECKER, *Das Urchristentum als gegliederte Epoche* (SBS, 155), Stuttgart, 1993, p. 94, 116. On Leidig and Thyen, see below, resp. pp. 319-320, 252-254, 262-266.

335. *TR* 47, p. 298.

from the three miracles to arrive at three short stories with a similar literary structure. For Becker, such an analysis seems to be controlled by the assumption that it is possible the reconstruct form-critical "pure" sources[336]. Finally, Becker considers the separation of 2,1ff. from its context a "Gewaltstrich": that the miracle is not followed by a discourse does not mean that it is not at its place in its context[337]. With regard to E. Leidig's objection to Bultmann's (cp. Becker's) reconstruction of SQ for ch. 4 (where v. 16 follows immediately after v. 9)[338], Becker thinks that the sequence can be understood very well against its Jewish background: after the amazed reaction of the woman (v. 9), Jesus now respects (v. 16) the Jewish custom that a man does not speak with a woman (v. 9)[339].

Later, in his 1980-1984 survey, Becker reacted to Neirynck's 1983 critique of the semeia hypothesis. Neirynck's criticisms, he says, concentrated too much on the three Galilean miracles (Heekerens) and their numbering in 2,11; 4,54 and 21,14[340]. Becker emphasizes that a critique of Heekerens's short signs source is not yet an attack of the semeia hypothesis in its usual form as proposed since Faure[341]. In addition, he assumes that Neirynck is only concerned with "formal" arguments of the hypothesis. Becker refers especially to the numbering of the signs and seems to abandon this argument[342], although, as noted by Neirynck, more than one defender of SQ had made the observation that "the strongest evidence for the existence of such a source is to be found in connection with the miracle stories themselves, i.e. the evidence of a

336. *Ibid.*, p. 298: "Das unbegründete Vorverständnis, formgeschichtlich reine Quellen erzielen zu müssen, diktiert das Gesetz der Analyse".

337. *Ibid.*, p. 298, with reference to his commentary (*Johannes*, I, 1979, p. 87 [105]).

338. LEIDIG, *Jesu Gespräch*, 1979, p. 7: "Von V. 9a wird zu V. 16 gesprungen. Dieser Sprung wirft Fragen auf. Wie kommt Jesus dazu, den Mann der Frau rufen zu lassen? Warum soll diese unwillige Frau, die nichteinmal bereit war, einen Trunk Wasser aus ihrem Krug zu reichen, auf diese Wendung des Gesprächs eingehen?".

339. *TR* 47, p. 298: "Da nach damaliger Sitte ein Mann eine Frau üblicherweise gar nicht anspricht, reagiert Jesus auf das Erstaunen der Frau (V. 9a), indem er der Sitte wieder ihr Recht gibt (V. 16). Also ergibt sich zwischen V.9a.16 – mit Bultmann – ein guter Zusammenhang, den jetzt V. 10-15 unterbricht".

340. *Das Johannesevangelium im Streit der Methoden (1980-1984)*, in *TR* 51 (1986) 1-78, pp. 22-23. For Neirynck's 1983 criticism, *Semeia-bron*, see below, pp. 320-324. Neirynck discusses Becker's reaction in the *Additional Note* to the English translation (*The Signs Source*, 1991) of his 1983 article; cf. *Evangelica II*, 1991, pp. 677-678, esp. 678.

341. *TR* 51, p. 22: "Wer H[eekerens] kritisiert, hat also noch lange nicht die sonst übliche Semeiaquelle hinreichend besprochen. Immerhin berufen sich jedoch alle, die eine Wunderquelle annehmen, seit Faure als einem Argument auf die Zählung der ersten beiden Wunder (2,11; 4,54), zu der jetzt 2,23; 4,45 quer stehen".

342. *Ibid.*, p. 23: "Aber offenbar gesteht N[eirynck] als Argumentation für literarische Schichtung überhaupt nur solche Beobachtungen zu, die sich ohne inhaltliche Wertung unmittelbar und formal auf der Textebene anbieten, wie z.B. eine Zählung".

numbered list"[343]. Becker now professes that this is not the only argument; the existence of SQ does not depends on that "formal" numbering[344]. He also objects that Neirynck neglects arguments with regard to the contents of the source: he cannot explain the aporia between the numbering in 2,11; 4,54 and the mention of other signs between the two Cana miracles (2,23; 4,45)[345], nor why the whole gospel, in which the discourses and not the miracle stories dominate, is summarized by the word σημεῖα in 20,30-31, even though the word σημεῖον does not appear in chs. 13–20, nor does he take notice of the tension between the heightening of the miraculous and the evangelist's criticism of miracle belief[346]. Indeed, Neirynck had concentrated his 1983 critique on the numbering of the signs (in three Galilean miracles) and 20,30-31, but it is less correct that he did not discuss other arguments. It seems that Becker, although he knows *Jean et les Synoptiques* (1979)[347], where additional criticism of the semeia hypothesis is provided, in both his surveys "skirts the more fundamental critique of the *beliebte* signs source"[348].

Like R. Schnackenburg and J. Becker, Joachim GNILKA, who declared for the semeia hypothesis already in 1980[349], generally follows the literary viewpoint of Bultmann in his short commentary on John for *Die Neue Echter Bibel* (1983)[350]. He thinks that "besides a pre-Johannine

343. NEIRYNCK, *Evangelica II*, 1991, p. 678. The quotation is from TIEDE, *The Charismatic Figure*, 1972, p. 279 (see above, p. 86 n. 69). Neirynck refers also to LINDARS (*Behind the Fourth Gospel*, 1972, p. 29; FT: 1975, p. 40) and justifies concentration on the argument of the numbering by asking: "Is it then not true that 'everyone knows that the main clue to the existence of the source is the numbering of the first two signs'?".
344. *TR* 51, p. 23: "Die Wundererzählung [sic] ist doch nur ein Anstoss zur Analyse unter anderen, und allein von der formalen Zählung hängt nicht die Existenz der Quelle ab (so sicher auch diese Zählung erklärt sein will)!".
345. *Ibid.*, p. 23: "Jede inhaltliche Argumentation, wie etwa die Spannung zwischen 2,11; 4,54 und 2,23; 4,45 oder die Frage nach der Möglichkeit, Joh 1–20 durch das Stichwort 'Semeia' zusammenfassen zu können, ist offenbar für ihn [Neirynck] eine subjektive Wertung und darf keine analytischen Folgen nach sich ziehen. In solchen Fällen darf man offenbar nur positivistisch feststellen: Der Autor, der so redet, hat darin keine Spannung empfunden, also hat der Interpret die Harmonie des Textes aufzuspüren und nicht die angebliche Spannung für literarkritische Folgerungen zu verwenden".
346. *Ibid.*, p. 23.
347. *TR* 47, p. 292.
348. NEIRYNCK, *Semeia-bron*, 1983, p. 28 n. 115 (ET: 1991, p. 677 n. 115). Cf. below, pp. 320-324.
349. J. GNILKA, *Zur Christologie des Johannesevangeliums*, in KASPER (ed.), *Christologische Schwerpunkte*, 1980, pp. 92-107, see esp. 98-99 (see below, pp. 135-136 n. 355).
350. *Johannesevangelium* (NEchB KNT, 1), Würzburg, 1983. – Reviews: cf. VAN BELLE, no. 1943. The shortness of the commentary has been criticized by A. FUCHS, in *SNTU/A* 10 (1985) 222-223, but praised by X. LÉON-DUFOUR, in *RSR* 73 (1985) 268-269, p. 269. See also J. BECKER, in *TR* 51 (1986), p. 37: "Ein neuerer Kommentar, der eine allgemeinverständliche und mehr elementare Auslegung des Joh bezweckt, ist dem

passion narrative the evangelist assimilated a written source which contained miracles of Jesus in a characteristic style"[351]. The "Semeia-quelle" contained seven Johannine signs[352] and was concluded with 20,30-31[353]. The miracle stories can be identified by place names (cf. J. Becker)[354] and especially by "a proper notion of miracle, which is not uncritically taken up in the gospel"[355]. In addition, Gnilka wonders

Modell von Schnackenburg/Becker gefolgt, der Kommentar von Gnilka". Becker classifies Gnilka's commentary under his sixth model of literary criticism (see above, p. 117 n. 253). See also BEUTLER, *Méthodes et problèmes*, 1990, pp. 22 n. 31, 24.

351. *Johannesevangelium*, p. 6. Also *kleinere Traditionseinheiten* (p. 6) and a *Logoslied* belonged to the *Vorlagen* of John (p. 6; cp. p. 13). In addition, the gospel was reworked, perhaps frequently, before its publication (p. 7); to this reworking Gnilka ascribes, among other things, 3,13ff.; 3,31ff.; 5,27-29; 6,51a-58; 12,44-50; chapters 15–17 and 21; and the transposing of chs. 5 and 6. The Fourth Gospel arose in a Johannine school, which presumably was situated in Syria (p. 8). – On the signs source, see also *Jesus von Nazaret. Botschaft und Geschichte* (HTKNT Supplementband, 3), Freiburg - Basel - Wien, 1990 (repr. 1993), pp. 118-119.

352. *Johannesevangelium*, p. 6. We cannot say that Gnilka gives a precise reconstruction: (1) For 2,1-11, cf. pp. 22-24, esp. 22. The evangelist is responsible for the following: the parenthesis in 2,6; the mention of the disciples in 2,2 (originally perhaps "brothers", cf. 2,12). The notice "on the third day" is "stilgemäss" (cf. 11,6) and does not come from the evangelist. Gnilka (p. 22) gives the following arguments for assigning the wine miracle to the σημεῖα-*Quelle*: first, the evangelist takes a different stance toward the σημεῖα than does the source (for the evangelist these are subordinated to the word); second, the evangelist's typical dualism is absent; third, difference in style; fourth, the numbering in 2,11 (cp. 4,54; see the conclusion of the source in 20,30-31). (2) For 4,46-54, cf. pp. 37-38: vv. 43-46a.48-49 are from the evangelist. (3) For 5,1-18, cf. pp. 39-41, esp. 39: vv. 17-18 are from the evangelist. (4) For 6,1-15, cf. pp. 46-47, esp. 46: vv. 2.6 (14-15?) are from the evangelist. Regarding the 12 baskets (v. 13) Gnilka notes: "Die 12 Körbe veranschaulichen die Mächtigkeit der Wundertat. Gleichzeitig deuten sie die Zwölfzahl der Jünger an – jeder sammelte eine Korb –, eine Tradition, die in SQ noch lebendiger als in JE war" (p. 47). (5) For 6,16-21, cf. p. 48: "E bezieht sie [die Seewandelgeschichte] aus der SQ". (6) For 9,1-12, cf. p. 75: vv. 3-4 and the "Offenbarungsformel" in v. 5 are from the evangelist. (7) For 11,1-16, cf. pp. 87-94, esp. 87-88. A traditional miracle story has been redacted in the source already, but to what extent is debatable: "Hat schon die SQ die Jünger mit der Tradition verbunden, die im 11. Kapitel nur in 1-16 und 54 genannt werden? 15 mit seiner uneingeschränkten Verbindung von Wunder und Glaube könnte dafür sprechen". From E come the motif of glory in v. 4, the day and light motif in vv. 9-10, and v. 2 ("übergreifende Klammerbemerkung"). For 11,17-44, cf. pp. 90-94, esp. 90. The earliest form of the raising narrative is recognizable in vv. 17.35.38b.39a.41a.43-44; from the redaction of SQ come the vivid portrayal of the sisters, the participation of the Jews, and the sisters' hurrying to the grave. Typical theological accents are from E, e.g., vv. 25-27.40.41b-42.

353. *Ibid.*, p. 156. The second ἵνα clause (20,31b) is from E.

354. *Ibid.*, p. 6. Cp., e.g., p. 22 (2,1). For Becker, see above, p. 120 n. 273.

355. *Ibid.*, p. 6. Cf. *Zur Christologie*, pp. 98-99, esp. 98: "Als Zeichen genügen die Wunder nicht sich selbst, sie haben Hinweisfunktion und sollen darauf aufmerksam machen, dass jetzt Offenbarung sich ereignet. Es kommt darauf an, das Zeichen im Zeichen zu sehen. ... Die Verbindung von Wunderzeichen und Offenbarungsreden ist der Redaktion des Evangelisten zuzuschreiben, weil die Wunderberichte des Johannesevangeliums wahrscheinlich einer zusammenhängenden Tradition, der sogenannten Semeiaquelle, entstammen und sicherlich eine von den Reden zunächst unabhängige

whether the source contained other narrative material, and in his com-
mentary assigns the ministry of the Baptist to the source[356]; contrary to
Bultmann, but in agreement with Becker, he ascribes not only the
Vorlage of 1,35-51 to the source, but also that of 1,19-28.29-34[357].

Like Becker and Gnilka, Pheme PERKINS (1990) accepts the evangelist's use of "a miracles source" and "an earlier acount of Jesus' passion
and traditions about the empty tomb and resurrection appearances of
Jesus"[358]. With regard to the signs source, she particularly notes: "The
miracle stories have probably been derived from a collection of Jesus'
miracles. Individual miracles may already have been elaborated with
discourse about their significance by Johannine Christians before they
were incorporated into the Gospel"[359].

Überlieferung darstellen". After the feeding miracle Jesus stresses "I am the Bread of
Life" (6,35); in the context of the healing of the blind man we hear, "As long as I am in
the world, I am the Light of the world" (9,5); and the raising of Lazarus is summarized
in "I am the Resurrection and the Life" (11,25). In Gnilka's view, the Johannine redaction has clearly reworked the miracle traditions for purposes of revelation: the Johannine
Jesus does not perform miracles because he has been asked, but on his own initiative
(2,4; 6,6; 9,3; 11,4). This does not mean, however, that the Johannine signs must be limited to the purpose of revealing Jesus' glory: "Sie geschehen an der Welt, an konkreten
Menschen. Sie vermögen gerade in ihrer Steigerung die Realität individueller Not ins
Bewusstsein zu heben"; cf. the man who lay sick for 38 years without help (5,5-7); the
man born blind (9,1); Lazarus, the only brother of his sisters (11,1ff.). In the last case
Jesus appears as a real person, weeping at the grave of his friend (11,35; cf. vv. 33.38).
For Gnilka this means: "Die Wundergeschichten insgesamt sind um der Weltzuwendung
der Offenbarung willen unentbehrlich, und sie stellen auch bei Johannes noch ein Stück
dieser Weltzuwendung dar" (p. 99).
    356. "Möglicherweise enthielt die SQ noch anderes Material, vor allem die
Täufergeschichte, so dass sie mit der Verteilung des Wirkens Jesu auf Galiläa und
Jerusalem eine evangelienähnliche Struktur besass, wobei allerdings nicht nur ein
Passionsbericht, sondern auch Hinweise auf die Passion Jesu fehlten" (*Johannesevan-
gelium*, p. 6).
    357. For 1,19-28, cf. pp. 17-18, esp. 18. E overstresses the witness character (v. 19a);
also from his hand is "die Rede von den Juden und der Wurde des Unbekannten (26b)".
For 1,29-34, cf. pp. 18-20, esp. 18: "Die Perikope wurde weitgehend vom E gestaltet.
Nur von ferne schimmert die SQ hindurch, die an dieser Stelle von der Tatigkeit des
Täufers und der Taufe Jesu berichtet haben dürfte". For 1,35-51, cf. pp. 20-22, esp. 20.
In SQ, the other disciple found either Philip (then the parallel with Andrew and Peter
would be complete), or (more probably) Andrew (cf. πρῶτον in v. 41). The other
disciple cannot be identified with Philip (contra BECKER, *Johannes*, I, 1979, p. 100;
[3]1991, pp. 119-120). Besides the redactional intervention in v. 43, E has also redacted
vv. 35-36 (the repetition of the "Lamb of God" acclamation) and fashioned the end of the
pericope with the addition of v. 51.
    358. P. PERKINS, *The Gospel according to John*, in *NJBC*, 1990, pp. 942-985, esp.
942b-943a. Also like Becker and Gnilka, she rejects Bultmann's *Offenbarungsreden*:
"Rather than assume such a source, it seems more plausible that the discourse material
reflects patterns and units of preaching that had been developed within the Johannine
community" (p. 943a).
    359. *Ibid.*, p. 942a-942b.

Analyzing Jn 2,1-11 in connection with 1,35-51, Knut BACKHAUS (1991)[360] contends against J. Becker and others[361] that the signs source reflects a positive relation between the Baptist circle and the Jesus movement rather than a polemical situation[362]. For the unity of these passages, Backhaus gives six arguments[363]. First, with regard to the immediate literary context, the Cana story is "Ziel- und Schlusspunkt" of 1,35-51. Thus, 1,35–2,11 can be described as "a story of the call of the Baptist's disciples"[364]. Second, in the narrative context, the disciples

360. K. BACKHAUS, Die "Jüngerkreise" des Täufers Johannes. Eine Studie zu den religionsgeschichtlichen Ursprüngen des Christentums (PTS, 19), Paderborn, 1991 (diss. Paderborn, 1989; dir.: J. Ernst), pp. 357-365: "Der Täuferkreis und SQ"; cp. Praeparatio Evangelii. Die religionsgeschichtlichen Beziehungen zwischen Täufer- und Jesus-Bewegung im Spiegel der sog. Semeia-Quelle des vierten Evangeliums, in TGl 81 (1991) 202-215, pp. 206-214; Täuferkreise als Gegenspieler jenseits des Textes. Erwägungen zu einer kriteriologischen Verlegenheit am Beispiel der Joh-Forschung, in TGl 81 (1991) 279-301 (without mention of the signs source). – On the "Semeia-Quelle" (SQ), see "Jüngerkreise", pp. 355-356, esp. 355: "Die einzige Quelle, die zumindest ihrer Existenz nach weithin anerkannt ist, ist die Semeia-Quelle"; cp. Praeparatio, p. 206. To the rejection of the semeia hypothesis by Schnelle (and Kümmel), he answers: "den hier vorausgesetzten Minimalbestand vermögen die Einwände Schnelles nicht zu erschüttern" ("Jüngerkreise", p. 355). He notes, however, that there is no consensus among the defenders of the hypothesis regarding the delimitation of the source. He distinguishes between the "maximalisierende Literarkritik" of Becker and the "two-signs hypothesis" ("Minimalbestand") of Heekerens (cp. Spitta and Temple), but throughout his work he never mentions the studies of Fortna! Review of "Jüngerkreise": D. KOSCH, in BZ 36 (1992) 267-268.

361. "Jüngerkreise", p. 357; Praeparatio, p. 206 (esp. n. 22). For Becker, see above, pp. 120 n. 272, 125 n. 302. Backhaus refers also to D.M. Smith (see below, p. 197 n. 254) and Heekerens (see below, pp. 259-260).

362. "Jüngerkreise", p. 366: "Sie [die SQ-Texte] sind eher missionarisch als apologetisch-polemisch orientiert; vor allem schlägt sich in ihnen eine bereits vollzogene Übergangsdynamik von den 'wider circles' der samaritanischen Täuferbewegung zu den frühen Kreisen der johanneischen Gemeinde nieder. Auch wenn der Lieblingsjünger nicht als Bindeglied zwischen beiden Gruppierungen beansprucht werden kann ..., erweist sie doch die Täuferbewegung in Samaria als ein Anfang des vierten Evangeliums". See also his criticism of Heekerens (p. 357).

363. "Jüngerkreise", pp. 359-360; Praeparatio, pp. 208-210. – For the attribution of 1,35-51 (without v. 43) to the signs source (cp. Bultmann, Becker, Gnilka, Kuhn, Schulz, and with hesitation Nicol), see "Jüngerkreise", pp. 230-249; cp. p. 361. Backhaus rejects Becker's attribution of 3,22-30 to SQ (cf. "Jüngerkreise", pp. 250-265; see esp. p. 250: "Joh 3,22–4,3 aber mit seiner 'Täuferpolemik' (entspricht) ganz dem Konzept des Evangelisten".

364. "Jüngerkreise", p. 359; Praeparatio, p. 208. He refers to several connections between the two pericopes: (1) 1,43 prepares the change of place in 2,1; (2) the σημεῖον of 2,1-11 is anticipated in 1,50-51; (3) the mention of the disciples in 2,2.11 refers back to the call of the Baptist's disciples; (4) the third day in 2,1 is prepared by the 1,43.35.29; (5) in 21,2, the only appearance of Nathanael in the Gospel after ch. 1, Nathanael is called ὁ ἀπὸ Κανὰ τῆς Γαλιλαίας; cp. 2,1. Note also that the aretalogical motif of Jesus' supernatural knowledge in 1,42.47.50 is in accordance with the christology of the signs source (cf. "Jüngerkreise", p. 232; Praeparatio, p. 208. For this motif, Backhaus rejects the θεῖος ἀνήρ typology: "Gewiss ist die sehr frag-

accompanying Jesus to the wedding in Cana (2,2.11) can be identified with the former disciples of the Baptist who followed Jesus. Jesus' promise (μείζω τούτων ὄψῃ in 1,50) is fulfilled in 2,11 (ταύτην ἐποίησεν ἀρχὴν τῶν σημείων ὁ Ἰησοῦς)[365]. Third, the larger context of the present gospel also legitimates the connection between the Cana story and the Baptist circle: three motifs (water: 1,26.31.33, cp. 3,23; καθαρισμός: 2,6, cp. 3,25; wedding: 2,1, cp. 3,29 ὁ φίλος τοῦ νυμφίου) are characteristic of the Baptist circle[366]. Fourth, the motif of wine as a symbol of the messianic time stands in opposition to the fasting of the Baptist's disciples (cp. Mk 2,18-22 par.)[367]. Fifth, the religion-historical background of the wine motif is to be found in Judaism and in the Baptist movement rather than in the Hellenistic Dionysus legend[368]. Sixth, the wine rule in 2,10 may be an explanation of the aporia of the chronological priority of John the Baptist to Jesus: the Jesus movement is indeed new, but this does not mean that it is inferior (1,15: ὁ ὀπίσω μου ἐρχόμενος ἔμπροσθέν μου γέγονεν, ὅτι πρῶτός μου ἦν; cp. vv. 27.30)[369].

According to Backhaus, Jn 2,1-11 (preceded by 1,35-51) expresses the change of the Baptist movement to the "Novum Christianum"[370]. The signs source does not react against a competing Baptist sect[371], but

---

würdige Hypothese einer hellenistisch geprägten ϑεῖος ἀνήρ-Christologie der SQ von diesem Motiv fernzuhalten. Es handelt sich hier aber um einen aretalogischen Sonder-fall, der sich an alttestamentlich-jüdischen Vorbildern orientiert und auch der synop-tischen Überlieferung vertraut ist; in die σημεῖον-Christologie der SQ fügt er sich passend ein".

365. *"Jüngerkreise"*, pp. 359-360; *Praeparatio*, pp. 208-209: "mit dem 'Anfang der Zeichen', der Offenbarung der δόξα Jesus und der πίστις der Jünger kommt die Dramatik der Berufungserzählung in ihr Ziel".

366. *"Jüngerkreise"*, p. 360; *Praeparatio*, p. 209.

367. *"Jüngerkreise"*, p. 360; *Praeparatio*, p. 209: "Die Jesus-Bewegung ist hier der neue Wein, der gerade in Ansehung des Fastens der Täuferschüler die alten Schläuche des Judentums zerreisst".

368. *"Jüngerkreise"*, p. 360; *Praeparatio*, p. 209.

369. *"Jüngerkreise"*, p. 360; *Praeparatio*, pp. 209-210, esp. 210: "Die Jesus-Bewe-gung ist zwar neu wie der gewandelte Wein, obschon doch, wie der biedere Speisemeister bemerkt, sonst nur Trunkenen das Neue zuzusagen pflegt. Aber gegen solch hausbak-kenes Menschenurteil steht die Wandlungsmacht des Messias. Gewiss, die Täuferbewe-gung war eher da, und doch: erst der neue Wein zeugt von der Herrlichkeit des Messias, denn er selbst steht auf der Seite des Neuen".

370. *"Jüngerkreise"*, pp. 360-361: "In summa vermuten wir also, dass Joh 2,1-12 [sic] auch auf die Verwandlung der Täuferbewegung in das Novum des Christentums abhebt. Insofern stimmt die Intention der Perikope mit der für Joh 1,35-51 ermittelten Darstellungsabsicht überein. Einerseits wird in beiden Perikopen die Transformation der Johannes- in die Jesus-bewegung *beschrieben*, andererseits diese Übergangsdynamik *missionarisch werbend* vorgestellt; zu dem letzteren Interesse passt also das Motiv des Geschenkwunders"; cp. *Praeparatio*, p. 210.

371. *"Jüngerkreise"*, p. 361; *Praeparatio*, p. 210.

deals with its own religious background[372]. For the source, the Baptist movement is Christianity's past (cf. 2,9: τὸ ὕδωρ οἶνον γεγενη-μένον)[373]. In other words, John the Baptist as the personification of the movement begun by him stands at the beginning of the Christian Gospel (see 3,30)[374]. Backhaus thinks that the relation between the Baptist movement and Johannine Christianity may have some root in Samaria (see 3,23)[375]. This is expressed in Jesus' comment in 4,37-38 (v. 38: ἄλλοι κεκοπιάκασι)[376].

372. *Praeparatio*, p. 210: "Nicht mit einer konkurrierenden Sekte setzt sich also die Semeia-Quelle auseinander, sondern mit ihrer eigenen religiösen Herkunftsgeschichte".

373. *Praeparatio*, p. 210: "In bestimmtem Sinn geht es der Erzählung sogar um die Identität beider Bewegungen. Denn das Christentum ist ja nichts anderes als das ὕδωρ οἶνον γεγενημένον. Die Täuferbewegung ist die Vergangenheit des Christentums; die Jesus-Bewegung ist die Erfüllung des Täufertums, in dem dieses positive, negative und supereminenter aufgehoben ist".

374. *"Jüngerkreise"*, pp. 361-362, esp. 362: "Jedenfalls setzt sich SQ nicht mit einer konkurrierenden Gemeinde, sondern mit den Ursprüngen der eigenen Gemeinschaft auseinander: Johannes ist auch hier der 'Anfang des Evangeliums', und es bietet sich in der Tat an, Joh 3,30 typologisch zu verstehen: 'die Mitgliederzahlen der johanneischen Gemeinde steigen auf Kosten der Täuferbewegung' [HEEKERENS, *Zeichen-Quelle*, 101]"; cp. *Praeparatio*, p. 211. According to Backhaus SQ must be dated before 80 A.D.: "So werden die weiteren Zirkel der täuferischen Umkehrbewegung im Blickfeld der Quelle stehen. Dem entspricht der religionsgeschichtliche Befund: In der Frühzeit fehlt von einer Täufersekte jede Spur; die umfassende Taufbewegung hingegen ist reich belegt. Am ehesten wird diese Phase der Fluktuation in einer Zeit anzusetzen sein, in der der johanneische Kreis wie die Täuferbewegung noch unter dem synagogalen Dach vereint waren, als vor dem Synagogalbann gegen den Kreis, den man heute gemeinhin um 80 datiert" (*Praeparatio*, p. 211; cp. *"Jüngerkreise"*, pp. 361-362).

375. *"Jüngerkreise"*, pp. 362-363; *Praeparatio*, pp. 211-213. Cp. Heekerens, who also thinks that the source originated in Samaria (see below, pp. 259 n. 36, 260 n. 39), cf. *"Jüngerkreise"*, pp. 362-363; *Praeparatio*, p. 212.

376. *"Jüngerkreise"*, pp. 363-365; *Praeparatio*, pp. 213-214.

CHAPTER IV

THE SEMEIA HYPOTHESES OF R.T. FORTNA AND W. NICOL

Many authors have adopted Bultmann's semeia hypothesis without any reply to the style-critical objections regarding the very possibility of such source reconstruction. But at least two scholars, R.T. Fortna and W. Nicol, have attempted to demonstrate that style criticism can even confirm the use of a signs source in the Gospel of John.

I. R.T. FORTNA: "THE GOSPEL OF SIGNS"

Inspired by the emergence of *Redaktionsgeschichte*, Robert T. FORTNA (1970) sought "to identify as objectively and distinctly as possible the exact form of a *Vorlage*" in order to study John's redaction of the source[1]. In a "Methodological Introduction", situating source criticism

---

1. R.T. FORTNA, *The Gospel of Signs: A Reconstruction of the Narrative Source Underlying the Fourth Gospel* (SNTS MS, 11), Cambridge, 1970, p. IX; diss. Union Theological Seminary, New York, 1965; dir. J.L. Martyn: *The Gospel of Signs. A Reconstruction of the Chief Narrative Source Used by the Fourth Evangelist*, slightly revised in the published text. – Fortna studied the Johannine redaction of the source in four subsequent articles: *Source and Redaction in the Fourth Gospel's Portrayal of Jesus' Signs*, in *JBL* 89 (1970) 151-166 (= *Signs*); *From Christology to Soteriology: A Redaction-Critical Study of Salvation in the Fourth Gospel*, in *Interpr* 27 (1973) 31-47 (= *Soteriology*); *Theological Use of Locale in the Fourth Gospel*, in *ATR SS* 3 (1974) 58-95 (= *Locale*); *Christology in the Fourth Gospel: Redaction-Critical Perspectives*, in *NTS* 21 (1974-75) 489-504 (= *Christology*); and in his 1988 monograph: *Predecessor* (see below, p. 213 n. 366). See also his article *Redaction Criticism, NT*, in *IDB SV*, 1976, pp. 733-735, esp. 734. For his article on Jn 18,13-27, see below, p. 216 n. 382. – Reviews of *Gospel of Signs*: cf. VAN BELLE, no. 1741 (see below, pp. 165-176; see also pp. 302-307). See also: KONINGS, *Joh. verhaal*, II, 1972, pp. 126-131 (Jn 6); SCHNACKENBURG, *Forschung*, 1974, pp. 273-274; TEEPLE, *Origin*, 1974, pp. 49-50; KYSAR, *Fourth Evangelist*, 1975, pp. 16-37, 67-70, 74-77; *ANRW* II, 25/3, 1985, pp. 2396-2398, 2399-2402; TEMPLE, *Core*, 1975, p. 41; COTHENET, *Le quatrième évangile*, 1977, pp. 184-186; *L'évangile selon saint Jean*, 1984, pp. 47-48; CARSON, *Current Source Criticism*, 1978, pp. 414-420; HOEFERKAMP, *Relationship*, 1978, pp. 44-49; CORSANI, *I miracoli*, 1983, pp. 24-30; HEEKERENS, *Zeichen-Quelle*, 1984, *passim*, esp. pp. 34-39; KÜMMEL, *Einleitung*, ²¹1984, p. 178; BEUTLER, *ANRW* II, 25/3, 1985, p. 2540; BITTNER, *Jesu Zeichen*, 1987, pp. 2-13; SCHNELLE, *Christologie*, 1987, pp. 168-182 (ET: 1992, pp. 150-164); KUHN, *Christologie*, 1988, pp. 49-50 (Jn 1,35-51); MARCHADOUR, *Lazare*, 1988, pp. 46-48 (Jn 11,1-45); WAGNER, *Auferstehung*, 1988, pp. 64-68 (Jn 11,1–12,19); LÜTGEHETMANN, *Hochzeit*, 1990, pp. 77-86 (Jn 2,1-11); WÖLLNER, *Zeichenglaube*, 1988, pp. 11-13; LINDARS, *Trends*, 1990, pp. 330-331; ASHTON, *Understanding*, 1991, pp. 86-88, 161, 163-164; BOTHA, *Jesus and the Samaritan Woman*, 1991, pp. 17-18; SLOYAN, *What Are They Saying about John?*, 1991, pp. 28-31; KOSKENNIEMI, *Apollonios von Tyana*, 1992, p. 142; SCHMITHALS, *Johannesevangelium*, 1992, p. 121.

within Johannine research, Fortna indicates "criteria for the source
analysis of Johannine narrative"[2]. As in Pentateuchal criticism, he distinguishes ideological, stylistic, and contextual criteria. He begins with
the miracle stories as the starting point of his source reconstruction. He
then expands the source with the passion and resurrection narratives and
other pre-Johannine material (1,6-7.19-34; 3,23-24; 1,35-50; 4,4-42;
6,67-71; 20,30-31)[3]. He himself acknowledges that his reconstructed
source "has a number of similarities to Bultmann's σημεῖα-*Quelle* (SQ)
but differs most notably in that it amounts not merely to a collection of
miracle stories but to a rudimentary gospel, complete with passion narrative"[4]. This Gospel of Signs has a definite structure, and its conclusion
(20,30-31) clearly indicates that it is the result of selection. It begins
with the testimony of the Baptist and the conversion of the first disciples
(1,6-7.19-34; 3,23-24; 1,35-50) as a prelude to the ministry of Jesus,
who, in the presence of his disciples, performs miracles which are
regarded as messianic deeds. They take place in Galilee and Judea
and culminate in the story of Jesus' death and resurrection (2,14-18;
11,47-53; 12,1-8; 12,12-15; fragments of 12,27; 13,(1b).2a.4-5.12-
14.18b.21b.26-27.37-38; 14,31b; 16,32b). All this is presented as
gospel, that is, a kerygma to be believed, stressing that Jesus' life and
ministry is a fulfillment of the scriptures. By comparison with the
Synoptic Gospels it is less complete on the teaching of Jesus. Each
episode is introduced and concluded by an itinerary notation. At the
center stand seven miracles: four in Galilee (the wine miracle, the
healing of the nobleman's son, the miraculous draught of fish, the
feeding miracle with the walking on the sea as an interlude) and three in
Jerusalem (the raising of Lazarus, the man born blind, and the para-

---

2. *Gospel of Signs*, pp. 1-25; cp. *Predecessor*, pp. 1-8.

3. *Gospel of Signs*, resp. pp. 27-109 ("The 'Signs Source'"), 111-158 ("The Passion
and Resurrection Narratives") and 159-200 ("Other Pre-Johannine Material"). Note that
Jn 12,37-38 does not belong to the source: "If the assertion of 12,37 is strange in Jn., it
is even stranger in a source that is purely concerned to show Jesus as winning faith on the
basis of signs. The possibility of not believing in signs is one which only John conceives"
(p. 199, see, however, below, p. 216 n. 381). – Fortna treats the style of the source in a
separate section (pp. 201-218), and then concludes the monograph with "The Character
of the Source" (pp. 219-234). We shall go into greater detail on these last two parts. In an
appendix Fortna brings together a continuous reconstruction of the source (pp. 235-245).

4. *Signs*, p. 151; for his characterization of the source, see *Gospel of Signs*, pp. 219-
234. Fortna speaks of a "gospel in the *narrower* sense"; cf. p. 221 n. 2: "As we have
reconstructed SQ, with its inclusion of a passion narrative, and in contrast to earlier discussion of a signs source..., it is clearly a gospel in the *narrower* sense"; with reference
to KOESTER, in *HTR* 61 (1968) 203-247, pp. 230-232 (= 1971, pp. 187-189). He returns in
detail to the inclusion of the passion narrative in 1975 and in 1988 (see below, pp. 217-
221, 233-235). See also Robinson's review (see below, pp. 172-174). – For the description of the source's structure given above, see *Gospel of Signs*, pp. 98-109 ("The Structure of the Signs Source"), 102-109 ("The Order and Interconnection of the Signs"), and
esp. 222. See also *Locale*, p. 60 (see below, p. 236 n. 519).

lytic)[5]. These two groups are each introduced by a story about Jesus meeting someone (Nathanael in the first and the Samaritan woman in the second) who, in the course of conversation, comes to believe. Preceding the cycle of signs are the three denials of the Baptist. "If the passion narrative is not so evidently structured, that is only because it is the most traditional and extensive of the units from which the source is made. But it begins, as does the series of signs, with a double confession of Jesus (1:49, 12:13; cf. 20:31), and it may not be accidental that the Jerusalem period (i.e., the last three signs together with the passion) begins and ends with accounts of resurrection (of Lazarus and Jesus, respectively)". The Galilean period likewise opens and closes with similar miracles: the wine miracle and the feeding miracle; the walking on the sea, as an epiphany miracle, separates the Galilean from the Judean section. The entire source is characterized editorially at beginning and end by balanced two-sentence units (1,6-7; 20,30-31).

The source was a written document (20,30-31) which John probably had before him when he wrote his gospel; it influenced him as to shape and content just as Mark influenced Matthew and Luke[6]. It had its origin in a Jewish-Christian milieu, for which there are various indications[7]: (1) Semitisms in a Greek text, which, according to Fortna, is not translation Greek; (2) lack of concern for the Gentile question on the one hand or polemic against the Torah on the other (John had to artificially introduce the Sabbath controversy into his source in chapters 5 and 9); (3) a non-deliberate use of the Old Testament (the Jewish scriptures are simply taken for granted, cf. 4,5-6). Fortna admits the difficulty of placing the background of the source within first-century Christianity, but he finds an analogy to the source's θεῖος ἀνήρ christology in that of the opponents of Paul in 2 Cor 10–13[8]. Regarding its geographical origin, a Syrian provenance is possible because of obvious contact with

5. The miracle stories were consecutively numbered (except for the walking on the sea) (*Gospel of Signs*, pp. 98-109, esp. 108-109; cp. *Signs*, p. 152 n. 4; *Locale*, p. 60):
[τοῦτο πρῶτον ἐποίησεν σημεῖον] ὁ Ἰησοῦς... (2,11)
τοῦτο [πάλιν] δεύτερον [ἐποίησεν σημεῖον] ὁ Ἰησοῦς... (4,54)
τοῦτο [ἤδη] τρίτον [ἐποίησεν σημεῖον] Ἰησοῦς... (21,14)
[τοῦτο τέταρτον ἐποίησεν σημεῖον ὁ Ἰησοῦς]... (6,14)
[τοῦτο πέμπτον ἐποίησεν ὁ Ἰησοῦς]... (11,45)
[τοῦτο ἕκτον ἐποίησεν σημεῖον ὁ Ἰησοῦς] (after 9,7)
[τοῦτο ἕβδομον (or ἔσχατον) ἐποίησεν σημεῖον ὁ Ἰησοῦς] (after 5,14).
6. *Gospel of Signs*, p. 223.
7. *Ibid.*, p. 223-224. With regard to (1), Fortna remarks that the audience of the signs source appears to have been bilingual: the source is interspersed with (a) Aramaic words which the author does not translate (e.g., Μεσσίας and Κηφᾶς); (b) Greek words to which the Semitic equivalent is added (e.g., 19,13.17); (c) certain words used interchangeably in Greek and Aramaic, e.g., Μεσσίας, χριστός, ῥαββ(ουν)ί, διδάσκαλος (p. 223).
8. Especially 2 Cor 11,13; 12,12; cf. 1 Cor 1,22; 12,19-20; Mk 13,22; Mt 7,22; Acts 2,22; see p. 224, with references to Koester, Georgi and Robinson in n. 1.

Palestinian traditions[9], but such a document could have originated in any part of the Hellenistic world. The source could be dated before 70 on the basis of 5,2 (the present tense ἐστίν) and 2,19, but these verses point only to the relatively early origin of the traditions and not necessarily to the date of their inclusion in the source. The conclusion (20,30-31; cp. 1,7c) explicitly states the purpose of the source: it is a missionary tract, probably directed toward potential Jewish converts to convince them that Jesus is the Messiah[10].

Although the source has close connections with the Synoptic tradition, the author of the source did not know the Synoptic Gospels in their canonical form. It is rather a parallel tradition, with a special relationship – though not necessarily on the literary level – with material peculiar to Luke. Despite several exceptions, the source as a whole displays a more developed tradition, as is evident from its novelistic tendency and the heightening of the miraculous. Not only does the source's author regard the miracles as proofs of Jesus' Messiahship, he also represents Jesus as taking the initiative. In his view, the miracles lead directly to faith[11].

The theology of the source is "frankly and simply christological"[12]. The central affirmation is that Jesus is the Christ, the Son of God, and that he alone possesses the Spirit (1,33). The miracles, then, are legitimizing signs of his messianic status. The appearance and witness of the Baptist stand solely in service of this christology. The joining of the passion narrative to Jesus' deeds was probably apologetically motivated for both the more traditional *justification* of the fact that the "crucified criminal" is the Messiah and the *proclamation* of that Messiahship. Toward that end, the Old Testament quotations in the source, all of which occur in the passion narrative, serve to demonstrate that "as the fulfillment of prophecy, the crucifixion is both necessary to and the confirmation of Jesus' status". In addition to Messiah, the fundamental title in the source, other titles appear: Son of God, Lamb of God, Rabbi (teacher), Prophet, God's Chosen One, King of the Jews, King of Israel(?), Savior of the World(?), (Elijah).

The miracles prove Jesus' Messiahship[13], perhaps because he is assumed to be the (quasi-messianic) Prophet-like-Moses (cf. 4,19; 6,14).

---

9. *Ibid.*, pp. 224-225. This is apparent from, among other things, "the detailed and fairly reliable knowledge of Palestinian geography shown by the source" (p. 228).

10. *Ibid.*, pp. 224-225; cp. *Signs*, p. 151; *Soteriology*, p. 32.

11. *Gospel of Signs*, pp. 226-228.

12. *Ibid.*, pp. 228-234, esp. 228. Apocalyptic and eschatological elements are wholly lacking. Neither are the miracles soteriological or eschatological, as are the Synoptic healing stories. The source focuses only on Jesus' power as Messiah and not on its cosmic consequences (pp. 228-229).

13. The miracles are not "signs" for the source in the same way as for the evangelist; they have no symbolic meaning. But they are really "signs" and not merely "miracles" in the sense of prodigies; they are signs of Jesus' person (p. 231 n. 4). See his article *Signs* (see above, p. 141 n. 1, and below, pp. 213 n. 370, 226-230).

But while parallels with Moses are not wholly lacking, they are not fully established. Fortna thinks rather that the miracles contain more general references to the great figures of the Old Testament like Elijah, Elisha, and perhaps even Joseph (in Gen). These heroes were apparently regarded by Hellenistic Jews as θεῖοι ἄνδρες, types of the Messiah. Yet for the signs source Jesus is not a "mere thaumaturge, only one among many θεῖοι ἄνδρες. He is rather the unique Messiah of Israel"[14]. Fortna particularly stresses the source's parallels with the Elijah-Elisha tradition[15]. In contrast to the evangelist, the author of the source took little interest in the origin of faith: the Baptist bears witness and immediately people follow Jesus (1,37; cp. 1,7); others see Jesus' deeds, or simply read about them, and believe in him as the Messiah (20,30-31). On account of its missionary interest in christology, other theological topics such as Spirit, Church, sacraments, ethics, and the ideas of salvation, forgiveness, grace, and sanctification have either no place or only passing mention. In this sense the source is a unique document in first-century Christianity.

In addition to this characterization of the signs source, Fortna devotes a separate discussion to stylistic arguments[16]. He first describes the source negatively by noting the absence of 32 of Ruckstuhl's 50 style characteristics[17]. This means that 64% of Ruckstuhl's characteristics of Johannine style do not appear in the Gospel of Signs. This percentage can be adjusted because Ruckstuhl's list needs further nuancing[18]. Thus for several terms a further distinction must be made[19]:

38. ἑλκύειν: 5/1
  - 38a. metaphorical: 2/0   6,44; 12,32
  - 38b. literal: 3/1/3   18,10; 21,6.11

---

14. *Gospel of Signs*, p. 231.

15. *Ibid.*, pp. 232-233.

16. *Ibid.*, pp. 201-218: "Part Four: Stylistic Tests of the Source's Purity and Integrity". The formula a + b / x + y represents the frequency of the style characteristic; a + b = the number of occurrences in John and the Johannine Epistles; x = the independent occurrences in the rest of the NT (not including Synoptic parallels); y = the Synoptic parallels to instances in x. The figures in parentheses include doubtful cases; "+0" before or after "/" is "omitted"; figures in square brackets represent instances in the Synoptic Gospels only. Any pre-Johannine instances are expressed by a figure following a second "/" – For Ruckstuhl's reaction to Fortna's stylistic tests, see below pp. 302-307.

17. These are numbers 3, 5, 7, 8, 10, 11, 12, 13, 14, 15, 18, 19, 20, 21, 22, 23, 25, 26, 27, 28, 29, 30, 31, 32, 33, 34, 36, 40, 41, 44, 46, and 47 (pp. 205-208). Fortna remarks that "some of these usages are by their nature appropriate only to the discourses" (p. 207).

18. *Ibid.*, pp. 208-211.

19. From these characteristics, Fortna (*Predecessor*, p. 209) now mentions only nos. 45c (n. 497), 45d (n. 498), and 45b (n. 499). See below, p. 218 n. 395.

39. ὀψάριον: 5/0
    39a. ὀψάριον (collective): 2/0   21,9.13
    39b. ὀψάρια: 3/0/3   6,9.11; 21,10
45. ἐκ (partitive): 31+3/26+3
    45a. τις (πολλοί, οὐδείς) ἐκ: 25(26)/[1]/0
        With τις or τινές: 6,64; 7,25.44.48.48; 9,16; 11,37.46.49; 12,20.
        Also included are instances where the pronoun is only implied:
        (1,24); 6,39; 7,40; 9,40; 16,17.
        With πολλοί: 4,39; 6,50; 7,31; 10,20; 11,19. 45; 12,42.
        With οὐδείς: 7,19; 16,5; 17,12; 18,9.
    45b. noun + ἐκ ("from among"): 4(6)/[8]/4(6)
        Cf. 3,1; 4,7; 6,(11).13; 18,3.(3). The instance in 6,11 is good if what
        follows (ὅσον ἤθελον) is to be taken substantively.
    45c. noun + ἐκ ("made of"): 3/[1]/3
        Cf. 2,15; 9,6; 19,2.
    45d. εἷς (δύο) ἐκ: 13(14)/[15+]/11(12)
        Cf. 1,35.40; 6,8.70.71; 12,2.(4); 13,21; 18,17.25.26; 21,2; two are
        not in the source: 7,50; 20,24. Fortna does not add this one to his list
        "because of the slight blurring", that is, it is found in both source and
        Johannine passages.

From these specifications Fortna is able to increase his list of missing
Johannine style characteristics from 32 to 39[20] and the proportion becomes
39:54[21]. But the ratio must be adjusted in a second way. Some of the
remaining characteristics are invalid, for "while the frequency of the characteristic in Jn is clearly out of proportion to the gospel's length in comparison with the rest of the NT, the usage is found often enough outside
the Johannine writings to account for a few instances in the source"[22]:

17. independent ἐκεῖνος ("he" or "she"): 44+6/11/(4)
    (in the source: 4,25; 18,17.25; 20,16)
37. πάλιν + δεύτερος: 2/2/(1)
    (in the source: 4,54 is doubtful)
42. πιστεύειν εἰς: 36+3/8(9)/1(2)
    (in the source: 2,11; [11,45])
48. ἐντεῦθεν: 5/6/3
    (in the source: 2,16; 14,31; 19,18)
50. πιάζειν: 8/4/2
    (in the source: 21,3.10)

And a sixth invalid characteristic is added because it is common enough, and
analogous to other expressions of time in the NT:

49. ὥρα ἐν ᾗ: 3/0/1
    (in the source: 4,52). If ὥρα ἵνα/ὅτε is idiomatic for John, this expression
    cannot be as well.

    20. By the addition of numbers 38a, 38b, 39a, 39b, 45a, 45b, and 45c.
    21. This last figure represents Ruckstuhl's 50 characteristics with the addition of num-
bers 38b, 39b, 45b, and 45c.
    22. *Gospel of Signs*, pp. 210-211, esp. 210.

Fortna thus arrives at the ratio 39:48. "This means that no less than 81% of the valid characteristics occur in Jn without blurring, that is either wholly in Johannine passages (as in most cases) or wholly in the source"[23]. The presence in the source of the remaining nine characteristics (nos. 1, 2, 4, 6, 9, 16, 24, 35, 43) is, according to Fortna, the result of John's imitation of the source's language or Johannine redaction of the source[24]. He concludes from the absence of "Johannine characteristics" that his reconstructed source is relatively pure[25].

For a positive description of the signs source, Fortna first gives a list of words which occur frequently in the NT (particularly in the Synoptics) and of which the use in John is restricted to the source[26]:

ἕτερος: 1/101/1	(19,37)
ἐνώπιον: 1/96/1	(20,30)
ἄρχεσθαι ποιεῖν τι: 1/77/1	(13,5)
ὑπό + acc.: 1/46/1	(1,48)
ἰσχύειν: 1/28/1	(21,6)
σύν: 3/127/3[4]	([11,33]; 12,2; 18,1; 21,3)
ἕκαστος: 3/82/3	(6,7; 16,32b; 19,23)
εὐθέως: 3/77/3	(5,9; 6,21; 18,27)
πρῶτον (adverbial): 3/[24]/3	(1,41; 2,10; 18,13)

The style of the source is thus more akin to that of the Synoptic Gospels than that of John, as is also apparent from the infrequent use of Ἰουδαῖος: 71/[11+5]/4(5) in 18,(12).33.39; 19,3.19; the frequency of the genitive absolute, and the absence of λέγειν πρός τινα[27].

Second, a few words that are infrequent in the NT occur in John but only in the source[28]:

κολυμβήθρα: 3/0/3	(5,2.7; 9,7)
ὑδρία: 3/0/3	(2,6.7; 4,28)
Μεσσίας: 2/0/2	(1,41; 4,25)
κῆπος: 3/1/3	(18,1.26; 19,41)
ῥάπισμα: 2/1/2	(18,22; 19,3)
ἀπό ("off", of distance): 2/1/2	(11,18; 21,8)
πρός + dative: 4/3/4	(18,16; 20,11.12.12)
κραυγάζειν: 6/3/5(6)	(11,43; 12,13; 18,40; 19,6.?12.15).

---

23. *Ibid.*, p. 211.
24. *Ibid.*, pp. 211-214.
25. "Far from demolishing our reconstruction, then, the stylistic tests would seem in the main to have verified it, and to suggest that while it may contain errors of detail, as reconstructed it is relatively pure" (p. 214).
26. *Ibid.*, pp. 214-215.
27. *Ibid.*, p. 215.
28. *Ibid.*, pp. 215-216.

Third, Fortna adds five characteristics from Ruckstuhl's list, but three of them in a more strict definition, and ascribes them to the signs source[29]:

4.   Ἱεροσόλυμα + article: 3(4)/0/2(3)
38b. ἑλκύειν (litteral): 3/1/3
39b. ὀψάρια: 3/0/3
45c. noun + ἐκ ("made of"): 3/[1]/3
50.   πιάζειν: 2/1/2.

Finally, a list of expressions "while not peculiar to the source in the NT, are characteristic of it and are largely if not wholly absent from the rest of Jn"[30]:

(a) introductory or resumptive ἦν (δέ) (τις): 11/7+2/10
    (2,6; 3,1; 4,6.46; 5,5; 6,10; 11,1.38; *12,20*; 19,41; 21,2)
(b) parenthetical or explanatory ἦν (δέ):
    (11,2.18; 18,10.13.*14*.28.40; 19,14.19.23)
(c) ὡς + numeral: 8/10/7(8)
    (1,39; 4,6; 6,10.19; 11,18; 19,14.[39]; 21,8)
(d) singular verb with double subject (often αὐτὸς καὶ ...):
    (1,35.45; 2,2.12; 4,*12*.53; 18,1b.15; etc.)
(e) οὖν after a command:
    (1,39; ?4,30; 6,10.(13); 9,7; 11,41; 21,6)
(f) εἷς (δύο) ἐκ: 12(13)/[15+]/10(11) [= 45d, above]
(g) noun + ἐκ ("from among"): 4(6)/[8]/4(6) [= 45b, above]
(h) ῥαββί(ουνί) addressed to Jesus: 9/5+1/4(5)
    (1,38.49; *3,2.26*; *4,31*; [6,25]; 9,2; *11,8*; 20,16)
(i) "come and see":
    (1,39.46; 4,29; 11,34)
(j) ἔχειν with expression of time: 4/0/3
    (5,5.6; *8,57*; 11,17; cf. κομψότερον ἔσχεν [4,52])
(k) ὄνομα αὐτῷ: 3/5(7)/3
    (1,6; 3,1; 18,10).

Fortna remarks that his analysis of style characteristics not only con-firms the existence of a narrative source but shows its integrity as well. The source's characteristic usages are not confined to one part of the source nor can they be grouped into two or more substrata; with but one exception (1,19-34), all the pericopes of the source contain at least one of these characteristics. Thus, in contrast to Bultmann's "cautious" supposition, the miracle stories and the passion narrative appear to constitute a single source. Fortna believes that he has "uncovered, how-ever inexactly in detail, a pre-Johannine stratum which had already a distinctive *literary* character imposed upon it"[31].

29. *Ibid.*, p. 216.
30. *Ibid.*, pp. 216-217. Johannine instances are cited in italics.
31. *Ibid.*, p. 217. With reference to Bultmann's literary theory Fortna remarks: "Bult-mann's distinction between SQ, and the other narrative sources which he lumps together

J. Louis MARTYN (1968) drew attention to Fortna's dissertation before its publication[32]; in 1970 he termed his student's analysis "in the main ... a solid working hypothesis", and examined the *Gospel of Signs* with regard to *Traditionsgeschichte* and *Religionsgeschichte*[33]. He hypothesizes that between the production of the signs gospel and the writing of the Fourth Gospel developments took place which had important influence on the way the evangelist redacted the *Gospel of Signs*. He acknowledges a wide range of possible developments offered by Johannine research[34], but chooses "a more inductive path ... to look for some of the intervening developments which seem fairly directly and simply reflected in the Evangelist's handling of SG"[35]. He thus probes the inter-

as EQ, is understandably cautious, but it is probably based on Faure's contention that chs. 1-12 have a different style (and thus a different source underlying them) than chs. 13–20" (p. 217 n. 3).

32. J.L. MARTYN, *History and Theology in the Fourth Gospel*, New York, 1968, p. 3 n. 7. In the second edition (1979), he has expanded this note into an excursus, presenting a "Bibliography Pertinent to the Hypothesis of a Signs Source" with a brief discussion of the development of the hypothesis and the alternatives proposed by its opponents (cf. pp. 164-168: "Excursus E").

33. *Source Criticism and* Religionsgeschichte *in the Fourth Gospel*, in *Jesus and Man's Hope* = *Perspective* 11/1 (1970) 247-273, p. 248 (= 1986, p. 100). Cf. *History and Theology*, ²1979, p. 166: "the Signs Source theory itself seems to me to enjoy a considerable degree of probability, especially as it has been developed in the extraordinarily careful analysis of Robert T. Fortna". See also *We Have Found Elijah*, in FS W.D. Davies, 1976, pp. 181-219, esp. 197-199 (= 1978, pp. 9-54, esp. 29-30); *Glimpses into the History of the Johannine Community*, in DE JONGE (ed.), *L'Évangile de Jean*, 1977 (²1987), pp. 149-175, esp. 156-157 (= 1978, pp. 90-121, esp. 98). – On Martyn, see NICOL, *Sēmeia*, 1972, pp. 12 n. 3, 14-15; BROWN, *Community*, 1979, pp. 171-174 (FT: 1983, pp. 187-191); LÉON-DUFOUR, *Où en est la recherche johannique?*, 1990, pp. 22-23; LINDARS, *Trends*, 1990, pp. 332-333; ASHTON, *Understanding*, 1991, pp. 11, 107-109; SLOYAN, *What Are They Saying about John?*, 1991, pp. 40-41; SCHMITHALS, *Johannesevangelium*, 1992, pp. 159-160; SMITH, *John among the Gospels*, 1992, p. 72; on the relation between Martyn and his student Fortna, see SMITH, *John among the Gospels*, 1992, p. 72 n. 100: "Fortna was Martyn's doctoral student and presumably worked out his dissertation proposal in conversation with him. Martyn clearly regards Fortna's work as profitable and probably correct, while not tying his own thesis to any single source reconstruction". See also p. 71 n. 98: "Fortna's work was completed before the publication of the first edition of Martyn's own book ... in 1968 but was published a couple of years later". For more information, see SMITH, in FS J.L. *Martyn*, 1990, pp. 275-294.

34. *Source Criticism*, pp. 248-252, esp. 252: "Were one proceeding on the basis of the present state of Johannine research, rather than following a more inductive path, several possibilities would demand attention. *Perhaps* between SG and 4G arose: a) a struggle with followers of John the Baptist; b) a hardening of battle lines between synagogue and church; c) inner-church problems, such as: (1) overemphasis on the anticipated glories of Jesus' future coming; (2) loss of a sense of contact with and memory of the earthly Jesus, with concomitant danger that Christianity might devolve into a mystery religion; (3) docetism; (4) growth of a hardening and institutionally oriented orthodoxy which pits itself with increasing fervor against the growth of Hellenistic enthusiasm in the church; (5) theological developments which are not truly christocentric". See Martyn's own scenario of developments in the Johannine community in *Glimpses*.

35. *Source Criticism*, pp. 252-253.

section of the signs gospel hypothesis with his own notion of intervening developments by posing three questions: (1) Who is Jesus[36]? (2) Can one follow Moses *and* Jesus[37]? (3) What is the significance of Jesus' death[38]?

In Martyn's view, the developments in (Johannine) Christian thought arose chiefly from Jewish opposition. He thinks there was a synagogue which, having expelled the messianic believers, stands in opposition to John's church. John attempted to respond to the opponents' objections by reshaping the signs gospel to correct deficiencies which had sparked the debate. It is difficult to give a precise outline of these opponents. Perhaps the synagogue was a strongly Pharisaic Jewish community which followed the lead of the Synod of Jamnia (cf. ἀποσυνάγωγος γενέσθαι). It seems that at least some of these Jewish opponents held the view that Moses was the θεῖος ἀνήρ par excellence and it was he who ascended into heaven, receiving the divine secrets. It is possible, too, that some of the opponents represent a form of Jewish *gnosis*[39]. For Martyn then, "John belongs in a dominantly Jewish-Christian milieu". Bultmann had suggested as much for the signs source, but "the same must be said about the Gospel itself. As one views the growth from SG to 4G, overt concern with Jewish questions become more, not less central"[40]. John continued to contend with Jewish opposition; nevertheless, he also continued to address himself, as the signs gospel did, to potential Jewish converts to Christianity[41].

II. W. NICOL: "THE SĒMEIA IN THE FOURTH GOSPEL"

Willem NICOL presented a dissertation on the signs source in 1972[42]. He considers the significance of the σημεῖα "an important key to the

36. *Ibid.*, pp. 253-260.
37. *Ibid.*, pp. 260-261.
38. *Ibid.*, pp. 261-267.
39. *Ibid.*, p. 267.
40. *Ibid.*, pp. 268-269.
41. *Ibid.*, p. 269: "The author of the Signs Gospel ... pens 'a textbook for potential Jewish converts' (Fortna). And John himself, in spite of the bitter Jewish opposition and persecution, holds that frontier still to be at least partially open". Cf. *Glimpses*, pp. 156-157 (= 1978, p. 98). – For further reactions to Fortna's *Gospel of Signs*, see below, pp. 165-176, 302-307.
42. W. NICOL, *The Sēmeia in the Fourth Gospel: Tradition and Redaction* (SupplNT, 32), Leiden, 1972 (diss. Kampen; dir. H. Ridderbos). – Reviews: cf. VAN BELLE, no. 1747 (see below, pp. 177-180). Other references to Nicol: SCHNACKENBURG, *Forschung*, 1974, p. 285; TEEPLE, *Origin*, 1974, pp. 50-51; KYSAR, *Fourth Evangelist*, 1975, pp. 16-37, 67-70, 72-75, 77; ANRW II, 25/3, 1985, pp. 2396-2399; CARSON, *Current Source Criticism*, 1978, pp. 414-420; HOEFERKAMP, *Relationship*, 1978, pp. 49-53; CORSANI, *I miracoli*, 1983, pp. 32-34; HEEKERENS, *Zeichen-Quelle*, 1984, *passim*; BEUTLER, ANRW II, 25/3, 1985, p. 2546; BITTNER, *Jesu Zeichen*, 1987, pp. 2-13; SCHNELLE, *Christologie*, 1987,

historical and theological problems of the Fourth Gospel" and in a brief introduction explains his application of the methods of literary (or source) criticism and form and redaction criticism[43]. Then, in three successive chapters, he treats the source-critical separation of the semeia traditions (S) and their Johannine redaction (J), the character of the semeia traditions, and the Johannine redaction of the semeia traditions[44].

1. Literary Criticism (Source Criticism)

After a summary but fairly complete review of "the history of the identification of the semeia source"[45], Nicol describes the most important arguments in favor of the signs source[46].

(a) Some pericopes are shorter and more Synoptic-like in form than the longer, typically Johannine narratives (chapters 4, 7, 9, 11, 18–19) which are dramatically constructed with "many short, powerful dialogue scenes in a lively sequence". The Synoptic-like form appears especially in 2,13-22; 12,1-11.12-19 and in the shorter miracle stories which have a basic three-part pattern: the illness, the healing, and the demonstration of the reality of the healing. This leads Nicol to postulate that "John

pp. 168-182 (ET: 1992, pp. 150-164); KUHN, *Christologie*, 1988, pp. 51-52 (Jn 1,35-51); LÜTGEHETMANN, *Hochzeit*, 1990, pp. 86-89 (Jn 1,1-11); WÖLLNER, *Zeichenglaube*, 1988, pp. 13-14; BOTHA, *Jesus and the Samaritan Woman*, 1991, pp. 18-19; SCHMITHALS, *Johannesevangelium*, 1992, pp. 125, 137; KOSKENNIEMI, *Apollonios von Tyana*, 1992, pp. 142-143; SMITH, *John among the Gospels*, 1992, p. 72. – See also W. NICOL, *The History of Johannine Research during the Past Century*, in *Neotestamentica* 6 (1972) 8-18 (without discussion of the semeia hypothesis). – Nicol's dissertation was directed by H. RIDDERBOS, who, in his own commentary, refers without enthusiasm to the semeia source: *Het evangelie naar Johannes. Proeve van een theologische exegese*, Kampen, 2 vols., 1987, 1992. Cf. I, p. 15 (cp. 13); see esp. pp. 120-121 (with reference to 2,1-11): "Others indeed are of the opinion that the evangelist, for traditional reasons, has drawn his miracle stories from a certain miracle (semeia) source in which all emphasis had been placed precisely on the historical reliability of the miracles, but that he himself would have taken a much more ambivalent attitude toward the miracles, which then would come to expression in the way he redacted them, completed them, etc. For him, then, only the spiritual meaning, which he attributed to the miracles, would have had value" (references to Nicol: I, pp. 33 n. 15, 65 n. 2, 66 n. 6, 68 n. 15, 121 n. 2, 122 n. 7, 127 n. 22, 136 n. 45, 204 n. 5, 206 nn. 11 and 12, 207 n. 16, 254 n. 23). Ridderbos does not accept the inconsistency of 4,54 with 2,23 and 4,45 on the level of Johannine redaction (cf. I, pp. 209-210); compare his discussion of 4,48 (p. 206). See also II, pp. 11 (with regard to the raising of Lazarus), 321 (with regard to 20,30-31). – On Ridderbos's commentary, see, e.g., MENKEN, *De christologie*, 1991, pp. 18-19 (ET: 1993, p. 296-297).

43. *Sēmeia*, pp. 1-8.

44. *Ibid.*, respectively pp. 9-40, 41-94, 95-149.

45. *Ibid.*, pp. 9-14. The historical review pays special attention to the rise of style criticism; the older authors (especially A. Schweizer) have been pushed too much to the background. In his short presentation, Nicol gives no specific discussion of the authors and he does not enter into their argumentation.

46. *Ibid.*, pp. 14-30.

received these pericopes from the same general stream of tradition from which the Synoptic Gospels grew"[47].

(b) "Because the results of style statistics can be fairly objective" he posits the existence of S especially on the basis of style criticism[48]. Beginning from Schweizer's observation that style characteristics appear very rarely in the so-called Synoptic-like pericopes of John (cf. Jeremias, Kümmel), Nicol presents Ruckstuhl's list (nos. 1-50) but, like Fortna, rejects no. 37 (πάλιν with δεύτερος) and no. 49 (ὥρα ἐν ᾖ). He adds a list of 32 characteristics, which he justifies by the different aim of his study. Unlike Schweizer and Ruckstuhl he does not consider "the possibility that a later redactor could have imitated John's style" and so includes even "imitable" traits, i.e., anything characteristic enough for John. In contrast to their interest in the *presence* of characteristics, Nicol finds their *absence* more significant, so "the more typical Johannine style characteristics we can gather, the better we can judge whether they are really scarce in the miracle stories"[49]. He presents all these style characteristics in a horizontal arrangement, verse by verse[50]. He then lists the averages of the total number of Johannine characteristics per verse for the different pericopes, derived by dividing the total number of characteristics in each pericope by the number of verses in it; Ruckstuhl's averages are given in parentheses. He divides the material into three groups: semeia source (S), Johannine narrative (JN) and Johannine discourse (JD)[51]:

1.	1,1-18	JD	1.6	(0.7)
2.	1,19-34	JN	1.2	(0.3)
3.	1,35-51	S	0.7	(0.5)
4.	2,1-12	S	0.7	(0.3)
5.	2,13-25	JN	1.3	(0.8)
6.	4,1-9.16-19.27-30.40	S	0.7	(0.6)
7.	4,10-15.20-24.31-39.41-42	JND	1.4	(0.5)
8.	4,43-45.48-49	JN	1.0	(0.6)
9.	4,46-47.50-54	S	0.6	(0.6)
10.	5,1-9	S	0.3	(0.1)

47. *Ibid.*, pp. 15-16. This, in any case, is clear in 4,46-54 and 6,1-25. Jn 5,2-9b could also be a "Synoptic" healing story: as in Lk 13,16 and Mk 5,25, the gravity of the illness is emphasized by stressing its duration (5,5); the short conversation between Jesus and the sick man (5,6-7) also appears in the Synoptics (Mk 1,40; 9,23-24). The strong emphasis on the man's helplessness is characteristic of the semeia traditions; the healing word (5,8) is identical to Mk 2,11, and the demonstration of healing (5,9) appears in Mk 2,12. Even the story of the man born blind resembles Synoptic healings of blind people and the raising of Lazarus contains a number of Synoptic characteristics.

48. *Ibid.*, pp. 16-27; cf. also p. 4.

49. *Ibid.*, p. 22.

50. He develops this using 1,1-51; 2,1-25; 4,1-54; 5,1-47; 6,1-71; 7,1-13; 9,1-41; 11,1-57; 12,1-19; 18,1-40 (pp. 19-21).

51. *Ibid.*, pp. 25-26.

11.	5,10-18	JN	2.1	(0.4)
12.	5,19-47	JD	1.9	(1.0)
13.	6,1-15	S+J	1.1	(0.7)
14.	6,16-21	S	0.7	(0.5)
14a.	6,22-25	S	0.75	(0.5)
15.	6,26-59	JD	2.4	(1.1)
16.	6,60-71	JN	1.3	(0.5)
17.	7,1-13	JN	1.8	(1.0)
18.	9,1-2.6-7	S	0.75	(0.5)
19.	9,3-5	JND	3.3	(0.3)
20.	9,8-41	JN	1.9	(1.0)
21.	11,7-10.18-32	JD	1.5	(0.7)
22.	11,1-6.11-17.33-34	S+J	1.0	(0.6)
23.	11,45-57	JN	1.9	(1.0)
24.	12,1-8.12-15	Trad.	0.4	(0.4)
25.	12,9-11.16-19	JN	2.0	(1.0)
26.	18,1-40	JN	2.0	(1.0)

Nicol observes that the two discourses in the list (nos. 12 and 15) have high averages (1.9 and 2.4 respectively). Five narrative pericopes (nos. 5, 16, 17, 20, 23) have a total average of 1.69 (Ruckstuhl 0.92), while that of the five short miracle stories (nos. 4, 9, 10, 14, 18) is 0.58 (Ruckstuhl 0.4). Johannine style characteristics thus occur 2.9 times more frequently (Ruckstuhl 2.3 times) in the former narratives than in the latter[52]. Nicol therefore concludes: "I contend that this cannot be ascribed to chance and must mean that in these five miracle stories there is evidence of the influence of a style different from that of John: he must have taken them from a tradition"[53]. Some Johannine style characteristics do occur in these miracle stories because John did not reproduce the source mechanically but gave a fairly faithful rendition from memory. According to Nicol, this was normal for New Testament times. For example, Lukan style appears in passages where the evangelist is following Mark or Q. In a footnote, he remarks that some Johannine style characteristics present in S may be accidental because they also appear in the rest of the New Testament[54]. A few typical expressions were bound to "slip into the source material" in addition to some conscious insertions. It should also be noted that Nicol rejects attempts to collect style characteristics of the

52. *Ibid.*, pp. 25-27.
53. *Ibid.*, p. 26.
54. *Ibid.*, p. 27 n. 2. The explanations of E. Hirsch (the later hand imitated the former one) and J. Becker (both had to some extent the same style because they belonged to the same congregation) are rejected by Nicol: "But with a few possible exceptions, these cannot be correct because in some passages there are practically no Johannine style characteristics". Cf. HIRSCH, in *ZNW* 43 (1950) 128-143, esp. pp. 129-130; BECKER, *Wunder*, 1970, p. 133 (= 1980, p. 439).

source itself. Bultmann may have been right that S bears a Semitic style, but that is hardly a criterion because the style of the whole Gospel has a Semitic hue. As for Fortna's list of 35 style characteristics for the *Gospel of Signs*, Nicol is unconvinced except for εὐθέως, Μεσσίας, πρός + dative, κραυγάζειν, and ἦν (δέ) (τις). The others are either too rare in the source or their absence from J is explicable by the fact that nearly all the Synoptic-like material in the Gospel is contained in the source[55].

(c) There are many aporias in the Gospel, which indicate that John was not written, as it were, in one sitting[56]. The process of composition appears to be incomplete as evidenced by seams which were not fully covered. Thus, if a σημεῖα source has been redacted, traces of it should also be recognizable. Nicol notes only a few basic ones: (1) The numbering of the signs (2,11 and 4,54) does not reckon with 2,23 and 4,45. Moreover, this count is not continued and seems to have no significance in the present Gospel. (2) Verse 4,48 seems to be a *corpus alienum* in the Johannine story. (3) Jn 20,30-31 refers to σημεῖα as if they have been described from beginning to end in the Gospel, even though none are mentioned after chapter 12. It is possible that the conclusion has been respectfully taken from a pre-existing source. (4) There seems to be a hiatus between 6,25 and 6,26 which divides the traditional miracle story from the discourse material. (5) The dialogue scenes in chapters 5 and 9 appear to be Johannine additions because they start with the theme of Sabbath-violation which is not integral to the miracle stories themselves. (6) In chapter 11 the conversation between Jesus and Martha "creates a few obvious aporias and seems to have been inserted into the traditional miracle story".

(d) A final argument, which Nicol accepts in association with the others, is the presence of ideological tensions within the Gospel[57]. According to S, the miracles are a legitimate basis for faith (2,11; 4,53; 6,14; 20,30-31), but John was critical of faith based on miracles (2,23; 6,26) and regarded the testimony of miracles as a "second best" route to belief (14,11; 10,38; 4,48).

On the basis of these four arguments, classic in determining a signs source but here brought together systematically, Nicol makes a distinction between S and J. In contrast to Fortna, he prefers not to give a "reconstruction" of S but a "separation", because he thinks a reconstruction is impossible. When he does present a precise delimitation of the text, it has more to do with his intention to trace John's redaction of

---

55. *Sēmeia*, p. 27 n. 2.
56. *Ibid.*, pp. 27-30.
57. *Ibid.*, p. 30.

his source as far as possible than with his precise knowledge about source and redaction[58]. To Nicol's S belong[59]:

1. 2,1-3. 4 (without γύναι, οὔπω ἥκει ἡ ὥρα μου). 5. 6 (without κατὰ τὸν καθαρισμὸν τῶν Ἰουδαίων κείμεναι). 7-8. 9 (without καὶ οὐκ ᾔδει ... ὕδωρ). 10. 11 (without καὶ ἐφανέρωσεν τὴν δόξαν αὐτοῦ).

2. 4,46-47. 50-54.

3. 5,2-3a. 5-9b.

4. 6,1-3. 5-11. 12 (without ἵνα μή τι ἀπόληται). 13. 14 (without ὁ ἐρχόμενος εἰς τὸν κόσμον). 15b.

5. 6,16-23 (only a few Johannine style characteristics appear and it is thus difficult to discover anything of J).

6. 6,22-25 (the basis of which comes from S).

7. 9,1-3a. 6-7.

8. 11,1-3. 6. 11b. 12-15. 17-19. 28-32 (this passage contains traditional elements and J is difficult to discern). 33-39. 41a. 43b-45.

9. 20,30-31a (12,37-38 is J!).

Perhaps the basic material for 1,35-51 is also from the signs source (v. 51 is J), as well as 4,5-9.16-19.28-30.40. Jn 4,25-26 appear to be J, but based on tradition.

2. *The Character of the Sēmeia Traditions*

(a) Nicol first studies the specific traits of S in comparison with the Synoptic Gospels[60]. S undoubtedly contains the most marvelous miracles of the New Testament; Jesus' miraculous power is more at center stage than in the Synoptics[61]. In contrast to the Synoptics (e.g., Mk 8,2 par.; Mt 14,14; 20,34; Lk 7,13), Jesus never performs a miracle out of

---

58. *Ibid.*, p. 4: "I have not attempted a full reconstruction of the source because this is impossible. My aim has not been to publish the text of the source but only to characterize it as far as possible in order to be able to evaluate John's reaction to it" (cp. pp. 4-5). Nicol limits himself: "It must also be clear that by 'sēmeia source' (S) I do not mean a source which contained only sēmeia. It would probably have contained more, even of the other narrative material in Jn. But I have limited myself to the miracles because they were probably an important and homogeneous core in the source so that the source criticism may be carried out with more certainty" (p. 6). For Fortna's reaction to Nicol's "separation", see below, pp. 163-165, esp. 165.

59. *Ibid.*, pp. 30-40.

60. *Ibid.*, pp. 41-48.

61. Lazarus is already in the tomb four days and yet is raised; a paralytic has been ill 38 years and is healed; Jesus changes a great quantity of water into wine; with the story of the walking on the sea comes a new miracle, the safe and immediate landing. It is not at all strange that S should contain such miraculous deeds: they were promised to Nathanael (p. 42).

compassion in this source. The sole aim of S is to demonstrate the unlimited power of Jesus. Thus, he performs the miracles on his own initiative and even takes it away from others by reacting in a manner different from the petitioner's expectation (2,4; 4,50; 11,6). Whereas in the Synoptics faith precedes the miracle, sometimes even as a condition (Mk 2,5; 5,34.36; 6,5-6; 7,29; 9,23; 10,52), in S faith is the natural result of the miracle and appears at the end of the miracle story (2,11; 4,53; 6,14a; 11,15.45). The divine Jesus stands above all human beings and needs no cooperation from them. For S, the miracles are authenticating signs of Jesus' Messiahship, realistically described so that all might believe[62]. The miracles are never called δυνάμεις (deeds of divine power in a wider eschatological context) and are not related to the coming of the Kingdom of God as in the Synoptics. Thus, S says little about the nature of Jesus' Messiahship; only *that* he is the Messiah[63].

(b) Regarding the history-of-religions background of S, Nicol reacts against the opinion that the source presented Jesus as a Hellenistic θεῖος ἀνήρ[64]. Many elements in the source give rise to the supposition of a Jewish background. He examines each pericope and the word σημεῖον to arrive at the following conclusions[65]:

1. The use of σημεῖον is Jewish[66]. In S it signifies "an event which is, by its miraculous character, a legitimizing sign of the Christ". This meaning of σημεῖον does not appear in Hellenism. Rather, if S intended to describe Jesus as a θεῖος ἀνήρ, one would expect words like θαῦμα, ἀρετή, and δύναμις. On the other hand, the Septuagint uses σημεῖον with this meaning to translate the Hebrew '*ot*, beginning with Exodus (Ex 4,8.8.9.17.28.30): God empowered Moses to perform signs that would authenticate his divine mission; these signs, worked by Moses, aim to awaken faith in those who see them (Ex 4,1.5.8.9.30; cp. Num 14,11). Likewise, σημεῖον is applied to the ten plagues (Ex 10,1-2; 11,9-10) and, after the Exodus, to all the mighty works of God to save Israel from Egypt (Num 14,11.22; Deut 4,34; 6,22; 7,19; 11,3; 26,8; 29,2; 34,11; Ps 77,43-52; 104,27-36; 136,9; Wis 10,14-20; Neh 9,10)[67]. In a certain sense, the recalling of God's mighty deeds at the Exodus was the center of Old Testament faith; they are the core of the creed in Deut 26,5-9. S has therefore termed Jesus' miracles "signs" by way of analogy to the spectacular Mosaic σημεῖα of God. Thus, these

---

62. *Ibid.*, p. 44: "The sole theme of S is that all should see the miracles as authenticating signs (sēmeia) of the Messiah and believe"; cp. p. 45: "The main theme dominates everything: Jesus is the Messiah".

63. *Ibid.*, pp. 46-48.

64. *Ibid.*, pp. 48-52.

65. *Ibid.*, pp. 53-68.

66. *Ibid.*, pp. 62-66.

67. *Ibid.*, p. 65.

signs are proofs of Jesus' divine mission: Jesus is the expected Messiah (ὁ χριστός: 20,31; 1,41; 4,29).

2. Many details in the source reveal the author's knowledge of the geography and customs of Palestine. The use of Aramaic words (like Cephas and Messiah) strengthen this. Nicol suggests, therefore, that "the first bearer(s) of this tradition must have been a Palestinian Jew – quite possibly John the son of Zebedee – and S can be regarded as an important and independent source to the life of Jesus of Nazareth"[68].

3. The Greek of S is Semitic. This is evidenced in the short sentence structure, with the verb at the beginning, and simple connections, i.e., with asyndeton, καί, δέ, or οὖν (never μέν)[69].

4. The quotations from the Septuagint (especially the Elijah-Elisha passages) point to a Jewish Sitz-im-Leben[70]. In itself, this is certainly not a conclusive argument (Philo also quoted the LXX), but it can indicate that the theology of the source is more Jewish than Hellenistic.

5. We find a number of Jewish ideas expressed in S[71]. For example, the notion of sin as the cause of illness (9,2) and the expectation of the eschatological prophet (6,14). A comparison of 4,46-54 with the rabbinic narrative of a healing at a distance (Berakoth 34b) undoubtedly reveals that the narrator of S is not far removed from the rabbinic mentality. Further, the title "Christ (Messiah)" is understood and applied in a very Jewish way.

On the basis of these characteristics, Nicol is even more inclined toward a Jewish Sitz-im-Leben for the signs source. He finds no Jewish parallels for only two traits: the duration of illness for 38 years (5,5) and the carrying of the bed (5,9). Otherwise, the so-called Hellenistic characteristics of the θεῖος ἀνήρ (supernatural knowledge and the power to work miracles) appear to be just as well, if not more, Jewish than Hellenistic[72].

(c) By examining the developmental tendencies of the Christian literature, Nicol attempts to situate the signs source within the primitive Christian tradition[73]. He thinks that S is perhaps younger than the Synoptic tradition[74]. If so, a number of S's characteristics can be explained

68. *Ibid.*, p. 66.
69. *Ibid.*, p. 67 (cp. Bultmann, see above, p. 27 n. 150).
70. *Ibid.*, p. 67.
71. *Ibid.*, p. 67.
72. *Ibid.*, pp. 51-52, 67-68.
73. *Ibid.*, pp. 68-77 (he refers to SANDERS, *Tendencies*, 1969).
74. In support of this notion are the following characteristics: (1) In 4,46-54: the mission terminology in 4,53 (cf. Acts 10,2; 11,14; 16,15.31; 18,8); it is not stated that the official is a Gentile – the debate over the Gentile mission was no longer so acute at the time of S (at the end of the first century); emphasis on the miraculous. (2) In 6,1-15: direct address is more frequent (6,10.12); παιδάριον and κριθίνους in v. 9 (absent from

from the later evolution of the church community[75]. The use of the word σημεῖα corresponds to the gradual evolution in the church toward characterizing Jesus' miracles as signs (Acts and Paul). Moreover, the theme of S, the view that miracles lead to faith (and not to amazement, as in the Synoptics) is also undoubtedly corroborated in Acts 9,42; 13,12 (cf. 9,35). The dominance of Jesus' power alone and the absence of Jewish-Christian ideas such as the Kingdom need not be put down to Hellenistic influence but are due to theological development within the church itself. If S is approaching John's "high" christology, then the absence of the Kingdom coincides with the dulling of eschatological expectations at the end of the first century[76].

(d) Nicol considers S a missionary book, written to convince Jews of Jesus' Messiahship[77]. S does not describe Jesus as the Davidic Messiah – from whom miracles were not expected[78] – but as the eschatological prophet who must justify his divine mission through signs[79]. Nevertheless, Nicol believes there is a broad base of evidence to say that the pos-

the Synoptics) reflect 2 Kgs 4; the concrete presentation of Jesus' dialogue with the disciples (Philip and Andrew are expressly named); the "Chorschluss" (6,14); emphasis on the initiative of Jesus and the helplessness of the disciples. (3) In the case of the walking on the sea the evidence may point in the opposite direction because the stilling of the storm is absent (perhaps it was introduced secondarily into Mk 6,51 under the influence of Mk 4,35-41). But in place of it S has the extra – particularly marvelous – miracle of the sudden landing. Moreover, the pericope is concluded by an extra scene (6,22-25) in which the reality of the miracle is demonstrated. (4) 1,35-50 could belong to S; it seems to demonstrate elements of later tradition: the disciples' immediate confession of Jesus as Messiah (cf. Mk 8,27ff). (5) In chapters 5 and 9, Jesus takes the initiative. (6) The "legendary" character of both the wine miracle and the raising of Lazarus points to later tradition (pp. 73-75).

75. *Ibid.*, p. 75.

76. *Ibid.*, pp. 75-76.

77. *Ibid.*, pp. 77-79. In ancient times miracles were frequently used as an aid in the missionary activity of Hellenistic religions (e.g., the cult of Sarapis). Likewise, Jewish missionaries performed miracles to convince and used miracle stories for propaganda (e.g., the Jewish Sibylline Oracles and Pseudo-Phocylides), and the later Church followed the same method (cf. the apocryphal Acts of the Apostles). From Paul (Rom 15,9; 2 Cor 12,12) and Acts (2,22; 10,38) we know that miracles were very important for the Christian mission. If these general observations indicate the purpose of S, according to Nicol, then the use of σημεῖον and χριστός in Acts is even more enlightening. The use of σημεῖον finds its origin in Ex 4; it is a sign that inspires belief, in Acts it is always used in the context of Jewish missionary work. Likewise the title χριστός is not a proper name but carries its original meaning of "Messiah" in its full sense. In contrast, Jesus is presented as κύριος to the Gentiles (Acts 10,36; 11,20; 16,15.31). According to Luke, who wrote Acts more or less at the same time that S was written, both terms belong to the Jewish mission. Nicol repeatedly refers to the mission terminology of 4,53 (cf. Acts 10,2; 11,14; 16,15.31; 18,8) and calls the conclusion of S (20,30-31) the conclusion of a "missionary book". Jn 1,35-50 and chapter 4 describe how other persons come to believe and reflect the "Sitz-im-Leben" of "a missionary interest".

78. *Ibid.*, pp. 79-81.

79. *Ibid.*, pp. 81-83.

sibilities for identifying the Messiah and the prophet lay inherent in Judaism. In addition, "the New Testament adds strong evidence that the Jews of the first century expected the coming of an eschatological prophet who would be authenticated by signs, and it is clear that the early Christian preachers made use of the possibility in Jewish thought of connecting this expectation with Messianic ideas by proclaiming Jesus, the Messiah, as final prophet"[80]. This would explain how S could proclaim the miracles of Jesus as authenticating σημεῖα of the Messiah. The entire christology of S is built upon the miracles-prophet-Messiah triangle: Jesus performs miracles like the eschatological prophet who can be identified with the Messiah[81]. In fact, S contains a good number of references to the prophet of the end-time (1,19-50; 4,19; 6,14; 9,17). The two eschatological figures, the prophet (Moses) and Elijah, are mentioned in S (in 1,21, connected with the title Messiah) and there are a number of allusions to the Elijah-Elisha cycle after that[82]. The best interpretation of S seems to come from not distinguishing too clearly between Elijah and Moses: "The two figures could become more or less amalgamated as prototypes of the eschatological prophet and founders of the Old Testament miracle tradition"[83]. The term σημεῖον is more associated with the Mosaic miracles, but the miracles of S are more referential to those in Kings, which, in turn, already show many parallels to Moses[84]. In view of Jewish expectation of miracles from God in the messianic time, the christology of S was simply: Jesus is a prophet like Elijah and Moses; he is therefore the Messiah[85].

After this description, Nicol thinks no further appeal should be made to the Hellenistic presentation of the θεῖος ἀνήρ for interpreting the christology of S, because the Jews, like all ancient Orientals, were just as interested in miracles. In contrast to the Synoptics, the miracles do not

80. *Ibid.*, pp. 83-84, 84-87, esp. 87.

81. *Ibid.*, pp. 87-94.

82. *Ibid.*, p. 89. Compare the multiplication of bread with 2 Kgs 4,42-44 (cf. the multiplication of oil, 2 Kgs 4,1-7), the raising of Lazarus with 1 Kgs 17 and 2 Kgs 4 (both concern a boy, cf. Jn 4,46-54), the wine miracle with 2 Kgs 2,19-25, washing oneself to be healed – Jn 9,7 (5,3) – with 2 Kgs 5,10. The absence of exorcisms is an *argumentum e silentio* for this comparison between Jesus and Elijah/Elisha.

83. *Ibid.*, p. 89, with a reference in n. 1 to MICHEL, *Anfang*, 1958, p. 19: "Die Vermehrung, die Verwandlung und die Auferweckung sind die drei Stoffe die an der Urzeit erinnern" (= 1986, p. 151).

84. Like Moses, Elijah also went to Horeb where God appeared (1 Kgs 19); like Moses at Marah, Elisha changed bad water to good (2 Kgs 2,19-25; cf. also, Moses' changing water into blood); Moses gave manna and Elisha multiplied bread; Moses crossed the Red Sea and Joshua, his successor, the Jordan, as did Elijah and his successor Elisha. In Jewish eschatological expectation, as well, Moses and Elijah are associated with one another (Pirque Maschiach 72; Rev 11,6; Mk 9,4) (pp. 89-90).

85. *Ibid.*, p. 90, with reference again to Michel (*Anfang*, p. 19): "Man hat Jesus als den endzeitlichen Moses und Elias angesehen, der die Wunder der Urzeit wieder lebendig machte" (= 1986, p. 151).

point to the coming of the Kingdom of God, but signify instead that the performer of the miracles, Jesus himself, *is* the End, the Kingdom of God. In S the title "Messiah" is then equivalent with the name of God: this has been perhaps most clearly rendered in the ἐγώ εἰμι formula of 6,20. In it, according to Nicol, S approaches the "high" christology of the Gospel of John itself[86].

3. *The Johannine Redaction of the Sēmeia Traditions*

(a) After comparing the interpretations of the evangelist's christology by Bultmann and Käsemann[87], Nicol describes John's (critical) interpretation of miracle faith[88]. The evangelist does not represent faith based on signs as an example for his readers[89]. He mentions faith in Jesus' miracles rather frequently, but adds critical objections denoting that this faith must be distinguished from higher faith (2,23 with its critique in 2,24; cf. 6,2.14 with 6,15.26.36; 4,45 with 4,44.48 and 6,66). The verb πιστεύειν in some cases refers to an initial interest in Jesus (compare 8,30-31 with 8,32-33.37.40.44; 4,39 with 4,42 – after they hear Jesus' word a deeper faith arises). The low quality of miracle faith is ridiculed especially in 12,42-43: they believe in the miracles but are afraid to confess their faith[90].

John also presents different stages of faith[91]. In chapter 9 the development of faith is dramatically described; in contrast to the Jews (12,42), the blind man confesses that Jesus is the Prophet (9,17) and the one come-from-God (9,33) so that he is excommunicated by the Jews. After a personal encounter and conversation with Jesus, he truly believes in the Lord (9,36-37). In chapter 3, as well, the process toward genuine faith is related. Like the blind man, Nicodemus confesses that Jesus has come from God (3,2, cf. 9,33); thus he is already further along than the Jews mentioned in 2,23. In 7,50 and 19,39 Nicodemus comes forth on Jesus' behalf. Yet John portrays him as still living in the "flesh" (3,6), as not understanding (3,4.7.9) and as unbelieving (3,12). He will not be saved if he has not been born anew in the Spirit (3,5), which means the same for Nicol as the personal encounter with Jesus in chapter 9, because Jesus comes in the Spirit (14,18). Also the Samaritan woman and her fellow villagers, impressed by Jesus' miraculous knowledge (4,19.29.30), believe to a certain degree, but come to a true faith only

86. *Ibid.*, pp. 90-94, esp. 92.
87. *Ibid.*, pp. 96-99.
88. *Ibid.*, pp. 99-106.
89. *Ibid.*, pp. 99-102.
90. "The conclusion is that the miracle faith of the masses is not held as an example for the reader. John does not call it unbelief, but neither does he regard it as true faith – much has still to happen to it" (p. 102).
91. *Ibid.*, pp. 102-103.

after a personal meeting and conversation with Jesus (4,42), again identical to receiving the Spirit (6,63)[92]. The same idea is expressed in the probably redactional verse 1,51: Nathanael, who believes on the basis of Jesus' miraculous knowledge (1,49), receives the promise that he will see even greater things (1,50). The evangelist adds 1,51, which Nicol interprets to mean that the growth of faith will not be accomplished by seeing more astonishing miracles but by insight into the deeper meaning of the miracles; by seeing the unity of Son and Father reflected in them (see further 6,31-32.51).

According to Nicol, all this does not really mean that faith in the miracles is completely worthless; the testimony of miracles is a "second best" way to faith[93]. John refers to it in 10,38 and 14,12: one should believe Jesus on the basis of his words, but if the hearers are not convinced, then a second possibility for belief exists – they can believe in Jesus on the basis of his works (10,25). It is also not intended that the miracles are weak witnesses; they are works of God (ἔργα). God knew the weakness of humans and gave the works, the Scriptures, and the appearance of John the Baptist as witnesses to Jesus (5,31-40, esp. v. 36). The miracles are secondary, because the word of Jesus alone is sufficient for faith (8,14; 20,29).

(b) John has interpreted the miracle stories symbolically[94]. He was convinced that he was giving the real meaning of the miracles Jesus intended. The symbolic interpretation was not imposed upon the tradi-

92. *Ibid.*, p. 102.
93. *Ibid.*, pp. 103-106.
94. *Ibid.*, pp. 106-113. This is especially evident in the wine miracle, the feeding miracle and the healing of the man born blind. In the wine miracle, from the very way in which the story is told, it is clear that we must see the wine as a symbol of the messianic time. For S the eschatological marriage between God and his people is consummated in Jesus. But John goes further than S. For him, the wine is not only a sign of the eschatological wine, but also of Jesus himself. According to 1,16 God's grace for the world has appeared "in fullness" in Jesus. This is probably expressed symbolically in the great quantity of wine. Jesus' grace is itself so great that the former Jewish religion has been abrogated (see the evangelist's addition κατὰ τὸν καθαρισμὸν τῶν Ἰουδαίων in 2,6). Finally the entire story is an illustration of 1,17: "For the law was given through Moses; grace and truth came through Jesus Christ". – John inserted ἵνα μή τι ἀπόληται into the bread miracle (6,12) in contrast to ἡ βρῶσις ἡ ἀπολλυμένη (6,27). The insertion of 6,4 is more important and prepares for the symbolic discourse on the eucharist as the Christian Passover: (1) as God gave manna during the Passover in Gilgal (Josh 5,10-12), so Jesus gives bread; (2) the discourse refers to Jesus' death in eucharistic terms; (3) also the mention that there was "plenty of grass" (6,10) refers to spring, the time of Passover. – In the healing of the blind man, the editorial ἀπεσταλμένος has a symbolic significance; Jesus is the true light, sent by the Father and gives true sight to humankind. – The thrice-mentioned "your son lives" in 4,50.51.53 can contain a reference to the spiritual ζωοποιεῖν of Jesus, discussed in chapter 5. – The same can apply to ἐγείρειν in 5,8 as a symbol of the spiritual ἐγείρειν of God in 5,21. – In 11,4 the reader is prepared for the symbolic meaning of the raising of Lazarus: in his hour, Jesus gives life to the world.

tion but derived from it. Nicol believes this was possible because the evangelist saw a unity between event and meaning. This unity is clarified for him in three seminal concepts: σημεῖα, ἔργον, and δόξα[95]. A σημεῖον is a demonstrative wonder, a miracle-with-meaning; δόξα signifies grace and truth, which is not revealed without the miracles; and ἔργον, a work of God, represents the meaning of both with equal weight. John employs all three to circle the essential truths continually, and so to plumb meditatively the unity between event and meaning. Nicol thinks that Hoskyns was right to maintain the unity of history and interpretation in the Gospel of John. "What Jesus *is* to the faith of the true Christian believer, he *was* in the flesh: this is the theme of the Fourth Gospel, and it is precisely this unity that constitutes the Problem of the Gospel". Dibelius, on the other hand, represents a perversion of John's intention when he claims that John expresses not what Jesus was but what Christians have in Jesus[96].

For Nicol, John contemplates the "blurred images" of the traditional miracle stories to discover the significant facts by which he can demonstrate what Jesus' miracles actually mean. Because he believes that Jesus' deeds are the eternal deeds of God, he finds in the narratives certain meaningful details which appear insignificant to us: e.g., the water jars (2,6); the abundance of grass = springtime (6,10). This symbolic interpretation rests on John's hermeneutical principle, based on his basic insight: the Word became flesh, and in this flesh the Son of God was revealed; in the earthly appearance of Jesus, therefore, there should be indications of this divinity.

(c) The ultimate meaning of the miracles according to John lay in the revelation of Jesus' δόξα[97]. During Jesus' earthly life the revelation of his δόξα was not completely understood (16,12) and so, throughout the farewell discourses, the disciples ask stupid questions (13,36-37; 14,4-5.8.22; 16,17-18.29). When the Spirit has been given to them, then he shall guide them (16,13), teach them all things, and bring all to remembrance (14,26). The δόξα, which was already revealed in the earthly life of Jesus, will then be revealed again by the Spirit so that the disciples might recognize the glorified Christ in the earthly Jesus[98]. John, inspired by the Spirit, felt himself qualified to interpret the miracle stories of S symbolically; his interpretation is not new, for the δόξα of the glorified Christ was already present in the miracles of the earthly Jesus[99]. Nicol

95. Σημεῖον (pp. 113-116), ἔργον (pp. 116-119), δόξα (pp. 119-122), conclusion (pp. 122-124).

96. *Ibid.*, p. 123. Cf. HOSKYNS, *The Fourth Gospel*, 1940, ²1947, pp. 34-35; DIBELIUS, in *RGG²* 3 (1929) 349-363, c. 350.

97. *Sēmeia*, pp. 124-137.

98. *Ibid.*, pp. 124-126.

99. *Ibid.*, p. 130.

posits therefore (contra Bultmann and Käsemann) that the δόξα *and* the σάρξ are equally real in Jesus' life[100]. For the evangelist both the history and the tradition are important. He could interpret these symbolically because there was a unity between event and meaning. This unity is revealed to him by the Spirit: there are two different phases in this revelation (before and after Jesus' exaltation), yet these two are essentially one, because in the historical Jesus both the δόξα and the σάρξ are actually present[101].

(d) John wrote in a Sitz-im-Leben different from that of S. The difference between them lies not so much in the distinction between a Hellenistic and a Jewish background, nor is it that one is more or less Jewish than the other. The significant difference is that S seems to have a missionary intention toward Jews, but John writes in a very hostile way about the Jews. This is because the relationship between Christians and Jews (especially under the influence of the leader of the Pharisees, Gamaliel II) was so strongly altered after the Synod of Jamnia that about 85-90 a complete break took place. In its time, S appealed within Judaism for belief in Jesus as Messiah; the Gospel of John reflects the break between church and synagogue[102].

III. REACTIONS TO THE WORKS OF FORTNA AND NICOL

We shall first note Nicol's reaction to Fortna, and then the most important reviews of both Fortna and Nicol.

1. *Nicol's Reaction to Fortna*

Nicol expresses several objections against Fortna's style criticism[103]. First, he does not agree with Fortna's method for demonstrating the stylistic purity of his "Gospel of Signs". It is remarkable at first glance that

---

100. *Ibid.*, p. 136: "Basic to the theology of John is that there was *really doxa* in the *sarx*. Bultmann denies that the *doxa* is real, and Käsemann, that the *sarx* is real. Against both it has to be maintained that the history and tradition was of vital importance to John. Although he may have treated it freely here and there, he had a basic theological appreciation of it because he regarded event and meaning as a unity. Bultmann broke this unity by situating the meaning behind the event. Käsemann does not deny the unity because he maintains, e.g., that the miracles are important both as works of power and as signs. But this 'unity' is not really a unity of event and meaning because it is situated above the sphere of historical reality. History has become docetic, and the 'unity' implies its partial dissolution in the dogma. This is too easy a unity. For John it was not so simple because there had to be a unity of meaning and *real* history. Therefore, he needed two phases for it, before and after Jesus' exaltation, and the Paraclete to weld them together".
101. *Ibid.*, pp. 136-137.
102. *Ibid.*, pp. 142-149, esp. 145.
103. *Ibid.*, p. 14.

32 of Ruckstuhl's 50 characteristics are wanting in Fortna's source, since Schweizer had already established that no more than three of his 33 characteristics were lacking in any of the literary strata identified by Spitta, Wendt, or Hirsch[104]. Under closer examination, "this method is surely not adequate to verify the reconstruction of an entire source":

(a) Fifteen of the 32 characteristics missing in Fortna's source do not appear in any narrative material in John; their absence from the source is meaningless. These are numbers 3-8, 10, 11, 21, 23, 25, 31-34, 41, 46.

(b) Fortna uses style characteristics as a circular argument: he uses them first to identify the source and then to verify the reconstructed source. Ratios like 32:50 can also occur with unacceptable source theories: 28 of Ruckstuhl's 50 characteristics are lacking in Bultmann's *Offenbarungs-reden*[105], which is generally rejected. Nicol concludes: "At least one conclusion can be drawn from the history: Ruckstuhl still has to be answered"[106].

Second, Fortna is not correct in adjusting the ratio so that 39 of 48 (instead of 32 of 50) occur in only one literary stratum[107].

(a) Nicol agrees with Fortna in only three cases: numbers 37 (πάλιν + δεύτερος) and 45 (partitive ἐκ) are too weak, and, strikingly enough, τις (πολλοί, οὐδείς) ἐκ occurs 25 times and never in the source.

(b) The remaining cases are unacceptable:

1. Referring to Fortna's division of ἑλκύειν (no. 38) into 38a "metaphoric" (Jn) and 38b "literal" (source), Nicol notes that the metaphoric sense cannot appear in the source, of course, "because the figurative sense which John gives to it can occur only in discourse material of which the source has none".

2. That ὀψάριον in the (singular) collective sense (no. 39a) occurs only in Johannine passages and the plural (no. 39b) only in the source is a meaningless observation: "the two Johannine occurrences could not have been plural because there the word is used not for fishes which can be counted but for fish as food (21:9,13), and the reverse holds good for the three source occurrences (6:9,11; 21:10)".

3. "Fortna's rejection of numbers 17, 42, 48, and 50 is unfounded because, although they do occur elsewhere in the New Testament, they are much more frequent in Jn. and are, therefore, typical of him". This means that the ratio 32:50 can only be altered to 31:48 (contra Fortna's 39:48), "which is not a significant difference".

104. SCHWEIZER, *Ego Eimi*, pp. 104-105 (see above, p. 46). For Fortna's stylistic tests, see above, pp. 145-148.
105. RUCKSTUHL, *Einheit*, pp. 213-214.
106. *Sēmeia*, p. 14.
107. *Ibid.*, p. 13 n. 3.

Third, Nicol cannot agree with Fortna's reconstruction of the source: "It is disappointing that the latest and most valuable book on Johannine source criticism again goes too far and becomes very hypothetical. Even where Bultmann finds exact reconstruction of the sēmeia source impossible, Fortna usually has no doubts about the precise wording of the source"[108]. The thesis that almost all the narrative material in the Gospel is taken from the source goes too far for Nicol, as does Fortna's reconstruction of the original order. Therefore, he chooses to speak of semeia traditions and selects the term "separation" instead of "reconstruction"[109]. Fortna responded to this critique in his discussion of Nicol's work[110].

2. *Reviews of R.T. Fortna: "The Gospel of Signs"*

Out of the many reviews of Fortna's book[111], we refer first to the brief notice by Eduard SCHWEIZER[112]. He remarks that, as Fortna himself acknowledged, the literary analysis remains questionable. The reconstruction of the *Gospel of Signs* seems improbable to him because such a document, consisting almost exclusively of miracles and an apologetic passion narrative, would be unique. The style characteristics that Fortna uses to delimit the source should be more closely examined. Joseph H. CREHAN[113] thinks that we can just as well attribute the aporias to the evangelist, who perhaps in later life reworked the gospel (cf. Lagrange)[114]. There is no aporia in 21,14 since the evangelist clearly writes that it was the third appearance *to the disciples*; there is thus no reason to place it after the second Cana miracle in the source.

Dwight Moody SMITH[115] admits that a source may well underlie Jn 1–12, but he thinks it an extremely difficult task to demonstrate its unity,

108. *Ibid.*, p. 5 n. 1.
109. See above, p. 155 n. 58.
110. See below, pp. 177-178, esp. 178 n. 158.
111. The most important reviews of Fortna's book are discussed below (pp. 165-176); in addition, see R. KYSAR, in *Perspective* 11 (1970) 334-336 (see below, p. 191 n. 214); M. REESE, in *AmEcclRev* 163 (1970) 142-143; F. BALCHIN, in *SEAJT* 12 (1971) 102; J. HIGGENS, in *RHE* 66 (1971) 967-969; L. LÓPEZ DE LAS HERAS, in *Studium* 12 (1971) 150-151; C. MATEOS, in *EstAg* 6 (1971) 129-130; S.S. SMALLEY, in *EvQ* 43 (1971) 50-51; B. JOHNSON, *Another Primitive Source?*, in *Encounter* 33 (1972) 393-399 (see the summary in *NTA* 17, 1973, no. 571r); E. KRENTZ, in *ConcTM* 43 (1972) 124-125; L.F. RIVERA, in *RevistBíb* 34 (1972) 187; P. ZARRELLA, in *ScuolC* 102 (1974) 349. See also E. RUCKSTUHL, *Johannine Language*, 1977 (GT: 1987) (cf. below, pp. 302-307).
112. E. SCHWEIZER, in *EvT* 30 (1970) 624-626, p. 626.
113. J.H. CREHAN, in *TS* 31 (1970) 757-759.
114. "Could not the Evangelist in old age, he [Lagrange] asked, have added bits and pieces to his own earlier composition, so as to leave signs of unevenness and dislocation? If he was an old man, could he not have died before finishing his revision and amplification? ... Where the *aporiai* are detected in subject matter rather than in style, Fortna's judgment does not inspire confidence" (pp. 757-758).
115. D.M. SMITH, in *JBL* 89 (1970) 498-501, pp. 500, 501. For Smith, see also above, pp. 53-54. In his later articles, Smith, under influence of Fortna, became less skeptical of the semeia source than in 1965 (see below, pp. 194-197, 241-242).

structure, and sequence. He wonders further why the evangelist rearranged the source, and whether it is not possible that the evangelist himself joined the miracle stories and the passion narrative. Jerome MURPHY-O'CONNOR[116], referring to 21,1-14, wonders at Fortna's attribution of this passage to John's *Vorlage*, since chapter 21 is generally viewed as the work of a final redactor. Murphy-O'Connor also finds Fortna's style-critical arguments less than convincing: "Likewise, Fortna tries hard to reinforce his position by verifying his conclusion in light of the criteria established by Ruckstuhl, but the value of this comparison is somewhat doubtful since, at least in two instances ..., the literary analysis has been influenced by Ruckstuhl's work. Anyway, the presentation is so difficult that I do not see how any clear conclusion can be drawn"[117]. He remarks that one can well assume that all the signs were numbered but that it is extremely problematic to reconstruct the order of the miracles; Fortna's reconstruction is pure conjecture. Again, one can accept that John was critical of the source's attitude toward the miracles, but Fortna must have wondered whether the evangelist understood the source correctly. It is a presupposition to assume that the author of the source had an opinion of miracles completely different from that of the evangelist. Donald MURPHY[118], in light of recent trends in exegesis, remains skeptical about source analysis: "This reviewer, with full admiration and gratitude for what Fortna has contributed, will simply suggest wherein he suspects opponents may find the Achilles' heel or unprotected heart of Fortna's thesis. Contemporary Gospel scholarship is magnificently harvesting the fruits of the insight that the canonical Gospels are unified works of art, wherein the meaning of parts can be determined only in view of the whole. ... Until far more scholarship born of this insight is devoted to discovering the overall meaning of the Fourth Gospel, there must remain the gnawing suspicion that source analysis such as that of Fortna is wasted effort. All too often in jousting with this book, this reviewer saw Fortna basing his analysis on highly challengeable presuppositions of meaning". Matthias RISSI[119] judges that the discovery that certain words and phrases are shared with the Synoptic Gospels is no indication of the source's style. He rejects Fortna's reconstruction of the *Gospel of Signs* as "an odd and rather meagre skeleton of narrations".

Charles Kingsley BARRETT[120] especially questions the argument from the aporias; he is convinced that John used sources and that we can trace indications of them, but this does not mean that we can reconstruct these

---

116. J. MURPHY-O'CONNOR, in *RB* 77 (1970) 603-606.
117. *Ibid.*, p. 605. Cf. FORTNA, *Gospel of Signs*, 1970, pp. 164,168.
118. D. MURPHY, in *RRel* 29 (1970) 927-928.
119. M. RISSI, in *Interpr* 25 (1971) 372-373.
120. C.K. BARRETT, in *JTS* 72 (1971) 571-574.

sources. In the second edition of his commentary, Barrett rejects the semeia source: "It must be plainly said that there is nothing at all incredible in the suggestion that there was available to John a source containing a sequence of miracle stories described as signs and intended to evoke faith in Jesus as a wonder-worker, though in 6.5-13; 6.16-21; and possibly in 4.46-54; 5.1-9 the Synoptic Gospels too may have contributed to John's narrative. It may have been so; but I see no evidence that proves, or indeed could prove, that it was so, or even that the hypothesis has such a weight of probability as to make it a valuable exegetical tool. To say this is not to deny the value of the observations made by Bultmann, Dr Fortna, and others, which suggest (among other things) that there were different views of the significance of the miracles of Jesus. Such different views did exist, and to examine and compare them is an important part of the historical and theological study of the gospel. But to say that they existed is not necessarily to say that one of them was to be found in a source and the other in the editorial work of the user of the source. It may well be that both existed in the mind of John himself"[121].

In a long review, Leonard SWEETNAM[122] especially criticizes Fortna's style-critical method: "he [Fortna] does admit it is 'only when the source has been completed, and correctly separated in detail from John's editorial work' that the stylistic distinctions between the source and the redaction will emerge clearly. This is strange, however, in view of the fact that one of the criteria for determining the pre-johannine material in the text of the gospel is the stylistic criterion. Consequently, the validity of the test of the source's purity and integrity on the basis of stylistic characteristics must be questioned"[123]. Moreover, Sweetnam points out that Fortna evades the question of the historical Jesus by making a distinction between "form" and "content", which for many in the Reformed tradition is unwelcome. Fortna's work demonstrates rather well the human dimension in the development of the *Gattung* "gospel" (cf. J.M. Robinson) and throws light upon the dynamic milieu in which the early church attempted to "generate an appropriate form for the witness to Jesus, the Christ"[124].

---

121. *The Gospel According to St John: An Introduction with Commentary and Notes on the Greek Text*, London - Philadelphia, PA, ²1978, pp. 18-19: "A Signs Source", esp. 19; cp. 20-21: "John's use of a Discourse Source is as unprovable as his use of a Signs Source; and the existence of the former is perhaps less probable than the existence of the latter" (GT: 1990, pp. 36-37, esp. 37; cp. p. 38). According to Barrett, on the basis of the word σημεῖον, only the two Cana miracles can be ascribed to the source: "The evidence ... suggests at most a 'Cana source' for the two miracles wrought there; there is nothing to suggest a more extended source based on signs" (p. 77).

122. L. SWEETNAM, in *CalvTJ* 6 (1971) 217-225.

123. *Ibid.*, pp. 224-225.

124. *Ibid.*, p. 226.

According to Marinus DE JONGE[125] the chief difficulty of Fortna's work is that the internal criteria can only be treated subjectively: "Mutatis mutandis, what Fortna himself says about 'ideological criteria' holds true here: 'For an author's thought ... may itself contain inner tensions which only appear to be contradictions' (p. 17). The only secure path here is comparison with other written data, preferably in each concrete case rather than one. Fortna's analysis is possible in theory, but in practice frequently hypothetical, and therefore this book is a stimulating but just as much an often disappointing tool for the study of the Gospel of John"[126]. De Jonge illustrates his point with reference to 20,30-31, which for Fortna, as for so many others, is the conclusion to the pre-Johannine source. De Jonge does not agree. (1) It is incorrect to speak of a "high christology" in the confession of Thomas and "the more primitive messianism" of 20,30. Elsewhere in the Gospel, namely 11,27 and in the discourse material, the title "Son" is used to elucidate the title "Christ". If 20,30 comes from the source, then should ὁ υἱὸς τοῦ θεοῦ be ascribed to redaction? (2) Fortna assigns only 20,31c (ἵνα πιστεύον-τες κτλ.) to Johannine redaction; the remainder of the conclusion (20,30-31b) belongs to the source. But Fortna should not escape the aporia that remains in his reconstruction: the word *semeion* still does not appear in the second part of the source. (3) There is also no perceivable difference in conceptions of faith between 20,29 and 20,30: "non-eyewitnesses after Thomas are directed to whatever is committed to writing by or on behalf of the eyewitnesses". (4) If the saying of Nicodemus in 3,2 is attributed to redaction, how can one assign 20,30-31 to the source? For de Jonge, the so-called tensions can be better explained as theological tensions within the gospel. These could indeed be due to the use of sources, but it does not seem possible to conclude from such tensions to a written source precisely delineated in form and content[127]. M. de Jonge concludes his review: "if 20,30-31 cannot be indicated with certainty as the conclusion of the signs gospel, then one of the arguments for the literary unity of the (supposedly written) source collapses"[128].

125. M. DE JONGE, in *NTT* 26 (1972) 91-94.
126. *Ibid.*, p. 93.
127. *Ibid.*, p. 93.
128. *Ibid.*, p. 94. See M. de Jonge's critique on reconstruction of the semeia source in *Signs and Wonders in the Fourth Gospel*, in BAARDA et al. (eds.), *Miscellanea Neotestamentica*, II, 1978, pp. 107-125, esp. 108 (= 1977, pp. 117-140, esp. 117-118): "But the arguments in favour of the existence of a pre-Johannine (or even early Johannine) Signs-source or Signs-Gospel with a clearly defined number of stories and a definite theology of its own, are not conclusive, and the question must be asked whether the distinction between the present Johannine redaction and the supposed presentation in the source really helps to explain the way in which the signs-stories and the statements about Jesus' works function in the present Gospel. All theories concerning a Signs-source have to assume that 'John' criticized his source, and yet incorporated it substantially in his own

Xavier JACQUES[129] further questions the purpose and method of Fortna's work: "one difficulty remains, nevertheless, which [Fortna] does not, in our view, convincingly resolve: the relative inadequacy of the means employed to the objective intended, that is, the miracle narratives (for in the source it is a question of 'miracles' more than signs). To be sure, one can conclude that this gospel, lacking so many themes found in the others, 'must have been unique in first-century Christian literature' (p. 234), but in view of such a conclusion, one could also call into question the initial presupposition of this study". According to Leo McMORROW[130], no one can overcome the hazard of subjectivity in distinguishing between Johannine and non-Johannine passages. Likewise, he judges that Fortna does not prove thoroughly enough the stylistic unity of the miracle stories among themselves or their connection with other narrative sections. The theological argument for the signs source is also too doubtful: if the evangelist had a totally different viewpoint from that of the source, why did he employ it as a whole and end his gospel with the conclusion from the source?

Wilhelm WILKENS[131] agrees with Fortna's source analysis for the most part but enumerates several instances which remain problematic for him. The list of characteristic expressions for the *Gospel of Signs* is "the most problematic of the entire work". Wilkens illustrates this on the basis of 1,38b.39, where only four characteristics of the source appear: ῥαββί, "come and see" (cf. 1,46; 11,34), οὖν after imperative, and ὡς *numerale* (cf. 4,6; 19,14). Such frequency points rather to the hand of the evangelist for Wilkens. Added to that is the frequently used μένω, which, according to J. Heise, appears to have "eine über den äusseren

---

work. The evangelist is always supposed to have been far more subtle than the people whose work he used; he rewrote considerable parts of the source(s) before him and yet did not do his work thoroughly enough. He left a clear Johannine stamp everywhere and yet we are able to reconstruct the state of his material before it received this stamp. Now, it is difficult to believe that the Johannine redaction left sufficient pre-Johannine traces to enable us to explain Johannine theology in terms of an explicit criticism of earlier theological tendencies, we must make an attempt to explain tensions and apparent inconsistencies in John's picture of Jesus' acts first and foremost on the level and within the framework of the very complicated and at the same time carefully balanced theology of the Johannine community as reflected in the Gospel itself". Cp. *John the Baptist and Elijah in the Fourth Gospel*, in *FS J.L. Martyn*, 1990, pp. 299-308, esp. 301-302: "But I remain very skeptical about the possibility of distinguishing between source material and late redaction with any degree of certainty. It is one thing to say that the Fourth Gospel presupposes earlier written and oral traditions (and will also have known material preserved in the Synoptic Gospels), but it is quite another matter to claim that we are still able to determine beyond reasonable doubt what the source employed in 1:19-51 contained" (his critique of Martyn's acceptance of Fortna's source in *Whe Have Found Elijah*, 1976; see above, p. 149 n. 33).

129. X. JACQUES, in *NRT* 94 (1972) 1102-1103, p. 1103.
130. L. McMORROW, in *IrTQ* 39 (1972) 306-310, pp. 306-308.
131. W. WILKENS, in *TZ* 28 (1972) 150-152.

Vorgang hinausgehende Bedeutung", and is more characteristic of the evangelist than the source. Against Fortna, who attributes 11,2 and 12,1-2 (cf. ἦν δέ in 11,2; εἷς ἐκ in 12,2) to the source, Wilkens holds that 12,1-2 is from the evangelist, "who intends a theological link with chapter 11 here", and that 11,2, which is usually described as a gloss, "forms the other member of the link". Thus, the evangelist very consciously used κύριος in 11,2: "The Lord, who will awaken Lazarus to life, is the one anointed for death by Mary". Also, 19,14 can hardly be ascribed to the *Gospel of Signs*: neither ἦν δέ nor ὡς *numerale* allows such a conclusion. With reference to the numbering of the signs, Wilkens remarks that "laying claim to 21,14 in support of the count is rather risky"; nor can he follow Fortna in choosing the reading of P[66] for 2,11: "πρώτην can just as well have been inserted secondarily for ἀρχήν with reference to 4,54". Finally, Wilkens points out that Fortna's pre-Johannine *Gospel of Signs* should not be confused with his own Johannine *Zeichenevangelium*. "My thesis of a *Johannine* signs gospel (inclined to the Johannine notion of signs) underlying the present gospel has been placed by Fortna alongside the thesis of a different *pre*-Johannine signs gospel SQ. This gives some cause for confusion. In view of the Johannine use of the idea 'sign' it would have been better to speak of a 'Gospel of Jesus' miracles' SQ. My argument occasionally brought against the SQ is not directed therefore against the thesis that the Fourth Evangelist worked with sources; rather against a hasty and, in my opinion, unjustified identification of a conception of 'Sēmeia' that is really Johannine with that of a pre-Johannine source. But Fortna knows very well how to differentiate between the two. Thus his work is to be welcomed"[132].

For Xavier LÉON-DUFOUR[133], a chief concern of Fortna's hypothesis is to place the pre-Johannine tradition (a real gospel for Fortna) alongside Mark at the origin of the gospel tradition. But, as Fortna himself admits, the hypothetical character of his reconstruction must be taken into account: "we touch here one of the risks of source criticism, which never leads to a satisfactory certainty, and one realizes that one might end up taking for certain what was the burden of proof at the beginning"[134]. The *Gospel of Signs*, in order to be accepted as a working hypothesis, must undergo supplementary testing. First, should the Fourth Gospel be considered a completed work? If not, can it be treated as having stylistic unity? Second, have not the aporias been ascertained by a logic that is not necessarily that of the text? For example, Fortna joins 2,3 to 2,5: Mary does not address Jesus, but the servants. This would already be suggested by the repetition of λέγει ἡ μήτηρ. Moreover, the sequence of events is not

132. *Ibid.*, p. 152.
133. X. LÉON-DUFOUR, in *RSR* 62 (1974) 290-291.
134. *Ibid.*, p. 291.

justifiable – how can Jesus perform the miracle which he has just refused? Fortna would have it that John inserted the dialogue between Jesus and his mother, with the very Johannine mention of the "hour". This argumentation is not at all convincing for Léon-Dufour: the hour is without doubt Johannine, but Jesus' attitude toward his relatives is surely pre-Johannine, even Synoptic. Thus he rejects the argument from aporias: "The incoherence in sequence only exists, in my opinion, in the insufficiency of the literary criticism applied here and in the logic which is hardly in accord with that of John. I am therefore forced to question the criterion of aporias, which in the end rests upon some unacceptable ideological conceptions". Third, one must explain not only the theological value of the reconstructed source, but also the work of the evangelist himself: "how then can it have resulted in the text which has a priori been judged 'incoherent'? In any case, it is necessary to come to the text as it is, or else the enterprise brings about a refuse pile of demolition and a construction in the air". Léon-Dufour admits the existence of sources but rejects such an expanded reconstruction as Fortna's *Gospel of Signs*[135].

According to Rudolf SCHNACKENBURG[136], Fortna's literary analyses should be given attention because they contain valuable data, but the entire reconstruction is hypothetical and problematic, especially because of the text rearrangements (e.g., the Samaritan woman's story between portions of the Lazarus narrative; the miraculous draught of fish among other Galilean miracles). Since, according to Fortna himself, a reconstruction of the source's account of the Last Supper is impossible, it can be wondered whether the evangelist borrowed his presentation of Jesus'

---

135. Léon-Dufour has only slight sympathy for the semeia hypothesis. At the ACEFB congress in 1973 and in his article on the Johannine σημεῖον, he did not mention it at all; cf. *Les miracles de Jésus selon Jean*, in ID. (ed.), *Les miracles*, 1977, pp. 269-286: *Autour du ΣHMEION johannique*, in *FS H. Schürmann*, 1977, pp. 363-377. In his commentary, *Lecture de l'évangile de Jean*, 3 vols., Paris, 1988, 1990, 1993, he mentions the signs source only incidentally. In connection with the numbering of the signs in 2,11 he notes that the hypothesis has known great success in Germany (cf. Faure, Bultmann, Schnackenburg) and in USA (cf. Fortna), and that at present it is being challenged by Heekerens (I, p. 212 n. 113). Regarding 5,1-9a, he speaks vaguely of "a source" (II, p. 20 n. 4: "La source du récit finit en 5,9a"). For 6,1-15 he accepts "diverses sources" (p. 99), but seems to reject the signs source: "La source prétendue des miracles se trouve ainsi mise en question" (p. 99 n. 10, with reference to Marguerat, 1990; see below, p. 344 n. 553). See also *Où en est la recherche johannique? Bilan et ouvertures*, in MARCHADOUR (ed.), *Origine et postérité*, 1990, pp. 17-41, esp. 24-25: "C'est la *Semeiaquelle* qui a la vie dure... Le désaccord des critiques sur cette *Semeiaquelle* signifie-t-il une erreur? Ce serait aller trop vite... Quel est l'avenir de la *Semeiaquelle*? La réponse pourrait être donnée grâce à un ouvrage d'ensemble, celui qu'a écrit W. Bittner"; cf. pp. 38-39, esp. 38: "La nature et la fonction des *signes* sont de mieux en mieux précisées, indépendamment de la fameuse *Semeiaquelle*".

136. R. SCHNACKENBURG, *Zur johanneischen Forschung*, in *BZ* 18 (1974) 272-287, pp. 273-274.

Passion and Resurrection from the same source. André FEUILLET, because of the stylistic unity of the Fourth Gospel, considers the semeia hypothesis a "conjecture fragile"[137].

James M. ROBINSON's reaction (1971) is of greater importance[138]. He first discusses the difficulty of establishing written sources in the Fourth Gospel[139]. The starting point for detecting a source in John lies in the two Cana stories (2,1-12a and 4,46-54)[140]. The next problem has to do with the extent of the source[141]. Fortna expanded Bultmann's signs source particularly by including the passion and resurrection narratives, plus 21,1-14 which Bultmann had attributed to the ecclesiastical redactor. Thus, he arrived at a signs gospel that contained almost a fifth of the present gospel. Fortna considered Bultmann's separation of two narrative sources (signs source and passion source) a result of the two-fold division of the gospel by Faure[142], which was disproved by the style criticism of Schweizer and his followers. On the basis of the source's style characteristics, Fortna himself tried to assign passages from the second part of John to the Gospel of Signs, but this is not very convincing[143]:

137. A. FEUILLET, Les christophanies pascales du quatrième évangile sont-elles des signes?, in NRT 97 (1975) 577-592, p. 578: "c'est l'hypothèse de la Sēmeia-Quelle défendue notamment par R. Bultmann et par R.T. Fortna et à laquelle Schnackenburg est favorable, mais que, pour notre part, nous rejetons: nous pensons en effet qu'il faut tenir compte de la présence dans l'ensemble du quatrième évangile d'un certain nombre de caractéristiques johanniques dont le relevé, dressé tout d'abord par E. Schweizer, a ensuite été repris et complété, notamment par E. Ruckstuhl".

138. J.M. ROBINSON, The Johannine Trajectory, in ID. – KOESTER, Trajectories, 1971, pp. 232-268, esp. 238-252; GT: 1971, pp. 216-250; cp. The Miracles Source of John, in JAAR 39 (1971) 339-348 (a review essay of Fortna's Gospel of Signs). On Robinson, see also above, pp. 69-70, 83-84.

139. The source is no longer extant. It is easier to detect sources for Matthew and Luke: we do possess one of their sources in the Gospel of Mark, and its existence facilitates the argument for the existence of Q by comparing Matthew and Luke. That John's sources no longer survive is not an argument against his use of them. In fact, only a small portion of ancient literature has come down to us. We know that other documents existed from the prologue of Luke, the testimony of Papias, and fragments and names of apocryphal gospels. Robinson remarks as well that source theory for the Fourth Gospel has been further hindered by exegetes who accept the dependence of John upon the Synoptics. The difficulty of reconstructing a source should not mean that the source did not exist; but from the establishment of the existence of a source, it follows logically that the attempt be made to reconstruct it. In the case of Markan studies, we encounter the same difficulty as with the Gospel of John (Johannine Trajectory, pp. 238-242; cp. Miracles Source, pp. 339-341).

140. Johannine Trajectory, pp. 242-246; Miracles Source, pp. 341-343.

141. Johannine Trajectory, pp. 247-252; Miracles Source, pp. 343-344.

142. FORTNA, Gospel of Signs, p. 217 n. 3. See above, pp. 148-149 n. 31.

143. Johannine Trajectory, pp. 247-248. For Fortna's reaction to Robinson, see below, p. 218 n. 393.

1. Of the list of nine style characteristics which occur in the rest of the New Testament and are rare in John (and limited there to the source), five occur only once and so cannot bind two sections; four occur three times each, at least once in the passion narrative and once in the signs sections, i.e., σύν, εὐθέως, ἕκαστος, and πρῶτον adverbially.

2. Of eight terms which are rare in the New Testament and occur only in the source in John, only one appears in both signs section and passion narrative, κραυγάζειν, and it is not lacking in the rest of the New Testament.

3. Of five traits from Ruckstuhl's list attributed by Fortna to the source, two occur only once in the passion section: no. 45c, noun + ἐκ "made of" (19,2) and no. 38b, ἑλκύειν meant literally (18,10 – the other two occurrences are in ch. 21). Fortna himself considers the latter irrelevant since it is dependent on subject matter.

4. Of the 11 traits not always peculiar to the Synoptics but also appearing elsewhere in the New Testament, and rare in John except for the source, six occur in the passion section as well as elsewhere in the source: (a) introductory or resumptive ἦν (δέ) (τις); (b) parenthetical or explanatory ἦν δέ; (c) ὡς with numeral; (d) singular verb with double subject; (g) noun + ἐκ, "from among"; and (k) ὄνομα αὐτῷ. In this list, Fortna includes two further traits which carry hardly any weight. The first (numeral + ἐκ) is so common in the Synoptics that Schweizer did not consider it distinctively Johannine; the second (ῥαββί/ῥαββουνί addressed to Jesus) flies in the face of the fact that John uses ῥαββί everywhere but 20,16.

From these considerations, Robinson concludes: "In sum, this total result seems to me (though not to Fortna) rather meager evidence to establish the inclusion within the miracle source of a passion and resurrection narrative"[144]. Robinson notes further that Fortna himself seems to recognize the independence of passion section and miracle stories since he considers the cleansing of the temple in the source a link which joined the cycle of miracle stories to a traditional passion narrative[145].

Robinson also compares Fortna's literary theory with that of Ernst Haenchen[146]. Both authors allow for more than miracle stories in the source or Ur-gospel; but Fortna calls his source a gospel "in the

144. *Ibid.*, p. 248. Cp. *Miracles Source*, p. 344.

145. *Johannine Trajectory*, p. 249; cf. FORTNA, *Gospel of Signs*, p. 146.

146. *Johannine Trajectory*, pp. 249-252; cp. *Miracles Source*, pp. 344-346. On the relationship between the two authors he observes: "Although the two works are basically independent of each other, Fortna is dependent upon Haenchen's numerous articles on the Fourth Gospel, and Haenchen had available Fortna's manuscript as he composed the final draft of his own commentary. The two have corresponded, both directly and through me, and have talked personally about their areas of agreement and disagreement, though with noticeable shift in positions" (*Johannine Trajectory*, p. 49).

narrower [sc. Synoptic] sense", while Haenchen refers to a non-Synoptic Ur-gospel, "a sort of crude version of the Gospel of Mark". A great deal of what Fortna assigns to his Gospel of Signs is vaguely attributed by Haenchen to a narrator or to tradition. Haenchen and Fortna agree in including passion and resurrection narratives in their source and both, therefore, regard this pre-Johannine tradition as a "gospel". They both admit only one written source for John and both consider it independent of the Synoptics. Fortna, however, is more inclined than Haenchen to see a Synoptic parallel in John as cause for assigning material to the source. For Haenchen, the evangelist is dependent on his source in a more oral and recollective way[147]; for Fortna, the relationship is more literary. Thus, the latter reconstructs the source word for word, whereas the former is elusive in precisely delimiting the source.

Fortna brings the theological position of the source closer to that of the evangelist than Haenchen does; thus, he speaks of a "Gospel of Signs" rather than a miracles source. Haenchen supposes a redactor who is responsible not only for chapter 21, the sacraments, and futuristic eschatology, but also for the presence of the Beloved Disciple and the few places where the present text depends on the Synoptics. Conversely, Fortna is skeptical about assigning certain passages to a redactor. Robinson concludes his comparison: "The similarity in basic trends, with the divergences of method and results, makes the post-Bultmannian development of Johannine source theory a fascinating and very promising enterprise. The outcome could be a sharp profile of the Fourth Evangelist which would bring into focus the other major aspects of Johannine research"[148].

Barnabas LINDARS (1971)[149] also formulated some objections against the semeia hypothesis. After a comparison of Becker with

147. See above, pp. 65-70.
148. *Johannine Trajectory*, p. 252; *Miracles Source*, p. 348.
149. B. LINDARS, *Behind the Fourth Gospel* (Studies in Creative Criticism), London, 1971, esp. pp. 27-42; FT: 1974, pp. 1-113, esp. 37-60; for the Spanish and Italian translations, and reviews, cf. VAN BELLE, no. 1761. On Lindars, see also SLOYAN, *What Are They Saying about John?*, 1991, pp. 41-42 and especially TUCKETT, in LINDARS, *Essays*, 1992, pp. XI-XVII. – In his commentary, *The Gospel of John* (NCB), London, 1972, pp. 46-48 ("The Question of Sources"), esp. 46 (note), Lindars refers to *Behind the Fourth Gospel* for a "detailed criticism" of the semeia hypothesis and summarizes the objections against "source analysis" as follows: "(i) Schweizer, Ruckstuhl and others have shown that John's style and diction run through the whole work. The scissors-and-paste method of source criticism cannot be used for John. (ii) The tradition of Synoptic type is not confined to the Signs, but occurs in sayings of Jesus in the Discourses, which are too important to be relegated to a secondary position. (iii) Some Signs and Discourses are so closely bound together that the Signs must be taken as the source for the Discourses, which have been built up from themes discovered in them by the evangelist (e.g. chapter 9 and 11)" (p. 47, with reference in n. 24 to SMITH, *Sources*, 1964; see above, p. 53 n. 70). At the 1975 Colloquium Biblicum Lovaniense, Lindars also referred to the presuppositions

Fortna[150], he remarks that a reconstruction like Fortna's depends upon the presupposition that there could have existed a complete gospel without any direct teaching of Jesus[151]. A second assumption is that John would have incorporated virtually all of his source in such a way that it can be reconstructed by simply distilling out the Johannine elements[152]. This is indeed possible but not very probable, since John is a highly creative writer. It is essential, therefore, to examine first his methods as a writer before attempting to determine the extent of his source. Lindars discovers many features characteristic of John in Fortna's source. Indeed, John has reproduced quite a bit of the source verbatim but never does so completely; he not only adds phrases, but often rewrites the text of the source, sometimes recasting the story itself in the process. It is also very unlikely that the miraculous draught of fish was in the source; in Lindars' opinion, chapter 21 was clearly composed by the evangelist after finishing the gospel and only added after his death. Fortna's view would require that the evangelist had left out this one item from his source, only to have it become the very thing he needed for a second redaction[153].

Lindars also questions the one-sided slant on christology which Fortna and Becker attribute to the source[154]. For the source, the miracles are demonstrative of Jesus' Messiahship. Though the passion narrative is included in Fortna's source, it apparently exerts no influence on the other material: there is no word about the passion, or suffering of any kind for Jesus or his disciples, until the passion narrative itself is reached. That nothing is said about the Church, the sacraments, the Spirit, ethics, ideas about salvation, forgiveness, and grace is remarkable for a primitive Christian document, seeing that these elements were generally present in the early Christian church. Referring to Becker's article, Lindars thinks it strange that the evangelist should take over the whole source, only to subject it to radical christological criticism. Perhaps the

---

of the semeia hypothesis: cf. *Traditions behind the Fourth Gospel*, in DE JONGE (ed.), *L'évangile de Jean*, 1977 (²1987), pp. 107-124 (= 1992, pp. 87-104). Thus, he expressly rejects the θεῖος ἀνήρ typology, with reference, for example, to Jn 4,46-54 (cf. p. 111 n. 16): "It must be pointed out, however, that both the concept and the title *theios anēr* are open to dispute in this connection. For in a Jewish circle it would have to mean a holy man or prophet, such as Moses, and it is doubtful if it could provide a bridge to a christology of the divinity of Jesus even if there were Hellenistic influence at work in the formation of the tradition except in a thoroughly pagan setting (cf. Acts 14,8-18)".

150. *Behind the Fourth Gospel*, pp. 28-31.

151. *Ibid.*, p. 31; cp. *Traditions*, pp. 113-123 (= 1992, pp. 93-103). See also *Discourse and Tradition: The Use of the Sayings of Jesus in the Discourses of the Fourth Gospel*, in *JSNT* 13 (1981) 83-101 (= 1992, pp. 83-101).

152. *Behind the Fourth Gospel*, pp. 32-33.

153. In Lindars' view, "Becker was much wiser not to ascribe this story to the Signs Source, in spite of its possible connection with the numbering of the signs" (p. 35).

154. *Ibid.*, pp. 35-38.

semeia hypothesis is not the correct way to explain the Johannine tradition; it does not offer us his tradition but a "pale ghost" of the Gospel
of John itself.

More recently, in *John* (New Testament Guides), Sheffield, 1990, pp. 32-33
("The Signs Source", esp. 32), Lindars formulates three objections: (1) "the
semi-pagan christology attributed to the source is unknown in the New Testament. It is really most improbable that the evangelist would engage in polemic
with the source at the same time as reproducing it almost word for word" (with
reference to Fortna, who "has abandoned the idea of a 'divine man' christology" in *Predecessor*; see below, pp. 221-222); (2) "the word *sēmeion* cannot be
used as a source criterion. It occurs more frequently in John's editorial writing
than in the material attributed to the source, and it does not carry a pejorative
sense, so that the contrast with *ergon* cannot be maintained"; (3) "the attempt
to reconstruct the source out of the text of the Gospel grievously underestimates
the extent of John's reworking of sources, and fails to establish convincing
criteria for deciding what belongs to the source". (Also cited by NEIRYNCK,
Evangelica II, 1992, p. 678.)

Lindars again utters his skepticism regarding the reconstruction of the signs
source in *Rebuking the Spirit: A New Analysis of the Lazarus Story of John 11*,
in *NTS* 38 (1992) 89-104 (= 1992, pp. 183-198; cp. the short version of this article with the same title in DENAUX, ed., *John and the Synoptics*, 1992, pp. 542-
547). See esp. p. 97 (= 1992, p. 191): "I have always felt that it is a mistake to
suppose that John has preserved what he found in the source almost intact,
because that seriously underestimates the extent of his rewriting and recasting of
his sources, which is everywhere apparent in the Gospel". Lindars thinks that
the source's phrase ἐνεβριμήσατο τῷ πνεύματι (11,33) means "rebuked the
spirit" (cf. the full analysis in *NTS*, pp. 92-96; = 1992, pp. 186-190), and in light
of Mk 1,23-26 and 9,25-29, he conjectures that "John's story retains traces of a
tradition of an exorcism by Jesus, in which the crippling effect of the spirit or
demon, and the new life resulting from the exorcism, have already been compared with death and resurrection, no doubt in connection with the use of the
story in catechesis"; John, however, "was not building directly on Mark" (ctr.
Neirynck; cf. p. 100; = 1992, p. 194). By way of conclusion, he stresses that his
"observations on the sources of the Lazarus story need to be taken into account
in further work on the theory of a Signs Source. It is one of the weaknesses of
current reconstructions of the source that it is supposed not to have included an
exorcism, simply because none is reproduced in John. But if it was a collection
of popular memories of Jesus it is altogether probable that at least one of the stories was of this type, seeing that casting out demons is such a prominent feature
of the Synoptic tradition" (p. 101; = 1992, p. 194).

His article on Jn 11 was for Lindars the impetus to undertake a new study on
Jn 4,46-53: *Capernaum Revisited: Jn 4,46-53 and the Synoptics*, in *FS F.
Neirynck*, III, 1992, pp. 1985-2000, esp. 1998 (= 1992, pp. 199-214, esp. 212).
He considers the story "a rare case where Synoptic criticism can be applied to
John almost on equal terms with the Synoptics", and thinks that it "is based on
a written form of the Centurion's Servant, similar to the forms which were
available in Matthew and Luke". Thus, "this pericope is a remarkable case in
which John gives positive help towards the recovery of the common source

behind Matthew and Luke" (see his tentative reconstruction on p. 1996; = 1992, p. 210). But the question, "Was John's source Q?", "must be left to Synoptic and Johannine scholars to ponder on future visits to Capernaum" (p. 2000; = 1992, p. 214). He repeats his skepticism regarding the signs source ("I agree with Neirynck in regarding it as very doubtful") and considers 4,54 "clearly editorial" (p. 1987; = 1992, p. 201). Further, he says that Fortna's reconstruction of the Signs Source for this pericope "fails to convince, because it depends on unsatisfactory criteria for isolating the source from the extensive rewriting and recasting which is characteristic of John" (p. 1987; = 1992, p. 201), but for 4,46-53, he stresses that John's "recasting of the narrative is much less drastic than in the Lazarus story, and the relation to the underlying source is accordingly much closer" (p. 1999; = 1992, p. 213).

As in these two articles, in his review of Fortna's *Predecessor*, in *ScotJT* 43 (1990) 526-527, Lindars stresses that in Johannine source criticism "the proper starting-point should be passages where there are clear links with the Synoptic tradition. John's source in any given instance was not necessarily identical with a Synoptic version, but the Synoptic parallel is the safest guide for reconstruction" (p. 527). Cp. *Some Recent Trends in the Study of John*, in *Way* 30 (1990) 329-338, p. 331: "Even if John is not directly dependent on any of the Synoptic Gospels (and this question still remains open), the words which he has in common with them give a first criterion for distinguishing source-words from the evangelist's own composition, if they differ from his normal vocabulary ... my new analysis of the Lazarus story shows that reconstruction of the source needs to be far more radical than Fortna is willing to allow. The value of this approach is that it gives a much clearer idea of John's techniques in handling his sources, which were similar to the Synoptic sources, and like them based on the general stock of oral traditions".

3. *Reviews of W. Nicol: "The Sēmeia in the Fourth Gospel"*

R. SCHNACKENBURG (1974) reacted very positively to Nicol's monograph[155]. R.T. FORTNA (1974) recognizes it as a major redaction-critical study[156], but depreciates Nicol's treatment of the source-critical criteria as "largely derivative and far too brief" and considers his handling of style characteristics, although more original and detailed, disappointing[157].

155. R. SCHNACKENBURG, *Zur johanneischen Forschung*, in *BZ* 18 (1974) 272-287, p. 285: "Das Buch ist nach Methode, Aufbau und Ergebnissen (mögen sie im einzelnen noch diskutabel sein) eine vorzügliche Arbeit, die auf der Höhe der Forschung steht und sie in guter Richtung vorantreibt".

156. R.T. FORTNA, in *JBL* 93 (1974) 119-121, p. 119.

157. *Ibid.*, p. 120: "Particularly disappointing is Nicol's application of the style-characteristics. He spends considerable energy extending Ruckstuhl's list, from 50 to 82 characteristics, but then proceeds to use them merely to locate points in the gospel at which, in conjunction with other criteria, we can expect to find Johannine redaction. Not only does this assume that all the characteristics belong to J rather than S, but it tells us nothing new: who now doubts, for example, that 2:4 or 4:48 contain evidence of John's hand? Presumably because he wants to avoid any danger of circularity, he has chosen to use the characteristics solely as criteria for source analysis, and not, as they were originally intended, to test the validity of a hypothetical source once reconstructed. That seems to me a wasted opportunity to apply the tool he has usefully refined".

If the source cannot be precisely reconstructed, says Fortna in response to Nicol's refusal to do so, then neither can a precise redaction-critical investigation like Nicol's be carried out[158]. Nicol gives no satisfactory explanation for including the narrative about the first disciples and the Samaritan woman, nor for excluding others that have been suggested as elements in a source. Fortna also criticizes the relevance of Nicol's "crude distinction" between Palestinian and Hellenistic thought in discussing the Sitz-im-Leben of S, especially when Nicol concludes that for S Jesus is the divine Messiah, which is probably a Jewish-Hellenistic notion. The most valuable portion of Nicol's work, for Fortna, is the description of the evangelist's redaction. He essentially agrees that John's symbolic interpretation of S arises from elements implicit in the source and from the evangelist's own "critical additions"[159]. According to Nicolaus WALTER (1974)[160], Nicol offers nothing new in his literary-critical chapter. Like Fortna, Walter thinks that the image of the Messiah in S, as Nicol describes it, and that of the divine revealer, the θεῖος ἀνήρ, are so closely related that the distinction is rather forced[161]. Nor is the description of the Sitz-im-Leben of S and J convincing. Walter does note the importance of Nicol's discussion of the evangelist's redaction[162].

Of more importance is the review of Georg RICHTER (1974)[163], who thinks Nicol has overvalued the significance of word statistics and has attributed to the evangelist all the passages which are now generally considered secondary (that is, from a second redaction)[164]. Richter otherwise agrees with Nicol's first and second chapters. He does remark that S may just as well have been directed toward already converted Jews who are in danger of losing their faith. In contrast to Nicol, he

158. *Ibid.*, p. 119.
159. *Ibid.*, pp. 120-121. Fortna does not agree with Nicol's description of the tension between event and meaning, "flesh" and glory.
160. N. WALTER, in *TLZ* 99 (1974) 826-828.
161. *Ibid.*, c. 827.
162. *Ibid.*, cc. 827-828. For Boismard's reaction to Nicol, see below, p. 275 n. 151.
163. G. RICHTER, *Zur sogenannten Semeia-Quelle des Johannesevangeliums*, in *MTZ* 25 (1974) 64-73 (= 1977, pp. 281-287). – On Richter, see MATTILL, Jr., in *TS* 38 (1977) 294-315; DAUER, in *FS J. Schneider*, 1986, pp. 62-83. See also BROWN, *Community*, 1979, pp. 174-176 (FT: 1983, pp. 191-193); KUHN, *Christologie*, 1988, pp. 271-286 (Jn 1,35-51); LÜTGEHETMANN, *Hochzeit*, 1990, pp. 93-97 (Jn 2,1-11); WÖLLNER, *Zeichenglaube*, 1988, pp. 15-17; BEUTLER, *Méthodes et problèmes*, 1990, p. 23; SCHMITHALS, *Johannesevangelium*, 1992, pp. 176, 187-188; SMITH, *John among the Gospels*, 1992, pp. 77-78.
164. *Semeia-Quelle*, p. 65 n. 8 (= 1977, p. 282 n. 8). Nicol does not recognize a secondary (anti-docetic) redaction by the evangelist. He ignores the tension between different valuations of the "flesh" or between present and future eschatology; these are either harmonized by Nicol or treated with a "not only ... but also" theology (pp. 67-68; = 1977, pp. 284-285).

gives a completely different description of the concept σημεῖον[165]. In his opinion, Nicol incorrectly understands and translates σημεῖον simply as "miracle". The σημεῖα in S are already miracles of a special nature, signs of the Messiah-prophet. Because exorcisms and leper-healings are not representative enough for the messianic time, S omits them. Nicol does not touch upon the lack of these miracles, although this is precisely a proof that Jesus was not described as θεῖος ἀνήρ, for whom exorcisms are characteristic. The signs have been "entmessianisiert" by the evangelist[166]. He does not give them a deeper significance; he uses them only to question the signs christology of S[167]. Elsewhere he uses the term ἔργον, which, as a christological term, does not indicate Jesus' Messiahship but his divinity and unity with the Father (5,36; 10,25ff.37ff.; 14,10ff.). According to S the "greater things" of 1,50 are Jesus' signs, but for the evangelist they are the eschatological functions of judgment and raising the dead (1,51; 5,20ff.); these are greater works than the signs (5,20). All this indicates that the evangelist, rather than deepening and building upon the concept σημεῖον, has abandoned the term and its content in favor of ἔργον. Contrary to Nicol, Richter thinks that already in S the signs are revelations of Jesus' δόξα (2,11 is entirely from S!); he is the Messiah who received the miracle-working power of God so that the signs are at the same time revelations of God's δόξα (11,4.40). For the evangelist, on the other hand, the signs have nothing to do with δόξα, but with Jesus' hour and return to the Father in the crucifixion. Δόξα is therefore not "the primary concept" of the evangelist in relation with σημεῖον, and the word is not used in connection with ἔργον. The evangelist speaks about Jesus' glory only in his pre-existence and in his return to the Father. Richter further remarks that in S not only do Jesus' signs illustrate his δόξα but also his majestic bearing (absent in the Synoptics, for example, in the temple-cleansing, the entry into Jerusalem, or the arrest). In this way, S replies to the traditional Jewish objection that Jesus cannot be the Messiah since he appeared without honor (ἄτιμος) and without glory (ἄδοξος) (JUSTIN, Dialogus, 32,1), while according to Jewish expectation the Messiah would reveal himself in splendor (ibid., 101,1). But the description by S does not imply, as Nicol thinks, that Jesus is divine; in the Jewish view, Jesus is a man among men (ibid., 48,1.3; 49,1; 67,2): he is the son of Joseph, he

---

165. Ibid., pp. 68-72 (= 1977, pp. 283-287).

166. In 2,4 the evangelist opposes the glorious character of the wine miracle and the signs in general (cp. 11,4). The healing at a distance is the impetus to a critique of S's view of faith (i.e., belief on the basis of signs). Beginning with Chapter 5 the messianic character is broken down in another way; the added discourses of Jesus give a different significance to the signs: they become spiritualized.

167. He does this in only three places: 4,48; 6,26.30. Nicol and others also count 2,23; 3,2; 6,2 and 7,31 among passages by the evangelist which likewise contain only criticism of S. 12,37 and 11,47 are certainly from S (contra Nicol).

does not come from God but from Nazareth (1,45.46). The evangelist opposes this: he proclaims Jesus' heavenly origin and communion with God. He does not eliminate S, Richter believes, because he could only proclaim a "new" belief in Christ by critiquing the "old" Jewish-Christian faith based on signs. Richter thinks that the evangelist was actually using the written source rather than citing it from memory, and perhaps even wrote his expansion on a copy of S itself.

Furthermore, John's *Vorlage* contained more than signs[168]. For that reason some authors choose another term in place of the title "signs source" to characterize the gospel that the evangelist knew within his community: σημεῖα (or *Signs*)-*Gospel*, *Grundschrift*, or simply *Gospel*[169]. Richter finds the term *Grundschrift* the most suitable, since John's *Vorlage* was not a gospel (the term itself is lacking and it contained no instruction by Jesus) but an apologetic text written to prove and defend Jesus' Messiahship[170]. Richter concludes his article with this consideration: if there had been a source "S" which contained only signs (as would appear from the numbering and the close of the gospel), this source would already have been used and redactionally reworked by the author of the *Grundschrift*[171].

IV. FURTHER STUDIES ON THE GOSPEL OF SIGNS

1. *H.M. Teeple: "The Literary Origin of the Gospel of John"*

Another study to be considered is that of Howard M. TEEPLE (1974)[172]. On the basis of the usage of certain terms, syntactical

---

168. To the *Vorlage* Richter assigns the testimony of the Baptist (1,19ff.; 3,2ff.), that of the disciples (1,35ff.), the Temple-cleansing (2,13ff.), the core of 4,1-42, 10,40-42, the arrest (18,1-11), the core of the passion narrative, and 20,1.11-18. All these passages have the same intention as the signs: they demonstrate Jesus' Messiahship (p. 72, esp. n. 18; = 1977, p. 287 n. 18).

169. Richter refers to Wellhausen (*Grundschrift*), Haenchen and Wilkens, J. Becker and Nicol himself (*Missionsevangelium*).

170. Cf. also *Der Vater und Gott Jesu und seiner Brüder in Joh 20,17. Ein Beitrag zur Christologie im Johannesevangelium*, in *MTZ* 24 (1973) 95-114, p. 95 (= 1977, pp. 266-280, esp. 267). On pp. 95-97 (= 1977, pp. 266-268) he gives a brief review of the origin of this hypothesis. There he also chooses the term *Grundschrift* (pp. 97 n. 12, 106 n. 50; = 1977, pp. 267 n. 12, 274 n. 50).

171. *Semeia-Quelle*, p. 73 (= 1977, p. 287). – Josef HAINZ, the editor of Richter's *Studien zum Johannesevangelium* (1977), is a fervent defender of the *Grundschrift* hypothesis; see his recent articles *Neuere Auffassungen zur Redaktionsgeschichte des Johannesevangeliums*, in HAINZ (ed.), *Theologie im Werden*, 1992, pp. 157-176; *"Zur Krisis kam ich in die Welt" (Joh 9,39). Zur Eschatologie im Johannesevangelium*, in KLAUCK (ed.), *Weltgericht und Weltvollendung*, 1994, pp. 149-163, and the dissertations of his students: Wagner (1988), Lütgehetmann (1990), and A. Link (1992). See below, resp. pp. 283-285, 285-286, 283-284 n. 186.

172. H.M. TEEPLE, *The Literary Origin of the Gospel of John*, Evanston, IL, 1974. – See the reviews by M.-É. BOISMARD, in *RB* 81 (1974) 467-468 and R. KYSAR, in *JBL* 93

constructions, and ideas, this author tries to indicate the various literary
layers in the Gospel of John. He pays particular attention to vocabulary[173]. For literary-critical delimitation of the signs source (S), Teeple
makes use of the following characterististics that appear almost exclusively in S: τέ, μετὰ τοῦτο, ὡς (in the sense of "about" with numbers),
τότε οὖν, πλοῖον (in place of πλοιάριον), ὄχλος with the verb in the
plural, compound subject with singular verb. There are also some traits
which, though not exclusive in S, are "quite characteristic": the use of
indefinite subjects, statements of specific passage of time and precise
measurements of quantity, personal names with the article (although Old
Testament names are anarthrous, presumably under influence of the Septuagint), the use of ἀπό in the expression "from a city". The following
elements never appear in S: "the Son", "the Son of Man", ἀναγκαῖόν
ἐστιν, ἀμὴν ἀμὴν λέγω ὑμῖν, μέλλω, πέμπω (for "send"), and
λόγος[174]. Like Fortna, Teeple admits elements from the Passion story
into the signs source, but no resurrection narratives[175]. The source would
have had a fairly late origin, as appears from the allusion to the destruction of the temple (11,48) as well as from the influence of Mark and
perhaps Matthew[176]. Various elements point to a relationship with Jewish Christianity[177]. Jesus is indeed the messianic prophet (4,19; 6,14;
7,40), and the Baptist is not (1,21). Like Jewish and Hellenistic pagan

(1974) 308-312; cf. THYEN, Literatur, p. 318: LÜTGEHETMANN, Hochzeit, 1990, pp. 93-
97; BOTHA, Jesus and the Samaritan Woman, 1991, pp. 19-20; SCHMITHALS, Johannesevangelium, 1992, pp. 184-185; SMITH, John among the Gospels, 1992, p. 75 n. 110. – In
his historical survey (pp. 1-116: Chapters 1-8), Teeple treats successively: "The Literary
Puzzle", "Hindrances to Solution", "The Question of Unity", "Source Theories", "Hel-
lenistic-Speech Theories", "John and Synoptic Tradition", "Redaction Theories", and
"Theories of Accidental Displacement". Then he presents his own literary theory
(pp. 117-252: Chapters 9-13), which is roughly comparable to Bultmann's (cf. p. 142). The
Gospel of John consists of four main literary strands (pp. 142-143): S (a signs source,
pp. 143-147), G (a semi-gnostic source of collected Hellenistic theological documents,
pp. 147-151), E (the work of an editor, pp. 152-160), and R (the work of a redactor,
pp. 160-164). In addition, Teeple also presupposes a Christian Gnostic Hymn in the
Prologue, a "post-resurrection stories source or sources" for Jn 20, a similar source or
sources for ch. 21, a possible Passion source (pp. 151-152), and a few scribal glosses
(p. 142). On pp. 164-248, he gives the entire gospel in translation, indicating the various
literary layers. How he arrives at his results is not always clear.
    173. Ibid., pp. 142-143 (vocabulary), 146, 148, 153, 160-161. The appendix (pp. 253-
260) offers a survey of syntax for the different literary layers.
    174. Ibid., pp. 145-146.
    175. Several characteristics of S appear in the Passion story: repetition of the article
(e.g., 18,10), compound subject with singular verb (18,1), and τότε οὖν for "then"
(19,1.16). Teeple thinks that the opinion of some (cf. Bultmann and Schnackenburg) that
the narrative source does not extend into the Passion story is due in part to "too much
influence from Faure's mistaken theory that the first half of John is completely different
from the second half" (p. 146).
    176. Ibid., p. 143.
    177. Ibid., pp. 143-144.

prophets, Jesus possesses a supernatural knowledge, which likewise leads to belief in his Messiahship (4,29.42)[178]. At the same time, Jesus is also portrayed as an ordinary human: he is the son of Joseph (1,45)[179]. Nevertheless, the author of S is not a Jewish Christian[180]. This would appear from the repeated pejorative use of "the Jews" in the Passion narrative. He is acquainted with the Jews' criticism of Christianity and tries to refute their objections. Against the claim that John the Baptist, and not Jesus, is the Messiah, he represents the Baptist denying this. He also disputes the claim that Jesus is not descended from David (7,41-49). To combat Jewish denials, S stresses the necessity of *believing* in Jesus as the Christ. It is no accident that S is so concerned with the signs. The Pharisees claimed that if Jesus were the Christ he would perform signs (Mk 8,11; Mt 12,38). According to Teeple, the historical Jesus apparently did no signs, for in Mk 8,12 we find Jesus' answer that no signs will be given. But S presents Jesus as a miracle worker and narrates seven miracles, of which the first two are specifically called "signs". The signs are of vital importance to S because they arouse faith in Jesus (2,11; 4,53); they also lead to his arrest (7,32a), and they form the central theme on which the book closes (20,30). S and Matthew, both written shortly after the Synod of Jamnia, regard the Pharisees as the chief opponents of Christianity. Only one passage portrays a Pharisee in a favorable light, namely Nicodemus (3,1-2). Although many Jews believed in Jesus, S still speaks hostilely about those who did not (11,46-50.54). S is obviously of later origin because of its doctrine that *belief in Jesus* is the basis of salvation, although Jesus himself and his disciples preached repentence, a concept that does not appear in S[181].

Teeple has recently taken up the semeia-hypothesis in his study on the origin of Christianity (1992)[182]. Especially in dialogue with J.L. Martyn

178. The Jewish character of the source also appears in the original name Simon used for Peter; Rabbi as the title for addressing Jesus; the use of Matthew's Gospel; the use of words like Messiah, Cephas, and the explanation of certain Semitic words. Like many other defenders of the semeia hypothesis, Teeple also believes that the author of the source wrote in a Semitized Greek, making frequent use of paratactic καί and ποιεῖν in a causative construction.

179. *Ibid.*, pp. 143-144.

180. *Ibid.*, p. 144.

181. *Ibid.*, p. 145.

182. TEEPLE, *How Did Christianity Really Begin? A Historical-Archaeological Approach*, Evanston, IL, 1992. Dealing with "Gnosticism" (pp. 498-527), Teeple notes: "The author of John displays a broad knowledge of the situation in his community. He knows and largely agrees with the Gnostics, but he also knows Jewish-Christian tradition (Synoptic Gospels, Gospel of Signs), the Christian controversy with the Jews, and the wide range of Christian doctrinal and polemic problems. He has mixed his variety of materials together instead of synthesizing them into a unity" (p. 516). For the Signs Source (= S), see, e.g., pp. 95 (on John the Baptist), 120 (2,1-11), 146 (ch. 18), 150 (6,15), 152 (18,13), 153 (2,15-16), 239 (on "Son of God" in 1,49; 11,27), 251 (on "Prophet-Messiah" in 4,25-26; 6,14), and esp. 428-430 (on ch. 5, 7, and 9) in his section

(and R.A. Culpepper)[183], he reads chs. 5, 7, and 9 on two levels: these chapters reflect what happened, on the one hand, during Jesus' lifetime, and, on the other, in the author's community. Some Jewish-Christian evangelists came to Alexandria[184] and may have brought with them the Gospel of Signs (or Signs Gospel)[185]. Its central theme was "we have found the Messiah" (1,41), which "surely reflects the evangelist's basic belief"[186]. In the Gospel of Signs, the author of Jn found material that he could use to deal with his own situation of excommunication or persecution[187].

2. The Spread of the Hypothesis

We take note of several other authors who, with reference to Fortna and/or Nicol, advocate the semeia hypothesis (in notes 189-204c)[188].

"Persecution" (pp. 423-550). As in 1972, he defends "a Semi-Gnostic Source" (= G) (see esp. pp. 513-517), a pre-Johannine "Christian Gnostic Hymn" at the basis of Jn 1,1-18.
183. *Ibid.*, p. 423; cp. p. 192. Teeple refers to MARTYN, *History and Theology*, [2]1979; CULPEPPER, *Anatomy*, 1983. He wrongly notes (p. 428) that Martyn did not recognize the Signs Source. Cf. above, pp. 149-150.
184. According to TEEPLE, *op. cit.*, p. 430, the Gospel of John was written by "a gentile Christian in a racially mixed church" and originated probably in Alexandria around A.D. 100 (p. 192; cp. p. 420; see below, n. 187).
185. The Gospel of Signs originated elsewhere "for, unlike much of the rest of John, it lacks Alexandrian thought and it emphasizes Samaria" (pp. 428-429).
186. *Ibid.*, p. 429; cp. p. 251.
187. *Ibid.*, p. 429. Teeple notes that "by the time the Benediction Against Heretics was promulgated by Gamaliel, the number of Jewish converts in Alexandria and elsewhere was alarming. The Benediction was enforced, and Jewish Christians were tried in the local Jewish court, the *Gerousia*, and expelled from the synagogue" (cf. 9,22; 12,42; 16,2) (p. 429). In the signs source, the crowd and the Pharisees say that Jesus "leads the crowd astray" (7,12.47). For Teeple, "even in the source the accusation fits the Christian apostles, and the same charge must have been made against the evangelists who came to Alexandria". The source's story of the healing of the blind man, which demonstrates that Jesus is a miracle-working Prophet-Messiah (9,13-17), has been taken up by the gentile Christian author of John, and in accord with his situation, the opponents has been changed from Pharisees to "the Jews" (9,18-22). When the excommunication did not stop the conversions, a further step was tried, i.e., the imposition of the death penalty (cf. 16,1-2). Jn 9,12.22 reflects the situation of the Johannine community: "the persecution forced the Jewish Christians out of the synagogues, so they met separately and thus formed a church. In Alexandria they must have met with gentile Christians in the safety of the gentile section of the city" (p. 430).
188. In addition to the other defenders of the hypothesis listed in nn. 506-517.

189. Charles H. TALBERT, *Artistry and Theology: An Analysis of the Architecture of Jn 1,19-5,47*, in *CBQ* 32 (1970) 341-366, p. 342 (in n. 7 he refers to Fuller and Fortna). See also p. 353 (the two Cana stories). – In his recent commentary, *Reading John: A Literary and Theological Commentary on the Fourth Gospel and the Johannine Epistles* (Reading the New Testament Series), New York, 1992 (see esp. pp. 59-284: "The Fourth Gospel"), Talbert does not explicitly deal with source criticism and, if I am right, never mentions the signs source. As editor of the series, Talbert notes in the *Preface* that the

volumes in this series "are concerned to understand large thought units and their relationship to an author's thought as a whole. The focus is on a close reading of the final
form of the text. The aim is to make one feel at home in the biblical text itself. The
approach of these volumes involves a concern both for *how* an author communicates and
what the religious point of the text is" (p. XI; see also p. 3). He reads the Fourth Gospel
as "a narrative theology" (p. 63) and stresses that the Gospel must be interpreted in its
canonical form: "Rearrangements are not to be attempted. Chapter 21 is to be considered
an integral part of the final text, as are the other passages believed by Bultmann to have
been editorial additions to an earlier version of John (e.g., 3:5, 'and water'; 5:28-29;
6:51c-58; 19:34b-35)" (p. 64). He thinks that the Fourth Gospel developed in different
stages over a long period (p. 103; cp. p. 62, with reference to R. KYSAR, *The Fourth
Evangelist and His Gospel*, 1975, pp. 38-66, 267-269), but does not enter into the discussion of the question.

190. George W. MACRAE, *The Fourth Gospel and Religionsgeschichte*, in *CBQ* 32
(1970) 13-24, p. 15 (= 1987, pp. 15-31, esp. 19): "But the existence of a signs-source has
withstood the test of analysis, so much so that its nature, extent and theology are now the
subject of much contemporary investigation". In reaction to Käsemann, MacRae contends
that John has minimized the miraculous, "even though he sometimes heightens the miracle stories to give emphasis to their symbolic content" (p. 16; = 1987, pp. 19-20). John
has not thrown the source aside because he wanted to transcend the Hellenistic θεῖος
ἀνήρ christology by emphasizing Jesus' unique relationship to his Father (p. 17; = 1987,
p. 21). – On MacRae, see ASHTON, *Understanding*, 1991, pp. 96-97; SMITH, *John among
the Gospels*, 1992, pp. 68-69.

191. Franz SCHNIDER – Werner STENGER, *Johannes und die Synoptiker. Vergleich
ihrer Parallelen* (BibH, 9), München, 1971, p. 72 n. 9. They refer especially to Fortna,
but observe that the semeia hypothesis comes into difficulty when the attempt is made to
include other material (e.g., the Passion story) in the signs source. They choose the term
"miracle source" because it is not certain whether the notion σημεῖον was already present in the source. See also SCHNIDER, *Jesus der Prophet* (OBO, 2), Freiburg/Schw.,
1973: the healing of the man born blind (p. 201) and the portrayal of Jesus as the eschatological prophet (1,21; 6,14) are from the source (pp. 223-224). But Schnider rejects the
Hellenistic θεῖος ἀνήρ interpretation of this title (p. 226). Cp. STENGER, *Die Auferwek-
kung des Lazarus (Johannes 11,1-45). Vorlage und johanneische Redaktion*, in *TTZ* 83
(1974) 17-37 (= 1990, pp. 181-201). He gives a brief description of the signs source with
a short historical review of the theory (pp. 17-19; = 1990, pp. 181-183); the *Grundlage*
of 11,1-45 is from the signs source (pp. 19-28; = 1990, pp. 183-191); John gives the story
a symbolic meaning and sees in the miracle a revelation of Jesus' glory (pp. 28-37; =
1990, pp. 191-201). More recently STENGER, *Biblische Methodenlehre* (Leitfaden Theologie, 18), Düsseldorf, 1987, pp. 162-167, accepted that Jn 4,46c-54 "dem Redaktor nicht
als Einzelüberlieferung vorlag, sondern schon Teil einer grösseren Quelle war" (p. 162).
For Stenger the story of John is not literarily dependent on the Synoptic versions of the
story in Mt 8,5-13 par. Lk 7,1-10 ("nicht literarisch abhängig, d.h. nicht aus unmittelbarer
Kenntnis des Textes der Synoptiker entstanden"), but this does not mean that there is
"überlieferungsgeschichtlich" no relationship at all (p. 165). Stenger considers two
possibilities (pp. 165-166; see his diagrams on p. 166): "Entweder hat es einmal eine
Texteinheit in mündlicher Überlieferung gegeben, die einerseits Aufnahme in die Logienquelle fand und andererseits unabhängig von Q auch das Traditionsmilieu erreichte,
innerhalb dessen die Quelle des Johannesevangelisten entstanden ist. Oder, als zweite
Möglichkeit: im Traditionsmilieu der Quelle des Johannesevangelisten waren die Synoptiker (oder einer von ihnen) zwar nicht literarisch, aber eventuell durch mündlichen Vortrag, vielleicht im Gottesdienst, bekannt und wirkten so als Ausgangspunkt sich erneut
bildender mündlicher Tradition, die schliesslich in der Quelle des Johannesevangeliums
ihren schriftlichen Niederschlag fand". The second possibility is similar to that of Dauer
(1984), but Dauer would see more of a literary relationship between the pre-Johannine

source and the Synoptics (see above, pp. 109-110). – On the work of Schnider and Stenger, especially with reference to Jn 6, see KONINGS, *Joh. verhaal*, III, 1972, pp. 710-721.

192. Helmut MERKEL, *Auf den Spuren des Urmarkus? Ein neuer Fund und seine Beurteilung*, in *ZTK* 71 (1974) 123-144, pp. 139-140. In criticism of "the secret gospel" proposed by M. Smith: "Auszugehen ist von der heute als gesichert anzusehenden Hypothese, dass Johannes die Wundergeschichten aus einer Quellenschrift entnommen hat". For his list of defenders of the hypothesis see p. 140 n. 71.

193. Ulrich B. MÜLLER, *Die Geschichte der Christologie in der johanneischen Gemeinde* (SBS, 77), Stuttgart, 1975, pp. 10-11, 12, 29, 32-33, 36, 45, 48. According to Müller, in 1,14.16 John used a "Logoslied" of the Johannine community (see pp. 13-22, esp. 17). It presents the incarnation of the heavenly Logos as the miracle-worker Jesus (pp. 22-26). This Logos hymn was marked by a christology of glory and, like the signs source (ctr. Fortna), it made no mention of Jesus' passion and death (pp. 27-31, esp. 29). The revelation of glory transmits grace to the believer, and the glory of the Logos is announced and can be seen especially in the miracle stories of the signs source (pp. 32-36, 36-41). Form-critically, this Logos hymn has its origin in the acclamations of the miracle stories (pp. 41-45). Regarding the history-of-religions background, Müller thinks that the christology of the Logos-miracle worker, which he sees as a combination of two christologies (the pre-existence and the miracle-worker christology) can be explained by a Hellenistic background (pp. 45-47). The Fourth Evangelist, who was concerned with the offense of Jesus' death and with his community's tendency to ignore that death, attempted to assert the facticity of Jesus' death; nevertheless, he still accepts the traditional christology of glory (pp. 49-52). – Reviews: cf. VAN BELLE, no. 4882. Cp. THYEN, in *TR* 42 (1977) 220-222; KYSAR, *ANRW* II, 25/3, 1985, 2440-2441; BEUTLER, *ANRW* II, 25/3, 1985, 2559. – See also U.B. MÜLLER, *Die Bedeutung des Kreuzestodes Jesu im Johannesevangelium. Erwägungen zur Kreuzestheologie im Neuen Testament*, in *KerDog* 21 (1975) 49-71, pp. 69-70; *Die Menschwerdung des Gottessohnes. Frühchristliche Inkarnationsvorstellungen und die Anfänge des Doketismus* (SBS, 140), Stuttgart, 1990, pp. 40-61 ("Die Inkarnation des Logos in John 1,14"), 62-83 ("Die Herausstellung der Göttlichkeit Jesu beim Evangelisten Johannes").

194. Raymond F. COLLINS, *Representative Figures of the Fourth Gospel*, in *DownR* 94 (1976) 26-46, 118-132, p. 40 (= 1990, pp. 1-45, esp. 19): "Traditionally, and with good reason, the substance of the narrative [4,46-54] has been assigned to the Signs-Source used by the evangelist in the composition of the Fourth Gospel". Cp. *Cana (Jn 2:1-12) – The First of His Signs or the Key to His Signs?*, in *IrTQ* 47 (1980) 79-95, p. 80 (= 1990, pp. 158-182, esp. 161), where Collins claims that "the story of the water-become-wine was taken over by the evangelist from his signs-source" (with reference to Bultmann and Fortna on p. 92 n. 6; = 1990, p. 161 n. 6). Cp. *Introduction to the New Testament*, Garden City, NY, 1983, p. 145. With reference to my historical survey he simply notes: "As a result of this lengthy discussion it would appear that contemporary Johannine scholarship has arrived at a consensus that John did make use of a Signs Source, even though the various authors do not exactly agree among themselves as to the content (did it contain the narrative of Jesus at the Sea of Tiberias, John 21:1-14, or not?) and the nature of the Source" (p. 145). There he mentions Bultmann, Fortna and Nicol (and the criticism of Schweizer and Ruckstuhl). See also *Miracles and Faith*, in NLENAYA ONWU (ed.), *New Testament Miracles in African Context*, 1989 (= 1990, pp. 183-197, esp. 185-187: "Source Criticism").

195. Hans-Martin SCHENKE – Karl-Martin FISCHER, *Einleitung in die Schriften des Neuen Testaments*. II. *Die Evangelien und die anderen neutestamentlichen Schriften*, Gütersloh, 1979, pp. 180-181. Like Bultmann, Schenke restricts the content of the signs source principally to the signs: "Die Hypothese einer Semeia-Quelle für das vierte Evangelium ist u.E. also wohlbegründet, kaum umgänglich und äusserst fruchtbar; sie ist auch der Teil von Bultmanns Quellentheorie, der fast allgemeine Anerkennung gefunden

hat" (p. 181, with reference to Faure, Bultmann, Käsemann, Haenchen [1955], Koester and J.M. Robinson; on the signs source, see also pp. 182, 190, 199-201, 203). Schenke seems inclined, however, to expand the source with other material. His starting point, of course, is the "vorjohanneische Erzählungszusammenhang" of the two Cana stories (cf. 2,11; 4,54) (pp. 180-181). He supposes that these two pericopes formed "eine fort-laufende, wohl schriftlich fixierte Erzählung" (p. 181), and, if 20,30-31 is to be consid-ered its conclusion, then Jn 20,24-29, together with other miracle stories, must also be assigned to this source: "Es spricht nun viel dafür, die Stelle 20,30f. in direktem Zusam-menhang mit 2,11 und 4,54 zu sehen. 20,30f. sieht aus wie der Schluss dieser Semeia-Sammlung. Dann musste aber wohl auch die unmittelbar vorhergehende Erzählung vom ungläubigen Thomas (20,24-29) in ihrem Grundbestand aus dieser Sammlung stammen. Von daher kann man es als wahrscheinlich ansehen, dass auch der Grundbestand der anderen Wundererzählungen des Vierten Evangeliums aus eben dieser Semeia-Sammlung stammt, die damit als besondere, durchgehend verwendete Quelle (sogenannte Semeia-Quelle) des Evangelisten erkannt wäre, eine Schrift, die, für sich betrachtet, als ein Evan-gelium vom Typ der Jesus-Aretalogie zu bestimmen ist" (p. 181, with reference to Koester and Robinson). Thus, Schenke does not give a precise delimitation of the signs source. Besides this, he also accepts a source for the passion narrative (p. 180) and he reckons with the possibility that John used a source for his discourses (pp. 181-182). Because he does not seem to join the signs source with the passion narrative in one pre-Johannine gospel as Fortna does (see Schenke's presentation of Fortna's hypothesis on pp. 199-200), it is not clear why Schenke assigns Jn 20,24-29 to the signs source.

196. Klaus WENGST, *Bedrängte Gemeinde und verherrlichter Christus. Der histori-sche Ort des Johannesevangeliums als Schlüssel zu seiner Interpretation* (BTSt, 5), Neukirchen-Vluyn, 1981, p. 102 n. 326 (cp. [2]1990, p. 190 n. 23): "Bei der Frage nach der Quellen des Evangelisten ist es weithin anerkannt, dass er eine 'Zeichenquelle' benutzte, die Wundergeschichten enthielt [with reference to my historical survey of 1975]. – Wie auch immer es sich mit einer möglichen 'Zeichenquelle' oder gar einem 'Zeichenevange-lium' verhalte, so ist doch so viel offenkundig, dass die Wundererzählungen dem Evan-gelisten vorgegeben sind. Die Annahme liegt am nächsten, dass er sie aus der eigenen Gemeindetradition aufgenommen hat". – On Wengst, see, e.g., LÉON-DUFOUR, *Où en est la recherche johannique?*, 1990, pp. 29-30; ASHTON, *Understanding*, 1991, pp. 196-198; SCHMITHALS, *Johannesevangelium*, 1992, pp. 160-161.

197. Schuyler BROWN, *The Origins of Christianity: A Historical Introduction to the New Testament* (The Oxford Bible Series), Oxford - New York, 1984, pp. 114-117: "The Gospel of Signs", esp. 114: "Just as Matthew's gospel is a revision of the Gospel of Mark, so the fourth and latest of the canonical gospels, attributed by tradition to John, represents a new edition of an earlier work, called 'The Gospel of Signs', because it cen-tres upon seven miracles of Jesus" (p. 114). He believes that this Gospel of Signs "comes from a community of Christian Jews, which is quite at home within Judaism", that it "shows no concern for the Gentile question and takes for granted the observance of the Torah", and that "the expectation which we find in the Synoptic tradition of Jesus return-ing in judgement as Son of man is notably absent" (p. 114). He agrees with Martyn that "the revision of the 'Gospel of Signs' by the Fourth Evangelist was occasioned by a trau-matic experience in the life of his community: its expulsion from the synagogue" (cf. 9,22; see pp. 114-115).

198. Hans WEDER, *Die Menschwerdung Gottes. Überlegungen zur Auslegungsproble-matik des Johannesevangeliums am Beispiel von Joh 6*, in ZTK 82 (1985) 325-360, p. 329 (= 1992, pp. 363-400, esp. 367: regarding ch. 6): "Will man die Wundergeschichten am Anfang des Kapitels genauer einordnen, so legt sich meines Erachtens die Annahme einer vorjohanneischen Quelle – der Semeiaquelle – nach wie vor am nächsten" (with reference to Fortna). – See also *Von der Wende der Welt zum Semeion des Sohnes*, in DENAUX (ed.), *John and the Synoptics*, 1992, pp. 127-145, esp. 128: "in unserem Zusam-menhang interessiert besonders die Semeia-Quelle, deren Existenz mit recht guter Wahr-

scheinlichkeit angenommen werden kann, auch wenn es wohl nicht möglich ist, ihren genauen Umfang abschliessend zu rekonstruieren". He refers (p. 128 n. 7) to J. Becker, Fortna (1970, 1988) and Schnackenburg, and rejects the criticism of Bittner: "Die neu-erliche Bestreitung dieser Quelle bei W.J. Bittner ... erfolgt weitgehend aus ideologiever-dächtigen Gründen", and he calls Hengel's and Marguerat's hypotheses of the origin of the Johannine miracle stories "eine mittlere Lösung". As in his 1985 article, Weder now accepts Hengel's view that "the Gospel, was not written down over a short period but grew relatively slowly in parallel to the development of the teaching of the school" (p. 127 n. 1; cf. HENGEL, *The Johannine Question*, 1989, p. 102; GT: 1993, p. 264). Also the trajectory of the theology of miracles can be traced in four stages (*Von der Wende*, pp. 129-144): (1) For Jesus (pp. 129-132; cp. 145), exorcisms and healings are under-stood as the eschatological turn of the eons (cf. Lk 11,20). They are events through which the future and transcendent kingdom of God breaks into the present time. (2) In the pre-Synoptic (i.e., pre-Markan) tradition (pp. 132-135; cp. 145), the miracles reveal Jesus' identity (see esp. Mk 1,24; 2,10; 4,38; 5,35; 9,17; 5,7.19; 7,28; 10,47-48). They have, at least implicitly, a christological point. In Q (Mt 11,2-6 par.), they qualify Jesus explicitly as eschatological Savior. (3) In the signs source (pp. 135-140; cp. 145), the miraculous is heightened, so that the miracle stories can be seen as "epiphany stories". They are cal-led, now for the first time, "signs". Revealing Jesus as Messiah and Son of God, they bring the disciples to believe that in him God's definitive messenger has come (cf. the conclusion of the source in 20,30-31). (4) The author of the Fourth Gospel takes the miracle theology of the signs source to a final conclusion (pp. 141-144; cp. 145). He explains the signs in discourses and discussions. For John the miracles not only "signify" Jesus as the Messiah, but they reveal the content of his Messiahship: he is the true bread of life and the resurrection. Thus, for the evangelist the signs show that the "turn of eons" has been incarnated in the Word made flesh. – According to Weder John is independent of the Synoptics; he thinks that neither the signs source nor John knew the Synoptic Gos-pels or the pre-Synoptic tradition. Both pre-Synoptic and pre-Johannine traditions are based on the older common tradition, but Weder does not specify further. – On Weder, see SMITH, *John among the Gospels*, 1992, pp. 186-188.

199. D.E.H. WHITELEY, *Was John Written by a Sadducee?*, in *ANRW* II, 25/3, 1985, pp. 2481-2505, esp. 2484-2488 ("The Sources of John"). With reference to Fortna and Becker, Whiteley notes that "the only source which can be identified with reasonable probability is the 'Signs Source'" (p. 2485). It seems, however, that he limits the content of the source. Thus, the two Cana miracles are "the only passages which can be safely ascribed to the signs source... It is hard to deny that these two passages come from a signs source". Further, he considers Jn 11,1-4 [sic], "the remains of a sign-story which the evangelist has used as a text for one of the most skilfully constructed sermons in the reli-gious literature of the whole world" (p. 2485). Besides the signs source, Whiteley reck-ons with two other sources. First, the recollections, written or oral, of John the Apostle, which he calls "the memoirs of the Apostle" (pp. 2485-2486). To these Whiteley ascribes: (a) ἐθεασάμεθα τὴν δόξαν αὐτοῦ in Jn 1,14; (b) the account of John the Bap-tist's mission; (c) the temple cleansing; (d) such verses as 13,16; 12,15; 13,20, that have Synoptic parallels (cf. Dodd); (e) the accounts of John the Baptist in 3,22-29, possibly the further account of the Baptist in 4,1f., and the account of the Samaritan woman; (f) other stories are: 6,1-15.16-25; the two fused parables of the shepherd and the door in Jn 10,1-6; (g) possibly also accounts of exorcisms, of the Passion and of the Resurrection ("If so, the evangelist has omitted the accounts of the exorcisms, and I suspect, has preferred to use his own memory of the lifting up of the Son of Man and his victory over the grave"; cf. p. 2486); (f) Second, the evangelist's "own memories". To these, Whiteley ascribes the Nicodemus episode and 5,8-9 (p. 2487).

200. Walter KLAIBER, *Die Aufgabe einer theologischen Interpretation des 4. Evan-geliums*, in *ZTK* 82 (1985) 300-324, p. 303: "Ein Teil der übernommenen Tradition lässt sich einer zusammengehörenden Überlieferungsschicht zuordnen, möglicherweise

sogar als schriftliche Quelle – etwa in Gestalt einer Semeia-Quelle oder eines Passionsberichtes – identifizieren".

201. Jerome H. NEYREY, *John's Christology of Revolt: John's Christology in Social-Science Perspective*, Philadelphia, PA, 1989. On pp. 122-130 ("Stage One: Missionary Propaganda"), Neyrey shows how in the first stage of John's christology the 'signs' material coheres with a preaching form and titles of low christology; he refers to his earlier attempt to distinguish the stages of Johannine development in *Christ Is Community: The Christologies of the New Testament* (GNS, 13), Wilmington, DE, 1985, pp. 142-192: "Chapter Five: The Christologies of John's Gospel", esp. 144-151: "Stage One: Missionary Christology". – Cf. MENKEN, *De christologie*, 1991, pp. 24-25; SLOYAN, *What Are They Saying about John?*, 1991, pp. 63-64.

202. Walter REBELL, *Gemeinde als Gegenwelt. Zur soziologischen und didaktischen Funktion des Johannesevangeliums* (BET, 20), Frankfurt/M - Bern - New York, 1987, pp. 56-58. Rebell accepts without criticism the semeia hypothesis of Bultmann: "Aus dem Joh-Ev in seiner Jetztgestalt lässt sich nach fast einhelliger Meinung der Forschung, die hier R. Bultmann folgt, eine Zeichen-Quelle herauslösen" (p. 56). With reference to the argumentation of Bultmann (*Johannesevangelium*, 1959, c. 842), he notes: "Diesen Argumenten lässt sich kaum widersprechen, und so ist Bultmanns Annahme einer Zeichen-Quelle im Joh-Ev (im Gegensatz zu seiner Annahme einer Quelle von Offenbarungsreden, die er ebenfalls im Evangelium finden will) weithin akzeptiert worden". He also refers to J. Becker and rejects O. Betz's criticism of the hypothesis: "Die Position von Betz kann dazu dienen, den Graben zwischen der Theologie der Quelle und der Theologie des Evangelisten nicht zu breit werden zu lassen, muss aber, aufs Ganze gesehen, zurückgewiesen werden (aufgrund der ... literarkritischen Argumente). Die Lektüre von O. Betz, Problem [see below, pp. 294-295 n. 264], hat bei J. Becker offenbar einen Lerneffekt ausgelöst: in seinem Kommentar (Evangelium 1, 112-120) reisst er den genannten Graben nicht mehr so weit auf wie in einem zuvor geschriebenen Aufsatz (Wunder)" (p. 57 n. 2). Rebell, however, notes that "Der Umfang der Zeichen-Quelle sehr verschieden bestimmt worden ist" (with reference to Bultmann, Becker, Gnilka, Richter, and Heekerens, as well as to Fortna and Wilkens; see pp. 57 nn. 3-4). He accepts without discussion that the source is influenced by the θεῖος ἀνήρ christology (p. 58, with in n. 2 references to Becker and Koester). – Cf. LÉON-DUFOUR, *Où en est la recherche johannique?*, 1990, p. 30.

203. Roger AUS, *Water into Wine and the Beheading of John the Baptist: Early Jewish-Christian Interpretation of Esther 1 in John 2:1-11 and Mark 6:17-29* (BJSt, 150), Atlanta, GA, 1988, p. 1, n. 2: "The evangelist most probably found most of 2:1-11 already in a source ... the so-called 'signs source'"; see esp. pp. 30-31: "The 'Signs Source'". According to Aus, the followers of John the Baptist were probably part of the audience to which a "mission tract" like the signs source was addressed (with reference to Fortna and D.M. Smith) (p. 30). Further, he thinks that "the signs source can only have arisen in a Jewish-Christian atmosphere and its author(s) and audience 'seem to have been bilingual'" (with reference to Fortna). He thinks that this would fit with his own description (pp. 7-24: "Jesus and the Wedding Imagery and Judaic Interpretations of Esther 1:1-8 as the Background of Jesus' Sign in John 2:1-11"): "The creator of John 2:1-11 not only was a Jewish Christian, but was also aware of both Hebrew and Aramaic, as well as Greek (LXX, perhaps also Philo and Psalm 23) haggadic traditions on Esther 1" (p. 30). Finally, Aus would count seven miracles in the signs source (2,1-11; 4,46-54; 5,1-9; 6,1-14; 6,15-25; 9,1-8; 11,1-45). According to him, "this has nothing to do with seven as the 'perfect number' in Judaism, but rather exclusively with 'signs'" (p. 30).

204a. John F. O'GRADY, *The Four Gospels and the Jesus Tradition*, New York - Mahwah, NJ, 1989, pp. 77-151: "Part III: The Heart of the Tradition: John". On the signs source, see p. 143.

204b. Paul HOFRICHTER, *Johannesevangelium*, in *NBL* 2 (1991) 359-369, c. 354, limits the source to the seven miracles of Jn 1–12 and stresses the enumeration of signs as argument of the hypothesis: "Da im Anschluss an das erste Zeichen in Kana zunächst 'viele Zeichen' in Jerusalem erwähnt werden, dann aber mit dem zweiten Zeichen weitergezählt wird, weist dies nachträglich vom 'Evangelisten' gestörte Zählung auf eine vorausliegende Quelle hin. Die Gesamtzahl von sieben erzählten Zeichen und der dazu passende Schluss in 20,30 stützen diese Vermutung". On Fortna, see c. 363.

204c. Alfons WEISER, *Theologie des Neuen Testaments. 2. Die Theologie der Evangelien* (Kohlhammer-Studienbücher Theologie, 8), Stuttgart, 1993, pp. 181-183, esp. 183: "Zu den verarbeiteten Quellen gehörten u.a. wahrscheinlich eine Semeiaquelle. [n. 232] Sie enthielt Wundererzählungen, als Einleitung Teile der Berufungsgeschichten (1,35-51) und als Abschluss Aussagen des Epilogs (20,30f)", with references to Bultmann, Heekerens, H.-J. Kuhn, and Lütgehetmann.

3. *Some Special Studies*

Not all authors just mentioned include the passion narrative, as Fortna and Teeple do. In fact, only a few follow them in this, and usually with hesitation. Robert KYSAR is as typical example. He spoke in favor of the "signs or miracles source" as early as 1973[205] and has repeated his outlook in several publications. He goes most into detail with his review of contemporary Johannine research in 1975[206]. According to Kysar, "the rich results of the pursuit of the source hypotheses are encouraging. That is, the early efforts at redaction criticism on the basis of the signs source hypothesis demonstrate, at least to my satisfaction, that source analysis may provide keys to a number of the forbidden chambers of Johannine thought and history"[207]. He has the following objections against the thorough and detailed source isolation (or reconstruction) of Teeple and Fortna:

1. "Fortna's claim to have reconstructed the signs gospel (in a tentative fashion, to be sure) is perhaps the most regrettable feature of his

205. R. KYSAR, *The Source Analysis of the Fourth Gospel – A Growing Consensus?*, in *NT* 15 (1973) 134-152. Kysar notes a consensus in the delimitation of the literary stages of John: "The evidence obtained from this survey [i.e., for Jn 6,1-53] is sufficient to suggest that a substantial agreement might indeed exist among the critics with regard to the entire gospel and that such consensus needs to be examined and utilized in further Johannine studies" (p. 152). In his overview (pp. 140-150) he has digested the source theories of Bultmann, Fortna, H. Becker, Wilkens, Hartke, Broome, Merlier, S. Schulz, and Boismard (pp. 136-139).

206. *The Fourth Evangelist and His Gospel: An Examination of Contemporary Scholarship*, Minneapolis, MN, 1975 (reviews: cf. VAN BELLE, no. 51). He pays special attention to "the three major investigations", i.e., Fortna, Nicol, and Teeple, to Schnackenburg's commentary, and to the redactional study of J. Becker, *Wunder*, 1970 (cf. pp. 13-37: "Recent Signs Source Analysis"). After an introduction (pp. 13-17), he discusses "The Methods of the Source Analyses" (pp. 17-24), "The Content of the Source Analyses" (pp. 25-29), "The Character of the Proposed Source" (pp. 29-33), "A Critical Appraisal of Source Analyses" (pp. 33-37). On Kysar, see BEUTLER, *Méthodes et problèmes*, 1990, p. 22; BOTHA, *Jesus and the Samaritan Woman*, 1991, p. 20; SMITH, *John among the Gospels*, 1992, p. 69.

207. *The Fourth Evangelist and His Gospel*, p. 33.

work" for he becomes too speculative and his reconstruction "imaginative"[208].

2. Kysar considers "Teeple and Fortna's arguments less convincing once they move beyond the simpler 'signs' material and begin to incorporate other narrative materials into their proposed sources"[209]. He himself would prefer a signs source in the "narrower sense"[210].

3. As for the use of style characteristics, it "is perhaps the most debatable and dangerous of the various criteria"[211]. For Kysar, style characteristics must "remain broad enough to recognize the validity of variation in the work of the source or the evangelist"[212].

208. *Ibid.*, p. 34. With Lindars, Kysar rejects "Fortna's basic assumption that the evangelist took over the proposed signs gospel almost in its entirety"; this is unlikely for such a "creative thinker and writer as the fourth evangelist" (p. 34). For Lindars, see above, pp. 174-177.

209. *Ibid.*, p. 34. Again, he refers to Lindars, who "has suggested that Fortna's hypothesis suffers the problem that his proposed 'signs gospel' supposes the existence of a kind of document for which we have no evidence in the early Christian movement, i.e., a purely narrative source comprised of miracle stories and the passion narrative".

210. *Ibid.*, p. 35: "A collection of signs would seem to have some greater degree of historical likelihood than does a collection of narrative materials which includes signs materials along with a passion account. In this sense the narrower (and more modest) hypotheses of Nicol, Becker, and Schnackenburg are to be preferred to those of Teeple and Fortna".

211. *Ibid.*, p. 35. He admits that "it is true that stylistic features provide confirmation of a source hypothesis but they cannot become the foundation of any such hypothesis" (p. 21). Moreover, there is always the danger that "the use of style characteristics tends to become circular, that is, they are used to separate the source materials and then to verify the integrity of the proposed source". This criticism applies especially to Teeple, who "fails to guard himself against the danger of this circularity, and in his case it seems particularly fatal due to the centrality of style criticism in his entire method" (p. 35), and to a lesser degree to Fortna, who "may have been charged with that tendency upon occasion, perhaps in his enthusiasm to isolate and reconstruct the entire signs gospel" (p. 35; he refers to Nicol's critique of Fortna [see above, pp. 163-165], and to McMorrow's review [see above, p. 169 n. 130]). For his part, Nicol "has taken such care not to employ the stylistic criteria in a circular manner that he has failed to use the criteria in a successfully supportive manner" (p. 35, with reference to Fortna's review of Nicol; see above, p. 177 n. 156). Further, Kysar particularly objects to the way in which Teeple uses this criterion: "If one were to accept the syntactical basis of the Teeple study, it would involve the judgment that the fourth evangelist was possessed of such a wooden style that he could effect few variations from the style the critic assigns him" (p. 35). Thus, for example, "Teeple's attention to such matters as the arthrous and anarthrous use of personal names ... and the differences between two connectives (*de* and *kai*) ... is paramount to pushing the stylistic criteria to their breaking point" (pp. 35-36).

212. *Ibid.*, p. 36. Kysar refers to his own review of TEEPLE, *Origin*, 1974 in *JBL* 93 (1974), p. 310, and to FREED, *Variations*, 1964, p. 197, with the remark: "While I would not want to suggest that such variation makes source analysis unnecessary or impossible (which Freed does not attempt to argue), it does seem that such an element of variation is realistic and must be taken into account with the use of any of the criteria for source separation" (*The Fourth Evangelist and His Gospel*, p. 36 n. 53).

4. Kysar also views the ideological criteria "with a certain suspicion, for they entail among other difficulties the question of why the evangelist would have used a source which held such different views from his own"[213]. This question especially "plagues Fortna's admirable attention to the aporias"[214].

5. Finally, Kysar questions the effectiveness of Nicol's form criticism[215], although he believes the use of form criticism within the framework of source criticism to be "a fascinating and promising enterprise"[216].

Kysar limits the semeia source to the miracle stories in his study *John, the Maverick Gospel* (1975)[217]. In his later *Forschungsberichte* (1977, 1983, 1985)[218], and in his article on John in *ABD* (1992)[219], he does not

213. *Ibid.*, p. 36, with reference to McMorrow (see above, p. 169 n. 130) and Lindars (see above, pp. 174-176).

214. *Ibid.*, p. 36: "How can one believe, on the one hand, that the evangelist was an astute enough theologian to sense the weaknesses of his signs gospel and subtly correct them and yet, on the other hand, was such an inferior editor that he left glaring flaws in the simple readability of his document?" (with reference to his own review of Fortna's *Gospel of Signs*, in *Perspective* 11, 1970, 334-336).

215. *Ibid.*, p. 37: "it is questionable whether Nicol has not extended himself beyond his method when he claims to isolate the signs material by detecting Synoptic-like forms but then includes as source material those Johannine accounts in which the form is not clearly evident or is present only by means of the critic's reconstruction to it (e.g., chapter 11)".

216. *Ibid.*, p. 37.

217. *John, the Maverick Gospel*, Atlanta, GA, 1976 (²1993), p. 13: "The tradition reached our evangelist in a number of forms. There may have been some written materials which the evangelist incorporated into his Gospel. More than likely this included a document concerned primarily with the signs of Jesus, and included narratives of the seven wondrous signs of Jesus" (cp., e.g., pp. 70, 72; ²1993, pp. 83, 85). In *John's Story of Jesus*, Philadelphia, PA, 1984, in which the "narrative plot line of the Gospel of John" is described, Kysar does not mention the signs source.

218. *Community and Gospel: Vectors in Fourth Gospel Criticism*, in *Interpr* 31 (1977) 355-366; he discusses the publications of the three or four previous years under the following categories: (1) the origin and nature of the Johannine Community (pp. 355-357); (2) traditions of the Johannine community (pp. 357-360); (3) the theology of the Fourth Gospel and his school (pp. 360-362); (4) the situation of the community (pp. 362-364); (5) special concerns of the Fourth Evangelist and his community (pp. 364-365). For the signs source he refers to Fortna and the positive reactions of Freed and Hunt, O'Rourke, D.M. Smith, and R. Schnackenburg (cf. p. 359 nn. 13-14), with the following consideration: "Fortna's redaction critical studies cannot *substantiate* his source theory, but they certainly do present a persuasive implementation of it. The ability of a source theory to produce a convincing and rational view of the Evangelist's redactional work is a powerful argument in favor of the theory" (p. 359). See also *The Gospel of John in Current Research*, in *RelStR* 9 (1983) 314-323, p. 315: "Sources and Tradition in the Gospel of John"; *The Fourth Gospel: A Report on Recent Research*, in *ANRW* II, 25/3, 1985, pp. 2389-2480, esp. 2398-2402: "Source Theories".

219. *John, The Gospel of*, in *ABD*, III, 1992, pp. 912-931, esp. 921a-922a: "Source Theories". See also his review of FORTNA, *Predecessor*, in *Interpr* 44 (1990) 186-187 (see below, p. 356 n. 629).

take a position, but neither does he share D.A. Carson's agnosticism[220]. He does stress that source criticism of the Fourth Gospel has not attained any harmony, and notes more particularly in 1985: "While a signs source of some kind seems to have considerable acceptance, there are still major differences. For example, did the signs source have the form of a collection of wonder stories as Becker, Nicol and Schnackenburg maintain, or did it fall roughly into the gospel genre with passion material as a part of its contents as Fortna, Teeple, and Temple would have us believe? Finally, we may simply ask if, given the formidable problems of source criticism of the FG, it is even possible to isolate with any precision the source materials? Still further debate among the source critics themselves and confirmation from others is needed before sufficient consensus is within reach"[221].

In the Introduction to his commentary (1986), Kysar places himself among the defenders of the signs source[222] and leaves open the possibility that the source may have contained other narrative materials[223]. In the commentary itself, however, he limits the source to the miracle stories (2,1-11; 4,46-54; 5,1-9; 6,1-13.16-21; 9,1-7; and 11,1-54[224]), and the conclusion (20,30-31)[225]. This source, like John's other sources[226], was probably a written document[227]. Kysar describes it as a "missionary tract

220. *RelStR* 9 (1983), p. 315. For Carson, see below, pp. 314-316.
221. *ANRW* II, 25/3, 1985, p. 2402. Cp. *ABD*, III, p. 921a, where he notes on source theories in general: "There is a considerable consensus today that the fourth evangelist employed tradition in the production of the gospel, but beyond that general agreement there is little in common among the various views proposed"; cp. p. 922a: "In general it must be concluded that the source analysis of the Fourth Gospel has been unsuccessful in delineating clear blocks of material which have been incorporated into the gospel from earlier documents. The enterprise has failed to influence scholarly treatment of the gospel in any comprehensive way". With regard to a signs source, however, he can speak of "the most widely held proposal for a literary source". He gives the following arguments: "the numbering of signs in 2:11 and 4:54"; "the reference to signs in the conclusion of the gospel"; and "the delicate and complicated attitude toward the role of signs in nurturing faith found throughout the gospel" (p. 921b; cp. p. 927b). After noting the differences in the reconstruction of the signs source, he must state: "Some such thesis is embraced by a large number of Johannine scholars, but by no means has agreement been reached on such a proposal" (p. 922a).
222. *John* (AugsbCNT), Minneapolis, MN, 1986, pp. 11-15: "Sources, Composition, and Setting", esp. 12: "However, a growing number contend, as I do, that among his sources was a collection of wonder stories concerning Jesus which we will call the *signs source*". Reviews: R.J. KARRIS, in *CBQ* 49 (1987) 344-345; T.F. JOHNSON, in *Interpr* 42 (1988) 202; D.A. CARSON, in *Themelios* 14 (1989), no. 1, 57.
223. "It may have contained some narrative materials beyond the simple accounts of wonder stories (e.g., the call of the disciples, 1,35-51). If it did not contain a *passion narrative*, then surely John employed another source which did" (p. 12).
224. *Ibid.*, p. 75.
225. "John may have adopted these verses from his signs source..." (p. 309).
226. Kysar thinks that besides the signs source and the passion narrative the evangelist employed a sayings source (p. 12).
227. "Each of these sources was probably written" (p. 13). Besides these John may also have incorporated "sayings and narratives which were still preserved in *oral* form".

employed in the Johannine community to evangelize among the Jews"[228]. The source supposed that "Jesus' wonders were persuasive evidence of his divine authority and therefore evoked faith"[229], a view which the evangelist nuanced (see, e.g., 4,48)[230]. Besides this tension between the two views on "sign", Kysar also employs the numbering[231] and style[232] as arguments for the existence of the signs source. He does not attempt any reconstruction of the source, and he refers only slightly to the signs source in the commentary proper[233].

– Regarding John's relationship with the Synoptics, Kysar clearly formulates his position: "This commentary, however, will suppose that there was no direct literary dependence and that similarities between John and any one of the Synoptics is best explained by the thesis that both depended on a common early Christian tradition. That thesis allows one to explain both the similarities and the differences between John and the Synoptics" (p. 12). Cp., e.g., p. 76 (on 5,8): "The words are parallel to those used in Mark 2:11 in the healing of the paralytic. This has given some interpreters evidence of John's use of the Markan story, but more likely there was interchange between the two healings in the pre-literary period of tradition"; p. 89 (on 6,1-15): "It is clear that in this narrative John employs a tradition related to but not identical with the Synoptic traditions...."; p. 90: "There is little to show that John has used one or more of the Synoptic accounts as the basis of this story and a great deal more to suggest that an independent tradition forms that basis"; p. 93 (on 6,16-21): "John employs a tradition related to, but independent of, the Synoptic tradition".

228. *Ibid.*, p. 12.

229. *Ibid.*, p. 47 (on 2,11). Cp. p. 73: "The signs source was probably a collection of wonder stories which sought to evoke faith in Jesus by narrating his wonders" (on 4,46-54).

230. "... this verse expresses John's suspicion of 'signs faith' (cf. 2:23-24). It has been suggested that this verse stands out in the story like an editorial insertion made in a narrative drawn for the most part from the signs source, and there is good reason to embrace that view" (p. 73). Cp. p. 47 (on 2,11): "In addition to qualifying the simplistic view of *signs* in his source and often giving the narratives symbolic value, John understands the signs as ambiguous events which point to the identity of Jesus only for those who dare to comprehend them in faith (in this case the *disciples*). Only on the condition of faith do they reveal Christ's glory. The result is a circular view: signs presuppose faith, yet they produce it". See further, e.g., Kysar's commentary on 20,29 (pp. 307-308).

231. "It is the appearance of these 'numbered signs' that has given some scholars a clue to the use of a signs source behind this gospel, and reconstructions of that source sometimes claim to find seven signs in John which may have come from the source" (pp. 74-75).

232. See his commentary on 20,30-31: it comes from the signs source because of "the appearance of *enôpion*, ... a word not found elsewhere in this gospel" (p. 309).

233. Besides the references cited above, see for example p. 44 (on 2,1): "John's time references seldom have clear symbolic significance, and it appears in this case that it may well have come from his signs source"; p. 90 (on 6,2): "John probably took v. 2 from his source, which may have included mention in general of many *signs*, and he did not intend the verse to have a specific reference in his narrative"; p. 92 (on 6,14-15): "The difference lies in the distinction between the role of the signs in John's source and his own view of the matter"; p. 93 (on 6,16-21): "The narrator exhibits little interest in the transition from the feeding story to this narrative, and it may be that they were already connected in the source John used as they are in Mark (6:30-52)"; p. 150 (on 9,8): "*The man who used to sit and beg* (v. 8) may have been part of John's source, a detail which he omitted in telling the healing but adds here (cf. Mark 10:46 and parallels)".

Dwight Moody SMITH is more important for the history of the semeia hypothesis. In his earlier studies (1964, 1965) he was rather reserved[234], but, as he notes in the *Preface* to his Collected Essays (1984)[235], he became less skeptical under the influence of Fortna's *Gospel of Signs*: "That John had narrative sources or traditions other than the Synoptic Gospels is, in my opinion, scarcely in doubt"[236]. With reference to Fortna, Bammel and Becker, he had stated this already in his article *Johannine Christianity* (1975): "The distinctive character of the Johannine narrative material within the Gospel strongly suggests a principal

234. See above, pp. 53-54.
235. D.M. SMITH, *Johannine Christianity: Essays on Its Setting, Sources, and Theology*, Columbia, SC, 1984, pp. IX-XV ("Preface"), esp. X: "Under the influence of Robert Fortna (*The Gospel of Signs*) I have become less skeptical of the *semeia*-source hypothesis than I was in 1965". For Smith's review of Fortna's *Gospel of Signs*, see above, p. 165 n. 115. In *Sources*, 1964, p. 349 (= 1984, p. 58), Smith noted that the signs source "has not been accorded wide acceptance" (see above, p. 71 n. 1), and in 1980 he could still say in a footnote: "It cannot be said that there is any wide consensus in favor of such a source"; cp. *John and the Synoptics*, 1980, p. 443 n. 39 (= 1984, p. 170 n. 39). Nevertheless, he became more positive in *The Milieu*, 1976, p. 164 (= 1984, p. 63): "Since the epoch-making commentary of Rudolf Bultmann, the hypothesis of a *semeia*- (or miracle) source has gained rather wide acceptance"; cp. *The Setting*, 1976, p. 231 (= 1984, p. 80): "The *semeia*-source has gained acceptance even among those who do not agree with Bultmann that, in adopting the source, the evangelist intended to correct or set aside its theology"; *Johannine Studies*, in EPP – MACRAE (eds.), *The New Testament and Its Modern Interpreters*, 1988, pp. 271-296, esp. 274: "A large number of scholars of varying points of view have found some form of the *sèmeia* source theory (which admittedly was not Bultmann's invention) useful in coming to terms with the Johannine miracle traditions".
236. *Johannine Christianity*, 1984, p. X. According to Smith, John does not depend on the Synoptics; cf. p. XIII: "Despite my willingness to concede that John may have known one or more of the Synoptics (a possibility which I have never denied), I remain essentially unconverted to the position of Neirynck, whose efforts to understand John as essentially derivative from the Synoptics seem to me to be much more plausible in the case of certain episodes from the passion and resurrection narratives than on consideration of the gospel as a whole. Thus I cannot accept his description of me as semi-converted (cf. *NTS* 30, 1984, p. 161); I fear I remain at most among the *seboumenoi* in the weaker sense of that term!". Cf. NEIRYNCK, *John and the Synoptics: The Empty Tomb Stories*, in *NTS* 30 (1984) 161-187, p. 161 (= 1992, pp. 571-599, esp. 572). See also Neirynck's reaction in his review of Smith's *Johannine Christianity*, in *ETL* 61 (1985) 400-402, p. 401. – On the relationship between John and the Synoptics, see esp. the Smith's articles in *JBL* 82 (1963) 58-64 (= 1984, pp. 97-105); *NTS* 26 (1979-80) 425-444 (= 1984, pp. 145-172); *PerspRelSt* 8 (1981) 201-218 (= 1984, pp. 106-127); *Bib* 63 (1982) 102-113 (= 1984, pp. 128-144); *FS E.E. Ellis*, 1987, pp. 166-180; *RExp* 85 (1988) 433-444, pp. 433-435; *FS P.W. Meyer*, 1990, pp. 74-89; *FS F. Neirynck*, III, 1992, pp. 1783-1797 (see p. 1793: on Bultmann's and esp. Fortna's redaction-critical analysis), and in DENAUX (ed.), *John and the Synoptics*, 1992, pp. 147-162 (cf. NEIRYNCK, *ibid.*, pp. 12-13). See now *John among the Gospels: The Relationship in Twentieth-Century Research*, Minneapolis, MN, 1992 (cf. NEIRYNCK, in *ETL* 68, 1992, 442-444). – On Smith, see further LINDARS, *Trends*, 1990, p. 330; SLOYAN, *What Are They Saying about John?*, 1991, pp. 38-39; KOSKENNIEMI, *Apollonios von Tyana*, 1992, p. 159; NEIRYNCK, *John and the Synoptics*, 1992, pp. 12-13, 15.

source (or sources) and one independent of the Synoptics"[237]. He studied the origin and character of the Johannine narrative sources or traditions more extensively in his two 1976 articles.

In *The Milieu of the Johannine Miracles Source*[238], Smith deals with "an unresolved contradiction or antinomy in Bultmann's treatment of the provenance of the *semeia*-source"[239]. On the one hand, Bultmann thought that the semeia source was composed "among Christians converted from among followers of John the Baptist, and that it was used originally as a mission document to persuade members of that sect to follow Jesus"[240]. On the other hand, he thought that the source presented a θεῖος ἀνήρ christology, which can be regarded as principally "an artifact of Hellenistic culture"[241]. For Smith, however, the two approaches are not incompatible. (a) His survey of recent research shows that the characteristics and functions associated with the θεῖος ἀνήρ were in some sense native to Hellenistic Judaism[242] and that "the source in the form we have it is addressed to Jews who are already 'Hellenistic'"[243]. (b) The absence of apocalyptic eschatology both in the source and in the gospel is also in accordance with Hellenistic Judaism[244]. (c) The source's expectation of a miracle-working eschatological prophet, like Moses and Elijah, existed in Palestinian Judaism and Samaritanism[245],

237. *Johannine Christianity: Some Reflections on Its Character and Delineation*, in *NTS* 21 (1975-76) 222-248, p. 229 (= 1984, pp. 1-36, esp. 11). See also p. 245 (= 1984, pp. 32-33): "That the miracle tradition of John embodies a θεῖος ἀνήρ Christology and that it existed in the form of a pre-Gospel collection which has a right to be called an aretalogy may be the case. ... What cannot be doubted, however, is the independence of the Johannine miracle tradition and its importance to Johannine Christianity. Probably the original reason for its importance, and the *sine qua non* for further developments, which there doubtless were, was the fact that Jesus actually had been a miracle worker. As such, he was neither the first nor the last of his type. When the evangelist took this miracle tradition up into his gospel he may be presumed to have endorsed its validity, however much he may have qualified and interpreted it" (with on p. 245 n. 3; = 1984, p. 32 n. 72, references to Koester, M. Smith, Achtemeier, and Tiede).

238. *The Milieu of the Johannine Miracle Source: A Proposal*, in *FS W.D. Davies*, 1976, 164-180 (= 1984, pp. 62-79).

239. *Ibid.*, pp. 164-168, esp. 168 (= 1984, pp. 63-67, esp. 67).

240. See above, p. 37 n. 193.

241. See above, pp. 35-36.

242. *The Milieu*, pp. 168-172 (= 1984, pp. 67-71). He refers to Georgi ("The possiblity that the *theios aner* figure or something like it could merge within Hellenistic Judaism has been impressively argued by D. Georgi"; cf. p. 169; = 1984, p. 67) and Tiede (pp. 169-170; = 1984, p. 68). Also according to KEE, in *JBL* 92 (1973) 402-433, "the existence of miracle workers whose activity was understood as divine empowerment ... [is] really not in question" (p. 170; = 1984, p. 69). Smith finds it noteworthy that Fortna and Nicol "in view of the recent tendency to find the *theios aner* in a (Hellenistic) Jewish matrix ... think the Johannine *semeia*-collection is Jewish-Christian in origin" (p. 171; = 1984, p. 69).

243. *The Milieu*, p. 172 (= 1984, p. 71).

244. *Ibid.*, p. 173 (= 1984, pp. 71-72).

245. *Ibid.*, pp. 173-175 (= 1984, pp. 72-74), with references to MARTYN, *History and Theology*, 1968, pp. 87ff.; [2]1979, pp. 102-128; MEEKS, *The Prophet-King*, 1967, pp. 48-

and "all the gospels reflect an early Christian or Christian-Jewish discussion about Elijah and the identity of Elijah *redivivus*, whether John or Jesus"[246]. From the exegesis of Jn 1,19-21 and 10,40, Smith finds it "tempting to conjecture that there is embedded in the Fourth Gospel a cycle of miracle stories which began with an account of the Baptist in which he explicitly denied that he was the miracle-working eschatological prophet (or Elijah, which amounts to about the same thing) and ended or reached an important culmination with the statement that John did no sign or miracle. Such a miracle source would have presented Jesus as a performer of signs, and thus confirmed his prophetic role, over against John, who could not claim that role because he performed no sign"[247]. This does not imply, however, that the θεῖος ἀνήρ figure and ideology are not present in the source and that the traditional σημεῖα are free of Hellenistic influence. Finally, Smith thinks that his proposal, which is "really an elaboration of Bultmann's suggestions in the light of more recent research", is enhanced by the following consideration: "a *semeia*-source would not have convinced Jews generally that the crucified Jesus was the Messiah. For that, a passion narrative or the equivalent would have been necessary. But a collection or cycle of miracle stories without a passion narrative is entirely credible against the background of a general expectation of a miracle-working prophet, and specifically as a mission tract directed to members of the Baptist sect as a means of convincing them to shift their loyalty to Jesus. Jesus, not John, was the miracle-working prophet-messiah"[248].

In *The Setting and Shape of a Johannine Narrative Source*[249], Smith gives a different presentation of the Sitz-im-Leben and content of the source. He proposes that the Fourth Gospel is dependent on a written source for its miracles and on a written source for its passion story[250],

---

49, 162-164, 302ff.; VERMES, *Jesus the Jew*, 1973, pp. 58-99; YOUNG, in *JBL* 68 (1949) 285-299.

246. *The Milieu*, p. 175 (= 1984, p. 74).

247. *Ibid.*, pp. 176-177 (= 1984, pp. 75-76).

248. *Ibid.*, pp. 177-178 (= 1984, pp. 76-77). Note that Smith does not give a precise delimitation of the source: "a comprehensive analysis of its content at this point is not my goal" (p. 177; = 1984, p. 76). That several Johannine miracle stories have "novelistic and epiphanic characteristics" (especially the "epiphany stories", e.g. 2,1-11; 2,12-22; 6,16-21) and therefore must be considered more Hellenistic than Jewish, cannot be adduced as an objection against his description of the source's Sitz-im-Leben: "In the first place, the Johannine stories have obviously been shaped by a strong christological, epiphanic interest, probably both in their formulation and in their collection. Certainly if their original purpose was to evangelize followers of John the Baptist, this is what one would expect. Secondly, it is not clear the *Novelle* is exclusively a Hellenistic, rather than Jewish, form" (p. 179; = 1984, p. 78).

249. *The Setting and Shape of a Johannine Narrative Source*, in *JBL* 95 (1976) 231-241 (= 1984, pp. 80-93).

250. *Ibid.*, pp. 231-234, esp. 234 (= 1984, pp. 80-84, esp. 84). Smith notes that "among scholars presently working on the problem of narrative sources in John some

and from Nicol's description of the Sitz-im-Leben of the semeia traditions (a missionary tract for Jews)[251] he concludes that these two sources were combined already in a pre-Johannine stage: "If the miracle narratives were directed to a Jewish audience with the missionary purpose of proving that Jesus was the Messiah, the questions of that audience would in all probability have necessitated the early addition of a passion narrative, if it had not been a part of the narrative source in the first instance"[252]. According to Smith, Jn 12,37-40(41), with its two testimonia to explain the Jewish rejection of Jesus or the Gospel, becomes intelligible as a transition between the two sources[253].

In 1984, Smith presents this double view of the Sitz-im-Leben as two stages in the development of the pre-Johannine Gospel: first, the miracle source or cycle directed to Baptist-disciples; second, a pre-Johannine Gospel, wherein the miracle source was combined with the passion source, directed to any Jews who would hear[254].

points of agreement have emerged, which may be stated in a decreasing order of probability as follows: (1) John used a passion narrative and (2) a tradition of miracle stories independent of the Synoptics; (3) the passion narrative was in written form; (4) the miracle stories had already been written down (5) in a single (or major) source document" (pp. 233-234; = 1984, pp. 83-84).

251. *Ibid.*, p. 235 (= 1984, pp. 85-86): "Perhaps most important for our purposes, he [Nicol] proposed a *Sitz im Leben* for the miracle material within the Johannine community by showing its predominantly Jewish character and, as he thinks, the absence of Hellenistic traits. He understands its milieu to be a Christian community in conflict with the synagogue but still conducting a mission among Jews. For this mission the *semeia*-source was composed; it was a missionary tract" (see above, pp. 158-160). – Nicol agrees with "J.L. Martyn's (and Fortna's) developing understanding of the setting from which the Fourth Gospel arose" (pp. 234-235, esp. 235; = 1984, pp. 85-86, esp. 86). Fortna supposes that the Gospel of Signs "originated and served a missionary purpose in the Christian mission to the synagogue" (see above, p. 144 n. 10), and his point of view "was developed in connection with the overall theory of J.L. Martyn regarding the origin of the Fourth Gospel in the synagogue controversy over the messianic claims advanced for Jesus" (see above, pp. 149-150).

252. *Ibid.*, pp. 240-241 (= 1984, p. 93); cp. p. 236 (= 1984, pp. 87-88): "Thus, for apologetic reasons a miracle source intended to convert Jews would have required a passion narrative designed to forestall such hostile questioning"; cp. *Johannine Christianity*, 1984, p. XI ("Preface").

253. *The Setting*, pp. 238-241, esp. 240 (= 1984, pp. 90-93, esp. 92): "The character and probably the traditional function of both testimonia correspond well with the proposal that they are the keystone of a primitive transition from signs to passion. Their use fits exactly the Jewish *Sitz im Leben* which Martyn, Fortna, and Nicol ascribe to the sign material, as well as the evident interests of the Johannine passion".

254. *Johannine Christianity*, 1984, p. XI, with the following comment: "My point is that a miracle source alone might have had a decisive impact among followers of the Baptist, whose leader, apparently *not* a miracle worker (John 10:40), had also been executed. On the other hand, once a missionary effort was directed to Jews generally, presumably a later development, the problem of the crucifixion of the messianic claimant would have to be addressed. At that point the addition of, or combination with, a passion narrative would have been a logical and necessary step". – For other references to the signs source, see SMITH, *John, Gospel of*, in *IDB SV*, 1976, pp. 482-486, esp. 483; *Sign in the NT*, in

In a style-critical study, Edwin D. Freed and Russell B. Hunt (1975)[255] react very positively to Fortna's Gospel of Signs. After examination of literary evidence in four areas[256], they express the wish that "perhaps before long NT scholars will come to acknowledge the use of a signs-source by the writer(s) of John in the same way that they admit the use of Q by the writers of Matthew and Luke"[257].

1. In his 1964 article on the Johannine variations, Freed had concluded that they "are so numerous and of so many different kinds, and so apparent throughout the gospel, that they could hardly be due to different sources or to different hands"[258]. Fortna, however, ignored Johannine variation almost entirely as a criterion for determining his source[259]. But for Freed and Hunt, "variations of the type discussed by Freed, when used as a criterion for source analysis, do, indeed, tend to confirm Fortna's hypothesis of a signs-source as he has isolated it"[260].

(a) They note that only two of more than two hundred types of variations listed by Freed appear in the Gospel of Signs, i.e., the variations in names and in the introductory formulas of Old Testament quotations. Regarding the first group, they remark that these "variations in names ... cannot be used to refute Fortna's source. A priori, we might expect variations in names to appear in the source as well as in the Johannine material; after all, names provide the best opportunity for brief redaction and imitation of the source and thus give occasion for stylistic blurring"[261].

IDB SV, 1976, pp. 824-825, esp. 825; John (ProclCom), Philadelphia, PA, 1976, pp. 106 n. 37, 65-66; The Presentation of Jesus in the Fourth Gospel, in Interpr 31 (1977) 367-378, pp. 368-369, 372 (= 1984, pp. 175-189, esp. 176-177, 181); Theology and Ministry in John, in SHELP – SUNDERLAND (eds.), Biblical Basis for Ministry, 1981, pp. 186-228 (= 1984, pp. 190-222, esp. 193).

255. E.D. Freed – R.B. Hunt, Fortna's Signs-Source in John, in JBL 94 (1975) 563-579. On this article, see Botha, Jesus and the Samaritan Woman, 1991, p. 24. – In The New Testament: A Critical Introduction, Belmont, CA, 1986, p. 201, Freed is more reserved regarding the semeia-hypothesis: "It is virtually impossible to identify the sources John may have used. There is a growing consensus, however, that he used a signs source for his treatment of Jesus' miracles, but not all agree that such a source was a kind of 'mini-gospel' or 'gospel in the narrower sense.' This is the view of R.T. Fortna, for whom the source consists of material on the Baptist, the call of disciples, seven miracles, including the catch of fish in chapter 21, the story of the Samaritan woman, and the passion narrative".

256. Fortna's Signs-Source, pp. 564-570: "Variations in the Source and Johannine Material", 570-572: "Hapaxlegomena in the Source and the Johannine Material", 572-574: "The Literary Relationship between the Source and the First Epistle of John", 574-577: "The Relationship of the Source to the Synoptics".

257. Ibid., pp. 577-579 ("Summary and Conclusions"), esp. 579.

258. Freed, Variations in the Language and Thought of John, in ZNW 55 (1964) 167-197, p. 196.

259. Fortna, Gospel of Signs, pp. 2 n. 3, 13 n. 4, 249.

260. Fortna's Signs-Source, p. 564.

261. Ibid., p. 565.

Regarding the second group, they "either assume, with Fortna, that variations in the formulas used to introduce quotations from the OT belonged originally to the source or that they were inserted later by the writer of J[ohannine] M[aterial], as also perhaps is the case of variations with names"[262].

(b) Moreover, Freed and Hunt point out that "not only are the variations in the source fewer in number than those in JM, but that they are also of less significance"[263]. So the variations in the following leading ideas do not occur in the source: glorification of Christ, judgment, life and eternal life, truth, Jesus baptizing, Jesus bearing witness, seeing God, coming to Jesus, Jesus' going away, being Jesus' disciples, and the hour coming.

(c) Also, the fifteen sayings which are repeated with variations, listed by T.F. Glasson, appear only in the Johannine material[264].

(d) Finally, they state that the title "Son of Man", for John only a variation for other christological titles, does not occur in the source[265].

Thus, according to Freed and Hunt, most of the evidence based on stylistic variations supports Fortna's Gospel of Signs, but the following pericopes should be eliminated from the source: 1,6.7.19-27.32-34; 1,35-50; 4,4-42; 21,2-14[266].

2. While Fortna thought that "John is as apt to use rare words as the source"[267], the examination of the *hapaxlegomena* listed by J.H. Bernard shows that "the tendency to display a high number of rare words is ... a characteristic feature of the source"[268].

---

262. *Ibid.*, pp. 565-566, esp. 566. Cp. FREED, *Variations*, pp. 176-179. See also FORTNA, *Gospel of Signs*, p. 218.

263. *Fortna's Signs-Source*, p. 566. Cp. FREED, *Variations*, pp. 179-199 ("leading ideas"), 188 ("contrasting and conflicting ideas").

264. *Fortna's Signs-Source*, p. 566. Cf. GLASSON, in *ExpT* 57 (1945-46) 111-112: 1,30 (cf. v. 15); 3,7 (cf. v. 3); 3,28 (cf. 1,20.23); 6,36 ("the reference is uncertain"); 6,65 (cf. v. 44); 8,52 (cf. v. 51); 9,23 (cf. v. 21); 11,40 (cf. vv. 25.26); 12,34 (cf. v. 32); 13,10 (cf. v. 11); 13,25 (cf. 21,20); 14,28 ("the reference is uncertain"; it may be to 14,3); 16,14 (cf. v. 15); 16,16 (cf. v. 17); 17,12 (cf. 18,9).

265. *Fortna's Signs-Source*, pp. 566-567, esp. 567. See FREED, *The Son of Man in the Fourth Gospel*, in *JBL* 86 (1967) 402-409. – Note that the test of variations applied to Bultmann's sources gives the following result: "Bultmann's signs- and passion-sources are stylistically differentiable from the evangelist's material, but his revelation-discourse source is not" (*Fortna's Signs-Source*, p. 567).

266. *Fortna's Signs-Source*, pp. 567-570.

267. FORTNA, *Gospel of Signs*, p. 83 n. 1.

268. *Fortna's Signs-Source*, pp. 570-572, esp. 572. See Table 1 (pp. 570-572). Cf. BERNARD, *John*, I, 1928, p. LXV. Regarding Bultmann's source criticism, Freed and Hunt note: "Bultmann's signs- and passion-sources also exhibit a significantly large number of *hapax legomena*. Bultmann's revelation-discourse source, by contrast, contains the same paucity of *hapax legomena* as J[ohannine] M[aterial]" (p. 572).

3. The existing stylistic, verbal, and theological parallels between the Fourth Gospel and 1 Jn, listed by R. Law, involve the Johannine material but not the Gospel of Signs[269].

4. Finally, Freed and Hunt show that, although much of the material in the source is similar to some of the miracle stories and passion narratives in the Synoptic Gospels, the differences seem to indicate that the source arose independently of the Synoptics. Moreover, they suppose, in the line of F.L Cribbs, that Luke may have had access to the source[270].

Mark L. APPOLD in his study on the "oneness motif" (1976) states that "there is little dispute that the Johannine semeion accounts have their roots in prior tradition"[271]. Indeed, "the numbering of the initial two miracles" (contrast 2,23; 4,45), "the inappropriateness of 20:30 as a closing to the Gospel in its present form", and "the presence of an inner tension in the Gospel between the two apparently conflicting views of the meaning of miracle ... have lent credibility to the widely accepted thesis that the form of John's given material was a signs source"[272]. Appold's aim is not the "determination of the scope, structural shape, and sequence" of the source[273], but "rather to trace out representative lines of development in the interaction between the evangelist's composition and his use of traditional material"[274]. Comparing the Johannine miracles stories with those of the Synoptics, Appold gives three "distinctive characteristics of the signs"[275]: "their demonstrative character in displaying the power of Jesus"[276]; "dramatic intensification" and

---

269. *Fortna's Signs-Source*, pp. 572-574. Cf. LAW, *The Tests of Life*, ³1914 (repr. 1968), pp. 341-345. Freed and Hunt conclude again that Bultmann's revelation-discourse source is not stylistically differentiable from the Johannine material (p. 574). Cp. above, p. 199 n. 265.

270. *Fortna's Signs-Source*, pp. 574-577, esp. 577. See Table 2 (pp. 576-577), which presents the agreements of Lk with Jn against Mk and Mt. Cf. CRIBBS, in *JBL* 90 (1971) 422-450, who suggested that the best explanation of the "Lukan agreements with John against both Matthew and Mark may have been due to Luke's familiarity with some form of the developing Johannine tradition or even to his acquaintance with an early draft of the original Gospel of John" (pp. 426-427). For Freed and Hunt this early Johannine tradition is "the signs source proposed by Fortna, or something very close to it" (*Fortna's Signs-Source*, p. 575).

271. M.L. APPOLD, *The Oneness Motif in the Fourth Gospel: Motif Analysis and Exegetical Probe into the Theology of John* (WUNT, 2/1), Tübingen, 1976 (diss. Tubingen, 1973), pp. 86-102: "Chapter IV: Oneness and the Semeia", esp. 87. – Reviews: cf. VAN BELLE, no. 4745. Cf. WÖLLNER, *Zeichenglaube*, 1988, pp. 14-15.

272. *The Oneness Motif*, p. 87.

273. *Ibid.*, pp. 87-88. For "the most recent attempts at a more precise delineation" of the source, he refers to "the carefully documented and researched studies" by Fortna and Nicol (p. 87 n. 4).

274. *Ibid.*, p. 88.

275. *Ibid.*, pp. 88-94: "Distinctive Characteristics of the Signs".

276. In contrast to the Synoptics, there is no emphasis on the healing the blind and raising the dead out of compassion (so Mt 20,34; Lk 7,13) and exorcizing demons as a

heightening of the miraculous[277]; and "the character of Jesus as wonder-worker"[278]. Against J. Becker, however, he rejects the idea that "the Hellenistic θεῖος ἀνήρ concept is the proper background for understanding the role ascribed to Jesus in the semeia"[279]. According to Appold, the source represented "a high christology". It considered the σημεῖα "demonstrative and intensified acts of divine power which derive from and point back to Jesus alone and so inspire the response to faith". This christology, however, is "not wholly congruent with the evangelist's theology of oneness"[280]. Therefore, he added a series of corrective additions and critical qualifications, which result from his christology[281]. First, the evangelist accepted the demonstrative power-character of the source's miracles; they are the works of God (5,17f.). Indeed, he not only incorporated and selected the most impressive and intensified miracles, but he also affirmatively reinforced their power and epiphany character through his own additions[282]. Second, for the evangelist also the signs are a basis for belief. Neither are they "merely concessions given in the face of human weakness" (so Bultmann), nor are they "simply inner-worldly phenomena which cause misunderstanding and oppose heavenly reality" (so Schottroff). For Appold, "they appear

sign of the inauguration of God's Kingdom (so Mk 1,15-28). In the source, "Jesus does not perform miracles in order to banish sin and evil. The miracles are not pointers to the eschatological kingdom work of God, but rather they call singular attention to the power of Jesus" (p. 88; cf. pp. 88-91).

277. *Ibid.*, p. 91; cf. pp. 91-92.

278. *Ibid.*, pp. 92-94. Against Becker, Appold affirms that "statements reflecting the humanity of Jesus play no functional or constitutive role either in the source or in the evangelist's redaction. The point of the traditional semeia material rather is to emphasize the status and power of Jesus. ... So wonderful are his works because of his uniqueness that they inspire the response to faith. The character or nature of Jesus sets the stage for this basic pattern: miracle-believing acclamation" (p. 92).

279. *Ibid.*, p. 92. He gives several reasons: (a) "The Hellenistic words for miracle – θαῦμα, ἀρετή, and δύναμις – are totally absent in John. The evangelist uses only σημεῖον and his interpretative addition ἔργον" (pp. 92-93). (b) "Whereas in Hellenistic literature, as well as for that matter in the Synoptics, the response to miracle is typically some measure of astonishment and amazement, these reactions are notably absent in the Johannine semeia events. There the response instead is regularly expressed in terms of belief or in a statement using one of the traditional eschatological titles" (p. 92). (c) "Furthermore, the θεῖος ἀνήρ affinity is hardly sufficient to explain the focal concentration in John on the one who does the miracle. The impression is gained in John that the initial purpose of the semeia is to direct all attention to him who worked them. The people and the situations in which they are presented, those who are healed or who witness one of the signs of Jesus have no independent function. They appear basically as stage props whose purpose is but to set the scene for an epiphany of the demonstrative power of Jesus. Correspondingly Jesus is never pictured as dependent on any one of the characters in the scene. Instead, he himself always takes the initiative and directs the course of action" (p. 94).

280. *Ibid.*, p. 94.

281. *Ibid.*, p. 94-102: "Critical Qualifications".

282. *Ibid.*, pp. 94-95, esp. 95.

as essential works consistent with the nature of Jesus and constitutively related to the structure of faith"[283]. Third, "although signs may well be a basis for faith, the evangelist is concerned that they may also be misunderstood and result in something less than genuine faith"[284]. He adopts the source's view of "the demonstrative power character of Jesus' miracles which evoke faith in him as an eschatological messianic figure", but "he develops at the same time a pronounced critique of miracle faith by insisting that a sign must be understood in terms of its real significance; otherwise it results in something less than authentic faith or even in outright unbelief"[285]. According to Appold, this means that "the evangelist refuses to isolate the miracles. They are important both as events and also for the significance and meaning which they are meant to convey. For John this is a 'both - and' and not an 'either - or'. The signs are not merely pictures and symbols. Neither are they dispensable occurrences for the witness of the Gospel nor are they merely legitimizing inner-worldly phenomena"[286].

Thus, the evangelist does not polemicize against his source, but rather "expands on accents already contained in the material, and in radicalizing its concerns he builds a critique against its inherent weaknesses"[287]. Appold calls this process "a kind of Johannine reductionism in which everything is virtually reduced to and concentrated on the point of contact between heavenly reality and the earthly sphere"[288]. The criterion by which the evangelist both adopts and criticizes the traditional semeia material is to be found in "the christological implications of the εἰς motif"[289]. Appold describes this as follows[290]. On the one hand, the evangelist can retain emphasis on the epiphany and demonstrative character of the semeia "because this is wholly consistent with [his] high christology where Jesus' glory is manifest to the world and displayed in his works which declare that he is sent from the Father (5,36) and that the Father may be seen in him (14,9)"[291]. On the other hand, the evangelist can criticize the faith inspired by the semeia, because according to him "it is not sufficient for faith to be directed to Jesus as to a Messiah or one of the eschatological figures. For John the accents must

283. *Ibid.*, p. 95.
284. *Ibid.*, pp. 95-99, esp. 95.
285. *Ibid.*, p. 99.
286. *Ibid.*, pp. 99-100.
287. *Ibid.*, p. 100.
288. *Ibid.*, p. 100.
289. *Ibid.*, p. 102: "Thus the semeia provide us with another major area demonstrating the scope and functional importance of the oneness motif in determining the shape and direction of the Fourth Gospel. In short, the christological implications of the εἰς motif appear here as the singularly most important and determinative factor in the formative process of the evangelist's adoption and adaptation of the semeia".
290. *Ibid.*, pp. 100-102.
291. *Ibid.*, pp. 101-102.

be fundamentally changed. Faith must relate to the absolute and only manifestation of God in the Son whose origin is from above and who is one with the Father"[292].

In the same year, Anitra Bingham KOLENKOW[293] has also argued for a pre-Johannine combination of the healing miracles and the passion, which she calls "a healing-controversy gospel"[294]. For Kolenkow, the verbal and structural parallels in Mc 2,1–3,6 and Jn 5,1-18 reveal their independence[295] and "their common use of a source which intentionally unites healing and the threat of death"[296]. There is also an implicit tie between healing and passion in the Sitz-im-Leben of the healing controversy, "since death is the penalty under Jewish law for the accusations of the healing controversy"[297]. From this, Kolenkow concludes that the death implication of the healing controversy "becomes the fulcrum of the healing-controversy gospel's tie between miracle and passion". To respond to the persecution of Christian healers by Jews, such a gospel presents Jesus as "a model Christian healer dying because he affirms his heavenly healing powers and the earthly emphasis of the Son of Man"[298].

Kolenkow seems to agree with Fortna that there are "Synoptic-like, non-Johannine style characteristics occurring both in the miracle and passion material"[299], although she "would not accept as pre-Johannine all of the specific word usages which Fortna thus defines"[300]. Further, she believes that Fortna's list of characteristics "suggest[s] the likelihood of a pre-Johannine source tying together miracle and passion"[301].

292. *Ibid.*, p. 102.

293. A.B. KOLENKOW, *Healing Controversy as a Tie between Miracle and Passion Material for a Proto-Gospel*, in *JBL* 95 (1976) 623-638, pp. 630, 633, 634, 638.

294. *Ibid.*, pp. 624-626: "Parallels in the Miracle and Passion Material of Mark and John: The Argument over Their Meaning for the Study of the Gospels".

295. *Ibid.*, pp. 626-630: "Healing Controversy as a Pre-Marcan Tie between the Miracles and the Passion".

296. *Ibid.*, p. 638.

297. *Ibid.*, p. 638; cf. pp. 630-634: "The 'Sitz im Leben' for a Healing Controversy and the Healing-Controversy Gospel".

298. *Ibid.*, p. 638. On pp. 634-638, Kolenkow describes "How Mark and John move from the intent of the healing-controversy gospel", i.e., that the healer must accept the burden of legal persecution; see p. 638: "John reflects and enlarges the motif of the healing that led to the passion from the posited source; the healed person is now persecuted as well as the healer. Mark separates what has been cause and effect in the source; another set of actions and additional controversies become more immediate catalysts of Jesus' arrest. He also changes the form and content of the controversy stories to show that the Jews had no legal reason to arrest Jesus".

299. *Ibid.*, p. 623 n. 2. See above, p. 147; cf. FORTNA, *Gospel of Signs*, pp. 214-215.

300. See above, p. 148; cf. FORTNA, *Gospel of Signs*, p. 217.

301. *Healing Controversy*, p. 623 n. 2. Kolenkow notes, however: "The present author would not accept as pre-Johannine all of the specific word usages which Fortna

But Kolenkow rejects his presentation of Jn 2,18-19 as a pre-Johannine tie between the miracles and the passion[302]; she sees it as a tie between passion and resurrection[303].

In his dissertation[304], Robert Theodore HOEFERKAMP (1978) studied the inconsistencies in the passages regarding the relation between σημεῖα and believing[305]: "It is difficult not to conclude that the passages which posit a direct correlation between signs and faith contradict those passages in which Jesus criticizes, minimizes, or rejects a faith based on signs"[306]. He thinks the evangelist employed a written signs source[307] and takes "Fortna's reconstruction of the Signs Gospel as a

thus defines". The use of εὐθέως (miracles: Jn 5,9; 6,21; passion: 18,27; John otherwise uses εὐθύς like Mark) is a sign of "a non-Marcan source even in passages where Mark and John are closest" (p. 625 n. 8; cp. FORTNA, Gospel of Signs, p. 52). Moreover, one should note "the unique agreements of Acts with John in Signs-Gospel material": (a) εὐθέως and κράβαττος in Jn 5 and Acts 9,33.34 (ctr. Lk): (b) ἄξιος and the singular ὑπόδημα in Jn 1,27 and Acts 13,25 (ctr. Lk; cp. BROWN, John, I, 1966, p. 52).

302. FORTNA, Gospel of Signs, p. 146.

303. Healing Controversy, p. 623 n. 2. On Jn 2,18-19, see also pp. 632-633 n. 37: "If the passion narrative already had a resurrection account (the expected reward for the righteous who do not perform miracles when they are killed by the unrighteous; cf. Mark 6:14; 2 Macc 14:43-46), the combined story of a healing controversy and death with resurrection would thus show the resurrection of the healer and his heavenly power. John 2:18-19 (emphasized by Fortna) may have been the fulcrum of the death and resurrection account in a pre-healing-controversy gospel (a testament urging endurance and promising reward)".

304. R.T. HOEFERKAMP, The Relationship between Sēmeia and Believing in the Fourth Gospel, diss. St. Louis, The Faculty of Christ Seminary-Seminex, 1978 (dir. R.H. Smith), pp. 171-201: "Chapter V: Summary and Conclusions". – Cf. DissAbstr. 40 (1979-80), no. 4, pp. 2131-2132; SBT 10 (1980) 139-140; see also ENGELBRECHT, in Neotestamentica 22 (1988) 139-161, pp. 149-150.

305. Compare, e.g., Jn 2,23-25; 4,48 and 7,1-9 with 2,11; 4,53 and 11,45. "Chapter I. Inconsistencies in the Relationship between Sēmeia and Believing" (pp. 1-24) gives the following classification of the passages that deal with the relationship between σημεῖα and πιστεύω: (a) "Direct correlation between signs and believing" (pp. 3-5): 2,11; 4,53; 11,45 (cf. vv. 15.47b-48); 12,10-11; 20,30-31; (b) "Inferential correlation between signs and believing" (pp. 5-11): 3,2; 6,2.14; 7,31; 8,30-31; 9,16.17-18.29.30-33; 10,40.41-42; 12,13.17-19; (c) "Jesus distrusts, criticizes, or rejects a faith based on signs" (pp. 11-15): 2,23-25; 4,48; 7,5; 20,29 (cf. v. 25); (d) "Jesus seems to approve of a certain type of viewing signs" (pp. 15-17): 6,26; 11,40 (cf. vv. 15-26); (e) "Jesus rejects the demand for a validating sign" (pp. 18-20): 2,18-19; 6,26.28-29; (f) "Signs lead, in some or many instances, to unbelief" (pp. 20-22): 11,46; 12,37.

306. Ibid., pp. 22-24, esp. 22-23.

307. Ibid., p. 55. "Chapter II. Attempts to Solve the Inconsistencies in the Relationship between Sēmeia and Believing" (pp. 25-56) deals with Bultmann, Käsemann, Wilkens, and "others who argue for the existence of a sēmeia source", esp. Schnackenburg, Haenchen, Fortna, and Nicol. – He gives the current argumentation for the existence of the signs source (p. 55): (a) "the style of the short miracle stories diverges significantly from the 'normal' Johannine style"; (b) Jn 20,30-31 is the conclusion of the source; (c) the numbering of the signs in 2,11; 4,54 (ctr. 2,23; 4,45); (d) 4,48 and 6,26 "attest a different understanding of the signs from that presupposed and articulated in the basic

tentative working model" for his analysis of the tradition and redaction of signs material[308].

(a) In the signs source there was, according to Hoeferkamp, "a clear-cut view of the relationship between signs and faith: Jesus performed many spectacular signs which were proof of his divine mission, that is, his Messiahship. Certain individuals accepted this proof of his Messiahship and gave their allegiance to Jesus: that is, they 'believed' in him"[309]. The nature of Jesus' Messiahship must be understood from the source's Old Testament background (Jesus is a prophet, like Elijah and Elisha) and from its Hellenistic θεῖος ἀνήρ concept[310]. The source was written within the Johannine community or in close connection with it in order to convert Jews to faith in Jesus as the Messiah[311].

(b) Because the evangelist incorporates the signs source, with its conclusion, into his Gospel, Hoeferkamp concludes that the evangelist, too, saw a positive relationship between signs and faith[312]. But he also "modified, corrected, shaped, and expanded upon the source which he employed"[313]. He does not deny that the signs prove Jesus' Messiahship, but "under his hand the signs acquire a christological concentration ...

miracle stories of John". – Regarding (a), Hoeferkamp refers (p. 55 n. 95) to "the caveat", which he noted in criticism of Nicol's use of style criticism (p. 51 n. 81): "A good number of these characteristics are vulnerable: some on the score of frequency – Nicol does not appear to adhere to the numerical canon he has set up; some on the score of vagueness: e.g., no. 68, chiasmus; no. 69, word separation; no. 76 'remarkable repetitions are also typical in John'". – Regarding (c), Hoeferkamp remarks: "Of course, as has been frequently observed, the fact that the first and second signs obviously belonged to a written source does not necessarily imply that the remaining signs of the Gospel belonged to the same source. However, the fact that the remaining signs display the same characteristics as the first two (for example, massiveness and legitimating nature and purpose) definitely indicates that they were originally part of the same source" (p. 55).

308. *Ibid.*, p. 56. "Chapter III. Tradition in the Fourth Gospel: Signs and Believing" (pp. 57-88) studies Jn 1,45-50; 2,1-11; 4,46-54; 5,1-9; 6,1-14; 6,15-25; 9,1-18; 11,1-45; 21,1-14; 20,30-31; further the "Old Testament Background" and "The Divine Man".

309. *Ibid.*, p. 57; cp. pp. 83, 171. See also p. 173, where Hoeferkamp characterizes the source's signs as "miracles in the sense of prodigies or wonders (*dunameis, terata*)".

310. *Ibid.*, pp. 83-88.

311. *Ibid.*, pp. 196-201. Hoeferkamp notes: "These converted Jews may have remained within the synagogue until the years 80 to 90, when the Pharisaic Jews who organized at Jamnia under Gamaliel II recognized the Christian missionary activity as a threat to Judaism and introduced the *Birkat ha-Minim* ... into the liturgical prayer *Schemone Es're* in order to be able to identify and expel the Jews who confessed Jesus as the Messiah" (p. 196).

312. *Ibid.*, p. 171; cp. pp. 57, 187. "Chapter IV. Redaction in the Fourth Gospel: Signs and Believing" (pp. 89-170) analyses Jn 1,51; 2,1-11.13-22.23-25; 3,1-2; 4,46-54; 5,1-18.19-47; 6,1-15a.15b-25.26-34.35-58; 9,1-41; 11,1-53; 12,37-41; 20,24-29.30-31; 21,1-14.

313. *Ibid.*, p. 89; cp. pp. 57, 181.

they become events-with-meaning. At the risk of some misunderstanding, we might say that the signs for John are not merely *historisch*, but above all *geschichtlich*"[314]. Thus, the signs are manifestations of Jesus' δόξα, which is the glory of his death by crucifixion[315]. They are not simply miracles as in the source, but real signs that speak (cf. Bultmann) about Jesus as giver of life through his death[316]. Hoeferkamp agrees with Brown[317] that there is in the Gospel of John no dichotomy between signs and words: "The signs ... awaken and deepen faith in Jesus by leading man – in the full corporeality of his being – to see the physical materiality of the sign and through the 'transparency' of the sign to hear Jesus' word"[318]. But at the same time the signs are ambivalent: as miracles-with-meaning (Nicol) the signs do not necessarily lead to faith[319]. According to John, Jesus criticizes the faith which is based on signs and wonders (4,48), but "he does not criticize the faith that begins with the sign and goes on to perceive its meaning as it points to Jesus"[320]. The Johannine explanation for the fact that the signs are not understood (12,37) is that "the Spirit has not yet been given, because Jesus had not yet been glorified" (7,39; cf. 20,22). The community of disciples after Easter lives in "the age of the Spirit-Paraclete" and the evangelist also writes from "the viewpoint of that age and as an instrument of the Paraclete" (14,26)[321]. It is the Paraclete who unveils the meaning of Jesus' deeds and words[322].

314. *Ibid.*, pp. 171-172.
315. See Jn 1,14; 2,11; 11,4.40 (cf. p. 172).
316. *Ibid.*, pp. 173-175, esp. 175.
317. BROWN, *John*, II, 1970, p. 1050. Cf. *Relationship*, p. 175.
318. *Ibid.*, p. 176. Cp. pp. 165-166. According to Hoeferkamp, however, the signs cannot be reduced to ῥήματα; he cites (p. 176) LIGHTFOOT, *John*, 1956, p. 40: "Each sign, together with the word accompanying the sign, refers directly or by implication to the Lord's whole work: His coming, His ministry in word and deed, His death, resurrection, exaltation" and refers to (p. 176 n. 10) Erdozain's criticism of "Bultmann's declaration that the meaning of signs is exhausted by saying that they are 'life-giving words'" (ῥήματα ζωῆς). Cf. ERDOZÁIN, *La función del signo*, 1968, p. 44: "The proper and specific element of the *signs*, by which they are differentiated from mere words or mere actions, is that the 'sign' is placed in a frontier zone between both. The 'sign' brings it about that the word which has spiritual and transcendent content (I am the life) becomes in a certain sense visible, and that the material and visible deed (bodily cure) acquires an invisible and transcendent dimension. The efficacy of the *signs* consists in bringing it about that the words of life be truly words of life, words in action which with tangible realism prolong the incarnation of the Word made flesh" (translation by Hoeferkamp, p. 176 n. 10).
319. *Relationship*, p. 178; cf. pp. 179-181.
320. *Ibid.*, p. 181.
321. *Ibid.*, p. 184.
322. *Ibid.*, pp. 184-186, esp. 186. Hoeferkamp develops the restrospective understanding of the signs in critical debate with Bultmann, Käsemann and Nicol; cf. pp. 187-195: "The Bearing of the Signs-Faith Relationship on Recent Positions and Controversy".

Hoeferkamp thinks that the Fourth Gospel was composed after the break between the synagogue and the Johannine community[323]. A great deal of the Gospel's material and also its modification of the traditional signs material can be explained "against the backdrop of hostility between the Johannine community and the synagogue around the year 90"[324]. But this does not explain why John had taken "the trouble to incorporate the signs source – supposedly produced in his community – into his Gospel"[325]. According to Hoeferkamp, we must postulate "a wider readership of the Gospel than envisioned by Martyn and his followers"[326]. With reference to Brown, he accepts that the Johannine community was increased by the entrance of Jews who had Samaritan sympathies[327] and of "Gentiles" ("Greeks")[328]. It was especially for these Greeks that John has incorporated the signs source: "Those Greeks who are members of the community are to be confirmed by the signs in their faith that they too are included in the magnetic field of Jesus' crucifixion"[329].

In 1987 Lamar COPE dealt with the relation of the "Signs Gospel" to the Synoptic Gospels[330]. He thinks that "the Johannine Signs Gospel is

323. *Ibid.*, p. 197. Cf. Martyn (see above, pp. 149-150).

324. *Ibid.*, p. 198.

325. *Ibid.*, p. 198.

326. *Ibid.*, p. 199.

327. *Ibid.*, p. 199. This second group which entered the Johannine community served as "catalyst" in the break with the synagogue. Cf. R.E. BROWN, in *Interpr* 31 (1977) 379-393, pp. 389-390 (= 1981, pp. 291-306): "one may posit that the second group in Johannine history consisted of Jews of peculiar anti-Temple views who converted Samaritans and picked up some elements of Samaritan thought, including a Christology that was not centered on a Davidic Messiah".

328. *Relationship*, pp. 199-201. See Jn 7,35; 12,20-23. Cf. BROWN, *art. cit.*, pp. 391-393.

329. *Relationship*, p. 201.

330. L. COPE, *The Earliest Gospel Was the "Signs Gospel"*, in *FS W.R. Farmer*, 1987, pp. 17-24. – Also in *Faith for a New Day: The New View of the Gospel of John*, St. Louis, MO, 1986, Cope accepted that "a very early 'Signs Gospel'" was used as a basis of the Fourth Gospel" (p. 15; cf. pp. 19-25). His arguments are the counting of signs (2,11; 4,54), the conclusion (20,30-31), and the consideration "that the miracle stories in John are units in themselves, differing from the material around them in vocabulary and style, and at times awkwardly connected to their contexts or interrupted by explanatory asides (e.g., 9:4)" (pp. 15-16, esp. 16). It is, however, "uncertain what the original Signs Gospel contained or whether every Johannine miracle story derived from it" (p. 16). The outline of the Signs Gospel was simple: "Jesus was shown to be the true Messiah by a recounting of his signs or mighty deeds or wonders" (p. 20; cp. p. 21). Cope refers to Fortna who "thinks that there were probably seven signs climaxed by the greatest wonder of all, the cross and resurrection" (p. 20) and that the source was introduced by 1,19-42. The author of the source used "the community's oral tradition" (p. 24). It was an early Christian-Jewish document, written in a community which "must have been in competition with the followers of John the Baptist" (pp. 21-22, esp. 21; cf. Jn 1,19-42) and which "clearly believed that it was possible to portray Jesus to their fellow

the earliest gospel that we know anything about, and that document may have influenced the development of the Synoptic Gospels both indirectly and directly"[331]. He explicitly accepts Fortna's hypothesis that "the evangelist responsible for 1–14, 17–20 (less some, but few, redactional glosses) started from an existing Signs Gospel which listed the mighty deeds of Jesus the Messiah, culminating in the mightiest deed of all, the resurrection"[332]. For Cope, the Signs Gospel is "an early, simplistic, Palestinian/Syrian Christian document aimed at convincing Jews to believe in Jesus Messiah"[333]; he characterizes it also as "a rudimentary gospel for it linked faith with some of the story of Jesus' life"[334]. This document was "the earliest gospel" for several reasons: "One, its use of the title Messiah is unqualified and simple... Two, its naive approach to apologetics suggests an early stage of development. For it, Jesus is Messiah by virtue of his mighty deeds. That is enough that you may believe and have life... Three, the Signs Gospel lacks any clear polemic against any opponents, Christian or Jewish, except perhaps the followers of the Baptist"[335]. Cope dates it around A.D. 55-60 and thinks that it circulated within Johannine Christianity in the period A.D. 55-70[336]. Thus, this

Jews as the promised Messiah/prophet like Moses" (pp. 22-25, esp. 24, with reference to MEEKS, *The Prophet King*, 1967). But after "the wrenching disaster of the Jewish war of A.D. 66-70 and its aftermath", and especially after the expulsion of the Christians from the synagogue, the Signs Gospel was called into question and became out-of-date (pp. 26-32; cp. 16). The problem of the Johannine community, which "by A.D. 85 ... had read, recited and revered the Signs Gospel for forty years" (p. 35), can be formulated thus: "How can we continue to believe in Jesus the Messiah if it divorces us from our roots, from the Judaism which we believe this faith fulfills?" (p. 34). In this new situation, "something more than the Signs Gospel's understated simplicity and Messianic faith was needed" (p. 34). Therefore, "in the decades A.D. 80-100 another Christian writer undertook a revision of the Gospel for that new day" (p. 16; cf. pp. 33-79; see also pp. 80-91, and esp. the scheme on p. 83). "John's revision of the Signs Gospel was a success among Christians for whom it was written" and it replaced the Signs Gospel in the first decade of the second century (pp. 82-83). In the following decades, however, "the use of the Johannine Gospel itself prompted questions and controversy", so that the gospel "underwent further revision before it became widely known in the manuscripts now available" (p. 83; cf. pp. 82-90). – On Cope, see LINDARS, *Trends*, 1990, p. 331; NEIRYNCK, *Evangelica II*, 1991, p. 650.

331. *The Earliest Gospel*, p. 17.

332. *Ibid.*, p. 18. To the critics of Fortna, Cope answers: "It is, however, important to note that his critics have objected to a Signs Gospel with a Passion narrative more on the basis of preconceived ideas of the Signs Gospel's content, or for reasons connected with an overriding concept of the development of the Fourth Gospel, than on linguistic or critical grounds. No one yet has advanced sound literary criteria for denying that the Signs Gospel contained a Passion narrative" (p. 18). Moreover, we find "the same characteristic disruptions in the text" (aporias) in both miracle stories and passion narrative, and the closing of the Signs Gospel (20,30-31) "is very difficult to explain if the Signs Gospel did not contain the death/resurrection story" (p. 18).

333. *Ibid.*, p. 19.

334. *Ibid.*, p. 19.

335. *Ibid.*, p. 19.

336. *Ibid.*, p. 19: "How early such a document may have come to be is of course only a guess at best. But the late forties or fifties seems likely. For, as R.E. Brown has argued,

document preceded any of the Synoptic Gospels and it may be possible that it "was well enough known among Christian Jews even beyond Johannine circles to have provided some of the impetus for the production of the earliest Synoptic Gospel, whether Matthew or Mark"[337]. More particularly, like Freed and Hunt, he thinks that it is "highly likely that Luke had access to an edition of the Signs Gospel and that fact accounts for the presence of the strong parallels between John and Luke"[338].

In his Leipzig dissertation, Heinz WÖLLNER (1988) also takes the position that the miracles stories were part of a larger book, which contained also the passion and resurrection narratives[339]. He does not call this pre-Johannine work a "Gospel" or "source", but referring to 20,30-31 he prefers the characterization "Zeichenbuch" or "Semeia-Buch"

a Signs document must represent a second stage in the communities' lives after the initial preaching which established those Johannine churches. For the sake of our consideration, then, any date before 60 will suffice, and a date of 55-60 seems to be a cautious and credible one".

337. *Ibid.*, p. 24. Cp. p. 20, where Cope notes that when the Signs Gospel is to be considered the original Christian gospel, "the classical problem, 'Did John know the Synoptics?,' has turned on its head. Now one must ask, 'Are there any indications that the Synoptic writers were familiar with the Johannine Signs Gospel at the stage before it was revised by the Fourth Evangelist?'". – For Cope, the work of F. Neirynck is "the only significant major dissent on John's independence of the Synoptics", but he rejects Neirynck's argumentation in *NTS* 30 (1984) 161-183: "by no means compelling" (p. 21 n. 9).

338. *The Earliest Gospel*, p. 24. Cp. pp. 22-23, esp. 23. This conclusion is, according to Cope, "step by step, the natural result of the research on John and on Luke over the last forty years" (p. 24). He refers especially (pp. 22-23) to CRIBBS, in *JBL* 90 (1971) 422-450, who proposed that "Luke was influenced by some early form of the developing Johannine tradition" (p. 450). For Fortna's reaction to Cope, see below, p. 222-223 n. 415.

339. H. WÖLLNER, *Zeichenglaube und Zeichenbuch. Ein literarkritischer Beitrag zur Entstehungsgeschichte des Johannesevangeliums*, diss. Leipzig, 1988 (dir. W. Wiefel), p. 1: "Es wird aufgewiesen, dass die Semeia-Erzählungen als Teil eines umfangreicheren Buches zu begreifen sind, das auch Passions- und Osterberichte enthalten hat und in 20,30f. eine programmatische Abschlusserklärung bot. Der Evangelist hat dieses Buch übernommen, ist ihm im literarischen Aufbau gefolgt, hat es aber theologisch tiefgreifend umgestaltet". Cf. SCHMITHALS, *Johannesevangelium*, 1992, p. 191. – The dissertation contains six chapters (pp. 5-20: "Einleitung"; 20-84: "Die Semeia-Erzählungen"; 84-107: "Das Semeia-Buch und die Passionsgeschichte"; 107-114: "Das Semeia-Buch und die Ostererzählungen"; 114-143: "Zeichen und Glaube – Funktion und Herkunft der weiteren Belege"; 143-151: "Semeia-Buch und Johannesevangelium"), three excursuses (pp. 24-25: "Zum δόξα-Begriff im JohEv"; 34-36: "Zu Verwendung und Hintergrund des Prophetentitels im JohEv"; 41-43: "Zur Gestalt und Funktion des Täufers im JohEv"), and ends with a bibliography (pp. 152-155) and a summary: "Thesen zur Dissertation" (10 pages), cited here: *Thesen*. – In the Introduction, Wöllner gives a historical survey (pp. 7-19: "Grundpositionen der SQ-Forschung im Anschluss an Bultmann"), and mentions the hypotheses of Haenchen, Wilkens, Schnackenburg, Schulz, J. Becker, Fortna, Nicol, Appold, Richter.

(= SB)[340]. Without giving a precise delimitation of SB, he attributes to it the following passages[341]: (*a*) the seven σημεῖα stories[342], i.e., four Galilean (2,1ff.; 4,46ff.; 6,1ff.; 6,16ff.)[343] and three Judean (5,1ff.; 9,1ff.; 11,1ff.)[344]; (*b*) the testimony of John the Baptist (1,19ff.), the calling of the disciples (1,35ff.), Jesus and the Samaritan woman (4,5ff.)[345]; (*c*) 7,11f.31f.37.38b.40-42.45-52 as a continuation of 5,1ff.[346]; (*d*) the passion and resurrection narratives[347]; (*e*) other SB material: the summaries in 2,23-25; 4,43-45; 6,2 and in 7,31; 10,42[348]; the witness of Nicodemus in 3,1f.[349]; the demand for a sign in 2,18 and 6,30[350]; Jesus' word in 12,30 (cp. "die kommentierende Äusserungen

340. *Zeichenglaube*, p. 1: "Die Bezeichnung 'Quelle' wird dem Umfang und der Bedeutung dieses Buches nicht gerecht; sie ist zu einseitig vom Blickwinkel des Evangelisten aus gebildet. Doch kann man auch nicht von einem 'Evangelium' sprechen. Es handelt sich bei dem Semeia-Buch um eine Schrift, die unter breiten Kreisen des jüdischen Volkes missionieren wollte und dazu das Kriterium der Zeichen benutzte. Sie ist nach 70 entstanden und verrät die Frontstellung zur pharisäischen Bewegung" (cp. *Thesen*, p. 3). On the Sitz-im-Leben, see also below, p. 212.

341. *Thesen*, p. 3: "Aufgabe und Ziel dieser Arbeit ist es, durch gezielte literarkritische Analyse im Blick auf die Zeichen-Glaube-Relation den Charakter und etwaigen Umfang des SB zu bestimmen. Eine wörtliche Gesamtrekonstruktion ist dabei nicht beabsichtigt". – For a continuous narrative description of the content and structure of SB, see also pp. 143-146.

342. They are all characterized as σημεῖα in the miracle stories themselves (2,11; 4,54; 6,14), or in the discussions and dialogues following the stories (6,26; 7,31; 9,16; 11,47; cp. ἔργον in 5,20 resp. 7,21). Cf. p. 20 (cp. *Thesen*, p. 4). Proper to them is "eine detailfreudige Erzählweise, die das Drastische des Wunders hervorhebt und alle Aspekte, auch die der menschlichen Not und Hilfsbedürftigkeit ausschliesslich auf die Demonstration der Wundermacht und messianischen Herrlichkeit Jesu hin ausrichtet. Alle Semeia-Erzählungen laufen für die beteiligten Personen auf die Frage hin, wer Jesus in ihren Augen ist und wie sie zu ihm stehen" (*Thesen*, pp. 4-5). Note that Wöllner also remarks the "auffällige formale Unterschiede" between the Galilean and Judean miracle stories. The Galilean stories in 2,1ff. and 4,46ff. "enthalten eine Zählung und damit einen rahmenden Abschluss (2,11; 4,54)"; cp. 6,1ff: "Auch die Speisungserzählung ist in sich gerundet und lässt in 6,14(15) einen typischen Abschluss erkennen". The Judean miracle stories serve to introduce extended dialogues and discourses (pp. 20-21; cp. *Thesen*, p. 5). On the delimitation of the Judean miracle stories, Wöllner notes: "Die literarkritische Analyse spricht gegen eine Beschränkung des SB auf die reine Wundererzählung. Die Auferweckung des Lazarus schliesslich führt über 11,45f. zum Todesbeschluss des Synedriums (11,47ff.)" (*Thesen*, pp. 5-6).

343. *Ibid.*, pp. 22-39 (cp. *Thesen*, p. 5). The enumeration of the signs in 2,11 and 4,54 is from the tradition taken up by SB (pp. 22-26, 27-28; cp. *Thesen*, p. 5).

344. *Ibid.*, pp. 55-74 (cp. *Thesen*, pp. 5-6).

345. *Ibid.*, pp. 39-55 (cp. *Thesen*, p. 5). Wöllner qualifies 1,35ff. and 4,5ff. as "ähnliche Erzählungen", because these pericopes contain the motif of Jesus' supernatural knowledge (1,47; 4,17-18), which is the reason for belief in Jesus, and present the same christological titles as in SB (p. 39; cp. *Thesen*, p. 5).

346. *Ibid.*, pp. 75-84 (cp. *Thesen*, p. 6).

347. *Ibid.*, pp. 84-107, 107-114 (cp. *Thesen*, pp. 6-7, 7-8). See below, pp. 211-212.

348. *Ibid.*, pp. 115-122 (cp. *Thesen*, p. 8).

349. *Ibid.*, pp. 122-126 (cp. *Thesen*, p. 8).

350. *Ibid.*, pp. 126-133 (cp. *Thesen*, p. 8).

Jesu" in 9,3; 11,4.15.40)[351] and the "Rahmenverse" of SB in 1,6f. and 20,30f.[352].

Wöllner points to several indications that for him evince a pre-Johannine connection between the miracle stories and the passion and resurrection narratives in the "Zeichenbuch"[353]. First, his analysis of the Judean miracle stories reveals, on the one hand, a growing attitude of persecution and hostility from the side of the Pharisees (cf. 5,16; 9,16ff.; 11,45-46), and, on the other hand, from the side of the crowd, belief in Jesus as the Messiah on the basis of his signs and his words (7,31.40f.)[354]. Second, the council of the chief priests and the Pharisees against Jesus (11,47ff.), the anointing at Bethany (12,1ff.) and the triumphal entry into Jerusalem (12,12ff.), which all are closely connected with the raising of Lazarus, are to be considered the introduction to the passion narrative[355]. Third, some common stylistic characteristics reveal the unity of miracle stories and passion narrative[356]. Fourth, in both the miracle stories and the passion narrative similar narrative and christological characteristics are present. Wöllner mentions especially 18,1ff. and 19,35.36-37[357]. Moreover, the description of Jesus in his passion as the one who takes the initiative is in accordance with the christology of the miracle stories[358]. Fifth, verses 12,37.38a.40.42 connect the miracle stories with the

351. *Ibid.*, pp. 133-136 (cp. *Thesen*, p. 8).

352. *Ibid.*, pp. 136-143 (cp. *Thesen*, pp. 8-9).

353. *Ibid.*, pp. 84-107 (cp. *Thesen*, pp. 6-7).

354. *Ibid.*, pp. 85-88 (cp. *Thesen*, p. 6). For the evangelist, Jesus' own testimony is the ground for the hostility of the "Jews" (cf. 5,18; 7,30; 8,59; 10,31.39; 19,7).

355. *Ibid.*, pp. 88-94 (cp. *Thesen*, p. 6).

356. *Ibid.*, pp. 94-96 (cp. *Thesen*, p. 6). Wöllner refers to the occurrences of κραυγάζειν (p. 95: "Anders als die synoptischen Parallelen und anders als der Evglist verwendet die Passionsgeschichte ein selteneres Wort, das zugleich auch im SB begegnet. Das ist ein signifikantes Merkmal, das für die Einheit beider Komplexe spricht"), ὑπηρέτης (p. 96: "Die Verwendung des Begriffs ὑπηρέτης an Stellen, wo die Synoptiker ὄχλος lesen, zeigt in den Passionsgeschichte eine Tendenz an, die aus SB zu erklären ist"), and χαμαί (p. 96: "im ganzen NT nur in 9,6 und 18,6").

357. *Ibid.*, pp. 96-102 (cp. *Thesen*, p. 7). Wöllner notes on 18,1ff.: "Die Betrachtung hat gezeigt, dass diese Verhaftungsszene eine ganze Anzahl von Analogien zum SB besitzt. Jesus repräsentiert hier das gleiche Muster, nach dem das Messiasbild der Semeia-Erzählungen gestaltet ist. Es besteht demnach viel Grund zu der Annahme, dass in 18,1ff. eine alte Tradition bereits vom SB aufgegriffen und umgestaltet worden ist" (p. 98); on 19,25.36-37: "Die Zitate in Kap. 19 [19,24.28.36.38] dürften indes alle auf das SB zurückgehen. Es ist auffällig, dass im johanneischen Kreuzigungsbericht vier Erfüllungszitate verwendet sind. Mt 27,35 zitiert lediglich Ps 22,19, wobei die schlecht bezeugte Zitationsformel spätere Angleichung an Joh 19,24 ist. (Das gilt auch für Mk 15,28 in Bezug auf Lk 22,37.) Dieses gesteigerte Verlangen nach Begründungen aus der Schrift lässt sich am besten aus dem legitimatorischen Bemühen des SB begreifen, 'allen' (1,7) die Messianität Jesu zu demonstrieren. Wenn die Schrifterfüllung durch einen Augenzeugen verbürgt ist, dann kann auch der Tod Jesu unter dem ἵνα πιστεύητε verkündigt werden. Im Hinblick auf die Schrifterfüllung wird aber auch der Augenzeuge selbst zu einem Teil des Geschehens: Er ist die Einlösung des ὄψονται in 19,37" (p. 101).

358. *Ibid.*, pp. 96-102 (cp. *Thesen*, p. 7).

passion. They must be read in connection with the unbelief of the Pharisees (cf. 12,19; 12,20-36 is added by the evangelist). The Scripture
quotation in 12,40 explains their unbelief[359]. Finally, considering the
Sitz-im-Leben of the miracle stories, Wöllner thinks it impossible that
such a missionary document could exist without apologetic mention of
the passion[360].

Wöllner characterizes SB as a book that narrates Jesus' work, death
and resurrection with the purpose of converting the Jewish people to
belief in Jesus as the promised Messiah[361]. All Jesus' actions are
described as σημεῖα, and those who saw them are themselves testimonies to his Messiahship. Thus, SB is an apologetic Jesus-book for
missionary use by evangelists to provoke belief in Jesus of Nazareth as
Messiah among the Jews [362]. The Pharisees, the leading religious party
after the catastrophe of 70 A.D., are the opponents in SB and presented
as those who persecuted and condemned Jesus to death. From this,
Wöllner concludes that SB was written after 70 A.D.[363].

The evangelist has profoundly reworked SB by adding the discourses
and dialogues throughout the Gospel[364]. Christology is also central in his
presentation; in opposition to SB, however, it is no longer presented in
an apologetic way but rather in a dualistic framework, in which the
invisible God is opposed to the fatal world. In this dualistic presentation,
Jesus is described as the pre-existent Son, who is sent by his Father to
the world in order to bring salvation and life. Those who believe in
Jesus, i.e., who see the Father, have eternal life. The evangelist no longer
considers the signs proofs of Jesus' Messiahship but rather pointers in
which the one who already believes recognizes Jesus as giver and gift of
life. Therefore, the evangelist added some critical additions regarding
belief in miracles as presented in SB[365].

---

359. *Ibid.*, pp. 102-106 (cp. *Thesen*, p. 7).
360. *Ibid.*, pp. 106-107 (cp. *Thesen*, p. 7).
361. *Ibid.*, pp. 143-147 (cp. *Thesen*, p. 9).
362. *Ibid.*, p. 146: "Das SB ist mehr als eine 'Sammlung von Wundergeschichten'. Es
ist aber auch kein Evangelium, das aus den Lebensvollzügen einer Gemeinde begriffen
werden kann. Es ist ein Buch, das sich an Juden wendet, um sie für Jesus zu gewinnen"
(cp. *Thesen*, p. 9). On the apologetic character of SB, see pp. 146-147 (cp. *Thesen*, p. 9).
363. *Ibid.*, p. 147: "Es spricht für die Annahme, dass das SB nach 70 geschrieben
wurde, als die Pharisäer das alleinige Sagen hatten, als religiös-nationale Erwartungen
durch den jüdischen Krieg zusammengebrochen, aber nicht vergessen waren, als der
Ausschluss von Jesusgläubigen aus der Synagoge eine schmerzliche, aber noch unab-
geschlossene Erfahrung war" (cp. *Thesen*, pp. 9-10).
364. *Ibid.*, pp. 147-151 (cp. *Thesen*, p. 10).
365. See, e.g., 20,31b (added to the conclusion of SB) and 2,24; 4,44.48; 6,15; 7,5;
12,37f.; 20,29).

4. R.T. Fortna: "The Fourth Gospel and Its Predecessor"

In 1988, R.T. Fortna published *The Fourth Gospel and Its Predecessor*[366], in which he makes use of his earlier reconstruction of the Gospel of Signs, "altered slightly in the light of subsequent discussion", and purposes "to return to 4G [= the Fourth Gospel] from the source and to understand both documents in ways that only a redaction-critical approach can afford"[367]. In Part I, Fortna distinguishes the pre-Johannine source from Johannine redaction in each pericope, gives a comment on each and shows how the separation was achieved[368]. In three excursuses, he studies the source's genre, its relation to the Synoptics, and sketches its character[369]. In Part II, he draws upon his earlier articles to synthetically examine the major categories of biblical theology and themes peculiar to Johannine thought in both source and gospel[370].

366. R.T. FORTNA, *The Fourth Gospel and Its Predecessor: From Narrative Source to Present Gospel*, Philadelphia, PA, 1988. – Reviews: F. NEIRYNCK, in *ETL* 65 (1989) 167-170; S.S. SMALLEY, in *ExpT* 100 (1989-1990) 30; M. FITZPATRICK, in *AustBR* 38 (1990) 84-85; D.W. KUCK, in *CurrTMiss* 17 (1990) 149; R. KYSAR, in *Interpr* 44 (1990) 185-188, pp. 186-187; B. LINDARS, in *ScotJT* 43 (1990) 526-527; J. PAINTER, in *Pacifica* 3 (1990) 344-346; F.F. SEGOVIA, in *CBQ* 52 (1990) 748-749; D.M. SMITH, in *JBL* 109 (1990) 352-355; C. NIEMAND, in *SNTU/A* 15 (1990) 176-178; G.M. BURGE, in *Themelios* 17 (1991), no. 1, 27; K. MATSUNAGA, in *Bib* 72 (1991) 282-286; H. THYEN, in *TLZ* 117 (1992) 34-38. See also BEUTLER, *Méthodes et problèmes*, 1990, p. 23; LÉON-DUFOUR, *Où en est la recherche johannique?*, 1990, p. 24; SCHNELLE, *Perspektiven*, 1990, p. 59: "R. Fortnas neuestes Buch knüpft stark an sein 'Gospel of Signs' an und nimmt leider die neuere Kritik an der 'Semeia-Quelle' nicht auf"; SLOYAN, *What Are They Saying about John?*, 1991, pp. 3-32; LINDARS, *Trends*, 1990, pp. 330-331; ASHTON, *Understanding*, 1991, pp. 86-88, 161; RUCKSTUHL – DSCHULNIGG, *Stilkritik*, 1991, pp. 214-215, 249 (see also below, pp. 309-312); SCHMITHALS, *Johannesevangelium*, 1992, p. 134; SMITH, *John among the Gospels*, 1992, pp. 71-72. For a criticism of Fortna's literary theory on Jn 18,28–19,16a, see SABBE, in DENAUX (ed.), *John and the Synoptics*, 1992, pp. 341-385, esp. 380-383 (= 1991, pp. 467-513, esp. 508-512). – Fortna used the term "predecessor" for the author of the pre-Johannine source already in his articles (see above, p. 141 n. 1); see, e.g., *Signs*, p. 153; *Soteriology*, p. 38; *Christology*, pp. 492, 493, 497, 504. – Before its publication, Fortna's new book was already mentioned by BROER, *Auferstehung*, 1987, p. 77 (regarding Jn 11,1-45).

367. *Predecessor*, p. XI. This purpose corresponds to his initial intention as expressed in the Foreword of the *Gospel of Signs*, p. IX ("In a later work I hope to apply to the source reconstructed below the redaction critical method which called it forth"). See above, p. 141 n. 1.

368. *Predecessor*, pp. 13-204: "Part One: The Narrative Source and Its Johannine Redaction".

369. *Ibid.*, pp. 205-220: "Excursuses: Studies in the Pre-Johannine Source" (205-216: "The Source's Genre"; 216-218: "The Source and the Synoptic Gospels"; 218-220: "The Character of the Source").

370. *Ibid.*, pp. 221-314: "Part Two: The Theological Development from Source to Present Gospel" (225-234: " A. Messiahship"; 235-250: "B. Signs and Faith"; 251-264: "C. Salvation"; 265-283: "D. The Death of Jesus"; 284-293: "E. Eschatology and Community"; 294-314: "F. Theological Locale: Jesus' Itinerary and 'the Jews'"). – For sections B, C, and F in this part, cf. *JBL* 89 (1970) 151-166 (= *Signs*); *Interpr* 27 (1973) 31-47 (= *Soteriology*); *ATR SS* 3 (1974) 58-95 (= *Locale*); see his references in *Prede-*

1. Fortna maintains his hypothesis that the Fourth Evangelist (= 4E) made use of the Signs Gospel (= SG), in which a Signs Source (= SQ) and the Passion Source (= PQ) were already combined[371], to write his Gospel (= 4G). SG has the following contents and structure:

The Opening: (*§ 1*) 1,6-7.19-34; (*§ 2*) 1,35-49;
The Signs of Jesus:
  The Signs in Galilee: (*§ 3*) 2,1-11; (*§ 4*) 2,12a; 4,46-54; (*§ 5*) 21,1-14;
              (*§ 6*) 6,1-25;
  The Signs in Jerusalem: (*§ 7*) 11,1-45; (*§ 8*) 9,1-8; (*§ 9*) 5,2-9;
Jesus' Death and Resurrection:
  The Culmination of the Signs: (*§ 10*) 2,14-19; (*§ 11*) 11,47-53;
                                Explanation: 12,37-40;
  The Prelude to the Passion: (*§ 12*) 12,1-8; (*§ 13*) 12,12-15; (*§ 14*) 13,1-20;
  The Passion: (*§ 15*) 18,1-12; (*§ 16*) 18,13-27; (*§ 17*) 18,28–19,16a;
              (*§ 18*) 19,16b-42;
  The Resurrection: (*§ 19*) 20,1-22;
The Closing: (*§ 20*) 20,30-31a.

Fortna contends that although his reconstructed pre-Johannine text is "hypothetical and at points questionable ... its existence and even wording are the subject of some scholarly consensus"[372], and he estimates his confidence in it as nearly seven on a scale of one to ten[373]. We note the main differences from his 1970 reconstruction[374]: (1) Jn 3,23-24 is omit-

---

cessor, pp. 235 n. 19, 251 n. 46, 294 n. 127. On several occasions, Fortna also refers to his article in *NTS* 21 (1974-75) 489-504 (= *Christology*). See above, p. 141 n. 1.

371. For Fortna's abbreviations, cf. *Predecessor*, pp. XV-XVI. For the argumentation of "A Combined Signs and Passion Source", see *ibid.*, pp. 208-214 (see below, pp. 217-221).

372. *Predecessor*, p. 10. Fortna has always stressed the hypothetical character of his reconstruction; see, e.g., *Soteriology*, p. 31; *Locale*, p. 60; *Christology*, p. 489; cp. *Gospel of Signs*, p. 221; cp. p. 217 (see above, p. 148-149 n. 31).

373. *Predecessor*, p. XII, in answer to CARSON, *Current Source Criticism*, 1978, p. 419 (see below, pp. 314-316), who estimated Fortna's "overconfidence" in the reconstruction to be about nine on the scale of one to ten. For Fortna (*Predecessor*, p. 223), the Fourth Evangelist has adapted the source in an extraordinary way "so as to leave reasonably intact (and therefore recoverable) the form and even much of the wording of the source – at the same time putting it to new use". Note that for 13,1-20 (§ 14) the source cannot be reconstructed. Cf. p. 149: "the material has evidently been so greatly rewritten, perhaps more than once – as, for example, the overloading and redundancy in vv. 1-3 seem to show – that reconstruction of the source now seems too tenuous to be practicable". In *Gospel of Signs*, pp. 157-158 (cp. p. 242), however, Fortna enumerated the following verses "where fragments of the source appear to be visible": 12,27; 13,(1b).2a.4-5.12-14.18b.21b.26-27.37-38; 14,31b; 16,32b. – Other "unrecoverable matter" could be derived (a) from SQ (*Predecessor*, p. 117): the tradition concerning Nicodemus in 3,1 and Peter's confession of Jesus in 6,67-70 (for 4,4ff., see below, p. 215 n. 379); or (b) from PQ (p. 149): Jesus' predictions of Judas' betrayal (6,70-71; 13,18.21-30), of Peter's denials (13,38), and of the disciples' "scattering" (16,32b); further elements of the Gethsemane tradition: Jesus' soul troubled (11,33; 13,21a), his tears (11,35), his prayer to the Father about his "hour" (12,27b), "Arise, let us be going" (14,31b); possibly the institution of the Eucharist (6,51c.53).

374. Some divergences from *Gospel of Signs* are explicitly noted by Fortna; cf. *Predecessor*, pp. 35 n. 61 (no. 1), 108 (no. 5), 137 n. 304 (no. 7), 162 n. 366 (no. 8), 186

ted (Jn 1)[375]. (2) Only the first, the second, and "perhaps" the third sign are now numbered[376]. (3) Fortna no longer mentions the conjectural addition after 4,50c and hesitates about 4,50c itself[377]. (4) The Synoptic-like elements in 6,2a ("And a great crowd followed him") and v. 15b (*cj.* "taking leave of them") are now cancelled[378]. (5) He no longer places the *Vorlage* of 4,2-42 between 11,15 and 17 as its original setting, nor indeed does he include it anywhere in SG[379]. (6) Jn 5,14b no longer concludes the story in the source[380]. (7) Jn 12,37-40, considered to be

n. 430 (no. 9). – The reconstruction of *The Signs Gospel* in R.L. MILLER (ed.), *The Complete Gospels: Annotated Scholars Version*, Sonoma, CA, 1992, pp. 175-193, written by Fortna, is based largely on *Predecessor*. The translation is that of SV (a number of words and phrases of the source, however, required a slight change, printed in italics). I noted some minor changes. (1) Fortna now assigns to the source: 1,19 ἐξ Ἱεροσολύμων; 1,48 (verse); 2,12 καὶ ἡ μήτηρ αὐτοῦ καὶ οἱ ἀδελφοὶ αὐτοῦ; 21,5 (verse); 21,7 ἦν γὰρ γυμνός; 21,8 οἱ δὲ ἄλλοι μαθηταὶ τῷ πλοιαρίῳ ἦλθον and σύροντες τὸ δίκτυον τῶν ἰχθύων; 6,5 and 7 "Philip"; 6,17b καὶ οὔπω ἐληλύθει πρὸς αὐτοὺς ὁ Ἰησοῦς; 6,21a ἤθελον οὖν λαβεῖν αὐτὸν εἰς τὸ πλοῖον; 11,4a ἀκούσας δὲ ὁ Ἰησοῦς εἶπεν; 11,32a ἡ οὖν Μαριὰμ ὡς ἦλθεν ὅπου ἦν Ἰησοῦς; 11,45b οἱ ἐλθόντες πρὸς τὴν Μαριάμ; 5,2 Ἑβραϊστί; 12,4 ὁ μέλλων αὐτὸν παραδιδόναι; 18,5b εἱστήκει δὲ καὶ Ἰούδας ὁ παραδιδοὺς αὐτὸν μετ᾽ αὐτῶν; 19,30 τοῦ Ἰησοῦ ἡ μήτηρ αὐτοῦ καί; 20,7 (verse); 20,13b (λέγει αὐτοῖς ὅτι ἦραν τὸν κύριόν μου, καὶ οὐκ οἶδα ποῦ ἔθηκαν αὐτόν); 20,14a ταῦτα εἰποῦσα ἐστράφη εἰς τὰ ὀπίσω, καί; 20,15a[β] γύναι, τί κλαίεις; 20,15b ἐκείνη δοκοῦσα ὅτι ὁ κηπουρός ἐστιν λέγει αὐτῷ· κύριε, εἰ σὺ ἐβάστασας αὐτόν, εἰπέ μοι ποῦ ἔθηκας. (2) He drops from the source: 1,29 ἴδε ὁ ἀμνὸς τοῦ θεοῦ; 21,2 ὁ λεγόμενος Δίδυμος. (3) Finally, Fortna changed the order: 11,47-53 / 2,14-19 / 12,37-40 (instead of 2,14-19 / 11,47-53 / 12,37-40); 19,25 (verse) stays after 19,24 (and no longer after 19,30), but τοῦ Ἰησοῦ ἡ μήτηρ αὐτοῦ καί is added. On the importance of some changes, see F. NEIRYNCK, in *ETL* 69 (1993) 421-424, p. 422.

375. Fortna's argument for his change of view: "The datum that John baptized the crowds collides with SG's focus on his role solely as witness. The verses are evidently an independent unit in 4E's tradition" (*Predecessor*, p. 35 n. 61).

376. For Fortna's reconstruction of the conclusion of each miracle story with a numbering of the sign in *Gospel of Signs*, see above, p. 143 n. 5. Fortna now reads for 2,11 in the source: "This [was] the beginning of the signs Jesus did..." (Lit., "Jesus did this beginning of signs..." (*Predecessor*, p. 50, esp. n. 103). For his reconstruction in 21,14: "This was the third [sign] Jesus [did] (before his disciples)", he gives the alternative: "the third time Jesus was shown to the disciples" (p. 68). However, regarding 6,14, Fortna notes: "Possibly this deed of Jesus was identified as either the third or fourth of Jesus' signs..., especially since it is still explicitly a 'sign' (v. 14), unlike some of the other miracles that nevertheless are attributable to SG" (p. 81 n. 186, with reference to *Gospel of Signs*, p. 105).

377. In *Gospel of Signs*, pp. 48, 237, Fortna reads καὶ ἰάθη ὁ παῖς ἐκείνη τῇ ὥρᾳ after 4,50. Cf. p. 42; see esp. 46.

378. *Ibid.*, pp. 237 (6,2), 238 (6,15); cp. pp. 63-64. See esp. 56, 61-62.

379. *Ibid.*, pp. 189-195, 238-239. See now his rejection in *Predecessor*, pp. 108-109, esp. 108 n. 241: "The present smooth transition between vv. 15 and 17 (even though now interrupted by the redactional parenthesis of v. 16) lacks all indication – such as a repetition of Jesus' name in v. 17 – that an intervening passage has been removed. At the pre-Johannine level a stay of two days in Samaria, when Jesus is already en route to Lazarus, is even more anomalous than is 11:6 now at the Johannine level".

380. *Gospel of Signs*, p. 54, 240; cp. p. 53. See, *Predecessor*, p. 117 n. 259, for the rejection of H.W. Attridge's hypothesis (see above, pp. 107-108): "Attridge ... holds with

completely Johannine in *The Gospel of Signs*, is now attributed to SQ (without ἔμπροσθεν αὐτῶν)[381]. (8) Only some vestiges of the original hearing remain in 18,19-23[382]. (9) He rejects his earlier suggestions of an original setting of 3,1 at 19,39[383].

2. In the first Excursus, Fortna considers the genre of the source (a) as a gospel, (b) as a combined signs and passion source, and (c) as an Early Jewish-Christian Gospel[384].

(a) He treats each part (SQ and PQ) separately. On the basis of both its form and content he states that "SQ was one of the first Christian Gospels to be written, purer, simpler, and thus almost certainly earlier than Mark"[385]. On the other hand, he thinks that PQ is not fundamen-

Bultmann that the whole of 5:2-16 derives from a pre-Johannine source, citing what he takes to be parallels in the Synoptics of healings that contain a scene of controversy with the authorities over Jesus' words and deeds; but in fact in none of the alleged parallels is the controversial detail (here, that it was the sabbath) introduced only after the healing takes place. Attridge goes on convincingly to connect parts of chap. 7 to the Johannine material beginning at 5:9b, but this only means that they belong to the same Johannine stage of these two obviously complex chapters".

381. Cf. *Predecessor*, pp. 128-139 (see also pp. 210, 215, 243, 268). Fortna (see p. 137 n. 304) changed his view on 12,37-40 (cf. *Gospel of Signs*, esp. p. 199; cp. *Signs*, p. 159) under influence of SMITH, *The Setting*, 1976 (= 1984). See above, pp. 196-197, and below, p. 219 nn. 397-398.

382. Cf. *Predecessor*, p. 162, with reference in n. 366 to his earlier article, *Jesus and Peter at the High Priest's House: A Test Case for the Question of the Relation between Mark's and John's Gospels*, in *NTS* 24 (1977-78) 371-383, p. 380: "In the exchange between the High Priest and Jesus (xviii.19-23) I am no longer inclined to attribute even tentatively most of the present text to the source. I now see the scene as primarily a Johannine creation, so that the source is not so easily reconstructed" (ctr. *Gospel of Signs*, pp. 117-122, 242). Cf. NEIRYNCK, *John and the Synoptics*, 1992, pp. 4 n. 10, 47.

383. *Predecessor*, p. 186 n. 430: "It seems to me likely that 4E drew the tradition about Nicodemus from his or her narrative source, but not necessarily that a part of 3:1 once appeared at this point in the source" (ctr. *Gospel of Signs*, pp. 132-134, 244).

384. *Predecessor*, pp. 205-216.

385. *Ibid.*, p. 206. Fortna gives the following description of the form: "As Bultmann already saw..., the Signs Source was an articulated narrative, from its opening introductory narratives onward. Similarly, it had an unusually explicit conclusion (20:30-31a), in which it refers to itself as a book (*biblion*) and comes formally to an end. Further, most of the individual stories, and very likely all, lead each to the next, in a carefully conceived geographic order for Jesus' performing of the signs, a minimal but unusually logical itinerary. In its relatively brief way, then, SQ by itself is comparable to the flow of the later Gospels, and indeed, compared to Mark at least, moves forward in a more controlled and consistent story line and has a tighter and more evident structure" (p. 205). SQ is also to be considered Gospel because it "announces the good news of Jesus the Messiah" (cf. 1,34.41.49; 20,30-31) (p. 206). For a comparison of SQ with Q, see pp. 206-207. – Note that Fortna designates "SQ alone, without passion narrative, as Gospel and therefore a Gospel" (p. 207); regarding the title of his earlier study, *Gospel of Signs*, he remarks: "I have come to realize that the evangelic character of SQ does not depend on the question of an attached passion narrative" (p. 207 n. 490, with reference to his article *Christology*, p. 501; see below, p. 220 n. 405).

tally a Gospel, for it "has the function of apologetic – not proclaiming but justifying, not good news but argumentation"[386]. However, by including the resurrection, "even PQ, separate from SQ, becomes in the end a kind of Gospel" (cf. 20,18)[387]. Thus, each part of SG was in some sense already Gospel and a Gospel[388].

(b) More explicitly than in his previous monograph[389], and now supported by D.M. Smith[390], Fortna tries to demonstrate that SQ and PQ were combined by the pre-Johannine author, and not at the Johannine level[391]. He gives four reasons.

386. *Predecessor*, p. 207. On the question "how could Jesus, if he was the Messiah, have died in the shocking and unacceptable way that he did?", see below, p. 233.

387. *Ibid.*, p. 207. According to Fortna, "the resurrection story was very likely not originally part of the passion tradition" (p. 207 n. 491).

388. *Ibid.*, p. 207: "It follows, then, that when SQ and PQ were combined, the sum would be still more both Gospel and a Gospel than each of them individually".

389. In *Gospel of Signs*, he mentioned particularly the stylistic overlaps between SQ and PQ (see his introduction to the analysis of the passion and resurrection stories, esp. p. 113): "The integrity of the source uncovered here with SQ will be an important issue of the tests we shall apply in pt. IV" (see above, pp. 145-148; cf. pp. 201-218: "Part Four: Stylistic Tests of the Source's Purity and Integrity"). Fortna (*Predecessor*, p. 208 n. 493) rejects the supposition that he started with the idea to reconstruct a combined Signs Gospel; in fact: "I stumbled upon the evidence, at first sight only telltale, that the two sources had been redactionally combined prior to the Johannine stage".

390. Fortna, *Predecessor*, p. 107 n. 492, notes that the combination of SQ and PQ in one source, "was one of the major objections, widely made, to TGOS [= *Gospel of Signs*]". But he now draws support from Smith, who in *Christianity*, 1975, "began to consider the hypothesis of a combined Gospel of signs and passion" and finally in *Setting*, 1976 "has moved to a clear assertion of the likelihood that signs and passion were combined prior to 4G" (*Predecessor*, pp. 207-208, n. 492). On Smith, see above, pp. 194-197.

391. *Predecessor*, pp. 208-214. – In his article *Christology*, pp. 498-500, Fortna treated the question of a combined signs and passion source "in a preliminary way". There also he mentioned first "the more obvious evidence of pre-Johannine stylistic consistency between signs and passion" (p. 499 n. 2; see also below, p. 218 n. 392). In addition, he gave five other considerations (pp. 499-500): (1) The use of the divine-man typology gives the author of the source "the possibility of adding to the aretalogical record of his impressive deeds an account also of his death" (p. 499). Fortna refers to TIEDE, *The Charismatic Figure*, 1972, pp. 491-492 (see above, p. 222). In *Predecessor*, p. 212 n. 514, Fortna no longer holds this position (see below, pp. 221-222). (2) The christological view of Jesus' death and resurrection in PQ (Jesus is "the one who dies according to OT prophecy" and his resurrection is his "own sign, a supreme act of self-presentation"; cf. 2,19) is "remarkably compatible with the christology of the signs stories – and notably different from John's own view" (p. 499). (3) The theme of belief on the disciples' part started from the beginning of SQ (1,35-50; 2,11). Thereafter, the disciples have no prominence, although the source ends "with the expectation that the signs done *enôpion tôn mathêtôn* will elicit faith in the later reader" (20,30-31). According to Fortna, "the anomaly is removed if the source contained a passion narrative, for with the resurrection our attention is directed again to the disciples, and the narrative ends on the note of their joy in perceiving Jesus' greatest sign (xx.20)" (p. 499). (4) "A *signs* source requires an apologetic of the crucifixion: how is Jesus still Messiah?". For Fortna,

A first indication is "the handful of *stylistic overlaps* between PQ and SQ"[392]. Fortna agrees with some critics who argue that these are meager[393]; nevertheless there are two kinds of evidence that "the same editorial hand appears to have reworked, and to that degree stylistically integrated, the two once-separate sources or bodies of tradition – and to have done so prior to the work of 4E"[394]. These are: (1) style elements characteristic of pre-Johannine material and found in both SQ and PQ; these represent in most cases Semitisms and are reminiscent of biblical language[395]; (2) some very common Synoptic-like elements which appear in SG (both SQ and PQ), but are found rarely in the Fourth Gospel[396].

"the apologetic of the cross is but an extension of the missionary purpose of the work as a whole" (p. 500). (5) Finally, "SG has a geographical unity". The signs "provide Jesus with a straightforward and logical itinerary, *culminating in Jerusalem*. There seems no reason for the author to have created an order out of independent, or at the most loosely collected, pericopes except in order to tell the story in some sense as it happened – that is, not for historical accuracy's sake but so as to lead up to the undeniable fact of Jesus' death in Jerusalem. Otherwise the signs done there might better have been omitted" (p. 500).

392. *Predecessor*, pp. 208-210, esp. 208. Cp. *Christology*, p. 499 n. 2 (see above, p. 217 [-218] n. 391).

393. *Predecessor*, p. 208. See esp. the criticism of J.M. Robinson (see above, pp. 172-174). For Fortna's interim answer to Robinson, see *Christology*, p. 499 n. 2: "I hope to give a more exhaustive presentation of the evidence in another place, but in the meantime I would maintain that some of the data I pointed to, while possibly 'meagre' in an absolute sense, are nevertheless hardly negligible, given the relative brevity of the source, and are just as telling as the stylistic data that show the signs to be integral among themselves". Fortna's style-critical argumentation in *Predecessor*, pp. 208-210, however, remains "meagre"; cf. HENGEL, *The Johannine Question*, 1989, p. 203 n. 72: "Fortna's new study ... is totally unsatisfactory... His own investigation of style ... is more than scanty" (GT: 1993, p. 241 n. 119).

394. *Predecessor*, p. 208. Note that for Fortna, "It appears that quite possibly the author of SQ is responsible for this stylistic overlap with PQ, since the style characteristics are usually more frequent in the signs than in the passion material, even though the latter is half again as long. That author has, then, adapted the preexisting passion tradition and only lightly retouched it when combining the two sources" (p. 210).

395. *Ibid.*, p. 208: "While not always peculiar to the source within the NT, yet they appear relatively rarely in the Synoptics and are largely or wholly absent from the rest of SG". The characteristics of this category are (pp. 208-209): (1) ἦν δέ: (a) as the opening of an explanatory parenthesis, and (b) ἦν δέ [τις] as introductory phrase, always without a predicate or participle; (2) various uses of ἐκ: 45c. Noun + ἐκ ("made of"); 45d. εἰς (δύο) ἐκ; 45b. Noun + ἐκ ("from among"); see above, p. 146; (3) ὡς with numeral; (4) οὖν after a command; (5) ὄνομα αὐτῷ; (6) Singular verb with double subject (often αὐτὸς καί). See above, p. 148. – Further in this category, Fortna notes "the interest of circumstantial detail of time and place and situation, a gratuitously 'factual' preoccupation (whether accurate or not)" (p. 209). He gives the following instances: (a) in SQ: 2,6 (λίθιναι ὑδρίαι ἕξ ..., χωροῦσαι ἀνὰ μετρητὰς δύο ἢ τρεῖς); 4,52 (ἐχθὲς ὥραν ἑβδόμην); 21,8 (ὡς ἀπὸ πηχῶν διακοσίων); 6,7 (διακοσίων δηναρίων ἄρτοι); 4,5-6 (5 εἰς πόλιν τῆς Σαμαρείας λεγομένην Συχὰρ... 6 ἦν δὲ ἐκεῖ πηγὴ τοῦ Ἰακώβ); (b) in PQ: 18,10 (Μάλχος); 18,15 (γνωστὸς τῷ ἀρχιερεῖ); 19,13 (Λιθόστρωτον, ... Γαββαθά); 19,20 (Ἑβραϊστί, Ῥωμαϊστί, Ἑλληνιστί); 19,39 (ὡς λίτρας ἑκατόν).

396. The caracteristics of this category are (pp. 209-210): (1) ἕκαστος instead of the Johannine πᾶς; (2) εὐθέως instead of the Johannine εὐθύς; (3) Adverbial πρῶτον

Second, Jn 12,37-40, which Fortna now ascribes to SG[397], is to be considered the *pre-Johannine link* between two kinds of material (SQ and PQ), of which the evangelist appears to be unaware[398].

Third, the *plot* or story-line is "still more telling in favor of the pre-Johannine combining of signs and passion"[399]. Fortna asserts that in the present gospel the discontinuity of signs and passion is due only to the separate origin of SQ and PQ[400]. For him the passion tradition would have to be incorporated into the miracle-working source, for "the contradiction between a self-revealing Messiah and the well-known fact that Jesus had suffered, and in fact had died an ignominious death, would be felt and found intolerable"[401]. To that contradiction the passion tradition in itself already contained the answer: it is apologetic and explains that according to the Scriptures the Messiah would suffer and die, "just as Jesus' Messiahship was demonstrated in SQ on the basis of underlying Old Testament expectations and prototypes"[402]. Further, "the resurrec-

instead of the uniquely Johannine equivalent τὸ πρῶτον; (4) σύν for the very frequent Johannine use of μετά; (5) πρωΐ(α) instead of the Johannine τῇ ἐπαύριον. See above, p. 147. – In his response to Ruckstuhl's critique that the 1970 reconstruction of the Gospel of Signs has a "pale face" (see below, pp. 302-307), Fortna concedes that his conclusions at that time "were in some ways hasty" (*Predecessor*, p. 210 n. 509). But, the fact that "Ruckstuhl diminishes the percentage of Johannine characteristics absent in the source ... only means that they are not to be used in asking the question of the distinctiveness of the source's style; in other words, that Ruckstuhl's original list of fifty characteristics must be reduced to twenty-six". According to Fortna, "the proportion of characteristics not found in the source remains significant, especially when we consider the likelihood that the Evangelist, perhaps unwittingly, will have imitated pre-Johannine style (e.g., the Semitic 'believe in,' with preposition instead of dative) or borrowed a usage in the source and elaborated it (e.g., taking the rare form *helkuein* ['draw'] and giving it metaphoric meaning; or the so-called partitive *ek* ['one of ...', 'a woman of ...,' 'officers of ...'] and making it into the distinctively Johannine phrase 'some [many, none] of ...'". He also notes that "the Evangelist's reuse of pre-Johannine material will have occasioned the insertion, again probably unconsciously, of typically Johannine particles (e.g., historical οὖν). This stylistic blurring is to be expected" (p. 210 n. 509). On Fortna's special attention to the particle οὖν, see NEIRYNCK, in *ETL* 65 (1989) 167-170, p. 169. – Further, Fortna remarks that "Ruckstuhl himself admits that the Gospel 'contains source material ... [which has not] been integrated into the world of Johannine thought and terminology' [*Einheit*, p. 141]. That it also has not 'kept the unmistakable signs of an independent pre-Johannine existence' is disproved by the distinctive style" (*Predecessor*, p. 210 n. 509).

397. See above, p. 216 n. 381.

398. *Predecessor*, p. 210.

399. *Ibid.*, pp. 210-213, esp. 210.

400. *Ibid.*, p. 211. In the present Gospel "there is a preparation for the shocking fact that the magisterial Jesus of the signs will be subjected to arrest and execution" (p. 211). See, e.g., the portrayal of the interrogation of the Baptist, the scattered references to Jesus' coming hour (from 2,4), and the repeated attempt to put Jesus to death (from 5,18).

401. *Ibid.*, p. 211; cp. *Christology*, p. 499 (see above, pp. 217-218 n. 391: argument 4).

402. *Predecessor*, pp. 211-212. Although Fortna considers the possibility that "one could imagine the pre-Johannine author of SQ to have penned it [PQ]", he maintains that "the tradition was available already to our author", "because the pre-Markan passion account demands the same genesis" (p. 211 n. 510).

tion not only helps to resolve the problem of the cross", but "becomes
– consistent with the signs tradition now prefixed to the passion story –
Jesus' chief sign, for he raises himself in accord with the promise he had
given" (2,18-19)[403]. Moreover, "SQ's original ending (20:30-31a) can
easily move to the end of the resurrection story" (Jesus' chief sign) to
become the closing of the combined SQ and PQ[404]. So, for Fortna, "the
only way to characterize the combined source's genre is to call it ... a
Gospel of signs. It is a Gospel of *signs*, since an account of Jesus' miracles, and especially his resurrection, remains the most obvious and explicit
function of the book. ... It is also a *Gospel* of signs in that by the signs the
good news of Jesus' Messiahship and his final overcoming of death is proclaimed; it is thus, in technical language, a thoroughly kerygmatic work"[405].

Fourth and finally, the strongest evidence is the fundamental *theological unity* in both SQ and PQ[406]. For SQ, "the theological theme in the
signs is a simple christology, the fact that Jesus is the Messiah"[407]. This
is also true, although less obviously, for PQ, "for Jesus' death is not
recounted for its own sake, and certainly not 'soteriologically' (as being
a redemption or any kind of salvation), but once again christologically,

403. *Ibid.*, p. 212; cp. *Christology*, p. 499 (see above, pp. 217-218 n. 391: argument 2).
404. *Predecessor*, p. 212. For Fortna, "the mention of the disciples as the audience for
the signs (20:30a) also makes sense at the end of the resurrection story, where the disciples figure so clearly; at the end of the signs, in most of which, after 2,11, they do not
appear at all, their mention – although tolerable and necessary for the closing purpose –
was not so natural" (p. 212 n. 512); cp. *Christology*, p. 499 (see above, pp. 217-218 n. 391:
argument 3).
405. *Predecessor*, pp. 212-213. – In *Christology*, pp. 498-504, Fortna exhaustively
treated the problem of the "Gattung" of SG and of the present Gospel. There he defines
SG, which contains both signs and passion (see his arguments described above, pp. 217-218
n. 391), not as "passion narrative with introduction" (cf. Mk), but rather as "an aretalogy-
with-sequel" (p. 501), culminating in the resurrection, the most important σημεῖον. For
Fortna, an aretalogy is "a narrative of the miraculous deeds of a god or hero", and he
attributes to it a kerygmatic purpose; for SG this means the proclamation of Jesus as
Messiah. SG is thus a Jewish aretalogy, having a missionary purpose. In short, it is a
Gospel. Although such a work does not require a passion narrative, Fortna thinks that SG
probably included one, so that the signs become all the more kerygmatic. Compared with
Mk, SG's *Gattung* "is different and somewhat more rudimentary, than Mark's – it is not,
as for Mark, a proclamation of the death of Jesus, but of the one who was Messiah *despite*
his death. It is, in short, still strictly christological" (p. 151). – On the other hand, Jn, with
its inclusion of the discourse material (esp. the farewell discourses "which are a kind of
a massive parenthesis"; cf. p. 503), is "neither passion-narrative-with-introduction nor
aretalogy-with-sequel, but *one continuous passion narrative*, that is, a single account of
Jesus' revelatory glorification via his death and resurrection" (p. 504).
406. *Predecessor*, pp. 213-214. Cf. *Christology*, p. 499 (see above, pp. 217-218 n. 391:
argument 2).
407. *Predecessor*, p. 213. Thus the miracles in SQ have become messianic signs. Note
that Fortna (p. 213 n. 516) distinguishes between "a miracle story" and "a sign episode":
"A miracle story per se (the literary form of *novelle*) is not the same as a sign episode,
which may but does not necessarily involve the same literary form; e.g., 2:1-11, at one
point a pronouncement story. A sign involves not only a miracle but an overt christological claim". Cp. *Christology*, p. 500 n. 3.

so as to demonstrate who Jesus is, namely, the one who dies according to OT prophecy"[408]. On the other hand, the unifying theology of 4G is not christological, but rather soteriological[409].

(c) For Fortna, SG is an early Christian-Jewish Gospel[410]. It is "Christian", because "it espouses belief in Jesus as the *christos*, the Messiah"; it is also "Jewish", because "the idea of Messiah is comprehensible only within Judaism"[411]. SG was written in Greek, for "Jews in the synagogue of the author's Greek speaking city"[412]; this fact "makes it no less Jewish". It was "a missionary tract", whose purpose was "to convince the readers that because of his signs Jesus is the Jewish Messiah" (20,30-31)[413]. It can be dated "in the 40s or possibly the 50s of the first century", and is thus "the earliest Gospel known to us"[414].

Note that Fortna in *Predecessor* no longer uses the characterization "an aretalogy with sequel" (see above, p. 220 n. 405) for SG: "The analogy of the Hellenistic 'aretalogy' about a 'divine man' (an account that could include both marvelous deeds and impressive death) is not of very much use (as I once held, 'Christology,' 501); for the death of Jesus at the pre-Johannine stratum is in itself anything but impressive or noble, even from the standpoint of the final resurrection" (p. 212 n. 154).

In *Christology*, pp. 490-494, Fortna defended on the one hand that SG, which is exclusively christological, had more affinity with the Hellenistic divine man concept than the present gospel (p. 491). This is supported by form-critical considerations: "The signs of Jesus are far more purely *novelistic* in their pre-Johannine than in their Johannine form" and "the source displays a thaumaturgic interest that the evangelist nowhere develops" (p. 491). In addition, the evangelist "makes of the miraculous event only an occasion for the revelatory discourse that he attaches to it" and "attention is particularly shifted away from the deed as such ... to its *theo*logical significance, namely the Father's presence in all the Son does" (p. 491). Also the portrait of the *courageous* suffering

408. *Predecessor*, p. 213.
409. *Ibid.*, p. 214. See below, pp. 231-232.
410. *Ibid.*, pp. 214-216, esp. 214. Following Martyn (*Glimpses*, 1977; = 1978), Fortna uses "Christian-Jewish" Gospel rather than the more common "Jewish-Christian", "to remind that the earliest Christian movement took place fully within Judaism" (*Predecessor*, p. 214, n. 518).
411. *Ibid.*, p. 215. For the Jewish character of SG, Fortna refers to NICOL, *Sēmeia*, 1972, pp. 66-67 (see above, pp. 156-157).
412. *Predecessor*, p. 215. For Fortna, "there is no clear evidence of translation from an earlier Semitic"; the audience of SG was "minimally bilingual, familiar with a number of Aramaic terms (*Rabbi, Messias, Cephas, Bethesda, Siloam, Thomas*) and also 'Hebrew' equivalents for Greek terms used (*Gabbatha, Golgotha*)" (p. 215). The evangelist inserted explanations or simple translations from Semitic terms into Greek (Teacher, Christ, Peter, 'sent', Didymus [or Twin]); the pre-Johannine author goes only from Greek back to Aramaic, using ὃ λέγεται Ἑβραϊστί; the evangelist writes (μεθ)ἑρμηνεύειν or ὃ λεγόμενος; see also pp. 76-77 n. 173. See above, p. 143 n. 7.
413. *Ibid.*, p. 215; cp. p. 235.
414. *Ibid.*, pp. 215-216, esp. 216 (cp. 206 n. 487).

and undaunted facing of *death*, for Tiede a second way of authenticating the status of divine men (see above, p. 217 n. 391), is closer to SQ than to the Fourth Gospel; for the predecessor, "the death of Jesus is as much his own act as God's, and thus calls attention to him in much the same way the signs do; and in the end, it is the necessary prelude to the greatest of his signs, his own resurrection"; by contrast, "John's redaction of the passion narrative seems ... to lack interest in the extraordinary nature of Jesus' death and particularly in the resurrection as a wonder following from it" (p. 492).

On the other hand, Fortna notes that "John has *heightened* some aspects of the portrait of Jesus that can be considered appropriate to the divine man" (p. 492). So, the evangelist (1) emphasized Jesus' foreknowledge (cf. 11,4; in the source: e.g., 4,18; 5,6); (2) stressed Jesus' *sovereignty*, particularly in face of adversity (cf. 8,59; 10,39; 18,36; 11,11.30; 20,17); (3) characterized Jesus by the sage's persuasive speech, for P.J. Achtemeier a characteristic of the θεῖος ἀνήρ (*Interpr* 26, 1972, p. 187; cp. TIEDE, *The Charismatic Figure*, 1972); and (4) finally, far more than the source, the evangelist portrays Jesus in epiphanic *self-disclosure* (2,11b; 6,17b; 18,6; cf. 19,5; 20,28) (*Christology*, p. 493).

Further, Fortna notes that some characteristics of the θεῖος ἀνήρ are absent in the source as well as in the present Gospel: (1) Jesus is not presented as an *example* for other men, he is not the one to be imitated; (2) "he performed no *thauma, teras, aretè,* or *dynamis*, such as one expects from a divine man" (with reference to NICOL, *Sēmeia*, 1972, pp. 62ff.); (3) neither for the predecessor nor for the evangelist was Jesus only a perfected human being; (4) the titles employed by the source (i.e., lamb of God, the one of whom Moses and the prophets wrote, the prophet, king of Israel [or the Jews], Messiah) and adopted by John do not point to a thaumaturge. Only υἱὸς τοῦ θεοῦ, used by both predecessor and evangelist, might be taken as a kind of paraphrase for θεῖος ἀνήρ, but Fortna immediately adds: "nevertheless, because of its unmistakable connection with these other titles [it] is clearly not meant as *a son of (a) God* but rather *the* chosen one of the only true God". Also the only title John adds, i.e., Son of Man, has "a meaning altogether detached from the divine man" (p. 494).

In the second Excursus, on the source and the Synoptic Gospels, Fortna states that "the best explanation for the complicated way that Synoptic-like material appears in 4G is that it derives from a roughly common tradition, mediated to 4E by SG". This means that "the situation for 4G is closely analogous to that for Matthew and Luke, SG and Mark in this case playing similar roles. That is, both 4G and the two later Synoptics derive from an earlier written source"[415].

415. *Ibid.*, pp. 216-218, esp. 218. – On p. 217 n. 526, he mentions the "Leuven school" for the hypothesis of John's literary dependence on the Synoptics. Note especially Fortna's rejection of my interpretation of 4,48 (cf. *Predecessor*, p. 65). Following Neirynck (*ETL* 60, 1984, pp. 372-374; = 1991, pp. 684-685; cp. *Jean et les Synoptiques*, 1979, pp. 110-111; = *ETL* 53, 1977, pp. 468-469) I interpreted (*ETL* 61, 1985, 167-169) 4,48 as an integral part of the story and as Jesus' reproach of the official for having faith inferior to the centurion's (cf. Mt 8,8: ἀλλὰ μόνον εἰπὲ λόγῳ). Fortna answers: "this fits the verse no better than the suggestion that it is not a criticism" (p. 65). See also

In the third Excursus, on the character of SG, Fortna paraphrases and expands the sketch he gave earlier in *The Gospel of Signs*[416]. SG was "written" and refers to itself as "a book" (cf. 20,30-31)[417]. That it originated in a Christian-Jewish milieu is "a safe assertion"[418]. It probably has a Syrian provenance[419].

3. In Part II, Fortna describes "how the theology shifts as we move from SG to the present Gospel"[420], regarding Messiahship, Signs and Faith, Salvation, the Death of Jesus, Eschatology and Community, and Theological Locale[421]. He thinks that "the overwhelming factor" in this theological development was "the powerful creativity" of the evangelist who made "dramatic new use of an older work"[422], and he agrees with J.L. Martyn that "the expulsion of 4E's Christian community from the synagogue has occasioned many of the differences between source and extant Gospel"[423].

below, pp. 239 n. 543, 377. – For Fortna's reaction to Cope's hypothesis that SG was possibly known and used by Luke (see above, pp. 207-209), cf. *Predecessor*, pp. 323-324: "This suggestion is more radical than I had dared to be and deserves further investigation. For example, if Luke is dependent on SG, then at points at which the Lukan and pre-Johannine traditions overlap ... more rather than less of the similarity between the two Gospels would be attribuable to SG, and my suggestion that not only SG but 4E too was influenced by pre-Lukan tradition would be unnecessary".

416. See *Predecessor*, pp. 218-220, esp. 218 n. 530; cp. *Gospel of Signs*, pp. 223-225. See above, pp. 143-144.

417. *Predecessor*, p. 219; see also p. 226 n. 1: "Many ancient documents, including some within the NT, were not intended to be read but to be listened to. But that the pre-Johannine author intends a reader (whether aloud or silently to oneself) is the best interpretation of 20:31a, even with its second-person plural"; *Christology*, p. 498 n. 4: "But the clear evidence of pre-Johannine interconnections among the various pericopes suggests an authored work, and the fact that it referred to itself as a 'book' (xx.30) point even more strongly in the same direction".

418. In *Predecessor*, p. 219, Fortna gives the same arguments as in *Gospel of Signs*, pp. 223-224. See above, pp. 143 n. 8, 144 n. 9.

419. *Predecessor*, pp. 219. Cp. above, pp. 142-143. For a summary of SG's theology, Fortna (p. 220) refers to his "earlier attempt" in *Gospel of Signs*, pp. 228-234; see above, pp. 144-145.

420. *Predecessor*, pp. 223-224 ("Introduction"), esp. 223.

421. See above, p. 213 n. 370.

422. *Predecessor*, p. 224. Note that Fortna does "not attempt to reconstruct the intervening events that influence the Evangelist's redaction of the source" (p. 224).

423. *Predecessor*, p. 224. Cf. MARTYN, *History and Theology*, 1968, ²1979 (see above, pp. 149-150). For references to Martyn, see also, e.g., *Predecessor*, pp. 110 n. 242, 111 (regarding ch. 9), 169 n. 379 (regarding 18,35b), 242 n. 35 (regarding the expression "seeing and yet not believing"; see below, p. 229 n. 462), 259 n. 60 (regarding duality in John). In *Gospel of Signs*, Fortna did not yet refer to Martyn; but see his review of WILKENS, *Zeichen*, 1969, in *JBL* 89 (1970) 457-462, pp. 461-462; *Signs*, p. 159 (esp. n. 28); *Locale*, p. 94 (esp. n. 100); *Christology*, p. 494 n. 2; *Jesus and Peter*, p. 380[-381] n. 7.

Messiahship. – According to Fortna, "for SG it is sufficient to demonstrate, in every way possible, *that* Jesus was the Messiah. The Johannine Gospel, on the other hand, has provided a wealth of meaning to *what it meant to be* Messiah"[424].

(a) Throughout both signs and passion traditions "runs a simple, fundamentally christological current"[425]. SQ's central christological impact lay in Jesus' signs interpreted as demonstrations of his Messiahship[426]. There is a similar christological concentration, although distinguishable, in PQ[427]. (1) The message is apologetic: Jesus suffered and died in order to fulfill the Scripture[428]. This presupposes PQ's starting point that Jesus is the Messiah. (2) Jesus' person is also the focus in his sayings[429]. (3) The use of the title "King of Israel"[430] is "consonant with this exclusively christological preoccupation in the passion story". (4) Finally, Jesus acts, as in SQ, like the Messiah[431].

(b) The evangelist first reaffirms and defends the source's christology that Jesus was a wonder-working Messiah[432]. Second, although the evangelist takes over the predecessor's theology, he never leaves it unchanged. So, he makes it clear what Messiahship means (it is not to be taken in a political or earthly sense; cf. 6,14-15; 18,36-37), and he corrects the source's christology in two passages on the Baptist[433].

424. FORTNA, *Predecessor*, pp. 225-234, esp. 234.
425. *Ibid.*, pp. 226-228, esp. 228.
426. *Ibid.*, p. 226. – This interest appears at once, in the first two sections of the pre-Johannine book (cf. 1,20-22.34.35-49) (p. 226). All titles used in SQ, i.e., Christ, Elijah, Prophet, Son of God, Lamb of God, King of Israel, convey one theological affirmation: that Jesus is the Messiah of Jewish expectation (pp. 228-229). In the miracles themselves, most often the reader can supply any one of the christological titles used in chapter one (see, however, the explicit statement in 6,14). But "belief is the paradigmatic response" (2,11c; 4,53b), "even when it is not named" (1,35-49; 2,5; 4,50). In the use of the word σημεῖον (2,11; 4,54), "Jesus' Messiahship is taken for granted by author and reader" (2,11; 21,1.14). The same idea is underscored by Jesus' supernatural knowledge (21,4) and by his unusual power (pp. 226-227).
427. See above, p. 144 and below, p. 233. Note, however, that the soteriological dimension is simply not present in the pre-Johannine source. See below, pp. 230-231.
428. *Predecessor*, p. 227; see also below, pp. 226, 233.
429. See, e.g., Jn 2,19; 12,7; 18,5.8.
430. See Jn 12,13; 18,33.37; 19,3.19; cp. 1,49.
431. *Ibid.*, p. 228: "He functions as prophet and judge in the Temple (2:13-22), refers to God as his Father (2:16), undergoes suffering without complaint (the background for this understanding of the event in Isaiah 53 is evident), and consequently even in the midst of his execution is somehow victorious over it. Most dramatic of all, he raises himself from death, the greatest of his miracles".
432. With the exception of the title Elijah, the Gospel takes up all titles from the source; and, one, Lamb of God, is emphasized, "by making the Baptist both reiterate and expand it [1,29]" (p. 229).
433. *Ibid.*, p. 229. – (a) For the source, Jesus is "sent from God" (1,6), for John he is "sent by the Father" (3,17; ch. 17). (b) The Baptist's testimony (1,7.32) seems to be

Third, the evangelist "greatly enhances and deepens the christology taken over from SG"[434]. SQ's wonderworking Messiah becomes "the speaker of revelatory words – the discloser of divine truth – and this role overshadows the thaumaturgic and even the self-revelatory function of the signs"[435]. In the source, there was no real typology. The evangelist, however, who suppresses the Elijah-title[436], emphasizes the Moses typology[437], probably because of the Church/Synagogue argument of the evangelist's own time (5,45-46; 6,32; 9,28-29)[438]. Moreover, he introduces into the narrative material a new title, i.e., "Son of Man" (1,50-51). Further, he intensifies Jesus' lordliness, stresses Jesus' sovereignty, his supremacy, and in the Johannine use of the term δόξα, Jesus' divine status and function is fully expressed (see esp. 1,14). Finally, by prefacing the Logos hymn to the opening of SG, the evangelist transforms a purely Jewish-messianic view of Jesus into a cosmic christology[439].

Regarding the so-called docetism, Fortna has taken a position in *Christology*, pp. 494-498. He first asks: "are the miraculous deeds of Jesus consistent with his humanity or do they rather display his divinity?" (p. 495). He disagrees with Becker, who considers the source as not docetic, and, thus, describes the source's miracles as "sole self-representation, not of a god, but of a man with divine power". For Fortna, however, "the pre-Johannine Jesus' self-sufficient ability to perform miracles, together with the faith in him it invariably produces, is an expression of something close to pure divinity". Thus, the source's christology cannot be reduced to "a portrait of Jesus' humanity" (p. 495). John has heightened the source's christology: "the unreal sound of Jesus' words, his remoteness from earthly concerns, the gulf between him and 'the Jews' – in these ways he [Jesus] seems, even more than the source, an *über die Erde schreitende Gott*" (p. 495). Moreover, John's redaction of the signs, although he does nothing to heigthen the miraculous *per se*, "creates an image of Jesus detached from those around him" (cf. 2,4; 4,48; 11,1ff.) (pp. 495-496).

Second, the Baptist, not Jesus, is described by the evangelist as a man sent from God. The evangelist emphasizes the differences between the two figures (1,8.20; 3,28-29; 10,41). Moreover, he adopts the pre-Johannine hymn's assertion: the Logos, to be identified as Christ (1,17), is θεός (1,1c), and, in

---

insufficient for the evangelist: only God can bear witness to Jesus (5,31-37). (c) In 3,13, John asserts that "no one has gone up into heaven except he who [first] came down from heaven, [namely] the Son of man". Thus, the figure of Elijah must fall away, "since Elijah is the one biblical figure who is reported to have already gone up into heaven and whose return from there is to be expected". Moreover, Jesus' origin goes back to the very beginning (1,1-2) and not to the time of early Israel like Elijah (p. 230).

434. *Ibid.*, p. 231.
435. *Ibid.*, p. 231.
436. See above, p. 224 n. 432.
437. *Ibid.*, p. 232; cp. p. 230.
438. *Ibid.*, p. 232.
439. *Ibid.*, pp. 233-234.

probably his own addition, he affirms that those who believe in his name are not
of earthly origin (1,12-13; cp. 3,3ff.). This means that John, in his use of both
SG and the Logos-hymn, underscores the divinity of Jesus on earth, implicit
already in the pre-Johannine narrative. And, although Fortna finds Käsemann's
corrective to the Bultmannian incarnationalism congenial, he does not accept the
use of the term docetic for John's theology (p. 496), because this seems "simplistic". According to Fortna, it is not a semantic matter. It involves first John's
conception of "the divine Jesus' involvement in human history". Here, Fortna
refers to the "historical" ἐγένετο ἄνθρωπος in 1,6 ("John the Baptist, while
still serving as an earthly foil to the heavenly Jesus, nevertheless in the present
gospel also anchors Jesus' earthly descent in time and space"; p. 496) and to
ἰδοὺ ὁ ἄνθρωπος in 19,5. Second, the use of the term "docetic" also involves
"Jesus' susceptibility to suffering". Fortna disagrees with Käsemann, who dismisses the passion account as unimportant (see above, p. 74 n. 16): "all the themes
pervading the gospel and coming to a climax in the crucifixion – most notably,
Jesus' 'hour', his 'glorification', and the completion (telein) of his work – are
plainly Johannine insertions into the older narrative material" (p. 497). In the
source, the death of Jesus is "treated apologetically, necessary in order to fulfil
scripture, and as but the prelude to the greatest of Jesus' signs, his resurrection"
(cp. above, p. 224). Fortna agrees with Martyn (Source Criticism, 1970, p. 262;
= 1986, p. 110): "to paraphrase Käsemann's statement about [the present gospel]
and apply it to SG, the passion comes into view only at the very end, is provided
with virtually no preparation, and is overshadowed by Jesus' signs which find
their proper climax in his resurrection". And what Becker (Wunder, 1970, p. 144;
= 1980, p. 456) says of a signs source without a passion narrative, is according to
Fortna also true for the Signs Gospel: "it was moving from a historical to a
mythological epiphany-christology". Fortna concludes: "In short, while John
heightens some docetic elements in the source, on the criterion of Jesus' implication in human history it is more at the pre-Johannine than the Johannine level that
we can speak of docetism" (p. 497). See also Predecessor, p. 234 n. 18, where he
notes with reference to his article Christology, "So the question of docetism is not
a very productive one: it oversimplifies and labels, ignoring the form of these
issues with which 4E has to deal, namely, ditheism" (p. 234 n. 18).

Signs and Faith. – Fortna proceeds from the view that both SG and
the Fourth Evangelist have the same basic insight: the signs or miracles
display Jesus' Messiahship; for both they are "the vehicle for faith in
that Messiahship"[440]. While this is simply assumed by SG, the evangelist takes special interest in it, "particularly in correcting in part what the
predecessor implies, and in greatly extending the question of the genesis
and character of faith"[441].

(a) In SG the term σημεῖον is fundamental (2,11; 4,54). In the Synoptics, "a sign is demanded as legitimation, and sometimes we learn that
those seeking the sign were 'testing' Jesus, perhaps even tempting

440. *Ibid.,* p. 235.
441. *Ibid.,* p. 235.

him"[442]. Although the author of SG is aware of this legitimizing function of a sign (2,18-19)[443], he considers the signs to be "positive and authentic"; for SG, they "constitute the whole of Jesus' activity"[444]. They do not point to the Kingdom, for example, but to Jesus. A sign is not "a miracle in the literal sense – an astounding deed, a 'wonder'"[445]; instead, signs are "pure demonstrations of Jesus' Messiahship"[446]. This means for SG that seeing the signs leads directly to faith (20,31a; cp. 2,11c; 4,53b; and possibly 6,14)[447].

(b) The evangelist reaffirmed and adopted the source's understanding of the signs as valid in itself[448]. But in the Fourth Gospel issues, wholly absent from SG, are raised about the genesis and validity of belief. John indeed uses the source's word σημεῖον (more frequently in fact, but mostly in the plural and along with the largely synonymous ἔργον)[449], so that Fortna can say that "there is on the 4E's part fundamental acceptance of the source's central statement, namely, its portrayal of Jesus' work as the doing of signs"[450]. How does the Fourth Evangelist proceed? In general, Fortna states that the Fourth Gospel "does not limit itself to the predecessor's understanding of the signs; on the contrary, at this very point it considerably expands and extends the source"[451]. First, the evangelist "clarifies what is only implicit in SG, namely that the sign is not to be taken either too seriously, as something in itself, or too casually, as merely a means to an end" (4,48; cp. 20,25; 6,26)[452]. Second, for the evangelist "a sign is not merely a demonstration of Jesus' Messiahship". He does not deny the basic assertion of SG, "but seeks to

442. *Ibid.*, p. 236. On the term σημεῖον, see also *Signs*, pp. 152-155.
443. On 2,18-19, cf. *Predecessor*, p. 236; *Signs*, pp. 156-157.
444. *Predecessor*, p. 236.
445. *Ibid.*, p. 236.
446. *Ibid.*, p. 236 (with reference to RICHTER, *Semeia-Quelle*, 1974, p. 69; = 1977, p. 284); cp. *Signs*, pp. 153-154; see above, p. 144 n. 13.
447. *Predecessor*, p. 237; with reference to J.M. Robinson (*Kerygma*, 1965, p. 138; 1971, p. 55; GT: 1965, p. 323): their effect is "direct, unambiguous, nonparadoxical, causal".
448. *Predecessor*, p. 237.
449. *Ibid.*, pp. 237-238. The Fourth Evangelist uses the word σημεῖον twelve times: 2,23; 3,2; 4,48; 6,2.26.30; 7,31; 9,16; 10,41; 11,47; 12,18.37; there are five surviving pre-Johannine instances: 2,11.18; 4,54; 6,14; 20,30 (*Predecessor*, p. 237 n. 21; cp. *Signs*, p. 152 n. 3, where 6,14 is pre-Johannine). For the emphasis on the great number of signs, see 7,31; 11,47; 12,37 (*Predecessor*, p. 237 n. 22; *Signs*, p. 152 n. 4). On the term ἔργον, see below, p. 228 n. 455.
450. *Predecessor*, p. 237; *Signs*, p. 152.
451. *Predecessor*, p. 237. For Fortna (*Signs*, p. 153), "the differences ... between John's use of σημεῖον and that of his source cannot be expressed by differing translations of the term ('miracle'/'sign'). For both authors, Jesus' deeds are significant acts. The difference appears rather in the answer each of the authors gives to the two questions about the nature of signs".
452. *Predecessor*, p. 237; *Signs*, p. 153.

break out of its limitations". He conveys all that the source presumed, "but also a deeper understanding – namely, of what it means that Jesus is the Messiah – an understanding, in short, of his divine sonship"[453]. Third, the evangelist "raises the question of the true author of the signs". The source attributes the signs to Jesus' own initiative and sees them as signs of his Messiahship; the fourth evangelist avers that Jesus' miraculous power lies in his divine origin and portrays the miracles as signs and works of God[454]. Therefore, he introduces a second term, ἔργον (4,34; 14,10; cp. 5,17), and so the signs of the Messiah have become expressions of the incarnation[455].

For the author of the source, seeing the signs leads directly to faith: "these [signs] are written that you may believe that Jesus is the Christ, the Son of God" (20,31a; cp. 2,11c; 4,53b; 6,14)[456]. The Fourth Gospel does not deny the relationship between σημεῖον and πιστεύειν, but criticizes those who demand a sign in order to believe (2,13-22)[457]. Such requests are incorrect according to the evangelist (2,4; 4,48; 7,3-8), yet in each of these cases Jesus proceeds to grant the request[458]. For Fortna, the key to the Fourth Evangelist's ambiguous attitude lies in the answer to *how the sign is requested and how it will be understood*; the evangelist clarifies this in 4,48 and 6,26[459]. Fortna summarizes the evangelist's posture with respect to the signs by quoting G. Hartmann: "Properly understood as signs, they evoke genuine faith; understood as arbitrary miracles, they create hardening"[460].

In several redactional verses (2,23; 4,48; 6,26; 7,3; see also 4,45; 6,23.30; 12,40) we read of "seeing signs"[461]. By introducing this

453. *Predecessor*, p. 238; *Signs*, p. 154. For John, in fact, the signs are not signs of Jesus' authority at all but of God's (5,19) (*Predecessor*, p. 238 n. 24; *Signs*, p. 154 n. 9). See also the evangelist's addition in 2,11: καὶ ἐφανέρωσεν τὴν δόξαν αὐτοῦ.

454. *Predecessor*, p. 238; *Signs*, p. 155. – Thus the works are "part of the total activity of God in Jesus; together with Jesus' words they stem from God (14:10)" (*Predecessor*, p. 238; cp. *Signs*, p. 155). According to Fortna (*Signs*, p. 155 n. 15), the title of the article by CERFAUX puts it aptly: *Les miracles, signes messianiques de Jésus et œuvres de Dieu, selon l'Évangile de saint Jean*, in *L'attente du Messie*, 1954, pp. 131-138 (= *Recueil*, II, 1954, pp. 41-50).

455. *Predecessor*, p. 238. In *Signs*, p. 155 n. 16, Fortna refers to MOLLAT, *Le semeion johannique*, in COPPENS et al. (eds.), *Sacra Pagina*, II, 1959, pp. 209-219 (= 1979, pp. 91-101).

456. *Predecessor*, p. 239; cp. *Signs*, pp. 155-156.

457. *Predecessor*, pp. 239-240; cp. *Signs*, pp. 156-157.

458. *Predecessor*, p. 240; *Signs*, p. 157.

459. *Predecessor*, pp. 240-241; *Signs*, pp. 157-158.

460. *Predecessor*, p. 241; cp. *Signs*, p. 158. Cf. HARTMANN, in *ZNW* 55 (1964) 197-220, p. 203 n. 17.

461. *Predecessor*, p. 242. Only in 6,14, is mention made of seeing a sign, for Fortna possibly the germ of 4E's enlargement; cp. however in SG "come and see" (1,39; 4,29; 11,34). For the Johannine elaboration of seeing a sign, Fortna indicates a Mosaic background (Deut 29,2-3; cp. Deut 6,22; 7,19). Cp. also the theme of seeing the glory: 1,14; 11,40; 12,41. Cf. *Ibid.*, p. 242 n. 34.

element into the σημεῖα-stories the evangelist describes the relation between seeing and believing in six combinations[462]. The author of the source pictured belief in a single way: as belief in Jesus as the Messiah. For the Fourth Gospel, however, faith is a complex phenomenon wherein several progressive stages or levels of faith can be distinguished[463]. He dramatizes this in chapter 4 (the Samaritan woman and her fellow townsfolk and the royal official) and chapter 9 (the man born blind). Jesus leads them all, in different ways and in several steps, from a less worthy to a more adequate faith. In ch. 11, a deeper example is found in Martha, who is led by Jesus to a believing that conveys the deepest seeing (Jesus as source of life itself).

According to Fortna, the Fourth Evangelist has expressed his understanding of faith most succinctly in the redactional insertion at 2,11b: καὶ ἐφανέρωσεν τὴν δόξαν αὐτοῦ. In this way he transforms the subsequent faith of the disciples: "What had been belief merely in what the sign had shown *about* Jesus (a quite sufficient faith in the source's

---

462. *Predecessor*, pp. 241-247; *Signs*, pp. 159-163. Fortna starts with the negative combinations. (a) The first combination is *seeing and yet not believing* (*Predecessor*, pp. 242-243; *Signs*, pp. 159-160). The possibility that people would not believe in the signs is simply not recognized by the SG. The evangelist's church, however, was confronted by a changed situation and the brute fact of unbelief (cf. J.L. Martyn) (*Predecessor*, p. 242; see above, pp. 149-150). Thus, he makes the failure of the signs an important theme of his gospel, referring to unbelief already in the Prologue (1,1-10) and using the Jews throughout the Gospel as a symbol of humanity's misunderstanding and rejection of Jesus (Jn 12,37-41) (*Predecessor*, pp. 242-243. On 12,37-43, now part of SG, see above, p. 216 n. 381. In *Signs*, pp. 159-160, he assigned these verses to the evangelist). (b) For John, the combination *not seeing and therefore not believing* raises the question of the second and third generation Christian's faith: "the refusal to believe without a sign" (4,48; 6,30; 20,25) (*Predecessor*, pp. 243-244; *Signs*, pp. 160-161). – Each of these negative combinations is matched by a positive counterpart. (c) The first is *seeing and therefore believing*. For John, seeing leads to faith on condition that the faith is genuine and understands the signs as real signs. Cf. 1,(50)-51; 6,40 (cf. vv. 2 and 4); see, however, the critique in 6,26 (cp. 2,23-25; 4,48) and 6,34. Cf. *Predecessor*, pp. 244-245; *Signs*, p. 161. (d) For John, *not seeing and yet believing* is the most important combination (*Predecessor*, pp. 245-246; *Signs*, pp. 161-162.). It is founded on the distinction he makes between the "seeing" of an eyewitness and that of the reader based on the testimony of the eyewitness (19,35; cf. 4,42). Those who see the signs are presented in the gospel (as in the source) as paradigms for the readers so that reading about the signs is in some sense seeing them. The Christian of the second and third generation *cannot* see the signs and is dependent on the witness of others. This circumstance can be a hindrance to faith and it is just this consequence that John wants to forestall. For him, "belief on the basis of concrete evidence is satisfactory, but belief without seeing is commendable" (20,24-29 esp. 20,29; cf. 13,17). (e-f) John poses still another way of combining the two words – reversing their order (*Predecessor*, pp. 246-247; *Signs*, pp. 162-163). The negative combination *not believing and therefore not seeing* is dramatized in chapter 9 where the metaphoric blindness of the Pharisees is presented as the result of their unbelief. They stand in contrast to the man born blind who is described at the end as *believing and therefore seeing*, whereby spiritual "vision" is to be understood (cf. 11,40; 1,18).

463. *Predecessor*, pp. 247-250; *Signs*, pp. 163-166.

terms) becomes full commitment *to* him on the basis of self-revelation"[464]. The real significance of *semeia*-faith thus lies in "the perception of Jesus as the ultimate sign, as the one sent from heaven to make God recognizable for us"[465]. The evangelist makes this clear in his redactional addition to the conclusion of the source: the signs are not only written that people may believe in Jesus, but also καὶ ἵνα πιστεύοντες ζωὴν ἔχητε ἐν τῷ ὀνόματι αὐτοῦ (20,31b)[466]. We cannot regard the Gospel of John as a "gospel of signs" like his source; it is rather a "gospel of salvation". For the author of the source the most important sign of Jesus was his resurrection, because it showed Jesus' Messiahship more decisively than all the others. For the evangelist, however, it is in his death that Jesus was glorified and by which he gives "life" (3,14f.; 12,32)[467]. Fortna treats this in the following section.

Salvation. – Fortna studies the evangelist's development of his concept of salvation from potentially soteriological elements in the SG[468].

(a) While the source is almost exclusively christologically oriented[469], we should recognize that, for its author, to believe in Jesus' Messiahship *is* to be saved[470]. The description of Jesus' public life is therefore not only a demonstration of his Messiahship but also a portrayal of what it means for the believer that the Messiah has come, so that citations of Messianic prophecy like Lk 4,18 and Mt 11,2-6 par. Lk 7,18-23 would not have been out of place in the signs gospel[471].

---

464. *Signs*, p. 165; *Predecessor*, p. 238.

465. *Predecessor*, p. 250; *Signs*, pp. 165-166.

466. *Predecessor*, p. 250; *Signs*, p. 166.

467. *Predecessor*, p. 250; *Signs*, p. 166.

468. *Predecessor*, pp. 251-264, esp. 251; *Soteriology*, pp. 31-47, esp. 33. See also *Christology*, p. 497.

469. *Predecessor*, pp. 251-257, esp. 257; *Soteriology*, pp. 32-38, esp. 33.

470. *Predecessor*, p. 253; *Soteriology*, p. 33; see the summary of SG's theology in *Gospel of Signs*, p. 228 (see above, pp. 144-145).

471. *Predecessor*, p. 255; *Soteriology*, p. 36. – The source's first two verses (1,6-7ac), which present the Baptist as sent from God so that all might believe, are missionary in Fortna's view, and presuppose a soteriological plan, set immediately into motion in the two following pericopes. Jn 1,19-34 shows how the Baptist prepares the way for the savior, and from 1,35-49 the reader perceives in the conversion of the first disciples that a Christian is one who follows Jesus and stays with him. The author of the SG specifically selected the seven miracles to display different aspects of salvation: (1) Three miracles result in an eschatological meal with Jesus and display the overabundant bounty he bestows: wine (ch. 2), bread (ch. 6), and fish (ch. 21); (2) the two healing stories (chs. 5 and 9) suggest a soteriological interpretation; and (3) in the two most dramatic miracles (chs. 4 and 11) Jesus is virtually, if not explicitly, presented as the giver of life. Outside the miracle stories proper, we also find implicit soteriology: Jesus reveals the truth (4,17-18, cf. v. 25). In 6,18ff. he brings comfort to the disciples who make their way in difficulty and anxiety. Cf. *Predecessor*, pp. 252-255; *Soteriology*, pp. 35-36.

To the question, "Who is saved?", the author of the source would answer: "Anyone who believes in Jesus as the Messiah"[472]. From the beginning the disciples are presented as paradigms[473]. By mentioning their presence at all the miracles[474], the author suggests that salvation is meant not only for the beneficiary of the miracle, but for all disciples, that is all believers, as well. The conversion of an entire household (4,53) and of the first disciples (ch. 1) should be understood in the same sense. The author of the source gave no answer, however, to the question, "How is salvation accomplished?". The SG contains a passion narrative but the death of Jesus is not at all treated soteriologically. Rather, Jesus' passion is handled entirely apologetically, and is at most used to portray Jesus' Messiahship in light of the rubric of prophecy fulfilled[475].

(b) Fortna describes John's redaction from the perspective of subjective soteriology, i.e., what salvation means from the human standpoint[476]. An examination of the terms σῴζειν, σωτηρία, and σωτήρ does not lead far in explaining the evangelist's theological distinctiveness in regard to the meaning of salvation[477]. Instead, the evangelist uses several metaphors for salvation, such as ζωή, χάρις, ἀλήθεια, and φῶς, of which the most important is φῶς αἰώνιον[478]. Further, he elaborated

472. *Predecessor*, pp. 255-256; *Soteriology*, pp. 36-37.

473. Cf. Jn 2,2.11.12a.

474. See esp. Jn 9,2; 11,7; 6,3.5.7.8.10.12; 21,2ff.; they are, however, not mentioned in 5,2-9. Cf. *Predecessor*, p. 255 n. 51; *Soteriology*, p. 36 n. 13.

475. *Predecessor*, p. 256; *Soteriology*, pp. 37-38. On the passion, see below, pp. 233-235.

476. *Predecessor*, pp. 257-264, esp. 257; *Soteriology*, pp. 38-45, esp. 38.

477. Fortna (*Predecessor*, p. 258; *Soteriology*, p. 38) refers to FOERSTER, in *TWNT* 7 (1964), p. 998 (ET: 1971, p. 997), who argued that "the theological distinctiveness of John's Gospel does not come to expression" in the use of such words.

478. The evangelist has added this metaphor at several places. He easily did so in the concluding lines of the source (20,31b: καὶ ἵνα πιστεύοντες ζωὴν ἔχητε ἐν τῷ ὀνόματι αὐτοῦ), not unexpected since he has stressed the idea repeatedly, e.g., in 3,15.36; 5,21; 6,33.47. Fortna finds a similar addition at 1,7b (ἵνα μαρτυρήσῃ περὶ τοῦ φωτός), taken from the hymnic *Vorlage* (1,4-5) where the light is none other than the life. This means that life, eternally coexisting with the Father, is light for humans, accessible to them only because God has sent his son. – In the narratives, as well, the notion of life is occasioned and suggested already in the source and subsequently expanded by the evangelist. Thus, after 4,50.51 he declares for the third time in 4,53a that the boy lives; the encounter with the Samaritan woman leads to the discourse on living water (4,10-15, cf. 7,37-38); the miracle of the loaves to the discourse on "enduring bread", the "bread of life" (6,26-51). And if the life/death contrast lay already in rudimentary form in the source, the evangelist clearly highlighted the spiritual meaning (see chapters 4 and 11). – The evangelist's most characteristic word for salvation, then, is life. It is not a quality or a state of being to which Jesus brings humans; Jesus himself is the life (11,25, cf. 14,6); he does not bring salvation, he is salvation. – Also the phrase χάρις καὶ ἀλήθεια (1,14.17) should be considered among John's metaphors for salvation. Grace does not appear again, but truth is a prominent word for John. From the statement of the Samaritan woman that Jesus revealed the truth about her entire life John develops the portrait of

his soteriology by a number of additions to the miracle stories[479]. At Cana, the amount of wine is no longer as important as the self-revelation of Jesus (2,11b); in the miracle of the loaves, he adds ἵνα μή τι ἀπόλη-ται (6,12) which points forward to the ensuing discussion about food that perishes (6,27) and to the promise that Jesus not lose any of his own (6,37; cf. 18,9). The two healing miracles (chapters 5 and 9) are transformed into occasions for controversy between Jesus and the Jews. Thereby, the point is no longer the salvation of the healed individual but that, in spite of these happenings, many do not believe and thus reject salvation. In 4,46ff. and 11,1ff., it is no longer of central importance that two individuals are rescued from death (see the apparent resistence of Jesus in 4,48; 11,6; cf. 2,4), but the metaphor of life: Jesus is life.

According to Fortna, to the question, "Who is saved?", the source would have answered: "The Jews in the Synagogue". But for the evangelist, who is no longer concerned with the Jewish/Gentile question, "the Jews" (a theological not an ethnic term) stand outside salvation; they represent the κόσμος (cf. 12,19) and stand opposite to Jesus' ἴδιοι, i.e., the Christians, who are saved because of their belief[480]. These two realms (the world and the ἴδιοι) are not in cosmological opposition to each other, for Jesus the Savior comes to the world, to the Jews and to Judea where he finds a home (4,44). John can declare at the same time that "salvation is from the Jews" (4,22) and that Jesus is "Savior of the world" (4,42)[481]. Anyone who believes and therefore shows that he does not belong to the world is saved[482]. For Fortna, it is not sufficient to say that salvation means "*redemption* from the world" (M. Lattke[483]) or that it is a question of a certain kind of *Entweltlichung*. The Johannine Jesus does not separate his own from the world; the world is rather the object of his mission (12,47; 16,33). "But since the world finally separates itself from the believers in the face of his coming, the locus of salvation is Jesus present with his own"[484].

Jesus bringing people to salvation by his teaching. Jesus himself is the truth (14,6; 18,37). – Still another metaphor of salvation is φῶς (8,12; 9,5; 12,46; cf. 1,4-5.9). In the Johannine redaction the story of the man born blind has become a story of conversion in which spiritual sight must be understood. This idea of seeing and believing appears throughout the gospel, with perhaps the most soteriological significance at the end of the prologue: "No one has ever seen God; the only Son, who is in the bosom of the Father, he has made him known" (1,18). Cf. *Predecessor*, pp. 258-261; *Soteriology*, pp. 39-42.

479. *Predecessor*, pp. 261-262; *Soteriology*, pp. 42-43.

480. *Predecessor*, pp. 262-263; *Soteriology*, pp. 43-44.

481. *Predecessor*, p. 263; *Soteriology*, p. 44. See below, pp. 237-238.

482. Salvation does not take place in the synagogue or in the world, even though that is where the revelation has taken place. Precisely where salvation occurs is harder to say, for John never uses the concept Church as a realm over against that of the world (*Predecessor*, p. 264; *Soteriology*, p. 44. See above, p. 145.

483. Lattke, *Erlöser und Erlösung im Johannesevangelium*, 1972. Cf. *Predecessor*, p. 264; *Soteriology*, p. 44.

484. *Predecessor*, p. 264; *Soteriology*, p. 44. On the time of salvation, see below, pp. 235-236.

The Death of Jesus. – (a) According to Fortna, "the death of Jesus plays no overarching role" in SG, and certainly not in SQ[485]. He presumes that even in PQ only "the inevitable succession of one event upon another, leading to the awful end" binds the episodes into one[486]. In SG, Jesus' death is "explained away by the resurrection"[487], and so already at the outset of the passion narrative (2,19; 12,7-8)[488]. Nevertheless, there is some theological reflection on the unavoidable fact of Jesus' death. For the Predecessor, it fulfills prophecy[489]. The same motif of divine necessity is conveyed by Jesus himself as PQ portrays him[490], and, in PQ, the death of Jesus has no salvific significance: "The good news that this Gospel proclaims is first and last Jesus' Messiahship, self-evident in his signs and even discernible at his execution"[491].

(b) Fortna claims that in the present Gospel Jesus is never shown in his lowliness at all[492]. For the evangelist, Jesus is from the beginning

485. *Predecessor*, pp. 265-273, esp. 265: "In the miracle stories there is no indication, or even hint, of the death that awaits the wonderworking Messiah, and equally in their preface (the witness of the Baptist and the conversion of the first disciples) we find no suggestion, like that in the Synoptic Gospels, that he who preceded Jesus or those who follow him will suffer the same fate as he".

486. *Ibid.*, pp. 265-266, esp. 265.

487. *Ibid.*, p. 273; cp. p. 266: "At the pre-Johannine level it is preeminently the events of Easter that make the death of Jesus tolerable: the resurrection reverses the crucifixion, it explains away Jesus' incomprehensive execution". Cp. *Christology*, pp. 503-504.

488. *Ibid.*, p. 266: "Thus, ... there is no theology of the approaching end but rather an attempt to come to terms with it by denying its finality. This perhaps reflects the earliest Christian responses to the events of that problematic Friday, once it had to be addressed theologically".

489. *Ibid.*, pp. 266-267: "the cross comes to make sense as part of the plan, the drama, that God was accomplishing in the appearance of his Messiah"; and so, "specific prophecies are assembled and cited to explain what takes place at the end of Jesus' life". According to Fortna, the device of prophecy fulfillment is used in the source at least five times; see Jn 2,17 (cf. Ps 69,10); 12,37-40 (cf. Isa 53,1; 6,10); 12,15 (cf. Zech 9,9); 19,24 (cf. Ps 22,19); 19,28 (cf. Ps 22,15; "more likely" Ps 69,21); 19,36 (cf. Ps 34,20 or Ex 12,46; Num 9,12; Zech 12,10). In addition, there are two other pre-Johannine occurrences of the motif of OT fulfillment: 20,9 (without any citation) and at the very beginning of SQ (1,23: "as the prophet Isaiah said"). See *ibid.*, pp. 266-272.

490. *Ibid.*, p. 272. See, e.g., 2,19; 12,7-8; 18,4-5.11.

491. *Ibid.*, p. 273. Regarding the charge placarded on the cross (19,40), Fortna notes: "This christological affirmation, though not only the thrust of the passion account, would have afforded the otherwise anomalous combining of the signs tradition or a Signs Source in the strict sense, with the passion tradition, to produce what we call SG, a combination that I believe to have occurred at the hands of the pre-Johannine author".

492. Noted in reaction to Käsemann. Fortna agrees with Käsemann that in the Fourth Gospel there is no passion journey up to Jerusalem "as a journey which leads from lowliness to glory" (cf. KÄSEMANN, *Jesu letzter Wille*, 1966, p. 19; ET: 1968, p. 7), but this does not yet mean that the passion account is "a mere postscript which had to be included" but which the Fourth Evangelist could not "fit ... organically into his work" (p. 7). Cf. MARTYN, *Source Criticism*, 1970, p. 262 (= 1985, p. 110), who observed that

"the incarnate Son of God, and his divine glory is always in view"[493]. In the first three episodes of the Johannine portrayal of Jesus' ministry "the death of Jesus is in some way singled out and pointed toward"[494]. In 2,1-11 by the theme of the hour; in 2,13-21, by the temple saying; in 3,1-14, by the verb ὑψόω (cp. 8,28; 12,32)[495]. By the repetition of the theme ὥρα[496] and the motif ὑψόω[497], the reader of the Fourth Gospel knows that "the crowning and unifying event in Jesus' manifestation to the world will be none other than his death"[498]. So he is "prepared to understand it both as divinely ordained, in line with SG, and as a glorification, a Johannine contribution"[499]. Further, in the Fourth Gospel, opposition to Jesus exists almost from the beginning of the Gospel[500], so that the outcome of the Sanhedrin (11,53) "sounds anticlimactic and redundant"[501]. But compared with SG "we glimpse something new of the Johannine understanding of Jesus' death"[502]. Caiaphas is depicted simply as "an unwitting player in the predestined drama" and his prophecy (11,51) is meant to convey to the reader a soteriological understanding: Jesus would die "for the nation", and not only for the nation but to gather the children of God[503]. Finally, Fortna analyzes three themes which prevail in the Johannine portrayal of Jesus' passion[504]: (1) the Fourth Gospel shows Jesus presiding magisterially over his passion[505]; (2) in this line, his death is characterized as none other than revealing his glory[506]; (3) in Jesus' death his victory over evil, which centers in "the Jews", is accomplished[507]. Fortna concludes: "The Gospel ... can be seen as *one extended passion narrative*. Both protagonist and

this is true not for the Fourth Gospel, but for the pre-Johannine source: "To paraphrase Käsemann's statement ... and apply it to SG, the passion comes into view only at the very end, is provided with virtually no preparation, and is overshadowed by Jesus' signs which find their proper climax in his resurrection". And Fortna adds only: "since it comprises roughly half of the hypothetical SG the passion narrative is somewhat more than appended postscript" (*Predecessor*, p. 274 n. 93).

493. *Ibid.*, p. 274.
494. *Ibid.*, p. 276.
495. *Ibid.*, pp. 274-276.
496. Cf. Jn 2,4; 7,30; 7,6-7a; 13,1. See *Predecessor*, pp. 276-278. For Fortna, the term καιρός is even more apt than ὥρα of 2,4 and 7,30 (p. 277 n. 96).
497. For ὑψόω, cf. Jn 3,14; 8,28; 12.32.24.
498. *Ibid.*, p. 278. See also *Christology*, p. 497: "Thus in the present gospel it is no longer the resurrection as such that carries the greater weight but Jesus' glorification on the cross, by which he draws all men to himself (xii.32)" (see also pp. 503-504).
499. *Predecessor*, p. 278.
500. Cf. Jn 5,16-18; 7,1.19.25; 8,59; 10,31; 11,8; cp. 12,10.
501. *Ibid.*, p. 279. Cf. the attempt to seize Jesus in 7,30; 10,39.
502. *Ibid.*, p. 279.
503. *Ibid.*, p. 280.
504. *Ibid.*, pp. 281-282.
505. *Ibid.*, pp. 281-282. Fortna refers to 18,4.8-9.23.32.36.38; 19,11.17.28a.28b.30.
506. *Ibid.*, p. 282. Fortna refers to 18,5-6.37 (cf. v. 20).
507. *Ibid.*, p. 282.

antagonists (Jesus and 'the Jews') convey from the beginning the meaning of that Friday. The portrayal of the death of Jesus is not at all 4G's concession to tradition but stands at the heart of its message. That death shows, christologically and soteriologically, what the good news is. For the first time – and here one must think of both Paul and the three other canonical Gospels, to say nothing of the pre-Johannine Gospel – 4E shows that Friday to be Good"[508].

Eschatology and Community. – Fortna thinks that "the eschatology in SQ is sufficient explanation for the rise of the so predominantly realized eschatology of 4G and of the discourses in particular"[509].

(a) In SQ, there is a "lack of any future expectation... Beneath the surface, however, there is clear enough evidence that in fact this pre-Johannine document is based on the premise of a realized eschatology. Jesus is the Christ, the One whose earthly appearance had so long been awaited. That he can be shown working the signs of the Messiah means, obviously if still unexplicitly, that the new age has now at last appeared"[510]. In PQ, Jesus' death is recounted "to show that there is no conflict with the fact of that Messiahship"[511]. Also in SG, "the future is simply not in view". But the joyous fact that Jesus is present (1,26b) as the Christ "is sufficient" and is "eschaton enough"[512]. This means that "the pre-Johannine author only hints at the eschatological implications of Jesus' Messiahship"[513]. Finally, Fortna notes that in SG "all attention to the nature and constitution of the eschatological community is missing"[514].

(b) According to Fortna, "the evangelist's radical extension of the source's christology ... has far-reaching eschatological results. If Jesus is now not simply the long-expected Christ but the eternal Son of God come down from the Father, all of history is fundamentally affected. Jesus ... represents the inbreaking of cosmic time into the merely earthly. His very appearance brings the old age to completion (to use non-Johannine language) and brings the glorious new age which had only been imagined in the futuristic eschatologies... In his life on earth Jesus has

508. *Ibid.*, p. 283.
509. *Predecessor*, pp. 284-293, esp. 286; on the eschatology, see also *Soteriology*, pp. 44-45.
510. *Predecessor*, pp. 286-287.
511. *Ibid.*, p. 287. On the death of Jesus, see above, pp. 233-235.
512. *Ibid.*, p. 287. Fortna refers to 1,34 ("This is the Son of God"); 1,43.43.45 ("We have found the Messiah ... Elijah ... [The Prophet]"); 4,42 ("This is truly the Savior of the world"); 6,14 ("... the Prophet who is to come into the world").
513. So, e.g., the wedding feast in 2,1-11 is perhaps to be understood as "symbolic of the messianic age"; cf. p. 288.
514. *Ibid.*, p. 288.

already, and once for all, appeared. In 4G the Incarnation replaces the Parousia. ... Thus, the locus of the christological event has radically moved from future to present, and the by-now-traditional order of ascent and descent is reversed"[515]. Jesus' hour, his time, is his death. But even the death is transformed by the Johannine perspective of a realized eschatology. This means that, for the Fourth Evangelist, no longer the resurrection (as in PQ, or a combined SG), but the cross is to be considered Jesus' chief sign (12,32)[516]. The author of the source hoped "that all might believe" (1,7), i.e., that "all Jews" would accept their long-awaited Messiah, so that "an Israel restored and consoled at last – would be the new community of faith"[517]. But by the time the Fourth Evangelist wrote, "Christians have been expelled from their spiritual home, exiled from Jewish faith and people". This means, for the evangelist, that the disciples represent a relatively small church and the body of Christians is but a sect over against the dominant Jewish religion; the Christians are surrounded by a foreign and hostile 'world'[518].

Theological Locale: Jesus' Itinerary and the Jews. – (a) According to Fortna, the source (SG) "follows a carefully conceived plan"[519]. (1) The seven signs happen to fall into two regional parts: four miracles in Galilee (chs. 2, 4, 21, 6) and three in Judea (chs. 11, 9, 5)[520]. (2) For the introduction of the source, i.e., the Baptist's testimony and the conversion of the first disciples, no topographical notice is given, but a northern locale is implied[521]. (3) Also "the events of Jesus' last days in their own way show a straightforward spatial logic"[522]. In sharp contrast to the present Gospel, however, "it is ... all the more striking that the reader is in no way asked to be aware of either Galilee or Judea as such, and never of their inhabitants in a symbolic way. Indeed, for SG all the

---

515. *Ibid.*, pp. 288-289.
516. *Ibid.*, pp. 289-290.
517. *Ibid.*, p. 291.
518. *Ibid.*, p. 292.
519. *Ibid.*, pp. 296-298, esp. 298; cp. *Locale*, pp. 60-66, esp. 60.
520. *Predecessor*, pp. 296-297; cp. *Locale*, p. 60. Fortna stresses that "when we speak of a dual ministry, then – one part in Galilee and the second part in Judea – we do so solely from the perspective of later Johannine redaction, or from our awareness of the geography of Palestine". For Fortna, "in the source there is simply a ministry of seven signs which happen to fall into two regional parts", but this does not mean that "the author of the source has no concern for itinerary" (*Predecessor*, p. 297). Fortna noted, however, in *Locale*, p. 60: "Beyond providing a coherent framework for the signs, the geographical notices appear to have had no significance to the author".
521. *Predecessor*, p. 297. Cf. Jn 1,44.45-46. Bethany-beyond-Jordan in 1,28 is supplied by the evangelist. Cp. *Locale*, p. 67.
522. *Predecessor*, p. 297; Fortna notes the following locations: "In the Temple (the Sanhedrin's meeting), out of Bethany, formal entry into the city, the Last Supper, a garden across the Kidron, the high priest's house, the Pretorium and Lithrostotos, Golgotha, a nearby garden tomb, the disciples' meeting place".

participants are simply taken for granted as Jewish, and so is the Christian movement itself"[523].

(b) For the evangelist, "the matter of geography is of central importance and its role is intricate"[524]. He changed "considerably" SG's structure by rearranging the signs and by interspersing them "with blocks of mostly new material"[525]. He has also made comments within the pre-Johannine stories and has supplied notices elsewhere[526]. So the Johannine topography, with its alternation of Judea on the one hand, with Galilee, Samaria, or Perea, on the other, is schematic, and everywhere has theological significance[527]. In sharp contrast to the Synoptic Gospels, who together have knowledge of fourteen regions of Palestine and its environs, the Fourth Evangelist mentions only the four named above[528]. Judea is by far the most prominent region in the Gospel[529]. It is primarily important because of the great prominence attached by the evangelist to its inhabitants, οἱ Ἰουδαῖοι[530]. It is obvious that the Fourth Evangelist identifies all Ἰουδαῖοι with Judea. For him, Judea is the πατρίς of Jesus (4,44) and this locale stands for the whole world, whose representatives are the Jews. Judea is Jesus' world, to which he came and belongs, yet it has rejected him and expelled his followers, so that he and his followers are no longer of the world. This must be understood, as J.L. Martyn has demonstrated, from the sociological situation in which the Fourth Gospel arose: "It reflects the intensive feelings of resentment, humiliation, and alienation of a group of Christian Jews who have been made to think of themselves as cast adrift from their spiritual

523. *Predecessor*, p. 298.

524. *Ibid.*, p. 298.

525. *Locale*, pp. 60-61; for a full description, see pp. 61-66.

526. *Locale*, p. 66; for a full description, see *Predecessor*, pp. 298-306; cp. *Locale*, pp. 66-81.

527. *Locale*, p. 82; *Predecessor*, p. 307.

528. *Locale*, p. 82; *Predecessor*, p. 307. – (a) Samaria and Perea across the Jordan are the two less important regions. The Johannine Jesus appears in Samaria only in ch. 4. But the symbolic meaning the evangelist gives to this region appears from Jn 8,48, where Jesus is accused by the Jews of being a Samaritan and of having a demon (cp. 7,20; see also 8,52; 10,20). For Fortna, it is important that Jesus denies the latter charge (8,49), but does not refuse the Samaritan identification. In ch. 4 the Samaritans, in sharp contrast to Nicodemus in ch. 3, come to believe in Jesus. For the evangelist, Samaria, just as Galilee, is a place of faith. The same may be said of "Perea across the Jordan", which is found only three times in the Gospel (1,28; 3,26; 10,40). Cf. *Predecessor*, pp. 307-308, *Locale*, pp. 82-84. – (b) The succession of Jesus' withdrawals "from Judea to Galilee" (1,43; 2,1.11; 4,43.45.46.54; 6,1) can be seen as a strong indication for Galilee's importance in the Fourth Gospel. Galilee is shown almost always in a favorable light. It is a center of belief and the Galileans are depicted as people of faith. For Jesus it is a place of refuge, a place of hiddenness (4,1.44; 7,1-13). Cf. *Predecessor*, pp. 308-310; *Locale*, pp. 84-89.

529. *Predecessor*, pp. 310-313, esp. 310; *Locale*, pp. 89-95, esp. 89.

530. They are named about fifty times in the Gospel, and the phrase is almost always a Johannine insertion. Cf. *Predecessor*, p. 311, esp. n. 168.

home, from their people, so that they can no longer think of themselves as Jews"[531].

In recent publications, R.T. Fortna has continued to defend the semeia hypothesis and has expressed particular disagreement with the "Leuven school". In a lecture on Jn 21 at the 1990 Leuven Colloquium, he asked which approach to reading the Fourth Gospel is most appropriate, diachronic or synchronic[532]. He considers two models for a diachronic reading: the "Leuven School" hypothesis, accepting that the Fourth Gospel is based on the Synoptic Gospels, and his own "semeia hypothesis", supposing that the Fourth Gospel is based on an independent source, i.e., the reconstructed signs source[533]. Both these perspectives consider gospel texts as "documents having a history of development that can illuminate both their sense and their significance"[534]. The synchronic reading, on the contrary, "does not depend on any theory of the passage's compositional origin, whether deriving from the Synoptic Gospels or the Signs Source. It takes clues solely from the text"[535] and interprets "the text as coherent in itself"[536]. Using the commentary of J. Mateos and J. Barreto as an example for such a synchronic reading of Jn 21[537], Fortna confesses that "he is not able to follow their interpretation with any conviction"[538] and he explicitly denies "that only a synchronic reading of the texts will suffice"[539]. According to him, the problem of such reading "is one of 'control' on imagination. Their interpretation is too ingenious, even when grounded in a reading of the gospel as a whole"[540]. But he suggests "appropriating what is persuasive in the synchronic approach"[541] to reject the diachronic reading: neither Neirynck's nor Goulder's interpretation of Jn 21 in the light of Lk 5 "sheds light on this intricate passage"[542]. For

---

531. *Predecessor*, p. 314; *Locale*, p. 94. On Martyn, see above, pp. 149-150.

532. *Diachronic/Synchronic: Reading John 21 and Luke 5*, in DENAUX (ed.), *John and the Synoptics*, 1992, pp. 387-399.

533. *Ibid.*, pp. 389-396.

534. *Ibid.*, p. 389.

535. *Ibid.*, pp. 396-398, esp. 398.

536. *Ibid.*, p. 397.

537. MATEOS – BARRETO, *El evangelio de Juan*, 1979, pp. 885-904.

538. *Diachronic/Synchronic*, p. 398.

539. *Ibid.*, p. 399.

540. *Ibid.*, p. 398.

541. *Ibid.*, p. 399.

542. *Ibid.*, pp. 389-391, 392, esp. 391 (with regard to Neirynck). Cf. NEIRYNCK, in *NTS* 36 (1990) 321-336 (= 1991, pp. 601-616; 616: Additional Note); GOULDER, *Luke a New Paradigm*, 2 vols., 1989, esp. I, pp. 323-328; see also *John 1,1–2,12 and the Synoptics. Appendix: John 2,13–4,54*, in DENAUX (ed.), *John and the Synoptics*, 1992, pp. 201-237, where Goulder, taking John's dependence on the Synoptics as working hypothesis, concludes for Jn 1,1–2,12 that "(i) John has copies of the three Synoptics to hand, and (ii) that he is involved in a struggle with Jewish Christians" (pp. 201-222, esp. 222). See also pp. 223-237, esp. 237 (with regard to 2,13–4,54).

Fortna, there are in Jn "virtually no verbatim similarities [with the Synoptic Gospels], beyond a number of words and the occasional phrase... There is much in common, but only very loosely so, and a comparison with the Synoptic Gospels will involve as much overly imaginative reading as a purely synchronic one"[543]. Therefore, he prefers his own diachronic reading: "Grant that for many it is *a priori* not convincing when one tries to reconstruct a pre-Johannine source and then, inter-Synoptic fashion, to undertake redaction-critical reading of Jn in the light of its alleged source. But in the case of the Fourth Gospel, just as perhaps of Mark, all the basis for supposing earlier material to underlie the present text is present within that very text. Its close reading reveals points at which a diachronic (or better, a stereoptic) perspective – the distinction between redaction and something redacted, something 'earlier' – will make the most sense of the text. When we find such a redactional moment, we will surely imagine what the text would have been like without it and therefore how its *presence* contributes to a new meaning"[544].

Finally, we must mention Fortna's *ABD* article on "Signs/Semeia Source"[545]. There, he particularly stresses that the semeia hypothesis has the advantage of explaining the aporias: "two discrete literary stages – best labeled 'pre-Johannine' and 'Johannine' respectively – are necessary and sufficient to account for the narrative aporias, which in effect are the 'seams' where earlier written material is adapted, without recasting, into a later format"[546]. By contrast, in the hypothesis that John is dependent on the Synoptics, the aporias remain unexplained. According to Fortna, "the connection of the Fourth Gospel to the Synoptics is to be explained by SQ's dependence on pre-Synoptic tradition – or even by dependence of the Synoptics themselves on SQ"[547]. Besides the aporias,

---

543. *Diachronic/Synchronic*, p. 399. Cp. *Predecessor*, p. 217: "If only the Synoptics lie behind 4G, only very loosely occasioning it, and not a parallel but distinct set of traditions or sources, we are helped very little to understand 4G better, to follow the method and meaning of 4E, by a comparison with them. One can only imagine how the author may have used them [the Synoptics], guess why it was done as it was. The ingenuity is in trying to show how 4E might have used the Synoptic material in this way or that, not in understanding from a careful comparison of source and present Gospel the resultant picture of Johannine theology. It is just the controls that redaction criticism provides that are lacking in the view of dependence on the Synoptics and that we need in coming to terms with the otherwise so subjective and elusive task of understanding the Johannine theology". See also Fortna's reaction to my note on Jn 4,48 in *ETL* 61 (1985) 167-169 (see above, pp. 222-223 n. 415, and below, p. 377).

544. *Diachronic/Synchronic*, p. 399; cp. p. 399 n. 48: "It is clear to me that the theory of independence of the Synoptic Gospels and the use of a source is, if not so ingenious, less hypothetical and more controlled. And in any case, it yields – what is in my view more important – a better understanding of the text before us".

545. *Signs/Semeia Source*, in *ABD*, VI, 1992, pp. 18-22.

546. *Ibid.*, pp. 18b-19a ("A. The Hypothesis and Its Advantages"), esp. 19a.

547. *Ibid.*, p. 19a, with reference to Cope's 1987 article. Cp. Fortna's reaction in *Predecessor*, p. 323 (see above, pp. 222-223 n. 415). With some other hypotheses in mind,

Fortna especially mentions the appearance of the word σημεῖον (and its positive or negative connection with faith)[548] and the numbering of signs[549] as indications which suggest "the survival of an older layer in the text of the present gospel"[550]. Surveying the history and the variations of the hypothesis[551], he enumerates his own "major innovations" to the theory: "an explicit consideration of method, particularly the choice of valid criteria for identifying the source (notably, 'contextual' ones); at some points a curtailment of what Bultmann assigned to SQ ..., at others an expansion (e.g., 1:6-7, 19-34; 21:1-14), and the discovery

he continues: "Further, the theory makes unnecessary the relative unmanageable view that in the narrative the author redacted a still fluid tradition (as perhaps did 'Mark') or that they developed gradually over many stages, as by a Johannine 'school'" (p. 19a).

548. "On the one hand, this term – and particularly its connection with faith – is used only rarely and negatively in the Synoptics and there never of the miracles Jesus has performed; and on the other hand, in the Fourth Gospel also 'signs-faith' sometimes comes in for criticism (e.g., 4:48; 6:26) but at other points – presumably pre-Johannine – is to be understood in an entirely positive sense" (p. 19b).

549. "Further, in the first part of the gospel there are what seem to be vestiges of a pattern of numbering the signs (2:11; 4:54). In fact, it is these miracle stories and others now unnumbered, together with Jesus' dialogues and long monologues ('discourses') now growing out of them, that alone comprise his public activity. What in the other gospels, and in far more diverse form, has been called his 'ministry' can only be described in this gospel as his self-presentation in the performing of signs and in extended talk about them" (p. 19b).

550. *Ibid.*, p. 19a-19b ("B. Grounds for Reconstructing SQ").

551. *Ibid.*, pp. 19b-20b ("C. History and Variations of the Hypothesis"). Bultmann "gave the classical statement to the Signs Source hypothesis" and "acknowledged several precursors, most notably Faure" (p. 19b). Fortna notes that not many agreed with Bultmann that "the audience for such a source would very likely have been members of the Baptist sect" (but see Smith in 1976) and that Bultmann "also included material that is not so confidently attributed to SQ" (p. 20a). Nevertheless it must be stated that "no one who has worked subsequently on the SQ hypothesis has been able to ignore Bultmann's ground-breaking work, and in principle it won wide acceptance, particularly in Germany and the United States" (p. 20a). Fortna especially mentions Wilkens, Schnackenburg and Brown, further D.M. Smith, Bammel, his own monographs, Martyn and "many others" such as J.M. Robinson, Reim, Kysar, Attridge, Corsani, Cope (p. 20a). Nicol "refined both Fortna's criteria (by the more explicit use of form criticism for the identification of pre-Johannine tradition) and the stylistic tests, and introduced a sketch of the Johannine redaction of the source" (cp. Fortna, 1974; Richter, 1977) (p. 20b). Temple (*Core*, 1974) and Teeple "produced extensive variations on the theory by including material that most proponents could not accept as pre-Johannine" (p. 20b). On Boismard's complex theory of the composition history of the gospel, he notes that "it is not easily falsified, but neither is it convincing to many" (with reference to Neirynck, 1979). Becker is "the most faithful follower of Bultmann" and "reasserted the original theory with relatively little change (only adopting from Fortna the inclusion of the Baptist pericope [1:19-35])". Finally, he mentions "a curtailed version of the hypothesis" proposed by Heekerens (cp. Temple 1962): "This more cautious approach would be valid if it weren't for the considerable evidence that the evangelist has extensively rearranged the miracle stories, necessitating a loss of any original enumeration beyond (strictly) the first two, the second retainable only via a contrived addition ('when he had come from Judea to Galilee')" (p. 20b).

of an ordering of the series of signs with a geographical consistency (cf. 2:12; 4:46; [21:1]; 6:1; etc.); above all, the combining of SQ with a revised form of Bultmann's passion source ..., resulting in a rudimentary gospel, a 'Gospel of Signs,' as basis for the present text; and application of the stylistic tests of the source's integrity ... and reproduction of the putative Greek text of the source"[552]. With regard to the stylistic criteria, however, he notes (in criticism of Teeple) that these "are rather the weakest of the handful available and that in any case one must look for an intersection of as many different criteria as possible to locate an aporia and assign strata"[553]. Fortna admits that "despite wide acceptance, the hypothesis has never been universally accepted"[554]. He does not, however, really answer the objections of "dissenters from the theory"[555].

Among reviews of Fortna's *Predecessor*, we mention the positive reaction of D.M. SMITH (1990)[556]. He agrees fully with the four "important aspects of Fortna's work"[557]: (1) "John's narrative tradition seems

552. *Ibid.*, p. 20a.
553. *Ibid.*, p. 20b; cp. p. 21a.
554. *Ibid.*, p. 20b-21a ("Major Objections"), esp. 20b.
555. Fortna discusses several forms of dissent. First, some "resist working backward from the present text for conservative reservations", for example, Ruckstuhl, Morris, and Carson (p. 20b); others, "especially in Britain seem to be antipathetic toward anything Bultmannian", e.g., Lindars (with "a frontal attack on Fortna, 1979, despite his own theory [1972] of a fixed tradition analogous to SQ"). According to Fortna, "in both groups there appear not infrequently the overly cautious phrase that it would be 'unsafe' to assume the theory (even as a working hypothesis, apparently)" (pp. 20b-21a). Second, he refers to the "Leuven School", which maintains that John is directly dependent of the Synoptics (esp. Neirynck), and to others, such as Busse and May (1980), who claim that he is dependent on "a looser body of tradition" (p. 21a). A third group "holds that the gospel is a product of a long process of development by a 'Johannine school' and cannot be seen as the product of two principal phases" (cf. Schnelle; cp. Richard, who rejects that the "creative fourth evangelist [would] employ at length and in detail such an uncongenial source"). Fourth, some, like Haenchen, accept the hypothesis, but "view its reconstruction as precarious at best, despite the aporias unique to this gospel" (p. 21a). Fifth, more radical reactions, like those of Schnelle and Carson hold "the aporias to be illusory, so that what is taken by others to be the collision of pre-Johannine and Johannine is simply the complexity of the author's subtle way of writing or of adapting a lengthy and no longer recoverable tradition" (p. 21a). Sixth, Fortna agrees with those who "object ... to the subjectivity of any reconstruction of a source based chiefly on stylistic criteria (such as that by Teeple" (p. 21a; cf. Schweizer, Ruckstuhl), but rejects Ruckstuhl's critique to Bultmann in 1951 and to Fortna in 1977. Finally, some object that "the similarity of SQ to the format of Mark betrays Johannine dependence on the Synoptics". Fortna answers: "In fact, the similarity is rather loose: a Galilean period of Jesus' activity, followed by a Judean". The combination of SQ with PQ "also bears little resemblance to Mark, where the theme of Jesus' passion is integrated with his deeds from the beginning and the passion is no longer apologetic [in contrast to Mark's underlying passion tradition]" (p. 21a).
556. D.M. SMITH, in *JBL* 109 (1990) 352-354. Most reviewers (see above, p. 213 n. 366), however, reacted negatively to Fortna's new monograph (see below, pp. 352-357). On SMITH, see also above, pp. 53-54, 165-166, 194-197.
557. *Ibid.*, p. 354.

independent of the Synoptic Gospels"; (2) "In showing by redaction-critical analysis *how* the evangelist might have redacted a written source, Fortna has made the *possibility* that he actually did seem a likelihood"[558]; (3) "his basic insight that where narrative and discourse are juxtaposed, the discourse more often than not presupposes the narrative, while the narrative does not presuppose the discourse for its intelligibility"; (4) "that the early narratives should have comprised a gospel, in the sense of a narrative of Jesus' ministry, is suggested by considerations of style, as well as the enumeration of certain signs, as Fortna has argued. Moreover, the joining together of traditional stories to form a continuous narrative seems a likely move. After a narrative of signs, a passion narrative would have been required, if indeed it did not already exist". Smith formulates five reservations and questions, however[559]. First, "it is oftentimes difficult to be persuaded by Fortna's detailed analysis, as ingenious as it may be". Second, "Fortna's insistence upon the evangelist's respect for his source leads one to ask whether it is a function of Fortna's own methods and results"[560]. Third, "a major historical question concerns the kind of Christian-Jewish milieu (Fortna's and Martyn's term) from which the source is said to have come... The picture of Judaism that is projected or presupposed is unusual, whether one thinks of this Christian-Jewish community that produced the Gospel or the audience addressed". Fourth, it is difficult to accept Fortna's description of the source's theology, which was limited to the claim that Jesus was the Messiah. Fifth, Fortna's redaction critical method "presents some problems, even if one affirms its goal, as recent studies in literary and rhetorical criticism, not to mention hermeneutics, have pointed out"[561]. For David W. KUCK, Fortna's "thesis as a whole is persuasive, for it offers a credible solution for many of the aporias"[562]. Fortna's reconstruction of the passion narrative, however, poses some problems, because "it is much harder to see the tension between source and redaction than it is in the miracle stories"[563].

558. For Smith, there is "a fundamental agreement" of Fortna's books (*Gospel of Signs* and *Predecessor*) with Dodd's *Historical Tradition*, "but Fortna has gone beyond Dodd in showing the plausibility of redaction-critical insights, and therefore of written sources" (p. 354).

559. *Ibid.*, pp. 354-355.

560. Smith remarks that Fortna is not able to reconstruct the source either for the account of the Last Supper, or for the story of the Samaritan woman, because the evangelist rewrote both sections. For Smith, "this possibility reduces confidence in our ability to make the kinds of minute judgments that Fortna's project induces – constrains – him to make". Moreover, we must also reckon with the possibility that the evangelist imitated the source.

561. Compare esp. Segovia's review (see below, pp. 355-356).

562. D.W. KUCK, in *CurrTMiss* 17 (1990) 149; but he adds: "Yet sometimes one wonders whether Fortna's ingenuity leaves too little room for the author's freedom to jar the reader".

563. *Ibid.*, p. 149.

5. U.C. von Wahlde: "The Earliest Version of John's Gospel"

Recently Urban C. VON WAHLDE (1989) proposed "The Earliest Version of John's Gospel"[564]. After discussing contextual aporias[565], and more specifically the occurrence of the "repetitive resumptive", which indicates where the literary seams occur[566], he sets out three types of criteria for "Recovering The Gospel of Signs"[567].

564. U.C. VON WAHLDE, *The Earliest Version of John's Gospel: Recovering the Gospel of Signs*, Wilmington, DE, 1989. – Reviews: R.A. CULPEPPER, in *RExp* 87 (1990) 337-338; P. PERKINS, in *TS* 51 (1990) 558; J.S. SIKER, in *BTB* 21 (1990) 130-131; S.S. SMALLEY, in *JTS* 41 (1990) 611-613. See also NEIRYNCK, *Evangelica II*, 1991, p. 650; SLOYAN, *What Are They Saying about John?*, 1991, pp. 33-38; SMITH, *John among the Gospels*, 1992, p. 72.

565. Under the heading "The Johannine Problem" (pp. 17-25) the author discusses the literary inconsistencies (or "aporias") of various sorts: sequence problems, contradiction or lack of consistency, shifts in terminology, the existence of passages which seem to occur in duplicate or near duplicate versions, and theological problems (pp. 17-20). He briefly reviews the solutions given to the Johannine problem (pp. 20-25) and mentions esp. the literary theories of Bultmann, Schnackenburg, Brown, Fortna, and Nicol (see also pp. 194-196: "Appendix C: Some Recent Proposals Regarding the Signs Material in John": Bultmann, Fortna, Boismard, Schnackenburg).

566. *Ibid.*, pp. 26-28. For the "repetitive resumptive", "framing repetition" or "resumptive repetition", which occurs in John in both narrative and discourse, von Wahlde can refer to his earlier articles in *CBQ* 38 (1976) 520-533 (narrative); *Bib* 64 (1983) 542-549 (discourse). See also BOISMARD, in DE JONGE (ed.), *L'évangile de Jean*, 1977 (^{2}1987), pp. 235-241; ID. – LAMOUILLE, *Jean*, 1977, pp. 12b-13a and *passim*. According to NEIRYNCK, *ETL* 56 (1980) 303-338 (= 1982, pp. 143-178, 178: "Note additionnelle"), the "Wiederaufnahme" is not necessarily an indication that the evangelist is working with primitive sources: "En effet, le problème du rédacteur en Jn 11,2 n'est plus le même si l'on accepte la dépendance envers Lc au niveau de l'évangéliste. C'est, je crois, l'hypothèse la plus vraisemblable. Il est beaucoup moins probable qu'on puisse reconstituer, comme le propose Boismard, un récit primitif pré-johannique" (pp. 56, 1980, 318-325, p. 323; = 1982, pp. 158-165, esp. 163).

567. *The Earliest Version*, pp. 28-65; cp. p. 12. In "Appendix B" (pp. 192-194) von Wahlde gives a "Summary Listing of Characteristics". – For von Wahlde, "the gospel in its present form is not a product of a single individual but rather the end-product of a series of editings" (p. 11). He presumes three stages in the composition (p. 13). After the first edition (the Signs Gospel), the second edition, written about 90 A.D., when the Johannine (i.e., a Jewish-Christian) community was expelled from the synagogue, "presents a more complex view of the reasons for belief and unbelief than that found in the earlier edition. This edition focused on the importance of the Spirit for belief and at the same time extended the basis for belief ... to more than just miracles" (p. 13). The third edition, written at about the same time as 1 Jn by someone other than the author of Jn but who clearly shared his theological viewpoint, "clarified the tradition as it was understood 'from the beginning,' removing ambiguities and producing the gospel in the form it stands today" (p. 14). Von Wahlde says he intends a "complete analysis" of the second and third editions in his commentary edited by Michael Glazier, Inc. (p. 14 n. 2), but he provides "A Glimpse at the Second edition of John" in Chapter 5 of the present work (pp. 176-188). – The author evaluates his work as follows: "This book presents a new set of evidence for distinguishing and separating from each other the material of these various editions. While in some ways this proposal is radically new (it shows with greater clarity the nature and extent of these various sets of material), in many ways the view provided here is not new" (p. 12). See also below, p. 248. For a summary of von

1. *Linguistic differences*. This first type concerns "the variation in vocabulary for the same realities in cases where this alternation is not due to changes in connotation or to stylistic variety"[568]. Under this heading, von Wahlde discusses the terms (1) for religious authorities[569]; (2) for miracle[570]; and (3) the use of 'Jews' to refer to Judeans[571]. He thinks that the words Φαρισαῖοι, ἀρχιερεῖς, and ἄρχων as designations for the religious authorities together with σημεῖον and ἔργον meaning "miracle" and Ἰουδαῖος meaning

Wahlde's literary theory, see his *The Johannnine Commandments: 1 John and the Struggle for the Johannine Tradition* (Theological Inquiries), New York - Mahwah, NJ, 1990, pp. 7-8: "A Note on the Literary History of the Johannine Tradition".

568. *The Earliest Version*, pp. 30-43; the quotation is from p. 28.

569. *Ibid.*, pp. 31-36, where von Wahlde follows his earlier article in *JBL* 98 (1979) 231-253. He distinguishes two sets of terms for religious authorities, which stem from separate authors. (a) The terms from the earliest version: Φαρισαῖοι (19 times: 1,24; 3,1; 4,1; 7,32.32.45.47.48; 8,13; 9,13.15.16.40; 11,46.47.57; 12,19.42; 18,3); ἀρχιερεῖς referring to a group (10 times: 7,32.45; 11,47.57; 12,10; 18,3.35; 19,6.15.21); ἄρχων in the sense of religious authority (4 times: 3,1; 7,26.48; 12,42). (b) from the second edition: οἱ Ἰουδαῖοι in "hostile sense" (37 times: 2,18.20; 5,10.15.16.18; 6,41.52; 7,1.11.13.15.35.35: 8,22.31.48.52.57; 9,18.22; 10,19.24.31.33; 11,8; 13,33; 18,12.14.31.36.38; 19,7.12.14.31.38; 20,19). For this meaning, see von Wahlde's earlier article in *NTS* 28 (1982) 33-60. – For Ἰουδαῖος meaning "Judean", see below, n. 571. – Note that the use of Ἰουδαῖος in the national or religious sense "seems to occur throughout the gospel and is not characteristic of one or the other edition of the Gospel. Nor is this use unique to the gospel of John" (*The Earliest Version*, p. 32). For this use, cf. the references to Jewish religious/national customs: 2,6; 19,40.42; to feasts: 2,13; 5,1; 6,4; 7,2; 11,55; or to their authorities: 3,1; 18,20; 19,21a; see also the references to individuals as "Jews" in a context which distinguishes them from non-Jews such as Samaritans or Romans (4,9.9.22; 18,35); the expression "King of the Jews" (18,33.39; 19,3.19.21b.c).

570. *Ibid.*, pp. 36-41, esp. 36: "In passages where the terms Pharisees, chief priests, and rulers occur, the miracles are referred to as signs (*sèmeia*). In passages were the authorities are referred to as Jews, the miracles are referred to as works (*erga*)". On p. 41, von Wahlde refers to Wendt, who "demonstrated that 'signs' occurred in the narrative, and 'works' occurred in the discourses" (see above, pp. 11-12). – Σημεῖον refers to the miracles in 2,11.23; 3,2; 4,48.54; 6,2.14.26; 7,31; 9,16; 10,41; 11,47; 12,18.37; 20,30. In 2,18 and 6,30 the term σημεῖον is used for "an apologetic sign" in the demand of the religious authorities (identified as Jews) for a sign. – Ἔργον is used first to refer to the miracles of Jesus. This use echoes the Old Testament usage: Jesus performs the works that the Father has given him. See 5,20.36; 7,3.21; 9,3.4 (?); 10,25.32.33.37; 14,10.11.12; 15,24. According to von Wahlde, 4,34; 5,17; 9,4; 17,4, where ἔργον or ἐργάζομαι refer "to the ministry as a whole", belong to this group. Second, ἔργον is used to refer "to human acts or deeds which are done to fulfill the request of another"; cf. 3,19.20.21; 6,28.29; 7,7; 8,39; regarding 9,4, von Wahlde notes: "9:4 may also be an example of this use. However it is at least possible that the use in 9:4 belongs to the 'Johannine' use to refer to miracles" (p. 38 n. 31). For the second use of ἔργον, see von Wahlde's earlier article in *NT* 22 (1980) 304-315.

571. *The Earliest Version*, pp. 42-43. Ἰουδαῖος meaning "Judean" "does occur in passages where the terms Pharisees, chief priests, and rulers occur" (p. 42; cp. p. 32 n. 15). Cf. 1,19; 3,25; 11,19.31.33.36.45.54; 12,9.11; 19,20; see also 3,22: εἰς τὴν Ἰουδαίαν γῆν.

"Judean" are used in the first edition of the gospel, whereas the term Ἰουδαῖος in a hostile sense and ἔργον meaning a human act are from the second edition. According to von Wahlde, "it should be noticed that using these terms as criteria is not possible if all instances of a given term are taken together indiscriminately", and he evaluates his own approach as follows: "Past attempts to use the two sets of terms for religious authorities and for miracles did not include such distinctions in a sufficiently thorough way. It is only recently that we have achieved a sufficiently nuanced sense of the difference in meanings given to the same terms by different authors. When these differences in meaning are attended to, then we have a sufficiently critical basis for separating the literary strata of the gospel"[572]. A secondary linguistic criterion is (4) the translation of place names and religious terms[573].

2. *Ideological differences or differences in thought*, which "refer to those elements of thought within the gospel which are not directly theological but which indicate the author's perspective on a particular topic"[574]. The following are enumerated: (5) stereotyped formulas of belief[575]; (6) tandem (or chain reaction) belief[576]; (7) concern for the quantity and quality of Jesus' signs[577]; (8) emphasis on the variety

572. *Ibid.*, p. 43.
573. *Ibid.*, pp. 44-46. For the translation of place names, see 5,2; 6,1; 9,7; 19,13.17; with the exception of 6,1 and 9,7, the place name is first given in Greek and then translated into Hebrew (Aramaic). For the translation of Jewish religious concepts, see 1,38.41.42; 2,23; 20,16; in these cases the concept is first given in Hebrew and then translated into Greek. – The translation is not a primary criterion, "since it does not occur in passages marked by the other distinctive vocabulary" (p. 43).
574. *Ibid.*, pp. 28-29 (cp. 46-57).
575. *Ibid.*, pp. 46-48, esp. 46: "This belief always occurs after the miracle rather than before it, is always as a result of 'signs', and occurs in either of two set forms: '... many of the (name of group) believed in him' or 'they (with or without the name of the group) believed in him'. In almost all cases there is explicit mention of the miracles as 'signs' – or other characteristics of the signs material". Cf. 2,11.23; 4,39.53; 7,31; 10,41-42; 11,45.52; 12,11; 12,42.
576. *Ibid.*, pp. 48-49, esp. 48: "That is, within the material of the first stratum of the Gospel, belief is often pictured as being 'passed' from one to another". Cf. 1,35-49; 4,28-30.39; 4,53; 11,45; 12,9-11; 12,17-18.
577. *Ibid.*, pp. 49-50, esp. 49: "In those passages where the miracles of Jesus are referred to as signs, there is a particular emphasis on the number and the greatness of signs. But such a concern is almost entirely absent from the material associated with the works". Cf. 3,2; 4,45; 7,32; 9,16; 10,40-42 (John did 'no' sign); 11,47; 12,37; 20,30. For the emphasis on the greatness of the miracles, see below, p. 249. In the material of the second edition, "the miracles do not seem to have any effect at all; they do not lead to belief as they did in the first edition"; cf. 5,20.36; 10,25.31-33.

of groups which come to belief in Jesus[578]; (9) reaction of the Pharisees to the signs[579]; (10) the increasing hostility of the Pharisees[580]; (11) the people's reaction to the authorities[581]; (12) division of opinion regarding Jesus[582]; (13) the predominance of narrative in the early edition[583].

3. *Theological differences*, such as (14) a belief based on the signs[584];

578. *Ibid.*, pp. 50-51. In the formulas of belief (see below, p. 249 n. 603), there is a striking diversity of groups: 2,11.23; 4,39; 7,31; 10,42; 11,45; 12,11 (see also v. 18).42; the variety of groups is more general in 1,35-49; 3,26; 4,1.45 (see also 6,2.14); 4,46-54; 12,20.42; 20,30-31.

579. *Ibid.*, pp. 51-53, esp. 51: "In the material of the first edition of the gospel, there is a repeated pattern whereby after an expression of belief by the common people, there is an immediate reaction on the part of the religious authorities. This is not present in the material of the second edition"; cf. 3,1-2 (following 2,23-25); 7,32 (following 7,31); 11,47-48 (following 11,45-46); 12,10 (following 12,9); 12,19 (following 12,18). For other examples of reaction by the authorities, see 7,45-52; 9,13.24.29.31; 11,57. In these cases, however, "the discussion does not follow so immediately upon the reaction of the people" (p. 52).

580. *Ibid.*, pp. 53-55, esp. 53: "In the material of the first edition of the gospel, the reaction of the authorities (Pharisees, etc.) grows in intensity throughout the gospel"; cf. 4,1-4; 7,32.45-52; 9,16; 11,47-50; 12,53; see also 11,54.55-57; 12,9.19; 18,1-3. In the second edition, however, "the hostility toward Jesus exhibits the same level of intensity from the beginning" (p. 53); cf. 2,18-22; 5,10-20 (esp. v. 18); cp. 7,1; 11,8; 8,59; 10,31.

581. *Ibid.*, pp. 55-56, esp. 55: "In the early edition there is a consistent portrayal of the authorities as fearing the reaction of the people, and the common people enter into debate with the authorities"; cf. 4,1-4; 7,32.45; ch. 9; 12,19. In the second edition, however, "the reverse is true: the people consistently fear the authorities and indeed are afraid to talk back to them" (p. 55); cf. ch. 5; 7,13; 9,18-23; 19,7-8.38; 20,19.

582. *Ibid.*, pp. 56-57, esp. 56: "In the signs material, there are repeated references to division among both the people and the authorities regarding Jesus. The authorities in particular are not sure what to make of Jesus"; cf. 7,45-52; 9,16; see also 7,31.40-44; 10,19-21; 11,45-50, for the division among the people (even though the vast majority of them believe in Jesus). In the second edition, however, "the authorities are presented as already set in their judgment about Jesus even before the events take place" (p. 56).

583. *Ibid.*, p. 57. Note that in the signs material Jn 3,1-2 and 9,40-41 are the only instances of dialogue between the authorities and Jesus in the entire public ministry. In the second edition, however, "the material is almost exclusively dialogue and discourse material and it is consistently (almost exclusively) between the Jews and Jesus" (2,18-22; 5,10-47; 6,30-59; 7,14-19.33-36; 8,13-29.48-59; 10,22-39).

584. *Ibid.*, p. 58. The concentration on the relationship between the miracles of Jesus and belief is a typical feature of the first edition of the gospel. In contrast to the Synoptics, belief occurs consistently after the miracle rather than before. Note also that the only significant factor in belief is the performance of signs. In the second edition, "the theology of works is somewhat similar to that of the 'signs' in that, repeatedly, Jesus points to his works as actions which should bring the 'Jews' to belief"; cf., e.g., 5,36; 10,25-39. But in this edition, "the belief on the basis of works is cast within a different framework. In the middle edition, the works are one of four 'witnesses' to Jesus"; cf. 5,31-40. Von Wahlde refers to his earlier article in *CBQ* 43 (1981) 385-404.

(15) belief presented as an easy affair[585]; (16) a traditional christology[586]; (17) the supernatural knowledge of Jesus[587].

In addition to these major categories, von Wahlde adds "other characteristics useful in the identification of the Signs Material": (18) the occurrence of terms only once in the Gospel[588]; (19) references to events narrated elsewhere in the signs material[589]; (20) geographical references which are quite specific and accurate[590]; (21) contrast with the surrounding theology[591]; (22) questions or statements with a response that is not consistent[592].

U.C. von Wahlde believes that these criteria, especially the major ones, are "sufficiently objective to avoid the charge of subjectivity" and enable him "to identify the material of the first and second editions of the gospel"[593]. He calls his approach "considerably different from that

585. *The Earliest Version*, pp. 58-59: "This should be clear from a review of the many stereotyped formulas of belief. Although there are now elements in the immediate context of these formulas to show the insufficiency of the belief based only on signs, within the first edition such immediate and spontaneous belief was looked upon as the only appropriate response to the tremendous miracles of Jesus". Belief in Jesus "is the response of the overwhelming majority of the people, from various sectors of society. In contrast, among the religious authorities, although there are some indications that a few believed in or were at least favorably disposed to Jesus, the overwhelming majority do not believe"; cf. 12,37.

586. *Ibid.*, pp. 59-60. In the first edition, there is "a presentation of belief within traditional Jewish messianic categories"; cf. the discussion about the meaning of the signs for the identity of Jesus: "from God" (3,2; 9,16); "a sinner" (9,16.24); "the prophet" (6,14; 7,52); "a prophet" (4,19; 9,17). The titles "Son of God" and "Christ" are also used in the second edition. For the high christology in the second edition, see esp. those verses which speak explicity of the identity of Jesus with God (the "I am" statements; 8,58) or of the equality of Jesus with God (5,18; 10,33).

587. *Ibid.*, p. 60: "In the early edition, the supernatural knowledge of Jesus is one of his signs demonstrating his power before the people"; cf. 1,42. 47-49; 4,16-19.25.39. In the second edition, however, "it is a christological statement indicating for the reader that Jesus was superior to everyone around him".

588. *Ibid.*, p. 61. U.C. von Wahlde calls this "a minor consideration ... because it is so ambigious... It is difficult to affirm that all such instances stem from the early edition, but some are so idiosyncratic that there can be little doubt that they come from the first edition". He refers to Dodd's discussion on the so-called "transitional passages" (*Tradition*, 1963, pp. 243-244; cp. p. 235). Cf. 1,19 (ἱερεῖς καὶ Λευίτας), 3,25 (μετὰ Ἰουδαίου and περὶ καθαρισμοῦ), 7,25 (τινες ἐκ τῶν Ἱεροσολυμιτῶν), 12,20 (Ἕλληνές τινες).

589. *The Earliest Version*, p. 62: "This criterion is also quite ambiguous and should not be considered as a major tool...".

590. *Ibid.*, p. 62: "While not a major tool in the analysis, such specific references occur so consistently within the signs material that they can be said to be a characteristic of it, while the anachronisms are typical of the material of the second edition".

591. *Ibid.*, p. 62: "This is the most difficult of the criteria to apply in a purely objective way".

592. *Ibid.*, pp. 62-63. Cf. the "broken responses" in 3,3.27; 4,15; 7,28.33; 12,23; 18,30.35.

593. *Ibid.*, p. 63.

taken by Fortna and other recent critics" and insists that his criteria are "seemingly more objective"[594]. Moreover, because in contrast to Fortna "the same criteria are applied consistently throughout the analysis", von Wahlde believes that his approach "results in an identification of signs material which is more precise, consistent, and complete than that of previous studies"[595]!

Like Fortna's Gospel of Signs, von Wahlde's Earliest Version of John's Gospel was "a document which treated the ministry of Jesus from the baptism of Jesus to the resurrection"[596], and, "although the first 'stratum' is not intact within the present gospel, nevertheless enough of it remains for us to be able to identify and describe its theological structure as well as its religious background and christology"[597]. It contains the following sections (secondary texts, those not identified by the primary criteria, are preceded by an asterisk *)[598]:

(1) 1,19-28; (2) 1,35-49 (without v. 43); (3) 2,1-11; (4) 2,23-3,2 (without 2,24-25); (5) 3,22-26; (6) 4,1-4; (7) 4,5-42 (without vv. 10-15.20-24.31-38.40-42); (8) 4,43-45 (without v. 44); (9) 4,46-54 (without v. 48); (10) 5,1-9; (11) 6,1-2; (12) 6,3-14 (without v. 6); (13) *6,16-21; (14) 7,25-27; (15) 7,31-32; (16) *7,40-44; (17) 7,45-52; (18) 9,1-41 (without vv. 2-5.18-23.35-41); (19) 10,19-21; (20) 10,40-42; (21) 11,1-45 (without vv. 2.4-5.7-10.15b-16.21-27.40-42); (22) 11,46-53 (without vv. 51-52); (23) 11,54-57; (24) *12,1-8; (25) 12,9-11; (26) 12,18-19; (27) *12,20-22; (28) 12,37-42; (29) 18,1-11 (without vv. 4-6.9); (30) *18,19-24; (31) 18,28-29.33-35; (32) 18,39–19,6a; (33) 19,13-16 (without vv. 14b-15a); (34) 19,17-25a; (35) *19,39-42; (36) 20,1.11.14-16; (37) 20,30-31.

In addition he adds two passages where the material from two strata is mixed: (13a) 6,26; (17a) 8,12-13; compare (28) 12,42[599]. In contrast to

---

594. *Ibid.*, p. 63. He uses the same procedure for identifying the material in the passion and resurrection stories, but there he will "rely more heavily on the presence of framing repetition, inconsistencies of sequence and shifts in theology as markers of editing" (pp. 63-64).

595. *Ibid.*, p. 65. He objects to Fortna: "Fortna's criteria did not lead him to ask about the presence of source material in, for example, chapter 7. Nor did the criteria used in the analysis of the signs themselves figure as prominently in the analysis of the passion and resurrection material. ... he frequently identified (as did Bultmann before him) the source material of the passion and resurrection by comparing it with the Synoptic accounts – a criterion which is at best indirectly related to those included among his original listing of criteria" (p. 65).

596. *Ibid.*, p. 13.

597. *Ibid.*, p. 14; see also p. 58 n. 67: "Parts of that first edition are of course missing from the gospel as we now have it".

598. *Ibid.*, pp. 66-155: "3. The Signs Material in John"; cp. pp. 190-191: "Appendix A: Texts of the Signs Material". In his reconstruction he follows the text from the RSV. Brief phrases belonging to a later edition are printed between [ ] and his modifications of the RSV translation between < >. The characteristics typical of the signs material are printed in boldface.

599. *Ibid.*, pp. 102 (6,26), 108-109 (8,12-13), 131 (12,42). See esp. p. 102 n. 82.

Fortna, von Wahlde thinks that the miracle of chapter 21 was most likely not part of the Gospel of Signs[600].

Three elements form the basic structure of the Gospel of Signs[601]. First, attention is directed to the magnitude of Jesus' signs by accenting their greatness in crescendo arrangement[602]. Second, and closely related, is the increasing reaction of belief by the common people[603]. Third, there is the increasing hostility of the religious authorities[604].

Further, the Gospel of Signs is characterized by a low christology, a Moses typology, and by a final recognition of Jesus as Messiah and Son of God[605]. This all means that the theology of the signs gospel is very Jewish: "It is written for Jews against a backdrop of the traditional view of Moses: Jesus was the Christ and the Son of God, but he was also the Prophet like Moses, who would save his people in the last days, just as Moses had saved them at the Exodus"[606]. This document "has close affinity with the Baptist movement" and "gives us details of the life of Jesus that we know from no other source"[607]. Moreover, it shows considerable familiarity with the customs and feasts of the Jews. Specifically, it identifies the places where the events took place[608].

Regarding the place of composition, von Wahlde thinks that, because of its emphasis on Judea, the Gospel of Signs was very likely a product of the Christian community there[609]. It was probably "a missionary (or kerygmatic) document" (cf. 20,30)[610], written sometime prior to 90 A.D., perhaps in the seventies or eighties[611]. The "signs community" was Jewish-Christian. The signs material itself tells us nothing about its author[612].

An interest in style criticism clearly appears in works on the signs source by Fortna, Nicol, Teeple, Freed (and Hunt), and von Wahlde.

600. *Ibid.*, pp. 154-155.
601. *Ibid.*, pp. 156-161.
602. *Ibid.*, pp. 157-160, esp. 158.
603. *Ibid.*, pp. 160-161. Cf. the statements of belief which demonstrate so regularly the reaction of the people: 2,23; 3,26; 4,1.39.43-45.53; 6,14; 7,31; 10,40-42; 11,45; 12,9.18-19.42. For von Wahlde, this is also "demonstrated by the repeated emphasis on the diverse social and geographical origins of believers": the people of Jerusalem (2,23; 7,31; 11,45; 12,9); various Judeans (3,26; 4,1; 10,40-42); Samaritans (4,39); people of Galilee (4,43.53; 6,14); the Greeks (12,20-22); the authorities (12,42). See also the final climax of the public reaction to Jesus in the words of the Pharisees in 12,19.
604. *Ibid.*, p. 161.
605. *Ibid.*, pp. 161-171.
606. *Ibid.*, p. 170.
607. *Ibid.*, p. 170.
608. *Ibid.*, p. 171.
609. *Ibid.*, pp. 171-172.
610. *Ibid.*, p. 171.
611. *Ibid.*, pp. 172-174 (cp. 13).
612. *Ibid.*, p. 174.

Bultmann's source theory onetime provided the occasion for the study of Johannine style characteristics by Schweizer and Ruckstuhl. That the recent studies on the semeia source have stimulated a renewed attention to Johannine language cannot be denied, even though the hypothesis itself is not always regarded positively and, as we shall see in Chapter V, alternative explanations of the miracle stories in John are being defended.

CHAPTER V

THE SEMEIA HYPOTHESIS CRITICIZED
IN RECENT RESEARCH

Although Fortna's *The Gospel of Signs* is one of the most cited monographs in Johannine studies, his theory of a pre-Johannine Gospel and especially his word-by-word reconstruction have undergone severe critique. Many will agree with M. de Jonge: "The present author is very skeptical about the possibility of delineating the literary sources in the Fourth Gospel and does not share the optimism displayed by some of his colleagues when they try to distinguish between sources and redaction"[1]. In this chapter I will review the opposition to the semeia hypothesis. In a first section I begin with the presentation of some alternative hypotheses.

I. ALTERNATIVE HYPOTHESES

1. *A Short Signs Source*

Some authors who reject Bultmann's or Fortna's semeia hypothesis accept a shorter source for at least the two Cana miracles. H. Thyen and his students renewed Spitta's suggestion that this short signs source was inserted into the Gospel by the Johannine redactor. G.R. Beasley-Murray ascribes the use of such a source to the evangelist. We can add here as well the "revival" of the hypothesis of Galilean interpolations into a Judean *Grundschrift* in the article of A. Mayer. We will conclude with M.W. Stibbe.

---

1. DE JONGE, *Jesus Stranger from Heaven*, 1977, p. VIII; also cited by ASHTON (ed.), *The Interpretation of John*, 1986, p. 13 (for M. de Jonge's reaction to Fortna's *Gospel of Signs*, see above, p. 168). See also M.M. THOMPSON, *The Humanity of Jesus*, 1988, p. 142 n. 2: "While I think it not unlikely that John had access to some sort of signs-source – i.e. a source, oral or written, which contained at least some of the miracles – I think it very unlikely that we can recover the exact boundaries of this source and discern its theology" (with reference to de Jonge, Barrett, and Lindars). On M.M. Thompson, cf. MENKEN, *De christologie*, 1991, p. 27 (ET: 1993, p. 308-309).

1. In his *Forschungsberichte* in *TR* (1974-1979) Hartwig THYEN[2] never published a section on the signs source[3], but his article on the Gospel of John in *TRE* (1988) contains a summary treatment of the hypothesis[4]. His position was already known from his annotations in previous articles. From 1974 on, he speaks very skeptically about the classic semeia hypothesis[5]. In his view, the examination of the arguments leads to a negative result[6]. There is no agreement on the reconstruction of the source. Moreover, texts attributed to the source show stylistical differences and are tradition-historically disparate. Further, the source's non-Johannine christology influenced by the Hellenistic θεῖος ἀνήρ concept, remains unproven (ctr. J. Becker, U.-B. Müller, H. Koester)[7]. Thyen pays most attention to 20,30-31 and the numbering of signs[8].

2. In his study *Sündenvergebung* (1970) he still accepted Bultmann's semeia hypothesis (see above, p. 105 n. 167). Thyen's most important contributions on Jn are: *Aus der Literatur zum Johannesevangelium*, in *TR* 39 (1974) 1-69, 222-252, 289-330; 42 (1977) 211-270; 43 (1978) 328-359; 44 (1979) 97-134; *Johannes 13 und die "Kirchliche Redaktion" des vierten Evangeliums*, in *FS K.G. Kuhn*, 1971, pp. 343-356; *Entwicklungen innerhalb der johanneischen Theologie und Kirche im Spiegel von Joh 21 und der Lieblingsjüngertexte des Evangeliums*, in DE JONGE (ed.), *L'évangile de Jean*, 1977 (²1987), pp. 259-299; *"Niemand hat grössere Liebe als die, dass er sein Leben für seine Freunde hingibt" (Joh 15,13). Das johanneische Verständnis des Kreuzestodes Jesu*, in *FS E. Dinkler*, 1979, pp. 467-481; *"Das Heil kommt von den Juden"*, in *FS G. Bornkamm*, 1980, pp. 163-184; *Johannesevangelium*, in *TRE* 17 (1988) 200-225. For his recent publications, see below, pp. 262-263 n. 66. – Cf. NEIRYNCK, *Semeia-bron*, 1983, pp. 9-10 (= ET: 1991, pp. 657-659); SCHNELLE, 1987, pp. 22-24 (ET: 1992, pp. 12-14); BEUTLER, *La recherche johannique*, 1990, pp. 20-21; LÜTGEHETMANN, *Die Hochzeit*, 1990, pp. 326-327; ZUMSTEIN, *La rédaction finale de l'évangile*, 1990, pp. 212-213; BEUTLER, *Méthodes et problèmes*, 1990, pp. 20-21, 23-24; SCHMITHALS, *Johannesevangelium*, 1992, pp. 194-196; NEIRYNCK, *John and the Synoptics*, 1992, p. 8; SMITH, *John among the Gospels*, 1992, pp. 136, 167-169.

3. See esp. *TR* 37, p. 225 (cp. 329); 42, p. 266 n. 1; *Johannes 13*, p. 344 n. 3. Thyen intended to deal with the signs source in section 4.21 of his *Forschungsbericht*, but in 1979 his survey ended with section 4.145. See HENGEL's comment in *Die johanneische Frage*, 1993, p. 244 n. 132: "War es eine Folge dieser begrüssenswerten *retractatio*, dass die Forschungsberichte über das 4. Evangelium in die Hände von Becker gegeben wurden?". On Thyen's *rectractio*, see below, pp. 262-266. For Becker's *Forschungsberichte*, see above, pp. 132-135.

4. *Johannesevangelium*, in *TRE* 17 (1988) 200-225, pp. 207-208 (section 5.2) for the "Semeia-Quelle"; see also pp. 203-205 ("4. Aporien im vierten Evangelium"), 205-208 ("5. Spannungen zwischen Quellen und ihre Bearbeitungen"), 208-211 ("6. Die Ursachen der Aporien und die Genese des Evangeliums").

5. *TR* 39, p. 329: "meine eigene Skepsis gegen die verschiedenen Quellentheorien und vor allem gegen die darin vielfach vorausgesetzte Art des literarischen Umgangs mit der Tradition"; he refers to, among others, Fortna, Nicol, Teeple, Becker, and Richter. In 1988, after a survey of the semeia hypothesis, he declares plainly: "Die Theorie einer alle Wundererzählungen des Evangeliums enthaltenden 'Semeia-Quelle' muss ... aufgegeben werden" (*TRE* 17, p. 207). Regarding the spread of the hypothesis, he notes: "Von allen Quellenhypothesen hat sich die der Semeia-Quelle am zähesten gehalten und erfreut sich wachsender Beliebtheit" (*ibid.*).

6. *TRE* 17, p. 207, with reference to Heekerens.

7. *Ibid.*, p. 207.

8. *TR* 39, pp. 224-227; 42, pp. 268-269; 43, p. 352; cp. *Johannes 13*, p. 344 (esp.

(a) The verses 20,30-31 do not speak of Jesus' Messiahship but of his identity with Christ (cp. 1 Jn 2,22[9]). They reflect the christological struggle in the Johannine Church (cf. 1 Jn 2,19) and must be read in connection with the story of the appearance to Thomas. According to Thyen, the (evangelist-)redactor is responsible for Jn 20,19-29.30-31; 21,1-25; he continues the christological theme of the macarism of 20,29 in vv. 30-31[10].

n. 3); *Entwicklungen*, pp. 260-261; *TRE* 17, p. 207. – In *TR* 39, p. 225, Thyen notes: "Das durchschlagendste Argument für die Zuweisung von Joh. 20,30f. zur Semeia-Quelle ... besteht in der Inkongruenz des Inhalts der Passage mit solchen Aussagen des Evangeliums, die gerade spezifisch johanneisch zu nennen sind. Denn das hier apostrophierte Verständnis der Semeia als der Epiphanie des Gottessohnes steht zu ihnen wie zu einer Anzahl von Wundergeschichten des Evangeliums in ihrer vorliegenden Gestalt in starker Spannung. Schon darum ist es nicht unbedenklich aus 20,31 unreflektiert den absichtsvoll definierten 'Zweck des Evangeliums' herauslesen zu wollen"; see also *TR* 42, pp. 268-269; 43, p. 352; for the aporia with ch. 21, see, e.g., *TRE* 17, p. 204: "Nirgends ist der Konsensus so gross wie in dem Urteil, nach dem eindrucksvollen ursprünglichen Buchschluss (20,30f) sei Joh 21 ein Nachtrag von anderer Hand"; cp. *Entwicklungen*, p. 260: "Dass Joh 20,30f ein resumierender 'Schluss' ist, steht ausser Frage, und muss für die Interpretation der Verse fruchtbar gemacht werden. Aber dass Joh 20,30f ein ursprünglicher 'Buchschluss' ist, der dann nach den sekundären Anfügung von Kapitel 21 durch einen anderen Autor durch den konkurrierenden Vers ungeschickt verdoppelt worden sein soll, ist eine blosse Hypothese mit der Prämisse vom Ungeschick jenes epigonalen 'Redaktors' (oder seiner Tabuehrfurcht vor dem fixierten Heiligen Text), die überzeugenderen Begründungen bedarf".

9. See also 1 Jn 5,5-12. Cp. the confession of the "antichrist" (cf. 1 Jn 2,18.22; 4,3; 2 Jn 7) in 1 Jn 2,22 ὅτι Ἰησοῦς οὐκ ἔστιν ὁ χριστός with Jn 20,31 ὅτι Ἰησοῦς ἐστιν ὁ χριστός. Cf. *TR* 39, pp. 225-226; *TR* 42, p. 269; *Entwicklungen*, pp. 260-261. With NEUGEBAUER, *Die Entstehung des Johannesevangeliums*, 1978, pp. 10-12, esp. 12, Thyen reads in 20,30 (cp. 19,35) πιστεύητε ... ἔχητε and translates 20,30-31 as follows: "Das ist geschrieben, damit ihr daran gläubig bleibet, dass Jesus der Christus, der Sohn Gottes ist, und damit ihr als gläubig Bleibende in seinem Namen (das) Leben behaltet"; cf. *TR* 39, p. 226; 42, p. 269; *Entwicklungen*, p. 260. This means in other words: "Das Buch ist also nicht primär in der missionarischen Absicht geschrieben, dass Heiden (oder Juden) zum Glauben an Jesus den messianischen Gottessohn *kommen*, sondern dazu, dass eine bedrohte Gemeinde bei dem wahren Glauben *bleibe*, dass *Jesus* und der messianische Gottessohn nicht nur partiell und zeitweise, sondern total identisch sind" (*Entwicklungen*, pp. 260-261).

10. See *Entwicklungen*, p. 261: "Diese nach 1 Joh 2,22 bezweifelte oder ausdrücklich geleugnete Identität wird durch die Lieblingsjüngerepisode (Joh 20,2-10), die Geistverleihung durch den mit dem Gekreuzigten identischen Auferstandenen (Joh 20,19-23; beachte besonders Vers 20!) und die unmittelbar vorausgehende Thomaserzählung (Joh 20,24-29) sichergestellt. Dabei weisen Joh 20,20 und die Thomasgeschichte nachdrücklich auf den Lanzenstich und das wahrhaftige Zeugnis des Lieblingsjünger zurück. Die Seligpreisung in Joh 20,29 darf nicht als Tadel des noch unvollkommenen Thomasglaubens angesehen werden, sondern sie gilt den ersten und allen späteren *Lesern* des Buches, die auf das wahrhaftige Zeugnis der Augenzeugen hin und nicht mehr, wie Thomas und die ersten Jünger, aufgrund der Autopsie glauben. Sie werden freilich nur dann das ewige Leben 'bewahren' (ἔχητε v. 31!), wenn sie an der totalen Identität von Jesus und dem messianischen Gottessohn festhalten und so im wahren Glauben 'bleiben'". Cp. *TR* 42, p. 269, with reference to LANGBRANDTNER, *Weltferner Gott*, 1977, p. 37. For Thyen's conception of the redactor, see also – *TR* 39, p. 226: "Geht es in Joh

(b) Thyen acknowledges the validity of Bultmann's "gewichtiges Argument" for the σημεῖα-*Quelle*[11]. The numbering in 2,11 and 4,54 and the connection apparent in 2,12 indicate that the two Cana miracles originally belonged together. But since only these two pericopes contain no Johannine style characteristics and are not followed by a revelatory discourse, only they could have originated in *one* source[12]. It cannot be concluded from 2,11 and 4,54 that the source contained more numbered signs. Furthermore, these verses do not contradict 2,23 and 4,45, because they stress that both miracles happened at Cana. Against Fortna, he does not consider 21,14 a "Quellenrudiment"; rather, the third appearance before the disciples (cf. 20,19-23.24-29), and here particularly before Peter, is narrated in 21,1-25[13].

Thyen himself was tempted by Spitta's hypothesis: the three miracle stories 2,1-11; 4,46-54; and 21,1-14 originally together in one source inserted into the *Grundschrift* by the Johannine redactor. Indications that Thyen was working in that direction are found in the dissertations of his students, first by W. Langbrandtner (1975) and at length by H.-P. Heekerens (1978)[14].

20,30f. aber um die Kontroverse um die Identität zwischen Jesus und dem Christus, dann besteht im Gegenteil der begründete Verdacht, dass die Stelle – statt Bestandteil einer älteren *Quelle* zu sein – zu den jüngsten Schichten des vierten Evangeliums, nämlich seiner 'johanneischen Redaktion' gehört"; cp. *Johannes 13*, pp. 343-345 and 356, where he already questioned the name "kirchlicher Redaktor" for the editor: "Wahrscheinlich nennte man ihn aber wohl zutreffender den 'vierten Evangelisten' und versuchte sein ganzes Buch – was immer es an Ungereimtheiten und literarischen Rätseln enthalten mag – als Autosemantikon für sich selber sprechen zu lassen. Allein im Dienste solcher Interpretation ist die Frage nach der gnostisierenden 'Grundschrift' und dem Mass ihrer Reinterpretation angebracht und sinnvoll". Cp. *Niemand*, pp. 469-470, 471-472. This does not mean, however, that there are no traditions or (possibly written) sources taken up in the Fourth Gospel; cf. *Das Heil*, p. 164.

11. *TRE* 17, p. 208. See also *TR* 39, p. 235 n. 1 (ctr. Schottroff); 42, p. 266 n. 1.

12. Referring to the use of γύναι in 2,4 and 19,26, he notes in *Entwicklungen*, p. 284: "War 2,1-11 in der Grundschrift vorgegeben, so könnte der Schöpfer von Joh 19,25-27 die Anrede nach diesem Vorbild kopiert haben. Das würde erst recht dann wahrscheinlich sein, wenn es der Autor von Joh 21 war, der die beiden Erzählungen vom Weinwunder in Kana (2,1-11) und von der Heilung des Sohnes des königlichen Beamten (4,46-54) nachträglich der Grundschrift eingefügt hat"; cp. p. 275 n. 42: "die Erzählung von 2,1-11 ..., die m.E. nicht der Anfang einer vorjohanneischen 'Semeia-Quelle' ist, sondern der Grundschrift zusammen mit 4,46-54 erst sekundär durch den Autor von 21 eingefügt wurde".

13. *TRE* 17, p. 208; cp. *Entwicklungen*, p. 264: "Es erscheint mir töricht, in dieser Notiz ein inkonsistentes Quellenrudiment erblicken und dem Autor anlasten zu wollen, er habe noch nicht bis drei zählen können. Es geht ihm ja um die Erscheinungen vor den *Jüngern* (20,19-23; 20,24-29; 21,1-25); und hier speziell um diejenigen vor *Petrus*. Was es um die Fusswaschung war, hat er nicht begriffen. *Dreimal* hat er danach seinen Herrn verleugnet, *dreimal* ist der ihm erschienen, und *dreimal* muss Petrus sich nun fragen lassen: 'Simon, Johannessohn, hast du mich lieb?'".

14. For his hypothesis Thyen refered to both students before the publication of their dissertations; see, e.g., *Entwicklungen*, p. 284 n. 65; *TR* 42, p. 266 n. 1.

Wolfgang LANGBRANDTNER (1975, 1977)[15] thinks that a gnostic *Grundschrift* lies at the basis of the Fourth Gospel[16]. This basic document, with a cosmological dualism, was not composed before 80 A.D.[17]. Its author probably used a written source only in Jn 1,1.3-13 and oral traditions elsewhere[18]. About 100 A.D., the Johannine redactor tried to correct the gnostic tendency of the *Grundschrift*. He stressed Jesus' earthly existence and physical resurrection, the ethical value of the commandments, sacramental practices, and the future aspect of the Gospel's eschatology[19]. Referring to Spitta, Langbrandtner contends that in 2,1-11 and 4,46-54 the redactor used a source that contained signs with a continuous numbering[20].

15. W. LANGBRANDTNER, *Weltferner Gott oder Gott der Liebe. Der Ketzerstreit in der johanneischen Kirche. Eine exegetisch-religionsgeschichtliche Untersuchung mit Berücksichtigung der koptisch-gnostischen Texte aus Nag-Hammadi* (BET, 6), Frankfurt/M - Bern, 1977 (diss. Heidelberg, 1975; dir. H. Thyen). On Thyen's influence, see pp. VIII-IX: "Diese Untersuchung hat ihren Anstoss in Vorlesungen und Übungen Prof. Thyens über das JohEv gefunden, wo die ersten tastenden Versuche dieser Richtung getan wurden; seine Meinung, die man aus dem Bericht der ThR 1974ff ersehen kann, ist im ersten Kapitel eingeflossen". – Cf. LÉON-DUFOUR, in *RSR* 68 (1980) 288-290; BROWN, *Community*, 1979, pp. 180-182 (FT: 1983, pp. 197-200); KUHN, *Christologie*, 1987, p. 59 (Jn 1,35-51); SCHNELLE, *Christologie*, 1987, pp. 20-22 (ET: 1992, pp. 9-11); LÜTGEHETMANN, *Hochzeit*, 1990, pp. 105-108 (Jn 2,1-12); SMITH, *John among the Gospels*, 1992, pp. 136, 165 n. 61.

16. *Weltferner Gott*, pp. 1-121: "Erstes Kapitel: Erhebung von zwei Theologien im Johannesevangelium auf Grund literarkritischer Analyse", see esp. 84-121: "Die Charakteristik der Theologie der Grundschrift und der Redaktion". On pp. 104-105, he gives the following reconstruction of the *Grundschrift*: (1) Introduction: 1,1.3-13; 1,19-21.25-26.28; 1,35-42.44-51; (2) The presentation of the crisis: 2,13b-16.18-20.23b-25; 3,1-10 (without ὕδατος καί in v. 5).12.13.31-36.14-19b; (3) Necessity of faith for salvation: 4,3a.4-21.23-45; 6,1-3 (without ἐπὶ τῶν ἀσϑ.).5-21.24-27a.b.28-39a.40a.b.41-44a.b.45-47.59-63; (4) Salvation for those who believe and the condemnation of the world: 5,1b-19.21-27.30-47; 7,15-22a.23-38.40-52; 8,12-59; (5) The believer in the hostile world: 9,1-21.24-41; 10,19-21.24-25.30-42; (6) The believer in the redemption by Jesus: 11,1-49a.c.50a.52b-57; (7) The claim of Jesus and the condemnation of the world: 12,1-13.17-23.27-32.34-36a.44-48a; (8) The salvation of the believers: 13,1(beginning).2 (beginning).3-10a.18-19.27-33; 14,1-12.16-19.22-31; (9) Passion and resurrection: 18,1-8.10-12.19-23.28-31.33-40; 19,1-24.28-33.36.38-42; 20,1.11-18.

17. *Ibid.*, p. 120. For a discription of the theology of the *Grundschrift*, see pp. 84-104.

18. *Ibid.*, p. 106.

19. For the redactor's theology, see pp. 106-121. For the date, see p. 120. – Langbrandtner attributes the following to the redaction (p. 106): 1,2.14-18.22-24.26b(ἐγὼ ... ὕδατι).27.29-34.43: 2,1-13a.17.21-23a; 3,5(ὕδατος καί).11.19c-21.22-30; 4,1.3b.22. 46-54; 5,20.28-29; 6,2(ἐπὶ τῶν ἀσϑ.).4.11(εὐχ.).22-23.27c.d.39b.40c.44c.48-58.60-61 (only the mention of the disciples).64-71; 7,1-14.22b.39; 9,22-23; 10,1-18.22-23.26-29; 11,49b(Καϊαφᾶς ... ἐκείνου).50b-52a(ὑπὲρ τοῦ λαοῦ ... μόνον, ἀλλ'); 12,14-16.24-26.33.36b-43.48b-50; 13,1(εἰδὼς ...).2(τοῦ διαβ. ...).10b-17.20-26.(in vv. 27.30 the mention of τὸ ψωμίον).34-38; 14,13-15.20-21; chs. 15-17; 18,9.13-18.24-27.32; 19,25-27.34-35.37; 20,2-10.19-31; ch. 21.

20. *Ibid.*, pp. 71-74, esp. 74: "vom R[edakt]or eingefügt ..., der sie wahrscheinlich aus einer Quelle entnommen hat, die in fortlaufender Zählung Jesuwunder berichtet". It is clear that he accepts "Bultmanns stärkstes Argument für die Semeiaquelle" (p. 74 n. 6)

Hans-Peter HEEKERENS (1978, 1984) deals more at length with the semeia hypothesis itself[21]. After a critique of Bultmann's argumentation he summarizes his own position in six points[22]: (a) An original connection between Johannine miracle stories can only be demonstrated for 2,1-11 and 4,46-54 (with 2,12 as transitional verse and the numbering in 2,11 and 4,54)[23]. (b) Only the first two miracle stories were originally numbered; it is an unproven postulate that all miracle stories were numbered[24]. (c) Only 2,1-11; 4,46-54; and 21,1-14 are relatively free of Johannine style characteristics; in other miracle stories it is difficult to distinguish between tradition and redaction[25]. (d) These three miracle stories are not followed by a discourse and they are not recalled in the rest of the Gospel[26]. (e) From a form-critical point of view, the "Vorlagen" of 2,1ff.; 4,46ff.; 5,1ff.; 6,1ff.; 9,1ff.; 11,1ff.; and 21,1ff.

for his own hypothesis. On p. 74 n. 7, Langbrandtner refers to Spitta ("aus einer Quelle, zu der auch c. 21 gehört"), but he does not consider 21,14 (cp. H. Thyen "kein Quellenrudiment" in *Entwicklungen*, p. 264; see above, p. 254 n. 13).

21. H.-P. HEEKERENS, *Die Zeichen-Quelle der johanneischen Redaktion. Ein Beitrag zur Entstehungsgeschichte des vierten Evangeliums* (SBS, 113), Stuttgart, 1984 (diss. Heidelberg, 1978; dir. H. Thyen). – Reviews: cf. VAN BELLE, no. 1744. See also LÜTGEHETMANN, *Hochzeit*, 1990, pp. 115-120 (Jn 2,1-11), and NEIRYNCK, in *ETL* 60 (1984) 367-375, p. 369 (= 1991, p. 681); LÉON-DUFOUR, *Où en est la recherche johannique?*, 1990, p. 24; BEUTLER, *Méthodes et problèmes*, 1990, p. 22; ASHTON, *Understanding*, 1991, p. 291; SCHMITHALS, *Johannesevangelium*, 1992, p. 125; SMITH, *John among the Gospels*, 1992, pp. 136, 165-167. – Heekerens presents his book as "die veränderte Fassung" of his dissertation with the same title. He did not update his bibliography (p. 9). (In the following notes, the pages of the dissertation are added within brackets.) Both publication and dissertation have six chapters: "Kritik der *Bultmann*schen-Semeia-Quellen-Hypothese" (pp. 17-43 [21-51]); "Das Problem von Joh 21,14" (pp. 45-47 [60-63]); "Analyse von Joh 21,1-11.12; 4,46-54 und 21,1-14" (pp. 49-94 [64-118]); "Die Zeichen-Quelle" (pp. 95-120 [119-148]); "Die redaktionelle Verarbeitung der Zeichen-Quelle" (pp. 121-130 [149-173]); "Zusammenfassung" (pp. 131-132 [174-179]). The introduction in the orginal dissertation (pp. 1-20) is much longer than in the published text (pp. 11-16). Section two in the dissertation deals with the "Entwicklung der alternativen Zeichen-Quelle-Hypothese" (with on pp. 52-58: "Vorläufer dieser Alternativ-Hypothese", and on pp. 58-63: "Die systematische Begründung der Zeichen-Quelle-Hypothese"; only pp. 59-63 correspond to the published text (pp. 45-47). – In his dissertation, Heekerens defended Jn 20,30-31 as part of the "Zeichen-Quelle", in contrast to his teacher Thyen: "Der Abschluss der Zeichen-Quelle (Grundbestand von Joh 20,30f.)" (pp. 145-148), but he changed his view in the publication (see below, p. 260 n. 43). On Heekerens' unpublished dissertation, see NEIRYNCK, *Semeia-bron*, 1983, pp. 10-11, 20-28 (ET: 1991, pp. 658-659, 666-672 and 677).

22. *Zeichen-Quelle*, pp. 17-43, esp. 42-43 [21-51, esp. 49-51]: "Schlussfolgerungen". In this section, he considers successively: "1. Traditionsgeschichtliche Überlegungen; 2. Literarkritische Argumentation; 3. Stilistische Beobachtungen; 4. Formgeschichtliche Betrachtung; 5. Redaktionsgeschichtliche Überlegungen; 6. Zur Christologie der postulierten Semeia-Quelle; 7. Schlussfolgerungen".

23. *Ibid.*, p. 42; cf. pp. 21-26, esp. 26 [49; cf. 25-31, esp. 26].

24. *Ibid.*, p. 42; cf. pp. 21-26, esp. 26 [49; cf. 25-31, esp. 26].

25. *Ibid.*, p. 42; cf. pp. 27-32, esp. 32 [49; cf. 31-38, esp. 38].

26. *Ibid.*, p. 42; cf. pp. 39-40, esp. 40 [49; cf. 46-48, esp. 47-48].

are "miracle stories"[27]. (f) From a tradition-critical point of view, Heekerens accepts the "broad consensus" that the Johannine miracle stories are independent from their Synoptic variants[28].

With Thyen and Langbrandtner[29], Heekerens thinks that (a) 2,1-12 and 4,46b-54 were secondarily inserted into the *Grundschrift* by the same hand who added ch. 21, i.e., the Johannine Redaction (JR); (b) the three miracle stories (2,1-12; 4,46-54; 21,1-14) were taken by JR from one source, the *Zeichenquelle* (ZQ)[30]. Against Bultmann[31], Heekerens asserts that not all the miracles in chs. 1–20 came from the source but only the two Cana stories, that 21,1-14 also belonged to the source, and that these miracles were not incorporated into the gospel by the evangelist but by a later redactor[32]. In disagreement with Temple, he assigns not only the two Cana miracles to the source but also 21,1-14 and thinks that these three were inserted not by the evangelist but by the final redactor[33]. Heekerens reconstructs ZQ as follows[34]:

27. *Ibid.*, p. 42; cf. pp. 32-39 [49; cf. 38-46].

28. *Ibid.*, p. 42; cf. pp. 19-21 [49; cf. pp. 23-25].

29. For Thyen, see esp. pp. 16 (nn. 23-25), 29 (nn. 50, 53, 55), 30 (n. 56), 143; other references to Thyen, see pp. 17 (n. 5), 39 (n. 88), 40 (n. 92), 46 (nn. 4, 6), 50 (nn. 4-5), 51 (nn. 6-9), 60 (n. 50), 61 (nn. 53, 55), 65 (n. 72), 71 (n. 101), 73 (nn. 111, 116), 74 (n. 121), 75 (nn. 126), 128, 129, 78 (n. 139), 81 (nn. 164-166), 86 (n. 177), 88 (nn. 186-187), 89 (n. 191), 92, 93, 106 (n. 51, 53), 107 (n. 59), 122 (n. 1), 123 (n. 7), 127 (nn. 15-16), 128 (nn. 18-19), 129 (n. 21), 132 (n. 2). For Langbrandtner, see esp. p. 13 (n. 16); other references to Langbrandtner: pp. 39 (n. 89), 60 (n. 50), 71 (n. 102), 73 (n. 111), 74 (n. 119), 75 (n. 127).

30. *Ibid.*, pp. 131-132 ("Zusammenfassung"), esp. 131; see also pp. 14-15 [174-179, esp. 174; 14]. Note that Heekerens consciously uses the term *Zeichen-Quelle* (ZQ) in distinction to Bultmann's σημεῖα-*Quelle* (cf. pp. 14, 43, 143). Heekerens also weighs the possibility that the miracles of Jn 5, 6, 9, and 11 stem from a common miracle collection "die dann wohl auch Markus benutzt haben dürfte" (see pp. 42-43).

31. *Ibid.*, p. 15: "Nun stellt diese Doppelhypothese, obschon in der Auseinandersetzung mit der neueren Literatur zum Johannesevangelium entstanden, doch kein völliges Novum dar. Wie könnte dies auf dem vielbeackerten Feld der johanneischen Forschung auch anders sein! Am nächsten steht ihr die von *F. Spitta* schon 1910 vertretenen Ansicht"; on p. 16 he also refers to Goguel. See also pp. 45, 132 [52-63, esp. 52; for Goguel see p. 52 n. 3, 59, 60].

32. *Ibid.*, p. 131; cp. p. 15 [174; cp. 61].

33. *Ibid.*, pp. 131-132; cp. pp. 13, 15 [176; cp. 52].

34. *Ibid.*, pp. 49-94 [64-118]: "Analyse von Joh 2,1-11.12; 4,46-54 und 21,1-14". After analysis of tradition and redaction of these three pericopes, Heekerens summarizes the result in fourteen points (pp. 91-94: "Zusammenfassung"; this summary is absent in his dissertation): (1) Against Ruckstuhl, Heekerens thinks that his analysis confirms the broad consensus that in Jn 2,1-12 and 4,46-54a distinction can be made between tradition and redaction, more precisely between source and redaction. This is also true for 21,1-14 (against Thyen). (2) The *Vorlage* of 21,1-14 is a miracle story (cp. Becker, Boismard – Lamouille, Dibelius, Fortna, Fuller, Goguel, Pesch, Schnackenburg and Spitta). (3) With Thyen, he accepts that the redactor composed the meal narrative under influence of Lk 24,13-35, thus rejecting Fortna's thesis that the original *Vorlage* of 21,1-14 already contained a meal as well as the thesis of a second *Vorlage* (so Becker, Boismard – Lamouille, Rissi, Pesch and Schnackenburg). (4) He agrees with Pesch that Lk 5,1-11 and

2,1-11.12

1 καὶ γάμος ἐγένετο ἐν Κανὰ τῆς Γαλιλαίας ... 2 ἐκλήθη δὲ καὶ ὁ Ἰησοῦς καὶ οἱ μαθηταὶ αὐτοῦ εἰς τὸν γάμον. 3 καὶ οἶνον οὐκ εἶχον, ὅτι σηνετελέσθη ὁ οἶνος τοῦ γάμου ... 7 λέγει αὐτοῖς ὁ Ἰησοῦς· γεμίσατε τὰς ὑδρίας ὕδατος. καὶ ἐγέμισαν αὐτὰς ... 8 καὶ λέγει αὐτοῖς· ἀντλήσατε νῦν καὶ φέρετε τῷ ἀρχιτρικλίνῳ. οἱ δὲ ἤνεγκαν. 9 ὡς δὲ ἐγεύσατο ὁ ἀρχιτρίκλινος ... φωνεῖ τὸν νυμφίον ... 10 καὶ λέγει αὐτῷ· πᾶς ἄνθρωπος πρῶτον τὸν καλὸν οἶνον τίθησιν καὶ ὅταν μεθυσθῶσιν τὸν ἐλάσσω· σὺ τετήρηκας τὸν καλὸν οἶνον ἕως ἄρτι. 11 [τοῦτο πρῶτον σημεῖον] ἐποίησεν ὁ Ἰησοῦς ἐν Κανὰ τῆς Γαλιλαίας ... 12 κατέβη εἰς Καφαρναοὺμ αὐτὸς ... καὶ οἱ μαθηταὶ αὐτοῦ ...

4,46b-54

46b ἦν δέ τις βασιλικὸς οὗ ὁ υἱὸς ἠσθένει ἐν Καφαρναούμ. 47 οὗτος ... ἀπῆλθεν πρὸς αὐτὸν καὶ ἠρώτα ἵνα ... ἰάσηται αὐτοῦ τὸν υἱόν ... 50 λέγει αὐτῷ ὁ Ἰησοῦς· πορεύου, ὁ υἱός σου ζῇ. ἐπίστευσεν ὁ ἄνθρωπος τῷ λόγῳ

21,1-14 go back to a common traditional miracle story. (5) For Jn 4,46-54 and Mt 8,5-13 par. Lk 7,1-10 (with Q as *Vorlage*), Heekerens also supposes a common tradition, not literary dependence. (6) Thus, there is no literary dependence between the *Vorlagen* of Jn 21,1-14 and Lc 5,1-11 on the one hand, and Jn 4,46-54 and Mt 8,5-13 par. Lk 7,1-10 on the other; JR, however, seems to be dependent upon the Lukan parallels. (7) For Heekerens, there is evidence of literary dependence on the Synoptics (esp. Lk) only in the verses which should be attributed to the redaction. This means that the same hand, i.e., JR, redacted Jn 4,46-54. (8) With Cullmann and Strathmann, Heekerens accepts the redactional reworking of Jn 2,1-11 into a narrative of the institution of the eucharistic wine. This is to be compared with the eucharistic discourse (ch. 6), also from JR (cp. Bultmann, Becker, Bornkamm, Haenchen, Käsemann, Koester, Langbrandtner, Lohse, Richter, Schulz, Thyen; but questioned by Ruckstuhl, Schweizer and Wilkens), and with the indication of the eucharistic meal in Jn 13, 21ff. (cp. Thyen). On the other hand, in GS there was no presentation of the eucharist. (9) Heekerens cannot accept that Jn 2,1-11 and 4,46-54 were inserted by the author of GS (*Grundschrift*), because these are the only miracles not used as an introduction to a discourse (cf. Fortna, Langbrandtner, Schnackenburg, Temple, Thyen) and because the cosmological dualism (under/above) constitutive for GS is absent in both pericopes (cp. Thyen). (10) He thinks that his distinction between tradition and redaction for 2,1-12; 4,46-54 and 21,1-14, is relatively precise. (11) This distinction is confirmed by the style-critical test. In the texts attributed to the source, there are no Johannine style characteristics as described by Nicol, Ruckstuhl, Schweizer, or Boismard-Lamouille, whereas these appear in the texts attributed to JR. (12) Apart from the Johannine characteristics that appear in the texts of GS and JR (Johannine sociolect), there are three characteristics that belong to the idiolect of JR: πάλιν δεύτερον in 4,54 (p. 52), εἶτα λέγει in 2,3 (p. 65), γύναι in 2,4 (p. 69). This confirms that the redaction of the source is to be attributed to JR. (13) In several places Heekerens prefers the text of ℵ*: 2,3 (p. 77 n. 137); 2,11 (pp. 25-26); 4,46 (p. 62 n. 61); 4,51 (p. 62 n. 62); 21,6 (pp. 89-90, esp. 90 n. 192). (14) Regarding the content, he thinks: *a.* ZQ contains only the three miracles mentioned above, the *Rahmensätze* included (2,11; 4,54; 21,14). *b.* Jn 2,12 is a transitional verse between 2,1-11 and 4,46-54; it is possible that there was a similar transitional verse between the second and third miracle. But this verse can no longer be detected in the present Gospel. *c.* The miracle stories are preserved largely in their original form. Perhaps before 21,3 in the source there was a sentence that mentioned the activity of the miracle worker (see pp. 94-95). *d.* Heekerens finally rejects Bultmann's thesis that the source was introduced with 1,35ff. and concluded with 20,30-31 (see below, p. 260 n. 43).

... καὶ ἐπορεύετο. 51 ... οἱ δοῦλοι ... ὑπήντησαν αὐτῷ καὶ ἤγγειλαν ὅτι ὁ παῖς αὐτοῦ ζῇ. 54 τοῦτο δὲ ... δεύτερον σημεῖον ἐποίησεν ὁ Ἰησοῦς...

21,3-14

21,3 ἐξῆλθον καὶ ἐνέβησαν εἰς τὸ πλοῖον, καὶ ἐν ἐκείνῃ τῇ νυκτὶ ἐπίασαν οὐδέν. 6 λέγει αὐτοῖς· βάλετε εἰς τὰ δεξιὰ μέρη τοῦ πλοίου τὸ δίκτυον, καὶ εὑρήσετε. οἱ δὲ ἔβαλον καὶ οὐκέτι αὐτὸ ἑλκύσαι ἴσχυον ἀπὸ τοῦ πλήθους τῶν ἰχθύων. 14 τοῦτο ἤδη τρίτον [σημεῖον ἐποίησεν] ὁ Ἰησοῦς...

Heekerens[35] thinks that ZQ probably originated in Samaria and must be dated before 50-60 A.D., the date of Q[36]. Regarding the history-of-religions background, he rejects the Hellenistic θεῖος ἀνήρ concept and accepts rather a Jewish background[37]. For the author of ZQ, Jesus is Elijah *redivivus*, a prophet like Moses, and thus Messiah, whereas the Baptist cannot lay claim to these titles[38]. ZQ's christology (especially its description of Jesus in contrast to the Baptist) indicates that the source

35. For the description of ZQ, see pp. 95-120 [119-148]: "Die Zeichen-Quelle".

36. *Ibid.*, pp. 95-96 [119-120]: "Die regionale Herkunft der Zeichen-Quelle". For the date, see p. 120 [128, where he dates ZQ between 50 A.D. and the beginning of the Jewish War]. – From the geography (Cana in 2,1; Capernaum in 2,12; 4,46; and the Sea of Galilee in 21,1-14), one can conclude that the traditional miracle stories originated in Galilee (cf. THEISSEN, *Wundergeschichten*, 1974, p. 245; ET: 1983, p. 247). The same may be true for the source (see κατέβη in 2,12 that presupposes a good knowledge of the Galilean geography). An exclusive binding of the miracle tradition with Galilee, however, cannot be maintained. Heekerens thinks that ZQ originated in Samaria: (a) the addition τῆς Γαλιλαίας to Κανά in 2,1 is only necessary if the source originated outside Galilee and is probably from ZQ's redactor; (b) there is nothing against Samaria as the origin of ZQ, because its socio-ecological, socio-economical, and socio-cultural context is very similar to that of Galilee (cf. THEISSEN, *Wundergeschichten*, 1974, pp. 244-256; ET: 1983, pp. 246-259).

37. *Zeichen-Quelle*, pp. 96-99 [129-132]: "Die religionsgeschichtliche Hintergrund der Zeichen-Quelle". With Boismard – Lamouille, Nicol, Reim, and Rissi, Heekerens identifies the background of ZQ with the Elijah-Elisha miracles (ctr. Bultmann). (a) Regarding Jn 2,1-11, he rejects (with Noetzel) Bultmann's Dionysus interpretation (cp. Linnemann, Haenchen, Schnackenburg) and refers to the wine as a symbol of the Messianic time (Gen 49,11; Is 25,6; Joel 4,18; Amos 9,13; see also Rissi's reference to Gen 27,27-29; cp. in the NT: Mt 22,1-14; 25,1-3; Lk 12,36; Mk 2,19; Jn 3,29). Moreover, there is no archaeological evidence for a Dionysus cult at Cana or in Galilee. Also, the references to January 6, as the day of the Dionysus feast (so Bultmann) or that of "Sol invictus", are irrelevant. The story can be compared with Elijah's flour and oil miracle 1 Kgs 17 (also a gift miracle); see esp. 1 Kgs 17,18 (cp. 2,4 τί ἐμοὶ καὶ σοί). (b) For Jn 4,46-54, Heekerens refers to the healing at a distance by the prayer of Hanina ben Dosa (see also Bultmann, Nicol, Rissi, Schnackenburg); this miracle by Hanina ben Dosa gives evidence that healings have their place in Judaism contemporary with the origin of the New Testament. Thus, it is not necessary to suppose a θεῖος ἀνήρ typology. Again, Heekerens refers to Elijah's story in 1 Kgs 17,17-24; see esp. 1 Kgs 17,23 (cp. 4,50: ὁ υἱός σου ζῇ). (c) The same Old Testament background may be accepted for 21,1-14, which, like Jn 2,1-11, is a gift-miracle. – For Heekerens's rejection of the θεῖος ἀνήρ typology, see also p. 41 [48-49].

38. *Ibid.*, pp. 99-106 [48-49]: "Die Christologie der Zeichen-Quelle". See also p. 41.

originated in the Johannine community when it was in conflict with the disciples of the Baptist; Heekerens stresses that the place of this confrontation was Samaria[39]. He argues as follows[40]: not only the Elijah title, but also the designation of a prophet like Moses is important for ZQ. The *Rahmenbemerkungen* in 2,11; 4,54 and 21,14 must be interpreted (with Boismard) in the light of Ex 4,1-9: like Moses, Jesus is presented as the one sent by God, legitimizing himself by three miracles, also called σημεῖα and also numbered as in Ex 4,8-9. Moreover, the presentation of Elijah and Elisha is typical for Samaritan theology[41]. ZQ is to be characterized as a *Missionsschrift*[42]. Its intention is perhaps reflected in Jn 20,30-31, but unlike many signs-source defenders (and in contrast to his own position in his dissertation) Heekerens does not believe these verses formed the conclusion of ZQ. He reads πιστεύητε in v. 31 and concludes that JR, who was familiar with ZQ's purpose, composed 20,30-31 when he incorporated the source into the gospel[43]. The three miracles have the same literary form[44]. The author of ZQ has taken them from the tradition almost without alteration; he is, however,

---

39. With reference to KIPPENBERG, *Garizim und Synagoge*, 1971, p. 306ff., Heekerens (p. 100 [132]), notes that the reference to a prophet like Moses (cf. Jn 1,21.25; 4,19; 6,14; 7,40), although not attested in Judaism contemporary to the New Testament, was vividly present in the Samaritan religion of Aramaic times. On 1,20-21, see also Heekerens's excursus "Die Auseinandersetzung der frühen johanneischen Gemeinde mit der Täuferbewegung in Samaria" (pp. 100-104 [133-137]).

40. *Zeichen-Quelle*, pp. 104-106 [138-139].

41. With reference to BUCHANAN, *The Samaritan Origin*, 1968, Heekerens notes: "Die Elija-Tradition war in Samaria wohl lebendiger als in Judäa, eine These, für die G.W. Buchanan auf zwei Fakten verweist: Elija war ein Nordreich-Prophet, und die Elija-Elischa-Geschichten der Königsbücher wurden in den judäischen Chronikbüchern übergangen. Ferner: die Erwartung 'eines Propheten wie Mose' ist eine exklusiv samaritanische Tradition, die dann freilich von christlichen Gruppen übernommen und auf Jesus übertragen wurde" (*Zeichen-Quelle*, p. 105 [138]). For this representation, see 6,14; 7,40; also 4,19, and perhaps also in 7,52 and 9,17; see also the citation of Deut 18,19 in Acts 3,22; 7,37. On Buchanan, see above, p. 91.

42. *Ibid.*, pp. 106-109 [139-145]: "Der Sitz im Leben der Zeichen-Quelle". Contrast diss. 1978: "Lehrschrift" (see below, n. 43).

43. In his dissertation (pp. 139-145, 145-148), Heekerens thought that Jn 20,30-31 "in seinem Grundbestand" belonged to ZQ and he then considered ZQ a "Lehrschrift". With Neugebauer, Schnackenburg, and Thyen, he reads πιστεύητε ("damit ihr gläubig bleibet"; see above, p. 253 n. 9) and reconstructed the source's ending as follows: 20,30 πολλὰ ... καὶ ἄλλα σημεῖα ἐποίησεν ὁ Ἰησοῦς ..., ἃ οὐκ ἔστιν γεγραμμένα ... 31 ταῦτα ... γέγραπται ἵνα πιστεύητε ὅτι Ἰησοῦς ἐστιν ὁ χριστὸς ... In the published version, he eliminates these verses from the source. Cf. *Zeichen-Quelle*, pp. 106-109, esp. 106: "H. *Thyen* indes hat mit der These, diese Verse [20,30-31] stammen aus der Feder der JR, allen literarkritischen und theologischen Begründungen, die für diese Hypothese in Feld geführt wurden, den Boden entzogen"; see his argumentation on pp. 106-108; cf. also p. 94. For a critique of Heekerens's first hypothesis, see NEIRYNCK, *Semeia-bron*, 1983, pp. 20-28 (= ET, 1991, pp. 669-677, with notation of the change in "Additional Note", p. 677).

44. *Zeichen-Quelle*, pp. 109-115 [123-124]: "Formgeschichtliche Betrachtung der Zeichen-Quelle". In his publication this section is more extensive, and he describes the

responsible for their order. The itinerary is clear: Jesus goes from Cana in Galilee through Capernaum to the shore of the Sea of Galilee[45]. The author of ZQ connected the first two miracles with 2,12[46]. Moreover, he concluded each miracle story with the numbering of signs to present Jesus as a prophet like Moses (2,11; 4,54; 21,14)[47]. As a collection of miracles, ZQ can be compared with the pre-Markan miracle source and the Old Testament collections of miracles performed by Moses and Elijah[48]. Regarding the language and style of ZQ[49], Heekerens states that the absence of Johannine characteristics confirms his literary analysis[50]. ZQ is written in a simple Greek and contains several Semitisms[51]: (1) the order "imperative, καί, future" (21,6)[52]; (2) the order "predicate, subject" (2.2.3.7.9.11.12; 4,46b.50a.50b.54; 21,14)[53]; (3) frequency of parataxis (with δέ: 2,2.8; 4,46b.54; 21,6; with καί: 2,1.3.7.8.10; 4,47.50.51; 21,3b.6)[54] and infrequency of hypotaxis (ἵνα: 4,47; ὅταν: 2,10; ὅτι: 2,3; 4,51; ὡς δέ: 2,9)[55]; (4) ἐκείνη as pleonastic pronoun (21,4)[56]; (5) the pleonastic ἐξῆλθον (21,3)[57]; (6) ζῆ (4,50)[58]; (7) the absence of constructions with the participle[59]. This description of ZQ

three miracle stories according to Theissen's approach and categories; cf. THEISSEN, *op. cit.*, 1974, pp. 53-125 (ET: pp. 43-118).

45. *Zeichen-Quelle*, pp. 113-115 [124].

46. *Ibid.*, p. 113 [124]. For the numbering of signs, see pp. 21-26, 45-47 [25-31, 58-63].

47. For a critique of the numbering as an argument for the signs hypothesis, see NEIRYNCK, *Semeia-bron*, 1983, pp. 12-17 (= ET: 1991, pp. 660-665).

48. *Zeichen-Quelle*, pp. 114-115 [124].

49. *Ibid.*, pp. 115-117 [120-123]: "Sprache und Stil der Zeichen-Quelle".

50. *Ibid.*, p. 115 [121]; cp. p. 93 (no. 11; see above, pp. [257-]258 n. 34).

51. *Ibid.*, pp. 115-116 [121-122]. To the characteristics mentioned [in the diss. nos. 1, 3, 4, 7-10], Heekerens also notes four other Aramaic characteristics (nos. 5, 6, 11, 12): (5) The name Ἰησοῦς, always with article. For JEREMIAS, in *TLZ* 74 (1949) 527-531, c. 530, this use of the article is an indication of the Aramaic origin, but not according to BLACK, *An Aramaic Approach*, ³1967, p. 93. Also for TEEPLE, *Origin*, 1974, p. 253, this is a characteristic of S (see above, p. 181). (6) Prolepsis of the pronoun in 4,46 (οὗ ὁ υἱός) and 4,47 (αὐτοῦ τὸν υἱόν). According to Black, typical for Aramaic. (11) Frequent use of the historic present (2,7a.8.9.10; 4,50; 21,6). According to BURNEY, *The Aramaic Origin*, 1922, p. 88, an Aramaism. (12) The imperfects ἐπορεύετο (4,50) and ἴσχυον (21,6) reflect Aramaic language, where the participle is connected with the main verb; cf. BURNEY, pp. 91-92. The last two characteristics are to be used "mit Vorsicht".

52. According to BEYER, *Semitische Syntax*, I, ²1968, p. 238 (cp. BULTMANN, *Johannes*, 1941, p. 542; ET: 1971, p. 700) one of the most frequent hypotactic constructions without conjunction in Semitic languages; it appears more in Aramaic than in Greek (BEYER, *op. cit.*, pp. 245, 251).

53. According to BLACK, p. 50 (cf. NORDEN, *Agnostos Theos*, 1913, p. 257), one of the most important Semitisms in the New Testament.

54. According to BLACK, pp. 61-69; BURNEY, pp. 49-56, parataxis is more frequent in Aramaic than in Greek.

55. Not noted in the dissertation.

56. According to BLACK, p. 96, typical of Aramaic.

57. Cf. BULTMANN, *Johannes*, 1941, p. 542 (ET: 1971, p. 700): "Semitism".

58. *Ibid.*, p. 153 n. 2 (ET: 1971, p. 208 n. 1): "semit. Sprachgebrauch".

responds to Bulmann's call to legitimitate the different layers of a recon-struction with distinctive characteristics for each layer[60]. Heekerens maintains that 21,1-14 reflects an older form of tradition than the *Vor-lage* of Lk 5,1-11, and that Jn 4,46-54 represents an older tradition than that in Q. Because Jn 2,1-11 is analogous in form to ZQ's two other mir-acles, he presumes also a very old tradition for this pericope[61].

ZQ was a document that circulated in the Johannine community and was inserted into the *Grundschrift* by JR at a moment when ZQ's mes-sage about Jesus as Messiah, originally intended for non-believers, was under discussion among the members of the community itself[62]. Because of this new historical situation, JR could not employ ZQ without change. Heekerens thinks that there is no *Wunderkritik* in JR, but rather an "Aufhebung", in the sense that earthly miracles are now interpreted in the light of the resurrection[63]. Moreover, for JR the miracles reflect the ecclesial situation[64]. Heekerens proposes further that JR, with knowl-edge of the Gospel of Luke, has inserted the miracles very consciously at appropriate places to achieve a contrast between Galilee (and Samaria), with Cana as center, and Judea, with Jerusalem as center. This geographical scheme reflects the historical situation of the Johannine community, which, after the disaster of the Jewish war, experienced a hostile relationship with Judaism and was expelled from the synagogue[65].

Meanwhile, Hartwig THYEN has retracted his former hypothesis of the Johannine redactor reworking a *Grundschrift*[66]. In his article on the shepherd discourse (1991), he summarizes his approach to the Fourth

---

59. Heekerens mentions esp. the absence of the genitive absolute (frequency in the Gospels: 160 times; cf. BURNEY, p. 57) and the aorist participle, followed by a finite verb, esp. ἀποκριθεὶς εἶπεν (frequency in the Gospels: 955 times: cf. BURNEY, p. 57).

60. *Zeichen-Quelle*, pp. 116-117 [123]; cp. pp. 27-32, esp. 27 [p. 31].

61. *Ibid.*, pp. 117-120 [124-128]: "Traditionsgeschichtliche Überlegungen"; see also pp. 19-21 [23-25].

62. *Ibid.*, pp. 121-130 [132-139]: "Die redaktionelle Verarbeitung der Zeichen-Quelle", esp. 121; see also p. 41 [48-49].

63. Thus, the first miracle takes place on Sunday and the second is to be seen as a pre-figuration of the resurrection (p. 121 [124]).

64. The story of the changing of water into wine becomes a story of the institution of the eucharistic wine, and in 4,46-54 the story may be seen (after the presentation of the Samaritan mission) as a legitimation of the mission to Galilee. Heekerens also suggests interpreting the servants of 4,52 as witnesses of Jesus' words and deeds, like the Beloved Disciple in ch. 21.

65. *Ibid.*, pp. 122-130, esp. 123, 124, 127.

66. He did this in several publications: *Johannes 10 im Kontext des vierten Evange-liums*, in BEUTLER – FORTNA (eds.), *The Shepherd Discourse*, 1991, pp. 116-134, 163-168; *Johannes und die Synoptiker. Auf der Suche nach einem neuen Paradigma zur Beschrei-bung ihrer Beziehungen anhand von Beobachtungen an Passions- und Östererzählungen*, in DENAUX (ed.), *John and the Synoptics*, 1992, pp. 81-107, esp. 81-84 ("Fünfzehn Jahre

Gospel in eight presuppositions[67]. We mention the most important:
(1) The Gospel of John, as it came to us, from 1,1 to 21,25 (!) is a literary unity[68]. (2) It is thus meaningless to name another person than the
author of ch. 21 "the Fourth Evangelist"[69]. (3) Not some hypothetical
"Vor- oder Nachgeschichte" of parts of the gospel, such as the "Prolog-
vorlage", signs source, or passion source, but the gospel text, its structural
value and the difference with other passages on the synchronic level of
the text as a whole reveal its meaning[70]. (4) As a literary *work*, the
Gospel of John is not to be regarded as the result of some anonymous
tradition- or redaction-historical growth that can be described, as if texts
like trees show annual rings, but it is rather the result of a production
process (ποίησις), in whose course it has become autonomous over
against the author's original intentions and the ostentatious relations to
the first readers' world[71]. (5) With Neirynck, Sabbe, and others, it must
be accepted that the Fourth Gospel presupposes the three Synoptic
Gospels themselves in their present (canonical) form[72]. Thyen again

---

später", in which he describes his *retractatio* of his former hypothesis, defended at the
1975 colloquium, cf. *Entwicklungen*, 1977) and pp. 85-93 (where he deals with "Die
Aporien der redaktionsgeschichtlichen Methode"; cp. his review of FORTNA, *Predecessor*, in *TLZ* 117, 1992, 34-39); *Die Erzählung von den bethanischen Geschwistern
(Joh 11,1–12,19) als "Palimpsest" über synoptischen Texten*, in *FS F. Neirynck*, III,
1992, pp. 2021-2050.
   67. *Johannes 10*, pp. 116-123.
   68. *Ibid.*, pp. 116-117 (no. 1), esp. 116; *Johannes und die Synoptiker*, pp. 84-85, 91;
TLZ 117, c. 37; *Die Erzählung*, pp. 2025-2027.
   69. *Johannes 10*, p. 117 (no. 2): "Meine eigenen ausgedehnten Wege durch das
Labyrinth johanneischer 'Literarkritik', 'Quellensuche' und 'Redaktionsgeschichte'
haben mich statt zu dem gesuchten 'ursprünglichen Johannesevangelium' und seinem
'Evangelisten' zu der Einsicht geführt, dass das Werk kohärent ist und es deshalb sinnlos
ist, irgend einen anderen als den Autor von Joh 21 den 'vierten Evangelisten' zu nennen"; *Johannes und die Synoptiker*, pp. 84-85, 91; *TLZ* 117, c. 37. This means that the
evangelist has created all the passages on the Beloved Disciple and Peter (ctr. *Entwicklungen*).
   70. *Johannes 10*, pp. 117-118 (no. 3), esp. 117. Thus he rejects his redaction-historical approach in *Entwicklungen*; cf. *Johannes und die Synoptiker*, pp. 81-85.
   71. *Johannes 10*, pp. 118-119 (no. 4), esp. 118.
   72. *Ibid.*, pp. 119-120 (no. 6), esp. 119: "Nicht nur aufgrund seines Ortes im Bibel-
kanon, sondern auch insofern ist Johannes der 'vierte Evangelist', als er unsere drei synoptischen Evangelien in ihrer überlieferten Gestalt voraussetzt, und nicht etwa nur ein
anonymes Analogon der 'synoptischen Tradition'". See esp. *Johannes und die Synoptiker*, pp. 89, 93-95; *TLZ* 117, c. 36; *Die Erzählung*, pp. 2021-2025. – Already at the
Leuven Colloquium of 1975, Thyen was convinced that the Johannine redaction was
influenced by Luke in Jn 21 (*Entwicklungen*, p. 263, on Lk 5,1-11; 24,41; see also *TR* 42,
p. 247; cp. pp. 226-227, 234) and that Lk 24,12 forms the basis of Jn 20,2-10 (*Entwicklungen*, p. 289; cp. *TR* 42, pp. 251-252). In the published text he added: "M.E. bedarf die
Frage 'Johannes und die Synoptiker' unter dieser Perspektive dringend erneuter Untersuchung" (*Entwicklungen*, p. 289; cp. *TR* 42, p. 252). See also *TRE* 17, p. 208, where
he could write: "So bahnt sich doch ein neuer Konsensus darüber an, dass jedenfalls der-

notes that the semeia hypothesis is "höchst unwahrscheinlich" and he agrees fully with the criticism of the hypothesis in Heekerens's mono-graph[73]. For Thyen, it is indeed impossible to prove the existence of one source which contained all the Johannine miracle stories: most of them originated from the Synoptics[74].

In his lecture at the Colloquium in Leuven, published in 1992, and in his review of Fortna's *Predecessor* in *TLZ*, Thyen illustrated the short-comings of Fortna's redaction-historical method[75]. First, he rejects the presupposition that the Johannine author treated his source "with far greater respect, so as to retain their original wording, than did the Matthean and Lukan author in reusing Mark"[76]. Second, one cannot push aside the view that John used the Synoptics and that John con-trolled the intertextual play with the works of his predecessors in a more sovereign manner than did Matthew and Luke with Mk[77]. Third, it is impossible to prove stylistically the pre-Johannine combination of SQ and PQ in the Signs Gospel[78]. Such genesis of the text is also

jenige, dem wir das Evangelium in seiner überlieferten Gestalt verdanken, die Synoptiker kannte und benutzte"; see also p. 215. Cf. NEIRYNCK, *John and the Synoptics*, 1992, p. 8; see also SMITH, *John among the Gospels*, 1992, pp. 167-169 ("Hartwig Thyen: A Note"), esp. 167: "In that scholar's [Thyen's] more recent utterances, he has made it unmistak-ably clear that he now not only believes that John knew Luke but fully embraces the results and perspective of Frans Neirynck, whose work he cites with hearty approval".

73. *Johannes 10*, p. 163 n. 1: "Nicht nur die Existenz von Bultmann's 'Offen-barungsreden-Quelle', sondern auch seine breit rezipierte und bis in die Kommentare hinein fast als 'Tatsache' gewertete Hypothese einer '*Semeia*-Quelle' ist mir höchst unwahrscheinlich".

74. *Ibid.*, p. 163 n. 1. Also with regard to Jn 1,1-18, Thyen notes that it becomes for him "immer unwahrscheinlicher" that the evangelist used a source, and he concludes: "Mit den vermeintlichen 'Quellen' steht dann natürlich auch die Basis für die Konstruk-tion einer 'johanneischen Entwicklungslinie' auf dem Spiel" (p. 163 n. 1). Cp. *Johannes und die Synoptiker*, 1992, p. 81. – The three other presuppositions not mentioned above are: (1) For the interpretation of the mythological history and destiny of the λόγος who became flesh, Bultmann's demythologization and existential interpretation is only a first – although necessary – step, but we need also, what Frye has called an "accommodation" to the mythological language. Cf. *Johannes 10*, pp. 119-120 (no. 4), esp. 119. Cf. FRYE, in MILLER - HADIDIAN (eds.), *Jesus and Man's Hope*, 1971, pp. 193-201, esp. 201ff. (2) It is a failure to interpret the Gospel of John as a product of a little esoteric sect at the bor-der of the "great church". Cf. *Johannes 10*, pp. 120-121 (no. 7); cp. *Johannes und die Synoptiker*, p. 81. (3) Finally, like the Johannine epistles, the Gospel of John reflects a sit-uation where Christians where expelled from the synagogue. They lost not only their social home but also the relative protection against the blasphemous demand that they participate in the imperial cult; they were thus exposed to the bloody consequences of refusal. Cf. *Johannes 10*, pp. 122-123 (no. 8), esp. 122.

75. *Johannes und die Synoptiker*, pp. 85-93; the text of these pages is presented in a slightly reworked form in his review of Fortna's *Predecessor*, in *TLZ* 117, 34-39.

76. *Johannes und die Synoptiker*, pp. 85-86; *TLZ* 117, c. 34.

77. John's intertextual play with the Synoptics can be compared with his play with OT texts. Cf. *Johannes und die Synoptiker*, p. 88; see also pp. 95-99 (for the model of such an intertextual reading Thyen refers, among others, to Kristeva; see p. 96 n. 41).

78. *Johannes und die Synoptiker*, p. 86; cp. p. 89 n. 17; *TLZ* 117, c. 35.

problematic with regard to the contents, because all signs in John are narrated in the light of the resurrection faith[79]. Fourth, Fortna fails when he takes "the all-but-intolerable tension between *narrative* and *discourse*" – the first being familiar to us from the other three Gospels, the second being Johannine – as the main starting point of his source criticism[80]. If one tests the result of such a source criticism with the stylistic criteria of Ruckstuhl-Dschulnigg, it becomes clear that there are no significant differences between the two layers Fortna distinguishes: the appearance, the distribution and the frequency of the Johannine characteristics are the same in both the signs source and the Johannine redaction[81]. Fifth, Fortna's reconstruction of the source's content is in fact very Synoptic-like, and, if we compare it with the present gospel, we must conclude that the Fourth Evangelist has handled the source with sovereign freedom. This means that Fortna's reconstruction is in contradiction with his own primary presupposition that the Fourth Evangelist handled his source with great respect[82]. Sixth, before Fortna can describe the genesis of the text from the narrative source to the present gospel, he needs to go first in the opposite direction, i.e., he has to reconstruct the source from the present gospel. Thyen cannot see how such a method can be controlled. Is it not so that the reconstruction of the Signs Gospel depends upon the guessing ingenuity of the constructor in combination with his knowledge of the Synoptic Gospels? Does not the semeia hypothesis need the presupposition of an ur-gospel independent from and older than the Synoptics and still other less plausible extra hypotheses[83]? Thyen concludes: "Fortna's Ur-gospel remains a pale homunculus, whose creator was unable to awake it to life"[84]. Seventh, Thyen rejects Fortna's interpretation of the Fourth Gospel because it does not explain the whole gospel with its specific plot, its peculiar combination of narratives and discourses and its dialectical unity of form and contents. Instead, Fortna essentially explains only the evangelist's presumed

79. *TLZ* 117, c. 35; Thyen adds: "Plausibel wäre die Konstruktion zudem nur, wenn F[ortna] die *vorösterliche* Entstehung seiner Zeichenquelle erweisen könnte".
80. *Johannes und die Synoptiker*, pp. 86-87; *TLZ* 117, c. 35. Cf. FORTNA, *Predecessor*, p. 1.
81. *Johannes und die Synoptiker*, p. 89 n. 17; *TLZ* 117, c. 35. For Ruckstuhl and Dschulnigg, see below, pp. 307-312.
82. *Johannes und die Synoptiker*, pp. 87-88; *TLZ* 117, cc. 35-36. See above, p. 264 n. 76.
83. *Johannes und die Synoptiker*, pp. 88-89; *TLZ* 117, c. 36.
84. *Johannes und die Synoptiker*, 1992, pp. 88-89; *TLZ*, 1992, c. 36. – Note that the expression "homunculus" was used by OVERBECK (*Das Johannesevangelium*, 1911, p. 243) in reaction to older source criticism: "Bei dem gegenwärtigen Stande der Quellenscheidung im Neuen Testament könnte ich mir wohl denken, dass auch die Frage zur Diskussion gestellt würde, ob nicht unter den Quellen des 4. Evangeliums auch ein vorkanonisches *Johannes*evangelium zu statuieren, aus ihm ein solches zu konstruieren und neben die ihm voranliegenden Synoptiker zu stellen sei. Da indessen dieses Joh.-Evangelium sonst, d.h. ausserhalb des 4. Evangeliums selbst spurlos ist und nur ein purer

interventions and additions to the narrative parts[85]. Finally, as in his article on Jn 10, Thyen pleads for a synchronic and intertextual reading of the whole gospel (ch. 21 included[86]) and proposes to read it as a text upon the texts of the Synoptic Gospels with which it "plays" and works in many ways[87]. For such a reading, Fortna's reconstruction of the signs source, even if it once existed and its existence could be proven by archaeological evidence, is meaningless[88].

2. Regarding source criticism, George R. BEASLEY-MURRAY (1987)[89], a former student of C.H. Dodd[90] and translator of Bultmann's commentary (1971)[91], is rather reserved; he thinks "in terms of *traditions* available to the evangelist rather than literary *sources*"[92]. For the semeia hypothesis, he refers to Bultmann, Becker, Fortna, and Nicol[93] and gives the following evaluation of the theory: on the one hand "not a few scholars view this proposal of a signs-source with a sympathetic eye, and some advocate it with enthusiasm", but on the other "resistance to the hypothesis remains widespread, especially on the European

gelehrter Evangelienhomunkulus gewesen sein könnte, so scheint mir das ganze Problem eine quellenkritische Spielerei, dergleichen neuerdings manche andere entstanden sind. Die ganze Konstruktion der Quelle wäre bodenlos". Overbeck has been cited recently by HENGEL, *The Johannine Question*, 1988, p. 86 (GT: 1993, p. 239).

85. *Johannes und die Synoptiker*, pp. 89-90; *TLZ* 117, c. 36.

86. Fortna does not answer the question whether ch. 21 is added by the evangelist or by someone else (cf. *Predecessor*, 1988, p. 246 n. 41).

87. *Johannes 10*, p. 120; *Johannes und die Synoptiker*, p. 96; *TLZ* 117, c. 36. In *Johannes und die Synoptiker*, he gives an intertextual reading of Jn 19,31-37 and Jn 20; cp. his intertextual reading of Jn 11,1–12,19 in *FS F. Neirynck*, 1992.

88. *Johannes und die Synoptiker*, p. 91; *TLZ* 117, cc. 36-37; see also the rejection of the semeia hypothesis in *Die Erzählung*, p. 2023 n. 7: "Trotz ihrer nahezu kanonischen Geltung sehe ich kein einziges ernstzunehmendes Argument für die Existenz dieser mutmasslichen *Semeiaquelle*".

89. G.R. BEASLEY-MURRAY, *John* (WBC, 36), Waco, TX, 1987. – Among the many reviews, see esp. R.A. CULPEPPER, in *RExp* 85 (1988) 566-567; U.C. VON WAHLDE, in *BTB* 18 (1988) 85-86; J. ZUMSTEIN, in *ÉTR* 63 (1988) 589-590; P.J. CAHILL, in *CBQ* 51 (1989) 144-145; R. KYSAR, in *JBL* 108 (1989) 732-733; B. LINDARS, in *JTS* 40 (1989) 189-192; F. NEIRYNCK, in *ETL* 65 (1989) 166-167; D. BALL, in *Themelios* 19 (1993-94) 13-14. See also LINDARS, *Trends*, 1990, pp. 329-330; SMITH, *John among the Gospels*, 1992, p. 68.

90. Beasley-Murray quotes Dodd's living voice (p. 10; cf. pp. X, XLII). Dodd's *Interpretation* and *Historical Tradition* are frequently cited, mostly with qualifying comment; see NEIRYNCK, in *ETL* 65, pp. 166-167.

91. See above, p. 24 n. 138.

92. *John*, pp. XXXVIII-XLII, esp. XLI, with reference to BARRETT, *John*, ²1978, p. 17 ("all source criticism of John is guesswork"; GT: 1990, p. 35; on Barrett, see above, pp. 166-167) and to CARSON, *Current Source Criticism*, 1978, who appeals for "a probing agnosticism regarding sources of the Fourth Gospel" (see below, p. 316 n. 402).

93. *John*, pp. XXXIX-XL. With respect to ch. 11, he also mentions Fuller and Schnackenburg (see p. 185). Nicol is misspelled throughout as Nichol. There is confusion between "signs source" and "the Book of Signs" in the Index (p. 426); cf. NEIRYNCK, in *ETL* 65, p. 167.

scene"[94]. Beasley-Murray notes three objections against the semeia hypothesis[95]: (1) The Gospel is a stylistic unity[96]. (2) "Some at least of the signs and discourses are woven together; they are so closely related they can hardly be viewed as two independent sources. In this connection it is noteworthy that along with the term 'sign' the term 'work' occurs in a related sense"[97]. (3) "We find some discourses introduced by significant miraculous acts"[98]. From these observations, he concludes: "All this raises the question whether the setting of the ministry of Jesus under the rubric of 'signs' (12:37 and 20:30) may have a more extensive significance than that commonly attributed to it, and whether therefore the separation from the rest of the Gospel of a source consisting of miracles only accords with the mind of the evangelist and with the structure of his Gospel"[99].

From the numbering of signs, however, Beasley-Murray thinks that "it is not impossible that the evangelist was acquainted with a source that contained the two signs of Cana"[100], and 2,12 was perhaps the link between the two[101]. He also notes: "the two Cana signs could well have circulated as twin narratives in the oral tradition of the Johannine communities"[102]. But from 2,11 and 4,54 it is difficult to postulate a signs source, "which included all the seven reproduced in the Fourth Gospel (plus a great deal more, according to Bultmann and Fortna)"[103]. Although he considers this not impossible, he thinks that "it is a large leap from vv 46 and 54 to that conclusion: the two statements primarily connect the *two* narratives"[104]. Finally, Beasley-Murray rejects 20,30-31 as the conclusion of the source[105].

---

94. *John*, p. XL.

95. *Ibid.*, p. XL; cp. p. 34: "The theory entails formidable difficulties".

96. Beasley-Murray (p. XL) refers to RUCKSTUHL, *Johannine Language*, 1977.

97. The latter not only refers to the miracles of Jesus, but embraces "the entire ministry of deed and word which God had commissioned him to achieve" (see 4,34; 9,4; 14,10; 17,4; see also 5,17.19-23, where Jesus' work consists in raising the dead and exercising judgment over mankind) (*John*, p. XL).

98. See chs. 5, 6, 9, 11. In contrast, the discourse of ch. 12 is introduced by two non-miraculous deeds. The discourses of chs. 3–4 are introduced by the the Changing of Water into Wine and the Cleansing of the Temple, whereas the discourse of chs. 7–8 "is conditioned by the presence of Jesus at the Feast of Tabernacles and its significant *rituals*, akin to which is the discourse given in chap. 10 at the Feast of Dedication" (p. XL).

99. *Ibid.*, p. XL.

100. *Ibid.*, p. 34; cp. p. 71.

101. *Ibid.*, p. 71: "If, as is often thought, 2:12 formed the introduction to the second miracle, the latter will have been seen in close proximity to the former".

102. *Ibid.*, p. 67.

103. *Ibid.*, p. 71.

104 *Ibid.*, p. 71.

105. *Ibid.*, p. 387; he calls Bultmann's interpretation "a questionable position to take". For Beasley-Murray, the σημεῖα refer to the resurrection appearances.

3. In 1988, Allan MAYER renewed the older interpolation hypothesis
of A. Schweizer and H. Delff: "If the Fourth Gospel went through several editions before reaching its final form (as maintained by Brown and
Lindars) it would not be difficult to envisage how at some stage the
Galilean source was merged into what was previously a basically
Judaean document"[106]. Mayer comes to this conclusion after studying
the influence of the Elijah-Elisha cycle on the Gospel of John, explaining that "although John seems to hint that Jesus is the prophet like
Moses, there is also a typological tendency to portray him as a prophet
like Elijah and Elisha"[107]. This tendency is clear in the three Galilean
miracles: (1) 2,1-12: cp. 1 Kgs 17,1-16; 2 Kgs 4,1-7; (2) 4,46b-54:
cp. 1 Kgs 17,17-24; 2 Kgs 4,7-37; (3) 6,1-15: cp. 2 Kgs 4,42-44[108].

Mayer thinks that the first two signs of Jesus in John originally
belonged to a common source[109]. They occur in the same order as
Elijah's first two miracles (1 Kgs 17), and this "may indicate that the
Elijah-Elisha typology was originally a concern of the source"[110].
Although Mayer does not agree with Temple in limiting the signs source
to these two miracles, he sees "no reason to suppose that all of John's
miracles shared a common origin"[111]. At any rate, he attributes the three
Galilean miracles to the source[112]. Along with the typology, they share
the following characteristics: 1. the Galilean setting; 2. the legendary
character; 3. after removing editorial intrusions (2,4; 4,48; 6,6), it
becomes evident that in the source Jesus performed miracles by request;
4. the three stories are self-contained[113]; 5. the miracles are called signs
at the end of each account (2,11; 4,54; 6,14) and a response of belief
among the witnesses is recorded. In the "Galilean signs source" Jesus
was portrayed as a northern prophet[114]. The order and continuity of the
source are parallel with the Elisha-cycle[115], but its "typology is more

106. A. MAYER, *Elijah and Elisha in John's Signs Source*, in *ExpT* 99 (1987-88) 171-173,
p. 173. Mayer mentions only Delff, however, as a predecessor: "The idea that the Galilean
portions of John were interpolations was suggested by Delff at the end of the last century"
(p. 173, n. 7), and refers for this to SANDAY, *Criticism*, 1905 (see above, p. 10 n. 49).

107. *Elijah*, p. 171.

108. *Ibid.*, pp. 171-172.

109. According to Mayer this is "an axiom of Johannine source criticism" (p. 172).

110. *Ibid.*, p. 172.

111. *Ibid.*, p. 172.

112. *Ibid.*, p. 172.

113. Mayer thinks that this is also the case for the bread miracle: "Although the bread
of life discourse follows the feeding, the fact that the crowd request a miraculous meal in
terms which indicate that they have not seen one (6:30-31) suggests that the discourse did
not grow from the narrative but had developed independently of it" (p. 172).

114. *Ibid.*, p. 172.

115. *Ibid.*, p. 172. The localisation of the second Galilean miracle at Cana (not Capernaum) is "a Johannine heightening of the miracle". In the source Jn 4,46b (καὶ ἦν τις
βασιλικὸς...) "quite naturally" followed from 2,12; 4,46b-54 was followed by 6,1.
Thus, the three signs are "stages in an eastward journey by a wandering prophet". The

concerned with showing Jesus to be the new Elijah"[116]. This typology is embraced by the evangelist (Jn 1,21)[117]. When the Galilean source was merged into the Judean document, the evangelist respected the order of the source[118].

4. We may conclude this survey of the short signs source with Mark W. STIBBE (1992)[119]. Against both Fortna and von Wahlde he objects that they "fail to see that there are differences between the Galilean miracles and the Judaean miracles in John"[120]. Therefore, he distinguishes

order of the source is the same as in 2 Kgs 4: (a) the miraculous alteration of a liquid (Jn 2,1-12; cp. 2 Kgs 4,1-7); (b) restoration of a son (Jn 4,46-54; cp. 2 Kgs 4,8-37); (c) feeding of a crowd (Jn 6,1-15; cp. 2 Kgs 4,42-42).

116. *Ibid.*, pp. 172-173.

117. Mayer (p. 173 n. 10) refers to B.P. ROBINSON, in *Scripture* 17 (1965) 104-105, who "has argued that John wished to represent Jesus as an Elijah-Elisha figure, citing the water to wine and feeding miracles, but comparing Jesus' first miracle to Elisha's first, the sweetening of the waters".

118. *Elijah*, p. 173.

119. M.W.G. STIBBE, *John as Storyteller: Narrative Criticism and the Fourth Gospel* (SNTS MS, 73), Cambridge, 1992. After a short Introduction (pp. 1-2), the monograph includes two parts. In the first part (pp. 3-92: "The Method of Narrative Criticism and the Gospel of John"), he deals with practical criticism (pp. 5-29), genre criticism (pp. 30-49), the social function of John's narrative (pp. 50-66), and, finally, with the narrative-historical approach to John's narrative (pp. 67-92). In the second part, he presents "An Application of the Method of Narrative Criticism to John 18–19" (pp. 93-196), with a chapter division corresponding to the first part. The monograph is a reworking of his dissertation (cf. p. XI-XII), *The Artistry of John: The Fourth Gospel as Narrative Christology*, diss. Nottingham, 1989 (dir. J. Muddiman). Cf. *DissAbstr* 50 (1989-90), no. 10, 3269. – Stibbe seeks to expose a false presumption on the part of German Johannine scholars – he refers especially to F.C. Baur, B. Bauer, J. Wellhausen, E. Schwartz, E. Hirsch, and H. Windisch – who "all insisted that John's gospel could not be history because John was a creative poet". According to Stibbe, "The gospel of John is a poetic history: it is a creative description of historical tradition in which the concrete reality of Jesus' life is by no means destroyed. By integrating aesthetic and historical criticism, I will open up the possibility of travelling from the narrative of Jesus' experience, through the narrative sources, to the narrative-shaped gospel" (cf. p. 2). Reviews: R.A. BURRIDGE, in *JTS* 44 (1993) 654-658; R.G. MACCINI, in *EvQ* 65 (1993) 165-167; C.R. KOESTER, in *CBQ* 55 (1993) 399-401.D. BALL, in *Themelios* 19 (1993-94), p. 16. – In his commentary, *John* (Readings: A New Biblical Commentary), Sheffield, 1993, Stibbe applied the method of narrative criticism to the whole gospel. See also his articles, *The Elusive Christ: A New Reading of the Fourth Gospel*, in *JSNT* 44 (1991) 20-39; *"Return to the Sender": A Structuralist Approach to John's Gospel*, in *Biblical Interpretation* 1 (1992) 189-206. Stibbe is the editor of *The Gospel of John as Literature: An Anthology of Twentieth Century Perspectives* (NTTS), Leiden, 1993.

120. *Ibid.*, pp. 82-84: "The signs gospel", esp. 84. According to Stibbe, there are two major differences: "In the first place, there are differences in geographical context: the Judaean miracles all occur in or around Jerusalem. In at least the case of Bethesda and Siloam, archaeology has revealed that the topography of these miracles reflects an accurate knowledge of Jerusalem before AD 70. Secondly, there are the differences in literary form: in the Judaean miracle narratives, the healing of the man born blind at Siloam, the raising of Lazarus very near Jerusalem, all lead on to controversy with the Jewish author-

between "two miracle traditions in John's gospel: a Galilean miracles source and the Judaean miracles in the Bethany gospel"[121], and thus rejects the signs gospel[122]. According to Stibbe, a second-generation follower of Jesus, whom he calls "John the storyteller", "took the Bethany gospel, a sign source [i.e., a collection of Galilean signs/miracles], and certain discourse sources (maybe other narrative sources too, such as a Samaritan tradition) and recast them into a carefully constructed story designed to address social needs in his church(es)"[123]. Regarding the sources of the gospel, Stibbe gives further information only about "the Bethany gospel", "the primary source behind John's story of Jesus"[124], to which he ascribes the following stories[125]: 1. John the Baptist's ministry around Bethany (1,19-42; 3,22ff.)[126]; 2. encounters between individuals (Nathanael in 1,43-51; Nicodemus in 3,1-15; 7,45-52; 19,38f.); 3. Jesus at the feasts in Jerusalem (5,1; 7,3-13; 10,22f.), in particular the passover visits (2,13; 13,1); 4. Lazarus himself (ch. 11; 12,1-11.17-19; 13,23-24; 18,15-18; 19,25-37; 20,3-4, ch. 21)[127];

---

ities. Unlike the Galilean miracles (except for the multiplication of the loaves in John 6), they lead into heated debates with the Jewish hierarchy and into discourse material which elaborates themes from the miracles" (p. 84). – Further, Stibbe objects that Fortna's second monograph does not take account of Lindars's critique against his *Gospel of Signs*: "Lindars showed how close to impossible it is to distinguish between tradition and redaction in John because the evangelist's style permeates every sentence of the gospel. Fortna has certainly not refined his method to take this into account" (pp. 83-84). With regard to von Wahlde's criteria for recovering the Gospel of Signs he notes: "although his basic approach distinguishing between two different understandings of the miracles and the Jewish hierarchy is innovative, the twenty other criteria he introduces for distinguishing between source and redaction are not convincing, and seriously undermine his method".

121. *Ibid.*, p. 84

122. *Ibid.*, p. 84: "I propose that there was no signs gospel, but that there was a collection of Galilean signs/miracles".

123. *Ibid.*, p. 86 (cp. p. 179).

124. *Ibid.*, p. 80.

125. *Ibid.*, p. 81. See also pp. 81-82, for a "hypothetical reconstruction of the ur-gospel centred upon Lazarus' reminiscences". Stibbe distinguishes two parts: "Part 1: The Jerusalem ministry of Jesus: (a) The preparatory ministry of John the Baptist in Bethany. (b) The calling of the first disciples, including Lazarus. (c) Encounters with Jerusalem-based individuals: Nathaniel and Nicodemus. Again witnessed by Lazarus. (d) Jerusalem-based miracles (Bethesda in ch. 5, Siloam in ch. 9, Bethany in ch. 11, though not necessary in this order). These miracles are set within Jesus' visits to the capital and were witnessed by Lazarus. (e) Conclusion to part 1. The controversy with the Jewish leaders in Jerusalem caused by these miracles finalized the plot to kill Jesus (material now in chapters 11 and 12). At the end of part 1, Lazarus' sister ominously anoints Jesus' feet. Part 2: The last days of Jesus in Jerusalem: (a) The entrance into Jerusalem and the cleansing of the temple. (b) The last supper, including institution narrative, Judas material, washing of disciples' feet and some last words of Jesus. (c) The arrest, trial and execution of Jesus. (d) The resurrection (the race to the empty tomb in John 20.3f.). (e) The conclusion to part 2".

126. He adds with reference to PARKER, in *JBL* 74 (1955) 257-261: "especially if this Bethany is being identified by John as the Bethany where Lazarus lived".

127. For the identification of Lazarus with the Beloved Disciple, see below, p. 271 n. 130.

5. Jerusalem-based miracles (5,1-15 at Bethesda; 9,1-34 at Siloam) "which clearly come from a different milieu from that other miracle stories"[128]; 6. the last supper ("the basis of the narrative and discourse in chapters 13 and 14") and passion/resurrection[129]. For Stibbe, the Bethany gospel provides us "valuable historical tradition ... which originates in the eye-witness of Lazarus of Bethany"[130]; it was a "primitive gospel which was already cast in narrative form", which Stibbe "boldly" calls the Gospel of Lazarus[131].

2. The Miracles Stories as Part of a "Grundschrift"

Some scholars, who deny the semeia hypothesis, hold that the Fourth Gospel went through several editions and suppose that the first of the editions must be considered a *Grundschrift* in which several traditions, including the Johannine miracle tradition, are combined[132]. Marie-Émile BOISMARD[133], for example, in his 1977 commentary[134] attributes the two

128. *John as Storyteller*, p. 81.

129. On chs. 18–19, see esp. Part II (pp. 93-196, esp. 179-189: "Narrative and source"). Stibbe proposes that "the passion source used by John was a narrative of the arrest, trial and death of Jesus deriving from the reminiscences of the BD" (p. 180), and he formulates two presuppositions which are implied in this value judgment: (1) "John's passion story is based on a source which existed independently from the pre-Synoptic passion traditions but which has some parallels with them" (p. 180; cp. p. 182: "John's passion source derived from a tradition independent of the written Synoptic passion narratives: the eye-witness tradition of the BD"); (2) "this tradition was very early on formed into a connected narrative. ... The source at John's disposal was already a narrative with a beginning, a middle and an end" (p. 182).

130. *Ibid.*, p. 81. See also pp. 77-80, where he argues that Lazarus is probably the Beloved Disciple. Cf. esp. p. 78: "It is my convinction that the gospel of John makes much better sense if we see John the elder as the author of the final work, and another candidate besides John bar Zebedee as the principal authority and eye-witness source behind him. This authority called 'the Beloved Disciple' can only be one person if John's story is read on its own terms and without any knowledge of the somewhat unreliable second-century traditions connecting him with John. ... He *has* to be Lazarus of Bethany, as a number of scholars, who have not been taken seriously enough, have stated" (with reference to KREYENBUHL, *Das Evangelium der Wahrheit*, 1900; EISLER, *The Enigma of the Fourth Gospel*, 1938; GARVIE, *The Beloved Disciple*, 1922; FILSON, in *JBL* 68, 1949, 83-88; ELLER, *The Beloved Disciple*, 1987).

131. *John as Storyteller*, p. 82.

132. Cf. MARTYN, *History and Theology*, ²1979, p. 165.

133. He thought in 1962 that Jn 2,1-11 and 4,46-54 originally belonged together, connected by Jn 2,12, and in 1972 presumed the existence of an ancient source with miracles, "un recueil de miracles" (although he began to hesitate about 4,46-54). See above, p. 56.

134. M.-É. BOISMARD – A. LAMOUILLE, *L'évangile de Jean. Commentaire* (Synopse des quatre évangiles en français, 3), Paris, 1977 (= *Jean*). In the Preface, Boismard notes: "Ce volume est le fruit d'une étroite collaboration avec le Père Arnaud Lamouille. Il est impossible de préciser ce qui revient à l'un ou à l'autre dans l'œuvre définitive. ... Pour sauvegarder l'unité de style de l'ensemble, j'ai assuré l'ultime rédaction de l'Introduction et des notes du Commentaire. Le Père Lamouille s'est attaché spécialement à perfectionner la liste des caractéristiques stylistiques et à rechercher les analogies de structure de

signs 2,1ff.; 4,46bff. together with 21,1ff.[135] to *Document C* (or *Jean I*), the oldest layer of the Fourth Gospel[136]. This primitive Gospel must be dated around 50 A.D.[137]; it was written in Palestine by a Christian who was related to Samaritan communities[138]. It may have been composed by the Beloved Disciple (whether he was John the apostle, the son of Zebedee, or Lazarus)[139]. Another writer, John the presbyter, mentioned

phrases dans les écrits johanniques; j'ai pris la responsabilité des options de critique textuelle signalées dans la première partie des notes" (p. 7). – Reviews: cf. Van Belle, no. 1917. See esp. F. Neirynck, *Jean et les Synoptiques. Examen critique de l'exégèse de M.-É. Boismard* (BETL, 49), Leuven, 1979; the first six sections (pp. 3-120) appeared already in *ETL* 53 (1977) 363-478: *L'évangile de Jean. Examen critique du commentaire de M.-É. Boismard et A. Lamouille* (with the collaboration of J. Delobel, T. Snoy, F. Van Segbroeck, G. Van Belle). See also Sabbe, in *ETL* 56 (1980) 125-131 (= 1991, pp. 389-395, 396-397: Additional Note); Brown, *Johannine Community*, 1979, pp. 178-179 (FT: 1983, pp. 195-196); Martyn, *History and Theology*, ²1979, p. 166; Léon-Dufour, in *RSR* 68 (1980) 280-283; Neirynck, *Semeia-bron*, 1983, *passim*, esp. pp. 9-10, 21-27 (= ET: 1991, *passim*, esp. pp. 657-658, 669-775); Heekerens, *Zeichen-Quelle*, 1984, p. 14; Cothenet, *L'évangile selon saint Jean*, 1984, pp. 51-52; Van Belle, *Parenthèses*, 1985, pp. 179-184; Kuhn, *Christologie*, 1988, pp. 56-58 (Jn 1,35-51); Wagner, *Auferstehung*, 1988, pp. 79-82 (Jn 11,1–12,19); Lütgehetmann, *Hochzeit*, 1990, pp. 97-105 (Jn 2,1-11); Morgen, *L'exégèse johannique*, 1989, pp. 246-247; Beutler, *Méthodes et problèmes*, 1990, pp. 17-19; Léon-Dufour, *Où en est la recherche johannique?*, 1990, p. 26; Ashton, *Understanding*, 1991, pp. 85-86, 161; Ruckstuhl – Dschulnigg, *Stilkritik*, 1991, pp. 39-43, 212-213, 248; Schmithals, *Johannesevangelium*, 1992, pp. 137, 190-191; Smith, *John among the Gospels*, 1992, pp. 69-70, 141-147. For a criticism of Boismard's literary theory on Jn 18,28–19,16a, see Sabbe, in Denaux (ed.), *John and the Synoptics*, 1992, pp. 341-385, esp. 375-379 (= 1991, pp. 467-513, esp. 503-508). – On Boismard's literary critical method, see the Introduction of his commentary, pp. 9a-11a ("I. L'énigme du quatrième évangile"), 11a-16a ("II. Comment résoudre l'énigme?"), 16a-70b ("III. Les divers niveaux rédactionnels". See also (in collaboration with A. Lamouille), *La vie des évangiles. Initiation à la critique des textes* (Initiations), Paris, 1980 (GT: 1980); on the significance of the resumption technique in literary criticism, see esp. Boismard's contribution at the Colloquium Biblicum Lovaniense XVIII (1975) in de Jonge (ed.), *L'évangile de Jean*, 1977 (²1987), 235-241; cf. Neirynck's reaction in *ETL* 56 (1980) 303-338 (= 1982, pp. 143-178).

135. *Jean*, pp. 100a-107b (Jn 2,1-12), esp. 103a, 103a-104b; pp. 146a-152b (Jn 4,46-54), esp. 146b-148a, 149b-150a; pp. 476a-485b (Jn 21,1-14), esp. 479b-480a, 482ab.

136. *Ibid.*, pp. 16a-25a (reconstruction and description of the content of *Doc C*), 45a-46a (comparison with the Synoptic tradition), 63b-64b (vocabulary and style of *Doc C*), 67a-68b (date, place of composition, author). See further, on "Les idées maîtresses", esp. pp. 48b-49a ("Le prophète, nouveau Moïse"), 51a ("Jésus est roi"), 51b ("Le Fils de l'homme"), and *passim*.

137. *Ibid.*, p. 67a-67b. He gives the following arguments: (a) It is older than *proto-Lc* (composed before 70 A.D.), who used *Doc C*; (b) it is also older than *Mc-intermédiaire* (composed around 60-65 A.D.), who fused it together with *Doc A* and *Doc B*; (c) its archaic character is confirmed by an internal analysis of the document.

138. *Ibid.*, pp. 67b-68a. Boismard's argumentation: (a) The author knows Palestinian geography very well, he cites the Bible in Hebrew, and, probably, wrote in Aramaic. (b) Samaritan influence is very clear. The first part of *Doc C* is situated in Samaria, its christology is dominated by Samaritian theology (the theme of Jesus, a prophet like Moses, the designation of Jesus as King), the first disciple, Philip, is probably to be identified with Philip who evangelized Samaria.

139. *Ibid.*, p. 68a-68b.

by Papias, subsequently produced editions of the Gospel and wrote the Epistles. He was a Jew and wrote the first edition in Palestine *ca* 60-65 A.D. (*Jean II-A*). He added new material and, under influence of the changing life-situation of the community, spoke pejoratively of the world and showed some opposition to the Jews[140]. In his second edition (*Jean II-B*), done *ca* 90 A.D., probably in Ephesus, he rearranged the order and added new material with knowledge of all three Synoptic Gospels and some Pauline letters. Persecution had left its trace in a strong aversion to "the Jews". Jesus is now presented as a pre-existent figure, clearly superior to Moses. Sacraments also came to the fore[141]. Finally, a third writer, *Jean III*, an unknown Jewish Christian of the Johannine school at Ephesus, was the final redactor early in the second century[142].

Document C as a whole can be compared with Fortna's Gospel of Signs[143]. It contained fives sections[144], of which the second sequence with the three numbered signs corresponds, as in Fortna's reconstruction, to Spitta's Galilean gospel document and Heekerens's *ZQ*:

1. In Samaria: John baptizes at Ainon (3,23-25). Testimony of John (1,19.21b.25-26.31-32.29). Call of the disciples (1,43b.45-49). Jesus and the Samaritan woman (4,5-7.9.16-18.28-30.40).

2. In Galilee: 4,43.45b. *The wedding at Cana* (2,1-3.6-8a.9b.11a). *The son of the royal official* (2,12; 4,46-47.50.54). Jesus and his brothers (7,1a.3-4.6a.9b). *The miraculous draught of fish* (21,1-4a.6.14a).

3. In Jerusalem at the Feast of Tabernacles: Entry of Jesus into Jerusalem (7,2.10; 12,12-13). The expulsion of the sellers in the temple (7,14; 2,14-16). The Greeks seek Jesus (12,20-23a.31.32.48). *The healing of a blind man* (8,59b; 9,1.6-7). Plot against Jesus (11,47a; 12,19b; 11,53-54).

140. *Ibid.*, pp. 25a-35a, 46a-47a, 64b-65a, 68a.
141. *Ibid.*, pp. 35a-44a, 47a-48a, 65b-67a, 68b-70a.
142. *Ibid.*, pp. 44a-45a, 48a-48b.
143. Cf. MARTYN, *History and Theology*, ²1979, p. 166: "one can notice that this source [*Doc C*] is in some regards comparable to Fortna's Signs Gospel". NEIRYNCK, *Jean et les Synoptiques*, pp. 15-16 (= *ETL* 53, pp. 376-377), compares Boismard's literary theory with those of Brown and Thyen. Stages 3, 4, and 5 of Brown's reconstruction (see above, p. 59 n. 105) can be compared with *Jn II-A*, *II-B* and *III*; Boismard differs from Brown (and most of the other recent commentators on Jn) "par sa thèse sur la dépendance envers les Synoptiques, située non pas au stade final d'un 'éditeur' de l'évangile, mais déjà au niveau de la deuxième rédaction par l'évangéliste même (II-B)". This can be compared with Thyen's hypothesis (1977): the *Redaktor* assimilates the orginal gospel, the *Grundschrift*, to the Synoptics, but "l'idée que Boismard se fait de l'indépendance de l'évangile primitif est toutefois moins rigide que celle de Thyen".
144. *Jean*, pp. 16a-19b (reconstruction of *Doc C* in French translation). Compare now *Doc C* with the reconstruction of "the pre-Johannine text" on the basis of John Chrysostom's homilies in BOISMARD – LAMOUILLE, *Un évangile pré-johannique*. I. *Jean 1,1–2,12*. II. *Jean 2,13–4,54* (ÉtB, n.s. 17-18, 24-25), Paris, 1993, 1994, four parts (see esp. vol. I/2, pp. 315-327: "Évangile pré-johannique: Reconstitution du texte"; vol. II/1, pp. 288-291 [on 4,46-54]: "Un récit devenu 'lucanien'?"). See F. NEIRYNCK, in *ETL* 69 (1993) 189-193, pp. 189-190.

4. At Bethany: *The resurrection of Lazarus* (11,1a.2b.4a.6b-7a.11b.17.29. 32b.33b.34.38-39.41a.43.44). The anointing at Bethany (12,2a.3a.4a.5.7a.8). Washing the disciples' feet (13,1b.4-5.12.17). Jesus announces his return (13,33; 14,1-3). Jesus' distress (12,23b.27-28; 14,30b.31b).

5. Passion and resurrection: The arrest of Jesus (18,1.3.12.13a). Peter's denial of Jesus (18,15a.c.18.25b.27b). Jesus before Annas (18,19.20a.c.21a.22a). Jesus before Pilate (18,28a.29-30.33b.37b; 19,4b.12a.6.16a). The death of Jesus (19,16b-18.23a.28-30.25b). The burial of Jesus (19,31.38b.c.40a.42b). The women and Peter at the tomb (20,1-3a.4b.5a.10). The appearance of Jesus to Mary Magdalene (20,11a.16a.18a). The appearance of Jesus to the disciples (6,19b; 20,20a; 6,20; 21,9.12-13).

Conclusion: 21,25.

This oldest layer of the Fourth Gospel was already a complete gospel, beginning with the Baptist's ministry and ending with the resurrection stories. It did not contain any of the great discourses of Jesus and related only five miracles or "signs"[145].

According to Boismard, it is difficult to distinguish the style of *Document C* from that of *Jean II*[146]. On the one hand, the text of *Document C* has been successively redacted in *Jean II-A* and *Jean II-B* (and further by *Jean III*), so that the texts attributed to *Document C* appears to us in the style of these later layers[147]. On the other hand, the whole Gospel originated in the same Johannine school, so that it must be accepted that there can be some unity in vocabulary and style[148]. Nevertheless, there

145. I.e., the wedding at Cana, the healing of the royal official's son, the miraculous draught of fish, the healing of a blind man, the resurrection of Lazarus. *Jn II-A* added the healing of the lame man and the multiplication of loaves from *Doc A*. Cf. p. 46a; cp. pp. 159a-159b, 159b-164a (Jn 5,5-9a), 178a-183a, 183b-184b (Jn 6,1-15); see Neirynck's critique in *Jean et les Synoptiques*, pp. 175-203: "VIII. Jean II-A et les Synoptiques", esp. 175-187: "Jean II-A et le Document A".

146. *Jean*, pp. 63b-64b. See also Boismard's general considerations on the use of stylistic criteria in source criticism on pp. 15a-16a. His "Liste des caractéristiques stylistiques" is given as "Appendice I" in his commentary (see pp. 491a-514b). Cp. Neirynck's discussion in *Jean et les Synoptiques*, pp. 41-70 (= *ETL* 53, pp. 400-429): "III. Les caractéristiques stylistiques", with an alphabetical classification of the characteristics in Greek (see pp. 45-66; = *ETL* 53, pp. 404-425, with the collaboration of G. Van Belle). In the following notes, the characteristics are first designated by Boismard's number and then within parentheses by the number in Neirynck's list. See below, pp. 405-420.

147. See, e.g., characteristic B1 (= 215) εἶπεν/εἶπον οὖν, extremely rare in *Doc C* (12,7; 18,25), but very frequent in *Jn II-B*. Cf. *Jean*, p. 63b.

148. See, e.g., the characteristics used in dialogues: B74 (= 53) ἀποκρίνομαι not followed by a *verbum dicendi*; B6 (= 54) ἀπεκρίθη καὶ εἶπεν; C12 (= 211) λέγει/λέγουσιν αὐτῷ + subject; A13 (= 295) οὖν ... καὶ ... καί, without change of the subject; B24 (= 293) order followed by its execution, repetition of the same verb with οὖν. See especially the expressions connected with a christological theme of *Doc C*, taken over by *Jn II-A* and *Jn II-B* (so the expressions connected with the theme of "Jesus as the new Moses"): B81 (= 346) ποιέω σημεῖα; B4 (= 141) ἔργον/ἔργα = miracle(s); B101 (= 345) ποιέω τὰ ἔργα; E2 (= 393) φανερόω. See also C19 (= 70) βασιλεύς of Christ; B7 (= 407) ἔρχεται + ὥρα + ἵνα/ὅτε/ἐν ᾗ" absolute; B50 (= 405) ὥρα, said of

are some characteristics and sentences typical of *Document C* and wholly absent in *Jean II* and *Jean III*[149]. Finally, a number of expressions in *Document C* are contrary to the style of *Jean II*[150].

According to Boismard, *Document C* presented Jesus particularly as a prophet like Moses (cf. Deut 18,18), a typology that is characteristic of Samaritan theology[151]. Boismard finds this typology in: (a) Jn 1,45 ("the man spoken of by Moses in the law"; cp. 1,19.21, where the Baptist denies that he is the prophet); see also 1,48 (cf. Lk 7,39) and 4,16-18, where Jesus demonstrates his quality as a prophet by his foreknowledge[152]; (b) passages which refer to biblical descriptions of Moses:

Christ; B102 (= 350) πορεύομαι, said of the death of Christ. See esp. the expressions of 13,33 (*Doc C*) taken over in 8,21-22 (*Jn II-A*) and 7,33-36 (*Jn II-B*), and in 14,19 and 16,16ff, the characteristics C15 (= 257) μικρόν; C21 (= 156) ζητέω, seek Jesus; A66 (= 390) ὅπου ἐγὼ ὑπάγω; B3 (= 104) ἐγώ, ὑμεῖς; B18 (= 149) ἔρχομαι ... ὑπάγω; B96 (= 199) κραυγάζω.

149. *Jean*, p. 64a. Cf. A130 (= 386) ὑδρία; A134 (= 40) ἀνθρακιά; A147 (= 322) ἡ οἰκία / ὁ οἶκος τοῦ πατρός μου; A155 (= 394) φανερόω ἐμαυτόν; C23 (= 131) πρὸς ἐμαυτόν. The following characteristics are taken over by a later layer immediately in the same context: A75 (= 44) ἀντλέω; A88 (= 253) μετὰ τοῦτο; A144 (= 241) μαρτυρέω μαρτυρίαν; B67 (= 270) ὀθόνιον. Cp. further 1,29 with 1,47; 4,5 with 11,54 and 19,17; 4,43 with 11,54; 4,46b-47 with 12,20-21; 4,46b with 11,1-2; 4,47 with 12,12; 1,29 with 20,1 and 21,9; 1,46 with 11,34; 12,3 with 13,4 and 18,3. See also the frequency of the impersonal plurals (cp. Mc), absent in *Jn II* and *Jn III*: 2,3a (*v.l.*); 2,7; 3,23 (twice); 7,3; 11,34.41; 12,2.4.

150. *Ibid.*, p. 64a-64b. (a) *Doc C* uses verbs of motion with the infinitive (4,7; 14,2; 21,3) (*Jn II* with ἵνα; cf. characteristic B76 = 175). In expressions such as 1,45 υἱὸν τοῦ Ἰωσήφ and 4,6 πηγὴ τοῦ Ἰακώβ, *Doc C* places the definite article before the proper name and not before the determined substantive (*Jn II* has the inverse position; cf. 1,40.42; 6,42), and in 11,6b reads ἐν ᾧ ἦν τόπῳ instead of ὁ τόπος ὅπου (= *Jn II*: characteristic B23 = 380; cf. 11,30; 19,41). (b) Entirely different from *Jn II* is the sentence in 7,6a: ὁ καιρὸς ὁ ἐμὸς οὔπω πάρεστιν. (c) *Doc C* prefers imperatives that follow each other without coordination: 4,16.29; 9,7; 21,12 (such a construction is wholly absent in *Jn II*). (d) Further, *Doc C* uses δέχομαι (4,45c) instead of the characteristic A25 (= 209) λαμβάνω τινά; ἐν παρρησίᾳ (7,4) instead of B21 (= 317) παρρησίᾳ; μετὰ τοῦτο instead of B29 (252) μετὰ ταῦτα; σύν (18,1; 21,3) instead of μετά (40 times); ἰσχύω (21,6) instead of δύναμαι (36 times); ἀπό + genitive ("because") instead of διά + accusative (26 times), ἐξετάζω (21,12) instead of C52 (= 150) ἐρωτάω.

151. *Ibid.*, pp. 48b-49a; cp. p. 67a. See also his review of NICOL, *Sēmeia*, 1972, in *RB* 81 (1974), p. 149, where he agrees with Nicol's presentation of the christology of S (Jesus is a prophet like Moses; cf. Deut 18,18): "Cette conclusion me semble parfaitement valable, bien que je ne sois pas parfaitement persuadé que tous les miracles racontés par Jean puissent provenir de cette source hypothétique". See further his *Rapports entre foi et miracles dans l'évangile de Jean*, in *ETL* 58 (1982) 357-364, pp. 358-360. He deals at length with this christology in *Moïse ou Jésus. Essai de christologie johannique* (BETL, 84), Leuven, 1988, pp. 1-71: "Jesus, le Prophète comme Moïse", esp. 70-71 (ET: 1993, pp. 1-68, esp. 66-67); cp. pp. 137-143: "Évolution de la christologie", esp. 137-138: "Le Document C" (ET: pp. 127-133, esp. 127-128).

152. *Jean*, p. 48a; cp. pp. 92b (Jn 1,45; 1,21), 133b (Jn 4,16-18); *Rapports*, p. 359; *Moïse*, pp. 25-44 ("La vocation de Nathanaël"), esp. 27-32 (1,45; cp. 1,20-21: pp. 9, 32, 70); ET: pp. 23-41, esp. 25-32; cp. 8, 29, 67.

7,3 ("the works you are doing"; cf. Num 16,28); 19,18 (Jesus crucified between two others; cf. Ex 17,8-13); 12,48 (Jesus announces judgement upon those who reject him; cf. Deut 18,19)[153]; (c) the three miracles at the beginning of Jesus' ministry (the Cana miracles and the miraculous draught of fish)[154], with their numbering in 2,11; 4,54; and 21,14, which correspond to the three signs Moses did to persuade the Hebrews that he was sent by God (Ex 4,1-9). In contrast to the Synoptics, *Document C* presents the miracles apologetically: they precede faith and demonstrate that Jesus is the prophet sent by God (7,4); people believe after seeing a miracle[155]. This apologetic presentation of miracles connected with the theme of Jesus as the new Moses appears also in *Jean II-A*, but more developed. So Boismard can attribute to *Jean II-A* texts assigned by others to the signs source: 6,14 and 12,37[156]. Note also that Boismard considers 20,30 as a text of *Jean II-B*, who redacted this verse under influence of 12,37 (*Jean II-A*) and 21,25 (*Document C*)[157]. (d) Finally, Boismard compares Jn 14,2-3 with Deut 1,29, and Jn 14,31c and 18,1 with Deut 2,13; Jesus is presented as the leader of the new and definitive Exodus who leads the people to the house of the Father[158].

---

153. *Jean*, p. 48b; cp. pp. 212b-213a (Jn 7,3), 441b-442a (Jn 19,18), 318a-318b (Jn 12,48); *Moïse*, pp. 53, 57-58, 138 (Jn 7,3), 12-15 (12,48), 20-22, 138 (19,18); ET: pp. 50, 54-55, 128 (7,3), 12-14 (12,48), 18-20, 128 (19,18).

154. *Jean*, p. 48b-49a; cp. pp. 20b-22b, 62a-62b, 103a-104b (Jn 2,1-12); *Rapports*, pp. 359-360; *Moïse*, pp. 44-62: "Les trois premiers signes" (ET: pp. 42-59). In *Jean*, p. 100a, Boismard reads in 2,11 τοῦτο πρῶτον σημεῖον ἐποίησεν (cp. Fortna: τ. π. ἐποίησεν σημεῖον, see above, p. 143 n. 5) and gives (pp. 101a, 146b, 477b) the following translations of the numbering of the three signs: 2,11 "Ce premier signe fit Jésus à Cana de Galilée"; 4,54 "Jésus fit de nouveau ce deuxième signe (à Capharnaüm)"; 21,14 "Ceci fut déja la troisième fois que Jésus fut manifesté". – See Neirynck's critique on the "numbering of signs" in *Jean et les Synoptiques*, pp. 122-174; cp. *Semeiabron*, pp. 12-17 (= ET, 1991, pp. 660-665); *Notes sur 21,14*, in *ETL* 64 (1988) 429-432 (= 1991, pp. 689-692). According to Boismard, three miracles were numbered in *Doc C*; he rejects Fortna's hypothesis of a numbering beyond these three (*Jean*, pp. 21b-22a).

155. *Jean*, pp. 48b-49a; *Rapport*, pp. 358-359; *Moïse*, pp. 66-68 (ET: pp. 62-65). In the Synoptics the miracles are presented more as consequences of faith: Mk 5,36; 9,23-24; 11,23; Mt 8,13; 9,28; Lk 8,50; see esp. the formula "your faith has cured you" in Mk 5,34; Mt 9,22; Lk 7,50; 8,48; 17,19 (*Jean*, pp. 48b-49a).

156. *Jean*, pp. 49a-49b; cp. pp. 183a-184b (6,14), 327a-328b (12,37). Thus for Boismard, the "primitive" theology of signs is present not only in *Doc C*, but also in *Jn II-A*; it was *Jn II-B* who criticized miracle faith. The instances of characteristic B81 (= 346) σημεῖον/σημεῖα ποιεῖν belong to three layers: from *Doc C*: 2,11; 4,54; *Jn II-A*: 2,23; 3,2; 6,2.14; 12,37; *Jn II-B*: 6,30; 7,31; 9,16; 10,41; 11,47; 12,18; 20,30. Note that Jn 4,46-54 played an important role in Boismard's interpretation of the relationship between miracles and faith, between seeing and believing in the Fourth Gospel (see above, pp. 56-57 n. 89).

157. *Jean*, pp. 474a-476b.

158. *Ibid.*, pp. 49b, 349a-349b (14,2-3), 404a-404b (14,31c; 18,1).

The commentary on John by Ernst HAENCHEN († 1975) was published posthumously by U. Busse in 1980, and appeared in English translation by R.W. Funk in 1984[159]. Despite his "healthy skepticism with respect to hazardous source theories", Haenchen would not defend the unity of the Fourth Gospel on the basis of stylistic and linguistic grounds[160]. In his view, the Fourth Gospel developed in three phases; we can distinguish: "(a) the author of the 'gospel of miracles,' which understands the 'signs' (σημεῖα) as miracles certifying faith; (b) an 'evangelist' who interprets the 'signs' (σημεῖα) as pointers, ...; and (c) an ecclesiastical 'supplementer,' or redactor, who appends the proclamation of the imminent end of the world, of the sacraments, and of an ethic that conceives of Christians as the elite among good men"[161]. With regard to the first phase of the gospel's composition, namely "the ur-gospel" or "the gospel of miracles", Haenchen seems to defend the same opinion as in

---

159. E. HAENCHEN, *Das Johannesevangelium*, ed. U. BUSSE ("Vorwort" by J.M. ROBINSON), Tübingen, 1980 (ET: 1984). – Reviews: cf. VAN BELLE, no. 1947. See also WÖLLNER, *Zeichenglaube*, 1988, pp. 7-8; MORGEN, *L'exégèse johannique*, 1989, pp. 249-250 n. 15; LINDARS, *Trends*, 1990, p. 329; SCHMITHALS, *Johannesevangelium*, 1992, p. 176; NEIRYNCK, *John and the Synoptics*, 1992, pp. 9-10; SMITH, *John among the Gospels*, 1992, pp. 65, 67. – Haenchen's commentary was already known in typescript. Cf. J.M. Robinson (see above, p. 69 n. 142), Richter (see below, p. 279 n. 168), Thyen (*TR* 42, 1977, p. 212; cp. pp. 227 and 242, n. 1; Thyen is quoted by J.M. Robinson in his Foreword to the commentary; cf. p. IX; ET: I, p. XIII), and MARTYN, *Glimpses*, 1977, p. 156 n. 19. – In 1977, two years after Haenchen's death (cf. SMEND, in *ZTK* 72, 1975, 303-309), Busse began to prepare the commentary for publication; for a description of his work as editor, see esp. BUSSE, *Ernst Haenchen*, 1981 (ET: 1984); *Vorwort des Herausgebers*, in HAENCHEN, *Johannes*, 1980, pp. XI-XVI (ET: I, pp. XV-XIX). From several manuscript versions of the commentary and from published texts Busse constructed a final edition, somewhat regretfully not a 'text-critical' edition but, as Becker calls it, "ein *mixtum compositum* aus Haenchen und Busse"; cf. BECKER, in *TR* 47 (1982), pp. 287-288, esp. 287. Cp. H.-J. KLAUCK, in *WissWeish* 44 (1981) 74-75; LINDARS, *Trends*, 1990, p. 329; ASHTON, *Understanding*, 1991, p. 44 n. 1. Note, however, that most reviewers consider Haenchen's commentary as "one of the great commentaries on the Fourth Gospel of the twentieth century, in spite of its flaws" (R. KYSAR, in *Interpr* 40, 1986, 69-72, p. 72) and agree that Busse has performed "a notable service to Johannine scholarship" (B. CHILTON, in *JSNT* 17, 1983, 115-116). Cp. D.M. SMITH, in *RelStR* 7, 1981, p. 353; ID., in *JBL* 102 (1983) 343-348, p. 348; F. NEIRYNCK, in *ETL* 57 (1981) 183-185, p. 184; X. JACQUES, in *NRT* 113 (1981) 894-895, p. 895; M. HASITSCHKA, in *ZKT* 104 (1982) 221-222, p. 222; G. SEGALLA, in *StPat* 29 (1982) 397-399, p. 389; F. GROB, in *RHPR* 63 (1983) 344-346, p. 345; X. LÉON-DUFOUR, in *RSR* 73 (1985) 261-264, pp. 261 and 264; U.C. VON WAHLDE, in *BTB* 15 (1985) 123-124, p. 123; P.J. JUDGE, in *LouvSt* 10 (1985) 291-292; P. PERKINS, in *CBQ* 48 (1986) 140-142, p. 142).

160. Cf. BUSSE, *Ernst Haenchen*, p. 140 (ET: p. 250). See HAENCHEN, *Johannesevangelium*, p. 78 (ET: I, p. 74): "A gospel as extensive as the Gospel of John cannot have been written without the use of sources".

161. *Johannesevangelium*, pp. 43-44 (ET: I, pp. 38-39; here Haenchen speaks about "the voices of various 'evangelists'" and about "three different authors"); cp. pp. 36-37 (ET: I, p. 33: "three hands"); pp. 262-263 (ET: I, p. 237: "three hands"; "three evangelists"); p. 286 (ET: I, p. 257: "three voices"); p. 290 (ET: I, p. 260: "three different hands"). See also BUSSE, *Ernst Haenchen*, p. 139 (ET: p. 250).

his article *Johanneische Probleme* (1959), in which he no longer
expressed himself so clearly in favor of the semeia hypothesis as he did
in his *Forschungsbericht* of 1955[162]. He starts with the observation that
"the evangelist made use of a source (*Vorlage*) whose theological
message differed from his own"[163]. By making this distinction between
the theology of the source and that of the evangelist, he opposes earlier
literary criticism: "Our thesis does not coincide with the earlier view,
often discussed, that a basic draft of the Gospel of John was developed
by means of further additions. At the basis of our view is the observation
that the theology of the evangelist differs from that of his source"[164].

162. See above, pp. 65-70. According to Robinson and Busse (see above, p. 70 n. 143)
Haenchen gradually would distance himself from this semeia hypothesis. In one place in
the commentary we find a very negative expression (see above, p. 70 n. 144). Moreover,
referring to the varying uses of the word σημεῖον, Haenchen concludes: "In view of the
diversity in the use of σημεῖον ('sign'), it is not possible, in my judgment, to maintain
the hypothesis that (almost) all narrative material in John stems from a 'signs' source. In
some miracle stories it is evident that older forms in the tradition preceded those versions
employed by the evangelist. As a consequence, the attempt to reconstruct literally the
original form of the story in question from the present text encounters greater difficulties
than one supposes, for the most part, when undertaking such reconstructions. One thinks,
for example, in this connection of the insertion of the sabbath-motif in John 5:9c and
9:14" (p. 102; ET, I, p. 89). See also below, p. 279 n. 168.

163. *Johannesevangelium*, p. 83 (ET: I, p. 77). Haenchen illustrates this in the case of
Jn 4,46-54 (pp. 83-84; ET: I, p. 78). In his overview of Jn 11,1-44, he refers specifically
to the problem created by the evangelist's use of the ur-gospel: "That the evangelist
found a 'gospel' that he alone knew how to read was at once his fortune and his misfor-
tune. This written gospel created by a great poet, a gospel that led from miracle to miracle, was created by someone for whom the divinity of Jesus was narrated palpably,
demonstrably. It was unfortunate for the evangelist that this 'gospel of miracles' used by
him as a pointer was nevertheless for him also a collection of actual miracle stories. In
that case, the miracles of Jesus were only events in the everyday world, events which did
not lead to God, only alleged proofs, like the story of Thomas without the last verse, a
verse which then corrects the faith of Thomas. It only became a book of the church when
a redactor restored the worst, that means, the highest, features of the message of the
evangelist to something like sound, normal Christianity; he of course did so by means of
additions, like those we so clearly discovered in chapter 5" (p. 419; ET: II, pp. 71-72).

164. *Ibid.*, p. 83 (ET: I, pp. 77-78). Cp. his reaction to Wilkens (see above, pp. 65-66).
This point of Haenchen's literary criticism has been attacked by D.M. SMITH, in *JBL* 102
(1983) 343-348, p. 348: "Yet I remain somewhat skeptical of the trustworthiness of theological criteria for source criticism, as certain as I am that John knew sources and has
been subjected to redaction. The theological wish too easily becomes father of the source-
critical thought"; cp. X. LÉON-DUFOUR, in *RSR* 73 (1985) 261-264, p. 263: "Je suis con-
vaincu que le critère concernant les récits de miracles, preuve ou signe, ne suffit pas à
établir l'existence d'une *Vorlage* dont on pourrait déterminer une certaine 'christologie'.
Or la tradition ainsi imaginée devient en fait pour l'auteur un document précis. Et comment oser parler de 'différentes christologies' en Jn (p. 103-109)? La christologie de
l'évangile johannique a sans doute été influencée par diverses traditions, mais elle a le
droit d'exister comme un tout, quitte à en montrer les divers aspects"; W.H. HARRIS, in
BS 143 (1986) 181-188, p. 182: "Many readers will disagree with Haenchen's presuppositions, particularly concerning the accuracy and validity of theological criteria for source
criticism". See also M. DE JONGE, in *NTT* 37 (1983) 150-153, p. 153: "Moet de erkenning

According to Haenchen, this source (tradition or "ur-gospel") and the evangelist's handling of it might be conceived as follows[165]:

1. "The Johannine narrative is independent of that represented by the Synoptics" (cf. Gardner-Smith and Noack)[166] and "John certainly did not know the Synoptics. He did not intend to supplement them, to improve them, or to replace them"[167].

2. Nevertheless, the evangelist has not freely created the narrative material, but made more or less free use of a tradition, a non-Synoptic gospel[168]. This tradition had "points of contact with the tradition taken up by the Synoptics", "exhibits the later, often already obviously

van de spanningsvolle eenheid van traditiemateriaal – evangelist – redactor niet tot de erkenning voeren, dat wij eigenlijk te maken hebben met twee redacties binnen de johan-neïsche gemeenten van traditiemateriaal dat daar langere tijd is overgeleverd, en dat wij bij onze exegese van de laatste definitieve redactie moeten uitgaan?".

165. Haenchen maintains his earlier rejection of the *Offenbarungsreden* (p. 102; ET: I, p. 90), with reference to his review of Bultmann's commentary (see above, p. 68 n. 134); see also, e.g., pp. 37-41 (ET: I, pp. 34-37, on Bultmann), 393-394 (ET: II, p. 51, on Jn 10), 401 (ET: II, p. 58, on Jn 11,9-10).

166. *Ibid.*, p. 80 (ET: I, p. 75). For Haenchen's references to Gardner-Smith, see above, pp. [65-]66 n. 125.

167. *Ibid.*, p. 263 (ET: I, p. 238). See above, p. 67 n. 130. Cp. also pp. 78-80, esp. 79 (ET: I, pp. 74-76, esp. 75). Cp., e.g., p. 263 (ET: I, p. 238, on Jn 4,46-54); p. 305 (ET: I, p. 274, on 6,1-15); p. 315 (ET: I, pp. 282-283, on 6,16-25). The presupposition that plays a certain role in the "Benutzungshypothese", namely that John used the Synoptics as Matthew and Luke used the Gospel of Mark, cannot be demonstrated: "a reading of John scarcely brings Mark to mind. Rather, the single evangelist with which John has frequent contact – and that is not close – is Luke" (p. 80; ET: I, p. 75).

168. Haenchen uses the following terminology to identify this gospel: (1) It is "a tradition"; see, e.g., pp. 106-107, 211, 261, 308; ET: I, pp. 95, 237, 276). More espe-cially "a tradition or writing with an entirely different theological posture"; see p. 106 (ET: I, p. 95). See also below, p. 280 n. 169. (2) Haenchen also speaks generally of "a source"; see, e.g., pp. 106 (ET: I, p. 95), 308 (ET: I, p. 276), 335-336 (ET: I, pp. 302-303), 362 (ET: II, p. 20), 427 (ET: II, p. 78). Sometimes he identifies the tradition with the "signs source"; see, e.g., pp. 129 ("Zeichenquelle"; ET: I, p. 119), 285 ("Zeichen-Quelle" and "Wunder-Quelle"; ET: I, p. 256), 308-309 ("Semeia-Quelle"; ET: I, pp. 276-277); in the ET it is always translated "signs source". (3) He prefers the term "gospel" however; see, e.g., pp. 211-212 (ET: I, p. 192), 574-575 (ET: II, pp. 212-213). So he speaks of "a written gospel" (see below, p. 280 n. 172) or "non-canonical gospel"; see, e.g., p. 332 (ET: I, p. 300). He uses especially "a 'gospel of miracles'" ("Wunderevangelium"); see, e.g., pp. 43-44 (ET: I, pp. 38-39), 211-212 (ET: I, p. 192), 262-263 (ET: I, p. 237), 333 (ET: I, p. 301), 419-420 ("Evangelium der Wunder"; ET: II, pp. 71-72), 427 (ET: II, p. 78). – Haenchen explains in a letter to G. Richter on January 12, 1973: "Er [the evangelist] hat es [the gospel of his community] meiner Meinung nach wörtlich übernommen, aber durch Hinzufügungen (und Auslassungen?) seiner eigenen Botschaft dienstbar gemacht". RICHTER, in *MTZ* 24 (1973), p. 96 n. 4 (= 1977, p. 267 n. 9), gives the following com-ment: "Haenchen meinte damals [in *TR* 23 (1955) 303-304; see above, p. 68 n. 132], dass der Evangelist dieses Evangelium seiner Gemeinde nur aus mündlicher Mitteilung (vom Hören im Gottesdienst) kannte, entscheidet sich aber jetzt ebenfalls für eine literarische Abhängigkeit".

'hackneyed' form"[169], lays more emphasis on the miraculous character than the Synoptic tradition[170], contained not only miracle stories but perhaps summaries as well[171], and presumably existed already in written form[172].

3. The signs (σημεῖα) were presented in the source as miracles certifying faith[173]. This appears clearly from the conclusion of the gospel,

169. See above, p. 66 n. 129. Against Bultmann's "σημεῖα-Quelle" he remarks: "If one attempts, as does Bultmann, to interpret the story of the feeding as a part of a 'signs source,' such an attempt has both positive and negative features. It is correct, in my opinion, to hold that this pericope contains a segment of tradition that the evangelist found in his source and which he reproduces relatively accurately; this piece of tradition reported a miracle that awakened faith. But one is thereby in danger of overlooking the fact that this piece of tradition does not represent the earliest form of the feeding story, but a developed and, at the same [time], abbreviated late form by virtue of the evolution of the tradition. One must not think of the evolution of the tradition like the growth of a spruce or fir. It is much more like the growth of a mighty oak with a great crown extending in all directions. The conception of the signs source, as Bultmann appears to hold it, tempts one to view the form of the source used by the Gospel of John as the original form and, at the same time, to forget the history of its tradition" (pp. 308-309; ET: I, pp. 276-277).

170. In the case of Jn 9,1-41, Haenchen remarks emphatically: "Insofar as we have Synoptic parallels as controls, the miraculous element in all the Johannine stories is heightened, and those stories without Synoptic parallels, like the healing of the man born blind (chap. 9) and the raising of Lazarus (chap. 11), eclipse all the miracles related in the Synoptics" (p. 384; ET: II, p. 42). Cp. above, p. 69 n. 137.

171. At 2,23-25 Haenchen observes: "If these 'summaries' [2,23; 4,45; 7,3.31; 11,47; 12,37; 20,30] were already contained in the 'gospel' used by the evangelist, then its character as a 'gospel of miracles' would have been further heightened: then the major individual miracles narrated would merely have been especially impressive examples of the miracle-working power of Jesus"; see pp. 211-212 (ET: I, p. 192). Cp. pp. 212-213 (ET: I, p. 193): "Perhaps one ought rather to say: the mention of 'many signs' in 12:37 and 20:30 may well have been taken over by the evangelist, but was not created by him. For him, the single miracle in 7:21 is sufficient: Jesus heals the paralytic by the pool of Bethzatha. The few miracles the evangelist has taken over are not meant to serve the legitimation of Jesus, to demonstrate his divine being. They can only point to his divine being as events which refer to an entirely different dimension. For that reason the evangelist does not require numerous miracles; they only prove something for those who have not yet perceived the 'qualitative distinction' between the divine and human spheres".

172. *Ibid.*, p. 313 (ET: I, p. 281; on 6,16-25: "The written source used by the evangelist"); p. 315 (ET: I, p. 282): "These peculiarities demonstrate that the evangelist is here following a written source of his own"; pp. 315-316 (ET: I, p. 283): "If our conjecture is correct that the evangelist found a written gospel in that community, a gospel that depicted Jesus as attested by many and impressive miracles, that is no reason to assume that the evangelist looked for other traditional material in the Synoptic style". See also above, pp. 68 n. 132, 278 n. 163. Elsewhere, however, Haenchen leaves open the question of the written character of the "gospel of miracles" (p. 105; ET: I, p. 94): "Thus, a priori, there is nothing against the view that one must also distinguish in the Gospel of John between the gospel tradition used – whether this was a written gospel we leave open – and the interpretation of that tradition".

173. *Ibid.*, p. 44 (ET: I, p. 39); cp. p. 102 (ET: I, p. 90). Cp. above, p. 68 nn. 133-134.

which the evangelist took over from the "ur-gospel"[174]. Jesus is pictured in the underlying tradition as the great miracle-worker whose mighty deeds demonstrate and authenticate his divinity[175], as a divine man (θεῖος ἀνήρ)[176].

4. The evangelist has employed this gospel of miracles; he believes in the reality of the miracles (ctr. Bultmann), but for him, in contrast to the author of the source, they only have meaning for Christians as 'signs' (σημεῖα)[177], i.e., "as pointers, through Jesus Christ, to the revelation of the invisible God, 'the Father of Jesus Christ', pointers whose meaning becomes visible for the first time only through the gift of the spirit at Easter"[178].

Ludger SCHENKE, who had referred to the "Zeichenquelle" in 1974[179], still accepted a signs source in his study on the bread miracles in

174. *Ibid.*, pp. 574-575 (ET: II, p. 212): "Verses 30f. probably formed the conclusion to the 'gospel' from which the evangelist selected, omitted things, and which he supplemented and improved. Not all of the deeds of Jesus are recorded in this book – for the source that means: not all the miracles; for the evangelist it means: not all the pointers – but only some of them. But the selection that the book contains ought to lead to faith in the Son of God".

175. *Ibid.*, p. 107 (ET: I, p. 95).

176. *Ibid.*, p. 34 (ET: I, p. 32: on 4,19); p. 211 (ET: I, p. 192: on 2,23-25); p. 336 (ET: I, p. 303); pp. 401-402 (ET: II, p. 59: on 11,11); p. 413 (ET: II, p. 67: on 11,43-44); p. 420 (ET: II, p. 72).

177. This idea recurs repeatedly in the commentary. In discussing the composition of the gospel, Haenchen formulates it thus: "the tradition utilized by John attempts to represent Jesus throughout as someone legitimated by miracles. In contrast, the evangelist has endeavored to transform this tradition of legitimizing [beweisenden] miracles into the doctrine of allusive [hinweisenden] signs" (p. 85; ET: I, p. 78; Funk notes in the translation [p. 79 n. 10]: "Haenchen is punning: transform the tradition of *beweisenden* miracles into the doctrine of *hinweisenden* signs"). Cp. p. 575 (ET: II, pp. 212-213).

178. *Ibid.*, p. 106 (ET: I, p. 95). Haenchen clarifies this understanding of σημεῖα ('signs') by reference to Gen 9,13ff.: "The LXX translates the Hebrew term *'ot* with σημεῖον (both mean 'sign'). This is the meaning of the term for the evangelist in the Fourth Gospel. It does not mean proof [Beweis] but pointer [Hinweis]" (see Funk' note in the ET, I p. 95, n. 2); cp. p. 190 (ET: I, p. 174, on 2,11): "The word σημεῖον, which is used to translate the Hebrew term *'ot* ('sign') in the LXX (e.g., Exod 4:8f., Isa 7:11,14) might have been understood as 'miracle' in the tradition embodied in this story. But the evangelist takes it as 'pointer' and thus as indicating something quite different; it is in this sense that he understands it as 'sign'"; p. 196 (ET: I, p. 179, on 2,1-11). On the Johannine doctrine of the signs as "pointers", see also pp. 105-109, esp. 107 (ET: I, pp. 94-97, esp. 95); p. 188 (ET: I, pp. 172-173, on 3,2-3); p. 212 (ET: I, p. 192, on the summaries); pp. 216-217 (ET: I, pp. 199-200, on 3,2-3); pp. 225-226 (ET: I, pp. 205-206, on 3,1-21); p. 258 (ET: I, p. 235: on 4,48); p. 261 (ET: I, p. 237, on 4,48); p. 276 (ET: I, p. 250, on 5,20); pp. 319-320 (ET: I, 289-290 on 6,26-59); pp. 332-336 (ET: I, pp. 300-303, on 6,26-59); p. 362 (ET: II, p. 20, on 7,39); p. 372 (ET: II, p. 30, on 8,41); p. 377 (ET: II, p. 38, on 9,3); p. 402 (ET: II, p. 60, on 11,15); p. 405 (ET: II, p. 62, on 11,23); p. 408 (ET: II, p. 64, on 11,26); pp. 419-420 (ET: II, pp. 71-72, on 11,1-44; see above, p. 278 n. 163); p. 422 (ET: II, pp. 74-75, on 11,45.47); pp. 427, 429 (ET: II, pp. 78, 80, on 11,45-54); p. 478 (ET: II, p. 127, on 14,23); p. 503 (ET: II, p. 152, on 17,7-8). On "The Johannine Σημεῖα", see below, pp. 379-404.

179. See above, p. 85 n. 63.

1983[180]. He presents a more complete literary-critical view of the Fourth Gospel in a series of articles beginning in 1985 and, most recently, he no longer believes the signs source existed[181]. According to Schenke[182], the redactor of the Fourth Gospel used a *Grundschrift* or *Grundevangelium*, i.e., the Gospel of his ("Johannine") community, that contained narrative material and some parts of the revelation discourses; it began with the call narratives and ended with the appearance stories. Its author is designated by the redactor, i.e. the author of the present gospel, as the "disciple whom Jesus loved". The redactor used this gospel as the

180. L. SCHENKE, *Die wunderbare Brotvermehrung. Die neutestamentliche Erzählungen und ihre Bedeutung*, Würzburg, 1983, pp. 81-86, esp. 85-86: "Der Wortlaut der mündlich überlieferten Speisungsgeschichte kann jedoch nicht mehr rekonstruiert werden. Wir setzen aber voraus, dass er in der Semeia-Quelle weitgehend bewahrt worden ist. Dort ist die Speisungsgeschichte auch mit der Seewandelperikope literarisch verknüpft worden. Ursprünglich war sie eine in sich abgerundete Erzählung, die keiner Fortsetzung bedurfte. Die Einleitung dürfte ursprünglich erzählt haben, dass Jesus sich 'danach nach Tiberias wegbegeben hat'. In dieser Formulierung ist ohne Zweifel der ursprüngliche Kontext der 'Semeia-Quelle' und ihr geographischer Rahmen berücksichtigt". Cp. *Das Szenarium von Joh 6,1-25*, in *TTZ* 92 (1983) 191-203. Here, Schenke also reckons with Synoptic influence. On Schenke, cf. BEUTLER, *Méthodes et problèmes*, 1990, p. 23; SCHMITHALS, *Johannesevangelium*, 1992, p. 128. – Under the direction of Schenke, Rosel BAUM-BODENBENDER wrote *Hoheit in Niedrigkeit. Johanneische Christologie im Prozess Jesu vor Pilatus (Joh 18,28–19,16a)* (FzB, 49), Würzburg, 1984 (diss. Mainz, 1982-83), defending an alternative to Dauer's hypothesis: "die Annahme einer *literarischen* Beziehung zwischen Joh und die Synoptikern (ist) unausweichlich" (p. 217). According to her, the Synoptic influences are to be situated on the level of the Johannine redaction and not on that of the pre-Johannine source. Reviews: cf. VAN BELLE, no. 4107; see A. DAUER, in *TRev* 81 (1985) 463-466; F. NEIRYNCK, in *ETL* 62 (1986) 427-430; A. FUCHS, in *SNTU/A* 12 (1987) 244-245. See also NEIRYNCK, *John and the Synoptics*, 1992, p. 7; SABBE, in DENAUX (ed.), *John and the Synoptics*, 1992, pp. 341-385, esp. 351-375 (= 1991, pp. 467-513, esp. 477-503).

181. *Die literarische Vorgeschichte von Joh 6,26-58*, in *BZ* 29 (1985) 68-89; this article is the sequel of *Die formale und gedankliche Struktur von Joh 6,26-58*, in *BZ* 24 (1980) 21-41, where Schenke considered the bread of life discourse a redactional composition whose final literary unity is the best starting point for an interpretation of its message; *Der "Dialog Jesu mit den Juden" im Johannesevangelium: Ein Rekonstruktionsversuch*, in *NTS* 34 (1988) 573-603; *Joh 7–10: Eine dramatische Szene*, in *BZ* 80 (1989) 172-192; *Die literarische Entstehungsgeschichte von Joh 1,19-51*, in *BibNot* 46 (1989) 24-57 (see below, p. 283 n. 183); *Das johanneische Schisma und die "Zwölf" (Johannes 6.60-71)*, in *NTS* 38 (1992) 105-121; *Das Johannesevangelium. Einführung – Text – Dramatische Gestalt* (UTB, 446), Stuttgart, 1992.

182. For a summary of his literary criticism, see *Vorgeschichte*, pp. 88-89, esp. 89; *Der "Dialog Jesu mit den Juden"*, pp. 573-574; *John 7–10*, pp. 189-190. Schenke sees his literary criticism not as "Auslegungsmethode", but as "Untersuchungsmethode"; cf. *Der "Dialog Jesu mit den Juden"*, p. 574: "Die literarkritischen Beobachtungen von Spannungen, Verdoppelungen und Brüchen aber sind Indikatoren und Hinweise auf diesen literarkritischen Prozess. Sie können den Blick freigeben auf das vom 'Evangelisten' verwendete Material, seine Quellen und Traditionen und so die Interpretation dieser literarisch sperrigen Schrift befruchten. Literarkritik ist dabei nicht Auslegungsmethode, sondern Untersuchungsmethode des vorliegenden Textes. Nur dessen Auslegung kann Aufgabe der Exegese sein"; *Das johanneische Schisma*, pp. 119-121.

framework for his own work. Besides the *Grundschrift*, he also adapted other written and oral traditional Johannine material (1,1-18, the "Bildworte" in ch. 10, chs. 15–17, 21,1-14, and perhaps 2,1-11 and 4,46-54)[183], and a "Dialog Jesu mit den Juden"[184].

In his dissertation on Jn 11,1–12,19[185], Josef WAGNER (1988) considers J. Becker's argumentation for the signs source more supportive of a *Grundschrift* as defended by G. Richter[186]. The passages that Becker

183. *Der "Dialog Jesu mit den Juden"*, p. 573 n. 4, with reference to Heekerens for the miracle of ch. 21 and the two Cana miracles. In *Joh 1,19-51*, p. 49 n. 84, he rejects the signs source: "Dass unsere rekonstruierte Erzählung den Anfang der 'Semeia-Quelle' gebildet hat (so Bultmann; Becker), glaube ich nicht, weil ich nicht mehr an derer Existenz glauben kann. Ich vermute eher, dass sie der Anfang eines ursprünglichen 'Evangeliums' ('Grundschrift', 'Grundevangelium') war (so die alte Literarkritik, aber auch Fortna). Doch kann dies hier offenbleiben".

184. To "The dialogue of Jesus with the Jews" he attributes: (a) "Die Eröffnung des Dialogs": 3,1-12; (b) "Das Kommen des Gesandten Gottes ist für die Welt Heil oder Gericht": 3,31-36; 3,13-15; 12,34-36; 3,16-21; 6,28-29; 12,44-50; (c) "Das Zeugnis des Gesandten Jesus": 8,13-19; 5,37-40; 7,15-19; 5,45-47; 6,30-33; 6,49-51; 6,36-46; (d) "Der Aufstieg des Gesandten Jesus": 6,60-64; 7,28-29; 7,33-36; 8,21-26; 8,31b-32; (e) "Der Unglaube der 'Juden'": 8,33-58; (f) "Der Abschluss des Dialogs": 10,31-39. See esp. *Der "Dialog Jesu mit den Juden"*, pp. 585-595 ("Rekonstruktion"); cp. *Vorgeschichte*, pp. 83-84; see also *Joh 7-10*, 1989, pp. 189-190; *Das johanneische Schisma*, p. 120.

185. J. WAGNER, *Auferstehung und Leben. Joh 11,1–12,19 als Spiegel johanneischer Redaktions- und Theologiegeschichte* (BibUnt, 19), Regensburg, 1988 (diss. Frankfurt/M, 1987; dir. J. Hainz). The dissertation contains five parts: "Einleitung" (pp. 12-28); "Probleme und Problemlösungsversuche" (pp. 29-94); "Literar- und redaktionskritische Analyse" (pp. 95-334); "Die traditionellen Stoffe" (pp. 335-395); "Die theologischen Akzente der drei literarischen Schichten und ihr 'Sitz' in der Geschichte der Gemeinde" (pp. 396-462). – Reviews: U. SCHNELLE, in *TLZ* 144 (1989) 275-276; G. ROCHAIS, in *CBQ* 52 (1990) 766-768; E. BEST, in *ExpT* 101 (1989-90) 284-285; X. LÉON-DUFOUR, in *RSR* 79 (1991) 312-313. – See also Wagner's article *Die Erweckung des Lazarus – Ein Paradigma johanneischer Theologiegeschichte*, in HAINZ (ed.), *Theologie im Werden*, 1992, pp. 199-217.

186. *Auferstehung*, pp. 347-361: "Stand die traditionelle Erzählung im Kontext einer Wundersammlung?", esp. 350. After a survey of "die wichtigsten 'Lösungsversuche'" (pp. 42-87: Schwartz, Wellhausen, Spitta, Wendt, Hirsch, Bultmann, Wilkens, Sass, Fortna, Schnackenburg, Nicol, Zwergel, Teeple, Boismard – Lamouille, Becker, and Kremer), Wagner notes that several exegetes supposed four stages in the composition of the Fourth Gospel (see esp. Wilkens, Richter, Teeple, Boismard – Lamouille) (p. 87); he is also convinced that the miracle tradition and the passion narrative were already combined before the redactional activity of the evangelist (p. 88). On Richter, see esp. pp. 89-94 ("Die Theorie G. Richters"). In his "Literar- und Redaktionskritische Analyse" Wagner uses Richter's terminology: "Grundschrift", "Evangelist" (E), and "Redaktion" (R). See his reconstruction for 11,1-12,19 on pp. 329-334. The *Grundschrift* used a pre-existent tradition (T) and a "Passionsbericht" (P). Cp. his article *Erweckung*, pp. 209-212. With reference to Wagner, SCHNELLE, *Perspektiven*, 1990, p. 59, notes: "Die Theorien G. Richters bilden teilweise unhinterfragt die Basis ganzer Monographien". See, e.g., W. Lütgehetmann's study on Jn 2,1-11 (see below, pp. 285-286). – Also Andrea LINK, *"Was redest du mit ihr?": Eine Studie zur Exegese-, Redaktions- und Theologiegeschichte von Joh 4,1-42* (BibUnt, 24), 1992 (diss. Frankfurt/M, 1991-92; dir.

attributes to the signs source are to be characterized as "Halbevangelium" or "Grundschrift ohne Passionsgeschichte"[187]. According to Wagner[188], Jn 20,30-31 is rather the conclusion of the *Grundschrift*; similarity in form and heightened miraculous character cannot prove that the miracles come from the same source; and, the numbering of signs can be explained within the *Grundschrift*: 4,54 indicates that this is the second miracle in *Cana*, so that there is no contradiction with 2,23; 3,2[189]. Wagner further rejects M. Smith's hypothesis that both John and Mark used a "common source" (see the geographical and chronological parallelism in Mk 6–10 and Jn 6–11), probably written in Aramaic, that was also the source of the *Secret Gospel of Mark*[190]. Wagner agrees with Brown that the author of the *Secret Gospel of Mark* may well have drawn upon John, at least from memory[191]. He also questions the existence of miracle collections with a θεῖος ἀνήρ christology, the so-called aretalogies, such as the pre-Markan miracle collection (with reference to H.C. Kee and K. Berger)[192]. Therefore, Wagner concludes that the author of the *Grundschrift* himself has used different traditional miracle stories, and he sees no reason to posit a σημεῖα-*Quelle*[193]. At most,

J. Hainz), works with "Richters Schichtenmodell als Arbeitshypothese" (pp. 176-177) for the analysis of 4,1-42. See pp. 179-195: "Die Bearbeitung der Redaktion (R)", 196-244: "Die Bearbeitung des Evangelisten (E)", 245-320: "Die Erzählung der Grundschrift", 320-324: "Die Redaktionsgeschichte im Überblick". Cp. *Botschafterinnen des Messias. Die Frauen des vierten Evangeliums im Spiegel johanneischer Redaktions- und Theologiegeschichte*, in HAINZ (ed.), *Theologie im Werden*, 1992, pp. 247-278.

187. After an enumeration of the content of SQ according to Becker, Wagner questions: "Sollte angesichts dieser Fülle von Stoffen, die zusätzlich und neben den Wundererzählungen Bestandteile der SQ sein sollen, nicht besser von einem 'Halbevangelium' – einer 'Grundschrift ohne Passionsgeschichte' die Rede sein?" (*Auferstehung*, p. 350).

188. *Ibid.*, pp. 351-352; cp. *Erweckung*, p. 213.

189. *Auferstehung*, pp. 351-352. He notes, however, that the style of Jn 2,1-11 and 4,46-54 differs from the other miracles and that they are not followed by discourses.

190. *Ibid.*, pp. 353-357. Cf. M. SMITH, *The Secret Gospel*, 1973 (GT: 1974); *Clement of Alexandria and the Secret Gospel of Mark*, 1973.

191. *Auferstehung*, pp. 356-357, esp. 357: "Obwohl auch H. Köster den Ergebnissen von Smith im wesentlichen zustimmt, möchte ich nicht mit einer derartigen Quelle rechnen, die Mk und Joh zugrunde gelegen haben könnte". Cf. R.E. BROWN, in *CBQ* 36 (1974) 466-485, pp. 474-485.

192. *Auferstehung*, pp. 358-360.

193. *Ibid.*, p. 361: "Ich möchte daher eher vermuten, erst der Autor der Grundschrift habe einzelne traditionelle Wundererzählungen in seine Schrift aufgenommen"; cp. pp. 357-358: "So darf gesagt werden, dass die SQ-Hypothese mit den im wesentlichen von R. Bultmann stammenden Begründungsversuchen zwar weiteste Verbreitung und Zustimmung in der Forschung fand (bei variierendem Umfang und unterschiedlicher theologischer Deutung), aber dennoch – rechnet man mit einer Grundschrift – auf schwachem Fundament steht". – Wagner's *Grundschrift* hypothesis is rejected by Stephanie M. FISCHBACH, *Totenerweckungen. Zur Geschichte einer Gattung* (FzB, 69), Würzburg, 1992 (diss. Würzburg, 1991; dir. H.-J. Klauck), pp. 237-268, with regard to 11,1-44. She prefers Becker's literary theory (p. 251 n. 18): "Unseren Überlegungen liegt vielmehr ein Modell von der Entstehung des Joh-Ev.s zugrunde, nach welchem der Evan-

the two Cana miracles and the two miracles of Jn 6,1-21, respectively, were already joined in the tradition[194].

Recently, Walter LÜTGEHETMANN (1990) has studied the first Cana miracle[195]. He describes its literary-critical history in three stages[196]. In the first stage, the sign of changing water into wine portrays Jesus as a miracle worker greater than Dionysus, with the missionary intention of convincing the followers of the wine god. Through the miracle, Jesus reveals his δόξα and legitimates his claim[197]. In the second stage, the

gelist Autor der Evangeliumsschrift ist und eine sog. Semeia-Quelle ... sowie den Passionsbericht vorfand. Eine sog. kirchliche Redaktion dürfte im Nachhinein noch den ein oder anderen eigenen Akzent gesetzt haben" (with reference to Becker's commentary). See also p. 261: "Mit grösserer Wahrscheinlichkeit ist die These einer schriftlichen Quelle von Wunder- resp. Semeiaerzählungen zu bejahen. Aus dieser Quelle stammt dann auch die Lazaruserzählung". After presentation of Becker's SQ (pp. 260-261; she is undecided, however, whether she would assign the Baptist's witness to SQ as Becker does) and rejection of Heekerens's hypothesis (p. 261), she proposes that the redactor of SQ adopted a traditional story (for a reconstruction of both stories, see pp. 258-259 and 262-263). The evangelist added to SQ the following verses: 4.5.7b-11a.13.16.18.19(only ἐκ τῶν Ἰουδαίων).20c-32a.33a(only Ἰουδαίους).36a(only Ἰουδαῖοι).37.40.41b-42c (pp. 253-259). V. 2 is from the ecclesiastical redactor (pp. 253-254). Regarding the relation of Jn 11 with Lk 16,19-31 (Lazarus), she notes: "So kann mit *R. Schnackenburg*, *J. Kremer*, und *J. Wagner* festgehalten werden, dass mit grösserer Wahrscheinlichkeit die konkrete Gestalt des Lazarus zuerst an der Wundergeschichte haftet und später erst der Arme aus dem Gleichnis mit diesem Lazarus identifiziert wurde" (p. 266). See also p. 267, on the relation between Jn 11 and Lk 10,38-42 (Mary and Martha): "Es steht zu vermuten, dass im Umfeld der SQ und ihrer Tradenten resp. Tradentinnen eine vorlk Variante der Erzählung von Lk 10,38ff bekannt war und der Redaktor der SQ das Namenspaar aufgriff und die Schwestern in die Erweckungserzählung integrierte, um die Überlieferung weiter ausbauen zu können" (p. 267).

194. *Ibid.*, p. 361.

195. W. LÜTGEHETMANN, *Die Hochzeit von Kana (Joh 2,1-11). Zu Ursprung und Deutung einer Wundererzählung im Rahmen johanneischer Redaktionsgeschichte* (BibUnt, 20), Regensburg, 1990 (diss. Frankfurt/M; dir. J. Hainz). The first part, with a survey of the present state of research (pp. 17-282: "Die Hochzeit zu Kana in der Sicht einzelner exegetischer Methoden"), contains four chapters: "Sprachwissenschaftliche Bearbeitungen" (pp. 18-40); "Literar- und redaktionskritische Lösungsversuche" (pp. 41-122); "Formkritische Betrachtungen" (pp. 123-133); "Traditions- und religionsgeschichtliche Untersuchungen" (pp. 134-282). The much shorter second part gives a "Versuch einer Neuinterpretation" (pp. 283-346) in three chapters: "Hinführung" (pp. 286-291); "Die christologische Ausrichtung der Hochzeit zu Kana" (pp. 292-316); "Zur literarkritischen und redaktionsgeschichtlichen Fragestellung" (pp. 317-346). In ch. 2 of the first part, Lütgehetmann gives a "Darstellung der wichtigsten Lösungsvorschläge" (pp. 41-120), in which he deals with Schwartz, Wellhausen, Spitta, Wendt, Hirsch, Bultmann, Parker, Wilkens, Temple, Brown, Fortna, Nicol, Teeple, Richter, Boismard – Lamouille, Langbrandtner, Becker, Busse – May, and Heekerens. – Cf. LÉON-DUFOUR, in *RSR* 79 (1991), pp. 310-312.

196. *Ibid.*, pp. 339-346. See also his article *Die Hochzeit von Kana – Der Anfang der Zeichen Jesu*, in HAINZ (ed.), *Theologie im Werden*, 1992, pp. 177-197.

197. *Die Hochzeit*, 1990, p. 339. On the Dionysus cult see pp. 261-272, esp. his conclusion on p. 271: "*Abschliessend lässt sich somit urteilen*, dass sich die Vorstellung einer Verwandlung von Wasser zu Wein im Dionysos-Glauben nachweisen lässt und dass diese

miracle story was taken into the Gospel, which served as a "Glaubens-
buch" for people who already believe. For the evangelist the miracle is
a sign of the incarnate Logos. From the beginning of his ministry, Jesus
reveals his δόξα, i.e., the glory of the incarnate Logos and the significance of salvation for believers[198]. In the third stage, a redactor tried to
limit the importance of the miracles and, instead, promoted the passion
as the basis for belief[199]. According to Lütgehetmann, this description of
the genesis of the miracle fits well with Becker's thesis that the evangelist used a *Vorlage*, SQ, that presents Jesus as θεῖος ἀνήρ[200]. He
disagrees with Richter and Wagner, who supposed a *Grundschrift* with
prophet-Messiah christology that was corrected by the evangelist into a
δόξα christology, presenting Jesus as Son of God and the One Sent from
the Father[201]. For Lütgehetmann, the redactor, not the evangelist, criticizes the miracles; for the evangelist they are symbols[202].

Further, Lütgehetmann gives several indications that Jn 2,1-11 was
already part of a larger composition[203]: the temporal indication of the
"third day" refers to ch. 1[204]; the θεῖος ἀνήρ christology of 2,1-11
fits well with that of 1,35-50 (cf. Kuhn)[205]; the numbering of signs
in 2,11 and 4,54 and the link 2,12 indicate that 2,1-12 was followed
by 4,46b-54[206]. He does not take a position, however, on whether
this greater unity was already part of a *Semeia-Quelle* or a *Grundschrift*[207].

Vorstellung alt genug war, um auf die Entstehung der Kana-Perikope eingewirkt haben zu
können. Wie sich ferner gezeigt hat, war der Dionysos-Glaube sowohl in Palästina als
auch in Syrien verbreitet, so dass anzunehmen ist, dass sich die joh Gemeinde auch mit
ihm auseinanderzusetzen hatte".

198. *Ibid.*, p. 339.
199. *Ibid.*, pp. 339-340.
200. *Ibid.*, p. 340. On Becker, see pp. 108-111.
201. *Ibid.*, pp. 340-342.
202. *Ibid.*, p. 341.
203. *Ibid.*, pp. 342-346.
204. *Ibid.*, pp. 343-344.
205. *Ibid.*, p. 344.
206. *Ibid.*, pp. 344-346.
207. *Ibid.*, p. 346: "Man könnte nun noch fragen, ob die Missionserzählung erst
vom Verfasser der bereits dem Evangelisten vorliegenden Erzählabfolge gebildet
wurde, oder ob sie von diesem bereits aus der Tradition aufgenommen werden konnte,
aber hierüber scheinen mir keine einigermassen gesicherten Aussagen möglich zu sein.
Die Frage schliesslich, ob es sich bei dieser Vorlage um eine Semeia-Quelle oder um
eine Grundschrift handelte, lässt sich m.E. auf dem gegenwärtigen Forschung gleich-
falls nicht beantworten. Festzuhalten bleibt aber, dass die Erzählung von der Hochzeit
zu Kana nicht erst redaktionell in eine Grundschrift (so Spitta zu Anfang dieses Jhdts.)
oder gar erst ins Evangelium (so jüngst Heekerens) eingefügt wurde, sondern selbst als
Teil der Vorlage des Evangelisten zum Urgestein des vierten Evangeliums zu rechnen
ist".

John ASHTON (1991) thinks in terms of "successive editions and reworkings" for the origin of the Fourth Gospel[208]. For Ashton, howewer, "it is obviously impossible to produce a totally convincing reconstruction", and ironically he adds: "the graveyards of New Testament scholarship are littered with discarded skeletons"[209]. He thinks of the signs source as "the earliest traceable literary production of the Johannine community"[210]: "the early stage is represented roughly by what remains of the so-called signs source"[211]. With regard to Fortna's work, Ashton mentions two great merits: "his clear enunciation of his methodological principles", and "his readiness to carry through his programme of reconstruction in detail"[212]. He agrees that "this makes him [Fortna] more vulnerable to criticism, but such vulnerability is not itself a fault"[213]. He formulates several objections to Fortna's method however[214]. First, "one of the inbuilt weaknesses" is "that it leaves out of account the discourse material"[215]. The second objection concerns his reconstruction: there is a problem with "the assumption that in adapting his source the evangelist proceeded by a simple method of addition and subtraction. In trying to reconstruct John's narrative source we are in much the same position as we would be if we were faced with the task of constructing the Gospel of Mark from, say, that of Luke. There is no

---

208. J. ASHTON, *Understanding the Fourth Gospel*, Oxford, 1991, pp. 245-246, esp. 246. See also pp. 162-166 ("A theory adopted") for Ashton's description of the Gospel's growth. According to him, the successive stages of composition correspond "to the changing situation of those for whom it was being written" (p. 162). Here, he largely depends on J.L. Martyn's hypothesis of the history of the Johannine community (cf. pp. 166-174; on Martyn, see above, pp. 149-150). On Boismard's multiple stage theory, Ashton notes: "Though Boismard is right in principle to marry his compositional theory to the story of the community's birth and development, there are far too many weak links in his long and elaborate chain" (p. 163; on Boismard, see above, pp. 271-276). – See already ASHTON, *Introduction: The Problem of John*, in ID. (ed.), *The Interpretation of John*, 1986, pp. 1-17, where he notes: "I believe it to be established beyond reasonable doubt that both the Johannine community and its book had a *history*. But this does not mean that it is possible to reconstruct this history with any certainty, or indeed with any plausibility" (p. 13). On the signs source, see esp. pp. 12-13. Ashton mentions (p. 12) Faure, Bultmann, Fortna and refers to Dodd, Barrett and M. de Jonge, "who have raised quizzical eyebrows at the efforts, first of Bultmann and subsequently of Martyn and his pupil Robert Fortna (1970), to distinguish between source and redaction" (p. 13). He cites de Jonge's point of view regarding the semeia hypothesis (1977, p. VIII; see above, p. 251 n. 1). On Ashton, see also above, p. 45. See also B. LINDARS, *John Ashton's Understanding of the Fourth Gospel*, in *ScotJT* 45 (1992) 245-251; D. BALL, in *Themelios* 19 (1993-94), p. 15.

209. *Understanding*, p. 246.

210. *Ibid.*, p. 279. Cp. p. 167: "the earliest discernable stratum of the Gospel".

211. *Ibid.*, p. 246.

212. *Ibid.*, pp. 86-88: "Signs-source theories", esp. 86.

213. *Ibid.*, p. 86.

214. *Ibid.*, pp. 86-88, 284; cp. p. 163.

215. *Ibid.*, p. 87.

reason to suppose that John (or the other preachers of his community) was any more anxious to preserve the precise wording of his source than Luke was. But a reconstruction of a hypothetical Mark along the same lines as Fortna's hypothetical Signs Gospel would leave us not with Mark, or anything approaching it, but with a woefully attenuated Luke"[216]. Third, Ashton has "some doubts concerning Fortna's attempt to reapply the stylistic criteria elaborated – and discredited – by Ruckstuhl"[217]. He refers to Lindars, who asserted that in Fortna's reconstructed text of the source features characteristic of John appear "again and again"[218]. Fourth, he rejects Fortna's "conviction that the document was not just a semeia source but a signs *Gospel*"[219]. By including the passion and resurrection narratives in the source, Fortna "removed much of the justification for the name 'Signs source'"[220]. Fifth, he rejects Fortna's "belief that the story of the miraculous draught of fishes in chapter 21 originally belonged to the source"[221].

Ashton's objections to Fortna do not lead him to the conclusion that "the hypothesis of a signs source is to be discarded altogether"[222]. He finds many of Faure's arguments "still valid"[223]. According to Ashton, the "signs-source" was "composed – presumably in Palestine – before the formation of the Johannine group as this is generally conceived nowadays"[224]. Regarding its content, "there are no high christological affirmations, but stories portraying Jesus as a wonderworker fulfilling the traditional Jewish expectation of a Messiah"[225]. "The cardinal affirmations of the signs source", whose conclusion was taken over by the evangelist (20,30-31a), can be summarized as follows: "We have found him of whom Moses wrote in the Law (the Prophet); we have found Elijah, who is to restore all things; we have found the Messiah and the

216. *Ibid.*, p. 87.
217. *Ibid.*, p. 87 n. 51. He rejects Fortna's division of Ruckstuhl's Johannine characteristic "partitive ἐκ" into four sub-categories (see above, p. 146). Considering two of them, (1) τις, τινές, πολλοί, or οὐδείς followed by ἐκ (which occurs frequently in John, i.e., the redactor of the source, never in the source itself), and (2) ἐκ with a numeral (εἷς or δύο) (common in the source, but found only twice in John), he says that "it is hard to agree with Fortna that we have here 'a telling state of affairs'" (cf. FORTNA, *Gospel of Signs*, 1970, p. 209).
218. *Understanding*, pp. 87-89, n. 51. Cf. LINDARS, *Behind the Fourth Gospel*, 1971, p. 33.
219. *Understanding*, p. 284; cp. p. 163.
220. *Ibid.*, p. 86. Moreover, by combining the signs source with the passion and resurrection narratives, "Fortna relinquishes the one argument that the opponents of the signs-source theory have found most difficult to refute – the reference, right at the end of the Gospel, to 'many other signs that are not written in this book' (20:30)" (p. 284).
221. *Ibid.*, p. 284.
222. *Ibid.*, p. 88.
223. *Ibid.*, p. 88; cp. p. 163.
224. *Ibid.*, p. 163.
225. *Ibid.*, p. 246, cp. p. 163.

Son of God"[226]. For Ashton, it does not matter "whether this source was a source in the proper sense of the term or whether it was in effect the first draft of what was later to become the Fourth Gospel"[227]. Ashton does not know "how the signs source continued", but he has "good reasons" for thinking how it began with 1,19–2,11 and, particularly in dialogue with Boismard, he gives a reconstruction of the source text for this section[228]. Finally, we note that Ashton is "unconvinced by the arguments of H.-P. Heekerens, who holds that the two Cana miracles (2:1-12 and 4:46b-54) derive from the same source and were added to the Gospel by a later redactor"[229].

In his study on the Fourth Gospel and the Johannine Letters, Walter SCHMITHALS (1992), after surveying the history of Johannine research[230], notices the failure of source criticism[231] and prefers the *Grundschrift* hypothesis to explain the aporias in the Fourth Gospel[232]. With regard to

226. *Ibid.*, p. 279.
227. *Ibid.*, p. 246. Cp. pp. 163-164: "Its extent remains uncertain, but is unlikely to have been as considerable as Fortna supposed".
228. *Ibid.*, pp. 280-291: "Excursus II: A Call to Faith (1:19-49)", esp. 284-286. He distinguishes three parts: (1) Ἡ Μαρτυρία (Testimony): 1,6.7 (without 7b: ἵνα πάντες πιστεύσωσιν δι' αὐτοῦ). 19 (Ashton puts καὶ αὕτη ἐστὶν ἡ μαρτυρία τοῦ Ἰωάννου, ὅτε within brackets, he reads ἀπέστειλαν πρὸς αὐτόν, and Λευῖται instead of Λευίτας). 20 (without ὡμολόγησεν¹ καὶ). 21.25.26 (without ἐγὼ βαπτίζω ἐν ὕδατι, Ashton reads στήκει instead of ἕστηκεν). 31 (without ἐγὼ ἐν ὕδατι). 32.34 (without κἀγὼ ἑώρακα, καὶ μεμαρτύρηκα ὅτι). 28. (2) Ἡ Ἀναγνώρισις (Discovery): 35-37. 38 (only οἱ δὲ εἶπαν αὐτῷ· ῥαββί ..., ποῦ μένεις;). 39 (Ashton puts τὴν ἡμέραν ἐκείνην· ὥρα ἦν ὡς δεκάτη within brackets). 40.41 (Ashton reads [πρῶτος] instead of πρῶτον, without ὅ ἐστιν μεθερμηνευόμενον χριστός). 42 (without ὅ ἑρμηνεύεται Πέτρος). Instead of v. 43a Ashton reads: καὶ ὁ Πέτρος εὑρίσκει Φίλιππον καὶ λέγει αὐτῷ· εὑρηκάμεν Ἐλείαν, ὃς ἀποκαταστήσει πάντα. 43b (καὶ λέγει αὐτῷ ὁ Ἰησοῦς· ἀκολούθει μοι). 44.45 (without καὶ οἱ προφῆται). 46-49. (3) Ἡ Φανέρωσις (Manifestation): 2,1-8.9 (without καὶ οὐκ ἤ"δει πόθεν ἐστίν, οἱ δὲ διάκονοι ἤ"δεισαν οἱ ἠντληκότες τὸ ὕδωρ).10.11 (instead of τὴν δόξαν αὐτοῦ Ashton reads ἑαυτόν).
229. *Ibid.*, p. 291.
230. W. SCHMITHALS, *Johannesevangelium und Johannesbriefe. Forschungsgeschichte und Analyse* (BZNW, 64), Berlin - New York, 1992. – Reviews: F. NEIRYNCK, in *ETL* 68 (1992) 166-168; U. SCHNELLE, in *TLZ* 118 (1993) 840-842; G. STRECKER – M. LAHBAHN, *Der johanneische Schriftenkreis*, in *TR* 59 (1994) 101-107. – In the first part, *Forschungsgeschichte* (pp. 1-214), Schmithals deals with the following problems: "Die äussere Bezeugung. Die altkirchliche Tradition. Die vorkritische Auslegung. Traditionelle historische Probleme. Die 'Echtheit' der johanneischen Schriften. Von Holtzmann bis Bultmann. Bultmanns Kommentar zum Johannesevangelium. Von Bultmanns Kommentar bis zur Gegenwart. Aufbau und Gliederung des Johannesevangeliums. Die Johannesbriefe. Die Hypothese einer johanneischen Schule". In the second part, *Analyse* (pp. 215-432), he proposes his own literary theory: "Die Lieblingsjünger-Redaktion. Der Prolog des Johannesevangeliums. Analyse der Johannesbriefe. Grundevangelium und Evangelium: Die Kriterien. Grundevangelium und Evangelium: Die Kritik. Zur Interpretation".
231. *Ibid.*, pp. 217-219.
232. *Ibid.*, pp. 218-219. See below, pp. 291-292. See also his article *Die Bedeutung der Evangelien in der Theologiegeschichte bis zur Kanonbildung*, in *FS F. Neirynck*, I,

the semeia hypothesis, he observes that its defenders do not agree on the delimitation of the source[233] and formulates several objections against its existence[234]. The seven miracles assigned to the source are very different in form[235]. The designated purpose of the source, i.e., the demonstration of Jesus' Messiahship, is also present in many other sections of the gospel, and 20,30-31 can be considered the conclusion of a more extensive work, a *Grundschrift*, in whose center the miracle stories are placed[236]. The distinction between tradition and redactional reworking cannot only be observed in the miracle stories (see, e.g., the classic example of 4,48-49), but also in other parts of the gospel[237]. That there are seven miracles in the gospel can be ascribed to the *Grundschrift* or the evangelist himself as well as to the signs source; and the same must be said about the numbering of the first two signs (2,11; 4,54), which are in fact the only miracles in Jn not followed by a discourse or interpretative dialogue[238]. The literary form of a miracle book is not found elsewhere in primitive Christianity or its environment: the free tradition of miracle stories and their collection in a pre- or para-Synoptic tradition

1992, pp. 129-157, esp. 151-154: "Das Johannesevangelium". Cf. pp. 153-154: "(ich) halte jene Erklärungsweise im Prinzip für berechtigt, die mit einer Grundschrift aus der Zeit des Aposynagogos und mit deren antignostischer Bearbeitung durch den Verfasser der Joh-Briefe rechnet. Jene Grundschrift hält sich offensichtlich im Rahmen einer Präexistenz- und Inkarnationschristologie und -soteriologie, wie sie auch der zum Prolog umgearbeitete Hymnus vorträgt, während die antidoketische Bearbeitung damit die Passionssoteriologie verbindet"; cp. p. 156.

233. *Johannesevangelium*, 1992, pp. 124-126: "Zeichen, Wunder- oder Semeiaquelle", esp. 125: "Vor allem diese Unsicherheit in der Abgrenzung der 'Zeichenquelle' gibt Anlass, ihre Existenz überhaupt zu bezweifeln, und in der Tat sind die für eine Zeichenquelle des JohEv vorgetragenen Beobachtungen wenig beweiskräftig". He refers to our historical survey (1975), and mentions (pp. 124-125) especially the following defenders of a signs source: Faure (and his predecessors: Renan, Soltau, Thompson), Windisch, Jeremias, Bultmann, Vielhauer (and further Käsemann, Schnackenburg, Conzelmann, Koester, Robinson, Reim, Richter, Marxsen, Schenke – Fischer, Gnilka, Smith, H.-J. Kuhn). For a more extensive source, including the narratives on John the Baptist and the passion and resurrection stories, he refers to Meyer, Haenchen, Fortna, Nicol, Teeple, Becker, Martyn and Wöllner, and for a short signs source, to Heekerens.

234. *Ibid.*, pp. 125-126. He refers to the critical observations made by Noack, Michaelis, Wilkens, Kümmel, Langbrandtner, Neirynck, Bittner, Schnelle, Thyen and Barrett.

235. According to Schmithals, Jn 6,1ff.; 6,16ff., and 4,46ff. "(folgen) dem synoptischen Typ" and are easily recognizable in their context; Jn 2,1-11 is also "formal geschlossen", but "(wirkt) gänzlich 'unsynoptisch'"; Jn 5,1ff.; 9,1ff. and 11,1ff. are "relativ formlos und ohne deutliche synoptische Parallelen" (p. 125).

236. *Ibid.*, p. 125. On 20,30-31 as conclusion of the *Grundevangelium*, see also p. 412.

237. *Ibid.*, p. 125. On 4,48-49, see also p. 342: "Der Hand des Evangelisten gehört ausserdem die schon oft als sekundäre Einlage identifizierte Wunderkritik in *V. 48* an, nach deren Einfügung *V. 49*, eine Dublette zu V. 47, erforderlich wurde, um mühsam wieder den Anschluss an die Vorlage zu gewinnen".

238. *Ibid.*, p. 125.

is doubtful[239]. The stylistic test of the delimitation of the signs source and its redaction by the evangelist has no conclusive force[240]. The fact that the evangelist has strongly reworked the signs source by combining it with the discourses does not sufficiently explain the aporias in the present gospel[241]. Finally, Schmithals stresses that the acceptance of the semeia hypothesis depends on the credibility of the whole literary-critical theory in which it is proposed[242].

Schmithals himself proposes three stages in the composition of the Fourth Gospel[243]. In the *first* stage, there was a *Grundevangelium*, composed at the end of the first century, intended to confirm the belief of the Christians expelled from the synagogue (ἀποσυνάγωγος), and to unify them. Its central theme concerns Jesus' Messiahship[244]. He reconstructs the *Grundevangelium* as follows (the asterisk indicates verses with a "Mischtext" of *Grundevangelium* and the evangelist's redaction)[245]:

---

239. *Ibid.*, pp. 125-126, with reference to his *Einleitung in die drei ersten Evangelien* (de-Gruyter-Lehrbuch), Berlin - Göttingen, 1985, pp. 298-318 ("Kritik der Formkritik"). See esp. p. 302 (on the pre-Markan collections): "Aber die Existenz solcher Sammlungen ist mehr als nur unwahrscheinlich ... und ein unbegründetes Hilfspostulat der Formgeschichte".

240. *Johannesevangelium*, p. 126. He notes that most defenders of the semeia hypothesis also reject the stylistic argumentation for the source. See also pp. 137-139: "Kritik der Literarkritik (Einheitlichkeit des JohEv; Stilkritik)".

241. *Ibid.*, p. 126.

242. *Ibid.*, p. 126 (he refers to the literary theories of Bultmann and Becker).

243. *Ibid.*, p. 219.

244. *Ibid.*, p. 219. See also pp. 421-422 ("Abfassungsverhältnisse. Das Grundevangelium"), 427-430 ("Theologie des Grundevangelisten").

245. For the distinction between the passages of the *Grundevangelium* and the additions by the evangelist, see pp. 320-420: "Grundevangelium und Evangelium: Die Kritik"; for the reconstruction of the original order, see esp. 413-420: "Relozierung des Grundevangeliums", with on pp. 417-418, the reconstruction as given in the text above. Note that for the reconstruction of the *Grundevangelium*, Schmithals has made several displacements (they are indicated in bold print). First, 4,4-39* is to be read after 6,1-35*. Second 15,18–16,23a* is placed before 14,18-31*. Third, (I) 2,14-16; 3,1-6.9-10, (II) 5,2-47*; and (III) chs. 7*–8*–9*–10* follow 12,12-13 (the only journey to Jerusalem in the *Grundevangelium*). On pp. 292-319, Schmithals gives 31 criteria for this distinction ("Grundevangelium und Evangelium: Die Kriterien"): "1. Christologische Hoheitstitel. 2. Die 'Ich-bin'-Formeln. 3. Das Verhältnis von 'Vater' und 'Sohn'. 4. Jesus als Menschensohn. 5. Die Leiblichkeit Christi. 6. Orts- und Zeitangaben. 7. Die Reisen Jesu in Palästina. 8. Der Name 'Jesus'. 9. Wunder und wunderbares Wissen. 10. Der Begriff 'Doxa'. 11. Martyria. 12. Glaube. 13. Gnosis. 14. Soteriologie. Jesus als Passalamm. 15. Polemik gegen pneumatisches Selbstbewusstsein. 16. Tradition gegen Enthusiasmus. 17. Die 'Juden' im Johannesevangelium. 18. Die Jünger Jesu. 19. Der 'Kosmos'. 20. Exklusivität und Universalität des Christuszeugnisses. 21. Der Heilige Geist. 22. Die Einheit der Gemeinde und das Bleiben in ihr. 23. Die Sünde. 24. Das Gericht. 25. Ethik. 26. Eschatologie. 27. Benutzung des Alten Testaments. 28. Hebräische Begriffe. 29. Stilmittel des Evangelisten. 30. Missverständnisse und Unverständnis. 31. Benutzung der synoptischen Überlieferung". On the date, see also below, pp. 293, 294.

(a) The prologue: 1,1-12b.13-18;

(b) The witness of the Baptist to the Jews: 1,19-21.25-27.33-34;

(c) The call of the disciples: 1,35*.36*.41*-42.45*.47-50;

(d) The miracle at Cana in presence of the disciples: 2,1*-3*.6-11;

(e) Jesus' work in Galilee: 4,46b.47*.50-54a; 6,1.3*.5-22.24b.25*-27a.34-35;

(f) Jesus in Samaria: (**2,13**)[246]; **4,4-7.9a.10-26.28-30.39b**;

(g) Jesus in Judea: 11,1*.4.6b-7a.11b-12.14-15.20-21.23-28*.29.32b-33*.34.38b-41a.43b-44;

(h) Jesus in Jerusalem: 12,12-13; **2,14-16; 3,1-6.9-10**; 12,42*-43;

(i) Healing of the paralytic and first conflict with the Jews: **5,2-19.21-24.33.36a.c.37-40.45-47; 7,12-13.21-24.31-33a; 10,14-15a.16.24-28; 7,45-52**;

(j) Healing of the blind man and last conflict with the Jews: **9,1*-3.6-35*.36-39a; 8,12b-14a.17-19; 10,19-21; 8,21-23a.38-39.41b-42a.44a.47.51-54a.56-59a**;

(k) Farewell to his disciples: 13,1a*.4-10a.12a.33; 14,1.2a.3.6b; **15,18.20b.c.23-24; 16,2-4a.16-17a.19-23a**; 14,18-19.27.30*.31b;

(l) Passion and resurrection: 18,1.3b*-5a.12b-13a.28*.29*-31; 19,7b-8*.9b-11.16*.28*.30b.38.41-42*; 20,1.11b-19.20b

(m) Conclusion of the book: 20,30-31.

For the *Grundevangelist*, the seven miracle stories were an essential witness to Jesus as Son of God in the dialogue with the synagogue[247]. They reveal Jesus' glory as Son of God (1,14; 2,11; 11,4.40; cp. 9,3; 12,43)[248] and are appropriate to inspire faith in Jesus' Messiahship (5,36; 9,3.29-33; 11,4.26f.; 10,25; 15,24; 20,30f.)[249]. Thus, it is no wonder that, compared with the Synoptic miracle stories, the miraculous is heightened in these stories. Moreover, the author of the *Grundevangelium* considered the miracles as signs and interpreted them in an existential way (2,1*-11; 3,2; 4,46-54; 5,21-24; 6,3.5-13.14f.16-21; 7,31; 9,1-3.6-38; 11,15.25-26.39-40; 12,42-43)[250]. This means, according to Schmithals, that for the *Grundevangelist*, as "a child of his time", reality and symbolism are in no way alternatives[251]. Jesus' miraculous foreknowledge is also used by the author of the *Grundevangelium* as a sign for Jesus' Messiahship (1,42.47.50; 4,16-19.29.39; 5,6; 6,15; 11,12.14-15; 13,1a.7; 16,4.19; 18,4; 19,28)[252].

---

246. On 2,13, Schmithals remarks: "Da auch im Grundevangelium die Reise nach Jerusalem mit einer entsprechenden Notiz eingeleitet worden sein dürfte, liegt die Annahme nahe, dass V. 13 schon im Grundevangelium stand und seinen Platz vor Joh 4,44ff hatte" (p. 328; cp. p. 414).

247. *Ibid.*, p. 302; cp. p. 304. The number seven indicates "das exemplarische der ausgewählten Wunder" (p. 302).

248. *Ibid.*, p. 303.

249. *Ibid.*, p. 302; cp. p. 304.

250. *Ibid.*, p. 302.

251. *Ibid.*

252. *Ibid.*

In the second stage, the evangelist, who was also the author of the Johannine Epistles, reworked the *Grundevangelium* around 140 A.D., giving it a new division and including additional material in an attempt to combat gnostic tendencies[253]. His reworking is anti-docetic, stressing that *Jesus* is the Messiah[254]. Consequently, miracle belief as such is problematic, because the miracles are not appropriate to illustrate the humanness of the Son of God[255]. Therefore, the evangelist added critical comments on miracle belief (2,23-25; 4,41-42.48-49; 20,29). In addition, belief for him is based on the preached word (1 Jn 1,1-4)[256]. He accepts, however, the symbolic character of the miracles, as proposed by the *Grundevangelist*, and expands it. Thus, for the evangelist, the resurrection of Lazarus refers to the physical resurrection[257]. The motif of Jesus' miraculous foreknowledge, as basis for faith, is also adopted by the evangelist. He enlarged it explicitly in 13,18-19; 14,29; 16,30[258]. Moreover, the evangelist uses this motif not only in the sense of the *Grundevangelist* but for many other purposes, especially to show Jesus' foreknowledge of the apostasy of heretics and their representative Judas Iskariot, and of Jesus' foreknowledge of his real death and physical resurrection (2,24-25; 6,43.61.64; 12,23.27; 13,3.11.18-19; 14,29; 16,30; 17,1; cp. 15,18ff.)[259]. Note that the evangelist also uses the term δόξα (and δοξάζω) in a similar way as the *Grundevangelist* (8,54; 12,28b; 13,31-32), but he does it with "subordinatianische Tendenz"[260] and with

253. The additions of the evangelist given in the order of the present gospel are (cf. pp. 320-420): 1,12c.22-24.38-32.35*.36*.37-40.41*.43-44.45*.46.51; 2,1*-3*.4-5.12.17-25; 3,7-8.11-21.22-36; 4,1-3.8.9.27.31-39a.40-46a.47*.48-49.54b; 5,1.20.25-32.34-35.36b.41-44; 6,2.3*.4.23-24a.25*.27b-33.36-62.64-71; 7,1-11.14-20.25-30.33b-44; 8,12a.14b-16.20.23b-37.40-41a.42b.44b-46.48-50.54b-55.59b; 9,1*.4.35*.39b-41; 10,1-13.15b.17-18.22-23.29-42; 11,1*.2-3.5-6a.7b-11a.13.16-19.22.28*.30-32a.33*.35-38a. 41b-43a.45-57; 12,1-11.14-41.42*.44-50; 13,1*.2-3.10b-11.12b-19.26b-32.34-35; 14,2b. 4-6a.7-17.20-26.30*.31a; 15,1-17.19.20a.20d.21-22.25-27; 16,1.4b-15.17b-18.23b-33; 17,1-26; 18,2.3a.b*.5b-12a.14b.19-23.28*.29*.32-40; 19,1-7a.8*.9a.12-15.16*.17-24a.28*.29-30a.31-37.39-40.42*; 20,20a.21-29.

254. *Ibid.*, p. 219. See also pp. 422-423 ("Abfassungsverhältnisse. Das Grundevangelium"), 431-432 ("Theologie des Evangelisten"). On the anti-gnostic/docetic reworking, see also SCHMITHALS, *Neues Testament und Gnosis* (Erträge der Forschung, 208), Darmstadt, 1984, pp. 96-123 ("II. Das Corpus Johanneum"), esp. 115-117 ("Die antignostische Bearbeitung des Johannesevangeliums"). For the rejection of the signs source, see esp. p. 121: "die Annahme einer besonderen 'Zeichenquelle', ohnedies unzureichend begründet, ist daneben nicht nötig".

255. *Johannesevangelium*, p. 303, rejects, however, Schnelle's interpretation (*Christologie*, pp. 87ff.) that "der Evangelist die Wunder wegen der Zuwendung Jesu zu den leiblichen Nöten der Menschen antidoketisch verstanden wissen will".

256. *Johannesevangelium*, p. 303; cp. p. 307.

257. *Ibid.*, p. 303; cp. pp. 315-316.

258. *Ibid.*, p. 303; cp. p. 317.

259. *Ibid.*, p. 303.

260. *Ibid.*, p. 303; cp. pp. 296-297.

his characteristic intention to show the δόξα of Jesus as the earthly-physical son of man[261].

In the third stage, the passages concerning the beloved disciple were added to the Gospel: 6,63(!); 13,20-26a.36-38; 16,12-13(!); 18,15-18.24-27; 19,24b-27; 20,2-11a; 21,1-25. He calls this stage the "LJ-Redaktion" (LJ = *Lieblingsjünger*) and dates it after 170 A.D. in connection with the formation of the canon in Montanistic circles[262].

II. Opposition to the Semeia Hypothesis

In 1972, Otto BETZ noted in reaction to Becker: "I must confess that the existence of such a Semeia-source seems to me no less questionable than that of the so-called Divine Man concept"[263]. Two years later, he dwelt at length on the signs source[264].

261. *Ibid.*, p. 303. As son of man Jesus dwelled before the creation of the world in the glory of his Father (6,62; 12,41; 17,5.24); he left this glory (17,5), is lifted up on the cross (3,14; 8,28; 12,32.34) and by his resurrection and ascension (6,62; 7,3ff.; 12,32-34; 13,3; cp. 14,4f.28; 16,17b) he is glorified again (7,39; 12,16.23.28; 13,31f.; 17,1.5.22), so that God is also glorified (13,31f.; 14,13; 17,1.4; cp. 15,8; 17,10.22). See also p. 298.

262. *Ibid.*, p. 219. See esp. pp. 220-259: "Die Lieblingsjünger-Redaktion". Cp. pp. 356, 389, 390, 398, 405, 407, 411. – With regard to the relationship of the Fourth Evangelist to the Synoptic Gospels (see esp. pp. 318-319: "Benutzung der synoptischen Überlieferung", Schmithals is "sur la même longueur d'onde" as Neirynck (cf. Neirynck's review in *ETL* 68, p. 167; cf. also Schmithals's article *Die Bedeutung der Evangelien*, p. 132). Cf. *Johannesevangelium*, p. 319: "Für den Evangelisten ist bemerkenswert, dass er das Grundevangelium in starkem Masse mit synoptischer Überlieferung anreichert. ... Das MtEv scheint der Evangelist gekannt zu haben ... Vor allem aber kennt der Evangelist und benutzt er häufig das lukanische Doppelwerk". Moreover, it is significant that Schmithals, in contrast to Boismard (Jn I and Jn II-A), also accepts contact with the Synoptics on the level of the *Grundevangelium*. Thus, Schmithals notes that the *Grundevangelist* knows the Synoptic tradition "auf literarischen Weg"; he knows "mit Sicherheit" (p. 421), "jedenfalls" (p. 319) "das MkEv bzw. dessen Grundschrift". With regard to 19,9b-10, he mentions a specific influence of the Markan *Grundschrift* (p. 319, 405-406). For Jn 15,20b, Schmithals refers to Mt 10,24, but he adds "oder dessen Vorlage" (p. 396), "oder ggf. der Spruchquelle des MtEv" (p. 318). Regarding the Gospel of Luke he hesitates between "sicher" oder "wahrscheinlich" (p. 319), and notes on the date of the Johannine *Grundevangelium*: "Sollte er jedoch auch Bekanntschaft mit dem LkEv verraten, müsste man die Abfassung des Grundevangeliums besser in den Anfang des 2. Jahrhunderts hinaufschieben" (p. 421). For the influence of the Synoptic Gospels on the *LJ-Redaktion*, see pp. 223, 225, 226, 228, 230, 232 and 240. For more information, see NEIRYNCK, in *ETL* 68, 1992, pp. 167-168.

263. O. BETZ, *The Concept of the So-Called "Divine Man" in Mark's Christology*, in *FS A.P. Wikgren*, 1972, pp. 229-240, esp. 240 (= 1987, pp. 273-284, esp. 284). See also *"Kann denn aus Nazareth etwas Gutes kommen?" (Zur Verwendung von Jesaja Kap 11 in Johannes Kap. 1)*, in *FS K. Elliger*, 1973, pp. 9-16, esp. 15-16 (= 1987, pp. 287-297, esp. 396-397: on Becker's analysis of Jn 1,35-51). On Betz, see KOSKENNIEMI, *Apollonios von Tyana*, 1992, pp. 135-136.

264. *Das Problem des Wunders bei Flavius Josephus im Vergleich zum Wunderproblem bei den Rabbinen und im Johannesevangelium*, in *FS O. Michel*, 1974, pp. 23-

First, he rejects Bultmann's and Becker's distinction between the source, which presents extremely heightened miracles, and the rest of the gospel, in which the evangelist understands the miracles as symbols and attacks the christology of the source[265]. Moreover, the σημεῖα cannot be defined as epiphanies (ctr. Becker)[266]. In fact, John never uses the Hellenistic concept ἐπιφάνεια, and the heightening of the Johannine σημεῖα is to be explained by their intention to show that Jesus is the one sent by God[267]. As in Josephus, the Johannine σημεῖον is related to belief and calls one to decision (2,11; 4,53; cp. 9,38)[268].

44, esp. 34-44 (= 1987, pp. 398-419, esp. 409-419): "Das Problem der Zeichen im Johannesevangelium". See also (in collaboration with W. GRIMM): *Wesen und Wirklichkeit der Wunder Jesu. Heilungen – Rettungen – Zeichen – Aufleuchtungen. Jes. 60,5 "Da wirst du Schauen und strahlen dein Herz wird beben und weit werden"* (ANTJ, 2), Frankfurt/M - Bern - Las Vegas, 1977, esp. pp. 120-151: "Die johanneischen Semeia"; art. *σημεῖον*, in *EWNT* 3 (1983) 565-575, cc. 572-573; ET: *EDNT* 3 (1992) 238b-241a, p. 240a-240b (see below, p. 299 n. 288); *"To Worship God in Spirit and Truth": Reflections on John 4,20-26*, in FS J.M. *Oesterreicher*, 1981, pp. 53-72, esp. 68 (= 1987, pp. 420-438, esp. 435): "It is not possible that the same scriptural texts serve as the basis for a part of the revelatory discourse (v. 23f), the *Semeia Source* (v. 25), the commentary of the evangelist (v. 21) and a gloss of the redactor (v. 22b). Such coincidences do not occur. In the Fourth Gospel we have before us the uniform work of John, the seamless robe of Christ"; *Die traditionsgeschichtliche Exegese als Beitrag zur theologischen Toleranz*, in BETZ, *Jesus, der Herr der Kirche*, 1990, pp. 407-424, esp. 419-420; see p. 420: "Aber auch die eher anerkannte christliche Semeia-Quelle muss als solche abgelehnt werden, genauso wie der für sie in Anspruch genommene Typos eines hellenistischen Theios Aner. Die 'Zeichen' im vierten Evangelium waren nicht etwa ursprünglich primitive Mirakel, die der Evangelist redaktionell seiner hochstehenden Christologie angepasst hat. Vielmehr standen sie von Anfang an ganz auf der Höhe der johanneischen Theologie, weil sie als ganze echt johanneisch sind. Dabei erhielten sie ihren theologischen Tiefgang durch eine stärkere Rückbindung an das Alte Testament. Das johanneische 'Semeion' wird zum zeichenhaften Hinweis auf den Christus, der sich durch das Wunder selbst bezeugt; die Entsprechung zu ähnlichen alttestamentlichen Geschichten macht die Zeichenhaftigkeit des Semeion aus. Die Wunder Jesu werden von den Taten Moses und der Gottesmänner Elia und Elisa her neu beleuchtet; dadurch erscheint Jesus als der bevollmächtigte Gesandte und Gottessohn".

265. *Problem*, p. 35 (= 1987, p. 410); cp. *Wesen*, p. 122: "Falsch ist die Scheidung zwischen dem naiven Wunderglauben einer hypothetischen Semeiaquelle und der Wunderkritik des Evangelisten. Es gibt keine solche Quelle; die in der Wundergeschichten erscheinende Christologie entspricht ganz der des übrigen Evangeliums".

266. *Problem*, p. 35 (= 1987, p. 410); see n. 50: "Der Begriff 'Epiphanie' wird bei der Exegese der neutestamentlichen Wunder zu viel und zu ungenau gebraucht".

267. *Ibid.*, p. 35 (= 1987, p. 410).

268. *Ibid.*, pp. 35-36 (= 1987, pp. 410-411). See also *Wesen*, pp. 148-151 (in discussion with Bultmann).

Second, Betz cannot accept the Hellenistic θεῖος ἀνήρ typology[269]: it is questionable that the titles Son of God[270] or prophet[271] were connected with the θεῖος ἀνήρ[272]; and the term σημεῖον is never mentioned in the Hellenistic aretalogies of divine men[273].

269. *Problem*, pp. 36-37 (= 1987, pp. 411-412). Cp. esp. *Concept*, p. 231 (= 1987, p. 275): "I must confess that I hesitate to follow the 'Divine Man' on his glorious ways into the New Testament"; cp. p. 240 (= 1987, p. 284; see above, p. 294 n. 263). See also *Nazareth*, p. 10 n. 9 (= 1987, p. 388 n. 9): "Er [θεῖος ἀνήρ] scheint mir – ähnlich wie der 'Gnostische Erlöser' – das künstliche Gebilde einer allzu rasch systematisierenden Religionswissenschaft zu sein. Dem sogenannten 'Göttlichen Menschen' fehlen sowohl ein fester Titel als auch die klar umrissenen Züge, die ein religionsgeschichtlicher Typus besitzen sollte". – With referrence to Betz, K. KERTELGE, *Die Wunder Jesu in der neueren Exegese*, in *TBer* 5 (1976) 71-105, pp. 91-94 ("Eine Theios-Anér-Christologie?"), also wonders if there existed θεῖος ἀνήρ christology: "Wenn es so etwas wie eine 'Theios-Anér-Christologie' in der urchristlichen Wunderüberlieferung gegeben hat, bleibt zu fragen, ob sie nicht von vornherein nur sektoralen Charakter haben konnte und darauf angewiesen war in eine umfassendere christologische Konzeption integriert zu werden" (p. 94; see n. 100 for reference to BETZ, *Concept*, p. 231, cited above). Two years before, however, Kertelge, with reference to Hahn, H.D. Betz, Koester, and Robinson, mentioned without criticism the θεῖος ἀνήρ christology and the pre-Markan and pre-Johannine collections of miracle stories. Cf. *Die Überlieferung der Wunder Jesu und die Frage nach dem historischen Jesus*, in ID. (ed.), *Rückfrage nach Jesus*, 1974, pp. 174-193, esp. 181: "Eine besondere Rolle spielte ... die Interpretation der Gestalt und Geschichte Jesu im Lichte der jüdischen Erwartung des 'eschatologischen Propheten' und, sich teilweise damit überschneidend, die sogenannte Theios-Aner-Christologie. Sie fanden Verwendung in der urchristlichen Missionsverkündigung und Katechese. Besonders die Katechese hat auf bestimmte Entsprechungen der Taten Jesu zu Überlieferungen des Alten Testaments unter verheissungsgeschichtlichem Gesichtspunkt Wert gelegt. In dieser Situation entstanden schon vor den Evangelien regelrechte Sammlungen von Wunderberichten, in denen die Taten Jesu eine der urchristlichen Verkündigung dienliche Deutung erlangten". For the signs source, he refers to Bultmann, Fortna, and Nicol; for the pre-Markan miracles collection(s), to H.-W. Kuhn and Achtemeier. In his earlier monograph, *Die Wunder Jesu im Markusevangelium. Eine redaktionsgeschichtliche Untersuchung* (SANT, 23), München, 1972, he only mentions the concept of θεῖος ἀνήρ to argue that the miracles of Jesus can only loosely be compared with the miracles in Mark. On Kertelge, see SNOY, in *RTL* 3 (1972) 449-466; 4 (1973) 58-101; SUHL, *Einleitung*, in ID. (ed.), *Der Wunderbegriff*, 1980, pp. 4, 14-15.

270. *Problem*, p. 36 (= 1987, p. 411). Betz refers to WÜLFING VON MARTITZ, art. υἱός, in *TWNT* 8 (1969) 338-340, p. 337 (ET: p. 338): "υἱὸς τοῦ θεοῦ als Hoheitstitel Jesu und einiger Gnostiker in frühchristlicher Zeit wird von modernen Gelehrten zuweilen mit der hellenistischen Vorstellung vom θεῖος ἀνήρ in Verbindung gebracht. Aber die Wurzeln dieser Vorstellung führen nicht in altgriechische Zeit".

271. *Problem*, p. 36 (= 1987, p. 411): "Neu ist Beckers These, auch der Titel 'der Prophet' passe zu dieser Vorstellung; den Beweis ist er schuldig geblieben. Schliesslich ist der Theios Aner für die Deutung der johanneischen σημεῖα keineswegs grundlegend, sondern im Gegenteil ganz entbehrlich; das hat W. Nicol in seinem besonnenen und gründlich bearbeiteten Buch 'The Sēmeia in the Fourth Gospel' gezeigt".

272. *Ibid.*, 1974, p. 36 (= 1987, p. 411): "Anderseits lässt sich kaum bestreiten, dass mit 'dem Propheten' Joh 6,14 der Erlöser wie Mose (Dtn 18,15-22) gemeint ist, ferner dass der johanneische 'Gottessohn' aus dem gemeinchristlichen Credo stammt".

273. *Ibid.*, pp. 36-37 (= 1987, pp. 411-412). Cp. *Wesen*, p. 122: "Irreführend ist ferner die Verbindung zum hellenistischen Wunderdenken, zumal dort das Wort 'Zeichen' für die Tat des Wundermannes gar nicht verwendet wird"; cp. p. 145 n. 218.

Third, the source's use of the word σημεῖον, and especially of the expression σημεῖα ποιεῖν, agrees with that of other passages in the Gospel[274]. For Betz, it is clearly a biblical expression and it recalls Moses' legitimating signs (Ex 4,17.30)[275]. Moreover, the term cannot be separated from the evangelist's use of ἔργα. This term refers to both words and acts of Jesus and describes the unity of the Son's work with that of the Father. For the evangelist, Jesus is more than a messenger who does σημεῖα[276].

Fourth, Betz cannot accept that there is a difference in christology between the passages attributed to the signs source and the rest of the gospel. The manner in which Jesus reveals his glory and wins belief in the miracles corresponds with that in the discourses and in the redactional verses of the evangelist[277]. For a late Judaic prophet, a σημεῖον and an ἐγώ εἰμι saying belong together[278], so it is difficult to conclude that they come from two different sources. Thus, the revealed unity of the Father and the Son is not limited to the discourses, but belongs to the miracles as well; this is already expressed in the emphatic use of σημεῖον and in such passages as 2,4 and 4,48[279].

Fifth, the unity of the gospel is also apparent from the Old Testament background. Jn 1,40-51 and 12,37, which belong to the signs source

274. *Problem*, p. 37 (= 1987, p. 412), refers to the use of σημεῖον(-α) ποιεῖν "in den abschliessenden Sätzen" (2,11; 4,54; 20,30); "in Feststellungen die von miterlebten Zeichen Jesu berichten" (6,2.14; 12,37). The expression σημεῖον(-α) ποιεῖν is predominant in the ten other cases: cp. 2,18 and 6,30 with Mk 8,11; in 3,2; 7,31; 11,47 Jesus' exceptional miraculous power is stated; in 10,41 it is said that John the Baptist did no signs. Further, 2,23 is to be compared formally with 12,37; for 12,18, see 6,2. See also *Wesen*, p. 124: "Uns scheint diese These [the semeia hypothesis] höchst fragwürdig zu sein, aus ziemlich einfachen Gründen. 1. Nicht nur der Begriff 'Semeion' kommt ausserhalb der joh. Wunderperikopen häufiger vor als innerhalb, sondern auch das für die Semeia charakteristische Wortfeld 'Zeichen bzw. Werke tun' – 'sehen' – 'glauben' (dass Jesus der Christus bzw. der Gesandte Gottes ist). ... 2. Gerade die Semeia-Elemente der joh. Wundergeschichten sind sprachlich, begrifflich und stilistisch, typisch johanneisch. 3. Einige der joh. Wunder, die angeblich der Zeichenquelle entstammen, haben gerade nichts Zeichenhaftes an sich. Wie sollten ausgerechnet die *Heilungs*wunder 4,46-54; 5,1-16; 9,1ff; 11,1ff eine Semeia-Schrift mit-konstituiert haben! Dieselbe Frage gilt für das Theophaniewunder 6,16-21". For the σημεῖον-concept, cf. pp. 124-127; see also p. 148.

275. *Problem*, p. 37 (= 1987, p. 412). For the analogy between Jesus and Moses, see Jn 1,17; 3,14; 6,30-32; 7,22; cp. Acts 7,35-39 (*Wesen*, pp. 126-127). Betz compares Jn 20,30-31 with Deut 34,10-12 and Ex 14,31 (pp. 125, 126).

276. *Problem*, pp. 37-38 (= 1987, pp. 412-413), refers to 5,1-20; 9,3-4; 10,25.32.37; 11,4. He notes that the raising of Lazarus, who was already three days in the tomb (11,17.39), takes the place of the sign of Jonah (cf. Mt 12,39-40); it refers to Jesus' resurrection, which is also considered a sign (20,30; cp. 2,18).

277. *Ibid.*, p. 38 (= 1987, p. 413), refers to 2,11; 4,53; cf. 12,37; 20,31, and compares these verses with 3,18; 5,24; 6,35.47; 7,38 in the discourses, and 2,23-24; 10,42; 12,42; 19,35, which are redactional.

278. See also the use of ἐγώ εἰμι in 6,20; 18,6.8 (*Problem*, p. 38; = 1987, p. 413).

279. *Ibid.*, p. 38 (= 1987, p. 413).

according to Bultmann and others, must be interpreted from Is 11,3 and 53,1 respectively, but passages such as Jn 2,23-25 and 5,30, which belong to the redaction, are also influenced by Is 11,3. Thus, it is difficult to ascribe them to different layers[280].

The theology of the source is diminished if one removes Jn 2,4 and 4,48 from their respective miracle stories. In doing so, one ascribes to the evangelist what belongs to the original story and consequently changes the σημεῖα into theological criticism of naive epiphanies. Jn 4,48 and 2,4 have the same function within their stories; they belonged to the original story and they can best be understood from the Elijah-Elisha tradition[281].

With respect to Jn 2,4, Betz refers to the Elijah tradition (esp. 1 Kgs 17,14), which is also used in Lk 4,25-26. The miracle of Cana is the beginning not only of the signs but of Jesus' public ministry, and so it takes the position of Lk 4,16-17. In Jesus' first appearance, the question of legitimation already comes to the fore (cp. Ex 4,27-31 and 7,1-13). In Jn 2,4 and Lk 4,16ff. there is a separation between Jesus and his relatives: "Human ties and obligations in no way influence Jesus' action; the miracle worker is bound to his own law and must listen to another voice"[282]. In Nazareth, Jesus makes his rejection understandable by referring to both Elijah and Elisha[283]: when a great famine lay over the whole country, Elijah was not sent to his own people, but to a widow at Sarepta in the territory of Sidon (Lk 4,25-26), and Elisha did not heal Israelites, but only the Syrian leper Naaman (Lk 4,27).

The allusion to the Elijah/Elisha tradition is found both in Jn 2,4 and 4,48[284]. (a) In both cases, Jesus refers to the peculiar realm of the man sent by God. Mary and the royal official were not criticized (see the plural in 4,48) and the miracle as such is not rejected or put into question. Rather, Jesus cautions against misinterpretation of the miracle. Through the person of the miracle worker one must perceive God working, lest one miss the real sense of a σημεῖον, i.e., the legitimation of the messenger and his mission. Thus, Jn 2,4 and 4,48 are not secondary additions but belong to the whole story on account of their Old Testa-

280. *Ibid.*, 1974, pp. 38-39 (= 1987, pp. 413-414); see also *Nazareth*, pp. 11-12 (= 1987, p. 390); *Wesen*, p. 145.

281. *Problem*, pp. 39-40 (= 1987, pp. 414-415). Betz's interpretation has been followed by NEIRYNCK, *Jean et les Synoptiques*, 1979, pp. 116-119 (= *ETL* 53, 1977, pp. 474-477). See below, p. 322 n. 425. For the presentation of "Jesus as the New Elisha", see also BOSTOCK, in *ExpT* 92 (1980-81) 39-41; cp. BRODIE, in *ExpT* 93 (1981-82) 39-42, who with regard to Jn 9 agrees with Bostock: "The complexity and coherence of the relationship of John 9 to 2 Kings 5 is such that, in my judgment, it can be explained by a conscious and systematic process. Bostock's suspicions appear to have been correct".

282. *Problem*, p. 40 (= 1987, p. 415), cites BULTMANN, *Johannes*, 1941, p. 81 (on 2,4; ET: 1971, p. 117).

283. *Problem*, p. 40 (= 1987, pp. 415). Cp. *Wesen*, pp. 121-122.

284. *Problem*, pp. 40-43 (= 1987, pp. 415-418).

ment background[285]. Jesus' first miracle is to be connected with Elijah's first miracle (cf. Lk 4,25-26). In both, the guest becomes the giver of salvation: Elijah assures that the oil in the jar (ὑδρία) will not give out (1 Kgs 17,12.14.16) and, when the wine ran out at Cana, Jesus changes the water of the jars (ὑδρίαι, Jn 2,7) into wine[286]. (b) The order of the first two Johannine miracles makes clear that their connection with the Elijah/Elisha tradition is not at all hypothetical[287]. Jn 4,46-54 is to be compared with Elijah's second miracle. In both stories, we find the expression ὁ υἱός σου ζῇ (Jn 4,50.51.53; 1 Kgs 17,23). The parallel is more apparent, because the healing in Jn 4 concerns the son of the royal official (and not his servant as in the Synoptic parallels) who is at the point of death (Jn 4,47.49; cp. 1 Kgs 17,17-20). Like the two miracles of Elijah, the first two miracles of Jesus happen at the same place. Regarding the numbering of the signs, which only makes sense in the present gospel where the two signs are separated by narrative and discourse material, Betz gives several explanations. The two signs can be numbered, because they occurred at the same place and are analogous to the two miracles of Elijah[288]. The numbering can be compared with Ex 4,8 (LXX): there the Lord said to Moses, ἐὰν δὲ μή πιστεύσωσίν σοι μηδὲ εἰσακούσωσιν τῆς φωνῆς τοῦ σημείου τοῦ πρώτου, πιστεύσουσίν σοι τῆς φωνῆς τοῦ σημείου τοῦ ἐσχάτου. The first of these signs is the changing of the water of the Nile into blood (Ex 7,14-25; cp. Jn 2,1-11); the last is the death of the first-born (Ex 12,29-30; cp. the opposite miracle in Jn 4,46-54)[289]. Finally, the allusion to the mission of Elijah and Elisha in Jn 2,4 and 4,48 (cp. Lk 4,25-27) also explains the numbering in Jn 2,11 and 4,54. The second miracle in Cana is not only to be interpreted in light of the Elijah miracle in 1 Kgs 17, but also in light of the story of Elisha, i.e., the healing of the Syrian Naaman mentioned in Lk 4,27 (see 2 Kgs 5,1-27). Jn 4,48 refers to this story. Naaman's preconception of the healing is contradicted by the instructions he

---

285. *Ibid.*, pp. 40-41 (= 1987, pp. 415-416).
286. *Ibid.*, p. 41 (= 1987, p. 416).
287. *Ibid.*, p. 41 (= 1987, p. 416).
288. *Ibid.*, pp. 41-42 (= 1987, pp. 416-417); see also *EWNT*, III, cc. 572-573 (ET: p. 240a): "Mit der Joh 2,11; 4,54 begonnenen und nicht weitergeführten Zählung der Zeichen wird an die beiden ersten Wunder Moses (Ex 4,8) und Elijas (1Kön 17) erinnert. Von daher gesehen stehen die Zeichen im Einklang mit der joh Theologie, weisen keine Brüche auf und verraten nichts von der Benützung einer primitiven, auf die Überbietung hellenistischer Wundermänner zielenden 'Semeia-Quelle'".
289. *Problem*, pp. 41-42 (= 1987, pp. 416-417). See also *Wesen*, p. 128: "Dass das erste Zeichen auf den Glauben der Jünger zielt, entspricht dem 'ersten' Zeichen von Ex. 4,8, das sich nur an Israel, noch nicht an den Pharao wendet"; p. 131: "Die Zählung 'das zweite Zeichen' weist natürlich nicht auf ein Zeichenevangelium hin – darin wäre sie höchst überflüssig –, sondern eher auf die Zählung der Zeichenwunder des Mose (Ex. 4,8): Wie im Joh-Evangelium werden in Ex. 4–11 nur die ersten beiden Semeia gezählt, obwohl weitere durchaus ins Auge gefasst werden (Ex. 4,9ff.)".

receives. He thought that Elisha would at least come out to him, invoke the Lord his God by name, wave his hands over the place and so rid him of the disease. But Naaman had to learn that a miracle of God can also happen in the absence of the miracle worker, so that one must hear the word and believe. This lesson has been taken up into Jesus' word to the royal official; thus Jn 4,48 gives an instruction on true belief in miracles[290]. Moreover, there are other parallels between Jn 4,46-54 and 2 Kgs 5,1-27. As Naaman finally complies with the command of Elisha to go and wash seven times in the Jordan (5,10.14), so the official obeys the command of Jesus to go (4,50)[291]. In both cases the miracle takes place in the absence of the miracle worker[292].

In addition to Freed & Hunt and Ruckstuhl[293], some other authors have applied stylistic tests to Bultmann's σημεῖα-*Quelle* or Fortna's Gospel of Signs. John J. O'ROURKE (1974) tried to determine whether there is any stylistic unity in the Gospel regarding the use of the historic present, characteristic both in Jn and Mk[294]. The 164 occurrences in Jn are distributed unevenly over the Gospel as a whole as well as within both the proposed σημεῖα-*Quelle* and the Gospel of Signs[295]. O'Rourke concludes that, with regard to that one stylistic criterion, these sources are not homogeneous. Nevertheless, since those reconstructions are worthy of consideration on other grounds, he presumes that "the lack of stylistic unity with regard to the historic present may indicate that such fine points of style do not provide reliable criteria in any attempt to discern sources", and that "the presence or absence of certain fine points of style is not a criterion for determining authorship or literary unity"[296]. In 1979, after discussing the asides in Jn according to the tenfold classification proposed by M.C. Tenney, O'Rourke thought that it is "impossible to determine whether or not a given aside already existed as such in a source which was then taken over without change into the Gospel as we now have it"[297].

In 1975, Nigel TURNER presented Bultmann's analysis of style in the discourses and the signs source and in the evangelist's additions, and

290. *Problem*, pp. 42-43 (= 1987, pp. 417-418). NEIRYNCK followed this interpretation in *Jean et les Synoptiques*, 1979, p. 110 (= *ETL* 53, 1977, p. 468); cp. *ETL* 60 (1984), p. 372. Cp. our notice in *ETL* 61 (1985) 167-169, p. 169 (for Fortna's reaction, see above, pp. 222-223 n. 415); see also ROBERGE, in *LavalTP* 45 (1989) 339-349, p. 345.

291. *Problem*, p. 43 (= 1987, p. 418).

292. *Ibid.*, pp. 42-43 (= 1987, pp. 418-419).

293. See above, pp. 198-200, and below, pp. 302-307.

294. J.J. O'ROURKE, *The Historic Present in the Gospel of John*, in *JBL* 93 (1974) 585-590, p. 585.

295. *Ibid.*, p. 587.

296. *Ibid.*, p. 588.

297. *Asides in the Gospel of John*, in *NT* 21 (1979) 210-219, p. 219. – Cf. VAN BELLE, *Parenthèses*, 1985, pp. 42-47; BJERKELUND, *Tauta Egeneto*, 1987, pp. 9-10.

concluded (with reference to Schweizer and Ruckstuhl): "The only permissible course is to ignore these divisions and to comment on the style of the Gospel as a unity"[298]. Michel ROBERGE (1975) studied several concluding notices at the end of narratives and discourses in the Fourth Gospel: 1,28; 2,11; 4,54; 6,59; 8,20; 10,6; 21,14[299]. Stylistically, they all begin with a demonstrative, have a similar construction, and are independent of the preceding context[300]. With regard to the content, these notices are mostly concerned with identifying places, counting episodes, or with the reactions of the witnesses or auditors. Note that he includes the numbering of signs, generally attributed to the signs source. For Roberge, all these remarks are the work of a secondary redactor[301].

After a short discussion of the "special Johannine sources", especially the signs source, Oscar CULLMANN (1975) remarks that while style criticism "does not exclude the possibility that the author of the Gospel used written sources, it does make problematical all attempts to *identify* their extent, despite Fortna's efforts in methodology and his attempts to contrast his statistics with those of Ruckstuhl"[302]. Therefore, he prefers "to speak of special Johannine traditions rather than of Johannine sources", and he believes that "the author will have known on the one hand a tradition *common* to *all* branches of early Christianity and made familiar to us through the Synoptic Gospels, and on the other a *separate*

---

298. Cf. N. TURNER, *Style* (J.H. Moulton's *Grammar*, IV), Edinburgh, 1976, pp. 64-67, esp. 67. On pp. 66-67, Turner notes: "We must leave the question open, concluding that if the evangelist used written sources, their distinctive character is not discernible through the finishing work which he or a subsequent editor accomplished on his material".

299. M. ROBERGE, *Notices de conclusion et rédaction du quatrième évangile*, in *LavalTP* 31 (1975) 49-53. – Cf. VAN BELLE, *Parenthèses*, 1985, p. 179.

300. *Notices*, pp. 49-50: "Caractéristiques littéraires"; pp. 50-52: "Caractéristiques de fond".

301. *Ibid.*, p. 53: "Si l'on tient compte de l'ensemble des traits que nous avons signalés, on est porté à penser que ce genre de notice, avec ses traits littéraires et narratifs caractéristiques remonte à une main rédactionnelle secondaire qui aura été en mesure de préciser cependant, dans plus d'un cas (sauf en x,6) le récit ou le discours. Il faut la chercher dans les milieux johanniques. Mais ces préoccupations topographiques et narratives en particulier (ἀρχὴν τῶν σημείων, πάλιν δεύτερον, τρίτον), en soulignent, pensons-nous, le moment récent".

302. O. CULLMANN, *Der johanneische Kreis. Sein Platz im Spätjudentum, in der Jüngerschaft Jesu und im Urchristentum. Zum Ursprung des Johannesevangeliums*, Tübingen, 1975, pp. 1-11: "Literarische Einheit, Quellen, Redaktion des Johannesevangeliums", esp. 7; cp. pp. 4-5; see also pp. 26-29: "Sprache, Stil, literarische Eigenart" (ET: 1976, pp. 1-11, esp. 7; cp. pp. 4-5, 25-29; FT: 1976, pp. 11-24, esp. 19; cp. pp. 15-16, 43-47). For the signs source, Cullmann refers to Faure, Bultmann, Fortna and Becker, and notes the criticism of DODD, *Interpretation*, 1953, on Bultmann's literary analysis, for "the close link between the miracles and the discourses". – Reviews: cf. VAN BELLE, no. 402. See also BROWN, *Community*, 1979, pp. 176-178 (FT: 1983, pp. 193-195); SLOYAN, *What Are They Saying about John?*, 1991, pp. 42, 45-46; SMITH, *John among the Gospels*, 1992, pp. 76-77.

tradition, of special interest to us, which came down to him in the particular circle to which he belonged"[303]. He refers to B. Noack[304], who called attention to the oral tradition, but Cullmann himself thinks that "we may at least reckon with the possibility that *in part* it may have already been given fixed form in writing"[305].

In his lecture at the *Colloquium Biblicum Lovaniense XXVI* (1975) Eugen RUCKSTUHL[306] reacted very negatively to Fortna's semeia hypothesis and more positively to that of Nicol[307].

1. Considering the history of Johannine criticism during the course of this century, Ruckstuhl states that most critics, even those who distinguish sources and redactional elaboration in the Fourth Gospel, "have acknowledged that the Fourth Gospel gives a strong impression of unity of language and style"[308]. In literary criticism, "the schemes which have been devised for distinguishing various strata in the Gospel do not agree with one another and thus do not inspire confidence in the theory"[309]. Regarding his list of fifty Johannine style characteristics, he notes that "perhaps all critics did not realize its nature, intention, and potential applicability"[310]. Therefore, he offers four comments. *First*, his list cannot be used "to assign passages and verses in Jn to a source or a second hand simply because none of the Johannine characteristics occurs in them", for it has not been designed "to include all the marks and

---

303. *Der johanneische Kreis*, pp. 7-8 (ET: p. 7; FT: p. 19).

304. *Ibid.*, p. 8 (ET: p. 8; FT: p. 19). See NOACK, *Tradition*, 1954 (see above, pp. 51-52).

305. Cullmann suggests the following process of literary composition (p. 10; ET: pp. 9-10; FT: p. 22): "1. The author, a strong personality, made use both of traditions belonging to the common legacy of early Christianity and of a number of special traditions, either written or in oral form, coming from the particular circles to which he belonged. We cannot rule out the possibility that he also included personal reminiscences as well as special traditions. 2. He was responsible for the main line of the work as we have it now. 3. A redactor or a group of redactors under the influence of the author and belonging to his circle revised or completed the whole work after his death".

306. E. RUCKSTUHL, *Johannine Language and Style: The Question of Their Unity*, in DE JONGE (ed.), *L'évangile de Jean*, 1977 (²1987), pp. 125-147; GT: 1987, pp. 304-331 (see above, p. 48 n. 42). On this translation, Ruckstuhl notes (*Einheit*, ²1987, p. 304): "Die Übersetzung ins Deutsche wurde von mir besorgt und erfolgte mehr in der Art einer flüssigen Übertragung. Eine Bearbeitung liegt insofern vor, als ich einige frühere Aussagen etwas weiter ausgeführt und verdeutlicht habe".

307. *Johannine Language*, pp. 125-129 (GT: pp. 304-309): "I. The style-critical method of Schweizer and Ruckstuhl: Remarks and criticism", 129-147 (GT: pp. 310-331): " II. The Signs Source today: A. Robert Fortna's Gospel of Signs; B. The Contribution of Willem Nicol".

308. *Ibid.*, p. 125 (GT: p. 304).

309. *Ibid.*, p. 125 (GT: p. 304). This idea was the impetus for Schweizer's style criticism in *Ego Eimi*, 1939, pp. 82-112 (see above, pp. 45-47).

310. *Johannine Language*, p. 127 (GT: p. 307).

features of Jn"[311]. *Second*, the list "was always intended to face the problem of style imitation and imitability". This means that "if it was possible to imitate any one of the characteristics, it is practically unthinkable that a later hand would have imitated an entire cluster of inconspicuous and unimportant characteristics, especially if there were several alternate ways of expressing oneself"[312]. *Third*, to Hirsch and Haenchen, who remark that some of Ruckstuhl's characteristics "are nothing but late Hellenistic idioms and phraseology"[313], Ruckstuhl answers that they have given no evidence[314]. He agrees, however, that "this is a serious problem". Neither Schweizer nor Ruckstuhl himself have made "a comparison with all koine documents and witnesses dating from the turn of the first century A.D."[315]. *Fourth*, he emphasizes that he "never denied the possibility of the evangelist's drawing the kernel of his narratives and discourses from sources and traditions at his disposal"[316]. The predominance of literary criticism and history-of-religions criticism at the time he wrote his dissertation was the reason "for

311. Ruckstuhl (p. 127; GT: p. 307) refers to NICOL, *Sēmeia*, 1972, pp. 22-27: "This would be a short circuit, as Nicol ... has clearly seen". Note that Ruckstuhl made a significant distinction between style characteristics and features: "the features being marks of a Johannine stamp which where either easy to imitate or were not too unusual in non-Johannine writings" (cf. *Einheit*, p. 185 n. 2, pp. 188-189; *Johannine Language*, p. 126; GT: p. 206).

312. *Johannine Language*, p. 127 (GT: p. 307).

313. *Ibid.*, p. 127 (GT: p. 307). Cf. HIRSCH, *Stilkritik*, 1950-51, p. 138; HAENCHEN, *Aus der Literatur*, 1955, p. 308: "Noch wichtiger ist das, was Hirsch (S. 138) zu Nr. 2 sagt, dem ἵνα epexegeticum ...: es ist nicht eine individuelle sondern eine spätgriechische Redeweise. Damit wird eine weitere Grenze der Schweizerischen Methode sichtbar, die auch noch andere wichtige 'johanneische' Merkmale betrifft: man muss zwischen dem Stil eines einzelnen Autors und dem einer bestimmten Schicht unterscheiden. So finden sich ... das johanneische ἐκεῖνος (Nr. 6 ...), das Asyndeton (Nr. 10 ...), übrigens auch die Anknüpfung von Hauptsätzen durch 'und', die als johanneisch gilt, genau so oft bei Johannes wie in der nicht literarischen Koine Epiktets. Dasselbs gilt von οὖν. Es zeigt sich hier, dass sich der johanneische Stil weithin von der nichtliterarischen Koine aus verstehen lässt". Ruckstuhl (*Johannine Language*, p. 128; GT: p. 308) answers: "A selective but extensive examination of the Johannine ἵνα epexegeticum, ἐκεῖνος, οὖν historicum and asyndeton epicum shows that there are hardly any true parallels to them in Epictetus. Indeed, how could there be parallels for our οὖν historicum and asyndeton epicum?". Ruckstuhl's selective examination also covered some other characteristics of his list: nos. 3 ἄν = ἐάν, 5. ἵνα epexegeticum, 7. inverting resumption, 10. unusual word separation, 12. καθὼς ... καί, and 22. σκοτία instead of σκότος, and he says: "In a series of chapters in several parts of Epictetus which were examined, instances of these style marks were not found with the only exception of ἄν = ἐάν, which seems to be rather frequent there" (p. 128 n. 14; GT: p. 308 n. 14).

314. *Ibid.*, p. 128 (GT: p. 308). Ruckstuhl's student, P. DSCHULNIGG, has studied the extra-NT parallels for the Markan style characteristics; cf. *Sprache, Redaktion und Intention des Markus-Evangeliums*, 1984 (²1986), pp. 82-83. On Dschulnigg, see NEIRYNCK's review in *ETL* 61 (1985) 393-395. See also RUCKSTUHL – DSCHULNIGG, *Stilkritik*, 1991, p. 30.

315. *Johannine Language*, p. 128 (GT: pp. 308-309).

316. *Ibid.*, p. 128 (GT: pp. 308-309).

the somewhat unfortunate wording of two statements": "aporias of the Fourth Gospel do not warrant a distinction among strata", and "criticism of earlier theories of sources and the establishment of Johannine literary unity litigate against the acceptance of any new source theories"[317]. Regarding the aporias, Ruckstuhl thinks that his view was "too cautious"; therefore he specifies: "I would still maintain that scholars are prone to engage in fancy or mere rational exercise when dealing with aporias. Jn certainly contains aporias and, unless they attest to inconsistency of thought, they point to the activity of different hands or different traditions adopted by the solitary author"[318]. With regard to source criticism, he underscores: "I certainly intended to advise against source reconstructions". But for Ruckstuhl, this does not mean that he excludes traditions behind the Fourth Gospel[319].

2. Against Fortna's use of style characteristics, Ruckstuhl asks: "Wasn't it a vicious circle to reconstruct a source by eliminating the expressions, phrases, and sentences with a Johannine ring, and then to test the result by means of our style characteristics?"[320]. With regard to Fortna's negative description of the style of the source, he states that it is better to say that only seven characteristics (not thirty-two!) do not appear in the Gospel of Signs[321]. Moreover, Ruckstuhl checks the correctness of the three steps by which Fortna tries "to modify the Schweizer-Ruckstuhl style-critical method and to weaken it as much as possible"[322]. (a) From the seven stylistic traits Fortna has created out of three, Ruckstuhl can only accept four, of which one appears exclusively in the source[323]. (b) Fortna's rejection of characteristics nos. 17, 37, 42, 48, 50, and 49 is not acceptable[324]. (c) The presence of characteristics no. 1, 2, 4, 6, 9, 16, 24, 35, 43 cannot be explained as "John's imitation of the source's language or Johannine redaction of the source", for Fortna "denies their importance in all the instances in which a characteristic is found in a smaller proportion in SQ than in Jn-SQ or vice-versa"[325]. Further, Ruckstuhl notes that he counted eighty-one instances of some twenty-one style characteristics of his list occurring in SQ:

317. *Ibid.*, pp. 128-129 (GT: p. 309). Cf. *Einheit*, pp. 218-219, esp. nos. 4 and 6.
318. *Johannine Language*, p. 129 (GT: p. 309).
319. *Ibid.*, p. 129 (GT: p. 309): "With reference to the Synoptic-type narratives in Jn [2,13-19; 4,46-54; 12,1-8.12-15], I suggested that the evangelist either drew from oral tradition or cited written traditions merely from memory. I claimed the same for other Johannine narratives as well. The reason for this suggestion was the probable dependence of these narratives on traditional material and their more or less dense Johannine stamp". Cf. *Einheit*, pp. 217-218, 219, resp. nos. 8 and 9. See also above, pp. 50 nn. 52-53.
320. *Johannine Language*, pp. 130-131, esp. 131 (GT: pp. 311-312, esp. 312).
321. See above, p. 145.
322. *Ibid.*, pp. 132-137 (GT: pp. 314-318).
323. See above, pp. 145-146.
324. See above, p. 146.
325. See above, p. 147.

nos. 1, 2, 4, 6, 9, 10, 16, 17, (22), 24, 35, (36), 37, 38, 39, 42, 43, 45, 48, 49, and 50; he comments: "This represents but a slight departure from Fortna's figures. The number of characteristics is ... quite normal, whereas the number of instances is relatively small. Considering the size of SQ (Jn-SQ = 3.7 times SQ) and the approximately 780 instances of Johannine characteristics, SQ should proportionately have 166 instances. ... The relatively small number of instances is the reason why joint occurrences of two or more characteristics are not frequent in SQ"[326]. Ruckstuhl counted "eight joint occurrences of two and three joint occurrences of three characteristics"[327].

Regarding Fortna's positive description of the source[328], Ruckstuhl first reacts against Fortna's assumption that the source's style is not neutral[329]. (a) Among the nine Synoptic-like words, five occur only once in his source (ἕτερος, ἐνώπιον, ἄρχεσθαι ποιεῖν τι, ὑπό + acc., ἰσχύειν). Therefore, Ruckstuhl does "not see their significance and force as a bit of style-critical evidence"[330]. The four other words (σύν, ἕκαστος, εὐθέως, and πρῶτον adverbial), all of which occur three times in Jn, always in the source, and which are frequent in the Synoptics or in the rest of the New Testament as well, cannot be considered style characteristics of the source for several reasons[331]. Further, the infrequency of the word Ἰουδαῖος, the frequency of the genitive absolute, and the absence of λέγειν πρός τινα are not an indication of the source's own style[332]. (b) Of the eight instances of words found only in the source, Ruckstuhl remarks, some of them are conditioned by the subject matter (ἀπό meaning "off, of distance"; πρός with dative indicating a place) or by the context (κραυγάζειν)[333]. From the features occurring in SQ which resulted from Fortna's dividing up several Johannine characteristics into two or three, Ruckstuhl accepts only no. 45c (noun + ἐκ = "made of")[334]; the subdivision of no. 50 (πιάζειν) is not significant[335]. (c) Ruckstuhl also disagrees with Fortna's proposed proof

326. *Ibid.*, p. 136 (GT: p. 318). The proportions are computed by presupposing Jn to comprise about 14,800 words, SQ 3,140.

327. Nos. 2+49, 4+45, 6+24, 6+43, 6+50, 22+24, 24+39, 38+39, 2+6+17, 2+9+17, 2+24+38. "On the basis of these joint occurrences, it was feasible to interlock eleven of thirteen characteristics, which occur together in one or two (twice) cases. Among these eleven characteristics are four of the first rank and two of the second" (p. 136; GT: p. 318).

328. *Ibid.*, pp. 137-141 (GT: pp. 319-323): "The source's own style". For Fortna, see above, pp. 147-148. For Fortna's reaction to Ruckstuhl, see above, pp. [218-]219 n. 396.

329. *Ibid.*, p. 137 (GT: p. 319).

330. *Ibid.*, pp. 137-138 (GT: pp. 319-320).

331. See above, p. 147.

332. See above, p. 147.

333. See above, p. 147.

334. See above, pp. 146, 148.

335. See above, p. 148.

that the Gospel of Signs is not stylistically colorless: "A survey of the phrases and idioms used by Fortna in his last attempt to present the source's style give a strong impression of a poor result. Almost all of the usages are distributed throughout both strata of the gospel or are confined to the source because of subject matter. In the latter case they are characteristic of the source but do not point to an author different from the evangelist"[336]. (d) Fortna could not "demonstrate that his source was not stylistically neutral, but that it was conspicuous by reason of its own stylistic features and marks and so stood out in relief against the style of the evangelist and his redaction of the Fourth Gospel"[337]. Ruckstuhl found exclusively in the source only eight or nine cases with thirty-two or thirty-five occurrences (σύν, εὐθέως, κραυγάζειν, noun + ἐκ = "made of", ὡς with numeral, noun + ἐκ = "from among", ἔρχεσθε καὶ ὄψεσθε, ὄνομα αὐτῷ). But for Ruckstuhl, "none of these features is so strong as to point to an individual author different from our evangelist". Therefore, "it seems preferable to speak of a source without stylistic colors of its own, except for the colors of Jn"[338]. (e) Ruckstuhl questions whether we can speak of a "Johannine narrative style"[339], and he concludes that "throughout the Johannine narrative material the language shows some identical coinage, that is different from the Synoptic coinage, and this identity of style suggests that all the Johannine narratives have passed through the medium of one personality who has somehow rethought and recast the traditional material at his disposal, though he did not imprint his stamp in identical fashion on all the narrative portions"[340].

3. Ruckstuhl approves both the procedure and the result proposed by Nicol in the first chapter of his book. He reaffirms his skepticism, however, about source reconstruction in general and about the existence of a signs source in particular: "I cannot deny the possibility of a Semeia-Quelle if I hold that our evangelist most likely drew on oral and written traditions. Nevertheless I am not sure that there ever existed a Semeia-Quelle which would have related just seven miracles. Am I wrong in guessing that we shall never know exactly what were the sources which our evangelist drew upon and how he drew upon them?"[341]. Moreover,

---

336. *Ibid.*, p. 141 (GT: p. 323).
337. *Ibid.*, p. 141 (GT: p. 324): "The source's pale face".
338. *Ibid.*, p. 141 (GT: p. 324).
339. *Ibid.*, pp. 141-145 (GT: pp. 324-328).
340. *Ibid.*, p. 145 (GT: p. 328). See Ruckstuhl's limited comparison of Johannine and Synoptic narrative language, a comparison first made in *Einheit*, pp. 100-104, with respect to Bultmann's source hypotheses, and adapted in *Johannine Language*, pp. 142-144 (GT: pp. 325-328), to an evaluation of Fortna's reconstructed source. For his comparison, Ruckstuhl singled out eight features, seven of which pertain to the narrative introductions to Synoptic and Johannine speeches and discourses.
341. *Ibid.*, p. 146 (GT: p. 330).

he agrees with Nicol that there is a difference between the short miracle stories and the narrative style of chs. 4, 7, 9, 11, 18 and 19. But we can not assume that the first are non-Johannine. For Ruckstuhl, they present "another kind of Johannine style"[342]. Finally, regarding the thirty-two style characteristics which Nicol added, Ruckstuhl notes: "He was quite aware that the intention of our list was quite different from the intention of his additional cluster of marks and that our standards of singling out Johannine characteristics had to be more severe than his. This implies that it is useful to distinguish two different lists, one of Johannine characteristics (*Stilkennzeichen*) and one of Johannine features (*Züge*) – a technical distinction which I proposed in my thesis which also made use of Johannine features"[343].

Ruckstuhl has not changed his view in his article on the idiolect and sociolect in Johannine literature (1987)[344]. He disagrees with H. Thyen, who thought that his list of style characteristics is "completely useless" for testing the literary-critical divisions of the Gospel[345]. After reviewing R.A. Culpepper's monographs and our study on the parentheses in the Fourth Gospel[346], he notes: "Culpepper's investigations and Van Belle's results certainly make it very improbable that the homogeneous outlook of the evangelist and the intentional structural unity which shapes the entire Gospel, will any longer permit the literary-critical acceptance of several hands. In so saying, I would not exclude the possiblity that the evangelist used sources for his work. But if that was the case, then they are recognizable only as traces. They must have been taken into the structural unity of the entire work and merged with it"[347].

In his new study (1991), RUCKSTUHL, in collaboration with Peter DSCHULNIGG, entirely revised the Schweizer/Ruckstuhl list (= R) of

342. *Ibid.*, pp. 146-147 (GT: pp. 330-331).

343. *Ibid.*, p. 147 (GT: p. 331).

344. *Zur Antithese Idiolekt – Soziolekt im johanneischen Schrifttum*, in *SNTU* A/12 (1987) 141-181 (= 1988, pp. 219-264). Cf. VAN BELLE, *Les parenthèses johanniques*, 1992, pp. 1922-1923.

345. THYEN, in *TR* 42 (1977), pp. 214-215.

346. CULPEPPER, *The Johannine School*, 1975 (diss. Duke University, 1974; dir. D.M. Smith); *Anatomy*, 1983; VAN BELLE, *Parenthèses*, 1985; *Les parenthèses johanniques*, 1992.

347. *Zur Antithese Idiolekt – Soziolekt*, p. 179 (= 1988, p. 261). Cp. HENGEL, *Question*, 1989, pp. 91, 210 n. 18 (GT: 1993, pp. 244-245, 279 n. 20); HEDRICK, *Authorial Presence*, 1990; see also his review of my *Parenthèses*, in *JBL* 106 (1987) 719-721. See my article *Les parenthèses johanniques*, 1992 pp. 1911-1915, 1921, 1922-1923. On the parentheses in John, see now also SEGALLA, *Evangelo e Vangeli*, 1993, p. 329; FABRIS, *Giovanni*, 1992, pp. 45-47; SCHENK, in *NTS* 38 (1992) 507-530, esp. p. 508 n. 6; ZUMSTEIN, in *FS F. Neirynck*, III, 1992, pp. 2119-2138, esp. 2123-2125; *LumV* 41 (1992), nº 209, 68-92, esp. pp. 74-75; FREY, *Erwägungen zum Verhältnis der Johannesapokalypse zu den übrigen Schriften des Corpus Johanneum*, in HENGEL, *Die johanneische Frage*, 1993, pp. 326-429, esp. 373[-374] n. 296.

Johannine characteristics[348]. Their new list (= R-D) can by characterized by three remarkable changes. First, the statistical comparison has been enlarged. It is no longer limited to the books of the New Testament, but includes 32 Hellenistic writings of the New Testament period[349]. Second, R-D could use the long list of 415 Johannine characteristics of Boismard-Lamouille (1977)[350]. Third, statistical criteria in the new list are refined[351]: (1) a minimum of three occurrences in Jn is required; (2) the number of occurrences in Mt, Mk, Lk, and Acts, taken individually, may not surpass the total number of instances in Jn; (3) the relative number of usages in each of the other books of the New Testament must be inferior to the number of occurrences in Jn; (4) the same criterion is used regarding the extra-biblical books. In his 1951 study, Ruckstuhl had classified the Johannine characteristics according to their declining importance in three categories (R 1-19, 20-31, 32-50). Now, there are still three groups, but the number of characteristics has been considerably enlarged (total: 153), and the classification in three categories has

348. E. RUCKSTUHL – P. DSCHULNIGG, *Stilkritik und Verfasserfrage im Johannesevangelium. Die johanneischen Sprachmerkmale auf dem Hintergrund des Neuen Testaments und des zeitgenössischen hellenistischen Schrifttums* (NTOA, 17), Freiburg/Schw. - Göttingen, 1991. – Reviews: F. NEIRYNCK, in *ETL* 67 (1991) 437-440; U. SCHNELLE, in *TLZ* 117 (1992) 917-919; C. NIEMAND, in *SNTU/A* 18 (1993) 262-264. See also VAN BELLE, *Les parenthèses johanniques*, 1992, pp. 1931-1932; HENGEL, *Die johanneische Frage*, 1993, pp. 122 n. 93, 242-242; SEGALLA, *Evangelo e Vangeli*, 1993, pp. 325-328. – The authors characterize their study as "vergleichende Stilkritik am Joh": "Sie erfasst die sprachlichen Eigentümlichkeiten des Ev. immer auch zahlenmässig und vergleicht sie in ihrer Häufigkeit mit anderen Schriften. Durch diese ihre Eigenart erweist sie sich als Stilkritik. Als solche diente sie unserer Absicht herauszufinden, ob im Joh eine von einem einzigen Verfasser geprägte Sprache vorliegt oder die Annahme verschiedener Texturheber des vorliegenden Ev. zutrifft" (p. 242; cp. pp. 19-20). The study contains seven chapters: "Einleitung" (pp. 10-22); "Das stilkritisch-statistische Verfahren" (pp. 23-43); "Die Verfasserschaft von Joh und 1-3 Joh" (pp. 44-54); "Auf der Suche nach Stilmerkmalen des Joh" (pp. 55-56); "Erarbeitung sprachlicher Eigentümlichkeiten des Joh" (pp. 57-173); "Auswertung der gesammelten Stilmerkmale des Joh" (pp. 174-241); "Rückschau und Zusammenfassung der Ergebnisse" (pp. 242-253).

349. Cf. pp. 59-63. They are (the abbreviations used are those of Ruckstuhl and Dschulnigg): ApkMos, Arr, Barn, CorpHerm, Did, Diod, DionChr, DionHal, Epikt, äthHen, Herm, Hier (El, Exz), Ign, JosAs, Bell, Iust, 1 Clem, ViAis, Lukian (somn., ver.hist., Philops, Peregr), 3 Makk, MusR, Nikol, Oen, EvPetr, Philod (Fr, Tod), Philo (VitCont, Flacc, LegGai), Plut, Polem, Polyk, Sus/Dan, TestAbr, TestXII.

350. See the annotated and alphabetically arranged presentation of this list in *ETL* 53 (1977) 400-429, esp. pp. 404-416 (= *Jean et les Synoptiques*, 1979, pp. 41-70, esp. 45-66). Cf. RUCKSTUHL – DSCHULNIGG, *Stilkritik*, p. 40 n. 50: "Die derart überarbeitete Liste ist als Arbeitsinstrument wesentlich brauchbarer und hilfreicher". From our list of Johannine characteristics appearing in parentheses (cf. *Parenthèses*, 1985, pp. 124-155) RUCKSTUHL – DSCHULNIGG borrowed three characteristics: A16 (ἔρχομαι ἵνα final), C18 (ἐρωτάω + ἵνα), and C59 (name of place + τῆς Γαλιλαίας). See pp. 79, 139-140, 161. Cf. VAN BELLE, *Les parenthèses johanniques*, 1992, p. 1932 n. 170.

351. *Stilkritik*, pp. 31-33. The fourth statistical criterion does not play a role in category C (characteristics C1-26).

become more formal (A1-26, B 1-65, C 1-26)[352]. Note, however, that Ruckstuhl-Dschulnigg have not retained the following nine characteristics of the earlier list: R3, 10, 21, 27, 28, 35, 36, 37, and 38[353].

With regard to the semeia hypothesis[354], Ruckstuhl and Dschulnigg especially study the sources reconstructed by Becker and Fortna. On the basis of their style criticism, they think that Becker's SQ cannot be proved[355]. *First*, they state that no one of the 26 A-characteristics appears alone in SQ[356]. Of the 65 B-characteristics, B50 ἦν ... Ἰωάννης ... βαπτίζων, which appears exclusively in the source (1,28; 3,23; 10,40), stands alone, unaccompanied by any other[357]. Two of those instances, however, are strongly connected with A-characteristics[358]: (1) with A21, ἦν δέ (καί) / ἦσαν δέ immediately followed by the subject[359] in 3,23: ἦν δὲ καὶ ὁ Ἰωάννης βαπτίζων ἐν Αἰνὼν ἐγγὺς τοῦ Σαλείμ; (2) with A17, ὁ τόπος ὅπου[360], in 10,40: καὶ ἀπῆλθεν πάλιν πέραν τοῦ Ἰορδάνου εἰς τὸν τόπον ὅπου ἦν Ἰωάννης τὸ πρῶτον

352. *Ibid.*, pp. 63-162: "Die Stilmerkmale des Johannesevangeliums erarbeitet und ausführlich dargestellt"; cp. pp. 164-168: "Übersichtslisten aller erarbeiteten Stilmerkmale des Joh". See also pp. 269-275: "Die joh. Stilmerkmale in alphabetischer Reihenfolge".

353. *Ibid.*, p. 173: "Aufgrund der von uns angewandten strengeren Kriterien für die Aufnahme sprachlicher Eigentümlichkeiten des Joh". For full comparison of the R-D list (1991) with the R list (1951), see F. NEIRYNCK, in *ETL* 67 (1991) 437-440. See also below, pp. 405-420: "Appendix II: Johannine Style Characteristics".

354. *Stilkritik*, p. 173. Ruckstuhl and Dschulnigg especially mention the following defenders: Faure (p. 11 n. 4), Bultmann (pp. 11-12), Schnackenburg, Fortna, J.M. Robinson, Nicol, Reim, Teeple, Vielhauer, Becker, Schenke – Fischer (p. 13), and for a short source with three Galilean miracles, Heekerens and Thyen (pp. 14-15). Referring to Bauer, Ruckstuhl, Noack, Cullmann and de Jonge, they conclude their survey with the observation that these authors "die Annahme von schriftlichen Quellen ablehnten oder mindestens die Möglichkeit einer einigermassen zuverlässigen Rekonstruktion verneinten. Sie gehen deshalb vornehmlich von der Verwendung mündlicher Überlieferung aus. Ihre Annahmen scheinen sich gegen das Ende unseres Jh. eher zu bewähren als diejenige von schriftlichen Quellen" (p. 15).

355. *Ibid.*, pp. 212-215: "Zur Gegenkontrolle des Vernetzungsverfahrens", esp. 213-214; see also pp. 238-241: "Zur Semeiaquelle und zum Passionsbericht im vierten Ev. nach dem Johanneskommentar von Jürgen Becker". Cp. pp. 248-249, 252. – As in *Einheit*, pp. 205-219 (cp. *Johannine Language*, pp. 136-137; GT: p. 318), Ruckstuhl and Dschulnigg pursue the "Verknüpfungstechnik/Verknüpfungsverfahren", i.e., the interlocking technique, in which they study how the different characteristics are interwoven ("die Vernetzung der Stilmerkmale") throughout the gospel and the literary layers as proposed by the proponents of source criticism. Cf. *Stilkritik*, pp. 174-241: "Auswertung der gesammelten Stilmerkmale des Joh", with on pp. 174-203: "Verteilübersicht über die Stilmerkmale des Joh", 204-215: "Schaubilder zur Vernetzung der Stilmerkmale im Joh", 216-241: "Zur Verteilung der Stilmerkmale über die verschiedenen Abschnitte des Joh".

356. *Ibid.*, p. 213.

357. *Ibid.*, p. 213; cf. p. 123 (B50).

358. *Ibid.*, p. 213-214, esp. 213, n. 13; cp. p. 248.

359. *Ibid.*, p. 213 n. 13; cf. pp. 82-83 (A21).

360. *Ibid.*, p. 213 n. 13; cf. pp. 79-80 (A17).

βαπτίζων. Because of this connection with an A-characteristic, the characteristic B50 cannot be considered an indication of SQ's style. It is rather an indication of the evangelist's own hand[361]. *Second*, the study of the distribution of the characteristics ("Verteilungsdichte der joh. Stilmerkmale") throughout the gospel and Becker's SQ also leads Ruckstuhl and Dschulnigg to reject SQ[362]. The following tables show the result of their statistical examination of Becker's literary theory[363].

TABLE I

Table I indicates for the whole gospel and for each literary layer[364] the number of lines in the N^{26} text[365], and the number of characteristics classified according to the division of the R-D list.

	Lines	Characteristics				
		A	B	A+B	C	A+B+C
Gospel	1786	604	480	1084	521	1605
SQ	267	117	36	153	90	243
SQ + *Umfeld*	454	177	80	257	139	396
Umfeld alone	187	60	44	104	49	153
PB	126.4	54	34	88	20	108
PB + *Umfeld*	364.8	171	93	264	72	336
Umfeld alone	238.4	117	59	176	52	228

---

361. *Ibid.*, pp. 213-214: "Es verweist wahrscheinlicher auf die Hand des Evangelisten"; cp. p. 248. See also p. 123: "Joh 10,40 schaut übrigens auf 1,28 zurück (vgl. besonders τὸ πρῶτον 10,40); ... Wiederum liegt ein deutlicher Hinweis auf eine die ganze Schrift gestaltende Redaktion vor, die von 10,40 über 3,23 auf 1,28 zurückblickt".

362. *Ibid.*, pp. 238-241; cp. p. 252.

363. *Ibid.*, pp. 239-240; cp. p. 252.

364. "SQ + Umwelt" means "die Abschnitten des Ev., aus denen die SQ ausgehoben wurde"; they are 1,19-51; 2,1-12; 3,22-30, 4,5-42; 4,46-54; 5,1-16; 6,1-25; 7,2-9; 9,1-34; 10,40-42; 11,1-44; 11,54; 12,37-38; 20,30-31. – "PB + Umwelt" means "die Abschnitten des Ev., aus denen der PB ausgehoben wurde"; they are 11,47–12,15 (without 11,54); 13,1-30; 18,1-40; 19,1-42; 20,1-29).

365. On the number of lines, Ruckstuhl and Dschulnigg (p. 238) note: "Da beide Schichten von Becker vielfach aus einzelnen Versstücken zusammengestellt wurden, war es notwendig, in einem eigenen Feinverfahren die Anzahl längengleicher Vollzeilen a. des Ev., b. der beiden Quellschichten und c. ihres Umfeldes zu ermitteln. Diese Anzahl Vollzeilen unterscheidet sich für das Ev. leicht von der unter 6.3.5 verwendeten Zeilenzahl (1776)"; cp. p. 252.

TABLE II

Table II shows for the whole gospel and for each literary layer the "Verteilungsdichte" (distribution frequency) of the characteristics. For obtaining the numbers of the "Verteilungsdichte", Ruckstuhl and Dschulnigg divide the number of Johannine lines by the number of characteristics (see Table I). In SQ, e.g., they count 267 lines and 243 characteristics; thus, the "Verteilungsdichte" is: 267 : 243 = 1.099. This means, according to their statistics, that there occurs one characteristic every 1.099 line.

	A	B	A+B	C	A+B+C
Gospel	2.957 (3)	3.72	1.648	3.428	1.1 (1)
SQ	2.282	7.42	1.745	2.967	1.099 (1)
SQ + *Umfeld*	2.565	5.675	1.767	3.266	1.146
Umfeld alone	3.117	4.25	1.798	3.816 (4)	1.222
PB	2.341	3.718 (4)	1.436	6.32	1.17 (1)
PB + *Umfeld*	2.133 (2)	3.923	1.382	5.067 (5)	1.086 (1)
Umfeld alone	2.038 (2)	4.041 (4)	1.355	4.585	1.046

From table II it becomes clear that there is no significant difference in the distribution of A-characteristics between the whole Gospel (2.957) and SQ + *Umfeld* (2.565). Moreover, the frequency in SQ is higher than in its *Umfeld* (resp. 2.282 and 3.177)[366]. With regard to the B-characteristics, their appearance is less frequent in SQ (7.42) than in the Gospel (3.72) and in the *Umfeld* of SQ (4.25), but for Ruckstuhl and Dschulnigg this can be by accident. Because the A- and B-characteristics are considered statistically more important than the C-characteristics, their combined frequency should not be disregarded. There is only a slight difference: Gospel 1.648; SQ 1.745; SQ + *Umfeld* 1.767; SQ's *Umfeld* alone 1.798. Therefore, Ruckstuhl and Dschulnigg conclude that the separation of SQ from its literary *Umfeld* and from the gospel as a whole is statistically impossible. It must rather be accepted that SQ stems from the same hand as the gospel and as the *Umfeld* of SQ. The supposition that SQ was reworked by the evangelist is also rejected by the authors[367]. After considering the last column of Table II, which shows that at least

366. Ruckstuhl and Dschulnigg explain this as follows: "Das dürfte damit zusammenhängen, dass SQ wesentlich Erzählung ist und die hier angetroffenen A-Merkmale überwiegend Erzählstoff prägen; im Umfeld von SQ spielt hingegen Redestoff mehrmals eine erhebliche Rolle wie etwa in 4,5-42 oder 9,1-34" (p. 240; cp. p. 252).

367. *Ibid.*, p. 241: "Auch die Vermutung, SQ habe einst ein eigenes Dasein gefristet, sei dann aber vom Evangelisten joh. überarbeitet worden, scheint angesichts der auffallend grossen Zahl unserer Merkmale in dieser Sicht eher abwegig, was auch durch die Ergebnisse unseres Vernetzungsverfahrens gestützt wird". Cp. p. 252.

one literary characteristic appears per each line of every literary layer, they state the Fourth Gospel must be considered a literary unity[368].

Also, with regard to Fortna's hypothetical Signs Gospel (SQ + PQ), as reconstructed in his *Predecessor* (1988), Ruckstuhl and Dschulnigg come to the conclusion that its existence cannot be proved by their stylistic test[369]. No one of the A- or B-characteristics appears exclusively in the Signs Gospel[370]. Moreover, they do not accept the style characteristics of the pre-Johannine material (both SQ and PQ), which Fortna enumerates to prove the existence of SG[371]: none of them is characteristic enough and, moreover, they also appear in the rest of the gospel, although not as frequently as in SG[372]. Further, the fact that 7 A-characteristics and 40 B-characteristics appear exclusively in parts which Fortna attributes to the Johannine redactor[373], cannot be considered a proof of the exactness of Fortna's reconstruction, because there are still 19 A-characteristics and 25 B-characteristics which appear in both the source and the Johannine redaction[374]. For Ruckstuhl and Dschulnigg, this can only mean that the evangelist was involved in Fortna's reconstructed signs gospel. Finally, they stress that the great number of B-characteristics which are absent from the source must be explained by the fact that Fortna was aware of their Johannine character and eliminated them from the source[375].

We may conclude that Ruckstuhl, as in his previous studies, maintains his position: it is impossible to reconstruct sources out of the Fourth Gospel, which is "a literary Unity"[376]. But this does not mean for Ruckstuhl that the evangelist has not used traditions, as he again defended in his study on ch. 6 for the *Festschrift Frans Neirynck*[377].

---

368. *Ibid.*, p. 241: "Diese Tatsache ist kaum zufällig und darf darum mit Recht wenigstens als Hinweis auf die literarische Einheit des vierten Ev. verstanden werden"; cp. p. 253.

369. *Ibid.*, pp. 214-215; cp. p. 249.

370. *Ibid.*, p. 214; cp. p. 249.

371. See above, pp. 218-219 nn. 395-396.

372. *Stilkritik*, p. 214 n. 17.

373. The 7 A-characteristics are: nos. 8, 11, 12, 15, 19, 23, 24. The 40 B-characteristics are: nos. 3, 4, 6, 7, 10, 15, 16, 18-22, 24, 25, 30, 31, 33, 36-41, 43, 44, 46, 47, 49-55, 57, 60, 61, 63-65. Cf. pp. 214 n. 18, 215 n. 19, cp. p. 249.

374. *Ibid.*, pp. 214-215; cp. p. 249.

375. *Ibid.*, p. 215; cp. p. 249. Also for the literary theory of Boismard and Lamouille, Ruckstuhl and Dschulnigg come to a similar conclusion: "Eine genaue Überprüfung der von Boismard/Lamouille 4 angenommenen Schichten des Joh zeigt, dass keines unserer A- oder B-Merkmale ausschliesslich in dem von ihnen festgehaltenen Grunddokument C oder allein in der Endfassung Jean III vorkommt. Deren Ausscheidung aus dem Joh als eigene Schichten ist sprachlich nicht gerechtfertigt. 22 unserer A-Merkmale (von 26) und 30 B-Merkmale (von 65) finden sich entweder in allen 4 oder wenigstens in 3 Schichten der genannten Forscher. Das zeigt, dass der von ihnen angenommene Evangelist (Jean II-A und B) sprachlich das ganze Joh mitbestimmt hat"; cp. pp. 213-214. On Boismard and Lamouille, see also pp. 39-43.

376. See above, n. 368.

377. *Die Speisung des Volkes durch Jesus und die Seeüberfahrt der Jünger nach Joh*

Johannes SCHNEIDER, in his commentary posthumously edited by Erich Fascher (1976), rejected the σημεῖα-*Quelle* of R. Bultmann and S. Schulz[378]. He calls the pre-Johannine miracles source "an audacious religion-historical reconstruction"[379]. In fact, he says, we know next to nothing about the community's situation, so that it is difficult to consider the "signs book" (*Zeichenbuch*) an "ecclesiastical source of pre-Johannine Christianity"[380]. Moreover, for Schneider, there is no compelling argument that John used a coherent written σημεῖα-*Quelle*[381].

Édouard COTHENET (1977) rejects Fortna's verse-by-verse reconstruction of the Gospel of Signs[382]. More specifically, he makes the following observations. First, it is difficult to accept a source without discourses; as Dodd noted, the close connection between the discourses and narratives in the present gospel is rather an indication that both stem from the same tradition. Second, is it possible to assign 21,1-14 to a written tradition, assert that it was not taken up by the evangelist, and then claim that it was added to the work of the evangelist by one of his disciples?

6,1-25 im Vergleich zu den synoptischen Parallelen, in *FS F. Neirynck*, III, 1992, pp. 2001-2019, esp. 2003: "Schon die starke Durchdringung von Joh 6,1-25 mit 38(39) Vorkommen von insgesamt 25 johanneischen Stilmerkmalen, die unter Anwendung strenger Kriterien ausgewählt wurden, weist mit erheblicher Wahrscheinlichkeit darauf hin, dass hier ein einziger Verfasser und überlegener Gestalter am Werk war, der nicht einfach einen oder mehr als einen synoptischen Paralleltext als Vorlage und Vorgabe vor sich hatte, sondern eher eine von den synoptischen Parallelen verschiedene, wenn auch verwandte Überlieferung verwendete, die ihm als Verkünder der christlichen Botschaft vertraut war. Das soll im Folgenden in verschiedener Weise weiter abgesichert werden". For his reaction to Vouga and Neirynck, who both accept dependence of John upon the Synoptics, see pp. 2018-2019.

378. J. SCHNEIDER, *Das Evangelium nach Johannes*, ed. E. FASCHER (THNT, Sonderband), Berlin, 1976; ²1978, pp. 28-29.

379. *Ibid.*, p. 29.

380. *Ibid.*, p. 29.

381. *Ibid.*, p. 29. See also p. 80 (on 2,1): "Die Annahme, dass Johannes die Zeitangabe in seiner 'Semeia-Quelle' vorgefunden und von daher übernommen hat, entbehrt der sicheren Grundlage"; p. 325 (on 20,30-31): "Doch ist die Semeia-Quelle eine sehr problematische Grösse, deren Existenz vermutet, aber nicht sicher nachgewiesen werden kann".

382. É. COTHENET, *Le quatrième évangile*, in GEORGE – GRELOT (eds.), *Introduction à la Bible. Édition nouvelle*, III/4, 1977, pp. 95-292, esp. 184-186. On Fortna's *Gospel of Signs*, he notes in general: "La démonstration de Fortna fait penser à un feu de paille qui projette de belles étincelles mais ne dure pas" (p. 185). On the σημεῖα-*Quelle*, see also pp. 104 (Bultmann and Fortna), 111-112 (Richter, Becker, Thyen and Fortna), 163-164 (Thyen's critique of the supposition that Jn 20,30-31 is the conclusion of the source). Cp. *L'évangile selon saint Jean*, in COTHENET et al., *Les écrits de S. Jean et l'épître aux Hébreux*, 1984, pp. 15-151, esp. 46-47 (Bultmann), 47-48 (Fortna), 135. Cothenet compares Fortna's *Gospel of Signs* with Boismard's *Document C* (p. 48). Regarding the so-called correction of the source's signs faith by the evangelist in 4,48 (cp. 20,29), he remarks: "En réalité cette explication n'est guère satisfaisante; si vraiment l'Évangéliste ne partageait pas le point de vue de la source des Signes, il l'aurait laissée de côté purement et simplement" (p. 135).

Third, is Fortna justified in making textual displacements to form a harmonious structure for his source (four signs in Galilee and three signs in Judea)? Finally, Cothenet cannot accept the hybrid character of the source. One could accept that John used a collection of miracles (so Schnackenburg), but that a source containing exclusively narrative material can be considered a gospel (*the Gospel of Signs*) is improbable. In early Christian literature, there are no examples of such a gospel. For Cothenet, at the basis of Fortna's method lies an "unwarranted postulate" (*un postulat gratuit*): he supposes that the evangelist John and the Gospel of Signs present two different theologies and that on the basis of these differences one can fully reconstruct the integral source[383].

In his 1978 article, Donald A. CARSON attacked the semeia hypothesis from several points of view[384]. After a survey of the source theories proposed by Bultmann, Becker, Schnackenburg, Nicol, Fortna, Teeple, and Temple, he states: "what is remarkable about the theories of the seven scholars surveyed is the extent to which they disagree both in their methods and their conclusions"[385]. He principally discusses Fortna's theory and formulates seven objections[386]. (1) That the numbering of signs in 2,11 and 4,54 comes from a collection of such numbered stories is possible "but not demonstrable, for when we inquire why John did not continue his numbering, the reasons are always less than convincing"[387]. (2) 21,1-14 cannot be considered the third sign of a source, "because it is explicitly referred to as the *third* resurrection appearance"[388].

383. *Le quatrième évangile*, pp. 185-186.

384. D.A. CARSON, *Current Source Criticism of the Fourth Gospel: Some Methodological Questions*, in *JBL* 97 (1978) 411-429. – On Carson, see LÉON-DUFOUR, *Où en est la recherche johannique?*, 1990, p. 25; NEIRYNCK, *John and the Synoptics*, 1992, pp. 11-12.

385. *Current Source Criticism*, pp. 414-420, esp. 419. Carson compares the literary theories of these authors regarding: (1) number and nature of sources; (2) nature of the "signs source"; (3) primary methodological tool; (4) subsidiary methods; (5) disallowed methodological tools. He gives the following appreciation: "Despite the fact that Bultmann's source theory can be seen as the progenitor of the others, it is no longer widely accepted. Of the remaining six, the work of Becker is too short to be very influential. Schnackenburg's reputation will rest on his contribution as commentator rather than on his success as a source critic, primarily because his source criticism is sufficiently innocuous that it can be discounted by the unconvinced without serious loss. Nicol's form critical approach is praised by Kysar as the most promising. ... Temple's work depends too much on highly subjective ideological criteria. The Teeple reconstruction will not find wide favor either. It shares most of Fortna's weaknesses and few of Fortna's strengths. The stylistic criteria are often singularly ill chosen, and in any case they neither guarantee the objectivity of this study (as he seems to think) nor constitute a sufficient basis for source criticism" (pp. 419-420).

386. *Ibid.*, pp. 420-428. He starts (pp. 420-421) with the critique of LINDARS, *Behind the Fourth Gospel*, 1971, pp. 27-42 (see above, pp. 174-176).

387. *Current Source Criticism*, p. 421.

388. *Ibid.*, p. 422. Carson's interpretation of the numbering in 21,14: "The inclusion of the number *may* be happenstance; or it may be designed to prove that the resurrected

(3) C. Goodwin's study of the Old Testament quotations has shown that the evangelist has freely handled them and that it is impossible to reconstruct the text of the Old Testament which the Fourth Evangelist used. So, "on what basis do we suppose that we are able to isolate hypothetical sources, when we must admit we could not isolate the demonstrable ones?"[389]. (4) Although source critics place a great emphasis on the need for consistency in their reconstructions, there is no agreement: "it is usually not long before a later critic points out that the resolution of one difficulty has led to the introduction of another". According to Carson, "rigid consistency is not only illusory, but in danger of destroying the known masterpiece (the gospel of John) for a speculative and disputed source"[390]. So Fortna bases his analysis on "contextual criticism", i.e., the aporias. But, for Carson, aporias "are very tricky things" and "some of them may only be in the mind of the beholder"; moreover, "even when a real one exists, it does not necessarily follow that its presence is a sure sign of a source, much less of a recoverable source"[391].

Jesus appeared more than once or twice; or, more plausibly, it may be designed to tie John 21 in a literary way to the previous chapter where the first two resurrection appearances to the disciples are recorded" (p. 422).

389. *Ibid.*, p. 422. Cf. GOODWIN, in *JBL* 73 (1954) 61-75. Carson remarks that FORTNA, *Gospel of Signs*, 1970, p. 12, tried to neutralize Goodwin's argumentation, noting that the Old Testament cannot be treated "in any sense analogous to a lost document which John might have followed". Carson agrees that there are some differences, "but to see the OT and the source as not *in any sense* analogous to one another is surely an overstatement. At least both (if the signs source *per se* ever existed) are *literary* sources". On the question: "Is John *a priori* more likely or less likely to treat a longer source as loosely as he does the OT?", Carson answers: "It is difficult to make an intelligent guess; but at least the OT quotations constitute hard *literary* evidence for what John does, and there is no *literary* evidence to the contrary, viz. that John on occasion copies extensive passages virtually verbatim from some source".

390. *Current Source Criticism*, p. 422. Cf. pp. 422-423: "Thus, Schnackenburg faults Wikenhauser's transpositions, J.M. Robinson criticizes Wilkens, D.M. Smith undermines Bultmann, and so on".

391. *Ibid.*, p. 423. See also *Selected Recent Studies of the Fourth Gospel*, in *Themelios* 14 (1989) 57-64, p. 62, where he notes on Culpepper's *Anatomy*, 1983: "Any approach, like this, that treats the text *as a finished literary product* and analyses it on that basis calls in question the legitimacy of the claim that layers of tradition can be peeled off the gospel in order to lay bare the history of the community. If aporias, say, can be integrated into the source-critical approach of R.T. Fortna, they can also be integrated into the literary unity of R.A. Culpepper. If aporias may be literary devices they are not *necessary* evidence of seams. In other words, Fortna and Culpepper in one sense represent divergent streams of contemporary biblical scholarship – so divergent, in fact, that a debate has begun about which approach to the text should take precedence. ... But the problem is deeper than mere precedence. If the material can be responsibly integrated into the unity Culpepper envisages, or something like it, what right do we have to say the same evidence testifies to *dis*unity, seams, disparate sources and the like? Conversely, if the latter are justified, should we not conclude that Culpepper's discovery of unity *must* be artificially imposed? The unforeseen benefit from this debate, then, is that it may free up the rather rigid critical orthodoxy of the day and open up possibilities that have illegitimately been ruled out of court".

(5) Fortna's stylistic criteria, both for the evangelist and for the source, "fail to provide the strength he ascribes to them"[392]. First, with reference to Kümmel, Carson notes that "the occurrence of an occasional word proves nothing. The sample is too small"[393]. Second, "some of the words or expressions Fortna adduces are qualified by a particular context"[394]. Third, "Fortna never checks out the opposite argument, viz. how many unlikely words *are* found in both the source and in the evangelist's contributions"[395]. Fourth, "the experience of writing teaches one that sometimes particular words and even certain syntactical arrangements congregate in clusters, and part of the polishing job is to thin them out"[396]. Fifth, "most source critics have never integrated into their work the findings that the Fourth Evangelist was given to repetitions *and variations*"[397]. Sixth, "it must be asked to what extent any stylistic unity found in the seven signs might be attributable to the artistry of the evangelist himself"[398]. (6) The argument of "the credibility of cumulative evidence ... can be abused by the selection of material which goes into the cumulation". "It must be set over against the cumulative counter evidence"[399]. (7) Finally, although the results of source criticism "are sometimes brilliant, usually stimulating, and often imaginative, ... it is doubtful if they are demonstrable, even in the limited sense of commanding sustained assent of their probability"[400]. This does not imply "that the Fourth Evangelist used no sources; it is *a priori* not unlikely that he did", but "it may be doubted that this has been *demonstrated* to any significant degree of probability; and it is certain that if they exist, these sources have not yet been isolated in a way which permits precise redaction criticism of the sort in which Fortna wishes to engage"[401]. Therefore, regarding source criticism of the Fourth Gospel, he considers "a probing agnosticism the best position to maintain"[402].

392. *Current Source Criticism*, p. 425. On pp. 425-427 Carson discusses Freed's and Hunt's article (1975; see above, pp. 198-200) and that by von Wahlde (1976; see above, p. 243 n. 566); for O'Rourke's article on the historic present (1974; see above, p. 300 n. 294), see p. 420 n. 34.

393. *Ibid.*, p. 425. Cf. KÜMMEL, *Introduction*, 1975, p. 214 n. 78 (see above, p. 59 n. 102).

394. See, e.g., κολυμβήθρα, ὑδρία, κῆπος, ῥάπισμα, ὀψάρια; cf. *Current Source Criticism*, p. 425 n. 52.

395. *Ibid.*, p. 425.

396. *Ibid.*, p. 425.

397. *Ibid.*, p. 425. Carson refers to FREED, *Variations*, 1964 (see above, p. 198 n. 258); MORRIS, *Studies in the Fourth Gospel*, 1969, esp. pp. 293-319: "Chapter Five: Variation – A Feature of Johannine Style"; CHANG, *Repetitions and Variations*, 1975.

398. *Current Source Criticism*, p. 425.

399. *Ibid.*, pp. 427-428.

400. *Ibid.*, p. 428.

401. *Ibid.*, p. 428.

402. *Ibid.*, p. 429; cp. pp. 411, 428. In *Recent Literature on the Fourth Gospel: Some Reflections*, in *Themelios* 9 (1983) 8-18, p. 9, Carson notes: "Source criticism no longer maintains the centre of the interest in Johannine research it once did", and to Attridge he

Stephen S. SMALLEY (1978)[403] accepts that sources obviously lie behind the Gospel of John, but "we do not know very much about their

objects: "this sort of work proceeds only by ignoring the detailed critiques of various source critical theories on John" (p. 9; he refers on p. 16 n. 21 to Ruckstuhl's 1977 article and to his own critique of 1978; on Attridge, see above, pp. 107-108). On the other hand, "redaction criticism of the fourth gospel still runs from strength to strength and by and large it is of the sort that makes many distinctions between source and redaction. In this sense source criticism continues apace; but ironically it is in some respects less disciplined than the slightly older source criticism it displaces, since much less is left to linguistic criteria (as in the justly famous work by Fortna) and much more to fairly subjective perceptions of shifts in theology or theme" (p. 9). According to Carson, "the continued impetus for this work stands beyond the desire to retrieve snippets from sources or to discern literary levels; the drive is to sketch in not only something of the beliefs and setting of the Johannine community but also to trace out its history and conceptual development" (p. 9). In *The Purpose of the Fourth Gospel: John 20:31 Reconsidered*, in *JBL* 106 (1987) 639-651, pp. 649-650, Carson rejects the signs source. First, he refers to his own 1978 article, in which he "attempted to assess the methodological viability of the source-critical approaches to the Fourth Gospel ... and came away dissatisfied" (p. 649). Second, "these two verses are fairly tightly tied to the preceding narrative by the twin uses of πιστεύω in 20:29, picked up in 20:30". Third, "now that the new criticism is being applied to John (notably by Culpepper), the problem of identifying aporias and therefore seams and sources is becoming increasingly problematic" (p. 649, with reference to CULPEPPER, *Anatomy*, 1983). See also his commentary *The Gospel According to John*, Leicester - Grand Rapids, MI, 1991, pp. 41-45: "The possibility of effective source criticism in John's Gospel", esp. pp. 41-42, where he notes: "Hengel rightly questions the likelihood that the evangelist took over something like the alleged 'Signs Source', which all sides admit (if it ever existed) boasted a theology radically different from that of the evangelist, and incorporated it so mechanically that it can be retrieved by contemporary scholarship" (on Hengel, see below, pp. 331-332). Review: D. BALL, in *Themelios* 19 (1993-94), p. 14. See now also *John*, in CARSON – MOO – MORRIS, *An Introduction to the New Testament*, 1992, pp. 135-179, esp. 152.

403. S.S. SMALLEY, *John: Evangelist and Interpreter*, Exeter, 1978; second printing, Nashville, TN, 1984. Reviews: cf. VAN BELLE, no. 302. – For the semeia hypothesis, see esp. pp. 104 (Bultmann), 106-108 ("Signs source research": Becker, Fortna, Nicol); see also pp. 113-118 ("Editions": Wilkens, Schnackenburg, Brown, Teeple), 119 ("Conclusion"), 123-124 (Windisch), 134-135, 176 (regarding 2,1-11: "a signs source?"). See esp. pp. 119-120, for Smalley's own "tentative proposals about the genesis of the Fourth Gospel". He supposes three stages: (1) "First, John the apostle (who was the beloved disciple) moved from Palestine to Ephesus, where he handed on orally to a disciple or disciples of his (much as by tradition Peter did to Mark), accounts of the deeds (mostly miracles) and sayings of Jesus, and of his death and resurrection. These accounts preserved information about the ministry of Jesus in both Judea and Galilee". (2) "Second, the disciple or the disciples of John (the nucleus of the Johannine church) committed to writing the traditions preserved by the beloved disciple. This was a first draft of the final Gospel, and consisted of a centre which narrated six miracles of Jesus (now treated as signs). ... With this centre were interwoven explanatory discourses, including the farewell discourse in its basic form, organised in a cyclic feast-sign-discourse pattern. At this stage what we now recognise as 'Johannine thought' emerges, by developing the seminal theological ideas handed on by the apostle himself. The material thus arranged by the writer(s), whom we may conveniently call the Fourth Evangelist(s), led into a passion narrative (excluding Jn 21). In addition an introduction to the work was composed, consisting of the present section John 1:19-51. This included traditions about John the Baptist which may have derived from the Baptist himself, possibly through John the apos-

original form and contents"[404]. More particularly, against the existence of a signs source, Smalley remarks first that "the attempt to isolate with any certainty a *single* source containing information about the miracles of Jesus and virtually no other part of the Christian tradition, is beset with difficulties on both formal and stylistic grounds. There is no firm evidence outside the SQ hypothesis (whatever form it has taken) that SQ (or S) existed". Moreover, Smalley finds it "notoriously speculative to determine the limits of the source by means of stylistic criteria"[405]. In addition, the notion that the Fourth Evangelist used a signs *Gospel* presents further complications. On the one hand, Smalley finds "it is very unlikely that a Gospel (in the canonical sense, at least) ever existed which contained narrative material but little if any teaching of Jesus (and in Nicol's view, no reference to the passion)"[406]. On the other hand he does not accept that "a creative writer and literary craftsman such as the Fourth Evangelist would adopt this 'mini-Gospel' as it stood, with no alteration except that which was involved in the publication of a 'new edition'"[407]. In 1989, in his review of Fortna's *Predecessor*, Smalley gives four reasons why "its thesis rests on insecure foundations": "First, it is unwise to separate narrative and discourse in John so sharply as Fortna does, and to find no place for sayings material in SG. Secondly, redaction need not always involve theological *change*. Thirdly, how do we *know* about the limits, the character or indeed the very existence of SG? What begins as a 'patently hypothetical reconstruction' becomes before long an established basis from which to work. Finally, Fortna does not properly face the issue of the purpose of John's Gospel, or indeed of the supposed SG. Only by addressing that question seriously, in my view, can sense be made of John's theology, and that of any of his predecessors"[408].

---

tle". (3) "Third, the Johannine church at Ephesus, after the death of the beloved disciple, published a finally edited version of the Gospel. This included a summary prologue (Jn 1:1-18), written last, based on a community hymn and now tied securely to the rest of the introductory first chapter, some editing of the discourses (especially marked in Jn 6 and 14–17; possibly the prayer of Jn 17, liturgically developed on the basis of an actual prayer of Jesus, was added at this stage); and an epilogue (Jn 21, incorporating for special reasons one additional sign from the collection preserved at the second stage). The whole Gospel thus assembled then carried an authenticating postscript (Jn 21,24f.)". Cp. *Keeping up with Recent Studies*. XII. *St John's Gospel*, in *ExpT* 97 (1985-86) 102-108, p. 105.

404. *John*, p. 119.

405. *Ibid.*, p. 108. Against Fortna, Smalley notes: "But the characteristics of 'Johannine style' are open to discussion; and in any case approximately one half of Fortna's stylistic features, by the *absence* of which he determines the limits of SG, do not appear in *any* Johannine narrative material – so that their absence from SG tells us nothing" (p. 108).

406. *Ibid.*, p. 108; cp. p. 119: Smalley similarly rejects Wilkens's *Grundevangelium*, "which was made up solely of signs and passion material" (p. 119).

407. *Ibid.*, p. 108, with reference to LINDARS, *Behind the Fourth Gospel*, 1971, pp. 31-34.

408. *ExpT* 101 (1989-90) 30. Cp. his reaction to U.C. von Wahlde's *The Earliest Version*, 1989, in *JTS* 41 (1990) 611-613, p. 612, where he notes that questions remain:

In her dissertation on Jn 4,1-42, Edeltraud LEIDIG (1979)[409] formulated several objections to the semeia hypothesis. If Jn 4,1-42 is to be assigned to the source, as Bultmann and Fortna thought, why is this pericope not numbered[410]? In fact, the numbering of signs in 2,11 and 4,54 does not come from the source, but is to be explained on the level of the evangelist's redaction: in 4,46 it is said that the second miracle (4,54), like the first, took place at Cana; the second miracle corresponds to the second miracle of Elijah; two miracles are also mentioned in Lk 4,25-27[411]; finally, the mission of Elijah and Elisha, mentioned in Lk 4,25-27 and referred to in Jn 2,4 and 4,48, may be considered decisive for the numbering in 2,11 and 4,54[412]. That 4,1-42 and 1,35-50, in which the theme of supernatural knowledge is expressed, fit well in the semeia source is questionable[413]. Fortna's precise reconstruction itself is doubt-

"First, von Wahlde's work in recovering John's original Gospel rests on a debatable premise: that John's Gospel started life as a document dealing chiefly with the *signs* which Jesus performed, and the response to them. ... However, this approach is questionable. I have elsewhere argued that all seven signs, including that in John 4, *can* be associated with a discourse. ... Moreover, does not von Wahlde lean rather too heavily on the sophisticated criteria which he unearths as his control? Granted also the redactional elements in John's Gospel, did the editing which von Wahlde detects necessarily take the detailed form outlined? I would accept, with Brown, Schnackenburg and others, that John's Gospel came to birth in broad stages. But I find it hard to think of the Fourth Evangelist(s) going through stage 1 (even supposing it were written!) with a fine toothcomb, *rejecting* material from that edition (p. 96 passim), and replacing it with extensive and deliberately nuanced passages to make an entirely different point. I see the history of the composition of the Fourth Gospel much more as an exercise in filling *out* what is already there in seminal form, rather than starting again virtually *de novo*".

409. E. LEIDIG, *Jesu Gespräch mit der Samaritanerin und weitere Gespräche im Johannesevangelium* (TDiss, 15), Basel, 1979; ²1981. See esp. pp. 2-14: "Die sogenannte 'Semeiaquelle'". – Reviews: cf. VAN BELLE, no. 2849. – Regarding the development of the Fourth Gospel, Leidig refers to Brown's five stages (see above, p. 59 n. 105): "Im Unterschied zu R. Bultmann nehmen wir an, dass Joh 21, das Nachtragskapitel, die Urzelle des Evangeliums war. Der Bericht von der Begegnung mit dem Auferstandenen am See Tiberias mit dem klärenden Wort über das Verhältnis des Petrus zu dem Jünger, den Jesus liebhatte (Joh 21,22f.), könnte am Anfang gestanden haben. In einer johanneischen Schule entstand dann durch den stattfindenden Lehrbetrieb das Evangelium, an dem eine Gruppe gleichgesinnter Leute arbeitete. Sie beriefen sich auf einen Augenzeugen und verstanden sich als seine Schüler; sie haben nach seinem Hinscheiden sein Lebenswerk herausgegeben" (p. 77).

410. *Jesu Gespräch*, p. 2: "Dieser Beweis verliert an Überzeugungskraft, sobald weiterer Stoff zwischen Joh 2,11 und 4,54 in der 'Semeiaquelle' untergebracht werden muss. Es stellt sich die berechtigte Frage, weshalb Joh 4,1-41 nicht mitgezählt wurde, wenn der Abschnitt in dieser Quelle gestanden haben soll. War die Anordnung in dieser Quelle anders, weshalb wurden dann nicht dritte, vierte und weitere Zeichen erwähnt?".

411. *Ibid.*, p. 256, with reference to BETZ, *Problem*, 1974, p. 42 (see above, pp. 298-299).

412. *Jesu Gespräch*, p. 256, with references (on p. 328 nn. 137-138) to BETZ, *Problem*, resp. pp. 42 and 41. Leidig notes: "Erst im Endzustand des Evangeliums werde die Zusammenhörigkeit der beiden Wundererzählungen durch den dazwischenliegenden Stoff etwas verdeckt" (p. 328 n. 139).

413. *Jesu Gespräch*, p. 2.

ful[414]. Leidig cites Lindars's critique: "My difficulty is that the theory presupposes too simple and rigid a distinction between the evangelist and his two main sources (Signs and Discourses)"[415]. It is debatable that such a source already existed as a book in the early church[416]. It is not at all proved that the concept of θεῖος ἀνήρ can be used[417].

In his lecture before the Royal Academy at Brussels in December, 1981, published in 1983, Frans NEIRYNCK took up the confrontation with the proponents of the signs source in the interest of defending the Fourth Evangelist's dependence upon the Synoptics[418]. After summarizing the argumentation for the existence of a source in five concise points, he

414. *Ibid.*, p. 3: "Bei dieser [Fortna's] Rekonstruktion gibt es im Unterschied zu R. Bultmann keine Stellen mehr, bei denen Unsicherheit herrscht. Schon diese Tatsache stimmt nachdenklich gegenüber diesem Versuch".

415. *Ibid.*, p. 4; on p. 13, she quotes BETZ, *Problem*, p. 37 n. 56: "Eine gute Kritik an der von Bultmann behaupteten Quellen des Johannesevangelium und speziell an R.T. Fortnas und J. Beckers Beiträgen zur Semeia-Quelle, wird von B. Lindars vollzogen, der mit Recht die synoptische Tradition als für Johannes massgeblich ansieht". Cf. LINDARS, *Behind the Fourth Gospel*, pp. 22-23; see above, pp. 174-176.

416. *Jesu Gespräch*, p. 11. Leidig notes this in connection with a comparison between Dodd's "The Book of Signs" and the "Semeiaquelle". She refers to DODD, *Tradition*, 1963, p. 8, who warns: "The early Church was not such a bookish community as it has been represented"; see also BARRETT, *John*, 1955, p. 16: "it is useless to speculate on the source whence the incidents were drawn, or even to say whether one source or several is involved, and whether the source (or sources) was written or oral" (cp. ²1978, p. 18; GT: 1990, p. 36); NOACK, *Tradition*, 1954, p. 42: "die wirklichen Quellen, aus denen die im Johannesevangelium enthaltene Überlieferung hervorquillt, (können) nicht als Quellen im Sinne der Literarkritik identifiziert werden".

417. *Jesu Gespräch*, pp. 11-13 (with reference to Nicol and O. Betz).

418. F. NEIRYNCK, *De Semeia-bron in het vierde evangelie. Kritiek van een hypothese*, in *AcAn (Letteren)* 45 (1983), no. 1, 1-28; ET: *The Signs Source in the Fourth Gospel: A Critique of the Hypothesis*, in *Evangelica II*, 1991, pp. 651-677 (678-679: "Additional Note"). See also *John 4,46-54: Signs Source and/or Synoptic Gospels*, in *ETL* 60 (1984) 367-375 (= 1991, pp. 679-687, 687-688: "Additional Note"), where in critique of Dauer (see above, pp. 109-110) and Heekerens (see above, pp. 256-262), Neirynck considers the story of the healing of the royal official's son in Jn 4,46-54 "a good illustration of Johannine 'relecture' of the synoptic gospels". We followed Neirynck's interpretation for 4,48 (see above, pp. 222-223 n. 415). – On Neirynck, see, e.g., BEUTLER, *Méthodes et problèmes*, 1990, pp. 18-19; SCHMITHALS, *Johannesevangelium*, 1992, pp. 8, 119, 125, 227; SMITH, *John among the Gospels*, 1992, pp. 147-158; BOISMARD, *Jean 4,46-54*, 1993. – See now also F. NEIRYNCK, *John and the Synoptics: 1975-1990*, in DENAUX (ed.), *John and the Synoptics*, 1992, pp. 3-62. In answer to Borgen's statement: "F. Neirynck rejects theories of 'unknown' and 'hypothetical' sources behind John, whether they are supposed to be written or oral" (cf. BORGEN, in *FS E.E. Ellis*, 1987, pp. 80-94, esp. 80; cp. DUNGAN (ed.), *The Interrelations of the Gospels*, 1990, pp. 408-437, esp. 409), Neirynck replies: "The truth is that I am skeptical with regard to the classic source theories such as the signs source and a continuous pre-Johannine passion narrative, or the combination of both in a *Grundschrift* or signs gospel. But I am not aware that I ever gave such an exclusiveness to the Synoptic Gospels as to exclude John's use of oral-tradition or source material" (p. 14).

takes issue with the interpretation of the evidence, beginning with the numbering of signs, "the strongest argument" for either the classic signs source hypothesis or the alternative theory of a source with three Galilean signs[419].

1. No one will contest that there is some kind of relation between Jn 2,11 and 4,54, Neirynck says, but just what these phrases meant for the evangelist is not as evident as is often supposed. Meanwhile, the use of τρίτον in Jn 21,14 bears a resemblance to that of δεύτερον in 4,54, but should that lead to seeing a continuance of the numbering of signs in a supposed source[420]? In Jn 21,14, first of all, the detection of redactional elements (ἐφανερώθη τοῖς μαθηταῖς, ἐγερθεὶς ἐκ νεκρῶν) does not point to such a source. Further, Fortna's difficulty with the adverbial phrase τοῦτο τρίτον as too clumsy – and his conclusion that it should be seen as a remnant of a different (adjectival) expression in the source – is "not to be taken too seriously". There is sufficient evidence that "like δεύτερον in v. 16 and τὸ τρίτον in v. 17, the τρίτον of v. 14,

419. *Semeia-bron*, pp. 5-7 (ET: pp. 653-656), where he summarizes "the classic argumentation for the existence of the signs source" in five points: "1. The numbering of the signs: Jn 2,11 and 4,54a; 2. The conclusion of the signs source: Jn 20,30-31; 3. The stylistic argument; 4. The form-critical argument; 5. The christology of the signs source". On the "alternative signs source" including the three Galilean miracles (cf. Spitta, Goguel; Thyen, Heekerens, Langbrandtner; cp. Boismard), see pp. 8-11 (ET: pp. 657-660). – In *The Apocryphal Gospels and the Gospel of Mark*, in SEVRIN (ed.), *The New Testament in Early Christianity*, 1989, pp. 123-175 (= *Evangelica II*, 1991, pp. 715-767 [768-772: Additional Notes]), Neirynck notes that M. Smith's hypothesis on the relation between the Secret Gospel of Mark and the Gospel of John, followed in some way by Koester, H.-M. Schenke, and Crossan, adds no additional supporting argument to the semeia hypothesis. According to him "the complexity of Synoptic and Johannine reminiscences and the combination of the parallels do not allow for the reconstruction of a pre-Markan or pre-Johannine source" (pp. 168-170, esp. 170; = 1991, pp. 760-762, esp. 762); cp. *The Historical Jesus: Reflections on an Inventory*, in *ETL* 70 (1994) 231-234, esp. p. 225 (against CROSSAN, *The Historical Jesus*, 1991, p. 312): "However, Crossan's argument is extremely weak: 'That common sequence could, of course, be sheer coincidence, but, at least hypothetically, I hold on to it as the only evidence we have for early collections of miracles...' (312). It is rather amusing that he sees redaction of the final author in 2,11 and 4,54 (editorial backwards linking, like 21,14) and so doing excludes from the collection the two Cana miracles which are the classic starting point of all Signs Source hypotheses" (see also above, p. 113 n. 234). See also BROWN, in *CBQ* 36 (1974), pp. 484-485; MERKEL, in *ZTK* 71 (1974), pp. 139-140 (see above, p. 185 n. 192); cp. *Das "geheime Evangelium" nach Markus*, 1987, p. 92; HEEKERENS, *Zeichen-Quelle*, 1984, pp. 20-21; KREMER, *Lazarus*, 1985, pp. 116-118, esp. 117; WAGNER, *Auferstehung*, 1988, p. 357.

420. *Ibid.*, pp. 12-17 (ET: pp. 660-665); see his conclusion on p. 17 (ET: p. 665): "Nothing in John suggests a numbering which must be further continued in the seven signs of a hypothetical signs source. Likewise, the opinion that the numbering is continued in a third sign in Galilee (21,14) is a fabrication of Johannine source criticism". On the numbering of signs, see also Neirynck's discussion with Boismard in *Jean et les Synoptiques. Examen critique de l'exégèse de M.-É. Boismard* (BETL, 49), Leuven, 1979, pp. 121-174: "VII. Les trois signes en Galilée". For Becker's reaction to Neirynck, see above, pp. 133-134.

preceded by τοῦτο can be connected with the verb: for the third time Jesus appeared, it was the third time that he appeared. The similarity with 4,54 is not such as to suggest an original version of 21,14 with τρίτον used as an adjective (added to σημεῖον)"[421]. In fact, the similarity between the two verses is of a different nature. In Jn 4,54 the construction τοῦτο ... δεύτερον σημεῖον is frequently understood adjectivally and compared with 2,11. But πάλιν δεύτερον can be interpreted adverbially: for the second time he did a sign[422]. As for 2,11, Neirynck points out that interpretations of ἀρχή as the "first" of the signs (even in early textual witnesses, perhaps with reference to an adjectival understanding of δεύτερον in 4,54) is an impoverishment of John's sense of the word[423]. The ἀρχή is a key notion for John (cf. 6,4; 15,27; 16,4b). The evangelist also characterizes the content of his gospel with the word σημεῖα (20,30). It therefore seems quite likely that this evangelist would give prominence to the ἀρχὴν τῶν σημείων "not so much as the first followed by the second, but as the ἀρχή, the prefiguration of all the other σημεῖα"[424]. In 4,54 (cf. v. 46a), the evangelist says this is the second Cana miracle, not the second in a series of miracles, and it is to be brought into relation with the first Cana miracle. This deliberate connection by the evangelist makes these two a separate pair, unlike the other Johannine miracles, each concluded with a special formula and neither leading into a discourse. The feeding miracle followed by a healing permits allusions to the Elijah and Elisha cycle, as well as to the characterization of the beginning of Jesus' ministry made in Lk 4,25-27[425].

421. *Semeia-bron*, p. 13 (ET: p. 661). On Jn 21,14, see also *Jean et les Synoptiques*, pp. 154-160; cp. *Note sur Jn 21,14*, in *ETL* 64 (1988) 429-432 (= 1991, pp. 688-692).

422. *Semeia-bron*, pp. 13-15 (ET: pp. 661-662). On Jn 4,54, see also *Jean et les Synoptiques*, pp. 166-173.

423. *Semeia-bron*, pp. 15-17 (ET: p. 661); *Jean et les Synoptiques*, pp. 160-166.

424. *Semeia-bron*, p. 16 (ET: pp. 664-665). Neirynck refers to BARRETT, *John*, 1955, p. 161 (²1978, p. 193; GT: 1992, p. 216): "ἀρχή may mean more than the first of a series; not merely the first sign, but the prefiguration of all the other σημεῖα" (with reference to Isocrates, *Panegyr.*, 38); MOLLAT, *L'évangile de Jean*, ³1973, p. 86 n. c: "l'archétype dans lequel est préfigurée et précontenue toute la série (des signes)"; DE LA POTTERIE, *La notion de "commencement"*, 1977, p. 391 n. 47 (IT: 1973; ²1986, p. 228 n. 48). Cp. ABBOTT, *Johannine Grammar*, 1906, pp. 287-288 (§ 2386); MICHEL, *Der Anfang*, 1958, p. 20 (= 186, p. 152): "der Ausgangpunkt einer Bewegung"; NICOL, *Sēmeia*, 1972, p. 114; OLSSON, *Structure and Meaning*, 1974, p. 100; RIDDERBOS, *Johannes*, I, 1987, p. 135; BITTNER, *Jesu Zeichen*, 1987, p. 93: "der Keim des Ganzen"; LÉON-DUFOUR, *Jean*, I, 1988, pp. 212-213 (he prefers the term "prototype", "qui désigne une réalité à la fois originelle et exemplaire"); CARSON, *John*, 1991, p. 175.

425. *Ibid.*, p. 17 (ET: p. 665); cp. *Jean et les Synoptiques*, pp. 116-119 (= *ETL* 53, 1977, pp. 474-477). Cf. above, p. 298 n. 281. For the connection of the two Cana miracles as deliberate composition of the evangelist, Neirynck refers to MOLONEY, in *Salesianum* 40 (1978) 817-843 (= 1980, pp. 185-213); cp. *The Word Became Flesh* (Theology Today Series, 14), Dublin – Cork, 1977, pp. 23-24; *The Living Voice of the Gospel*, New York – Mahwah, NJ, 1986, pp. 203-220, esp. 211-218 (see also pp. 175-178); *Belief in the Word*, 1993, pp. 192-197. See also Wilkens (cf. above, p. 65 nn. 123-124).

2. Neirynck is especially critical of Heekerens's association of Jn 21,1-14 with 2,1-11 and 4,46-54. His reconstruction of v. 14 is suspect, and "a story reduced to 21,3b.6 is completely indefensible: it can be taken entirely from Lk 5,1-11". Neirynck would easily concede that 21,14 is a parenthetical remark: "In the middle of the story, the title from v. 1 is resumed and made more precise (in v. 14), and then the story continues. ... The τρίτον ... seems to complete the introductory verse (v. 1) and to join the appearance story of Jn 21 to the appearances to the disciples first in 20,19-23 and then (πάλιν) in 20,26-29"[426].

3. Finally, Neirynck discusses the concluding formula at 20,30-31, considered a chief literary indicator of the source besides the numbering. He prefers to see a "provisional conclusion followed by an epilogue" (much like 1 Jn 5,13) on the level of the evangelist[427]. For most supporters of the signs source, these verses formed the conclusion of the source and are a pointer to the source's "inferior" conception of the relation between signs and faith. Boismard, however, assigns these verses to the evangelist (Jn II-B), under influence of 12,37 (Jn II-A) and 21,25 (Doc C). It is striking that Boismard, more than anyone, stresses the "primitive" sign theology of the source documents[428]. It is also emphasized, particularly by Boismard, that Jesus' miracles are never called σημεῖα in the Synoptics and that the word, therefore, must go back to a unique source that contained miracles as legitimating signs of Jesus, like those of Moses in Exodus. Neirynck would recall that the notion of legitimating "sign" does indeed appear in the Synoptics. Furthermore, it may be formally correct to observe that faith precedes the miracle in the Synoptics and follows it in John's supposed source, but "the notion that miracles legitimate the prophet is not absent in the Synoptic Gospels. The *Chorschluss* of the miracle stories expresses what John renders in more abstract language as πιστεύειν εἰς αὐτόν (2,11), πιστεύειν εἰς τὸ ὄνομα αὐτοῦ (2,23)"[429]. Neirynck acknowledges a

426. *Semeia-bron*, pp. 17-20, esp. 20 (ET: pp. 665-668, esp. 668); cp. *Jean et les Synoptiques*, pp. 122-160; see also *John 21*, in *NTS* 36 (1990) 321-336, pp. 325-329 (= 1991, pp. 501-616, esp. 604-609).
427. *Semeia-bron*, pp. 20-28 (ET: pp. 668-677). – Neirynck reacts against DE JONGE, *De brieven van Johannes*, p. 224, who considered 1 Jn 5,13 "a typical transitional verse" that concludes 5,5-12 and introduces the following section 5,14-21. Neirynck cites H. ALFORD, who notes with reference to F. Düsterdieck: "an anticipatory close of the Epistle" (cf. 1,4). On the reading ἵνα πιστεύητε meaning "that you might continue to believe...", cf. *Semeia-bron*, pp. 22-24 (ET: pp. 669-672). See also DE KRUIJF, in *Bijdragen* 36 (1975) 439-449; CARSON, in *JBL* 106 (1987) 639-651; FEE, in *FS F. Neirynck*, vol. III, 1992, 2193-2205. On 20,30-31, see further LATTKE, in *ZNW* 78 (1987) 288-292; ROBERTS, in *JTS* 38 (1987) 409-410.
428. On Boismard, see above, pp. 271-276, esp. 275-276.
429. *Semeia-bron*, p. 27 (ET: pp. 675-678). – With regard to the legitimating sign, Neirynck compares (a) Lk 11,29 Q σημεῖον ζητεῖ (in Mk 8,11 introduced by ζητοῦντες παρ᾽ αὐτοῦ σημεῖον ἀπὸ τοῦ οὐράνου, cf. Mt 16,1, and in Mt 12,38 introduced by

double level of "seeing signs" and "believing" in John's Gospel, but a source-critical distinction is not the correct way to comprehend this ambivalence. Indeed, it must even be admitted by signs source proponents that John could take the terminology from his source – and use it in his own sense. "This is precisely ... what makes borrowing from a source so difficult to prove". In the end, we are still left with interpreting the word σημεῖα in 20,30 in its context. Some, like Schnackenburg, are prepared to broaden the Johannine concept of σημεῖον. But, says Neirynck, this evacuates the argument for the signs source[430].

For Howard Clark KEE (1983), the reconstruction of the signs source is impossible: "Serious but inconclusive efforts have been made to reconstruct a source of signs, which is conjectured to have been utilized by John in compiling his gospel. Even if John did draw on written sources, which cannot be demonstrated but is not unlikely, he has so thoroughly integrated his material as to present a remarkably consistent point of view, particularly in relation to the miracles of Jesus"[431]. According to F.F. BRUCE (1983) "the signs and the discourses are too interdependent to be sorted out into separated sources"[432]. In their NT Introduction (1983), Georg STRECKER and Udo SCHNELLE rejected both Bultmann's σημεῖα-Quelle and Fortna's Gospel of Signs[433]. They have maintained this opinion in later works[434].

διδάσκαλε, θέλομεν ἀπὸ σοῦ σημεῖον ἰδεῖν) with Jn 6,30 τί οὖν ποιεῖς σὺ σημεῖον, ἵνα ἴδωμεν καὶ πιστεύσωμέν σοι; τί ἐργάζῃ; (b) Mk 11,28 (and par.) ἐν ποίᾳ ἐξουσίᾳ ταῦτα ποιεῖς with John's explicitation in 2,18 τί σημεῖον δεικνύεις ἡμῖν ὅτι ταῦτα ποιεῖς; Moreover, "in the Synoptic Gospels the request for a sign is refused" and "there is also a warning against the σημεῖα καὶ τέρατα of the false prophets (Mk 13,22)".

430. *Ibid.*, p. 28 (ET: p. 678).

431. H.C. KEE, *Miracle in the Early Christian World: A Study in Sociohistorical Method*, New Haven, CT - London, 1983, p. 226, with references to Smith (*Composition*, 1965) and Kümmel.

432. F.F. BRUCE, *The Gospel of John: Introduction, Exposition and Notes*, Grand Rapids, MI, 1983, p. 5 (with reference to Bultmann); for Fortna, see p. 22 n. 15.

433. G. STRECKER – U. SCHNELLE, *Einführung in die neutestamentliche Exegese* (UTB, 1253), Göttingen, 1983, p. 65; [3]1989, p. 69: "Weithin durchgesetzt hat sich die Annahme einer besonderen Passionstradition bei Johannes, während die beiden anderen von Bultmann postulierten Quellenschichten [Zeichenquelle, Quelle von Offenbarungsreden] Kritik hervorriefen. ... Auch eine mehrere Wundergeschichten umfassende Zeichenquelle, von R. Fortna zu einem ganzen Evangelium ausgeweitet, lässt sich nicht wirklich nachweisen".

434. STRECKER, *Die Anfänge der johanneischen Schule*, in *NTS* 32 (1986) 31-47, p. 32. Referring to the hypotheses of a σημεῖα-Quelle (Bultmann, followed by J.M. Robinson and Corsani), a "Gospel of Signs" (Fortna) or a "Grundschrift" (Langbrandter and Richter), he questions: "Sind die Quellenschriften, die R. Bultmann und seine Nachfolger vermuteten, literarkritisch eindeutig von den späteren Schichten abzusetzen?". Cp. *Neues Testament* (Urban Taschenbücher, 422; Grundkurs Theologie, 2), Stuttgart, 1989, p. 45; *Literaturgeschichte des Neuen Testaments* (UTB, 1682), Göttingen, 1992, pp. 206-

In his study on parallelism Peter F. ELLIS (1984)[435] tested J. Gerhard's hypothesis that "the Gospel was not the work of many but of one author, that it was a unified manuscript from beginning to end, and that it was written according to the laws of parallelism rather than the laws of narrative"[436]. Ellis became convinced of Gerhard's supposition and, regarding source criticism, he notes: "whatever the postulated sources, whether written or oral, John has so Johannized his material from

231 ("Das Johannesevangelium"), esp. 210: "Wenn auch der Evangelist Traditionen aufgenommen hat, die literarkritisch zu ermitteln sind, so ist als anerkennenswerter Kern der Grundschrifthypothesen i.w. nur die Tatsache festzuhalten, dass die Abfassung des JohEv die synoptischen Evangelien voraussetzt. Dabei ist die Unterscheidung von verschiedenartigen mündlichen und schriftlichen Traditionen im Vorstadium der Komposition des vierten Evangeliums eine bisher nur unzureichend bewältigte traditions- und redaktionsgeschichtliche Aufgabe. Selbstverständlich ist das JohEv nicht allein auf der Stufe der Endredaktion zu interpretieren; denn hierdurch würde übersehen werden, welche Bedeutung vorgegebene Traditionen für die Arbeit des Redaktors haben". On the signs source, see pp. 206-210 ("Quellenhypothesen zum Johannesevangelium"), esp. 208: "Auch die Annahme der 'Semeia-Quelle' hat in jüngerer Zeit begründeten Widerspruch erfahren. So wurde durch U. Schnelle die Einheit von 'Doxa und Wunder' in der Theologie des vierten Evangelisten, die auch die 'Semeia Jesu' umgreift, nachgewiesen"; see also p. 225: "Sind formgeschichtliche Parallelen zu der rekonstruierten Semeia-Quelle nicht zu belegen [with reference to Schnelle], so zeichnet sich zudem der ihr zugewiesene Wunderstoff durch traditions- und religionsgeschichtliche Divergenzen aus". (On Schnelle, see below, pp. 335-341.) Also in his article *Schriftlichkeit oder Mündlichkeit der synoptischen Tradition? Anmerkungen zur formgeschichtlichen Problematik*, in *FS F. Neirynck*, I, 1992, pp. 159-172, esp. 170-171, Strecker rejects the hypothesis of a "Grundschrift", "für die man entweder eine ausgearbeitete σημεῖα-Quelle oder eine Kombination aus einer messianologisch-christologischen Schrift der Täufertradition, σημεῖα-Quelle und Passions- und Ostergeschichten oder eine gnostische Grundschrift in Anspruch nimmt". He notes: "Darüber hinaus ist gegen diese Hypothese geltend zu machen, dass die vermutete Grundschrift weder formgeschichtlich noch literaranalytisch zu rekonstruieren ist und die hiermit sich als Konsequenz ergebende Vermutung von weiteren Redaktionen oft zu schematisch begründet wird. Sie müssten aus kurzen Textabschnitten, Versen oder einzelnen Wörtern erhoben werden, ohne dass ein anderer Zusammenhang als der gegebene Kontext vorausgesetzt werden kann. Dagegen ist zu fragen, was einen Redaktor überhaupt zu einer Rezension einer Grundschrift veranlasst haben sollte, wenn er mit ihrer Theologie grundsätzlich nicht übereinstimmte und sie durch seine Eingriffe erheblich verändern musste. Hypothetisch bleibt auch die Vermutung von akuten, externen oder internen Konflikten, die den Anlass für die verschiedenen redaktionellen literarischen Ebenen gebildet haben sollen; denn eine akute Auseinandersetzung etwa über die Christologie oder zu anderen kontrovers theologischen Themen in der johanneischen Schule sind für den Verfasser des Johannesevangeliums nicht nachzuweisen; dieser nimmt vielmehr eine vermittelnde, die divergierenden Tendenzen der johanneischen Schule überbrückende Position ein".

435. P.F. ELLIS, *The Genius of John: A Composition-Critical Commentary on the Fourth Gospel*, Collegeville, MN, 1984. – Cf. CULPEPPER, in KAESTLI *et al.* (eds.), *La communauté johannique et son histoire*, 1990, pp. 97-120, esp. 110-113; SLOYAN, *What Are They Saying about John?*, 1991, pp. 95-96; VAN BELLE, *Les parenthèses johanniques*, 1992, p. 1923.

436. *The Genius*, p. ix. Cf. John GERHARD, *The Literary Unity and the Compositional Methods of the Gospel of John*, diss. Washington, DC, The Catholic University of America, 1975.

tradition that any clear indications of distinct source materials have been so homogenized as to be virtually undetectable. It is much more probable that the Gospel as a whole is a pristine theological creation flowing from a genius theologian who required no sources beyond the broad oral traditions of the community in which he lived"[437]. In the same year, Vern S. POYTHRESS delineated some rough rules for the use of the principal conjunctions δέ, οὖν, καί, and asyndeton in the Gospel of John[438] and applied them as a test to the literary history of the Fourth Gospel to conclude that only Jn 7,53–8,11 deviates from the normal Johannine pattern[439]. The test also shows that it is not possible to separate sources, such as the signs source[440].

In a study of double-meaning expressions in the Fourth Gospel, Earl RICHARD (1985) rejected the signs-source hypothesis: "source conclusions and reconstructions, especially of the *Sēmeia*-Source, leave much to be desired in regard to methodology"[441]. He considers such expressions "characteristically Johannine" and part of the evangelist's dialectical vision and method[442]. "Since, repeatedly, those devices are related to traditions similar to those found in the Synoptics, one might postulate, in lieu of a Sign-Source, that John shared a common Jesus tradition with the other evangelists"[443]. Three years later, in his monograph on the christological concept of New Testament authors, he notes, in reference to Ruckstuhl's 1977 article and his own 1985 rejection of the "alleged

437. *The Genius*, pp. 3-4: "The Sources of the Gospel", esp. 4.

438. V.S. POYTHRESS, *The Use of the Intersentence Conjunctions* De, Oun, Kai, *and Asyndeton in the Gospel of John*, in *NT* 26 (1984) 312-340.

439. *Testing for Johannine Authorship by Examining the Use of Conjunctions*, in *WestTJ* 46 (1984) 350-369, pp. 361-362; cp. pp. 353-355, esp. 355.

440. *Ibid.*, pp. 355-358, esp. 358; cp. p. 356 (with reference to Turner, see above, pp. 300-301).

441. E. RICHARD, *Expressions of Double Meaning and Their Function in the Gospel of John*, in *NTS* 31 (1985) 96-112, pp. 105-107, esp. 107.

442. *Ibid.*, p. 107. According to Richard, the expressions of double meaning can be categorized as "misunderstanding, irony, use of technical terms (in a general context), ambiguous terms (in a specific context), figurative expressions, Christological titles, and double meanings that transcend particular literary techniques" (p. 97).

443. *Ibid.*, p. 107. Using Nicol's reconstruction, Richard (p. 106) notes the following "'expressions of double meaning', which allegedly would derive from the Sign-Source": the verb "sleep" in 11,11ff., irony in 11,16 and 2,10, the verb "follow" in 1,37.38.40.43, and εὐχαριστέω in 6,11.23. With regard to 11,11ff. (cp. Mk 5,39), however, "One might prefer, with Lindars, to see here and elsewhere in the Fourth Gospel not the use of a *Semeia*-Source but of the Jesus tradition"; with regard to 2,10 (cp. Mk 2,22 par.; Lk 5,39 and other passages of wedding imagery), "it seems preferable to appeal to the Jesus tradition as the ultimate source of the passage under discussion"; for 1,37-43, "there is contact between the Johannine device and the Jesus tradition, i.e. 'to follow' means 'to become a disciple' as in Mark 2.14 *passim*"; and on 6,11.23, he notes: "Source critics routinely attribute this verse to the Sign-Source. Contact, however, between this episode in John and the Jesus tradition, whether the multiplication stories or the Last Supper narratives, points in another direction" (pp. 106-107).

signs source": "Such a theory has many weaknesses. First, it is crucial to answer the following question: why should the admittedly creative fourth evangelist employ at length and in detail such an uncongenial source? Secondly, on the level of methodology, the linguistic and stylistic criteria used to isolate such a source are the most subject to criticism, for these are inadequate and lead to overly subjective reconstructions of the source. Instead linguistic study, originally formulated as a critique of Bultmann's proposals, convincingly demonstrates that there exists in John unity of style and argues strongly against much recent work done on the source"[444].

It was already clear in 1957 that John A.T. ROBINSON did not accept the semeia hypothesis[445]. In his Bampton Lectures on "The Priority of John", posthumously edited by J.F. Coakley in 1985, he dwells more at length on the semeia hypothesis[446]. With Dodd, he accepts that, if the Synoptic Gospels are eliminated as sources behind the Fourth Gospel, there are "no grounds for positing other written sources behind the Gospel of John"[447]. Although Robinson is impressed by Fortna's monograph, he rejects the semeia hypothesis[448]. (1) Against the text rearrangement, he posits Barrett's "sane judgment" on Bultmann: "I take it that if the gospel makes sense as it stands it can generally be assumed that this is the sense it was intended to make. That it may seem to me to make better sense when rearranged I do not regard as adequate reason for abandoning an order which undoubtedly runs back into the second century – the order, indeed, in which the book was *published*"[449]. (2) Robinson considers the attempt to isolate a source from its subsequent editorial treatment "a highly subjective exercise"[450]. (3) He agrees

---

444. *Jesus: One and Many. The Christological Concept of New Testament Authors*, Wilmington, DE, 1988, pp. 187-231, esp. 197.

445. See above, pp. 61-62.

446. *The Priority of John*, ed. J.F. COAKLEY, London, 1985. He treats the semeia hypothesis in the section "The Long Shadow of Dependence" (pp. 10-23, esp. 14-23), within the first chapter: "I. The Presumption of Priority" (pp. 1-35). – Reviews: cf. VAN BELLE, nos. 1731-1732; see esp. J.F. COAKLEY, in *Mowbrays Journal* 123 (1985) 1-2; P. GRELOT, *Problèmes critiques du IVe évangile*, in *RB* 84 (1987) 519-573, who provides an extended review of Robinson's book. See also C.St.M. STEWART, *John A.T. Robinson on the Priority of John*, Leuven, 1987 (S.T.L. thesis; dir. F. Neirynck); LINDARS, *Trends*, 1990, p. 330; SLOYAN, *What Are They Saying about John?*, 1991, pp. 42-45; SMITH, *John among the Gospels*, 1992, pp. 74-75.

447. *Priority*, p. 14. See also p. 21: "that he [John] depended on sources, of whatever kind, would appear quite unproven".

448. *Ibid.*, p. 15. In n. 43 Robinson also refers to Becker, Nicol, and Wilkens and to Ruckstuhl's analysis of Fortna's and Nicol's monographs.

449. BARRETT, *John*, ²1978, p. 22 (GT: 1990, p. 40). Cf. *Priority*, p. 15.

450. He notes (p. 16): "The most charitable verdict [on Fortna's hypothesis] is perhaps one that Fortna himself has passed on another, yet more elaborate and complex analysis of Johannine sources ... by M.-É. Boismard and A. Lamouille: 'I am not persuaded that such a multi-stage theory can be verified ... all the while admitting that it is

with Fortna that there are many *aporiai*, roughnesses, and disconnec-
tions in the gospel, but "the eye of the critic for 'contradictions' where
the ordinary reader has for centuries observed none often makes one
wonder whether they are being read in rather than read out"[451]; "more
than this is required to establish different 'hands' or 'sources'"[452]. (4) He
thinks, too, that style criticism has shown that it is impossible to establish different hands in the present gospel[453]. Teeple's attempt "to see in
the internal variations of vocabulary and syntax within the *distinctive*
Johannine style the evidence for (four) separate hands" is subjective[554].
(5) Regarding Fortna's reconstruction of the *Gospel of Signs*, he agrees
with B. Lindars that it is only "a pale ghost of John's theology"[455] and
with W.H. Brownlee that it is "sometimes so dull that it sounds more
like an abstract, than an original composition"[456]. Robinson himself supposes that John's material was developed in various stages, but this does
not mean that we can discover or isolate them[457]. He thinks that "there
is every reason to suppose, as Eusebius said a long time ago, that the
Gospel of John was put together out of 'unwritten preaching' material,
composed for apologetic, catechetical and liturgical purposes, and may
well have gone through different editions and redactions (whether by
one hand or more)"[458]. For Robinson, this is "entirely compatible with

probably equally incapable of falsification'"; cf. R.T. FORTNA, *The Relation of the
Narrative and Discourse in the Fourth Gospel: An Approach to the Question*. A Paper
Prepared for the Fourth Gospel Seminar of the Society for New Testament Studies at
Durham, August 1979.

451. *Priority*, p. 17, with reference in n. 53 to LINDARS, *Behind the Fourth Gospel*,
1971, p. 5 and KÜMMEL, *Introduction*, 1975, p. 210. For Robinson "some at least of the
self-corrections appear to be a deliberate part of the author's method" (p. 17; cf. 5,31
cp. 8,14; 8,16; cf. 11,25-26).

452. *Priority*, p. 17.

453. *Ibid.*, pp. 18-19, esp. 18: "But the overwhelming impression, borne out by a
number of detailed studies, is of the massive unity and consistency of the Johannine style.
If it does not make source-analysis impossible, it makes it extremely precarious". Robinson refers to the studies of Schweizer, Menoud, and Ruckstuhl and quotes MEEKS, in *JBL*
91 (1972) 44-72, p. 48 (= 1986, pp. 141-173, esp. 144): "The major literary problem of
John is its combination of remarkable stylistic unity and thematic coherence with glar-
ingly bad transitions between episodes at many points. The countless displacement,
source, and redaction theories that litter the graveyards of Johannine research are voluble
testimony to this difficulty". Robinson agrees again with PARKER, *Two Editions*, p. 304
(see above, p. 61).

454. *Priority*, pp. 19-20, esp. 20.

455. *Priority*, p. 20; cf. LINDARS, *Behind the Fourth Gospel*, 1971, pp. 78-79 (FT:
p. 113).

456. BROWNLEE, in CHARLESWORTH (ed.), *John and Qumran*, 1972, pp. 166-194, esp.
181 n. 55. Robinson also rejects the literary theory of Temple: "Yet a recent attempt to
do this and isolate an original and *very* primitive Aramaic 'core' is equally arbitrary and
has failed to win serious scholarly support" (*Priority*, p. 21).

457. *Ibid.*, p. 21.

458. EUSEBIUS, *HE*, III,24,7.

the hypothesis he was his own tradition, and stood in an internal rather than external relation to it"[459].

For Jacob KREMER (1985)[460] the evangelist used a written or oral tradition in Jn 11,1-46[461], but this does not mean that we can reconstruct a source or a basic narrative[462]. Regarding the origin of the tradition, Kremer considers several possibilities ("eine rein urkirchliche Bildung"[463], "Weiterbildung einer ursprünglichen Heilungsgeschichte"[464], or a "Bericht von Zeugen"[465]) and proposes the following alternative[466]: either a healing story has developed very early into a resurrection miracle, or an act of Jesus has been understood from the very beginning as a raising from death[467]. George MLAKUZHYIL (1987) remarks that source critics of the Fourth Gospel "are not agreed either about the number and relative importance of the criteria to be used for the detection of the source or about the number and content of the sources"[468]. Regarding

459. *Priority*, p. 21.

460. J. KREMER, *Lazarus. Die Geschichte einer Auferstehung. Text, Wirkungsgeschichte und Botschaft von Joh 11,1-46*, Stuttgart, 1985. – Reviews: cf. VAN BELLE, no. 3506; see esp. X. LÉON-DUFOUR, in *RSR* 75 (1987) 78-81; A. FUCHS, in *SNTU/A* 12 (1987) 240-243. See also WAGNER, *Auferstehung*, 1988, pp. 85-87.

461. *Lazarus*, p. 108: "Die vorliegende Lazarusgeschichte weist unverkennbar Anzeichen dafür auf, dass der Evangelist eine ihm vorgegebene schriftliche oder mündliche Nachricht über eine Totenerweckung im Blick auf einen bestimmten Leserkreis und mit einigen Worten wiedergegeben hat. Manche Spannungen und Unebenheiten, auf die schon die synchrone Untersuchung stiess, finden damit eine gute Erklärung".

462. *Ibid.*, p. 108: "Ob und inwieweit eine übernommene 'Quelle' oder gar 'ein Grundbericht' noch rekonstruiert und einer bestimmten Gemeindesituation zugeordnet werden kann, ist allerdings angesichts des einheitlichen Stils und des Fehlens sonstiger Belege dafür höchst fraglich"; cp. pp. 90-91: "Die skizzierten Versuche, eine schriftliche Quelle oder gar einen 'Grundbericht' aus dem vorliegen Text von Joh 11,1-46 herauszuschälen, bleiben letztlich sehr fragwürdige Hypothesen, vor allem wegen des einheitlichen Stils der ganzen Perikope". On pp. 83-91 ("Rekonstruktion schriftlicher Quellen") Kremer gives Becker's reconstruction of SQ (pp. 86-87) and the "Urform der Erzählung" (pp. 88-89); he compares these with the reconstructions of Bultmann and Schnackenburg (p. 86 n. 123) and of Boismard-Lamouille (pp. 90-90). For the argumentation of the "Zeichenquelle", see pp. 87-88. On the semeia hypothesis, see also p. 45 (with reference to Bultmann, Schnackenburg, Becker, Fortna, Nicol).

463. *Ibid.*, pp. 95-105.

464. *Ibid.*, pp. 105-107.

465. *Ibid.*, pp. 107-108.

466. *Ibid.*, p. 109: "Als mögliche Ausgangspunkte für das Entstehen unserer Überlieferung kommen daher vor allem folgende in Betracht: erstens eine Krankenheilung, die bald als Totenerweckung weitererzählt wurde, oder zweitens eine Tat Jesu, die von Anfang an damaligem Verstehen gemäss als Totenerweckung beurteilt wurde".

467. See also *Der arme Lazarus. Lazarus, der Freund Jesu. Beobachtungen zur Beziehung zwischen Lk 16,19-31 und Joh 11,1-46*, in *FS J. Dupont*, 1985, pp. 571-584.

468. G. MLAKUZHYIL, *The Christocentric Literary Structure of the Fourth Gospel* (AnBib, 117), Rome, 1987 (diss. Pontifical Gregorian University; dir. A. Vanhoye). See pp. 1-16: "Difficulties against the Literary Unity and Structure of the Fourth Gospel", esp. 10 (with reference to KYSAR, *The Fourth Evangelist and His Gospel*, 1975, p. 24). – Reviews: J. BECKER, in *TLZ* 113 (1988) 895-896; X. LÉON-DUFOUR, in *RSR* 77 (1989)

the signs source, in particular, he notes that "a consensus seems to be emerging among the source critics"[469]; but for Mlakuzhyil they "have still to explain how an intelligent evangelist could have left the glaring aporias in the final text of the Gospel"[470]. He thinks that "if the evangelist used some sources, he has reworked them so much that a scissor-and-paste method cannot be applied to the Fourth Gospel to recapture the original sources, because 'the creative composition places the precise underlying traditions beyond recovery'"[471]. He considers at least some of the aporias to be "creations of the critics themselves", and cites the enumeration of the two Cana signs as an example[472]. Mlakuzhyil thinks that there is no aporia[473]: the changing of water into wine is not called "the first sign", but the "beginning of the signs"; the signs that Jesus did in Jerusalem (cf. 2,23; 4,45; see also 3,2) are only mentioned in passing; in 4,54 it is said that this second sign too, like the first, was done on Jesus' return from Judea into Galilee. Gary M. BURGE (1987)[474] notes three objections against the signs-source hypothesis: "outside the hypothesized source in John there is no other evidence for it"; "Johannine features cannot be determined with precision"[475]; and "it is doubtful if such a miracle source would have existed without teachings and discourses by Jesus, presenting him purely as a divine man"[476]. Later, in his review (1991) of Fortna's *Predecessor*, Burge remarks that "much of Fortna's redactional spadework seems like guesswork"[477]. For Burge, it seems difficult to verify Fortna's reconstruction: "Could someone else sift the same material with utterly different results? Truth is, one gets the

264-266; G. SEGALLA, in *Bib* 70 (1989) 286-290; F.F. SEGOVIA, in *CBQ* 51 (1989) 192-194; S.S. SMALLEY, in *JTS* 40 (1989) 192-194; U.C. VON WAHLDE, in *BTB* 20 (1990) 41-42. See also MENKEN, *De christologie*, 1991, pp. 22-23 (ET: 1993, pp. 302-303).

469. *Structure*, p. 10. He refers to Bultmann, Becker, Fortna, Teeple, Nicol, and Schnackenburg (pp. 9 n. 31, 10 n. 34) and for a critique of the semeia hypothesis to D.M. Smith, Barrett, Cullmann, Lindars, Neirynck, and Ruckstuhl (cp. E. Schweizer and Menoud) (p. 10 n. 33).

470. *Ibid.*, p. 10, with reference to KYSAR, *The Fourth Evangelist and His Gospel*, 1975, p. 36 (see above, p. 191).

471. *Structure*, p. 11; cf. LINDARS, *Behind the Fourth Gospel*, 1971, p. 54.

472. *Structure*, p. 11.

473. *Ibid.*, p. 11, with reference (n. 40) to NEIRYNCK, *Jean et les Synoptiques*, 1979, pp. 173-174.

474. G.M. BURGE, *The Anointed Community: The Holy Spirit in the Johannine Tradition*, Grand Rapids, MI, 1987, p. 78 n. 115; on the signs source see also p. 75 n. 108. – Among the many reviews, see esp. U. SCHNELLE, in *TLZ* 113 (1988) 594-596; F. SEGOVIA, in *CBQ* 50 (1988) 711-712; S.S. SMALLEY, in *ExpT* 99 (1987-88) 311-312; X. LÉON-DUFOUR, in *RSR* 77 (1989) 272-274; M.R. MANSFIELD, in *JBL* 108 (1989) 158-160; B. LINDARS, in *JTS* 40 (1989) 189-192.

475. *Anointed Community*, p. 78 n. 115: "despite Fortna"; with reference to E. Schweizer and Ruckstuhl.

476. *Ibid.*, p. 78 n. 118 (contra Becker).

477. *Themelios* 17 (1991), no. 1, p. 27, with regard to rearranging of the source material vis-à-vis the present gospel.

haunting feeling that Professor Fortna has found themes in the text which are as much *his* as anyone's. But this will always be the danger in thorough-going redaction criticism like this. Separating the source from the redactor is often more art than science. And if beauty of art is really in the eye of the beholder, then the success of Fortna's results will depend entirely on who is doing the viewing"[478].

In his article on the Wine Miracle (1987), Martin HENGEL finds the existence of a semeia source "very questionable"[479]. For him, such a source is "a scholarly phantom", and "the self-evident manner with which it is presupposed by various authors does not render it more convincing"[480]. Considering the great stylistic unity of the Gospel of John, it is impossible to reconstruct such "a foreign body" as a signs source within the gospel. Moreover, "how can one expect that such a theologically wilful evangelist, ... should have mechanically taken over such statements as 2:11 or 20:30f. (which are decisive for the construction and structure of his Gospel) from a source which was entirely alien?"[481]. Further, the enumeration of the signs in 2,11 and 4,54 cannot be used as an argument for the signs source, for in these verses the geographical location is emphasized (4,54; cf. 2,1.11) and it is "absurd" to see an opposition to 2,23 and 3,2[482]. The ambivalence or doubtful character of the miracle narrative and of the miracle worker (see 8,48) is also an indication against a "pure" signs source, i.e., a collection of miracles without any reference to the teaching and the passion of Jesus; for Hengel, "such basically sterile listings of ϑαυμάσια as purported ἀληϑῆ διηγήματα (Lucian) concerning a ϑεῖος ἀνήρ were of little use as 'missionary writings' to awaken faith in non-believers", and "standing at the end of the Passion and Resurrection narrative, John 20:31 was certainly

478. *Ibid.*, p. 27.
479. M. HENGEL, *The Interpretation of the Wine Miracle at Cana: John 2:1-11*, in HURST – WRIGHT (eds.), *The Glory of Christ*, 1987, pp. 84-112, esp. 90-95: "the Semeia-Source Theory as a Solution?". See p. 87 n. 17: "the very questionable existence of a Semeia-source"; cp. p. 95 (on Jn 2,1-11): "the Semeia-source theory does not illuminate the interpretation of this 'mysterious' text; it obscures both it and the understanding of the whole Gospel, since the miracle occurs in a passage which is decisive for the entire work. The theory, in other words, only *displaces* the problem: what was objectionable to the old interpretation is now attributed to a *written* source. Thus all that was excessive and miraculous now appears unaltered in the source, while the profound editorial additions are attributed to the evangelist". On Hengel's article, see SLOYAN, *What Are They Saying about John?*, 1991, pp. 48-49; SMITH, *John among the Gospels*, 1992, pp. 181-182; NEIRYNCK, *John and the Synoptics*, 1992, pp. 6, 20-21.
480. *Wine miracle*, pp. 90 n. 27, 91-92.
481. *Ibid.*, p. 92.
482. *Ibid.*, p. 87 n. 18: "The effect of the σημεῖα of Jesus in Jerusalem to some extent 'loses its power' through the previous demand of the Jews in 2:18 for a legitimating sign (cf. 6:30). They do not lead to authentic faith (cf. 2:24f.). This explains the reproachful answer of Jesus in 4:48, to which the 'royal official' replies with authentic faith".

not the mechanically applied conclusion of such a document"[483]. Thus, for Hengel, "the assumption of a 'signs source' ... only causes difficulties for the understanding of the Gospel"[484], and regarding source criticism in general, he thinks that "except for the Gospels we know already, we can *reconstruct* no written sources with sufficient certainty"[485]. Therefore, like B. Olsson, he interprets 2,1-11 as a *Johannine* text and, thus, as a unity[486]. In his Stone Lectures at Princeton Theological Seminary in 1987, published in 1989, Hengel similarly rejected the signs source: "The existence of a signs source with a *theios anèr* christology supposedly contrary to the Fourth Gospel cannot be demonstrated in terms either of style or of the history of religion. For the Fourth Gospel the 'signs' are not an alien body but a basic ingredient of its picture of Jesus"[487]. He considers the possibility that "the teacher (and his pupils) collected miracles of Jesus" and that such "a collection of miracle stories (or more) could have been kept in written form for the school", but he adds immediately that this is already hypothetical and that "if there was such a collection (or collections), this was no alien body nor an independent 'Gospel'"[488].

J. ENGELBRECHT (1988)[489] notes that there is no agreement regarding the semeia hypothesis: "One does get the idea that the Fourth Evangelist

483. *Ibid.*, p. 107; cp. p. 108: "The collections of miracles of healing were interesting as means of propaganda in places where new, miraculous cures were constantly carried out. A Semeia-source would therefore be significant at best as a 'primer' or 'stimulus' for the miracle-workers in their own group. But, while testimony of the antimontanistic Apollonius [Eus., *HE* 5. 18. 14] even speaks of an awakening from the dead which was attributed to the Ephesian John, there is nevertheless much more to be said against such an independent document than for it".

484. *Ibid.*, p. 92 n. 30.

485. *Ibid.*, p. 92: "He [the author or authors] knew Mark and Luke at least, presumably discussed them in the 'school', took some things over in a more or less altered way and, critical on the whole, detached himself from them". Cp. *The Johannine Question* (see below, n. 487), p. 102: "As literary 'sources' of which the author takes account without really being dependent on them in the strict sense we should look primarily to the earlier Synoptic Gospels, above all Mark and Luke: the development of the Fourth Gospel took place in antithesis to the Synoptic tradition"; see also p. 91 (GT: 1993, pp. 264, cp. 245-246).

486. *Wine Miracle*, p. 83; cf. pp. 95-104: "John 2:1-11 Regarded as Unity".

487. *The Johannine Question*, London - Philadelphia, PA, 1989, pp. 91-92 (GT: 1993, pp. 246-247). For Hengel's "own attempt at a solution" of the Johannine problem, see pp. 102-108 (GT: pp. 264-274). – Reviews: E. BAMMEL, in *JTS* 42 (1991) 666-668; R.A. CULPEPPER, in *JBL* 110 (1991) 536-537; J.L. HOULDEN, in *Theology* 93 (1990) 480-481.

488. *The Johannine Question*, p. 92 (GT: p. 247-248). Cp. p. 102 (GT: p. 265): "The seven signs in the Gospel are a selection from a more extensive collection of the signs of Jesus in the school. They are regarded as a necessary part of the activity of Jesus and do not derive from an alien source. They also illustrate the anti-docetic tendency of the Gospel: the miracles are the work of the creator of the physical world who is going to his death; at the same time they have a deeper 'spiritual' meaning".

489. J. ENGELBRECHT, *Trends in Miracle Research*, in *Neotestamentica* 22 (1988) 139-161, pp. 149-150. Engelbrecht mentions Bultmann, Becker, Fortna, Teeple, Hoeferkamp

was uncomfortable with the kind of faith evoked by miracles. But how he revised the view of his source materials is something that redaction critics do not agree on ..., it seems that none of the proposed source theories approaches the status of widespread acceptance. Therefore further debate can be expected with regard to the sources employed and the utilisation thereof"[490].

In his doctoral dissertation on σημεῖον in the Fourth Gospel (1988)[491], Wolfgang J. BITTNER "joins a strong current movement rejecting a proposed pre-Johannine Signs-source or gospel"[492]. He especially criticizes Bultmann's, Becker's, and Heekerens's arguments for the semeia hypothesis[493].

1. Regarding Bultmann, Bittner first treats his tradition-historical observations. There are parallels to some of the Johannine miracle stories in the Synoptic tradition; Bultmann compared these and concluded that the Johannine miracle stories are literarily independent of the Synoptics, and he therefore posited a common written source for these narratives, the so-called σημεῖα-*Quelle*[494]. But for Bittner, the observation of literary independence allows only to conclude that both John and the Synoptics had contact with some common tradition[495]. Second, the most important argument for the semeia hypothesis, the numbering of the signs, can be explained from the present Johannine text. There is no contradiction between 2,11 and 4,54 on the one hand and 2,23 on the other: the signs in Galilee are opposed to the signs in Jerusalem[496]. Third, the style-critical observations of Schweizer and Ruckstuhl make it impossible to reconstruct sources behind the Fourth Gospel. The so-

---

and Boismard as proponents of the signs source and for criticism refers to Neirynck (1983 and 1984: "This critique coincides with the question of Synoptic influence on John's Gospel"; cf. p. 149), Dauer and Heekerens ("studies which criticise the signs source hypothesis along the same line as Neirynck").

490. *Ibid.*, p. 152, with reference to KYSAR, *ANRW*, II, 25/3, 1985, esp. pp. 2441-2442 and 2398-2402 (see above, p. 192 n. 221).

491. W.J. BITTNER, *Jesu Zeichen im Johannesevangelium. Die Messias-Erkenntnis im Johannesevangelium vor ihrem jüdischen Hintergrund* (WUNT, 2/26), Tübingen, 1987 (diss. Basel, 1986; dir. M. Barth). See also *Geschichte und Eschatologie im Johannesevangelium*, in STADELMANN (ed.), *Glaube und Geschichte*, 1986, pp. 154-180. – Reviews of *Jesu Zeichen*: B. LINDARS, in *JTS* 39 (1988) 199-200; R.E. BROWN, in *CBQ* 51 (1989) 147-148; M.M. THOMPSON, in *JBL* 108 (1889) 735-737; R. RIESNER, in *TLZ* 114 (1989) 30-31; X. LÉON-DUFOUR, in *RSR* 77 (1989) 271-272. See also ID., *Où en est la recherche johannique?*, 1990, p. 25; KOSKENNIEMI, *Apollonios von Tyana*, 1992, p. 160; SMITH, *John among the Gospels*, 1992, p. 73 n. 103.

492. R.E. BROWN, in *CBQ* 51 (1989) 147-148, p. 147.

493. *Jesu Zeichen*, pp. 2-14: "Die Semeiaquellen-Hypothese". See above, pp. 24-40 (Bultmann), pp. 116-135 (Becker) and below, pp. 256-262 (Heekerens).

494. *Ibid.*, p. 5.

495. *Ibid.*, p. 5.

496. *Ibid.*, pp. 5-6; cp. p. 10.

called "distinctive style characteristics", which Bultmann notes, are only indications of different traditional material and not of different sources[497] Fourth, that the Johannine miracles belong to a common source because they all have a common form (Gattung) is to be refuted[498]: (a) from the observation of form-critical similarity one cannot conclude that these stories came from a source and still less that they belonged to the same source; (b) moreover, it is purely hypothetical to suppose that a source contains only reports which are form-critically parallel. Fifth, the observation that discourses are built upon the miracle stories as commentaries does not mean that the miracle stories are subordinate to the discourses; nor is this an indication that the miracle stories all belonged to the same source. In addition, it must be observed that the first two miracles are not followed by discourses[499].

2. Bittner agrees with Becker that the style-critical argument cannot be used to delimit a signs source. But he refutes Becker's three arguments from content[500]. First, for Bittner, it is unproven that the discourses are the most important material in the Fourth Gospel, so that the claim that they are not in the purview of 20,30-31 and that, therefore, these verses are originally the conclusion of the signs source is misguided[501]. Second, is it not a presupposition to say that the extremely heightened miracles do not harmonize with sayings which relativize the miracles? Third, regarding the numbering of signs, Bittner refers to his critique of Bultmann[502]. Bittner especially criticizes the presupposition of the semeia hypothesis that there is a strong contradiction between the θεῖος ἀνήρ christology of the signs source and the Johannine christology[503].

3. Heekerens's study shows some progress for Bittner. Nevertheless, he does not understand why Heekerens, after a critique of Bultmann's argumentation, still maintains a source and does not speak of traditions. What is necessary, and this is the point of Bittner's study, is an explanation of the origin and use of the word σημεῖον[504].

In his study on Jn 11 Alain MARCHADOUR (1988)[505] criticizes the literary analyses of Spitta, Bultmann, Wilkens, Fortna, Schnackenburg,

---

497. *Ibid.*, p. 7.

498. *Ibid.*, p. 8.

499. *Ibid.*, pp. 8-9.

500. *Ibid.*, pp. 9-13.

501. *Ibid.*, p. 10. For the Johannine character of 20,30-31, see pp. 197-225.

502. See above, p. 333 n. 496.

503. *Ibid.*, pp. 11-13, esp. 12-13, with reference to BERGER, *Hellenistische Gattungen*, 1985, pp. 1230-1231.

504. *Jesu Zeichen*, pp. 13-14, esp. 14.

505. A. MARCHADOUR, *Lazare. Histoire d'un récit. Récits d'une histoire* (LD, 132), Paris, 1988. – Reviews: É. CUVILLIER, in *ÉTR* 63 (1988) 467-468; X. LÉON-DUFOUR, in *RSR* 77 (1989) 277-279; J.J. O'ROURKE, in *CBQ* 51 (1989) 160. See also MORGEN, *L'exégèse johannique*, 1989, p. 255.

and Boismard and Lamouille[506] and objects that these authors start from two presuppositions: that a σημεῖα-*Quelle* existed[507] and that a miracle story had a clearly defined form[508]. For Marchadour, the literary-critical hypothesis has its limits[509]. First, the reconstruction of the signs source, based on the inner tensions of the present gospel, remains hypothetical[510]. Second, literary criticism is able to detect evidences of linguistic, stylistic, and theological ruptures in a text that seems homogeneous, but it must be said that in most of these cases the narrative logic is unrecognized[511]. Finally, source critics do not accept that narrative and discourse belong to the same narrative strategy[512].

Of more importance for the history of the semeia hypothesis is the study of Udo SCHNELLE on antidocetic christology in the Fourth Gospel (1987)[513].

506. *Lazare*, pp. 33-63: "Le texte et sa préhistoire", esp. 40-54. For a concise survey of the semeia hypothesis, see pp. 34-37; Marchadour mentions Bultmann, Wilkens, and Fortna.

507. *Ibid.*, p. 56. He refers to C.H. Weisse (1838), who distinguished between narratives and discourses (see above, pp. 2 n. 4, 12 n. 61), and to Heekerens for a recent presentation of the signs source. Marchadour objects to Fortna: "On peut s'interroger sur la légitimité de telles procédures qui cherchent à réduire par tous les moyens les aspérités d'un récit, au risque de perdre de vue la logique qui a inspiré le récit premier" (p. 48); cp. his critique of Schnackenburg: "Mais on peut déjà s'interroger sur le statut narratif de ce genre de squelette, s'il a jamais existé. Le récit actuel 'est une construction dramatique pleine de suspense', selon Schnackenburg. Comment cela peut-il se concilier avec une histoire rédactionnelle complexe, faite d'introductions successives d'éléments narratifs, de discours, de commentaires et même de personnages nouveaux? *A priori*, c'est difficile à imaginer" (p. 50).

508. *Ibid.*, pp. 56-57. Most authors presume that the miracle stories must be very simple and correspond to those in the Synoptics, but for Marchadour it is clear that "un récit comme la résurrection de Lazare n'a pas grand-chose à voir avec une telle grille".

509. *Ibid.*, pp. 57-63.

510. *Ibid.*, pp. 57-60, esp. 60: "nous n'avons pas encore trouvé des témoins qui viendraient donner à la théorie historico-critique l'appui décisif qui jusqu'ici lui fait défaut. Tirons-en la conclusion que les reconstitutions présentées plus haut resterons invérifiables et improbables". The *Secret Gospel of Mark* (M. Smith), which Boismard uses to reconstruct the primitive story of Jn 11, is rejected by Marchadour as intermediary text, "parce que ce récit est une sorte de mosaïque formée à partir d'éléments synoptiques et aussi johanniques" (p. 59).

511. *Ibid.*, p. 60. He cites ALTER, *The Art of Biblical Narrative*, 1981, p. 20: "There is no point, to be sure, in pretending that all the contradictions among different sources in the biblical texts can be happily harmonized by the perception of some artful design. It seems reasonable enough, however, to suggest that we may still not fully understand what would have been perceived as a real contradiction by an intelligent Hebrew writer of the early Iron Age, so that apparently conflicting versions of the same event set side by side, far from troubling their original audience, may have sometimes been perfectly justified in a kind of logic we no longer apprehend".

512. *Lazare*, p. 61, with reference to the study of ch. 6 by the GROUPE D'ENTREVERNES, *Signes et paraboles*, 1977; DODD, *Tradition*, 1963, p. 230; VAN DEN BUSSCHE, *Structure*, 1958, p. 93.

513. U. SCHNELLE, *Antidoketische Christologie im Johannesevangelium. Eine Unter-*

The author emphatically rejects the signs source and believes that the evangelist took the miracle stories from separate traditions and made them subservient to his antidocetic christology[514]. The evangelist does not criticize the miracles, but maintains that faith arises from the revelation of God's δόξα by the Incarnate Son[515]. After studying the context, tradition and redaction, and the interpretation of each miracle story, Schnelle raises eight objections against a σημεῖα-*Quelle*[516].

1. The main clue for the existence of the signs source, the numbering of the first two signs, is by no means valid. For Schnelle, these verses are from the evangelist. He numbered the signs in *Cana* to indicate the beginning and the end of Jesus' first public ministry; this numbering does not contradict the summaries in 2,23 and 3,2 because there the

suchung zur Stellung des vierten Evangeliums in der johanneischen Schule (FRLANT, 144), Göttingen, 1987 (ET: 1992). – Reviews: J. BECKER, in *TRev* 84 (1988) 370-372; C. WOLFF, in *TLZ* 113 (1989) 818-820; LÉON-DUFOUR, in *RSR* 77 (1989) 274-275; A. FUCHS, in *SNTU/A* 15 (1990) 179; R. McIVER, in *JSNT* 51 (1993) 126. See also MORGEN, *L'exégèse johannique*, 1989, pp. 252-253; LÉON-DUFOUR, *Où en est la recherche johannique?*, 1990, p. 30; ASHTON, *Understanding*, 1991, pp. 74 n. 24, 162; MENKEN, *De christologie*, 1991, pp. 25-27 (ET: 1993, pp. 307-308); KOSKENNIEMI, *Apollonios von Tyana*, 1992, p. 159; SCHMITHALS, *Johannesevangelium*, 1992, pp. 193-194; NEIRYNCK, *John and the Synoptics*, 1992, p. 7.

514. See esp. pp. 87-194 (ET: pp. 74-175): "Der sichtbare Christus: Wunder und johanneische Christologie". For analysis of 2,1-11; 4,46-54; 5,1-9ab; 6,1-15; 6,16-25; 9,1-41; 11,1-44; 20,20-31; 20,24-29, see pp. 87-161 (ET: pp. 74-144), and of the concepts σημεῖον and ἔργον, see pp. 161-167 (ET: pp. 144-150).

515. *Ibid.*, *passim*; see, e.g., p. 94 (ET: p. 81, on 2,1-11): "Die Offenbarung der Doxa im Wunder ruft Glauben hervor. Dieses Geschehen vollzieht sich exemplarisch beim ersten Wunder an den Jüngern. Johannes demonstriert an ihnen in einer völlig undualistischen Terminologie sein Verständnis von Wunder und Glaube: Nicht der Glaube schaut das Wunder, sondern durch die Offenbarung der Doxa des Inkarnierten im Wunder entsteht Glaube. Weil das Wunder Offenbarungsort der Doxa des sarkinischen Jesus ist, kann es zum Glauben führen. Hier wird das christologische Interesse des Evangelisten sichtbar: Johannes ist weder an einem mirakulösen Glauben noch an einer Abwertung der Wunder interessiert, sondern einzig und allein an der Darstellung der Doxa des Inkarnierten und damit der Realität der Inkarnation". Cf. pp. 182-194 (ET: pp. 164-175): "Das johanneische Verständnis der Wunder Jesu"; pp. 192-192 (ET: pp. 173-175): "Die Bedeutung der Wunder für die johanneische Christologie".

516. *Ibid.*, pp. 168-182 (ET: pp. 150-164): "Einwände gegen die Annahme einer 'Semeia-Quelle'". See also pp. 105-108 (ET: pp. 91-93): "Exkurs: Die Wundererzählung im Johannesevangelium", with a list of defenders and opponents of the semeia hypothesis on p. 105[-106], n. 105 (ET: p. 91[-91] n. 105); see above, pp. 71-72. – Against Becker, who points to the Sayings Source (Q) as a support for the plausibility of a Johannine source criticism (see above, p. 119 n. 266), SCHNELLE, *Christologie*, 1987, p. 18 n. 51 (ET: 1992, p. 8 n. 51) states: "Hier aber liegt ein entscheidender methodischer Unterschied! Die Logienquelle als ein Pfeiler synoptischer Quellenkritik ist nur rekonstruierbar, weil es eine Doppelüberlieferung gibt. Bei Johannes hingegen kommen keine Doppelüberlieferungen vor, so dass man ausschliesslich auf werkimmanente Angaben angewiesen ist und der Gefahr eines methodischen Zirkelschlusses kaum entrinnen kann" (cp. *Perspektiven*, 1990, p. 60 n. 14).

signs in *Jerusalem* are meant[517]. Against Spitta, Fortna, and Heekerens, who interpret the numbering in 21,14 as an enumeration of the third sign in the source, Schnelle replies that 21,14 is from a post-evangelist redaction and refers to the appearances in 20,19-23.24-29[518].

2. Jn 20,30-31, the so-called close of the signs source, is from the evangelist. He uses the concept σημεῖον to pregnantly formulate the quality of the revelation that appears in Jesus' ministry, which provokes and deepens faith[519].

517. *Ibid.*, p. 168 (ET: p. 151); cp. pp. 92 (ET: p. 79, on 2,11), 100 (ET: p. 87, on 4,54). See also pp. 106-108 (ET: pp. 91-93), where Schnelle mentions five explanations of the inconsistencies for the numbering in 2,11 and 4,54 with 2,23 and 4,45: (1) The numbering is a characteristic of the source. Schnelle objects: "Dann aber muss gefragt werden, warum sie bei zwei endet. Die Auskunft der Leser könne selbst bis sieben zählen, ist keine wirkliche Antwort auf diese Frage. Zudem hat die Analyse der ersten beiden Wundergeschichten ergeben, dass Joh 2,11; 4,54 redaktionell sind" (p. 106; ET: pp. 92-93). (2) Jn 4,46-54 narrates the second miracle, so there is no inconsistency with the summaries. Schnelle objects: "Aber auch bei dieser Lösung bleibt die Frage, warum die Zählung in 4,54 endet, denn es werden noch mehrere Wunder erzählt" (p. 107; ET: p. 93). (3) John introduced the numbering of the signs. Schnelle objects: "Wiederum muss gefragt werden, warum er nur die beiden ersten Wunder erzählt" (p. 107; ET: p. 93). (4) Because the two miracles are located at Cana, they are numbered in the *Vorlage* as the first and second miracle in Cana. So the numbering is traditional and consciously related to these miracles in Cana. Schnelle objects: "Gegen diese Lösung spricht, dass nach der vorangegangenen Analyse Joh 2,11 und 4,54 redaktionell sind" (p. 107; ET: p. 93). (5) The numbering is from the evangelist. He numbered the signs to stress the beginning and the end of Jesus' first public ministry. Moreover, he is clearly interested in Cana as a special place of Jesus' revelation. Schnelle accepts this explanation: "Für diese letzte Erklärung spricht einmal der eindeutig redaktionelle Charakter von Joh 2,11; 4,54; ausserdem besteht kein Widerspruch zu den summarischen Wundererwähnungen in Joh 2,23 und 4,45 (die nicht in Kana, sondern sehr bewusst im feindlichen Jerusalem spielen), und zudem kann die Zählung der Kanawunder als kompositorisches Mittel des Evangelisten verstanden werden (die beiden Wunder Jesu in Kana als Anfangs- und Endpunkt des ersten öffentlichen Auftretens Jesu). Schliesslich entsprechen 2,11, 4,54 der joh. Methode der nachträglichen Explikation (vgl. Joh 2,17; 7,39; 11,13; 12,16.33)" (p. 107; ET: p. 93).

518. *Ibid.*, p. 168 (ET: p. 151).

519. *Ibid.*, p. 168 (ET: p. 151). Cp. pp. 152-156, esp. 154 (ET: pp. 135-139, esp. 138). See, however, Becker's rejection of Schnelle's stylistic argumentation: "Wer allerdings (dabei noch weitgehend nur formal-statistisch) Joh 20,30f. mit dem Joh und 1–3 Joh vergleicht und dann folgert, in 20,30f. spräche E und nicht die SQ (so Schnelle), hat stillschweigend aus einem Soziolekt (Joh und 1–3 Joh haben verschiedene Autoren) eine individuelle Sprache von E gemacht, weiter für die SQ vorab behauptet, sie müsse frei sein von allen Spracheigentümlichkeiten des joh Soziolektes, und endlich das Joh flächig benutzt, als sei hier von vornherein eine literarische Schichtung indiskutabel" (*Johannes*, vol. II, ³1991, pp. 754-755). – Cp. THYEN, in *TR* 42 (1977), p. 214, who remarked against Ruckstuhl that with his list of style characteristics no distinction can be made between the "Idiolekt" of an individual author and the "Soziolekt" of the Johannine school. See also, e.g., LORENZINI, in *VetChrist* 18 (1981) 453-469, pp. 456-460 and PORSCH (see above, p. 111). RUCKSTUHL, *Zur Antithese Idiolekt-Soziolekt*, 1987, pp. 178-181, esp. 179 (= 1988, pp. 261-264, esp. 261-262) agrees that there existed something like a sociolect of the Johannine Community, used in its proclamation- and

3. Regarding the tradition-historical background, Schnelle maintains that the evangelist has taken up the miracle stories from apparently different traditions. He distinguishes between special traditions of the Johannine school (for 2,1-11; ch. 9; ch. 11) and traditions of a Synoptic type (5,1-9a.b; 4,46-54) and for 6,1-25 he accepts literary dependence upon Mk 6,32-52[520]. The history-of-religions background is very complex. Schnelle supposes an Old Testament and Jewish background as well as a Hellenistic and pagan one. So, it is impossible to assign the pre-Johannine miracles tradition to a coherent tradition-historical and history-of-religions background[521].

4. From the style-critical point of view, it is difficult to maintain a σημεῖα-*Quelle*. For Schnelle, style criticism of the miracle stories allows us to conclude only that they go back to traditional material[522]. We note here Schnelle's remarks on the use of Schweizer's and Ruckstuhl's style-critical method[523]. (a) It is impossible to characterize an author's style in contrast to other authors. Words, expressions, and constructions can also be considered Johannine if they appear in other books of the New Testament[524]. (b) Moreover, it is insufficient to compare the style of the Gospel of John with the New Testament alone. Many "Johannine" style characteristics also appear in the Koine. By extending the comparable texts, the number of Johannine characteristics will be reduced[525]. (c) Not only the "idiolect" of the evangelist (or of his traditions), but also the Johannine "sociolect" must be considered, for it is possible that within the Johannine school a group-language was developed[526]. (d) Johannine style

---

mission-activity. But for him, there is little evidence that others collaborated with the leader of this circle in the redaction of the four Johannine works: the whole sociolect of the Johannine circle has been taken up in the literary activity of the author.

520. *Ibid.*, pp. 169-171 (ET: pp. 151-154). He notes on 2,1-11: "eine ausgesprochene Sondertradition der joh. Schule" (p. 169; cp. pp. 92-93, esp. 93; ET: p. 151; cp. pp. 79-80, esp. 80); on ch. 9: "eine Sondertradition aus der joh. Schule" (p. 169; cp. p. 133; ET: p. 152; cp. pp. 117-118); on ch. 11: "eine weitere joh. Sondertradition" (p. 169; cp. pp. 149-150; ET: p. 152; cp. pp. 133-134); on 5,1-9a: "eine joh. Sondertradition synoptischen Typs" (p. 169; cp. pp. 110-111; ET: p. 152; cp. pp. 96-97); on 4,46-54: "eine gemeinsame Überlieferung mit Mt 8,5-13 / Lk 7,1-10. ... Wenn auch keine literarische Abhängigkeit nachzuweisen ist, so sind die traditionsgeschichtliche Berührungen unverkennbar" (p. 170; cp. pp. 101-104, esp. 104; ET: 152; cp. pp. 87-91, esp. 90); on 6,1-25: "traditionsgeschichtlich und literarisch von Mk 6,32-52 abhängig" (p. 170; cp. pp. 119-122, esp. 122; pp. 126-130, esp. 129-130; ET: p. 153; cp. pp. 105-107, esp. 107; pp. 111-115, esp. 114-115).

521. *Ibid.*, p. 170 (ET: pp. 153-154).

522. *Ibid.*, pp. 171-177, esp. 177 (ET: pp. 154-160, esp. 159-160).

523. *Ibid.*, pp. 172-173 (ET: pp. 155-156).

524. *Ibid.*, p. 172 (ET: p. 155)

525. *Ibid.*, p. 172 (ET: p. 155), with reference to COLWELL, *The Greek of the Fourth Gospel*, 1931.

526. *Ibid.*, pp. 172-173 (ET: p. 155); Cf. THYEN, in *TR* 39 (1974), p. 299; 42 (1977), p. 214; HEEKERENS, *Zeichen-Quelle*, 1984, pp. 27-32. See above, pp. 337-338 n. 519.

criticism always runs the risk of a logical circle. The method is analytical as well as synthetic. On the one hand, characteristics are used to identify the different layers within the Gospel, and on the other, to verify the results[527]. (e) The conclusive force of style criticism depends essentially upon the text exegetes ascribe to a postulated source; style criticism is more conclusive when the text of the source is more extended[528]. (f) Extensive literary-critical and tradition-historical theories, which are style-critically founded, cannot depend on words which occur only once, twice, or three times in the whole Gospel[529]. (g) When texts are clearly different stylistically from other texts in the Gospel, this is a first indication that they are traditional. For Schnelle, what appears to be pre-Johannine tradition cannot be attributed *a priori* to a source. One can only speak of a coherent source if the text is free of Johannine style characteristics and, moreover, if the source itself contains its own characteristics. Schnelle objects that Fortna cannot demonstrate either a characteristic style for the source or the unity of the miracles and passion tradition on the pre-Johannine level[530]. He agrees with Nicol's observation, however, that five miracle stories (2,1-12; 4,46-47.50-54; 5,1-9; 6,16-21; 9,1-2.6-7) contain only a few Johannine characteristics and that, therefore, these can be ascribed to John's tradition, but he adds that this does not mean that John employed a continuous source[531].

5. There is no parallel to the literary form of the σημεῖα-*Quelle*. Schnelle rejects the term aretalogy, for it can hardly be used as an indication for a literary form[532].

---

527. *Christologie*, p. 173 (ET: p. 155).

528. *Ibid.*, p. 173 (ET: p. 155). Schnelle gives 21,1-14 as an example: "Bei R. Fortna spielt Joh 21,1-14 für den Nachweis eines einheitlichen Stils der 'Semeia-Quelle' eine wichtige Rolle. Lehnt man die Zugehörigkeit dieser Wundergeschichte zum ursprünglichen JE ... ab, so verliert seine Stilanalyse erheblich an Überzeugungskraft". On 21,1-14; see esp. pp. 30-31 (ET: pp. 19-20).

529. *Ibid.*, p. 173 (ET: p. 155).

530. *Ibid.*, pp. 173-174 (ET: pp. 156-157). See pp. 174-176 (ET: pp. 157-159) for the rejection of Fortna's "Stylistic Tests of the Source's Purity and Integrity" (see above, pp. 145-148).

531. *Ibid.*, pp. 176-177 (ET: p. 159).

532. *Ibid.*, p. 177-179, esp. 179 (ET: pp. 160-161, esp. 161). Regarding the use of the term aretalogy, Schnelle notes: "Ist es schon fragwürdig, die Wundergeschichten des Markusevangeliums als formgeschichtliche Parallele heranzuziehen, so ist darüber hinaus der von R. Reitzenstein geprägte Terminus 'Aretalogie' sehr problematisch, denn in der klassischen Philologie bezeichnet Aretalogie nicht die Form, 'sondern den Inhalt und den Zweck sehr verschiedener literarischer Gattungen'. Aretalogische Motive finden sich in Hymnen, Briefen, Weihinschriften und Romanen, 'von einer festliegenden literarischen Gattung kann man allerdings nie sprechen'. Deshalb sollte auf den Begriff 'Aretalogie' im Sinn einer festen formgeschichtlichen Gattung verzichtet werden" (p. 179; ET: p. 161). Schnelle refers to ESSER, *Formgeschichtliche Studien*, 1969, p. 101: "von einer festliegenden literarischen Form kann man allerdings nie sprechen". See also KEE, in *JBL* 92 (1973), pp. 402, 411-412; BERGER, in *ANRW* II, 25/2, 1984, p. 1228; MARGUERAT, *La*

6. Even the number of miracle stories in John counters the signs-source hypothesis. The number seven is clearly a Johannine concept; it indicates the fullness of revelation in Jesus. Moreover, the evangelist has taken up the miracles from the Johannine school tradition and integrated them very well into his composition[533].

7. If a signs source ever existed, one should expect that the concept σημεῖον played an important role in the source. But of the seventeen times the word occurs in John, it is used fifteen times by the evangelist. It appears to be traditional only in 2,18 and 6,30. The word σημεῖον is in fact central to John's christology: it pregnantly demonstrates Jesus' revelatory activity[534].

8. Finally, Schnelle does not understand why the evangelist should have employed the signs source if, as most defenders of the semeia hypothesis suppose, the source's christology was opposed to his own. The tension in theology can also appear within the separate pericopes; moreover, it must first be demonstrated that the source possessed a coherent christology[535]. According to Schnelle, it is improbable that the source was written to prove Jesus' Messiahship for Jewish readers, because the portrayal of the Messiah as a miracle worker would not have been convincing for such readers[536]. Further, the missionary intention is

---

"source des signes", 1990, p. 85 (see below, p. 346 n. 562); TIEDE, in *ABD*, I, 1992, pp. 372-373, esp. 372: "The term 'aretalogy' was used rarely in antiquity and possessed no specific literary or oral form"; STRECKER (see above, pp. 324-325 n. 434).

533. *Ibid.*, pp. 179-180 (ET: pp. 161-162). On p. 180 (ET: p. 162) he rejects Fortna's reconstruction of the order: "Methodisch ist dieses Vorgehen als willkürlich zu bezeichnen. Fortna analysiert acht Wundergeschichten, behauptet dann aber, die 'Quelle' habe nur sieben enthalten. Er postuliert eine 'ursprüngliche' Reihenfolge der Wunder, ohne in die Erzählungen selbst auf vorjoh. Ebene ein geographisches Schema nachweisen zu können". For the importance of the number seven in the Gospel of John, Schnelle refers to HOLTZMANN, *Theologie*, II, ²1991, p. 459; WINDISCH, *Erzählungsstil*, 1923 (ET: 1993); LOHMEYER, in *ZNW* 27 (1928) 11-36, p. 12; RENGSTORF, art. ἑπτά, in *TWNT* 2 (1935) 623-631 (ET: *TDNT* 2, 1964, pp. 627-635); DODD, *Interpretation*, 1953, pp. 297-389 (FT: 1975, pp. 381-491); GRUNDMANN, *Zeugnis*, 1961, p. 13. Cp. also ABBOTT, *Johannine Grammar*, 1906, pp. 463-465 (§§ 2624-2627); FIEBIG, in *GKG* 64 (1928) 126-132; HIRSCH, *Das vierte Evangelium*, 1936; DEFOURNY, in *CMechl* 11 (1937) 359-367; BOISMARD, *LumV* 1 (1961), n° 1, 95-114, esp. pp. 99-105; *Le Prologue*, 1953, pp. 136-138; *Du Baptême à Cana*, 1956, pp. 14-15; (& LAMOUILLE), *Jean*, 1977 (see "Index alphabétique", esp. 558, under "Sept"); QUIÉVREUX, in *RHPR* 33 (1953) 123-165; LIGHTFOOT, *St. John's Gospel*, 1956, pp. 11-26. See, however, the reaction of BULTMANN, *Johannes*, 1941, p. 78 n. 2 (ET: 1971, p. 112 n. 3): "Von der Bedeutung der Siebenzahl für Joh kann ich nichts bemerken"; cp. NEIRYNCK's reaction to BOISMARD in *Jean et les Synoptiques*, 1979, pp. 142-143 n. 275.

534. *Ibid.*, p. 180; cp. pp. 161-166, 181 (ET: p. 162; cp. pp. 144-148, 163).

535. *Ibid.*, pp. 181-182, esp. 181 (ET: pp. 163-164, esp. 163). See also p. 36 (ET: p. 25): "Weshalb übernehmen die einzelnen Redaktionen ihre Vorlagen, wenn sie mit deren Theologie nicht übereinstimmen? Warum entfalten sie nicht ausschliesslich ihre eigene Theologie?".

536. *Ibid.*, p. 181 (ET: p. 163). Cp. p. 188 n. 173 (ET: p. 103 n. 173). Schnelle refers

only apparent in 4,53, and the pre-Johannine miracle traditions were not characterized by the expectation that Jesus was a prophet like Moses. The expansive depiction of miracles is also redactional[537]. Finally, the absence of theological concepts such as dualism, eschatology, or the christology of the One-Sent is due to the literary form of the miracles and is therefore no indication for source material[538].

In his 1988 review of Carl J. Bjerkelund's study on the "Präzisierungssätze" (1987)[539], Schnelle again rejects the semeia hypothesis. He objects that Bjerkelund does not clearly treat the literary-critical consequences of his investigation. More particularly, he notes: "Consequences for source theories can be drawn from this work, for if Jn 2,11; 4,54 are comments by the evangelist then the main argument for a 'Zeichenquelle', the numbering, falls by the way"[540].

to STRACK-BILLERBECK, *Kommentar*, vol. I, 1922, pp. 593-596; LOHSE, *RGG*[3] 6 (1962), c. 1834; NICOL, *Sēmeia*, 1972, 79-80 (see above, p. 158); SCHWEIZER, *Jesus Christus*, 1968 ([2]1970; [3]1972), p. 127 (ET: 1975, p. 127; FT: 1975, p. 157); MARTYN, *History and Theology*, [2]1978, pp. 95-100; KLAUSNER, *Messianic Idea*, pp. 502-508; and VIELHAUER, *Erwägungen*, 1964, p. 159 (= 1965, p. 203). See also DELLING, *Botschaft und Wunder*, 1961, p. 390; cp. DE JONGE, in *NTS* 12 (1972-73) 246-270; *ETL* 49 (1973) 160-177 (= 1977, pp. 77-116, 49-76).

537. *Christologie*, p. 181; cp. pp. 182-185 (ET: p. 163; cp. pp. 164-167).

538. *Ibid.*, pp. 181-182 (ET: pp. 163-164).

539. C.J. BJERKELUND, *Tauta Egeneto. Die Präzisierungssätze im Johannesevangelium* (WUNT, 40), Tübingen, 1987. Bjerkelund examines a special group of "Randbemerkungen" or "Fussnoten": the Johannine *Präzisierungssätze*, "die wir so bezeichnet haben, weil sie sich auf die vorangehenden Aussagen beziehen und diese präzisieren" (p. 2). His list includes: 1,28; 2,11; 2,21-22; 4,54; 6,59; 7,39; 8,20, 10,6; 11,51; 12,16; 12,33; 12,41. Bjerkelund concludes: "die P-Sätze (stammen) aus ein- und derselben Traditionsschicht. ... Unsere Untersuchung unterstreicht die Bedeutung des Evangelisten für die Gestaltung des Evangeliums" (pp. 147, 148-149). On 2,11 and 4,54, see pp. 76-80, 83-87. For a comparison of this monograph with our study on the parentheses (see Bjerkelund's reference on pp. 5-6, n. 2), see F. NEIRYNCK, *Parentheses in the Fourth Gospel*, in *ETL* 65 (1989) 119-123, p. 122; see also VAN BELLE, *Les parenthèses johanniques*, 1992, pp. 1925-1927.

540. *TLZ* 113 (1988) 185-186, p. 186. – Schnelle again criticizes the signs source in *Perspektiven der Johannesexegese*, in *SNTU/A* 15 (1990) 59-72, p. 60: "Weder einzelne 'Quellenschriften' (z.B. die sogen. 'Semeia-Quelle') noch eine durchgehende 'Grundschrift' lassen sich methodisch exakt rekonstruieren. Da es keine Parellelüberlieferungen gibt, müssen ausschliesslich werkimmanenten Anhaltspunkte herangezogen werden. Sprachliche oder theologische Eigentümlichkeiten angeblicher 'Quellen' lassen sich aber nicht überzeugend herausarbeiten, wodurch die subjektive Einschätzung des Exegeten ein methodisch nicht mehr kontrollierbares Gewicht bekommt". Cp. his criticism in *Johannes und die Synoptiker*, in *FS F. Neirynck*, III, 1992, pp. 1799-1814, esp. 1801-1802. Dealing with the literary form "gospel", he refers to the hypotheses of Wilkens ("Grundevangelium"), Haenchen ("Wunderevangelium") and Fortna ("Zeichenevangelium"), who all accept that John found this literary form before him, but he adds immediately: "Die Plausibilität dieser Argumentation hängt natürlich an der Frage, ob es ein solches 'Zeichenevangelium' jemals gab!". Fortna's prejohannine combination of SQ and PQ in the signs gospel (SG) "lässt sich aber stilistisch nicht nachweisen" (with reference to J.M. Robinson, and his own observations in *Christologie*) and its existence is doubted by

In his commentary, Gerald Stephan SLOYAN (1988) is rather hesitant to accept sources and prefers to speak of "traditions"[541]. According to him the evangelist, or first author, adopted a "sayings tradition", a "signs tradition", a "final-days tradition", and a "risen-life tradition". He edited his own work in stages and the final editor gave us the gospel as we have it in hand[542]. Three years later, reviewing the Johannine scholarship in the last two decades, Sloyan seems to hold the same position: "The search for written sources which the next to last writer, the evangelist, might have employed continues, but not with the earlier assurance that tradition and redaction is the way that Jn, like the Synoptics, came to be"[543]. More particularly, he rejects U.C. von Wahlde's literary criticism: "In the source question, Von Wahlde's separating of a later edition of the signs gospel from the earliest edition ... promises to explain too much"[544].

Commenting on the first Cana miracle, J. Ramsey MICHAELS (1989) notes that "much has been written about a miracle and signs source used by the author of this Gospel" but he rejects the numbering of signs in 2,11 and 4,54 as an argument for the signs source: "the numbering of Jesus' miracles stops at two. The two Cana miracles form a pair distinct from all the rest. Neither of them gives rise to discourse or controversy. Both do exactly what the Gospel writer wants miracles to do. They lead

---

several authors: "Zudem wird in der neuesten Forschung die Existenz einer 'Zeichenquelle' immer mehr problematisiert, so dass ein 'Zeichenevangelium' als mögliche Vorstufe des Johannesevangelium entfällt" (p. 1802; with references to Bittner, Schnelle, Marguerat, Ruckstuhl-Dschulnigg, and Neirynck). According to Schnelle, John has taken up the literary form "Gospel" from Mark (p. 1805), in the passion narrative he used Markan compositional elements and integrated Lukan motifs (p. 1813). As in *Christologie*, he thinks that John orginated from several traditions: "Er wollte die Synoptiker weder verdrängen noch kritisieren oder überarbeiten. Vielmehr schuf er auf der Basis umfangreicher Traditionen ein Evangelium, das aus sich selbst verstanden werden will" (p. 1813). The similarities between John and the Synoptics must be explained by "Berührungen im vorredaktionellen Bereich", and "die von Johannes aufgenommenen Stoffe" which are "mit den Synoptikern verwandt, aber nicht annähernd identisch". For Schnelle, "Nähe erklärt sich aus dem Zusammenfliessen verschiedener Ströme mündlicher oder schriftlicher Überlieferung" (p. 1813), but he adds: "Wenn aber die johanneischen Traditionen die Synoptiker voraussetzen, sie damit in der johanneischen Schule rezipiert wurden, ist nicht einzusehen, warum der Evangelist Johannes sie nicht gekannt und aufgenommen haben soll" (p. 1814). In n. 72 (p. 1814), he reacts against Dauer: "Hier liegt m.E. die Hauptschwäche der Arbeiten von A. Dauer, der wiederholt ... eine Abhängigkeit johanneischer Traditionen von den Synoptiker konstatiert, dann aber dennoch mit der These einer 'Zwischenstufe' bzw. 'Quelle' eine Kenntnis der Synoptiker durch den Evangelisten ausschliesst".

541. G.S. SLOYAN, *John* (Interpretation), Atlanta, GA, 1988, p. 3.
542. *Ibid.*, pp. 4-5.
543. *What Are They Saying about John?*, New York – Mahwah, NJ, 1991, p. 97. Cf. pp. 28-49 ("The Question of Sources", with a presentation of the theories of Fortna, von Wahlde, Smith, Martyn, Lindars, J.A.T. Robinson, Cullmann, and Culpepper).
544. *Ibid.*, p. 97.

people to believe in Jesus and through faith in him to gain life (see 20:31)"[545]. Michaels, however, clearly accepts that it is "certain" that the evangelist "did not write in a vacuum but had a number of traditions available to him: for example, his own recollections as an eyewitness of much that happened, and collections of Jesus' sayings and miracles preserved orally or in writing"[546].

Also Kenneth GRAYSTON (1990) seems to be rather hesitant with respect to source theories. He notes that "it may be" that "the writer used various *sources* in composing the Gospel"[547], and regarding the "signs-source" and the "discourse-source", he says: "they might do something for the exegesis of the Gospel but little to explain its literary oddities"[548]. For Grayston, "the literary problems are not caused by accident or by inept use of sources, but by the need to try first this way, then that way to communicate the truth of the Gospel to Christians in need of help. The sometimes rough and unfinished state of the Gospel as we now read it is not evidence that the final editor overlooked necessary revisions, but that any edition of the Gospel must be responsive to the needs of its readers"[549] Thus, according to Grayston, "the most defensible and fruitful view is that the Gospel was composed in stages out of various components"[550]. He distinguishes[551]: (1) "A traditional passion narrative retold to display the dominating role of Jesus, with one explanatory passage (18.34-35) in typically Johannine style". (2) "A collection of narratives from various backgrounds: the Jewish Christians of Judaea and some from Galilee, former followers of John the Baptist, and Samaritan converts"; the evangelist made "flexible use of this material"[552]. (3) "At an early stage of composition, the end of ch. 14 may have moved at once to the beginning of ch. 18. John 13–14 is the final gathering of Jesus with 'his own who were in the world', and this

---

545. J.R. MICHAELS, *John* (NIBC, 4), Peabody, MA, 1989, p. 48. See also p. 80 (on 4,46-54).

546. *John*, p. 12. The evidence that he used Mark's Gospel is "far from conclusive". Michaels goes on to say: "For the most part, he seems to have written independently of the others, drawing on the same kinds of traditions – in some cases the very same traditions – that they used but putting these traditions to work in his own distinctive way to produce a unique portrait of Jesus" (p. 12).

547. K. GRAYSTON, *The Gospel of John* (Epworth Commentaries), London, 1990, p. xx.

548. *Ibid.*, p. xxi.

549. *Ibid.*, pp. xxii-xxiii.

550. *Ibid.*, pp. xxi.

551. *Ibid.*, pp. xxi-xxii.

552. Regarding the signs, Grayston notes: "There may be signs in this long section (1.19–12.50) that what we now read is the end result of earlier attempts to arrange the material in various ways; and it can be argued that some features were added to guard against unsatisfactory attitudes inside the Johannine community for which the Gospel was composed".

is the necessary farewell discourse". (4) Chapter 17. (5) Chapters 15 and 16 were provided, statements about the "advocate" were added to ch. 14, and references to the Spirit in 1,19–12,50 "were carefully subordinated to Jesus" in order to maintain the Johannine community "against hostility from outside and controversy within". (6) "A lively resurrection narrative in John 20". (7) Chapter 21, with "supplementary stories and instruction (vv. 2-19) which might equally well have appeared earlier in the Gospel".

According to Daniel MARGUERAT (1990) the semeia hypothesis does not take into account the diversity of the Johannine miracle stories[553]. With reference to Heekerens, Bittner, and Schnelle, he formulates the following objections against the semeia hypothesis[554]. (a) To postulate a christology concentrated on the miraculous and then to collect texts that correspond to this canon in order to reconstruct a source is begging the question[555]. Even if the signs source is limited to the miracle stories of chs. 1–12, it still contains a great diversity of literary forms[556]. (b) Regarding style, Marguerat agrees with Fortna and Nicol that the absence of Johannine characteristics is an indication of the traditional character of a text, but this does not immediately mean that we have

---

553. D. MARGUERAT, La "source des signes" existe-t-elle? Réception des récits de miracle dans l'évangile de Jean, in KAESTLI et al. (eds.), La communauté johannique, 1990, pp. 69-93, esp. 93. – In the same volume, C. RINIKER, Jean 6,1-21 et les évangiles synoptiques (pp. 41-67, esp. 59), defends that "la tradition johannique est clairement secondaire, plus tardive que la tradition synoptique. ... Cette tradition, l'évangéliste l'a eue à sa disposition sous une forme écrite" (cp. p. 60). On Marguerat contrast Riniker, see ZUMSTEIN, in the same volume, pp. 359-374, esp. 372-373.

554. La "source des signes", pp. 75-89: "La source des semeia: critique de l'hypothèse". For the references to Heekerens, Bittner, and Schnelle, see p. 77 n. 28.

555. Ibid., pp. 77-78: "La forme littéraire", esp. 77: "Postuler une christologie centrée sur le miraculeux, et collecter les textes répondant à ce canon pour constituer une source: l'opération, de mon point de vue, frise la pétition du principe".

556. Marguerat distinguishes between healing narratives (4,46-54; 5,1-9; 9,1-7; 11,32-44), gift miracles (2,1-11; 6,1-15), and a miracle of recognition (6,16-21), and sees no reason to assign all of them to the same source (p. 78). Against Heekerens's "Zeichen-Quelle", he notes: "Même la limitation d'une Zeichen-Quelle à trois récits (Jn 2, Jn 4 et Jn 21) ... ne fonde pas encore une certitude". He formulates four objections: "(1) les trois récits envisagés ne sont pas homogènes du point de vue de l'arrière-fond religieux; (2) son argument contextuel (ces récits ne sont pas suivis d'un discours christologique) devrait conduire à annexer Jn 6,16-21, pour la même raison; (3) la numérotation des deux premiers signes (2,11; 4,54) ne peut englober 21,14 qu'au prix d'une manipulation textuelle et en quittant la localisation à Cana; (4) Jn 21 ne relève pas de la même couche rédactionnelle que le corps de l'évangile". Moreover, Marguerat remarks that we have learned from Synoptic source criticism that Mt and Lk borrowed the miracle stories from different sources, and even in Johannine exegesis scholars like Boismard – Lamouille accept several sources (or traditions) for the miracle stories. With reference to Schnelle, he notes against Nicol (Sēmeia, 1972, pp. 15-16): "mais prouver la provenance traditionnelle ne fonde pas encore la thèse de l'unicité d'une source, qui doit avoir pour elle un 'Sitz im Leben' reconstituable" (p. 78 n. 34).

detected a homogeneous source with a style[557]. (c) Further, Marguerat does not think Fortna proves a clear geographical itinerary (from Galilee to Golgotha) for the source. His relocation of the healing of the lame man is especially debatable[558]. (d) The christological features of the supposed signs source, i.e., emphasis on the miraculous, Jesus' supernatural knowledge, and the miracles-signs as manifestations of divine glory, are also typical of the evangelist[559]. Moreover, "there is no divorce between belief and miracles" because the negative verdict on the unbelief of the people (12,37) can be interpreted instead as an invitation to belief[560]. Thus, σημεῖον is an "ambivalent concept" in John[561]. (e) Finally, the Johannine miracle stories do not belong to one particular religious tradition (Jewish or Hellenistic), but they go back to different traditions

557. *La "source des signes"*, pp. 79-80: "Le vocabulaire et le style". Marguerat thinks that the language of the group or school (sociolect) dominates individual language (idiolect). Therefore, in contrast to Schnelle (see above, p. 339 n. 530), he does not think that the presence of Johannine style characteristics in the miracle stories necessarily means that there is no signs source.

558. *Ibid.*, pp. 80-81: "Quelle structure?". For the place of the miracle of ch. 5 in Fortna's Gospel of Signs, see above, pp. 143 n. 5, 214.

559. *Ibid.*, pp. 81-85: "La question de la cohérence théologique"; cp. p. 93. For Marguerat, the heightening of the miraculous is traditional in the miracles of chs. 2, 6 and 9; but in those of chs. 4, 5, and 11 it must be ascribed to the evangelist. For the motif of Jesus' supernatural knowledge he refers especially to 5,6; cp. (a) 2,19-21; 4,35; 8,21; 13,1.19; 18,4.32; 19,28; (b) 16,19; (c) 6,15; 8,40; (d) 1,47-48; 2,24-25; 5,42; 6,64; 13,38. On the signs as revelation of the divine glory, he notes against Becker who considered the miracles of the source "Zeichen im Sinne der Transparenz der göttlichen Herrlichkeit Jesu" (*Johannes*, I, 1979, p. 118; ³1991, p. 140): "Mais de part et d'autre, dans la tradition et dans la rédaction, la δόξα est manifestée par l'agir de Jésus; elle se concrétise ici dans la croix, là dans le pouvoir thaumaturgique du Fils" (*La "source des signes"*, p. 83); see 1,14; 5,44; 7,18; 8,50.54; 11,4; 12,28; 13,31; 17,1-5.22.24.

560. *Ibid.*, pp. 83-84, esp. 84: "Ce verdict négatif porté sur l'incroyance de la foule devant l'activité de Jésus est une invitation faite au lecteur à nourir sa foi du récit des σημεῖα de Jésus. D'un divorce entre le croire et les signes, il n'est pas question ici". For John's critique on the signs, see esp. 4,48; 6,30. But with reference to SCHNELLE, *Christologie*, 1988, pp. 161-166 (ET: 1992, pp. 144-148; see above, p. 337), Marguerat notes that sign can lead to belief; cf. 2,23; 6,26; 7,31; 11,45.48; 12,11; see also 12,37-40 ("le fait que les σημεῖα accomplis devant la foule ne l'aient pas conduite à la foi est évalué comme un déficit"); 10,40-42. All these passages may be compared with 2,11 and 6,14. See also his reaction to Becker: "faut-il donc recevoir le quatrième évangile comme l'exposé de deux théologies qui s'excluent réciproquement? Notre étude montre que le rapport de l'évangéliste à la tradition (multiforme) des miracles est certes fait de critique, mais aussi d'*assentiment*" (p. 93).

561. *La "source des signes"*, pp. 84-85, esp. 85: "Il peut être dégradé et lié à une foi appelée au dépassement (2,23-24; 3,2-3). Mais l'évangéliste peut aussi en faire la dénomination synthétique de l'action révélatrice de Jésus (7,31; 12,37)". Thus, with reference to Schnelle (*Christologie*, pp. 164-165; ET: pp. 147-148), Marguerat rejects Becker's attempt to attribute the positive occurrences of σημεῖον to the source, and the negative occurrences to the evangelist: "la valorisation positive ou négative de σημεῖον ne coïncide pas avec un partage de couches littéraires" (p. 85).

preserved within the Johannine circle[562]. From an analysis of ch. 5, Marguerat concludes that the evangelist has taken up the miracle traditions to illustrate the symbolism of his discourses[563].

In his dissertation on Jn 12,35-50, published in 1990, Roman KÜH-SCHELM rejects the argumentation for the attribution of 12,37-38 to the signs source[564]. First, against Bultmann and Becker, who maintained that the two Isaiah quotations (vv. 37.40) can hardly have been written by one hand (the former is quoted literally from the LXX, while the latter does not use the LXX)[565], Kühschelm remarks that vv. 40-41 also quote the LXX literally (καὶ ἰάσομαι αὐτοῖς), and that, moreover, the evangelist has adopted the LXX-version of Is 53,1 (τίς ἐπίστευσεν) in his own summary (v. 37 οὐκ ἐπίστευον)[566]. Thus, it seems difficult to suppose, as Becker does, that all passages in which the Old Testament

---

562. *Ibid.*, pp. 85-87: "La quête de l'arrière-fond religieux". He distinguishes (pp. 85-86, esp. 86; cp. pp. 87, 93) a stream of tradition close to the Synoptics behind the miracles in chs. 4 and 6, and one more peculiar to the Johannine circle for those of chs. 2, 5, 9, and 11. See also pp. 87-89: "Plusieurs traditions plutôt qu'une source", esp. 87: "L'idée que la réception des récits de miracle s'est opérée par la relecture d'une source de semeia ne s'impose donc pas. Plutôt que d'une source documentaire unique, ne faut-il pas plutôt parler de *traditions diverses dans leur origine*, soit proches du fonds synoptique, soit autonomes? La tradition johannique des miracles présente en effet ... un paysage plus diffus que ne le conçoit le modèle d'une seule source – plus diffus, hétérogène et pluriel. L'attribution forfaitaire des récits de miracle chez Jean à une même source constitue une entreprise réductrice, que la diversité formelle, théologique et idéologique des textes incriminés conduit à ne pas ratifier. Il ne faut pas parler d'une source, mais de plusieurs courants traditionnels auxquels Jean a puisé". For the rejection of a θεῖος ἀνήρ christology and of the literary form aretalogy, he refers to Berger (p. 85).
563. *Ibid.*, pp. 72-75: "L'exemple de Jean 5"; pp. 89-92: "La réception des récits de miracles". Marguerat concludes: "les miracles offrent à la symbolique des discours johanniques une matérialité, une concrétisation historique, bref une incarnation à laquelle l'évangéliste n'a pas voulu renoncer"; cp. p. 93: "la réception des récits de miracle dans l'évangile indique *une trajectoire théologique* qui ne conduit pas des miracles aux discours de révélation, mais l'inverse. C'est à partir du canon herméneutique que constitue la haute christologie des discours que la tradition des miracles a été accueillie et relue. La réception des miracles dans l'évangile révèle la pratique pastorale de l'évangéliste, et sa conviction que les gestes de Jésus assurent à la symbolique des discours une indispensable incarnation".
564. R. KÜHSCHELM, *Verstockung, Gericht und Heil. Exegetische und bibeltheologische Untersuchung zum sogenannten "Dualismus" und "Determinismus" in Joh 12,35-50* (BBB, 76), Frankfurt/M, 1990 (diss. Wien, 1989-90; dir. J. Kremer), pp. 125-127, esp. 127: "Aufgrund unserer synchronen Vorarbeiten, die Beziehungen von V. 37-38 nach hinten wie vorne aufzeigten, dürfen wir resümieren: Da die literarkritischen Indizien für die Herkunft aus einer Semeiaquelle o.ä. überzogen scheinen bzw. auf einem (textlinguistisch) überholten Präjudiz beruhen, bleibt die Herkunftsfrage keineswegs 'hypothetisch', sondern ist zugunsten des Evangelisten zu entscheiden" (in reaction to BERGMEIER, *Glaube als Gabe nach Johannes*, p. 230: "Die Quellenfrage bleibt für 12,37f m.E. hypothetisch"). – Reviews: A. FUCHS, in *SNTU/A* 15 (1990) 173-174; X. LÉON-DUFOUR, in *RSR* 79 (1991) 291-293; R. SCHNACKENBURG, in *BZ* 35 (1991) 272-274.
565. *Verstockung*, p. 126.
566. *Ibid.*, p. 127.

quotation resembles the LXX do not stem from the evangelist[567]. Second, the presence of the ἵνα ... πληρωθῇ formula, used in the Gospel from 12,38 on, cannot be considered a valid source-critical criterion[568]. Third, while Bultmann and others consider the summary which mentions only the signs un-Johannine, because the evangelist is principally concerned with the theology expressed in the discourses and because the summary does not fit very well with Jesus' appeal of vv. 35-36a[569], Kühschelm maintains that the evangelist is interested in both words (v. 36) and deeds (v. 37)[570]. Fourth, against the notion that vv. 37-38 agree with the signs-source theology[571] – the verses explain explicitly the unbelief in the signs by reference to the Old Testament –, Kühschelm argues that these verses are more in line with the evangelist's criticism of miracle faith (cf., e.g., 4,48)[572]. Finally, Kühschelm stresses that a stylistic analysis of the verses shows the hand of the evangelist[573].

In the same year, without referring explicitly to the semeia hypothesis, Thomas M. DOWELL thinks that "in order to understand the Fourth Gospel there is no need for any source other than the Synoptic tradition"[574]. According to him, "far from being capricious and inexplicable, the additions, subtractions, and other modifications which were made to the Synoptic Gospels are intelligible as the deliberate response of an unknown Christian writer to Jewish challenges"[575]. Thus, e.g., in order to escape the charge that Jesus "casts out demons by the prince of demons" (Mt 9,34), John gives no exorcisms, and, although he does not ignore this charge, he undermines it "by repeating over and over again that God, the Father of Jesus, is the source of the supernatural power" (3,2; 5,19-21.36; 9,3-4; 10,24-25.31-32.37-38; 14,10)[576]. Further, Dowell considers 20,30-31 "an apologetic statement to a community which knows the Synoptic tradition. The writer is saying that he knows all those other stories which he has chosen to neglect, and

---

567. Cf. BECKER, *Johannes*, II, 1981, p. 409 ([3]1991, p. 476).

568. In reaction to Faure; cf. *Verstockung*, pp. 126 and 127.

569. *Ibid.*, p. 126.

570. *Ibid.*, p. 127: "Dass nach der 'Rede' V. 35-36c gerade das Semeia-Wirken Jesu in V. 37a resümiert wird, könnte auch für den Evangelisten sprechen, der Worte und Wunder häufig und absichtsvoll einander zuordnet".

571. *Ibid.*, p. 126.

572. *Ibid.*, pp. 126-127: "Der Inhalt spricht eher für die dem Evangelisten auch sonst geläufige (vgl. etwa 4,48) Korrektur und Kritik blossen Wunderglaubens" (with, in n. 33, references to Lona, Appold, and Fortna).

573. *Ibid.*, p. 127: "Der summarische Hinweis auf Jesu Wunderwirken ist ebenso Indiz für den Hauptverfasser wie stilistische Details von V. 37 (gen. abs., τοσοῦτος, ἔμπροσθεν, πιστεύειν εἰς), zumal objektive Kriterien für eine Zugehörigkeit zur Semeiaquelle hier nicht zu erbringen sind".

574. T.M. DOWELL, *Jews and Christians in Conflict: Why the Fourth Gospel Changed the Synoptic Tradition*, in *LouvSt* 15 (1990) 19-37, p. 36.

575. *Ibid.*, p. 20.

576. *Ibid.*, p. 28.

that he is also including new stories"[577], such as 2,1-11 and the raising of Lazarus. The first has no Synoptic parallel, but the second "seems to be inspired by the Synoptic material"[578]. Dowell repeated his thesis at the Leuven colloquy on "John and the Synoptics"[579]. Referring to 2,1-11 and 18,13-24, he argues, "There is, however, no need to limit the sources to the Synoptics and the [Jewish] arguments. His task of giving credibility to his account would be easier if he incorporated non-Synoptic material which was familiar to his readers and hearers"[580].

John W. PRYOR (1992) is "not at all convinced that John made use of a signs source for his gospel", and that Jn 20,30-31 (or parts of them) "formed the original conclusion to it. But even if they were the ending to a signs source, John has relocated them to the ending of his gospel"[581]. Regarding the signs in Jn, Pryor stresses that "John does have a positive attitude to them: they are a demonstration of the Messianic status of Jesus", and referring to Bittner, he states that "there is nothing unhistorical in John's theology of signs which bear witness to [Jesus'] status as Davidic Messiah"[582]. He thinks that "only two people need to be considered as being involved in the writing"[583]. First is the beloved disciple, who was "a South Palestinian disciple of Jesus" and "a witness to *some* of the incidents in the gospel". He was the "founding father of the communities behind the Johannine writings". Pryor calls him John or the evangelist. On the basis of "his own recollections, general oral tradition, and written accounts (perhaps even one or more of the Synoptic gospels), he created "over a period of many years ... the narratives and discourses which make up the gospel" with 20,30-31 as the conclusion. Second, "John worked with a faithful pupil/disciple", "an amanuensis collaborator". Pryor attributes to him the references to the Beloved Disciple ("though it is uncertain whether this was during

577. *Ibid.*, p. 28.
578. *Ibid.*, p. 28. Cf. Lk 10,38-42 and 16,19-31.
579. *Why John Rewrote the Synoptics*, in DENAUX (ed.), *John and the Synoptics*, 1992, pp. 453-457, esp. 457: "John's Gospel can be understood as the one-sided, idealized response to Jewish arguments based on the Synoptics; *this is sufficient* to explain satisfactorily the similarities and differences. When the Synoptic accounts were being challenged, John wrote to encourage Christians and strengthen their faith in the claim that 'Jesus is the Christ, the Son of God' (20,31, cf. Mt 16,16; 26,63)" (italics mine; instead of the italicized words the paper delivered at the Colloquy read: "no other sources are required...").
580. *Ibid.*, p. 457.
581. J.W. PRYOR, *John: Evangelist of the Covenant People. The Narrative and Themes of the Fourth Gospel*, London, 1992, p. 204 n. 223. – Cf. D. BALL, in *Themelios* 19 (1993-94), p. 14.
582. *Ibid.*, p. 136.
583. For his own literary theory see *ibid.*, pp. 3-4.

the initial writing of the gospel or after the BD's death") and 21,1-23 as well as a reference to his own person in 21,24-25. He is thus "responsible for the final form of the Fourth Gospel"[584].

Especially with reference to Bittner and Schnelle, Klaus-Michael BULL (1992) rejects Bultmann's semeia hypothesis and prefers to speak of a "Wundertradition"[585]. First, he finds it improbable that there was already a connection between the miracles tradition and the term σημεῖον at a pre-Johannine literary level. The starting-point for the evangelist's christological use of σημεῖον was not the signs source but the Old Testament[586]. Second, the tradition-historical background of the Johannine miracle stories is so heterogeneous that it is difficult to accept that the evangelist used a continuous "Semeia-Quelle"[587]. Moreover, the

584. *Ibid.*, p. 4. Pryor also mentions "five stages from Jesus to the Gospel of John": "1. Jesus – his authoritative words and deeds; 2. Traditions of Jesus known to the BD – either from his own memory or from oral and written traditions; 3. The BD's theological reflection upon and shaping of the traditions into narratives and discourses; 4. The BD's decision to write a gospel based on his theological reflections of many years; 5. The final editor's completion of the task" (p. 4).

585. K.-M. BULL, *Gemeinde zwischen Integration und Abgrenzung. Ein Beitrag zur Frage nach dem Ort der joh Gemeinde(n) in der Geschichte des Urchristentums* (BET, 24), Frankfurt/M - Bern - New York - Paris, 1992 (diss. Rostock, 1990-91; dir. H.-F. Weiss), pp. 79-92: "Die Wundertradition im Johannesevangelium und ihre Aufnahme durch den Evangelisten"; see p. 105: "Der Evangelist setzt einen breiten Traditionsstrom voraus, der die irdische Wirksamkeit Jesu und seine Passion im Rahmen judenchristlicher Überlieferung versteht. Hier is zuallererst an die Wundertradition zu denken, die die Erwartung eines (eschatologischen) Propheten wie Mose aufnimmt, bzw. Züge der Messiaserwartung (nach Is 11) auf Jesus übertragt".

586. *Ibid.*, pp. 80-85, see esp. 85: "Als Fazit dieses ersten Gedankenganges lässt sich festhalten, dass eine dem Evangelisten auf der literarischen Ebene vorgegebene Verknüpfung von Wundertradition und 'σημεῖον' nicht wahrscheinlich ist. Die traditionsgeschichtliche Fragestellung zeigte hingegen, dass der Terminus 'σημεῖον' auf dieser Ebene durchaus in den Kontext der Wundertradition gehört. Darüber hinaus zeigte sich eine schon im Alten Testament zu belegende Verbindung zwischen 'σημεῖον' und letztgültiger Gottesoffenbarung. Hier boten sich dem Evangelisten Anknüpfungspunkte für seine christologische Verwendung des Begriffs".

587. *Ibid.*, pp. 85-87. For 6,1-15, Bull notes "ein starker Einfluss alttestamentlicher Vorstellungen" (p. 85); he refers to Ex 16,1-36; Num 11,6-9; Deut 8,3-16; 1 Kings 17,7-16; 2 Kings 4,42-44, but concludes: "Dominierend sind aber die Bezugnahmen auf die Exodustradition, so dass es durchaus sachgemäss scheint, wenn der Evangelist gerade hier die Diskussion um den Titel ὁ προφήτης anklingen lässt" (p. 86). "Weniger deutlich sind die alttestamentlichen Bezüge" in 2,1-11 and 4,46-54; but he refers to 1 Kings 17 and, for the numbering, to the masoretic text of Ex 4,8. For Bull, however, "es wäre allerdings ein Kurzschluss, wollte man die gesamte Wundertradition des Johannesevangeliums von der Erwartung des endzeitlichen Propheten (nach Dtn 18,15.18 oder Mal 3,1.23f) her verstehen. Das verbieten schon das Fehlen aller typologischen Anspielungen in den übrigen Wundergeschichten". For the other miracle stories, Bull refers to the influence of Jes 11,2-31; 42,1.6-7 and 61,1-2 (see esp. Jn 7,31; 9,22; 11,27; 20,31): "Ausgehend von diesem Befund, möchte ich annehmen, dass die Wundertradition, die der Evangelist in sein Evangelium aufnahm, schon vor ihm durch eine Tradition überformt bzw. sogar erst hervorgebracht worden ist, die in Jesus den (davidischen) Messias sah" (p. 87).

argument from the numbering of signs must be rejected and the assumption that there was a source in which all miracles were numbered is "ein reines Postulat"[588]. But for Bull this does not mean that John had no literary sources; he reckons with "eine schriftliche Vorlage" for at least the miracle stories of chs. 2, 4, and 6[589]. Third, with regard to belief in signs, Bull rejects the presumed tension between the source and the evangelist[590]. (a) In the conclusion of the gospel, the evangelist clearly established a positive relation between signs and belief; this means that we cannot ascribe similar formulations (2,11b.23; 6,2) to a source. The evangelist himself stressed the epiphanic character of the miraculous (2,3b-5; 9,2-5; 11,4.40.42), regards the signs as revelation of Jesus' δόξα, which is the δόξα τοῦ θεοῦ, and he emphazises Jesus' miraculous foreknowledge (5,6; 6,6.15a; 11,11)[591]. (b) Moreover, the evangelist equates the σημεῖα with the ἔργα τοῦ θεοῦ (9,3; 5,17-23.36)[592]. According to him, the signs reveal Jesus as the eschatological prophet-like-Moses and as Messiah. Because these terms, however, can be politically misinterpreted (6,14-15), he complements the christological title ὁ χριστός, used by preference in his community, by the title υἱὸς τοῦ θεοῦ (e.g., 1,49; 11,27; 20,31). This christological title seems to him the most appropriate to express the character of the one sent by God[593]. Finally, Bull thinks that for the evangelist belief is impossible without signs (so 4,48), but they do not lead unambiguously to belief (11,35)[594].

For the rejection of the semeia hypothesis in recent Johannine research, see also:

---

588. *Ibid.*, pp. 87-88.

589. *Ibid.*, pp. 88-89, esp. 89: "Der gemeinsame Traditionshintergrund der Wundererzählungen in Joh 2; 4 und 6 ... gibt zu der Vermutung Anlass, dass es sich nicht um zwei Quellen, sondern nur um eine gehandelt habe, aber das läss sich nicht beweisen". With regard to ch. 6, he remarks: "In Kap. 6 is besonders auffällig dass die Abfolge Speisungsgeschichte – Seewandel genau der bei Mk entspricht"; to this *Vorlage*, Bull also attributes Peter's confession, but he notes: "aber gerade an dieser Stelle haben so viele Hände mitgewirkt, dass eine sichere Entscheidung darüber nicht möglich scheint" (p. 88). With regard to the miracle stories of ch. 2 and 4, he notes that the redactional additions (2,1b.3b-5.9b.c?; 4,46a.48-49.52-53) are so easily separable from the tradition that he must accept "eine schriftliche Vorlage" in which 2,12 was already the link between the two miracle stories. He also considers the possibility that 5,1-16 comes from a "schriftliche Vorlage". But in the other miracles stories "fehlen eindeutige Indizien für schriftliche Vorlagen völlig. Sollte es dergleichen dennoch gegeben haben, halte ich eine auch nur halbwegs sichere Rekonstruktion für unmöglich" (p. 89).

590. *Ibid.*, pp. 89-92.

591. *Ibid.*, p. 90.

592. *Ibid.*, p. 90.

593. *Ibid.*, p. 91.

594. *Ibid.*, pp. 91-92.

595. François Vouga, *The Johannine School: A Gnostic Tradition in Primitive Christianity?*, in *Bibl* 88 (1988) 371-385, esp. p. 381: "The *Semeia-Quelle* probably never existed"; cp. *Le quatrième évangile comme interprète de la tradition synoptique: Jean 6*, in Denaux, *John and the Synoptics*, 1992, pp. 261-279, esp. 270-271: "Le postulat de cet évangile des signes n'explique en effet ni le manque d'unité formelle des récits de miracles johanniques, ni leur rapport littéraire remarquablement variables aux parallèles synoptiques. Il n'explique guère non plus le fait que la discussion herméneutique de la rédaction johannique sur les signes s'inscrive dans la continuité thématique et conceptuelle directe des évangiles synoptiques. Il s'ensuit qu'à cette hypothèse devrait en être préférée une autre qui répond de surcroît aux exigences du principe déjà mentionné d'économie des hypothèses, et qui est tout simplement celle-ci: c'est la rédaction johannique qui a composé la séquence des sept signes. Pour ce faire, elle a repris quatre scénarios de la tradition synoptique, dont un double (Jn 4,46-54; 5,1-9a; 6,1-21; 9,6-7), parce qu'ils étaient susceptibles, entre autres, d'une interprétation métaphorique à partir des theologumena de la tradition johannique (Jésus est la vie, le pain descendu du ciel et la lumière du monde). Elle les a encadrés de deux compositions de son cru, construites en forme de dialogues (Jn 2,1-11; 11,1-44). La liberté dont la rédaction johannique use avec sa documentation ne fait guère difficulté: comme on l'a vu déjà, une telle liberté est attestée à l'intérieur de la tradition synoptique elle-même par Luc, qui réécrit en grande partie les récits de miracles qu'il reprend pourtant, selon les consensus largement admis, de Marc. Un autre précurseur de cette liberté est sans doute l'évangile de Marc lui-même, dont le mot-à-mot des traditions est souvent bien difficile à reconstituer. La difficulté que l'hypothèse d'une dépendance littéraire des récits de signes johanniques par rapport aux évangiles synoptiques doit prendre en compte n'est pas la liberté de la rédaction johannique à l'égard de ses sources, mais, au contraire et bien plutôt, la fidélité qu'elle conserve partiellement à leur égard, en particulier en Jn 5,1-9a et 6,1-21". See also p. 279 n. 20

596. Anthony Tyrrell Hanson, *The Prophetic Gospel: A Study of John and the Old Testament*, Edinburgh, 1991, who stresses that John's narrative is heavily influenced by the Old Testament, mostly from the Septuagint but also sometimes by the targumic traditions, notes (pp. 9-11, esp. 9): "The main objection to the theory of a separate signs-source, as contrasted with the tradition that merely included miracle stories, is that the signs in the Gospel seem to be of such diverse origins"; see also p. 10: "we can quote weighty authority for the view that there never was a 'signs-source' and that it is a fruitless task to seek different theologies in different alleged sources behind the Gospel", with references to de Jonge, Olsson, Lindars, Hengel, and Vouga.

597. Margaret Davies, *Rhetoric and Reference in the Fourth Gospel* (JSNT SS, 69), Sheffield, 1992, pp. 260-261, esp. 261: "Recents attempts by Fortna (1970) and Nicol (1972) to define the signs source are not convincing (see Ruckstuhl 1977)".

598. Jeffrey A. Trumbower, *Born from Above: The Anthropology of the Gospel of John* (HUT, 29), Tübingen, 1992 (diss. Chicago, IL, 1989: dir. H.D. Betz), pp. 61-62, esp. 62: "The claim about the evangelist's understanding of the signs can be made independently of the decision taken with regard to the 'signs' source".

599. Johan Konings, *The Dialogue of Jesus, Philip and Andrew in John 6,5-9*, in Denaux (ed.), *John and the Synoptics*, 1992, pp. 523-534, describes the dialogue in 6,5-9 as "a coherent Johannine redaction based on the Synoptic feeding stories and the OT narratives of Moses and Elisha, which explain most of the differences between John and the Synoptic narration" (p. 533). For Konings, "Synoptic dependence is fairly certain" for Jn 6,5-7 (pp. 528-531), but he concedes that "the question is not so clear" for 6,8-9 (pp. 531-533). Nevertheless, he thinks that "it is still less hypothetic to explain John from the Synoptic texts than to postulate a para- or pre-Synoptic document. The Elisha-reminiscences can better be situated at the level of the redaction than of the source" (p. 533). In reaction to the semeia hypothesis, Konings stresses that the reference to the miracle-prophet Elisha, generally considered a trait of the source, "may be the concern of the

redactor, who tries to show how the greatest of prophets, uniting in himself Moses, Elijah, Elisha etc., has been misunderstood by the people (6,14-15)" (p. 533). Also the solemn opening words in 6,5, which express very well the initiative and sovereignty of Jesus' action, are for Konings "the work of the redactor rather than a source characteristic" (p. 528). For the rejection of the θεῖος ἀνήρ presentation in the semeia hypothesis see p. 529. On p. 526 n. 23, Konings refers to his earlier article, *The Pre-Markan Sequence in Jn, VI: A Critical Re-Examination*, in SABBE (ed.), *L'évangile selon Marc*, 1974 (²1988), pp. 147-177, in which he has demonstrated, with respect to the feeding miracle and the walking on the sea, that the order postulated by Achtemeier, Keck, Kertelge, and H.-W. Kuhn for pre-Markan aretalogies cannot be established with any certainty by reference to Jn 6; the scheme of Jn 6, in fact, betrays the influence of the Synoptic Gospels (Mark and Matthew) in their redactional state. Therefore, he concludes: "We can say that no convincing stylistic or theological indications are found in the Fourth Gospel in favor of a pre-Johannine collection of miracles characterized by a θεῖος ἀνήρ christology. So John offers no support for the hypothesis that Mark was acquainted with an analogous collection. Rather than finding in the Fourth Gospel a witness for the pre-redactional stages of the synoptic tradition, we believe that John has often brought to fulfillment a development already perceptible in the synoptic gospels" (p. 176).

600. Thomas L. BRODIE, *The Quest for the Origin of John's Gospel: A Source-Oriented Approach*, New York – Oxford, 1993, pp. 25-29, esp. 26: "There are two fundamental flaws in the various efforts to reconstruct a sign source: they do not use reliable criteria, and above all, they do not sufficiently consider whether the predecessor was Mark"; cp. *The Gospel according to John: A Literary and Theological Commentary*, New York, 1993, p. 231.

601. Ismo DUNDERBERG, *Johannes und die Synoptiker. Studien zu Joh 1–9* (AASF DHL, 69), Helsinki, 1994, p. 191: "Da Joh 4.46b-54 und Joh 6 laut dieser Untersuchung nicht auf die vorjoh Tradition zurückzuführen sind, ist zugleich die traditionelle Semeiaquellenhypothese in Frage gestellt. Doch ist die Möglichkeit nicht von der Hand zu weisen, dass den beiden Heilungsgeschichten der Grundschrift (Joh 5,1-18*; 9.1-41*) eine Quellenschrift zugrundeliegt. In jedem Fall ist die einfache Heilungsgeschichte in Joh 5,2-9c* schon vor dem Verfasser der Grundschrift mit der Sabbatthematik erweitert worden (Joh 5,9d-16)".

To conclude our survey of the opponents of the semeia hypothesis, it is worthy of note that most reviewers of Fortna's *Predecessor*, although they appreciate and praise Fortna's work as "an excellent and highly sophisticated application of redaction critical method"[602], have rejected his reconstruction of the signs source. Besides the negative reactions noted above[603], we can refer to John PAINTER

---

602. F.F. SEGOVIA (see below, p. 355 n. 625), p. 749. Cp., e.g., R. KYSAR (see below, p. 356 n. 629), p. 187: "Still, Fortna has masterfully defended and elaborated his contention for a source for the composition of the Fourth Gospel"; K. MATSUNAGA (see below, p. 356 n. 630), p. 283: "There is no doubt that this book demonstrates scholarly ability and solid discipline as Fortna undertakes to prove his thesis that the Fourth Gospel depended on 'the gospel of signs'"; J. PAINTER (see below, p. 353 n. 604), p. 346: "In spite of these differences, I greatly admire his [i.e., Fortna's] book"; D.M. SMITH, in *JBL* 109 (1990) 352-355, p. 355: "we are clearly in debt to Fortna for the product of mature scholarship, which effectively raises many important questions about the theology and interpretation of the Fourth Gospel, as well as its redaction-history".

603. See above, pp. 330-331 (Burge), 176-177 (Lindars), [214-]215 n. 374, [218-]219 n. 396 (Neirynck), 309-312 (Ruckstuhl), 317-318 (Smalley), and 262-266 (Thyen). See the positive reaction, however, of D.M. Smith (see above, pp. 241-242) and D.W. Kuck (see above, p. 242).

(1990)[604]. Painter does not agree with Fortna's claim that the evangelist's great respect for his source "gave rise to the seams in the Gospel, providing the redaction critic with the opportunity of recovering the source, following the same path as the original readers of the Gospel. They started with knowledge of the source and read the Fourth Gospel (4G) as the legitimate interpretation of it"[605]. But Painter points out the inconsistency of Fortna's argument. It seems in fact to be the first reader's respect for the source that limited the evangelist[606]. Nevertheless, Fortna says that in rewriting the source, the evangelist "is willing at points to break with the source's theology, qualifying, even correcting it boldly"[607] and to modify its order radically[608]. The evangelist even rewrites sections so radically that reconstructions are impossible[609]. For Painter, "these qualifications surely put the recovery of the source in jeopardy"[610]. Further, he discusses Fortna's starting point, "the all-but-intolerable tension between *narrative* and *discourse*"[611] and objects that Fortna does not even consider the possibility "that the evangelist is largely responsible for the discourses, developing them freely on the basis of the narrative source and making use of other fragments of tradition"[612] but simply concludes that

604. J. PAINTER, in *Pacifica* 3 (1990) 344-346, pp. 344-345. See also the discussion on "The Signs Source" in *The Quest for the Messiah: The History, Literature and Theology of the Johannine Community*, Edinburgh, 1991, pp. 80-87 (on Fortna, see esp. 81-82). On pp. 82-84, he especially discusses von Wahlde's monograph and particularly rejects his two primarily linguistic criteria (two separate terms for the Jewish authorities and for Jesus' miracles), which von Wahlde considers an "objective" basis for his source criticism: "The main point to be made is that von Wahlde's so called 'objective criteria' are far from objective. He has not here even limited himself to formal characteristics. In each instance value judgments are involved determining the criteria and, as has been shown, serious objections can be raised concerning each of his two 'primary linguistic criteria'. The reason for this failure is that von Wahlde is mistaken (in my view) in thinking that the versions of Jn were produced by different 'authors'". Review: P.W. ENSOR, in *EvQ* 65 (1993) 163-165.

605. *Pacifica* 3, p. 344. Cf. FORTNA, *Predecessor*, p. 6.

606. *Pacifica* 3, p. 344. Cf. FORTNA, *Predecessor*, p. 56 n. 119: "At the very least, 4E [= the Fourth Evangelist] knows the respect paid to it by the pre-Johannine author's readers, so as not to dare openly to rewrite it".

607. FORTNA, *Predecessor*, p. 56, 8, 223.

608. *Ibid.*, p. 79 n. 179. With regard to the insertion of Jn 21,1-14 as the third sign in the source, Painter (*The Quest for the Messiah*, p. 81), says that this cannot be proved "with any degree of certainty on the basis of evidence": "His [Fortna's] hypothesis presupposes a rather inept evangelist who allowed the numbering of the first two signs to remain while excluding the third and removing the numbering on the remaining signs. He also referred to other signs which upset the numbering of the first two (Jn 2.23-25; 3.2). It seems easier to refer to the two numbered signs simply as the two Cana signs. They are numbered because of the focus on Cana which the evangelist wishes to highlight" (pp. 81-82).

609. FORTNA, *Predecessor*, pp. 149, 162, 164.

610. *Pacifica* 3, pp. 344-345, esp. 345.

611. FORTNA, *Predecessor*, p. 1.

612. *Pacifica* 3, p. 346. Cp. *The Quest for the Messiah*, p. 86: "Bultmann's (and Fortna's) theory concerning the signs source breaks down because it presupposes that the

"so far a precise way to explain the discourses' provenance and development has not been found"[613]. For Painter, "the evangelist was working freely with source material developing themes in various ways, via sign and sign elaborated by dialogue or discourse, or by discourse alone"[614]. Painter concludes that Fortna's "book has tended to make the signs source hypothesis less persuasive"[615]; he does not think that "anything like SG ever existed"[616]. Painter's own position would be that the evangelist used a "Synoptic-like" tradition, the term Fortna uses to describe the tradition underlying SG[617]. Working with this tradition, the evangelist "shaped the Gospel in a situation very much like Fortna (and Martyn) have described"[618]. For Painter, "the Gospel itself was shaped in a number of stages, one of theses prior to the breach with the synagogue, and another subsequent to that event"[619], but he stresses that in the first stage, in contrast to Fortna's SG, narrative and discourse were already united[620].

Christoph NIEMAND (1990) considers the list of stylistic links between PQ and SQ too small and "wenig aussagekräftig" to prove that the two

narrative source was free from discourse. While this was probably true of independent narrative stories it seems highly likely that narrative and discourse were woven together from the beginning of the Johannine development. Rather than a Signs Gospel the evangelist appears to have begun with a loose collection of traditional-stories, perhaps mainly miracle stories". See also pp. 90-91.

613. FORTNA, *Predecessor*, p. 3.

614. *The Quest for the Messiah*, p. 91.

615. *Pacifica* 3, p. 346.

616. *Ibid.*, p. 346.

617. *Ibid.*, p. 346; cp. *The Quest for the Messiah*, pp. 86-87: "Thus the view that the evangelist was working with Synoptic-like tradition (including miracle stories) and, in a number of stages, weaving it into its present form is an alternative to the distinctive signs source hypothesis"; p. 86: "Rather than a Signs Gospel the evangelist appears to have begun with a loose collection of tradition stories, perhaps mainly miracle stories". Painter summarizes his own approach on pp. 90-93; see esp. 90: "An alternative to an approach based on the delineation of various sources is to recognize the source of the Synoptic tradition in the BD and to allow for its distinctive character being formed in the history of the Johannine community through the interpretative influence of the evangelist". For his older studies on Jn, in which he has been building his hypothesis, see below, n. 619 and *Bibliography*.

618. *Pacifica* 3, p. 346.

619. *Ibid.*, p. 346. Cp. *NTS* 35 (1989) 421-450, p. 422: "The evidence suggests that a series of editions expanded the Gospel in various ways". Painter worked this out in several articles: *AustBR* 28 (1980) 21-38; *NTS* 27 (1980-81) 525-543; *AustBR* 31 (1983) 45-62; *NTS* 30 (1984) 460-474; *JSNT* 28 (1986) 31-61; *AustBR* 35 (1987) 28-34; *NTS* 35 (1989) 421-450: BEUTLER – FORTNA, *The Shepherd Discourse*, 1991, pp. 53-74.

620. *Pacifica* 3, p. 346. In the first edition of the gospel, the evangelist made significant use of the quest story genre, which "was eminently suitable in appealing to those the evangelist perceived as searchers for the truth" and the rejection story genre. Cf. *The Quest for the Messiah*, p. 86. See esp. his articles in *JSNT* 36 (1989) 17-46; 41 (1991) 33-70; DENAUX (ed.), *John and the Synoptics*, 1992, pp. 498-506; *FS F. Neirynck*, III, 1992, pp. 1869-1887.

layers had already been joined, as Fortna claims, when the fourth evangelist used them[621]. Moreover, Niemand thinks that Fortna's reconstruction of the pre-Johannine tradition is too simple and too hypothetical[622]. More particularly, he rejects his description of the theology of both the source and the Johannine redaction. According to Fortna, the source's theology is simple and univocal, whereas that of the redaction contains all Johannine themes[623]. Such an opposition between a *minimum* and a *maximum*, however, does not give a real differentiated picture of Johannine theology and community, and, therefore, Niemand prefers the models which describe the origin of the gospel in multiple stages[624]. Fernando F. SEGOVIA (1990) takes issue with the use of aporias as the basic key to the separation of the layers: "not all aporias are equally evident or convincing"[625]. Further, he cannot accept that "the early stages of the Fourth Gospel included only narrative material"; Fortna's over-emphasized distinction between narrative and discourse, the former being "earthly" and "unspiritual", the latter being "unearthly" and "spiritual", is "far more problematic than helpful"[626]. For Segovia, "the resulting contrast of the two narratives in question, source and redaction, is given too neat an either/or formulation: the former is simple, extremely focused, and unidimensional; the latter is quite complex, open-ended, and multidimensional". He also objects that "the literary

621. C. NIEMAND, in *SNTU* 15 (1990) 176-178, p. 177.

622. "Bei einem Gesamtentwurf zum Verständnis des vierten Evangeliums, der in so hohem Masse *konstruktiv (konstruiert?)* und synthetisch ist und wo die verschiedensten Einzelbeobachtungen und Einzelbefunde so mutig-vereinfachend in das gewählte Modell integriert werden wie hier, entsteht gleichermassen 'Verärgerung' wie Bewunderung: Zu schnell schreitet der Autor von einer kritisierbaren Entscheidung zur darauf aufbauenden nächsten!". But he adds: "Andererseits, will man in der gegenwärtigen differenzierten Forschungslage ... nicht überhaupt auf Gesamtdarstellungen verzichten, *muss* die kühne Grosszügigkeit des konstruktiven Modells erlaubt sein" (p. 178).

623. "In allen Bereichen wird die Position der Quelle praktisch als völlig linear und univok angenommen und auf das Mindestmass des im joh Rahmen möglichen reduziert. ... Demgegenüber steht das voll entwickelte Feld der joh Themen – mit all seinen Aporien – auf der Stufe des Evangelisten: Aber zu *dieser* Erkenntnis, dass sich jegliche Vollgestalt *ab ovo* entwickelt, hätte man weder Literar- noch Redaktionskritik gebraucht!" (p. 178). Niemand especially refers to Fortna's description of the source's "single-minded christology" and its notion of faith (cf. *Predecessor*, pp. 226-228 and 235-237).

624. *SNTU* 15, p. 178 (with reference to the commentaries of Brown, Schnackenburg and Becker). In *Die Fusswaschungserzählung des Johannesevangeliums. Untersuchungen zu ihrer Entstehung und Überlieferung im Urchristentum* (Studia Anselmiana, 114), Roma, 1993 (diss. Linz), pp. 409-410, Niemand distinguishes three stages in the composition of the Gospel: "die älteste Tradition", "die joh Erstbearbeitung", "die joh Letztbearbeitung". On his skepticism with regard to source reconstructions, see p. 412: "Bezüglich des Versuches, solche Traditionskerne [e.g., 13,4-5.9-10abc preceded by 'eine verlorene Einleitung'] *untereinander* zu grösseren Quellenschriften und Vorlagdokumenten zu verbinden, bin ich skeptischer".

625. F.F. SEGOVIA, in *CBQ* 52 (1990) 748-749, p. 749.

626. *Ibid.*, p. 749. Cf. FORTNA, *Predecessor*, pp. 1-2; cp. p. 3.

question of genre is pursued in an extremely theological fashion: that which 'proclaims' the good news is gospel, a category which further admits of degrees depending on the extent and nature of the proclamation involved". After asking whether such a detailed knowledge of the gospel's process of composition is necessary to understand the text, Segovia concludes that the overall proposal of Fortna's book strikes him "as ultimately too massive, too problematic, too unnecessary – especially now when the discipline finds itself in the very midst of the literary critical explosion"[627]. Also, Michael FITZPATRICK (1990) is not convinced of the existence of the signs source. With reference to Lindars he regards the source "a 'pale ghost' of the Gospel itself"[628]. In line with his earlier skepticism toward Fortna's source theory, Robert KYSAR (1990), who defends a signs source "in the narrower sense", notes: "Critics will challenge many of Fortna's distinctions between source and redaction and his heavy dependence on the aporias as a criterion for detecting source and redaction. His methodology may also be faulted insofar as he sometimes gives too little attention to the discourses of the Fourth Gospel in determining how the Fourth Evangelist differed from the author of the source"[629]. For Kikuo MATSUNAGA (1991), Fortna's SG, in which SQ and PQ were already joined together, is "not self-evident"[630]. The crucial problem for him is that PQ was based on the glory of the Cross and not on humiliation and redemption as in the paradosis of 1 Cor 15,3-4 and in the Gospel of Mark. This would mean that there were "in the first fifty or sixty years of the early church ... two streams of Christian circles (churches); one had its center in the redemptive interpretation of the Cross and the other in the glorious interpretation of the Cross" and that the Fourth Evangelist "united the two streams into one and the 'early catholic Church' ('Frühkatholizismus')". According to Matsunaga, "we have to be cautious" about such a dichotomy[631] and such a description of the origin of the Fourth Gospel according to the Hegelian pattern, thesis-antithesis-synthesis[632]. Moreover, Matsunaga

---

627. *CBQ* 52, p. 749. For Segovia's recent studies from the "new" literary-critical point of view, see the *Bibliography*.

628. M. FITZPATRICK, in *AustBR* 38 (1990) 84-85, p. 85. For Lindars, see above, pp. 174-177.

629. R. KYSAR, in *Interpr* 44 (1990) 186-187, p. 187. On Kysar, see also above, pp. 189-193.

630. K. MATSUNAGA, in *Bibl* 72 (1991) 282-286, p. 284.

631. Matsunaga notes that "such a dichotomy fits well with the conflict between Paul and his opponents in the congregation at Corinth" (p. 285).

632. *Ibid.*, p. 285. Matsunaga agrees that there is "a tension between the beloved disciple, whose witness is the authority of this Gospel, and Peter" and that "it is possible that the Johannine church was different from churches which depended on the authority of Peter or the Twelve Apostles", but he finds it "difficult to suppose any hostility between the beloved disciple and Peter or between the Johannine church and the Petrine church as far as the text of the JG is concerned" (p. 285).

cannot accept that SQ and PQ, and therefore SG, had no eschatological concern. For him, "it would seem that the eschatological scheme was potentially laid in the sign-story itself"[633].

---

633. *Ibid.*, p. 286. For Matsunaga, the concept of Jesus' divine sonship, proved by the nature of sign as messianic event, "was closely connected with the Old Testament and the Jewish messianic expectation".

CHAPTER VI

EVALUATION OF THE SEMEIA HYPOTHESIS

I. THE HYPOTHESIS SUMMARIZED

The roots of Johannine source criticism can be traced to J.C.R. Ecker-mann (1796)[1], who perceived a tension between narratives and discourses and hypothesized that John the disciple wrote down Jesus' discourses and, after John's death, one of his disciples added narratives and a chronological framework. Like Eckermann, Weisse and Wendt thought that the discourses are the oldest part of the Gospel. Beginning with J.M. Thompson the situation was reversed. He considered the narrative portions in chs. 1–12 the oldest element in the Gospel: the evangelist used a narrative gospel source with 20,30-31 as its conclusion. Thompson's source can be compared with E. Meyer's *Sonderquelle* and with W. Bauer's theory that the evangelist used a written non-Synoptic tradition. The pre-Johannine source was more clearly defined by Faure as a *Wunderbuch* and was given its "classic form" by Bultmann as part of his complex literary theory. The opinion that the narratives are incompatible with the discourses led Bultmann to the assumption that the evangelist used a σημεῖα-*Quelle* and a passion source for the narrative parts and an *Offenbarungsreden* source for the discourses. For Bultmann, the σημεῖα-*Quelle* was primarily a *collection* of seven miracles lying behind the narrative material of the first part of the Gospel (chs. 1–12): **2,1-11.12; 4,46-54; 5,1-18; 6,1-15.16-21; 9,1-41; 11,1-44**; the source concluded with **12,37-38** and **20,30-31**. Several later authors limit the source to these miracle stories. Schnackenburg, however, included **21,1-14** and he even thought that the source could have had two accounts of a miraculous draught of fish. Moreover, he believed, like Faure, Broome, and Buchanan, that the source contained still other miracles not taken up by John. Some proponents of the semeia hypothesis, however, think that the source did not contain one or two of the seven stories in John: 2,1-11 (Mack, Crossan); 4,46-54 (Crossan); 5,1-18 (Reim, Crossan); 6,1-21 (Faure, Broome); 11,1-44 (Bammel, Mack).

Bultmann himself expanded the source with the *Vorlage* of **1,35-50** (see also Hartke, Fortna, Becker, Nicol, Schulz, Teeple, Reim, von

---

1. For references to the authors mentioned in the first part of this chapter, the reader can consult the Index of Names (the numbers in bold print in the Index refer to the pages where the authors are discussed).

Wahlde, Gnilka, H.-J. Kuhn, Wöllner, Ashton, Backhaus; cp. before Bultmann: Spitta, Meyer); **4,4-42** (Hartke, Fortna, Becker, Nicol, Teeple, Gnilka, Wöllner, von Wahlde; cp. Soltau, Meyer, Bauer); **7,1-13** (Hartke, Becker, Teeple; cp. Bauer); and **7,19-24** (Hartke, Becker, Teeple, Attridge, Kotila, H. Weiss; cp. Faure, Bauer). He hesitated to include **10,40-42**, but for Bammel, this passage is "the very end" of the source, which dealt with the Baptist and his circle. For Becker, too, the source treats the relation with the rival Baptist community and he includes 10,40-42 (Hartke, Teeple, Smith, von Wahlde) together with **1,19-34** (cp. Hartke, Fortna, Reim, Teeple, Smith [1,19-21], Gnilka, von Wahlde, Ashton) and **3,22-30** (Hartke, Teeple, von Wahlde). Other passages added to the source are: **1,6-7** (Hartke, Fortna); **3,1-2** (Hartke, Fortna 1970, Teeple, von Wahlde; cp. Soltau, Meyer); **4,43-45** (Hartke, Becker, Wöllner, von Wahlde; cp. A. Schweizer, Delff, Meyer); **6,22-24** (Fortna, Hartke, Nicol, Teeple, von Wahlde; cp. A. Schweizer, Delff); **7,31-32.40-52** (Hartke, Teeple, Attridge, Kotila, von Wahlde). Some, however, proposed a "short" signs source, containing only the two Cana miracles: **2,1-11.12** and **4,46-54** (Jeremias, E. Schweizer, Temple, Merlier, Boismard 1962, Michel, Kümmel, R.E. Brown, Siegman, Marxsen, Beasley-Murray).

Already A. Schweizer (1841) considered the Galilean pericopes to be interpolated by the redactor into the pre-existent Judean Gospel. His theory was further developed by Delff, who extended the Galilean pericopes to a gospel book of a popular Galilean tradition. Spitta, followed by Goguel, renewed Schweizer's interpolation theory: the three Galilean miracles from an older Galilean gospel document, **2,1-11.12; 4,46-54; 21,1-14**, were inserted into the *Grundschrift* by the Redactor. More recently, this hypothesis was taken up by Thyen, Langbrandtner and Heekerens, and Mayer resumed the theory of the Galilean miracles (cp. Stibbe's "Galilean miracle source"). Temple thought that the evangelist inserted a "two-sign-source" or "Cana-sign-source" (**2,1-11; 4,46-54**) into his main gospel source, the *Core*.

Fortna has expanded the signs source by combining an earlier stratum of the passion and resurrection narratives (chs. **18–20**) with the pre-Johannine miracle tradition to form a *Gospel of Signs* or *Signs Gospel*. This gospel describes the life of Jesus from beginning to passion and resurrection. It is a "mini-Gospel", however, because Jesus' discourses are lacking. In fact, Fortna combined Bultmann's two sources, the σημεῖα-*Quelle* and the passion source, into one source. He has been followed by Martyn, D.M. Smith, Hoeferkamp, Cope, von Wahlde, and Wöllner (cp. Teeple, who did not include the resurrection stories). The content of Fortna's *Gospel of Signs* can be compared with Wilkens's *Zeichenevangelium*. The two hypotheses should not be confused, however. Attempting to combine Wellhausen's hypothesis of a

Grundevangelium with the recognition of the gospel's stylistic unity, Wilkens considered the Fourth Gospel the work of one author, accomplished in three phases. So the *Zeichenevangelium* is not a source but a *Grundschrift* that the same author reworked twice. Moreover, Wilkens's literary theory is to be compared with those of Richter, Boismard, Haenchen, Schenke, Wagner, Lütgehetmann, and Schmithals, who all proposed some kind of *Grundschrift* or *Grundevangelium* in which miracles were already combined with the passion and resurrection narratives. None of them accept the signs source in its classic form. Unlike Wilkens, however, they do not attribute the basic document and its successive elaborations to the evangelist, but to different writers all working within the Johannine school or community which is characterized by some unity in vocabulary and style.

*

Bultmann did not give a word-by-word reconstruction, but his σημεῖα-*Quelle* can be described rather well on the basis of the disparate notations in his commentary. Fortna proclaimed a high degree of confidence in the precise wording and order of his reconstructed source, but found himself unable to reconstruct the source's text for 13,1-20. Moreover, he mentions "unrecoverable matter" which could derive from SQ or from PQ. Likewise, Hartke, Teeple, Heekerens and von Wahlde present a word-by-word reconstruction (cp. Temple for the material attributed to the *Core*, Boismard for *Document C*, and Schmithals for the *Grundschrift*). An exact reconstruction is impossible for Nicol, who prefers to give a "separation" rather than a "reconstruction". Schnakkenburg, Schulz, Becker and Gnilka provide only a vague indication of verses that can be ascribed to the source.

Although some defenders of the theory (e.g., Wegner) leave open the question whether the source was written or oral, for most it appears from the conclusion of the source that it was a written document, a book of miracles (cf. 20,31: ἐν τῷ βιβλίῳ τούτῳ). This was already explicitly stated by Faure: he named the "Wunderquelle" a "Quellenschrift" or "Wunderbuch". Similarly, Windisch and Bauer thought that the older non-Synoptic material used by the evangelist was composed in written form. For Bultmann, too, the σημεῖα-*Quelle* was a literary source, and after him, several scholars characterized the source as "Quellenschrift" (e.g., Merkel, Vielhauer), "Zeichen/Semeiabuch" (H.-J. Kuhn, Wöllner), "Wunder/Semeiabüchlein" (Reim) or "Book of Signs" (Fuller, Perrin). This last label, however, should not be confused, as, e.g., in Beasley-Murray's commentary, with Dodd's designation "Book of Signs" for the first part of the Gospel (Jn 2,1–12,50). Hartke spoke of the "Zeichenevangelium" as a "Missions*schrift*" (cp. Nicol: "a missionary writing or book"; D.M. Smith and Kysar: "a missionary tract"; Aus: "mission tract"; von Wahlde: "a missionary or kerygmatic document"), and Fortna labeled the *Gospel of Signs* a "text book" (cp. Martyn). Whereas Haenchen supposed that the evangelist had only oral recollection of the (written) Gospel used in the liturgy of his own community, Fortna presumed that John probably had the *Gospel of Signs* before him when he wrote his gospel. Richter also thinks that the evangelist was actually using the written source rather than citing from memory, and he even suggested that the evangelist wrote his expansion on a copy of S itself. Another outlook is that of Koester, who defined the signs source as one of the earlier written documents and, influenced by Georgi, compares it with the letters of recommendation used by Paul's opponents (see below).

Jn 20,30-31 seems to indicate that the author of the source selected his material and that the source was not a mere collection of signs (and other narrative material) but had a definite structure. Faure, Bultmann, and Schnackenburg gave only vague indications about the source's order, but Becker and especially Fortna have stressed that the source was "far from a haphazard document". After his analysis of the miracle stories, Fortna pointed out several "indications of a *pre-Johannine editorial shaping* common to all the signs [that] suggest that a single source lies immediately behind them, and not simply oral tradition"[2]. Observations on the source's redaction can also be found in works of Gnilka, Heekerens, Cope, Wöllner and von Wahlde, among others. Thus, for example, it has been stressed that the source is marked by a careful geographical itinerary, which Becker and Fortna compared with Mark's Galilee/Judea division: Jesus performed seven miracles, four in Galilee (2,1-11; 4,46-54; [21,1-14, cf. Fortna]; 6,1-14; [6,15b-21.(22.25), not numbered by Fortna]) and three in Judea (5,1-18; 9,1-41; 11,1-44). Further, the first two miracles are closely connected not only by their location in Cana and the linking verse (2,12), but also by their numbering (2,11; 4,54; see below). There is a growing supernatural character in the miracles, from the first, water changed into wine, to the last, the raising of Lazarus (see, e.g., Broome, Schnackenburg, von Wahlde). Similarly, there is an increasing reaction of belief by the common people and an increasing hostility on the part of the religious authorities (see, e.g., Wöllner, von Wahlde). For Fortna, followed by Cope, the seven miracles are climaxed by the greatest σημεῖον of all, Jesus' resurrection. Fortna also detected the same redactional techniques in both SQ and PQ: both parts start with a double confession of Jesus, respectively in 1,49 (σὺ εἶ ὁ υἱὸς τοῦ θεοῦ, σὺ βασιλεὺς εἶ τοῦ Ἰσραήλ) and 12,13 (εὐλογημένος ὁ ἐρχόμενος ἐν ὀνόματι κυρίου, καὶ ὁ βασιλεὺς τοῦ

---

2. *Gospel of Signs*, 1970, p. 99.

Ἰσραήλ; cp. 20,31 Ἰησοῦς ἐστιν ὁ χριστὸς ὁ υἱὸς τοῦ θεοῦ); the three denials of the Baptist (1,20-21) correspond to the three denials of Peter (18,17.25.27); there is a double-sentence unit at the beginning (1,6-7) and at the end (20,30-31a). For some authors, the signs source is patterned according to the Elijah/Elisha cycle (see, e.g., Buchanan) or to the miracle cycle of Wisdom 11,2-19,22 (Ziener).

*

Jesus' initiative and the heightening of the miraculous indicated for Bultmann and most defenders of the hypothesis that the source represented an advanced stage in the development of gospel tradition in comparison with the Synoptics. So, for instance, Haenchen thought that the "Wunderevangelium" represents a "later, often already obviously 'hackneyed' form", and Käsemann called it a tradition "which has to some extent run wild". Bultmann compared the signs source with the supposed pre-Markan miracle cycle(s). This has been elaborated especially by J.M. Robinson and Koester. For them, it is beyond doubt that earlier written documents were an intermediate stage between free transmission and written gospels. They describe the pre-Markan and pre-Johannine miracle collections as aretalogies which presented Jesus as θεῖος ἀνήρ with the purpose of promoting Jesus as the Messiah (cf. Jn 20,30-31; cp. Sir 43,27; 1 Macc 9,22). They advance Georgi's suggestion that these collections can be compared with the letters of recommendation of Paul's opponents (2 Cor 3,1). Moreover, for Koester, the content and sequence of several miracle stories in Mark and John (and also in the Secret Gospel of Mark) share enough in common to conclude that the miracle sources of Mark and John were different versions of the same literary collection. Becker also thought that the special relation of SQ with the Markan tradition is to be explained "traditionsgeschichtlich". On the other hand, Fortna originally defined his Gospel of Signs as "a rudimentary gospel" and spoke of "an aretalogy with sequel" (1975) but no longer finds this characterization appropriate in 1988.

For some authors the signs source had some relation with the Lukan tradition. In his 1964 reaction to Boismard, Schnackenburg claimed that the parallels to Luke in Jn 4,46-54 belonged to the source and he supposed that Luke possibly used a source similar to the σημεῖα-Quelle. Fortna also thought the Gospel of Signs had a special relationship, though not necessarily on the literary level, with the material peculiar to Luke. Further, Freed and Hunt have taken up Cribbs's suggestion that Luke was familiar with some form of the developing Johannine tradition or an early draft of the original Gospel of John: for them, this tradition is Fortna's Gospel of Signs or something very close to it. Cope, like

Freed and Hunt, thought that Luke had access to an edition of the Signs Gospel, but Fortna notes that this suggestion is "more radical" than he "had dared to be". Moreover, with references to the parallels with the Elijah/Elisha miracles in both the Johannine tradition and the material peculiar to Luke, Reim concluded that Luke and John probably used a similar collection of miracle stories. For some authors, however, the signs source is dependent on the final redaction of the Synoptic Gospels. Thus Dauer, rejecting his earlier hypothesis of a non-Synoptic Johannine tradition, now explains the pre-Johannine story of Jn 4,46-54a as "a free rendering of Mt 8,5-13 making use of narrative elements from Lk 7,1-10". For Teeple, S displays in various passages the influence of the Gospel of Mark and possibly of the Gospel of Matthew.

*

With regard to the Sitz-im-Leben, the signs source is generally situated within the context of religious propaganda: the author sought to evoke faith in Jesus as Messiah and Son of God. Faure defined the *Wunderbuch* as an apologetic tract with a missionary interest and Bultmann considered it a part of religious propaganda. The source has been called especially a "*Missions*schrift" (Hartke, Fortna, Martyn, Nicol, Smith, Kysar, Aus). According to Fortna and Nicol (cp. Boismard), there are several indications of the source's missionary interest: its conclusion in 20,30-31, the stress on signs leading to faith, the "missionary terminology" in 4,53 (cf. Acts 10,2; 11,14; 16,15.31; 18,8), and passages such as Jn 1,35-50 and ch. 4, which describe extensively how other persons come to believe. Georgi, J.M. Robinson and Koester (cp. Tiede, H.-W. Kuhn) situated the source in the circle of Christian-Jewish itinerant missionaries who had adopted the pattern of Hellenized Jewish propaganda. Like other aretalogies, the signs source promoted a religion, particularly in competition with other missionaries (cp. Becker). The "heightened" miracles in the source as well as the Isaian "hardening" motif in Jn 12,38-40 (cf. Is 6,9) point to this field of competition.

J.M. Robinson and Richter especially stressed the apologetic scope of the source (cp. Faure): it was written to prove and defend Jesus' Messiahship. Especially Fortna, followed by D.M. Smith and Wöllner, believed that the joining of PQ with SQ was apologetically motivated: it sought to justify the death of Jesus and so relieve the seemingly intolerable contradiction that a self-revealing, miracle-performing Messiah should suffer an ignominious death. In his second monograph, Fortna stressed this apologetic scope even more. Koester and Backhaus, however, strongly rejected the term "apologetic".

In his dissertation, Heekerens suggested the source was a "Lehrschrift", but he changed his mind and in the published text he calls it a "Missionsschrift" for (Samaritan) Christians to strengthen their faith in Jesus as Messiah against the objections of the disciples of John the Baptist. Without further considerations, Lona considered the purpose of the *Semeia-Quelle* "catechetical".

Faure thought that the miracle book was perhaps a reply to the objections of the Jews or to the Baptist's disciples concerning Jesus' Messiahship. Both possibilities have been further defended. On the one hand, Bultmann thought that the source would have originated in the circle of former Baptist disciples. This view has been taken up by Teeple, Smith, Becker, Heekerens, and Cope: by presenting Jesus as a miracle worker, the source confirmed his prophetic role over against John who performed no signs. Backhaus vigourously rejected this idea that the source was directed against a competing Baptist sect and prefers a missionary (rather than apologetic or polemic) Sitz-im-Leben.

Fortna and Nicol defended Faure's first proposition: the source was written to convince Jews of Jesus' Messiahship. For Nicol, the Jewish Sitz-im-Leben of the signs source is clear. The so-called Hellenistic characteristics of the θεῖος ἀνήρ (supernatural knowledge and the power to work miracles) appear to be just as well, if not more, Jewish than Hellenistic. Fortna and Walter were critical, however, of Nicol's "crude distinction" between Palestinian and Hellenistic thought in discussing the Sitz-im-Leben of S. Further, the addition of the passion narrative to the signs source (Fortna, Smith, Kolenkow, Wöllner) as well as the healing controversies in chs. 5 and 9 (Kotila) are to be understood within a Jewish context.

*

Only a few proponents of the signs source try to determine the date of the source. Bultmann, for instance, gave no date and Becker also found it difficult to determine. In 1970, Fortna dated the Gospel of Signs either before or after the Jewish war, but in 1988, he imagines for SG "a dating in the 40s or possibly the 50s of the first century – roughly contemporary with Q" (cp. Boismard, who dates *Document C* around 50 A.D.). For Cope 55-60 A.D. is a "cautious and credible date". An even earlier date (43/44 A.D.) was proposed by Hartke. Several authors, however, suggested a later date. For Nicol, S was written at the same time that Luke composed the Acts of the Apostles. Teeple thought that S should be dated after 75 A.D., and for Dauer the date of the source must be later than the final redaction of the Synoptic gospels. According to von Wahlde, 70-80 A.D. is perhaps "not unreasonable". Similarly, Wöllner dates the *Zeichenbuch* after the catastrophe of 70 A.D., whereas Backhaus thinks that SQ must be dated before 80 A.D. (cp. Schmithals who situates the *Grundschrift* at the end of the first century).

With regard to the source's place of origin, Becker and Heekerens identified it with Samaria since it was there that the Christian mission encountered opposition from the Baptist's disciples. This was supported by, e.g., Backhaus and Koch and this view can be compared with Boismard's proposal with regard to *Document C*: it was written in Palestine by a Christian who was related to Samaritan communities. For Fortna, a Syrian provenance is possible because of obvious contact with Palestinian traditions (cp. Cope: "a Palestinian/Syrian Christian document"), although such a document could have originated in any part of the Hellenistic world. Haenchen thought that the Johannine (non-Synoptic) tradition as well as the completed Gospel, probably originated on the frontier between Syria and Palestine, more particularly in a small community outside the main stream of development. Ashton places the source's origin in Palestine. For Hartke, however, the *Zeichenevangelium* was written in Jerusalem, and for von Wahlde, the Gospel of Signs was very likely a product of the Christian community in Judea.

*

We can summarize the classic argumentation for the signs source in five points (Neirynck)[3]. They are different in nature: there are two literary (source-critical) arguments, and one each from the stylistic, form-critical and ideological (christological) point of view.

1. The "main clue" to the existence of the signs source is the numbering of the first two signs in 2,11 and 4,54. The concluding notation to the healing of the official's son in 4,54 (τοῦτο δὲ πάλιν δεύτερον σημεῖον) refers to that of the wine miracle in 2,11 (ταύτην ἐποίησεν ἀρχὴν τῶν σημείων), but seems to ignore the many signs Jesus performed in the meantime in Jerusalem, referred to in 2,23 (θεωροῦντες αὐτοῦ τὰ σημεῖα ἃ ἐποίει; cp. 3,2 οὐδεὶς γὰρ δύναται ταῦτα τὰ σημεῖα ποιεῖν ἃ σὺ ποιεῖς) and 4,45 (πάντα ἑωρακότες ὅσα ἐποίησεν ἐν Ἱεροσολύμοις ἐν τῇ ἑορτῇ). For defenders of the signs source, this inconsistency or "aporia" means that the evangelist has taken the numbering from a source without adapting it to his own redaction. A. Schweizer and Windisch considered the possibility that 6,1-14 was numbered. Meyer and especially Bultmann presumed that all the other miracles in the source were also numbered. Defenders of the semeia hypothesis have reacted to this suggestion in two directions: Fortna, on the one hand, reconstructs a conclusion with numbering for every sign in the source; Becker, on the other hand, labels Bultmann's postulation that the source would have had a continuous count an "unproven assertion" and remarks that after the numbering of the first

3. See above, p. 321 n. 419.

two miracles (cp. Ex 4,7-9) the reader of SQ could be expected to count to seven. Some scholars, however, assign the numbering at 2,11 and 4,54 to a short signs source that contained just the two Cana miracles. Since Spitta, some detected a "third sign" in 21,1-14, with a third numbering in v. 14: τοῦτο ἤδη τρίτον ἐφανερώθη Ἰησοῦς... Other defenders of the signs source, such as Windisch and Conzelmann, do not accept the numbering of signs as evidence for the hypothesis, and even Becker, in his reply to Neirynck, seems to abandon this argument for the existence of the source.

2. Since many Johannine scholars consider Jn 21 an appendix, they think the evangelist originally ended his gospel at 20,30-31:

30 πολλὰ μὲν οὖν καὶ ἄλλα σημεῖα ἐποίησεν ὁ Ἰησοῦς
         ἐνώπιον τῶν μαθητῶν αὐτοῦ,
     ἃ οὐκ ἔστιν γεγραμμένα ἐν τῷ βιβλίῳ τούτῳ·

31 ταῦτα δὲ γέγραπται
         ἵνα πιστεύσητε ὅτι Ἰησοῦς ἐστιν ὁ χριστὸς ὁ υἱὸς τοῦ θεοῦ,
         καὶ ἵνα πιστεύοντες ζωὴν ἔχητε ἐν τῷ ὀνόματι αὐτοῦ.

It is surprising that the evangelist characterized the content of his book (v. 31 ταῦτα δὲ γέγραπται, v. 30 ἃ οὐκ ἔστιν γεγραμμένα ἐν τῷ βιβλίῳ τούτῳ) with the term σημεῖα (signs which Jesus performed: ἐποίησεν ὁ Ἰησοῦς), as though he had been relating signs from the beginning of the gospel to its end. The evangelist narrated Jesus' last sign in ch. 11, and he refers to the miracles only two times in chs. 13–20, but with the word ἔργα (14,11; 15,24). The term σημεῖα, used for the last time in 12,37 (τοσαῦτα δὲ αὐτοῦ σημεῖα πεποιηκότος ἔμπροσθεν αὐτῶν οὐκ ἐπίστευον εἰς αὐτόν), does not seem to include Jesus' words and discourses, which are so important for John. From these inconsistencies, the defenders of the signs source conclude that the term σημεῖα and the conclusion formula is not appropriate for the whole gospel but rather for a collection of miracles. Therefore, they think that the evangelist used in 20,30-31 the concluding formula of the source as the conclusion of his own work.

Faure regarded the whole of 20,30-31 (preceded by 12,37) as the conclusion of the *Wunderbuch* (cp. Teeple). Bultmann, Fortna, Nicol, Becker and most proponents of the semeia hypothesis attribute the second ἵνα-clause to the evangelist: καὶ ἵνα πιστεύοντες ζωὴν ἔχητε ἐν τῷ ὀνόματι αὐτοῦ. In his 1964 article, and in the first volume of his commentary, Schnackenburg considered only 20,30 to be the conclusion of the source, but in the third volume he attributes verse 31 (without the second ἵνα-clause) to the source. Nevertheless, he allows for the strong possibility that ἐνώπιον τῶν μαθητῶν αὐτοῦ (v. 30) may have been added by the evangelist. Thyen, Heekerens (1984) and Boismard do not accept the secondary character of chapter 21, and consider 20,30-31 as the provisional conclusion of the gospel that can be compared with 1 Jn 5,13, likewise a provisional conclusion followed by an epilogue (5,14-21).

3. From the very beginning, stylistic considerations have played an important role in the semeia hypothesis. Older source critics noted the distinctive vocabulary and style in the respective parts they attributed to the evangelist and the interpolator (A. Schweizer), in the narrative parts and discourses (Wendt), or in chs. 1–12 (and 20,30-31) and chs. 13–21 (Thompson, Faure). Bultmann mentioned the characteristics each time he ascribed a pericope to the σημεῖα-*Quelle*. Its style is clearly distinguishable from the language of both the Evangelist and the *Redenquelle* as well as from the miracle stories of the Synoptic tradition, and is especially characterized by Semitisms, which indicate for Bultmann that the source was written in Greek by a Greek-speaking Semite. This is a common opinion (see, e.g., Hartke, Fortna, Schulz, Koester, Heekerens). More recently, von Wahlde considered "linguistic differences" the basis upon which literary analysis of the Fourth Gospel must be founded and thought them more objective than those which have been used previously in the literary analysis of the Fourth Gospel.

After Schweizer's and Ruckstuhl's attacks on Johannine source criticism, most signs source defenders have acknowledged that the stylistic unity of the Fourth Gospel makes it difficult to reconstruct sources and that the style-critical argument must converge with other evidence. Becker even gave up the use of style criticism as a decisive means of source analysis. Authors such as Ziener, Temple, Schnackenburg, Conzelmann, and Vielhauer, on the other hand, consider the complete or near complete absence of Johannine characteristics in some passages an indication for the signs source. Fortna, Nicol, and Teeple, each in his own way, have attempted to demonstrate that style criticism can even confirm the use of a signs source in the Gospel of John. Moreover, Fortna tried to indicate the stylistic unity between SQ and PQ (cp. Teeple and Wöllner). Finally, Thyen and Heekerens accept that Ruckstuhl's list has demonstrated the stylistic homogeneity and unity of the gospel, but they do not believe that it can be used to control the literary-critical hypotheses. For them, it is not possible to distinguish between the "Idiolekt", i.e., the language of an individual author, and the "Soziolekt", i.e., the language of the Johannine school.

4. Since the source primarily contains miracle stories, the form of the narrative is another criterion. First, the proponents of the semeia hypothesis isolate the miracle stories from other narrative material and from the discourses in the Gospel of John and contend that the miracle stories have a similar pattern. From this they conclude that all the miracles stem from the same source. Second, it is said that the miracles

in Jn are more miraculous than those in the Synoptics (Bultmann, followed by all defenders; see, e.g., Becker: "die Wunder sind massiv
gesteigert"); they can be characterized as "novelistic miracle stories"
(Tiede), "epiphany stories" (D.M. Smith, Koester and Becker). This
heightening of the miraculous does not harmonize with the evangelist's
supposed critical attitude toward miracles (see already, before Bultmann,
A. Schweizer and Meyer). Third, in contrast with the Synoptics, where
faith frequently precedes, often even as a condition for the miracle, faith
is rather regarded as a natural result of the miracle (2,11; 4,53; 6,14;
11,15.45).

For some authors, such as Schnackenburg, Martyn, and Nicol, the
form of the miracle story is even a decisive criterion for assigning a
Traditionsvorlage to the source. Therefore, Schnackenburg rejected
Bultmann's attempt to extend the presumed source beyond the miracle
stories. Fortna, from his side, noted that he finds it "all the more
surprising, in one of the fathers of the Synoptic form criticism, that Bultmann never adequately discusses the issues involved in the form criticism of John, or perhaps even fully recognizes its possibilities"[4].
Finally, Heekerens, who rejected Fortna's attempt to describe the pre-
Johannine shaping of *all* miracle stories in Jn, agreed with Schnackenburg that a "signs source" cannot contain material other than miracle
stories. He thinks, however, that only the three miracle stories in Galilee
(2,1-11.12; 4,46-54; 21,1-14) have a similar form, and he describes
them according to G. Theissen's approach and categories. For the other
miracles he suggested another "miracles source".

5. The ideological criterion is the last argument for the semeia
hypothesis, and, according to Fortna, it is the "readiest" and "earliest"
to have been applied to the Johannine literary question. It concerns
mainly the theology and christology of the signs. On the one hand, signs
source proponents always suppose that there is a contradiction in the
Fourth Gospel between the passages that posit a direct correlation
between signs and faith (e.g., 2,11; 4,53; 6,14; 20,30-31) and those in
which faith based on signs is criticized, minimized, or even rejected
(e.g., 2,23; 4,48; 6,26). For these scholars, the evangelist considered
belief in miracles inferior, a second best coming to faith (14,11; 10,38;
4,48). They suppose that if the first passages can be attributed to the
signs source, then this ideological aporia is explained. On the other
hand, they think that the source presents a lower messianism, whereas
the Johannine redaction reflects a higher christology. Since Bultmann,
the source's "lower" christology has most frequently been described
as a Hellenistic θεῖος ἀνήρ christology. In order to prove his Messiahship, Jesus is presented as a miracle worker, as all-knowing, and

---

4. *Gospel of Signs*, 1970, p. 25 n. 2.

always taking the initiative: his actions cannot be determined by others, not even by his relatives (2,3-6; 4,50; 5,6; 6,5; 9,6; 11,6; 21,4). These characteristics of the θεῖος ἀνήρ led Bultmann, and others, to ascribe narrative passages other than miracle stories to the source (Jesus' supernatural knowledge in 1,35-49, esp. vv. 47.50, and 4,4-42, esp. vv. 17-18; Jesus taking the initiative in 7,1-10, esp. v. 6). For John Jesus' miracles are not proofs but signs, symbols or pointers to the unique event of salvation: Jesus, who performs the ἔργα τοῦ θεοῦ.

II. The Hypothesis Criticized

It is one thing to say that the Fourth Gospel presupposes earlier traditions, oral and possibly written, but it is quite another to reconstruct the Gospel's source verse-by-verse and word-by-word, and to recover its original order[5]. Proponents of the semeia hypothesis themselves do not agree on the contents of the source. Some propose a signs source that contains exclusively miracle stories, others a source with additional narrative material, sometimes including the passion and resurrection narratives (the *Gospel of Signs*)[6]. Still others suggest a short source (the two Cana miracles), sometimes followed by 21,1-14. There is also significant divergence in reconstructing individual sections. Furthermore, some perceive the signs source as one of the sources in Jn, others consider it the principal source used by the evangelist or by the author of the *Grundschrift*, while some think the short source was interpolated into the Gospel by a later redactor. For critics of the theory, such disagreement does not inspire confidence in the semeia hypothesis in particular and in Johannine source criticism in general[7]. Reconstructions are too hypothetical because distinctions between Johannine and non-Johannine elements are frequently too subjective[8].

---

5. Cp. de Jonge (pp. 168-169 n. 128).

6. Especially this pre-Johannine combination of the miracles (signs source) with the passion and resurrection narratives has been criticized. See Schnackenburg and J.M. Robinson. Cp., e.g., Ashton, Barrett, Crehan, de Jonge, Feuillet, Jacques, Léon-Dufour, Lindars, Matsunaga, McMorrow, Murphy, Murphy-O'Connor, Rissi, E. Schweizer, Sweetnam, and Wilkens.

7. Cf. de Jonge (p. 251 n. 1), Ruckstuhl (p. 302 n. 309), Carson (pp. 315 n. 390, 316-317 n. 402), Neirynck (p. 320 n. 418). See also, e.g., Kysar (p. 192 n. 221), Ashton (p. 287 n. 209), Schmithals (p. 290 n. 233). Cp. Jeremias (p. 42 n. 7).

8. See, e.g., Carson (p. 315 n. 389, with reference to Goodwin), Burge (p. 331 n. 478). See esp. Thyen's (pp. 264 n. 76, 265 n. 82) and Painter's (p. 353 nn. 605-610) reaction to Fortna, who claims that the Fourth Evangelist treated his source(s) with great respect (*Predecessor*, 1988, p. 6).

The fact that the source is no longer extant is not *a priori* an argument against John's use of a signs source[9]. But is there a literary parallel for such a source? Was it an aretalogy which presented Jesus as θεῖος ἀνήρ? Authors like Gundry, Betz, Schneider, Berger, and especially Schnelle[10] offer a number of critical considerations. First, the analogy of pre-Markan miracle collection(s) is a circular argument because studies on a pre-Markan catena of miracles frequently appeal to a pre-Johannine signs source for support[11]. Second, it is not certain that in Hellenistic-Roman times there was a fixed literary form called "aretalogy". At best, "aretalogical" tendencies can be found within various literary forms[12]. Third, instead of Hellenistic terms (θαῦμα, ἀρετή, δύναμις), the supposed source uses the Septuagint word σημεῖον[13]. Fourth, it is questionable whether the source could have presented Jesus as θεῖος ἀνήρ, since there are doubts about this concept in Hellenistic literature[14]. Fifth, it is doubtful that the titles son of God or prophet were connected with the θεῖος ἀνήρ concept[15]. Even some defenders of the signs source reject the Hellenistic θεῖος ἀνήρ and interpret the miracles against an Old Testament (and Jewish) background alone[16]. It seems that "Jesus' miracles look more like salvific miracles such as we meet in the OT"[17].

There is no unanimity with regard to the source's date, its place of origin, or its Sitz-im-Leben. With respect to the latter, Schnelle, e.g., has pointed out that a missionary Sitz-im-Leben is apparent only in 4,53[18]

9. Cf. J.M. Robinson (p. 172 n. 139). Becker compared the reconstruction of SQ with that of the Q-source. See, however, the reaction of Schnelle (p. 336 n. 516).

10. See above, p. 79 n. 35 (Grundry, Berger), pp. 294-300 (Betz), p. 313 n. 379 (Schneider), pp. 339-340 n. 532 (Schnelle).

11. See above, p. 85 n. 63.

12. Cf. Schnelle (p. 339 n. 532). Cp. Marguerat (p. 346 n. 562).

13. Cf. Nicol (p. 156), Appold (p. 201 n. 279), Fortna (p. 222). Cp. Betz (p. 296 n. 273).

14. Cf. GALLAGHER, *Divine Man or Magician?*, 1982, p. 177.

15. Cf. Betz with reference to Wülfing von Martitz (p. 296 nn. 270-271). See also VAN OYEN, *De studie van de Marcusredactie*, 1993, pp. 266-267, referring in nn. 1036-1039 to, among others, Holladay (1977), Betz (1972, 1977), Gallagher (1982), Blackburn (1991), and Koskenniemi (1992). See also above, p. 79 n. 35.

16. See esp. Ziener (pp. 87-90), Noetzel (p. 91), Buchanan (p. 91), Reim (pp. 92-93), Nicol (pp. 156-157), Heekerens (p. 259), Mayer (pp. 268-269), Scott (pp. 90-91). See also Fortna in *Predecessor* (see above, p. 221). Cp. Boismard (pp. 275-276).

17. GUNDRY, *Recent Investigations*, 1974, p. 116. See esp. Betz (pp. 297-300), Clark (p. 90), Schnelle (p. 338 n. 521), Konings (pp. 351-352 n. 599). See also Bostock and Brodie (p. 298 n. 281), Sahlin, Enz, R.H. Smith and Kiley (pp. 87-88 n. 76), and Hanson (p. 351 n. 596). For the explicit Old Testament citations in the Fourth Gospel, see FREED, *Old Testament Quotations*, 1965, the recent studies by Menken (cited in the *Bibliography*); SCHUCHARD, *Scripture within Scripture*, 1992; MERCIER, *La mémoire de l'Écriture dans le quatrième évangile*, 1994.

18. Cf. pp. 340-341.

and that Jewish readers would not have been convinced by a miracle-working Messiah[19].

*

Several objections can be made to each of the arguments advanced in favor of a pre-Johannine source for the miracles in John. Of course, the arguments must be considered in convergence with each other; but the enumeration of unproven assertions cannot legitimate the theory. We consider each of them.

1. "Nothing in John suggests a numbering that must be further continued in the seven signs of a hypothetical signs source"[20]. Jn 2,11 and 4,54 are not incongruent with 2,23; 3,2; 4,45. With ἀρχή in 2,11 the evangelist gives prominence to this primary sign and with πάλιν δεύτερον in 4,54 he brings the second Cana miracle into relation with the first one[21]. Moreover, the close connection between the two Cana stories can be explained as deliberate composition by the evangelist[22] and related to the Elijah-Elisha cycle of miracles[23]. The continuation of the counting of miracles in 21,14 neglects that τοῦτο ... τρίτον in 14 is connected with the verb ἐφανερώθη (and Jn 20): "it was the third time that he appeared"[24]. The Johannine character of 2,11; 4,54 (and 21,14) is confirmed by the presence of Johannine characteristics and the evangelist's ability to make parenthetical remarks[25]. It should not be surprising, therefore, that even some defenders of the signs source attribute 2,11 and 4,54 to the redaction of the evangelist[26].

19. Cf. pp. 340-341 n. 536.

20. NEIRYNCK, *Semeia-bron*, 1983, pp. 12-17, esp. 17 (ET: 1991, pp. 660-665, esp. 665). A continuous numbering is also not accepted by Becker (p. 119 n. 265) and Boismard (p. 276 n. 154).

21. Cf. p. 322.

22. See Moloney, cited by Neirynck (p. 322 n. 425). Cp. Wilkens (p. 65 nn. 123-124).

23. See Betz (pp. 298-300), followed by Neirynck (p. 322 n. 425).

24. NEIRYNCK, *Semeia-bron*, 1983, pp. 12-13, 17 (ET: pp. 660-661, 665). See pp. 321-322.

25. For the Johannine characteristics in 2,11; 4,54, and 21,14, see esp. NEIRYNCK, *Jean et les Synoptiques*, 1979, pp. 121-174, esp. 154-173; *Semeia-bron*, pp. 12-17 (ET: pp. 660-665); VAN BELLE, *Parenthèses*, 1985, pp. 67, 73, 103; BITTNER, *Zeichen*, 1987, pp. 92-99, 135; SCHNELLE, *Christologie*, 1987, pp. 91-92, 100, 168 (ET: 1992, pp. 78-79, 87, 151). With reference to Stange, Tenney, O'Rourke, Schnackenburg, Konings, Olsson and Roberge (p. 301), I considered 2,11; 4,54 and 21,14 examples of the group of parentheses called "notices de conclusion": 1,28; 2,11; 4,54; 6,59; 7,9; 8,20.30, 10,6; 12,36; 12,37-43; 20,30-31; 21,14; 21,24-25 (cf. *Parenthèses*, 1985, p. 111: no. 13). Cp. Ruckstuhl (p. 50), Bjerkelund (p. 341 n. 539), and Schnelle (p. 341 n. 540). See also above, p. 307 n. 347.

26. See esp. Windisch (pp. 20-21) and Conzelmann (pp. 75-76 n. 24).

2. There are several reasons why 20,30-31a need not be seen as the conclusion of a source. First, these verses can be considered "a provisional conclusion followed by an epilogue" (Jn 21), comparable with 1 Jn 5,13[27]. Second, although the use of σημεῖα in 20,30 is striking, this does not mean that it comes from a source. In source reconstructions that include the passion and resurrection stories the word σημεῖον still does not appear in the second part of the source[28]. On the basis of the word σημεῖον only the two Cana narratives could be assigned to the signs source[29]. Betz, Neirynck, and Schnelle have shown that it seems difficult to assign the instances of σημεῖα (ποιεῖν) to different literary layers[30]. Moreover, it is not quite correct to claim that the Synoptic Gospels never refer to miracles as σημεῖα and that in John the word comes from one source which contained miracles as legitimizing signs like the σημεῖα in Exodus[31]. Although in John the word σημεῖον primarily refers to a miracle performed by Jesus, the evangelist can describe the content of his work with σημεῖα ποιεῖν in 20,30[32]. Third, Bittner's and Schnelle's analyses of the evangelist's language and style have convincingly demonstrated that the first conclusion of the Gospel in 20,30-31 does not go back to a pre-Johannine signs source[33]. Some defenders of the source, such as Bammel, Conzelmann and Schottroff, came to the same conclusion[34].

3. The stylistic criteria for isolating sources are the weakest. Most critics, even those who distinguish sources and redactional elaboration in the Fourth Gospel, have accepted the Fourth Gospel's unity of language and style[35]: it seems to be a "seamless robe"[36] out of which different literary layers can hardly be separated. Especially E. Schweizer, Jeremias, Menoud, Ruckstuhl (and Dschulnigg), and Schnelle have shown against Bultmann's and Fortna's literary theories that Johannine characteristics are nearly evenly distributed throughout the Gospel and that they offer no evidence for source reconstructions. Against Fortna's attempt to

27. NEIRYNCK, *Semeia-bron*, 1983, p. 22 (ET: 1991, p. 670); cp., e.g., BOISMARD – LAMOUILLE, *Jean*, 1977, p. 475. See above, p. 323 n. 427.

28. Cf. de Jonge (p. 168).

29. See, e.g., D.M. Smith (p. 54) and Barrett (p. 167 n. 121).

30. Betz (p. 297 n. 274), Neirynck (pp. 323-324), Schnelle (p. 337). According to Schnelle only 2,18 and 6,30 (the demand for a sign) are traditional (p. 340 n. 534).

31. See esp. Neirynck (pp. 323-324) against Schnackenburg (p. 379 n. 1).

32. Cf. pp. 398-404.

33. SCHNELLE, *Christologie*, 1987, pp. 152-154 (ET: 1992, pp. 135-138; see above, p. 337); BITTNER, *Jesu Zeichen*, 1987, pp. 197-225 (p. 334 n. 501); cp. NEIRYNCK, *Semeia-bron*, 1983, pp. 20-28 (ET: 1991, pp. 668-677) (pp. 323-324). On 20,30-31 as "notice de conclusion", see above, p. 372 n. 25.

34. Conzelmann (pp. 75-76 n. 24), Bammel (p. 102 nn. 151-152), Schottroff (p. 104 n. 166).

35. See Ruckstuhl (p. 302 n. 308).

36. See above, p. 118 n. 261.

show the literary unity of the *Gospel of Signs*[37], one may note his logical error: Fortna uses the Johannine style characteristics to separate the Johannine material and to discover the Gospel of Signs, and then, in his test for the presence of Johannine characteristics in the source, comes to the conclusion that his source is free of such characteristics. Further, the absence of Johannine characteristics in some narrative parts of the Fourth Gospel (miracle stories and the passion narrative) does not prove that these passages belong to a source, and, still less, as Fortna claims, to *one* source[38]. It can be no more than an indication that John possibly used traditional material[39]. In addition, in most cases this absence is meaningless, because the characteristics do not appear in any narrative material in John[40]. Finally, Fortna's description of the source's own style is not sufficient to prove the existence of a source and, still less, a pre-Johannine combination of the signs source and the Passion narrative in a signs gospel[41].

The literary features used by Freed and Hunt in support of Fortna's Gospel of Signs are doubtful and cannot be used to test the narrative parts[42]. (1) If one tests the purity of Fortna's *Gospel of Signs* with characteristics which are typically Johannine – and variation is indeed such a characteristic – it appears that the source contains no such variations[43]. (2) The high number of *hapaxlegomena* cannot be considered a characteristic of the source, because they have to do with the particular circumstances at hand, and, therefore, are not valuable for testing the source either[44]. (3) It is obvious that the stylistic, verbal, and theological parallels between the Fourth Gospel and 1 Jn involve characteristics found in the Johannine material but not in the Gospel of Signs, because they occur mostly in the discourses[45].

Fortna and other source critics assign the asides, remarks, comments, or parentheses to both the source and the evangelist. In my study *Les parenthèses dans l'évangile de Jean*, I could conclude that parenthesis is a mark of the evangelist's work and provides no ground for theories of composite origin or (post-evangelist) redaction. I came to that conclusion

37. For the rejection of Fortna's stylistic test, see esp. Nicol (pp. 163-165), Murphy-O'Connor (p. 166), Sweetnam (p. 167), J.M. Robinson (pp. 172-174), Kysar (p. 190), Hengel (p. 218 n. 393), Cullmann (p. 301 n. 302), Ruckstuhl (pp. 302-312), Carson (p. 316), Smalley (p. 318 n. 405), Schnelle (p. 339). Cp. Klijn and Morris (see pp. 61-62), J.A.T. Robinson (pp. 61-62; cp. p. 328 n. 453, with reference to Parker).

38. See Schnelle (p. 339).

39. See, e.g., Bittner (pp. 333-334), Schnelle (p. 339). See also, e.g., Noack (p. 52) and Nicol (p. 155 n. 58).

40. See Nicol (p. 164), Ruckstuhl (p. 304), Smalley (p. 318 n. 405).

41. See esp. J.M. Robinson (pp. 172-174); cp. Thyen (p. 264 n. 78).

42. See above, pp. 198-200.

43. Cf. Carson (p. 316 n. 397).

44. Carson, with reference to Kümmel (p. 316 nn. 393-394).

45. CARSON, *Current Source Criticism*, 1978, p. 427.

by consideration of grammar and style, and of the Gospel's narrative art as well[46]. Also the distribution of the historic present (O'Rourke), the principal conjunctions (Poythress), the phenomenon of parallelism (Ellis), and the double meaning expressions (Richard) in John's Gospel do not confirm Fortna's Gospel of Signs or any source theory. In addition, the occurrence of the "repetitive resumptive", "framing repetition", or "Wiederaufnahme", also mentioned by Fortna, is not necessarily an indication that the evangelist is working with primitive sources[47].

4. Opponents of the semeia hypothesis, such as Bittner, Marchadour, and Marguerat, consider the form-critical argument a *petitio principii*[48]. If analysis begins with the rigid distinction between narrative and discourse, one can suppose *a priori* that "some sort of *signs* source theory would necessarily be among the first prospects to emerge"[49]. From the form-critical similarity of some stories in Jn one cannot conclude that these stories came from *a* source and still less that they belonged to the *same* source. It is only after the attribution of the discourses and the dialogue scenes to the evangelist (or another source) that the proponents of the semeia hypothesis obtain "a synoptic-like" form. The short synoptic-like form is obvious only in 2,1-11 and 4,46-54, and these are the only two miracles not followed immediately by discourses. Therefore, authors such as Brown and Temple think that only these miracles should be ascribed to a source. Moreover, is it necessary to attribute the divergences from the Synoptics to the signs source or to a further developed tradition? In John's christology the heightening of the miraculous and the emphasis on the materiality of the miracles are important features[50]. One may remark that the *Chorschluss* of the Synoptic miracle stories can be compared with John's more abstract language in 2,11 (πιστεύειν εἰς αὐτόν) and 2,23 (πιστεύειν εἰς τὸ ὄνομα αὐτοῦ)[51].

Likewise, the tradition-historical argument, i.e., the presumption that the Johannine miracle stories are independent of the Synoptics, does not permit the conclusion that they all come from the same source. For some critics, e.g., Bittner, Schnelle, Marguerat, and Hanson, the material taken up in the signs source is "traditionsgeschichtlich" heterogeneous. They maintain that the evangelist borrowed the miracle stories from apparently different traditions[52].

46. *Parenthèses*, 1985, pp. 206-210 (p. 307 n. 347). On Fortna, see *ibid.*, pp. 174-176; *Les parenthèses johanniques*, 1992, p. 1927 n. 145.

47. See above, p. 243 n. 566.

48. Cf. Bittner (p. 334), Marchadour (p. 335), Marguerat (p. 344). Cp. already Dibelius (p. 41). See also Schmithals (p. 290 n. 235).

49. CARSON, *Current Source Criticism*, 1978, p. 419.

50. See below, pp. 391-394.

51. See above, p. 323.

52. Bittner (p. 333), Schnelle (p. 338), Marguerat (pp. 345-346), Hanson (p. 351 n. 596). Cp. Bull (p. 349 n. 587).

5. Several critics have rejected the "ideological criterion". Indeed, it is strange that the evangelist would use the whole source, including Jn 20,30-31 that accords neither with his intention nor with the content of the gospel, only to subject it to radical criticism[53]. One may agree that there is a double level of "seeing signs" and "believing", but "it seems incorrect to comprehend this in a source-critical distinction"[54]. Other explanations can be suggested. One can agree with Schnelle and M.M. Thompson that there is no "Wunderkritik" in the Fourth Gospel[55]. The characteristics attributed to the so-called θεῖος ἀνήρ christology of the signs source belong in fact to the evangelist's own interest[56].

In general, the two indications, which make it impossible for many critics to regard the Fourth Gospel as a consistent work, namely "the all-but-intolerable tension between *narrative* and *discourse*"[57] and the presence of the so-called aporias[58], do not necessarily lead to the acceptance of a signs source. First, it should be noted that a rigid distinction between narrative and discourse does not reckon with the interrelationship and unity of both as "a literary skill of the author"[59]. Second, an aporia is not "a sure sign of a source, much less of a recoverable source"[60].

*

On the basis of these remarks, I am inclined to refuse the semeia hypothesis as a valid working hypothesis in the study of the Fourth Gospel. It is to be emphasized, however, that the theory itself has stimulated Johannine research in many branches, e.g., the study of the Gospel's redaction and structure, its theology of signs and christology, its religion-historical background, and especially its style. In criticism of the hypothesis, alternative explanations of the origin of the Fourth Gospel have been proposed. I mention particularly the revival of the

---

53. See, e.g., Noack (p. 52), Filson (p. 84), Murphy-O'Connor (p. 166), McMorrow (p. 169), Lindars (pp. 174-175), Kysar (p. 191), Cothenet (p. 314), Kee (p. 324), Hengel (p. 331), Bittner (p. 334 n. 503), Schnelle (p. 340), Marguerat (p. 345).
54. NEIRYNCK, *Semeia-bron*, 1983, p. 28 (ET: 1991, p. 676).
55. See below, pp. 394-398, esp. 398.
56. See below, p. 394.
57. FORTNA, *Predecessor*, 1988, p. 1; cp. p. 3; cp. *Gospel of Signs*, 1970, p. 22; D.M. Smith (pp. 194-195); LINDARS, *Behind the Fourth Gospel*, 1971, pp. 16-17 (FT: 1974, pp. 20-22); *John*, 1990, p. 27.
58. Cf. above, p. 142.
59. KYSAR, *John, The Gospel of*, 1992, p. 916a.
60. CARSON, *Current Source Criticism*, 1978, p. 423 (see above, p. 315 n. 391).

Grundschrift hypothesis and the reopening of the debate on John's dependence on the Synoptics. Tracing Johannine parallels to the Synoptics, however, is labeled "uncontrolled imagination" by Fortna[61], and he thinks that "theories of Johannine dependence on the Synopsis [sic] ... ignore the sometimes small but telling differences that betray not literary dependence but the variation of parallel but distinct tradition"[62]. One may reply that in Fortna's semeia hypothesis, "the question of a *literary dependence upon the present Synoptic Gospels* is not seriously taken into consideration"[63] and that in some instances his reconstruction of the pre-Johannine source is so similar to the text of the Synoptics that "it is difficult to recognize its *raison d'être*"[64].

61. FORTNA, *Predecessor*, 1988, pp. 65, 218.
62. *Ibid.*, p. 65.
63. SABBE, *The Trial*, 1992, p. 383 (= 1991, p. 511).
64. NEIRYNCK, *John and the Synoptics*, 1992, p. 42 (with reference to the pre-Johannine source behind 20,3-10 in comparison with Lk 24,12).

THE JOHANNINE ΣΗΜΕΙΑ

The word σημεῖον plays an important role in the discussion on the signs source. It occurs 16 times in the first part of the Fourth Gospel (up to the concluding notation at 12,37) and not again until 20,30. In the Synoptic Gospels the miracles of Jesus are never called σημεῖα. Therefore the defenders of the signs source assume that "John used a Christian source which had σημεῖα for the miracles of Jesus, instead of the Synoptic δυνάμεις, with the same general use"[1]. In this Appendix, I shall study especially the relationship between σημεῖον and ἔργον, the unity of signs and discourses, the characteristics of the Johannine σημεῖα, the theme of seeing signs and believing, and the meaning of σημεῖα in Jn 20,30-31.

From the large number of studies on signs (and works) (cf. MALATESTA, nos. 2673-2681; VAN BELLE, nos. 5687-5710, 5765-5767), I mention especially the following articles and monographs (for full references see the *Bibliography*): BERTRAM, art. ἔργον, ἐργάζομαι, in *TWNT* 2 (1935) 631-649, pp. 639, 642, 646-647, 649 (ET: 1964, pp. 635-652, esp. 642-643, 645, 649-650, 651); CERFAUX, *Les miracles*, 1954 (= 1954, pp. 41-50); CHARLIER, *La notion de signe*, 1959; MOLLAT, *Le semeion johannique*, 1959 (= 1979, pp. 91-101); FORMESYN, *Le Sèmeion johannique*, 1962; RIGA, *Signs of Glory*, 1963; RENGSTORF, art. σημεῖον, in *TWNT* 7 (1964) 199-261, pp. 241-257 (ET: 1971, pp. 200-261, esp. 243-257); HOFBECK, *Semeion*, 1966; ²1970; ERDOZÁIN, *La función del signo*, 1968; WILKENS, *Zeichen und Werke*, 1969; BECKER, *Wunder*, 1970 (= 1980, pp. 435-461, 461-463); INCH, *Apologetic Use of 'Signs'*, 1970; RIEDL, *Das Heilswerk Jesu*, 1973; BETZ, *Problem*, 1974, pp. 34-44 (= 1987, pp. 409-419); *Wesen*, 1977, pp. 120-151; LÉON-DUFOUR, *Autour du ΣΗ-ΜΕΙΟΝ johannique*, 1977 (*Les miracles*, 1977); DE JONGE, *Signs and Works*, 1978 (= 1977, pp. 117-140); HOEFERKAMP, *The Relationship*, 1978; HEILIGEN-THAL, art. ἔργον, in *EWNT* 2 (1981) 123-127, cc. 124-125 (ET: 1991, pp. 49-51, esp. 50); *Werke als Zeichen*, 1983; BOISMARD, *Rapports*, 1982; BETZ, art. σημεῖον, in *EWNT* 3 (1983) 569-574 (ET: 1992, pp. 238-241); NEIRYNCK, *Semeia-bron*, 1983, pp. 20-28 (ET: 1991, pp. 668-677); REINHARTZ, *John 20:30-31*, 1983, pp. 20-53: "The Meaning of *sēmeia* in 20,30" (cp. pp. 209-210); GROB, *Faire l'œuvre de Dieu*, 1986, pp. 46-74; BITTNER, *Jesu Zeichen*, 1987; SCHNELLE, *Christologie*, 1987, pp. 161-167, 180 (ET: 1992, pp. 144-150, 162); COLLINS, *Miracles and Faith*, 1989 (= 1990, pp. 183-197).

See further the excursuses and sections in the following commentaries and monographs: BERNARD, *John*, I, 1928, pp. CLXXVI-CLXXXVI; BARRETT, *John*,

---

1. Cf. SCHNACKENBURG, *Johannesevangelium*, I, 1965, p. 355 (ET: 1968, p. 526).

1955, pp. 62-65 (²1978, pp. 75-78); SCHNACKENBURG, *Johannesevangelium*, I, 1965, pp. 344-356 (ET: 1968, pp. 515-528); BROWN, *John*, I, 1966, pp. 525-532; E. SCHWEIZER, *Ego Eimi*, 1939, pp. 138-140; DODD, *Interpretation*, 1953, pp. 141-143; TRAETS, *Voir Jésus*, 1967, pp. 132-145; BOICE, *Witness and Revelation*, 1970, pp. 88-100; FORTNA, *Gospel of Signs*, 1970, pp. 20 n. 1, 36, 146, 198 n. 4, 231 n. 4; *Predecessor*, 1988, pp. 235-250 (cp. *Signs*, 1970); WEAD, *The Literary Divices*, 1970, pp. 12-29; MORRIS, *John*, 1971, pp. 684-691; SELONG, *Cleansing*, III, 1971, pp. 198-201; KONINGS, *Joh. verhaal*, III, 1972, pp. 294-298; SMALLEY, *John*, 1978, pp. 86-88; NICOL, *Sēmeia*, 1972, pp. 113-119 (see also pp. 139-142: "Theological Literature on the Sēmeia"); KYSAR, *The Fourth Evangelist*, 1975, pp. 222-233, esp. 225-227; ALBRECHT, *Zeugnis durch Wort und Verhalten*, 1977, pp. 133-166; BURGE, *The Anointed One*, 1987, pp. 74-81; M.M. THOMPSON, *Humanity*, 1988, pp. 53-86, 142-147; WAGNER, *Auferstehung*, 1988, pp. 289-292; MORRIS, *Jesus is the Christ*, 1989, pp. 1-19; LÜTGEHETMANN, *Die Hochzeit*, 1990, pp. 216-238; DAVIES, *Rhetoric and Reference*, 1992, pp. 221-224.

1. Σημεῖον and Ἔργον in the Gospel of John

In the Fourth Gospel the miracles can be called either σημεῖα or ἔργα; both terms are largely synonymous[2]. Σημεῖον, however, seems to be "a somewhat narrower term" than ἔργον[3].

1. Σημεῖον ("sign") is "one of the most characteristic and important words of the gospel"[4]. It occurs 17 times in the Fourth Gospel and refers primarily to Jesus' miracle working (but see also 10,41: Ἰωάννης μὲν σημεῖον ἐποίησεν οὐδέν). Regarding the persons who use the word, the instances may be divided into four groups[5]: (*a*) seven times on the lips of the Jews (or the crowd): 2,18; 3,2; 6,30[6]; 7,31; 9,16; 10,41;

---

2. See below, p. 386 n. 41.
3. BROWN, *John*, I, 1966, p. 528.
4. BARRETT, *John*, 1955, p. 63 (²1978, p. 77; GT: 1990, p. 91); BETZ, *Wesen*, 1977, p. 124.
5. Cf. CERFAUX, *Les miracles*, 1954, p. 132 (= 1954, p. 42); CHARLIER, *La notion de signe*, 1959, p. 435; FORMESYN, *Le Sèmeion johannique*, 1962, pp. 882-883; RENGSTORF, in *TWNT* 7 (1964), pp. 245-246 (ET: 1971, p. 247); HOFBECK, *Semeion*, ²1970, p. 72; NICOL, *Sēmeia*, 1972, p. 113; LÉON-DUFOUR, *Les miracles*, 1977, p. 276; DE JONGE, *Signs and Works*, 1978, pp. 120-121 (= 1977, pp. 131-132); REINHARTZ, *John 20:30-31*, 1983, pp. 24, 50; GROB, *Faire l'œuvre de Dieu*, 1986, pp. 48-49.
6. In 2,18 and 6,30, a sign is requested for legitimation (see below, p. 387 nn. 45-46). On this, see BARRETT, *John*, 1955, p. 64 (²1978, p. 76; GT: 1990, p. 93); RENGSTORF, in *TWNT* 7 (1964), p. 242 (ET: 1971, p. 244); SCHNACKENBURG, *Johannesevangelium*, I, 1965, pp. 346-347 (ET: 1968, p. 517); BROWN, *John*, 1966, pp. 527-528; HOFBECK, *Semeion*, ²1970, pp. 72, 81-90; MORRIS, *John*, 1972, p. 685; BETZ, *Problem*, 1974, p. 37 (= 1987, p. 412); *EWNT* 3 (1983), c. 572 (ET: 1992, p. 240); THOMPSON, *Humanity*, 1988, pp. 68-69; LÜTGEHETMANN, *Die Hochzeit*, 1990, p. 218. – According to SCHNELLE, *Christologie*, 1987, pp. 161-166, 181 (ET: 1992, pp. 144-148, 163), all σημεῖα passages, with the exception of 2,18 and 6,30 (the demand for a sign) are Johannine (see esp. pp. 161, 165;

11,47; once in an objection uttered by the highpriests and Pharisees (11,47), and once used by Nicodemus (3,2); (*b*) four times as the object of the crowd's perception: 2,23; 6,2.14; 12,18; (*c*) four times in the commentary of the narrator: 2,11; 4,54; 12,37; 20,30; (*d*) twice in the mouth of Jesus: 4,48[7]; 6,26.

In John σημεῖον has the same meaning as δύναμις in the Synoptic Gospels[8]. Five of the seven miracles are designated by the word σημεῖον[9]: the changing of water into wine (2,11), the healing of the official's son (4,54), the feeding of the five thousand (6,14.26), the healing of the man born blind (9,16), and the raising of Lazarus (12,18; cp. 11,47). The healing of the lame man is not characterized by the word σημεῖον but by the term ἔργον (7,21; cp. 5,20.36)[10]. Only the walking on the sea is not designated by either σημεῖον or ἔργον[11]. Moreover,

ET: pp. 145, 148), cp. p. 180 (ET: p. 162): "Σημεῖον als prägnante Benennung des irdischen Offenbarungswirkens Jesu ist ein zentraler Begriff der Christologie des 4. Evangelisten. Auch dieses Ergebnis spricht gegen das Vorhandensein einer vorjoh. 'Semeia-Quelle'" (see above, p. 337). For the Synoptic background of 2,18 and 6,30, cf. esp. NEIRYNCK, *Semeia-bron*, 1983, p. 27 (ET: 1991, pp. 675) (see above, pp. 323-324 n. 429); cp. SELONG, *Cleansing*, III, 1971, pp. 201-209; VOUGA, *Jean 6*, 1992, p. 267.

7. NICOL, *Sēmeia*, 1972, p. 113 (esp. n. 1) classifies 4,48 under category b. On the expression σημεῖα καὶ τέρατα, see below, p. 387 n. 47.

8. Cf. RENGSTORF, in *TWNT* 7 (1964), p. 243 (ET: 1971, p. 245); BROWN, *John*, I, 1966, p. 526 (cp. Jn 5,19); HOFBECK, *Semeion*, [2]1970, p. 158 (he remarks: "An der Stelle des Nomen tritt das Verbum δύνασθαι", cf. 3,2; 5,19.30; 6,52; 9,16; 10,21; 11,37); see pp. 158-159 for the distinction between the Synoptic miracles and the Johannine signs: "Nach den Syn weisen δυνάμεις Jesu auf die kommende Gottesherrschaft. ... Joh dagegen identifiziert Jesus mit den Reich Gottes. ... Jesus erscheint nicht mehr nur mit den δυνάμεις des künftigen Gottesreiches ausgestattet, sondern in ihm ist das Reich Gottes in der Welt wesenhaft anwesend. Die Heilsgaben erscheinen nicht mehr losgelöst vom Spender, sondern Jesus selbst ist das Licht, die Wahrheit und das Leben"; MORRIS, *John*, 1972, p. 684; SCHNELLE, *Christologie*, 1987, p. 161 (ET: 1992, p. 144); BURGE, *The Anointed One*, 1987, p. 78, refers to the parallel use of δύναμιν/σημεῖον ποιέω Mk 6,5 and Jn 10,41. Comparing the Johannine miracles with those of the Synoptics, BEASLEY-MURRAY, *John*, 1987, p. 33, notes: "Our evangelist goes one step further in viewing the miracles as *parables* of the kingdom which comes through the total work of the Son of God". On the Johannine σημεῖα as "parables", see RIGA, *Signs of Glory*, 1963.

9. Cf. BERNARD, *John*, I, 1928, p. CLXXVII; RENGSTORF, in *TWNT* 7 (1964), p. 244 (ET: 1971, p. 246); SCHNACKENBURG, *Johannesevangelium*, I, 1965, p. 345 (ET: 1968, p. 516); HOFBECK, *Semeion*, [2]1970, pp. 91-147; WEAD, *The Literary Devices*, 1970, p. 19; REINHARTZ, *John 20:30-31*, 1983, pp. 24-26; SCHNELLE, *Christologie*, 1987, p. 161 (ET: 1992, p. 144); LÜTGEHETMANN, *Die Hochzeit*, 1990, p. 220.

10. Cf. SCHNACKENBURG, *Johannesevangelium*, I, 1965, p. 345 (ET: 1968, p. 516); WEAD, *The Literary Devices*, 1970, pp. 21-22; DE JONGE, *Signs and Works*, 1978, p. 117 (= 1977, p. 128); SCHNELLE, *Christologie*, 1987, p. 161 (ET: 1992, p. 145); LÜTGEHETMANN, *Die Hochzeit*, 1990, p. 220. According to RENGSTORF, in *TWNT* 7 (1964), p. 244 (ET: 1971, p. 246), this miracle "is adduced more as an example in 6:2"; cp. REINHARTZ, *John 20:30-31*, 1983, pp. 26, 32.

11. Cf. BERNARD, *John*, I, 1928, pp. CLXXVII, 185 (for Bernard, the evangelist "not intended to record 'any miracle'"); SCHNACKENBURG, *Johannesevangelium*, I, 1965, p. 345 (ET: 1968, p. 516); WEAD, *The Literary Devices*, 1970, p. 22; SMALLEY, *John*,

σημεῖον is used several times in the plural to indicate Jesus' miracle activity in general, without telling a particular story[12]: 2,23; 3,2; 6,2.14(*v.l.*).26; 7,31; 9,16; 11,47; 12,37; 20,30 (cp. 10,41)[13]. Moreover, in the instances where σημεῖον appears as a summary mention of Jesus' miracle working, the crowd believes because of the miracles or do not believe in spite of them[14].

The concept σημεῖον "has a distinctive theological contour and ... leads us to the heart of Johannine theology"[15]. It is a christological notion. For John, the "σημεῖα and the person of the one who does them cannot be separated"[16]; "the σημεῖα pose questions about Jesus' appearance" (cf. 6,14) and call for decision[17]. They are a means to

1978, pp. 86-87, who notes that the walking on the sea "cannot be regarded as a sign in the same sense as the others". For REINHARTZ, *John 20:30-31*, 1983, p. 26, "Jesus' walking on the water is perhaps included in the reference in 6,26: '... you seek me not because you saw signs...'" (cp. p. 38); cp. LÜTGEHETMANN, *Die Hochzeit*, 1990, pp. 220-221.

12. RENGSTORF, in *TWNT* 7 (1964), p. 244 (ET: 1971, p. 245); SCHNACKENBURG, *Johannesevangelium*, I, 1965, p. 345 (ET: 1968, p. 516); HOFBECK, *Semeion*, ²1970, pp. 73-77 (2,23; 3,2; 6,2; 7,31); SCHNELLE, *Christologie*, 1987, p. 161 (ET: 1992, pp. 144-145).

13. In 2,23; 3,2; 6,2.26, and 9,16 other miracles, especially healing narratives, which are not related by the evangelist, are to be supposed. Sometimes there is mention of the great number (11,47; 12,37; 20,30). Cf. SCHNACKENBURG, *Johannesevangelium*, I, 1965, pp. 345-346 (ET: 1968, p. 516) (see above, p. 98). Cp. BERNARD, *John*, II, 1928, p. 685 (on Jn 20,30); REINHARTZ, *John 20:30-31*, 1983, pp. 28-29.

14. Cf. 2,23; 6,2; 7,31; (10,41); (11,47); 12,37; 20,30. See, e.g., BARRETT, *John*, 1955, p. 64 (²1978, p. 76; GT: 1990, p. 92); BETZ, *Wesen*, 1977, p. 134 n. 208; *EWNT* 3 (1983), c. 572 (ET: 1992, p. 240); SCHNELLE, *Christologie*, 1987, pp. 161, 167 (ET: 1992, pp. 144-145, 150).

15. SCHNACKENBURG, *Johannesevangelium*, I, 1965, p. 346 (ET: 1968, p. 517); WILKENS, *Zeichen und Werke*, 1969, p. 83: "Der Semeia-Begriff ist vielmehr ein Zentralbegriff der johanneischen Theologie"; NICOL, *Sēmeia*, 1972, p. 115: "The sēmeia should provide us with a key to the basic hermeneutical principle of John"; BITTNER, *Zeichen Jesu*, 1987, p. 285: "Von dieser Beobachtung her wird die Tatsache, dass Johannes den Terminus σημεῖον für die Taten Jesu, nicht nur gebraucht, sondern geradezu ins Zentrum seiner Jesusdarstellung und der Aussageabsicht seines Evangeliums stellt, erst recht auffallend"; LÜTGEHETMANN, *Die Hochzeit*, 1990, p. 221.

16. RENGSTORF, in *TWNT* 7 (1964), p. 243 (ET: 1971, p. 245); SCHNACKENBURG, *Johannesevangelium*, I, 1965, p. 354 (ET: 1968, p. 525): "So erweist sich die christologische Bedeutsamkeit der joh. σημεῖα als ihr tiefster Sinn, ihr unverwechselbare Eigenart und ihre theologische Mitte"; HOFBECK, *Semeion*, ²1970, p. 68: "Das Vollbringen von σημεῖα ist ausschliesslich auf die Person Jesu, des Offenbarers, beschränkt. Der Begriff σημεῖον trägt damit vor allem christologische Bestimmtheit" (cp. pp. 69, 72, 98-101, 166, 167-178); BOICE, *Witness and Revelation*, 1970, p. 90; KYSAR, *The Fourth Evangelist*, 1975, pp. 226-227; BURGE, *The Anointed One*, 1987, p. 79.

17. RENGSTORF, in *TWNT* 7 (1964), p. 242 (ET: 1971, p. 243); cp. CHARLIER, *La notion de signe*, 1959, p. 437: "Le σημεῖον est un geste posé (ποιέω) par le Christ, et dont la vue (ὁράω) conduit à la foi (πιστεύω). Cette définition semble d'autant moins hasardeuse qu'elle est à peu près celle de l'Évangéliste ... (XX, 30)"; CERFAUX, *Les miracles*, 1954, p. 131 (= 1954, p. 42): "Éveiller la foi profonde, ... tel est le rôle des miracles johanniques. En déterminant plus exactement ce rôle, nous pénétrons dans les profondeurs de la christologie, car les miracles 'révèlent' le Christ. Dans notre Évangile

reveal Jesus' true nature, his δόξα (2,11; 11,4.40)[18]. At first sight, in all 17 instances, "the signs are important works of Jesus, performed in the sight of his disciples, miracles, in fact, which of their nature should lead to faith in Jesus the Messiah, the Son of God" (cf. 20,30-31)[19].

2. Ἔργον is the alternative word for miracle in Jn[20]. "When the Johannine Jesus himself refers to what John calls σημεῖον He consistently uses the word ἔργον"[21]. Like σημεῖον, this is "a specifically

apparaît une théorie très consciemment élaborée: les miracles nous permettent de 'contempler' la divinité du Christ"; WILKENS, *Zeichen und Werke*, 1969, pp. 47-49, 55-59; BOICE, *Witness and Revelation*, 1970, p. 91; MORRIS, *John*, 1972, p. 688; BETZ, *Problem*, 1974, p. 36 (= 1987, p. 410-411): "Das σημεῖον ist bei Johannes, wie bei Josephus, auf den *Glauben* angewiesen; es stellt in die Entscheidung, scheidet den Menschen, und nur wenige glauben (2,11; 4,53; vgl. 9,38). Darum findet sich eine Akklamation nur in Joh 6,14f, wo sie abgelehnt wird"; DE JONGE, *Signs and Works*, 1978, p. 122 (= 1977, p. 111): "A σημεῖον is a demonstration which aks for reaction" (cp. p. 120; = 1977, p. 131); SCHNELLE, *Christologie*, 1987, p. 161; cp. p. 167 (ET: 1992, pp. 144-145, 150); REINHARTZ, *John 20:30-31*, 1983, p. 45: "In conclusion, the signs can be described as revelatory of Jesus' true identity and the appropriate response to them as faith in, or approach to, Jesus".

18. CHARLIER, *La notion de signe*, 1959, p. 435: "le σημεῖον est l'indice que son auteur est ἀπὸ ou μετὰ θεοῦ" (3,2; 9,33); cp. FORMESYN, *Le Sèmeion johannique*, 1962, p. 883; SCHNACKENBURG, *Johannesevangelium*, I, 1965, p. 347 (ET: 1968, pp. 517-518): "die joh. σημεῖα im vollen und tiefen Sinn gehen ganz und gar von Jesus aus, sind untrennbar an sein Offenbarungswirken im Auftrag des Vaters gebunden und können nur im Glauben aufgenommen und verstanden werden"; WILKENS, *Zeichen und Werke*, 1969, p. 49; HOFBECK, *Semeion*, ²1970, p. 68, 98-101. On δόξα, see below, p. 389 n. 61.

19. SCHNACKENBURG, *Johannesevangelium*, I, 1965, p. 344 (ET: 1968, p. 515); RENGSTORF, in *TWNT* 7 (1964), pp. 249-251 (ET: 1971, pp. 250-252). With the exception of ch. 6, the disciples do not play a great role in the miracle stories. They are, however, always supposed to be present as witnesses of Jesus' wonderful works (see 15,27 καὶ ὑμεῖς δὲ μαρτυρεῖτε, ὅτι ἀπ᾽ ἀρχῆς μετ᾽ ἐμοῦ ἐστε). In the miracle stories they are mentioned in 2,2.11 (cf. 2,12); 6,3.8.12.16.22.24; 9,2; 11,7.8.12.54; see also 7,3. Cp. 20,30 especially with 2,11 and 11,15 (καὶ χαίρω δι᾽ ὑμᾶς ἵνα πιστεύσητε) (cf. SCHNELLE, *Christologie*, 1987, p. 153; ET: 1992, p. 237). For the disciples as witnesses of the miracles, cf. BERNARD, *John*, II, 1928, p. 685 (he supposes that "the witnesses of the 'signs' were not only the Twelve, but disciples generally", p. 685); THOMAS, in *BS* 125 (1968), pp. 256-257 (he pointed out that in 20,30 the evangelist relates the content of his gospel to signs performed in presence of Jesus' *disciples*). See also BULTMANN, *Johannes*, 1941, p. 541 n. 2 (ET: 1971, p. 698 n. 2); BROWN, *John*, II, 1970, p. 1060; CARSON, *John*, 1991, p. 175.

20. THÜSING, *Erhöhung*, 1960, p. 74; WILKENS, *Zeichen und Werke*, 1969, p. 84; HOFBECK, *Semeion*, ²1970, p. 148: "'Ἔργα können auch synonym zu σημεῖα sein" (cp. p. 155); NICOL, *Sēmeia*, 1972, p. 116; SCHNELLE, *Christologie*, 1987, p. 167 (ET: 1992, p. 150): "Parallelbegriffe sind σημεῖα und ἔργα nur insofern sie beide das Wunderwirken Jesu bezeichnen". For the interpretation of σημεῖα in 20,30-31, see below, pp. 398-404.

21. RENGSTORF, in *TWNT* 7 (1964), p. 246 (ET: 1971, p. 248); WILKENS, *Zeichen und Werke*, 1969, pp. 83-88, esp. p. 83; MORRIS, *John*, 1972, p. 690; REINHARTZ, *John 20:30-31*, 1983, pp. 24, 50. Only in 7,3, is the word used by others. See CERFAUX, *Les miracles*, 1954, p. 132 (= 1954, p. 42); BROWN, *John*, 1966, p. 526.

Johannine usage"[22]. Of the 27 instances in Jn, ἔργον occurs 17 times meaning miracle[23], but in contrast to σημεῖον it is always used in discourse material: 3 times in the singular (7,21; 10,32b.33) and 14 times in the plural (5,20.36.36; 7,3; 9,3.4; 10,25.32a.37.38; 14,10.11.12; 15,24). In all these instances (except 14,10), as with σημεῖον, Jesus is the one who does the ἔργον/α. The miracles as works of Jesus have revelation quality as well as a legitimation function (cp. Mt 11,2-6) and are clear expressions of the unity of the Father with the Son (4,34; 5,36; 6,28-29; 9,4; 10,25.32.37; 14,10; 17,4)[24]. The Son fulfills the ἔργα τοῦ θεοῦ[25], does the will of the one who sent him. Thus, the works testify that the Father has sent the Son[26].

Jesus' words can also be presented as works (5,36-38; 8,28; 14,10; 15,22-24)[27]. In 4,34 and 17,4 ἔργον means "the total life-work of Jesus, i.e., the revelation of the Father, i.e., the works as well as the words"[28]. But this does not mean that in Jn there is an identity between words and works/signs of Jesus (so Bultmann)[29]. From 10,32-38 and 14,8-12 it appears that the evangelist clearly distinguishes both meanings[30].

22. RENGSTORF, in *TWNT* 7 (1964), p. 246 (ET: 1971, p. 248).

23. See BOISMARD's Johannine characteristic B4 ἔργον/ἔργα = miracle(s) (= NEIRYNCK no. 141 and RUCKSTUHL C42). See also RENGSTORF, in *TWNT* 7 (1964), p. 246 (ET: 1971, p. 247); NICOL, *Sēmeia*, 1972, p. 116; MORRIS, *John*, 1972, p. 689; BETZ, *Problem*, 1974, p. 37 (= 1987, p. 412); *Wesen*, 1977, pp. 132-133; HEILIGENTHAL, *Werke als Zeichen*, 1983, pp. 139-142; SCHNELLE, *Christologie*, 1987, p. 166 (ET: 1992, p. 149).

24. BERTRAM, in *TWNT* 2 (1935), p. 639 (ET: 1964, pp. 642-643); WILKENS, *Zeichen und Werke*, 1969, p. 85; BETZ, *Problem*, 1974, p. 37 (= 1987, p. 412); SCHNELLE, *Christologie*, 1987, p. 166 (ET: 1992, p. 149).

25. WILKENS, *Zeichen und Werke*, 1969, p. 86.

26. Cp. BARRETT, *John*, 1955, p. 63 (²1978, p. 75; GT: 1990, p. 91): "The works make visible both the character and the power of God, and at the same time that in Christ he is active in a unique way"; WILKENS, *Zeichen und Werke*, 1969, p. 86.

27. WILKENS, *Zeichen und Werke*, 1969, pp. 86-88; NICOL, *Sēmeia*, 1972, p. 115 (ctr. Bernard, Hoskyns, and Barrett, who say the ἔργα are miracles); RIEDL, *Das Heilswerk Jesu*, 1973, pp. 43-183; SCHNELLE, *Christologie*, 1987, p. 166 (ET: 1992, p. 149).

28. WILKENS, *Zeichen und Werke*, 1969, p. 85; NICOL, *Sēmeia*, 1972, p. 116; cp. BROWN, *John*, 1966, p. 527; HOFBECK, *Semeion*, ²1970, pp. 68, 72, 147; MORRIS, *John*, 1972, p. 689-690; HEILIGENTHAL, *EWNT* (1981), c. 124 (ET: 1991, p. 50); SCHNELLE, *Christologie*, 1987, p. 166 (ET: 1992, p. 149); DE JONGE, *Signs and Works*, 1978, p. 122 (= 1977, p. 133).

29. Against BULTMANN, *Theologie*, 1958, p. 413 (= ET: II, 1955, p. 60): "*die Werke Jesu – als Ganzes einheitlich gesehen: sein Werk – sind seine Worte*", see SCHNELLE, *Christologie*, 1987, p. 166 (ET: 1992, p. 149). Cp. CERFAUX, *Les miracles*, 1954, p. 138 (= 1954, p. 49): "Il faut cependant reconnaître que Jésus se révèle de deux manières bien différentes, tantôt par ses déclarations, tantôt par ses œuvres (la valeur théologique de celles-ci requérant d'ailleurs des explications du révélateur)".

30. WILKENS, *Zeichen und Werke*, 1969, p. 54: "Es geht nicht an, die Semeia als blosse Bilder, Symbole, verba visibilia zu interpretieren"; cp. p. 87; DE JONGE, *Signs and Works*, 1978, p. 124 (= 1977, p. 136): "R. Bultmann's often quoted saying, 'The works of Jesus (or, seen collectively as a whole: his work) are his words'..., is one-sided and wrong".

In other instances where ἔργον does not denote primarily a miracle, the subject can be the Father (5,20; 14,10; cp. 5,17; 10,32), or the disciples (14,12), who continue the works of Jesus and will do greater works than Jesus has done because the exalted Christ will work through the disciples. Or it can be people in general (3,19.20.21), the crowd (6,28.29), the κόσμος (7,7), Abraham (8,39), or the devil (8,41)[31]. The ethical quality of these works depends on whether they are done in God (3,21; 6,28.29; 8,39; 14,12) or whether they are derived from the devil or the world (3,19.20; 7,7; 8,41)[32].

Thus ἔργον does not mean "miracle" only and it is not restricted to Jesus' activity[33]. The σημεῖα exclusively mean the revelatory *acts* of Jesus; the ἔργα also mean revelatory *words*[34]. Moreover, the σημεῖα are limited to the public activity of Jesus, whereas the ἔργα also concern the works of the glorified (exalted) Christ[35]. Furthermore, while σημεῖον is mainly a christological concept which expresses the visual revelation of Jesus' δόξα that provokes faith or unbelief, ἔργον has a wider meaning. It can mean the whole revelatory work of Jesus and refers especially to Jesus' divine mission[36]. The unity of the Father and the Son becomes manifest in the ἔργα. From this point of view, ἔργον is a soteriological concept[37]. But when it refers to the works of the disciples, it is used in an ecclesiological sense[38]. Finally, when speaking of the ἔργα πονηρά/ἀγαθά of the people, the evangelist uses it in an *ethical* sense[39].

---

31. BERTRAM, in *TWNT* 2 (1935), pp. 642, 646-647 (ET: 1964, pp. 645, 650); HOFBECK, *Semeion*, ²1970, p. 67 (cp. p. 68); MORRIS, *John*, 1972, p. 688; SCHNELLE, *Christologie*, 1987, pp. 166-167 (ET: 1992, pp. 149-150).

32. HOFBECK, *Semeion*, ²1970, p. 67; MORRIS, *John*, 1972, p. 688; SCHNELLE, *Christologie*, 1987, p. 167 (ET: 1992, p. 150).

33. SCHNELLE, *Christologie*, 1987, p. 167 (ET: 1992, p. 150).

34. DE JONGE, *Signs and Works*, 1978, p. 123 (= 1977, p. 134): "All Jesus did *and said* on earth is summed up in the word ἔργον"; SCHNELLE, *Christologie*, 1987, p. 167 (ET: 1992, p. 150).

35. SCHNACKENBURG, *Johannesevangelium*, I, 1965, pp. 349, 352-353 (ET: 1968, pp. 520, 523-524); HOFBECK, *Semeion*, ²1970, p. 69; SCHNELLE, *Christologie*, 1987, p. 167 (ET: 1992, p. 150).

36. SCHNELLE, *Christologie*, 1987, p. 167 (ET: 1992, p. 150).

37. SCHNACKENBURG, *Johannesevangelium*, I, 1965, p. 349 (ET: 1968, p. 520): "Die 'Werke' sind stärker messianisch, die 'Zeichen' ganz und gar christologisch orientiert, obwohl sich bei Joh beides nie trennen lässt"; HOFBECK, *Semeion*, ²1970, pp. 69, 72, 156-157; SCHNELLE, *Christologie*, 1987, p. 167 (ET: 1992, p. 150).

38. HOFBECK, *Semeion*, ²1970, pp. 69, 72; SCHNELLE, *Christologie*, 1987, p. 167 (ET: 1992, p. 150).

39. HOFBECK, *Semeion*, ²1970, p. 67; SCHNELLE, *Christologie*, 1987, p. 167 (ET: 1992, p. 150). See BOISMARD's Johannine characteristic B58 ἔργα πονηρά (= NEIRYNCK no. 143).

3. Although the evangelist distinguishes between σημεῖον and ἔργον[40], "the overlap among the usage of the terms suggests that there is no intention in the Gospel to differentiate sharply among them"[41]. By using ἔργα (χριστοῦ/θεοῦ), however, he has not rejected, or even restricted, but deepened the exclusive christological meaning of the σημεῖα as a precise indication for the revelatory activity of the Incarnate One[42]. The interchangeability of the two terms is apparent, even within the same chapter (cp. 7,3 with v. 31; 9,3-4 with v. 16; 10,25.32.37-38 with v. 41; 12,37 with 15,24)[43]. In addition, the two terms occur in similar constructions, which in most instances are mentioned in the lists of Johannine characteristics:

(a) Of the 17 instances, σημεῖον occurs 14 times in the construction ποιέω σημεῖον/σημεῖα, 5 times in the singular (4,54; 6,14.30; 10,41; 12,18) and 9 times in the plural (2,11; 2,23; 3,2; 6,2; 7,31; 9,16; 11,47; 12,37; 20,30)[44]. The

40. HOFBECK, *Semeion*, [2]1970, p. 69; SCHNELLE, *Christologie*, 1987, p. 167 (ET: 1992, p. 150). See above, p. 384.

41. Cf. REINHARTZ, *John 20:30-31*, 1983, p. 32.

42. WILKENS, *Zeichen und Werke*, 1969, p. 86; MORRIS, *John*, 1972, p. 690-691: "Perhaps it would be true to say that where John sees miracles from one point of view as σημεῖα, activities pointing men to God, from another point of view he sees them as ἔργα, activities which take their origin in God. But because they originate with God they have a revelatory function and they also point men to God. Therefore John can look for faith on the basis of the 'works' just as much as on the basis of 'signs'. ἔργον for him is the fuller word. It includes what we could call the 'natural' activities of Jesus as well as the 'supernatural'. It reminds us that these are all of a piece, that Jesus' whole life was consistently spent in doing the will of God and in accomplishing His purpose. Not only in the miracles, but in all His life He was showing forth God's glory"; BURGE, *The Anointed One*, 1987, p. 79: "The signs reveal the oneness and unity of God and Jesus in all that Jesus does. The signs are proof that the Father is working through Jesus. They authenticate the revelation of the Son. The signs are John's conscious theological effort toward a oneness christology. John's special use of work (ἔργον) supports and develops this aspect further"; RIGA, *Signs of Glory*, 1963, p. 423: "*Sēmeia* have as their deeper explanation the fact that they are the works (*erga*) of the Father performed by Christ". The unity between the two expressions, designating the miracles, is very well expressed in the title of Cerfaux's article: "Les miracles, signes messianiques de Jésus et œuvres de Dieu, selon l'Évangile de Jean"; BETZ, *Problem*, 1974, p. 37 (= 1987, p. 412): "Das σημεῖον wird eingebettet in das Wirken von Vater und Sohn (vgl. 5,1-20; 9,3f). Andererseits wird das Werk Jesu zum Zeichen, weil es als Taterweis von Vater und Sohn die messianische Sendung Jesu aufzeigt"; cp. p. 38 (= p. 413): "Die Offenbarungseinheit von Vater und Sohn ist nicht auf die johanneischen Reden beschränkt, sondern schon vom Begriff σημεῖον her auch in den Wundern vorausgesetzt; an Stellen wie Joh 2,4 und 4,48 wird sie darüberhinaus ausdrücklich betont". Cp. FORTNA (see above, p. 228 n. 453).

43. SCHNACKENBURG, *Johannesevangelium*, I, 1965, p. 347 (ET: 1968, p. 518). Moreover, DE JONGE, *Signs and Works*, 1978, p. 121 (= 1977, p. 132), notes: "in 7:3 the use of τὰ ἔργα σου is parallel to that of σημεῖα in 20:30"; REINHARTZ, *John 20:30-31*, 1983, pp. 28-30.

44. See BOISMARD's Johannine characteristic B81 (= NEIRYNCK no. 346 and RUCK-STUHL C43). See also, e.g., CERFAUX, *Les miracles*, 1954, p. 133 (= 1954, p. 43); CHARLIER, *La notion de signe*, 1959, p. 435; FORMESYN, *Le Sèmeion johannique*, 1962, p. 883; RENGSTORF, in *TWNT* 7 (1964), p. 243 (ET: 1971, p. 245); HOFBECK, *Semeion*, [2]1970,

three other occurrences of σημεῖον have to do with the request or demand for a sign (2,18: τί σημεῖον δεικνύεις ἡμῖν, ὅτι ταῦτα ποιεῖς;)[45], the search for Jesus (6,26: ζητεῖτέ με οὐχ ὅτι εἴδετε σημεῖα ἀλλ' ὅτι ἐφάγετε ἐκ τῶν ἄρτων καὶ ἐχορτάσθητε)[46], and with the Septuagint construction σημεῖα καὶ τέρατα (4,48)[47]. – Ἔργον is also used with ποιέω in 5,36; 7,3.21; 10,25.37; 14,10.12; 15,24 (in 5,36; 10,25 and 14,12: τὰ ἔργα ἃ ἐγὼ ποιῶ; see also 8,39.41; 17,4)[48]; compare the characteristic ἐργάζομαι τὰ ἔργα (3,21; 6,28; 9,4)[49] and τελειόω τὸ ἔργον (4,34; 17,4)[50]. In 5,20; 10,32 the verb δείκνυμι is used[51].

(b) In several instances, the word σημεῖον is connected with *verba videndi*: (a) ὁράω (or εἶδον)[52] in 4,48 (ἴδητε); 6,2 (*v.l.* ἑώρων TR T V N[25]); 6,14 (ἰδόντες); 6,26 (εἴδετε); 6,30 (ἴδωμεν); (b) θεωρέω[53] in 2,23 (θεωροῦντες); 6,2 (ἐθεώρουν). In 12,18 another verb of perception is used (ἀκούω)[54]. Moreover, the use of ἔμπροσθεν αὐτῶν in 12,37 and ἐνώπιον τῶν μαθητῶν in 20,30 may be interpreted in the same line[55]. Together with θεάομαι and βλέπω

p. 67 n. 5; WEAD, *The Literary Devices*, 1970, p. 19; KONINGS, *Joh. verhaal*, III, 1972, pp. 293-294; NICOL, *Sēmeia*, 1972, p. 115; BETZ, *Problem*, 1974, p. 37 (= 1987, p. 412); *Wesen*, 1977, pp. 128, 131, 132; WAGNER, *Auferstehung*, 1988, pp. 286-289; COLLINS, *Miracles and Faith*, 1990, p. 30; REINHARTZ, *John 20:30-31*, 1983, pp. 30-33.

45. For the use of the verb δείκνυμι, see also below, n. 51.

46. Cp. BOISMARD's Johannine characteristic A59 τί ζητεῖς/ζητεῖτε (cf. Jn 1,38, 4,27; 18,4.7; 20,15) (= NEIRYNCK no. 157 and RUCKSTUHL B12). Other characteristics with ζητέω: Boismard C21 ζητέω: to search for Jesus (= NEIRYNCK no. 156); BOISMARD C28 δόξαν ζητέω (= NEIRYNCK no. 92); BOISMARD B79 ζητέω ἀποκτεῖναι (= NEIRYNCK no. 56 and RUCKSTUHL B22).

47. For σημεῖα καὶ τέρατα, see Deut 29,2; 34,11; Jer 32,21; Bar 2,11; Dan 3,31 (99), etc.; Mk 13,22 par Mt 24,24; Acts 2,19.22.43; 4,30; 5,12; 6,8; 7,36; 14,3; 15,12; Rom 15,19; 2 Cor 12,12; 2 Thess 2,9; Heb 2,4. See, e.g., CERFAUX, *Les miracles*, 1954, p. 133 (= 1954, p. 43); RENGSTORF, in *TWNT* 7 (1964), pp. 242-243 (ET: 1971, pp. 244-245); BROWN, *John*, 1966, p. 527; GROB, *Faire l'œuvre de Dieu*, 1986, pp. 63-64. For the history of the expression, see S.V. McCASLAND, *Signs and Wonders*, in *JBL* 76 (1957) 149-152.

48. See BOISMARD's Johannine characteristic B101 ποιέω τὰ ἔργα (= NEIRYNCK no. 345). See also RENGSTORF, in *TWNT* 7 (1964), p. 246 (ET: 1971, p. 248); BETZ, *Wesen*, 1977, p. 133.

49. See BOISMARD's Johannine characteristic A112 (= NEIRYNCK no. 142 and RUCK-STUHL C7). See also CERFAUX, *Les miracles*, 1954, p. 132 (= 1954, p. 42).

50. See BOISMARD's Johannine characteristic A159 τελειόω τὸ ἔργον / τὰ ἔργα (= NEIRYNCK no. 375 and RUCKSTUHL C37).

51. CHARLIER, *La notion de signe*, 1959, p. 435; HOFBECK, *Semeion*, ²1970, p. 67 n. 5; BETZ, *Wesen*, 1977, p. 133.

52. CHARLIER, *La notion de signe*, 1959, p. 435; RENGSTORF, in *TWNT* 7 (1964), p. 242 (ET: 1971, p. 243); HOFBECK, *Semeion*, ²1970, p. 67 n. 3.

53. RENGSTORF, in *TWNT* 7 (1964), p. 242 (ET: 1971, p. 243); HOFBECK, *Semeion*, ²1970, p. 67 n. 3.

54. HOFBECK, *Semeion*, ²1970, p. 67 n. 3. See esp. LAMMERS, *Hören und Glauben*, 1966, pp. 49-62.

55. Ἐνώπιον occurs in Jn only at 20,30. BOISMARD – LAMOUILLE consider it a Lukan characteristic of *Jn II-B* (*Jean*, 1977, p. 475a; cp. p. 66a). Cp. BERNARD, *John*, II, 1928, p. 685; BARRETT, *John*, 1955, p. 478 (²1978, p. 575; GT: 1990, p. 550). But the Johannine character may be clear from 1 Jn 3,22 and 3 Jn 6 (35 times in the Apocalypse) (cf. SCHNELLE, *Christologie*, 1987, p. 153; ET: 1992, p. 136). Moreover, its use in 20,30

these verbs of seeing play an important role in John[56]. – Ἔργον is also accompanied with a verb of seeing in 7,3 (θεωρέω)[57]; compare the use of φανερόω in 9,2-3 (cp. 3,21)[58].

(c) Whether implicitly or explicitly, faith based on signs (cf. 6,26 ὅτι) is connected with all 17 instances of σημεῖον. In 10 instances, the verb πιστεύω occurs immediately in the context[59]: 2,11.23; 4,48.54 (cp. v. 53); 6,30; 7,31; 10,41 (cf. v. 42); 11,47 (cf. vv. 45.48); 12,37; 20,30. Compare the use of ἀκολουθέω (6,2), ζητέω (6,26), ὑπαντάω (12,18)[60]. – The term ἔργον is also connected with the verb πιστεύω in 5,38 (cf. v. 36); 6,29; 7,3; 10,25.37.38; 14,10.11.

is to be compared with the use of ἔμπροσθεν in 12,37. Ἔμπροσθεν is used 5 times in Jn, but, as NEIRYNCK has noted, means "before (the eyes of) someone" only in 12,37 (*Jean et les Synoptiques*, 1979, p. 163 n. 353). Thus, the occurrence of ἐνώπιον (τῶν μαθητῶν αὐτοῦ) (20,30) alongside ἔμπροσθεν (αὐτῶν) (12,37) can be regarded as one of the many Johannine variations. See esp. BITTNER, *Jesu Zeichen*, 1977, p. 221, who notes: "Der Blick in die Septuagint zeigt das beide [ἔμπροσθεν/ἐνώπιον] auf dieselben hebräischen Äquivalente zurückgehen" (with reference to JOHANNESSOHN, *Präpositionen*, 1926, pp. 194-196, 359-361).

56. RENGSTORF, in *TWNT* 7 (1964), p. 242 (ET: 1971, p. 243): "Das joh σημεῖον ist etwas, das man sehen kann u[nd] im Grunde auch sehen soll". See BOISMARD's Johannine characteristics B82 ἑώρακα, perfect tense (= NEIRYNCK no. 285); A40 ὁράω/θεάομαι + μαρτυρέω (= NEIRYNCK no. 286); B54 ὁράω/θεωρέω/θεάομαι (God, the Father) (= NEIRYNCK no. 287); C77 ἴδε (= NEIRYNCK no. 167); B68 ὁράω + πιστεύω, same subject (= NEIRYNCK no. 337); C41 θεωρέω + substantive + participle (= NEIRYNCK no. 164). See also RUCKSTUHL's characteristic C17 ἴδε/ἴδετε + another imperative (which differs from Boismard C77 = NEIRYNCK 286). See also CULLMANN, *Εἶδεν καὶ ἐπίστευσεν*, 1950; PHILLIPS, *Faith and Vision in the Fourth Gospel*, 1957; WENZ, *Sehen und Glauben*, 1961; FORMESYN, *Le Sèmeion johannique*, 1962, p. 883; HOFBECK, *Semeion*, ²1970, pp. 67, 178-179; TRAETS, *Voir Jésus*, 1967, pp. 132-145; HAHN, *Sehen und Glauben*, 1972; KYSAR, *The Fourth Evangelist*, 1975, pp. 231-232; WAGNER, *Auferstehung*, 1988, pp. 285-286; C. KOESTER, *Hearing, Seeing, and Believing in the Gospel of John*, 1989.

57. HEILIGENTHAL, *Werke als Zeichen*, 1983, p. 140: "Die in Joh 7,3 vorliegende Verbindung von ἔργον und θεάομαι [sic] gehörte in die Wundertradition (vgl. Joh 6,30; 15,24), wobei φανερόω (7,4) die Funktion der Wundertaten bestimmt. Denn die Taten werden getan, um sich der Welt zu offenbaren (vgl. Joh 3,21; 9,3)"; REINHARTZ, *John 20:30-31*, 1983, pp. 54-71: "The Johannine view of Signs-Faith"; cp. pp. 210-211;

58. HEILIGENTHAL, *Werke als Zeichen*, 1983, p. 139 n. 14. – See BOISMARD's characteristic E2 φανερόω (= NEIRYNCK no. 393). On this characteristic, see NEIRYNCK, *Jean et les Synoptiques*, 1979, pp. 156-158; *Semeia-bron*, 1983, pp. 12-13 (ET: 1991, pp. 660-661), and *Note sur Jn 21,14*, 1988, pp. 431-432 (= 1991, pp. 691-692). See also BOISMARD's Johannine characteristic A 155 φανερόω ἐμαυτόν (= NEIRYNCK no. 394); cp. the 1951 list of RUCKSTUHL (no. 28, no longer considered a Johannine characteristic in 1991).

59. CHARLIER, *La notion de signe*, 1959, pp. 435, 436-438; FORMESYN, *Le Sèmeion johannique*, 1962, p. 883; HOFBECK, *Semeion*, ²1970, p. 67 n. 4; see esp. pp. 178-192: "'Zeichen' und Glauben"; WEAD, *The Literary Devices*, 1970, p. 19; GROB, *Faire l'œuvre de Dieu*, 1986, pp. 51-56; WAGNER, *Auferstehung*, 1988, pp. 281-285; COLLINS, *Miracles and Faith*, 1990, p. 191.

60. On ζητέω, see above, pp. 380 n. 6, 387 n. 46.

(d) Both σημεῖα and ἔργα are closely connected with the Johannine theme of δόξα (2,11: σημεῖον) and the verb δοξάζω (17,4-5: ἔργον)[61].

(e) John has verbs with the same root as σημεῖον and ἔργον: resp. σημαίνω and ἐργάζομαι. The first verb occurs only three times and always in the Johannine expression σημαίνων ποίῳ θανάτῳ (12,33; 18,22; 21,19)[62]. The second verb occurs eight times, three in the construction ἐργάζομαι τὰ ἔργα, as noted above[63]. In addition, in 6,30 the two word-groups are used in close connection with each other (τί οὖν ποιεῖς σὺ σημεῖον, ἵνα ἴδωμεν καὶ πιστεύσωμέν σοι; τί ἐργάζῃ;)[64]. Compare also μὴ πλείονα σημεῖα ποιήσει said by the crowd in 7,31 with μείζονα τούτων δείξει αὐτῷ ἔργα said by Jesus in 5,20[65].

These similarities in the usage of the two terms make it difficult to assign them to two different literary layers: the signs source (σημεῖον) and the evangelist (ἔργον)[66].

2. The Unity of Signs and Discourses

There is not only an interrelationship between the words σημεῖον and ἔργον but also an interrelationship between narrative (miracle story) and discourse: "The sign provides the basis for the discourse which spells out the nature of the Son's relationship to the Father"[67]. For John, the signs are revelatory of the glory of God inasmuch as they show God's power at work through the person of Jesus. That power can be defined as life-giving power that involves the physical universe and the

61. BETZ, Wesen, 1977, p. 128; LÜTGEHETMANN, Die Hochzeit, 1990, pp. 238-261. See BOISMARD's Johannine characteristics C28 δόξαν ζητέω (= NEIRYNCK no. 92); B88 to see the glory (of Christ) (= NEIRYNCK no. 93); B9 δοξάζω, said of Jesus (= NEIRYNCK no. 94); B41 ὁ υἱὸς τοῦ ἀνθρώπου + ὑψόω/δοξάζω/ἀναβαίνω (= NEIRYNCK no. 388). See also, e.g., CHARLIER, La notion de signe, 1959, pp. 435, 440-444; RIGA, Signs of Glory, 1963, pp. 410-416; NICOL, Sēmeia, 1972, pp. 119-122; GROB, Faire l'œuvre de Dieu, 1986, pp. 56-59; BURGE, The Anointed One, 198, pp. 80-81.
62. See BOISMARD's characteristic A127 (= NEIRYNCK no. 363 and RUCKSTUHL B54). See also, e.g., E. SCHWEIZER, Ego Eimi, 1939, pp. 138-139; HOFBECK, Semeion, ²1970, p. 67 n. 2; MORRIS, John, 1972, pp. 686, 688; GROB, Faire l'œuvre de Dieu, 1986, p. 53.
63. See above, p. 387 n. 49.
64. BETZ, Wesen, 1977, p. 132; DE JONGE, Signs and Works, 1978, p. 121 (= 1977, p. 132); REINHARTZ, John 20:30-31, 1983, p. 32.
65. RENGSTORF, in TWNT 7 (1964), p. 246 (ET: 1971, p. 247).
66. See A. SCHWEIZER (p. 3 n. 13), WENDT (p. 12 n. 59), J.M. THOMPSON (p. 16 nn. 99-102), FAURE (p. 19).
67. M.M. THOMPSON, Humanity, 1988, p. 58, on Jn 5. See also BETZ, Problem, 1974, p. 38 (= 1987, p. 413): "In den johanneischen Wundern offenbart Jesus seine Herrlichkeit (2,11) und gewinnt den Glauben an seine Sendung und seine Person (2,11; 4,53, vgl. 12,37; 20,31; Ant 2,274). Genau das Gleiche gilt von den Reden (3,18; 5,24; 6,35.47; 7,38 u.a), aber auch von den redaktionellen Sätzen des Evangelisten (2,23f; 10,42; 12,42; 19,35)"; VOUGA, Jean 6, 1992, pp. 261-267. See also D.A. LEE, The Symbolic Narratives of the Fourth Gospel: The Interplay of Form and Meaning (JSNT SS, 95), Sheffield, 1994.

elements necessary for life (bread, water, wine, healing of the human body, restoration of life). In the miracle stories, the evangelist narrates Jesus' life-giving power; in the discourses, he explains what can be grasped from seeing a sign[68].

The Fourth Evangelist uses different literary techniques to comment on the signs[69]: (a) an interpretative discourse can follow the sign (chs. 5 and 6); (b) dialogues and discourses can be intricately interwoven with the narrative (chs. 9 and 11; cp. ch. 4); (c) the narrative can anticipate the discourse (2,1-11; 4,46-54)[70]. M.M. Thompson rightly notes: "The discourses attached to the signs are not extraneous appendages, but grow out of the very particular reality of the signs themselves. When Jesus feeds five thousand people, he is revealed as 'the bread of life'; when he opens the eyes of a blind man, he reveals himself to be 'light of the world'; and in raising Lazarus, he manifests the validity of his claim to be 'resurrection and life'"[71].

Thus, in the Gospel of John "the events themselves, the Johannine σημεῖα, are symbolic acts"[72]. The whole gospel, "narrative and dis-

---

68. Especially DODD, *Interpretation*, 1953, pp. 297-389, has stressed that in the seven episodes of "the Book of Signs" (Jn 1–12) "the discourses ... serve to elucidate the significance of the narrative" (p. 291). "The Book of the Passion" (Jn 13–20; cf. pp. 390-443) is "constructed on a pattern broadly similar to that of each individual episode of the Book of Signs", with the difference, however, that "the narrative follows the discourses, instead of the discourses following the narrative, as is the general rule in the Book of Signs" (p. 290). Cp., e.g., WREDE, *Charakter und Tendenz*, ²1933, pp. 5-7, esp. 6: "Und die Reden stehen nicht etwa bloss neben den Geschichten, sie knüpfen ja so manchmal an sie an, sie wachsen aus ihnen hervor"; E. SCHWEIZER, *Ego Eimi*, 1939, pp. 139-140; BROWN, *John*, I, 1966, p. 525; cp. pp. CXL-CXLI; SMALLEY, *John*, 1978, pp. 86-92; THOMPSON, *Humanity*, 1988, pp. 56-63; MORRIS, *Jesus is the Christ*, 1989, pp. 20-42; BARTON, in *Theology* 96 (1993) 289-302, esp. p. 296.

69. THOMPSON, *Humanity*, 1988, p. 57; *John, Gospel of*, 1992, p. 379. On John as creative writer, see DODD, *Interpretation*, 1953, p. 389, who remarked on the composition of the Book of Signs: "which I take to be characteristic of the creative mind to which we owe the composition of the Fourth Gospel"; cp. SELONG, *Cleansing*, 1971, pp. 124-125; MORRIS, *Jesus is the Christ*, 1989, p. 42; VOUGA, *Jean 6*, 1992, pp. 261-267.

70. THOMPSON, *Humanity*, 1988, p. 141 n. 11, remarks: "Jesus' discourse with Nicodemus about new life may belong with the changing of water into wine. There are thematic links between the story of the healing of the official's son, with its emphasis on Jesus' hour to give life (4:50-53), and the discourse about the Son's life-giving authority in 5:19-47 (5:21,25-26)". According to SMALLEY, *John*, 1978, p. 89, the "discourse concerning the living water of life (4,7-26) looks backwards to the discussion with Nicodemus about new birth through water and Spirit (3:5), and forwards to the new life given at a distance to the official's son"; cp. MORRIS, *Jesus is the Christ*, 1989, pp. 25-26.

71. THOMPSON, *Humanity*, 1988, p. 62; cp. BETZ, *Problem*, 1974, p. 38 (= 1987, p. 413): "Das 'Ego Eimi' des Offenbarers, das in den Reden soteriologisch entfaltet ist, wird auch im Wunder vom Seewandel sowohl offenbarend als auch soteriologisch verkündigt (6,20); in dieser Bedeutung erscheint es auch in der Leidensgeschichte (18,6.8). Wie das Beispiel der spätjüdischen Propheten zeigt, gehören das σημεῖον und das Ego eimi fest zusammen; von daher is es unsachgemäss, sie auf verschiedenartige Quellen zu verteilen".

72. CULPEPPER, *Anatomy*, 1983, p. 185.

course, [is] bound together by an intricate network of symbolism" and
depicts "a world in which phenomena – things and events – are a living
and moving image of the eternal, and not a veil of illusion to hide it, a
world in which the Word is made flesh"[73]. By combining the discourses
with the signs, the evangelist shows that "they are to be understood
symbolically"[74]. Because of this unity between narrative and discourse,
we question the existence of a pre-Johannine source without discourses[75]
and consider it improbable that the miracle stories and the discourses are
attributable to independent sources: "The evangelist saw both narrative
and discourse as important for the purpose of his work, but varied the
relationship between the two in a provocative and unmonotonous
way"[76].

3. The Characteristics of the Johannine Σημεῖα

1. In John, we find the most marvelous miracles of the New Testament. In their greatness Jesus manifests his divinity. The trend to
emphasize the miraculous as such and to picture Jesus with an unlimited
power is clear in every miracle story[77]:

(a) Jesus produced about 120 gallons of wine (2,6) and the steward, ignorant of
the miracle, testifies to the good quality of wine (2,9-10). (b) At Cana, Jesus
heals the official's son, who was at the point of death (4,47.49; compare
Lk 7,2), from afar by the word alone, and immediately. It is narrated in detail
how the father realized that his son recovered in the same hour that Jesus spoke
the healing word, and he and his house came to a full faith (4,52-53). Compared
with the parallel story in Mt 8,5-13 and Lk 7,1-10, there is a *Steigerung* of
distance. (c) Jesus healed a man paralyzed for thirty-eight years (5,5). (d) From
a handful of bread and fishes (6,9) is fed a multitude so large that even two
hundred denarii would not buy enough bread (6,7.10). (e) In the story of the
walking on the sea an extra miracle, not mentioned by the Synoptics, is told: the
boat was still in the middle of the stormy sea, but when the disciples took Jesus
aboard, all problems were solved "and suddenly the boat reached the land they
were making for" (6,21). (f) Jesus healed a man, blind from his birth (9,1).

73. DODD, *Interpretation*, 1953, p. 143; cp. CULPEPPER, *Anatomy*, 1983, p. 185.
74. CULPEPPER, *Anatomy*, 1983, p. 185; cp. THOMPSON, *Humanity*, 1988, p. 62.
75. See, e.g., LINDARS (see above, p. 175), THYEN (p. 265), SMALLEY (p. 318),
COTHENET (p. 313), LEIDIG (p. 320), BRUCE (p. 324), MARCHADOUR (p. 335) KÜHSCHELM
(p. 347), KYSAR (p. 356), PAINTER (pp. 353-354), SEGOVIA (p. 355). Note that PERKINS
supposes that the miracles of the signs source were already elaborated with discourses
before they were incorporated into the gospel (p. 136).
76. KYSAR, *John, The Gospel of*, 1992, p. 916ab.
77. SCHNELLE, *Christologie*, 1987, p. 183 (ET: 1992, p. 165), with reference to H.J.
HOLTZMANN, *Lehrbuch der neutestamentlichen Theologie*, II, ²1911, p. 459. Thus, I disagree with COLLINS, *Miracles and Faith*, 1990, p. 192, who notes: "It is likewise clear
that the author of the Fourth Gospel was not particularly interested in accentuating the
'wonder' element of signs. ... They hardly accentuate Jesus' power as wonder worker".

(*g*) He raises Lazarus, whom he found already dead four days (11,17). (*h*) The miraculous catch of fish is described vividly: the net is full of large fish, a hundred and fifty of them, and even so the net did not break (21,6.11).

2. The "heightening" of the miraculous is related to the tendency to depict Jesus as acting on his own initiative. In three miracles, Jesus rebukes the requests addressed to him (2,4; 4,48; 11,6) and keeps the initiative in hand by reacting differently than expected. In all other miracle stories, Jesus takes the full initiative (cp. 7,6-10.14)[78]. This characteristic can be compared with other passages where "John ... records Jesus' interlocutors operating at a purely human, natural level, while Jesus himself transcends their demands or expectations"[79] (cf. 3,3-4; 4,15; 5,6-7; 6,32-33; 11,22-24; see also 8,59; 10,39; 11,11.30; 18,36; 20,17).

3. Not only the miracle, but also Jesus' supernatural knowledge and omniscience are pointers to his divinity[80]. We find these characteristics in the miracle stories (cf. 5,6; 6,6.15a; see also 4,50; 11,11.14-15), where the motif is linked with the tendency to depict Jesus as taking the initiative. Also outside the miracle stories, the motif of Jesus' supernatural knowledge appears again and again: Jesus knows his destiny (2,19.21; 3,14; 4,35; 6,64.70; 8,21.40; 12,23.27; 13,1.3.11.7.18-19.38; 14,29; 16,4; 17,1; 18,4.32; 19,28; cp. 15,18-26), he knows what his disciples think (16,19; cp. 6,43.61), he knows human beings and what is in their hearts (2,24-25; 5,42; 6,64), he teaches the Scriptures, although he has not studied (7,15), he knows Peter (1,42) and Nathanael (1,47-48), and is informed about the past life of the Samaritan woman (4,16-19.29.39). What Jesus' knowledge means is expressed in the disciples' confession in 16,30: νῦν οἴδαμεν ὅτι οἶδας πάντα καὶ οὐ χρείαν ἔχεις ἵνα τίς σε ἐρωτᾷ· ἐν τούτῳ πιστεύομεν ὅτι ἀπὸ θεοῦ ἐξῆλθες

---

78. Cf. KONINGS, *Joh. verhaal*, III, 1972, pp. 384-386; SCHNACKENBURG, *Johannes-evangelium*, I, 1965, p. 334 (ET: 1968, p. 329); WILKENS, *Zeichen und Werke*, 1969, pp. 46-47: "Jesus, der in den Zeichen souverän Handelnde"; GROB, *Faire l'œuvre de Dieu*, 1986, p. 61; BLACKBURN, *Miracles and Miracle Stories*, 1992, p. 556. – The evangelist stresses that Jesus is acting independently of all human instigation in 4,46-54 and 2,1-12 (cp. 11,1-44) by the following pattern common throughout the gospel: (1) Someone (respectively Mary and the royal official) comes with a request (2,3; 4,47; cp. 11,3); (2) Jesus seems to refuse the request (2,4; 4,48; cp. 11,6); (3) The questioner persists (2,5; 4,49); (4) Jesus grants the request. Cf. BROWN, *John*, 1966, p. 194; THOMPSON, *Humanity*, 1988, pp. 71-72. See esp. MOLONEY, in *Salesianum* 40 (1978), p. 826 (= 1980, pp. 190-191); GIBLIN, in *NTS* 26 (1979-80) 197-211; PAINTER, in *JSNT* 36 (1989), pp. 23-24, 27-28; 41 (1991), pp. 50-52, 65-68.

79. CARSON, *John*, 1991, p. 170 (on 2,3-4), with reference to GOURGUES, in *NRT* 108 (1986), pp. 174-191, esp. 179-180.

80. SCHNELLE, *Christologie*, 1987, p. 184 (ET: 1992, pp. 165-166); BLACKBURN, *Miracles and Miracle Stories*, 1992, p. 555.

(cp. 21,17). This emphasis on Jesus' marvelous foreknowledge is parallel to his performing of miracles and indicative of his divinity. This is a conscious motif used by the evangelist throughout the Gospel[81].

4. The greatness of the miracles reveals not only Jesus' divinity, but also his humanity[82]. In narrating each miracle the evangelist stresses the "solidly material aspect", the facticity, the reality of the signs[83]:

(a) In the first Cana miracle, the reality of the wonder is demonstrated not only by the quantity of the water changed into wine (six stone jars, holding each twenty or thirty gallons; cf. 2,6), but also by the testimony of the steward of the feast, ignorant of the miracle, who tasted and praised the quality of the wine (2,9-10). (b) In the second Cana miracle, the servants of the royal official confirmed that the son recovered in the same hour that Jesus spoke the healing word (4,51-53). (c) After Jesus' healing word, the man at the pool called Bethzatha who was ill for thirty-eight years (5,5) was healed at once, took up his pallet and walked (5,8-9). (d) At the feeding of the five thousand (6,10), not even two hundred denarii would have bought enough bread for each person to get a little (6,8), but from five barley loaves and two fish (6,9), the multitude is sated, and the disciples filled twelve baskets with leftover fragments (6,12-13). (e) The reality of Jesus' walking on the sea is especially demonstrated in 6,22-25. (f) The identity of the man born blind (9,1) with the man who recovered his sight is explicitly stated in 9,9.20.25.30. (g) At the raising of Lazarus it is explicitly said by Martha that Lazarus was really dead: "Lord, by this time there will be an odor, for he has been dead four days", but after Jesus' word (11,43), in the presence of the people standing by (11,42), the dead man came out, his hands and feet bound with bandages and his face wrapped with a cloth, and Jesus commanded them to unbind him and to let him go (11,44). (g) In 21,1-14, it is noted that the disciples are not able to haul the net (21,6), for it contained one hundred and fifty-three large fishes (21,11).

By narrating the reality of Jesus' deeds the evangelist makes Jesus' δόξα visible, and thus the signs eminently illustrate the incarnation of the Logos (1,14)[84].

81. SCHNELLE, Christologie, 1987, p. 184 (ET: 1992, p. 166).

82. For the expression "solidly 'material' aspect", see SCHNACKENBURG, Johannesevangelium, I, 1965, p. 354 (ET: 1968, p. 525) (see below, p. 398 n. 107); cp. THOMPSON, Humanity, 1988, p. 56, 62, 63.

83. SCHNELLE, Christologie, 1987, pp. 184-185 (ET: 1992, pp. 166-167). See also WREDE, Charakter und Tendenz, ²1933, pp. 6-7; E. SCHWEIZER, Ego Eimi, 1939, p. 139-140; WILKENS, Zeichen und Werke, 1969, pp. 30-45, esp. 30, 44-45 (n. 325), 49. Cp. CULLMANN, Εἶδεν καὶ ἐπίστευσεν, 1950, p. 55: "Il n'y a par conséquent aucune contradiction lorsque l'évangile insiste d'une part sur la nécessité de voir physiquement, et d'autre part sur celle de croire. En réalité, cette juxtaposition correspond à toute la pensée du quatrième Évangile ainsi qu'au but qu'il poursuit".

84. CERFAUX, Les miracles, 1954, p. 135 (= 1954, p. 46): "Les miracles de l'évangile continuaient ceux de l'Ancien Testament et, comme ceux-là, manifestaient la gloire de Dieu, mais désormais présente parmi nous dans le Christ: 'nous avons vu sa gloire, la

The defenders of the semeia hypothesis attribute these characteristics of the Johannine σημεῖα – the heightening of the miraculous, the tendency to depict Jesus as acting on his own initiative, Jesus' supernatural knowledge and omniscience, and the stress on the "solidly material aspect" – to the so-called θεῖος ἀνήρ christology. But O. Betz and Bittner, among others, argue that the extremely heightened miracles belong in fact to the evangelist's own interest[85]. In fact, some defenders of the signs source think that John does not contradict his source, and authors like Käsemann, Lona, and Appold even stress that the evangelist himself wholly accepts the heightening of the miraculous[86]. Fortna, as well, thinks "John has *heightened* some aspects of the portrait of Jesus that can be considered appropriate to the divine man"[87].

4. *Seeing Signs and Believing*

There is a double level of "seeing signs" and "believing", but "it seems incorrect to comprehend this in a source-critical distinction"[88]. Other explanations can be proposed. Some authors think that the evangelist portrays various "stages of faith" in the reaction of the people to Jesus' miracles[89]. In such an interpretation, the evangelist does not reject or denigrate faith on the basis of signs, but he considers it inadequate or provisional; it is a first step towards a deeper and more mature discipleship[90]. Recently, Schnelle and M.M. Thompson have pointed out that John

---

gloire qui appartient au Fils unique du Père' (ι,14)"; MOLLAT, *Le semeion johannique,* 1959, p. 217 (= 1979, p. 101): "Les *semeia* sont pour Jean les gestes du Verbe fait chair demeurant parmis nous, ils sont 'signes' du Fils de Dieu"; THOMPSON, *Humanity,* 1988, p. 70: "The relationship between signs, seeing, glory and faith which is evident in 2:11 is the same as that expressed in 1:14: Jesus manifested his glory to those who had eyes to see"; SCHNELLE, *Christologie,* 1987, p. 185 (ET: 1992, p. 167): "Die Wunder sind gleichermassen Ausdruck der Göttlichkeit und Menschlichkeit Jesu. Der Evangelist betont beides und kann gerade deshalb Wunder und Doxa miteinander verbinden, insofern die Inkarnation nicht der Verlust, sondern das Sichtbarwerden der Doxa Jesu ist (Joh 1,14)" (cp. p. 188; ET: pp.169-170).
   85. BETZ (see above, p. 295), BITTNER (p. 334).
   86. KÄSEMANN (see above, pp. 74-75), LONA (p. 109), APPOLD (p. 201).
   87. FORTNA, *Christology,* 1973, p. 492 (see above, p. 222).
   88. NEIRYNCK, *Semeia-bron,* 1983, p. 28 (ET: 1991, p. 676). For literature on seeing signs and believing, see above, p. 388 n. 56.
   89. See, e.g., CULLMANN, *Εἶδεν καὶ ἐπίστευσεν,* 1950; CERFAUX, *Les miracles,* 1954, pp. 133-135 (= 1954, pp. 44-46); ROUSTANG, *Les moments de l'acte de foi,* 1958; GRUNDMANN, *Verständnis und Bewegung des Glaubens,* 1960; SCHNACKENBURG, *Johannesevangelium,* I, 1965, pp. 519-522 (ET: 1968, pp. 569-573); BROWN, *John,* I, 1966, pp. 530-531; BARON, *La progression des confessions de foi,* 1968; NICOL, *Sēmeia,* 1972, pp. 99-106; MOLONEY, *From Cana to Cana,* 1978, pp. 820-821, 841-843 (= 1990, pp. 186-187, 201-202); *Johannine Theology,* 1990, p. 1425; *Belief in the Word,* 1993, pp. 192-197.
   90. THOMPSON, *Humanity,* 1988, p. 63.

in fact always views the concept σημεῖον positively and that we cannot speak of a "Wunderkritik" in the Fourth Gospel[91]. A sign can provoke faith or unbelief. From two important passages, the conclusion of the first sign (2,11) and the first conclusion of the whole gospel (20,30-31), we learn what signs effect: as revelations of Jesus' δόξα they evoke faith; on seeing a σημεῖον follows πιστεύειν εἰς Ἰησοῦν Χριστόν[92]. This "un-dualistic" connection between seeing and believing is explicitly present in Jn 2,11.23; 4,53; 6,14; 7,31; 9,35-38; 10,40-42; 11,15.40.45; 12,11; 20,8.25.27.29a and supposed in 4,39; 6,2; 9,16; 12,18. Belief in Jesus Christ as Son of God is not only the purpose of the Gospel but also the intention of the incarnation in general (1,7.12) and thus also of the whole history of salvation. He who believes in Jesus Christ has eternal life (3,15.16.36; 5,24; 6,35.40.47.69; 7,38); he who does not believe is con-demned (3,18)[93]. Miracles, however, lead also to unbelief. This is explic-itly noted in the summary statement at the end of Jesus' public life, with reference to Is 53,1 (12,37-38)[94]. John illustrates in the signs the essence of unbelief: in face of the σημεῖα unbelief is to deny the undeniable fact that Jesus Christ is the Son of God[95]. The link between miracle and unbe-lief demonstrates that according to the evangelist the miracles do not work in a magical way. In spite of their revelatory character, their materiality, and their reality, they still demand a decision from human beings. Insofar as miracles can lead equally to faith or to disbelief, they are an essential part of the whole ministry of Jesus, which, as a whole, leads to faith or to disbelief (see, e.g., 5,47; 6,36.64; 8,45.46; 10,25.26; 16,9)[96]. The signs have the same twofold effect as the incarnation (1,11-12)[97].

---

91. SCHNELLE, *Christologie*, 1987, pp. 182-194, esp. 194 (ET: 1992, pp. 164-175, esp. 175): "Eine grundsätzliche joh. Wunderkritik existiert nicht!" (against SCHOTTROFF, *Der Glaubende*, 1970, p. 256) (cp. below, p. 396 n. 101); THOMPSON, *Humanity*, 1988, pp. 52-86, 142-147, esp. 56-63, 143; *John, Gospel of*, 1992, pp. 379-380. See also LOADER, *The Chri-stology of the Fourth Gospel*, 1989, p. 216: "The criticism is not an attack on miracles or on miracle based faith in itself, but it does attack a form of such faith which fails to draw the right conclusions". Referring to SCHNIDER – STENGER, *Johannes und die Synoptiker*, 1971, p. 83 ("Man glaubt nicht, weil man gesehen hat, sondern man sieht, weil man glaubt, und weil man glaubend sieht, glaubt man"), TRUMBOWER, *Born from above*, 1992, p. 62, contin-ues: "In other words, the signs are not completely rejected; the author, after all, incorpo-rated them into his gospel. Rather, correct understanding of the signs already presupposes correct belief, and for the believer, encounter with the signs points to Jesus' true identity (his whence/whither, John 8:15-16). This claim about the evangelist's understanding of the signs can be made independently of the decision taken with regard to the 'signs' source".

92. SCHNELLE, *Christologie*, 1987, pp. 186-188, esp. 187-188 (ET: 1992, pp. 168-170, esp. 169).

93. *Ibid.*, p. 188 (ET: 1992, p. 169).

94. Cf. KÜHSCHELM, *Verstockung*, 1991, pp. 167-178; SCHUCHARD, *Scripture*, 1992, pp. 91-106. Cp. BITTNER (see below, p. 396 n. 98).

95. SCHNELLE, *Christologie*, 1987, p. 189 (ET: 1992, p. 170).

96. *Ibid.*, p. 189.

97. Cf. MOLLAT, *Le semeion johannique*, 1959, p. 212 (= 1979, p. 95).

Thus for John the signs themselves always have a positive meaning: "Where the signs do not produce faith (9,16; 11,47-53; 12,37), the fault lies neither with the insufficiency of signs nor with the inadequacy of the faith they produce, but rather with the individuals who stubbornly refuse to see"[98]. Nevertheless, there are some passages were John seems to reject the signs and faith arising from them (see, e.g., 2,23-25; 4,48). It cannot be denied that the Johannine Jesus for some reason found faith based on signs unsatisfactory. But, as M.M. Thompson rightly notes with regard to 2,23-25, "the problem is *not* with signs, but with the faith of the 'many'; they are not criticized for believing *because* they saw signs. ... What is disparaged in 2,23-25 is not faith which grows out of signs, but faith which does not abide in the commitment of discipleship"[99]. Jn 4,48 is not a "critical insertion" by which the evangelist "wants to correct the naive faith in miracles, such as is exhibited by the Synoptic tradition"[100], and it surely does not contain a "Wunderkritik"[101], for this verse leads to a greater miracle (healing at a distance) than the one requested[102].

98. THOMPSON, *Humanity*, 1988, p. 80. See also REINHARTZ, *John 20:30-31*, 1983, p. 47: "This negative response is engendered by an incorrect interpretation and understanding of Jesus and his works"; cp. p. 54 and esp. p. 211 (on 20,29 and 4,48): "The passages ... do not express a critical attitude towards sign-faith"; BITTNER, *Jesu Zeichen*, 1987, pp. 195-196 (with regard to 12,37): "Damit steht auch für dieses Vorkommen des Terminus σημεῖα fest, dass der Evangelist die Zeichen Jesu positiv wertet. Auch hier erscheint als ihre Funktion, die Menschen zum Glauben zu führen. Dass es zu diesem Ergebnis während der öffentlichen Wirksamkeit Jesu nicht gekommen ist, liegt nicht daran, dass Zeichen dafür nicht tauglich wären. Die Ursache des Scheiterns wird von Johannes theologisch bestimmt. Gott selbst hat nach seinem in der Schrift niedergelegten Willen diese geschichtliche Etappe unter ein konkretes Urteil gestellt, das in der Periode der öffentlichen Wirksamkeit Jesu geschichtlich konkret geworden ist". See also p. 281: "Die Ursachen, die zur fehlenden Erkenntnis führen, liegen für Johannes nicht in den Möglichkeiten, die der Erkenntnis durch ihren Gegenstand gegeben sind, sondern auf der Seite des Menschen, der diese Erkenntnis verweigert". Cp. KÄSEMANN (see above, p. 75); FORMESYN, *Le Sèmeion johannique*, 1962, p. 891 n. 121: "la foi qui s'appuie sur les σημεῖα, n'est pas nécessairement fausse ou imparfaite. S'il y a reproche de Jésus, c'est à cause des dispositions déficientes de ceux qui demandent le signe".

99. THOMPSON, *Humanity*, diss. 1985, p. 180. – THOMPSON, *Humanity*, 1988, p. 64 (cp. p. 80), with reference to CULPEPPER, *Anatomy*, 1983, p. 116, who notes on the difference between the disciples (2,11) and the many (2,23): "Both begin with a signs-faith, but the disciples have already shown a willingness to 'follow' Jesus (1:37, 38, 40), and they remember what Jesus said (2:22). Faith which does not lead to following is therefore inadequate. 'Abiding' is the test of discipleship (cf. 8:31)"; cp. pp. 85-86.

100. BULTMANN, *Johannes*, 1941, p. 153 (ET: 1971, p. 207).

101. SCHNELLE, *Christologie*, 1987, p. 105 (ET: 1992, p. 91); cp. BETZ, *Problem*, 1974, pp. 38-44 (= 1987, p. 413-419; see above, pp. 298-300); *Wesen*, 1977, p. 135 n. 208a; REINHARTZ, *John 20:30-31*, 1983, p. 61: "Both 4:48 and 20:29 may be interpreted in a way that does not at all contradict the positive evaluation of signs-faith which is evident in other passages of the Gospel". Cf. pp. 61-69 (20,29), 69-71 (4,48). See also THOMPSON, *Humanity*, 1988, p. 76.

102. Ctr. FORTNA (see above, pp. 222-223 n. 415). Following NEIRYNCK, I proposed in 1985 to read 4,48 in light of John's possible dependence on the Synoptic parallels

The evangelist's positive interpretation of the signs and his stress on their "solidly material aspect" as described above cannot be labeled in terms of a lower christology or messianism which contrasts with John's higher logos doctrine[103]. Indeed, the miracles cannot be isolated from the center of Johannine christology, i.e., the presence of the ultimate revelation of the Father in the incarnation of the Son[104]. Although the purely

(Mt 8,5-13; Lk 7,1-10). Unlike the centurion (see esp. Mt), the official does not ask a healing at a distance but he asks that Jesus καταβῇ καὶ ἰάσηται αὐτοῦ τὸν υἱόν. He clearly does not believe, like the centurion, that Jesus could heal by his word alone (cf. Mt 8,7 ἀλλὰ μόνον εἰπὲ λόγῳ), not even when he repeats his request (v. 49). It is Jesus' word in v. 50a (πορεύου· ὁ υἱός σου ζῇ) that finally leads him "to believe without seeing" (v. 50b ἐπίστευσεν ὁ ἄνθρωπος τῷ λόγῳ ὃν εἶπεν αὐτῷ ὁ Ἰησοῦς καὶ ἐπορεύετο; cp. v. 53 ἐν ἐκείνῃ τῇ ὥρᾳ ἐν ᾗ εἶπεν αὐτῷ ὁ Ἰησοῦς, ὁ υἱός σου ζῇ) and to go away (v. 50 καὶ ἐπορεύετο; cp. v. 51 καταβαίνοντος) without Jesus, who does not come down as he requested (v. 47 ἠρώτα ἵνα καταβῇ; cp. v. 49 κατάβηθι). Cf. NEIRYNCK, Jean et les Synoptiques, 1979, p. 110 (= ETL 53, 1977, p. 468); John 4,46-54, pp. 371-372 (= 1991, pp. 683-684); VAN BELLE, Jn 4,48 et la foi du centurion, pp. 167-169, esp. 169. That Jesus addresses the royal official in the plural, cannot be an objection to the unity of the passage, for elsewhere in the Gospel the plural is used when the speaker or addressee is a representative of a larger group. Cp., e.g., the use of the plural in 3,2 and 3,11-12 (cf. NEIRYNCK, Jean et les Synoptiques, 1979, p. 116 n. 197; = ETL 53, 1977, p. 474 n. 197). Also with regard to Jesus' word to Thomas in 20,29, "it seems clear that the evangelist is not so critical of faith based on seeing". Thus, "it does not seem justified to draw many conclusions about 4,48 from this pericope, particularly with reference to the evangelist's critique of a supposed source". Cf. JUDGE, A Note on 20,29, 1992, p. 2192.

103. CARSON, John, 1991, p. 663, rejecting the view of the defenders of the signs source that 20,30-31 expressed a "somewhat 'lower' view of christology than what is articulated in the preceding two verses (vv. 28-29)", notes: "This is a serious misunderstanding of the Fourth Gospel. In John, the nature of Jesus' deity is profoundly and repeatedly tied to the exposition of his sonship ..., which is linked with his messiahship. If one must use the somewhat question-begging categories 'higher' and 'lower', it is not that 'Son of God' has been dragged lower by its connection with 'Messiah', but that 'Messiah' has been raised higher by its connection with 'Son of God'". Carson refers to DE JONGE, Signs and Works, 1978 (= 1977, pp. 117-140) and cites BEASLEY-MURRAY, John, 1987, p. 388: "The content of Christological faith in v 31 is not to be viewed as a lower Christology than that of Thomas' confession, but must be understood in its light and filled out by it".

104. The miracles testify to the unity of the Son with the Father. Jesus does the works which the Father has granted him to accomplish and the miracles are nothing else than the ἔργα τοῦ θεοῦ (5,19-20.36; 6,29.30; 7,3.21; 9,3b-5; 10,25.32ff.38; 14,10-11; 15,24). In 9,3b-5 the evangelist links Jesus' miracle working with his salvation activity as a whole, which is described as ἔργον in 4,34; 17,4. Jesus is legitimated in the miracles because they testify to his unity with the Father. The one who performs such works can only come from God (9,16.30.33; 11,42), and God must be with him (3,2). The works point to Jesus' origin (πόθεν in 9,30) and verify him as the messenger of the Father. Because the Son and the Father are One (10,30: ἐγὼ καὶ ὁ πατὴρ ἕν ἐσμεν; cp., e.g., 8,28; 12,45; 14,9), the Son received from the Father the power over all flesh to give eternal life (17,2; cp. 10,28-30). Jesus uses this power when he rescues the royal official's son from the point of death (4,47c.49) and when he raises Lazarus from death (11,20-27). Cf. SCHNELLE, Christologie, 1987, p. 186 (ET: 1992, pp. 167-168). See esp. APPOLD, The Oneness Motif, pp. 86-102 ("Chapter IV: Oneness and the Semeia") (see above, pp. 202-203).

symbolic interpretation is only rarely defended now[105], it is still current in Johannine exegesis to argue that the signs in John are pointers to a higher reality, that they evoke only a preliminary belief, and that they are in fact of lesser value for the christology of the evangelist. If one agrees with Schnelle and Thompson that John himself "treats the materiality of signs ... as crucial to understanding Jesus" and that signs are not irrelevant for faith"[106], then we are not compelled to postulate a signs source whose theology of signs the evangelist transforms. Both the material and symbolic aspect of the signs belong to his proper interest[107].

5. *The Meaning of Σημεῖα in Jn 20,30-31*

In 20,30-31 the Johannine redactor distinguishes (μὲν ... δέ) the "many other signs ..., which are not recorded in this book (v. 30: πολλὰ μὲν οὖν καὶ ἄλλα σημεῖα ..., ἃ οὐκ ἔστιν γεγραμμένα ἐν τῷ βιβλίῳ τούτῳ) from "those here written" (v. 31: ταῦτα δὲ γέγραπται). Most authors agree that ταῦτα does not restate the immediately preceding ἐν τῷ βιβλίῳ τούτῳ but refers to σημεῖα[108]. With respect to the meaning

105. SCHNELLE, *Christologie*, 1987, p. 192 (ET: 1992, p. 174).

106. THOMPSON, *Humanity*, 1988, p. 63.

107. See esp. SCHNACKENBURG, *Johannesevangelium*, I, 1965, p. 354 (ET: 1968, pp. 524-525): "So werden wir schliesslich dahin geführt, einen inneren Zusammenhang zwischen der Inkarnation und der durch sie ermöglichten und eingeleiteten Offenbarung Jesu Christi in 'Zeichen' anzunehmen. Das wird aber noch auf eine andere Weise bestätigt, nämlich durch die Art und Struktur der σημεῖα selbst. Es ist schon lange aufgefallen, dass sie trotz ihres Symbolgehaltes nach der joh. Darstellung auch eine massive 'Materialität' besitzen; sie geschehen recht 'dinglich' am Stoff dieser Welt und stehen fest umrissen an ihrem geschichtlichen Ort. Auf ihren Ereignischarakter, ihre Bezeugbarkeit und Unbezweifelbarkeit legt der Evangelist ebenso entschieden Wert wie auf ihre symbolische Aussagekraft; sie sollen ja auch (als 'Werke') 'Zeugnisse' für den Glauben und wider den Unglauben werden, erhalten also fast eine juristische Geltung wie besonders die wiederholten Verhöre des Blindgeborenen (Kap. 9) zeigen. Diese in die Augen springende Eigenart der joh. σημεῖα, die wir darum nicht im einzelnen nachzuweisen brauchen hat eine unübersehbare Analogie in der Person des inkarnierten Logos selbst: So hoch der Logoshymnus die Geistigkeit und Göttlichkeit des Logos preist, ebenso hart setzt er daneben die Tatsache seiner 'Fleisch'-Werdung. Ähnlich besitzen die σημεῖα eine materielle 'Erscheinungsform' und verbergen darunter doch einen tief geistigen, näherhin christologischen Sinn. Das dürfte schon darum keine 'zufällige' Strukturähnlichkeit sein, weil die σημεῖα eben von diesem menschgewordenen Gottessohn und von ihm allein gewirkt werden und weil sie ihn in seiner göttlichen Herrlichkeit und Heilsmacht enthüllen, also Offenbarungszeichen für ihn und nichts anderes sind".

108. Cf. BROWN, II, 1970, p. 1056: "The neuter plural *tauta* can refer to 'signs' or more generally to all 'the things' in the Gospel". For C.H. DODD, *Note on John 21,24*, in *JTS* 4 (1953) 212-213, p. 212, ταῦτα refers to the σημεῖα: "The *tauta* of 20,31, by which the understanding of 21,24 has perhaps been insensibly affected, is not properly pronominal: *ta semeia* is to be supplied from the context". Cp. GROSHEIDE, 1950, vol. II, p. 547: "Ταῦτα, de in het voorafgaande vermelde, dus in de eerste plaats de σημεῖα, die de opstanding betreffen". According to BOISMARD – LAMOUILLE, *Jean*, 1977, p. 746a, how-

of σημεῖα (and ταῦτα), however, several interpretations have been proposed.

1. Some scholars have taken the σημεῖα of 20,30 in exclusive, or at least pre-eminent reference to the appearances in ch. 20, as signs or proofs of the resurrection (*documenta resurrectionis*, τεκμηρία: cf. Acts 1,3), from which it would follow that vv. 30-31 are the conclusion of only the resurrection narrative (20,1-29), not of the Gospel.

For this exegesis MEYER, *Johannes*, [3]1856, pp. 508-509; [5]1869, p. 661 (ET: II, 1884, p. 386) and WEISS ([6]1880, p. 677; [7]1886, p. 696[-697] n. **; [8]1893, p. 619 n. *; [9]1902, p. 528 n. *) refer to CHRYSOSTOM, THEOPHYLACT, EUTHYMIUS ZIGABENUS (first proposition), RUPERT OF DEUTZ, LUTHER, BEZA, CALOVIUS, MALDONATUS, SEMLER, and several others, including SCHLEIERMACHER, KUINOEL, LÜCKE, OLSHAUSEN, LANGE, BAUR, EWALD. See also, e.g., the commentaries of TOLETUS, MCRORY (1908, p. 359), GROSHEIDE (II, 1950, p. 359), HOSKYNS (1940; [2]1947, p. 549), MICHAELS (1989, p. 348), BEASLEY-MURRAY (1987, p. 387). That the expression πολλὰ καὶ ἄλλα σημεῖα refers to the appearances of the Risen Lord (ch. 20) or even to the resurrection of Jesus is rejected by, e.g., RENGSTORF, in *TWNT* 7 (1964), pp. 253-254 (ET: 1971, pp. 200-261, esp. 243-257). See also BROWN, *John*, II, 1970, p. 1059: "If we think that the evangelist thought of the post-resurrectional appearances as signs, there is no evidence that he thought of the resurrection itself as a sign, or that the main events of The Book of Glory, the passion and death of Jesus, were on the level of signs".

2. For others, σημεῖα refers to the miracles as well as to the resurrection appearances: "In xx 30-31 John probably does not mean to exclude the signs described in chs. i-xii..., but he must mean also to include the apparances to the disciples in xx 1-28 that led them to confess Jesus as Lord. The similarity between xx 25 and iv 48 ... indicates that John thinks of the appearances as signs" (Cf. BROWN, II, p. 1058).

In reaction to the first interpretation, MEYER ([3]1856, p. 509; [5]1869, p. 661; ET: II, 1884, p. 386) and WEISS ([6]1880, pp. 677-678; [7]1886, p. 696[-697] n. **; [8]1893, p. 619 n. *; [9]1902, p. 528-529 n. *) note: "dem entspricht weder das allgemeine und absolute σημεῖα an sich, noch das Prädikat πολλὰ κ. ἄλλα, da Christus auch nach unserem Evang. jedenfalls nur einzelne Male erschienen ist ..., noch endlich ἐποίησεν und ἐν τῷ βιβλ. τούτῳ, welches zeigt, dass Joh. den Inhalt *seines ganzen Evangeliums* im Auge hat". For the view that the word σημεῖα also means the miracles Meyer and Weiss refer to EUTHYMIUS ZIGABENUS (second

---

ever, ταῦτα refers to the whole book: "Dès le v. 31, il revient à une formule plus générale. Le pronom 'ces (choses)' ne désigne pas seulement les 'signes', mais aussi les paroles de Jésus et plus exactement tout le contenu du livre que Jean II-B vient d'écrire". Cp. SCHWANK, cited by Brown (p. 1056): "Schwank thinks that the latter is meant, but the contrast between signs not written down and signs that have been written down is too obvious to overlook".

proposition), CALVIN, JANSENIUS, WOLF, BENGEL, LAMPE, THOLUCK, DE WETTE, FROMMANN, MAIER, BAUMGARTEN-CRUSIUS, LUTHARDT, HILGENFELD, GODET, BAEUMLEIN, SCHOLTEN, HENGSTENBERG ("der richtig bemerkt, dass die Erscheinungen des Auferstandenen in diese σημεῖα eingeschlossen sind"), KEIL, and SCHANZ. See also CYRIL OF ALEXANDRIA, OECOLAMPADIUS, GROTIUS, ERASMUS, BRENZ, CORNELIUS A LAPIDE, CALMET, BENGEL, NATALIS ALEXANDER, and further KLOTUFAR (1862, p. 314), VON BURGER (1868, p. 510), BEELEN (1869, pp. 680-681), CORLUY (1878; ²1880; ³1889, p. 540), PLUMMER (1880; repr. 1923, p. 366), WESTCOTT (1881, p. 297), FILLION (1887, p. 375), O. HOLTZMANN (1887, pp. 148, 303), H.J. HOLTZMANN (1891, p. 201; ²1893, p. 225; ³1908, ed. W. BAUER, p. 307), KNABENBAUER (1898; ²1906, p. 587), CEULEMANS (1901, p. 293), HORN (*Kapt. 21*, 1904, pp. 9-16), BELSER (1905, p. 543), ZAHN (1908, pp. 686-687), BAUER (1912, p. 184; ²1925, p. 227; ³1933, pp. 233-234), MACGREGOR (1928, pp. 366-367), KEULERS (1936, p. 453; ²1951, p. 351), THÜSING (*Erhöhung*, 1960 [²1970], pp. 268-269), TRAETS (*Voir Jésus*, 1961, p. 133), HULL (1970, p. 370), LINDARS (1972, p. 617), TENNEY (1981, p. 196), J.R. MICHAELS (1989, p. 196), BLANQUART (*Le premier jour*, 1991, p. 151), PRYOR (1992, p. 91).

3. Other commentators particularly note that, although the word σημεῖα primarily means "*miraculous signs*, by which Jesus has proved Himself to be the Messiah, the Son of God" (30,31; cp. 12,37), the evangelist has widened the concept: "the signs form the distinguishing characteristic in the working of Jesus (cp. 10,41), and the historical basis, with which the rest of the contents (particularly the discourses) are connected" (Meyer) so that with ταῦτα, *sc.* σημεῖα, "the evangelist has in view the contents of his entire Gospel" (Nicol).

According to MEYER (³1856, p. 508), the σημεῖα of v. 30 are "Wunderzeichen, durch welche er sich als der Messias, der Gottessohn, ausgewiesen hat (V. 31). Dem entspricht der Schluss des Anhangs 21,25. ... Mit Recht konnte Joh., auf sein nunmehr beendigtes βιβλίον zurücksehend, als dessen Inhalt a potiori die σημεῖα, welche Christus gethan, anführen, da diese das unterscheidende Characteristicum im Wirken Jesu (vrgl. 10,41.) und die geschichtliche Grundlage bilden, an welche der übrige Inhalt (meist auch die Reden) sich anschliesst" (cp. ⁵1869, pp. 660-661; ET: II, 1884, p. 386; see also WEISS (⁶1880, pp. 677; ⁷1886, p. 696; ⁸1883, p. 619; ⁹1902, p. 528). Cp. NICOL (*Sēmeia*, 1972, p. 115).

Also for the following commentators, σημεῖα may comprehend the words of Jesus: GODET (1865; ⁴1903, III, p. 516; ET: 1886, p. 995; DT: 1871, p. 629), BALJON (1902, p. 331), LAGRANGE (1925, p. 519), BOUMA (1927, p. 207), DURAND (1927, p. 519), TILLMANN (1921; ⁴1931, p. 340), BULTMANN (1941, pp. 346, 541; ET: pp. 452, 698), LENSKI (1942, p. 1395), WIKENHAUSER (1948, p. 285; DT: 1964, p. 425), SMELIK (1957, p. 293), VAN DEN BUSSCHE (1960, p. 193; FT: 1967, p. 555), RIGA (*Signs of Glory*, 1963, p. 402), SCHNEIDER (1976, ²1978, p. 326-327), MOLLA (1977, p. p. 281), KÜHSCHELM (*Verstockung*, 1991, p. 172), RUCKSTUHL (*Joh 6,1-25*, 1992, p. 2003 n. 6), THYEN (*Joh 11,1–12,19*, 1992, p. 2033 n. 11).

This third interpretation has been also defended by Schnelle, rightly I think, in reaction to the semeia hypothesis: "If the use of σημεῖον in v. 30 is conditioned by the agreement between the function of the miracle stories in awakening faith, on the one hand, and the goal of the whole Gospel, on the other hand, we can discern here both a continuity and an expansion in the use of the concept of σημεῖον. John consciously alludes to his interpretation of the miracle traditions, but at the same time he uses σημεῖον as a tool for interpreting his whole description of the words and deeds of Jesus, in order to prepare for the statement of the purpose of his Gospel in v. 31. Σημεῖον at this point becomes the hermeneutical key to the Fourth Gospel"[109].

For defenders of the signs source the term σημεῖα is not especially fitting as a summation of the whole gospel but seems to be the appropriate term for a collection of miracles. They remark, however, that the evangelist used the end of the source "in his own way"[110] and are inclined to accept that he broadened the meaning of σημεῖα. Thus, Schnackenburg notes: "the term σημεῖον, which until now, was firmly tied to the earthly (miracle-) deeds of Jesus, is broadened; yet it can be said with W. Nicol: 'The concept sēmeion is widened to include the appearances ... [it] has acquired striking elasticity'"[111]. Schnackenburg does not go as far as Nicol in extending the σημεῖα to "all that the Gospel of John preaches about Jesus, both the works and the words"[112], but it can be asked whether, in allowing the widening of the concept at all, he "has not evacuated the argument for the signs source"[113].

Already Conzelmann, who accepted the signs source, considered all of Jn 20,30-31 to be Johannine (ctr. Bultmann). Every occurrence of the word σημεῖον "has been inserted by the evangelist at a later stage"[114]. Becker does not share Conzelmann's opinion and considers the word σημεῖα in 20,30-31 "the impetus for separating sources"[115]. According to him, the evangelist is not at all concerned with the concept of signs in 20,30-31 and has only introduced it "under pressure from the semeia

---

109. SCHNELLE, *Christologie*, 1987, p. 155 (ET: 1992, p. 139). – Nicol's interpretation is rejected by SCHNACKENBURG, *Johannesevangelium*, III, 1975, p. 402 (ET: 1982, p. 337); see also BECKER, *Johannes*, II, 1981, p. 633: "E kommt es bei der Übernahme aus der SQ nicht darauf an, ob sich sein Evangelium unter dem Begriff des Zeichens erfassen lässt. Letztmals zeigt er in solchen Äusserlichkeiten eine gewisse Gleichgültigkeit. Darum ist es fehl am Platz, von 20,30 her nachträglich zu fragen, ob die Kreuzigung oder die österlichen Erscheinungen oder gar die Reden für E auch Zeichen sein sollen"; cp. ³1991, pp. 755-756 (see below, p. 402 n. 120).
110. SCHNACKENBURG, *Johannesevangelium*, III, 1975, p. 405 (ET: 1982, p. 339).
111. *Ibid.*, p. 402 (ET: 1982, p. 337). Cf. NICOL, *Sēmeia*, 1972, p. 115.
112. SCHNACKENBURG, *Johannesevangelium*, III, 1975, p. 402 (ET: 1982, p. 337).
113. NEIRYNCK, *Semeia-bron*, 1983, p. 28 (ET: 1991, p. 677).
114. See above, p. 75.
115. See above, p. 127 n. 313.

source"[116]. He does not accept that the whole Gospel can be summarized by the term σημεῖα. It is only by the addition to the concluding formula of the source in 20,31b (καὶ ἵνα πιστεύοντες ζωὴν ἔχητε ἐν τῷ ὀνόματι αὐτοῦ) that the evangelist looks to the whole revelatory activity of the Son[117]. But can the christological claim in 20,31a be separated from its soteriological meaning in 20,31b? In the third edition of his commentary (1991)[118], Becker still fervently argues against Schnelle[119] that all options for a larger meaning of σημεῖα are "pure postulates"[120]. Nevertheless, the four arguments he gives to support his position are not convincing[121]:

1. Σημεῖον occurs only in chs. 1–12 and never in 13–20 (except 20,30) and means exclusively a miracle of the earthly Jesus. – It is true that for John σημεῖον is a miracle, but from its first use in the Gospel it becomes clear that it is also a miracle with meaning, pointing to a higher reality, the revelation of the δόξα (2,11). This meaning is explained troughout the Gospel in a double way: by the discourses closely connected with the miracles and by the use of the largely parallel term ἔργον. Therefore, the meaning of the σημεῖα may be broadened: with σημεῖα in 20,30 the evangelist indicates Jesus' whole activity, his incarnation of Son of God, as revelation of the Father.

2. The Ecclesiastical Redactor, using 20,30-31, consciously avoids the term σημεῖα and prefers ταῦτα to summarize Jesus' whole activity: καὶ ὁ γράψας ταῦτα (21,24)[122]. – Dodd, followed by Roberts, remarked

116. BECKER, *Johannes*, II, 1981, p. 633: "unter dem Druck der SQ".
117. *Johannes*, II, ³1991, p. 757. See also above, p. 367.
118. *Johannes*, II, ³1991, pp. 753-757, esp. pp. 755-756.
119. SCHNELLE, *Christologie*, 1987, pp. 154-155 (ET: 1992, p. 138-139). See above, p. 337.
120. *Johannes*, II, ³1991, pp. 753-757, esp. pp. 755-756. Against Bittner (*Jesu Zeichen*, p. 287; cf. pp. 197-225), who defends that "Johannes den Terminus σημεῖον für die Taten Jesu verwenden kann, das Verständnis der Sendung aber, das mit dieser Bezeichnung sonst verbunden ist, ausdrücklich zurückweist: Jesus ist nicht der eschatologische Prophet. Er ist als der davidische Messias, der Sohn Gottes zu erkennen, zu glauben und zu bekennen", Becker remarks: "Dazu ist zu sagen, dass keines der vier Evangelien so von den Wundern redet, schon gar nicht das Joh. Wer wie E sofort am Anfang (2,18ff.23-25; 3,1-5) und am Schluss (20,29) den Wunderglauben (nicht ablehnt, aber) differenziert kritisiert und sonst fast keine Gelegenheit auslässt, bei Aufnahme einer Wundertradition die Problematik von Glaube und Wunder zu behandeln, der wird nicht so glatt 20,30f. schreiben können. Es heisst auch, die Verhältnisse im Joh umzudrehen, wenn man die Quantität und Qualität der öffentlichen Reden Jesu und des Abschnittes Joh 13–20 so einschätzt, dass angesichts des Ranges der Wunder eine Schlussbemerkung wie 20,30 in Ordnung sei" (³1991, p. 756).
121. *Ibid.*, p. 755.
122. *Ibid.*, p. 755: "Tatsache ist, dass die KR in 21,25 [= 21,24] auf dieses Wort [= σημεῖα] verzichtet, obwohl sie bewusst 20,30f. verarbeitete. Sie sagt: '... diese Dinge... geschrieben hat...'. Das ist formaler, aber korrekt".

that τούτων and ταῦτα in 21,24 do not refer to the entire Gospel as does ταῦτα in 20,31, but to the immediately preceding incident, or perhaps to ch. 21 as a whole[123].

3. In Early Christianity more appropriate expressions were used to summarize the complete exposition of Jesus' life. Becker refers to Acts 1,1 (περὶ πάντων, ... ὦν ἤρξατο ὁ Ἰησοῦς ποιεῖν τε καὶ διδάσκειν); Lk 24,19 (ἐν ἔργῳ καὶ λόγῳ; cp. Acts 7,22: ἐν λόγοις καὶ ἔργοις); see also Mt 28,20 (πάντα ὅσα ἐνετειλάμην ὑμῖν). From 15,22.24 it appears that the Johannine community also knows analogous expressions, noting the revelation in words before the revelation in works. – It may be striking that John uses the term σημεῖα to summarize the whole activity of Jesus. But Becker, I think, does not reckon with John's language: as elsewhere in the narrative parts, where he is summarizing Jesus' activity, John uses σημεῖα (ποιεῖν) in 20,30-31, whereas in the discourses the concept ἔργον is used for the same purpose[124].

4. Becker thinks that John would be the only one in Early Christianity who describes the whole activity of Jesus by the term σημεῖα. This is all the more striking since the meaning of the passion and resurrection is explained in the discourses of chs. 13–17. – If in 4,34 and 17,3, when Jesus is speaking, John uses ἔργον to summarize the whole activity of Jesus, both deeds and words, why, when he is expressing himself as an author, can he not use the largely synonymous word σημεῖα to indicate his whole Gospel? This is precisely, I think, John's own contribution to early christian thinking: since the miracles are the privileged signs of Jesus' incarnation and revelation of the Father, the term σημεῖα may mean Jesus' whole revelatory activity. As we noted above, the narratives and the discourses in John are intrinsically interwoven and form a unity. The absence of the term σημεῖον in the second part of the Gospel should not be an objection: chs. 13–17 deal with Jesus' last discourses, and according to Johannine habit the term ἔργον is used; chs. 18–20 describe the fulfillment of Jesus' revelation, his exaltation on the cross and resurrection, and although John does not refer to the passion as a σημεῖον, we may suppose that σημεῖα in 20,30 also refers to this fulfillment[125].

123. DODD, in *JTS* 4 (1953), p. 212; cp. C. ROBERTS, *John 20:30-31 and 21:24-25*, in *JTS* 38 (1987) 409-410, p. 409.

124. See above, pp. 380-389.

125. For some authors Jn 20,30-31 also referred to the crucifixion. Cf. CARSON, *John*, 1991, p. 661: "But to place this conclusion here suggests that the greatest sign of them all is the death, resurrection and exaltation of the Incarnate Word, the *significance* of which has been carefully set forth in the farewell discourse"; cp., e.g., LOISY, *Le quatrième évangile*, 1903, p. 922; LIGHTFOOT, *John*, 1956, p. 335; BARRETT, *John*, 1955, p. 65 (²1978, p. 78; GT: 1990, p. 94); MOLLAT, *Le semeion johannique*, 1959, p. 209 (= 1979, p. 91); CHARLIER, *La notion de signe*, 1959, pp. 435, 444-447. This is rejected by SCHNACKENBURG, *Johannesevangelium*, I, 1965, p. 350 n. 1 (ET: 1968, p. 520 n. 1) and BROWN, *John*, II, 1970, p. 1059.

Conclusion. Authors like Becker, who see 20,30-31 as the end of a pre-Johannine signs source, do not sufficiently explain "why the evangelist revives the σημεῖον concept at the very end of his account, when elsewhere it refers primarily to concrete miracle stories"[126]. It seems impossible that John wrote this important first conclusion of his work without reflection. The term σημεῖα in 20,30 has become the hermeneutical key to the whole Gospel and does not allow for a source-critical conclusion. Defenders of the signs source have overlooked, it seems to me, two important aspects of Johannine writing: the unity between narrative and discourse and John's use of synonymous expressions. By stressing this unity, I would not deny John's use of traditional material but to some extent, I think, this material can be found in the Synoptic tradition and, as suggested in recent studies, in the Synoptic Gospels themselves.

126. SCHNELLE, *Christologie*, 1987, pp. 154-155 n. 341 (ET: 1992, p. 138 n. 341).

JOHANNINE STYLE CHARACTERISTICS

When studying the signs source in Jn, it is useful to have at hand a list of the Johannine style characteristics. The catalogue below is a cumulative list including all characteristics listed by Ruckstuhl (1951, 1991)[1] and Nicol (1972)[2]. The characteristics are given in the order and with the numbers of Neirynck's alphabetical rearrangement of the *Liste des caractéristiques johanniques* in Boismard-Lamouille (1977)[3]. Numbers of additional items are followed by the letters a, b, c, etc.

The description of each characteristic is followed by the number of Ruckstuhl's 1991 list (A1-26, B1-65, C1-62; a dash is used to indicate that the characteristic is not mentioned) and, if applicable, the number in Ruckstuhl's 1951 ([2]1987) list (R[1-50]) or Nicol's list (N[51-82]). The total number of occurrences in John is given within parentheses before the enumeration of the instances[4]. Words in small print placed in alphabetical order (with arrow) refer to occurrences in one or more characteristics.

---

1. RUCKSTUHL, *Einheit*, 1951, pp. 190-210: "Die Liste der johanneischen Eigentümlichkeiten", esp. 203-205; [2]1987, pp. 291-303: "Liste der johanneischen Stilmerkmale mit allen Belegstellen aus dem johanneischen Schrifttum". Ruckstuhl distinguishes three categories: (1) the most important Johannine characteristics (R1-19); (2) less important characteristics, but useful in combination with others (R20-31); (3) characteristics only useful in critique of source hypotheses (R32-50).

RUCKSTUHL – DSCHULNIGG, *Stilkritik und Verfasserfrage*, 1991, pp. 63-162: "Die Stilmerkmale des Johannesevangeliums erarbeitet und ausführlich dargestellt"; cp. pp. 164-168: "Übersichtslisten aller erarbeiteten Stilmerkmale des Joh" and pp. 269-275: "Die joh. Stilmerkmale in alphabetischer Reihenfolge". The number of characteristics has been considerably enlarged (total: 153) in three groups: A1-26, B1-65, C1-62. Cf. NEIRYNCK, in *ETL* 67 (1992) 437-440.

2. NICOL, *Sèmeia*, 1972, pp. 16-27, esp. 22-24: "Additions to Ruckstuhl's List" (nos. 51-82).

3. BOISMARD – LAMOUILLE, *Jean*, 1977, pp. 491-514. Boismard's list contains 416 characteristics, classified in six categories: A1-167, B1-102, C1-85 (the Gospel and the Johannine Epistles compared with the rest of the New Testament), D1-6, E1-16, F1-38 (the Gospel compared with the Synoptic Gospels and the Acts). Cf. NEIRYNCK, *Jean et les Synoptiques*, 1979, pp. 45-66 (= *ETL* 53, 1977, pp. 404-425), with references to the B-L list, corrected and annotated. Cp. VAN BELLE, *Parenthèses*, 1985, pp. 124-155, where the Johannine characteristics occurring in the "parentheses" are listed.

4. The number of occurrences given here are those of Ruckstuhl and Nicol (or Boismard). For the identification of the occurrences, see Ruckstuhl ([2]1987), Boismard (1977), and Ruckstuhl-Dschulnigg (1991). For comparison of the characteristics in the lists of Schweizer, Ruckstuhl (1951), and Nicol with Boismard's list see the footnotes in Neirynck's list. References to ABBOTT, *Johannine Vocabulary*, 1905, pp. 195-239, nos. 1707-1728, are also included there.

Three comparative tables are appended to the list: the numbers of Ruckstuhl's first list, Nicol's list, and Ruckstuhl's second list compared with the numbers of the list below[5].

JOHANNINE STYLE CHARACTERISTICS

ἀγάπαω → μαθητής 235a

9a ἄγω: ἄγωμεν C57 (4) 11,7.15.16; 14,31.

10a αἰτέω τι C47 (4) 14,13.14; 15,16; 16,23.

11 αἰών: εἰς τὸν αἰῶνα – N[61] (12) see no. 13 (6), add: 6,51.58; 8,35[bis]; 12,34; 14,16. — Cf. p. 48 n. 38.

13 οὐ μὴ ... εἰς τὸν αἰῶνα B20 R[20] (6) 4,14; 8,51.52; 10,28; 11,26; 13,8. — Cf. pp. 145 n. 17, 312 n. 373.

ἀληθῶς → οὗτος 307a

28 ἀλλά: οὐ ..., ἀλλ᾽ ἵνα (elliptic) A19 R[13] (4) 1,8; 9,3; 13,18; 14,30-31. — Cf. pp. 32[-33] n. 169, 145 n. 17, 312 n. 373.

30 οὐ περὶ ... ἀλλὰ περί B57 (3) 10,33; 17,9.20. — Cf. p. 312 n. 373.

31 οὐχ ὅτι ... ἀλλ᾽ ὅτι C31 R[14] (2) 6,26; 12,6. — Cf. p. 145 n. 17.

33 ἄλλος: (ὁ) ἄλλος μαθητής / οἱ ἄλλοι μαθηταί C48 (8) 18,15.16; 20,2.3.4.8 / 20,25; 21,8.

→ λέγω (ἔλεγον) 218

35 ἁμαρτία: ἁμαρτία (sing.) + pers. pron. (gen. plur.) B43 (3) 8,21; 9,41; 15,22. — Cf. p. 312 n. 373.

36 ἁμαρτίαν ἔχω B30 (4) 9,41; 15,22.24; 19,11. — Cf. p. 312 n. 373.

37 ἀμὴν ἀμήν C45 R[40] (25) 1,51; 3,3.5.11; 5,19.24.25; 6,26.32.47.53; 8,34.51.58; 10,1.7; 12,24; 13,16.20.21.38; 14,12; 16,20.23; 21,18. — Cf. pp. 48 n. 38, 77, 145 n. 17, 181.

38 ἄν: ἄν τις/τι – R[3.(47)] (5) 5,19; 13,20; 16,23; 20,23[bis]. — Cf. pp. 47 n. 33, 48 n. 40, 145 n. 17, 164, 303 n. 313, 309.

39 εἰ, ... ἄν – N[57] (11) 4,10; 5,46; 8,19.42; 9,41; 11,21.32; 14,28; 15,19; 18,30.36.

40 ἀνθρακιά – R[35] (2) 18,18; 21,9. — Cf. pp. 275 n. 49, 304, 305, 309.

42a ἄνθρωπος of Jesus – N[73] (15) 4,29; 5,12; 7,46; 8,40; 9,11.16[bis].24; 10,33; 11,47.50; 18,14.17.29; 19,5.

43 ἀνοίγω τοὺς ὀφθαλμούς C54 (9) 9,(10).14.17.21.26.30.32; 10,21; 11,37.

48 ἀπέρχομαι: ἀπέρχομαι πρός τινα C49 (4) 4,47; 6,68; 11,46; 20,10.
→ ὑπάγω 389

49-50 ἀπό: ἀπ᾽ ἐμαυτοῦ / ἀπὸ σεαυτοῦ / ἀφ᾽ ἑαυτοῦ B19 R[31] (13) 5,30; 7,17.28; 8,28.42; 10,18; 14,10 / 18,34 / 5,19; 7,18; 11,51; 15,4; 16,13. — Cf. pp. 47 n. 33, 48 n. 38, 145 n. 17, 164, 312 n. 373.

---

5. In Tables I and II the numbers in Schweizer's list (s[1-33]) are also mentioned and the characteristics added by Jeremias (= J) and Menoud (= M) are marked as well. Cf. SCHWEIZER, *Ego Eimi*, 1939, pp. 82-112, esp. pp. 103-105; JEREMIAS, *Literarkritik*, 1939, cc. 35, 37, 40-41; MENOUD, *L'évangile de Jean*, 1943; ²1947, p. 16.

50a Proper name + (ὁ) ἀπό + name of place C58 (6) 1,44.45; 11,1; 12,21; 19,38; 21,2. — Cf. p. 138 n. 164.

52 ἀποθνῄσκω: ἤμελλεν/ἔμελλεν ἀποθνῄσκειν B35 (4) 4,47; 12,33; 18,32 / 11,51.

53 ἀπεκρίθη (asyndetic/οὖν) (αὐτῷ/αὐτοῖς) ([ὁ] Ἰησοῦς / other name/noun or pronoun) as introduction of direct discourse A2 N⁶² (40) 1,49; 3,5; 5,7; 6,7.68.70; 7,20.46.47; 8,19.34.49.54; 9,3.11.25.27; 10,25.32.33.34; 11,9; 12,34; 13,26.36.38; 16,31; 18,5.8.20.23. 34.35.36.37; 19,7.11.15.22; 21,5. — Cf. pp. 274[-275] n. 148.

54 ἀποκρίνομαι: ἀπεκρίθη (asyndetic/οὖν) καὶ εἶπεν (+ analogous finite forms) as introduction of direct discourse A3 R¹⁶ (30) 1,48.50; 2,18.19; 3,3.9.10.27; 4,10.13.17; 5,19; 6,26.29.43; 7,16. 21.52; 8,14.39.48; 9,20.30.34.36; 12,30; 13,7; 14,23; 18,30; 20,28. — Cf. pp. 48 nn. 38 and 40, 58, 274[-275] n. 148, 304, 305.

56 ἀποκτείνω: ζητέω ἀποκτεῖναι B22 (7) 5,18; 7,1.19.20.25. 8,37.40. — Cf. pp. 312 n. 373, 387 n. 46.

59 ἀποσυνάγωγος B65 (3) 9,22; 12,42; 16,2. — Cf. pp. 291, 312 n. 373.

66 ἀρχιερεύς: οἱ ἀρχιερεῖς καὶ οἱ Φαρισαῖοι B23 (5) 7,32.45; 11,47.57; 18,3. — Cf. p. 101 n. 145.

ἀρχών → κόσμος 195

68 αὐτός: αὐτός/αὐτοί taking up a *casus pendens* – N⁷⁹ (10) 1,12; 4,14; 5,36; 6,39; 7,38; 12,49; 15,2ᵇⁱˢ; 17,2; 18,11.
→ ἀποκρίνομαι 53 → ἵνα 176

ἀφίημι → ὑπάγω 389

βαπτίζω → Ἰωάννης 181a

70a Γαλιλαία: name of place + τῆς Γαλιλαίας C59 (5) 2,1.11; 4,46; 12,21; 21,2. — Cf. pp. 259 n. 36, 308 n. 350.

γάρ → οὔπω 303

γεννάομαι → εἰμί 108

γίνομαι → μαθητής 235 → σχίσμα 370

73a γινώσκω + indirect question B21 (8) 2,25; 7,17.27.51; 10,6; 11,57; 13,12.28. — Cf. p. 312 n. 373.

77 γογγύζω περί + gen. B47 (3) 6,41.61; 7,32. — Cf. p. 312 n. 373.

79 γραφή: ἵνα ἡ γραφὴ πληρωθῇ B28 (4) 13,18; 17,12; 19,24.36. — Cf. pp. 18-19, 26 n. 145, 198, 347.

80 γράφω: ἔστιν/ἦν γεγραμμένον(-α) A20 (9) 2,17; 6,31.45; 10,34; 12,14; 20,30 / 12,16; 19,19.20.

83 γύναι (of Jesus' mother) – R²⁷ (2) 2,4; 19,26. — Cf. pp. 37 n. 196, 47 n. 33, 145 n. 17, 254 n. 12, [257-]258 n. 34, 309.

84 δαιμόνιον ἔχω (said of Jesus) B38 (5) 7,20; 8,48.49.52; 10,20. — Cf. p. 312 n. 373.

δέ → εἰμί 116, 118 → νῦν 269 → λέγω 218, 226

δεύτερος → πάλιν 310a

85 διά: διὰ τοῦτο ... ὅτι – N⁵¹ (7) 5,16.18; 8,47; 10,17; 12,18.39; 15,19.

86   διὰ τοῦτο + λέγω + ὅτι B25 (4) 6,65; 9,23; 13,11; 16,15. — Cf.
         p. 312 n. 373.
         → ἵνα 176 → Ἰουδαῖος 180 → πιστεύω 331

89   Δίδυμος: Θωμᾶς (...) ὁ λεγόμενος Δίδυμος B56 (3) 11,16; 20,24;
         21,2.
         δίδωμι → ἐντολή 135 → ζωή 160

95   δύναμαι: οὐ δύναμαι (...) ποιεῖν (...) οὐδέν C34 (4) 5,19.30; 9,33;
         15,5.

96   πῶς δύναμαι + infinitive B6 (6) 3,4.9; 5,44; 6,52; 9,16; 14,5.
         — Cf. p. 312 n. 373.

97-98 ἐάν: οὐ (μὴ) ..., ἐάν μή B3 R[44] (16) 3,2.3.5.27; 4,48; 5,19;
         6,44.53.65; 7,51; 12,47; 13,8; 15,4[bis]; 16,7; 20,25. — Cf. pp. 47 n. 33, 145
         n. 17, 312 n. 373.

99   ἐὰν (μή) τις C19 R[47] (19) 3,3.5; 6,51; 7,17.37; 8,51.52; 9,22.31;
         10,9; 11,9.10.57; 12,26[bis].47; (13,20); 14,23; 15,6. — Cf. p. 145 n. 17.
         ἑαυτοῦ → ἀπό 49

100   Ἑβραϊστί C9 (5) 5,2; 19,13.17.20; 20,16.

102   ἐγγὺς ἦν / ἦν ... ἐγγύς A25 (7) 2,13; 19,20.42 / 6,4; 7,2; 11,18.55. — Cf.
         p. 101 n. 145.

104-105 ἐγώ: ἐγώ, ὑμεῖς B32 (25) 4,32.38; 5,34; 7,8.34.36; 8,15.21.
         22.23[bis].38.49; 10,25-26; 13,14.15.33; 14,3.19.20; 15,5.14.16; 16,27; 19,6.
         — Cf. pp. [274-]275 n. 148.

106   (ἐ)μέ, ὑμᾶς C36 (8) 7,7; 12,30; 15,9.16.18.20; 16,27; 20,21.
         → πέμπω 323
         εἰ → ἄν 38 → νῦν 269

108, 72 εἰμί: εἰμὶ ἐκ (in metaphorical sense) / γεννάομαι ἐκ C44 R[46]
         (23) 3,31[bis]; 8,23[quater].44.47[bis]; 10,26; 15,19[bis]; 17,14[bis].16[bis]; 18,37 / 1,13;
         3,5.6[bis].8; 8,41. — Cf. pp. 145 n. 17, 164.

115a The periphrastic construction of ἐστὶν + article + present par-
         ticiple (singular) − N[80] (12) 1,33; 4,10.37; 5,12.32.45; 6,33.63.64;
         8,54; 9,8; 14,21.

116   ἦν δέ (καί) / ἦσαν δέ immediately followed by the subject
         A21 (20) 1,44; 3,1.23; 5,5.9; 6,10; 9,14; 11,1.2.18.38; 13,30; 18,10.14.
         18.25.40; 19,14.23 / 12,20. — Cf. pp. 101 n. 145, 148, 154, 170, 173, 309.

118   ἦν/ἦσαν δέ + temporal note C16 (8) 5,9; 6,4; 7,2; 9,14; 11,55;
         13,30; 18,28; 19,14. — Cf. p. 28.

118a ἤμην + adverb of place (with the exception of ὅπου ἦν)
         A22 (15) 2,1.6; 3,23; 4,6; 5,5; 6,22; 11,15.18.21.32; 19,20.42; 20,26;
         21,2.8.
         → γράφω 80 → ἐγγύς 102 → Ἰωάννης 181a → μαθητής 235 → ὅπου
         284 → οὗτος 307a → πόθεν 342 → σχίσμα 370 → τόπος 381 → ὥρα 408
         εἰς → αἰών 11, 13 → ἑορτή 139a → ἴδιος 170 → πιστεύω 332

121a ἐκ: ἐκ partitive B9 R[45] (23) 1,24; 3,1.25; 6,39.60.[66]; 7,19.31.40; 9,40;
         10,20.26; 11,19.45; 12,9.42; 16,5.17; 17,12; 18,9.17.25; 21,2. — Cf.

pp. 145 n. 19, 146, 164, 148, 170, 173, 218 n. 395, [218-]219 n. 396, 288 n. 217, 305, 306.

123   ἐκ τούτου, from that moment – R³⁶ (2) 6,66; 19,12.

→ εἰμί 108 → ἔρχομαι 147a → λαλέω 204

124   ἐκεῖνος: ἐκεῖνος/ἐκείνη, used absolutely B1 R¹⁷ (42) 1,8.18.33; 2,21; 3,28.30; 4,25; 5,11.19.35.37.38.43.46; 6,29; 7,11; 8,42.44; 9,9.11. 12.25.36.37; 10,1; 13,25.26.27.30; 14,21.26; 15,26; 16,8.13.14; 18,17.25; 19,21.35 / 11,29; 20,15.16. — Cf. pp. 27 n. 147, 31 n. 165, 52 n. 63, 145 n. 17, 146, 164, 303 n. 313, 304, 305, 309.

128   ἐκεῖνος/κἀκεῖνος taking up a *casus pendens* A15 N⁷⁹ (12) 1,18.33; 5,11.37; 9,37; 10,1; 12,48; 14,21.26; 15,26 / 6,57; 14,12. — Cf. p. 312 n. 373.

129   ἕλκω – R³⁸ (5) 6,44; 12,32; 18,10; 21,6.11. — Cf. pp. 145, 146 n. 20, 148, 164, 173, [218-]219 n. 396, 305.

ἐμαυτός → ἀπό 49 → ἔχω 154 → ποιέω 343

ἐμός → Adjectif possessif 412

ἐν → ἑορτή 139b → ἔχω 154 → ἡμέρα 162 → κρυπτός 201 → οὗτος (τούτῳ) 305 → σαββάτον 361a → σχίσμα 370 → τόπος 381 → ὥρα 407

133   ἐντεῦθεν B8 R⁴⁸ (6) 2,16; 7,3; 14,31; 18,36; 19,18ᵇⁱˢ. — Cf. pp. 146, 164, 304, 305.

135   ἐντολή: ἐντολὴν/ὰς δίδωμι B64 (3) 12,49; 13,34 / 11,57. — Cf. p. 312 n. 373.

136a   ἐντολή + ἵνα B63 (3) 11,57; 13,34; 15,12. — Cf. p. 312 n. 373.

→ τηρέω 378

139a   ἑορτή: εἰς τὴν ἑορτήν B34 (7) 4,45; 7,8ᵇⁱˢ.10; 11,56; 12,12; 13,29.

139b   ἐν τῇ ἑορτῇ C11 (4) 2,23; 4,45; 7,11; 12,20.

ἐργάζομαι → ἔργον 142

141   ἔργον (miracle) C42 N⁵⁴ (17) 5,20.36ᵇⁱˢ; 7,3.21; 9,3.4; 10,25.32ᵇⁱˢ. 33.37.38; 14,10.11.12; 15,24. — Cf. pp. 162, 179, 227, 244 n. 570, 274[-275] n. 148, 297, 367, 383-389, 384 n. 23, 397 n. 104, 403.

142   ἐργάζομαι τὰ ἔργα C7 N⁵⁴ (3) 3,21; 6,28; 9,4. — Cf. pp. 387, 389.

→ τελειόω 375

145   ἔρχομαι: ὁ ἐλθών/οἱ ἐλθόντες as attribute A9 (5) 7,50; 12,12; 19,39; 20,8 / 11,45.

147a   ἔρχομαι ἐκ B10 (5) 3,31; 4,54; 6,23; 7,41; 12,28. — Cf. p. 312 n. 373.

→ ἵνα 175 → οὔπω 304

150   ἐρωτάω: to question C20 (16) 1,19.21.25; 5,12; [8,7]; 9,2.15.19.21; 16,5.19.23.30; 18,19.21ᵇⁱˢ. — Cf. pp. 50 n. 51, 275 n. 150.

150a   ἐρωτάω + ἵνα C18 (5) 4,47; 17,15.20-21; 19,31.38. — Cf. pp. 95 n. 110, 308 n. 350.

151   ἐρωτάω περί τινος, to petition on someone's behalf C62 (4) 16,26; 17,9ᵇⁱˢ; 17,20.

ἐσχάτος → ἡμέρα 162

154 ἔχω: ἔχω ἐν ἐμαυτῷ C25 (5) 5,26ᵇⁱˢ.42; 6,53; 17,13.

→ ἁμαρτία 36 → δαιμόνιον 84 → ζωή 161

157 ζητέω: τί/τίνα ζητεῖς/ζητεῖτε (without complement) B12 (5) 1,38; 4,27; 18,4.7; 20,15. — Cf. pp. 101 n. 145, 387 n. 46.

→ ἀποκτείνω 56

160 ζωή: ζωὴν δίδωμι C35 (3) 6,33; 10,28; 17,2.

161 ζωὴν ἔχω C40 (14) 3,15.16.36; 5,24.26ᵇⁱˢ.39.40; 6,40.47.53.54; 10,10; 20,31.

ἡμεῖς → οἶδα 275

162 ἡμέρα: (ἐν) τῇ ἐσχάτῃ ἡμέρᾳ C10 R³² (7) 6,39.40.44.54; 7,37; 11,24; 12,48. — Cf. pp. 145 n. 17, 164.

→ μένω 249a

θάνατος → σημαίνω 363

Θωμᾶς → Δίδυμος 89

167a ἴδε/ἴδετε + another imperative C17 (5) 1,46; 4,29; 7,52; 11,34; 20,27. — Cf. p. 388 n. 56.

170 ἴδιος: εἰς τὰ ἴδια C50 (3) 1,11; 16,32; 19,27.

171 Ἱεροσόλυμα: τὰ Ἱεροσόλυμα C14 R⁴ (4) 2,23; 5,2; 10,22; 11,18. — Cf. pp. 101 n. 145, 148, 164, 304, 305.

172 Ἰησοῦς: Proper name οὖν + participle + finite verb A6 (11) 4,6; 6,15; 11,32.38; 12,3; 18,3.4.10; 19,13.26; 21,7.

→ ἀποκρίνομαι 53

174 ἵνα: epexegetic ἵνα/ὅτι A14 R⁵ (14) (a) οὗτος ἐστιν ..., ἵνα/ὅτι (6): 6,29.39.40.50; 17,3 / 3,19; (b) ἐν τούτῳ ..., ἵνα (3): 4,37; 9,30; 15,8; (c) analogous instances (5): 4,34; 13,35; 15,13; 16,19; 18,39. — Cf. pp. 145 n. 17, 164, 303 n. 313.

175 ἔρχομαι ἵνα (final) A16 (15) 1,7.31; 3,20.21; 5,40; 6,15; 9,39; 10,10ᵇⁱˢ; 11,19; 12,9.46.47ᵇⁱˢ; 18,37. — Cf. p. 275 n. 150, 308 n. 350.

176 ἵνα ... δι' αὐτοῦ/αὐτῆς (at the end of a phrase) B48 (3) 1,7; 3,17; 11,4.

→ ἀλλά 28 → γραφή 79 → ἐντολή 136a → ἐρωτάω 150a → πληρόω 339 → ὥρα 407

179a Ἰουδαῖος: οἱ Ἰουδαῖοι (plural) – N⁵⁵ (67) see no. 180 (3), add: 1,19; 2,6.13.18.20; 3,1; 4,9b.22; 5,1.10.15.16.18; 6,4.41.52; 7,1.2.11.15.35; 8,22.31.48.52.57; 9,18.22ᵇⁱˢ; 10,19.24.31.33; 11,8.19.31.33.36.45.54.55; 12,9.11; 13,33; 18,12.14.20.31.33.36.38.39; 19,3.7.12.14.19.20.21ᵗᵉʳ.31.40.42. — Cf. pp. 237, 244 n. 569.

180 διὰ τὸν φόβον τῶν Ἰουδαίων B53 (3) 7,13; 19,38; 20,19. — Cf. p. 312 n. 373.

Ἰούδας → Σίμων 364

Ἰσκαριώτης → Σίμων 364

181 ἵστημι: εἱστήκει/εἱστήκεισαν B26 (7) 1,35; 7,37; 18,5.16; 20,11 / 18,18; 19,25.

181a Ἰωάννης: ἦν (...) Ἰωάννης (...) βαπτίζων B50 (3) 1,28; 3,23; 10,40. — Cf. pp. 309, 312 n. 373.

182 καθώς: καθὼς ..., καί (= οὕτως) A8 R^{12} (6) 6,57; 13,15.33; 15,9; 17,18; 20,21. — Cf. pp. 145 n. 17, 303 n. 313, 312 n. 373.

καί → ἀποκρίνομαι 54 → ἀρχιερεύς 66 → εἰμί 116 → ἐκεῖνος 128 → καθώς 182 → μή 256 → οὖν 295

186a καρδία: ἡ καρδία/τὴν καρδίαν (singular) preceded by a pers. pron. in gen. plur. B13 (5) 14,1.27; 16,22 / 12,40; 16,6.

→ ταράσσομαι 370a

187 καρπός: καρπὸν φέρω C52 (8) 12,24; 15,2^{ter}.4.5.8.16.

191 κόσμος – N^{66} (78) see no. 195 (3), add: 1,9.10^{ter}.29; 3,16.17^{ter}.19; 4,42; 6,14.33.51; 7,4.7; 8,12.23^{bis}.26; 9,5^{bis}.39; 10,36; 11,9.27; 12,19.25.31a. 46.47^{bis}; 13,1^{bis}; 14,17.19.22.27.31; 15,18.19^{quinquies}; 16,8.20.21.28^{bis}.33bis; 17,5.6.9.11^{bis}.13.14^{ter}.15.16^{bis}.18bis.21.23.24.25; 18,20.36^{bis}; 18,37; 21,25. — Cf. pp. 32, 167, 385.

195 ὁ ἀρχὼν τοῦ κόσμου C60 (3) 12,31b; 14,30; 16,11.

199 κραυγάζω B14 (6) 11,43; 12,13; 18,40; 19,6.12.15. — Cf. pp. 147, 154, 173, 211 n. 356, [274-]275 n. 148, 305, 306.

201 κρυπτός: ἐν κρυπτῷ B52 (3) 7,4.10; 18,20. — Cf. p. 312 n. 373.

204 λαλέω: λαλέω ἐκ B44 (3) 3,31; 8,44; 12,49. — Cf. p. 312 n. 373.

206 λελάληκα ὑμῖν (in the direct discourse of Jesus) B31 (10) 6,63; 8,40; 14,25; 15,3.11; 16,1.4.6.25.33. — Cf. p. 312 n. 373.

207 ταῦτα λαλέω – N^{71} (13) 8,26.28.30; 12,36; 14,25; 15,11; 16,1.4.6. 25.33; 17,1.13.

209 λαμβάνω τινα (to receive or to recognize someone personnally) B37 R^{23} (7) 1,12; 5,43^{bis}; 13,20^{quater}. — Cf. pp. 48 n. 40, 145 n. 17, 164, 275 n. 150, 312 n. 373.

211 λέγω: λέγει/λέγουσιν (asyndetic/οὖν) + dative + someone (as introduction to the direct discourse) A4 (52) 1,46.48; 2,[4].7; 4,7.9.[11].17.19.21.25.26.34.50; 5,8; 6,8; 7,6; 8,39; 11,8.23.24.39.40.44; 13,8.9.10.27.(29).36.37; 14,5.6.8.9.22; 18,17.38; 19,6.10.15; 20,15.16.17. 29; 21,3.5.10.12.(15).[17].22. — Cf. pp. 274[-275] n. 148.

218 ἄλλοι (δὲ) ἔλεγον A24 (7) 7,12.41; 9,9^{bis}.16; 10,21; 12,29. — Cf. p. 312 n. 373.

222 ὁ λόγος (...) ὃν εἶπεν A18 (7) 2,22; 4,50; 7,36; 12,38; 15,20; 18,9.32. — Cf. pp. 18-19, 26 n. 145, 198, 347.

223-225 τοῦτο/ταῦτα + verb of saying B2 N^{71} (41) 2,22; 4,18; 5,34; 6,6.59; 7,9.39; 8,[6].26.28.30; 9,6.22; 11,11.28.43.51; 12,33.36.41; 13,21; 14,25; 15,11; 16,1.4^{bis}.6.25.33; 17,1.13; 18,1.22.34.38; 20,14.18.22; 21,19^{bis}.

226 τοῦτο δὲ εἶπεν/ἔλεγεν – N^{71} (7) 7,39; 11,51; (12,6); 21,19 / 6,6; [8,6]; 12,33.

228a λέγειν τινά meaning saying something about someone – N^{77} (7) see no. 230 (3), add: 1,15; 6,71; 8,27; 10,35.

229 ὑμεῖς λέγετε ὅτι B11 (5) see no. 230 (3), add: 4,20.35.

230 ὃν (...) ὑμεῖς λέγετε ὅτι B45 (3) 8,54; 9,19; 10,36.

→ ἀποκρίνομαι 54 → διά 86 → Δίδυμος 89 → πῶς 359

λόγος → λέγω 222 → πληρόω 339 → τηρέω 377

235 μαθητής: εἰμὶ/γίνομαι μαθητής C22 (7) 8,31; 9,28ᵇⁱˢ; 13,35; 19,38 / 9,27; 15,8.

235a ὁ μαθητής (...) ὃν ἠγάπα/ἐφίλει C61 (4) 19,26; 21,7.20 / 20,2. — Cf. p. 19 n. 115.

→ ἄλλος 33

238 μαρτυρέω – N⁶⁵ (33) see no. 240 (17), add: 1,32.34; 3,11.26.28.32; 4,39.44; 5,33; 12,17; 13,21; 15,27; 18,23.37; 19,35; 21,24.

240 μαρτυρέω περί τινος B33 R³⁰ (17) 1,7.8.15; 2,25; 5,31.32ᵇⁱˢ. 36.37.39; 7,7; 8,13.14.18ᵇⁱˢ; 10,25; 15,26. — Cf. pp. 145 n. 17, 312 n. 373.

242 μαρτυρία (14) – N⁶⁵ (14) 1,7.19; 3,11.32.33; 5,21.32.34.36; 8,13.14.17; 19,35; 21,24. — Cf. p. 48 n. 38.

μέλλω → ἀποθνήσκω 52

244 μέντοι: οὐ(δεὶς) μέντοι B59 R²⁶ (4) 4,27; 7,13; 20,5; 21,4. — Cf. p. 145 n. 17.

249a μένω + ἡμέρα C12 (4) 1,39; 2,12; 4,40; 11,6.

253 μετά: μετὰ τοῦτο C6 R⁴³ (4) 2,12; 11,7.11; 19,28. — Cf. pp. 30 n. 162, 58, 181, 275 n. 149, 275 n. 150, 304, 305.

μεταβαίνω → ὑπάγω 389

256 μή: μὴ (interrogative) καί + pers. pron. A5 (7) 6,67; 7,47.52; 9,27.40; 18,17.25.

→ αἰών 13 → ἐάν 97, 99

257 μικρός, indicating the time B7 R³⁴ (11) 7,33; 12,35; 13,33; 14,19; 16,16ᵇⁱˢ=17ᵇⁱˢ=19ᵇⁱˢ.18. — Cf. pp. 145 n. 17, 164, [274-]275 n. 148, 312 n. 373.

264 νίπτω C51 (13) 9,7ᵇⁱˢ.11ᵇⁱˢ.15; 13,5.6.8ᵇⁱˢ.10.12.14ᵇⁱˢ.

265 νόμος + with a term indicating the appartenance C24 (5) 7,51; 8,17; 10,34; 15,25; 18,31.

269 νῦν: εἰ ... νῦν δέ B24 (5) 8,39-40; 9,41; 15,22.24; 18,36. — Cf. p. 312 n. 373.

ὁ → αἰών 11, 13 → ἄλλος 33 → ἀνοίγω 43 → ἀπό 50a → ἀποκρίνομαι 53 → ἀρχιερεύς 66 → Γαλιλαία 70a → γραφή 79 → Δίδυμος 89 → εἰμί 115a → ἑορτή 139a, 139b → ἔργον 142 → ἔρχομαι 145 → ἡμέρα 162 → ἴδιος 170 → Ἱεροσόλυμα 171 → Ἰουδαῖος 179a, 180 → καρδία 186a → κόσμος 195 → λέγω 222 → μαθητής 235a → οὗτος 307a → πέμπω 323 → πληρόω 339 → πρῶτος 357 → σαββάτον 361a → τόπος 380, 381 → τρώγω 383 → ψυχή 404 → Adjectif possessif 412

271a οἶδα: οἶδα + indirect question C29 (22) 2,9; 3,8; 4,10; 5,13; 6,6.64; 7,27.28; 8,14ᵇⁱˢ; 9,21ᵇⁱˢ.25.29.30; 12,35; 13,18; 14,5; 15,15; 16,18; 20,2.13.

272 οἴδαμεν (without particle) ὅτι C4 (8) 3,2; 4,42; 9,20.24.29.31; 16,30; 21,24.

275 ὑμεῖς οὐκ οἴδατε / ἡμεῖς οὐκ οἴδαμεν B4 (7) see no. 276 (3), add: 8,14; 9,30; 11,49 / 9,21. — Cf. p. 312 n. 373.

276 ὃν/ἣν ὑμεῖς οὐκ οἴδατε B46 (3) 1,26; 7,28 / 4,32. — Cf. p. 312 n. 373.

284 ὅπου: ὅπου ἦν/ἦσαν C15 (8) 1,28; 6,62; 7,42; 10,40; 11,32; 12,1; 18,1 / 20,19.

→ εἰμί 118a → τόπος 380

ὁράω → ἴδε 167a

ὅς → λέγω 222, 230 → μαθητής 235a → οἶδα 276 → πᾶς 415a → ὥρα 407

ὅτε → ὥρα 407

288a ὅτι: the subordinating use of ὅτι ("because" ... at the beginning of a sentence) – N[78] (5) 1,50; 8,45; 15,19; 16,6; 20,29.

→ ἀλλά 31 → διά 85-86 → ἵνα 174 → λέγω 229-230 → πιστεύω 334 οὐ → αἰών 13 → ἀλλά 28, 30-31 → δύναμαι 95 → ἐάν 97-98 → μέντοι 244 → οἶδα 275-276 → οὐδείς 289a → πώποτε 358

289a οὐδείς: οὐκ ... οὐδείς (or inflexions) – N[59] (16) 5,19.22.30; 6,63; 8,15; 9,33; 11,49; 12,19; 14,30; 15,5; 16,23.24; 18,9.31; 19,11.41. — Cf. pp. 47 n. 33, 48 n. 40.

→ δύναμαι 95 → μέντοι 244

290 οὐδέπω B58 (3) 7,39; 19,41; 20,9.

292 οὖν: οὖν narrativum A1 R[2] (166) (a) finite verb + οὖν (115): 1,22.39; 2,18.20; 3,25; 4,5.9.28.33.46.48.52[bis].53.; 5,10.19; 6,10.11.13.21.28.30a.32. 34.41.52.53.67; 7,3.6.15.16.25.28.30.33.35.45.47; 8,13.19.21.22.24.25.28.31. [41].[52].57.59; 9,7.10a.16.17.18.20.24.25.26; 10,7.24.[39]; 11,3.12.16.21.36. 41.47.56; 12,2.7.9.17.28.34.35; 13,6.24.27; 16,17.18; 18,11.16.17.24.25.28. 29.31.33.37.40; 19,5.10.15.16b.21.24a.32.38.40; 20,2.3.6.10.20.21.25; 21,5. 6.7a.11.23; (b) subject + οὖν (32): 4,6; 6,14.15.(60); 7,11.40.43; 9,8;11,20. 31.32.33.38.(45).53.54; 12,1.3.19.29; 18,3.4.10.12.19; 19,13.20.23.26.29b. 31; 21,7b; (c) πάλιν οὖν (4): 8,12; 9,15; 18,7.27; (d) ὅτε οὖν (9): 2,22; 4,45; 6,24; 13,12.31; 19,6.8.30; 21,15; (e) ὡς οὖν (6): 4,1.40; 11,6; 18,6; 20,11; 21,19. — Cf. pp. 27, 157, [218-]219 n. 396, 303 n. 313, 304, 305, 326.

295 οὖν ... καὶ + finite verb ... καὶ + finite verb (same subject) A10 (12) 1,39; 4,28; 9,7; (11,33-34); [13,12]; 18,10; 18,12-13.16.33; 20,2.6.8. — Cf. pp. [274-]275 n. 148.

301 τότε οὖν narrativum C13 R[1] (4) 11,14; 19,1.16; 20,8. — Cf. pp. 181, 304, 305.

→ ἀποκρίνομαι 54 → Ἰησοῦς 172 → λέγω 211

302 οὔπω C5 N[70] (11) see nos. 303 (3) and 304 (4), add: 2,4; 7,6.8; 8,57.

303 οὔπω γάρ C3 (3) 3,24; 7,39; 20,17.

304 οὔπω ἐληλύθει B39 (4) 6,17; 7,30; 8,20; 11,30. — Cf. p. 312 n. 373.

305 οὗτος: ἐν τούτῳ – N[53] (4) 4,37; 9,30; 13,35; 15,8.

307a οὗτός ἐστιν ἀληθῶς ὁ + christological title C32 (3) 4,42; 6,14; 7,40.

307b οὗτός, taking up a *casus pendens* N[79] (14) 1,33; 3,26.32; 5,19.38; 6,46; 7,18; 8,26.28; 9,31; 10,25; 14,13; 15,5.19.

τοῦτο → διά 85-86 → ἐκ 123 → λαλέω 207 → λέγω 223-226 → μετά 253

οὕτως → καθώς 182

ὀφθαλμός → ἀνοίγω 43

308 ὀψάριον C55 R³⁹ (5) 6,9.11; 21,9.10.13. — Cf. pp. 146, 148, 164, 305, 316.

310a πάλιν + δεύτερον – R³⁷ (2) 4,54; 21,16. — Cf. pp. 3, 146, 152, 164, [257-] 258 n. 34, 301 n. 301, 303 n. 313, 304, 305, 309, 321-322, 366, 372.

314 παρά: (εἰμὶ) παρά, of Jesus – N⁶⁴ (8) 6,46; 7,29; 9,16.33; 16,27; 17,8.

316 παροιμία – R²¹ (4) 10,26; 16,25ᵇⁱˢ.29. — Cf. pp. 145 n. 17, 164, 309.

317 παρρησία: παρρησίᾳ A12 R¹⁹ (7) 7,13.26; 10,24; 11,14.54; 16,25; 18,20. — Cf. pp. 145 n. 17, 275 n. 150, 312 n. 373.

πᾶς → Collectif neuter 415a

323 πέμπω: ὁ πέμψας με (and analogous expressions) C41 N⁸¹ (27) 1,(22).33; 4,34; 5,23.24.30.37; 6,38.39.44; 7,16.18.28.33; 8,16.18.26.29; 9,4; 12,44.45.49; 13,16.20; 14,24; 15,21; 16,5.

325 πέραν + gen. C1 (8) 1,28; 3,26; 6,1.17.22.25; 10,40; 18,1. — Cf. p. 101 n. 145.

περί → ἀλλά 30 → γογγύζω 77 → ἐρωτάω 151 → μαρτυρέω 240
Πέτρος → Σίμων 364-365

327 πιάζω B62 R⁵⁰ (8) 7,30.32.44; 8,20; 10,39; 11,57; 21,3.10. — Cf. pp. 146, 164, 304, 305.

331 πιστεύω + διά B5 N⁵² (6) 1,7; 4,39.41.42; 14,11; 17,20.

332 πιστεύω εἴς τι(να) C39 R⁴² (36) 1,12; 2,11.23; 3,16.18ᵇⁱˢ.36; 4,39; 6,29.35.40; 7,5.31.38.39.48; 8,30; 9,35.36; 10,42; 11,25.26.45.48; 12,11.36.37.42.44ᵇⁱˢ.46; 14,1ᵇⁱˢ.12; 16,9; 17,20. — Cf. pp. 47, 48 nn. 38 and 40, 146, 164, 304, 305, 347 n. 573, 375.

334 πιστεύω ὅτι (that) C38 (14) 4,21; 6,69; 8,24; 9,18; 11,27.42; 13,19; 14,10.11; 16,27.30; 17,8.21; 20,31.

339 πληρόω: ἵνα ὁ λόγος (...) πληρωθῇ B27 (4) 12,38; 15,25; 18,9.32. — Cf. pp. 18-19, 26 n. 145, 198, 347.

→ γραφή 79 → χαρά 402

340 πλοιάριον C56 (4) 6,22.[23].24; 21,8.

πνεῦμα → ταράσσομαι 370a

342 πόθεν + εἰμί C28 (7) 2,9; 7,27ᵇⁱˢ.28; 9,29.30; 19,9.

343 ποιέω ἐμαυτόν + attribute C27 (5) 5,18; 8,53; 10,33; 19,7.12.

346 ποιέω σημεῖον/σημεῖα C43 (13) 4,54; 6,14.30; 10,41; 12,18 / 2,23; 3,2; 6,2; 7,31; 9,16; 11,47; 12,37; 20,30. — Cf. pp. 101 n. 145, 274-[275] n. 148, 297 n. 274, 386.

→ δύναμαι 95

ποῖος → σημαίνω 363
πορεύομαι → ὑπάγω 389

353 ποῦ ὑπάγω C30 (7) 3,8; 8,14ᵇⁱˢ; 12,35; 13,36; 14,5; 16,5.

πρός → ἀπέρχομαι 48

357 πρῶτος: τὸ πρῶτον B60 N⁵⁸ (3) 10,40; 12,16; 19,39. — Cf. p. 312 n. 373.

358 πώποτε: οὐ ... πώποτε B61 R³³ (4) 1,18; 5,37; 6,35; 8,33. — Cf. pp. 145 n. 17, 164, 312 n. 373.

359 πῶς: πῶς σὺ λέγεις B51 (3) 8,33; 12,34; 14,9. — Cf. pp. 218-219 n. 396, 312 n. 373.

→ δύναμαι 96

360 ῥαββί/ῥαββουνί, vocative (for Jesus) C23 (8) 1,49; 3,2; 4,31; 6,25;
9,2; 11,8 / 1,38; 20,16. — Cf. pp. 101 n. 145, 143 n. 7, 148, 169, 173, 182
n. 178, 221 n. 412.

361a σάββατον: ἐν (τῷ) σαββάτῳ C2 (5) 5,16; 7,22.23^bis; 19,31.

σεαυτοῦ → ἀπό 49

363 σημαίνω: σημαίνων ποίῳ θανάτῳ B54 (3) 12,33; 18,32; 21,19. —
Cf. pp. 312 n. 373, 389 n. 62.

σημεῖον → ποιέω 346

364 Σίμων: Ἰούδας Σίμωνος Ἰσκαριώτου B55 (3) 6,71; 13,2.26. — Cf.
p. 312 n. 373.

365 Σίμων Πέτρος A13 R^24 (17) 1,40; 6,8.68; 13,6.9.24.36; 18,10.15.25;
20,2.6; 21,2.3.7.11.15. — Cf. pp. 304, 305.

367 σκοτία for σκότος B17 R^22 (8) 1,5^bis; 6,17; 8,12; 12,35^bis.46; 20,1. — Cf.
pp. 3, [9-]10 n. 46, 145 n. 17, 303 n. 313, 305.

368a σύ after the verb C21 (8) 1,21; 4,19; 6,30; 8,48; 12,34; 17,5; 18,37;
19,9.

→ πώς 359

370 σχίσμα (...) ἐγένετο/ἦν ἐν + dative B49 (3) 7,43; 10,19 / 9,16. — Cf.
p. 312 n. 373.

370a ταράσσομαι (passive) connected with καρδία / πνεῦμα / ψυχή
B40 (4) 14,1.27 / 13,21 / 12,27. — Cf. p. 312 n. 373.

375 τελειόω τὸ ἔργον/τὰ ἔργα C37 (3) 4,34; 17,4 / 5,36. — Cf. p. 387 n. 50.

377 τηρέω: τηρέω τὸν λόγον (sing.) C26 (7) 8,51.52.55; 14,23; 15,20^bis;
17,6.

378 τηρέω τὰς ἐντολάς C46 (4) 14,15.21; 15,10^bis.

τίθημι → ψυχή 404

τίς → ζητέω 157

τις → αἰτέω 10a → ἄν 38 → ἀπέρχομαι 48 → ἐάν 99 → ἐρωτάω 151 →
λαμβάνω 209 → λέγω 228a → μαρτυρέω 240 → πιστεύω 332 →
ὑπαντάω 389a

380 τόπος: ὁ τόπος ὅπου A17 (7) 4,20; 6,23; 10,40; 11,30; 19,(17-18).20.41.
— Cf. pp. 275 n. 150, 309.

381 εἰμὶ ἐν τῷ τόπῳ B29 (4) 5,13; 6,10; 11,30; 19,41.

τότε → οὖν 301

383 τρώγω: ὁ τρώγων C53 (5) 6,54.56.57.58; 13,18.

ὑμεῖς → ἐγώ 104-106 → λαλέω 206 → λέγω 229-230 → οἶδα 275-276

389,350,254 ὑπάγω: ὑπάγω / πορεύομαι / ἀπέρχομαι / ἀφίημι /
μεταβαίνω (used for Jesus' death) C33 R^29,41 (27) ὑπάγω (17) in
7,33; 8,14^bis.21bis.22; 13,3.33.36^bis; 14,4.5.28; 16,5^bis.10.17; πορεύομαι (6)
in 14,2.3.12.28; 16,7.28; ἀπέρχομαι (2) in 16,7^bis; ἀφίημι (1) in 16,28;
μεταβαίνω (1) in 13,1. — Cf. pp. 47, 74 n. 16, 109, 145 n. 17, 164, [274-]
275 n. 148.

→ ποῦ 353

389a ὑπαντάω τινί (to meet someone; not in a hostile sense) C8 (4)
4,51; 11,20.30; 12,18.

393 φανερόω – N^{72} (9) see no. 394 (3), add: 1,31; 2,11; 3,21; 9,3; 17,6; 21,14.
394 φανερόω ἐμαυτόν – R^{28} (3) 7,4; 21,1a.(1b). — Cf. pp. 145 n. 17, 275 n. 49, 309.
Φαρισαῖος → ἀρχιερεύς 66
φέρω → καρπός 187
396 φιλέω – N^{82} (13) 5,20; 11,3.36; 12,25; 15,19; 16,27^bis; 20,2.15.16.17^ter.
→ μαθητής 235a
φόβος → Ἰουδαῖος 180
402 χαρά, subject of πληροῦσθαι B36 (4) 3,29; 15,11; 16,24; 17,13. — Cf. p. 312 n. 373.
404 ψυχή: τίθημι τὴν ψυχήν/τὰς ψυχάς B41 R^{25} (8) 10,11.15.17.(18bis); 13,37.38; 15,13. — Cf. pp. 145 n. 17, 164, 312 n. 373.
→ ταράσσομαι 370a
405 ὥρα, said of Jesus – N^{67} (10) see no. 406 (5, without 16,21), add: 12,23.27^bis; 16,32; 17,1. — Cf. pp. 234, 274-275 n. 148.
406 ὥρα + possessive (gen.) B15 R^{18} (6) 2,4; 7,30; 8,20; 13,1; 16,4.21. — Cf. pp. 145 n. 17, 312 n. 373.
407 ὥρα ἵνα / ὥρα ὅτε / ὥρα ἐν ᾗ B16 $R^{15,49}$ (9) 12,23; 13,1; 16,2.32 / 4,21.23; 5,25; 16,25 / 5,28. — Cf. pp. 145 n. 17, 146, 152, 274[-275] n. 148, 304, 305, 312 n. 373.
408 ὥρα ἦν ὡς + number B42 (3) 1,39; 4,6; 19,14.
ὡς → ὥρα 408
412 Adjective possessive, placed after the substantive, with duplication of the article A11 R^{8} (29) ἐμός in 3,29; 5,30^bis; 6,38; 7,6; 8,16.31.37.43^bis.56; 10,26.27; 12,26; 14,15.27; 15,9.11.12; 17,13.24; 18,36^quater; σός in 17,17; 18,35; ὑμέτερος in 7,6; 8,17. — Cf. pp. 47 n. 33, 48 n. 40, 164, 312 n. 373.
412a *Asyndeton epicum* A7 R^{6} (102) (a) the instances mentioned by S^{10} (cp. R^{6}) (38): 1,39.40.42.45.47; 2,17; 4,6.7.30.50; 5,12.15; 6,23; 7,32.41; 8,27; 9,9^bis.13.35.40; 10,21.22; 11,35.44; 12,22^bis.29; 13,22.23; 16,19; 18,25; 19,29; 20,18.26; 21,3.13.17; (b) finite form of ἀποκρίνομαι or ἀπεκρίθη καὶ εἶπεν (64): 1,26.48.49.50; 2,19; 3,3.5.9.10.27; 4,10.13.17; 5,7; 6,7.26.29.43.68.70; 7,20.21.46.52; 8,14.19.33.34.39.48.49.54; 9,3.27.30.34; 10,25.32.33.34; 11,9; 12,30; 13,7.8.26.36.38; 14,23; 16,31; 18,5.8.20. 23.30.34.35.36.37; 19,7.11.15.22; 20,28; 21,5. — Cf. pp. 157, 164, 303 n. 313, 304, 305, 326.
413 Definitions: τοῦτό ἐστιν ... ἵνα/ὅτι/substantive – N^{56} (7) ἵνα (6) in 6,29.39.40.50; 15,12; 17,3; ὅτι (1) in 3,19.
414 Misunderstanding – N^{63} (13) 2,19-21; 3,3-5; 4,10-14.32-34; 6,33-35; 7,33-36; 8,21-23.56-57; 11,11-14.23-26; 12,34; 13,8-10; 14,4-6.
415a Collective neuter in the singular A23 R^{11} (8) 3,6^bis; 6,37.39^bis; 10,29; 17,2.24. — Cf. pp. 145 n. 17, 164, 312 n. 373.
415b Noun + article, with complement, as attribute A26 R^{9} (8) 2,23; 6,27; 7,2; 8,44; 11,13; 13,1; 18,1.17. — Cf. pp. 304, 305.

416a *Wiederaufnahme* B18 R[7] (29) 1,1; 3,12.20-21.31.32-33; 5,31-32; 6,46.57; 8,15-16.18; 9,28; 10,4-5.38; 12,35-36; 13,31; 14,1.11.20; 15,2.4.9.10; 16,27-28; 17,1.10.11.16.23; 18,36. — Cf. pp. 145 n. 17, 164, 243 n. 566, 303 n. 313, 312 n. 373.

416b Word separation – N[69] (56) (a) substantive and genitive (resp. ἐκ + gen.) (30): 1,49; 2,15; 3,19; 4,39; 6,60; 7,38.44; 8,34; 9,5.28^{bis}.40; 10,2; 11,32.49.51; 12,11.31.47; 13,6.14.28; 18,17.22; 19,20^{bis}.21.32.35; 20,23; 21,12; (b) substantive and adjective (11): 5,20; 6,23.55^{bis}; 7,12.50; 10,32; 11,17.47; 19,14.29; (c) substantive and pronoun (9): 4,23; 5,14; 7,46; 9,16; 10,41; 12,18.37; 18,38; 21,15; (d) substantive and apposition (2): 6,27; 19,20; (e) verb and subject/object/other determination (4): 7,44; 11,15; 12,37; 17,5. — Cf. pp. [204-]205 n. 307.

416c Unusual word separation – R[10] (12) 4,39; 5,20; 7,12.38.44; 10,32; 11,15; 12,11.18.37; 17,5; 19,20. — Cf. pp. 145 n. 17, 164, 303 n. 313, 305, 309.

416d The genitive before article + noun – N[60] (5) 2,15; 8,17; 10,5; 15,10; 19,32.

416e *Chiasmus* – N[68] (23) 1,1; 3,12.20-21.31.32-33; 5,31-32; 6,37.46; 7,18.22-23; 8,15-16.18; 10,4-5.14-15.38; 12,35.35-36; 13,31; 14,1; 15,2.4; 16,27-28; 18,36. — Cf. pp. [204-]205 n. 307.

416f Grammatical parataxis for logical hypotaxis, one of the typical Semitic characteristics – N[74] (14) 1,10.11; 7,21.22.26.34.36; 8,52.57; 9,34; 10,12; 11,8; 14,9; 16,22.

416g Conditional parataxis in a subordinate clause (also Semitic) – N[75] (13) 3,12; 5,24; 6,26.30.36.40.50.57.58; 9,30; 12,47; 15,10; 20,29.

416h Remarkable repetitions – N[76] — Cf. pp. [204-]205 n. 307.

I. Ruckstuhl's 1951 List (^{2}1987)

R^{1-50} compared with (1) Schweizer's list (S^{1-33}) and those of Jeremias (J) and Menoud (M), (2) Ruckstuhl's 1991 list (A1-26, B1-65, C1-62), and (3) the list printed above (nos. 1-416)

R^1	S^4	C13	301		R^{27}	J		83
R^2	S^3	A1	292		R^{28}			394
R^3			38		R^{29}		C33	254
R^4		C14	171		R^{30}		B33	240
R^5	S^2	A14	174		R^{31}	S^{21}	B19	49-50
R^6	S^{10}	A7	412a					
R^7	S^{11}	B18	416a		R^{32}	S^{24}	C10	162
R^8	S^1	A11	412		R^{33}		B61	358
R^9	S^7	A26	415b		R^{34}		B7	257
R^{10}	S^{12}		416c		R^{35}			40
R^{11}		A23	415a		R^{36}			123
R^{12}	S^9	A8	182		R^{37}			310a
R^{13}	S^8	A19	28		R^{38}	S^{26}		129
R^{14}		C31	31		R^{39}	S^{27}	C55	308
R^{15}		B16	407		R^{40}	M	C45	37
R^{16}	M	A3	54		R^{41}	S^{22}	C33	350, 389
R^{17}	S^6	B1	124		R^{42}	J	C39	332
R^{18}	J	B15	406		R^{43}		C6	253
R^{19}	S^{25}	A12	317		R^{44}	S^{16}	B3	97-98
					R^{45}	S^{13}	B9	121a
R^{20}		B20	13		R^{46}	S^{14}	C44	108, 72
R^{21}			316		R^{47}	S^{15}	C19	99
R^{22}	S^{20}	B17	367		R^{48}		B8	133
R^{23}	S^{23}	B37	209		R^{49}		B16	407
R^{24}		A13	365		R^{50}	S^{29}	B62	327
R^{25}	S^{28}	B41	404					
R^{26}	S^{17}	B59	244					

II. Nicol's 1972 List

N^{51-82} compared with (1) Schweizer's list (S^{1-33}), and (2) the list above (nos. 1-416)

N^{51}		85		N^{61}		11
N^{52}		331		N^{62}		53
N^{53}		305		N^{63}		414
N^{54}		141-142		N^{64}		314
N^{55}		179a		N^{65}		242, 238
N^{56}		413		N^{66}		191
N^{57}	S^{31}	39		N^{67}		405
N^{58}		357		N^{68}	S^{33}	416e
N^{59}	S^{18}	289a		N^{69}	S^{32}	416b
N^{60}	S^{30}	416d		N^{70}		302

N^{71}	207, 223-226		N^{77}	228a
N^{72}	393		N^{78}	288a
N^{73}	42a		N^{79}	68, 128, 307b
N^{74}	416f		N^{80}	115
N^{75}	416g		N^{81}	323
N^{76}	416h		N^{82}	396

III. RUCKSTUHL'S 1991 LIST

A1-26, B1-65, C1-62 compared (1) with R^{1-50} (1951, ^{2}1987) and (2) the list above (nos. 1-416).

Label	R	No.
A1	R^{2}	292
A2		53
A3	R^{16}	54
A4		211
A5		256
A6		172
A7	R^{6}	412a
A8	R^{12}	182
A9		145
A10		295
A11	R^{8}	412
A12	R^{19}	317
A13	R^{24}	365
A14	R^{5}	174
A15		128
A16		175
A17		380
A18		222
A19	R^{13}	28
A20		80
A21		116
A22		118a
A23	R^{11}	415a
A24		218
A25		102
A26	R^{9}	415b

Label	R	No.
B1	R^{17}	124
B2		223-225
B3	R^{44}	97-98
B4		275
B5		331
B6		96
B7	R^{34}	257
B8	R^{48}	133
B9	R^{45}	121a
B10		147a
B11		229
B12		157
B13		186a
B14		199
B15	R^{18}	406
B16	$R^{15,49}$	407
B17	R^{22}	367
B18	R^{7}	416a
B19	R^{31}	49-50
B20	R^{20}	13
B21		73a
B22		56
B23		66
B24		269
B25		86
B26		181
B27		339
B28		79
B29		381
B30		36
B31		206
B32		104-105
B33	R^{30}	240
B34		139a
B35		52
B36		402
B37	R^{23}	209
B38		84
B39		304
B40		370a
B41	R^{25}	404
B42		408
B43		35
B44		204
B45		230
B46		276
B47		77
B48		176
B49		370
B50		181a
B51		359
B52		201
B53		180
B54		363
B55		364
B56		89
B57		30
B58		290
B59	R^{26}	244
B60		357
B61	R^{33}	358
B62	R^{50}	327
B63		136a
B64		135
B65		59

Label	R	No.
C1		325
C2		361a
C3		303
C4		272
C5		302
C6	R^{43}	253
C7		142
C8	389a	
C9		100
C10	R^{32}	162
C11		139b
C12		249a

C13	R[1]	301	C30		353	C47		10a
C14	R[4]	171	C31	R[14]	31	C48		33
C15		284	C32		307a	C49		48
C16		118	C33	R[29,41]	389,350,254	C50		170
C17		167a	C34		95	C51		264
C18		150a	C35		160	C52		187
C19	R[47]	99	C36		106	C53		383
C20		150	C37		375	C54		43
C21		368a	C38		334	C55	R[39]	308
C22		235	C39	R[42]	332	C56		340
C23		360	C40		161	C57		9a
C24		265	C41		323	C58		50a
C25		154	C42		141	C59		70a
C26		377	C43		346	C60		195
C27		343	C44	R[46]	108,72	C61		235a
C28		342	C45	R[40]	37	C62		151
C29		271a	C46		378			

BIBLIOGRAPHY

Abbreviations

Periodicals, Series, and Encyclopedias

AASF   Annales Academiae Scientiarum Fennicae (Helsinki)

AASF DHL   Annales Academiae Scientiarum Fennicae. Dissertationes Humanarum Litterarum (Helsinki)

AB   The Anchor Bible (Garden City, NY)

ABD   FREEDMAN, D.N. (ed.), *The Anchor Bible Dictionary*, 6 vols., New York – London, 1992.

AcAn (Letteren)   *Academiae Analecta. Mededelingen van de Koninklijke Academie voor Wetenschappen, Letteren en Schone Kunsten van België: Klasse der Letteren*, Brussel.

ALBO   Analecta Lovaniensia Biblica et Orientalia (Leuven)

AmEcclRev   *The American Ecclesiastical Review* (Washington, DC)

AnBib   Analecta Biblica (Roma)

AnGreg   Analecta Gregoriana (Roma)

AnJapB   *Annual of the Japanese Biblical Institute* (Tokyo)

ANRW II   TEMPORINI, A. – HAASE, W. (eds.), *Aufstieg und Niedergang der Römischen Welt. Geschichte und Kultur Roms im Spiegel der neueren Forschung. II. Prinzipat.* Vol. 25/1-6: *Religion (vorkonstantinisches Christentum: Leben und Umwelt Jesu; Neues Testament [Kanonische Schriften und Apokryphen])*, Berlin – New York, 1982 (25/1); 1984 (25/2); 1985 (25/3); 1987 (25/4); 1988 (25/5-6).

Ant   *Antonianum* (Roma)

ANTJ   Arbeiten zum Neuen Testament und Judentum (Frankfurt – Bern – Las Vegas, NV – New York)

AOAT   Alter Orient und Altes Testament (Kevelaer – Neukirchen-Vluyn)

ArchTGran   *Archivo teológico Granadino* (Granada)

AssSeign   *Assemblées du Seigneur* (Bruges – Paris)

ATR   *Anglican Theological Review* (Evanston, IL)

ATR SS   *Anglican Theological Review. Supplementary Series* (Evanston, IL)

ATANT   Abhandlungen zur Theologie des Alten und Neuen Testaments (Zürich)

ATDan   Acta Theologica Danica (Århus – Leiden)

AugsbCNT   Augsburg Commentary on the New Testament (Minneapolis, MN)

AustBR   *Australian Biblical Review* (Melbourne)

AzT   Arbeiten zur Theologie (Stuttgart)

BBB   Bonner Biblische Beiträge (Bonn)

BET   Beiträge zur biblischen Exegese und Theologie (Frankfurt – Bern – New York – Paris)

BETL	Bibliotheca Ephemeridum Theologicarum Lovaniensium (Leuven)
BEvT	Beiträge zur evangelischen Theologie (München)
BFCT M	Beiträge zur Forderung christlicher Theologie. 2. Reihe: Sammlung wissenschaftlicher Monographien (Gütersloh)
BGBE	Beiträge zur Geschichte der biblischen Exegese (Tübingen)
BHBib	Bibliotheca Hispana Biblica (Madrid)
BHT	Beiträge zur historischen Theologie (Tübingen)
Bib	*Biblica. Commentarii Periodici Pontificii Instituti Biblici* (Roma)
BibH	Biblische Handbibliothek (München)
BibKi	*Bibel und Kirche* (Stuttgart)
BibLeb	*Bibel und Leben* (Düsseldorf)
Bible Bhashyam	*Bible Bhashyam: An Indian Biblical Quarterly* (Kottayam, Kerala, India)
BibNot	*Biblische Notizen* (München)
BibUnt	Biblische Untersuchungen (Regensburg)
Bijdragen	*Bijdragen. Tijdschrift voor Filosofie en Theologie* (Meppel)
BJSt	Brown Judaistic Studies (Atlanta, GA)
BJRL	*The Bulletin of the John Rylands University Library of Manchester* (Manchester)
BNTC	Black's New Testament Commentaries (London)
BS	*Bibliotheca Sacra* (Dallas, TX)
BSt	Biblische Studien (Neukirchen-Vluyn)
BTB	*Biblical Theology Bulletin* (Jamaica, NY)
BTrans	*The Bible Translator* (London)
BTSt	Biblisch-theologische Studien (Neukirchen-Vluyn)
BVC	*Bible et vie chrétienne* (Maredsous)
BWANT	Beiträge zur Wissenschaft vom Alten und Neuen Testament (Stuttgart)
BZ	*Biblische Zeitschrift* (Paderborn)
BZNW	Beihefte zur Zeitschrift für die neutestamentliche Wissenschaft (Berlin – New York)
CalvTJ	*Calvin Theological Journal* (Grand Rapids, MI)
CBQ	*The Catholic Biblical Quarterly* (Washington, DC)
CMech	*Collectanea Mechliniensia* (Mechelen)
CNEB	The Cambridge Bible Commentary. New English Bible (Cambridge)
CoBRA	Collectanea Biblica et Religiosa Antiqua (Brussel)
Collationes	*Collationes. Vlaams tijdschrift voor theologie en Pastoraal* (Gent)
Communio (Spain)	*Communio. Commentarii internationales de Ecclesia et Theologia* (Sevilla)
ConBibNT	Coniectanea Biblica. New Testament Series (Lund)
ConcTM	*Concordia Theological Monthly* (St. Louis, MO)
CRB	Cahiers de la Revue biblique (Paris)
CTAP	Cahiers théologiques de l'actualité protestante (Neuchâtel – Paris)

CurrTMiss	*Currents in Theology and Mission* (Chicago, IL)
CW	*Christliche Welt* (Gotha)
CwH	Calwer Hefte zur Förderung biblischen Glaubens und christlichen Lebens (Stuttgart)
Dabar	"Dabar". Studi biblici e giudaistici (Genova)
DBI	COGGINS, R.J. – HOULDEN, J.L. (eds.), *A Dictionary of Biblical Interpretation*, London – Philadelphia, PA, 1990.
DissAbstr	*Dissertation Abstracts International.* A: *The Humanities and Social Sciences* (Ann Arbor, MI)
DivThom	*Divus Thomas* (Piacenza)
DLZ	*Deutsche Literaturzeitung* (Berlin)
DownR	*The Downside Review* (Bath)
EDNT	BALZ, H. – SCHNEIDER, G. (eds.), *Exegetical Dictionary of the New Testament*, 3 vols., 1990, 1991, 1992. → EWNT
EET	Einführung in die evangelische Theologie (München)
EHNT	Exegetisches Handbuch zum Neuen Testament (Münster)
EHS	Europäische Hochschulschriften (Bern – Frankfurt – New York – Paris)
EKL	FAHLBUSH, E. – LOCHMAN, J.M. – MBITI, J. – PELIKAN, J. – VISCHER, L. (eds.), *Evangelisches Kirchenlexikon [EKL]. Internationale theologische Enzyklopädie.* Dritte Auflage (Neufassung), 1986–.
ErfTSt	Erfurter theologische Studien (Leipzig)
EstAg	*Estudio agustiniano* (Valladolid)
EstE	*Estudios eclesiásticos. Revista teológica de investigación e información* (Madrid)
ÉtB	Études bibliques (Paris)
ÉtHPR	Études d'histoire et de philosophie religieuses (Paris)
ÉTR	*Études théologiques et religieuses* (Montpellier)
ETL	*Ephemerides Theologicae Lovanienses* (Leuven)
EV	*Esprit et vie* (Langres)
EvQ	*The Evangelical Quarterly* (Exeter)
EvT	*Evangelische Theologie* (München)
EWNT	BALZ, H. – SCHNEIDER, G. (eds.), *Exegetisches Wörterbuch zum Neuen Testament*, 3 vols., Stuttgart, 1980, 1981, 1983. → EDNT
Exp	*The Expositor* (London)
ExpT	*The Expository Times* (Edinburgh)
FRLANT	Forschungen zur Religion und Literatur des Alten und Neuen Testament (Göttingen)
Forum	*Forum. Foundations & Facets* (Sonoma, CA)
FTS	Freiburger Theologische Studien (Freiburg – Basel – Wien)
FzB	Forschung zur Bibel (Würzburg)
FZPT	*Freiburger Zeitschrift für Philosophie und Theologie* (Freiburg/Schw.)

GGA	*Göttingische gelehrte Anzeigen* (Göttingen)
GKG	*Geisteskampf der Gegenwart* (Gütersloh)
GL	*Geist und Leben* (München)
GNS	Good News Studies (Wilmington, DE)
GPM	*Göttinger Predigtmediationen* (Göttingen)
GTT	*Gereformeerd Theologisch Tijdschrift* (Kampen)
Hermeneia	Hermeneia: A Critical and Historical Commentary on the Bible (Philadelphia, PA)
HeythJ	*The Heythrop Journal* (London)
HNT	Handbuch zum Neuen Testament (Tübingen)
HTCNT	Herder's Theological Commentary on the New Testament (New York) → HTKNT
HTKNT	Herders theologischer Kommentar zum Neuen Testament (Freiburg – Basel – Wien) → HTCNT
HTR	*Harvard Theological Review* (Cambridge, MA)
HTS	Harvard Theological Studies (Philadelphia, PA)
HUT	Hermeneutische Untersuchungen zur Theologie (Tübingen)
ICC	The International Critical Commentary (Edinburgh)
IDB	BUTTRICK, G.A. *et al.* (eds.), *The Interpreter's Dictionary of the Bible*, New York – Nashville, TN, 1962.
IDB SV	CRIMM, K. *et al.* (eds.), *The Interpreter's Dictionary of the Bible. Supplementary Volume*, Nashville, TN, 1976.
Interpr	*Interpretation: A Journal of Bible and Theology* (Richmond, VA)
IrTQ	*The Irish Theological Quarterly* (Maynooth)
JAAR	*Journal of the American Academy of Religion* (Atlanta, GA)
JAC	*Jahrbuch für Antike und Christentum* (Münster)
JBL	*Journal of Biblical Literature* (Atlanta, GA)
JBL MS	Journal of Biblical Literature. Monograph Series (Philadelphia, PA)
JNES	*Journal of Near Eastern Studies* (Chicago, IL)
JSNT	*Journal for the Study of the New Testament* (Sheffield)
JSNT SS	Journal for the Study of the New Testament. Supplement Series (Sheffield)
JSOT	*Journal for the Study of the Old Testament* (Sheffield)
JSOT SS	Journal for the Study of the Old Testament. Supplement Series (Sheffield)
JTS	*The Journal of Theological Studies* (Oxford)
JTSouthAfr	*Journal of Theology for Southern Africa* (Rondebosch)
KEK	Kritisch-exegetischer Kommentar über das Neue Testament (Göttingen)
KerDog	*Kerygma und Dogma* (Göttingen)
KerkT	*Kerk en Theologie* (Den Haag)
LavalTP	*Laval théologique et philosophique* (Québec)

LD	Lectio Divina (Paris)
LoB	Leggere oggi la Bibbia (Brescia)
LouvSt	*Louvain Studies* (Leuven)
LouvTPMS	Louvain Theological and Pastoral Monographs (Leuven)
LSSK T	Det Lærde Selskabs Skrifter. Teologiske Skrifter. Publications de la Société des Sciences et des Lettres d'Aarhus. Série de théologie (København)
LTK²	HÖFER, J. – RAHNER, K. (eds.), *Lexikon für Theologie und Kirche*, 10 vols., Freiburg, 1957-1965; *Register*, 1967.
LumV	*Lumière et Vie* (Paris)
MSU	Mitteilungen des Septuaginta-Unternehmens (Göttingen – Berlin)
MTZ	*Münchener theologische Zeitschrift* (München)
NAWG PH	*Nachrichten der Akademie der Wissenschaften zu Göttingen. Philosophisch-historische Klasse* (Berlin)
NBL	GÖRG, M. – LANG, B. (eds.), *Neues Bibel-Lexikon*, Zürich, 1988-.
NCB	The New Century Bible (London)
NEchB NT	Die Neue Echter Bibel. Kommentar zum Neuen Testament mit der Einheitsübersetzung (Würzburg)
Neotestamentica	*Neotestamentica: Journal of the New Testament Society of South Africa* (Pretoria)
NIBC	New International Biblical Commentary (Peabody, MA)
NICNT	The New International Commentary on the New Testament (Grand Rapids, MI)
NJBC	BROWN, R.E. – FITZMYER, J.A. – MURPHY, R.E. (eds.), *The New Jerome Biblical Commentary*, Englewood Cliffs, NJ, 1990.
NKZ	*Neue kirchliche Zeitschrift* (Erlangen)
NRT	*Nouvelle revue théologique* (Tournai)
NT	*Novum Testamentum* (Leiden)
NTA	*New Testament Abstracts* (Cambridge MA)
NTAbh	Neutestamentliche Abhandlungen (Münster)
NTD	Das Neue Testament Deutsch (Göttingen)
NTLi	The New Testament Library (London)
NTOA	Novum Testamentum et Orbis Antiquus (Freiburg/Schw. – Göttingen)
NTS	*New Testament Studies* (Cambridge)
NTT	*Nederlands theologisch tijdschrift* ('s-Gravenhage)
NTTS	New Testament Tools and Studies (Leiden)
OBO	Orbis Biblicus et Orientalis (Freiburg/Schw.)
ÖTKNT	Ökumenischer Taschenbuchkommentar zum Neuen Testament (Gütersloh – Würzburg)
Pacifica	*Pacifica: Australian Theological Studies* (Brunswick East, Victoria)

PBSB NT	Petite bibliothèque des sciences bibliques. Nouveau Testament (Paris)
Perspective	*Perspective: A Journal of Pittsburgh Theological Seminary* (Pittsburgh, PA)
PerspRelSt	*Perspectives in Religious Studies* (Macon, GA)
PKZ	*Protestantische Kirchenzeitung für das evangelische Deutschland* (Berlin)
PrM	*Protestantische Monatshefte* (Leipzig)
ProclCom	Proclamation Commentaries: The New Testament Witness for Preaching (Philadelphia, PA)
PTS	Paderborner theologische Studien (Paderborn)
QDisp	Quaestiones disputatae (Freiburg – Basel – Wien)
RB	*Revue biblique* (Jérusalem – Paris)
RechBib	Recherches bibliques (Bruges – Paris)
RelStR	*Religious Studies Review* (Waterloo, Ont)
RevistBíb	*Revista Bíblica* (Buenos Aires)
RExp	*Review and Expositor. The Faculty Journal of the Southern Baptist Theological Seminary* (Louisville, KY)
RHE	*Revue d'histoire ecclésiastique* (Leuven)
RHPR	*Revue d'histoire et de philosophie religieuses* (Strasbourg)
RHR	*Revue de l'histoire des religions* (Paris)
RGG	SCHIELE, F.M. – ZSCHARNACK, L. (eds.), *Die Religion in Geschichte und Gegenwart. Handwörterbuch für Theologie und Religionswissenschaft*, 5 vols., Tübingen, 1909-1913; 2. Auflage, 1927-1932; 3. Auflage (ed. K. GALLING), 6 vols., 1957-1962; W. WERBICK, *Registerband*, 1965.
RNT	Regensburger Neues Testament (Regensburg)
RRel	*Review for Religious* (St. Louis, MO)
RSPT	*Revue des sciences philosophiques et théologiques* (Paris)
RSR	*Recherches de science religieuse* (Paris)
RThom	*Revue Thomiste* (Toulouse)
RTL	*Revue théologique de Louvain* (Louvain-la-Neuve)
RTP	*Revue de théologie et de philosophie* (Lausanne)
RTQR	*Revue de théologie et des questions religieuses* (Montauban)
RVV	Religionsgeschichtliche Versuche und Vorarbeiten (Berlin – New York)
SANT	Studien zum Alten und Neuen Testament (München)
SBA	Stuttgarter biblische Aufsatzbände (Stuttgart)
SBB	Stuttgarter biblische Beiträge (Stuttgart)
SBF/LA	*Studium Biblicum Franciscanum/Liber Annuus* (Jerusalem)
SBL DS	Society of Biblical Literature. Dissertation Series (Missoula, MT – Chico, CA)
SBL SBSt	Society of Biblical Literature. Sources for Biblical Study (Missoula, MT – Chico, CA)
SBS	Stuttgarter Bibelstudien (Stuttgart)

SBT	*Studia biblica et theologica* (Pasadena, CA)
SCHNT	Studia ad Corpus Hellenisticum Novi Testamenti (Leiden)
ScotJT	*Scottish Journal of Theology* (Edinburgh)
Scripture	*Scripture: Quarterly of the Catholic Biblical Association* (London)
ScuolC	*La scuola cattolica* (Venegono Inferiore, Varese)
SEAJT	*South East Asia Journal of Theology* (Singapore)
SecCent	*The Second Century: A Journal of Early Christian Studies* (Abilene, TX)
Semeia	*Semeia: An Experimental Journal for Biblical Criticism* (Atlanta, GA)
SF	Studia Friburgensia (Freiburg/Schw.)
SGV	Sammlung gemeinverständlicher Vorträge und Schriften aus dem Gebiet der Theologie und Religionsgeschichte (Tübingen)
SHAW PH	Sitzungsberichte der Heidelberger Akademie der Wissenschaften. Philosophisch-historische Klasse (Heidelberg)
SHR	Studies in the History of Religions. Supplements to *Numen* (Leiden)
SJLA	Studies in Judaism and Late Antiquity (Leiden)
SK	Schriften zur Katechetik (München)
SKK NT	Stuttgarter Kleiner Kommentar. Neues Testament (Stuttgart)
SNTA	Studiorum Novi Testamenti Auxilia (Leuven)
SNTS MS	Society for New Testament Studies. Monograph Series (Cambridge)
SNTU	*Studien zum Neuen Testament und seiner Umwelt* (Linz)
SSA	Deutsche Akademie der Wissenschaften zu Berlin. Schriften der Sektion für Altertumswissenschaft (Berlin)
StBT	Studies in Biblical Theology (London)
StEv	ALAND, K. *et al.* (eds.), *Studia Evangelica: Papers Presented to the International Congress on "The Four Gospels in 1957" Held at Christ Church, Oxford, 1957* (TU, 73; 5/18), Berlin, 1959.
StNT	Studien zum Neuen Testament (Gütersloh)
StNTIW	Studies of the New Testament and Its World (Edinburgh – Philadelphia, PA, 1986)
StPat	*Studia Patavina. Rivista di scienze religiose* (Padova)
StudTheol	*Studia Theologica* (Oslo)
StudRel/SciRel	*Studies in Religion/Sciences religieuses* (Waterloo, Ont.)
SUNT	Studien zur Umwelt des Neuen Testaments (Göttingen)
SupplNT	Supplements to Novum Testamentum (Leiden)
TBer	*Theologische Berichte* (Zürich)
TBl	*Theologische Blätter* (Leipzig)
TDiss	Theologische Dissertationen (Basel)
TDNT	KITTEL, G. – FRIEDRICH, G. (eds.), *Theological Dictionary of the New Testament*, trans./ed. G.W. BROMILEY, 10 vols., Grand Rapids, MI, 1964-1976. → TWNT

TdT	Themen der Theologie (Stuttgart)
TGegw	*Theologie der Gegenwart* (Münster)
TGl	*Theologie und Glaube* (Paderborn)
Themelios	*Themelios: An International Journal for Theological and Religious Studies Students* (Leicester)
Theology	*Theology* (London)
THKNT	Theologischer Handkommentar zum Neuen Testament (Berlin)
TJb(T)	*Theologische Jahrbücher* (Tübingen)
TLZ	*Theologische Literaturzeitung* (Leipzig)
TR	*Theologische Rundschau* (Tübingen)
TRev	*Theologische Revue* (München)
TRE	KRAUSE, G. – MÜLLER, G. (eds.), *Theologische Realenzyklopädie*, Berlin – New York, 1976-.
TS	*Theological Studies* (Washington DC)
TSK	*Theologische Studien und Kritiken* (Hamburg)
TT	*Tijdschrift voor Theologie* (Nijmegen)
TTod	*Theology Today* (Princeton, NJ)
TTZ	*Trierer theologische Zeitschrift* (Trier)
TWNT	KITTEL, G. – FRIEDRICH, G. (eds.), *Theologisches Wörterbuch zum Neuen Testament*, 10 vols., Stuttgart, 1933-1979. → TDNT
TU	Texte und Untersuchungen zur Geschichte der altchristlichen Literatur (Berlin)
TVers	*Theologische Versuche* (Berlin)
TW	Theologische Wissenschaft. Sammelwerk für Studium und Beruf (Stuttgart)
TyndB	*Tyndale Bulletin* (Cambridge)
TZ	*Theologische Zeitschrift* (Basel)
UNT	Untersuchungen zum Neuen Testament (Leipzig)
UTB	Uni-Taschenbücher (Tübingen, etc.)
VetChrist	*Vetera Christianorum* (Bari)
VF	*Verkündigung und Forschung. Theologisches Jahresbericht* (München)
Way	*The Way: Contemporary Christian Spirituality* (London)
WBC	Word Biblical Commentary (Waco, TX)
WdF	Wege der Forschung (Darmstadt)
WestTJ	*Westminster Theological Journal* (Philadelphia, PA)
WissWeish	*Wissenschaft und Weisheit* (Mönchengladbach)
WMANT	Wissenschaftliche Monographien zum Alten und Neuen Testament (Neukirchen-Vluyn)
WUNT	Wissenschaftliche Untersuchungen zum Neuen Testament (Tübingen)
YPR	Yale Publications on Religion (New Haven, CT – London)

ZdZ	*Die Zeichen der Zeit. Evangelische Monatschrift für Mitarbeiter der Kirche* (Berlin)
ZKG	*Zeitschrift für Kirchengeschichte* (Stuttgart)
ZNW	*Zeitschrift für die neutestamentliche Wissenschaft und die Kunde der älteren Kirche* (Berlin – New York)
ZSysT	*Zeitschrift für systematische Theologie* (Berlin)
ZTK	*Zeitschrift für Theologie und Kirche* (Tübingen)
ZWT	*Zeitschrift für wissenschaftliche Theologie* (Jena)

Other Abbreviations

ACFEB	Association catholique de française pour l'étude de la Bible.
c(c).	column(s)
ch(s).	chapter(s)
cp.	compare
ctr.	*contra*
dir.	director, directed by
diss.	dissertation
ed(s).	editor(s), edited by, edition
DT	Dutch Translation
ET	English Translation
et al.	and others
FS	Festschrift
FT	French Translation
GT	German Translation
impr.	impression
IT	Italian Translation
Lief.	Lieferung
NF	Neue Folge
n(n).	note(s), footnote(s)
no(s).	number(s)
p(p).	page(s)
par.	parallel(s)
repr.	reprint(ed)
rev.	revised
ser.	series
SBL	Society of Biblical Literature
SNTS	Society for New Testament Studies
TR	Textus Receptus
trans.	translator, translated by
vol(s).	volume(s)

MALATESTA	MALATESTA, E., *St. John's Gospel 1920-1965*, 1967.
VAN BELLE	VAN BELLE, G., *Johannine Bibliography 1966-1985*, 1988.

MISCELLANEA, FESTSCHRIFTEN, AND COLLECTED ESSAYS

In both the footnotes and the bibliography collected essays of the same author are given by the author's name, other collected works by the name(s) of the editor(s), a short title and the year of publication. Festschriften are indicated by the name of the honoree preceded by the letters FS and followed by the year of publication.

ANDERSON, B.W. (ed.), *The Books of the Bible*. Vol. II: *The Apocrypha and the New Testament*, New York, 1989. → Culpepper
ASHTON, J. (ed.), *The Interpretation of John* (Issues in Religion and Theology, 9), Philadelphia, PA – London, 1986. → Ashton, Bornkamm, Martyn, Meeks

BAARDA, T. – KLIJN, A.F.J. – VAN UNNIK, W.C. (eds.), *Miscellanea Neotestamentica. Studia ad Novum Testamentum praesertim a sociis sodalicii Batavi c.n. Studiosorum Novi Testamenti conventus anno MCMLXXVI quintum lustrum feliciter complentis suscepta* (SupplNT, 47-48), 2 vols., Leiden, 1978. → de Jonge
BAARLINK, H. (ed.), *Inleiding tot het Nieuwe Testament*, Kampen, 1989. → den Heyer
BETZ, O., *Jesus, der Messias Israels. Aufsätze zur biblischen Theologie I* (WUNT, 42), Tübingen, 1987.
—— *Jesus, der Herr der Kirche. Aufsätze zur biblischen Theologie II* (WUNT, 52), Tübingen, 1990.
BEUTLER, J. – FORTNA, R.T. (eds.), *The Shepherd Discourse of John 10 and Its Context* (SNTS MS, 67), Cambridge, 1991. → Painter, Sabbe, Thyen
BORNKAMM, G., *Geschichte und Glaube*, 2 vols. (Gesammelte Aufsätze, 3-4; BEvT, 48, 53), München, 1968, 1971.
—— *Studien zum Neuen Testament*, München, 1985.
[Bornkamm, G.] LÜHRMANN, D. – STRECKER, G. (eds.), *Kirche. Festschrift für Günther Bornkamm zum 75. Geburtstag*, Tübingen, 1980. → Thyen
BOURG, D. – COULOT, C. – LION, A. (eds.), *Variations johanniques* (Parole présente), Paris, 1989. → Grosjean, Kristeva, Marchadour, Morgen
BRAUN, F.-M. (ed.), *L'évangile de Jean. Études et problèmes* (RechBib, 3), Paris, 1958. → Braun, Menoud, Van den Bussche
BROER, I. – WERBICK, J. (eds.), *"Auf Hoffnung hin sind wir erlöst" (Röm 8,24). Biblische und systematische Beiträge zum Erlösungsverständnis heute* (SBS, 128), Stuttgart, 1987. → Broer
BULTMANN, R., *Exegetica. Aufsätze zur Erforschung des Neuen Testaments*, ed. E. DINKLER, Tübingen, 1967.
[Bultmann, R.] DINKLER, E. (ed.), *Zeit und Geschichte. Dankesgabe an Rudolf Bultmann zum 80. Geburtstag*, Tübingen, 1964. → Vielhauer

CERFAUX, L., *Recueil Lucien Cerfaux. Études d'exégèse et d'histoire religieuse*, vol. II (BETL, 7), Gembloux, 1954.
CHARLESWORTH, J.H. (ed.), *John and Qumran*, London, 1972; repr. (Christian Origins Library), 1992. → Brownlee
—— (ed.), *Jews and Christians: Exploring the Past, Present and Future* (Shared Ground among Jews and Christians. A Series of Explorations, 1), New York, 1990. → D.M. Smith

CLINES, D.J.A. – GUNN, D.M. – HAUSER, A.J. (eds.), *Art and Meaning: Rhetoric in Biblical Literature* (JSOT SS, 19), Sheffield, 1982. → Webster

COLLINS, R.F., *These Things Have Been Written: Studies on the Fourth Gospel* (LouvTPM, 2), Leuven, 1990.

COPPENS, J. – DESCAMPS, A. – MASSAUX, É. (eds.), *Sacra Pagina. Miscellanea biblica congressus internationalis catholici de re biblica*, vol. II (BETL, 13), Gembloux, 1959. → Mollat

CORLEY, B. (ed.), *Colloquy on New Testament Studies: A Time for Reappraisal and Fresh Approaches*, Macon, GA, 1983. → Koester

CROSS, F.L. (ed.), *Studies in the Fourth Gospel*, London, 1957. → Phillips

[Cullmann, O. = I] CHRIST, F. (ed.), *Oikonomia. Heilsgeschichte als Thema der Theologie. Oscar Cullmann zum 65. Geburtstag gewidmet*, Hamburg, 1967. → Rissi

[Cullmann, O. = II] BALTENSWEILER, H. – REICKE, B. (eds.), *Neues Testament und Geschichte. Historisches Geschehen und Deutung. Oscar Cullmann zum 70. Geburtstag*, Zürich – Tübingen, 1972. → Hahn, Schnackenburg

CULPEPPER, R.A. – SEGOVIA, F.F. (eds.), The Fourth Gospel from a Literary Perspective. — *Semeia* 53 (1991) I-VI, 1-212. → Beutler, Culpepper, Kysar, O'Day, Segovia, Staley, Tolbert, Wuellner

[Davies, W.D.] HAMERTON-KELLY, R. – SCROGGS, R. (eds.), *Jews, Greeks and Christians: Religious Cultures in Late Antiquity. Essays in Honor of William David Davies*, Leiden, 1976. → Martyn, D.M. Smith

DE JONGE, M., *Jesus: Stranger from Heaven and Son of God. Jesus and the Christians in Johannine Perspective*, ed./trans. J.E. Steely (SBL SBSt, 11), Missoula, MT, 1977.

—— (ed.), *L'évangile de Jean. Sources, rédaction, théologie* (BETL, 44), Gembloux – Leuven, 1977; repr. 1987. → Boismard, de Jonge, Lindars, Martyn, Neirynck, Painter, Ruckstuhl, Sabbe, Schnackenburg, Thyen

[de Jonge, M.] DE BOER, M.C. (ed.), *From Jesus to John: Essays on Jesus and New Testament Christology in Honour of Marinus de Jonge* (JSNT SS, 84), Sheffield, 1993. → Menken, D.M. Smith

DE LA POTTERIE, I., *Studi di cristologia giovannea* (Dabar, 4), Genova, 1973 (²1986).

[Delekat, F.] WOLF, E. – MATTHIAS, W. (eds.), *Libertas Christiana. Friedrich Delekat zum 65. Geburtstag* (BEvT, 26), München, 1957.

DELOBEL, J. (ed.), *Logia. Les paroles de Jésus – The Sayings of Jesus. Mémorial Joseph Coppens* (BETL, 59), Leuven, 1982. → Sabbe

[Delorme, J.] PANIER, L. (ed.), *Le temps de la lecture. Exégèse biblique et sémiotique. Recueil d'hommages pour Jean Delorme* (LD, 155), Paris, 1993. → Marguerat

DENAUX, A. (ed.), *John and the Synoptics* (BETL, 101), Leuven, 1992. → Bammel, Barrett, Boismard, Dauer, Denaux, Dowell, Fortna, Geiger, Goulder, Konings, Lindars, Neirynck, Painter, Roth, Sabbe, D.M. Smith, Thyen, Verheyden, Vouga, Weder

[Dinkler, E.] ANDRESEN, C. – KLEIN, G. (eds.), *Theologica crucis – signum crucis. Festschrift für Erich Dinkler zum 70. Geburtstag*, Tübingen, 1979. → Thyen

DUNGAN, D.L. (ed.), *The Interrelations of the Gospels: A Symposium Led by M.-É. Boismard – W.R. Farmer – F. Neirynck, Jerusalem 1984* (BETL, 95), Leuven, 1990. → Borgen, Neirynck

[Dupont, J.] *À cause de l'évangile. Études sur les Synoptiques et les Actes offertes au P. Jacques Dupont, O.S.B., à l'occasion de son 70ᵉ anniversaire* (LD, 123), Paris, 1985. → Kremer

[Elliger, K.] GESE, H. – RÜGER, H.-P. (eds.), *Wort und Geschichte. Festschrift für Karl Elliger zum 70. Geburtstag* (AOAT, 18), Kevelaer – Neukirchen-Vluyn, 1973. → Betz

[Ellis, E.E.] HAWTHORNE, G.F. – BETZ, O. (eds.), *Tradition and Interpretation in the New Testament. Essays in Honor of E. Earle Ellis for His 60th Birthday*, Grand Rapids, MI – Tübingen, 1987. → Borgen, D.M. Smith

EPP, E.J. – MACRAE, G.W. (eds.), *The New Testament and Its Modern Interpreters* (SBL The Bible and Its Modern Interpreters, 3), Philadelphia, PA – Atlanta, GA, 1988. → D.M. Smith

[Evans, C.] HOOKER, M. – HICKLING, C. (eds.), *What about the New Testament? Essays in Honour of Christopher Evans*, London, 1975. → Lohse

[Farmer, W.R.] SANDERS, E.P. (ed.), *Jesus, the Gospels, and the Church. Essays in Honor of William R. Farmer*, Macon, GA, 1987. → Cope

[Goguel, M.] *Aux sources de la tradition chrétienne. Mélanges offerts à M. Maurice Goguel à l'occasion de son soixante-dixième anniversaire* (Bibliothèque théologique), Neuchâtel – Paris, 1950. → Cullmann

GREEN, J.B. – MCKNIGHT, S. – MARSHALL, I.H. (eds.), *Dictionary of Jesus and the Gospels*, Downers Grove, IL – Leicester, 1992. → Blackburn, M.M. Thompson

GROUPE D'ENTREVERNES, *Signes et paraboles*, Paris, 1977. → Kristeva

[Gunkel, H.] SCHMIDT, H. (ed.), ΕΥΧΑΡΙΣΤΗΡΙΟΝ. *Studien zur Religion und Literatur des Alten und Neuen Testaments, Hermann Gunkel zum 60. Geburtstage, dem 23. Mai 1922 dargebracht* (FRLANT, 36/1-2), Göttingen, 1923. 2 vols. → Windisch

HAENCHEN, E., *Gott und Mensch* (Gesammelte Aufsätze, 1), Tübingen, 1965.
—— *Die Bibel und Wir* (Gesammelte Aufsätze, 2), Tübingen, 1968.

HAINZ, J. (ed.), *Theologie im Werden. Studien zu den theologischen Konzeptionen im Neuen Testament*, Paderborn, 1992. → Hainz, Link, Lütgehetmann, Wagner

HEDRICK, C.W. – HODGSON, R., JR. (eds.), *Nag Hammadi, Gnosticism & Early Christianity*, Peabody, MA, 1986. → MacRae

HURST, L.D. – WRIGHT, N.T. (eds.), *The Glory of Christ in the New Testament: Studies in Christology in Memory of George Bradford Caird*, Oxford, 1987. → Hengel

HYATT, J.P. (ed.), *The Bible in Modern Scholarship. Papers Read at the 100th Meeting of the Society of Biblical Literature, December 28-30, 1964*, Nashville, TN - New York, 1965. → Filson, J.M. Robinson, Stanley

[Jülicher, J.] *Festgabe für Adolf Jülicher zum 70. Geburtstag*, Tübingen, 1927. → Bultmann

KÄSEMANN, E., *Exegetische Versuche und Besinnungen*, 2 vols., Göttingen, 1960, 1964.
—— *New Testament Questions of Today* (NTLi), London, 1969.
KAESTLI, J.-D. – POFFET, J.-M. – ZUMSTEIN, J. (eds.), *La communauté johannique et son histoire. La trajectoire de l'évangile de Jean aux deux premiers siècles* (Le monde de la Bible), Genève, 1990. → Beutler, Culpepper, Marguerat, Riniker, Zumstein
KASPER, W. (ed.), *Christologische Schwerpunkte* (Patmos Paperback), Düsseldorf, 1980. → Gnilka
KERTELGE, K. (ed.), *Rückfrage nach Jesus. Zur Methodik und Bedeutung der Frage nach dem historischen Jesus* (QDisp, 63), Freiburg – Basel – Wien, 1974. → Kertelge
[Kilpatrick, G.D.] ELLIOTT, J.K. (ed.), *Studies in New Testament Language and Text: Essays in Honour of George D. Kilpatrick on the Occasion of His Sixty-fifth Birthday* (SupplNT, 44), Leiden, 1976. → Reim
KLAUCK, H.-J. (ed.), *Weltgericht und Weltvollendung. Zukunftsbilder im Neuen Testament* (QDisp, 150), Freiburg – Basel – Wien, Herder, 1994. → Hainz
[Köberle, A.] MICHEL, O. – MANN, U. (eds.), *Die Leibhaftigkeit des Wortes. Theologische und seelsorgliche Studien und Beiträge als Festgabe für Adolf Köberle zum sechzigsten Geburtstag*, Hamburg, 1958. → Michel
[Kuhn, K.G.] JEREMIAS, G. – KUHN, H.-W. – STEGEMANN, H. (eds.), *Tradition und Glaube. Das frühe Christentum in seiner Umwelt. Festgabe für Karl Georg Kuhn zum 65. Geburtstag*, Göttingen, 1975. → Thyen

LEIMGRUBER, S. – SCHOCH, M. (eds.), *Gegen die Gottesvergessenheit. Schweizer Theologen im 19. und 20. Jahrhundert*, Basel – Freiburg – Wien, 1990. → Flückiger
LÉON-DUFOUR, X. (ed.), *Les miracles de Jésus selon le Nouveau Testament* (Parole de Dieu), Paris, 1977. → Léon-Dufour
LINDARS, B., *Essays on John*, ed. C.M. TUCKETT (SNTA, 17), Leuven, 1992. → Tuckett
[Lindars, B.] CARSON, D.A. – WILLIAMSON, H.G.M. (eds.), *It Is Written: Scripture Citing Scripture. Essays in Honour of Barnabas Lindars, SSF*, New York, 1988. → Carson
LIVINGSTONE, E.A. (ed.), *Studia Biblica 1978. II. Papers on the Gospels. Sixth International Congress on Biblical Studies, Oxford 3-7 April 1978* (JSNT SS, 2), Sheffield, 1980. → Moloney
LOHSE, E., *Die Vielfalt des Neuen Testaments. Exegetische Studien zur Theologie des Neuen Testaments*, Göttingen, 1982.
LONGENECKER, R.N. – TENNEY, M.C. (eds.), *New Dimensions in New Testament Study*, Grand Rapids, MI, 1974. → Gundry, Lane

MACRAE, G.W., *Studies in the New Testament and Gnosticism*, ed. D.J. HARRINGTON – S.B. MARROW (GNS, 26), Wilmington, DE, 1987.
MARCHADOUR, A. (ed.), *Origine et postérité de l'Évangile de Jean. XIIIe congrès de l'ACFEB Toulouse (1989)* (LD, 143), Paris, 1990. → Léon-Dufour, Marchadour, Zumstein
MARTYN, J.L., *The Gospel of John in Christian History: Essays for Interpreters* (Theological Inquiries. Studies in Contemporary Biblical and Theological Problems), New York – Toronto, 1978.

[Martyn, J.L.] FORTNA, R.T. – GAVENTA, B.R. (eds.), *The Conversation Continues: Studies in Paul & John. In Honor of J. Louis Martyn*, Nashville, TN, 1990. → de Jonge, Fuller, Lindars, D.M. Smith

MAYS, J.L. (ed.), *Interpreting the Gospels*, Philadelphia, PA, 1981. → R.E. Brown

MCCONNELL, F. (ed.), *The Bible and the Narrative Tradition*, Oxford, 1986. → Foster

MCGINLAY, H. (ed.), *The Years of John*, Melbourne, 1985. → Moloney

METZGER, B.M. – COOGAN, M.D. (eds.), *The Oxford Companion to the Bible*, New York – Oxford, 1993.

[Meyer, P.W.] CARROLL, J.T. – COSGROVE, C.H. – JOHNSON, E.E. (eds.), *Faith and History: Essays in Honor Paul W. Meyer* (Scholars Press Homage Series), Atlanta, GA, 1990. → D.M. Smith

MICHEL, O., *Dienst am Wort. Gesammelte Aufsätze*, ed. K. HAACKER, Neukirchen-Vluyn, 1986.

[Michel, O.] BETZ, O. – HAACKER, K. – HENGEL, M. (eds.), *Josephus-Studien. Untersuchungen zu Josephus, dem antiken Judentum und dem Neuen Testament Otto Michel zum 70. Geburtstag gewidmet*, Göttingen, 1974. → Betz

MILLER, D.G. – HADIDIAN, D.Y. (eds.), *Jesus and Man's Hope [Pittsburgh Theological Seminary Festival on the Gospels]* (A Perspective Book), 2 vols., Pittsburgh, PA, 1970, 1971. → R.E. Brown, Frye, Martyn, J.M. Robinson, Schnackenburg → Perspective

MILLER, R.J. (ed.), *The Complete Gospels: Annotated Scholars Version*, Sonoma, CA, 1992. → Fortna

MOLLAT, D., *Études johanniques* (Parole de Dieu), Paris, 1979.

[Morris, L.] BANKS, R.J. (ed.), *Reconciliation and Hope: New Testament Essays on Atonement and Eschatology Presented to Leon Lamb Morris on His 60th Birthday*, Grand Rapids, MI, 1974, 36-52. → Painter

MOULE, C.F.D. (ed.), *Miracles: Cambridge Studies in Their Philosophy and History*, London, 1965. → Bammel

NEIRYNCK, F., *Evangelica. Gospel Studies – Études d'évangiles. Collected Essays*, ed. F. VAN SEGBROECK (BETL, 60), Leuven, 1982 [= *Evangelica I*].

— *Evangelica II: 1982-1990. Collected Essays*, ed. F. VAN SEGBROECK (BETL, 99), Leuven, 1991 [= *Evangelica II*].

— (ed.), *L'évangile de Luc. The Gospel of Luke*. Revised and enlarged version of "L'évangile de Luc. Problèmes littéraires et théologiques" (BETL, 32), Leuven, 1989. → Judge

[Neirynck, F.] VAN SEGBROECK, F. – TUCKETT, C.M. – VAN BELLE, G. – VERHEYDEN, J. (eds.), *The Four Gospels 1992. Festschrift Frans Neirynck* (BETL, 100), Leuven, 1992. 3 vols. → Borgen, Fee, Freed, Freyne, Judge, Koch, Kremer, Lindars, Menken, Painter, Ruckstuhl, Sabbe, Smit Sibinga, Schmithals, Schnackenburg, Schnelle, D.M. Smith, Strecker, Thyen, Trocmé, Van Belle, Vorster, Zumstein

NEUSNER, J. (ed.), *Religions in Antiquity. Essays in Memory of Erwin Ramsdell Goodenough* (SHR, 14), Leiden, 1968. → Buchanan

NLENAYA ONWU (ed.), *New Testament Miracles in African Context*, Nsukka, 1989. → Collins

OBERLINNER, L. (ed.), *Auferstehung Jesu – Auferstehung der Christen. Deutungen des Osterglaubens* (QDisp, 105), Freiburg – Basel – Wien, 1986. → Nützel

[Oesterreicher, J.M.] FINKEL, A. – FRIZZELL, L. (eds.), *Standing before God: Studies on Prayer in Scriptures and Tradition with Essays. In Honor of John M. Oesterreicher*, New York, 1981. → Betz

[Reicke, B.] WEINRICH, W.C. (ed.), *The New Testament Age: Essays in Honor of Bo Reicke*, Macon, GA, 1984. → Ruckstuhl

RENGSTORF, K.H. (ed.), *Johannes und sein Evangelium* (WdF, 82), Darmstadt, 1973.

RICHTER, G., *Studien zum Johannesevangelium*, ed. J. HAINZ (BibUnt, 13), Regensburg, 1977.

RIGAUX, B. (ed.), *L'attente du Messie* (RechBibl, 1), Bruges, 1954. → Cerfaux

RISTOW, H. – MATTHIAE, K. (eds.), *Der historische Jesus und der kerygmatische Christus. Beiträge zum Christusverständnis in Forschung und Verkündigung*, Berlin, 1960, [2]1961, [3]1964. → Delling

ROBINSON, J.A.T., *Twelve New Testament Studies* (StBT, 34), London, 1962.
—— *Twelve More New Testament Studies*, London, 1984.

ROBINSON, J.M., *The Problem of History in Mark and Marcan Studies*, Philadelphia, PA, 1982.
—— *Messiasgeheimnis und Geschichtsverständnis. Zur Gattungsgeschichte des Markusevangeliums*, trans. K. Fröhlich – U. Berger (Theologische Bücherei, 81. Neues Testament), München, 1986.
—— & KOESTER, H., *Trajectories through Early Christianity*, Philadelphia, PA, 1971.
GT: *Entwicklungslinien durch die Welt des frühen Christentums*, Tübingen, 1971.

[Robinson, J.M.] GOEHRING, J.E. – HEDRICK, C.W. – SANDERS, J.T. – BETZ, H.-D. (eds.), *Gospel Origins & Christian Beginnings: In Honor of James M. Robinson* (Forum Fascicles, 1), Sonoma, CA, 1990. → Hedrick

RUCKSTUHL, E., *Jesus im Horizont der Evangelien* (SBA, 3), Stuttgart, 1988.

SABBE, M. (ed.), *L'évangile selon Marc. Tradition et rédaction* (BETL, 34), Gembloux – Leuven, 1974; [2]1988. → Konings, J.M. Robinson, van Cangh
—— *Studia Neotestamentica. Collected Essays* (BETL, 108), Leuven, 1991.

"Salvation Today" in exegetischer Sicht: Ein deutscher Beitrag. Ökumenischer Rat der Kirchen Kommission für Weltmission und Evangelisation. Biblische Konsultation, Bossey, 1972. → Lattke

SCHLIER, H., *Das Ende der Zeit. Exegetische Aufsätze und Vorträge*, Freiburg – Basel – Wien, 1971.

SCHMAUCH, W. (ed.), *In Memoriam Ernst Lohmeyer*, Stuttgart, 1951. → Bultmann

SCHNEEMELCHER, W. (ed.), *Neutestamentliche Apokryphen in deutscher Übersetzung. I. Evangelien*, vol. I, Tübingen, [5]1987. → Merkel

[Schneider, J.] *Die Kraft der Hoffnung. Gemeinde und Evangelium. Festschrift für Alterzbischof DDr. Josef Schneider*, Bamberg, 1986. → Dauer

SCHREINER, J. – DAUTZENBERG, G. (eds.), *Gestalt und Anspruch des Neuen Testaments*, Würzburg, 1969. → Dautzenberg

[Schürmann, H.] SCHNACKENBURG, R. – ERNST, J. – WANKE, J. (eds.), *Die Kirche des Anfangs. Festschrift für Heinz Schürmann zum 65. Geburtstag* (ErfTSt, 38), Leipzig, 1977. → de la Potterie, Léon-Dufour

SCHÜSSLER FIORENZA, E. (ed.), *Aspects of Religious Propaganda in Judaism and Early Christianity* (University of Notre Dame Center for the Study of Judaism and Christianity in Antiquity, 2), Notre Dame, IN – London, 1976. → Georgi

SCHULZ, H.J. (ed.), *Jesus in His Time*, Philadelphia, PA, 1967. → Georgi

SCHWEIZER, E., *Neotestamentica. Deutsche und Englische Aufsätze 1951-1963. German and English Essays 1951-1963*, Zürich – Stuttgart, 1963.

[Sevenster, J.N.] *Studies in John: Presented to Professor Dr. J.N. Sevenster* (SupplNT, 24), Leiden, 1970. → de Jonge

SEVRIN, J.-M. (ed.), *The New Testament in Early Christianity / La réception des écrits néotestamentaires dans le christianisme primitif* (BETL, 86), Leuven, 1989. → Neirynck

SHELP, E.E. – SUNDERLAND, R. (eds.), *Biblical Basis for Ministry*, Philadelphia, PA, 1981. → D.M. Smith

SINT, J. (ed.), *Bibel und zeitgemässer Glaube*. Band II: *Das Neue Testament*, Klosterneuburg, 1967. → Schlier

SMITH, D.M., *Johannine Christianity: Essays on Its Settung, Sources, and Theology*, Columbia, SC, 1984.

[Smith, M.] NEUSNER, J. (ed.), *Christianity, Judaism and Other Greco-Roman Cults. Studies for Morton Smith at Sixty*. Part One: *New Testament* (SJLA, 12/1), Leiden, 1975. → Meeks

[Söhngen, G.] RATZINGER, J. – FRIES, H. (eds.), *Einsicht und Glaube. FS G. Söhngen*, Freiburg – Basel – Wien, 1962. → Schlier

STADELMANN, H. (ed.), *Glaube und Geschichte. Heilsgeschichte als Thema der Theologie*, Giessen – Basel – Wuppertal, 1986. → Bittner

STENGER, W., *Strukturale Beobachtungen zum Neuen Testament* (NTTS, 12), Leiden, 1990.

STIBBE, M.W.G. (ed.), *The Gospel of John as Literature: An Anthology of Twentieth-Century Perspectives* (NTTS, 17), Leiden, 1993. → Culpepper, Muilenburg, Windisch

SUHL, A. (ed.), *Der Wunderbegriff im Neuen Testament* (WdF, 245), Darmstadt, 1980. → Becker, Suhl

La théologie au risque de l'histoire. Colloque de théologie du Centre de formation théologique (1er, 2 et 3 octobre 1992), Grand Séminaire de Montréal (Communauté et ministères, 4), Montréal, 1994. → Mercier

VAN UNNIK, W.C., *Sparsa Collecta: The Collected Essays of W.C. van Unnik*. Part One: *Evangelica, Paulina, Acta* (SupplNT, 29), Leiden, 1973.

VIELHAUER, P., *Aufsätze zum Neuen Testament* (Theologische Bücherei, 31). München, 1965.

WEDER, H., *Einblicke ins Evangelium. Exegetische Beiträge zur neutestamentlichen Hermeneutik. Gesammelte Aufsätze aus den Jahren 1980-1991*, Göttingen, 1992.

WENHAM, D. – BLOMBERG, C.L. (eds.), *Gospel Perspectives*. Vol. V: *The Miracles of Jesus*, Sheffield, 1986. → Blackburn

[Wikgren, A.P.] AUNE, D.E. (ed.), *Studies in New Testament and Early Christian Literature. Essays in Honor of Allen P. Wikgren* (SupplNT, 33), Leiden, 1972. → Betz

ZUMSTEIN, J., *Miettes exégétiques* (Le monde de la Bible, 25), Genève, 1991.

MONOGRAPHS AND ARTICLES

* Studies on the signs source hypothesis and other pertinent literature

ABBOTT, E.A., *Johannine Vocabulary: A Comparison of the Words of the Fourth Gospel with Those of the Three* (Diatessarica, 5), London, 1905; repr. Farnborough, 1968.
—— *Johannine Grammar* (Diatessarica, 6), London, 1906; repr. Farnborough, 1968.
* ACHTEMEIER, P.J., Toward the Isolation of Pre-Markan Miracle Catenae. — JBL 89 (1970) 265-291.
* —— The Origin and Function of the Pre-Marcan Catenae. — *JBL* 91 (1972) 198-221.
—— Gospel Miracle Tradition and the Divine Man. — *Interpr* 26 (1972) 174-197.
—— The Lucan Perspective on the Miracles of Jesus: A Preliminary Sketch. — *JBL* 94 (1975) 547-562.
—— Mark as Interpreter of the Jesus Traditions. — *Interpr* 32 (1978) 339-352.
—— "He Taught Them Many Things": Reflections on Marcan Christology. — *CBQ* 42 (1980) 465-481.
ALBRECHT, E., *Zeugnis durch Wort und Verhalten untersucht an ausgewählten Texten des Neuen Testaments* (TDiss, 13), Basel, 1977. – Diss. Basel, 1977 (dir. B. Reicke).
ALFORD, H., *The Greek Testament: With a Critically Revised Text: A Digest of Various Readings: Marginal References to Verbal and Idiomatic Usage: Prolegomena: And a Critical and Exegetical Commentary*. Vol. I: *The Four Gospels*, London, 1849, [7]1874; repr. Chicago, IL, 1958.
ALTER, R., *The Art of Biblical Narrative*, New York, 1981.
* ALTHAUS, P., Review of BULTMANN, *Johannes* [1941]. — *Deutsches Pfarrerblatt*, January 1943.
AMMON, C.F. VON, *Docetur Johannem evangelii auctorem ab editore huius libri fuisse diversum*, Erlangen, 1811.
* APPOLD, M.L., *The Oneness Motif in the Fourth Gospel: Motif Analysis and Exegetical Probe into the Theology of John* (WUNT, 2/1), Tübingen, 1976.
* ASHTON, J., Review of BULTMANN, *John* [1971]. — *HeythJ* 13 (1972) 196-197.
—— Introduction: The Problem of John. — ID. (ed.), *The Interpretation of John*, 1986, 1-17.
* —— *Understanding the Fourth Gospel*, Oxford, 1991.
* ATTRIDGE, H.W., Thematic Development and Source Elaboration in John 7:1-36. — *CBQ* 42 (1980) 160-170.

* Aus, R., *Water into Wine and the Beheading of John the Baptist: Early Jewish-Christian Interpretation of Esther 1 in John 2:1-11 and Mark 6:17-29* (BJSt, 150), Atlanta, GA, 1988.

* Backhaus, K., *Die "Jüngerkreise" des Täufers Johannes. Eine Studie zu den religionsgeschichtlichen Ursprüngen des Christentums* (Paderborner theologische Studien, 19), Paderborn, 1991. – Diss. Paderborn, 1989 (dir. J. Ernst).
* —— Praeparatio Evangelii. Die religionsgeschichtlichen Beziehungen zwischen Täufer- und Jesus-Bewegung im Spiegel der sog. Semeia-Quelle des vierten Evangeliums. — *TGl* 81 (1991) 202-215.
* —— Täuferkreise als Gegenspieler jenseits des Textes. Erwägungen zu einer kriteriologischen Verlegenheit am Beispiel der Joh-Forschung. — *TGl* 81 (1991) 279-301.
Bacon, B.W., *The Fourth Gospel in Research and Debate: A Series of Essays on Problems Concerning the Origin and Value of the Anonymous Writings Attributed to the Apostle John*, London – Leipzig, 1910.
Baljon, J.M.S., *Commentaar op het Evangelie van Johannes*, Utrecht, 1902.
Ball, D., Some Recent Literature on John: A Review Article. — *Themelios* 19 (1993-94) 13-18.
* Bammel, E., John Did no Miracle. — Moule (ed.), *Miracles*, 1965, 179-202.
* —— The Baptist in Early Christian Tradition. — *NTS* 18 (1971-72) 95-128.
* —— Die Tempelreinigung bei den Synoptikern und im Johannesevangelium. — Denaux (ed.), *John and the Synoptics*, 1992, 507-513.
Baron, M., La progression des confessions de foi dans les dialogues de saint Jean. — *BVC* 82 (1968) 32-44.
* Barrett, C.K., *The Gospel according to St John: An Introduction with Commentary and Notes on the Greek Text*, London, 1955, ²1978.
GT: *Das Evangelium nach Johannes. Eingeleitet und erklärt*, trans. H. Bald (KEK, Sonderband), Göttingen, 1990.
* —— Review of Bultmann, *John* [1971]. — *ExpT* 83 (1971-72) 185.
* —— Review of Fortna, *Gospel of Signs* [1970]. — *JTS* 72 (1971) 571-574.
—— The Place of John and the Synoptics within the Early History of Christian Thought. — Denaux, A. (ed.), *John and the Synoptics*, 1992, 63-79.
Barton, S., The Believer, the Historian and the Fourth Gospel. — *Theology* 96 (1993) 289-302.
* Bauer, W., *Das Johannesevangelium erklärt* (HNT, 2/2), Tübingen, 1912, ²1925, ³1933.
* —— Das Johannesevangelium und die Johannesbriefe. — *TR* 1 (1929) 135-160.
Baum-Bodenbender, R. *Hoheit in Niedrigkeit. Johanneische Christologie im Prozess Jesu vor Pilatus (Joh 18,28–19,16a)* (FzB, 49), Würzburg, 1984. – Diss. Mainz, 1982-83 (dir. L. Schenke).
Baumgarten-Crusius, L.F.O., *Theologische Auslegung der Johanneischen Schriften*, 2 vols., Jena, 1843, 1845.
Baur, F.C., *Kritische Untersuchungen über die kanonischen Evangelien, ihr Verhältniss zu einander, ihren Charakter und Ursprung*, Tübingen, 1847.
—— *Vorlesungen über Neutestamentliche Theologie*, ed. F.F. Baur, Leipzig, 1864.
* Beasley-Murray, G.R., *John* (WBC, 36), Waco, TX, 1987.

—— *Gospel of Life: Theology in the Fourth Gospel*, Peabody, MA, 1991.

BECKER, A., Über die Komposition des Johannesevangeliums. —— *TSK* 62 (1889) 117-140.

BECKER, H., *Die Reden des Johannesevangeliums und der Stil der gnostischen Offenbarungsrede* (FRLANT, 68; NF 50), Göttingen, 1956.

* BECKER, J., Wunder und Christologie. Zum literarkritischen und christologischen Problem der Wunder im Johannesevangelium. —— *NTS* 16 (1969-70) 130-148; = SUHL (ed.), *Der Wunderbegriff*, 1980, 435-461, 461-463 ("Nachtrag [1979]").

* —— *Das Evangelium nach Johannes*. I. *Kapitel 1–10*. II. *Kapitel 11–21* (ÖTNT, 4/1-2; Siebenstern, 505-506), Gütersloh – Würzburg, 1979, 1981; ²1984, 1985; ³1991 ("überarbeitete Auflage").

* —— Aus der Literatur zum Johannesevangelium (1978-1980). —— *TR* 47 (1982) 279-301, 305-347.

* —— Das Johannesevangelium im Streit der Methoden (1980-1984). —— *TR* 51 (1986) 1-78.

—— *Das Urchristentum als gegliederte Epoche* (SBS, 155), Stuttgart, 1993.

BEELEN, J.T., *Het Nieuwe Testament onzes Heeren Jesus Christus*. I. *De vier evangeliën*, Brugge, 1869; repr. 1891.

BELSER, J.E., *Das Evangelium des heiligen Johannes übersetzt und erklärt*, Freiburg, 1905.

* BERGER, K., *Exegese des Neuen Testaments. Neue Wege vom Text zur Auslegung* (UTB, 658), Heidelberg, 1977.

* —— Hellenistische Gattungen im Neuen Testament. —— *ANRW* II, 25/2, 1984, 1031-1432, 1831-1885 ("Register").

—— *Formgeschichte des Neuen Testaments*, Heidelberg, 1984.

—— *Einführung in die Formgeschichte* (UTB, 1444), Tübingen, 1987.

—— *Hermeneutik des Neuen Testaments*, Gütersloh, 1988.

BERGMEIER, R., *Glaube als Gabe nach Johannes. Religions- und theologiegeschichtliche Studien zum prädestinatianischen Dualismus im vierten Evangelium* (BWANT, 112), Stuttgart, 1980. – Diss. Heidelberg (dir. K.G. Kuhn).

BERNARD, J.H., *A Critical and Exegetical Commentary on the Gospel according to St. John* (ICC), 2 vols., Edinburgh, 1928.

BERTRAM, G., art. Ἔργον, ἐργάζομαι, κτλ. —— *TWNT* 2 (1935) 631-649; ET: *TDNT* 2 (1964) 635-652.

* BETZ, O., The Concept of the So-Called "Divine Man" in Mark's Christology. —— *FS A.P. Wikgren*, 1972, 229-240; = ID., *Jesus, der Messias Israels*, 1987, 273-284.

* —— "Kann denn aus Nazareth etwas Gutes kommen?" (Zur Verwendung von Jesaja Kap. 11 in Johannes Kap. 1). —— *FS K. Elliger*, 1973, 9-16; = ID., *Jesus, der Messias Israels*, 1987, 388-397.

* —— Das Problem des Wunders bei Flavius Josephus im Vergleich zum Wunderproblem bei den Rabbinen und im Johannesevangelium. —— *FS O. Michel*, 1974, 23-44; = ID., *Jesus, der Messias Israels*, 1987, 398-419.

* —— & GRIMM, W., *Wesen und Wirklichkeit der Wunder Jesu. Heilungen – Rettungen – Zeichen – Aufleuchtungen. Jes. 60,5 "Da wirst du schauen und strahlen dein Herz wird beben und weit werden"* (ANTJ, 2), Frankfurt – Bern – Las Vegas, NV, 1977.

— *Wie verstehen wir das Neue Testament?*, Wuppertal, 1981.

* — "To Worship God in Spirit and Truth": Reflections on John 4,20-26. — *FS J.M. Oesterreicher*, 1981, 53-72; = ID., *Jesus, der Messias Israels*, 1987, 420-438.

* — art. Σημεῖον. — *EWNT* 3 (1983) 569-574; ET: *EDNT* 3 (1992) 238-241.

* — Die traditionsgeschichtliche Exegese als Beitrag zur theologischen Toleranz. — ID., *Jesus, der Herr der Kirche*, 1990, 407-424.

BEUTLER, J., Literarische Gattungen im Johannesevangelium. Ein Forschungsbericht 1919-1980. — *ANRW* II, 25/3, 1985, 2506-2568.

— Méthodes et problèmes de la recherche johannique aujourd'hui. — KAESTLI *et al.* (eds.), *La communauté johannique*, 1990, 15-38.

— Response from a European Perspective. — *Semeia* 53 (1991) 191-202.

BEYER, K., *Semitische Syntax im Neuen Testament. I. Satzlehre*, 1 (SUNT, 1), Göttingen, 1962, ²1968.

BITTNER, W.J., Geschichte und Eschatologie im Johannesevangelium. — STADELMANN (ed.), *Glaube und Geschichte*, 1986, 154-180.

* — *Jesu Zeichen im Johannesevangelium. Die Messias-Erkenntnis im Johannesevangelium vor ihrem jüdischen Hintergrund* (WUNT, 2/26), Tübingen, 1987. – Diss. Basel, 1986 (dir. M. Barth).

BJERKELUND, C.J., *Tauta Egeneto. Die Präzisierungssätze im Johannesevangelium* (WUNT, 40), Tübingen, 1987.

BLACK, M., *An Aramaic Approach to the Gospels and Acts*, Oxford, 1946, ²1950; ³1967 (with an Appendix on *The Son of Man*, by G. VERMES). ET: *Die Muttersprache Jesus. Das Aramäische der Evangelien und der Apostelgeschichte*, trans. G. Schwarz (BWANT, 115; 6/15), Stuttgart, 1982.

* BLACKBURN, B., "Miracle Working ΘΕΙΟΙ ΑΝΔΡΕΣ" in Hellenism (and Hellenistic Judaism). — WENHAM – BLOMBERG (eds.), *The Miracles of Jesus*, 1986, 185-218.

* — *Theios Anēr and the Markan Miracle Traditions: A Critique of the* Theios Anēr *Concept as an Interpretative Background of the Miracle Traditions Used by Mark* (WUNT, 2/40), Tübingen, 1991. – Diss. Aberdeen, 1986 (dir. I.H. Marshall).

* — Miracles and Miracle Stories. — GREEN – MCKNIGHT – MARSHALL (eds.), *Dictionary of Jesus and the Gospels*, 1992, 549-564.

BLANK, J., *Krisis. Untersuchungen zur johanneischen Christologie und Eschatologie*, Freiburg, 1964.

BLANQUART, F., *Le premier jour. Étude sur Jean 20* (LD, 146). Paris, 1991.

* BLAUERT, H., *Die Bedeutung der Zeit in der johanneischen Theologie. Eine Untersuchung an Hand von Joh 1–17 unter besonderer Berücksichtigung des literarkritischen Problems*, diss. Tübingen, 1953. Cf. *TLZ* 78 (1953) 689-690.

BOICE, J.M., *Witness and Revelation in the Gospel of John* (The Christian Student's Library, 8), Exeter, 1970.

BOISMARD, M.-É., Le chapitre XXI de saint Jean. Essai de critique littéraire. — *RB* 54 (1947) 473-501.

— *Le Prologue de saint Jean* (LD, 11), Paris, 1953.

— *Du Baptême à Cana (Jean, 1,19–2,11)* (LD, 18), Paris, 1956.

— L'évangile aux quatre dimensions. Introduction à la lecture de saint Jean. — *LumV* 1 (1961), n° 1, 95-114.

* —— Saint Luc et la rédaction du quatrième évangile (Jn, IV, 46-54). — *RB* 69 (1962) 185-211.

* —— Le lépreux et le serviteur du centurion. — *AssSeign* 17 (1962) 29-44.

—— Les traditions johanniques concernant le Baptiste. — *RB* 70 (1963) 5-42.

* —— Guérison du fils d'un fonctionnaire royal (Jn 4,46b-53). — *AssSeign* 75 (1965) 26-37.

* —— in collaboration with A. LAMOUILLE and P. SANDEVOIR, *Commentaire* (Synopse des quatre évangiles en français, 2), Paris, 1972.

* —— Review of NICOL, *The Sēmeia* [1972]. — *RB* 81 (1974) 149.

* —— & LAMOUILLE, A., in collaboration with G. ROCHAIS, *L'évangile de Jean. Commentaire* (Synopse des quatre évangiles en français, 3), Paris, 1977.

—— Un procédé redactionnel dans le quatrième évangile: la Wiederaufnahme. — DE JONGE (ed.), *L'évangile de Jean*, 1977 (²1987), 235-241.

—— & LAMOUILLE, A., *La vie des évangiles. Initiation à la critique des textes* (Initiations), Paris, 1980.
GT: *Aus der Werkstatt der Evangelisten. Einführung in die Literarkritik*, trans. M.-T. Wacker, München, 1980.

* —— Rapports entre foi et miracles dans l'évangile de Jean. — *ETL* 58 (1982) 357-364.

* —— *Moïse ou Jésus. Essai de christologie johannique* (BETL, 84), Leuven, 1988.
ET: *Moses or Jesus: An Essay in Johannine Christology*, trans. B.T. Viviano (BETL, 84A), Leuven, 1993.

* —— Jean 4,46-54 et les parallèles synoptiques. — DENAUX (ed.), *John and the Synoptics*, 1992, 239-259.

—— & LAMOUILLE, A., *Un évangile pré-johannique*. Vol. I: *Jean 1,1–2,12*. Vol. II: *Jean 2,13–4,54* (ÉtB, n.s. 17-18, 24-25), 4 parts, Paris, 1993, 1994.

BORGEN, P., John and the Synoptics. — DUNGAN (ed.), *The Interrelations of the Gospels*, 1990, 408-437.

—— John and the Synoptics: A Reply. — *Ibid.*, 451-458.

—— John and the Synoptics: Can Paul Offer Help? — *FS E.E. Ellis*, 1988, 80-94.

—— The Independence of the Gospel of John: Some Observations. — *FS F. Neirynck*, 1992, vol. III, 1815-1833.

* BORNKAMM, G., Formen und Gattungen. II. Im NT. — *RGG*³ 2 (1958) 999-1005.

* —— Zur Interpretation des Johannes-Evangeliums. Eine Auseinandersetzung mit Ernst Käsemanns Schrift "Jesu letzter Wille nach Johannes 17". — *EvT* 28 (1968) 8-25; = ID., *Geschichte und Glaube*, vol. I, 1968, 104-121; = ID., *Studien zum Neuen Testament*, 1985, 118-135.
ET: Towards the Interpretation of John's Gospel: A Discussion of The Testament of Jesus by Ernst Käsemann. — ASHTON (ed.), *The Interpretation*, 1986, 79-98.

* —— *Bibel. Das Neue Testament. Eine Einführung in seine Schriften im Rahmen der Geschichte des Urchristentums* (TdT, 9), Stuttgart – Berlin, 1971; repr. in ID. – H.W. WOLFF, *Zugang zur Bibel. Eine Einführung in die Schriften des Alten und Neuen Testaments* (TdT, 7, 9), Stuttgart – Berlin, 1980 (pp. 175-336).
ET: *The New Testament: A Guide to Its Writings*, trans. R.H. Fuller – I. Fuller, Philadelphia, PA, 1973; London, 1974.

* — Die Heilung des Blindgeborenen. Johannes 9. — *Geschichte und Glaube*, vol. II, 1971, 65-72 (reworked edition of *GPM*, vol. VI/3, 1952).

BOSTOCK, D.G., Jesus as the New Elisha. — *ExpT* 92 (1980-81) 39-41.

BOTHA, J.E., *Jesus and the Samaritan Woman: A Speech Act Reading of John 4:1-42* (SupplNT, 65), Leiden, 1991.

BOUMA, C., *Het evangelie naar Johannes* (Korte verklaring der heilige Schrift met nieuwe vertaling), 2 vols., Kampen, 1927, ²1933.

BOUSSET, W., Ist das vierte Evangelium eine literarische Einheit? — *TR* 12 (1909) 1-12, 39-64.

* BRASHLER, J., *A Form-Critical Analysis of the Miracle Stories in Fortna's Reconstructed "Gospel of Signs"*, Course Papers, Claremont Graduate School and University Center, 1969.

BRAUN, F.-M., *Évangile selon Jean traduit et commenté* (La sainte Bible, 10), Paris, 1935, ²1946.

— Conclusions. — ID. (ed.), *L'évangile de Jean*, 1958, 249-258.

— *Jean le théologien et son évangile dans l'Église ancienne* (ÉtB), Paris, 1959.

BRODIE, T.L., Jesus as the New Elisha: Cracking the Code. — *ExpT* 93 (1981-82) 39-42.

* — *The Quest for the Origin of John's Gospel: A Source-Oriented Approach*, New York – Oxford, 1993.

— *The Gospel according to John: A Literary and Theological Commentary*, New York – Oxford, 1993.

BROER, I., Auferstehung und ewiges Leben im Johannesevangelium. — ID. – WERBICK (eds.), *"Auf Hoffnung hin sind wir erlöst"*, 1987, 67-94.

BROMBOSZCZ, T., *Die Einheit des Johannes-Evangeliums*, Katowice, 1927.

BROOKE, A.E., *A Critical and Exegetical Commentary on the Johannine Epistles* (ICC), Edinburgh, 1912.

* BROOME, E.C., The Sources of the Fourth Gospel. — *JBL* 63 (1944) 107-121.

* BROWN, R.E., *The Gospel according to John: Introduction, Translation, and Notes* (AB, 29-29A), 2 vols., Garden City, NY, 1966, 1972.

* — Jesus and Elisha. — *Perspective* 12 (1971) 85-104.

* — The Gospel of John. — MILLER – HADIDIAN (eds.) *Jesus and Man's Hope*, vol. II, 1971, 349-351.

* — Review of BULTMANN, *John* [1971]. — *TTod* 28 (1971-72) 517-519.

* — The Relation of the "Secret Gospel of Mark" to the Fourth Gospel. — *CBQ* 36 (1974) 466-485.

— Johannine Ecclesiology. The Community's Origins. — *Interpr* 31 (1977) 379-393; = MAYS (ed.), *Interpreting the Gospels*, 1981, 291-306.

— *The Community of the Beloved Disciple*, New York – Ramsey – Toronto; London, 1979.
  GT: *Ringen um die Gemeinde. Der Weg der Kirche nach den johanneischen Schriften*, trans. B. Michl, Salzburg, 1982.
  FT: *La communauté du disciple bien-aimé*, trans. F.M. Godefroid (LD, 115), Paris, 1983.

— *The Epistles of John. Translated with Introduction, Notes, and Commentary* (AB, 30), Garden City, NY, 1982.

— *The Death of the Messiah: From Gethsemane to the Grave. A Commentary on the Passion Narratives in the Four Gospels* (The Anchor Bible Reference Library), New York, 1994.

* BROWN, S., *The Origins of Christianity: A Historical Introduction to the New Testament* (The Oxford Bible Series), Oxford – New York, 1984.

BROWNLEE, W.H., Whence the Gospel according to John. — CHARLESWORTH (ed.), *John and Qumran*, 1972, 166-194.

* BRUCE, F.F., *The Gospel of John: Introduction, Exposition and Notes*, Grand Rapids, MI, 1983.

* BUCHANAN, G.W., The Samaritan Origin of the Gospel of John. — NEUSNER (ed.), *Religions in Antiquity*, 1968, 149-175.

* BULL, K.-M., *Gemeinde zwischen Integration und Abgrenzung. Ein Beitrag zur Frage nach dem Ort der joh Gemeinde(n) in der Geschichte des Urchristentums* (BET, 24), Frankfurt – Bern – New York, 1992. – Diss. Rostock, 1990-91 (dir. H.-F. Weiss).

* BULTMANN, R., *Die Geschichte der synoptischen Tradition* (FRLANT, 29; NF 12), Göttingen, 1921, [2]1931 ("neubearbeitete Auflage"), [3]1957 ("3. durchgesehene Auflage"); *Ergänzungsheft*, 1958, [2]1962 ("2. verbesserte Auflage"), [3]1966, [4]1971 (G. THEISSEN – P. VIELHAUER).
ET: *The History of the Synoptic Tradition*, trans. J. Marsh, Oxford, 1963, [2]1968.
FT: *L'histoire de la tradition synoptique. Suivie du complément de 1971*, trans. A. Malet, Paris, 1973.

—— Das Johannesevangelium in der neuesten Forschung. — *CW* 41 (1927) 502-511.

—— Analyse des ersten Johannesbriefes. — *FS A. Jülicher*, 1927, 138-158; = *Exegetica*, 1967, 105-123.

—— Hirsch's Auslegung des Johannes-Evangeliums. — *EvT* 4 (1937) 115-142.

* —— *Das Evangelium des Johannes* (KEK, 2), Göttingen, 1941 (10th ed. in the series), [11]1950, [12]1952, [13]1953, [14]1956, [15]1957, [16]1959, [17]1962, [18]1964, [19]1968, [20]1978, [21]1986; *Ergänzungsheft*, 1950, 1957 ("Neubearbeitung"), 1966. → Meyer, Weiss
ET: *The Gospel of John: A Commentary*, trans. G.R. Beasley-Murray, Oxford, 1971.

—— Die kirchliche Redaktion des ersten Johannesbriefes. — SCHMAUCH (ed.), *In Memoriam Ernst Lohmeyer*, Stuttgart, 1951, 189-201; = *Exegetica*, 1967, 381-393.

* —— Zur johanneischen Tradition. — *TLZ* 80 (1955) 521-526.

* —— Johannesevangelium. — *RGG*[3] 3 (1959) 840-850.

* —— *Theologie des Neuen Testaments*, Tübingen, [1948/1951/]1953, [2]1954, [3]1958, [4]1959, [5]1965, [8]1980 ("durchgesehene, um Vorwort und Nachträge wesentlich erweiterte Auflage", ed. O. MERK; UTB, 630).
ET: *Theology of the New Testament*, trans. K. Grobel, 2 vols., London, 1952, 1955.

—— *Die drei Johannesbriefe* (KEK, 14), Göttingen, 1967, [2]1969.
ET: *The Johannine Epistles: A Commentary on the Johannine Epistles*, trans. R.P. O'Hara – L.C. McGaughy – R.W. Funk, ed. R.W. FUNK (Hermeneia), Philadelphia, PA, 1973.

* BURGE, G.M., *The Anointed Community: The Holy Spirit in the Johannine Tradition*, Grand Rapids, MI, 1987.

* —— Review of FORTNA, *Predecessor* [1988]. — *Themelios* 17 (1991), n° 1, 27.

—— *Interpreting the Gospel of John* (Guides to New Testament Exegesis, 5), Grand Rapids, MI, 1993.

BURGER, C.H.A. VON, *Das Evangelium nach Johannes*, Nördlingen, 1868.

BURNEY, C.F., *The Aramaic Origin of the Fourth Gospel*, Oxford, 1922.

BUSSE, U., Ernst Haenchen und sein Johanneskommentar. Biographische Notizen und Skizzen zu seiner johanneischen Theologie. — *ETL* 57 (1981) 125-143; = *ALBO* V, 5.
ET: Ernst Haenchen and His Commentary on John: Biographical Notes and Sketches of His Johannine Theology. — HAENCHEN, *John*, vol. II, 1984, 240-253.

* CARSON, D.A., Current Source Criticism of the Fourth Gospel: Some Methodological Questions. — *JBL* 97 (1978) 411-429.

—— Understanding Misunderstandings in the Fourth Gospel. — *TyndB* 33 (1982) 59-91.

* —— Recent Literature on the Fourth Gospel: Some Reflections. — *Themelios* 9 (1983) 8-18.

* —— The Gospel of John in Current Research. — *RelStR* 9 (1983) 314-323.

* —— The Purpose of the Fourth Gospel: John 20:31 Reconsidered. — *JBL* 106 (1987) 639-651.

—— John and the Johannine Epistles. — *FS B. Lindars*, 1988, 245-264.

* —— Selected Recent Studies of the Fourth Gospel. — *Themelios* 14 (1989) 57-64.

* —— *The Gospel according to John*, Leicester – Grand Rapids, MI, 1991.

* —— & MOO, D.J. – MORRIS, L., *An Introduction to the New Testament*, Leicester, 1992.

CERFAUX, L., Les miracles, signes messianiques de Jésus et œuvres de Dieu, selon l'Évangile de saint Jean. — RIGAUX (ed.), *L'attente du Messie*, 1954, 131-138; = *Recueil Lucien Cerfaux*, 1954, 41-50.

CEULEMANS, F.C., *Commentarius in Evangelium secundum Joannem cui succedit Synopsis chronologica quatuor evangeliorum*, Mechelen, 1901.

CHANG, P.S.-C., *Repetitions and Variations in the Gospel of John*, diss. Strasbourg, 1975 (dir. M-A. Chevallier).

CHARLES, R.H., *A Critical and Exegetical Commentary on the Revelation of St. John* (ICC), 2 vols., Edinburgh, 1928.

CHARLIER, J.-P., La notion de signe (ΣΗΜΕΙΟΝ) dans le IVᵉ évangile. — *RSPT* 43 (1959) 434-448.

* CLARK, D.K., Signs in Wisdom and John. — *CBQ* 45 (1983) 201-209.

CLEARY, M., Raymond Brown's View of the Johannine Controversy: Its Relevance for Christology Today. — *IrTQ* 48 (1992) 292-304.

CLEMEN, C., *Die Entstehung des Johannesevangeliums*, Halle a.S., 1912.

COAKLEY, J.F., Some Thoughts on the Priority of John. — *Mowbrays Journal* 123 (1985) 1-2.

* COLLINS, R.F., Representative Figures of the Fourth Gospel. — *DownR* 94 (1976) 26-46, 118-132; = ID., *These Things*, 1990, 1-45.

* —— Cana (Jn. 2:1-12) – The First of His Signs or the Key to His Signs? — *IrTQ* 47 (1980) 79-95; = ID., *These Things*, 1990, 158-182.

* —— *Introduction to the New Testament*, Garden City, NY, 1983.

* —— Miracles and Faith. — NLENAYA ONWU (ed.), *New Testament Miracles in African Context*, 1989; = ID., *These Things*, 1990, 183-197.

COLWELL, E.C., *The Greek of the Fourth Gospel: A Study of Its Aramaisms in the Light of Hellenistic Greek*, Chicago, IL, 1931.

—— & TITUS, E.L., *The Gospel of the Spirit: A Study of the Fourth Gospel*, New York, 1952.

* CONZELMANN, H., Jesus Christus. — *RGG*[3] 3 (1959) 619-653.

* —— *Grundriss der Theologie des Neuen Testaments* (EET, 2), München, 1967, [2]1968 ("zweite durchgesehene Auflage").
ET: *An Outline of the Theology of the New Testament*, trans. J. Bowden (NTLi), London, 1969.

* —— & LINDEMANN, A., *Arbeitsbuch zum Neuen Testament* (UTB, 52), Tübingen, 1975, [9]1988 ("überarbeitete und erweiterte Auflage").
ET: *Interpreting the New Testament: An Introduction to the Principles and Methods of N.T. Exegesis*, trans. S.S. Schatzmann, Peabody, MA, 1988.

* COPE, L., *Faith for a New Day: The New View of the Gospel of John*, St. Louis, MO, 1986.

* —— The Earliest Gospel Was the "Signs Gospel". — *FS W.R. Farmer*, 1987, 17-24.

COPPENS, J., L'analyse critique du IVe évangile. — *ETL* 18 (1941) 180-182.

CORLUY, J., *Commentarius in Evangelium S. Joannis in usum praelectionum*, Gent, 1878, [2]1880, [3]1889.

* CORSANI, B., *I miracoli di Gesù nel quarto vangelo. L'ipotesi delle fonte dei segni* (Studi biblici, 65), Brescia, 1983.

* COTHENET, É., Le quatrième évangile. — A. GEORGE – P. GRELOT (eds.), *Introduction à la Bible. Édition nouvelle. III. Introduction critique au Nouveau Testament. Vol. IV: La tradition johannique*, Paris, 1977, 95-292.

—— L'évangile de Jean. — *RThom* 78 (1978) 625-633.

* —— L'évangile selon saint Jean. — É. COTHENET – L. DUSSAUT – P. LE FORT – P. PRIGENT, *Les écrits de S. Jean et l'épître aux hébreux* (PBSB NT, 5), Paris, 1984, 15-151.

CREDNER, K.A., *Einleitung in das Neue Testament*. Erster Theil, Halle, 1836.

* CREHAN, J.H., Review of FORTNA, *Gospel of Signs* [1970]. — *TS* 31 (1970) 757-759.

* CRIBBS, F.L., St. Luke and the Johannine Tradition. — *JBL* 90 (1971) 422-450.

CROSSAN, J.D., *Four Other Gospels: Shadows on the Contours of Canon*, Minneapolis, MN – Chicago, IL – New York, 1985.

—— *The Cross That Spoke: The Origins of the Passion Narrative*, San Francisco, CA, 1988.

* —— *The Historical Jesus: The Life of a Mediterranean Jewish Peasant*, San Francisco, CA, 1991.

CULLMANN, O., Εἶδεν καὶ ἐπίστευσεν. La vie de Jésus, object de la "vue" et de la "foi" d'après le quatrième évangile. — *FS M. Goguel*, 1950, 52-61.

* —— *Der johanneische Kreis. Sein Platz im Spätjudentum, in der Jüngerschaft Jesu und im Urchristentum. Zum Ursprung des Johannesevangeliums*, Tübingen, 1975.
ET: *The Johannine Circle. Its Place in Judaism, among the Disciples of Jesus and in Early Christianity: A Study in the Origin of the Gospel of John*, trans. J. Bowden, London – Philadelphia, PA, 1976.
FT: *Le milieu johannique. Sa place dans le judaïsme tardif, dans le cercle des disciples de Jésus et dans le Christianisme primitif. Étude sur l'origine de l'évangile de Jean* (Le monde de la Bible), Neuchâtel – Paris, 1976.

CULPEPPER, R.A., *The Johannine School: An Evaluation of the Johannine School Hypothesis Based on an Investigation of the Nature of Ancient Schools* (SBL DS, 26), Missoula, MT, 1975. – Diss. Duke University, 1974 (dir. D.M. Smith).

— The Narrator in the Fourth Gospel: Intratextual Relationships. — *SBL 1982 Seminar Papers*, 1982, 81-96.

— Anatomy of the Fourth Gospel: A Study in Literary Design (Foundations and Facets: New Testament), Philadelphia, PA, 1983.

— Story and History in the Gospels. — *RExp* 81 (1984) 467-478.

— The Gospel of John and the Jews. — *RExp* 84 (1987) 273-288.

— The Theology of the Gospel of John. — *RExp* 85 (1988) 417-432.

— John. — ANDERSON (ed.), *The Books of the Bible*, vol. II, 1989, 203-228.

— L'application de la narratologie à l'étude de l'évangile de Jean. — KAESTLI et. al. (eds.), *La communauté johannique*, 1990, 97-120.

— Un exemple de commentaire fondé sur la critique narrative: Jean 5,1-18. — *Ibid.*, 1990, 135-151.

ET: John 5,1-18: A Sample of Narrative Critical Commentary. — STIBBE (ed.), *The Gospel of John as Literature*, 1993, 193-207.

— The Johannine *Hypodeigma*: A Reading of John 13. — *Semeia* 53 (1991) 133-152.

* DAUER, A., *Die Passionsgeschichte im Johannes-Evangelium. Eine traditionsgeschichtliche und theologische Untersuchung zu Joh 18,1–19,30* (SANT, 30), München, 1972. – Diss. Würzburg, 1968-69 (dir. R. Schnackenburg).

* — *Johannes und Lukas. Untersuchungen zu den johanneisch-lukanischen Parallelperikopen: Joh 4,46-54/Lk 7,1-10 – Joh 12,1-8/Lk 7,36-50; 10,38-42 – Joh 20,19-29/Lk 24,36-49* (FzB, 50), Würzburg, 1984.

— Review of BAUM-BODENBENDER, *Hoheit in Niedrigkeit* [1984]. — *TRev* 81 (1985) 463-466.

— Schichten im Johannesevangelium als Anzeichen von Entwicklungen in der (den) johanneischen Gemeinde(n) nach G. Richter. Darstellung und Kritik. — *FS J. Schneider*, 1986, 62-83.

— Spuren der (synoptischen) Synedriumsverhandlung im 4. Evangelium. Das Verhältnis zu den Synoptikern. — DENAUX (ed.), *John and the Synoptics*, 1992, 307-339.

* DAUTZENBERG, G., Die Geschichte Jesu im Johannesevangelium. — SCHREINER – ID. (eds.), *Gestalt und Anspruch*, 1969, 229-248.

DAVIDSON, S., *An Introduction to the New Testament: Containing an Examination of the Most Important Questions Relating to the Authority, Interpretation and Integrity of the Canonical Books, with Reference to the Latest Inquiries*. Vol. II: *The Acts of the Apostles to the Second Epistle to the Thessalonians*, London, 1849.

DAVIES, M., Which is the Best Commentary? XI. The Fourth Gospel. — *ExpT* 99 (1987-88) 73-78.

* — *Rhetoric and Reference in the Fourth Gospel* (JSNT SS, 69), Sheffield, 1992.

DE BOER, M.C., Narrative Criticism, Historical Criticism, and the Gospel of John. — *JSNT* 47 (1992) 35-48.

DECOURTRAY, A., La conception johannique de la foi. — *NRT* 81 (1959) 561-576.

DEFOURNY, P., Au sujet de la composition du quatrième évangile. — *CMechl* 11 (1937) 359-367.

DE JONGE, M., *De brieven van Johannes* (De Prediking van het Nieuwe Testament), Nijkerk, 1968.

* —— Review of FORTNA, *Gospel of Signs* [1970]. — *NTT* 26 (1972) 91-94.

—— The Use of the Word χριστός in the Johannine Epistles. — *FS J.N. Sevenster*, 1970, 66-74.

—— Jewish Expectations about the "Messiah" according to the Fourth Gospel. — *NTS* 19 (1972-73) 246-270; = ID., *Jesus: Stranger from Heaven and Son of God*, 1977, 77-116.

—— Jesus as Prophet and King in the Fourth Gospel. — *ETL* 49 (1973) 160-177; = ID., *Jesus: Stranger from Heaven and Son of God*, 1977, 49-76.

—— Introduction. — ID. (ed.), *L'évangile de Jean*, 1977 (²1987), 13-18.

* —— Signs and Works in the Fourth Gospel. — BAARDA *et al.* (eds.), *Miscellanea Neotestamentica*, vol. II, 1978, 107-125; = ID., *Jesus: Stranger from Heaven and Son of Man*, 1977, 117-140.

—— & VAN DUYNE, H.M.J., *Taal en teken. Ontmoetingen met Jezus in het evangelie van Johannes*, Nijkerk, 1978.

* —— John the Baptist and Elijah in the Fourth Gospel. — *FS J.L. Martyn*, 1990, 299-308.

DE KRUIJF, T.C., "Hold the Faith" or "Come to Believe"? A Note on John 20,31. — *Bijdragen* 36 (1975) 439-449.

DE LA POTTERIE, I., La notion de "commencement" dans les écrits johanniques. — *FS H. Schürmann*, 1977, 379-403; = ID., *Studi*, 1973 (²1986), 217-238.

* DELFF, H., *Grundzüge der Entwicklungsgeschichte der Religion dargestellt*, Leipzig, 1883.

* —— *Die Geschichte des Rabbi Jesus von Nazareth. Kritisch begründet, dargestellt und erklärt*, Leipzig, 1889.

—— *Das vierte Evangelium. Ein authentischer Bericht über Jesus von Nazareth, wiederhergestellt, übersetzt, und erklärt*, Husum, 1890.

—— *Neue Beiträge zur Kritik und Erklärung des vierten Evangeliums. Supplement zu der Schrift "Das vierte Evangelium, ein authentischer Bericht über Jesus von Nazareth"*, Husum, 1890.

—— Noch einmal das vierte Evangelium und seine Authenticität. — *TSK* 65 (1892) 72-104.

DELLING, G., Botschaft und Wunder im Wirken Jesu. — RISTOW – MATTHIAE (eds.), *Der historische Jesus und der kerygmatische Christus*, 1960, 389-402.

DEMKE, C., Der sogenannte Logos-Hymnus im johanneischen Prolog. — *ZNW* 58 (1967) 43-68.

DENAUX, A., John and the Synoptics. Colloquium Biblicum Lovaniense XXXIX (1990). — *ETL* 67 (1991) 196-203; = Introduction. — ID. (ed.), *John and the Synoptics*, 1992, XIII-XXII.

DEN HEYER, C.J., Het evangelie naar Johannes. — BAARLINK (ed.), *Inleiding*, 1989, 150-165.

DE WETTE, W.M.L., *Kurze Erklärung des Evangeliums und der Briefe Johannes* (Kurzgefasstes exegetisches Handbuch zum Neuen Testament, I/3), 1837, ³1846, ⁵1863 (ed. B. BRÜCKNER).

* —— *Lehrbuch der historisch-kritischen Einleitung in die kanonischen Bücher des Neuen Testaments* (Lehrbuch der historisch-kritischen Einleitung in die

Bibel Alten und Neuen Testaments, 2), Berlin, ⁵1848 ("fünfte, verbesserte und vermehrte Ausgabe), ⁶1860 ("sechste, verbesserte und vermehrte Ausgabe", ed. H. MESSNER – G. LÜNEMANN).

DIBELIUS, M., *Die Formgeschichte des Evangeliums*, Tübingen, 1919, ²1933 ("zweite, neubearbeitete Auflage), ³1959 ("dritte, durchgesehene Auflage" with a "Nachtrag" by G. IBER"), ⁴1961, ⁵1966, ⁶1972.
    ET: *From Tradition to Gospel*, trans. B.L. Woolf, New York, 1935; (The Library of Theological Translations), Greenwood, SC – London, 1971.
—— Johannesevangelium. — *RGG*² 3 (1929) 349-363.
* —— Ein neuer Kommentar zum Johannes-Evangelium. — *TLZ* 67 (1942) 257-264.

DODD, C.H., The First Epistle of John and the Fourth Gospel. — *BJRL* 21 (1937) 129-156.
—— Note on John 21,24. — *JTS* 4 (1953) 212-213.
—— *The Interpretation of the Fourth Gospel*, Cambridge, 1953.
—— *Historical Tradition in the Fourth Gospel*, Cambridge, 1963.
    FT: *La tradition historique du quatrième évangile*, trans. M. et S. Montabrut (LD, 128), Paris, 1987.

DORMEYER, D., *Das Neue Testament im Rahmen der antiken Literaturgeschichte* (Die Altertumswissenschaft), Darmstadt, 1993.

* DOWELL, T.M., Jews and Christians in Conflict: Why the Fourth Gospel Changed the Synoptic Tradition. — *LouvSt* 15 (1990) 19-37.
* —— Why John Rewrote the Synoptics. — DENAUX (ed.), *John and the Synoptics*, 1992, 453-457.

DSCHULNIGG, P., *Sprache, Redaktion und Intention des Markus-Evangeliums. Eigentümlichkeiten der Sprache des Markus-Evangeliums und ihre Bedeutung für die Redaktionskritik* (SBB, 11), Stuttgart, 1984, ²1986. – Diss. Luzern, 1983-84 (dir. E. Ruckstuhl).
—— Die Berufung der Jünger Joh 1,35-51 im Rahmen des vierten Evangeliums. — *FZPT* 36 (1989) 427-447.
    → Ruckstuhl

DUKE, P.D., *Irony in the Fourth Gospel*, Atlanta, GA, 1985.

DUNDERBERG, I., *Johannes und die Synoptiker. Studien zu Joh 1–9* (AASF DHL, 69), Helsinki, 1994.

DURAND, A., *Évangile selon saint Jean traduit et commenté* (Verbum Salutis), Paris, 1927.

* EASTON, B.S., Review of BULTMANN, *Johannes* [1941]. — *ATR* 22 (1940) 223-224; *JBL* 65 (1946) 73-81.
—— Bultmann's RQ Source. — *JBL* 65 (1946) 143-156.

ECKERMANN, J.C.R., *Über die eigentlich sichern Gründe des Glaubens an die Hauptthatsachen der Geschichte Jesu und über die wahrscheinliche Entstehung der Evangelien und der Apostelgeschichte* (Theologische Beiträge, 5/2), Altona, 1796, 106-256.

EISENBEIS, W., *A Translation of the Greek Expressions in the Text of "The Gospel of John: A Commentary by Rudolf Bultmann"*, Lanham, MD, 1982.

EISLER, R., *The Enigma of the Fourth Gospel: Its Author and Its Writer*, London, 1938.

ELLER, V., *The Beloved Disciple: His Name, Story, His Thought*, Grand Rapids, MI, 1987.

* ELLIS, P.F., *The Genius of John: A Composition-Critical Commentary on the Fourth Gospel*, Collegeville, MN, 1984.

* ENGELBRECHT, J., Trends in Miracle Research. — *Neotestamentica* 22 (1988) 139-161.

ENZ, J.J., The Book of Exodus as a Literary Type for the Gospel of John. — *JBL* 76 (1957) 208-215.

ERDOZÁIN, L., *La función del signo en la fe según el cuarto evangelio. Estudio crítico exegético de las perícopas Jn IV,46-54 y Jn XX,24-29* (AnBib, 33), Rome, 1968.

—— La fe, adhesión personal a Cristo, según el cuarto evangelio. — *EstE* (1990) 443-455.

ESSER, D., *Formgeschichtliche Studien zur hellenistischen und frühchristlichen Literatur unter besonderer Berücksichtigung der vita Apollonii des Philostrat und der Evangelien*, diss. Bonn, 1969.

EVANG, M., *Rudolf Bultmann in seiner Frühzeit* (BHT, 74), Tübingen, 1988.

EVANS, C.A., On the Quotation Formulas in the Fourth Gospel. — *BZ* 26 (1982) 79-83.

—— *To See and Not Perceive: Isaiah 6.9-10 in Early Jewish and Christian Interpretation* (JSNT SS, 64), Sheffield, 1989.

FABRIS, R., *Giovanni* (Commenti biblici), Roma, 1992.

* FAURE, A., Die alttestamentlichen Zitate im 4. Evangelium und die Quellenscheidungshypothese. — *ZNW* 21 (1922) 99-121.

* —— Das 4. Evangelium im Muratorischen Fragment. (Ein nicht genug beachteter Bericht über die Entstehung des Johannesevangeliums). — *ZSysT* 19 (1942) 143-149.

FEE, G.D., On the Text and Meaning of Jn 20,30-31. — *FS F. Neirynck*, 1992, vol. III, 2193-2205.

FESTUGIÈRE, A.-J., *Observations stylistiques sur l'évangile de S. Jean* (Études et commentaires, 74), Paris, 1974.

* FEUILLET, A., Les christophanies pascales du quatrième évangile sont-elles des signes? — *NRT* 97 (1975) 577-592.

FIEBIG, P., Zur Form des Johannesevangelium. — *GKG* 64 (1928) 126-132.

FILLION, L.-C., *Évangile selon S. Jean. Introduction critique et commentaire* (La Sainte Bible), Paris, 1887, 1904.

FILSON, F.V., Who Was the Beloved Disciple? — *JBL* 68 (1949) 83-88.

* —— Response to James M. Robinson's "Kerygma and History in the New Testament". — HYATT (ed.), *The Bible*, 1965, 160-165.

* FISCHBACH, S.M., *Totenerweckungen. Zur Geschichte einer Gattung* (FzB, 69), Würzburg, 1992. – Diss. Würzburg, 1991 (dir. H.-J. Klauck).

FITZPATRICK, M., *The Structure of St. Mark's Gospel. With a Reconsideration of the Hypothesis of Pre-Markan Collections in Mk 1–10*, 2 vols., diss. Leuven, 1975 (dir. F. Neirynck).

* —— Review of FORTNA, *Predecessor* [1988]. — *AustrBR* 38 (1990) 84-85.

FLÜCKIGER, F., Alexander Schweizer (1808-1888). Vermittler zwischen Glaube und Wissen. — LEIMGRUBER – SCHOCH (eds.), *Gegen die Gottesvergessenheit*, 1990, 68-85.

FOERSTER, W., art. Σῴζω und σωτηρία im Neuen Testament. — *TWNT* 7 (1964) 989-999: ET: in *TDNT* 7 (1971) 989-998.

FORMESYN, R., Le Sèmeion johannique et le Sèmeion hellénistique. — *ETL* 38 (1962) 856-894; = *ALBO* V, 7.

* FORTNA, R.T., *The Gospel of Signs: A Reconstruction of the Narrative Source Underlying the Fourth Gospel* (SNTS MS, 11), Cambridge, 1970. – Diss. New York, Union Theological Seminary, 1965 (dir. J.L. Martyn).

* —— Wilhelm Wilkens's Further Contribution to Johannine Studies: A Review Article. — *JBL* 89 (1970) 457-462.

* —— Source and Redaction in the Fourth Gospel's Portrayal of Jesus' Signs. — *JBL* 89 (1970) 151-166.

* —— From Christology to Soteriology: A Redaction-Critical Study of Salvation in the Fourth Gospel. — *Interpr* 27 (1973) 31-47.

* —— Theological Use of Locale in the Fourth Gospel. — *Gospel Studies in Honor of Sherman Elbridge Johnson*; = *ATR SS* 3 (1974) 58-95.

* —— Review of NICOL, *The Sēmeia* [1972]. — *JBL* 93 (1974) 119-121.

* —— Christology in the Fourth Gospel: Redaction-Critical Perspectives. — *NTS* 21 (1974-75) 489-504.

* —— Redaction Criticism, NT. — *IDB SV*, 1976, 733-735.

* —— Jesus and Peter at the High Priest's House: A Test Case of the Relation between Mark's and John's Gospels. — *NTS* 24 (1977-78) 371-383.

* —— Sayings of the Suffering and Risen Christ. — *Forum* 3 (1987), n° 3, 63-69.

* —— *The Fourth Gospel and Its Predecessor: From Narrative Source to Present Gospel*, Philadelphia, PA, 1988; Edinburgh, 1989.

* —— Diachronic/Synchronic: Reading John 21 and Luke 5. — DENAUX (ed.), *John and the Synoptics*, 1992, 387-399.

* —— Signs/Semeia Source. — *ABD*, vol. 6, 1992, 18-22.

* —— The Signs Gospel. — MILLER (ed.), *The Complete Gospels*, 1992, 175-193.

FOSTER, D., John Comes Lately: The Belated Evangelist. — McCONNELL (ed.), *The Bible and the Narrative Tradition*, 1985, 113-131.

FREED, E.D., Variations in the Language and Thought of John. — *ZNW* 55 (1964) 167-197.

—— *Old Testament Quotations in the Gospel of John* (SupplNT, 11), Leiden, 1965.

—— The Son of Man in the Fourth Gospel. — *JBL* 86 (1967) 402-409.

* —— & HUNT, R.B., Fortna's Signs-Source in John. — *JBL* 94 (1975) 563-579.

* —— *The New Testament: A Critical Introduction*, Belmont, CA, 1986.

—— Jn 1,19-27 in Light of Related Passages in John, the Synoptics, and Acts. — *FS F. Neirynck*, 1992, vol. III, 1943-1961.

FREY, J., Erwägungen zum Verhältnis der Johannesapokalypse zu den übrigen Schriften des Corpus Johanneum. — HENGEL, *Die johanneische Frage*, 1993, 326-429.

FREYNE, S., Locality and Doctrine: Mark and John Revisited. — *FS F. Neirynck*, III, 1889-1900.

FRYE, R.M., A Literary Perspective for the Criticism of the Gospels. — MILLER - HADIDIAN (eds.), *Jesus and Man's Hope*, vol. II, 1971, 193-221.

* FULLER, R.H., *Interpreting the Miracles*, London, 1963; repr. 1968.

GT: *Die Wunder Jesu in Exegese und Verkündigung*, trans. F.J. Schierse ("mit einem Vor- und Nachwort") (Theologische Perspektiven), Düsseldorf, 1967, ²1968.

DT: *Interpretatie van de wonderen van Jezus*, trans. K. Van Dun, Antwerpen – Utrecht, 1971.
* —— *The Foundations of New Testament Christology*, London – New York, 1965; repr. (Fontana Library), 1972.
* —— *A Critical Introduction to the New Testament* (Studies in Theology, 55), London, 1966.
—— Lower and Higher Christology in the Fourth Gospel. (An Imaginary Dialogue between J. Louis Martyn and the Late John A.T. Robinson with Reginald H. Fuller as Moderator). — *FS J.L. Martyn*, 1990, 357-365.

GABRIEL, A., Faith and Rebirth in the Fourth Gospel. — *Bible Bhashyam* 16 (1990) 205-215.
* GALLAGHER, E.V., *Divine Man or Magician? Celsus and Origen on Jesus* (SBL DS, 64), Missoula, MT, 1982. – Diss. Chicago (dir. J.Z. Smith).
GARCÍA-MORENO, A., La historicidad de los evangelios. Boletín bibliográfico (1980-1990). — *Scripta Theologica* 22 (1990) 927-955.
—— Autenticidad e historicidad del IV Evangelio. — *Scripta Theologica* 23 (1991) 13-67.
GARDNER-SMITH, P., *Saint John and the Synoptic Gospels*, Cambridge, 1938.
GARVIE, A.E., *The Beloved Disciple: Studies in the Fourth Gospel*, London, 1922.
GEIGER, G., Die ΕΓΩ ΕΙΜΙ-Worte bei Johannes und den Synoptikern. Eine Rückfrage nach dem historischen Jesus. — DENAUX (ed.), *John and the Synoptics*, 1992, 466-471.
GENUYT, F., L'économie des signes. — *LumV* 41 (1992), n° 209, 19-35.
* GEORGI, D., *Die Gegner des Paulus im 2. Korintherbrief. Studien zur religiösen Propaganda in der Spätantike* (WMANT, 11), Neukirchen-Vluyn, 1964. ET: *The Opponents of Paul in Second Corinthians* (StNTIW), Edinburgh – Philadelphia, PA, 1986.
—— Forms of Religious Propaganda. — SCHULZ (ed.), *Jesus in His Time*, 1967, 124-131.
* —— The Records of Jesus in the Light of Ancient Accounts of Revered Men. — *SBL 1972 Seminar Papers*, 1972, vol. II, 527-542.
* —— Socioeconomic Reasons for the "Divine Man" as Propagandistic Pattern. — SCHÜSSLER-FIORENZA (ed.), *Aspects of Religious Propaganda*, 1976, 27-42.
GERHARD, J., *The Literary Unity and the Compositional Methods of the Gospel of John*, diss. Washington, DC, The Catholic University of America, 1975.
GIBLET, J., Développements dans la théologie johannique. — DE JONGE (ed.), *L'évangile de Jean*, 1977 (²1987), 45-72.
GIBLIN, C.H., Suggestion, Negative Response, and Positive Action in St John's Portrayal of Jesus (John 2.1-11.; 4.46-54.; 7.2-14.; 11.1-44.). — *NTS* 26 (1979-80) 197-211.
GIRARD, M., La composition structurelle des sept "signes" dans le quatrième évangile. — *StudRel/SciRel* 9 (1980) 315-324.
GLASSON, T.F., Inaccurate Repetitions in the Fourth Gospel. — *ExpT* 57 (1945-46) 111-112.
* GNILKA, J., Zur Christologie des Johannesevangeliums. — KASPER (ed.), *Christologische Schwerpunkte*, 1980, 92-107.

* —— *Johannesevangelium* (NEchB NT, 1), Würzburg, 1983.

* —— *Jesus von Nazaret. Botschaft und Geschichte* (HTKNT Supplementband, 3), Freiburg – Basel – Wien, 1990; durchgesehene und erweiterte Sonderausgabe, 1993.

GODET, F.L., *Commentaire sur l'évangile de saint Jean* (Bibliothèque théologique), 2 vols., Paris, 1864, 1865; 3 vols., Neuchâtel, ⁴1902, 1903.
  ET: *Commentary on John's Gospel*, New York, 1886; repr. Grand Rapids, MI, 1978.
  DT: *Kommentaar op het evangelie van Johannes*, trans. P.J. Gouda Quint, 2 vols., Utrecht, 1866, 1871.

GOGUEL, M., *Les sources du récit johannique de la passion*, Paris, 1910.

* —— *Introduction au Nouveau Testament*. II. *Le quatrième évangile*, Paris, 1923.

—— Les sources des récits du quatrième évangile sur Jean-Baptiste. — *RTQR* 20 (1911) 12-44.

—— Le rejet de Jésus à Nazareth. — *ZNW* 12 (1911) 321-324.

—— Notes d'histoire évangélique. III. La venue de Jésus à Jérusalem pour la fête des tabernacles (Jn. 7). — *RHR* 83 (1921) 123-162.

—— La formation de la tradition johannique d'après B.W. Bacon. — *RHPR* 14 (1934) 415-439.

GOODWIN, C., How Did John Treat His Sources? — *JBL* 73 (1954) 61-75.

GOULDER, M.D., *Luke a New Paradigm*. I. *The Argument. Commentary: Luke 1.1–9.50*. II. *Commentary: Luke 9.51–24.53* (JSNT SS, 20), 2 vols., Sheffield, 1989.

—— John 1,1–2,12 and the Synoptics. Appendix: John 2,13–4,54. — DENAUX (ed.), *John and the Synoptics*, 1992, 201-237.

GOURGUES, M., Marie, la "femme" et la "mère" en Jean. — *NRT* 108 (1986) 174-191.

GRANT, F.C., *The Gospels: Their Origin and Their Growth*, London, 1957.

* GRAYSTON, K., *The Gospel of John* (Epworth Commentaries), London, 1990.

GREEN-ARMYTAGE, A.H.N., *John Who Saw: A Layman's Essay on the Author of the Fourth Gospel*, London, 1952.

GRELOT, P., Problèmes critiques du IVᵉ évangile. — *RB* 94 (1987) 519-573.

GREGORY, C.R., *Wellhausen und Johannes* (Versuche und Entwürfe, 3), Leipzig, 1910.

GRILL, J., *Untersuchungen über die Entstehung des vierten Evangeliums*, 2 vols., Tübingen, 1902, 1923.

GROB, F., *Faire l'œuvre de Dieu. Christologie et éthique dans l'Évangile de Jean* (ÉtHPR, 68). Paris, 1986.

* GROBEL, K., Review of BULTMANN, *Johannes* [1941]. — *JBL* 59 (1940) 434-436.

GROENEWALD, E.P., The Christological Meaning of John 20:31. — *Neotestamentica* 2 (1968) 131-140.

GROSHEIDE, F.W., *Het heilig evangelie volgens Johannes* (Kommentaar op het Nieuwe Testament, 4), 2 vols, Amsterdam, 1950.

GROSJEAN, J., Le style johannique. — BOURG et al. (eds.), *Variations johanniques*, 1989, 127-136.

GRUNDMANN, W., Verständnis und Bewegung des Glaubens im Johannes-Evangelium. — *KerDog* 6 (1960) 131-154.

—— *Zeugnis und Gestalt des Johannesevangeliums. Eine Studie zur denkerischen und gestalterischen Leistung des vierten Evangelisten* (AzT, 7), Berlin, 1960; Stuttgart, 1961.

—— *Der Zeuge der Wahrheit. Grundzüge der Christologie des Johannesevangeliums*, ed. W. WIEFEL, Berlin, 1985.

GUERIKE, H.E.F., *Historisch-kritische Einleitung in das Neue Testament*, Leipzig, 1843.

GUILDING, A., *The Fourth Gospel and Jewish Worship: A Study of the Relation of St. John's Gospel to the Ancient Jewish Lectionary System*, Oxford, 1960.

* GUNDRY, R.H., Recent Investigations into the Literary Genre "Gospel". —— LONGENECKER – TENNEY (eds.), *New Dimensions*, 1974, 97-114.

* HAENCHEN, E., Aus der Literatur zum Johannesevangelium. — *TR* 23 (1955) 295-335.

—— *Die Apostelgeschichte. Neu übersetzt und erklärt* (KEK, 3), Göttingen, 1956 (10th ed. in the series), [12]1959 ("durchgesehene und erweiterte Auflage"), [14]1965 ("neu durchgesehene und verbesserte Auflage"), [15]1968. ET: *The Acts of the Apostles. A Commentary*, trans. from the 14th German ed., Philadelphia, PA, 1971.

* —— Faith and Miracle. — *StEv*, 1959, 495-498.

* —— Johanneische Probleme. — *ZTK* 56 (1959) 19-54; = ID., *Gott und Mensch*, 1965, 78-113.

—— Probleme des johanneischen "Prologs". — *ZTK* 60 (1963) 305-334; = ID., *Gott und Mensch*, 1965, 114-143.

—— "Der Vater, der mich gesandt hat". — *NTS* 9 (1962-63) 208-216; = ID., *Gott und Mensch*, 1965, 68-77.

* —— Das Johannesevangelium und sein Kommentar. — *TLZ* 89 (1964) 881-898; = ID., *Die Bibel und Wir*, 1968, 206-234.

* —— Gott und Mensch (Zur ergänzenden Einführung in die folgenden Aufsätze). — ID., *Gott und Mensch*, 1965, 1-28.

—— *Der Weg Jesu. Eine Erklärung des Markus-Evangeliums und der kanonischen Parallelen* (Sammlung Töpelmann, 2/6), Berlin, 1966, [2]1968 (durchgesehene und verbesserte Auflage, de Gruyter Lehrbuch).

* —— *Das Johannesevangelium. Ein Kommentar aus den nachgelassenen Manuskripten*, ed. U. BUSSE, Tübingen, 1980 (Preface by J.M. ROBINSON). ET: *John 1/2. A Commentary on the Gospel of John, Chapters 1–6/7–21*, trans. R.W. Funk, ed. R.W. FUNK – U. BUSSE (Hermeneia), Philadelphia, PA, 1984.

HAHN, F., *Christologische Hoheitstitel. Ihre Geschichte im frühen Christentum*, Göttingen, 1963, [2]1964.

—— Sehen und Glauben im Johannesevangelium. — *FS O. Cullmann II*, 1972, 125-141.

—— art. Χριστός. — *EWNT* 3 (1983) 1147-1165; ET: *EDNT* 3 (1992) 478-487.

HAINZ, J., Neuere Auffassungen zur Redaktionsgeschichte des Johannesevangeliums. — HAINZ (ed.), *Theologie im Werden*, 1992, 157-176.

—— "Zur Krisis kam ich in die Welt" (Joh 9,39). Zur Eschatologie im Johannesevangelium. — KLAUCK (ed.), *Weltgericht und Weltvollendung*, 1994, 149-163.

* HANSON, A.T., *The Prophetic Gospel: A Study of John and the Old Testament*, Edinburgh, 1991.

HARNACK, A. VON, Zum Johannesevangelium. — *Erforschtes und Erlebtes*, Giessen, 1923, 36-43.

* HARTKE, W., *Vier urchristliche Parteien und ihre Vereinigung zur apostolischen Kirche* (SSA, 24), 2 vols., Berlin, 1961.

HARTMANN, Gerhard, *Der Aufbau des Markusevangeliums. Mit einem Anhang: Untersuchungen zur Echtheit des Markusschlusses* (NTAbh, 17/2-3), Münster, 1936.

HARTMANN, Gert, Die Vorlage der Osterberichte in Joh 20. — *ZNW* 55 (1964) 197-220.

HASLER, V., Glauben und Erkennen im Johannesevangelium. Strukturale und hermeneutische Überlegungen. — *EvT* 50 (1990) 279-296.

* HAUFE, G., *Vom Werden und Verstehen des Neuen Testaments. Eine Einführung*, Gütersloh, 1968.

* —— Einführung in das Johannes-Evangelium. — *ZdZ* 24 (1970) 265-271.

HEDRICK, C.W., Authorial Presence and Narrator in John: Commentary and Story. — *FS J.M. Robinson*, 1990, 74-93.

* HEEKERENS, H.-P., *Die Zeichen-Quelle der johanneischen Redaktion. Ein Beitrag zur Entstehungsgeschichte des vierten Evangeliums* (SBS, 113), Stuttgart, 1984. – Diss. Heidelberg, 1978 (dir. H. Thyen).

HEILIGENTHAL, R., *Werke als Zeichen. Untersuchungen zur Bedeutung der menschlichen Taten im Frühjudentum, Neuen Testament und Frühchristentum* (WUNT, 2/9), Tübingen, 1983.

—— art. Ἔργον. — *EWNT* 2 (1981) 123-127; ET: *EDNT* 2 (1991) 49-51.

HEISING, A., Exegese und Theologie der alt- und neutestamentlichen Speisewunder. — *ZKT* 86 (1964) 80-96.

—— *Die Botschaft der Brotvermehrung. Zur Geschichte und Bedeutung eines Christusbekenntnisses im Neuen Testament* (SBS, 15), Stuttgart, 1966.
DT: *De boodschap van de broodvermenigvuldiging. Bijdrage tot de geschiedenis en zin van een Christus-getuigenis in het Nieuw Testament*, trans. D. Antheunis (De christen in de tijd, 39), Antwerpen, 1968.

HENAUT, B.W., John 4:43-54 and the Ambivalent Narrator: A Response to Culpepper's *Anatomy of the Fourth Gospel*. — *StudRel/SciRel* 19 (1990) 287-304.

* HENGEL, M., The Interpretation of the Wine Miracle at Cana: John 2:1-11. — HURST – WRIGHT (eds.), *The Glory of Christ*, 1987, 84-112.

* —— *The Johannine Question*, trans. J. Bowden, London – Philadelphia, PA, 1989.
GT: *Die johanneische Frage. Ein Lösungsversuch. Mit einem Beitrag zur Apokalypse von J. FREY* (WUNT, 67), Tübingen, 1993.

HENGSTENBERG, E.W., *Das Evangelium des heiligen Johannes erläutert*, 3 vols., Berlin, 1863.

HILGENFELD, A., Das Johannes-Evangelium nicht interpolirt. — *ZWT* 11 (1868) 434-455.

HIRSCH, E., *Studien zum vierten Evangelium. (Text/Literarkritik/Entstehungsgeschichte)* (BHT, 11), Tübingen, 1936.

—— *Das vierte Evangelium in seiner ursprünglichen Gestalt verdeutscht und erklärt*, Tübingen, 1936.

—— Stilkritik und Literaranalyse im vierten Evangelium. — *ZNW* 43 (1950-51) 128-143 [Abgeschlossen am 24. März 1942].

* HOEFERKAMP, R.T., *The Relationship between* Sēmeia *and Believing in the Fourth Gospel*, diss. St. Louis, MO, Christ Seminary-Seminex, 1978 (dir. R.H. Smith). – Cf. *DissAbstr* 40 (1979-80), n° 4, 2131-2132; *SBT* 10 (1980) 139-140.

* HOERNLE, E.S., *The Record of the Loved Disciple together with the Gospel of St. Philip. Being a Reconstruction of the Sources of the Fourth Gospel*, London, 1931.

* HOFBECK, S., *Semeion. Der Begriff des "Zeichens" im Johannesevangelium unter Berücksichtigung seiner Vorgeschichte* (Münsterschwarzacher Studien, 3), Münsterschwarzach, 1966, ²1970.

HOFRICHTER, P., Johannesevangelium. — *NBL*, Lief. 8, 1992, 359-369.

* HOLLADAY, C.R., Theios aner *in Hellenistic-Judaism: A Critique of the Use of This Category in New Testament Christology* (SBL DS, 40), Missoula, MT, 1977.

HOLLERAN, J.W., Seeing the Light: A Narrative Reading of John 9. I. Background and Presupposition. II. Narrative Expositions. — *ETL* 69 (1993) 5-26, 354-382.

HOLTZMANN, H.J., *Lehrbuch der neutestamentlichen Theologie* (Sammlung Theologischer Lehrbücher), vol. II, Freiburg – Leipzig, 1987, ²1911.

—— *Lehrbuch der historisch-kritischen Einleitung in das Neue Testament*, Freiburg, ³1892 ("dritte verbesserte und vermehrte Auflage").

—— *Evangelium, Briefe und Offenbarung des Johannes* (Handcommentar zum neuen Testament, 4), Freiburg, 1891, ²1893 (Tübingen), ³1908 (*Evangelium des Johannes*, ed. W. BAUER).

—— Hugo Delff und das vierte Evangelium. — *ZWT* 26 (1893) 503-507.

HOLTZMANN, O., *Das Johannesevangelium untersucht und erklärt*, Darmstadt, 1887.

HORN, K., *Abfassung, Geschichtlichkeit und Zweck vom Evang. des Johannes, Kap. 21. Ein Beitrag zur johanneischen Frage*, Leipzig, 1904.

HOSKYNS, E.C., *The Fourth Gospel*, ed. F.N. DAVIS, London, 1940, ²1947.

HOWARD, W.F., *The Fourth Gospel in Recent Criticism and Interpretation*, London, 1931, ²1935, ³1945, ⁴1955 (rev., ed. C.K. BARRETT).

HULL, W.E., *John* (The Broadman Bible Commentary, 9), London, 1970.

IBUKI, Y., Viele glaubten an ihn. Auseinandersetzung mit dem Glauben im Johannesevangelium. — *AnJapB* 9 (1983) 128-183.

INCH, M., Apologetic Use of "Signs" in the Fourth Gospel. — *EvQ* 42 (1970) 35-43.

* JACQUES, X., Review of FORTNA, *Gospel of Signs* [1970]. — *NRT* 94 (1972) 1102-1103.

JACQUIER, E., *Histoire des livres du Nouveau Testament. IV. Les écrits johanniques*, Paris, ³1908, ⁵1923.

* JEREMIAS, J., Ein bisher unbekanntes Evangelienfragment. Einblicke in die Arbeitsweise eines alten Evangelisten. — *TBl* 15 (1936) 38-45.

* —— Johanneische Literarkritik. — *TBl* 20 (1941) 33-46.

* —— Review of BULTMANN, *Johannes* [1941]. — *DLZ* 64 (1943) 414-420.

—— Die aramäische Vorgeschichte unserer Evangelien. — *TLZ* 74 (1949) 527-531.

—— Joh. 6,51c-59 – Redaktionell? — *ZNW* 44 (1952-53) 256-257.

—— *Der Prolog des Johannesevangeliums (Johannes 1,1-18)* (CwH, 88), Stuttgart, 1967.

JOHANNESSOHN, M., *Der Gebrauch der Präpositionen in der Septuaginta* (MSU, 3/3), Berlin, 1926.

* JOHNSON, B., Another Primitive Source? — *Encounter* 33 (1972) 393-399.

JOHNSON, L.T., *The Writings of the New Testament: An Interpretation*, London, 1986.

* JUDGE, P.J., Luke 7,1-10: Source and Redaction. — NEIRYNCK (ed.), *L'évangile de Luc. The Gospel of Luke*, 1989, 473-490.

—— A Note on Jn 20,29. — *FS F. Neirynck*, 1992, vol. III, 2183-2192.

JUNCKER, A., *Zur neuesten Johanneskritik. Vortrag gehalten auf dem theologischen Ferienkursus in Königsberg i. Pr. am 17 Oktober 1911*, Halle a. S., 1912.

* KÄSEMANN, E., Review of BULTMANN, *Johannes* [1941]. — *VF* 1942-46 (ed. 1947) 182-201.

* —— Aus der neutestamentlichen Arbeit der letzten Jahre. — *VF* 1947-48 (ed. 1950) 195-223.

* —— Ein neutestamentlicher Überblick. — *VF* 1949-50 (ed. 1951-52) 181-218.

* —— Ketzer und Zeuge. Zum johanneischen Verfasserproblem. — *ZTK* 48 (1951) 292-311; ID., = *Exegetische Versuche und Besinnungen*, vol. I, 1960, 168-214.

* —— Aufbau und Anliegen des johanneischen Prologs. — *FS F. Delekat*, 1957, 75-99; = ID., *Exegetische Versuche und Besinnungen*, vol. II, 1964, 155-180.
   ET: The Structure and Purpose of the Prologue to John's Gospel. — ID., *New Testament Questions of Today*, 1969, 138-167.

* —— Neutestamentliche Fragen von heute. — *ZTK* 54 (1957) 1-21; = ID., *Exegetische Versuche und Besinnungen*, vol. II, 1964, 11-31.
   ET: New Testament Questions of Today. — ID., *New Testament Questions of Today*, 1969, 1-22.

* —— Review of HOWARD, *The Fourth Gospel* [⁴1955, ed. BARRETT] and BARRETT, *The Gospel according to John* [1955]. — *GGA* 211 (1957) 145-160; = ID., *Exegetische Versuche und Besinnungen*, vol. II, 1964, 131-155.

* —— Wunder. IV. Im N.T. — *RGG*³ 6 (1962) 1835-1837.

* —— *Jesu letzter Wille nach Johannes 17*, Tübingen, 1966, ²1967.
   ET: *The Testament of Jesus: A Study of the Gospel of John in the Light of Chapter 17*, trans. G. Krodel (NTLi), Philadelphia, PA, 1968.

* KAMPHAUS, F., *Von der Exegese zur Predigt. Über die Problematik einer schriftgemässen Verkündigung der Oster-, Wunder-, und Kindheitsgeschichten*, Mainz, 1968, ²1968. – Diss. Münster, 1967 (dir. T. Filhaut).
   DT: *De paasverhalen*, trans. H. Biezeno (Van exegese tot verkondiging, 1), Boxtel, 1970 (= 1968, 23-112).
   DT: *De wonderverhalen in de evangelies*, trans. H. Biezeno (Van exegese tot verkondiging, 3), Boxtel, 1971 (= 1968, 115-208).

KECK, L.E., Mark 3:7-12 and Mark's Christology. — *JBL* 84 (1965) 341-358.

—— The Introduction to Mark's Gospel. — *NTS* 12 (1965-66) 352-370.

* KEE, H.C., Aretalogy and Gospel. — *JBL* 92 (1973) 402-422.

* —— *Miracle in the Early Christian World: A Study in Socio-historical Method*, New Haven, CT – London, 1983.

—— *Medicine, Miracle and Magic in New Testament Times* (SNTS MS, 55), Cambridge, 1986.

—— Miracle in Biblical World. — *DBI*, 1990, 461-465.

KEIL, C.F., *Commentar über das Evangelium des Johannes*, Leipzig, 1881.

KEMPER, F., Zur literarischen Gestalt des Johannesevangeliums. — *TZ* 43 (1987) 247-264.

KERTELGE, K., *Die Wunder Jesu im Markusevangelium. Eine redaktionsgeschichtliche Untersuchung* (SANT, 23), München, 1972.

* —— Die Überlieferung der Wunder Jesu und die Frage nach dem historischen Jesus. — ID. (ed.), *Rückfrage nach Jesus*, 1974, 174-193.

* —— Die Wunder Jesu in der neueren Exegese. — *TBer* 5 (1976) 71-105.

KEULERS, J., *Het evangelie van Johannes* (De boeken van het Nieuwe Testament, 3), Roermond – Maaseik, 1936, ²1951.

* KILEY, M., The Exegesis of God: Jesus' Signs in John 1–11. — *SBL 1988 Seminar Papers*, 1988, 555-569.

KIPPENBERG, H.G., *Garizim und Synagoge. Traditionsgeschichtliche Untersuchungen zur samaritanischen Religion der aramäischen Periode* (RVV, 30), Berlin – New York, 1971.

* KIRBY, J.C., Review of BULTMANN, *John* [1971]. — *StudRel/SciRel* 1 (1971) 140.

* KLAIBER, W., Die Aufgabe einer theologischen Interpretation des 4. Evangeliums. — *ZTK* 82 (1985) 300-324.

KLAUSNER, J., *The Messianic Idea in Israel from Its Beginning to the Completion of the Mishnah*, trans. from the 3rd Hebrew ed. by W.F. Stinespring, London, 1955.

KLIJN, A.F.J., *Inleiding tot het Nieuwe Testament* (Aula, 66), Utrecht – Antwerpen, 1961.

—— *De wordingsgeschiedenis van het Nieuwe Testament* (Aula, 207), Utrecht – Antwerpen, 1965.
ET: *An Introduction to the New Testament*, Leiden, 1980.

KLOTUFAR, L., *Commentarius in Evangelium Sancti Joannis concinnatus*, Wien, 1862.

KNABENBAUER, I., *Commentarius in Quatuor S. Evangelia Domini N. Iesu Christi. IV. Evangelium secundum Ioannem* (Cursus Scripturae Sacrae, I/4), Paris, 1898, ²1906.

* KNOCH, O., *Begegnung wird Zeugnis. Werden und Wesen des Neuen Testaments* (Biblische Basis Bücher, 6), Kevelaer – Stuttgart, 1980.

* KOCH, D.-A., *Die Bedeutung der Wundererzählungen für die Christologie des Markusevangeliums* (BZNW, 42), Berlin – New York, 1975. – Diss. Göttingen, 1973 (dir. H. Conzelmann).

—— Inhaltliche Gliederung und geographische Aufriss im Markusevangelium. — *NTS* 29 (1983) 145-166.

—— Der Täufer als Zeuge des Offenbarers. Das Täuferbild von Joh 1,19-34 auf dem Hintergrund von Mk 1,2-11. — *FS F. Neirynck*, 1992, vol. III, 1963-1984.

—— Source Criticism, New Testament. — *ABD*, vol. 6, 1992, 165-171.

KOESTER, C., Hearing, Seeing, and Believing in the Gospel of John. — *Bib* 70 (1989) 327-348.

KOESTER, C.G., R.E. Brown and J.L. Martyn: Johannine Studies in Retrospect. — *BTB* 21 (1991) 51-55.

* KOESTER, H., Häretiker im Urchristentum. — *RGG*³ 3 (1959) 17-21.

* —— *ΓΝΩΜΑΙ ΔΙΑΦΟΡΟΙ*: The Origin and Nature of Diversification in the History of Early Christianity. — *HTR* 58 (1965) 279-315; = ROBINSON – KOESTER, *Trajectories*, 1971, 114-157.

GT: *ΓΝΩΜΑΙ ΔΙΑΦΟΡΟΙ*. Ursprung und Wesen der Mannigfaltigkeit in der Geschichte des frühen Christentums. — *ZTK* 65 (1968) 160-203; = ROBINSON – KOESTER, *Entwicklungslinien*, 1970.

* —— One Jesus and Four Primitive Gospels. — *HTR* 61 (1968) 203-247; = ROBINSON – KOESTER, *Trajectories*, 1971, 158-204.

GT: Ein Jesus und vier ursprüngliche Evangeliengattungen. — ROBINSON – KOESTER, *Entwicklungslinien*, 1970, 147-190.

—— Grundtypen und Kriterien frühchristlicher Glaubensbekenntnisse. — ROBINSON – KOESTER, *Entwicklungslinien*, 1970, 191-215.

ET: The Structure of Criteria of Early Christian Beliefs. — ROBINSON – KOESTER, *Trajectories*, 1971, 205-231.

—— Conclusion: The Intention and Scope of Trajectories. — ROBINSON – KOESTER, *Trajectories*, 1971, 269-279.

—— Aprocyphal and Canonical Gospels. — *HTR* 73 (1980) 105-130.

* —— *Einführung in das Neue Testament im Rahmen der Religionsgeschichte und Kulturgeschichte der hellenistischen und römischen Zeit* (de Gruyter Lehrbuch), Berlin – New York, 1980.

ET: *Introduction to the New Testament*. Vol. I: *History, Culture and Religion of the Hellenistic Age*. Vol. II: *History and Literature of Early Christianity*, Philadelphia, PA – Berlin – New York, 1982.

* —— History and Development of Mark's Gospel (From Mark to *Secret Mark* and "Canonical" Mark). — CORLEY (ed.), *Colloquy*, 1983, 35-57 (59-85: "Seminar Dialogue with Helmut Koester").

* —— Überlieferung und Geschichte der frühchristlichen Evangelienliteratur. — *ANRW* II, 25/2, 1984, 1463-1542.

—— The History-of-Religions School, Gnosis, and Gospel of John. — *StudTheol* 40 (1986) 115-136.

* —— Johannesevangelium. — *EKL*, vol. II (Lief. 2), 1988, 840-843.

* —— *Ancient Christian Gospels: Their History and Development*, London – Philadelphia, PA, 1990.

KOHLER, H., *Kreuz und Menschwerdung im Johannesevangelium. Ein exegetisch-hermeneutischer Versuch zur johanneischen Kreuzestheologie* (ATANT, 72), Zürich, 1987.

* KOLENKOW, A.B., Healing Controversy as a Tie between Miracle and Passion Material for a Proto-Gospel. — *JBL* 95 (1976) 623-638.

—— Relationships between Miracle and Prophecy in the Greco-Roman World and Early Christianity. — *ANRW* II, 3/2, 1980, 1470-1506.

—— "Divine Men" and Society. — *Forum* 2 (1986), n° 4, 85-92.

* KONINGS, J., *Het johanneïsch verhaal in de literaire kritiek. Historiek. Dossier van Joh., I–X. Redactiestudie van Joh., VI, 1-21*, 3 parts (6 vols.), diss. Leuven, 1972 (dir. F. Neirynck).

* —— The Pre-Markan Sequence in Jn, VI: A Critical Re-Examination. — Sabbe (ed.), *L'évangile selon Marc*, 1974 (^{2}1988), 147-177.

* —— The Dialogue of Jesus, Philip and Andrew in John 6,5-9. — Denaux (ed.), *John and the Synoptics*, 1992, 523-534.

* Koskenniemi, E., *Apollonios von Tyana in der neutestamentlichen Exegese. Forschungsbericht und Weiterführung der Diskussion*, Turku, 1992; (WUNT, 2/61), Tübingen, 1994. – Diss. Åbo, 1992 (dir. J. Thurén).

* Kotila, M., *Umstrittener Zeuge. Studien zur Stellung des Gesetzes in der johanneischen Theologiegeschichte* (AASF DHL, 48), Helsinki, 1988. – Diss. Helsinki (dir. H. Räisänen).

* Kremer, J., *Lazarus. Die Geschichte einer Auferstehung. Text, Wirkungsgeschichte und Botschaft von Joh 11,1-46*, Stuttgart, 1985.

* —— Der arme Lazarus. Lazarus, der Freund Jesu. Beobachtungen zur Beziehung zwischen Lk 16,19-31 und Joh 11,1-46. — *FS J. Dupont*, 1985, 571-584.

—— "Nimm deine Hand und lege sie in meine Seite!". Exegetische, hermeneutische und bibeltheologische Überlegungen zu Joh 20,24-29. — *FS F. Neirynck*, 1992, vol. III, 2153-2181.

Kreyenbühl, J., *Das Evangelium der Wahrheit. Neue Lösung der johanneischen Frage*, 2 vols., Berlin, 1900, 1905.

Kristeva, J., Des signes au sujet. — Bourg et al. (eds.), *Variations johanniques*, 1989, 147-155.

Krüger-Velthusen, W., *Das Leben Jesu*, Eberfeld, 1872.

* Kuck, D.W., Review of Fortna, *Predecessor* [1988]. — *CurrTMiss* 17 (1990) 149.

Kügler, J., *Der Jünger, den Jesus liebte. Literarische, theologische und historische Untersuchungen zu einer Schlüsselgestalt johanneischer Theologie und Geschichte. Mit einem Exkurs über die Brotrede in Joh 6* (SBB, 16), Stuttgart, 1988. – Diss. Bamberg, 1987 (dir. P. Hoffmann).

* Kühschelm, R., *Verstockung, Gericht und Heil. Exegetische und bibeltheologische Untersuchung zum sogenannten "Dualismus" und "Determinismus" in Joh 12,35-50* (BBB, 76), Frankfurt, 1990. – Diss. Wien, 1989-90 (dir. J. Kremer).

* Kümmel, W.G., *Einleitung in das Neue Testament*, Heidelberg, ^{12}1963, ^{17}1973. ET: *Introduction to the New Testament*, trans. from the 14th rev. ed. [1965] by A.J. Mattill, Jr., in collaboration with the author (NTLi), London – New York, 1966; repr. 1970.
ET: *Introduction to the New Testament*, rev. ed., trans. from the 17th German edition by H.C. Kee, Nashville, TN, 1975; repr. 1984.

—— *Das Neue Testament im 20. Jahrhundert. Ein Forschungsbericht* (SBS, 50), Stuttgart, 1970.

* Kuhn, H.-J., Joh 1,35-51 – Literarkritik und Form. — *TTZ* 95 (1987) 149-155.

* —— *Christologie und Wunder. Untersuchungen zu Joh 1,35-51* (BibUnt, 18), Regensburg, 1988. – Diss. Trier, 1985-86 (dir. J. Eckert).

* Kuhn, H.-W., *Ältere Sammlungen im Markusevangelium* (SUNT, 8), Göttingen, 1971. – Diss. Heidelberg, 1969 (dir. K.G. Kuhn).

Kuinoel, C.T., *Commentarius in libros Novi Testamenti historicos*. Vol. III: *Evangelium Iohannis*, Leipzig, 1807, ^{2}1817, ^{3}1825.

* KYSAR, R., Review of FORTNA, *Gospel of Signs* [1970]. — *Perspective* 11 (1970) 334-336.
* —— The Source Analysis of the Fourth Gospel – A Growing Consensus? — *NT* 15 (1973) 134-152
* —— *The Fourth Evangelist and His Gospel: An Examination of Contemporary Scholarship*, Minneapolis, MN, 1975.
* —— *John, the Maverick Gospel*, Atlanta, GA, 1976; Louisville, KY, ²1993.
—— Community and Gospel: Vectors in Fourth Gospel Criticism. — *Interpr* 31 (1977) 355-366.
* —— The Gospel of John in Current Research. — *RelStR* 9 (1983) 314-323.
* —— *John's Story of Jesus*, Philadelphia, PA, 1984.
* —— The Fourth Gospel: A Report on Recent Research. — *ANRW* II, 25/3, 1985, 2389-2480.
* —— *John* (AugsbCNT), Minneapolis, MN, 1986.
* —— Review of FORTNA, *Predecessor* [1988]. — *Interpr* 44 (1990) 186-187.
—— Johannine Metaphor – Meaning and Function: A Literary Case Study of John 10:1-8. — *Semeia* 53 (1991) 81-111.
* —— John, The Gospel of. — *ABD*, vol. 3, 1992, 912-931.

LAGRANGE, M.-J., Où en est la dissection littéraire du quatrième évangile? — *RB* 33 (1924) 321-342.
—— *Évangile selon saint Jean* (ÉtB), Paris, 1925.
LAMMERS, K., *Hören, Sehen und Glauben im Neuen Testament* (SBS, 11), Stuttgart, 1966.
* LANE, W.L., Theios Anèr Christology and the Gospel of Mark. — LONGE-NECKER – TENNEY (eds.), *New Dimensions*, 1974, 144-161.
* LANGBRANDTNER, W., *Weltferner Gott oder Gott der Liebe. Der Ketzerstreit in der johanneischen Kirche. Eine exegetisch-religionsgeschichtliche Untersuchung mit Berücksichtigung der koptisch-gnostischen Texte aus Nag-Hammadi* (BET, 6), Frankfurt – Bern – New York, 1977. – Diss. Heidelberg (dir. H. Thyen).
LATTKE, M., Erlöser und Erlösung im Johannesevangelium. — *"Salvation Today"*, Bossey, 1972, 17-27.
—— Joh 20,30f. als Buchschluss. — *ZNW* 78 (1987) 288-292.
LAW, R., *The Tests of Life: A Study of the First Epistle of John*, ³1914; repr. Grand Rapids, MI, 1968.
LEE, D.A., *The Symbolic Narratives of the Fourth Gospel* (JSNT SS, 95), Sheffield, 1994.
* LEIDIG, E., *Jesu Gespräch mit der Samaritanerin und weitere Gespräche im Johannesevangelium* (TDiss, 15), Basel, 1979. – Diss. Basel (dir. B. Reicke).
LÉON-DUFOUR, X., *Les évangiles et l'histoire de Jésus* (Parole de Dieu, 1), Paris, 1963.
    GT: *Die Evangelien und der historische Jesus*, Aschaffenburg, 1966.
    ET: *The Gospels and the Jesus of History*, trans./ed. J. McHugh, New York – Tournai.
* —— Review of FORTNA, *Gospel of Signs* [1970]. — *RSR* 62 (1974) 290-291.
* —— Autour du ΣΗΜΕΙΟΝ johannique. — *FS H. Schürmann*, 1977, 363-377.

* —— Les miracles de Jésus selon Jean. — ID. (ed.), *Les miracles de Jésus*, 1977, 269-286.

* —— Bulletin d'exégèse du Nouveau Testament. L'évangile de Jean. — *RSR* 75 (1987) 77-96; 77 (1989) 261-280.

* —— Lecture de l'évangile selon Jean. I. *Chapitres 1–4*. II. *Chapitres 5–12*. III. *Les adieux du Seigneur (chapitres 13–17)* (Parole de Dieu, 26, 28, 31), Paris, 1988, 1990, 1993.

* —— Où en est la recherche johannique? Bilan et Ouvertures. — MARCHADOUR (ed.), *Origine et postérité*, 1990, 17-41.

LÉMONON, J.P., Chronique johannique (1881-1992). — *LumV* 41 (1992), n° 209, 95-104.

LENSKI, R.C.H., *The Interpretation of St. John's Gospel*, Columbus, OH, 1942.

LEROY, H., *Rätsel und Missverständnis. Ein Beitrag zur Formgeschichte des Johannesevangeliums* (BBB, 30), Bonn, 1968.

* LEVIE, J., Review of BULTMANN, *Johannes* [1941]. — *NRT* 73 (1951) 876.

LEVIN, S., The Early History of Christianity in Light of the "Secret Gospel" of Mark. — *ANRW* II, 25/6, 1988, 4271-4293.

—— Thoughts on Two Extracanonical Gospels. — *Semeia* 49 (1990) 155-168.

LIGHTFOOT, R.H., *St. John's Gospel: A Commentary*, ed. C.F. EVANS, London – Oxford – New York, 1956; paperback ed., 1960.

* LINDARS, B., *Behind the Fourth Gospel* (Studies in Creative Criticism), London, 1971.
> FT: *Au-delà du quatrième évangile*, trans. J. Winandy. — ID. – B. RIGAUX, *Témoignage de l'évangile de Jean* (Pour une histoire de Jésus, 5), Paris, 1974, 1-113.

* —— *The Gospel of John* (NCB), London, 1972.

* —— Review of BULTMANN, *John* [1971]. — *Theology* 75 (1972) 149-150.

* —— Traditions behind the Fourth Gospel. — DE JONGE (ed.), *L'évangile de Jean*, 1977 (²1987), 107-204; = LINDARS, *Essays*, 1992, 33-50.

—— Discourse and Tradition: The Use of the Sayings of Jesus in the Discourses of the Fourth Gospel. — *JSNT* 13 (1981) 83-101; = ID., *Essays*, 1992, 113-129.

* —— Review of FORTNA, *Predecessor* [1988]. — *ScotJT* 43 (1990) 526-527.

* —— *John* (New Testament Guides), Sheffield, 1990.

* —— Some Recent Trends in the Study of John. — *Way* 30 (1990) 329-338.

* —— Rebuking the Spirit: A New Analysis of the Lazarus Story of John 11. — *NTS* 38 (1992) 89-104; = ID., *Essays*, 1992, 183-198; abbreviated in DENAUX (ed.), *John and the Synoptics*, 1992, 542-547.

* —— Capernaum Revisited: Jn 4,46-53 and the Synoptics. — *FS F. Neirynck*, 1992, vol. III, 1985-2000; = LINDARS, *Essays*, 1992, 199-214.

—— John Ashton's *Understanding the Fourth Gospel*. — *ScotJT* 45 (1992) 245-251.

LINDEMANN, A. → Conzelmann

* LINK, A., *"Was redest du mit ihr?". Eine Studie zur Exegese-, Redaktions- und Theologiegeschichte von Joh 4,1-42* (BibUnt, 24), 1992. – Diss. Frankfurt, 1991-92 (dir. J. Hainz).

* —— Botschafterinnen des Messias. Die Frauen des vierten Evangeliums im Spiegel johanneischer Redaktions- und Theologiegeschichte. — HAINZ (ed.), *Theologie im Werden*, 1992, 247-278.

LINNEMANN, E., Die Hochzeit zu Kana und Dionysus. Oder das unzureichende der Kategorien Übertragung und Identifikation zur Erfassung der religionsgeschichtlichen Beziehungen. — *NTS* 20 (1973-74) 408-418.

LIPS, H. VON, Anthropologie und Wunder im Johannesevangelium. Die Wunder Jesu im Johannesevangelium im Unterschied zu den synoptischen Evangelien auf dem Hintergrund johanneischen Menschenverständnisses. — *EvT* 50 (1990) 296-311.

LOADER, W.R.G., The Central Structure of Johannine Christology. — *NTS* 30 (1984) 188-214.

— *The Christology of the Fourth Gospel: Structure and Issues* (BET, 23), Frankfurt – Bern – New York, 1989.

LOHFINK, G., Das Weinwunder zu Kana. Eine Auslegung von Joh 2,1-12. — *GL* 57 (1984) 169-182.

LOHMEYER, E., Über Aufbau und Gliederung des vierten Evangeliums. — *ZNW* 27 (1928) 11-36.

— *Das Evangelium nach Markus übersetzt und erklärt* (KEK, 1/2), Gottingen, [10]1937, [11]1951 ("nach dem Handexemplar des Verfassers durchgesehene Auflage mit Ergänzungsheft").

LOHSE, E., Wunder. III. Im Judentum. — *RGG*[3] 6 (1962) 1834.

* — *Die Entstehung des Neuen Testaments* (TW, 4), Stuttgart – Berlin – Köln – Mainz, 1972.

* — Miracles in the Fourth Gospel. — *FS C. Evans*, 1975, 64-75; = LOHSE, *Die Vielfalt*, 1982, 45-56.

LOISY, A., *Le quatrième évangile*, Paris, 1903, [2]1921.

* LONA, H.E., Glaube und Sprache des Glaubens im Johannesevangelium. — *BZ* 28 (1984) 168-184.

LORENZINI, E., La problematicità dell'unità linguistica giovannea secondo il metodo dello Schweizer. — *VetChrist* 18 (1981) 453-469.

LOUW, J.P., On Johannine Style. — *Neotestamentica* 20 (1986) 5-12.

LÜCKE, F., *Commentar über das Evangelium des Johannes* (Commentar über die Schriften des Evangelisten Johannes), 2 vols., Bonn, 1820, 1824; [2]1833, 1834; [3]1840, 1843.

* LÜHRMANN, D. *Das Markusevangelium* (HNT, 3), Tübingen, 1987.

* — Faith, New Testament. — *ABD*, vol. 2, 1992, 749-758.

* LÜTGEHETMANN, W., *Die Hochzeit von Kana (Joh 2,1-11). Zu Ursprung und Deutung einer Wundererzählung im Rahmen johanneischer Redaktionsgeschichte* (BibUnt, 20), Regensburg, 1990. – Diss. Frankfurt (dir. J. Hainz).

* — Die Hochzeit von Kana – Der Anfang der Zeichen Jesu. — HAINZ (ed.), *Theologie im Werden*, 1992, 177-197.

* LUTHARDT, C.E., *Das johanneische Evangelium nach seiner Eigenthümlichkeit geschildert und erklärt*. Erste Abtheilung, Nürnberg, 1852.

MACGREGOR, G.H.C., *The Gospel of John* (The Moffatt New Testament Commentary), London, 1928.

* MACK, B.L., *A Myth of Innocence: Mark and Christian Origins*, Philadelphia, PA, 1988.

* MACRAE, G.W., The Fourth Gospel and Religionsgeschichte. — *CBQ* 32 (1970) 13-24; = ID., *Studies*, 1987, 15-31.

—— Gnosticism and the Church of John's Gospel. — HEDRICK – HODGSON, JR. (eds.), *Nag Hammadi*, 1986, 89-96.

MAIER, A., *Commentar über das Evangelium des Johannes*, 2 vols., Karlsruhe – Freiburg, 1843, 1845.

MALATESTA, E., *St. John's Gospel 1920-1965: A Cumulative and Classified Bibliography of Books and Periodical Literature on the Fourth Gospel* (AnBib, 32), Rome, 1967.

* —— Review of BULTMANN, *John* [1971]. — *BTB* 2 (1972) 93-94.

* MARCHADOUR, A., *Lazare. Histoire d'un récit. Récits d'une histoire* (LD, 132), Paris, 1988.

* —— Lazare: du silence à la parole. — BOURG *et al.* (eds.), *Variations johanniques*, 1989, 175-189.

* —— *La fécondité d'un texte* [Jn 11]. — ID. (ed.), *Origine et postérité*, 1990, 173-182.

* MARGUERAT, D., La "source des signes" existe-t-elle? Réception des récits de miracle dans l'évangile de Jean. — KAESTLI *et al.* (eds.), *La communauté johannique*, 1990, 69-93.

—— L'évangile de Jean et son lecteur. — *FS J. Delorme*, 1993, 305-324.

MARSH, J., *The Gospel of John* (The Pelican Gospel Commentaries), Harmondsworth, 1968.

MARTY, F., Le signe, épreuve du croire. — *LumV* 41 (1992), nº 209, 5-18.

* MARTYN, J.L., *History and Theology in the Fourth Gospel*, New York – London, 1968; Nashville, TN, ²1979 ("revised and enlarged").

* —— Source Criticism and *Religionsgeschichte* in the Fourth Gospel. — MILLER – HADIDIAN (eds.), *Jesus and Man's Hope*, vol. I, 1970, 247-273; = ASHTON (ed.), *The Interpretation*, 1986, 99-121.

* —— We Have Found Elijah. — *FS W.D. Davies*, 1976, 181-219; = MARTYN, *The Gospel of John in Christian History*, 1978, 9-54.

* —— Glimpses into the History of the Johannine Community: From Its Origin through the Period of Its Life in Which the Fourth Gospel Was Composed. — DE JONGE (ed.), *L'évangile de Jean*, 1977 (²1987), 149-175; = MARTYN, *The Gospel of John in Christian History*, 1978, 90-121.

* MARXSEN, W., *Einleitung in das Neue Testament. Eine Einführung in ihre Probleme*, Gütersloh, 1963, ²·³1964, ⁴1978 ("völlig neu bearbeitete Auflage").
ET: *Introduction to the New Testament: An Approach to Its Problems*, trans. G. Buswell, Philadelphia, PA, 1968.

MATEOS, J. – BARRETO, J., *El evangelio de Juan. Análisis lingüístico y comentario exegético* (Lectura del Nuevo Testamento, 4), Madrid, 1979.

* MATSUNAGA, K., Review of FORTNA, *Predecessor* [1988]. — *Bib* 72 (1991) 282-286.

MATTILL, A.J., JR., Johannine Communities behind the Fourth Gospel: Georg Richter's Analysis. — *TS* 38 (1977) 294-315.

* MAYER, A., Elijah and Elisha in John's Signs Source. — *ExpT* 99 (1987-88) 171-173.

McCAUGHY, L.C., *Toward a Descriptive Analysis of EINAI as a Linking Verb in New Testament Greek* (SBL DS, 6), Missoula, MT, 1972.

* McMORROW, L., Review of FORTNA, *Gospel of Signs* [1970]. — *IrTQ* 39 (1972) 306-310, esp. pp. 306-308.

MCPOLIN, J., *John* (New Testament Message, 6), Wilmington, DE – Dublin, 1979.

MCRORY, J., *The Gospel of St. John with Notes, Critical and Explanatory*, Dublin, ³1908.

MEEKS, W.A., *The Prophet-King: Moses Traditions and the Johannine Christology* (SupplNT, 14), Leiden, 1967.

— The Man from Heaven in Johannine Sectarianism. — *JBL* 91 (1972) 44-72; = ASHTON (ed.), *The Interpretation*, 1986, 141-173.

— "Am I a Jew?" Johannine Christianity and Judaism. — *FS M. Smith*, vol. I, 1975, 163-186.

MEIER, J.P., *A Marginal Jew: Rethinking the Historical Jesus*. I. *The Roots of the Problem and the Person* (AB Reference Library), New York – London, 1991.

MENDNER, S., Johanneische Literarkritik. — *TZ* 8 (1952) 418-434.

MENKEN, M.J.J., The Old Testament Quotation from Isa 40,3 in John 1,23. — *Bib* 66 (1985) 190-250.

— The Provenance and Meaning of the Old Testament Quotation in John 6:31. — *NT* 30 (1988) 39-56.

— The Old Testament Quotation in John 6,45: Source and Redaction. — *ETL* 64 (1988) 164-172.

— Die Form des Zitates aus Jes 6,10 in Joh 12,40. Ein Beitrag zum Schriftgebrauch des vierten Evangelisten. — *BZ* 32 (1988) 189-209.

— Die Redaktion des Zitates aus Sach 9,9 in Joh 12,15. — *ZNW* 80 (1989) 193-209.

— The Translation of Psalm 41.10 in John 13.18. — *JSNT* 40 (1990) 61-79.

— De christologie van het vierde evangelie. Een overzicht van resultaten van recent onderzoek. — *NTT* 45 (1991) 16-33. ET: The Christology of the Fourth Gospel: A Survey of Recent Research. — *FS M. de Jonge*, 1993, 292-320.

— The Old Testament Quotation in John 19,36: Sources, Redaction, Background. — *FS F. Neirynck*, vol. III, 1992, 2101-2118.

— The Textual Form and the Meaning of the Quotation from Zech 12:10 in John 19,37. — *CBQ* 55 (1993) 494-511.

* MENOUD, P.-H., Le problème johannique. — *RTP* 29 (1941) 236-256; 30 (1942) 155-175; 31 (1943) 80-101.

* — *L'évangile de Jean d'après les recherches récentes* (CTAP, 3), Neuchâtel – Paris, 1943, ²1947.

* — Les études johanniques de Bultmann à Barrett. — BRAUN (ed.), *L'évangile de Jean*, 1958, 11-40.

MERCIER, R., La mémoire de l'Écriture dans le quatrième évangile. — *La théologie au risque de l'histoire*, 1994, 113-131.

* MERKEL, H., Auf den Spuren des Urmarkus? Ein neuer Fund und seine Beurteilung. — *ZTK* 71 (1974) 123-144.

— Das "geheime Evangelium" nach Markus. — SCHNEEMELCHER (ed.), *Neutestamentliche Apokryphen*, vol. I, ⁵1987, 89-92.

* MERLIER, O., *Le quatrième évangile. La question johannique*, Athens, 1961.

— *Itinéraires de Jésus et chronologie dans le quatrième évangile* (Études néotestamentaires, 11), Paris, 1961.

METZGER, B.M., *A Textual Commentary on the Greek New Testament: A Companion Volume to the United Bible Societies' Greek New Testament (Third Edition)*, London – New York, 1971.

MEYER, A., Die Behandlung der johanneischen Frage im letzten Jahrzehnt. — *TR* 2 (1899) 255-263, 295-305, 333-345.

—— Johanneische Literatur. — *TR* 5 (1902) 316-333, 497-507; 7 (1904) 473-484, 519-531.

—— Das Johannesevangelium. — *TR* 9 (1906) 302-311, 340-359, 381-397.

—— Die Johanneische Literatur. — *TR* 13 (1910) 15-26, 63-75, 94-100, 151-162; 15 (1912) 239-249, 278-293, 295-305.

* MEYER, E., *Ursprung und Anfänge des Christentums. I. Die Evangelien*, Stuttgart – Berlin, 1921.

MEYER, H.A.W., *Kritisch-exegetisches Handbuch über das Evangelium des Johannes* (KEK, 2), Göttingen, 1834, ^{2}1852, ^{3}1856, ^{4}1862, ^{5}1869.
ET: *Critical and Exegetical Handbook to the Gospel of John*, trans. from the 5th ed. of the German by W. Urwick, rev. and ed. by F. CROMBIE (Critical and Exegetical Commentary on the New Testament, 2), 2 vols., Edinburgh, ^{2}1883-1884.

MEYER, M.W., The Youth in the Secret Gospel of Mark. — *Semeia* 49 (1990) 129-153.

* MICHAELIS, W., *Einleitung in das Neue Testament. Die Entstehung, Sammlung und Überlieferung des Neuen Testaments*, Bern, 1946, ^{2}1954.

* MICHAELS, J.R., *John* (NIBC, 4), Peabody, MA, 1989.

* MICHEL, O., Der Anfang der Zeichen Jesus (Joh 2,11). — *FS A. Köberle*, 1958, 15-22; = MICHEL, *Dienst am Wort*, 1986, 148-153.

MICHIELS, R., De opwekking van Lazarus. — *Collationes* 5 (1975) 433-447.

MIRANDA, J.P., *Die Sendung Jesu im vierten Evangelium. Religions- und theologiegeschichtliche Untersuchungen zu den Sendungsformeln* (SBS, 87), Stuttgart, 1977.

* MLAKUZHYIL, G., *The Christocentric Literary Structure of the Fourth Gospel* (AnBib, 117), Rome, 1987. – Diss. Rome, Pontifical Gregorian University (dir. A. Vanhoye).

MOELLER, H.R. – KRAMER, A., An Overlooked Structural Pattern in New Testament Greek. — *NT* (1961-62) 25-35.

MOFFATT, J., *An Introduction to the Literature of the New Testament* (International Theological Library), Edinburgh, 1911, ^{2}1912, ^{3}1918.

MOLLA, C.F., *Le quatrième évangile*, Genève, 1977.

MOLLAT, D., L'évangile selon saint Jean. — ID. – BRAUN, *L'évangile et les épîtres de saint Jean* (La Sainte Bible traduite en français sous la direction de l'École biblique de Jérusalem), Paris, 1953, 7-198; ^{2}1960, 7-193; ^{3}1973, 7-227.

—— Le semeion johannique. — COPPENS *et al.* (eds.), *Sacra Pagina*, vol. II, 1959, 209-218; = MOLLAT, *Études johanniques*, 1979, 91-101.

MOLONEY, F.J., *The Word Became Flesh* (Theology Today Series, 14), Dublin – Cork, 1977.

* —— From Cana to Cana (Jn 2:1–4:54) and the Fourth Evangelist's Concept of Correct (and Incorrect) Faith. — *Salesianum* 40 (1978) 817-843; = LIVINGSTONE (ed.), *Studia Biblica 1978*, vol. II, 1980, 185-213.

—— The First Days... from Cana to Cana (John 1:19–4:54). — McGINLAY (ed.), *The Years of John*, 1985, 9-17; = Reading John 1:19 to 4:54: A Question of Faith. — ID., *The Living Voice of the Gospel*, 1986, 203-220.

—— *The Living Voice of the Gospel*, New York – Mahwah, NJ, 1986.

—— Johannine Theology. — *NJBC*, 1990, 1417-1426.

—— *Belief in the Word: Reading John 1–4*, Minneapolis, MN, 1993.

MORGEN, M., L'exégèse johannique à l'heure actuelle. Quelques orientations. — BOURG et al. (eds.), *Variations johanniques*, 1989, 243-263.

—— *Afin que le monde soit sauvé. Jésus révèle sa mission de salut dans l'évangile de Jean* (LD, 154), Paris, Cerf, 1993.

MORRIS, L., *The Gospel according to John: The English Text with Introduction, Exposition and Notes* (NICNT), Grand Rapids, MI, 1971.

—— *Studies in the Fourth Gospel*, Grand Rapids, MI, 1969.

—— *Jesus is the Christ: Studies in the Theology of John*, Grand Rapids, MI – Leicester, 1989.

MÜLLER, P.-G., *Lexikon exegetischer Fachbegriffe* (Biblische Basis Bücher, 1), Stuttgart – Kevelaer, 1985.

IT: *Lessico della scienza biblica*, ed. M. MASINI (LoB, 3/11), Brescia, 1990.

* MÜLLER, U.B., *Die Geschichte der Christologie in der johanneischen Gemeinde* (SBS, 77), Stuttgart, 1975.

* —— Die Bedeutung des Kreuzestodes Jesu im Johannesevangelium. Erwägungen zur Kreuzestheologie im Neuen Testament. — *KerDog* 21 (1975) 49-71.

—— *Die Menschwerdung des Gottessohnes. Frühchristliche Inkarnationsvorstellungen und die Anfänge des Doketismus* (SBS, 140), Stuttgart, 1990.

* MUHLACK, G., *Die Parallelen von Lukas-Evangelium und Apostelgeschichte* (Theologie und Wirklichkeit, 8), Frankfurt, 1979.

MUILENBURG, J., Literary Forms in the Fourth Gospel. — *JBL* 51 (1932) 40-53; = M.W.G. STIBBE (ed.), *The Gospel of John as Literature*, 1993, 65-76.

MULDER, H., Ontstaan en doel van het vierde evangelie. — *GTT* 69 (1969) 233-258.

MUÑOZ LEÓN, D., Panorama de un cuarto de siglo de Bibliografía sobre el Evangelio de San Juan. — RABANOS ESPINOSA – MUÑOZ LEON, *Bibliografía joánica*, 1990, 13-40.

* MURPHY, D., Review of FORTNA, *Gospel of Signs* [1970]. — *RRel* 29 (1970) 927-928.

* MURPHY-O'CONNOR, J., Review of FORTNA, *Gospel of Signs* [1970]. — *RB* 77 (1970) 603-606.

* MUSSNER, F., *Die Wunder Jesu. Eine Einführung* (SK, 10), München, 1967.

NAUCK, W., *Die Tradition und der Charakter des ersten Johannesbriefes* (WUNT, 3), Tübingen, 1953.

NEIRYNCK, F., The "Other Disciple" in Jn 18,15-16. — *ETL* 51 (1975) 113-141; = ID., *Evangelica I*, 1982, 335-363 (363-364: Additional Notes).

—— L'évangile de Marc. À propos du commentaire de R. Pesch. — *ETL* 53
* (1977) 153-181; 55 (1979) 1-42; = *ALBO* V, 42, Leuven, 1979; = ID., *Evangelica I*, 1982, 491-561.

—— John and the Synoptics. — DE JONGE (ed.), *L'évangile de Jean*, 1977 (²1987), 73-106; = *Evangelica I*, 1982, 365-400.

* —— with the collaboration of J. DELOBEL, T. SNOY, G. VAN BELLE and F. VAN SEGBROECK, L'évangile de Jean. Examen critique du commentaire de M.-É. Boismard et A. Lamouille. — *ETL* 53 (1977) 363-478.

* —— *Jean et les Synoptiques. Examen critique de l'exégèse de M.-É. Boismard* (BETL, 49), Leuven, 1979 (3-120 = *ETL* 53 [1977] 363-478).

—— L'*epanalepsis* et la critique littéraire. À propos de l'évangile de Jean. — *ETL* 56 (1980) 303-338; = ID., *Evangelica I*, 1982, 143-178 (178: Note additionnelle).

* —— De Semeia-bron in het vierde evangelie. Kritiek van een hypothese. — *AcAn (Letteren)* 45 (1983), n° 1, 1-28.
ET: The Signs Source in the Fourth Gospel: A Critique of the Hypothesis. — ID., *Evangelica II*, 1991, 651-677 (650, 677-678: Additional Note).

—— & VAN SEGBROECK, F., *New Testament Vocabulary: A Companion Volume to the Concordance* (BETL, 65), Leuven, 1984.

—— John and the Synoptics: The Empty Tomb Stories. — *NTS* 30 (1984) 161-187; = ID., *Evangelica II*, 1991, 571-597 (597, 600: Additional Note).

* —— John 4,46-54: Signs Source and/or Synoptic Gospels. — *ETL* 60 (1984) 367-375; = ID., *Evangelica II*, 1991, 679-687 (687-688: Additional Note).

* —— Note sur Jn 21,14. — *ETL* 64 (1988) 429-432; = ID., *Evangelica II*, 1991, 689-692.

* —— Review of FORTNA, *Predecessor* [1988]. — *ETL* 65 (1989) 167-170.

—— Review of RUCKSTUHL, *Die literarische Einheit* [1987]. — *ETL* 65 (1989) 170-171.

—— The Apocryphal Gospels and the Gospel of Mark. — SEVRIN (ed.), *The New Testament in Early Christianity*, 1989, 123-175; = NEIRYNCK, *Evangelica II*, 1991, 715-767 (768-772: Additional Notes).

—— Parentheses in the Fourth Gospel. — *ETL* 65 (1989) 119-123; = ID., *Evangelica II*, 1991, 693-697 (697-698: Additional Note).

—— John and the Synoptics: A Response to P. Borgen. — DUNGAN (ed.), *The Interrelations of the Gospels*, 1990, 438-450; = NEIRYNCK, *Evangelica II*, 1991, 699-711: "John 5,1-18 and the Gospel of Mark: A Response to P. Borgen" (712: Additional Note).

* —— John 21. — *NTS* 36 (1990) 321-336; = ID., *Evangelica II*, 1991, 601-616 (616: Additional Note).

—— The Anonymous Disciple in John 1. — *ETL* 66 (1990) 1-37; = ID., *Evangelica II*, 1991, 617-649 (649: Additional Note).

—— John and the Synoptics: 1975-1990. — DENAUX (ed.), *John and the Synoptics*, 1992, 3-62.

—— Review of RUCKSTUHL – DSCHULNIGG, *Stilkritik und Verfasserfrage* [1991]. — *ETL* 67 (1992) 437-440.

—— The Historical Jesus: Reflections on an Inventory. — *ETL* 70 (1994) 221-234.

NEUGEBAUER, F., *Die Entstehung des Johannesevangeliums. Altes und Neues zur Frage seines historischen Ursprungs* (AzT, I/36), Stuttgart, 1978.

* NEWMAN, B.M., JR., Review of BULTMANN, *John* [1971]. — *BTrans* 24 (1973) 336-337.

* NEYREY, J.H., *Christ Is Community: The Christologies of the New Testament* (GNS, 13), Wilmington, DE, 1985.

* —— *John's Christology of Revolt: John's Christology in Social-Science Perspective*, Philadelphia, PA, 1989.

—— "My Lord and My God": The Divinity of Jesus in John's Gospel. — *SBL 1986 Seminar Papers*, 1986, 152-171.

NICHOLSON, G.C., *Death as Departure: The Johannine Descent-Ascent Schema* (SBL DS, 63), Chico, CA, 1983. – Diss. Vanderbilt University, 1980 (dir. J.R. Donahue).

* NICOL, W., *The Sēmeia in the Fourth Gospel: Tradition and Redaction* (SupplNT, 32), Leiden, 1972. – Diss. Kampen (dir. H. Ridderbos).

—— The History of Johannine Research During the Past Century. — *Neotestamentica* 6 (1972) 8-18.

NIELSEN, H.K., *Heilung und Verkündigung. Das Verständnis der Heilung und ihres Verhältnisses zur Verkündigung bei Jesus und in der ältesten Kirche* (ATDan, 22), Leiden, 1987.

* NIEMAND, C., Review of FORTNA, *Predecessor* [1988]. — *SNTU* 15 (1990) 176-178.

—— *Die Fusswaschungserzählung des Johannesevangeliums. Untersuchungen zu ihrer Entstehung und Überlieferung im Urchristentum* (Studia Anselmiana, 114), Roma, 1993. – Diss. Linz, 1993.

* NOACK, B., *Zur johanneischen Tradition. Beiträge zur Kritik an der literarkritischen Analyse des vierten Evangeliums* (LSSK T, 3), København, 1954.

* NOETZEL, H., *Christus und Dionysos. Bemerkungen zum religionsgeschichtlichen Hintergrund von Johannes 2,1-11* (AzT, 1), Stuttgart, 1960.

NORDEN, E., *Agnostos Theos. Untersuchungen zur Formengeschichte religiöser Rede*, Leipzig – Berlin, 1913.

NÜTZEL, J.M., "Komm und sieh" – Wege zum österlichen Glauben im Johannesevangelium. — OBERLINNER (ed.), *Auferstehung Jesu*, 1986, 162-189.

O'DAY, G.R., *Irony and the Johannine Theology of Revelation: An Investigation of John 4*, diss. Graduate School of Emory University, 1983 (dir.: W.A. Beardslee).

—— *Revelation in the Fourth Gospel: Narrative Mode and Theological Claim*, Philadelphia, PA, 1986.

—— Narrative Mode and Theological Claim: A Study in the Fourth Gospel. — *JBL* 105 (1986) 657-668.

—— *The World Disclosed: John's Story and Narrative Preaching*, St. Louis, MI, 1987.

—— "I Have Overcome the World" (John 16:33): Narrative Time in John 13–17. — *Semeia* 53 (1991) 153-166.

* O'GRADY, J.F., *The Four Gospels and the Jesus Tradition*, New York – Mahwah, NJ, 1989.

OLMSTEAD, A.T.E., The Chronology of Jesus' Life. — *ATR* 24 (1942) 1-26.

—— Could an Aramaic Gospel Be Possible? — *JNES* 1 (1942) 41-75.

—— *Jesus in the Light of History*, New York, 1942.

OLSHAUSEN, H., *Erklärung des Evangeliums Johannes* (Biblischer Commentar über sämmtliche Schriften des Neuen Testaments, II/1), Köningsberg, 1832, ³1838, ⁴1861 (ed. A. EBRARD).

OLSSON, B., *Structure and Meaning in the Fourth Gospel: A Text-Linguistic Analysis of John 2:1-11 and 4:1-42* (ConBibNT, 6), Lund, 1974.

* ONUKI, T., Die Semeia-Quelle im Johannesevangelium, eine formgeschichtliche Studie. — *Journal of Religious Studies* (Japanese Association for Religious Studies) 225 (1975) 1-14 [in Japanese].

* O'ROURKE, J.J., The Historic Present in the Gospel of John. — *JBL* 93 (1974) 585-590.

* —— Εἰς and ἐν in John. — *BTrans* 25 (1974) 139-142.

* —— Asides in the Gospel of John. — *NT* 21 (1979) 210-219.

OVERBECK, F., *Das Johannesevangelium. Studien zur Kritik seiner Erforschung*, ed. C. BERNOUILLI, Tübingen, 1911.

* PADILLA, C., *Los milagros de la "Vida de Apolonio de Tiana". Morfología del relato de milagro y géneros afines* (Estudios de Filología Neotestamentaria, 4), Córdoba, 1991.

PAINTER, J., Eschatological Faith in the Gospel of John. — *FS L.L. Morris*, Grand Rapids, MI, 1974, 36-52; cp. ID., *The Quest for the Messiah*, 1991, 327-348.

* —— *John: Witness and Theologian*, London, 1975.

—— Surveying the Fourth Gospel. — *JTSouthAfr* 20 (1977) 41-53.

—— Christ and the Church in John 1,45-51. — DE JONGE (ed.), *L'Évangile de Jean*, 1977, 359-362.

—— *Reading John's Gospel Today*, Atlanta, GA, 1978.

—— The Church and Israel in the Gospel of John: A Response. — *NTS* 25 (1978-79) 103-122.

—— Johannine Symbols: A Case Study in Epistemology. — *JTSouthAfr* 27 (1979) 26-41.

—— Glimpses of the Johannine Community in the Farewell Discourses. — *AustBR* 28 (1980) 21-38.

—— The Farewell Discourses and the History of Johannine Christianity. — *NTS* 27 (1980-81) 525-543.

—— Christology and the Fourth Gospel: A Study of the Prologue. — *AustBR* 31 (1983) 45-62.

—— Christology and the History of the Johannine Community in the Prologue of the Fourth Gospel. — *NTS* 30 (1984) 460-474.

—— John 9 and the Interpretation of the Fourth Gospel. — *JSNT* 28 (1986) 31-61; cp. ID., *The Quest for the Messiah*, 1991, 175-213.

—— C.H. Dodd and the Christology of the Fourth Gospel. — *JTSouthAfr* 59 (1987) 42-56.

—— Text and Context in John 5. — *AustBR* 35 (1987) 28-34; cp. ID., *The Quest for the Messiah*, 1991, 175-213.

—— Tradition and Interpretation in John 6. — *NTS* 35 (1989) 421-450; cp. ID., *The Quest for the Messiah*, 1991, 215-244.

—— Quest and Rejection Stories in John. — *JSNT* 36 (1989) 17-46; cp. ID., *The Quest for the Messiah*, 1991, 129-173.

* —— Review of FORTNA, *Predecessor* [1988]. — *Pacifica* 3 (1990) 344-346.

—— Quest Stories in John 1-4. — *JSNT* 41 (1991) 33-70; cp. ID., *The Quest for the Messiah*, 1991, 129-173.

—— Tradition, History and Interpretation in John 10. — BEUTLER – FORTNA (eds.), *The Shepherd Discourse*, 1991, 53-74; cp. ID., *The Quest for the Messiah*, 1991, 287-311.

* —— *The Quest for the Messiah: The History, Literature and Theology of the Johannine Community*, Edinburgh, 1991, ²1993.

—— Quest Stories in John and the Synoptics. — DENAUX (ed.), *John and the Synoptics*, 1992, 498-506; cp. ID., *The Quest for the Messiah*, 1991, 129-173.

—— The Enigmatic Johannine Son of Man. — *FS F. Neirynck*, 1992, vol. III, 1869-1887.

PANCARO, S., *The Law in the Fourth Gospel. The Torah and the Gospel, Moses and Jesus, Judaism and Christianity according to John* (SupplNT, 42), Leiden, 1975.

PARKER, P., Bethany beyond Jordan. — *JBL* 74 (1955) 257-261.

—— Two Editions of John. — *JBL* 75 (1956) 303-314.

* PERKINS, P., The Gospel according to John. — *NJBC*, 1990, 942-985.

—— Johannine Traditions in Ap. Jas. (NHC I,2). — *JBL* 101 (1982) 403-414.

* PERRIN, N., *The New Testament: An Introduction. Proclamation and Parenesis, Myth and History*, New York, 1974, ²1982 (& D.C. DULING, ed. R. FERM).

—— *A Modern Pilgrimage in New Testament Christology*, Philadelphia, PA, 1974.

PESCH, R., *Das Markusevangelium*. I. Teil: *Einleitung und Kommentar zu Kap. 1,1–8,26* (HTKNT, 3/1), Freiburg – Basel – Wien, 1976, ³1980 ("Nachtrag"), ⁴1984 ("2. Nachtrag").

—— Das Weinwunder bei der Hochzeit zu Kana (Joh 2,1-12). Zur Herkunft der Wundererzählung. — *TGegw* 24 (1981) 219-225.

* PETZKE, G., *Die Traditionen über Apollonius von Tyana und das Neue Testament* (SCHNT, 2), Leiden, Brill, 1970. – Diss. Mainz, 1968.

* —— Die historische Frage nach den Wundertaten Jesu. Dargestellt am Beispiel des Exorzismus Mark. ix. 14-29 par. — *NTS* 22 (1975-76) 180-204.

PHILLIPS, G.L., Faith and Vision in the Fourth Gospel. — CROSS (ed.), *Studies in the Fourth Gospel*, 1957, 83-96.

PLUMMER, A., *The Gospel according to St John* (The Cambridge Bible for Schools and Colleges), Cambridge, 1880; repr. 1923.

* POKORNÝ, P., *Die Entstehung der Christologie. Voraussetzungen einer Theologie des Neuen Testaments*, Stuttgart, 1985.

* PORSCH, F., *Johannes-Evangelium* (SKK NT, 4), Stuttgart, 1988.

* POYTHRESS, V.S., The Use of the Intersentence Conjunctions *De, Oun, Kai*, and Asyndeton in the Gospel of John. — *NT* 26 (1984) 312-340.

* —— Testing for Johannine Authorship by Examining the Use of Conjunctions. — *WestTJ* 46 (1984) 350-369.

PRICE, J.L., *The New Testament: Its History and Theology*, New York, 1987.

* PRYOR, J.W., *John: Evangelist of the Covenant People. The Narrative and Themes of the Fourth Gospel*, London, 1992.

QUIÉVREUX, F., La structure symbolique de l'évangile de saint Jean. — *RHPR* 33 (1953) 123-165.

RABANOS ESPINOSA, R. – MUÑOZ LEÓN, D., *Bibliografía joánica. Evangelio, Cartas y Apocalípsis, 1960-1986* (BHBib, 14), Madrid, 1990.

* RÄISÄNEN, H., *Die Mutter Jesu im Neuen Testament* (AASF, B/247), Helsinki, 1969, ²1989.

RAVASI, G. *et al.*, *Fede e cultura dal Vangelo di Giovanni* (Teologia Viva), Bologna, 1986.

* REBELL, W., *Gemeinde als Gegenwelt. Zur soziologischen und didaktischen Funktion des Johannesevangeliums* (BET, 20), Frankfurt – Bern – New York, 1987.

* REIM, G., *Studien zum alttestamentlichen Hintergrund des Johannesevangeliums* (SNTS MS, 22), Cambridge, 1974. – Diss. Oxford, 1967 (dir. G.D. Kilpatrick).
—— Johannes 21 – ein Anhang? — *FS G.D. Kilpatrick*, 1976, 330-337.
—— Probleme der Abschiedsreden. — *BZ* 20 (1976) 117-122.
* —— Joh 9 – Tradition und zeitgenössische messianische Diskussion. — *BZ* 22 (1978) 245-253.
—— Targum und Johannesevangelium. — *BZ* 27 (1983) 1-13.
—— Johannesevangelium und Synagogegottesdienst. Eine Beobachtung. — *BZ* 27 (1983) 101.
—— Joh 8,44 Gotteskinder/Teufelskinder. Wie antijudaistisch ist "die wohl antijudaistischste Äusserung des NT"? — *NTS* 30 (1984) 619-624.
—— Jesus as God in the Fourth Gospel: The Old Testament Background. — *NTS* 30 (1984) 158-160.
—— Zur Lokalisierung der johanneischen Gemeinde. — *BZ* 32 (1988) 72-86.
—— Nordreich – Südreich. Der vierte Evangelist als Vertreter christlicher Nordreichtheologie. — *BZ* 36 (1942) 235-240.
REINHARTZ, A., *John 20:30-31 and the Purpose of the Fourth Gospel*, diss. Hamilton (Ontario), McMaster University, Department of Religious Studies, 1983 (dir. E.P. Sanders). — Cf. *DissAbstr* 44 (1983-84) 3095.
—— Jesus as Prophet: Predicative Prolepses in the Fourth Gospel. — *JSNT* 36 (1989) 3-16.
REITZENSTEIN, R., *Hellenistische Wundererzählungen*, Leipzig, 1906, ³1974 (Darmstadt).
* REMUS, H.E., Miracles, New Testament. — *ABD*, vol. 4, 1992, 856-869.
* RENGSTORF, K.H., art. Σημεῖον. — *TWNT* 7 (1964) 199-261; ET: *TDNT* 7 (1971) 200-261.
* RENNER, R., *Die Wunder Jesu in Theologie und Unterricht*, Lahr/Schwarzwald, 1966.
* RICHARD, E., Expressions of Double Meaning and Their Function in the Gospel of John. — *NTS* 31 (1985) 96-112.
* —— *Jesus: One and Many. The Christological Concept of New Testament Authors*, Wilmington, DE, 1988.
RICHARDSON, A., Sign in the NT. — *IDB*, 1962, 346-347.
RICHTER, G., Die Deutung des Kreuzestodes Jesu in der Leidensgeschichte des Johannesevangeliums (Joh 13–19). — *BibLeb* 9 (1968) 21-36; = ID., *Studien*, 1977, 58-73.
—— Blut und Wasser aus der durchbohrten Seite Jesu (John 19,34b). — *MTZ* 21 (1970) 1-21; = ID., *Studien*, 1977, 120-142.
—— Die Fleischwerdung des Logos im Johannesevangelium. — *NT* 13 (1971) 81-126; 14 (1972) 257-276; = ID., *Studien*, 1977, 149-198.
—— Der Vater und Gott Jesu und seiner Brüder in Joh 20,17. Ein Beitrag zur Christologie im Johannesevangelium. — *MTZ* 24 (1973) 95-114; = ID., *Studien*, 1977, 266-280.
* —— Zur sogenannten Semeia-Quelle des Johannesevangeliums. — *MTZ* 25 (1974) 64-73; = ID., *Studien*, 1977, 281-287.
* RIDDERBOS, H.N., *Het evangelie naar Johannes. Proeve van een theologische exegese*. I. *Hoofdstuk 1–10*. II. *Hoofdstuk 11–21*, Kampen, 1987, 1992.
RIEDL, J., *Das Heilswerk Jesu nach Johannes* (FTS, 93), Freiburg – Basel – Wien, 1973.

RIESENFELD, H., Zu den johanneischen ἵνα-Sätzen. — *StudTheol* 19 (1965) 213-220.

RIGA, P., Signs of Glory: The Use of "Semeion" in St. John's Gospel. — *Interpr* 17 (1963) 402-424.

RINIKER, C., Jean 6,1-21 et les évangiles synoptiques. — KAESTLI *et al.* (eds.), *La communauté johannique*, 1990, 41-67.

* RISSI, M., Die Hochzeit in Kana (Joh 2,1-11). — *FS O. Cullmann I*, 1967, 76-92.

— Review of FORTNA, *Gospel of Signs* [1970]. — *Interpr* 25 (1971) 372-373.

* ROBERGE, M., Notices de conclusion et rédaction du quatrième évangile. — *LavalTP* 31 (1975) 49-53.

— Jean 6,26 et le rassasiement eschatologique. — *LavalTP* 45 (1989) 339-349.

ROBERT, R., Un examen critique de l'exégèse de M.-É. Boismard. — *RThom* 83 (1983) 625-638.

ROBERTS, C., John 20:30-31 and 21:24-25. — *JTS* 38 (1987) 409-410.

ROBINSON, B.P., Christ as a Northern Prophet in St. John. — *Scripture* 17 (1965) 104-105.

ROBINSON, J.A.T., Destination and Purpose of St. John's Gospel. — *NTS* 6 (1959-60) 117-131; = ID., *Twelve New Testament Studies*, 1962, 107-125.

— Elijah, John and Jesus: An Essay in Detection. — *NTS* 4 (1957-58) 263-281; = ID., *Twelve New Testament Studies*, 1962, 28-52.

* — The New Look on the Fourth Gospel. — *StEv*, 1959, 338-350; = ID., *Twelve New Testament Studies*, 1962, 94-106.

— The Relation of the Prologue to the Gospel of St John. — *NTS* 9 (1962-63) 120-129; = ID., *Twelve More New Testament Studies*, 1984, 65-76.

* — *The Priority of John*, ed. J.F. COAKLEY, London, 1985.

* ROBINSON, J.M., Recent Research in the Fourth Gospel. — *JBL* 78 (1959) 242-246.

* — Kerygma and History in the New Testament. — HYATT (ed.), *The Bible*, 1965, 114-150; = ID. – KOESTER, *Trajectories*, 1971, 20-70.

GT: Kerygma und Geschichte im Neuen Testament. — *ZNW* 62 (1965) 294-337; = ID. – KOESTER, *Entwicklungslinien*, 1970, 20-66.

* — On the Gattung of Mark (and John). — MILLER – HADIDIAN (eds.), *Jesus and Man's Hope*, vol. I, 1970, 99-129; = ID., *The Problem of History in Mark*, 1982, 11-39.

GT: Zur Gattung des Markusevangeliums. — ID., *Messiasgeheimnis und Geschichtsverständnis*, 1989, 126-148.

* — The Miracles Source of John. — *JAAR* 34 (1971) 339-348.

* — The Johannine Trajectory. — ID. – KOESTER, *Trajectories*, 1971, 232-268.

* — The Literary Composition of Mark. — SABBE (ed.), *L'évangile selon Marc*, 1974 (²1988), 11-19 (19-20: Additional Note).

GT: Zur Komposition des Markus-Evangeliums. — ID., *Messiasgeheimnis und Geschichtsverständnis*, 1989, 107-114.

ROLOFF, J., *Neues Testament* (Neukirchener Arbeitsbücher), Neukirchen-Vluyn, 1977.

ROTH, W., Mark, John and Their Old Testament Codes. — DENAUX, A. (ed.), *John and the Synoptics*, 1992, 458-465.

ROUSTANG, F., Les moments de l'acte de la foi et ses conditions de possibilité. Essai d'interprétation du dialogue avec la Samaritaine. — *RSR* 46 (1958) 344-378.

RUCKSTUHL, E., Literarkritik am Johannesevangelium und eucharistische Rede (Joh. 6,51c-58). — *DivThom* 23 (1945) 153-190, 301-333.

* —— *Die literarische Einheit des Johannesevangeliums. Der gegenwärtige Stand der einschlägigen Forschungen* (SF, NF 3), Freiburg/Schw., 1951. Second edition: Mit einem Vorwort von M. HENGEL. Im Anhang: *Liste der johanneischen Stilmerkmale mit allen Belegstellen aus dem johanneischen Schrifttum. – Sprache und Stil im johanneischen Schrifttum. Die Frage ihrer Einheit und Einheitlichkeit* (NTOA, 5), Freiburg/Schw. – Göttingen, 1987.

—— Joh. 6,51c-59 – Redaktionell? — *ZNW* 44 (1952-53) 256-257.

* —— Johannine Language and Style: The Question of Their Unity. — DE JONGE (ed.), *L'évangile de Jean*, 1977 (²1987), 125-147.
GT: Sprache und Stil im johanneischen Schrifttum. Die Frage ihrer Einheit und Einheitlichkeit. — ID., *Die literarische Einheit*, ²1987, 304-331.

—— Kritische Arbeit am Johannesprolog. — *FS B. Reicke*, 1984, vol. II, 442-452; = ID., *Jesus im Horizont der Evangelien*, 1988, 265-276.

—— Der Jünger, den Jesus liebte. — *SNTU* 11 (1986) 131-167; = ID., *Jesus im Horizont der Evangelien*, 1988, 355-395, 400-401 ("Nachtrag").

* —— Zur Antithese Idiolekt-Soziolekt im johanneischen Schrifttum. — *SNTU* 12 (1987) 141-181; = ID., *Jesus im Horizont der Evangelien*, 1988, 219-264.

* —— & DSCHULNIGG, P., *Stilkritik und Verfasserfrage im Johannesevangelium. Die johanneischen Sprachmerkmale auf dem Hintergrund des Neuen Testaments und des zeitgenössischen hellenistischen Schrifttums* (NTOA, 17), Freiburg/Schw. – Göttingen, 1991.

* —— Die Speisung des Volkes durch Jesus und die Seeüberfahrt der Jünger nach Joh 6,1-25 im Vergleich zu den synoptischen Parallelen. — *FS F. Neirynck*, 1992, vol. III, 2001-2019.

SABBE, M., The Arrest of Jesus in Jn 18,1-11 and Its Relation to the Synoptic Gospels: A Critical Evaluation of A. Dauer's Hypothesis. — DE JONGE (ed.), *L'évangile de Jean*, 1977 (²1987), 203-234; = SABBE, *Studia Neotestamentica*, 1991, 355-388 (387-388: Additional Note).

—— John and the Synoptists: Neirynck vs. Boismard. — *ETL* 56 (1980) 125-131; = ID., *Studia Neotestamentica*, 1991, 389-395 (396-397: Additional Note).

—— Can Mt 11,27 and Lk 10,22 Be Called a Johannine Logion? — DELOBEL (ed.), *Logia*, 1982, 363-371; = SABBE, *Studia Neotestamentica*, 1991, 399-408 (409: Note).

—— The Footwashing in Jn 13 and Its Relation to the Synoptic Gospels. — *ETL* 57 (1982) 279-308; = ID., *Studia Neotestamentica*, 1991, 409-438 (439-441: Additional Note).

—— John 10 and Its Relationship to the Synoptic Gospels. — BEUTLER – FORTNA (eds.), *The Shepherd Discourse*, 1991, 75-93, 156-161; = SABBE, *Studia Neotestamentica*, 1991, 443-464 (465-466: Additional Note).

* —— The Trial of Jesus before Pilate in John and Its Relation to the Synoptic Gospels. — DENAUX (ed.), *John and the Synoptics*, 1992, 341-385; = SABBE, *Studia Neotestamentica*, 1991, 467-513.

474   BIBLIOGRAPHY

—— The Johannine Account of the Death of Jesus and Its Synoptic Parallels (Jn 19,16b-42). — *ETL* 70 (1994) 34-64.

SAHLIN, H., *Zur Typologie des Johannesevangeliums* (Uppsala Universitets Årsskrift, 1950/4), Uppsala – Leipzig, 1950.

SANDAY, W., *The Criticism of the Fourth Gospel: Eight Lectures on the Morse Foundation, Delivered in the Union Seminary, New York, in October and November, 1904*, Oxford – London, 1905.

SANDERS, E.P., *The Tendencies of the Synoptic Tradition* (SNTS MS, 9), Cambridge, 1969.

SANDERS, J.N. – MASTIN, B.A., *A Commentary on the Gospel according to St John* (BNTC), London, 1968.

* SASS, G., *Die Auferweckung des Lazarus* (BSt, 51), Neukirchen-Vluyn, 1967. DT: *De opwekking van Lazarus. Een uitleg van Johannes 11*, trans. M. Sanders (De christen in de tijd, 46), Antwerpen, 1969.

SCHANZ, P. *Commentar über das Evangelium des heiligen Johannes*, Tübingen, 1885.

SCHENK, W., Interne Strukturierungen im Schluss-Segment Johannes 21: Συγγραφή + σατυρικόν/ἐπίλογος. — *NTS* 38 (1992) 507-530.

* SCHENKE, H.-M. – FISCHER, K.-M. (with H.-G. BETHGE - G. SCHENKE), *Einleitung in die Schriften des Neuen Testaments. II. Die Evangelien und die anderen neutestamentlichen Schriften*, Gütersloh, 1979.

—— The Mystery of the Gospel of Mark. — *SecCent* 4 (1984) 65-82.

* SCHENKE, L., *Die Wundererzählungen des Markusevangelium* (SBB, 5), Stuttgart, 1974.

* —— Die formale und gedankliche Struktur von Joh 6,26-58. — *BZ* 24 (1980) 21-41.

* —— *Die wunderbare Brotvermehrung. Die neutestamentlichen Erzählungen und ihre Bedeutung*, Würzburg, 1983.

* —— Das Szenarium von Joh 6,1-25. — *TTZ* 92 (1983) 191-203.

* —— Die literarische Vorgeschichte von Joh 6,26-58. — *BZ* 29 (1985) 68-89.

* —— Der "Dialog Jesu mit den Juden" im Johannesevangelium: Ein Rekonstruktionsversuch. — *NTS* 34 (1988) 573-603.

* —— Joh 7–10: Eine dramatische Szene. — *BZ* 80 (1989) 172-192.

* —— Die literarische Entstehungsgeschichte von Joh 1,19-51. — *BibNot* 46 (1989) 24-57.

* —— Das johanneische Schisma und die "Zwölf". — *NTS* (1992) 105-121.

* —— *Das Johannesevangelium: Einführung – Text – dramatische Gestalt* (Urban-Taschenbucher, 446), Stuttgart – Berlin – Köln, 1992.

SCHENKEL, D., Über die neuesten Bearbeitungen des Lebens Jesu. — *TSK* 13 (1840) 736-808.

SCHIERSE, F.J., *Einleitung in das Neue Testament* (Leitfaden Theologie, 1), Düsseldorf, 1978.

SCHILLE, G., Traditionsgut im vierten Evangelium. — *TVers* 12 (1981) 77-89.

SCHLIER, H., Glauben, Erkennen, Lieben nach dem Johannesevangelium. — *FS G. Söhngen*, 1962, 98-111; = ID., *Besinnung auf das Neue Testament. Exegetische Aufsätze und Vorträge II*, Freiburg, 1964, 279-293 (FT: cf. VAN BELLE, no. 5507).

* —— Johannes 6 und dat johanneische Verständnis der Eucharistie. — J. SINT (ed.), *Bibel und zeitgemässiger Glaube*, vol. II, 1967, 69-95; = SCHLIER, *Das Ende der Zeit*, vol. II, 1971, 102-123.

* SCHMITHALS, W., *Neues Testament und Gnosis* (Erträge der Forschung, 208), Darmstadt, 1984.

—— *Einleitung in die drei ersten Evangelien* (de Gruyter-Lehrbuch), Berlin – New York, 1985.

* —— *Johannesevangelium und Johannesbriefe. Forschungsgeschichte und Analyse* (BZNW, 64), Berlin – New York, 1992.

* —— Die Bedeutung der Evangelien in der Theologiegeschichte bis zur Kanonbildung. — *FS F. Neirynck*, 1992, vol. I, 129-157.

* SCHNACKENBURG, R., *Das erste Wunder Jesu (Joh 2,1-11)*, Freiburg, 1950.

—— *Die Johannesbriefe. Auslegung* (HTKNT, 13/3), Freiburg – Basel – Wien, 1953, ²1963, ⁵1975.

* —— Johannesevangelium. — *LTK²* 5 (1960) 1101-1105.

* —— Zur Traditionsgeschichte von Joh 4,56-54. — *BZ* 8 (1964) 58-88.

* —— *Das Johannesevangelium* (HTKNT, 4/1-4), 4 vols., Freiburg – Basel – Wien, 1965, 1971, 1975, 1984.

I. Teil: *Einleitung und Kommentar zu Kap. 1–4*, 1965, ²1967, ³1972 (525-536: "Erster Nachtrag zum I. Band"), ⁴1978 (537-548: "Zweiter Nachtrag zum I. Band"), ⁵1981.

II. Teil: *Kommentar zu Kap. 5–12*, 1971, ²1977 (545-557: "Nachtrag zum II. Band"), ³1980.

III. Teil: *Kommentar zu Kap. 13–21*, 1975, ²1976, ³1979, ⁴1982 (471-484: "Nachtrag zum III. Band").

IV. Teil: *Ergänzende Auslegungen und Exkurse*, 1984 (pp. 185-234: "Nachträge zu den Kommentarbänden").

ET: *The Gospel according to St John* (HTCNT), New York, 1968, 1980, 1982.

Volume One: *Introduction and Commentary on Chapters 1–4*, trans. K. Smyth, New York, 1968.

Volume Two: *Commentary on Chapters 5–12*, trans. C. Hastings – F. McDonagh – D. Smith – R. Foley, New York, 1980.

Volume Three: *Commentary on Chapters 13–21*, trans. D. Smith – G.A. Kon, New York, 1982.

—— On the Origin of the Fourth Gospel. — MILLER – HADIDIAN (eds.), *Jesus and Man's Hope*, vol. I, 1970, 223-246.

* —— Zur johanneischen Forschung. — *BZ* 18 (1974) 272-287.

—— Joh 12,39-41. Zur christologischen Schriftauslegung des vierten Evangelisten. — *FS O. Cullmann II*, 1972, 167-177; = ID., *Das Johannesevangelium*, vol. IV, 1984, 143-152.

* —— Entwicklung und Stand der johanneischen Forschung seit 1955. — DE JONGE (ed.), *L'évangile de Jean*, 1977 (²1987), 19-44; = SCHNACKENBURG, *Das Johannesevangelium*, vol. IV, 1984, 9-32.

* —— Zur Redaktionsgeschichte des Johannesevangeliums. — ID., *Das Johannesevangelium*, vol. IV, 1984, 89-102.

—— Synoptische und johanneische Christologie. Ein Vergleich. — *FS F. Neirynck*, 1992, vol. III, 1723-1750.

* —— *Die Person Jesu Christi im Spiegel der vier Evangelien* (HTNT Supplementband, 4), Freiburg – Basel – Wien, 1993.

* SCHNEIDER, J., *Das Evangelium nach Johannes*, ed. E. FASCHER (THKNT, Sonderband), Berlin, 1976, ²1978.

* SCHNELLE, U., *Antidoketische Christologie im Johannesevangelium. Eine Untersuchung zur Stellung des vierten Evangeliums in der johanneischen Schule* (FRLANT, 144), Göttingen, 1987.
ET: *Antidocetic Christology in the Gospel of John: An Investigation of the Place of the Fourth Gospel in the Johannine School*, trans. L.M. Maloney, Minneapolis, MN, 1992.

—— Paulus und Johannes. — *EvT* 47 (1987) 212-228.
* —— Review of BJERKELUND, *Tauta Egeneto* [1987]. — *TLZ* 113 (1988) 185-186.
* —— Perspektiven der Johannesexegese. — *SNTU* 15 (1990) 59-72.
—— Johannes und die Synoptiker. — *FS F. Neirynck*, 1992, vol. III, 1799-1814.
→ Strecker

SCHNIDER, F., *Jesus der Prophet* (OBO, 2), Freiburg/Schw., 1973.
* —— & STENGER, W., *Johannes und die Synoptiker. Vergleich ihrer Parallelen* (BibH, 9), München, 1971.

SCHOEPS, H.-J., *Theologie und Geschichte des Judenchristentums*, Tübingen, 1949.

* SCHOLTEN, J.H., *Het evangelie naar Johannes. Kritisch historisch onderzoek*, Leiden, 1864.
GT: *Das Evangelium nach Johannes. Kritisch-historische Untersuchung*, trans. H. Lang, Berlin, 1867.

* SCHOTTROFF, L., *Der Glaubende und die feindliche Welt. Beobachtungen zum gnostischen Dualismus und seiner Bedeutung für Paulus und das Johannesevangelium* (WUNT, 37), Neukirchen-Vluyn, 1970.

SCHUCHARD, B.G., *Scripture within Scripture: The Interrelationship of Form and Function in the Old Testament Citations in the Gospel of John* (SBL DS, 133), Atlanta, GA, 1992. – Diss. Union Seminary; dir. M. Rissi)

SCHULZ, S., *Komposition und Herkunft der johanneischen Reden* (BWANT, 81), Stuttgart, 1957.
—— *Untersuchungen zur Menschensohn-Christologie im Johannesevangelium. Zugleich ein Beitrag zur Methodengeschichte der Auslegung des 4. Evangeliums*, Göttingen, 1957.
* —— *Die Stunde der Botschaft. Einführung in die Theologie der vier Evangelisten*, Hamburg – Zürich, 1967, ²1970.
* —— *Das Evangelium nach Johannes übersetzt und erklärt* (NTD, 4), Göttingen, 1972 (12th ed. in the series), ³1978. → Strathmann

SCHULZE, J.D., *Der schriftstellerische Charakter und Werth des Johannes, zum Behuf der Specialhermeneutik seiner Schriften untersucht und bestimmt. Voran ein Nachtrag über die Quellen der Briefe von Petrus, Jakobus und Judas, und über das Verhältniss dieser Briefe zu andern neutestamentlichen Schriften*, Weissenfels – Leipzig, 1803, ²1811.

SCHWARTZ, E., *Aporien im vierten Evangelium* (NAWG PH), Berlin, 1907, 342-372 (I); 1908, 115-148 (II), 149-188 (III), 497-560 (IV).

* SCHWEGLER, A., Die neueste Johanneïsche Literatur. — *TJb(T)* 1 (1842) 140-170, 288-309.

SCHWEITZER, A., *Von Reimarus zu Wrede. Eine Geschichte der Leben-Jesu-Forschung*, Tübingen, 1906.
ET: *Quest of the Historical Jesus: A Critical Study of Its Progress from Reimarus zu Wrede*, trans. W. Montgomery, London, 1910, ²1911; repr. 1936.

Geschichte der Leben-Jesu-Forschung. Zweite, neu bearbeitete und vermehrte Auflage des Werkes "Von Reimarus zu Wrede", Tübingen, 1913.

* SCHWEIZER, A., *Das Evangelium Johannes nach seinem innern Werthe und seiner Bedeutung für das Leben Jesu kritisch untersucht*, Leipzig, 1841.

—— *Die christlichen Glaubenslehre nach den protestantischen Grundsätzen*, 2 vols., Zürich, 1863, 1869.

* —— Das Johannesevangelium. Eine Erwiederung. — *PKZ* (1864), no. 17 (Sonnabend, 23. April), 362-363.

* SCHWEIZER, E., *Ego Eimi. Die religionsgeschichtliche Herkunft und theologische Bedeutung der johanneischen Bildreden, zugleich ein Beitrag zur Quellenfrage des vierten Evangeliums* (FRLANT, NF 38), Göttingen, 1939, ²1965.

* —— Die Heilung des Königlichen: Joh. 4,46-54. — *EvT* 11 (1951-52) 64-71; = ID., *Neotestamentica*, 1963, 407-415.

ET (summarized): Orthodox Proclamation: The Reinterpretation of the Gospel of John by the Fourth Evangelist. — *Interpr* 8 (1954) 387-409.

—— *Jesus Christus im vielfältigen Zeugnis des Neuen Testaments* (Siebenstern, 126), 1968, ²1970, ³1972.

ET: *Jesus*, trans. D.E. Green (NTLi), London, 1971.

FT: *La foi en Jésus Christ. Perspectives et langages du Nouveau Testament*, trans. M. Roy (Parole de Dieu), Paris, 1975.

* —— Review of FORTNA, *Gospel of Signs* [1970]. — *EvT* 30 (1970) 624-626.

* —— *Theologische Einleitung in das Neue Testament* (Grundrisse zum Neuen Testament. NTD Ergänzungsreihe, 2), Göttingen, 1989.

—— Johannes 6,51c-58 – vom Evangelisten übernommene Tradition? — *ZNW* 82 (1991) 274.

* SCOTT, M., *Sophia and the Johannine Jesus* (JSNT SS, 71), Sheffield, 1992. – Diss. Durham, 1990 (dir. J.D.G. Dunn).

SCROGGS, R., *Christology in Paul and John: The Reality and Revelation of God* (Proclamation Commentaries), Philadelphia, PA, 1988.

SEGALLA, G., *Panorama letterario del Nuovo Testamento* (LoB, 3/6), Brescia, 1986.

—— *Evangelo e Vangeli. Quattro evangelisti, quattro Vangeli, quattro destinatari* (La Bibbia nella storia, 10), Bologna, 1993.

* SEGOVIA, F.F., Review of FORTNA, *Predecessor* [1988]. — *CBQ* 52 (1990) 748-749.

—— Towards a New Direction in Johannine Scholarship: The Fourth Gospel from a Literary Perspective. — *Semeia* 53 (1991) 1-22.

—— The Journey(s) of the Word of God: A Reading of the Plot of the Fourth Gospel. — *Semeia* 53 (1991) 23-54.

—— The Final Farewell of Jesus: A Reading of John 20:30–21:25. — *Semeia* 53 (1991) 167-190.

SELONG, G., *The Cleansing of the Temple in Jn. 2,13-22: With a Reconsideration of the Dependence of the Fourth Gospel upon the Synoptics*, 3 vols., diss. Leuven, 1971 (dir. F. Neirynck).

* SIEGMAN, E.F., St. John's Use of the Synoptic Material. — *CBQ* (1968) 182-198.

* SLOYAN, G.S., *John* (Interpretation: A Bible Commentary for Teaching and Preaching), Atlanta, GA, 1988.

* —— *What Are They Saying about John?*, New York – Mahwah, NJ, 1991.

SMALLEY, S.S., The Sign in John XXI. — *NTS* 20 (1973-74) 275-288.

* —— *John: Evangelist and Interpreter*, Exeter, 1978; repr. Nashville, TN, 1984.

* —— Keeping up with Recent Studies. XII. St John's Gospel. — *ExpT* 97 (1985-86) 102-108.

* —— Review of FORTNA, *Predecessor* [1988]. — *ExpT* 101 (1989-90) 30.

* —— Review of VON WAHLDE, *The Earliest Version of John's Gospel* [1989]. — *JTS* 41 (1990) 611-613.

—— John, The Gospel according to. — METZGER – COOGAN (eds.), *The Oxford Companion to the Bible*, 1993, 373-377.

SMELIK, E.L., *Het evangelie naar Johannes. De weg van het Woord* (De Prediking van het Nieuwe Testament), Nijkerk, 1948, ²1956, ³1965, ⁴1973, ⁵1977.

SMEND, F., Die Behandlung alttestamentlicher Zitate als Ausgangspunkt der Quellenscheidung im 4. Evangelium. — *ZNW* 24 (1925) 147-150.

SMEND, R., Ansprache am Sarge Ernst Haenchens. In der Universitätskirche Münster am 6. Mai 1975. — *ZTK* 72 (1975) 303-309.

SMIT SIBINGA, J., Towards Understanding the Composition of John 20. — *FS F. Neirynck*, III, 2139-2152.

SMITH, D.M., John 12:12ff. and the Question of John's Use of the Synoptics. — *JBL* 82 (1963) 58-64; = ID., *Johannine Christianity*, 1984, 97-105.

* —— *The Composition and Order of the Fourth Gospel: Bultmann's Literary Theory* (YPR, 10), New Haven, CT – London, 1965.

* —— The Sources of the Gospel of John: An Assessment of the Present State of the Problem. — *NTS* 21 (1963-64) 336-351; = ID., *Johannine Christianity*, 1984, 39-61.

* —— Review of FORTNA, *Gospel of Signs* [1970]. — *JBL* 89 (1970) 498-501.

* —— Johannine Christianity: Some Reflections on Its Character and Delineation. — *NTS* 21 (1974-75) 222-248; Introduction: Johannine Christianity. — ID., *Johannine Christianity*, 1984, 1-36.

* —— The Milieu of the Johannine Miracle Source: A Proposal. — *FS W.D. Davies*, 1976, 164-180; = ID., *Johannine Christianity*, 1984, 62-79.

* —— The Setting and Shape of a Johannine Narrative Source. — *JBL* 95 (1976) 231-241; = ID., *Johannine Christianity*, 1984, 80-93.

* —— John, Gospel of. — *IDB SV*, 1976, 482-486.

* —— Sign in the NT. — *IDB SV*, 1976, 824-825.

* —— *John* (ProclCom), Philadelphia, PA, 1976, ²1986 (rev. ed.).

—— The Presentation of Jesus in the Fourth Gospel. — *Interpr* 31 (1977) 367-378; = ID., *Johannine Christianity*, 1984, 175-189.

—— John and the Synoptics: Some Dimensions of the Problem. — *NTS* 26 (1979-80) 425-444; = ID., *Johannine Christianity*, 1984, 145-172.

—— B.W. Bacon on John and Mark. — *PerspRelSt* 8 (1981) 201-218; = ID., *Johannine Christianity*, 1984, 106-127.

—— Theology and Ministry in John. — SHELP – SUNDERLAND (eds.), *Biblical Basis for Ministry*, 1981, 186-228; = SMITH, *Johannine Christianity*, 1984, 190-222.

—— Preface. — ID., *Johannine Christianity*, 1984, IX-XV.

—— John and the Synoptics. — *Bib* 63 (1982) 102-113; = *John and the Synoptics*: de Solages and Neirynck. — ID., *Johannine Christianity*, 1984, 128-144.

—— John, the Synoptics, and the Canonical Approach to Exegesis. — *FS E.E. Ellis*, 1987, 166-180.

—— The Life Setting of the Gospel of John. — *RExp* 85 (1988) 433-444.

—— Johannine Studies. — Epp – MacRae (eds.), *The New Testament and Its Modern Interpreters*, 1988, 271-296.

—— John and the Synoptics in Light of the Problem of Faith and History. — *FS P.W. Meyer*, 1990, 74-89.

—— Judaism and the Gospel of John. — Charlesworth (ed.), *Jews and Christians*, 1990, 76-96, 97-99.

* —— The Contribution of J. Louis Martyn to the Understanding of the Gospel of John. — *FS J.L. Martyn*, 1990, 275-294.

* —— Review of Fortna, *Predecessor* [1988]. — *JBL* 109 (1990) 352-355.

—— The Problem of John and the Synoptics in Light of the Relation between Apocryphal and Canonical Gospels. — Denaux (ed.), *John and the Synoptics*, 1992, 147-162.

* —— *John among the Gospels: The Relationship in Twentieth-Century Research*, Minneapolis, MN, 1992.

—— John and the Synoptics and the Question of Gospel Genre. — *FS F. Neirynck*, 1992, vol. III, 1783-1797.

—— Historical Issues and the Problem of John and the Synoptics. — *FS M. de Jonge*, 1993, 253-267.

* Smith, M., Prolegomena to a Discussion of Aretalogies, Divine Men, the Gospels and Jesus. — *JBL* 90 (1971) 174-199.

* —— *Clement of Alexandria and a Secret Gospel of Mark*, Cambridge, MA, 1973.

* —— *The Secret Gospel: The Discovery and Interpretation of the Secret Gospel according to Mark*, New York, 1973.
    GT: *Auf der Suche nach dem historischen Jesus. Entdeckung und Deutung des geheimen Evangeliums im Wüstenkloster Mar Saba*, trans. O. Weith, Frankfurt/M – Berlin – Wien, 1974.

* —— Clement of Alexandria and Secret Mark: The Score at the End of the First Decade. — *HTR* 74 (1982) 449-461.

Smith, R.H., Exodus Typology in the Fourth Gospel. — *JBL* 81 (1962) 329-342.

Smitmans, A., *Das Weinwunder von Kana. Die Auslegung von Jo 2,1-11 bei den Vätern und heute* (BGBE, 6), Tübingen, 1966. – Diss. Tübingen, 1964-65 (dir. K.H. Schelkle).

Snoy, T., *La marche de Jésus sur les eaux. Étude de la rédaction marcienne*, STD diss. Leuven, 1967 (dir. F. Neirynck).

—— La rédaction marcienne de la marche sur les eaux (Mc VI, 45-52). — *ETL* 44 (1968) 205-241, 433-481; = *ALBO* IV, 44-45.

—— Les miracles dans l'évangile de Marc. Examen de quelques études récentes. — *RTL* 3 (1972) 449-466; 4 (1973) 58-101.
    → Neirynck

Soltau, W., *Unsere Evangelien. Ihre Quellen und ihr Quellenwert vom Standpunkt de Historikers aus betrachtet*, Leipzig, 1901.

—— Zum Problem des Johannesevangeliums. — *ZNW* 2 (1901) 140-149.

—— Die Entstehung des vierten Evangeliums. — *TSK* 81 (1908) 177-202.

—— Zum Johannesevangelium. Die Kritiker am Scheideweg. — *PrM* 13 (1909) 436-437.

—— Welche Bedeutung haben die synoptischen Berichte des IV. Evangeliums für die Feststellung seines Entstehens. — *ZWT* 52 (1910) 33-66.

—— Der eigenartige dogmatische Standpunkt der Johannesreden und seine Erklärung. — *ZWT* 52 (1910) 341-358.

—— Thesen über die Entwicklung einer johanneischen Literatur. — *ZWT* 53 (1911) 167-170.

—— Kannte der 4. Evangelist den Lieblingsjünger? — *TSK* 88 (1915) 371-380.

—— Das Problem des Johannesevangeliums und der Weg seiner Lösung. — *ZNW* 16 (1915) 24-53.

—— Die Reden des vierten Evangeliums. — *ZNW* 17 (1916) 49-60.

—— Die synoptische Grundlage der johanneischen Reden. — *ZNW* 17 (1916) 49-60.

—— Die Verwandtschaft zwischen Evangelium und dem 1. Johannesbrief. — *TSK* 89 (1916) 228-233.

* —— *Das vierte Evangelium in seiner Entstehungsgeschichte dargelegt* (SHAW PH, 7/6), Heidelberg, 1916.

* SPITTA, F., *Das Johannes-Evangelium als Quelle der Geschichte Jesu*, Göttingen, 1910.

STALEY, J.L., *The Print's First Kiss: A Rhetorical Investigation of the Implied Reader in the Fourth Gospel* (SBL DS, 82), Atlanta, GA, 1988. – Diss. Graduate Theological Union, 1985 (dir.: W.B. Herzog, III).

—— Stumbling in the Dark, Reaching for the Light: Reading Character in John 5 and 9. — *Semeia* 53 (1991) 55-80.

STANGE, E., *Die Eigenart der johanneischen Produktion. Ein Beitrag zur Kritik der neueren Quellenscheidungshypothesen und zur Charakteristik der johanneischen Psyche*, Dresden, 1915.

* STANLEY, D.M., Response to James M. Robinson's "Kerygma and History in the New Testament". — HYATT (ed.), *The Bible*, 1965, 151-159.

STANTON, G.N., *The Gospels and Jesus* (The Oxford Bible Series), Oxford, 1989.

STANTON, V.H., *The Gospels as Historical Documents. III. The Fourth Gospel*, Cambridge, 1920.

* STAUFFER, E., Review of BULTMANN, *Johannes* [1941]. — *ZKG* 62 (1943-44, ed. 1947) 347-352.

* STENGER, W., Die Auferweckung des Lazarus (Johannes 11,1-45). Vorlage und johanneische Redaktion. — *TTZ* 83 (1974) 17-37; = ID., *Strukturale Beobachtungen*, 1990, 181-201.

* —— *Biblische Methodenlehre* (Leitfaden Theologie, 18), Düsseldorf, 1987. ET: *Introduction to New Testament Exegesis*, trans. D.W. Scott, Grand Rapids, MI, 1993.

STEWART, C.St.M., *John A.T. Robinson on the Priority of John*, STL diss. Leuven, 1987 (dir. F. Neirynck).

STIBBE, M.W.G., The Elusive Christ: A New Reading of the Fourth Gospel. — *JSNT* 44 (1991) 20-39.

—— "Return to the Sender": A Structuralist Approach to John's Gospel. — *Biblical Interpretation* 1 (1992) 189-206.

* —— *John as Storyteller: Narrative Criticism and the Fourth Gospel* (SNTS MS, 73), Cambridge, 1992. – Diss. University of Nottingham, 1989 (dir. J. Muddiman).

—— *John* (Readings: A New Biblical Commentary), Sheffield, 1993.

—— A Tomb with a View: John 11.1-44 in Narrative-Critical Perspective. — *NTS* 40 (1994) 38-54.

STRACHAN, R.H., Spitta on John XXI. — *Exp*, 8th ser., 4 (1912) 363-369, 554-561.

STRACK, H.L. – BILLERBECK, P., *Kommentar zum Neuen Testament aus Talmud und Midrasch*, vol. I-VI, München, 1922-1961.

STRATHMANN, H., *Geist und Gestalt des vierten Evangeliums. Fünf Lehrbriefe zur Einführung*, Göttingen, 1946.

—— *Das Evangelium des Johannes übersetzt und erklärt* (NTD, 4), Göttingen, [6]1951 (first ed. by Strathmann), [7]1954, [8]1955, [9]1959, [10]1962, [11]1968. → Schulz

* STRAUSS, D.F., *Das Leben Jesu kritisch bearbeitet*, 2 vols., Tübingen, 1835, 1836.
  ET: *The Life of Jesus Critically Examined*, ed. P.C. HODGSON, trans. G. Eliot, Philadelphia, PA, 1972.

* —— *Das Leben Jesu für das deutsche Volk bearbeitet*, Leipzig, 1864.
  FT: *Nouvelle vie de Jésus*, trans. A. Nefftzer – C. Dollfus, 2 vols., Paris, s.d.

—— Vorrede zu den Gesprächen von Ulrich von Hutten. — *Gesammelte Schriften*, vol. VII, [3]1877 (original ed.: 1860).

* STRECKER, G. – SCHNELLE, U., *Einführung in die neutestamentliche Exegese* (UTB, 1253), Göttingen, 1983, [3]1989.

* STRECKER, G., Die Anfänge der johanneischen Schule. — *NTS* 32 (1986) 31-47.

* —— *Neues Testament* (Urban Taschenbücher, 422; Grundkurs Theologie, 2), Stuttgart, 1989

* —— Schriftlichkeit oder Mündlichkeit der synoptischen Tradition? Anmerkungen zur formgeschichtlichen Problematik. — *FS F. Neirynck*, 1992, vol. I, 159-172.

* —— *Literaturgeschichte des Neuen Testaments* (UTB, 1682), Göttingen, 1992.

—— & LAHBAHN, M., Der johanneische Schriftenkreis. — *TR* 59 (1994) 101-107.

STREETER, B.H., *The Four Gospels: A Study of Origins Treating the Manuscript Tradition, Sources, Authorships, & Dates*, London, 1924.

* STUHLMACHER, P., Review of NOETZEL, *Christus und Dionysos* [1960]. — *VF* 1960-62 (ed. 1965) 242-243.

SUGGIT, J.N., John 2:1-11: The Sign of Greater Things to Come. — *Neotestamentica* 21 (1987) 141-158.

SUHL, A., Einleitung. — ID. (ed.), *Der Wunderbegriff*, 1980, 1-38.

* SWEETNAM, L., Review of FORTNA, *Gospel of Signs* [1970]. — *CalvTJ* 6 (1971) 217-225.

* TALBERT, C.H., Artistry and Theology: An Analysis of the Architecture of Jn 1,19-5,47. — *CBQ* 32 (1970) 341-366.

—— *Reading John: A Literary and Theological Commentary on the Fourth Gospel and the Johannine Epistles* (Reading the New Testament Series), New York, 1992.

TAYLOR, M.J., *John: The Different Gospel. A Reflective Commentary*, New York, 1983.

TEEPLE, H.M., *The Mosaic Eschatological Prophet* (JBL MS, 10), Philadelphia, PA, 1957.

—— Methodology in Source Analysis of the Fourth Gospel. — *JBL* 81 (1962) 279-286.

* —— *The Literary Origin of the Gospel of John*, Evanston, IL, 1974.

* —— *How Did Christianity Really Begin? A Historical-Archaeological Approach*, Evanston, IL, 1992.

* TEMPLE, S., A Key to the Composition of the Fourth Gospel. — *JBL* 80 (1961) 220-232.

* —— The Two Signs in the Fourth Gospel. — *JBL* 81 (1962) 169-174.

* —— *The Core of the Fourth Gospel*, London, 1975.

TENNEY, M.C., *The Gospel of John* (The Expositor's Bible Commentary, 9), Grand Rapids MI, 1981.

THEISSEN, G., *Urchristliche Wundergeschichten. Ein Beitrag zur formgeschichtlichen Erforschung der synoptischen Evangelien* (StNT, 8), Gütersloh, 1974.
ET: *The Miracle Stories of the Early Christian Tradition*, trans. F. McDonagh (StNTIW), Edinburgh – Philadelphia, PA, 1983.

THEOBALD, M., *Die Fleischwerdung des Logos. Studien zum Verhältnis des Johannesprologs zum Corpus des Evangeliums und zu 1 Joh* (NTAbh, NF 20), Münster, 1988. – Diss. Regensburg, 1985 (dir. F. Mussner).

THOLUCK, A.F., *Commentar zu dem Evangelio Johannis*, Hamburg, 1827, ²1828, ³1837.

THOMAS, W.H.G., The Purpose of the Fourth Gospel. — *BS* 125 (1968) 254-262.

* THOMPSON, J.M., Accidental Disarrangements in the Fourth Gospel. — *Exp*, 8th ser., 9 (1915) 421-437.

* —— Is John XXI an Appendix? — *Exp*, 8th ser., 10 (1915) 139-147.

* —— The Structure of the Fourth Gospel. — *Exp*, 8th ser., 10 (1915) 512-526.

* —— The Composition of the Fourth Gospel. — *Exp*, 8th ser., 11 (1916) 34-46.

* —— Some Editorial Elements in the Fourth Gospel. — *Exp*, 8th ser., 14 (1917) 214-231.

* THOMPSON, M.M., *The Humanity of Jesus in the Fourth Gospel*, Philadelphia, PA, 1988; = *The Incarnate Word: Perspectives on Jesus in the Fourth Gospel*, Peabody, PA, 1993. – Diss. Duke University, 1985 (dir. D.M. Smith).

* —— John, Gospel of. — GREEN – MCKNIGHT – MARSHALL (eds.), *Dictionary of Jesus and the Gospels*, 1992, 368-383.

THÜSING, W. *Die Erhöhung Jesu und Verherrlichung Jesu im Johannesevangelium* (NTAbh, 21/1-2), 1960, ²1970.

* THYEN, H., *Studien zur Sündenvergebung im Neuen Testament und seinen alttestamentlichen und jüdischen Voraussetzungen* (FRLANT, 96), Göttingen, 1970.

* —— Aus der Literatur zum Johannesevangelium. — *TR* 39 (1974) 1-69, 222-252, 289-329; 42 (1977) 211-270; 43 (1978) 328-359; 44 (1979) 97-134.

* —— Johannes 13 und die "Kirchliche Redaktion" des vierten Evangeliums. — *FS K.G. Kuhn*, 1975, 343-356.

* —— Entwicklungen innerhalb der johanneischen Theologie und Kirche im Spiegel von Joh 21 und der Lieblingsjüngertexte des Evangeliums. — DE JONGE (ed.), *L'évangile de Jean*, 1977 (²1987), 259-299.

* —— "Niemand hat grössere Liebe als die, dass er sein Leben für seine Freunde hingibt" (Joh 15,13). Das johanneische Verständnis des Kreuzestodes Jesu. — *FS E. Dinkler*, 1979, 467-481.

* —— "Das Heil kommt von den Juden". — *FS G. Bornkamm*, 1980, 163-184.

* —— Johannesevangelium. — *TRE* 17 (1988) 200-225.

* —— Johannes 10 im Kontext des vierten Evangeliums. — BEUTLER – FORTNA, (eds.), *The Shepherd Discourse*, 1991, 116-134, 163-168.

* —— Johannes und die Synoptiker. Auf der Suche nach einem neuen Paradigma zur Beschreibung ihrer Beziehungen anhand von Beobachtungen an Passions- und Östererzählungen. — DENAUX (ed.), *John and the Synoptics*, 1992, 81-107.

* —— Review of FORTNA, *Predecessor* [1988]. — *TLZ* 117 (1992) 34-39.

* —— Die Erzählung von den bethanischen Geschwistern (Joh 11,1–12,19) als "Palimpsest" über synoptischen Texten. — *FS F. Neirynck*, 1992, vol. III, 2021-2050.

—— Ich bin das Licht der Welt. Das Ich- und Ich-Bin-Sagen Jesu im Johannesevangelium. — *JAC* 35 (1992) 19-46.

* TIEDE, D.L., *The Charismatic Figure as Miracle Worker* (SBL DS, 1), Missoula, MT, 1972. – Diss. Harvard, 1970 (dir. H. Koester).

* —— Religious Propaganda and the Literature of the Early Christian Mission. — *ANRW* II, 25/2, 1984, 1705-1729.

* —— Aretalogy. — *ABD*, vol. 1, 1992, 372-373.

TILLMANN, F., *Das Johannesevangelium übersetzt und erklärt* (Die heilige Schrift des Neuen Testamentes, 3), Bonn, 1916, [2]1921, [3]1922, [4]1931.

TIMMINS, N.G., Variation in Style in the Johannine Literature. — JSNT 53 (1994) 47-64.

TOBLER, E., *Vom Missverstehen zum Glauben. Ein theologisch-literarischer Versuch zum vierten Evangelium und zu Zeugnissen seiner Wirkung* (EHS, 23/395), Bern – Frankfurt – New York – Paris, 1990. – Diss. Zürich, 1989-90.

TOLBERT, M.A., A Response from a Literary Perspective. — *Semeia* 53 (1991) 203-212.

TRAETS, C., *Voir Jésus et le Père en lui selon l'évangile de saint Jean* (AnGreg, 159), Rome, 1967.

TROCMÉ, É., Jean et les Synoptiques: l'exemple de Jn 1,15-34. — *FS F. Neirynck*, 1992, vol. III, 1935-1941.

TRUDINGER, P., A "Hot" Apology for the "Cool Gospel". — *DownR* 103 (1985) 66-75.

* TRUMBOWER, J.A., *Born from above: The Anthropology of the Gospel of John* (HUT, 29), Tübingen, 1992. – Diss. Chicago (dir. H.D. Betz).

TUCKETT, C.M., Barnabas Lindars' Work on John. — LINDARS, *Essays*, 1992, XI-XVII.

TURNER, M. – BURGE, G.M., The Anointed Community: A Review and Response. — *EvQ* 62 (1990) 253-268.

* TURNER, N., *Style (J.H.* MOULTON, *A Grammar of New Testament Greek*, Vol. IV), Edinburgh, 1976.

* VAN BELLE, G., *De Semeia-bron in het vierde evangelie. Ontstaan en groei van een hypothese* (SNTA, 10), Leuven, 1975. – STL diss. Leuven, 1974 (dir. F. Neirynck).

– Reviews: *Academische Tijdingen* 10 (1975), n° 7, 19; *EV* 87 (1977) 174; *JBL* 95 (1976) 174; *NTA* 20 (1976) 242; M.-É. BOISMARD, *RB* 86 (1979)

153; R.F. Collins, *LouvSt* 6 (1976-77) 188-189; J. Coppens, *ETL* 52 (1976) 231; M. de Jonge, *NTT* 30 (1976) 225-226; A. Denaux, *Collationes* 7 (1977) 507-508; K. Grayston, *ExpT* 87 (1975-76) 261; J. Helderman, *GTT* 77 (1977) 207-208; X. Léon-Dufour, *RSR* 64 (1976) 448; J. Ponthot, *RTL* 7 (1976) 378; J. Reiling, *KerkT* 30 (1979) 84; L. Sabourin, *BTB* 6 (1976) 311; M.W. Schoenberg, *CBQ* 38 (1976) 264-265; S. van Tilborg, *TT* 16 (1976) 217.

── The Text of John in N²⁶. ── *ETL* 56 (1980) 417-426; = Id., *Les parenthèses*, 1985, 231-339.

── *Les parenthèses dans l'évangile de Jean. Aperçu historique et classification. Texte grec de Jean* (SNTA, 11), Leuven, 1985. – STD diss. Leuven, 1987 (dir. F. Neirynck).

* ── Jn 4,48 et la foi du centurion. ── *ETL* 61 (1985) 167-169.

── *Johannine Bibliography 1966-1985: A Cumulative Bibliography on the Fourth Gospel* (BETL, 82; CoBRA, 1), Leuven – Brussel, 1988.

── Bibliographia Academica F. Neirynck. ── *FS F. Neirynck*, 1992, vol. I, 3-47.

── Les parenthèses johanniques. Un premier bilan. ── *FS F. Neirynck*, 1992, vol. III, 1901-1933.

→ Neirynck

van Cangh, J.-M., Les sources de l'évangile: les collections prémarciennes de miracles. ── *RTL* 3 (1972) 76-85.

── La multiplication des pains dans l'évangile de Marc. Essai d'exégèse globale. ── Sabbe (ed.), *L'évangile selon Marc*, 1974 (²1988), 309-346.

Van den Bussche, H., La structure de Jean i–xii. ── Braun (ed.), *L'évangile de Jean*, 1958, 61-109.

── *Het vierde evangelie* (Woord en beleving), Tielt – Den Haag, 1959, 1960, 1955, 1960. I. *Het Boek der Tekens. Verklaring van Johannes 1–5*, 1959. II. *Het Boek der Werken. Verklaring van Johannes 5–12*, 1960. III. *Jezus' woorden aan het afscheidsmaal. Verklaring van de hoofdstukken 13–17 van het Sint-Jansevangelie*, 1955. IV. *Het Boek der Passie. Verklaring van Johannes 18–21*, 1960.

FT: *Jean. Commentaire de l'Évangile spirituel* (Bible et vie chrétienne), Bruges, 1967.

ET: *The Gospel of the Word*, trans. M. Marta – J.C. Guinness, 1968.

Van Oyen, G., *De summaria in Marcus en de compositie van Mc 1,14-8,26* (SNTA, 12), Leuven, 1987. – STL diss. Leuven, 1987 (dir. F. Neirynck).

── *De studie van de Marcusredactie in de twintigste eeuw. Met een bijdrage tot de verklaring van de broodwonderen*, STD diss., 2 vols., Leuven, 1993 (dir. F. Neirynck).

── *De studie van de Marcusredactie in de twintigste eeuw* (Verhandelingen van de Koninklijke Academie voor Wetenschappen, Letteren en Schone Kunsten van België. Klasse der Letteren, Jaargang 55, 1993, Nr. 147; SNTA, 18), Brussel – Leuven, 1993.

van Tilborg, S., *Johannes* (Belichting van het bijbelboek), Boxtel – Leuven – Brugge, 1988.

van Unnik, W.C., The Purpose of St John's Gospel. ── *StEv*, 1959, 382-411; = Id., *Sparsa Collecta*, vol. I, 1973, 35-63.

Verheyden, J., P. Gardner-Smith and "The Turn of the Tide". ── Denaux (ed.), *John and the Synoptics*, 1992, 423-452.

VERMES, G., *Jesus the Jew: A Historian's Reading of the Gospels*, London, 1973.

VIELHAUER, P., Erwägungen zur Christologie des Markusevangeliums. — *FS R. Bultmann*, 1964, 155-169; = ID., *Aufsätze zum Neuen Testament*, 1965, 199-214.

* —— *Geschichte der urchristlichen Literatur. Einleitung in das Neue Testament, die Apokryphen und die Apostolischen Väter*, Berlin – New York, 1975.

* VÖGTLE, A., Wunder im N.T. — *LTK*² 10 (1965) 1255-1261.

VON WAHLDE, U.C., A Redactional Technique in the Fourth Gospel. — *CBQ* 38 (1976) 520-533.

—— The Terms for Religious Authorities in the Fourth Gospel: A Key to Literary Strata? — *JBL* 98 (1979) 231-253.

—— Faith and Works in Jn vi 28-29. Exegesis or Eisegesis? — *NT* 22 (1980) 304-315.

—— The Witnesses to Jesus in John 5:31-40 and Belief in the Fourth Gospel. — *CBQ* 43 (1981) 385-404.

—— The Johannine 'Jews': A Critical Survey. — *NTS* 28 (1982) 33-60.

—— *Wiederaufnahme* as a Marker of Redaction in Jn 6,51-58. — *Bib* 64 (1983) 542-549.

—— Literary Structure and Theological Argument in Three Discourses with the Jews in the Fourth Gospel. — *JBL* 103 (1984) 575-584.

* —— *The Earliest Version of John's Gospel: Recovering the Gospel of Signs*, Wilmington, DE, 1989.

—— *The Johannine Commandments: 1 John and the Struggle for the Johannine Tradition* (Theological Inquiries), New York – Mahwah, NJ, 1990.

VORSTER, W.S., The Growth and Making of John 21. — *FS F. Neirynck*, 1992, vol. III, 2207-2221.

* VOUGA, F., The Johannine School: A Gnostic Tradition in Primitive Christianity? — *Bibl* 88 (1988) 371-385.

* —— Le quatrième évangile comme interprète de la tradition synoptique: Jean 6. — DENAUX (ed.), *John and the Synoptics*, 1992, 261-279.

WAGNER, G., *An Exegetical Bibliography of the New Testament*. Vol. III: *John and 1, 2, 3 John*, Macon, GA, 1988.

* WAGNER, J., *Auferstehung und Leben. Joh 11,1–12,19 als Spiegel johanneischer Redaktions- und Theologiegeschichte* (BibUnt, 19), Regensburg, 1988.

* —— Die Erweckung des Lazarus – Ein Paradigma johanneischer Theologiegeschichte. — HAINZ (ed.), *Theologie im Werden*, 1992, 199-217.

* WALTER, N., Die Auslegung überlieferter Wundererzählungen im Johannes-Evangelium. — *TVers* 2 (1970) 93-107.

* —— Review of NICOL, *The Sēmeia* [1972]. — *TLZ* 99 (1974) 826-828.

WEAD, D.W., *The Literary Devices in John's Gospel* (TDiss, 4), Basel, 1970. – Diss. Basel (dir. B. Reicke).

WEBER, M., *Authentia capitis ultimi evangelii Johannei, hujusque evangelii totius, argumentorum internorum usu, vindicata*, Halle, 1823.

WEBSTER, E.C., Pattern in the Fourth Gospel. — CLINES *et al.* (eds.), *Art and Meaning*, 1982, 230-237.

* WEDER, H., Die Menschwerdung Gottes. Überlegungen zur Auslegungsproblematik des Johannesevangeliums am Beispiel von Joh 6. — *ZTK* 82 (1985) 325-360; = ID., *Einblicke*, 1992, 363-400.

* —— Von der Wende der Welt zum Semeion des Sohnes. — DENAUX (ed.), *John and the Synoptics*, 1992, 127-145.

* WEGNER, U., *Der Hauptmann von Kafarnaum (Mt 7,28a; 8,5-10.13 par Lk 7,1-10). Ein Beitrag zur Q-Forschung* (WUNT, 2/14), Tübingen, 1985. – Diss. Tübingen, 1982-83 (dir. M. Hengel).

WEGSCHEIDER, J.A.L., *Versuch einer vollständigen Einleitung in das Evangelium des Johannes*, Göttingen, 1806.

WEISER, A., *Theologie des Neuen Testaments. 2. Die Theologie der Evangelien* (Kohlhammer-Studienbücher Theologie, 8), Stuttgart, 1993.

WEISS, B., *Kritisch-exegetisches Handbuch über das Evangelium des Johannes* (KEK, 2), Göttingen, ⁶1880, ⁷1886, ⁸1893, ⁹1902. → Meyer

—— *Das Johannesevangelium als einheitliches Werk geschichtlich erklärt*, Berlin, 1912.

WEISS, H., The Sabbath in the Fourth Gospel. — *JBL* 110 (1992) 311-321.

WEISS, J., *Das älteste Evangelium. Ein Beitrag zum Verständnis des Markus-Evangeliums und der ältesten evangelischen Überlieferung*, Göttingen, 1903.

WEISSE, C.H., *Die evangelische Geschichte kritisch und philosophisch bearbeitet*, 2 vols., 1838.

—— *Die Evangelienfrage in ihrem gegenwärtigen Stadium*, Leipzig, 1856.

WELCK, C., *Erzählte 'Zeichen'. Die johanneischen Wundergeschichten literarisch untersucht. Mit einem Ausblick auf Joh 21*, diss. Bethel, 1991 (dir. A. Lindemann).

WELLHAUSEN, J., *Erweiterungen und Änderungen im vierten Evangelium*, Berlin, 1907.

—— *Das Evangelium Johannis*, Berlin, 1908; repr. ID., *Evangelienkommentare*. Mit einer Einleitung von M. HENGEL, Berlin – New York, 1987, 601-746.

* WENDT, H.H., *Die Lehre Jesu. I. Die evangelischen Quellenberichte über die Lehre Jesu*, Göttingen, 1885, ²1901.
ET: *The Teaching of Jesus*, trans. J. Wilson, 2 vols., Edinburgh, 1893.

* —— *Das Johannesevangelium. Eine Untersuchung seiner Entstehung und seines geschichtlichen Wertes*, Göttingen, 1900.
ET: *The Gospel according to St. John*, Edinburgh, 1902.

—— *Die Schichten im vierten Evangelium*, Göttingen, 1911.

WENGST, K., *Der erste, zweite und dritte Brief des Johannes* (ÖTKNT, 16; Siebenstern, 502), Gütersloh – Würzburg, 1978.

* —— *Bedrängte Gemeinde und verherrlichter Christus. Der historische Ort des Johannesevangeliums als Schlüssel zu seiner Interpretation* (Biblisch-theologische Studien, 5), Neukirchen-Vluyn, 1981.
New ed.: *Bedrängte Gemeinde und verherrlichter Christus. Ein Versuch über das Johannesevangelium*, München, ²1990, ³1990, ⁴1992.

WENZ, H., Sehen und Glauben bei Johannes. — *TZ* 17 (1961) 17-25.

WESTCOTT, B.F., *The Gospel according to St. John: The Authorized Version with Introduction and Notes* (The Speaker's Commentary), Cambridge, 1881; repr. Grand Rapids, MI, 1958.

—— *The Gospel according to St John: The Greek Text with Introduction and Notes*, 2 vols., London, 1908; repr. (in one volume) Grand Rapids, MI, 1980.

WETTER, G.P., *"Der Sohn Gottes"*. *Eine Untersuchung über den Charakter und die Tendenz des Johannes-Evangeliums. Zugleich ein Beitrag zur Kenntnis der Heilandsgestalten der Antike* (FRLANT, 26; NF 9), Göttingen, 1916.

WHITACRE, R.A., *Johannine Polemic: The Role of Tradition and Theology* (SBL DS, 67), Chico, CA, 1982. – Diss. Cambridge, 1982 (dir. M.D. Hooker).

* WHITELEY, D.E.H., Was John Written by a Sadducee? — *ANRW* II, 25/3, 1985, 2481-2505.

WIKENHAUSER, A., *Das Evangelium nach Johannes übersetzt und erklärt* (Regensburger Neues Testament, 4), Regensburg, 1948, ²1957, ³1969.

DT: *Het evangelie volgens Johannes*, trans. L. Witsenburg (Het Nieuwe Testament met Commentaar, 4), Antwerpen, 1964.

WILKENS, J., *Die Individualität der synoptischen Evangelien*, diss. Münster, 1926.

—— *Johannes 2,1-11 unter dem Gesichtspunkt der Entmythologisierung*, ungedrucktes Referat vor der Dozentenarbeitsgemeinschaft der kirchlichen Hochschule Wuppertal, 1951.

* WILKENS, W., *Die Entstehungsgeschichte des vierten Evangeliums*, Zollikon, 1958. – Diss. Basel (dir. O. Cullmann).

—— Die Abendmahlszeugnis im vierten Evangelium. — *EvT* 18 (1958) 354-370.

* —— Die Erweckung des Lazarus. — *TZ* 15 (1959) 22-39.

* —— Evangelist und Tradition im Johannesevangelium. — *TZ* 16 (1960) 81-90.

* —— *Zeichen und Werke. Ein Beitrag zur Theologie des 4. Evangeliums in Erzählungs- und Redestoff* (ATANT, 55), Zürich, 1969.

* —— Review of FORTNA, *Gospel of Signs* [1970]. — *TZ* 28 (1972) 150-152.

WILLEMSE, J.J.C., *Het vierde evangelie. Een onderzoek naar zijn structuur*, Hilversum – Antwerpen, 1965. – Diss. Nijmegen.

WIND, A., Ontstaan en doel van het vierde evangelie. — *GTT* 71 (1971) 1-17.

—— Destination and Purpose of the Gospel of John. — *NT* 14 (1972) 26-69.

* WINDISCH, H., Der Johanneische Erzählungsstil. — *FS H. Gunkel*, 1923, vol. II, 174-213.

ET: John's Narrative Style. — STIBBE (ed.), *The Gospel of John as Literature*, 1993, 25-64.

* —— *Johannes und die Synoptiker. Wollte der vierte Evangelist die älteren Evangelien ergänzen oder ersetzen?* (UNT, 12), Leipzig, 1926.

—— Die Absolutheit des Johannesevangeliums. — *ZSysT* 5 (1927) 3-54.

WITKAMP, L.T., The Use of Traditions in John 5,1-18. — *JSNT* 25 (1985) 19-47.

—— *Jezus van Nazareth in de gemeente van Johannes. Over de interactie van traditie en ervaring*, diss. Kampen, 1986 (dir. H. Baarlink).

* WÖLLNER, H., *Zeichenglaube und Zeichenbuch. Ein literarkritischer Beitrag zur Entstehungsgeschichte des Johannesevangeliums*, diss. Leipzig, 1988 (dir. W. Wiefel).

WREDE, W., *Charakter und Tendenz des Johannesevangeliums* (SGV, 37), Tübingen, 1903, ²1933.

* WÜLFING VON MARTITZ, P., Υἱός im Griechischen. — *TWNT* 8 (1969) 335-340; ET: *TDNT* 8 (1972) 335-340.

WUELLNER, W., Putting Life back into the Lazarus Story and Its Reading: The Narrative Rhetoric of John 11 as the Narration of Faith. — *Semeia* 53 (1991) 113-132.

YOUNG, F.W., Jesus the Prophet: A Re-examination. — *JBL* 58 (1949) 285-299.

ZAHN, T., *Das Evangelium des Johannes ausgelegt* (Kommentar zum Neuen Testament, 4) Leipzig, [1-2]1908, [3-4]1912, [5-6]1921.
—— Das Evangelium des Johannes unter den Händen seiner neuesten Kritiker. — *NKZ* 22 (1911) 28-58, 83-115.
* ZIENER, G., Weisheitsbuch und Johannesevangelium. — *Bib* 38 (1957) 396-418; 39 (1958) 37-60.
* —— Johannesevangelium und urchristliche Passafeier. — *BZ* 2 (1958) 263-274.
ZUMSTEIN, J., L'évangile johannique: une stratégie du croire. — *RSR* 77 (1989) 217-232; = ID., *Miettes exégétiques*, 1991, 237-252.
—— La communauté johannique et son histoire. — KAESTLI *et al.* (eds.), *La communauté johannique*, 1990, 359-374.
—— Visages de la communauté johannique. — MARCHADOUR (ed.), *Origine et postérité*, 1990, 87-106; = ZUMSTEIN, *Miettes exégétiques*, 1991, 281-297.
—— L'interprétation johannique de la mort du Christ. — *FS F. Neirynck*, 1992, vol. III, 2119-2138.
—— Le signe de la croix. — *LumV* 41 (1992), n° 209, 68-92.
* ZWERGEL, N., *Die Erweckung des Lazarus Joh 11,1-44. Wachstumsprozess und Sinn der johanneischen Darstellung*, diss. Würzburg, 1972.

INDEXES

INDEX OF AUTHORS

The Index includes a selection of authors mentioned in Chapters I-V and in Appendix I (pp. 1-357, 379-404). Pages where the author is specially studied are in heavy type. References to the footnotes are added in superscript to the page numbers.

SELECTED INDEX OF BIBLICAL REFERENCES

Passages Attributed to the Signs Source in John

Negative or restrictive reactions to the signs-source hypothesis are marked with an asterisk.

1,6-7	100 142 199* 211 214 240 289[228] 360
1,19-34	92-93 100 119 121 136 142 168-169[128]* 196 199* 210 214 240 248 289[228] 360
1,35-50	15 17 29 50* 54* 92-93 94* 100 103* 112 114[239] 119 121 124 136-139 142 155 168-169[128]* 189[204c] 192[223] 199* 210 214 248 286* 289[228] 297-298* 319* 359-360
2,1-11.12	2-4 6-10* 10 13-15 17 19 21 30 46 47 51* 54-60 81 82 88 91 92 93-94[103] 95-97 100 104[164] 107[181] 108-110 113* 122 135[352] 137-139 142 155 170-171* 188[203] 192 210 214 248 254 255 258 267 268 285-286* 297-300* 289[228] 323* 332* 338* 339* 359* 360
2,13-21	46 58 100 142 210 214
2,23-25	210 248
3,1-2(15)	13 17 100 210 216* 248 360
3,22-26(30)	100 122 124 248 360
3,23-24	142 214-215*
4,1-42	13 17 22 30 50* 54* 81 93* 94* 100 100[138]* 114[239] 122 133 142 155 199* 210 215* 248 319-320* 360
4,43-45	2-4 6-10* 10 81 122 210 248 360
4,46-54	2-4 6-10* 10 14-15 17 19 21 31 54-60 81-84 88 92 93-94[103] 95-97 100 104-105[166] 105[170] 107[181] 108-110 113 122 135[352] 142 155 167* 176-177* 184-185[191] 188[203] 192 210 214 215 222-223[415]* 248 254 255 258-259 267 268 298-300* 313[382]* 323* 331* 333* 338* 339* 351[595]* 359* 360
5,1-9(18)	3 13 17 19 22 31 54* 81 82 88 93* 93-94[103] 96 98 100 106 107[181] 108 112 113 123 135[352] 142-143 155 167* 192 203 210 214 215 248 338* 339* 351[595]* 352[601]* 359*
6,1-21	2-4 6-10* 10 19* 22 31 54* 55[80] 77* 81 82 88 92 93-94[103] 96 98 100 103[158] 105[170] 107[181] 108 109 111* 113 122 123 135[352] 142 155 167* 188[203] 192 210 214 215* 248 268 312-313[377]* 338* 351[595]* 351-352[599]* 359*
6,22-25	10 31 155 214 360
6,26	248
6,30	210
6,67-71	142
7,1-13.14	22 32 54* 123 210 360
7,19-24	19 32 93* 107-108 112 360
7,25-27	248
7,31-32	107-108 112 210 248 360
7,37.38b	210
7,40-42(44)	210 248

BIBLIOTHECA EPHEMERIDUM THEOLOGICARUM LOVANIENSIUM

LEUVEN UNIVERSITY PRESS / UITGEVERIJ PEETERS LEUVEN

SERIES I

* = Out of print

*1. *Miscellanea dogmatica in honorem Eximii Domini J. Bittremieux*, 1947.

*2-3. *Miscellanea moralia in honorem Eximii Domini A. Janssen*, 1948.

*4. G. PHILIPS, *La grâce des justes de l'Ancien Testament*, 1948.

*5. G. PHILIPS, *De ratione instituendi tractatum de gratia nostrae sanctificationis*, 1953.

6-7. *Recueil Lucien Cerfaux. Études d'exégèse et d'histoire religieuse*, 1954. 504 et 577 p. FB 1000 par tome. Cf. *infra*, n°s 18 et 71 (t. III).

8. G. THILS, *Histoire doctrinale du mouvement œcuménique*, 1955. Nouvelle édition, 1963. 338 p. FB 135.

*9. *Études sur l'Immaculée Conception*, 1955.

*10. J.A. O'DONOHOE, *Tridentine Seminary Legislation*, 1957.

*11. G. THILS, *Orientations de la théologie*, 1958.

*12-13. J. COPPENS, A. DESCAMPS, É. MASSAUX (ed.), *Sacra Pagina. Miscellanea Biblica Congressus Internationalis Catholici de Re Biblica*, 1959.

*14. *Adrien VI, le premier Pape de la contre-réforme*, 1959.

*15. F. CLAEYS BOUUAERT, *Les déclarations et serments imposés par la loi civile aux membres du clergé belge sous le Directoire (1795-1801)*, 1960.

*16. G. THILS, *La «Théologie œcuménique». Notion-Formes-Démarches*, 1960.

17. G. THILS, *Primauté pontificale et prérogatives épiscopales. «Potestas ordinaria» au Concile du Vatican*, 1961. 103 p. FB 50.

*18. *Recueil Lucien Cerfaux*, t. III, 1962. Cf. *infra*, n° 71.

*19. *Foi et réflexion philosophique. Mélanges F. Grégoire*, 1961.

*20. *Mélanges G. Ryckmans*, 1963.

21. G. THILS, *L'infaillibilité du peuple chrétien «in credendo»*, 1963. 67 p. FB 50.

*22. J. FÉRIN & L. JANSSENS, *Progestogènes et morale conjugale*, 1963.

*23. *Collectanea Moralia in honorem Eximii Domini A. Janssen*, 1964.

24. H. CAZELLES (ed.), *De Mari à Qumrân. L'Ancien Testament. Son milieu. Ses Écrits. Ses relectures juives* (Hommage J. Coppens, I), 1969. 158*-370 p. FB 900.

*25. I. DE LA POTTERIE (ed.), *De Jésus aux évangiles. Tradition et rédaction dans les évangiles synoptiques* (Hommage J. Coppens, II), 1967.

26. G. THILS & R.E. BROWN (ed.), *Exégèse et théologie* (Hommage J. Coppens, III), 1968. 328 p. FB 700.

27. J. COPPENS (ed.), *Ecclesia a Spiritu sancto edocta. Hommage à Mgr G. Philips*, 1970. 640 p. FB 1000.

28. J. COPPENS (ed.), *Sacerdoce et célibat. Études historiques et théologiques*, 1971. 740 p. FB 700.

29. M. DIDIER (ed.), *L'évangile selon Matthieu. Rédaction et théologie*, 1972. 432 p. FB 1000.
*30. J. KEMPENEERS, *Le Cardinal van Roey en son temps*, 1971.

SERIES II

31. F. NEIRYNCK, *Duality in Mark. Contributions to the Study of the Markan Redaction*, 1972. Revised edition with Supplementary Notes, 1988. 252 p. FB 1200.
32. F. NEIRYNCK (ed.), *L'évangile de Luc. Problèmes littéraires et théologiques*, 1973. *L'évangile de Luc – The Gospel of Luke*. Revised and enlarged edition, 1989. X-590 p. FB 2200.
33. C. BREKELMANS (ed.), *Questions disputées d'Ancien Testament. Méthode et théologie*, 1974. *Continuing Questions in Old Testament Method and Theology*. Revised and enlarged edition by M. VERVENNE, 1989. 245 p. FB 1200.
34. M. SABBE (ed.), *L'évangile selon Marc. Tradition et rédaction*, 1974. Nouvelle édition augmentée, 1988. 601 p. FB 2400.
35. B. WILLAERT (ed.), *Philosophie de la religion – Godsdienstfilosofie. Miscellanea Albert Dondeyne*, 1974. Nouvelle édition, 1987. 458 p. FB 1600.
36. G. PHILIPS, *L'union personnelle avec le Dieu vivant. Essai sur l'origine et le sens de la grâce créée*, 1974. Édition révisée, 1989. 299 p. FB 1000.
37. F. NEIRYNCK, in collaboration with T. HANSEN and F. VAN SEGBROECK, *The Minor Agreements of Matthew and Luke against Mark with a Cumulative List*, 1974. 330 p. FB 900.
38. J. COPPENS, *Le messianisme et sa relève prophétique. Les anticipations vétérotestamentaires. Leur accomplissement en Jésus*, 1974. Édition révisée, 1989. XIII-265 p. FB 1000.
39. D. SENIOR, *The Passion Narrative according to Matthew. A Redactional Study*, 1975. New impression, 1982. 440 p. FB 1000.
40. J. DUPONT (ed.), *Jésus aux origines de la christologie*, 1975. Nouvelle édition augmentée, 1989. 458 p. FB 1500.
41. J. COPPENS (ed.), *La notion biblique de Dieu*, 1976. Réimpression, 1985. 519 p. FB 1600.
42. J. LINDEMANS & H. DEMEESTER (ed.), *Liber Amicorum Monseigneur W. Onclin*, 1976. XXII-396 p. FB 1000.
43. R.E. HOECKMAN (ed.), *Pluralisme et œcuménisme en recherches théologiques. Mélanges offerts au R.P. Dockx, O.P.*, 1976. 316 p. FB 1000.
44. M. DE JONGE (ed.), *L'Évangile de Jean. Sources, rédaction, théologie*, 1977. Réimpression, 1987. 416 p. FB 1500.
45. E.J.M. VAN EIJL (ed.), *Facultas S. Theologiae Lovaniensis 1432-1797. Bijdragen tot haar geschiedenis. Contributions to its History. Contributions à son histoire*, 1977. 570 p. FB 1700.
46. M. DELCOR (ed.), *Qumrân. Sa piété, sa théologie et son milieu*, 1978. 432 p. FB 1700.
47. M. CAUDRON (ed.), *Faith and Society. Foi et Société. Geloof en maatschappij. Acta Congressus Internationalis Theologici Lovaniensis 1976*, 1978. 304 p. FB 1150.

48. J. KREMER (ed.), *Les Actes des Apôtres. Traditions, rédaction, théologie*, 1979. 590 p. FB 1700.
49. F. NEIRYNCK, avec la collaboration de J. DELOBEL, T. SNOY, G. VAN BELLE, F. VAN SEGBROECK, *Jean et les Synoptiques. Examen critique de l'exégèse de M.-É. Boismard*, 1979. XII-428 p. FB 1400.
50. J. COPPENS , *La relève apocalyptique du messianisme royal*. I. *La royauté – Le règne – Le royaume de Dieu. Cadre de la relève apocalyptique*, 1979. 325 p. FB 1000.
51. M. GILBERT (ed.), *La Sagesse de l'Ancien Testament*, 1979. Nouvelle édition mise à jour, 1990. 455 p. FB 1500.
52. B. DEHANDSCHUTTER, *Martyrium Polycarpi. Een literair-kritische studie*, 1979. 296 p. FB 1000.
53. J. LAMBRECHT (ed.), *L'Apocalypse johannique et l'Apocalyptique dans le Nouveau Testament*, 1980. 458 p. FB 1400.
54. P.-M. BOGAERT (ed.), *Le Livre de Jérémie. Le prophète et son milieu. Les oracles et leur transmission*, 1981. 408 p. FB 1500.
55. J. COPPENS, *La relève apocalyptique du messianisme royal*. III. *Le Fils de l'homme néotestamentaire*, 1981. XIV-192 p. FB 800.
56. J. VAN BAVEL & M. SCHRAMA (ed.), *Jansénius et le Jansénisme dans les Pays-Bas. Mélanges Lucien Ceyssens*, 1982. 247 p. FB 1000.
57. J.H. WALGRAVE, *Selected Writings – Thematische geschriften. Thomas Aquinas, J.H. Newman, Theologia Fundamentalis*. Edited by G. DE SCHRIJVER & J.J. KELLY, 1982. XLIII-425 p. FB 1400.
58. F. NEIRYNCK & F. VAN SEGBROECK, avec la collaboration de E. MANNING, *Ephemerides Theologicae Lovanienses 1924-1981. Tables générales. (Bibliotheca Ephemeridum Theologicarum Lovaniensium 1947-1981)*, 1982. 400 p. FB 1600.
59. J. DELOBEL (ed.), *Logia. Les paroles de Jésus – The Sayings of Jesus. Mémorial Joseph Coppens*, 1982. 647 p. FB 2000.
60. F. NEIRYNCK, *Evangelica. Gospel Studies – Études d'évangile. Collected Essays*. Edited by F. VAN SEGBROECK, 1982. XIX-1036 p. FB 2000.
61. J. COPPENS, *La relève apocalyptique du messianisme royal*. II. *Le Fils d'homme vétéro- et intertestamentaire*. Édition posthume par J. LUST, 1983. XVII-272 p. FB 1000.
62. J.J. KELLY, *Baron Friedrich von Hügel's Philosophy of Religion*, 1983. 232 p. FB 1500.
63. G. DE SCHRIJVER, *Le merveilleux accord de l'homme et de Dieu. Étude de l'analogie de l'être chez Hans Urs von Balthasar*, 1983. 344 p. FB 1500.
64. J. GROOTAERS & J.A. SELLING, *The 1980 Synod of Bishops: «On the Role of the Family». An Exposition of the Event and an Analysis of its Texts*. Preface by Prof. emeritus L. JANSSENS, 1983. 375 p. FB 1500.
65. F. NEIRYNCK & F. VAN SEGBROECK, *New Testament Vocabulary. A Companion Volume to the Concordance*, 1984. XVI-494 p. FB 2000.
66. R.F. COLLINS, *Studies on the First Letter to the Thessalonians*, 1984. XI-415 p. FB 1500.
67. A. PLUMMER, *Conversations with Dr. Döllinger 1870-1890*. Edited with Introduction and Notes by R. BOUDENS, with the collaboration of L. KENIS, 1985. LIV-360 p. FB 1800.

68. N. LOHFINK (ed.), *Das Deuteronomium. Entstehung, Gestalt und Botschaft / Deuteronomy: Origin, Form and Message,* 1985. XI-382 p. FB 2000.
69. P.F. FRANSEN, *Hermeneutics of the Councils and Other Studies.* Collected by H.E. MERTENS & F. DE GRAEVE, 1985. 543 p. FB 1800.
70. J. DUPONT, *Études sur les Évangiles synoptiques.* Présentées par F. NEIRYNCK, 1985. 2 tomes, XXI-IX-1210 p. FB 2800.
71. *Recueil Lucien Cerfaux,* t. III, 1962. Nouvelle édition revue et complétée, 1985. LXXX-458 p. FB 1600.
72. J. GROOTAERS, *Primauté et collégialité. Le dossier de Gérard Philips sur la Nota Explicativa Praevia (Lumen gentium, Chap. III).* Présenté avec introduction historique, annotations et annexes. Préface de G. THILS, 1986. 222 p. FB 1000.
73. A. VANHOYE (ed.), *L'apôtre Paul. Personnalité, style et conception du ministère,* 1986. XIII-470 p. FB 2600.
74. J. LUST (ed.), *Ezekiel and His Book. Textual and Literary Criticism and their Interrelation,* 1986. X-387 p. FB 2700.
75. É. MASSAUX, *Influence de l'Évangile de saint Matthieu sur la littérature chrétienne avant saint Irénée.* Réimpression anastatique présentée par F. NEIRYNCK. Supplément: *Bibliographie 1950-1985,* par B. DEHAND-SCHUTTER, 1986. XXVII-850 p. FB 2500.
76. L. CEYSSENS & J.A.G. TANS, *Autour de l'Unigenitus. Recherches sur la genèse de la Constitution,* 1987. XXVI-845 p. FB 2500.
77. A. DESCAMPS, *Jésus et l'Église. Études d'exégèse et de théologie.* Préface de Mgr A. HOUSSIAU, 1987. XLV-641 p. FB 2500.
78. J. DUPLACY, *Études de critique textuelle du Nouveau Testament.* Présentées par J. DELOBEL, 1987. xxvii-431 p. FB 1800.
79. E.J.M. VAN EIJL (ed.), *L'image de C. Jansénius jusqu'à la fin du XVIIIᵉ siècle,* 1987. 258 p. FB 1250.
80. E. BRITO, *La Création selon Schelling. Universum,* 1987. XXXV-646 p. FB 2980.
81. J. VERMEYLEN (ed.), *The Book of Isaiah – Le Livre d'Isaïe. Les oracles et leurs relectures. Unité et complexité de l'ouvrage,* 1989. X-472 p. FB 2700.
82. G. VAN BELLE, *Johannine Bibliography 1966-1985. A Cumulative Bibliography on the Fourth Gospel,* 1988. XVII-563 p. FB 2700.
83. J.A. SELLING (ed.), *Personalist Morals. Essays in Honor of Professor Louis Janssens,* 1988. VIII-344 p. FB 1200.
84. M.-É. BOISMARD, *Moïse ou Jésus. Essai de christologie johannique,* 1988. XVI-241 p. FB 1000.
84ᴬ. M.-É. BOISMARD, *Moses or Jesus: An Essay in Johannine Christology.* Translated by B.T. VIVIANO, 1993, XVI-144 p. FB 1000.
85. J.A. DICK, *The Malines Conversations Revisited,* 1989. 278 p. FB 1500.
86. J.-M. SEVRIN (ed.), *The New Testament in Early Christianity – La réception des écrits néotestamentaires dans le christianisme primitif,* 1989. XVI-406 p. FB 2500.
87. R.F. COLLINS (ed.), *The Thessalonian Correspondence,* 1990. XV-546 p. FB 3000.
88. F. VAN SEGBROECK, *The Gospel of Luke. A Cumulative Bibliography 1973-1988,* 1989. 241 p. FB 1200.

89. G. Thils, *Primauté et infaillibilité du Pontife Romain à Vatican I et autres études d'ecclésiologie,* 1989. xi-422 p. FB 1850.
90. A. Vergote, *Explorations de l'espace théologique. Études de théologie et de philosophie de la religion,* 1990. xvi-709 p. FB 2000.
91. J.C. de Moor, *The Rise of Yahwism: The Roots of Israelite Monotheism,* 1990. xii-315 p. FB 1250.
92. B. Bruning, M. Lamberigts & J. Van Houtem (eds.), *Collectanea Augustiniana. Mélanges T.J. van Bavel,* 1990. 2 tomes, xxxviii-viii-1074 p. FB 3000.
93. A. de Halleux, *Patrologie et œcuménisme. Recueil d'études,* 1990. xvi-887 p. FB 3000.
94. C. Brekelmans & J. Lust (eds.), *Pentateuchal and Deuteronomistic Studies: Papers Read at the XIIIth IOSOT Congress Leuven 1989,* 1990. 307 p. FB 1500.
95. D.L. Dungan (ed.), *The Interrelations of the Gospels. A Symposium Led by M.-É. Boismard – W.R. Farmer – F. Neirynck, Jerusalem 1984,* 1990. xxxi-672 p. FB 3000.
96. G.D. Kilpatrick, *The Principles and Practice of New Testament Textual Criticism. Collected Essays.* Edited by J.K. Elliott, 1990. xxxviii-489 p. FB 3000.
97. G. Alberigo (ed.), *Christian Unity. The Council of Ferrara-Florence: 1438/39 – 1989,* 1991. x-681 p. FB 3000.
98. M. Sabbe, *Studia Neotestamentica. Collected Essays,* 1991. xvi-573 p. FB 2000.
99. F. Neirynck, *Evangelica II: 1982-1991. Collected Essays.* Edited by F. Van Segbroeck, 1991. xix-874 p. FB 2800.
100. F. Van Segbroeck, C.M. Tuckett, G. Van Belle & J. Verheyden (eds.), *The Four Gospels 1992. Festschrift Frans Neirynck,* 1992. 3 volumes, xvii-x-x-2668 p. FB 5000.

Series III

101. A. Denaux (ed.), *John and the Synoptics,* 1992. xxii-696 p. FB 3000.
102. F. Neirynck, J. Verheyden, F. Van Segbroeck, G. Van Oyen & R. Corstjens, *The Gospel of Mark. A Cumulative Bibliography: 1950-1990,* 1992. xii-717 p. FB 2700.
103. M. Simon, *Un catéchisme universel pour l'Église catholique. Du Concile de Trente à nos jours,* 1992. xiv-461 p. FB 2200.
104. L. Ceyssens, *Le sort de la bulle Unigenitus. Recueil d'études offert à Lucien Ceyssens à l'occasion de son 90ᵉ anniversaire.* Présenté par M. Lamberigts, 1992. xxvi-641 p. FB 2000.
105. R.J. Daly (ed.), *Origeniana Quinta. Papers of the 5th International Origen Congress, Boston College, 14-18 August 1989,* 1992. xvii-635 p. FB 2700.
106. A.S. van der Woude (ed.), *The Book of Daniel in the Light of New Findings,* 1993. xviii-574 p. FB 3000.
107. J. Famerée, *L'ecclésiologie d'Yves Congar avant Vatican II: Histoire et Église. Analyse et reprise critique,* 1992. 497 p. FB 2600.

108. C. BEGG, *Josephus' Account of the Early Divided Monarchy (AJ 8, 212-420). Rewriting the Bible*, 1993. IX-377 p. FB 2400.
109. J. BULCKENS & H. LOMBAERTS (eds.), *L'enseignement de la religion catholique à l'école secondaire. Enjeux pour la nouvelle Europe*, 1993. XII-264 p. FB 1250.
110. C. FOCANT (ed.), *The Synoptic Gospels. Source Criticism and the New Literary Criticism*, 1993. XXXIX-670 p. FB 3000.
111. M. LAMBERIGTS (ed.), avec la collaboration de L. KENIS, *L'augustinisme à l'ancienne Faculté de théologie de Louvain*, 1994. VII-455 p. FB 2400.
112. R. BIERINGER & J. LAMBRECHT, *Studies on 2 Corinthians*, 1994. XX-632 p. FB 3000.
113. E. BRITO, *La pneumatologie de Schleiermacher*, 1994. XII-649 p. FB 3000.
114. W.A.M. BEUKEN (ed.), *The Book of Job,* 1994. X-465 p. FB 2400.
115. J. LAMBRECHT, *Pauline Studies: Collected Essays,* 1994. XIV-465 p. FB 2500.
116. G. VAN BELLE, *The Signs Source in the Fourth Gospel: Historical Survey and Critical Evaluation of the Semeia Hypothesis,* 1994. XIV-503 p. FB 2500.

ORIENTALISTE, KLEIN DALENSTRAAT 42, B-3020 HERENT